CONTROL OF THE MEDIA
IN THE
UNITED STATES

GARLAND REFERENCE LIBRARY
OF SOCIAL SCIENCE
(VOL. 456)

CONTROL OF THE MEDIA IN THE UNITED STATES
An Annotated Bibliography

James R. Bennett

GARLAND PUBLISHING, INC. • NEW YORK & LONDON
1992

© 1992 James R. Bennett
All rights reserved

Library of Congress Cataloging-in-Publication Data

Bennett, James R., 1932–
   Control of the media in the United States : an annotated
bibliography / James R. Bennett.
     p.   cm. — (Garland reference library of social science ; vol. 456)
   Includes indexes.
   ISBN 0–8240–4438–X (alk. paper)
   1. Mass media—Censorship—United States—Bibliography.
2. Communication policy—United States—Bibliography. I. Title.
II. Series: Garland reference library of social science ; v. 456.
Z5634.U6B46   1992
[P96.C4]
016.3633'1'0973—dc20   91–26064
                                                                         CIP

Printed on acid-free, 250-year-life paper
Manufactured in the United States of America

To all independent investigative writers, scholars, magazines, book publishers, and organizations devoted to free inquiry and diversity, adversaries of dominating power and a passive public and press.

"Domination filters through a thousand capillaries of transmission, a million habitual meanings." Richard Ohmann, <u>Politics of Letters</u>

"There is little merit in hiding reality . . . however harsh it may be. 'We the people' will never build a better social order unless we first understand what we have been, what we are, and what we can become." Arthur Selwyn Miller, <u>The Modern Corporate State</u>

"The yearning for democracy comes with wanting to be an actor, not just an object, in the decision of one's fate, and the sense that all is not fore-ordained." Flora Lewis

CONTENTS

General Introduction	xi
List of Periodicals Cited with Acronyms	xix
Bibliographies and Indexes	1

I. The Structures of the Corporate State — 5
- Introduction — 6
- A. The Master Institutions — 9
  1. Corporate State — 9
  2. Corporations and Finance — 25
  3. Government: The Presidency — 33
  4. Government — 41
     a. Military — 41
     b. Intelligence — 48
  5. Anticommunism — 55
- B. The Secondary Institutions — 65
  1. Law — 65
  2. Education — 68
  3. Religion — 74
  4. Science and Technology — 77
  5. Medicine — 79
  6. Sports — 83

II. The Media Complex — 87
- Introduction — 88
- A. The Media — 92
  1. General — 92
  2. News — 126
  3. Corporations — 172
  4. Government — 189
- B. Advertising and Public Relations — 247
  1. The Mass Consumption System — 247
  2. Product Advertising — 269
  3. Corporate Image and Advocacy Advertising — 287
  4. Children and Advertising — 298
  5. Political Advertising (Campaigning) — 301
- C. Electronic Media — 310
  1. Commercial Broadcasting — 310
     a. Regulation — 310
     b. General — 318
     c. Television — 331
        (1) General — 331
        (2) Entertainment — 353
        (3) News — 368
        (4) Cable — 409
        (5) Children — 411
        (6) Religion — 418
  2. Public and Subscriber Broadcasting — 420

         3. Film and Theater   429
            a. Economics   429
            b. Entertainment and News   432
         4. Computers   449
      D. Print Media   454
         1. News Agencies/Wire Services   454
         2. General: Newspapers and Magazines   460
         3. Newspapers   470
            a. General   470
            b. Individual   490
            c. The New York Times   511
         4. Magazines   525
            a. General   525
            b. Individual   529
         5. Books   540
         6. Government and Corporate Reports   549
      E. Art and Music   562
         1. Art   562
         2. Music   564

III. Alternatives   569
     Introduction   570
     A. Media   577
     B. Advertising   604
     C. Broadcasting, Film, Video   606
     D. Print   626
     E. Art, Music, Literature   645

Author Index   649

Subject Index   685

ACKNOWLEDGMENTS

The reference, reserve, documents, and circulation staffs of the Mullins Library at the University of Arkansas were always supportive, particularly the interlibrary loan staff. Special thanks to Jennifer Hammer, Patsy Moore, and Elizabeth McKee. My library assistants, Angela Woodward, David Jennings, and (again) Ken Smedley, provided intelligent, reliable, and cheerful work of all kinds. They shared the search of this bibliography for a diverse public dialogue instead of a consciousness industry and an empowered citizenry rather than a hierarchy of domination.

GENERAL INTRODUCTION

Media Research

Cohen and Young describe four types of mass media research, which also apply to discourses and media of all kinds, the subject of this bibliography: "the first deals with questions of ownership and control; the second with the actual processes of selection and manufacturing of news; the third with the images and content eventually presented; and the fourth with the effects of this presentation" (491). This bibliography presents research on all of these aspects of communication, with particular emphasis upon their interrelationship as process. Ownership and control are perceived by the majority of the contributors as the fundamental condition of the other three categories and inseparable from them. Many theories dispute the nature of media content; each of these four areas has produced its own interpretations. In the field of news, for example, Herbert Gans has proposed four theories to explain news frames: 1) reflection or event-centered theories, claiming that news mirrors the world; 2) journalist-centered theories, "which explain the news as a product of professional news judgments"; 3) organizational theories, the conditions set by the finances, the commercial imperatives, the formal and informal rules of the journalism business; and 4) theories which locate news selection outside of and prior to professional training and news organizations, especially in the system of the dominant political power and ideology. All of these theories apply broadly to all media--the influences of the world out there, of professionalism, of bureaucracy, and of corporate and government and other sources of power--, and all are reflected in this bibliography, but the last is given special attention. Extrapolating from Gans on the news, media contents are "the exercise of power over the interpretation of reality" (80).

The Way Things Are and Might Be

This bibliography sets forth many of the dimensions and details of the United States corporate state. It is not the entire structure, which is too vast to be encompassed in one bibliography, and the system is always in a process of metamorphosis. Just as we do not yet understand everything about the human mind and body, but we steadily expand what is known about aging, cancer, or memory, while new diseases and epidemics appear, so we continue to increase our knowledge of the steel industry, the Pentagon, or television, while existing institutions evolve or disappear and new appear.

But it is a process with a direction, according to Arthur Selwyn Miller, who provides a gross anatomy that is both historical and systemic:

The giant corporation--that authoritarian, bureaucratic, and hierarchical private government--grows and spreads its influence. Political power moves to the national government, and within Washington to the executive branch and the national security managers. These growing concentrations of power need and increasingly support each other. An elite of top management and old wealth dominates the decision-making process, with the aid of the universities and the acquiescence of labor leadership. Big government, big business, big labor, and big universities come together in a symbiotic relationship that allows a small elite to run the whole system (Introduction, xiii).

Corporations, wealth, the national government, the executive branch, the National Security Council, Pentagon, CIA, with university and labor--this is "the monolith whose legal and constitutional foundations" Miller analyzes.

But something is missing, something important, from this description of the decision-making system, though its existence is implied, perhaps because Miller assumed its inevitability; I mean the systems of discourses that are the subject of this bibliography, the media. Budd and Ruben in Beyond Media make a useful distinction between the process of mass communication and mass media technologies as the basis for a broad model of communication technologies and institutions that depend upon mass communication for survival. "This extended view includes such activities as architecture, religion, popular art, museums, libraries, legitimate theater, restaurants, and political image-making" (Preface). I have followed this approach as far and as much as I could, since the corporate state reaches into all modes of communication from comic strips to public schools.

This complex web of mass media technologies in the mass communication process of the US corporate state functions both to perpetuate the status quo and simultaneously, as the press/ Fourth Estate, to balance and correct it. John Schaar describes the two activities--critical analysis of the way things are and utopian projection of the way things might be-- in practical terms. There is "the widespread feeling that we as a people, a culture, are messing up. A lot of our standard ways of doing and thinking, from welfare to warfare, are working badly, and we are making a lot of trouble for others and ourselves. Giving thought to what we are doing might reduce the damage and confusion" (9). But "giving thought" must include not only exposure of damage and confusion, of "messing up," but must enable us to envision a reconstituted society. Political theory "also always studies what might be other than it is," and this stresses "engagement, responsibility, action" (10). Like Miller's, Schaar's "guiding themes are authority, equality, justice, and citizenship," since "little in our culture encourages growth towards political adulthood" (1-2).

Daniel Fusfield believes we have only three options: "a slide into fascist authoritarianism" (from Watergate to Contragate); "continuation of the corporate state with some reforms to make it a little less malign" (militarism, unemployment, deficit and debt); or "democratic socialism" (redistributing wealth, decentralizing government and corporations, demilitarizing) (Miller xvi). (He omits a fourth option: continuation of the corporate state without reform.) Katznelson and Kesselman explain these options by a model of three ideologies. The dominant ideology, the "official creed," has "more power in the United States than in any other capitalist democracy" (29): 1) materialism, consumerism, and possessive individualism; 2) procedural democracy; 3) personal or private freedom; 4) patriotism; and 5) technology (30-32). The accommodationist ideology perceives a multitude of deficiencies in the US and would remedy them by bringing pressure to bear on the ruling authorities. It accepts the basic system, including acceptance of inequality and injustice, but would ameliorate conditions (48-50). The radical ideology goes beyond the accommodationist by the analysis of social evils as a manifestation of systematic structural failure--the problems linked and cumulative and therefore beyond piecemeal reform. The radical finds support among those who believe the ruling elites manipulate reform for their advantage, allowing only so much as to quiet opposition without significantly altering their privileges. This ideology has received such a relentless attack from the representatives of the dominant ideology, beginning with the Espionage Act of 1917, that it is virtually shattered as an alternative today (50-57).

In an argument basically like Miller's and Katznelson and Kesselman's regarding the arrangement of power in the US, but with more emphasis upon government autonomy, Gordon Clark and Michael Dear in State Apparatus believe that the US "system of structured political discourse," embodying "proper" political behavior and delegitimizing competing political views and behavior, facilitates capitalist accumulation and social control (Ch. 5). But state legitimacy based upon the interests of privileged individuals and groups creates conflicts and crises unresolved by recourse to consumerism to satisfy ideals (Ch. 8). The complicity of the corporate state in reproducing economic and political inequality clashes with ideals of equity and social justice, and undermines consensual claims by the ruling elites. "In the absence of a strong moral claim of legitimacy . . . the state's only recourse, apart from outright violence, is to a consumption-based politics" (xi).

But these realities do not leave Clark and Dear in dismay over the possibility of achieving equity and justice. Rather they conceive of the state as a potential instrument of these values (Ch. 9). "It cannot be assumed that the state will be resistant to social justice in every instance. There are many examples of the state leading social change, particularly in Western Europe" (xi). The governments of Spain and especially Portugal recently "led social reform, initiated greater equality, and fundamentally changed the underlying social order and even the national constitutions," without the impetus of a popular revolt and "against sections of the ruling elite" (187). In the US, Volunteers In Service To America (VISTA) mobilized poor Appalachian communities against other state agencies (186). While law is recognized as a powerful instrument "in the reproduction of the capitalist system," at the same time it is not "simply, or even solely, the domain of the elites." In addition to the interests of power, law embodies ideals of a good society which "give precedence to individual consent" (x). Thus these authors seek legitimacy for the corporate state in an alternative vision of the state as a potentially "liberating agent of social justice" (194). Theirs is no Pollyanna hopefulness, however. They find "few other examples of liberating crisis-oriented state apparatus" in the US, and they acknowledge that "most support the <u>status quo</u>" and some (the CIA, for example) support repression.

In the literary tradition can be found strong support at least for a vision of emancipation from manifold bondages and in defense of a more just society. From Melville, Brooks and Henry Adams, and Twain, to Dreiser and Steinbeck, to Pynchon and Doctorow writers have rejected nationalism and acquisitiveness in search of an authentic foundation for authority and loyalty in individuals and institutions. Instead of cynicism, rapacious competition, acquisitive individualism, racism, sexism, and imperialism, many of our intellectuals defended whatever sustained genuine freedom and justice, whether in personal lives or in institutions.

Similarly, Steven Shiffrin in <u>The First Amendment, Democracy, and Romance</u> looks both to Emerson and Whitman and to the state apparatus of the Supreme Court in the future to defend speech for all through a vital respect for dissenters. Like Clark and Dear, Shiffrin fully recognizes how much the ideal differs from reality, how much freedom of speech has "been subtly denigrated in recent first amendment theory and seriously abused in practice" (5-6, see Curry, Demac). He knows the history of newspaper failure to defend dissenters from political and social orthodoxies (see Lofton). But he also believes that the best of the nation is revealed by contrast to the repression of dictatorships--Nazis, El Salvador --, and that the foremost foundation for that vision is the First Amendment, which to Shiffrin affirms above all "the protection of dissent and its nurturance." That vision is earliest and best expressed by Ralph Waldo Emerson in his Divinity School Address of 1838, whose ringing denunciation of illegitimate authority and convention and demand for individuals to speak out against them serves Shiffrin for his own defense of dissenters, the unorthodox, individualists, rebels. In the frame of the argument of Clark and Dear's <u>State Apparatus</u>, a Supreme Court imbued with the spirit of this First Amendment vision would become a more consistent agency for equity and justice.

These realities and these hopes are represented in this bibliography. In 1986 a few more than three million or 1.6% of the population possessed a net worth of $3.8 trillion, 28.5% of the nation's personal wealth, and controlled $4.3 trillion, up over a trillion dollars since 1984 ("America's"). In 1982, according to Ben Bagdikian in <u>The Media Monopoly</u>, 50 corporations controlled most of the media business; by 1987 the number was 27. And his book is packed with illustrations of how this power is employed in the interests of the media corporations. Clark and Dear move from a description of the A, B, and C vocabularies of the "Newspeak" of George Orwell's novel <u>1984</u>, which were designed not only to make dissenting speech impossible but to eradicate dissenting thought, to the recognition that the state is actively and massively "engaged in the linguistic structuring of political and social reality" (84). The dominant elites use language and information to gain "power and control through the coercion and domination" which access to political language and the media permits them (102).

Despite these sobering realities, many of the authors cited in this bibliography express ideals of a future US founded upon discourses and media responsive to the real diversity of needs and interests throughout the nation. Clark and Dear ask: "If the state is in fact autonomous, if it can create its own legitimacy through clientism and control of the interpretive organs of society and, if it has its own objectives of reproduction and power, how is it different from organized crime (such as the Mafia)?" (188). The readings in this bibliography describe a corporate state ominously separate from the democratic political process intended to direct it (Parts I and II), but they also suggest how, because it is not the Mafia, the state might still be guided toward equity and justice through more diverse, democratic education and media (Part III).

Arrangement

Part I presents some 550 books in corroboration and elaboration of Miller's conception of the connections of concentrated power, from Standard Oil to environmental damage to the White House to technology and education, and of Schaar's conviction that people lack "a feeling of being at home in a place they have helped make and where their voices matter" (14). (Numerous additional details were provided in my earlier bibliography, <u>Control of Information in the United States</u>.)

Part II encompasses the specific subject of this bibliography, the role of all discourses and media in the big business/ big government symbiotic relationship. Here will be found over 3,500 books and articles not only on NBC as a corporation within a larger corporation (RCA) within a larger corporation (GE) but on the contribution <u>Saturday Evening Post</u> stories made to the acceptance of such a concentration of power and the values that power assumes. A journalism that functions mainly as a major, but still one more, institution of the corporate state is called "statist" by Robert Manoff. In contrast is "civil" journalism, the voice of individual citizens. Manoff sees a connection between statist journalism and a strong antidemocratic current in which leaders, managers, and administrators run the government and the media.

Part III counteracts and balances I and II, offering almost 600 works on alternatives to the dominant institutions that either already exist and might be expanded or might be created new. On the assumption that diversity and competition of ideas are essential to democracy, the reformers in Part III defend, for example, the independent voices of subscriber-

supported radio or advocate expanded investigative reporting and documentaries and critical journalistic reviews, or they recommend a new public broadcasting system composed of divergent political ideologies, while the radicals attack the institutions themselves--commercialism, militarism, inequality.
   The bibliography contains almost 5000 entries. However, I have omitted much. A separate section on education, discourse, and media had to be dropped because of space. Self-censorship, so important to social control and ideological hegemony, is very difficult to study. As Bagdikian observes, "No one can know how many editors of books, magazines, broadcasts, screenplays, and newspapers . . . think about possible damage to the parent corporation [and to themselves!] and act accordingly." I consider the evidence of this bibliography, therefore, only the tip of the iceberg; my chief hope is that it will inspire expanded investigation of the corporate state.

Bibliographical Methods
   Although I did survey several indexes and bibliographies, which are listed at the beginning of the bibliography, my chief method was the examination of magazines. (The list of journals surveyed and their acronyms follows this introduction). I did not depend upon the mainstream indexes because they tend to survey mainstream journals, which means that they are part of the phenomena of discourse control under study by this bibliography. For example, after ten years of publication, Mother Jones was still not indexed by one of the most often-consulted library reference books in the US, the Reader's Guide to Periodical Literature. The Reader's Guide indexed the Family Handyman and the National Review, but not MJ, perhaps because the review of the magazine in Magazines for Libraries slammed its "soap box defense of everyone's rights and privileges" (Hochschild). The only index I could rely upon for a relatively full listing of magazines seriously skeptical and systematically investigative of the nexus of power is The Alternative Press Index (and see the Inland [Book Company] Subject Catalog). I also surveyed Dissertation Abstracts International under the topics of Cinema, Communication, and Journalism.
   I have emphasized post-World War II events and scholarship, since that is the period of reaction against the economic reforms of the 1930s, the accelerated concentration of economic power, and the rise of the Cold War, but also of significant advances in civil rights and electronic communications. I have further sought to make the bibliography as current as possible. For example, of the approximately 846 entries in the commercial broadcasting section (items 2116-2961), 575 were published between 1980 and 1991, and of the 77 entries in the general section on newspapers and magazines (3270-3346), 62 were published during this past decade.
   Finally, I have followed James Harner's "commentary" approach to annotating in On Compiling an Annotated Bibliography. Instead of a paraphrase, I generally state what each item is about, often reduced succinctly to the thesis.

Works Cited

"America's 3.3 Million Wealthiest Control $4.3 Trillion." *AG* (August 23, 1990) 1C.

Bagdikian, Ben. *The Media Monopoly.* Boston: Beacon, 1987.

Budd, Richard W., and Brent D. Ruben, eds. *Beyond Media: New Approaches to Mass Communication.* Rochelle Park, NJ: Hayden, 1979.

Clark, Gordon, and Michael Dear. *State Apparatus: Structures and Language of Legitimacy.* Boston: Allen & Unwin, 1984.

Cohen, Stanley, and Jock Young, eds. *The Manufacture of News.* Beverly Hills: Sage, 1981.

Gans, Herbert. *Deciding What's News.* New York: Pantheon, 1979.

Hochschild, Adam. "Of Indexes and Editors." *MJ* 12.5 (June-July 1987) 8.

Katznelson, Ira, and Mark Kesselman. *The Politics of Power.* 2nd ed. New York: Harcourt Brace Jovanovich, 1979.

Lofton, John. *The Press as Guardian of the First Amendment.* Columbia, SC: U of South Carolina P, 1980.

Manoff, Robert K. "Reporters Covering the Government All Too Often Succumb to the Urge to Run It." *Deadline* 4.2 (Mar.-Apr. 1989) 7-8.

Miller, Arthur S. *The Modern Corporate State.* Westport: Greenwood, 1976.

Schaar, John. *Legitimacy in the Modern State.* New Brunswick: Transaction, 1981.

Shiffrin, Steven. *The First Amendment, Democracy, and Romance.* Cambridge, MA: Harvard UP, 1990.

MASTER LIST OF PERIODICALS IN ALPHABETICAL ORDER BY ACRONYM

AA	Advertising Age
AAA	American-Arab Affairs
AAPSS	American Academy of Political and Social Science Annals
A&S	Administration and Society
ABAJ	American Bar Association Journal
Academe	Academe (formerly AAUP Bulletin)
AC	Against the Current
ACon	Atlanta Constitution
Adbusters	Adbusters Quarterly
AF	American Film
AFJ	Armed Forces Journal
AFS	Armed Forces and Society
AG	Arkansas Gazette
AHV	Agriculture and Human Values
AJ	Amicus Journal
AJS	American Journal of Sociology
Alert!	Alert! Focus on Central America
ALR	Akron Law Review
AltM	Alternative Media
AM	Atlantic Monthly
AmT	American Teacher
AN	Akwesasne Notes
AP	American Psychologist
APSR	American Political Science Review
Aquarian	Aquarian Times (later Aquarian, 1969-1985?)
AQ	American Quarterly
AR	Antioch Review
ArT	Army Times
AS	American Studies
ASE	Alternative Sources of Energy
ASR	American Sociological Review
AT	Arkansas Traveler
Au	Audubon
AULR	American U Law Review
AUR	Air University Review
AWPR	Atlas World Press Review
BAS	Bulletin of the Atomic Scientists
BB	Bulletin of Bibliography
BCAS	Bulletin of Concerned Asian Scholars
Bf	Blackfriars
BG	Boston Globe
BI	Barricada Internacional
BJS	Berkeley Journal of Sociology
BP	Black Panther (1969-1983)
BPEJ	Business and Professional Ethics Journal
BPP	Bulletin of Peace Proposals
Br	Broadcasting
BR	The Brookings Review
BRJ	Bill of Rights Journal
BS	Brazilian Studies
BSR	Business and Society Review

BSun	The Baltimore Sun
BT	Business Today
Bth	Breakthrough
BULR	Boston U Law Review
Buncombe	Buncombe: A Review of Baltimore Journalism (1972)
BW	Business Week
CA	Communication Abstracts
CAA	Central American Alert
CAB	Central American Bulletin
CAIB	Covert Action Information Bulletin
C&C	Christianity and Crisis
CAR	Central American Report
CarlJR	Carleton Journalism Review (1977-1980)
CC	Common Cause Magazine
CCR	Center for Constitutional Rights
CCRev	The Critical Communication Review
CE	College English
CEAF	The CEA Forum
CFL	Conservation Foundation Newsletter
Change	Change: The Magazine of Higher Learning
Channels	Channels: The Business of Communications
ChC	Christian Century
CHE	Chronicle of Higher Education
ChJR	Chicago Journalism Review (1968-1975)
CHQ	The Churchman's Human Quest (now The Human Quest)
Cineaste	Cineaste
CJ	Cinema Journal
CJC	Canadian Journal of Communications
CJPST	Canadian Journal of Political & Social Theory
CJR	Columbia Journalism Review
CL	Civil Liberties
CLR	Civil Liberties Review (1973-1979)
CLRv	Columbia Law Review
CM	The Center Magazine
CMC	Chicago Media Critic
CMJ	Critical Mass Journal (later, Critical Mass Energy Journal) (1977-1983)
CMon	Communication Monographs
CN	Censorship Notes
CNN	CCCO News Notes
Com	Commentary
ComLR	Communication Law Review
Comm	Communication
CommR	Communication Research
CongQ	Congressional Quarterly
CongR	Congressional Record
Cont	Contemporaries
ContM	Contemporary Marxism
Conv	Convergence
Count	Counterattack
CP	Communication Perspectives
CQ	Communication Quarterly (formerly Today's Speech)
CR	Consumer's Reports
CRPV	Current Research on Peace and Violence
Cs	Counterspy (now The National Reporter)

CS	Critical Sociology (formerly The Insurgent Sociologist)
CSM	Christian Science Monitor
CSMC	Critical Studies in Mass Communication
CSoc	Contemporary Sociology
CSQ	Clinton St. Quarterly
CSSJ	Central States Speech Journal
CSt	Cultural Studies
Ct	Cubatimes (1974-1985)
CT	Chicago Tribune
CUF	Columbia U Forum
CulC	Cultural Critique
Current	Current: For People in Public Telecommunications
CW	The Catholic Worker
CY	Communication Yearbook
Daedalus	Daedalus: Journal of the American Adademy of Arts & Sciences
DAI	Dissertation Abstracts International
DC	Daily Camera
Deadline	Deadline: The Press and the Arms Race
Discourse	Discourse: Journal for Theoretical Studies in Media and Culture
Dissent	Dissent
DJ	The Democratic Journalist
DM	The Defense Monitor
DMN	Dallas Morning News
DP	Denver Post
DS	Dollars & Sense
EA	Environmental Action
E&P	Editor and Publisher
Ed	Edcentric (1971-1979)
EF	Educational Forum
EIJ	Earth Island Journal
EJ	English Journal
EL	Educational Leadership
ELJ	Emory Law Journal
ER	Educational Record
ERev	Evergreen Review
Esq	Esquire
ETC	Etcetera
EW	Education Week
Extra!	Extra! A Publication of FAIR
FA	Foreign Affairs
FC	Film Comment
FCBJ	Federal Communications Bar Journal
FCNL	FCNL Washington Newsletter
Feed	Feedback
Fel	Fellowship
FemS	Feminist Studies
FfA	Facts for Action
FI	Free Inquiry
FICR	Freedom of Information Center Report
FM	Focus Midwest (1962-1984)
FoM	Food Monitor (1976-1984) (1986-)
For	Fortune

ForP	Foreign Policy
Forum	Forum: The Newsletter of People for the American Way
FP	First Principles: National Security and Civil Liberties
FS	Free Speech
FSN	Freedom of Speech Newsletter
FSULR	Florida State U Law Review
FSY	Free Speech Yearbook
FTC	FTC Watch
Fu	The Futurist
Gaz	Gazette: International Journal for Mass Communication Studies
GIQ	Government Information Quarterly
GLJ	Georgetown Law Journal
GR	The Green Revolution
Granma	Granma
GrE	Greenpeace Examiner
Green	Greenpeace
GS	Grand Street
Gu	Guatamala!
Guard	The Guardian
GZ	Ground Zero
HA	Health Affairs
HAM	Harvard Alumni Magazine
Har	Harper's Magazine
HBR	Harvard Business Review
HC	Hartford Courant
HCLQ	Hastings Constitutional Law Quarterly
HER	Harvard Educational Review
HI	Humanities International
HiS	Humanities in Society
HJR	Hawaii Journalism Review (1971-1973)
HL	Health Letter
HLJ	Hastings Law Journal
HLR	Harvard Law Review
HR	Human Rights
HRLJ	Human Rights Law Journal
HS	Humanities in the South
Hum	The Humanist
IBCB	Interracial Books for Children Bulletin (1966-1985?)
IC	Index on Censorship
IFSW	I.F. Stone's Weekly (later I.F. Stone's Bi-Weekly) (1953-1971)
IJIC	International Journal of Intelligence & Counterintelligence
IJWP	International Journal on World Peace
ILJ	Indiana Law Journal
IM	Index Magazine
Independent	The Independent Film and Video Monthly
Inq	Inquiry (1978-1982)
IPSN	International Peace Studies Newsletter
IPSR	International Political Science Review
IR	Islamic Revolution

IREJ	The Investigative Reporters and Editors Journal
IRPV	Instant Research on Peace and Violence (now Current Research on Peace and Violence)
IS	The Insurgent Sociologist (now Critical Sociology)
IST	Issues in Science and Technology
ItS	Inside the System
ITT	In These Times
IW	Industry Week
JA	Journalists' Affairs
JACR	Journal of Applied Communications Research
JAE	Journal of Aesthetic Education
JAH	Journal of American History
JAR	Journal of Advertising Research
JBE	Journal of Business Ethics
JC	Jump Cut: A Review of Contemporary Media
JCA	Journal of Contemporary Asia
JCH	Journal of Community Health
JCI	Journal of Communications Inquiry
JE	Journalism Education
JEE	Journal of Economic Education
JEL	Journal of Economic Literature
JFAS	Journal of the Federation of American Scientists
JFV	Journal of Film and Video
JH	Journalism History
JIA	Journal of International Affairs
JM	Journalism Monographs
JMME	Journal of Mass Media Ethics
JN	Journalists Newsletter (1970)
JoB	Journal of Broadcasting and Electronic Media (formerly Journal of Broadcasting)
JoC	Journal of Communication
JoCS	Journal of Communication Studies
JPC	Journal of Popular Culture
JPHP	Journal of Public Health Policy
JPR	Journal of Peace Research
JPS	Journal of Palestine Studies
JQ	Journalism Quarterly
JSH	Journal of Social History
JSR	Journal of Social Reconstruction
JUFVA	Journal of the University Film and Video Association (formerly Journal of the University Film Association)
JW	Justice Watch (formerly Justice Department Watch) (1972-1985; 1986- intermittently)
LAER	Latin America and Empire Report
L&S	Language and Style
LAP	Latin American Perspectives
LARR	Latin American Research Review
LASAF	Latin American Studies Association Forum
LAT	Los Angeles Times
LAWR	Latin American Weekly Report
LC-J	Louisville Courier-Journal
LCP	Law and Contemporary Problems
Link	The Link

LJ	Library Journal
LOOT	Lies of Our Times (1990-)
Lucha	Lucha/Struggle
Mam	Mesoamerica
M&M	Media and Methods
M&V	Media and Values
MC	The Media Critic
MCRY	Mass Communication Review Yearbook
MCS	Media, Culture and Society
MedF	Media File
Media	Mediactive
MedM	Media Monitor
MedW	MediaWatch (1976-1981)
MEF	Middle East Forum
MEI	Middle East Insight
MEN	Mother Earth News
MER	Middle East Reports (formerly Merip Reports)
MGW	Manchester Guardian Weekly
MH	Miami Herald
MilR	Military Review
MJ	Mother Jones
MJR	Montana Journalism Review (1958-1979)
MLR	Michigan Law Review
MM	Multinational Monitor
MO	The Minority of One (1959-1968)
MonR	Monthly Review
MORE	MORE (1971-1978)
MQR	Michigan Quarterly Review
MR	Monthly Review
MRev	Military Review
Multilingua	Multilingua: Journal of Cross-Cultural Communication
Na	The Nation
NA	The Nonviolent Activist
NACLA	NACLA: Report on the Americas
NaR	The National Reporter (formerly CounterSpy)
NaRev	National Review
NB	Nation's Business
NCLR	North Carolina Law Review
NCTE	National Council of Teachers of English
NCTVN	National Coalition on Television Violence News
NEAT	The NEA Today
NewT	New Times
NicP	Nicaraguan Perspectives
NIF	Newsletter on Intellectual Freedom
NJ	National Journal
NL	New Leader
NLR	Nebraska Law Review
NMA	Not Man Apart
NM&L	The News Media and the Law
NMPN	The New Manhattan Project Newsletter
NmR	Nieman Reports
NNN	No Nuclear News (1977-1984)
NO	National Observer
NOR	New Oxford Review

NP	New Politics
NPS	New Political Science
NR	New Republic
NRDCN	Natural Resources Defense Council Newsline
NRJ	Newspaper Research Journal
NS	New Statesman
NSEN	New Schools Exchange Newsletter (1969-1976)
NT	Nuclear Times
NuA	Nutrition Action
Nuc	Nucleus
NULR	Northwestern U Law Review
NUT	New University Thought (1960-1971)
NWCR	Naval War College Review
NY	The New Yorker
NYRB	New York Review of Books
NYSJM	New York State Journal of Medicine
NYT	The New York Times
NYTM	New York Times Magazine
NYTRB	New York Times Review of Books
NYUJLP	New York U Journal of International Law and Politics
OAH	OAH Newsletter
Ob	The Observer
OLR	Oregon Law Review
ON	Organizing Notes (1977-1983)
OOB	Off Our Backs
ORK	Our Right to Know
OT	Oakland Tribune
OWR	Old Westbury Review
Pa	Parade
PA	Political Affairs
PacS	Pacific Spectator
Pan	Pandora
P&C	Peace and Change: A Journal of Peace Research
P&S	Physics and Society
PaR	Partisan Review
PAR	Propaganda Analysis Review
Pb	Playboy
PC	Public Citizen
PCME	Popular Culture and Media Events
PCP	Political Communication and Persuasion
PDK	Phi Delta Kappan
PE	Politics and Education (1978-1980)
PI	Philadelphia Inquirer
PJR	Philadelphia Journalism Review (1971-1974)
Plow	Plowshare
PLR	Pepperdine Law Review
Pn	Panorama
PO	Public Opinion
PolSQ	Political Science Quarterly
POQ	Public Opinion Quarterly
PoR	Policy Review
PoV	Point of View (1968-)
PP	Political Psychology
Pr	The Press

PR	Propaganda Review
Practice	Practice: The Journal of Politics, Economics, Psychology, Sociology, and Culture
PRev	Peace Review
PRJ	Public Relations Journal
Prog	The Progressive
PS	Political Studies
PSQ	Presidential Studies Quarterly
PTR	Public Telecommunications Review (1973-1980)
PuAR	Public Affairs Review
PubI	Public Interest
QJS	Quarterly Journal of Speech
QRD	Quarterly Review of Doublespeak
QREB	Quarterly Review of Economics and Business
QRFS	Quarterly Review of Film Studies
RA	Report on the Americas (NACLA)
RadA	Radical America
RadS	Radical Software
RadSc	Radical Science Journal (UK, 1974-)
Rain	Rain: Journal of Appropriate Technology
Ram	Ramparts (1962-1968)
R&C	Race and Class
Recon	Recon
Rep	The Reporter (1949-1968)
RHR	Radical History Review
RKFA	The Right to Know and the Freedom to Act
RMN	Rocky Mountain News
Rn	Reason
RoP	Review of Politics
RP	Radical Philosophy
RR	Rhetoric Review
RRJ	Ryerson Review of Journalism
RS	Rolling Stone
RSCJ	Review of Southern California Journalism (1971-1975)
RSQ	Rhetoric Society Quarterly
RT	Radical Teacher
RW	Revolutionary Worker
SAIS	SAIS Review
Sal	Salvanet: Newsletter of Crispaz
S&D	Socialism and Democracy
S&S	School and Society
SANE	Sane World
SAR	Soviet-American Review
Sc&S	Science and Society
Science	Science
SCLR	Santa Clara Law Review
ScP	Science for the People
ScR	School Review
Screen	Screen
SD	Seven Days (1977-1980)
SDY	San Diego Union
SE	Screen Education
Sem	Seminar
SEP	Saturday Evening Post

SF	Social Forces
SFBG	San Francisco Bay Guardian
SFC	San Francisco Chronicle
SFE	San Francisco Examiner
SFJR	San Francisco Journalism Review
Signs	Signs
SJMN	San Jose Mercury News
SL	Studies on the Left
SLJR	St. Louis Journalism Review
SLP-D	St. Louis Post-Dispatch
SLULJ	St. Louis U Law Journal
SM	Stanford Magazine
SMCJ	Southwestern Mass Communication Journal
SocP	Social Policy
SocPr	Social Praxis
SocR	Socialist Review
Soj	Sojourners
SP	Social Problems
SPE	Studies in Political Economy
SP-I	Seattle Post-Intelligencer
SPLCR	Student Press Law Center Report
SQ	The Sociological Quarterly
SR	Saturday Review
SSCJ	Southern Speech Communication Journal
SSN	Space and Security News
SSQ	Social Science Quarterly
ST	Social Text
STP	Social Theory and Practice
TA	Thought and Action: The NEA Higher Education Journal
TCJR	Twin Cities Journalism Review (1972-1977)
TE	Today's Education
Telos	Telos: A Quarterly Journal of Critical Thought
Thorn	Thorn: Connecticut Valley Media Review (1971)
TLS	Times Literary Supplement
TM	This Magazine (formerly This Magazine Is About Schools)
TO	Texas Observer
TOv	Take Over
TQ	Television Quarterly
TR	Technology Review
TRA	Television/Radio Age
Trans	Transaction
TS	Today's Speech (now Communication Quarterly)
TSoc	Theory & Society
TVG	TV Guide
TW	Tulsa World
TxM	Texas Monthly
TynR	Tyndall Report
UCLAE	UCLA Education
UCLALR	UCLA Law Review
UM	The Unsatisfied Man: A Review of Colorado Journalism (1970-1974)
Unity	Unity
UR	Utne Reader

USNIP	U.S. Naval Institute Proceedings
USNWR	U. S. News and World Report
Voice	A Voice of the Voiceless
VS	Vital Speeches
VV	Village Voice
W&D	Works and Days
WC	Written Communication
WH	Whole Earth
Win	Win (1965-1984)
Wit	The Witness
WJR	Washington Journalism Review
WJSC	Western Journal of Speech Communication
WLR	Wisconsin Law Review
WM	Washington Monthly
WoP	World Politics
WorkP	Working Papers (1973-1983)
World	The World: Journal of the Unitarian Universal Association
WP	Washington Post
WPF	World Policy Forum
WPJ	World Policy Journal
WPR	World Press Review
WQ	Wilson Quarterly
WRH	Washington Report on the Hemisphere
WS	The Washington Spectator (formerly Washington Watch)
WSJ	Wall Street Journal
WULQ	Washington U Law Quarterly
Wv	Worldview
YLJ	Yale Law Journal
Z	Z (formerly Zeta)

Control of the Media
in the
United States

BIBLIOGRAPHIES AND INDEXES

These are general in content; specific subject bibliographies appear with their category.

Alternative Press Index. Baltimore: Alternative Press Center, 1969.
The index to alternative and radical publications. [Indispensable to research on media control.]

Arts and Humanities Citation Index. Philadelphia: Institute for Scientific Information, 1978.
The 1986 issue indexed approximately 1,300 journals fully and another 5,600 partially.

Bennett, James R. Control of Information in the United States. Westport, CT: Meckler, 1987. 587.
The 2,943 entries bring "together research on the system as a whole, the network from banks and White House and Pentagon to education and the media." The main sections are "Anticommunism and Anti-Sovietism," "The Complex" (the interlocking powers), "Corporations," "Government," "Pentagon," "Intelligence Agencies," and "Global." Subsections under each chapter heading enumerate aspects of the topic. Indexed by author and subject (3,700 topics).

Bennett, James R. "Domination of Information in the United States: An Annotated Bibliography of Selected Books." BoB 43.2 (1986) 82-99.
Almost 200 entries divided into six categories: the complex, anti-communism, corporations, government, military, intelligence establishment. [Some of these books are included in the present collection.]

Bosmajian, Haig A. Censorship, Libraries, and the Law. New York: Neal-Schuman, 1983. 217.
Compilation of school library censorship cases.

Communication Abstracts. Beverly Hills, CA: Sage, 1978.
Quarterly.
Each issue offers about 250 abstracts of articles from about 100 journals and 50 recent books.

Dissertation Abstracts International. Ann Arbor, MI: U Microfilms International, 1938.
The major source of information on doctoral dissertations worldwide; appears in two major segments, A, "The Humanities and Social Sciences," and B, "The Sciences and Engineering."

Dorman, William A., Robert Karl Manoff, and Jennifer Weeks. American Press Coverage of U.S.-Soviet Relations, the

Soviet Union, Nuclear Weapons, Arms Control, and National Security: A Bibliography. New York: Center for War, Peace, and the News Media, 1988. 102.
Lists "more than 1,000" books and articles dating from 1965 dealing either with the performance of the press in these areas or modifying conditions (i.e. secrecy, censorship). Divided into six chapters: "The News Media and U.S. Foreign and Defense Policy," "Control of Information," "The Media and the Nuclear Question," "The Media and the Soviet Union," "Propaganda and Disinformation," and "The Media and the Vietnam War."

Free Speech Yearbook. Annual Bibliography.

Hoffmann, Frank. Intellectual Freedom & Censorship: An Annotated Bibliography. Metuchen, NJ: Scarecrow, 1989. 244.
Nine hundred entries arranged in five parts: theoretical foundations, court cases, four professions especially involved, individuals and groups either pro or anti censorship, cases in the mass media. Each section introduced with a historical essay. Name and subject indexes.

Humanities Index. New York: Wilson, 1975.
The leading cumulative index to English-language periodicals in the humanities. Previous to 1975 a part of Social Sciences and Humanities Index (1965-1974). Available through WILSONLINE and the CD-ROM Search System, WILSONDISC.

Index to Journals in Communication Studies Through 1985.
Annandale, VA: Speech Communication Assoc., 1987. 645.
Indexes fifteen journals: QJS, CM, etc.

The Left Index. Santa Cruz, CA: Reference & Research Services P, 1982.
A "quarterly index to periodicals of the left" organized by authors and topics, but also includes book reviews and journals. No. 4 gives a cumulated subject index. In 1986 indexed 83 journals mainly small press, most published in US, Great Britain, or Australia.

LLBA, Linguistics & Language Behavior Abstracts, 1985. (Formerly Language & Language Behavior Abstracts, 1967-1984.)
Includes a very brief section on mass media that includes advertising, but most items (April 1990) on foreign countries.

Maier, Mark, and Dan Gilroy, eds. Reading Lists in Radical Social Science. New York: Monthly Review/Union for Radical Political Economics, 1982. 179.
The lists range "from short introductory course outlines to more detailed graduate level course syllabi," organized by subject matter: Marxism and Methodology, the State, Women, Labor, the Corporation, Racism, Law, etc. This collection is the fourth in a series dating back to 1971, formerly titled Reading Lists in Radical Political Economics.

BIBLIOGRAPHIES AND INDEXES

Marxism and the Mass Media: Toward a Basic Bibliography. 7 vols. New York: International General, 1976 (Bagnolet, France: International Mass Media Research Center).
"An ongoing bibliographic research series to provide a global, multi-lingual annotated documentation of past and current marxist studies on all aspects of communications. Each issue contains more than 500 entries indexed by subject, author, and country."

Marxism and the Mass Media: Toward a Basic Bibliography, 6-7. Bagnolet, Fr.: International Mass Media Research Center, 1980. 122.
Part of a continuing series for "a global multilingual annotated bibliography of marxist, left and critical studies on all aspects of communication and culture." One hundred sixty-six entries containing 516 texts with subject, author, and country indexes.

McCoy, Ralph. Freedom of the Press: An Annotated Bibliography. Carbondale: Southern Illinois UP, 1968. 526.
An "annotated bibliography of some 8,000 books, pamphlets, journal articles, films, and other material relating to freedom of the press in English-speaking countries, from the beginning of printing to the present." Supplement (1979).

Skidmore, Gail, and Theodore Spahn. From Radical Left to Extreme Right: A Bibliography of Current Periodicals of Protest, Controversy, Advocacy or Dissent. 3rd ed., rev. Metuchen, NJ: Scarecrow, 1987. 491.
The second edition contained 1,324 periodicals in three volumes; this edition contains only 280 in one.

Social Sciences Citation Index. Philadelphia: Institute for Scientific Information, 1973.
International, interdisciplinary, enables user to identify related writings (reviews, etc.) by indicating sources in which a work by a given author has been cited. A subject search may also be made. Covers about 2,000 journals.

Social Sciences Index. New York: Wilson, 1975.
Previously part of Social Sciences and Humanities Index (1965-1974). Available online through WILSONLINE and the CD-ROM Search System, WILSONDISC.

Source Collective, ed. The Source Catalog: No. 1, Communications. Chicago: Swallow, 1971. 120.
About 1400 annotated entries of US left and movement groups organized by subject: mass media, art, music, theatre, film, TV, video, radio, periodicals, printing, libraries, and community communications. Alphabetical index.

I. THE STRUCTURES OF THE CORPORATE STATE   1-545

Introduction

A. The Master Institutions   1-414
   1. Corporate State   1-108
   2. Corporations and Finance   109-166
   3. Government: The Presidency   167-221
   4. Government   222-334
      a. Military   222-271
      b. Intelligence   272-334
   5. Anticommunism   335-414

B. The Secondary Institutions   415-545
   1. Law   415-436
   2. Education   437-478
   3. Religion   479-497
   4. Science and Technology   498-511
   5. Medicine   512-530
   6. Sports   531-545

THE STRUCTURES OF THE CORPORATE STATE

INTRODUCTION

Arthur Selwyn Miller gives a broad description of a corporation that includes not only the business corporation but "such a congeries of institutions as the church, the university, the 'think tank,' the union, cities (municipal corporations), the foundation, modern guilds (for example, the American Bar Association and American Medical Association), political parties, cartels--the list is long," most of which are "controlled by oligarchies" (20). These groups of private power are closely intertwined with government power, a complex and sometimes conflicting alliance Miller labels "corporativism," especially "the fusion of political and economic power" (29). The US has become corporate America; its economy is "dominated by the supercorporation, which finds a ready ally in the rise of 'positive' government" (35).

Although corporativism was not envisioned by the Constitution, and the Supreme Court said in 1905 that corporations are "incorporated for the benefit of the public" (38), after the Civil War the corporation shifted from a public agency to "an institution for purely private gain" (40). Miller's undertaking is to explain how corporativism became "living" law in a profound alteration of the Constitution, and how it was and is promulgated and enforced by a "flow of decisions" by private and public officials which constitute the "legal nexus between political and economic power" (31). His basic explanation is that economic power means social and political power, that "law follows power," and that law functions "to compel adherence to the values of those who hold economic wealth" (41). This influence extends to the Supreme Court. Two early cases, for example, <u>Fletcher v. Peck</u> and the <u>Dartmouth College Case</u>, illustrate how litigation was employed to persuade the Court to advance corporations and property rights (42-43), which in <u>Fletcher</u> protected fraud over ethics and public welfare and "'paved the way for the Robber Barons'" (44). The gradual capture by corporations of the due process guaranteed in the Fourteenth Amendment for freed slaves and other human "persons" is another notable example. Economic pressure brought favorable rulings; despite "the myth to the contrary, government intervention in economic affairs has always been the norm in American history--but to help, not to regulate, business enterprise" (44).

A parallel argument is constructed by Reynolds and Henslin in <u>American Society</u>. In the Preface to their book, they describe the US as structured upon "master" and "secondary" institutions. The master institutions deal with the economic, political, and military orders. "We assume, as did C. Wright Mills, that it is within the upper echelons of these three institutions that the real power in American society resides" and that "the highest reaches of the economic, military, and

THE STRUCTURES OF THE CORPORATE STATE 7

political orders interlock and overlap to form a military-industrial-political complex or what Mills termed The Power Elite." But while recognizing the "near-symbiotic nature of the relationship between these three institutions, we argue the thesis that the economic institution is the master institution of American society."

This economic power is no "free market" society, which is only a "social fiction" serving ruling interests. It is, rather, "a market society dominated by a few corporate giants." We live in a society "whose principal form of social organization remains . . . the short-term, depersonalized, specific, and atomistic contract but whose dominant structural feature has become the ascendancy of large-scale, bureaucratic organizations. In short, we live in a corporate capitalistic society of organizational bureaucracy."

The secondary institutions deal with US society's scientific, religious, medical, educational, familial, and legal institutions. The economic, political, and military institutions have "either relegated" the subordinate institutions "to a position of minor importance" or have "made them subservient to the needs of the military-industrial-political complex." These "secondary institutions generally serve the needs and follow the dictates of American society's economic order and have become, in our words, mere appendages to the [corporate bureaucratic] market."

I have modified their formulation in several ways, most conspicuously by concentrating upon an institution not discussed in their book--the media appendage. Anticommunism (especially Sovietphobia) as a dominant institution augments their conception of an interlocking economic-political-military order, as do the intelligence establishment and sports enlarge their secondary institutions. The additions of anticommunism and intelligence emphasize what some historians refer to as the US National Security State. The family is not included, for the reason they adduce, that families are produced by and are agencies of "surrounding economic, political, and class structure" (Gronseth). Although no separate topics designate the institutions of classism, racism, sexism, and homophobia, selections may be found throughout the bibliography (see Index). Thus their model is altered only by extension and emphasis, into a corporate-government-military-anticommunist-media complex.

Part I presents a selection of books only. (The rest of the bibliography contains books and articles, moving from the institutional foundations to the subject of this bibliography --the interconnecting complex of media and discourse control.) The books in Part I treat the underlying power structures of the nation, the below-the-surface iceberg of influences. These books augment the arguments and evidence presented by Miller and the writers in Reynolds and Henslin. All of these master and secondary structures recur again and again in all of the categories and processes described in Part II, where the discourses and media, the channels, of mediation are shown to be inseparable from the structures of power. America, Inc. and Power, Inc. by Mintz and Cohen in Part I are indivisible from Schiller's Culture, Inc. in Part II. The primary and secondary institutions not only practice buying and selling, managing government bureaus, and building a military machine, but they also produce and distribute communications through the manifold media available in a Western industrial democracy today.

Arthur S. Miller warns that the imperatives of the master and secondary institutions will produce continued uniformity, particularly since people prefer material prosperity over individualism and freedom. Many of the books in Part I offer programs to counter power and to defend individual autonomy, in the ongoing struggle not only for formal authority over decisions but for effective control.

THE MASTER INSTITUTIONS (1-414)

I. A. 1. CORPORATE STATE (1-108)

1. Aronowitz, Stanley. False Promises; the Shaping of American Working Class Consciousness. New York: McGraw Hill, 1973. 465.
Part I discusses the new developments in working class life and labor with emphasis on the emerging new worker. Part II explains the historical development of the working class, particularly its ethnic, sexual, racial, and skill divisions, and their relations with trade unions.

2. Ballard, Hoyt, and G. William Domhoff, comps. C. Wright Mills and "The Power Elite." Boston: Beacon, 1968. 278.
Brings together fifteen "of the most thoughtful and representative" of the reviews of Mills' book, which in 1956 "reopened the study of the upper reaches of American society."

3. Barnet, Richard J. Roots of War. New York: Atheneum, 1972. 350.
"The thesis of this book is that war is a social institution, that America's permanent war can be explained primarily by looking at American society, and that America's wars will cease only if that society is changed" (5). Part I explores the leaders and bureaucratic structures (Pentagon, CIA, etc.), Part II the economic roots of foreign policy (business expansion, etc.), and Part III the public.

4. Bell, Daniel, ed. The Radical Right. Garden City, NY: Doubleday, 1963. 394.
The New American Right expanded and updated. The original idea for the first volume "arose in 1954 in a faculty seminar" on McCarthyism. The fourteen essays in this new collection discuss such topics as class, status, intellectuals, conservatism, the John Birch Society, intolerance, radical right, McCarthyism, Sovietphobia, and other issues of the 1960s.

5. Blaxall, Martha, and Barbara Reagan, eds. Women and the Workplace: The Implications of Occupational Segregation. Chicago: U of Chicago P, 1976. 326.
Has two objectives: "(1) to analyze occupational segregation as an interlocking set of institutions with sociological, psychological, and economic aspects and with deep historical roots; and (2) to consider what policy changes might be needed to achieve a society free from denial of job opportunities on the basis of sex" (ix).

6. Blumenthal, Sidney. The Rise of the Counter-Establishment. New York: Times, 1986. 383.
Traces the development of the conservative movement into a vast network of aggressive institutions, think tanks,

journals, and foundations that have transformed the national debate on foreign and domestic policy. They wage battle on every front for their goal of a "conservative nation."

7. Bodenheimer, Thomas, and Robert Gould. Rollback! Right-wing Power in U.S. Foreign Policy. Boston: South End, 1989. 272.

"Rollback" refers to the Right's long objective and fundamental US foreign policy since 1947 of moving beyond US Cold War "containment" policy to overthrowing governments perceived to be unfriendly to US interests. The book penetrates the "delusion" of US "defensive and selfless role in world affairs," which was actually "one of unprecedented ambition and global commitment" (Foreword by Richard Falk, ix) "seeking above all else as much space as possible for capitalist expansion" (xii).

8. Caldicott, Helen, M.D. Missile Envy: The Arms Race and Nuclear War. Rev. ed. New York: Bantam, 1986. 346.

The chapter on "The Iran Triangle" examines the military-industrial-scientific-presidential-congressional complex pushing the arms buildup; the next chapter studies the pathology of the war system--lust for power, paranoia about the Soviets, rapacious greed by military industries, and fascination with technology, etc.

9. Chambliss, William. On the Take: From Petty Crooks to Presidents. Bloomington: Indiana UP, 1978. 269.

A picture of "ubiquitous" corruption and crime in US politics and business.

10. Chomsky, Noam, and Edward Herman. The Political Economy of Human Rights. 2 vols. I: The Washington Connection and Third World Fascism. II: After the Cataclysm: Postwar Indochina and the Reconstruction of Imperial Ideology. Boston: South End, 1979. 441 and 392.

Vol. I a history and analysis of US organization, sponsorship, and protection of a neo-colonial system of client states ruled mainly by terror and serving the interests of a small local and foreign business and military elite. Vol. II about the cover-up of US culpability in Vietnam and the effort to rebuild its worldwide intervention.

11. Colen, Donald. The ABCs of Armageddon: The Language of the Nuclear Age. New York: World Almanac, 1988. 208.

In alphabetical order the linguistic "nonsense" that is "bankrupting the nation and shaping a future" that "promises only Apocalypse." The US, "a nation of packagers," has for 40 years "wrapped the whole subject of nuclear strategy in an inexplicable, sometimes obscene language."

12. Cook, Blanche W. The Declassified Eisenhower: A Divided Legacy. Garden City, NY: Doubleday, 1981. 432.

Eisenhower "intended to destabilize communism worldwide, eradicate New Deal 'socialism' domestically, and globalize

THE MASTER INSTITUTIONS

American business and America's values," and his success is measured by its "repression and reaction." But there is a co-legacy--his fear that the anti-communist crusade could transform the nation "into a dictatorship--militarily burdened, financially exhausted, politically destroyed." Thus, he warned against the inordinate growth of the military-industrial complex (viii).

13. Curry, Richard O., ed. *Freedom at Risk: Secrecy, Censorship, and Repression in the 1980s.* Philadelphia: Temple UP, 1988. 423.

Twenty-five essays on fourteen topics: the First Amendment, censorship and secrecy, the OMB, the Morison case, national security and seditious libel, the McCarran-Walter Act, the USIA, disinformation, drug testing, FBI surveillance, conspiracy trials, the Sanctuary Movement, the Reagan administration and the courts, and attacks on the media. The book exposes "a reactionary and authoritarian tradition that is as deeply ingrained in American society and politics as is the spirit of light and progress" (4).

14. Dahl, Robert. *Controlling Nuclear Weapons: Democracy Versus Guardianship.* Syracuse, NY: Syracuse UP, 1985. 128.

The "tragic paradox" of the nuclear age is that decisions about nuclear weapons "largely escaped" the democratic process (3), decided, often in secret, by military and civilian experts. But Dahl questions reliance upon experts, since many nuclear issues require a moral perspective more than specialized knowledge. [See Gans, Schell, Sigal, and Tuchman on "experts."]

15. Danielson, Michael. *The Politics of Exclusion.* New York: Columbia UP, 1976. 443.

On class, race, education, and income divisions in the US.

16. Davis, Kenneth, ed. *Arms, Industry and America.* New York: Wilson, 1971. 232.

A series of essays which analyze the impact of militarized technology upon "social, cultural, political, and economic institutions," and upon individual lives (3). The concluding section is divided into 6 essays which offer rational solutions to the US government's pre-emptive war policies.

17. Demac, Donna. *Liberty Denied: The Current Rise of Censorship in America.* New York: PEN American Center, 1988. 175.

Chapters on censorship in public schools and libraries, in corporations and media, government surveillance, harassment, secrecy, bureaucratic restrictions on information, government controls on press, media, and travel, restrictions on academic and scientific research, etc. Now "arbitrary power is budding in America as never before in our peacetime history" (Foreword by Walter Karp). "Today the United States faces the significant challenge of restoring the traditions of free speech and diversity of information that have been eroded in the 1980s" (164). [Also see her Keeping America Uninformed (1984).]

18. Dixon, Marlene. Omens of Darkness: The Rise of Reaction in the United States. San Francisco, CA: Synthesis, 1985. 304.
Revival of a virulent Cold War ideology, nuclear provocation of the Soviet Union, the militarization of Central America, increased repression in the name of "law and order," etc.

19. Domhoff, G. William. The Bohemian Grove and Other Retreats: A Study in Ruling-Class Cohesiveness. New York: Harper & Row, 1974. 250.
Description of three "upper-class watering holes," which "increase the social cohesiveness of America's rulers": Bohemian Grove, Rancheros Visitadores, and Roundup. Lengthy (112-245) list of "the most prominent men who were members of two or more of six social clubs and three policy-planning groups between the years 1965 and 1970."

20. Domhoff, G. William. Fat Cats and Democrats: The Role of the Big Rich in the Party of the Common Man. Englewood Cliffs, NJ: Prentice-Hall, 1972. 203.
"The purpose of this book is to examine the rich men who support the Democratic Party in order to show that their presence and activities contradict the image of the Democrats as the party of the common man" (12).

21. Domhoff, G. William. The Higher Circles: The Governing Class in America. New York: Random House, 1970. 367.
Analysis of the upper class as both a social and a political force, an often invisible affluent hierarchy of influence over government.

22. Domhoff, G. William, ed. Power Structure Research. Beverly Hills, CA: Sage, 1980. 270.
Ten essays dealing with basic questions of the distribution and exercise of power.

23. Domhoff, G. William. The Powers that Be: Processes of Ruling Class Domination in America. New York: Vintage, 1979. 206.
Describes the numerous methods and processes through which the power elite seek to shape a consensus.

24. Domhoff, G. William. Who Rules America? Englewood Cliffs, NJ: Prentice-Hall, 1967. 184.
"It will be shown that there is a national upper class made up of rich businessmen and their families, an 'American business aristocracy,'" as Baltzell calls it. This class controls foundations, universities, mass media, opinion molding associations, the executive branch of the federal government, the regulatory agencies, the federal judiciary, the military, the CIA, and the FBI.

THE MASTER INSTITUTIONS

25. Domhoff, G. William. <u>Who Rules America Now?: A View for the '80s</u>. Englewood Cliffs, NJ: Prentice-Hall, 1983. 230.
 A sequel to <u>Who Rules America?</u> adding further evidence and synthesis of the proposition that a "relatively fixed group of privileged people" dominates the economy and government.

26. Domhoff, G. William, and Thomas Dye, eds. <u>Power Elites and Organizations</u>. Beverly Hills, CA: Sage, 1987. 292.
 Thirteen studies of power structures, specifically the relationships between elites and organizations, with essays on minorities in corporations and government, elite domination of private institutions, corporate elites and education, and related topics.

27. Draper, Theodore. <u>Present History</u>. New York: Random House, 1983. 458.
 Punctures diverse official doctrines and myths: U.S. intervention in Vietnam was not motivated by ideals, Jeane Kirkpatrick's distinction between authoritarian and totalitarian regimes as a justification for U.S. support of friendly dictatorships is illogical, the State Department's document classifying system is partly intended to manipulate and distort history, etc.

28. Dugger, Ronnie. <u>On Reagan: The Man and His Presidency</u>. New York: McGraw-Hill, 1983. 617.
 Chapter titles suggest the point of view, for example, corporations: "A Wholesale Giveaway to Private Interests," "Riding Down the Marxist Income Tax," "Big Money and Big Business in the White House," "Uranium, Plutonium, and Bechtel."

29. Dugger, Ronnie. <u>The Politician: The Life and Times of Lyndon Johnson</u>. New York: Norton, 1982. 514.
 Johnson successfully exploited post-WWII commercialism, corporate rapacity, and anti-communism.

30. Dye, Thomas R. <u>Who's Running America?: The Reagan Years</u>. 3rd ed. Englewood Cliffs, NJ: Prentice-Hall, 1983. 285.
 Traces national policy planning to corporate and personal wealth channeled into universities, foundations, etc. in cooperation with legal, governmental, media, and other institutions.

31. Dye, Thomas, and Harmon Zeigler. <u>The Irony of Democracy: An Uncommon Introduction to American Politics</u>. 7th Ed. Monterey, CA: Brooks/Cole, 1987. 506.
 A refutation of the pluralistic theory of U.S. government and a formulation of the U.S. as elitist: "only a tiny handful of people make decisions that shape the lives of all of us." Chapter 6 deals with "Elite-Mass Communication: Television, the Press, and the Pollsters." "Communication in the American political system flows downward from elites to masses."

32. Easlea, Brian. Fathering the Unthinkable: Masculinity, Scientists and the Nuclear Arms Race. London: Schocken, 1987. 240.
Demonstrates how the atomic bomb project and the discourse of the early nuclear physicists, strategists, and SAC commanders were rife with overt images of competitive male sexuality.

33. Edsall, Thomas B. The New Politics of Inequality. New York: Norton, 1984. 287.
Describes a major power shift in recent years in favor of the privileged and rich.

34. Ericson, Edward L. American Freedom and the Radical Right. New York: Ungar, 1982. 117.
Examines the right-wing extension of conservatism and its war against communism, secular humanism, godlessness, etc.

35. Ferguson, Thomas, and Joel Rogers. Right Turn: The Decline of the Democrats and the Future of American Politics. New York: Hill & Wang, 1986. 276.
Focuses on the powerful elite who run the Democratic Party and who have pushed it rightward: "principally capital-intensive and multinationally oriented big business and its allies among urban real-estate magnates, military contractors, and portions of the media. This elite and not the public turned rightward, for the public "actually moved slightly leftward since Reagan assumed office" regarding "social welfare, New Deal concerns, civil rights, relations with the Soviet Union, and U.S. military intervention abroad" (196).

36. Ferguson, Thomas, and Joel Rogers, eds. The Hidden Election: Politics and Economics in the 1980 Presidential Campaign. New York: Pantheon, 1981. 342.
Studies of the processes by which mainly economic interests dominate elections.

37. Forster, Arnold, and Benjamin R. Epstein. Danger on the Right. New York: Random, 1964. 294.
A survey of the many manifestations of the right wing at that time.

38. Gandy, Oscar. Beyond Agenda Setting: Information Subsidies and Public Policy. Norwood, NJ: Ablex, 1982. 243.
Explains how the corporate/government complex of interests influences policy by subsidizing information sources--health, education, science, etc.

39. Ganley, Oswald, and Gladys Ganley. To Inform or to Control? The New Communications Networks. New York: McGraw, 1982. 250.
Communication innovations and information resources serve US national interests, particularly business, which continues to converge with government.

40. Ginger, Ann Fagan, and David Christiano, eds. The Cold
War Against Labor: An Anthology. 2 vols. Berkeley,
CA: Meiklejohn Civil Liberties Institute, 1987. 915.
The Cold War had two fronts--to defeat the Soviet Union and
to suppress progressive movements in the US and the world. In
the US the war produced by 1955 "tens of thousands" of
victims, the most notable of which were Ethel and Julius
Rosenberg. These volumes focus on the repression of unions
and union members since WWII.

41. Ginsberg, Benjamin. The Captive Public: How Mass Opinion Promotes State Power. New York: Basic, 1986. 272.
Secrecy is less important to modern democratic states for
control because they can manage public opinion through public
relations. And they can even dispense with favorable opinion
by obfuscating already immensely complex issues beyond the
capacity of the general public to understand (220-4).

42. Goldstein, Robert. Political Repression in Modern
America: From 1870 to the Present. Boston: G.K.
Hall, 1978. 682.
Repression is a significant element in the history of the
US, employed to shape thought and behavior whenever normal
controls fail. Many radical movements have been crushed.

43. Graebner, William. The Engineering of Consent:
Democracy and Authority in Twentieth-Century America.
Madison: U of Wisconsin P, 1987. 262.
"In the half century before the Great War" the US created a
"new structure or system of authority," operating "on groups
rather than individuals." This new "democratic social engineering" employed "YMCA clubs, Boy Scout patrols, Bible study
classes," schools and families that gave the feeling of participation when, in fact, choice among alternatives was limited.

44. Green Mark, et al. The Closed Enterprise System. New
York: Grossman, 1972. 488.
Examines destructiveness of unregulated monopoly capitalism.

45. Green, Mark, and Michael Waldman. Who Runs Congress?.
4th ed. New York: Dell, 1984. 432.
Corporate power over Congress and presidency is
intensifying.

46. Greenberg, Edward. The American Political System: A
Radical Approach. 4th ed. Boston: Little, Brown,
1986. 384.
About "the reality of business control of the workplace and
of the conditions of daily existence of most Americans; the
treatment of citizens of a democratic country as mere factors
of production; the vast extent of the economic, political, and
social role of concentrated private economic power; the close
collaboration of business and governments at all levels in the
United States; the pro-corporate bias in the letter and the
administration of the law; the public policy continuities

between Democratic and Republican administrations through the years; and the unequal distribution of political power" (11).

47. Gronseth, Erik. "The Familial Institution: The Alienated Labor-producing Appendage." *American Society: A Critical Analysis*. Ed. Larry Reynolds and James Henslin. New York: McKay, 1973. 248-293.
Calls into question the desirability of the nuclear family so cherished in US myths, for he finds repression and "perverted social relations at the marrow" of nuclear families, which function "largely in the interest" of state capitalist imperatives.

48. Gross, Bertram. *Friendly Fascism: The New Face of Power in America*. New York: Evans, 1980. 410.
Examines the "Big Business-Big Government" partnership as it becomes more authoritarian. Part I traces the roots of the development, Part II sketches its many faces. Part III in four chapters suggests how it may be stopped and reversed through "True Democracy."

49. Grove, Gene. *Inside the John Birch Society*. Greenwich, Conn: Fawcett, 1961. 160.
Anecdotal account of the beliefs and behavior of the leader of the John Birch Society, Robert Welch.

50. Hamelink, Cees. *Finance and Information: A Study of Converging Interests*. Norwood, NJ: Ablex, 1983. 170.
The subject of the author's *The Corporate Village* (transnational corporate control of communications) is here focused upon the information-industrial-banking complex.

51. Herman, Edward. *The Real Terror Network: Terrorism in Fact and Propaganda*. Boston: South End, 1982. 252.
Reveals the hypocrisy of western influence concerning national and international class interests. US nurtured Third World states are often mass murderers and torturers with a small, capitalist elite class controlling the government.

52. Hertsgaard, Mark. *Nuclear Inc.: The Men and Money Behind Nuclear Energy*. New York: Pantheon, 1983. 339.
A history of the struggles among corporations for control of the nuclear industry during the '50s and '60s and the winners' struggles with setbacks in the 1970s. This account is connected with the government sponsorship of nuclear power, a conglomeration the author calls "America's Atomic Brotherhood."

53. Huber, Joan, and William Form. *Income and Ideology: An Analysis of the American Political Formula*. New York: Free, 1973. 226.
The widespread doctrine that poverty is a matter of individual responsibility comes in for close analysis, as do the "dominant ideology of American stratification": "equality, success, and democracy."

THE MASTER INSTITUTIONS

54. Hunt, Michael. <u>Ideology and U.S. Foreign Policy</u>. New Haven: Yale UP, 1987. 256.

Three interrelated ideological strands have shaped US foreign policy: 1) national mission to promote liberty abroad, 2) classification of peoples in racial, class, and ethnic hierarchies, and 3) hostility toward revolutions. The author considers this ideology bankrupt, as proven by the Vietnam War, and he argues for a new "republican" ideology and foreign policy based upon the realization of a just and equitable society at home.

55. Jansen, Sue. <u>Censorship: The Knot That Binds Power and Knowledge</u>. New York: Oxford UP, 1988. 282.

Knowledge and emancipation or repression emerge out of human struggles, particularly for power. "The powerful require knowledge to preserve, defend, and extend their advantage." They "use this power to generate and enforce definitions of words and of social reality that enhance their sovereignty. . . They do not just control access to podium, presidium, or press room. They also determine the rules of evidence, shape the logic of assertion, define the architecture of arguments" (6-7). Censorship is thus constitutive as well as regulative (7-8). In modern liberal, industrial societies, the ideal of a "free market of ideas" has been "replaced under corporate capitalism by market censorship both at home and abroad," and freedom is really the freedom of multi-national corporations from proper restrictions (11).

56. Jezer, Marty. <u>The Dark Ages: Life in the United States, 1945-1960</u>. Boston: South End, 1982. 335.

A chronicle of US domestic and global repression under the Cold War and the military-industrial complex, and resistance during the 1960s.

57. Johansen, Robert. <u>The National Interest and the Human Interest: An Analysis of U.S. Foreign Policy</u>. Princeton, NJ: Princeton UP, 1980. 517.

On the contradictions in foreign policy, both affirming and undermining self-determination and pluralism.

58. Karp, Walter. <u>Indispensable Enemies: The Politics of Misrule in America</u>. New York: Saturday Review, 1973. 308.

The main problem is the oligarchy of the two main collusive parties, which promotes global intervention, corporations, and special interests. The final chapter suggests how to break up the Democratic-Republican syndicate.

59. Katznelson, Ira, and Mark Kesselman. <u>The Politics of Power: A Critical Introduction to American Government</u>. 2nd ed. New York: HBJ, 1979. 435.

Focuses upon the relationship between capitalism and politics and the fundamental inequalities that result from the requirements of capitalism, relegating "democracy largely to the sphere of selecting government officials."

60. King, Dennis. *Lyndon LaRouche and the New American Fascism*. New York: Doubleday, 1989. 415.

This neo-Nazi with ties to the CIA, FBI, the Pentagon, local police red squads, wealthy conservatives, GOP leaders, and even the Ku Klux Klan, built his power on a crusade against evil leftists, liberals, environmentalists and other perceived evil enemies of the state. Yet the "media consistently avoided" the subject.

61. Klatch, Rebecca. *Women of the New Right*. Philadelphia: Temple UP, 1987. 247.

Analyzes the various alliances and configurations of conservative women: social conservatives, traditional family values, laissez-faire economic conservatives, supporters of increased military spending, anti-communists, anti-secular humanists, anti-government.

62. Knelman, F.H. *America, God and the Bomb: The Legacy of Ronald Reagan*. Rev. Vancouver, Canada: New Star, 1987. 478.

A "substantially" revised and augmented edition of *Reagan, God and the Bomb*, published in 1985. The Reagan administration in alliance with the combined forces of the right wing had as its central objective the destruction of the Soviet Union. And the legacy of Reagan's creation of "the technological infrastructure to wage nuclear war" affects all the world and all aspects of life.

63. Knoll, Erwin, and Judith McFadden, eds. *American Militarism 1970*. New York: Viking, 1969. 150.

Papers from the 1969 "Congressional Conference on the Military Budget and National Priorities" clarify the basic issues of the militarization of American society. The book also examines concrete proposals for restoring democratic control over the military budget.

64. Kornbluh, Peter. *Nicaragua: The Price of Intervention: Reagan's Wars Against the Sandinistas*. Washington, DC: Institute for Policy Studies, 1987. 287.

The "wars" refer to the covert, economic, military, and domestic (propaganda) wars, in separate chapters.

65. LaFeber, Walter. *Inevitable Revolutions: The U.S. in Central America*. New York: Norton, 1984. 378.

An explanation of why US domination of Central America by a system of neodependency failed to improve life in the region and produced "massive revolution."

66. Landau, Saul. *The Dangerous Doctrine: National Security and U.S. Foreign Policy*. Boulder, CO: Westview Press/ PACCA, 1988. 201.

Secrecy, exploitation of fear in general and of the Soviet Union specifically, and manipulation of language for confusion and anxiety have served US leaders to suppress debate and dissent on foreign policy.

THE MASTER INSTITUTIONS

66a. Lens, Sidney. *The Day before Doomsday.* Boston: Beacon, 1977. 273.
Lens addresses the potential for human obliteration inherent in the nuclear arms race, and he gives us the facts needed in order to reverse the orientation toward global militarization.

67. Lens, Sidney. *The Forging of the American Empire.* New York: Crowell, 1971. 462.
American policies are dominated by imperial interests which revolve around "such mundane things as land, commerce, markets, spheres of influence, investments, or strategic threats from other nations that might threaten land, commerce, markets, etc."

67a. Lens, Sidney. *The Military Industrial Complex.* Philadelphia: United Church, 1970. 183.
The present military-industrial complex has upset the tradition of Congressional control of the military and now threatens the nation with a political monopoly many times more ominous than economic monopolies" (34).

68. Lloyd, Cynthia, and Beth Niemi. *The Economics of Sex Differentials.* New York: Columbia UP, 1979. 355.
Analyzes all facets of women's secondary economic status.

69. Lowi, Theodore. *The Politics of Disorder.* New York: Basic, 1971. 193.
On the system of repression.

70. May, Lary, ed. *Recasting America: Culture and Politics in the Age of Cold War.* Chicago: U of Chicago P, 1989. 310.
After World War II "a corporate order was fully legitimized" by "the promise of classless consumption" that however masked "the continuing reality of class, race, and psychological repression" and the steady decline of the "progressive ethos" traditionally geared to reforming capitalism for the general good. Anti-communism was another major factor in the post-1945 consensus that "legitimized the new corporate order" in an "ideology of abundance" (11).

71. McIntyre, Thomas, with John Obert. *The Fear Brokers.* Introduction by Senator Mark Hatfield. New York and Philadelphia: Pilgrim, 1979. 350.
Former Senator McIntyre unveils the forces and personalities of the emerging New Right across the nation, focusing particularly on his own state of New Hampshire. Details the intensification of xenophobia, chauvinism, national egotism, and hyperpatriotism in the U.S. Anti-communism and Sovietphobia are treated passim, especially in Chapter 18, "'Americans' and 'Americanism.'"

72. Melman, Seymour. *Pentagon Capitalism: The Political Economy of War.* New York: McGraw, 1970. 290.
A diagnosis of the many-dimensional military-industrial

complex and its negative effects on the American economy and society. The Pentagon's priorities have become the leading cause of war and domestic decline.

73. Miles, Michael W. The Odyssey of the American Right. New York: Oxford UP, 1980. 371.

Section II deals with the McCarthy Era, III with the New Right, Nixon, etc. A history of the powerful rightist forces in modern US.

74. Miller, Arthur S. Democratic Dictatorship: The Emergent Constitution of Control. Westport: Greenwood, 1981. 268.

Deepening problems in the world and in the US, the extension of technology, and other factors increase the likelihood of the demise of liberal democracy and the continued extension of authoritarianism, regimentation, and repression, the "Constitution of Control." The press cannot be expected to counter the process, since "the media are not the nemesis of government; they are its surrogates" (104).

75. Miller, Arthur S. The Modern Corporate State: Private Governments and the American Constitution. Westport: Greenwood, 1976. 269.

"Miller sketches a chilling future. The giant corporation--that authoritarian, bureaucratic, and hierarchical private government--grows and spreads its influence. Political power moves to the national government, and within Washington to the executive branch and the national security managers. These growing concentrations of power need and increasingly support each other. Big government, big business, big labor, and big universities come together in a symbiotic relationship that allows a small elite to run the whole system" (Introduction by Daniel Fusfeld xiii).

75a. Mills, C. Wright. The Power Elite. New York: Oxford UP, 1959. 423.

The US power elite is composed of "warlords, the corporate chieftains, the political directorate."

76. Mintz, Morton, and Jerry Cohen. America, Inc.: Who Owns and Operates the United States. New York: Dial, 1971. 424.

Government functions to serve corporate power. Remedies: antitrust, federal chartering, etc.

77. Mintz, Morton, and Jerry Cohen. Power, Inc.: Public and Private Rulers and How to Make Them Accountable. New York: Viking, 1976. 831.

Examines the numerous ways "the powerful in both public and private sectors avoid accountability." The 47 chapters deal with such topics as secrecy, conflict of interest, unaccountability.

78. Mosco, Vincent, and Janet Wasko, eds. The Political

THE MASTER INSTITUTIONS

Economy of Information. Madison, WI: U of Wisconsin P, 1988. 334.
The title refers to "how power is used to shape the production, distribution, and use of information as a commodity." Much of the book studies "how corporations are making information a marketable commodity, how the state advances that process, the implications for access to information and the wider class structure, and the impact on the workplace and the home" (4). In the Introduction, Mosco expounds the idea of the "Pay-per Society," in which "new technology makes it possible to measure and monitor more and more of our electronic communication and information activities. Business and government see this potential as a major instrument to increase profit and control" (5). But this system exacerbates class divisions, problems of civil and human rights, and the threat of global warfare (10).

79. Oakley, Ann. Women's Work: The Housewife, Past and Present. New York: Pantheon, 1974. 275.
A study of "women's unpaid work role in the home" in Britain and the US, in the context of the "myth of the division of labour by sex" that equates "femininity and domesticity."

80. O'Brien, Conor Cruise. God Land: Reflections on Religion and Nationalism. Cambridge: Harvard UP, 1988. 112.
Broadly about the destructive consequences of the alliance of religion and nationalism. Discusses the move toward belief in the "deified nation" during the Reagan presidency, as illustrated by the National Prayer Breakfast, the Museum of Air and Space, and other manifestations of growing militarism.

81. Packard, Vance. The Naked Society. New York: McKay, 1964. 369.
Part I, "The Mounting Surveillance," Part II, "Some Specific Areas of Assault" (upon students and teachers, invasion of privacy, computer data, etc.), Part III, "Assaults on Traditional Rights of Free Citizens" (of dissent, from police mistreatment, etc.), Part IV, "If Personal Liberty Is to Be Sustained" (remedies to a Bill of Rights under siege).

82. Parenti, Michael. Democracy for the Few. New York: St. Martin's, 1974. 307.
The central theme is that "our government represents the privileged few rather than the needy many and that elections, political parties and the right to speak out are seldom effective measures against the influences of corporate wealth." Chapters on leaders and lobbyists, Congress, the presidency, government bureaucracy, the media, etc.

83. Parenti, Michael. Power and the Powerless. New York: St. Martin's, 1978. 238.
"The subject of this book is power in American society or, specifically, the relationship of power to social structure, political consciousness, and powerlessness: how and for whom

power is organized and what its institutionalized roots are; how power serves interest and how it defines interest; why certain social alternatives are chosen and others ignored; how change and protest are contained; how in the face of all inequities and abuses the prevailing social order maintains itself" (v). Chapter 11 focuses upon the class interest of Institutions: press, religion, unions, universities, science, arts, and sports. "By omission and commission, complicity and docility, the [mainstream] media seldom stray from the ideological fold" (150).

84. Pell, Eve. <u>The Big Chill: How the Reagan Administration, Corporate America, and Religious Conservatives Are Subverting Free Speech and the Public's Right to Know</u>. Boston: Beacon, 1984. 269.
Traces the ways the Reagan administration, corporations, and rightist religious sects are attacking First Amendment freedoms through secrecy, censorship, suppression, intimidation, bannings, libel suits, and sheer domination of access by their combined positions of power.

85. Piven, Frances, and Richard Cloward. <u>Why Americans Don't Vote</u>. New York: Pantheon, 1988. 312.
"Well-to-do electorates based on low turnouts" have contributed to "American exceptionalism"--"the comparative absence of class-based, left wing identities and political organization, and the consequent hegemony of bourgeois political parties, discourse, and definitions of political choice."

86. Raskin, Marcus. <u>The Politics of National Security</u>. New York: Transaction, 1979. 211.
How the US became a National Security State with all its destructive consequences.

87. Reardon, Betty. <u>Sexism and the War System</u>. New York: Teachers College P, 1985. 110.
Argues that sexism and violence have a systemic relationship with the current militarization of our planet. In order to reverse and halt the arms race, peace activists and feminists must work together.

88. Reich, Charles. <u>The Greening of America</u>. New York: Random, 1970. 399.
The corporate state is a single vast corporation consisting of large industrial organizations, the educational system, policy institutions, etc., with government as coordinator. The author hopes for a society more open to diversity.

89. Reynolds, Larry, and James Henslin, eds. <u>American Society: A Critical Analysis</u>. New York: McKay, 1973. 337.
Three "master" institutions rule the country--economic, political, and military--, with the economic the most powerful.

90. Robinson, William I., and Kent Norsworthy. <u>David and Goliath: The U.S. War Against Nicaragua</u>. New York:

THE MASTER INSTITUTIONS

Monthly Review, 1987. 400.
On the Reagan administration's efforts to destroy the Sandinista government.

91. Rogin, Michael P. "Political Repression in the United States." "Ronald Reagan," the Movie. Berkeley: U of California P, 1987. 44-80.
"Addresses racial, class, and sexual conflict" and "institutional power" to connect "countersubversive mentality to political repression and institution building." A history of U.S. political demonology and suppression of "alien" groups and ideas from the Indians to the communists.

92. Saloma, John S. III. Ominous Politics: The New Conservative Labyrinth. New York: Hill & Wang, 1984. 177.
Examines the recent emergence of a new conservative coalition, including massive efforts to turn the tide of public discourse in favor of the right: conservative think-tanks, attempts to influence and transform the mainstream media, and politically active televangelists.

93. Savage, Robert, James Combs, and Dan Nimmo, eds. The Orwellian Moment: Hindsight and Foresight in the Post-1984 World. Fayetteville, AR: U of Arkansas P, 1989. 180.
Eight essays focus mainly on Orwell's hatred of totalitarianism. A few of the essays in whole or part apply his opposition to the US: the hardening wrought by the Cold War, Secretary of State Haig's doublespeak, polls, and in one essay "the control of consciousness by mass media" that could lead to "Media Fascism."

94. Schaar, John. Loyalty in America. Berkeley: U of California P, 1957. 217.
The concept of loyalty has been drastically altered in recent years from actions alone to actions and thought, from loyalty as individualism to loyalty and disloyalty by association, and from loyalty as independence to loyalty as conformity.

95. Schlesinger, Arthur M., Jr. A Thousand Days; John F. Kennedy in the White House. Boston: Houghton Mifflin, 1965. 1087.
Describes the undue influence of military-industrial-complex --super patriots, arms makers, demagogues, Pentagon--in resorting "to massive military violence" to resolve conflict.

96. Sennett, Richard, and Jonathan Cobb. The Hidden Injuries of Class. New York: Knopf, 1973. 275.
Workers in this society have few ways to validate themselves as people, to earn dignity and respect, other than the indirect one of buying things. [See Aronowitz, False Promises.]

97. Shoup, Laurence. The Carter Presidency and Beyond: Power and Politics in the 1980s. Palo Alto, CA:

Ramparts, 1980. 319.
Explains the real power wielders as they operated during the Carter administration: The Trilateral Commission, etc.

98. Smythe, Dallas. "On the Political Economy of C^3I." Communication and Domination: Essays to Honor Herbert I. Schiller. Ed. Jorg Becker, et al. Norwood, NJ: Ablex, 1986. 66-75.

"Division into 'military' and 'civilian' aspects of society is no longer admissible," because the "contemporary, monopoly capitalist society is run by a military-civilian industrial complex (MCIC), not a military industrial complex" (54).

99. Suall, Irwin. The American Ultras: The Extreme Right and the Military Industrial Complex. New York: New America, 1962. 65.

"Ultras" derives from the French generals who tried to overthrow DeGaulle over Algerian independence. In the US the combination of military leaders with right-wing corporate executives threatens democracy.

100. Taylor, John. Circus of Ambition: The Culture of Wealth and Power in the Eighties. New York: Warner, 1989. 240.

The open worship of money, a culture of greed, produced a decade more ruthless and corrupt than ever before in a nation which prefers profits over ethics.

101. Vyner, Henry, M.D. Invisible Trauma: The Psychological Effects of the Invisible Environmental Contaminants. Lexington, MA: Lexington/Heath, 1988. 219.

Analyzes the major studies of the psychosocial effects of ionizing radiation and toxic chemicals. Chapter 18, "The Institutional Denial of Invisible Threat," demonstrates that both public and private institutions deny existing health threats "until a preponderance of evidence rendered the threat undeniable" (178), as in the cases of uranium mining, nuclear weapons testing, and Love Canal toxic wastes.

102. Wasserman, Harvey. Killing Our Own: The Disaster of America's Experience with Atomic Radiation. New York: Dell, 1982. 368.

US atomic development is a radiation "litany of death" for our own citizens, from Hiroshima to Three Mile Island.

103. Weisberg, Barry. Beyond Repair: The Ecology of Capitalism. Boston: Beacon, 1971. 201.

The US corporate state is an environmental disaster.

104. Weissman, Steve, ed. Big Brother and the Holding Company: The World Behind Watergate. Palo Alto, CA: Ramparts, 1974. 350.

Watergate was no aberration but one aspect of the concerted effort to build the Republican Party/conservative/right-wing coalition.

THE MASTER INSTITUTIONS 25

105. Wills, Garry. Reagan's America: Innocents at Home. Garden City, NY: Doubleday, 1987. 472.
An attempt to explain Ronald Reagan in terms of national dreams. "He is . . . what Hollywood promoters used to call 'fabulous.' We fable him to ourselves," and we draw security from his youthful "All-American" "lack of inner division" and his role as icon of national myths. For example, Chapter 41 explores Reagan as the embodiment of the myth of individualism in a corporate world which recognizes "a social discipline of standardization." Reagan "makes this absurdity believable."

106. Wolfe, Alan. The Limits of Legitimacy: Political Contradictions of Contemporary Capitalism. New York: Free P, 1977. 432.
Examines "the effects capitalism has had on democracy and vice versa," especially the boundaries established to restrict democracy for the benefit of a narrow accumulating elite. The solution to present inequality is economic democracy: giving people "the same voice in making investment and allocation decisions as they theoretically have in more directly political decisions," the "democratization of accumulation."

107. Zeitlin, Maurice, ed. American Society, Inc. Chicago: Markham, 1970. 527.
Thirty-nine conflicting essays centering on the issue of whether freedom and democracy are possible under the domination of highly developed capitalism. The essays discuss such topics as ownership, inequality, poverty, and power.

108. Zelinsky, Wilbur. Nation Into State: The Shifting Symbolic Foundations of American Nationalism. Chapel Hill, NC: U of North Carolina P, 1988. 350.
Traces the symbolic history of US from nation to state and Americanism as a civil religion. Nationalism and statism have become the US religion, as reflected in its flag and eagle, monuments, museums and parks, the varied physical apparatuses of the state, heroes, villains, place-names, holidays, countless commemorative acts, world's fairs, countless political rituals, patriotic organizations, sports, and many other symbols and symbolic acts.

I. A. 2. CORPORATIONS AND FINANCE (109-166)

109. Ackerman, Frank. Reaganomics: Rhetoric vs. Reality. Boston: South End, 1982. 166.
Shows how the Reagan administration favors the rich and powerful, how the short-term economic benefits of the military buildup means long term disaster--runaway deficits, declining quality of life, etc.

110. Adams, James R. The Big Fix: Inside the S&L Crisis. New York: Wiley, 1989. 308.
Behind every corrupt banker was a con man, a political

fixer, and sometimes a US Senator. The "thrift" executives acted like they had a license to steal.

111. Agger, Ben. Fast Capitalism: A Critical Theory of Significance. Urbana, IL: U of Illinois P, 1989. 191.
In the nineteenth century, books stood apart from the world, enabling readers to comprehend the world's totality and thus to remake it. But now the fast pace of our economic system has eroded both book culture and critical commentary. He sets forth Marxism and feminism as strategies to reverse the trend toward thoughtlessness.

112. Barnet, Richard, and Ronald Muller. Global Reach: The Power of the Multinational Corporations. New York: Simon, 1974. 508.
"The global corporation is the first institution in human history dedicated to centralized planning on a world scale. Because its primary purpose is to organize and to integrate economic activity around the world in such a way as to maximize global profit, the global corporation is an organic structure in which each part is expected to serve the whole. Thus in the end it measures its successes and its failures . . . by the growth in global profits and global market shares" (14).

113. Bennett, James R. "American Literature and the Acquisitive Society, Background and Criticism: A Bibliography." BoB 30 (1973) 175-184; 37 (1980) 1-15, 53-71.
US imaginative writers have provided traditionally a searching critique of the business ethos.

114. Bowlby, Rachel. Just Looking: Consumer Culture in Dreiser, Gissing and Zola. London: Methuen, 1985. 160.
Counters the belief of some historians that the department store served as an agent of women's liberation by showing how the institutions of consumer culture, and the department store in particular, were instruments of class power and male domination.

115. Brodeur, Paul. Outrageous Misconduct. New York: Pantheon, 1985. 357.
For fifty years Johns-Manville Corporation stifled disclosure of the danger of asbestos.

116. Burroughs, Bryan, and John Helyar. Barbarians at the Gate: The Fall of RJR Nabisco. New York: Harper & Row, 1990. 528.
The fight to control RJR Nabisco during October and November of 1988, with $25 billion at stake, gives a glimpse of the decline of US capitalism into egregious greed, rapacity, and irresponsible and unaccountable power.

117. Clairmonte, Frederick, and John Cavanaugh. Merchants of Drink. Malaysia: Consumers' Association of Penang

(c/o Third World Network, 87 Cantonment Road, Penang 10250), 1988. 190.
The story of the modern beverage industry and how a few powerful transnational conglomerates, locked in battle for monopoly, tap, fabricate, package, advertise, market, and price what we drink. The result is not a fall in product prices, greater consumer choice, fairer distribution of income, but cartelizing, so that now the $500 billion global beverage market is fully in the grip of fifty conglomerates, five of which control one half of the market.

118. Cockburn, Alexander. "The Boss." Corruptions of Empire. London, New York: Verso, 1987. 217-23.
A review of The Annenbergs: The Salvaging of a Tainted Dynasty by John Cooney and "the various ways criticism can be quelled."

119. Copetas, A. Craig. Metal Men: Marc Rich and the 10-Billion-Dollar Scam. New York: Putnam's, 1985. 224.
The story of commodity trader Marc Rich's accumulation of $10 billion in assets while avoiding income taxes.

120. Curti, Merle, and Roderick Nash. Philanthropy in the Shaping of American Higher Education. New Brunswick: Rutgers UP, 1965. 340.
Wealthy individuals and corporations gained ascendant influence over universities by their gifts, service on boards of trustees, etc.

121. Danielian, Noobar. A. T. & T.: The Story of Industrial Conquest. New York: Vanguard, 1939. 460.
Competition in inventions and acquisition of patents resulted in monopolies in use and exploitation by the division of fields through agreement among the contesting industries (GE, GM, Du Pont, AT&T). "This is highly reminiscent of the competition for colonies among the power before the World War, which resulted in the partition of unoccupied territory for exclusive possession."

122. Edwards, Richard C., Michael Reich, and Thomas E. Weisskopf. 2nd ed. The Capitalist System: A Radical Analysis of American Society. Englewood Cliffs, NJ: Prentice Hall, 1978. 546.
Indicts the exploitation of the US by monopoly capitalism and urges an alternative.

123. Etzioni, Amitai. Capital Corruption: The New Attack on American Democracy. New York: Harcourt, 1984. 337.
About the subversion of representative democracy by the "new plutocracy" of concentrated wealth. Final section suggests remedies.

124. Farhang, Mansour. U.S. Imperialism: From the Spanish-American War to the Iranian Revolution. Boston, MA: South End, 1981. 190.

Behind US imperialism Farhang places corporate capitalism, both defined as "the cult of every person for himself or herself," which is "a principal source" of misery, exploitation, and dependence in the world.

125. Ferguson, Thomas, and Joel Rogers, eds. The Hidden Election: Politics and Economics in the 1980 Presidential Campaign. New York: Pantheon, 1981. 342.

On the structures of power behind the Carter and Reagan campaigns.

126. Galbraith, John K. The New Industrial State. 3rd ed., rev. Boston: Houghton Mifflin, 1978. 438.

Examines "the world of great corporations--a world in which people increasingly served the convenience of those organizations which were meant to serve them" and in which "markets were more and more accommodated to the needs and convenience of the great business organizations" (ix). The large industrial corporation "can manage its consumers--and, by inference" the Pentagon, and weapons producers instruct the public on military needs and "not the reverse" (xiii).

127. Glaberman, Martin, and George Rawick. "The Economic Institution." American Society: A Critical Analysis. Ed. Reynolds and Henslin. New York: McKay, 1973. 25-65.

Analyzes the rise of state capitalism and its consequences of global imperialism, worker exploitation, inequality, poverty, automation, and insecurity--i.e., of perpetual disturbance and change.

128. Green, Mark, Michael Waldman, and Robert Massie, Jr., eds. The Big Business Reader: On Corporate America. Rev. New York: Pilgrim, 1983. 514.

Forty-eight essays divided into twelve sections on the consumer, labor, natural resources, community, politics, government, regulation, etc., the final section on alternatives. The corporation, the dominant institution of the US, pervades "government politics, communications, foundations, athletics," and the family and religion.

129. Hall, Ross Hume. Food for Nought: The Decline in Nutrition. New York: Harper, 1974. 292.

The aim of the food industry is to induce an ever-increasing consumption of fabricated products.

130. Heilbroner, Robert. Business Civilization in Decline. New York: Norton, 1976. 127.

Capitalism will end "within a century" because its expansion is "an exponential process" requiring "continuously increasing quantities of resources and spewing forth continuously increasing quantities of wastes," until the environment is overloaded, "consuming all its nutrients or poisoning it by the waste products associated with growth" (102-103).

THE MASTER INSTITUTIONS

131. Herman, Edward. *Corporate Control, Corporate Power.* London: Cambridge UP, 1981. 432.
Studies "the centralizing tendencies and effects of corporate and financial power," and argues that "corporations have remained faithful to their basic objective, which is to maximize profits, and that they continue to be relatively impervious" to their "responsibility for the public welfare" (xii).

132. Kanter, Rosabeth. *Men and Women of the Corporation.* New York: Basic, 1977. 348.
If "people's attitudes and behaviors take shape out of the experiences they have in their work," then "the corporation is the quintessential contemporary people-producer," since it employs "a large proportion of the labor force." The author explores "how people-production happens in all large bureaucracies" by focusing upon one manufacturing firm.

133. Kefauver, Estes. *In a Few Hands; Monopoly Power in America.* New York: Pantheon, 1965. 239.
Indicts monopoly capitalism.

134. Kotz, David. *Bank Control of Large Corporations in the United States.* Berkeley: U of California P, 1978. 217.
The "giant corporation is the central economic institution in Modern U.S. capitalism" and bankers are the "major group that controls large corporations." "The power held by the leading bankers should be of concern to economists interested in the market behavior of large corporations, to anti-trusters interested in the sources of market power, and to anyone else interested in the concentration of economic power in present-day capitalism."

135. Lappé, Frances, and Joseph Collins. *Food First: Beyond the Myth of Scarcity.* Boston: Houghton, 1977. 466.
Opposes corporate agribusiness and advocates a democratized food system.

136. Lasch, Christopher. *Haven in a Heartless World: The Family Besieged.* New York: Basic, 1977. 230.
Examines the realities of home and family life and of established social science studies of the family. "The sanctity of the home is a sham in a world dominated by giant corporations and by the apparatus of mass promotion." Lasch affirms the possibility of change.

137. Lernoux, Penny. *In Banks We Trust.* Garden City, New York: Anchor/Doubleday, 1984. 310.
A world-ranging story of corruption at the highest levels of the banking establishment--how bankers endanger US depositors by gambling on quick profits, how they evade laws designed to ensure safety for the depositors, how they work with organized crime, the CIA, and Latin-American dictators, and why regulators fail to perform their oversight responsibilities.

138. Lundberg, Ferdinand. The Rich and the Super-Rich: A Study in the Power of Money Today. New York: Stuart, 1968. 1009.
On the oligarchy of the rich who run the country through their money, institutions, and agents.

139. Lydenberg, Steven, et al. Rating America's Corporate Conscience. Reading, MA: Addison-Wesley, 1986. 499.
"A provocative guide to the companies behind the products you buy every day." [See Moskowitz.]

140. Maggin, Donald. Bankers, Builders, Knaves, and Thieves: The $300 Million Scam at ESM. Chicago: Contemporary, 1989. 288.
Beginning in 1985 sixty-eight banks in Ohio failed because of fast and loose deals with securities, and one of the largest and most respected auditing firms in the nation was caught falsifying accounts.

141. McCartney, Laton. Friends in High Places: The Bechtel Story: The Most Secret Corporation and How It Engineered the World. New York: Simon & Schuster, 1988. 273.
A history of a powerful engineering company, builder of nuclear energy plants, oil and gas developer, political wheeler and dealer.

142. McGovern, James. The Oil Game. New York: Viking, 1981. 239.
On the power of oil companies to dominate policies and direct attitudes.

143. Meeting the Corporate Challenge: A Handbook on Corporate Campaigns. Amsterdam: Transnational Information Exchange Report 18/19, 1985. 77.
An attempt to illuminate the "monumental changes . . . that affect the way work is organized, the goods we purchase, the ownership of land, the depletion of resources and the role of women and minorities in the global assembly line," because of transnational corporations. Part 1 Corporate Strategies, Part 2 Counterstrategies (eight case studies).

144. Mokhiber, Russell. Corporate Crime and Violence: Big Business Power and the Abuse of the Public Trust. San Francisco, CA: Sierra Club, 1988. 450.
After documenting thirty-six cases of corporate crime, Mokhiber proposes a fifty point program which argues for the need to discuss publicly the consequences of corporate abuse of the population.

145. Moskowitz, Milton, et al., eds. Everybody's Business: An Almanac. The Irreverent Guide to Corporate America. New York: Harper & Row, 1980. 916.
A reference book about American businesses. [See Lydenberg.]

THE MASTER INSTITUTIONS 31

146. Munson, Richard. The Power Makers. Emmaus, PA: Rodale, 1985. 260.
A critical history of the electrical industry.

147. Nash, Bruce, and Allan Zullo. The Misfortune 500: Featuring the Business Hall of Shame. New York: Pocket, 1988. 210.
"More than 50,000 companies go belly-up every year and tens of thousands of other corporations screw up in some fashion. Nevertheless, blunders don't get the attention they deserve."

148. Nielsen, Waldemar. The Big Foundations. New York: Columbia UP, 1972. 475.
Examines the largest foundations, headed by corporate and financial leaders.

149. Pizzo, Stephen, Mary Fricker, and Paul Muolo. Inside Job: The Looting of America's Savings & Loans. New York: McGraw-Hill, 1989. 443.
Rampant fraud contributed greatly to the possibly $300 billion missing from the S&Ls. A network of S&L executives, con men, and mobsters capitalized on lack of oversight created by Reagan administration deregulation to fleece the public.

150. Reece, Ray. The Sun Betrayed: A Report on the Corporate Seizure of U.S. Solar Energy Development. Boston: South End, 1979. 234.
Analyzes all aspects of the takeover.

151. Ridgeway, James. The Last Play: The Struggle to Monopolize the World's Energy Resources. New York: New American, 1973. 373.
The takeover of natural resources by a few oil companies and utilities.

152. Rifkin, Jeremy. Common Sense II: The Case Against Corporate Tyranny. New York: Bantam, 1975. 111.
Denounces the control of the US by a few corporations and wealthy individuals who have appropriated the land and resources for their own profit. The corporate fourth branch of government has eclipsed the other three. Calls for a change to a "democratic economy": Chapter 18 provides "A Declaration of Economic Independence."

153. Robbins, William. The American Food Scandal: Why You Can't Eat Well on What You Earn. New York: Morrow, 1974. 280.
The food industry systematically deceives the consumers.

154. Role of Giant Corporations. Hearings Before the Subcommittee on Monopoly of the Select Committee on Small Business, U.S. Senate, 91st Cong., 1st Sess. 4 vols. Washington: GPO, 1969-1972.
Surveys the "ever greater power in ever fewer hands."

155. Russett, Bruce M., and Elizabeth C. Hanson. Interest and Ideology: The Foreign Policy Beliefs of American Businessmen. San Francisco: Freeman, 1975. 296.
Capitalism and anticommunism/conservatism produce aggressive foreign policies. Businessmen, military officers, and numerous Republican Party leaders are "the most hawkish of the American elite."

156. Sampson, Anthony. The Sovereign State of ITT. Greenwich, CT: Fawcett, 1974. 335.
ITT's irresponsible history and the need for strong government oversight.

157. Schiller, Herbert. Culture, Inc.: The Corporate Takeover of Public Expression. New York: Oxford UP, 1989. 201.
Examines the increasing power of corporations over all economic and social activity and the consequent danger to "democratic existence, focusing on the increasing ownership and direction of informational systems by a small number of corporations, which have been given First Amendment protection. All information and creative activities, large (network TV) or small (local parades) have come under the influence of varying degrees of the transnational corporate system. The "corporate-sponsored, mass media history machine . . . churns out products that are processed and calibrated to corporate specifications," reality "as seen from the top of the social pyramid" (7).

158. Schiller, Herbert. Who Knows: Information in the Age of the Fortune 500. Norwood, NJ: Ablex, 1981. 187.
New technologies are being turned over to corporations, which already dominate the production and distribution of information.

159. Seldes, George. One Thousand Americans. New York: Boni and Gaer, 1948. 312.
Big Business oligarchies own and run the US.

160. Stevenson, Russell, Jr. Corporations & Information: Secrecy, Access & Disclosure. Baltimore: John Hopkins UP, 1980. 226.
Analyzes the excessive secrecy in corporations and suggests ways to expand access for the public good.

161. Talbot, David, and Richard Morgan. Power and Light: Political Strategies for the Solar Transition. New York: Pilgrim, 1981. 262.
Denounces corporate control of energy resources and advocates renewable energy sources.

162. Vanneman, Reeve, and Lynn W. Cannon. The American Perception of Class. Philadelphia: Temple UP, 1987. 363.
Opposes earlier psychologizing of workers and class conflict and blaming the victims for their subordination. Demonstrates

THE MASTER INSTITUTIONS

that US workers are class conscious because of the strength of US business to overwhelm or redirect any challenge from below. No other working class has faced such a formidable opponent.

163. Webster, Frank, and Kevin Robins. <u>Information Technology: A Luddite Analysis</u>. Norwood, NJ: Ablex, 1986. 375.

The "creation of needs is essential to the continuation of capitalist production" (212). The increasingly "integrated information network allows large corporations to orchestrate decentralized productive and administrative units <u>as if</u> they were centralized" (333). Public opinion polls report a growing sense of alienation and mistrust, but this is producing instead of dissent and resistance only resignation and withdrawal. [See Jennifer Slack.]

164. Whelan, Elizabeth M. <u>A Smoking Gun: How the Tobacco Industry Gets Away with Murder</u>. Philadelphia: Stickley, 1984. 244.

Foreword by former Surgeon General Luther Terry, M.D., recalls the report of January 11, 1964, conclusively linking smoking with many diseases and the failure of the report to stop smoking, partly because of "the economic clout of the tobacco industry." The book "explores the political, economic and social forces which have made the tobacco industry so powerful--and smoking our leading cause of premature death."

165. Woodmansee, John, et al. <u>The World of a Giant Corporation: A Report from the GE Project</u>. Seattle: North Country, 1975. 84.

A study of GE because "a few hundred of the largest corporations now hold decisive economic power" and GE "is the sixth largest" in the world and "the most diversified." Some of the topics: GE and the military-industrial complex, GE and unions, GE and women, GE and monopoly/prices, public relations and image advertising, changing the corporate system: economic democracy, converting from the war machine, and federal chartering.

166. Zilg, Gerard Colby. <u>Du Pont Dynasty</u>. Secaucus, NJ: Lyle Stuart, 1984. 968. (Expanded from <u>Du Pont: Behind the Nylon Curtain</u>, 1974).

Exposé of the Du Pont empire: labor repression, international power, anticommunism as a tool for both, etc. The first edition was censored by its publisher on the demand of Du Pont.

I. A. 3. GOVERNMENT: THE PRESIDENCY (167-221)
(See II.A.4.)

167. Adato, Michelle, et al. <u>Safety Second: The NRC and America's Nuclear Power Plants</u>. Bloomington, IN: Indiana UP, 1987. 194.

As evidenced by its behavior before, during, and after the

Three Mile Island accident, the Nuclear Regulatory Commission is more concerned with special interests than with public safety.

168. Allman, T.D. Unmanifest Destiny: Mayhem and Illusion in American Foreign Policy--From Monroe Doctrine to Reagan's War in El Salvador. Garden City, NY: Dial/ Doubleday, 1984. 468.
The author condemns the nationalistic illusion that the whole world should be "virtuous" like America in order to "save" nations from the "scourge of communism." He points out several actualities, such as Cambodia, Vietnam, but especially Central America, where the US used its power to destroy countries, not save them.

169. Atkinson, Max. Our Masters' Voices: The Language and Body Language of Politics. New York: Methuen, 1984. 203.
Explores the language, verbal and nonverbal, which politicians use to attract, persuade, and gain a positive response from their audiences.

170. Bennett, James R. "Presidential Control of Information: A Bibliography." ORK (1986-87).
Almost 200 entries on President Reagan published serially in four parts beginning with the Spring 1986 issue. [Only significant books are repeated in this collection, annotations shortened.]

171. Brownstein, Ronald, and Nina Easton. Reagan's Ruling Class: Portrait of the President's Top 100 Officials. Washington, DC: Presidential Accountability Group, 1982. 747.
A generally negative picture of Reagan's executive branch, who are mostly white, male, middle-class, middle-aged, wealthy, successful people who favor the rich, expand military at the expense of social programs, and cut regulatory social functions of government.

172. Burchett, Wilfred. Shadows of Hiroshima. London: Verso, 1983. 123.
Chapter 3 on the news suppression of the effects of the Hiroshima and Nagasaki bombings by the U.S. government, "on a vast scale and in a monstrous cause."

173. Chomsky, Noam. The Chomsky Reader. Ed. James Peck. New York: Pantheon, 1987. 492.
Exposes the self-righteous beliefs and consequences of US imperialism and violence, with special attention to aggression, war crimes, and genocide in Asia and Central America, while at home protest against these crimes is controlled by engineered consent.

174. Commager, Henry S. The Defeat of America: Presidential Power and the National Character. New York: Simon,

THE MASTER INSTITUTIONS 35

1974. 163.
Fanatical anticommunism led the US to oppose liberation movements and to expand its military power throughout the world. These depredations were equally damaging domestically, for anticommunism eroded the Constitution and Bill of Rights, especially in increasing the arrogance of the presidency.

175. [Cancelled]

176. Demac, Donna. Keeping America Uninformed: Government Secrecy in the 1980s. New York: Pilgrim Press, 1984. 180.
Ten chapters on the Reagan campaign to curtail information to the public: OMB, regulatory agencies, Congress, media, science, statistics, libraries, secrecy. Chapter eleven gives a Directory of Public Organizations fighting back.

177. Drew, Elizabeth. Politics and Money: The New Road to Corruption. New York: Macmillan, 1983. 166.
The rising expense of campaigning is corrupting the politicians and the political system.

178. Dunaway, David. How Can I Keep From Singing: Pete Seeger. New York: McGraw-Hill, 1981. 386.
Partly an account of the government's attempts to suppress Seeger's political views. One of the first musicians in US history to be investigated for sedition, a clash with the House Committee on Un-American Activities began seven years of court battle. Blacklisted, picketed, and stoned by conservative groups, Seeger survived to sing his message of socialism, peace, and justice.

179. Epstein, Edward Jay. Agency of Fear: Opiates and Political Power in America. New York: Putnam's, 1977. 261.
Nixon's "war on heroin" was the rationale for creating several new law enforcement agencies outside of constitutional frameworks in an attempt to achieve virtually a coup d'état.

180. The Final Report of the Select Committee on Presidential Campaign Activities, U.S. Senate. Washington: GPO, 1974. 1250.
The investigation of illegal activities by the Nixon administration during the 1972 presidential campaign.

181. Goldston, Robert. The American Nightmare: Senator Joseph R. McCarthy & the Politics of Hate. Indianapolis: Bobbs-Merrill, 1973. 202.
McCarthyism was "a political device to smash the old New Deal coalition, cunningly employed by certain unscrupulous politicians," "an outlet for the paranoia of the lunatic fringe of the extreme right," a means to political power for McCarthy, and "a flight from reality" on the part of the public.

182. Halperin, Morton, and Daniel Hoffman. Freedom vs. National Security, Secrecy, and Surveillance. New York: Chelsea, 1977. 594.
Assesses several court decisions which have limited the rights of all American citizens by perpetuating secrecy and deceit on all levels of US government in the name of national security.

183. Hersh, Seymour. The Price of Power: Kissinger in the Nixon White House. New York: Summit, 1983. 698.
The anti-democratic machinations of Nixon and Kissinger.

184. [Cancelled]

185. Higgs, Robert. Crisis and Leviathan: Critical Episodes in the Growth of American Government. New York: Oxford UP, 1987. 350.
Traces the expansion of the federal government in the twentieth century, arguing that political and other interests have exploited a series of crises to legitimize government power.

186. Katz, Steven. Government Secrecy: Decisions Without Democracy. Washington, DC: People for the American Way, 1987. 104.
Documents the growing secrecy throughout the federal government and its dangers to US democracy. "Excessive government secrecy threatens our health, our safety, and most importantly our democracy." Exposes "the machinations of secrecy from the life-long censorship of government employees to the Pentagon's 'Black Budget'--secret even from Congress."

187. Klare, Michael, and Peter Kornbluh, eds. Low-Intensity Warfare: Counterinsurgency, Proinsurgency, and Antiterrorism in the Eighties. New York: Pantheon, 1988. 250.
In pursuit of global dominance through counter-revolution, two campaigns are being waged by the US: 1) suppression of national liberation movements threatening allies and support of liberation movements threatening Soviet allies, which includes propaganda, and 2) a "hearts and minds" political campaign at home "to garner grass-roots support for renewed interventionism."

188. Kurland, Philip. Watergate and the Constitution. Chicago: U of Chicago P, 1978. 261.
On the excessive power now located in the executive branch and especially the White House.

189. Kutler, Stanley. The Wars of Watergate: The Last Crisis of Richard Nixon. New York: Knopf, 1990.
Compares Haldeman's and Ehrlichman's notes of their conversations with Nixon and other evidence at the National Archives to demonstrate decisively Nixon's early and continuing direction of Watergate crimes and cover-up (from rev., book not inspected).

THE MASTER INSTITUTIONS   37

190. Ladd, Bruce. Crisis in Credibility. New York: New
      American Library, 1968. 247.
   The book "deals exclusively with three practices of the
executive branch--secrecy, lying, and news management."
Ladd's conclusion: our system of government no longer enables
the free flow of ideas in the marketplace of democracy because
the presidency has become too powerful and arrogant.

191. Leggett, John G. "The Political Institution."
      American Society: A Critical Analysis. Ed. Reynolds
      & Henslin. New York: McKay, 1973. 66-108.
   The state is the most powerful "ideology-producing institution" by regulation and dissemination of information by
elites, which in the US means businessmen and their subordinates. The essay focuses on "both content of themes and forms
of dissemination used to control populations" by inducing them
to internalize views favored by the state (68). Resistance or
revolution by the people occurs when state myths are no longer
accepted.

192. Lockard, Duane. The Perverted Priorities of American
      Politics. New York: Macmillan, 1971. 337.
   A study of unequal power and its consequences in war,
poverty, and other dysfunctions. The opening chapter exposes
the narrowly concentrated political and economic authority in
the country; subsequent chapters discuss the party system,
federalism, Congress, the judiciary, and the presidency and
bureaucracy. The final chapter turns to "What is to Be Done?"
with remedies that "work within the existing system."

193. Marshall, Jonathan, Peter D. Scott, and Jane Hunter.
      The Iran-Contra Connection: Secret Teams and Covert
      Operations in the Reagan Era. Boston: South End,
      1987. 313.
   Argues that the Iran-Contra scandal is an outgrowth of a
long history of covert activities. What is presented in The
Tower Commission Report as bureaucratic alienation is here
exposed in its historical and institutional roots. "The
policies embodied in both the arms sales and the diversion of
funds for a variety of dirty purposes were carried out by
powerful transnational networks of individuals and organizations long associated with rabid anti-communism." (Preface by
Richard Falk, viii). "Unlike the rosy picture accepted by
most Americans, Reaganism has undermined constitutionalism in
structural ways" (x).

194. Mathews, Anthony S. The Darker Reaches of Government:
      Access to Information about Public Administration in
      the U.S., Britain, and South Africa. Berkeley: U of
      California P, 1978. 245.
   Situates the US between Sweden and South Africa in regard to
open government.

195. Mayer, Jane, and Doyle McManus. Landslide: The
      Unmaking of the President, 1984-1988. Boston:

Houghton Mifflin, 1988. 468.
Studies Reagan's second term, an administration that mistook a landslide reelection for an unlimited mandate that resulted in numerous disasters: the inside staff rivalries, Nancy's power, the Iran-Contra scandal, obsession with secrecy and deception, especially a failure of presidential leadership.

196. McGaffin, William, and Erwin Knoll. *Anything But the Truth: The Credibility Gap--How the News is Managed in Washington*. New York: Putnam's, 1968. 250.
Government "secrecy, deception, and distortion of the news" are "grave and growing."

197. McMahan, Jeff. *Reagan and the World: Imperial Policy in the New Cold War*. New York: Monthly Review, 1985. 300.
On Reagan's foreign policies: two chapters on arms buildup; four chapters on Third World interventionism; front and end chapters on imperial policy; appendix on the Kissinger report on Central America. He analyzes nuclear weapons as instruments of coercion and arms control as exercises in public relations. The chapters on interventionism expose the discrepancies between avowed humanitarian aims and real military aggression.

198. McQuaid, Kim. *The Anxious Years: America in the Vietnam-Watergate Era*. New York: Basic, 1989. 350.
Treats Tet, Chicago, and Watergate as landmarks of a single military, social, and political disaster that continues today with the Iran-Contra crimes.

199. McWilliams, Carey. *Witch Hunt: The Revival of Heresy*. Boston: Little, Brown, 1950. 361.
Witch hunts function to "control men's thoughts and to police their loyalties," a regression "clearly evident" in the US "today."

200. Mollenhoff, Clark. *Washington Cover-Up*. New York: Doubleday, 1962. 239.
Mainly about the Truman and Eisenhower administrations' secrecy and deceit.

201. Nelson-Pallmeyer, Jack. *War Against the Poor: Low Intensity Conflict and Christian Faith*. Maryknoll, NY: Orbis, 1989. 125.
Discusses Low-Intensity Conflict (LIC), a relatively new approach to US intervention which "victimizes the poor through terrorism, exploitation, the use of elections for undemocratic purposes, and disinformation campaigns." LIC, in using many aspects of warfare to slow or stop social change in the Third World, contradicts democratic values and Christian faith while protecting national interests.

202. Orman, John M. *Presidential Secrecy and Deception: Beyond the Power to Persuade*. Westport, CT: Greenwood, 1980. 239.

THE MASTER INSTITUTIONS

"The focus of this book is secrecy and covert presidential power as they relate to presidential deception, with selected covert programs in the Kennedy, Johnson, Nixon, and Ford administrations being examined."

203. Peterzell, Jay. Reagan's Secret Wars. Washington, DC: Center for National Security Studies, 1984. 100.
The Reagan administration's belief that covert action should be a routine rather than an exceptional instrument of US foreign relations severely limits the operations of public debate and discourse in guiding foreign policy.

204. Prados, John. Presidents' Secret Wars: CIA and Pentagon Covert Operations Since World War II. New York: William Morrow, 1986. 480.
An assessment of the secret wars (covert operations, clandestine operations, special operations, paramilitary operations) perpetrated by the president, the CIA, and the Pentagon designed to intervene in the affairs of other nations and to alter the course of global politics.

205. Relyea, Harold, et al. The Presidency and Information Policy. New York: Center for the Study of the Presidency, Proceedings, 4.1 (1981) 216.
Seven essays include security vs. the right to know, the Carter White House information management, executive privilege, presidential libraries, and the president and the media.

206. Rourke, Francis. Secrecy and Publicity: Dilemmas of Democracy. Baltimore: Johns Hopkins UP, 1966. 236. (Orig. pub. 1961).
The ability of leaders to control communications and manipulate public opinion "has now opened up an avenue through which the gap between totalitarian and democratic government can progressively be narrowed, as modern dictators gradually substitute persuasion for coercion" (vii). The 9 chapters are divided into "Secrecy in American Bureaucracy" and "The Power of Publicity."

207. Schandler, Herbert Y. The Unmaking of a President: Lyndon B. Johnson and Vietnam. Princeton, NJ: Princeton UP, 1977. 419.
How President Johnson's authority as president was dissolved.

208. Scheer, Robert. With Enough Shovels: Reagan, Bush & Nuclear War. New York: Random House, 1983. 285.
Interviews of government officials discovered their "appalling ignorance" about nuclear bombs and war.

209. Schell, Jonathan. The Time of Illusion. New York: Knopf, 1976. 393.
An analysis of the Nixon administration in the context of the Vietnam War. Parts of the book discuss Nixon's offensive against the press.

210. Shawcross, William. Sideshow: Kissinger, Nixon and the Destruction of Cambodia. New York: Simon, 1979. 467.
An account of the secret, falsified, illegal, and unconstitutional bombings of Cambodia during the Vietnam War.

211. Sklar, Holly. Washington's War on Nicaragua. Boston: South End, 1988. 472.
A survey of the Reagan-Bush administration's fanatical obsession to destroy the Sandinista government by demonizing and destabilizing the government through propaganda, invasion by mercenary army, covert operations, and economic sanctions.

212. Smith, Myron, Jr., comp. Watergate: An Annotated Bibliography of Sources in English, 1972-1982. Metuchen, NJ: Scarecrow, 1983. 329.
Index: see "Press Coverage" and "Television Coverage."

213. Stockman, David. The Triumph of Politics: How the Reagan Revolution Failed. New York: Harper, 1986. 422.
The author was Reagan's first budget director, who tried but failed to explain the rising deficit to the anti-tax president. Stockman shows Reagan as an intellectually vacuous person tied to a few simple conservative ideas.

214. Vaughn, Stephen. Holding Fast the Inner Lines: Democracy, Nationalism, and the Committee on Public Information. Chapel Hill: U of North Carolina P, 1980. 397.
During WWI the CPI was the US government's first large-scale propaganda agency, also known as the Creel Committee. "The CPI proved spectacularly successful in mobilizing public opinion behind the country's participation in the World War of 1917-18." The author explores the extent to which the CPI weakened or strengthened democracy in the US.

215. The Watergate Hearings: Break-in and Cover-Up. Proceedings of the Senate Select Committee on Presidential Campaign Activities as Edited by the Staff of "The New York Times." New York: Viking, 1973. 886.
With a narrative, a chronology, and index.

216. Wattenberg, Martin. The Decline of American Political Parties, 1952-1980. Cambridge, MA: Harvard UP, 1984. 160.
Some causes: increase of candidate imagery and as cognitive object with decrease of party, growth of PACs and other non-party financing, presidential nomination rule changes that undercut party leaders and raise influence of candidate. Parties matter because "pure candidate-domination of elections is a recipe for domination of the political order by the haves at the expense of the have-nots" (xiii).

217. White, Ralph. Nobody Wanted War. New York: Doubleday Anchor, 1970. 347.

THE MASTER INSTITUTIONS

Attempt to identify the psychological foundations of war, particularly the Vietnam War. The last 3 chapters attempt to explain why we must change our perceptions and ways of thinking and how to accomplish such a major task.

218. White, Theodore. Breach of Faith: The Fall of Richard Nixon. New York: Atheneum, 1975. 373.
Of all the US political myths, the "crowning myth" is the presidency as upholder of "equal justice under law" and "due process of law." Nixon and his subordinates broke that myth.

219. Wise, David. The Politics of Lying: Government Deception, Secrecy, and Power. New York: Vintage, 1973. 614.
Part I offers many examples of lying by government officials; Part II deals mainly with the excessive "security" classification system; Part III is about Nixon's public relations; Part IV manipulation of the press; and V remedies.

220. Woodward Bob, and Carl Bernstein. The Final Days. New York: Simon & Schuster, 1976. 529.
An account of the Nixon White House crimes.

221. Zinn, Howard, and Noam Chomsky, eds. The Pentagon Papers: Critical Essays. Vol. 5. Boston: Beacon P, 1972. 341.
Various explorations of secret and illegal activities during the Vietnam War, of the publication of the government's secret plans, and of the government's attempt to prevent their publication and to prosecute those involved.

I. A. 4. a. GOVERNMENT: MILITARY (222-271)

222. Ackley, Charles. The Modern Military in American Society: A Study in the Nature of Military Power. Philadelphia: Westminster, 1972. 400.
Examines the "deepening patterns of rationalized violence," the effects of a "garrison state" mentality, etc.

223. Ambrose, Stephen, and James Barber, Jr. The Military and American Society: Essays & Readings. New York: Free, 1972. 322.
On the impact on US society of "the most powerful Armed Forces the world has ever known."

224. Bender, David, ed. The American Military: Opposing Viewpoints. St. Paul, MN: Greenhaven, 1983. 227.
Chapter 2, "Is the U.S. a Militaristic Society?"

225. Bennett, James R. Grassroots Militarism: A Model for Community Research. Eureka Springs, AR: Center on War & the Child, 1989. 30.
A study of militarism and its alternatives in one county in Arkansas, the structures and processes that reflect and con-

tribute to militarism or which oppose it on the local level.

226. Betts, Richard. Soldiers, Statesmen, and Cold War Crises. Cambridge, MA: Harvard UP, 1977. 292.
Responsibility for US Cold War decisions divided equally between military and civilian leaders.

227. Boyer, William. Education for Annihilation. Honolulu: Hogarth, 1972. 162.
A study of the militaristic mind-set which exists in America and pervades the American social, economical, and political institutions. "The war system is described as a cultural system in which people have been taught to embrace a way of life that supports military threat systems, so they find it hard to understand what they are doing and even harder to extricate themselves" (Intro.). The concluding chapter outlines solutions which could transform the present day war system into a rational, educational, survival, peace system.

228. Clotfelter, James. The Military in American Politics. New York: Harper, 1973. 244.
On the powerful influence of the military establishment over both foreign and domestic policies.

229. Coffin, Tristram. The Armed Society: Militarism in Modern America. Baltimore: Penguin, 1964. 287. (First published as The Passion of the Hawks: Militarism in Modern America. New York: Macmillan, 1964. 280.)

230. Coffin, Tristram. The Passion of the Hawks: Militarism in Modern America. New York: Macmillan, 1964. 280.
Chapter 2 summarizes the history and aspects of US militarism and subsequent chapters expand the topics. "There is no evidence that we are peace-loving or ever have been."

231. Cook, Fred. The Warfare State. New York: Macmillan, 1962. 376.
Traces rising ascendance of the military through a permanent war economy, constant propaganda of foreign threat, etc.

232. Donovan, James A., Col. Militarism, U.S.A. New York: Scribner's, 1970. 265.
On the immense power and influence of the vast military establishment of the Pentagon, armed forces, industry, secrecy, propaganda, money, etc.

233. Emerson, Steven. Secret Warriors: Inside the Covert Military Operations of the Reagan Era. New York, Putnam's, 1988. 256.
Covert operations were organized 1980-1987 by the Pentagon and Army through the National Security Council to circumvent Congressional oversight. The NSC "became a de facto center for unauthorized covert operations," leading to violations of laws and involving the US in international crises.

THE MASTER INSTITUTIONS

234. Falk, Richard, and Samuel Kim, eds. The War System: An Interdisciplinary Approach. Boulder, CO: Westview, 1980. 659.
   This anthology analyzes the causes of war and the contributing factors which cultivate the war system of all levels of society. The editors believe war can be eliminated if we understand all the facets of a war system and the most fundamental beliefs, values, attitudes, and myths which make up US consciousness.

235. Fitzgerald, A. Ernest. The Pentagonists: An Insider's View of Waste, Mismanagement, and Fraud in Defense Spending. Boston, MA: Houghton Mifflin, 1989, 344.
   This famous whistle blower (High Priests of Waste, 1972) gives a history of military programs in the 1970s and 1980s that were corrupt, badly managed, and politically motivated. Especially during the Reagan years much of the trillions of dollars was wasted on graft and defective weapons.

236. Fulbright, J. William. The Pentagon Propaganda Machine. New York: Vintage/Random House, 1970. 166.
   The incursions of the military in our civilian system "have subverted or muffled civilian voices within the executive branch, weakened the constitutional role . . . of Congress, and laid an economic and psychological burden on the public that could be disastrous" (157).

237. Galbraith, John K. How to Control the Military. Garden City, NY: Doubleday, 1969. 69.
   Shows how a few powerful men in the Pentagon, the defense industries, and Congress have succeeded in reversing America's basic constitutional processes, and sets forth ten ways to reestablish civilian and constitutional control over the military establishment.

238. Gerson, Joseph. The Deadly Connection: Nuclear War & U.S. Intervention. Foreword by Bishop Thomas Gumbleton. Philadelphia: New Society, 1986. 253.
   Explores "the relationship between U.S. nuclear policy and past, present, and future U.S. military intervention around the globe" in terms of diminishing resources, exploitation of the Third World, corporate expansion, and the maintenance of "a war system."

239. Heise, Juergen. Minimum Disclosure: How the Pentagon Manipulates the News. New York: W.W. Norton, 1979. 221.
   Analysis of Pentagon-media relationships which provides an in-depth analysis of why the media respond feebly to military power and do not question the status quo. Heise focuses especially on how the military controls bad news through centralized review, public relations, constant appeal to "national security," etc.

240. Hersh, Seymour. Cover-Up. New York: Random House,

1972. 305.
Analyzes both the Army's attempt to white-wash the My Lai 4 massacre and the military system that produced it.

241. Kaku, Michio, and Daniel Axelrod. To Win a Nuclear War: The Pentagon's Secret Strategy. Boston: South End, 1986. 350.
On US nuclear war brinkmanship, first strike plans, and other secret intentions of "winning" a nuclear war.

242. [Cancelled]

243. Knoll, Erwin, and Judith McFadden, eds. American Militarism, 1970: A Dialogue on the Distortion of Our National Priorities and the Need to Reassert Control over the Defense Establishment. New York: Viking, 1969. 150.
An edited transcript of the Congressional Conference on the Military Budget and National Priorities (1969), which discussed the militarization of the US, arms control, the Vietnam War, and related subjects. Epilogue by Senator J. William Fulbright.

244. Knoll, Erwin, and Judith McFadden, eds. War Crimes and the American Conscience. New York: Holt, 1970. 208.
An edited transcript of the Congressional Conference on War and National Responsibility (1970), a discussion of war crimes, including US war crimes in Vietnam.

245. Lapp, Ralph. Kill & Overkill--The Strategy of Annihilation. New York: Basic, 1962. 197.
Criticizes dangerous over-building of weapons and secrecy. Last chapter recommends 5 steps to turn around US nuclear policies and increase security: eliminate first strike weapons, cease producing new bombs, declare space off limits, etc.

246. Lifton, Robert J. Home from the War. New York: Simon and Schuster, 1973. 478.
The author uses the Vietnam War as a psychological model to explain the mythology of war and its immeasurable relationship with the expanding militarization of American society. The last two chapters explain ways in which Americans can change and heal our warring attitudes.

247. Loory, Stuart H. Defeated: Inside America's Military Machine. New York: Random House, 1973. 405.
The "defeat" is to US as a nation by the immense military-industrial bureaucracy that is suffocating the country politically and economically.

248. Manno, Jack. Arming the Heavens: The Hidden Military Agenda for Space, 1945-1995. New York: Dodd, 1984. 245.
By the fifties all the armed services and the CIA had secret space-war programs. By the time the public knew about the

THE MASTER INSTITUTIONS

military's space plans the momentum carried Reagan's Star Wars proposal. In Chapter 18 Manno urges the people to oppose the militarization of space and to seek international treaties.

249. McGaffin, William, and Erwin Knoll. Scandal in the Pentagon: A Challenge to Democracy. Greenwich, CT: Fawcett, 1969. 192.
Decries the pervasive militarization of the nation.

250. Melman, Seymour. The Permanent War Economy: American Capitalism in Decline. New York: Simon and Schuster, 1974. 384.
Military spending has led us to ignore the areas of capital investment that would revive our economy and the civilian control of the economy that would expand social justice. [Melman also authored Pentagon Capitalism (1970) and The War Economy of the United States (1971).]

251. Mollenhoff, Clark. The Pentagon: Politics, Profit, and Plunder. New York: Putnam's, 1967. 450.
An exposé of the "colossal multi-million dollar propaganda machine" whose power is so omnipresent that its ideology is often accepted without question.

252. Nelkin, Dorothy. The University and Military Research: Moral Politics at M.I.T. Ithaca and London: Cornell UP, 1972. 195.
Students and faculty opposition in 1969 to M.I.T.'s Instrumentation Laboratory, which worked for the Pentagon and NASA.

253. Nisbet, Robert. The Present Age--Progress and Anarchy in Modern America. New York: Harper & Row, 1988. 145.
Militarization--the growth of the military establishment into a globalized imperial power--produced today's state centralization and pervasive bureaucracy.

254. Perry, Mark. Four Stars: The Inside Story of the Forty-Year Battle Between the Joint Chiefs of Staff and America's Civilian Leaders. Boston, MA: Houghton Mifflin, 1989. 412.
A history from creation of the JCS to the end of the Reagan administration, focusing on the rebellion of the Chiefs in August 1967 over how the Vietnam War was being fought as a watershed in the political struggle over the influence of the JCS.

255. Prados, John. Pentagon Games: Wargames & the American Military. New York: Harper & Row, 1987. 81.
Surveys the history of war games, our inadequate knowledge about war, how wargames are created and performed, and "the danger of the mystique of wargames." Also contains three games designed by the author on bureaucratic politics, the process of research and development, and the Vietnam War.

256. Raymond, Jack. *Power at the Pentagon*. New York: Harper & Row, 1964. 363.
A report on the increasingly uncontrollable Pentagon power. As the U.S. increases military influence to secure national interest, we alter and endanger every aspect of our society.

257. Reardon, Betty. *Sexism and the War System*. New York: World Policy Institute, 1985. 136.
Militarism promotes sexism among other anti-social behaviors. Urges fusion of feminist and peace scholarship.

258. Rising, Richard. "The Military Institution." *American Society: A Critical Analysis*. Ed. Reynolds and Henslin. New York: McKay, 1973. 109-141.
"The basic *fact* . . . of the twentieth century has been the inexorable growth and development of the American Empire, backed as always by military might" (110). Domestically the military has extended so far into the economic, political, and social structure that increased totalitarian control is a "very real prospect."

259. Rodberg, Leonard, and Derek Shearer, eds. *The Pentagon Watchers: Students Report on the National Security State*. Garden City, NY: Doubleday, 1970. 416.
Ten essays on the military-industrial complex, one on Pentagon propaganda.

260. Russett, Bruce, and Alfred Stepan, eds. *Military Force and American Society*. New York: Harper & Row, 1973. 371.
Explores "the causes and effects of an expanding political role for the American armed forces and the increasing reliance by civilians on military methods." Sections on "Politicization of the Military," "Militarization of the Polity," and "The New Politics of National Security," which is an extensive bibliography (196-371).

261. Stapp, Andy. *Up Against the Brass*. New York: Simon & Schuster, 1970. 192.
The author's account of his fight to create a union for US soldiers, in opposition to the Vietnam War and the Army's anti-democratic practices. By 1970 he headed the American Servicemen's Union of 8,000.

262. Swomley, John, Jr., ed. *Militarism in Education*. Washington, D.C.: National Council Against Conscription, 1950. 80.
Militarization increasing.

263. Swomley, John, Jr. *The Military Establishment*. Boston: Beacon, 1964. 266.
Chapters 1-8 on the struggle against universal military training (UMT), 9-15 on diverse aspects of military influence.

THE MASTER INSTITUTIONS

264. Swomley, John, Jr. **Press Agents of the Pentagon.** Washington, D.C.: National Council Against Conscription, 1953. 55.
Pentagon propaganda has played a significant part in producing the immense military machine.

265. Tirman, John, ed. **The Militarization of High Technology.** Cambridge, MA: Ballinger, 1984. 247.
The military machine has subverted commercial development and the nation's economic competitiveness.

266. Trofimenko, Genrikh. **U.S. Military Doctrine.** USSR: Progress, 1986. 222.
"Falsifying the 'Enemy's' Intentions and Image: The American Way of Justifying the Arms Race" (130-146): US leaders systematically falsified data about the actual state of the US/SU strategic balance in order to frighten Congress and the public and to justify building more and more weapons.

267. Wells, Ronald, ed. **The Wars of America: Christian Views.** Grand Rapids, MI: Eerdmans, 1981. 280.
On 8 major US wars from the Revolution to World Wars I and II, the Korean, and the Vietnam Wars, and the tension between Christian love and Christian responsibility to the state.

268. Wieseltier, Leon. **Nuclear War, Nuclear Peace.** New York: New Republic/Holt, 1983. 109.
Condemns doctrines of Reagan and the nuclear hawks.

269. Yakovlev, A. **On the Edge of an Abyss: From Truman to Reagan, The Doctrines and Realities of the Nuclear Age.** USSR: Progress, 1985. 400.
Centers on the psychological conditioning of the US people to accept growing militarism and foreign intervention. "Americans are accustomed to deception, cynicism and demagogy in politics." Behavior is stereotyped and "cluttered with myths" of "defense" which are in reality policies of worldwide interventionism.

270. Yarmolinsky, Adam. **The Military Establishment: Its Impacts on American Society.** New York: Harper, 1971. 434.
The power of the military in government and business and its propaganda machine. The military establishment is "the single most powerful and pervasive establishment in our society."

271. Yarmolinsky, Adam, and Gregory Foster. **Paradoxes of Power: The Military Establishment in the Eighties.** Bloomington: Indiana UP, 1983. 154.
Examines the paradoxes of deterrence, limited response, military bureaucracy, and peaceful policy under the topics of civilian policy makers, the structure of the military establishment, the impacts on the economy and the society at large, civilian control, and alternatives.

I. A. 4. b. GOVERNMENT: INTELLIGENCE (272-334)

272. Agee, Philip. *Inside the Company: CIA Diary.* New York: Stonehill, 1975. 639.
Revelations of the "huge and sinister" CIA.

273. Bamford, James. *The Puzzle Palace: A Report on America's Most Secret Agency.* New York: Houghton, Mifflin; England: Penguin, 1983. 655.
Examines the National Security Agency and the use and abuse of technological espionage and surveillance. NSA's "potential to violate the privacy of American citizens is unmatched" (473).

274. Beck, Melvin. *Secret Contenders: The Myth of Cold War Counterintelligence.* New York: Sheridan, 1985. 192.
Partly about CIA efforts to convince the public that the US is engaged in a war against an implacable enemy, which serves US policy by justifying any action, no matter how unconstitutional, wasteful, or counterproductive. An exposé of the mystique the CIA has spent so much money and time creating.

275. Bennett, James R. "The Agencies of Secrecy." NaR 9 (Winter 1986) 41-47.
A bibliographical guide to U.S. intelligence agencies, 143 books and articles.

276. Berman, Jerry J., and Morton H. Halperin, eds. *The Abuses of the Intelligence Agencies.* Washington, DC: Center for National Security Studies, 1975. 185.
Further information about the continuing violations of laws and Constitution by the intelligence agencies.

277. Blackstock, Nelson. *COINTELPRO: The FBI's Secret War on Political Freedom.* New York: Vintage, 1976. 216.
The FBI's counterintelligence program (Co-Intel-Pro) against socialists and protesters of the Vietnam War was illegal and unconstitutional.

278. Borosage, Robert L, and John Marks, eds. *The CIA File.* New York: Grossman, 1976. 236.
Eleven papers examine domestic and global covert operations as violations of Constitution, law, and ethics.

279. Chernyavsky, V., ed. *The CIA in the Dock: Soviet Journalists on International Terrorism.* Trans. Cynthia Carlile. Moscow: Progress, 1983. 176.
The CIA employs both ideological and terrorist tactics against both socialist and Third World liberation governments to further US imperialist objectives.

280. Churchill, Ward, and Jim Vander Wall. *Cointelpro Papers: Documents from the FBI's Secret Wars Against Dissent in the United States.* Boston: South End, 1990. 320.

THE MASTER INSTITUTIONS

Compiles hundreds of FBI documents which reveal that the Black Panthers, the American Indian Movement (AIM), and a host of other domestic organizations over the past seventy years have been victims of the US political police. [See same authors' Agents of Repression.]

281. Cook, Fred. The FBI Nobody Knows. New York: Macmillan, 1964. 436.
By a "monumental propaganda effort," Hoover and the FBI "have made themselves sacrosanct." Consequently, the "police state looms on the horizon" (414).

282. Cowan, Paul, Nick Egleson, and Nat Hentoff. State Secrets: Police Surveillance in America. New York: Holt, 1974. 333.
The "machinery of fear" continues to compel obedience and conformity--bugging, informers, grand juries, data banks, etc.

283. Donner, Frank. The Age of Surveillance: The Aims and Methods of America's Political Intelligence System. New York: Knopf, 1980. 554.
A critique of the long domestic political espionage system against dissent by the FBI and other agencies.

284. Donner, Frank. Protectors of Privilege: Red Squads & Police Repression in Urban America. Berkeley: U of California P, 1990. 496.

285. Frazier, Howard, ed. Uncloaking the CIA. New York: Free, 1978. 288.
The CIA is the "gravedigger of liberty at home as well as abroad" in the name of "national security" but in the service of the corporate state.

286. Garrison, Omar V. Spy Government: The Emerging Police State in America. New York: Stuart, 1967. 277.
Government agencies on all levels are increasingly intruding in the lives of ordinary people.

287. Garrow, David. The FBI and Martin Luther King, Jr.: From "Solo" to Memphis. New York: Norton, 1981. 320.
Explains FBI pursuit of King throughout the 1960s.

288. Garwood, Darrell. Under Cover: Thirty-Five Years of C.I.A. Deception. New York: Grove, 1985. 309. (Orig. American Shadow. Stafford, VA: Dan River, 1980).
Chronicles CIA illegalities at home and abroad.

289. Halperin, Morton, and Daniel Hoffman. Freedom VS. National Security: Secrecy and Surveillance. New York and London: Chelsea, 1977. 594.
On the increasing violations of constitutional rights by government officials in the name of national security.

290. Halperin, Morton, et al. The Lawless State: The Crimes of the U.S. Intelligence Agencies. Harmondsworth, Eng.: Penguin, 1976. 328.
Exposes the abuses by intelligence agencies in secret and largely unaccountable. The final section suggests ways to curb their illegitimate power.

291. Intelligence Activities. Hearings Before the Select Committee to Study Governmental Operations with Respect to Intelligence Activities of the U.S. Senate, 94th Cong., 1st Session. 7 vols. Washington: GPO, 1975.
The Church Committee Hearings.

292. Intelligence Activities. Hearings Before the Select Committee to Study Governmental Operations with Respect to Intelligence Activities of the U.S. Senate, 94th Congress, 1st Sess. Vol. 1: "Unauthorized Storage of Toxic Agents." Washington: GPO, 1975. 245.
Exposes illegal CIA biological poisons.

293. Intelligence Activities. Hearings Before the Select Committee to Study Governmental Operations with Respect to Intelligence Activities of the U.S. Senate, 94th Cong., 1st Sess. Vol. 2: "Huston Plan." Washington: GPO, 1975. 403.
Exposes the illegal and unconstitutional domestic spying operation of the Nixon administration.

294. Intelligence Activities. Hearings Before the Select Committee to Study Governmental Operations with Respect to Intelligence Activities of the U.S. Senate, 94th Congress, 1st Sess. Vol. 3: "Internal Revenue Service." Washington: GPO, 1975. 124.
On the illegal political activities of the IRS.

295. Intelligence Activities. Hearings Before the Select Committee to Study Governmental Operations with Respect to Intelligence Activities of the U.S. Senate, 94th Congress, 1st Sess. Vol. 4: "Mail Opening." Washington: GPO, 1975. 260.
Investigates the illegal and unconstitutional surveillance of mail.

296. Intelligence Activities. Hearings Before the Select Committee to Study Governmental Operations with Respect to Intelligence Activities of the U.S. Senate, 94th Congress, 1st Sess. Vol. 5: "The National Security Agency and Fourth Amendment Rights." Washington: GPO, 1975. 165.
On the NSA as a political spying arm of the presidency.

297. Intelligence Activities. Hearings Before the Select Committee to Study Governmental Operations with

THE MASTER INSTITUTIONS 51

> Respect to Intelligence Activities of the U.S.
> Senate, 94th Congress, 1st Sess. Vol. 6: "Federal
> Bureau of Investigation." Washington: GPO, 1975.
> 1000.

Reveals illegal and unconstitutional activities of the FBI.

298. Intelligence Activities. Hearings Before the Select
Committee to Study Governmental Operations with
Respect to Intelligence Activities of the U.S.
Senate, 94th Congress, 1st Sess. Vol. 7: "Covert
Action." Washington: GPO, 1975. 230.

On unconstitutional and illegal CIA activities abroad.

299. Foreign and Military Intelligences: Final Report, Book
I. United States Senate, Select Committee to Study
Governmental Operations with Respect to Intelligence
Activities. 94th Congress, 2nd Session. Washington:
GPO, 1976. 651.

The Church Committee Report. Also see Book IV, Supplementary Detailed Staff Reports on Foreign and Military Intelligence. (N.B. Nos. 299 & 300 constitute one Report.)

300. Intelligence Activities and the Rights of Americans.
Final Report, Book II. United States Senate, Select
Committee to Study Governmental Operations with
Respect to Intelligence Activities. 94th Congress,
2nd Session. Washington: GPO, 1976. 396.

The Church Committee Report. Also see Book III, Supplementary Detailed Staff Reports on Intelligence Activities and the Rights of Americans.

301. Johnson, Loch. America's Secret Power: The CIA in a
Democratic Society. New York: Oxford UP, 1989. 344.

A study of both domestic and foreign activities, for in reality "they are often closely linked." Part II examines the major dangers posed by CIA foreign operations. Part III "examines the most chilling threat posed by secret intelligence agencies: their use against the very citizens they are meant to protect." Chapters 8 and 9 explore the CIA in universities and media.

302. Johnson, Loch. A Season of Inquiry: The Senate
Intelligence Investigation. Lexington: UP of
Kentucky, 1985. 317.

On the Church Committee's investigations of unconstitutional and illegal activities of the intelligence agencies and presidents, and the failure to establish a permanent framework of oversight and accountability for the future.

303. Keller, William. The Liberals and J. Edgar Hoover:
Rise and Fall of a Domestic Intelligence State.
Princeton, NJ: Princeton UP, 1989. 215.

Explores "the ideological moorings of the national security state"--for example, the "thoroughgoing institutionalization of official secrecy on a grand scale" that threatens the

"viability of democratic and republican forms of governance."
At the heart of the US liberal state is a drive for conformity, a system of "defenses against those individuals, organizations, movements, and ideologies that appear to challenge or pose a potential threat to its continued sovereignty."

304. Kim, Young, ed. The Central Intelligence Agency: Problems of Secrecy in a Democracy. Lexington, MA: D.C. Heath, 1968. 113.
Details the dangers of the CIA to constitutional government.

305. Lee, Martin, and Bruce Shlain. Acid Dreams: The CIA, LSD, and the Sixties Rebellion. New York: Grove, 1985. 343.
On CIA involvement in creating the US drug culture.

306. LeMond, Alan, and Ron Fry. No Place to Hide. New York: St. Martin's, 1975. 278.
The increasing surveillance of the populace by government and business.

307. Lowenthal, Max. The Federal Bureau of Investigation. New York: Sloane, 1950. 559.
On how the FBI developed into a political police.

308. Marchetti, Victor and John Marks. The CIA and the Cult of Intelligence. New York: Knopf, 1974; Dell, 1980. 377.
Exposes the interlocking complex of secret power by the "political aristocracy" seeking world power.

309. McGehee, Ralph. Deadly Deceits: My Twenty-Five Years in the CIA. Berkeley: Meiklejohn Civil Liberties, 1983. 250.
The CIA is "the covert arm of the President's" foreign policy, and disinforming the public is one of its chief purposes.

310. Mitgang, Herbert. Dangerous Dossiers: Exposing the Secret War Against America's Greatest Authors. New York: Fine, 1988. 331.
On the 50-year espionage campaign waged by the CIA, FBI, and other intelligence agencies against some of our most famous and popular writers, from Hemingway to Galbraith.

311. Morgan, Richard E. Domestic Intelligence: Monitoring Dissent in America. Austin: U of Texas P, 1980. 194.
On police state spying and harassment of citizens.

312. O'Reilly, Kenneth. "Racial Matters": The FBI's Secret File on Black America, 1960-1972. New York: Free P, 1989. 456.
Ordered by successive administrations to enforce the federal civil rights law, J. Edgar Hoover undermined that enforcement and pursued a surveillance agenda aimed instead at black America. Spying on black groups, provoking bloody conflicts

THE MASTER INSTITUTIONS 53

between the Black Panther Party and rival black nationalist groups, compiling endless "agitator" and "rabble rouser" indices, recruiting an army of more than 7,000 ghetto informants, the FBI was an adversary, instead of a protector, of civil rights.

313. O'Reilly, Kenneth. *Hoover and the Un-Americans: The FBI, HUAC, and the Red Menace.* Philadelphia: Temple UP, 1983. 411.
Describes the FBI as a political police determined to conform the US to Hoover's Sovietphobic ideology. Together the FBI and HUAC made deep injuries to freedom.

314. Oseth, John M. *Regulating United States Intelligence Operations: A Study in Definition of the National Interest.* Lexington: U of Kentucky P, 1985. 236.
Contrasts the Ford, Carter, and Reagan administrations, the latter particularly encouraging intelligence subversion of civil liberties.

315. Poelchau, Warner. *White Paper Whitewash: Interviews with Philip Agee on the CIA and El Salvador.* New York: Deep Cover, 1981. 206.
An analysis of the widely reported but spurious "captured documents" which alleged a communist plot against the government of El Salvador, backed up by analysis of several cases of false documentation and false press stories prepared by the CIA.

316. Powers, Richard Gid. *Secrecy and Power: The Life of J. Edgar Hoover.* New York: Free, 1987. 624.
An account of the FBI head's rise to power, explaining Hoover's view that the agency should do more than enforce the law--it should also be a watchdog of traditional values. "For Hoover, the specter of Communism was more than the shadow of the real-life Communist. . . . Anticommunism had a positive value as a defense of American values whether or not there still were any Communists."

317. Powers, Thomas. *The Man Who Kept the Secrets: Richard Helms & the CIA.* New York: Knopf, 1979. 393.
Operation Chaos (246), Huston Plan (248), Watergate (250), etc. (see Index), secrecy passim. Former CIA director Helms was convicted of perjury for lying to a Senate committee about an operation in Chile.

318. *Presidential Campaign Activities of 1972. Hearings Before the Select Committee on Presidential Campaign Activities of the U.S. Senate, 93rd Cong., 1st Sess.* 26 vols. Washington: GPO, 1973-74.
The Watergate Hearings.

319. Prouty, Leroy Fletcher. *The Secret Team: The CIA and Its Allies in Control of the United States and the World.* Englewood Cliffs, NJ: Prentice, 1973. 496.

How secrecy and anticommunism corrupt the CIA and government.

320. Rositzke, Harry. The CIA's Secret Operations. New York: Reader's Digest/Crowell, 1977. 286.
The CIA is "a pillar of the Imperial Presidency."

321. Rowan, Ford. Technospies: The Secret Network That Spies on You--and You. New York: Putnam's, 1978. 262.
Studies the dangerous "growth of sophisticated surveillance systems" by government agencies and corporations designed to "watch and listen to us." The danger is totalitarianism: the FBI's COINTELPRO operations, the CIA's Operation CHAOS, the IRS's punishing political "enemies," the Army's collecting information on dissidents, all seeking to "enforce discipline" not on law-breakers but "on a restive society."

322. Stockwell, John. In Search of Enemies: A CIA Story. New York: Norton, 1978. 285.
How the CIA lied to Congress and "actively propagandized the American public, with cruel results."

323. Theoharis, Athan, ed. Beyond the Hiss Case: The F.B.I., Congress and the Cold War. Philadelphia: Temple UP, 1982. 423.
Ten essays examine FBI "abuse of power."

324. Theoharis, Athan. Spying on Americans: Political Surveillance from Hoover to the Huston Plan. Philadelphia: Temple UP, 1978. 331.
The steadily illegal expansion of the FBI to investigate and harass citizens regarding their loyalty and orthodoxy.

325. Theoharis, Athan, and John Cox. The Boss: J. Edgar Hoover and the Great American Inquisition. Philadelphia: Temple UP, 1988. 489.
"Hoover had more to do with undermining American constitutional guarantees than any political leader before or since" (17). This biography traces Hoover's life from his childhood to his death in 1972, with particular attention to the secret files maintained by him in his office, the illegal wiretaps, bugs, burglaries, of his lifetime of illegal efforts to crush beliefs contrary to his own. "Hoover made a mockery of the American Constitution."

326. Turner, Stansfield. Secrecy and Democracy: The CIA in Transition. Boston: Houghton Mifflin, 1985. 304.
By a former Director of the CIA. Reveals the struggles among the components of the intelligence agencies.

327. Ungar, Sanford. FBI: An Uncensored Look Behind the Walls. Boston, Toronto: Little, Brown, 1975. 682.
Covers all aspects--secrecy, disinformation, COINTELPRO, etc.

THE MASTER INSTITUTIONS   55

328. Watters, Pat, and Stephen Gillers, eds. Investigating
      the FBI: A Tough, Fair Look at the Powerful Bureau,
      Its Present and Its Future. New York: Doubleday,
      1973. 518.
   Tom Wicker in his "Introduction" argues that the most important theme of the conference was the development of the FBI's counterespionage mission in the 1930s into "a pervasive system of political surveillance in America."

329. Wise, David. The American Police State: The Government
      Against the People. New York: Random House, 1976.
      437.
   On the development of unconstitutional and illegal political police.

330. Wise, David, and Thomas Ross. The Espionage Establishment. New York: Random House, 1967. 308.
   On the intelligence agencies outside of constitutional and legal accountability and restraint.

331. Wise, David, and Thomas Ross. The Invisible Government.
      New York: Random House, 1964. 375.
   Describes the interlocking hidden and often illegal machinery that carries out US policies "in the Cold War."

332. Woodward, Bob. Veil: The Secret War of the CIA. New
      York: Simon and Schuster, 1987. 543.
   Under William Casey's leadership, the CIA was the instrument of the bigoted anticommunist Reagan/ right wing ideology, often circumventing legal and constitutional restraints.

333. Wyden, Peter. Bay of Pigs: The Untold Story. New
      York: Simon and Schuster, 1979. 352.
   On the CIA's failed attempt to invade Cuba.

334. Yakovlev, N. CIA Target: The USSR. Trans. Victor
      Schneierson and Dmitry Belyavsky. USSR: Progress,
      1982. 279.
   On the covert US campaign to defeat the SU.

I. A. 5. ANTICOMMUNISM (335-414)

335. Haynes, John E. Communism & Anti-Communism in the
      United States: An Annotated Guide to Historical
      Writings. New York: Garland, 1987. 321.
   Introd. bib. essay; 37 major categories; over 2000 books, articles, and dissertations.

336. Alperovitz, Gar. Atomic Diplomacy: Hiroshima and
      Potsdam. New York: Simon, 1965. 317. Rpt. Penguin,
      1985. 426.
   US post-World War II Sovietphobic containment crusade began at Hiroshima in 1945.

337. Anatomy of Anti-Communism. New York: Hill and Wang, 1969. 138.
Anticommunism is failing and will prove to have been destructive to the world and to the US.

338. Anderson, Jack, and Ronald May. McCarthy: The Man, the Senator, the "Ism." Boston: Beacon, 1952. 431.
The secret to McCarthy's success was his understanding that many people craved simple answers to complex problems.

339. Andrews, Bert. Washington Witch Hunt. New York: Random, 1948. 218.
Anticommunist hysteria undermines constitutional protections.

340. Arevalo, Juan J. Anti-Kommunism in Latin America: An X-Ray of the Process Leading to a New Colonialism. New York: Stuart, 1963. 224.
"Kommunism" refers to the fake "communism" fabricated by the US in order to control Latin America through client states. The final chapter denounces journalists for betraying freedom of the press by following the official US line. The author was president of Guatemala when he was overthrown by the CIA and the United Fruit Company.

341. Austin, Anthony. The President's War: The Story of the Tonkin Gulf Resolution and How the Nation was Trapped in Vietnam. Philadelphia: Lippincott, 1971. 368.
Out of anticommunist zeal, President Johnson and a handful of his Cabinet and staff lied to Congress and the public about the alleged North Vietnamese attack on US destroyers, in order to legitimate the war.

342. Barth, Alan. The Loyalty of Free Men. New York: Viking, 1951. 253.
On account of the "Red Scare," toleration and civil liberties are eroding.

343. Belfrage, Cedric. The American Inquisition, 1945-1960. Indianapolis: Bobbs, 1973. 316.
A history of McCarthyism and anti-communism for over a decade and its repressive consequences.

344. Belknap, Michal R. Cold War Political Justice: The Smith Act, the Communist Party, and American Civil Liberties. Westport, Conn: GP, 1977. 322.
The political trial and imprisonment of Communist Party leaders under the Smith Act have damaged the civil liberty of all citizens.

345. Bentley, Eric, ed. Thirty Years of Treason: Excerpts from Hearings Before the House Committee on Un-American Activities, 1938-1968. New York: Viking, 1971. 991.

THE MASTER INSTITUTIONS 57

Part of the record of Congress' efforts to enforce conformity.

346. Beres, Louis. America Outside the World: The Collapse of U.S. Foreign Policy. Lexington: Lexington, 1987. 172.

Sovietphobia, "our contrived hatred" of the SU, has placed the US "outside the world," the freedom granted to citizens "routinely transmuted into obedience," absorbed by the state, while the media "make thinking almost impossible."

347. Bernstein, Carl. Loyalties: A Son's Memoir. New York: Simon and Schuster, 1989. 262.

Looks at what the loyalty hearings--the forerunner to the McCarthy trials--did to the lives of innocent people practicing their rights as citizens. Both of Bernstein's parents invoked the Fifth Amendment when asked about their membership in the Communist Party; his lawyer father defended many of those accused of disloyalty.

348. Bottome, Edgar. The Balance of Terror: Nuclear Weapons and the Illusion of Security, 1945-1985. Rev. Boston: Beacon, 1986. 291.

US responded to world changes by increasingly militarizing and nuclearizing its foreign policy.

349. Brown, Ralph S. Loyalty and Security. New Haven: Yale UP, 1958. 524.

Abuses by the federal loyalty program.

350. Carleton, Don. Red Scare! Right-Wing Hysteria, Fifties Fanaticism, and Their Legacy in Texas. Austin: Texas Monthly, 1985. 390.

Second Red Scare of 1950s in Houston, Texas.

351. Carr, Robert K. The House Committee on Un-American Activities, 1945-1950. Ithaca, NY: Cornell UP, 1952. 489.

On the first six years of the House Un-American Activities Committee, its damage to constitutional liberties, and the failure of the press to resist.

352. Caute, David. The Great Fear: The Anti-Communist Purge Under Truman and Eisenhower. New York: Simon and Schuster, 1978. 697.

An account of the great eruption of enforced conformity of thought and action during this period and the attack on First Amendment freedoms of openness, accessibility, communication, thought, association, and the right to know in a democracy.

353. Clubb, O. Edmund. The Witness and I. New York: Columbia UP, 1975. 314.

A victim of the anticommunist hysteria and persecution tells his story.

354. Cohen, Stephen F. Sovieticus: American Perceptions and Soviet Realities. New York: Norton, 1985. 160.
Partly about Sovietphobia in government and press.

355. Cook, Fred J. The Nightmare Decade: The Life and Times of Senator Joe McCarthy. New York: Random, 1971. 626.
About a decade of bigotry and its supreme demagogue.

356. Cox, Arthur M. The Myths of National Security: The Peril of Secret Government. Boston: Beacon, 1975. 231.
National security, Sovietphobia, and secrecy the triad subversives of constitutional, accountable government.

357. Cox, Arthur M. Russian Roulette: The Superpower Game. New York: Times, 1982. 248.
Sovietphobia and falsehoods and exaggerations about the Soviet "threat" fuel militarism and the drive for military supremacy.

358. deMause, Lloyd. Reagan's America. New York and London: Creative Roots, Inc., 1984. 193.
Month by month history of Reagan years probing Reagan's and the American people's motives for anti-communism, imperialism, etc. Numerous cartoons.

359. Feuerlicht, Roberta. Joe McCarthy and McCarthyism: The Hate That Haunts America. New York: McGraw-Hill, 1972. 160.
Senator McCarthy's five-year campaign of anti-Soviet and anticommunist bigotry was only the most blatant manifestation of "McCarthyism," which preceded him and continues today.

360. Fried, Richard. Men Against McCarthy. New York: Columbia UP, 1976. 428.
Focuses on strategies of the Democrats to counter McCarthy.

361. Fried, Richard. Nightmare in Red: The McCarthy Era in Perspective. New York: Oxford UP, 1990. 243.
Locates McCarthy "chronologically in the continuum of twentieth-century anti-Communist politics" with its deep roots in American culture, flourishing long before 1950 and continuing afterward.

362. Garrison, Jim, and Pyare Shivpuri. The Russian Threat: Its Myths and Realities. London: Gateway, 1983. 344.
Examines the "threat" and its exaggeration based upon fear and ignorance.

363. Goldston, Robert C. The American Nightmare: Senator Joseph R. McCarthy and the Politics of Hate. Indianapolis: Bobbs-Merrill, 1973. 202.
Paranoia about global communist power and "plots and treason at home."

THE MASTER INSTITUTIONS

364. Goodman, Walter. *The Committee: The Extraordinary Career of the House Committee on Un-American Activities.* New York: Farrar, 1968. 564.
   The Committee hunted down communists and radicals, but its larger target was the reforms of the New Deal and the liberal spirit in general.

365. Griffith, Robert. *The Politics of Fear: Joseph R. McCarthy and the Senate.* Lexington: Kentucky UP, 1970. 362.
   On the failure of the Senate to curb McCarthy's bigotry.

366. Griffith, Robert, and Athan Theoharis, eds. *The Specter: Original Essays on the Cold War and the Origins of McCarthyism.* New York: New Viewpoints, 1974. 368.
   Twelve essays analyze anticommunism in political institutions --"interest groups, parties, the presidency, Congress."

367. Halliday, Fred. *The Making of the Second Cold War.* London: Schocken, 1983. 280.
   Sovietphobia of the 1970s and 1980s.

367a. Heale, M.J. *American Anticommunism: Combatting the Enemy Within, 1830-1970.* Baltimore: Johns Hopkins UP, 1990. 256.
   On the deep roots of anticommunism leading to attacks on workers in the Haymarket Riot and to the witch hunts of Senator McCarthy.

368. Herken, Gregg. *The Winning Weapon: The Atomic Bomb in the Cold War, 1945-1950.* New York: Knopf, 1980. 425.
   US monopoly and secrecy of the bomb immediately after WWII caused many great harms.

369. Hoffmann, Stanley. *Dead Ends: American Foreign Policy in the New Cold War.* Cambridge, MA: Ballinger, 1983. 299.
   On the inadequacy of anticommunism and Sovietphobia as a basis of foreign policy.

370. Horne, Gerald. *Black & Red: W.E.B. DuBois & the Afro-American Response to the Cold War, 1944-1963.* Albany: State U of New York P, 1986. 457.
   DuBois' later years were a consistent evolution of his civil rights and anticolonial ideas despite threats of McCarthyism--his ouster from the NAACP, the Justice Department's indictment of him as a foreign agent, etc.

371. Horowitz, David. *The Free World Colossus: A Critique of American Foreign Policy in the Cold War.* New York: Hill, 1965. 451.
   The Truman Doctrine of containment established 1945-7 caused the Cold War and Soviet "threat" as part of US global counter-

revolutionary policy.

372. Investigation of Senator Joseph R. McCarthy. Hearings Before the Subcommittee of Privileges and Elections of the Committee on Rules and Administration. U.S. Senate, 82nd Congress on S. Res. 187 to Investigate Senator Joseph R. McCarthy to Determine Whether Expulsion Proceedings Should be Instituted Against Him. Part I, Sept. 28, 1951, May 12-16, 1952. Washington, DC: GPO, 1952. 320.

373. Ivie, Robert. Cold War Rhetoric: Strategy, Metaphor, and Ideology. New York: Greenwood, 1990.

374. Joël, Judith, and Gerald Erickson, eds. Anti-Communism: The Politics of Manipulation. Minneapolis, MN: Marxist Educational P, 1987. 193.
The eight articles share "two central ideas": "Anticommunism harms all people," and it is "fomented by deliberate design and used to further reactionary and antipeople purposes" (7).

375. Kahn, Albert E. The Game of Death: Effects of the Cold War on Our Children. New York: Cameron & Kahn, 1953. 256.
The effects have been extremely harmful.

376. Kahn, Albert E. High Treason: The Plot Against the People. New York: Lear, 1950. 372.
On ruling elite methods of domination, especially the anticommunist crusade.

377. Kaplan, Fred. The Wizards of Armageddon. New York: Simon, 1983. 452.
The Rand Corporation was an important cause of US Sovietphobia, arms buildup, and militarism.

378. Kovel, Joel. Against the State of Nuclear Terror. Boston: South End; London: Pan, 1984. 240.
Analyzes the roots of the global nuclear confrontation in US political and psychological culture, the technocratic state, and sets forth specific steps people can take to end it.

379. Kull, Steven. Minds at War: Nuclear Reality and the Inner Conflicts of Defense Policymakers. New York: Basic, 1988. 352.
Interviews with US and Soviet leaders reveal the unreality and contradictions propelling the arms race and justifying a mind-set based on winning a nuclear war.

380. Kutler, Stanley. The American Inquisition: Justice and Injustice in the Cold War. New York: Hill & Wang, 1982. 285.
The unprecedented political repression of the late 1940s and 1950s inspired by the Cold War.

381. Lens, Sidney. The Futile Crusade: Anti-Communism as American Credo. Chicago: Quadrangle, 1964. 256.
   The long history of US Sovietphobia and its global and domestic destructiveness.

382. Lewis, Lionel. Cold War on Campus: A Study of the Politics of Organization Control. New Brunswick, NJ: Transaction, 1988. 358.
   Studies the cases of 128 faculty members whose appointments were lost or threatened between 1947 and 1956 as a result of their political beliefs and activities. The villains in this process were college and university administrators who victimized individual faculty out of fear of damage to their institution. The result was that the institutions became not guardians of liberty but instruments of repression.

383. Lipsitz, George. Class and Culture in Cold War America: "A Rainbow at Midnight." New York: Praeger, 1981. 254.
   World War II "permanently altered economic and political power relations within American society, and produced a totalitarian oligarchy of the major interest groups. The elite that emerged from the war held unprecedented control over government and the economy, and it used its power to narrow rather than widen popular aspirations for control over their own lives" (2-3).

384. Matusow, Allen J., ed. Joseph R. McCarthy. Englewood Cliffs, NJ: Prentice, 1970. 181.
   McCarthy's anticommunist crusade thrived in the virtual absence of internal communist threat.

385. May, Elaine Tyler. Homeward Bound: American Families in the Cold War Era. New York: Basic, 1988. 284.
   Sovietphobia and arms race contributed significantly to the retreat to the security of the home, consumerism, and conservative politics and norms. Traces popular images of women and the family through the media, especially movies.

386. McMahan, Jeff. Reagan and the World: Imperial Policy in the New Cold War. New York: Monthly, 1985. 300.
   Reagan administration's military, economic, and propaganda campaign against the SU, their allies, and Third World revolutionary movements.

387. Meranto, Philip, et al. Guarding the Ivory Tower: Repression and Rebellion in Higher Education. Denver, CO: Lucha, 1985. 182.
   Contrary to official national and educational public relations, universities are not hospitable to dissidents, many of whom have been driven out of academe. A history of the 1960s and '70s.

388. Miliband, Ralph, et al., eds. The Uses of Anti-Communism. New York: Monthly, 1985. 372.

Fourteen essays on anti-communism world wide, 5 of them wholly or mainly about the US, including: "Anti-Communism and American Intervention in Greece," "Anti-Communism and the Korean War, 1950-53," "Waging Ideological War: Anti-Communism and US Foreign Foreign Policy in Central America," "Anti-Communism in Guatemala: Washington's Alliance with Generals and Death Squads," etc.

389. Mills, C. Wright. The Causes of World War Three. New York: Simon, 1958. 172.
Causes: that war is inevitable, US threatening nuclear war, the "doctrine of violence," etc.

390. Mitchell, David. 1919: Red Mirage. New York: Macmillan, 1970. 385.
The year 1919 witnessed an extreme eruption of Sovietphobia.

391. Oshinsky, David. A Conspiracy So Immense: The World of Joe McCarthy. New York: Free, 1983. 597.
McCarthy's delusory, paranoid anticommunism simplified the nation's problems.

392. Parenti, Michael. The Anti-Communist Impulse. New York: Random, 1969. 333.
The credo, ideology or religion of the US is anticommunism.

393. Paterson, Thomas. Meeting the Communist Threat: Truman to Reagan. New York: Oxford UP, 1988. 317.
A history of why and how US leaders particularly have exaggerated the Communist threat, and the tenacity of US belief in threats from abroad. This inquiry is made in order to explain why the US has "undertaken, from the 1940s to the present, global interventionism, the containment doctrine, nuclear arms expansion, covert activities," etc. and "activities that have violated their professed ideals of self-determination, democracy, and opportunity" (xi).

394. Rader, Melvin. False Witness. Seattle: U of Washington P, 1969. 209.
Anticommunist repression at the U of Washington.

395. Redekop, John. The American Far Right: A Case Study of Billy James Hargis and Christian Crusade. Grand Rapids, MI: Eerdmans, 1968. 232.
An account of another force in the anticommunist fear campaign for repression at home and expansion abroad.

396. Reeves, Thomas. The Life and Times of Joe McCarthy: A Biography. New York: Stein, 1982. 819.
McCarthy was only part of the larger "second Red Scare" for which others were more to blame.

397. Rogge, O. John. Our Vanishing Civil Liberties. New York: Gaer, 1949. 287.
The so-called "Communist threat" has seriously eroded civil

liberties (summarized pp. 275-77), when the real threat comes from the corporate and political leaders who would destroy the Bill of Rights while pursuing their own gain. "Let us make our own testament of loyalty to the Bill of Rights, to the Fourteenth Amendment."

398. Rogin, Michael P. The Intellectuals and McCarthy: The Radical Spectre. Cambridge, MA: M.I.T., 1967. 366.
Right-wing Republicans distinguished from reform movements.

399. Rosenzweig, Robert, with Barbara Turlington. The Research Universities and Their Patrons. Berkeley: U of California P, 1982. 151.
The authors advocate expanded government, corporate, and university linkage, citing as a model for cooperation The National Council for Soviet and East European Research, an "independent organization of scholars" funded in the past by the Pentagon and now by the CIA.

400. Rovere, Richard H. Senator Joe McCarthy. New York: Harcourt, 1959. 280.
Analyzes McCarthy as another dangerous expression of a totalitarian tendency.

401. Sanders, Jane. Cold War on the Campus; Academic Freedom at the University of Washington, 1946-64. Seattle: U of Washington P, 1979. 243.
Account of the anticommunist witchhunt at U.W.

402. Sanders, Jerry. Peddlers of Crisis: The Committee on the Present Danger and the Politics of Containment. Boston: South End, 1983. 371.
Analyzes another of the many forces of the Sovietphobic, militaristic right wing.

403. Scales, Junius Irving, and Richard Nickson. Cause at Heart; A Former Communist Remembers. Athens, GA: U of Georgia P, 1987. 427.
"Junius Scales spent the first two decades of his adult life fighting against racism and for democratic rights in the South. Harassed by J. Edgar Hoover's FBI, condemned by a court system fevered with McCarthyism, he became a test case for America's commitment to freedom of speech and thought" (publisher's description).

404. Schrecker, Ellen. No Ivory Tower: McCarthyism and the Universities. New York: Oxford UP, 1986. 437.
"The extraordinary facility with which the academic establishment accommodated itself to the demands of the state may well be the most significant aspect of the academy's response to McCarthyism." The government, not some fringe group of right-wing fanatics, initiated the movement to eliminate Communism from American life. "It let the universities handle the second stage and get rid of the targeted individuals. . . . It was, in many respects, just another step in the integration of

American higher education into the Cold War political system" (340).

405. Schultz, Bud and Ruth Schultz. It Did Happen Here: Recollections of Political Repression in America. Berkeley: U of California P, 1989. 427.
Interviews of victims of government repression. "The primary focus of this book is on techniques, on the ways government discriminates against political dissenters."

406. Selcraig, James. The Red Scare in the Midwest, 1945-55: A State and Local Study. Ann Arbor, MI: UMI Research P, 1982. 208.
The paranoia fed on an obsession with conformity ("loyalty"), which pervaded state and local institutions.

407. Stone, I. F. The "I.F. Stone's Weekly" Reader. Ed. Neil Middleton. New York: Vintage, 1974. 321.
Twenty-three of the essays deal with the harm done to the US and to the world by McCarthyism and the Cold War.

408. Theoharis, Athan. Seeds of Repression: Harry S. Truman and the Origins of McCarthyism. Chicago: Quadrangle, 1971. 238.
US militaristic foreign policy was paralleled by repression domestically, out of fear of SU subversion, which was almost entirely unfounded in reality.

409. Watkins, Arthur V. Enough Rope. Englewood Cliffs, NJ: Prentice, Hall and Utah UP, 1969. 302.
The story of the censure of Senator Joe McCarthy by his colleagues.

410. Weisberger, Bernard. Cold War, Cold Peace: The United States and Russia Since 1945. New York: American Heritage/Houghton, 1984. 341.
Surveys the detrimental effects of the Cold War.

410a. Whitfield, Stephen J. The Culture of the Cold War. Baltimore: Johns Hopkins UP, 1990. 261.
On the 1950s, when US power and paranoia reached new heights.

411. Wilcox, Clair, ed. Civil Liberties Under Attack. Freeport, NY: Books for Libraries, 1968. 155.
Groundless fears of Soviet subversion have undermined civil liberties.

412. Williams, William A. The Tragedy of American Diplomacy. 2nd ed. New York: Delta, 1971. 312.
US enmity toward the SU has led to US imperialism abroad, including opposition to revolutionary movements.

413. Wittner, Lawrence S. Cold War America: From Hiroshima to Watergate. New York: Praeger, 1974. 403.

THE SECONDARY INSTITUTIONS

Anticommunism and corporate profits lead the country domestically and globally, instead of a concern for "war, poverty, and freedom."

414. Wofsy, Leon, ed. Before the Point of No Return. New York: Monthly Review, 1986. 146.
Twenty-five pieces providing "an exchange of views on the Cold War, the Reagan doctrine, and what is to come."

THE SECONDARY INSTITUTIONS (415-545)

I. B. 1. LAW (415-436)

415. Martin, Fenton, and Robert Goehlert. The U.S. Supreme Court: A Bibliography. Washington, DC: Congressional Q, 1990. 800.
More than 9,000 entries organized by seven areas (equal rights, regulation, economics, etc.), plus biographical listings and subject and author indexes.

416. Auerbach, Jerold. Unequal Justice: Lawyers and Social Change in Modern America. New York: Oxford UP, 1976. 395.
By 1925 the legal profession had become almost completely stratified. The elite used their powerful positions to ensure their continued "ascendancy in professional life and to the economic institutions of industrial capitalism which they served."

417. Carp, Robert, and Ronald Stidham. Judicial Process in America. Washington, DC: Congressional Q, 1989. 393.
Delineates the contexts in which judges and lawyers function, how they approach and make decisions, including the impact of the Reagan era.

418. Eisenstein, Zillah. The Female Body & the Law. Berkeley, CA: U of California P, 1988. 245.
Discusses wide range of feminist thought, outlines the legal history of the inequality of women and focuses on the "phallocentricism" at the heart not only of traditional but liberal law. For the author the body, especially the pregnant body, must be the referent (which is not the same as the gender constructed "mother's body").

419. Green, Mark, and Bruce Wasserstein, eds. With Justice for Some: An Indictment of the Law by Young Advocates. Boston: Beacon, 1970. 400.
Thirteen essays on inequalities in the legal system. Despite a legal system "designed largely for the powerful to contend among themselves or against the weak--the myth of equal justice moves on" (Ralph Nader ix).

420. Kairys, David, ed. The Politics of Law: A Progressive Critique. New York: Pantheon, 1982. 321.

Places the law, its institutions, and individual actors "in their social and historical contexts," in contrast to the prevailing idealized model of law as a system of preexisting, clear, and predictable principles.

421. Kennedy, Duncan. "Legal Education as Training for Hierarchy." The Politics of Law: A Progressive Critique. Ed. David Kairys. New York: Pantheon, 1982. 40-64.

A significant part of the training in law school is "ideological training for willing service in the hierarchies" of the corporate state.

422. Kunstler, William. And Justice for All. Dobbs Ferry, NY: Oceana, 1963. 239.

The trials of Leo Frank, the Scottsboro boys, Sacco and Vanzetti, Mary Surratt, Alger Hiss, Corliss Lamont, Tom Mooney, Scopes, Herricks.

423. Lefcourt, Robert, ed. Law Against the People: Essays to Demystify Law, Order and the Courts. New York: Random House, 1971. 400.

Most of the essays argue that the law as an institution is an instrument of the corporate-government establishment designed to deceive and oppress--to control--the people, and the lawyer is part of this machinery.

424. Miller, Arthur S. The Supreme Court and American Capitalism. New York: Free P, 1968. 259.

"The importance of the government-business relationship to the American people cannot be overestimated. Government and business are the key institutions of the nation." Concludes the Supreme Court "has little or no real power" in economic matters. Some chapter titles: "Corporate America," "Constitutional Doctrine and the Consolidation of Corporate Power."

425. Nader, Ralph, and Mark Green, eds. Verdicts on Lawyers. New York: Crowell, 1976. 341.

Twenty-three essays connected by Nader's concern for the myth of equality under the law "whose repeated invocation cloaks its hollow reality" (vii).

426. Polan, Diane. "Toward a Theory of Law and Patriarchy." The Politics of Law: A Progressive Critique. Ed. David Kairys. New York: Pantheon, 1982. 294-303.

A Marxist/feminist critique of the legal perpetuation of patriarchy, concluding that elimination of patriarchy must precede elimination of sexist laws.

427. Quinney, Richard, ed. Criminal Justice in America: A Critical Understanding. Boston: Little, Brown, 1974. 448.

The traditional American view of legal society produces "a mystified conception of reality" and promotes injustice. The book develops a Marxist theory of criminal law.

THE SECONDARY INSTITUTIONS   67

428. Rome, Edwin, and William H. Roberts. Corporate and
     Commercial Free Speech: First Amendment Protection of
     Expression in Business. Westport: Quorum, 1985. 269.
  A chronicle of the Supreme Court's evolution from denying
First Amendment protection for commercial speech in 1942 to
reversing itself in 1978 in First National Bank of Boston v.
Bellotti, which increased corporate propaganda power signi-
ficantly.

429. Schiller, Herbert. "The Corporation & the Law."
     Culture, Inc.: The Corporate Takeover of Public
     Expression. New York: Oxford UP, 1989. 46-65.
  Recent Supreme Court protections of corporate commercial
speech are "the latest stage in the historical, judicial
accommodation to and promotion of property rights" (49) and
"the adaptation of the law to the needs of an information-
using corporate economy" (50). These legal changes that benefit mainly the commercial interest of the few were produced
"under the pretext of serving the general interest" (51).

430. Schwartz, Herman. Packing the Courts: The Conservative
     Campaign to Rewrite the Constitution. New York:
     Scribners, 1988. 242.
  How the Reagan Administration succeeded in packing the lower
courts with conservative ideologues as part of its long-range
effort to gut the Constitution. [Studies of the discourses of
these judges should be forthcoming.]

431. Shaskolsky, Leon. "The Legal Institution: The Legiti-
     mizing Appendage." American Society: A Critical
     Analysis. Ed. Larry Reynolds and James Henslin. New
     York: McKay, 1973. 294-337.
  The main function of law is "the enhancement of the interests of those dominant groups in society that have access to
the power structure, including the institutions where law is
legislated, adjudicated, and enforced" (297).

432. Sherrill, Robert. "Hogging the Constitution: Big
     Business and Its Bill of Rights." Performance and
     Reality: Essays from "Grand Street." Ed. Ben
     Sonnenberg. New Brunswick: Rutgers UP, 1989. 233-
     251. (Orig. pub. Fall 1987).
  The First Amendment was inverted when the Supreme Court
granted free speech rights to corporations as "persons." "The
First Amendment belongs to human beings and the press, and it
should be secured for their use only."

433. Smigel, Erwin. The Wall Street Lawyer: Professional
     Organization Man! New York: Free P, 1964. 369.
  "Competition is keen for both the preferred lawyers and the
preferred clients. The Wall Street firms easily win this
contest." They are thus able to influence government and
business policy. "Their main function is to preserve the
status quo" favorable to big business.

434. Spence, Gerry. With Justice for None: Destroying an
     American Myth. New York: Times Books, 1989. 370.
   Examines "how the crimes of nonliving corporations cost the
rest of us ten times more than all the crimes of all the
street thugs and mobsters and crooks and scam artists
combined" and "how law schools have become factories producing
replacement parts for the large corporate-law machines, and
judges have become the high priests of the marketplace,
beholden too often to the new king, corporate America. . . .
This is the key--the commoditization of America." Part Two
offers remedies to bring about law schools, lawyers, judges,
and law that serve people instead of corporations. "Perhaps
the greatest betrayal of America was the giveaway of our
airways to the commercial corporations of America" (298).

435. Tushnet, Mark. "Corporations and Free Speech." The
     Politics of Law: A Progressive Critique. Ed. David
     Kairys. New York: Pantheon, 1982. 253-261.
   "Corporations dominate the media," and the Supreme Court's
Bellotti decision in 1980 made it extremely difficult for
government to regulate corporate speech in the public interest. Behind this ruling lies the "deep structure of capitalist
ideology" that "all products of human activity" are "commodities." This deep structure is revealed in 3 influential doctrines: "the corporation as person," "the free marketplace of
ideas," and "money talks." "Someday a political movement may
be able to recapture the older sense of corporations as creations of public power and as subject to public control" (260).

436. Witt, Elder. Guide to the U.S. Supreme Court. 2nd ed.
     Washington, DC: Congressional Q, 1989. 1060.
   A history from 1790 through the July 1989 term.

I. B. 2. EDUCATION (437-478)

437. Apple, Michael, ed. Culture and Economic Reproduction
     in Education: Essays on Class, Ideology and the
     State. Boston: Routledge, 1982. 362.
   The books by Apple analyze the complex ways schools reproduce the economic and cultural status quo of race, gender, and
class.

438. Apple, Michael. Education and Power: Reproduction &
     Contradiction in Education. Boston: Routledge, 1982.
     218.

439. Apple, Michael. Ideology and Curriculum. Boston:
     Routledge, 1979. 203.

440. Apple, Michael, and Lois Weis, eds. Ideology and
     Practice in Schooling. Philadelphia: Temple UP,
     1983. 286.

441. Aronowitz, Stanley, and Henry Giroux. Education Under

THE SECONDARY INSTITUTIONS 69

Siege: The Conservative, Liberal and Radical Debate Over Schooling. Hadley, MA: Bergin, 1985. 256.
Analyzes the rightward drift in educational policy and calls for emancipating democratic schooling.

442. Beck, Hubert. Men Who Control Our Universities: The Economic and Social Composition of Governing Boards of Thirty Leading American Universities. New York: King's Crown, 1947. 229.
University trustees reflect the structure of power in society at large.

443. Berlowitz, Marvin, and Frank Chapman, Jr., eds. The United States Educational System: Marxist Approaches. Minneapolis: Marxist Educ., 1980. 221.
Fourteen essays. A working-class oriented critique.

444. Blits, Jan, ed. The American University: Problems, Prospects and Trends. Buffalo, NY: Prometheus, 1985. 180.
Ten essays on the effects of demands of an increasingly technological society, industry-university research ties, the takeover of computer technology, etc.

445. Bowles, Samuel, and Herbert Gintis. Schooling in Capitalist America: Educational Reform and the Contradictions of Economic Life. New York: Basic, 1976. 340.
Education both increases the productive capacity of workers and defuses and depoliticizes potential class conflict in the production process, thus serving the social, political and economic status quo.

446. Burt, Samuel. Volunteer Industry Involvement in Public Education. Lexington, MA: Heath, 1970. 203.
The authors advocate industry-education cooperation for "the better management of people, things, and ideas."

447. Carnoy, Martin. Education as Cultural Imperialism. New York: McKay, 1974. 378.
The main function of education is to transmit the social and economic structure "from generation to generation." The final chapter sets forth alternative program and goals.

448. Carnoy, Martin, ed. Schooling in a Corporate Society: The Political Economy of Education in America. New York: McKay, 1975. 374.
Pictures US education's real goal to perpetuate an unequal system in which mobility is achieved by only a limited number of people, "while the majority are held in place." For example, Marcus Raskin describes the system as a "channeling colony" that teaches children how to behave in a hierarchical world.

449. Carnoy, Martin, and Henry M. Levin. Schooling and Work in the Democratic State. Stanford, CA: Stanford UP,

1985. 307.
Explores the conflict between the two functions of education in America: the creation of students who will fit nicely into the capitalist machine, and the preparation of students for participation in a democracy.

450. Connery, Robert, ed. The Corporation and the Campus. New York: Praeger, 1970. 187.
Papers presented at a conference whose purpose is to "stimulate the widest possible voluntary support of colleges and universities, especially by business."

451. Dixon, Marlene. Things Which Are Done in Secret. Montreal: Black Rose, 1976. 290.
Universities are taught mainly by conservative professors serving corporate interests.

452. Farber, Jerry. The Student As Nigger. New York: Pocket, 1970. 142.
Because the government controls through indoctrination in the schools, police repression is seldom employed; both serve the military-industrial state.

453. Giroux, Henry. Ideology, Culture, and the Process of Schooling. Philadelphia: Temple UP, 1981. 168.
The struggle for critical thinking in the schools is part of the "larger struggle to contest the power concentrated in the capitalist state."

454. Giroux, Henry. Theory and Resistance in Education: A Pedagogy for the Opposition. Hadley, MA: Bergin, 1983. 304.
Studies how an alternative to the workplace of daily school routines can be developed to increase critical autonomy in students.

455. Giroux Henry, and David Purpel, eds. The Hidden Curriculum and Moral Education: Deception or Discovery? Berkeley, CA: McCutchan, 1983. 425.
The hidden curriculum refers to the underlying unequal structures of economic relationships reflected in the schools and functioning as social control. These writers want an education that "stimulates moral thought and growth rather than fixating it," that enables the young "to choose in accord with an ethic of rights and responsibilities--to be actively valuing persons in their interrelationships rather than passive objects of a controlling society" (4).

456. Greer, Colin. The Great School Legend: A Revisionist Interpretation of American Public Education. New York: Basic, 1972. 206.
The public schools are designed for the middle-class and cannot end poverty, the end of which depends upon a national policy of full employment. Calls for an education for critical thinking, democratic participation, and humanness.

THE SECONDARY INSTITUTIONS 71

457. Hartnett, Rodney. College and University Trustees: Their Backgrounds, Roles and Educational Attitudes. Princeton, NJ: Educ. Testing Serv., 1969. 71.
A negative profile of trustees.

458. Hook, Sidney, et al., eds. The University and the State: What Role for Government in Higher Education? Buffalo: Prometheus, 1978. 296.
One contributor writes that federal patronage makes major universities vulnerable; e.g., Columbia University is "now acutely and critically dependent on the federal government." Another describes how faculty members adapt their research projects to the availability of federal money.

459. Howard, John A., and H. Bruce Franklin. Who Should Run the Universities? Washington: Am. Enterprise Inst., 1969. 243.
A debate between conservative Howard and Marxist Franklin. Franklin argues that because conflict on the campus derives from a fundamental antagonism against the power elite of the US, it will continue. Howard in contrast blames the unrest upon faculties' preoccupation with their own academic freedom and a lack of concern for the students' usefulness to society.

460. Kaplan, Craig, and Ellen Schrecker, eds. Regulating the Intellectuals: Perspectives on Academic Freedom in the 1980s. New York: Praeger, 1983. 260.
Essays on limitations on dissent and academic freedom in the universities under corporate and government domination.

461. Karabel, Jerome, and A.H. Halsey. Power and Ideology in Education. New York: Oxford UP, 1977. 670.
The authors focus on the relations of capitalism and class bias as the major determinants in shaping the US educational system and research. The editors share a "political vision of a classless educational system" dedicated to a "common culture." One traces his roots to a "Christian pragmatic, piecemeal, and democratic road to socialism," while the other "has been deeply influenced by both the American New Left and continental Marxism" (vi).

462. Kozol, Jonathan. The Night is Dark and I Am Far From Home. Boston: Houghton, 1975. 208.
Indicts the indoctrination and conformity of schools.

463. Krueger, Marlis, and Frieda Silvert. Dissent Denied: The Technocratic Response to Protest. New York: Elsevier, 1975. 194.
Studies the takeover of New York's City College South Campus by black and Puerto Rican students in 1969 as a focus for an examination of control of dissent in higher education.

464. MacIver, Robert. Academic Freedom in Our Time. New York: Columbia UP, 1955. 329.
Studies the assaults on academic freedom by representatives

of orthodoxy.

465. Patrick, Kenneth, and Richard Eells. Education and the Business Dollar. New York: Macmillan, 1969. 313.
The authors advocate "the construction of a living government-business-education relationship that will explore new fields of investment, new kinds of participation, and a new division of the chores essential to a balanced and unmortgaged education community."

466. Piliawsky, Monte. Exit 13: Oppression & Racism in Academia. Boston: South End, 1982. 252.
"Because colleges perform the vital task of training the country's future employees, the capitalist elite demands the power to determine the course of higher education. The ruling class exercises this control through its domination of the boards of trustees of colleges" (xii). See "The Purging of Dissident Professors at U.S. Universities."

467. Ridgeway, James. The Close Corporation, America's Universities in Crisis. New York: Random, 1968. 273.
Analyzes the government-military-corporate-academic complex.

468. Shor, Ira. Critical Teaching and Everyday Life. Boston: South End, 1980. 270.
An effort to reconceive education in a country dominated by corporate values, needs, and organization. "One of the unacknowledged realities is that mass higher education is the largest warehouse in America. Surplus labor is stored there and regimented."

469. Shor, Ira. Culture Wars: School & Society in the Conservative Restoration, 1969-1984. Boston: Routledge, 1986. 238.
A defense of education against the "conservative restoration" now occurring, against "those who would turn the school and its teachers and students into appendages of industry" and right-wing forces. In addition to occupational literacy, schools should teach "critical literacy" which instead of indoctrinating students with the dominant ideology, teaches them that education is the product of "power and inequality."

470. Sinclair, Upton. The Goose-Step: A Study of American Education. Pasadena, CA: Pub. by author, 1923. 488.
The conformist education in America examined by Sinclair is indicated by the title and by these titles selected from the ninety-three chapters: "Interlocking Directorates," "The University of the House of Morgan," "Free Speech But--," "The Dean of Imperialism," "The University of the Lumber Trust," "The Bolshevik Hunters."

471. Smith, David N. Who Rules the Universities? An Essay in Class Analysis. New York: Monthly Review, 1974. 295.
Universities are controlled by the corporate-government-

THE SECONDARY INSTITUTIONS

military complex. Parts 1-3 present the case of ruling class control, Part 4 ways to end it.

472. Spring, Joel. <u>Education and the Rise of the Corporate State</u>. Boston: Beacon, 1972. 206.
"Since 1900 the power of schooling has tended to be in the hands of businessmen, political leaders, and professional educators who have been instrumental in the development of the modern corporate state" (149).

473. Vaughan, Ted. "The Educational Institution: The Indoctrinating Appendage." <u>American Society</u>. Ed. Reynolds and Henslin. New York: McKay, 1973. 225-247.
Fundamental inquiry into the rationality and rectitude of the US corporate system is systematically suppressed in universities, which function as appendages of the political and economic system.

474. Veblen, Thorstein. <u>The Higher Learning in America: A Memorandum on the Conduct of Universities by Business Men</u>. New York: Hill, 1967 (orig. 1918). 209.
The essential academic issue centers on "the claims of science and scholarship on the one hand and those of business principles and pecuniary gain on the other" (35). Ch. 2 on governing boards, 3 on the administration, 4 on prestige, etc.

475. Wiggin, Gladys. <u>Education and Nationalism: An Historical Interpretation of American Education</u>. New York: McGraw, 1962. 518.
An admiring appraisal of education as a central agency in the training of nationalistic citizen.

476. Wilson, David A., ed. <u>Universities and the Military</u>. Philadelphia: American Academy of Political and Social Science, 1989. 202.
Special issue of <u>The Annals of the American Academy of Political and Social Science</u>. "Nothing has had the overall force of the defense establishment in redirecting basic and applied research, in putting limits on the free exchange of intelligence, and in dampening discussion of the merits of research that has policy implications, or in converting scientists into policy advocates and scholars into entrepreneurs" (Richard Adams, 28). Vera Kistiakowsky suggests the military's most striking impact lies in its influence on the careers and attitudes of the students trained to place contracts and disciplinary advancement ahead of conscience and social vision and reform. Julian Cooper finds significant parallels between US and SU military R&D.

477. Wise, Arthur. <u>Legislated Learning: The Bureaucratization of the American Classroom</u>. Berkeley: U of California P, 1982. 219.
Analysis of the values of order, efficiency, and uniformity in education, the result of following the corporate industrial model.

478. Wolf-Wasserman, Miriam, comp. Demystifying School: Writings and Experiences. New York: Praeger, 1974. 355.

People in power or who seek power have long covered up "what goes on in the schoolroom and the Oval Room" by spinning out myths. For example: schools were not so much a melting pot as a "sorting board"; public education was not so much a highway to opportunity as a "series of barriers." The author calls for us "to recognize that schools are part of a system of power and profits" (8).

I. B. 3. RELIGION (479-497)

479. Bartelt, David. "The Religious Institution: The Opium-Producing Appendage." American Society: A Critical Analysis. Ed. Larry Reynolds and James Henslin. New York: McKay, 1973. 171-197.

Focuses on religion's "commitment to and support of the corporate state" in consequence of which it deflects real problems "into ultimate ones." Religion "celebrates the image of egoistic, marketplace man" through its "privatized" separation from the real economic and social conditions of the nation.

480. Bruce, Steve. The Rise and Fall of the New Christian Right: Conservative Protestant Politics in America 1978-1988. Oxford: Clarendon, 1988. 210.

Explains the origins of the movement, how supporters were mobilized ("a story about leadership"), and the social and political structures within which the mobilization occurred.

481. Conway, Flo, and Jim Siegelman. Holy Terror: The Fundamentalist War on America's Freedoms in Religion, Politics and Our Private Lives. New York: Dell, 1984. 496.

The fundamentalist/conservative drive for power threatens the principle of separation of church and state. The fundamentalist right "has mushroomed in its reach and power" and is no temporary aberration.

482. Diamond, Sara. Spiritual Warfare: The Politics of the Christian Right. Boston: South End, 1989. 292.

Despite setbacks of the collapse of Jimmy Swaggart and Jim Bakker, the Christian Right is a major force in both Congress (especially the Republican Party) and the White House, for it has built a network of organizations that reaches everywhere across the country. Its strength derives also from its participation in the broad coalition known as the New Right, whose aim, which it shares with the Republican Party, is to turn back the social gains of the New Deal and the 1960s--supporting tax exemption for religious colleges, opposing abortion and birth control, opposing civil rights for gays and lesbians, supporting the Contras in Nicaragua, supporting prayer in public schools, Sovietphobia, etc.

THE SECONDARY INSTITUTIONS

483. Ezcurra, Ana Marie. *The Vatican and The Reagan Administration*. New York: Circus, 1986. 182.
The convergence between the Vatican and the Reagan administration means a more coordinated political, economic, and military attack on those Christian leaders who have given their lives for the poor. Particularly is this true in Nicaragua.

484. Finnerty, Adam D. *No More Plastic Jesus: Global Justice and Christian Lifestyle*. Maryknoll, NY: Orbis, 1977. 223.
The present economic system is controlled "by a handful of rich and powerful people whose unbridled pursuit of continued profits and dividends is going to bring us all to ruin" (75). The author examines the imminent dangers of consumption, pollution, global waste, military spending, poverty, classes, etc., and the remedies offered by the Simple Living Movement, the Shakertown Pledge, and the churches, all in search of a movement for global justice.

485. Flake, Carol. *Redemptorama: Culture, Politics, and the New Evangelicalism*. Garden City, NY: Anchor/Doubleday, 1984. 300.
On evangelicalism and the status of women, sports, "Christian capitalism," TV evangelism, popular music, political issues and movements, the struggle between theocratic and democratic purposes, between the Scriptures and secular texts, etc. Chapter 6, "The Stations of the Cross: The Electronic Kingdom," Chapter 7, "Selling the Word: The Christian Publishing Industry," Chapter 8, "Making a Joyful Noise: The New Christian Music."

486. Gottlieb, Robert, and Peter Wiley. *America's Saints: The Rise of Mormon Power*. New York: Harcourt Brace Jovanovich, 1987. 280.
Despite the extraordinary secrecy of the church, the authors have pieced together a comprehensive account of the Mormon wealth and political power.

487. Halsell, Grace. *Prophecy and Politics: Militant Evangelists on the Road to Nuclear War*. Westport, CT: Lawrence Hill, 1986. 210.
Jerry Falwell, Jimmy Swaggart, Jim Bakker, Pat Robertson, and other televangelists are eagerly awaiting a nuclear Armageddon in Israel that will bring about the Second Coming of Christ. Halsell offers an account of this doomsday belief system and its impact on US policy in the Middle East.

488. Harrell, David. *Pat Robertson: A Personal, Religious, and Political Portrait*. San Francisco: Harper & Row, 1987, 246.
Part I gives a biographical sketch of Robertson and a short history of the Christian Broadcasting Network (CBN), Part II explains his most important religious views--charismatic, evangelical, Southern Baptist, and Part III analyzes the

evolution of those views and the strengths and weaknesses of his candidacy for president.

489. Hertzke, Allen. Representing God in Washington: The Role of Religious Lobbies in the American Polity. Knoxville: U of Tennessee P, 1988. 260.
Religious lobbying has had and continues to have considerable effect on public policy.

490. Jorstad, Erling. Evangelicals in the White House: The Cultural Maturation of Born Again Christianity, 1960-1981. New York: Edwin Mellen, 1981. 171.
About the widespread born again evangelical revival and its extension into politics, particularly its "spirited participation in the national political campaign of 1980," showing "how sophisticated, organized and pragmatic they could be in using the election of specific candidates to further their specific tenets of morality."

491. Lader, Lawrence. Politics, Power, and the Church: The Catholic Crisis & Its Challenge to American Pluralism. New York: Macmillan, 1987. 273.
Account of development of Catholic power in the US and its use of that power to suppress dissent and to propagandize its doctrines. US bishops have sought public funds for church schools in violation of the Constitution, have tried to impose Catholic medical and sexual ethics on doctors and the public, have censored and expelled nuns and priests who differed from the Vatican on liberation theology, birth control, abortion, sanctuary, and participation in politics, have allied with right-wing Protestant Fundamentalists, etc. Chapter eight of the sixteen chapters deals with the media, "Money, Power, and the Media": "money and media control have proved to be the foundation of the Fundamentalist-Catholic alliance and have brought it to a peak of power" (120).

492. Liebman, Robert, and Robert Wuthnow, eds. The New Christian Right: Mobilization and Legitimation. New York: Aldine, 1983. 256.
Many Christian groups joined with a variety of secular New Right groups in an increasingly successful effort to coordinate legislative battles and to air political issues from a conservative perspective. Chapters on the Moral Majority, PACs, the Southern Baptist clergy, etc. Chapter 7 on the struggle to define the US focuses upon "seizing access to symbol production" to "create an alternative world."

493. Moen, Matthew. The Christian Right and Congress. Tuscaloosa: U of Alabama P, 1989. 234.
An account of the systematic efforts of conservative Christians to influence Congress during the Reagan administration.

494. Noll, Mark A. Religion and American Politics: From the Colonial Period to the 1980s. New York: Oxford UP, 1990. 401.

THE SECONDARY INSTITUTIONS

Six essays on the twentieth century.

495. Pell, Eve. *The Big Chill: How the Reagan Administration, Corporate America, and Religious Conservatives Are Subverting Free Speech and the Public's Right to Know.* Boston: Beacon, 1984. 269.
   The late 1970s and early 1980s were marked by a government hostile to free speech, a religious Right seeking to police the nation's reading matter, and a corporate sector trying to intimidate critics through libel suits. A compendium of recent transgressions against the First Amendment.

496. Reese, Thomas, S.J. *Archbishop: Inside the Power Structure of the American Catholic Church.* New York: Harper, 1989. 401.
   Examines the hierarchy of churchmen who wield great social and political power not only among Catholics but in US society at large.

497. Smith, Charles M. *The Pearly Gates Syndicate, or How to Sell Real Estate in Heaven.* Garden City, NY: Doubleday, 1971. 220.
   Treats the church as a business corporation which has buried the message of Jesus (and St. Francis, Wesley, et al.) in enterprise.

I. B. 4. SCIENCE AND TECHNOLOGY (498-511)

498. Aitken, Hugh G. *Taylorism at Watertown Arsenal: Scientific Management in Action 1908-1915.* Cambridge: Harvard UP, 1960. 269.
   A study of the Taylor system of management as it was installed in a particular manufacturing plant, and the reactions to the system. The system of scientific management is the idea "that human activity could be measured, analyzed, and controlled by techniques analogous to those that had proved successful when applied to physical objects."

499. Arditti, Rita, Pat Brennan, and Steve Cavrak, eds. *Science & Liberation.* Boston: South End, 1980. 398.
   Five essays on "The Myth of the Neutrality of Science," seven on "Science and Social Control," five on "Working in Science," and eight on "Towards a Liberating Science." "The purpose of this book is to discuss the role of science and scientists in maintaining social oppression and to present ideas and concrete examples . . . toward a new science."

500. Dickson, David. *The New Politics of Science.* New York: Pantheon, 1984. 404.
   Presidents, the military, Congress, bankers, industry, the universities, and the science community have cooperated in orienting science almost exclusively around the profit motive rather than needs of the larger population. The final chapter proposes a "democratic Strategy for Science."

501. Gellhorn, Walter. Security, Loyalty, And Science.
    Ithaca: Cornell UP, 1950. 300.
  The Sovietphobic national security obsession has resulted in
the slashing of scientific, human, and democratic values:
censorship, secrecy, militarization of scientific research and
technology, loyalty oaths and screening, black lists, restriction of the interchange of ideas, etc.

502. Goggin, Malcolm L., ed. Governing Science and Technology in a Democracy. Knoxville: U of Tennessee P,
    1986. 314.
  The contributors explore the processes by which current
science and technology policy is made, analyze the deficiencies, and propose practical reforms to give citizens a greater
voice in decisions about their own and their nation's future.

503. Greenberg, Daniel S. The Politics of Pure Science.
    New York: NAL, 1967. 303.
  Traces the growth of the post-WWII symbiosis of government
and basic research, pushed partly by hot and cold wars.

504. Haber, Samuel. Efficiency and Uplift: Scientific
    Management in the Progressive Era 1890-1920.
    Chicago: U of Chicago P, 1964. 181.
  A history of the "efficiency craze." "Efficiency provided a
standpoint from which those who had declared allegiance to
democracy could resist the leveling tendencies of the principles of equality" (xii).

505. Haberer, Joseph. Politics and the Community of Science.
    New York: Van Nostrand Reinhold, 1969. 337.
  "Scientists have almost always been pliant partners, willing
under almost any conditions to accommodate to a given political order." This "disjuncture between power and responsibility" is "cause for grave concern." Historical case studies
reveal the inherently political nature of science. Ch. 9
focuses upon the atomic bomb, Ch. 10-11 on Dr. Robert Oppenheimer. The last chapter emphasizes the strong methodological
ethic of scientists in contrast to their weak social ethic.

506. Harding, Sandra, and Jean F. O'Barr, eds. Sex and Scientific Inquiry. Chicago: U of Chicago P, 1987. 317.
  Fifteen essays from Signs examine the social structure of
science and technology, their misuses, abuses, and biases, the
sexual meaning of science, etc. The essays were chosen "to
demonstrate the wide range of the feminist critique of the
natural sciences."

507. National Commission on Research. Industry and the
    Universities: Developing Cooperative Research
    Relationships in the National Interest. Washington:
    Aug., 1980.
  Recommends increased industry-university cooperation in
research and development. [Implications for autonomy and
control not critically explored.]

THE SECONDARY INSTITUTIONS   79

508. Nelkin, Dorothy. Science as Intellectual Property: Who
         Controls Research? New York: Macmillan, 1984. 130.
   As the concept of research as property expands, the scientist increasingly encounters dilemmas of rights, regulations, secrecy, and many other problems. Academic science has been a public resource, a repository for ideas, and a source of relatively unbiased information. Industrial connections blur the distinctions between corporations and the university, "establishing private control over a public resource" (29).

509. Noble, David. America By Design: Science, Technology, and the Rise of Corporate Capitalism. New York: Knopf, 1977. 384.
   "The primary thesis of this book is that the history of modern technology in America is of a piece with that of the rise of corporate capitalism." It was "a change without a change," for it maintained the "basic social relations of capitalist society" of owner and controller vs. worker. The author accounts for this dynamism within status quo by explaining the professional engineers as management agents of corporate capital. The engineers "consciously undertook to structure the labor force and foster the social habits demanded by corporate capitalism" (xxiv). Thus "modern technology became a class-bound phenomenon, the racing heart of corporate capitalism" (xxv).

510. Price, Don K. The Scientific Estate. Cambridge: Harvard UP, 1967. 323.
   Traces the rise of technocracy (the scientific-technological revolution) and its assimilation by the techno-corporate-state. Urges scientists to "play an active role in government, and politicians to take a sympathetic interest in science" (278).

511. Smith, Dusky L. "The Scientific Institution: The Knowledge-producing Appendage." American Society: A Critical Analysis. Ed. Larry Reynolds and James Henslin. New York: McKay, 1973. 145-170.
   Science and technology have been merged with humanism (compassion) in the interests of "marketeering interests" so that people at home and abroad can be frightened or destroyed for their "own good," particularly so that poverty and denial of human potential "can be maintained without guilt" (166).

I. B. 5. MEDICINE (512-530)

512. Berman, Edgar, M.D. The Solid Gold Stethoscope. New York: Ballantine, 1976. 209.
   Examines the medical establishment's specializations, privilege, political conservatism, and power.

513. Brown, J.H.U. The High Cost of Healing: Physicians and the Health Care System. New York: Human Sciences, 1985. 213.

A study of "the quality and cost of care, dealing primarily with the physician," whose education "does not deal with cost reduction or cost control" but with using "all of the armamentarium of care" and "lavishly."

514. Cook, Fred J. *The Plot Against the Patient.* Englewood Cliffs, NJ: Prentice-Hall, 1967. 373.

Focuses upon the wonders of modern medicine confronted by "pyramiding and virtually insupportable costs," and "the creaking, antiquated, horse-and-buggy system of financing." The US offers the best medical care in the world, if you can pay for it.

515. Ehrenreich, Barbara, and John Ehrenreich. *The American Health Empire: Power, Profits, and Politics.* New York: Random House, 1970. 279.

The US health system "is not in business for people's health" partly because of distorted national priorities (the swollen military budget) and partly because of the health industry itself, which is the subject of the book.

516. Goldsmith, Jeff. *Can Hospitals Survive? The New Competitive Health Care Market.* Homewood, IL: Dow Jones-Irwin, 1981. 240.

"This book is about the transition of the current organization of health services from autonomous hospitals and physicians to corporate structures rivaling those in industry and business" (vii). At the time of his book "the total health services enterprise" in the US was "more than $220 billion a year, around $1,000 for every person in the country" (viii).

517. Harmer, Ruth M. *American Medical Avarice.* New York: Abelard-Schuman, 1975. 333.

Examines doctors rich on Medicaid fees, the inequities of the fee-for-service system and inadequate insurance, the myth of self-policing, etc. Chapter 16 compares US to other countries. Chapter 17 recommends changes: decreasing power of AMA, increasing influence of all health care professionals, addition of consumer representatives to all professional associations, councils, etc., elimination of all profit-seeking businesses from councils, etc. "A primary goal should be to remove medicine from the marketplace" (285).

518. Illich, Ivan. *Medical Nemesis: The Expropriation of Health.* New York: Pantheon, 1976. 294.

Indicts social and cultural "iatrogenesis," disabling of all kinds caused by society and its institutions. Medical institutions and medical practitioners damage and oppress people by depriving them of the capacity for autonomous choices and activities not only in regard to health but in other aspects of their lives. "The medical establishment has become a major threat to health" (3).

519. Lasko, Keith, M.D. *The Great Billion Dollar Medical Swindle.* Indianapolis: Bobbs-Merrill, 1980. 237.

THE SECONDARY INSTITUTIONS 81

Chapter 15, "There's No Business Like Health Business," summarizes the extraordinarily high and rapidly rising cost of the health care business, the equally high profits of doctors, kickbacks, the $4 billion tax deductible continuing medical education (CME) rip-off, success measured by income, etc. Chapter 16 offers 21 specific remedies for the "money-hungry American medical establishment." "The major reform needed" "is the removal of the profit motive from medicine" (226), to be accomplished by a national health service.

520. Mintz, Morton. By Prescription Only: A Report on the Roles of the United States Food & Drug Administration, the American Medical Association, Pharmaceutical Manufacturers, and Others in Connection with the Irrational & Massive Use of Prescription Drugs that May Be Worthless, Injurious, or Even Lethal. 2nd ed., rev. Boston: Houghton, 1967. 446. (Rev. The Therapeutic Nightmare, Houghton, 1964).

Indicts "those pharmaceutical companies and medical advertising agencies where drug testing has been falsified," the "massive efforts" that "continue to be made to deceive and mislead physicians about prescription drugs," the AMA, and the US Senate for failing its watchdog function.

521. Navarro, Vicente. Medicine Under Capitalism. New York: Neale Watson, 1976. 230.

Indicts the medical profession. Part I: "the same political and economic forces that determine the nature of capitalism and imperialism also determine the underdevelopment of health and health resources." Part II discusses Ivan Illich's views. Part III the "political economy of medical care." Part IV on class, power, and health care.

522. Pelligrino, Edmund. Humanism and the Physician. Knoxville: U of Tennessee P, 1979. 248.

Explores the concept of medical humanism, the interaction between medicine and the humanities, medicine and ethics, with the aim of encouraging educated physicians rather than trained technicians.

523. Physicians for the Twenty-First Century: The GPEP Report: Report of the Panel on the General Professional Education of the Physician and College Preparation for Medicine. Washington, DC: Assoc. of American Medical Colleges, 1984.

Criticizes the profound imbalance in medical and pre-medical education between hard science and humanities and other disciplines that could bring a broader perspective to bear on clinical practice.

524. Reynolds, Janice. "The Medical Institution: The Death & Disease-producing Appendage." American Society: A Critical Analysis. Ed. Larry Reynolds and James Henslin. New York: McKay, 1973. 198-224.

The "medical helping professions form a privileged and autonomous cartel" in isolation from and unaccountable to the consumers or government. Services and drugs are expensive and for many scarce, and preventive medicine is neglected. A chief cause of these problems is the fee-for-service model of US medicine. Remedies suggested are: national health service, active participation in medical institutions by patients and laypersons, high standard of living for low-income citizens.

525. Schorr, Daniel. Don't Get Sick in America. Nashville: Aurora/CBS, 1970. 224.
A "more complete report" of the investigation of health care presented in two CBS Reports documentaries, "Health in America." The reports and the book present "the difficulty that Americans find in gaining access" to affordable medicine, why the wealthiest nation is not the healthiest, why medical care in the US is so expensive.

526. Shapiro, Martin, M.D. Getting Doctored. Philadelphia: New Society, 1987. 221.
Central perspective that the problems of medicine are linked to problems in society as a whole, especially alienation and authoritarianism, through which dehumanization and social irresponsibility thrive. Begins with medical schools' reinforcement of destructive forms of power and authority in the profession as a whole, moves to the negative effects of technology and sub-specialization, and the deliberate mystification of the public.

527. Siler, William, et al. Death by Prescription. Nashville, TN: Sherbourne/Charter House, 1978. 263.
Despite consumer expenditures of $120 billion in 1975 to stay well, the longevity of the males in the US "dropped from eleventh to fortieth place" worldwide, because of the "oligarchic power" of the health establishment and the ignorance and passivity of the public. Chapter 9, "What Is to Be Done?" discusses procedural and structural changes of the "vast and monolithic professional edifice."

528. Starr, Paul. The Social Transformation of American Medicine. New York: Basic, 1982. 514.
A dual history, "first, the rise of professional sovereignty; and second, the transformation of medicine into an industry and the growing, though still unsettled, role of corporations and the state." From "the standpoint of the profession, the challenge was initially to establish its authority and control of the market, then to keep it as large organizations and government threatened to intervene."

529. Waitzkin, H.B., and B. Waterman. The Exploitation of Illness in Capitalist Society. New York: Bobbs Merrill, 1974. 129.
A call for radical change, because health care contributes to the stratification of people. Since health care is a right of all citizens, it should be equally available to all.

THE SECONDARY INSTITUTIONS

530. Wohl, Stanley, M.D. The Medical Industrial Complex. New York: Crown, 1984. 218.
The author traces "the transformation of American medicine from an art and a science to a business for profit," the "spectacular rise of a large number of Wall Street-listed companies that have in the last few years become giant health care providers on a national scale."

I. B. 6. SPORTS (531-545)

531. Cady, Edwin H. The Big Game: College Sports and American Life. Knoxville: U of Tennessee P, 1978. 254.
A sympathetic appraisal of college athletics calling "for care, for renewal, for redemption." Since corruption never slackens, as in society at large, reform must be tireless. Athletics "needs to be liberated from the 'gate' and made independent of the things for which the media and show biz hate themselves" (233).

532. Dickey, Glenn. The Jock Empire: Its Rise & Deserved Fall. Radnor, PA: Chilton, 1974. 235.
From the president of the US to the Little Leagues, sports permeate the nation: stadiums, parades, million dollar players, multimillion dollar owners, celebrity sportscasters, male chauvinism, commercialism. Above all the "Winning Is Everything Syndrome which is the basis of the Watergate affair."

533. Freedman, Warren. Professional Sports and Antitrust. New York: Quorum, 1987. 147.
Economics of professional sports.

534. Hauser, Thomas. The Black Lights: Inside the World of Professional Boxing. New York: McGraw Hill, 1986. 257.
Economics of boxing.

535. Hoch, Paul. Rip Off the Big Game: The Exploitation of Sports by the Power Elite. Garden City, NY: Doubleday, 1972. 222.
The problems in US sports result from monopoly capitalism and are not the inevitable development of competitive sport; much of the book praises athletes and sportswriters who have maintained humanistic values against a dehumanizing system. A sample chapter is "Socialization for Consumption" in which sports owners systematically manipulate a "booming market in players and fans" for profits. "Sports watching is still one of the most powerful socializers for the habit of passive consumption around" (132).

536. Klatell, David, and Norman Marcus. Sports for Sale: Television, Money, and the Fans. New York: Oxford UP, 1988. 253.
They "explain, rather than judge the business of television sports, accepting as we do the innately commercial orientation

of both television and sports." They show the connections among sports, money, fans, cable and network, corporate marketing campaigns, and TV manipulation of sporting events for profit, even manufacture of events.

537. Levine, Peter. A.G. Spalding & the Rise of Baseball: The Promise of American Sport. New York: Oxford UP, 1985. 184.
This biography of the country's first sports superstar is viewed "as a microcosm of the rise of industrialism in the U.S." In a time of "tremendous disruptions," baseball provided law, order, efficiency, team play, specialization of skills, and courage as essential to immigrant assimilation into the "American Way of Life" and the Dream of Success. Levine's largest context is capitalism's transformation and control of all aspects of daily life into profitable systems.

538. Lipsky, Richard. How We Play the Game: Why Sports Dominate American Life. Boston: Beacon, 1981. 189.
Focuses upon the political and symbolical implications and importance of sporting events, team allegiance, socialization, heroism, and language. "As our representatives," for example, "the athletes sacrifice for 'good' principles of social order," and "our heroes are ready to do battle with the enemy" (22), and "victory defines success with a clarity seldom achieved in the real world" (23).

539. Lipsyte, Robert. SportsWorld: An American Dreamland. New York: Quadrangle, 1975. 292.
SportsWorld is the name that Lipsyte uses to represent the owners and corporations, television executives and journalists who organize, sell, and propagandize spectator sports.

540. Novak, Michael. The Joy of Sports. End Zones, Bases, Baskets, Balls, & the Consecration of the American Spirit. New York: Basic, 1976. 357.
People seek sports out of needs similar to attraction to religion--a hunger for authority, stability, order, community, transcendence. Sports provide the public a civil or secular religion which satisfies the needs in ways denied to institutionalized religion in the US.

541. Roberts, Randy, and James S. Olson. Winning Is the Only Thing: Sports in America Since 1945. Baltimore: Johns Hopkins UP, 1989. 259.
A book about "America's misplaced emphasis on sports" since World War II and the uses of sports for "the highest economic, political, and personal stakes." Underlying this national obsession are scandals, corruption, greed, drugs, crime, racism, and politics. One chapter is about "The World that Hiroshima Created: The Olympics Games and the Cold War," on how athletic stars became cold warriors against the SU. Two chapters explain how television "changed the nature of sports" under the pressure of commercialized entertainment for great profits. One chapter analyzes the economics of sports. Etc.

THE SECONDARY INSTITUTIONS

542. Scott, John V. The Role of Athletics in American Higher Education. Oakland, CA: Other Ways, 1969. 111.
"Professionalized" sports contribute to authoritarianism, conformity, obedience, and military precision at the expense of self-expression.

543. Smith, Ronald. Sports and Freedom: The Rise of Big-time College Athletics. New York: Oxford UP, 1988. 290.
A history of "the four major sports in the first half-century of intercollegiate athletics": crew, baseball, football, and track and field. Three themes are emphasized: the early commercialization of sports, the conflict between freedom and authority (as control moved from the students, to the faculty, to the institution, to independent organizations), and contrast with the British ideal of amateurism. "The professional model with a strong commercial base resulted" in the US.

544. Telander, Rick. The Hundred Yard Lie: The Corruption of College Football and What We Can Do About It. New York: Simon and Schuster, 1989. 223.
Attacks the exploitation of student-athletes at the expense of education. Winning, money, and entertainment replace knowledge, truth, and integrity in college athletics.

545. Whitford, David. A Payroll to Meet: A Story of Greed, Corruption, and Football at SMU. New York: Macmillan, 1989. 221.
Athletics at SMU reflects the culture at large.

II. THE MEDIA COMPLEX 546-4171

Introduction

A. The Media 546-1662
   1. General 546-765
   2. News 766-1087
   3. Corporations 1088-1214
   4. Government 1215-1662

B. Advertising and Public Relations 1663-2115a
   1. The Mass Consumption System 1663-1818
   2. Product Advertising 1819-1952
   3. Corporate Image and Advocacy Advertising 1953-2034
   4. Children and Advertising 2035-2057
   5. Political Advertising (Campaigning) 2058-2115a

C. Electronic Media 2116-3219
   1. Commercial Broadcasting 2116-2961
      a. Regulation 2116-2182
      b. General 2183-2275
      c. Television 2276-2961
         (1) General 2276-2448
         (2) Entertainment 2449-2550
         (3) News 2551-2885
         (4) Cable 2886-2899
         (5) Children 2900-2942
         (6) Religion 2943-2961
   2. Public and Subscriber Broadcasting 2962-3034
   3. Film and Theater 3035-3185
      a. Economics 3035-3052
      b. Entertainment and News 3053-3185
   4. Computers 3186-3219

D. Print Media 3220-4126
   1. News Agencies/Wire Services 3220-3269
   2. General: Newspapers and Magazines 3270-3346
   3. Newspapers 3347-3817
      a. General 3347-3511
      b. Individual 3512-3696
      c. The New York Times 3697-3817
   4. Magazines 3818-3946
      a. General 3818-3847
      b. Individual 3848-3946
   5. Books 3947-4026
   6. Government and Corporate Reports 4027-4126

E. Art and Music 4127-4171
   1. Art 4127-4146
   2. Music 4147-4171

THE MEDIA COMPLEX

INTRODUCTION

How media function in general solidarity with the dominant elites and institutions is the main subject of this bibliography. The explanation is complex obviously, especially because it is inseparable from US history. Wilbur Zelinsky in <u>Nation Into State</u> traces the gradual evolution of this country from a "nation" into a "state," the corporate state. During this long development of nationalism and statism, numerous "eidolons" and physical symbolical apparatuses of the nation-state accumulated: the flag and eagle, monuments, museums, parks, placenames, holidays, commemorative acts, pilgrimages, world's fairs, political rituals, hereditary and patriotic organizations, patriotic historiography, popular and high arts, songs, oratory, documents, the national anthem, the pledge of allegiance, birthdays and funerals of leaders, sports, heroes and heroines, villains, celebrities, and cemeteries (224-5). Early personal military and political heroes "came to share the stage with captains of industry and finance and with wizards of technology," who eventually were joined by "stars of the worlds of sport and entertainment." Gradually also "we have moved in the direction of the impersonal, abstract eidolon . . . a trend most notably exemplified by the [statist] glorification of the [sacerdotal] presidency." The evolution from nation to state is "concisely symbolized by the way in which Uncle Sam has displaced Miss Liberty as the favored national icon" (66).

In order to understand why so few reservists refused the presidential order to go to Saudi Arabia in the summer of 1990, or why the Whirlpool Company's "Eagle" ad on TV was so effective, or why televised sports are so popular and so lucrative, or why media coverage of Central America so closely adheres to official policy, one must be aware of this growth of patriotic symbols into the US civil religion of "Americanism" (232-45). (And be aware too of the confiscation of the word "American" from the other Americas for the exclusive designation of the US.)

Nationalism and statism have replaced the conventional Christian dogma as the chief set of beliefs and rituals understood as transcendent, providentially destined, and capable of arousing the deepest emotions (233-34). There is "a truly uncanny similarity between the workings of the fully mature statist civil religion" of the US and "the operations of orthodox Christianity during its heyday" (242). National heroes, martyrs, and villains "have preempted the emotional space once occupied by the Holy Trinity, the saints, and Satan and his imps"; the flag has become "a literally holy object, the equivalent of the cross or communion wafer" (243). "Thus there is literally no aspect of a fully constituted supernatural church that lacks its direct counterpart in the

American civil religion" (245). A look back at the wars and rhetoric against Native Americans since the Powhatan confederacy resistance uprising of 1622 to the vanquishing of all resistance (Cadwalader and Deloria) is to see a history of foreign wars and rationalizing discourse against non-White developing countries: African slavery, conquering the Philippines, the Mexican War, and most recently the Vietnam War. Whether racism or divine purpose was the chief motive (Svaldi), or rapacity or imperialism (Parenti), from the Pequoit massacre by the Puritans in 1637 to the My Lai 4 massacre by Charlie Company in 1968 or the killings of Nicaraguans by the CIA's Contras during the 1980s, the superior, "civilized" US has often dealt violently with treacherous or deficient "colored enemies" (complexly intertwined with religious and secular philanthropy, from Christian schools to the Peace Corps).

And these horrific violations of ethics and law, grounded in economic reality, in profit and competition (ranchers, traders, oilmen), were transformed into adventure myths by the media—a cowboy tall in the saddle, a lonely sheriff against outlaws (Limerick). The doctrine of Manifest Destiny, its symbols, and its media representations have been transmuted into the Truman Doctrine or Bush's New World Order but they still energize military adventures and the media that transmit them: Korea, Guatemala, Vietnam, Nicaragua, El Salvador, Libya, Granada, Panama, Iraq (see I. A. and II. A., and Control of Information).

Not only in foreign but in domestic policy, discourses and media have followed official myths, policies, and economic power. From Nicholas Johnson to Ben Bagdikian, anxiety has deepened, in Johnson's words, over "the dreadful significance of the ownership structure of the mass media in America" (49) (in reference to the proposed ITT-ABC merger of 1966) in regard to the integrity of news reporting. To Eric Sevareid, participating in a news program at a network is like "'being bitten to death by ducks'" (53). In his last broadcast for ABC, Edward P. Morgan declared that "'every major facet'" of the press "'pulls its punches to save a supermarket of commercialism'" (59). But not only in the journalism of news does centralized power reveal itself through direct or (mainly) self-censorship, the prevailing organization of power dominates "every phase of culture" through "overt propaganda in political rhetoric . . . advertising, and public relations and through the often unconscious absorption of capitalist ideology by creators and consumers in all aspects of the culture of everyday life" (Lazere 6-7). According to Herbert Schiller, the corporate control of consciousness has achieved its fullest development in the US, and it is a power that reaches throughout the world.

Jacques Ellul distinguishes between political propaganda and sociological propaganda (62-70). Political propaganda is the familiar usage, any direct attempt to reinforce or change the behavior of the public. Sociological propaganda is more general, "the penetration of an ideology" through "a general climate, an atmosphere that influences people imperceptibly," through customs, habits, the "persuasion from within," until people not only adopt the outlook as if freely chosen, but they actively participate in its maintenance and reproduction as though originating with them, as though natural. Donald McIntosh divides the subject of power into three kinds: persuasion, coercion, and force. Persuasion is the appeal to reason. Coercion operates through sanctions, ranging from the threat of violence to the subtlest forms of flattery, to bring about agreement. Propaganda, the use of irrational appeals (political campaigns, advertising), is a form of coercion that aims to induce internalized sanctions (patriotism, fear). From the point of view of many of those wielding power, a perfect educational system would produce perfect assimilation of their norms and rules. The ultimate aim of the entire system of political and social propaganda, and of persuasion, coercion, and force, is the voluntary acceptance of the legitimacy of the reigning system of power.

Antonio Gramsci's idea of hegemony has gained adherents increasingly in recent years as, in the words of Todd Gitlin in The Whole World Is Watching, "the most comprehensive theoretical approach" (252) to understanding the exercise of power over the interpretation of reality. Gramsci spent eleven years in a Fascist prison writing about why the working class accepted Mussolini. His explanation included force, but it was much more complex than that. The ruling factions and their apparatus can and do use force to compel the population, but more importantly they can successfully project their own interests into the common sense and everyday practice of the majority of the people. They can engineer mass consent to the established order. Hegemony exists when the alliance of dominant groups possesses the power not only to coerce but to win the consent of the subordinated groups. And in the liberal-capitalist state, consent predominates (253). The dominant economic and political classes cannot produce the hegemonic ideology directly, but must depend upon mass media and education--the journalists, teachers, bureaucrats, advertisers, entertainers, executives, and managers of the corporations and government--to indoctrinate consent. The cultural industry and the educational system function as the chief institutions for legitimating the established hierarchy of power (254-55).

But in a democratic society such a complicated arrangement cannot be a perfect machine; hegemonic ideology conflicts with alternative values and programs. Yet this very diversity, the relative autonomy even of subordinate sectors--the great extent of personal freedom in the US particularly--functions to legitimate the system as a whole (255). "Indeed, the hegemonic ideology of bourgeois culture is extremely complex and absorptive; only by absorbing and domesticating conflicting values, definitions of reality, and demands on it, in fact, does it remain hegemonic" (256).

Timothy Luke had apparently not read Zelinsky's Nation Into State, though his Screens of Power might be read as an extension of the other book's history of US ideological symbols. Luke had read, however, Gramsci's Selections from the Prison Notebooks. New transnational economic and technological forces are producing "the complete commodification of all aspects" of life. The "substance and form" of the new electronic technologies, from TV to computers, function as new projections of "power and ideology" within "consumption communities." Organized elites "reveal their biases most directly in the electronic imagery and technology underpinning contemporary mass consumption and production" (4). This is the new information society, and Luke's project is to examine why it distorts human activity and how it can be resisted (4-5).

Why do people obey? In answer Luke draws upon Raymond Williams and Richard Ohmann. Domination works on many complex levels throughout all the practices of living in a particular society, shaping perceptions and energy and the sense of reality for most people (when successful). Our "everyday experience in the various mediascapes" makes the system appear basically reasonable, natural, right. The eidolons of US statism seem common sense. "'Domination filters through a thousand capillaries of transmission, a million habitual meanings.'"

Works Cited

Cadwalader, Sandra, and Vine Deloria, Jr., eds. The Aggressions of Civilization: Federal Indian Policy Since the 1880s. Philadelphia: Temple UP, 1984.

Ellul, Jacques. Propaganda: The Formation of Men's Attitudes. New York: Vintage, 1973 (Knopf, 1965).

Gramsci, Antonio. Selections from the Prison Notebooks. Trans. and ed. Quintin Hoare and Geoffrey N. Smith. New York: International, 1971.

Johnson, Nicholas. How to Talk Back to Your TV Set. Boston: Little, Brown, 1967.

Limerick, Patricia. The Legacy of Conquest: The Unbroken Past of the American West. New York: Norton, 1987.

McIntosh, Donald. "Power and Social Control." APSR 57 (1963) 619-31.

Parenti, Michael. The Sword and the Dollar: Imperialism, Revolution, and the Arms Race. New York: St. Martin's, 1989. Chapter 8, "The Mythology of Interventionism."

Schaar, John. Legitimacy in the Modern State. New Brunswick: Transaction, 1981.

Schiller, Herbert. Culture, Inc.. New York: Oxford UP, 1989.

Svaldi, David. Sand Creek and the Rhetoric of Extermination: A Case Study in Indian-White Relations. Lanham, MD: U P of America, 1989.

THE MEDIA (546-4171)

II. A. 1. GENERAL (546-765)

546. Abel, Elie, ed. What's News: The Media in American Society. San Francisco: Inst. for Contemporary Studies, 1981. 296.
On media monopoly and chains, news as entertainment and business, advertising, new technologies, First Amendment, economics of media, candidate images on network news, business news, etc. In "The Last Word" he summarizes problems and suggests remedies.

547. Achenbach, Joel. "Creeping Surrealism: Does Anybody Really Know What's Real Anymore?" UR 30 (Nov.-Dec. 1988) 112-116.
"Lies have been raised to an art form in this country" with "such unparalleled virtuosity" that it's difficult "to tell the genuine from the fake."

548. Aldrich, Pearl. The Impact of Mass Media. Rochelle Park, NJ: Hayden, 1975. 179.
The media represent the "commercial-military-governmental complex" (5).

549. Altheide, David. Media Power. Beverly Hills, CA: Sage, 1985. 288.
Studies the media's power to create social reality by creating cognitive and cultural patterns which structure people's perceptions. From the production process to the mode of expression, each medium's format contributes to the totality of social reality. Thus traditional discussions of "objectivity" are naive.

550. Altheide, David, and Robert P. Snow. Media Logic. Beverly Hills, CA: Sage, 1979. 256.
On media as culture, entertainment, news, politics, religion, sports, etc. Analyzes how social institutions are transformed by the media because they have "adopted a media logic and specific media formats as their own institutional strategies and thus have become part of the total media culture" (16).

551. Andrae, Thomas. "From Menace to Messiah: The History and Historicity of Superman." American Media & Mass Culture. Ed. Donald Lazere. Berkeley: U of California P, 1987. 124-138.
Examines various versions of Superman's ahistorical exploits, since the 1950s a defender of "the American way of life."

551a. Angus, Ian, and Sut Jhally, eds. Cultural Politics in Contemporary America. New York: Routledge, 1989. 388.

THE MEDIA

Twenty-four essays discuss how interlocked politics, the consumer society, and the media are shaping the culture.

552. Aronowitz, Stanley. "Mass Culture and the Eclipse of Reason: The Implications for Pedagogy." American Media & Mass Culture. Ed. Donald Lazere. Berkeley: U of California P, 1987. 465-474.

Urges "the free play of critical political thought as a means of overcoming the reflex conservatism induced by illiteracy and mass culture" (416).

553. Bagdikian, Ben. The Effete Conspiracy and Other Crimes By the Press. New York: Harper, 1972. 159.

Examines conglomerates, monopolies, absentee ownership, press agentry and free advertising, suppression of news, presidential manipulation of news, presidential intimidation of media, ombudsmen, Agnew and Nixon, Lyndon Johnson, TV and the president, Pentagon Papers, DuPont newspapers, etc.

554. Barber, James David. The Pulse of Politics: Electing Presidents in the Media Age. New York: Norton, 1980. 342.

Part of the book is about the enormous power the media--especially TV--have to advance or retard a presidential candidate, and the ability or inability of various candidates to exploit that power. "If the journalists are the new kingmakers, the candidates are the new storytellers, active plotters of dramas they hope will win for them" (8). But journalists can hold candidates and presidents to reality and facts, they can provide analysis of the character of each leader, and they can test the individuals' values and how they connect to groups that might form a government.

555. Barsamian, David. "Interviewing Michael Parenti." Zeta 2.1 (Jan. 1989) 100-104.

The author of Inventing Reality discusses the way ruling class domination is ignored by the media, the little real diversity of opinion, how the appearance of objectivity is maintained by "false balancing," how "framing" is more useful than outright lying in propaganda, and problems faced by alternative media.

556. Becker, Jörg, et al., eds. Communication and Domination: Essays to Honor Herbert I. Schiller. Norwood, NJ: Ablex, 1986. 278.

The twenty-six essays deal with topics ranging from information technology, cultural domination and resistance, to the new international information order and the democratization of communication.

557. Benét, James. "Conclusion: Will Media Treatment of Women Improve?" Hearth and Home: Images of Women in the Mass Media. New York: Oxford UP, 1978. 266-271.

It will improve if women gain more financial and executive control of the media.

558. Bennett, W. Lance. "Myth, Ritual, and Political Control." JoC 30.4 (1980) 166-179.
Myths, with their attendant values and beliefs, structure public opinion and political processes as we can see through the rejection of options outside the boundary of myth-sanctioned choices. The very things we criticize--melodrama or personal imagery--are often the core cultural structures for the ritual enactment of the myths.

559. Berger, Arthur A. Media Analysis Techniques. Beverly Hills: Sage, 1989. 160.
The first section (14-110) introduces semiological, psychoanalytic (Freudian), Marxist, and sociological theories. The second section (112-159) applies the perspectives to the public arts. Annotated bibliography follows each chapter.

560. Berger, Arthur A. Seeing Is Believing: An Introduction to Visual Communication. Mountain View, CA: Mayfield, 1989. 189.
A study of TV, film, cartooning, typography, cave pictographs, etc., from a highly personal perspective as a text for undergraduates.

561. Berger, Arthur A. Television as an Instrument of Terror: Essays on Media, Popular Culture, and Everyday Life. New Brunswick, NJ: Transaction, 1980. 214.
Twenty-six essays on a variety of topics, such as pop culture, politics in comics, advertising, The Six Million Dollar Man, sex and advertising.

562. Bird, George L., and Frederic E. Merwin, eds. The Press and Society: A Book of Readings. New York: Prentice-Hall, 1951. 655.
A comprehensive collection covering twenty-seven topics: big business, press agents, propaganda, press freedom, suppression of news, advertising, syndicates, editorials, crusading newspapers, etc.

563. Birkhead, Herbert. "Presenting the Press: Journalism & the Professional Project." U of Iowa, 1982. 363. DAI 43.4 (Oct. 1982) 960-A.
The professionalization of journalism was more than a search for "occupational identity and prestige" but involved a "focus on public service" through "objectivity and standardization."

564. Black, George. The Good Neighbor: How the United States Wrote the History of Central America and the Caribbean. New York: Pantheon, 1988. 200.
Covers song lyrics, postage stamps, cartoons, advertisements, news photographs, travel brochures, and many other discourses to expose the US neurosis regarding Latin America--the use of an entire region for behavior forbidden at home.

565. Blewett, Mary H. "Machines, Workers, and Capitalists: The Interpretation of Textile Industrialization in

New England Museums." History Museums in the United States: A Critical Assessment. Ed. Warren Leon and Roy Rosenzweig. Urbana: U of Illinois P, 1989. 262-293.
The New England textile-history museums serve as a model for the combination of "the history of technology and the history of industrial workers," though more can be done to see "industrial capitalism in systemic ways that apply to contemporary American economic problems."

566. Bonk, Kathy. "Money, Media, and 'Electability.'" M&V 44 (Summer-Fall 88) 8-9.
Uses press reaction to Pat Schroeder's tentative presidential candidacy to illustrate biases working against fair coverage of women and minorities.

567. Bosmajian, Haig A. The Language of Oppression. Washington: Public Affairs P, 1974. 156.
Examines the language of bigotry: anti-Semitism, white racism, Indian derision, sexism, and war. Language can be used "to dehumanize human beings and to 'justify' their suppression and even their extermination."

568. Boylan, James. "The Big Numbers." CJR 17.3 (1978) 78-79.
The Mass Media, by Sterling and Haight, provides not only "copious numbers about media finances, control, audiences, content, and employment," but also analyzes the limitations of their figures.

569. Boylan, James. "Whose Press Is Free?" CJR 22.6 (1984) 53-54.
Journalists generally are ethnocentric and support the ruling elites.

570. Breed, Warren. "Mass Communication and Sociocultural Integration." People, Society, and Mass Communications. Ed. Lewis Dexter and David White. New York: Free, 1964. 595.
The media, by affirming common ultimate values and by avoiding exposing structural flaws in the major institutions, are a continuing source of consensus.

571. Brown, Thomas. JFK: History of an Image. Bloomington: Indiana UP, 1988. 150.
Examines the ways in which Kennedy has been portrayed in the popular and scholarly media, particularly as the result of his assassination: "it is the circumstances of Kennedy's death rather than the events of his life that have elevated him to a primary place in the political consciousness of Americans" (2).

571a. Budd, Richard, and Brent Ruben. Beyond Media: New Approaches to Mass Communication. Rochelle Park, NJ: Hayden, 1978. 292.

In an attempt to broaden the view of what constitutes mass communication, they argue for inclusion of architecture, religion, popular art, museums, and libraries.

572. Buhle, Paul, ed. Popular Culture in America. Minneapolis: U of Minnesota P, 1987. 271.
Thirty-three previously published essays (1975-1983) "rooted in the social experience of the 1960s." In his Introduction Buhle comments: "Never has the real past . . . seemed more distant or its Reaganesque evocation more blatantly deceitful." "The writers in this volume condemn the manipulative qualities of commercial culture." Some titles: "The Politics of Boys' Sports Novels," "Prime Time Jesus," "Hegemony and Me."

573. Bunce, Dick. "The Crisis in Political Publishing." SocR 15.4-5 (1985) 7-12.
On the increase of right-wing media.

574. Burnham, Philip. "Corrupted by Condescension: The Museum of Westward Expansion Rationalizes the Obsession of Manifest Destiny." SLJR 20.127 (June 1990) 12-13.
Under the arch in St. Louis the Museum of Westward Expansion gives a nationalistic, Manifest Destiny version of history.

575. Burroughs, William. Ah Pook Is Here and Other Texts. London: Calder, 1982. 157.
In two essays the novelist defends imagination against Control and then in a third essay imagines a device to disrupt illusory media programs.

576. [Cancelled]

577. Casty, Alan, ed. Mass Media and Mass Man. New York: Holt, 1968. 260.
"I have collected materials that focus on the media as processors and conveyors of culture and information. In their dual role, the mass media create and shape not only the values, tastes, attitudes, and the art and entertainment experiences of their audience, but also the patterns of fact and opinion about the world of that audience."

578. Chaffee, Steven, and Michael Petrick. Using the Mass Media: Communication Problems in American Society. New York: McGraw-Hill, 1975. 264.
Part II deals with "Public Information": the courts, schools, military, and corporate public relations. For example, Chapter 8, "The Military and Its Public," attempts to explain "why most of us find it so hard to learn how it operates." Authors assume a free media market with minimal social and political biases.

579. Chaney, David. "The Symbolic Form of Ritual in Mass Communication." Communicating Politics. Ed. Peter

Golding, et al. New York: Holmes & Meier, 1986. 115-132.
Rituals promoted by the established media reaffirm existing political arrangements. A "rhetoric of democratic egalitarianism paradoxically displays the form of institutionalized power as private participation in rituals of consensus" (132).

580. "Charity Games by PD, Channel 8." PoV 1.13 (Jan. 13, 1969) n.p.
Instead of investigating the political economy of the Mannington Mine disaster after 78 miners died, the Cleveland Plain Dealer and Channel 8 made "self-seeking" promotion drives for charity for the dependents of the dead miners.

581. Chisman, Forrest P. "New Directions and Developments." JoC 26.2 (Spring 1976) 91-94.
Updates research on the "agenda-setting functions" of mass communication by previewing the new series of integrative studies by the Social Science Research Council (SSRC).

582. Chomsky, Noam. "The Agenda of the Doves." Zeta (Sept. 1988) 8-30.
Analysis of how "policy flows from institutional structures of power and domination" and how "tactical choices fall within the narrow bounds of this elite consensus" (8). Looks at governmental, media, and scholarly expressions of this consensus, particularly dissent within the bounds.

583. Chomsky, Noam. "American Media and Foreign Policy." IR (Feb. 1980) 10-19.
Analyzes the media as an agency of the state for indoctrination of a narrow framework of values within which debate is possible.

584. Chomsky, Noam. "The Manufacture of Consent" (1984). The Chomsky Reader. New York: Pantheon, 1987. 121-136.
"Propaganda is to democracy what violence is to totalitarianism. The techniques have been honed to a high art, far beyond anything that Orwell dreamt of" (136).

585. Chomsky, Noam. Necessary Illusions: Thought Control in Democratic Societies. Boston: South End, 1989. 422.
Far from performing a watchdog role, the "free press" serves the needs of those in power. Manifold measures are employed "to deprive democratic political structures of substantive content, while leaving them formally intact," especially the ideological institutions that "channel thought and attitudes within acceptable bounds, deflecting any potential challenge to established privilege and authority before it can take form and gather strength" (vii). "I will primarily be concerned with one aspect: thought control, as conducted through the agency of the national media and related elements of the elite intellectual culture" (viii). Five essays 1-136; Appendices 137-355; Notes 357-412.

586. Christensen, Jack. "The Study of Meaning." M&M 10
(Sept. 1973), 35-37, 53-58.
On ways teachers can educate students about thought control.

587. Christians, Clifford, Kim Rotzoll, and Mark Fackler.
Media Ethics: Cases and Moral Reasoning. 2nd ed.
New York: Longman, 1987. 332.
Examines eighty-two specific cases: cable tv, Watergate, exploitation movies, etc. [Complements Johannesen's Ethics in Human Communication on theoretical issues.]

588. Cirino, Robert. We're Being More Than Entertained.
Honolulu: Lighthouse Press, 1977. 224.
The controllers of the messages are the owners of communication technology, whose purpose is to make a profit. The author analyzes Kojak, All My Children, the Los Angeles Times sports page, Playboy, Let's Make a Deal, Top 40, Tournament of Thrills, Sesame Street, Guardians of the Galaxy (comic book), radio news, Paul Conrad's cartoons, and network live coverage. He proposes a new broadcasting system which represents all major political viewpoints--socialist, liberal, conservative, libertarian--called the United States Broadcasting Corporation (USBC).

589. "City Club Talk." PoV (Dec. 22, 1968) Special Issue, n.p.
Hunger and other massive problems disturb our nation, but the media assist government and corporations to limit dissent and free speech.

590. Clark, David G., and William B. Blankenburg. "The Peculiarities of Freedom: Truth and Freedom Grapple! Cast of Thousands!" You & Media. San Francisco, CA: Canfield, 1973. 103-118.
Examines the relationship between free speech and social responsibility, which they define as "libertarianism with a conscience."

591. Clark, David G., and William B. Blankenburg. You & Media: Mass Communication and Society. San Francisco, CA: Canfield, 1973. 275.
The media "make decisions that have enormous influence on our lives but of which we know very little. They set our priorities for discussion of the day's events with our friends. They tell us what to eat, what to wear, what opinions are socially acceptable, what actions are likely to be successful" (vii). And media perspectives have too often been arrogantly restricted to those of "upper-middle-class mercantilism" (ix). At the end the authors suggest remedies based on the hope that the media might represent "a kind of second government for all Americans."

592. Cockburn, Alexander. "The Network." Corruptions of Empire. London: Verso, 1987. 261-64.
The adherence of the government and mainstream media to

peanuts violence against the US is contrasted to the real, massive violence committed by nations allied to and supported by the US. Establishment writers are "captive intellectuals of the state indulging in a spectacular trahison des clercs, nourishing the Reaganite vision."

593. Cockburn, Alexander, and Richard McKerrow. "Black Holes." LOOT 1.7 (July 1990) 14-15.
Evidence of a tendency by the media to forget the students killed at Jackson State in 1970.

594. Cooper, Thomas. "Fictional 1984 & Factual 1984: Ethical Questions Regarding the Control of Consciousness by Mass Media." The Orwellian Moment. Ed. Robert Savage, James Combs, and Dan Nimmo. Fayetteville, AR: U of Arkansas P, 1989. 83-107.
Lists 17 dangers in the US, divided into eleven "lesser" and six "terminal" tendencies, the latter operative when the first combine into "Media Fascism."

595. Cox, Harvey. "The Consciousness Industry: A Theological View of the Media." PTR 1 (Oct. 1973) 8-15.
Biblical vs. mass media concepts of communication.

596. Cunningham, Ben. "The Press and Civil Liberties." RSCJ 8 (July 1973) 9-10.
On the press's failure to defend Cedric Belfrage and other journalists disliked by the government or the majority. The problem with US news people is their commitment to the "acceptable-unacceptable" syndrome regarding civil liberties, based upon fear, enmity, and nationalism.

597. Cunningham, Ben. "The Press and the Cold War." RSCJ 4 (Apr. 1972) 5-6.
Praises James Aronson's The Press and the Cold War for revealing how the US press helped perpetuate Cold War mythology and hysteria which have been catastrophic for the nation and world.

598. Curran, James, Jake Ecclestone, Giles Oakley, and Alan Richardson. Bending Reality: The State of the Media. London: Pluto, 1986. 243.
Although the essays deal with the British media, they apply also to the US. For example, the contributors believe that the airwaves belong to the public and should serve public not commercial interests, and that political campaigns by the people to gain control of media are necessary.

599. Curran, James, Michael Gurevitch, and Janet Woollacott, eds. Mass Communication and Society. Beverly Hills: Sage, 1979 (1977). 478.
Designed originally for the British Open University Course "Mass Communication and Society," intended for a wide, interdisciplinary audience. Thus the collection "concentrates on the relationship between systems of production, the division

of labour and systems of domination and control" in the media.

600. Darnovsky, Marcy, Claude Steiner, Charles Rappleye, and Frederic Stout. "What Is Propaganda, Anyway?" PR 5 (Summer 1989) 6-13.
Former and current editors of Propaganda Review offer definitions of propaganda and explain its function in US culture.

601. Dennis, Everette. Reshaping the Media: Mass Communication in the Information Age. Newbury Park, CA: Sage, 1989. 210.
Assesses impact of cable TV, satellite transmissions, VCRs, computers, data bases, etc. on existing media and consumers.

602. Diamond, Edwin. Good News, Bad News. Cambridge, MA: MIT P, 1978. 263.
A series of reports constituting a "press watch" conducted by the News Study Group at MIT 1975-77, continuing the research published in The Tin Kazoo, which focused upon TV. Good News studies also newspapers and magazines, especially focusing upon the 1976 presidential campaign and media performance. In his final pages Diamond makes a strong appeal for more investigative journalism.

603. Doob, Leonard. Public Opinion and Propaganda. 2nd ed. Hamden, CT: Archon, 1966. 612.
A social sciences effort to describe these aspects of the modern world, with "only one thesis to advocate: public opinion and propaganda are intimately related because they both involve phases of human behavior." Draws examples "from three fields: politics, business, and war."

604. Dorfman, Ariel. "The Infantilizing of Culture." American Media & Mass Culture. Ed. Donald Lazere. Berkeley: U of California P, 1987. 145-156.
Right-wing "sentimentality" throughout US history "has rationalized racism and imperialism" (103).

605. Downing, John, Ali Mohammadi, and Anabelle Sreberny-Mohammadi. Questioning the Media: A Critical Introduction. Newbury Park: Sage, 1990. 385.
Twenty-five essays in 5 parts: I "Introductory Perspectives," II "Media, Power, and Control," III "Audiences and Users," IV "Information Technologies," V "Mass Culture and Popular Culture." Treats current communications research as an "arena of debate." The editors' aim is to enable readers to "understand better how the media are connected with economic forces, political processes, and cultural values and products."

606. Downs, Hugh. "Rating the Media." CM 11.2 (1978) 17-22.
Reviews the findings of the Hutchins Commission in 1947, applies its criteria for a "free and responsible press" to today's media, finds them lacking in most areas. Urges more funding for PBS.

THE MEDIA 101

607. Dynes, Wayne. Homosexuality: A Research Guide. New York: Garland, 1987. 853.
Section I.H., "Press and Media," includes books and articles on the treatment of homosexuality in both mainstream and gay-lesbian press. I.G., "Libraries and Archives," treats special problems posed for cataloguing and collecting materials.

608. Efron, Edith. The Apocalyptics: Cancer and the Big Lie: How Environmental Politics Controls What We Know About Cancer. New York: Simon & Schuster, 1984. 589.
The "apocalyptics" are Rachel Carson and other scientists who have exaggerated, she argues, the dangers of environmental and especially industrial and synthetic pollutants. Epilogue discusses media coverage.

609. Ehrlich, Howard J. "The Politics of News Media Control." IS 4 (1974) 31-43.
Describes the corporate-government-media complex.

610. Eliasoph, Nina. "Measuring the American Mind." PR 2 (Summer 1988) 10-14.
A skeptical look at polls. Powerful groups and institutions manipulate via polls.

611. Emery, Edwin, and Michael Emery. The Press and America: An Interpretive History of the Mass Media. 5th ed. Englewood Cliffs, NY: Prentice-Hall, 1984. 774.
Chapter 23, "Television Takes Center Stage"; Ch. 24, "Challenge and Dissent" (1960s); Ch. 25, "A Crisis of Credibility" (1970s); Ch. 26, "The Surviving Newspaper Press"; Ch. 27, "Media Technology: The Challenge of the 1980s."

612. Emery, Michael, and Ted Smythe, eds. Readings in Mass Communication: Concepts and Issues in the Mass Media. 2nd ed. Dubuque, IA: Brown, 1972. 552.
Sections on "Increasing [Public] Access to the Mass Media," "Increasing [Citizen] Control of the Mass Media," "Increasing Protection for Sources of News," "Increasing 'Relevance' of Reporting Practices" (i.e., muckraking), "Creating Alternative Media for Minorities," etc. (eleven in all containing over fifty selections).

613. English, Robert, and Jonathan Halperin. The Other Side: How Soviets and Americans Perceive Each Other. New Brunswick and Oxford: Transaction, 1987. 155.
Exploration of how history, the media, books, and films influence SU and US perceptions of each other.

614. Entman, Robert M., and David L. Paletz. "Media and the Conservative Myth." JoC 30.4 (1980) 154-165.
The media depicted an increasingly conservative political climate during the 1970s by confusing a general political distrust with a rejection of "big government" programs in an atmosphere of pack journalism.

615. "Environmental Reporting." MJR 18 (1975) 20-34.
Seven speeches given at an Environmental Reporting Seminar at the U of Montana in 1974.

616. Ewen, Stuart. All Consuming Images: The Politics of Style in Contemporary Culture. New York: Basic, 1988. 306.
Studies the union of economic power and images in the US in advertising, architecture, fashion, packaging, corporate image, and political propaganda to show how the images we consume end up consuming us. The dissociation of images from experience and the substitution of images for substance permeates our society, creating a nation "in which style has emerged as the predominant expression of meaning" (271). [See Ewen's Captains of Consciousness.]

617. Fackler, Paul. "The Hutchins Commissioners & the Crisis in Democratic Theory, 1930-1947." U of Illinois, 1982. 408. DAI 43.3 (Sept. 1982) 576-A.
The Commission on Freedom of the Press, chaired by Robert M. Hutchins, made forceful defense of Social Responsibility Theory. This theory derived especially from the classical and Christian humanists on the Commission, who sought "a moral base for freedom of speech" and democracy.

618. Fejes, Fred. "The U.S. in Third World Communications: Latin America 1900-1945." JM 86 (Nov. 1983) 1-29.
Media imperialism in Latin America, complete by 1945.

619. Ferguson, Marjorie, ed. Public Communication, The New Imperatives: Future Directions for Media Research. Newbury Park, CA: Sage, 1990. 256.
Contributors investigate how new technologies, regulatory policies, and changes in ownership have affected today's media and the democratic process.

620. Fisher, Glen. American Communication in a Global Society. Norwood, NJ: Ablex, 1979. 165.
A government official assesses global communication trends and processes toward establishing government policies for the future. Some conclusions: First and Third World communications gap will grow, fear of US threat to national sovereignties will also grow, US citizens abroad will expand.

621. Fonzi, Gaeton. Annenberg: A Biography of Power. New York: Weybright and Talley, 1970. 246.
Life of father Mo and son Walter. Walter Annenberg owned the Philadelphia Inquirer, Triangle Publications (New York Morning Telegraph, Daily Racing Form, Screen Guide, Radio Guide, TV Guide, Seventeen), TV and radio in six cities, and largest stockholder in Penn Central. Many pages describe Annenberg's manipulation of the Inquirer's news columns for personal and sometimes vindictive ends. An exposé of the relationship between big money, politics, and big media.

THE MEDIA

621a. Fore, William. <u>Mythmakers: Gospel, Culture and the Media</u>. New York: Friendship, 1990. 150.
Attacks the dominant capitalist, materialistic culture and its powerful myth-maker, the media, particularly TV. Documents the ways TV has brainwashed the public with its myths of consumerism, western superiority, the "American Way of Life," etc. Urges the churches in the US and Canada to pioneer in media education.

622. Forester, John, ed. <u>Critical Theory and Public Life</u>. Cambridge, MA: MIT, 1985. 337.
Assesses "issues of power, policy, ideology, and political action in ways informed by Jurgen Habermas's critical communications theory of society." Especially relevant is Part III, which "analyzes the constitution of everyday practical judgments by considering the institutional development of the news media and the phenomenological character of consumer choices."

623. Fox, Florence. "Kolliers Konquers the Kremlin." CHQ 202.4 (July-Aug. 1988) 9-12.
Thought controllers have manipulated media into portraying Russia as a military threat and conditioned the public to the inevitability of war. Examples include the Feb. 15, 1987, ABC "Amerika," depicting US ten years after a Soviet takeover.

623a. Francois, William. <u>Mass Media Law and Regulation</u>. Columbus, OH: Grid, 1982. 732.
Discusses First Amendment, libel, prior restraint, freedom of information, subpoena power, reporter privilege, antitrust laws, and media concentration.

624. Franklin, H. Bruce. <u>War Stars: The Superweapon & the American Imagination</u>. New York: Oxford UP, 1988. 256.
Traces in fact and media of all kinds the history of the pursuit of a weapon so terrible it could end war by defeating all enemies and establishing US hegemony forever--a torpedo, a ray, aerial warfare, the atom bomb. President Reagan's 1983 "Star Wars" speech promising the public a shield against missiles was one more instance in a long line of illusory magic shields designed to save the world by terrorizing it.

625. Friedman, Barbara. "Consumer Reporting [in St. Louis] Spotty." SLJR 18.114 (Mar. 1989) 1, 6.
Few of the Better Business Bureau fraud alert press releases are printed by newspapers, TV, and radio, and those that are usually are innocuous.

626. Fussell, Paul. <u>Wartime: Understanding and Behavior in the Second World War</u>. New York: Oxford UP, 1989. 330.
Partly an analysis of ignorance and evasion of the realities of the war as the result of systematic euphemism and the deceits of Hollywood, Madison Avenue, and government propaganda.

627. Gambill, Joel. "Hugo Black: The First Amendment & the Mass Media." Ph.D. diss., Southern Illinois U, 1973.

295. DAI 34 (1974) 5895-A.
A study of Supreme Court Justice Hugo Black's "staunch support for freedom of the press . . . in more than one hundred cases" covering a period of thirty-four years, 1937 to 1971.

628. Gerard, Jeremy. "Can the Press Do the Right Thing? II. Hurting Words, Fighting Words." CJR 29.2 (July-Aug. 1990) 25-27.
Analyzes homophobia in the media.

628a. Gerbner, George, Larry P. Gross, and William H. Melody, eds. Communications Technology and Social Policy: Understanding the New 'Cultural Revolution.' New York: Wiley, 1973. 573.
A collection of forty-one essays, divided into six interrelating sections, dealing with the vast changes in communications. In particular, examines issues and problems associated with directing the new technologies toward accomplishing public interest objectives. Essays by Nicholas Johnson, Bertram Gross, Herbert Schiller, et al.

629. Gerbner, George, and Marsha Siefert, eds. World Communications: A Handbook. New York: Longman, 1984. 527.
Fifty-four essays on "U.S. Television Coverage of Foreign News," "Transnational Advertising: The Latin American Case," "International Circulation of U.S. Theatrical Films and Television Programming," "Remote Sensing by Satellite: Global Hegemony or Social Utility," etc.

630. Ghareeb, Edmund, ed. Split Vision: The Portrayal of Arabs in the American Media. Rev. Washington, DC: American-Arab Affairs Council, 1983. 402.
Although the media have "sought to discontinue pejorative characterizations of ethnic groups, Arabs, and as a result Arab-Americans, still suffer from malevolent and inaccurate characterization" (xv).

631. Giffard, Anthony. Unesco and the Media. New York: Longman, 1989. 288.
History and analysis of US press coverage of US withdrawal from Unesco and "the successful manipulation of the news media by a few Washington officials" (xi), especially State Department spokesman, Gregory Newell, a "conservative ideologue" (xiii). The withdrawal was actually an attack on the U.N. itself, long a right-wing goal. This larger story was meagerly exposed by the press, and the public "never received a fair chance to weigh the evidence pro and con" (xiv) (from the Foreword by Leonard Sussman).

632. Gitlin, Todd. "Making Democracy Safe for America." CJR 18.6 (1980) 53-58.
By neglecting protest movements or treating them as "a sideshow," the press cuts the political process off at the grass roots and "limits the ability of American democracy to renew itself."

THE MEDIA

633. Glessing, Robert, and William P. White, eds. "Politics, Censors, and Media." Mass Media: The Invisible Environment Revisited. Chicago: SRA, 1976. 172-207.
Five essays on the institutional power blocs and Nixon, TV in election campaigns, public broadcasting, etc.

634. Golding, Peter, Graham Murdock, and Philip Schlesinger. Communicating Politics: Mass Communications and the Political Process. New York: Leicester UP/Holmes & Meier, 1986. 241.
Eleven essays explore the damage done to democracy by "the proliferation of highly commercialized distribution technologies, the growth of the strong state and the assault upon the 'public sphere.'" The developing technologies are not expanding democratic choice and public control, but in fact are diminishing public control.

635. Goldsmith, Barbara. "The Meaning of Celebrity." NYTM (Dec. 4, 1983) 74-82, 120.
The US preference for illusion has increased during the past twenty years through the power of TV.

636. Goldstein, Richard. Reporting the Counterculture. Boston: Unwin Hyman, 1989. 173.
About the culture of the Sixties politics: influence of the media, psychedelics, the New Left, rock music, etc., written at the time and now collected. He "exhumes" the New Journalism of the Sixties because journalism now is too impersonal, too standardized. The dissenters of the Sixties call us again to "assert the distinction between culture and commodity."

637. Goodman, Ellen. At Large. New York: Summit, 1981. 245.
A few of the articles, originally published in BG, deal with power and the media. For example, with the Three Mile Island nuclear reactor melt-down for illustration and Sissela Bok's Lying for background, Goodman comments on the rise of official lying.

638. Goodman, Ellen. Keeping in Touch. New York: Summit, 1985. 313.
Several of these articles, previously published in BG, treat various media. For example, "Say Good-Bye to Self-Doubt" (1981) analyzes President Reagan's patriotic West Point speech that urged the public to stop criticizing the country. "Nuclear Follies: I" (1982) examines the "dippy" civil defense pamphlets published by the Federal Emergency Management Agency (FEMA).

639. Greenfield, Patricia. Mind and Media: The Effects of Television, Video Games, and Computers. Cambridge, MA: Harvard UP, 1984. 210.
Studies the relationship between media and the development of children, in nine chapters on electronic literacy, TV and reality, TV and education, comparing print, radio, and TV,

video games, computers, etc. Electronic media can be damaging: commercials manipulate defenseless children, watching TV can be deadening, etc. But if used wisely, if adults guide children to watch critically and learn from what they watch, the electronic media can have "great positive potential" (2).

640. Gregory, Richard. No More Lies: The Myth and the Reality of American History. Ed. James McGraw. New York: Harper, 1972. 372.
Analyzes white superiority myths that permeate society and media.

641. Gross, Gerald, ed. The Responsibility of the Press. New York: Fleet, 1966. 416.
Thirty-one chapters discuss TV, print, book industry, film, syndicates, student press, etc.

642. Gurevitch, Michael, Tony Bennett, James Curran, and Janet Woollacott, eds. Culture, Society and the Media. London: Methuen, 1982. 317.
Eleven essays divided into three sections. The first presents major theoretical traditions; the second ownership, internal organization, and institutions in the Third World; and the third is on control of communications systems, political effects, and reporting race. Mainly British experience and derived from the Open University course on "Mass Communication and Society."

643. Haight, Timothy. "The New American Information Order." The Critical Communications Review: Volume II: Changing Patterns of Communications Control. Ed. Vincent Mosco and Janet Wasko. Norwood, NJ: Ablex, 1984. 101-117.
Argues that "the alienation of the worker from information is necessary for capitalist social relations to continue."

644. Halberstam, David. The Powers That Be. New York: Knopf, 1979. 771.
Hundreds of interviews provide the basis for an anecdotal study of "the rise of media power" in the 20th century through the combination of strong individuals and new economic forces. Focuses on CBS, Time, Inc., WP, and LAT.

645. Hall, Stuart. "Culture, the Media, and the 'Ideological Effect.'" Mass Communication and Society. Ed. James Curran et al. Beverly Hills, CA: Sage, 1979. 315-348.
A Marxist explanation of how "the discourses of the media become systematically penetrated and inflected" by the dominant capitalist ideology and by the interests of the ruling class alliances.

646. Hall, Stuart. "The Rediscovery of 'Ideology': Return of the Repressed in Media Studies." Culture, Society & the Media. Ed. Michael Gurevitch, et al. London:

Methuen, 1982. 56-90.
Charts the major paradigm-shift from "mainstream" sociological studies of the media to "critical," with their "profound differences in theoretical perspective and in political calculation," a shift from behavioural to ideological perspective.

647. Hamilton, Charles V. "Why Blacks Should Distrust the Mass Media." RSCJ 3 (Feb. 1972) 10-12.
The media feed on conflict, using and abusing the black community for their own profitable purposes.

648. Hellmann, John. American Myth and the Legacy of Vietnam. New York: Columbia UP, 1986. 241.
From Caputo's A Rumor of War and Herr's Dispatches to Coppola's Apocalypse Now and Lucas's Star Wars, the "American story" of "carrying forth their revolutionary heritage into the frontier of the emerging nations" became a nightmare of a lost crusade which American writers explored "as a symbolic landscape inverting America's frontier mythos."

649. Herman, Edward. "Orwell, Reagan, Doublethink & Deception." AltM 14.4 (Spring 1984) 15-25.
Reaganspeak flourishes in the "corporate-elite-rightwing"-Sovietphobic US with a compliant press: "the mass media serve as a collective Big Brother" (25).

650. Herman, Edward, and Gerry O'Sullivan. The "Terrorism" Industry: The Experts and Institutions That Shape Our View of Terror. New York: Pantheon, 1990. 312.
A full-scale "terrorism" industry manufactures an image of the terrorist to legitimate policies and power: government, think tanks, foundations, lobbying organizations, private experts, and the mass media. A chief purpose of the "terrorism threat" is to mobilize support for intelligence and military expenditures at a time of declining Soviet "threat."

651. Herner de Schmelz, Irene. Tarzan, el hombre mito. Mexico City: Secretaria de Educaci on Publica, 1974. 191.
Tarzan as mythic figure of US culture: the "self-made man," racist, sexist, imperialist.

652. Hiebert, Ray, Donald Ungurait, and Thomas Bohn. Mass Media II: An Introduction to Modern Communication. 2nd ed. New York: Longman, 1979. 536.
The editors have prepared the book to "develop a critical attitude toward the mass media," to enable "all consumers of mass communication to be critically aware of the problems and processes of mass media." Thus it examines communication models, philosophies and systems, economics, advertising, network TV, diverse media, the Gatekeeper role, regulators, filters, audiences, feedback, book publishing, newspapers, magazines, movies, radio, TV and other media.

653. Hilgartner, Stephen, Richard Bell, and Rory O'Connor.

Nukespeak: Nuclear Language, Visions and Mindset.
San Francisco: Sierra Club, 1982. 282. (Reissued as
Nukespeak: The Selling of Nuclear Technology in
America. Harmondsworth: Penguin, 1983.)
On the government-corporate propaganda campaign to sell
nuclear power and arms to the public, until mindsets were
established that limited consideration of alternatives.

654. Hitchens, Christopher. Prepared for the Worst:
Selected Essays and Minority Reports. New York: Hill
& Wang, 1988. 357.
A collection of articles most of which "were written in a
period of calamitous cynicism"--the 1980s and Reaganism. In
the US "the saturnalia took the form of an abysmal chauvinism,
financed by MasterCard and celebrating a debased kind of
hedonism" (4). The author affirms the values of "secularism,
libertarianism, internationalism, and solidarity."

655. Honey, Maureen. Creating Rosie the Riveter: Class,
Gender, and Propaganda during World War II. Amherst:
U of Mass. P, 1984. 251.
Attempts to explain why women's successful performance of
male jobs during WWII failed to legitimize women's entry into
nontraditional occupations after the war, why the media's
legitimation of female entry into male work failed to supplant
the traditional image of women as homemakers, and how the
"strong figure of Rosie the Riveter" became "transformed into
the naive, dependent, childlike, self-abnegating model of
femininity in the late forties and 1950s" (1-2).

656. Hook, Glenn. "Making Nuclear Weapons Easier to Live
With: The Political Role of Language in
Nuclearization." JPR 22.1 (1985) 67-77.
Those with the most power are able to dominate by defining
the terms in which we speak about nuclear issues.

657. Horton, James O., and Spencer R. Crew. "Afro-Americans
and Museums: Towards a Policy of Inclusion." History
Museums in the United States: A Critical Assessment.
Ed. Warren Leon and Roy Rosenzweig. Urbana: U of
Illinois P, 1989. 215-236.
"In the 1980s the contributions and experiences of black
people still are often excluded from the public presentation
of our nation's history" (215).

658. Hudson, Michael C., and Ronald Wolfe, eds. The
American Media and the Arabs. Washington, DC: Center
for Contemporary Arab Studies, 1980. 103.
Chapter 11, "The Media and the Arabs: Room for Improvement,"
summarizes "the inadequate reporting, unbalanced commentary,
and negative stereotyping that does seem to characterize the
treatment of the Arabs" (91). He recommends 2 steps to promote the American media's treatment of the Arabs: 1) monitoring of negative stereotyping and 2) increased efforts to
educate all the news media personnel. (See Ghareeb).

THE MEDIA

658a. "Intellectual Freedom Bibliography." Newsletter on Intellectual Freedom. Ongoing in every issue.

659. "It's Not Every Day." PoV (Feb. 10, 1969) special no.
Media are failing to respond to the needs of people, but fill themselves with irrelevant news and ads and refuse to permit criticism of the media.

660. Jamieson, Kathleen, and Karlyn Campbell. The Interplay of Influence: Mass Media & Their Publics in News, Advertising, Politics. Belmont, CA: Wadsworth, 1983. 287.
A textbook which studies the mass media from a rhetorical perspective, analyzing the patterns of choice that determine media influence and also examining the ways that corporations, government, and the public in turn influence such choices.

661. Jeffords, Susan. The Remasculinization of America: Gender and the Vietnam War. Bloomington, IN: Indiana UP, 1989. 215.
The crisis in Vietnam reveals emphatically the pervasiveness and power of patriarchal values. "The specific aim of this study is to elucidate the gendered structure of representations of the Vietnam War in America through readings of films, personal narratives, criticism, novels, essays, and short stories" with the purpose of changing "the structures that support and enforce the paradigms of gender."

662. Johannesen, Richard. Ethics in Human Communication. 3rd ed. Prospect Heights, IL: Waveland, 1990. 343.
Contains materials for assessing communication ethics and for making ethical judgments on such topics as lying, intentional ambiguity and vagueness, emotional appeals, advertising, propaganda, racist and sexist language, and ghostwriting. A twenty-three page bibliography.

663. Johnson, Paul. "Trivialization of News May Do Us In." AG (July 8, 1990) 8G.
On the steady decline of knowledge about the world by youth.

664. Jowett, Garth. "Propaganda and Communication: The Reemergence of a Research Tradition." JoC 37.1 (Winter 1987) 97-114.
Review of new books that signal a revival of interest in the role of propaganda as a tool of mass persuasion. Among other books, discusses Craig Campbell's Reel America and World War I, Honey's Creating Rosie the Riveter, Marchand's Advertising the American Dream, Pope's The Making of Modern Advertising, Schudson's Advertising, the Uneasy Persuasion, and Ginsberg's The Captive Public.

665. Joyce, James A. "Neurotic Myths of Defense." MO 5.3 (Mar. 1963) 4-5.
False dichotomies of communist and anti-communist and good

and evil, the language of "defense" (= war), "victory," and the "incessant press and radio war-propaganda" have led to the Warfare State.

666. Keracher, John. *The Head-Fixing Industry.* Chicago: Kerr, 1955 (1935). 52.
School, press, movies, radio, and TV as institutions of indoctrination.

667. Krassner, Paul. *How a Satirical Editor Became a Yippie Conspirator in Ten Easy Years.* New York: Putnam, 1971. 319.
The creator of *The Realist* magazine tells story after story about the language distortions, misinformation, lying, censorship, and general nonsense during the 1950s and 60s satirized in his magazine.

668. Kraus, Sidney, and Dennis Davis. *The Effects of Mass Communications on Political Behavior.* State College, PA: Pennsylvania State UP, 1976. 308.
"Our purpose is to provide" readers "with a review of and commentary on what is known about the field, what is not yet known, what ought to be known, and how we measure, assess, and evaluate the effects of mass communication on political behavior."

668a. Kunzle, David. "Introduction to *How to Read Donald Duck.*" *American Media & Mass Culture.* Ed. Donald Lazere. Berkeley: U of California P, 1987. 516-529.
Locates capitalist and imperialist values in Disney's production of the American Dream and in US culture in general.

669. Lang, Gladys. "The Most Admired Woman: Image-Making in the News." *Hearth and Home: Images of Women in the Mass Media.* Ed. Gaye Tuchman, et al. New York: Oxford UP, 1978. 147-160.
The most admired women are "satellites of men with high status." This stereotype helps explain the treatment of women in the press corps.

670. "The Latin American Spirit: Art & Artists in the United States, 1920-1970." El Paso Museum (& other galleries), 1989. *ITT* 13.18 (Mar. 29 -Apr. 4, 1989) 18-19.
Reveals the pressures of colonization and decolonization.

671. Lazere, Donald, ed. *American Media and Mass Culture: Left Perspectives.* Berkeley: U of California P, 1987. 618.
The 40 essays relate cultural production to its social, political, and economic contexts (Shirley Temple and Superman during the Depression), analyze the creation and power of ideology (definition of woman developing in romance novels), and reveal the multifarious ways corporations control cultural priorities. Cultural analyses grouped by such categories as "Ideology in Perception, Structure and Genre" and "Moments of

THE MEDIA

Historical Consciousness" on Frank Capra, rock, soap operas, Daffy Duck, public access cable, advertising, and other mass media topics. The book "is intended to demonstrate that the bulk of American mass cultural media, and of scholarship in the field, is equally one-sided in favor of capitalism" (19).

672. Lazere, Donald. "Conservative Media Criticism: Heads I Win, Tails You Lose." American Media & Mass Culture. Ed. Donald Lazere. Berkeley: U of California P, 1987. 81-96.
On conservative exaggeration of a "leftward shift in the media" (82). [See Drier.]

673. Lee, Hyo-Seong. "Overcoming Reified & Administered Communication: A Critical Analysis of Theodor W. Adorno's Theory of the Culture Industry." Northwestern U, 1987. 419. DAI 48 (1987) 4-A.
Examines Adorno's thesis that cultural institutions under monopoly capitalism are apparatuses for an "administered world" and that only autonomous individuals and art could break through capitalist power for social change.

674. Leon, Warren, and Roy Rosenzweig, eds. History Museums in the United States: A Critical Assessment. Urbana: U of Illinois P, 1989. 333.
This is "the first book-length critical assessment of historical museums" in the US. The essays examine the why of history exhibits by considering constraints that shape museums, including power, museums being "leery of material that might offend either major donors or the communities in which they are located. . . . Such financial and institutional concerns may produce distorted or sanitized versions of the past" (xix).

674a. Lindblom, Charles E. Inquiry and Change: The Troubled Attempt to Understand and Shape Society. New Haven, CT: Yale UP, 1990.
Public apathy and ignorance derive from many causes, including the use of media and education for indoctrination.

675. Lipsitz, George. Time Passages: Collective Memory and American Popular Culture. Minneapolis: U of Minnesota P, 1990. 306.
Mass media have "worked insidiously to legitimate exploitative social hierarchies, to colonize the body as a site of capital accumulation, and to inculcate within us the idea that consumer desire is the logical center of human existence," but new technology offers possible "resistance and revolution" (vii). Chapters on network TV in the 1950s and the program Mama, rock music, films, etc.

676. Lutz, William, ed. Beyond Nineteen Eighty-Four: Doublespeak in a Post-Orwellian Age. Urbana, IL: NCTE, 1989. 220.
Eighteen essays "explore the kinds and extent of doublespeak in our world." Lutz gives a method for analyzing 4 kinds of

doublespeak; Weingartner discusses how the counterfeit overwhelms the authentic; Lazere analyzes disinformation; Ohmann works on the semantics of foreign policy discourse; etc.

677. Lutz, William. Doublespeak: From Revenue Enhancement to Terminal Living--How Government, Business, Advertisers, and Others Use Language to Deceive You. New York: Harper, 1989. 290.
Analyzes all the kinds of doublespeak discussed in the pages of QRD: advertising, government, military, medical, education, statistics, polls, TV political ads, etc. Also lists all winners of the George Orwell Award and the Doublespeak Award.

678. Lyons, Gene. The Higher Illiteracy: Essays on Bureaucracy, Propaganda, and Self-Delusion. Fayetteville: U of Arkansas P, 1988. 268.
Sixteen essays written over an eleven-year period about "the intellectual disorder Orwell in 1984 called 'collective solipsism,'" which derives from public and private "self-aggrandizing bureaucracies" and their jargon and cant (Introduction).

679. MacDougall, A. Kent, ed. The Press: A Critical Look from the Inside. Princeton, NJ: Dow Jones, 1972. 172.
Anthology of WSJ articles on the press, a small contribution to the scarce criticism of the press by the press: Reader's Digest, UPI and AP, WP, etc.

680. Macqueen, Graeme. "Nuclearism and the Credibility Gap." The Name of the Chamber Was Peace. Downsview, Ont.: U of Toronto P, 1988. 172.
"Treats the instability of power based on lies. Colonialism and patriarchy, as described in world nuclear politics, are here associated with their characteristic lies" (quoted from promotional brochure).

680a. Mahoney, Eileen. "American Empire and Global Communication." Cultural Politics in Contemporary America. New York: Routledge, 1989. 37-50.
"American power has been extended globally through control of communication technology and international regulation especially since the Second World War" (15).

681. Maltby, Richard, ed. Passing Parade: A History of Popular Culture in the Twentieth Century. New York: Oxford UP, 1989. 256.
A survey of the ways popular culture has been packaged, sold, and consumed since 1900: movies, fashion, design, advertising, popular music, dance, sports, TV, popular magazines and newspapers, fads, etc. Examines popular media as the organization of desire; for example, the motives, interests, and economics of the fashion industry and the "reassertion of impractical and decorative femininity" after WWII.

682. Marvin, Carolyn. "Delivering the News of the Future." JoC 30.1 (1980) 10-20.

THE MEDIA

Given the gradual convergence of electronic and print media technologies, Marvin discusses the role of private concentration and government regulation in regard to freedom of the press.

683. Mattelart, Armand. Multinational Corporations and the Control of Culture: The Ideological Apparatuses of Imperialism. Trans. Michael Chanan. New Jersey: Humanities, 1979. 304.
Explores the foundations of corporate domination over cultural production, the mass media, and all electronic information systems, in alliance with government.

684. Mattelart, Armand. Transnationals and the Third World: The Struggle for Culture. South Hadley, MA: Bergin, 1983. 184.
On the media power of multinational corporations over host countries.

685. Mattelart, Armand, and Seth Siegelaub, eds. Communication and Class Struggle: 1. Capitalism, Imperialism. New York/Bagnolet, Fr.: International General, 1979. 445.
First of two volumes analyzing the relation between the practice and theory of communication within the context of class struggle. Sixty-four essays in Vol. 1.

686. McAnany, Emile, Jorge Schnitman, and Noreene Janus, eds. Communication and Social Structure: Critical Studies in Mass Media Research. New York: Praeger, 1981. 341.
Twelve essays on theory, US mass communication (children's TV, FCC and minority ownership, etc.) and global telecommunications.

687. McCarthy, Eugene. America Revisited: 150 Years After Tocqueville. Garden City, NY: Doubleday, 1978. 256.
The eleven chapters "compare and contrast the America of 1978 with that which existed in 1831." Chapter 7 on the media discusses concentration, equal time, etc., and advocates First Amendment freedom and diversity.

688. McCombs, Maxwell E., and Donald L. Shaw. "Structuring the 'Unseen Environment.'" JoC 26.2 (Spring 1976) 18-28.
The media establish the unseen boundaries of political discussion, containing debate by assigning relative importance.

689. Medhurst, Martin, et al. Cold War Rhetoric: Strategy, Metaphor, and Ideology. New York: Greenwood, 1990. 225.
Diverse approaches (eleven essays) to the analysis of Cold War discourse, placing rhetoric at the center of debate and analysis since the authors see it as "a central defining characteristic of Cold War" as a rhetorical war "fought with

words, speeches, pamphlets, public information (or disinformation) campaigns, slogans," etc. Bibliog. 209-217.

690. "Media and Culture." ETC. 34.2 (June 1977) 131-238.
Special number on "the meaning and implications of modern communications technology" and a call to general semanticists to make the "transforming power of new media" a "central concern."

691. "Mediawatch." MJ 12.5 (1987) 21.
The trend toward monopolization and conglomerization of the mass media has created a less critical media climate.

692. Mehra, Achal. Free Flow of Information: A New Paradigm. Westport, CT: Greenwood, 1986. 225.
US and Western "free-flow" doctrine of international communication largely impelled by "ideological and economic expediency" (155) "has perpetuated and entrenched a one-way flow of communications, which undermines national sovereignty and promotes cultural and economic imperialism" (148).

693. Melosh, Barbara. "Speaking of Women: Museums' Representation of Women's History." History Museums in the United States: A Critical Assessment. Ed. Warren Leon and Roy Rosenzweig. Urbana: U of Illinois P, 1989. 183-214.
Women's history in museums is part of the process of "incorporation and accommodation that constantly renews and fortifies dominant ideology" (183) and "amounts to censorship" (205).

694. Merrill, John, and Ralph Lowenstein. Media, Messages, and Men: New Perspectives in Communication. 2nd ed. New York: Longman, 1979. 264.
Recognizes control throughout; e.g., advertising determines media content not by direct censorship but by advertisers' ability to choose or reject programs for sponsorship, avoiding the controversial (73-5), and media impact on government "must be within the limitations of existing political philosophy . . . must be 'tolerated' by the system, thereby making the media no more than a part of the system" (153).

695. Miège, Bernard. The Capitalization of Cultural Production. New York/Bagnolet, Fr.: International General, 1989. 165.
A systematic explanation of the advancing industrialization and commercialization of culture and information as a process of three competitive "logics": the publishing model (books, records, films, cassettes), the flow model (broadcasting), the written press model (newspapers, magazines).

695a. "Missing Voices. Women & the Media." Extra! 4.2 (Mar.-Apr. 1991).
Twelve articles on rape and abortion coverage, tobacco advertising, NYT representation of women, etc.

THE MEDIA   115

696. Modleski, Tania, ed. Studies in Entertainment: Critical Approaches to Mass Culture. Bloomington: Indiana UP, 1986. 210.
Provides especially a feminist "critical view of mass cultural production," the essays focusing on "a unit larger than the discrete single work: rock 'n' roll music, television sound, television news, advertisements, popular novels for women, fashion, contemporary horror films, and so on" (xiii). The writers "have opened up spaces in which to think about and work for genuine cultural change" (xviii).

696a. Monaco, James, ed. Celebrity: The Media as Image Makers. New York: Delta, 1978. 258.
"Increasingly our lives are acted out in a social sea of celebrityhood; we are submerged in such images--based to some extent on fact, but also pervasively fictional." Thirty-four essays.

697. Monaco, James, ed. Media Culture: Television, Radio, Records, Books, Magazines, Newspapers, Movies. New York: Dell, 1978. 335.
Twenty-six selections on "The Situation," "The People," "The Product," and "The Effect," plus an extensive (81-316) appendix on media ownership. Sample titles: "The Silverman Strategy," "Kanned Laffter," "The Making of a Television Series," "What TV Does to Kids." Preface stresses the "vast sea of images, sounds, and language" that makes it difficult to distinguish between fact and fiction, and the commercial basis of the media in which maximum financial gain is the primary goal.

698. Moore, Linda Wright. "Can the Press Do the Right Thing? 1. How Your News Looks to Us." CJR 29.2 (July-Aug. 1990) 21-24.
Analyzes racism in the media.

699. Morrow, Frank S. "The U.S. Power Structure and the Mass Media." Diss., U of Texas at Austin, 1984. 553.
Combines Power Elite and Marxist approaches to describe the power system. The Ruling Cartel controls the core economic organizations--the corporations and largest financial institutions. The cartel dominates the country's political institutions by key decision-making positions, financing political campaigns, and by its network of idea and educational controls (think tanks, foundations, corporations, universities, etc.). These mechanisms establish the range of discourse presented by the media, shielding the populace from knowing the realities of control. "Thus, ruling class hegemony is maintained."

700. Mosco, Vincent, and Janet Wasko. The Critical Communications Review. Vol. II: Changing Patterns of Communications Control. Norwood, NJ: Ablex, 1984. 299.
Chapters deal with information flows and transnational capitalism, communications and the nuclear peace movement, advertising and global markets, the "new American information order," the Cuban-US radio war, etc. "The articles explore

the consequences of the ongoing restructuring of communication systems . . . in the revitalization of the capitalist system."

701. Mosco, Vincent, and Janet Wasko. Popular Culture and Media Events. Norwood, NJ: Ablex, 1985. 323. (CCRev 3).
Twelve essays "challenge the notion that the creation of culture is solely the province of elites" (x). Part I, "History: Popular Culture, Commodity Culture," five essays discuss "the process of making popular culture" and "efforts to turn popular cultural productions into mechanized, profitable commodities." Part II, "Media Events: Stars and Star Wars," four essays discuss media coverage of Olympic boycotts, Academy Awards telecasts, rock music, and video games and US militarism. Part III, "The Public Sphere and Social Struggle," three essays strive to create "a democratic public culture."

702. Mueller, Claus. "Class as the Determinant of Political Communication." American Media & Mass Culture. Ed. Donald Lazere. Berkeley: U of California P, 1987. 431-440.
Explains "the restricted linguistic and cognitive codes typical of mass media content and reception," deficiencies in analytic and synthetic reasoning (409).

703. Mueller, Claus. The Politics of Communication: A Study in the Political Sociology of Language, Socialization, and Legitimation. New York: Oxford UP, 1973. 226.
"Government constraints on political communication, the mobilization of bias by powerful interests, and the commercial character of the media create a situation where news items that would invite challenges of the status quo are either omitted or embedded in interpretations which depreciate them" (100). Consumerism substitutes for autonomy and social responsibility (178).

704. Nimmo, Dan. Subliminal Politics: Myths and Mythmakers in America. Englewood Cliffs, NJ: Prentice, 1980. 256.
Part One examines the reigning myths in the US past and present. Part Two focuses on "who the mythmakers of America are and how they do it." Ch. 4 the "politicians and the people who promote them into public figures," 5 "the media of popular entertainment and how popular culture contributes to political mythmaking," 6 "public affairs reporting," 7 the social scientists "who also contribute to mythmaking," and finally the fundamental myths which constitute the US "supermyth."

705. Nimmo, Dan, and James Combs. "Fantasies of the Arena: Popular Sports and Politics." Mediated Political Realities. New York: Longman, 1983. 124-140.
Sports reflect and reinforce national values--heroism, patriotism, winning: "the American way of life" (130). These fantasies are exploited to the fullest by the mass media:

sportswriters, broadcasters, newspaper sports pages, sports magazines, etc.

706. Nimmo, Dan, and James Combs. Mediated Political Realities. New York: Longman, 1983. 240.
The "vast bulk of political reality that most of us take for granted (whether we are private citizens or public officials) consists of a combination of fantasies created and evoked by group and mass communication." I on "mass mediated political realities": TV crisis reporting, election campaigns, popular culture, celebrities, Hollywood, sports. II on "group mediated political fantasies": groupthink, pack journalism, religion and politics, etc.

707. Ohlgren, Thomas H., and Lynn M. Berk, eds. The New Languages: A Rhetorical Approach to the Mass Media and Popular Culture. Englewood Cliffs, NJ: Prentice, 1977. 395.
Designed for undergraduate liberal arts courses. Forty-six selections divided into five sections on "Popular Culture and the Mass Media," "Commercial and Public Propaganda," "The Language of Print," "The Language of Film," and "The Languages of Television and Radio."

708. Ohmann, Richard. Politics of Letters. Middletown, CT: Wesleyan UP, 1987. 321.
Analysis of the ways in which English teachers, writers, journalists, and professional literary people participate in the hegemonic process and in mediating relations between the other two classes: the bourgeoisie and the proletariat.

709. O'Neill, Terry, and Bruno Leone, eds. Censorship: Opposing Views. St. Paul, MN: Greenhaven, 1985. 234.
Opposing arguments divided by topics--limits to free speech, news regulation, national security, schools, pornography.

710. Paletz, David, and Robert Entman. Media, Power, Politics. New York: Free, 1981. 308.
Powerful institutions and individuals dominate the media and through them create "quiescent mass loyalty."

711. Paletz, David, and Paul Feldman. "Little Investigation." JoC 36.4 (Autumn 1986) 179-180.
Review of Philip Lawler's The Alternative Influence: The Impact of Investigative Reporting Groups on America's Media (1984), which alleges that leftists are taking over the mass media. "Instead of systematic data showing what articles appeared when, in which media outlets, we are treated to innuendo, tenuous links, and conspiracy theory."

712. Pember, Don. Mass Media in America. 2nd ed. Chicago: Science Research, 1977. 389.
A survey of mass communications: government, corporations, TV, film, radio, etc. Because they are businesses "the same perverse rules that dictate successful business practices

(usually defined as showing a profit on the bottom line) in the automobile industry . . . even in the corner grocery store, also dictate much of the operation of the mass media in America."

713. Phelan, John. Mediaworld: Programming the Public. New York: Seabury, 1977. 169.
Argues that Mill's "marketplace of ideas" metaphor has become literal: issues are now a saleable product to be sold by government, corporate, and media bureaucrats. Public opinion and popular culture are reprocessed by the media so that all three are joined in a "Mediaworld." The traditional forum of views based on values and philosophies has given way to personalities competing for popularity ("melodoxy").

714. Raboy, Marc, and Peter Bruck, eds. Communication For and Against Democracy. Montreal: Black Rose, 1989. 230.
Papers presented at the 1988 Union for Democratic Communications conference in Ottawa discuss communication as an instrument of domination or for human emancipation: mainstream media, grassroots communications strategies, military uses of new communication technologies, globalization of mass-mediated culture, limitations of TV, etc.

715. Randall, Margaret. Albuquerque: Coming Back to the U.S.A. Vancouver, Can.: New Star, 1986. 350.
Throughout the book Randall comments on media as instruments of state power. [Beginning in 1985 the INS attempted to expel her from the country, but she was finally granted residence in 1989.]

716. Real, Michael. Mass Mediated Culture. Englewood Cliffs, NJ: Prentice, 1977. 289.
This book examines the methods, messages and "the priorities of the mass-consciousness industry that programs" the culture "and the quality of the total ecosystem that results from it." Six chapters offer case studies on Disney, the Super Bowl, Marcus Welby, Nixon political campaigning, Billy Graham, and the Aymara Indians as a "control" study. Central thesis: "mass-mediated culture primarily serves the interests of the relatively small political-economic power elite that sits atop the social pyramid. It does so by programming mass consciousness through an infrastructural authoritarianism that belies its apparent superstructural egalitarianism."

717. Real, Michael. Super Media: A Cultural Studies Approach. Newbury Park: Sage, 1989. 282.
Reviews previous traditions of media research, explains how issues of personal consciousness, bias, and politics are best understood through cultural studies, which extend from text, representation, conflict, and ideology, to hegemony. Extensive case studies: Olympics, Hollywood films, superpower politics, transnational TV programs, the Cold War, Bill Cosby and ethnicity, gender in movie directing, etc.

THE MEDIA   119

718. Reeves, Jimmie. "Television Stardom: A Ritual of
      Social Typification and Individualization." Media,
      Myths, and Narratives: Television and the Press. Ed.
      James W. Carey. Newbury Park: Sage, 1988. 146-160.
   Ritual analysis explains "how media stardom assists in the
production, repair, and transformation of social reality,"
star as both "commodity and communication," "the hero celebrated in the news, the news anchor, the talk show host, the
sports star, the movie star, and the popular series character
as being different forms of the same complex phenomenon"
(147).

719. Rogin, Michael P. "Ronald Reagan," the Movie and Other
      Episodes in Political Demonology. Berkeley: U of
      California P, 1987. 366.
   Nine essays on the "countersubversive" ("political demonology") tradition "at the center of American politics," "the
creation of monsters as a continuing feature of American
politics by the inflation, stigmatization, and dehumanization
of political foes"--Indians, blacks, Catholics, communists,
etc. Chap. 1, "Ronald Reagan, the Movie," "analyzes the
formation of President Reagan through his Hollywood roles"
into the demonologist president; etc.

720. Rosenberg, Emily. Spreading the American Dream:
      American Economic and Cultural Expansion, 1890-1945.
      New York: Hill and Wang, 1982. 258.
   "In the twentieth century, in ever more complex ways, the
government helped citizens export American influence, while
private businesses and groups, in turn, helped the government
fulfill the expansive national interest. . . . Throughout,
economic and cultural expansion were closely related" (230).

721. Ross, Andrew. No Respect: Intellectuals and Popular
      Culture. New York: Routledge, 1989. 269.
   Essays on "the immense political stakes of popular culture,"
which affirms the "American way of life" of capitalist
consumption and militarism but in a complex "historically
fractious relationship between intellectuals and popular
culture" which appeals to both authority and opposition.
Chapters on the Rosenberg letters, the rhetoric of containment
of communism, pornography, etc.

722. Rubin, Bernard, ed. Questioning Media Ethics. New
      York: Praeger, 1978. 308.
   Contributors deal with illustrative issues, cases, and arguments; for example, the image of the press in motion pictures,
standards for education of journalists.

723. Rusher, William. The Coming Battle for the Media:
      Curbing the Power of the Media Elite. New York:
      Morrow, 1988. 228.
   "It is the thesis of this book that in recent decades the
principal media in the United States, responding to liberal
intellectual trends once dominant but now much less so, have

allied themselves with those political forces promoting liberal policies (meaning primarily the Democratic party), and have placed news reportage at the service of those policies" (9).

724. Russett, Bruce, and Donald Deluca. "'Don't Tread on Me': Public Opinion and Foreign Policy in the Eighties." PolSQ 96.3 (Fall 1981) 381-400.
Public and media shift rightward.

725. Sale, Kirkpatrick. SDS. New York: Random House, 1973. 752.
A history of Students for a Democratic Society in exhaustive detail in contrast to the alarmed media coverage of the time.

726. Salter, Liora. "Two Directions on a One-way Street: Old and New Approaches in Media Analysis in Two Decades." Studies in Communications. Ed. T. McCormack. Greenwich, CT: JAI, 1980. 85-118.
Analysis of media instrumentality in a system of power should be supplemented by studies of the relation between media content, audience response, and citizen action.

727. Sandman, Peter M., David M. Rubin, and David B. Sachsman, eds. Media: An Introductory Analysis of American Mass Communications. Englewood Cliffs, NJ: Prentice-Hall, 1972. 434.
Part II "Responsibility" about ethics (media codes, etc.), internal control (gatekeeping), monopoly control (chains, abuses of concentration, etc.), advertiser control, source control, government control (law), and public control. Part III discusses the various media including advertising. Part IV is about coverage--of government, crimes and demonstrations, war and national security, race, and specialized news.

728. Sandman, Peter M., David M. Rubin, and David B. Sachsman, eds. Media Casebook: An Introductory Reader in American Mass Communications. Englewood Cliffs, NJ: Prentice-Hall, 1972. 184.
The US system of mass communications has three characteristics ("pervasive influence, freedom of the press, and big-business journalism") and four functions ("to entertain, to inform, to influence, and to make money"). The primary goal is to make money, and the functions to entertain and to influence derive and depend upon it (attracting advertisers and audiences). "The only function they can safely ignore is information, and ignore it they often do" (2-3).

729. Schement, Jorge, and Leah A. Lievrouw, eds. Competing Visions, Complex Realities: Social Aspects of the Information Society. Norwood, NJ: Ablex, 1987. 167.
Part I gives three interpretations of the information society, the editors emphasizing the continuing corporate capitalist and industrial context. Part II includes six essays on the institutions of the information society: education, technology, law, etc. In their Introduction and Part III

THE MEDIA   121

the authors discuss six characteristics of the information
society, beginning with "informational materialism, or information as an economic commodity" (3-).

730. Schiller, Herbert. Communication and Cultural Domina-
        tion. White Plains, NY: M.E. Sharpe, 1976. 126.
  The selling of ideas and tastes throughout the world is
essential to the US marketing system.

731. Schiller, Herbert. The Mind Managers. Boston: Beacon
        Press, 1973. 214.
  "The odds are that the illusion of informational choice is
more pervasive in the United States than anywhere else in the
world. The illusion is sustained by a confusion, deliberately
maintained by the information controllers, that mistakes abundance of media with diversity of content." Chapter 1 presents
five myths exploited by ruling groups, Chapters 2-3 on the
"knowledge industry," Chapter 4 TV Guide, National Geographic,
and Disney, 5 polling, 6 global, etc.

732. Schiller, Herbert, and Joseph Phillips, eds. Super
        State: Readings in the Military-Industrial Complex.
        Chicago: U of Illinois P, 1970. 373.
  Chapter 6, "The Military-Industrial Complex and Communica-
tions," and Chapter 7, "Science and the Universities in the
Military-Industrial Complex."

733. Schneir, Walter, and Miriam Schneir. "Beyond Westmore-
        land: The Right's Attack on the Press." Freedom at
        Risk: Secrecy, Censorship, and Repression in the
        1980s. Ed. Richard O. Curry. Philadelphia, PA: Temple
        UP, 1988. 341-354. (Na 240 [Mar. 30, 1985] 361-67).
  A survey of the "New Right's war against the mass media"
during the 1970s and '80s.

734. Schrank, Jeffrey. Snap, Crackle, and Popular Taste:
        The Illusion of Free Choice in America. New York:
        Dell, 1977. 192.
  People are increasingly susceptible to control because
genuine freedom of autonomous choice has been replaced by the
"feeling of freedom," which is manipulated by ads and mass
media via consumer products and packaged entertainment.

735. Schrank, Jeffrey. Understanding Mass Media. Skokie,
        IL: National Textbook, 1975. 260.
  Designed as a text for undergraduate Language Arts elective
courses. Readings on TV, advertising, film, comics and cartoons, news media, newspapers, magazines, radio, records,
media control, future media. A media literacy text to reveal
"the special techniques of media persuasion" and thereby to
minimize "the ability of the media to deceive."

736. Schulz, Muriel. "Minority Writers: The Struggle for
        Authenticity and Authority." Language and Power.
        Ed. Cheris Kramarae, Muriel Schulz, and William

O'Barr. Beverly Hills: Sage, 1984. 206-217.
Minority literature continues outside of the mainstream because readers of the dominant class refuse to accept it as authoritative and authentic.

737. Seiden, Martin. Who Controls the Mass Media? Popular Myths and Economic Realities. New York: Basic Books, 1974. 246.
"It is with the audience and not the media that the power resides."

737a. Seldes, George. Never Tire of Protesting. New York: Stuart, 1968. 288.
Much of the contents about the failure of the media to inform the people sufficiently for democratic participation. One extensive section on repression of McCarthyism.

738. Seldes, Gilbert. The Great Audience. New York: Viking, 1950. 299.
This book raises questions about mass media that others do not ask due to "passive acceptance," by viewing it as propaganda--a "means of making us feel and think and act as we do."

739. Sholle, David. "An Archaeology of Critical Studies of the Media." Ohio U, 1986. 372. DAI 47 (1986) 1523-A.
Studies Marxist critiques of the mass media using Michel Foucault's archaeological method. These "critical studies" share a "double-problematic" that prevents them from creating a "coherent, total theory," a limitation practitioners attempt to overcome by "a theory of emancipation."

740. Signorielli, Nancy, and Michael Morgan, eds. Cultivation Analysis: New Directions in Media Effects Research. Newbury Park, CA: Sage, 1989. 272.
On the influences on the production of mass media content, the major patterns of images, values, facts, and lessons in media messages, the molding of audiences' conception of social reality, etc.

741. Silverman, Debora. Selling Culture: Bloomingdale's, Diana Vreeland, and the New Aristocracy of Taste in Reagan's America. New York: Pantheon, 1986. 175.
The managers of US "media culture" sought "novel images for consumer sales" and a suppression of "history and historical consciousness." This movement has close connections with Ronald and Nancy Reagan, whose leadership was "dedicated to public relations, image making, and the obliteration of the past." Mrs. Vreeland's costume shows of aristocratic China and France for the New York Metropolitan Museum of Art mirrored Ronald Reagan's extreme "freedom with facts" that have become "a significant force in national life" (Preface).

742. Slack, Jennifer. "The Information Revolution as Ideology." MCS 6 (1984) 247-256.
Explores the present information hegemony and appeals for a

THE MEDIA

more democratic system.

743. Smith, Stephen A. Myth, Media, and the Southern Mind. Fayetteville, AR: U of Arkansas P, 1985. 207.
Examines the changing myths of the South in chronological order through a wide range of media: formal addresses, country music, personal correspondence, tourist advertising, newspapers, TV, films, fiction, etc.

744. Smythe, Dallas. Dependency Road: Communications, Capitalism, Consciousness, and Canada. Norwood, NJ: Ablex, 1981. 347.
Explains how capitalism and its communications system made Canada culturally dependent upon the US.

745. Snow, Robert P. Creating Media Culture. Beverly Hills, CA: Sage, 1983. 261.
Chapters on theory, newspapers, novels and magazines, radio, TV, film, and power, based upon the belief that "media tailors information according to linguistic criteria, sees issues and events through particular perspectives, and even creates events or culture out of these perspectives" (213).

746. Sobel, Robert. The Manipulators: America in the Media Age. Garden City, NY: Anchor/Doubleday, 1976. 458.
Tells how "mass intellectuals" have manipulated the people via the five information and entertainment industries: newspapers, radio, movies, television, and college. "In the twentieth century there emerged in America a new culture, based upon play rather than work, organized around consumption instead of production--and concerned more with images than reality" (xii-xiii). Since power in this culture derives from "the ability to make people see the world the way you want them to," control of the media became essential.

747. Stanley, Robert H., and Charles S. Steinberg. The Media Environment: Mass Communications in American Society. New York: Hastings House, 1976. 281.
"Examines the content, structure and control of the communications media . . . particularly newspapers, motion pictures, and radio and television," asking such questions as "Who controls America's vast information and entertainment apparatus? In what ways does the economic posture of the media affect content?" "What passes for in-depth analysis of urban crises, government surveillance, military insurgency, corporate expansion, and other social, political and economic problems is fundamentally superficial." Part of the cause of this superficiality is "the communication industry's consumer-pleasing economic posture" (12).

748. Stein, Robert. Media Power. Who Is Shaping Your Picture of the World? Boston: Houghton Mifflin, 1972. 265.
Calls for serious thought by all about the system of "pervasive communication" and "those who decide what we see, hear

and read," who are "sitting astride a great source of power over our lives" (xvi). Among subjects covered: TV news, media as business, celebrities, the New Journalism and the underground press.

749. Susman, Warren. Culture as History: The Transformation of American Society in the Twentieth Century. New York: Pantheon, 1984. 321.
Argues that intellectuals can be understood only in cultural context which in the US is dominated by popular culture, and that this culture has moved from a focus on production and scarcity to a focus on consumption and abundance. This evolving culture he explains through a Broadway play, Bruce Barton's advertising campaigns, the New York World's Fair, and other media.

750. Terry, Janice J. Mistaken Identity: Arab Stereotypes in Popular Writing. Washington, DC: Arab Affairs Council, 1985. 135.
"Exposes the dehumanization of an ethnic group which, despite the raised consciousness of the present generation, is still considered fair game for bigotry" (publisher's description).

751. Thayer, Lee, ed. Ethics, Morality and The Media: Reflections on American Culture. New York: Hastings, 1980. 302.
Nineteen essays on advertising and public relations (several), polling, doublespeak, TV, etc., and conversations with eight commentators, all asking questions about the right and wrong of the consciousness industry.

752. Tichi, Cecelia. Shifting Gears: Technology, Literature, Culture in Modernist America. Chapel Hill: U of North Carolina P, 1987. 310.
The "story of American writers' efforts [from the 1890s through the 1920s] to reinvigorate imaginative literature in accordance with the terms of a new world" of technology, engineering, efficiency and speed. "Materially that world appeared to them to be a system of component parts, and human beings its designers."

753. Tinney, James S., and Justine Rector, eds. Issues and Trends in Afro-American Journalism. Lanham, MD: UP of America, 1980. 363.
Twenty-seven essays covering both print and electronic media deal with some history but mainly with current black concerns regarding the media, such as race in TV news, news jobs, and TV and self-esteem of Blacks.

754. Tuchman, Gaye. "Introduction: The Symbolic Annihilation of Women by the Mass Media." Hearth and Home: Images of Women in the Mass Media. New York: Oxford UP, 1978. 3-38.
Summary of the subject of the book, "the tyranny of media

THE MEDIA

messages limiting [women's] lives to hearth and home."

755. Tuchman, Gaye, Arlene Daniels, and James Benét, eds. Hearth and Home: Images of Women in the Mass Media. New York: Oxford UP, 1978. 333.
Fifteen essays on "the interaction between the media and public opinion in the press for equality between the sexes," including both "the portrayal of women in the media and the place of women in media production." Topics: women on prime-time TV, magazine heroines, newspaper women's pages, sex-typing and children's TV, etc.

756. Tunstall, Jeremy. The Media are American. New York: Columbia UP, 1977. 352.
Sixteen chapters mainly about British and US media in four parts: I "News, Entertainment, Advertising . . . And Imperialism?" II "British Commonwealth, English Language . . . Anglo-American Cartel?" III "1945: American Media Conquest," IV "The End of Empire?" Weighs the issue of media imperialism (e.g. 262-3), the argument summarized in Chapter 16, "The Media Are American."

757. Tunstall, Jeremy. "Media Imperialism?" American Media & Mass Culture. Ed. Donald Lazere. Berkeley: U of California P, 1987. 540-554.
Examines a growing body of studies "of the spread to other countries of American industry--through film, popular music, television, other communications technologies, sports and sporting equipment--and the effect on foreign economies and national cultures" (477).

758. Tunstall, Jeremy, and David Walker. Media Made in California: Hollywood, Politics, and the News. Oxford: Oxford UP, 1981. 204.
Power structure, products, and impact of California media reveal national media characteristics: economic concentration, interlocking ownership, exclusion of minorities and poor, personalization and localization of politics, etc.

759. Turow, Joseph. Media Industries: The Production of News & Entertainment. New York: Longman, 1984. 213.
Turow sets up a hierarchical model of "power roles" of a mass media industry from producer to public, the most important relationship between the producers of the media material and their "patrons" (advertisers, etc.). Suggests that public advocacy organizations may pressure producers to reform through addressing the other power roles (government, investor, distributor, etc.)

760. Voelker, Francis H., and Ludmilla A. Voelker, eds. Mass Media: Forces in Our Society. 3rd ed. New York: Harcourt, Brace, Jovanovich, 1978. 470.
The over seventy selections are divided into four parts: a historical overview; a wide coverage of print and electronic media; the media performing their roles as informers, enter

tainers, and persuaders; and impact on society and the future. Each section in Parts 2 and 3 concludes with a "mini-case study": Daniel Schorr, violence, accessibility, social issues in entertainment, and comics.

761. Walley, David. "Hopeless Halberstam." AM 11.2 (1979) 21-22.
An attack on David Halberstam's The Powers That Be (1979). The book lacks critical context or synthesis; it is "sanitized press release journalism" by a member of the "old boy network."

762. Weart, Spencer. Nuclear Fear: A History of Images. Cambridge: Harvard UP, 1988. 535.
Compendious study of origins and processes of fear and aggression through nuclear weapons and energy. Examples: President Eisenhower's Cold War civil defense/armaments campaign, which received "whole-hearted cooperation from the American press and other [ideological] institutions" (131). But images and symbols of fear were also employed by seekers of alternatives to force in foreign policy, because "the structure of imagery embraced opposites: mad scientists and victims, world doom and a Golden Age, death and life" (423).

763. Webster, Duncan. Looka Yonder: The Imaginary America of Populist Culture. London: Routledge, 1988. 271.
Examines the ideology and political impact of populist films, music, books, and events.

764. Wenner, Lawrence, ed. Media, Sports, and Society. Newbury Park, CA: Sage, 1989. 320.
Analyzes mediated sports, the communication of sport, the relationship between media and society, media organizations, sports journalists, audience, etc.

765. Wilson, Clint, and Felix Gutierrez. Minorities and Media: Diversity and the End of Mass Communication. Beverly Hills, CA: Sage, 1985. 247.
A summary history of four US racial groups (blacks, Hispanics, native Americans, and Asians) within TV, film, radio, newspapers, and magazines, an overview of the representation of these minorities in media advertising, a history of minority advocacy in US mass media, and a discussion of the future of mass communication in the US in regard to minorities.

II. A. 2. NEWS (766-1087)

766. McKerns, Joseph, comp. News Media and Public Policy: An Annotated Bibliography. New York: Garland, 1985. 171.
Focuses on coverage of government and government reaction to the media, including attempts to control the media and their impact on setting agenda, mainly during the 1970s and early 1980s.

THE MEDIA

767. Abourezk, James. "The Relentless Israeli Propaganda Machine." Penthouse (Feb. 1978) 122-23.
Excoriates the media for "pack journalism" in presenting Israel as underdog against the Arabs and for distorting the coverage of Israel's bombing of South Lebanon.

768. Adler, Renata. Reckless Disregard. New York: Knopf, 1986. 256.
Though CBS News and Time may not have been guilty of libel (in suits brought by Gen. Westmoreland and Ariel Sharon, respectively), they both were guilty of bad journalistic practice.

769. "Air War Targets Salvadoran Civilians: U. S. Media Keep Silent." NicP 11 (Fall 1985) 34-35.
The bloody rightist President Duarte is reported as a moderate.

770. Al-Karni, Ali. "Mass Media and Social Conflict: A Comparative Content Analysis of the Austin (Minnesota) Strike and the Egyptian Food Riots." U of Minnesota, 1987. 178. DAI 48 (1988) 2185-A.
Both systems disseminated "negative images about the [protest] movements," aiming at "delegitimizing the issues and actors of movements."

770a. "All the News That's Fit to Print." Humanist 50.6 (Nov.-Dec. 1990).
Special number on media with articles by Dan Rather and Michael Parenti, and an interview of Noam Chomsky. Chomsky believes that the US media "constitute the most awesome propaganda system in world history."

771. Altheide, David, and Robert P. Snow. "Media News." Media Logic. Beverly Hills: Sage, 1979. 61-102.
This chapter three and chapters four and five explain how news has become a part of mass media formats dependent upon entertainment values in pursuit of ratings for profit. The mass media have transformed journalism into "the third, and perhaps the second, estate" (17).

772. Altschull, J. Herbert. Agents of Power: The Role of the News Media in Human Affairs. New York: Longman, 1984. 355.
Discusses the First Amendment, the rise of the commercial press, advertising, muckraking, the ideological press: socialist, capitalist, and Third World, media responsibility: Hutchins Commission, UNESCO, etc. His basic purpose is to analyze aspects of the conflictual, Us vs. Them mode of news reporting and to honor journalists who have transcended simplicities and stereotypes.

773. Andersen, Roberta. "The United States Press Coverage of Conflict in the Third World: The Case of El Salvador." U of California, Irvine, 1986. 197. DAI 47 (1986) 698-A.
TV news and news photograph distortions and bias derive not only from formal and organizational constraints but from "ideological hegemony functioning within the media." News stories contain "cultural themes and values, and a marked status quo bias."

774. Archer, Jules. The Plot to Seize the White House. New York: Hawthorne, 1974. 256.
Story of the plot to overthrow the US government in 1934 and efforts by officials to suppress testimony. The role the press played in trying to suppress news about the plot and to ridicule General Smedley Butler, who exposed it, is also told. George Seldes and John Spivak receive high praise for their struggle to uncover the coverup.

775. Armstrong, Dave. "The Great S & L Robbery." Z (June 1990) 108-116.
Executive fraud and theft, sometimes involved with mobsters and the CIA, and the lack of government regulation were the main causes of the estimated $300 billion S & L scandal. But the mainstream media continue to fail to investigate and expose the corruption.

776. Arnett, Peter. "Tet Coverage: A Debate Renewed." CJR 16.5 (1978) 44-48.
Braestrup's criticism of press coverage of the North Vietnamese and Vietcong Tet offensive is not convincing.

777. Arno, Andrew, and Wimal Dissanayake, eds. The News Media in National and International Conflict. Boulder, CO: Westview, 1984. 250.
Fifteen essays on the influence exerted by and on the media. For example, Donohue, et al., claim in "Media Evaluations and Group Power" that coverage generally is more favorable for dominant organizations. Other essays argue that media organizations are constrained either by technological conditions or by cultural values and ideological frames. An essay on "The Role of the Media in the U.S.-Iranian Conflict," for example, assesses the "cultural nearsightedness" of the nationalistic US press.

778. Aronson, James. "The Media and the Message." The Pentagon Papers: Critical Essays. The Senator Gravel Edition, Vol. V. Boston: Beacon, 1972. 41-59.
Lack of historical perspective and knowledge, commitment to an ideal of "objectivity," and patriotic nationalism and anticommunism undermined efforts of US journalists and media to inform the public adequately about the Vietnam War.

THE MEDIA

779. Aronson, James. Packaging the News: A Critical Survey of Press, Radio, TV. New York: International, 1971. 109.
Chapters 1 and 2 describe the increase of newspaper chains, the decrease of competing newspapers, and the increase of standardization, which tend "to insure that all persons who read newspapers will be similarly influenced. . . . It follows that they will think alike, and their thinking will be encouraged to defend the 'national interest,'" which is defined primarily by businessmen (15). Other chapters deal with government intimidation, Sovietphobia, the black press, the radical press, etc.

780. Aronson, James. The Press & the Cold War. Rev. ed. Joanne Dolinar, ed. New York: Monthly Review, 1990. 342.
Contains three new chapters covering the 1970s and 1980s further pursuing his thesis that the US press has operated in complicity with the government in perpetuating the Cold War.

781. Banks, Jack. "The Contradiction of a 'Free Press': An Analysis of U.S. Press Coverage of UNESCO." M.S. thesis, U of Oregon, 1984. 276.
Media were biased.

782. Bartimole, Roldo. "The Censors, Again." PoV 4.8 (Oct. 25-30, 1971) 3-4.
Investigative reporter Bartimole was denied access to respond to a WKYC-Radio endorsement of United Torch.

783. Bartimole, Roldo. "Media Assume Job of Silencing Any Dissent by Filtering Out Thorny Community Conflict." PoV 4.10 (Nov. 22-27, 1971) 3-4.
Cleveland media suppress firings within the media and conflict in politics.

784. Beckstrom, Maja. "Out of Sight, Out of Mind." UR 30 (Nov.-Dec. 1988) 28-29.
US coverage of South Africa has withered since 1985 not only because of government censorship but because of US journalistic complicity.

785. Bedford, Michael. "Covering the Philippines: Aquino Gets the Teflon Treatment." Extra! 2.7/8 (Summer 1989) 59.
"The U.S. media have consistently been kind to Philippine President Corazon Aquino," despite reports by Amnesty International and others that the use of torture by government forces is increasing.

786. Bennett, James R. "Soviet Scholars Look at U.S. Media." JoC 36.1 (1986) 126-32.

Analyzes Soviet scholarship dealing with US imperialism. Their consolidation of published information challenges the complacent myth of the US "free press."

787. Bennett, W. Lance. News: The Politics of Illusion. 2nd ed. New York: Longman, 1988. 216.
Written to point out "where our mass information system does not serve the ideals of American democracy, while offering constructive suggestions for improving the situation." Mass media news "remains our only broadly shared window on reality," yet it has profound flaws. It maintains "power and privilege while limiting popular participation" in politics. It provides "at best, a superficial and distorted image of society." Government officials and economic interests dominate information and are minimally accountable. As for the media, "as long as the distribution of power is narrow and decision processes are closed, journalists will never be free of their dependence on the small group of public-relations experts, official spokespersons, and powerful leaders whose self-serving pronouncements have become firmly established as the bulk of the daily news." The author calls for, "instead of running a messenger service for the rich and powerful, the media could become a forceful voice in their own right or even on the people's behalf. At the very least . . . journalists would be trained and empowered to analyze and 'decode' the daily propaganda to help people figure it out" (Introduction).

788. Bennett, W. Lance, and Murray Edelman. "Toward a New Political Narrative." JoC 35.4 (1985) 156-171.
News stories are structured in ways that validate established perspectives. New news plots must break official stereotypes by a "critique of material conditions" behind the standard narrative closures.

789. Bensky, Larry. "The Morning After." Na 247.4 (Aug. 13-20, 1988) 135-37.
Criticizes the media for their failure to investigate and expose the Reagan administration's covert operations and criticizes several new books on the subject for not attending to that failure.

790. Bensman, David. "The Downside of the G. M. Contract." Na 239 (Nov. 3, 1984) 440-442.
The media were silent about the negative aspects of the auto contract.

791. Berle, A.A., Jr. "Loose Thinking on Latin America.' CJR 1.2 (1962) 11-13.
"Unreliable reporting, failure to report adequately, and slanted news complicate US relations with Latin American governments and aggravate their problems, especially as the Cold War there deepens."

792. "Biowarfare Research Up Tenfold." SLJR 16.102 (May 1988) 12-13.
Biological war research is increasing, but the media has neglected the issues of university involvement and treaty violation.

793. Bird, S. Elizabeth, and Robert W. Dardenne. "Myth, Chronicle, and Story: Exploring the Narrative Qualities of News." Media, Myths, and Narratives: Television and the Press. Ed. James W. Carey. Newbury Park: Sage, 1988. 67-86.
Journalists tend to "speak in one narrative voice. Within the existing news paradigm, they frame the problem of 'the impulse to moralize reality' in terms of fact/fiction or true/false dichotomies" (82).

794. Black, Edwin R. Politics and the News: The Political Functions of the Mass Media. Toronto: Butterworths, 1982. 272.
Nine chapters on such topics as "The Manufacture of News" and "Politics Between Elections." The chapter on "The Struggle for Dominance" covers economic interests, censorship, news management, punishing the press, and related subjects.

795. Blanchard, Eric. "The Poor People and the 'White Press.'" CJR 7.3 (1968) 61-65.
The press reported the Poor People's Campaign negatively and in general reports the poor and poverty inadequately. But the situation seems to be improving.

796. Bleifuss, Joel. "The Rich Get Richer" & "See No Evil, Hear No Evil." ITT 13.17 (Mar. 22-28, 1989) 5.
The national media are not reporting the increasing gap between the rich and the poor adequately.

797. Bond, Patrick. "In Coverage of Wright's Wrongs, Savings & Loan Scandal Submerged." Extra! 2.1 (July-Aug. 1988) 3-4.
Reporting has focused on Wright's petty misdeeds, "while downplaying the far more important story about Wright's role in pressuring members of Congress and a federal banking agency on behalf of some Texas bankers who were in financial trouble."

798. Bond, Patrick. "S & L Coverage Ignores Root Causes and Progressive Solutions." Extra! 2.5 (Mar.-Apr. 1989) 6.
Media coverage of the savings and loan bailout has generally failed to place blame for the thrifts' collapse where it belongs (on Reagan's economic policies and resulting over-investment).

799. Bonner, Raymond. "A One-Sided Press." Na 239 (Dec. 8, 1984) 604-5.
Press distortions about Central America "favor the Administration's policies"--e.g., the biased reporting of the elections in El Salvador and Nicaragua.

800. Boot, William. "NASA and The Spellbound Press." CJR 25.2 (1986) 23-29.
"Dazzled by the glamour of man-in-space, the press kept ignoring hints of the disaster to come."

801. Boot, William. "Star-spangled News Package." CJR 25.3 (1986) 18-21.
Decries the jingoism of the news accounts of the Statue of Liberty's face lift.

802. Boss, Donna. "Justice: 'Why Don'tya Come Up 'n Film Me Sometime?'" UM 3.2 (Oct. 1972) 8-9.
Appeals for adequate news coverage of the judicial branch.

803. Braestrup, Peter. Battle Lines: Report of the Twentieth Century Fund Task Force on the Military and the Media. New York: Priority, 1985. 178.
Written after the exclusion of journalists during the invasion of Grenada, the report seeks to "restore the cooperative attitude that has marked military-media relations in the past." The press should be allowed "accurate, independent reporting of battle," within established guidelines. The bulk of the book is a background paper by Braestrup (15-142).

804. Braestrup, Peter. Big Story: How the American Press and Television Reported and Interpreted the Crisis of Tet 1968 in Vietnam and Washington. Vol. I. Boulder, CO: Westview, 1977. 740.
Condemns media reporting of the Tet offensive. [See Chomsky, Hallin, and others.]

805. Bram, Steven. "Cruise Missile Crashes in Canada, A Crashing Bore to U.S. Press." Deadline 1.2 (1986) 6-7.
This important story was little reported.

806. Brenner, Daniel, and William Rivers, eds. Free But Regulated: Conflicting Traditions in Media Law. Ames, IA: Iowa State UP, 1982. 283.
Thirteen essays on diverse legal topics: concepts underlying legal problems of the mass media, practices of the law, future pathways, etc. In general the contributors' free speech perspective is that of a competitive marketplace; Brenner in the final essay suggests ways to improve the marketplace of ideas.

807. Brinkley, David. Washington Goes to War. New York:

Knopf, 1988. 286.
An account of Washington, D.C., during World War II, with considerable attention to the press. Chapter 7, "Press Lords and Reporters," gives anecdotes of press conflicts with President Roosevelt.

808. Broder, David. Behind the Front Page: A Candid Look at How the News Is Made. New York: Simon and Schuster, 1987. 393.
Critical analysis of problems of contemporary journalism, especially those associated with the reporting of politics from Washington, D.C., including a detailed study of politics and practices of all presidents from Eisenhower to Reagan. Specific examples of misreporting by taking incidents out of context, by misjudging characters, by exaggerating and distorting false alarm investigations, and by consumer fraud. Explanation of development of "clique," "pack," "precision," and "horse race" journalism and the flaws produced by these developments.

809. Brodhead, Frank, and Edward S. Herman. "The KGB Plot to Assassinate the Pope: A Case in Free World Disinformation." CAIB 19 (Spring-Summer 1983) 13-24.
Cites the supposed KGB connection with Pope assailant Mehmet Ali Agca as an example of the way the news media are used in "mobilization of bias"; analyzes the methods used to "sell" the phony plot to the public.

810. Brown, Cynthia. "Strong Arming the Hispanic Press." CJR 19.2 (1980) 51-54.
A look at how in New York, the nation's largest Hispanic community, anti-Castro Cuban exile extremists are "censoring the news media--sometimes with bombs."

811. Brumberg, Abraham. "'Sham' and 'Farce' in Nicaragua?" Dis 32 (1985) 226-236.
Analyzes the democratic 1984 election in Nicaragua, showing the lies about it by the Reagan administration and the failure of the press to report it accurately.

812. Bunzl, Martin. "Manipulating Wounded Knee with Media Misunderstanding." TCJR 2.6 (July-Aug. 1974) 12-13.
The media have generally failed to report the real complexities of the trial of Russell Means and Dennis Banks (American Indian Movement leaders charged with felonies allegedly committed at the Sioux Pine Ridge Reservation).

813. Burke, Chris. "Central America Coverage: The Bias Persists." Extra! 2.1 (July-Aug. 1988) 10.
"US reporting on Central America continues to focus on negatives in Nicaragua while worse repression in El Salvador, Guatemala and Honduras receives far less attention."

814. Burkett, Warren. News Reporting: Science, Medicine, and High Technology. Ames: Iowa State UP, 1986. 160.
A how-to-do-it book. Chapter 7, "Science Writing and Public Interest"; Chapter 9, "Controls on Science News," etc.

815. "The Business of News." Gannett Center Journal (Spring 1987).
The first issue of this new quarterly features many articles by journalists, press critics, and media scholars on the relationship between the press and profits and how it affects the way the news is presented.

816. Caldicott, Helen. "Helen Caldicott on Tactics." BAS 42.5 (1986) 45-6.
On underreporting and misrepresentation of the nuclear freeze movement, because journalists rely on officials and experts.

817. Carey, John. "How Media Shape Campaigns." JoC 26.2 (Spring 1976) 50-57.
Based on a four-week survey of three national television networks, magazines, and newspapers just before the 1974 congressional elections, the study finds that media attention consistently focused on campaign tactics for winning and defeating the opponent.

818. Chafets, Ze'ev. Double Vision: How the Press Distorts America's View of the Middle East. New York: Morrow, 1985. 349.
US journalists have not told the truth about Arab countries because they have been denied "real access" to and have been physically intimidated by those countries. And the news media refuse to disclose the influences on their work (refuse to be openly and publicly self-critical) in regard to reporting the Middle East, "thus abandoning 'the public's right to know' for the more businesslike slogan of 'caveat emptor'" (23).

819. Chirot, Daniel. "Getting the Story - Missing the Point." Deadline 4.5 (Nov.-Dec. 1989) 3-4, 15.
Coverage of President Bush's East European trip July 1989 was intensive but superficial because the media "failed to integrate an analysis of regional history and past American policy." The immediate crisis was reported but not the "historical legacies" likely to dominate future directions.

820. Chomsky, Noam. "After 'Pinksville.'" The Chomsky Reader. New York: Pantheon, 1987. 259-263.
The atrocity at Song My by US soldiers was not reported by the press until pressure by the November Mobilization, but enormously worse and similarly underreported was the "virtual war of extermination against helpless peasants," of which Song My was a tiny manifestation.

THE MEDIA

821. Chomsky, Noam. "East Timor" (1985). The Chomsky Reader. New York: Pantheon, 1987. 303-311.
The massacre by the Indonesian government of some 200,000 people in East Timor by 1979, which was supported by the US government, has been self-censored by the US mainstream press.

822. Chomsky, Noam. "East Timor: The Press Cover-up." Inq 2.5 (1979) 9-15.
The media pay no attention to the US-backed slaughter in East Timor by the Indonesian government.

823. Chomsky, Noam. "The Fledgling Democracies." The Culture of Terrorism. Boston: South End, 1988. 225-49.
US support of terrorism by its client states and the atrocities committed by those dictatorships are little reported by US media, while all of Nicaragua's failings (many caused by the US/contra invasion) receive media attention.

824. Chomsky, Noam. "The Old and the New Cold War." The Chomsky Reader. New York: Pantheon, 1987. 207-19.
The old and the new Cold War is a continuous system in which both the US and the Soviet Union mobilize their populations "against victims within what they take to be their respective domains." The threat of the other is part of the system used to justify global intervention, and manipulation of foreign news has helped sustain it.

825. Chomsky, Noam. Pirates and Emperors: International Terrorism in the Real World. New York: Claremont Research, 1986. 174.
Examines how the media frame international issues, especially the subject of terrorism, in accordance with national policies reinforced by suppression of history. For example, he contrasts the small amount of violence by "retail terrorists" constantly reported and inflated by the media to the US government's enormously more destructive violence in El Salvador, Nicaragua, and elsewhere, which is played down by the media.

826. Chomsky, Noam. "Reporting Indochina: The News Media and the Legitimation of Lies." SocP 4.2 (1973) 4-19.
The press generally supports or reflects official policies and doctrines regarding the Vietnam War.

827. Chomsky, Noam. "The Threat of a Good Example." The Culture of Terrorism. Boston: South End, 1988. 217-222.
Fear that Nicaragua might be admired by other countries inspires support of the contras and "gross misrepresentation," as in the distortion of a speech by Tomás Borge, a fraud "reported by the press without comment."

828. Cirino, Robert. Power to Persuade: Mass Media and the News. New York: Bantam, 1974. 246.

Provides, through case studies, insight into the processes of news production, covering areas such as bias, placement of news stories, censorship, advertiser control, news priorities, and hiring and firing of personnel. The author seeks to empower the consumer citizen.

829. Cirino, Robert. "The Story of Hunger: Anyone Interested?" Don't Blame the People. New York: Vintage, 1971. 1-5.
Inadequate media coverage of hunger.

830. Clarke, Peter, and Eric Fredin. "Newspapers, TV and Political Reasoning." POQ 42 (1978) 143-160.
Compares media information; e.g., multiple newspapers in a city enhances political awareness.

831. Clurman, Richard. Beyond Malice: The Media's Years of Reckoning. New Brunswick, NJ: Transaction, 1988. 306.
Concerned with both the self-righteousness of giant media corporations and the backlash of politicians and other leaders that might lead to a decline in investigative reporting. Focuses upon two cases--the suit against CBS by General William Westmoreland and the suit against Time, Inc., by Israeli General Ariel Sharon. Urges media to "report energetically and critically on themselves and on each other just as they do on the rest of the world," and to make available to the public "adequate ways to reply after the press has spoken."

832. Cockburn, Alexander. "Adventures in the Peace Trade." ITT 12.37 (Sept. 28-Oct. 4, 1988) 17.
Justice Department arrest of representatives of a group which trades with Nicaragua, in spite of the World Court ruling that the embargo was illegal, "has gone largely unreported" by the US media.

833. Cockburn, Alexander. "After the Contra Vote." Corruptions of Empire. London: Verso, 1987. 427-29.
The Reagan administration is violating Article 6 of the Nuremberg Laws, the UN Charter (Art. 2, Sec. 3 and 4), and the OAS Treaty (Chap. 3, Art. 15) in its aid to the contras, but the media offer little awareness of these violations.

834. Cockburn, Alexander. "After the Press Bus Left: The Case of Guatemala." ITT 12.27 (June 8-21, 1988) 16-17.
Detailed analysis of the wretched US media coverage averaging only two critical news stories per year since 1955 for a country in which more than 50,000 civilians have been murdered by government security forces during the past five years.

835. Cockburn, Alexander. "The Assassination of Ben Linder." Corruptions of Empire. London: Verso, 1987. 460-63.

Mainstream reporting of the murder of Linder by the contras was incompetent.

836. Cockburn, Alexander. "Bad Start." Corruptions of Empire. London: Verso, 1987. 355-57.
Contrasts media criticism of the Sandinistas with the lack of criticism of US conquest of Nicaragua and its installation and support of Somoza's dictatorship.

837. Cockburn, Alexander. "The Beirut Massacre and the US Press." Corruptions of Empire. London: Verso, 1987. 292-93.
The press was complicit in the atrocities. "The US press assisted for years in that confiscation of identity and humanity which, for those Palestinian men, women and children, culminated in that final confiscation of life."

838. Cockburn, Alexander. "Blood and Ink." Corruptions of Empire. London: Verso, 1987. 212-216.
During 1980 the press generally misinformed the public about El Salvador, giving the erroneous impression that the extreme right-wing were committing the assassinations and massacres, when the government and its army were the right wing.

839. Cockburn, Alexander. "A Blunt Proposal." ITT 11.16 (1987) 17.
The US official press ignored a story which surfaced in Mexico about a US ambassador's proposal that a phony attack on Costa Rica by Sandinistas be used as justification for American military action against Nicaragua.

840. Cockburn, Alexander. "Can the Press Save the Presidency?" ITT 11.16 (1987) 17.
Despite the glaring abuses of the Reagan administration and growing public disenchantment with the man and his policies, the official press portrays the president in a positive light.

841. Cockburn, Alexander. "The Captive Press." Na 240.11 (Mar. 23, 1985) 328-9.
President of Nicaragua Daniel Ortega's recent peace proposal presented to a delegation of US Catholic bishops was either ignored or distorted by the media.

842. Cockburn, Alexander. "The Gospel According to Ali Agca." Corruptions of Empire. London: Verso, 1987. 397-98.
Major media reported uncritically the false allegation that the Bulgarian government was behind the plot to kill the Pope.

843. Cockburn, Alexander. "Haiti, Before and After." ITT 10.24 (1986) 12.
US media are virtually silent about continued Haitian police

brutality and US aid to its government.

844. Cockburn, Alexander. "His Place in History." Na 241.18 (Nov. 30, 1985) 574.

"The weeks leading up to the summit . . . produced some of the most preposterous news coverage in my memory" by its presentation of President Reagan as someone who "wished to be remembered in history as a man of peace."

845. Cockburn, Alexander. "Is Press Awakening to Reagan's Deceptions?" Corruptions of Empire. London: Verso, 1987. 442-44.

The press "is now showing some signs of coming to life" regarding an administration that has constantly managed news and practiced disinformation.

846. Cockburn, Alexander. "Lying by Silence." ITT 13.13 (Feb. 15-21, 1989) 17.

From misrepresentation by coverage the mainstream media now misrepresent by withdrawing attention from Nicaragua, even though US spy flights over Nicaragua have significantly increased.

847. Cockburn, Alexander. "Newspeak US-Style." NSS 2.44 (Apr. 7, 1989) 22-23.

Focuses on the means by which the US media isolate popular struggles here and abroad from the acceptable mainstream. The striking machinists of Eastern Airlines and the rebels of the FMLN in El Salvador are cast as "intransigent" or extremists who threaten the public: greedy corporate heads and death-squad wielding politicians are shown as moderate compromisers.

848. Cockburn, Alexander. "Pestilent Mendicant." ITT 12.37 (Sept. 28-Oct. 4, 1988) 17.

Denounces media neglect of the systemic causes of homelessness in the US.

849. Cockburn, Alexander. "Their Miners and Ours - II." Na 249.12 (Oct. 16, 1989) 410-411.

On media suppression of the strike by miners at the Pittston mines in Virginia, while giving ample attention to strikes in the SU.

850. Cockburn, Alexander. "Them." Na 248.13 (Apr. 3, 1989) 438-39.

Reporting on the Eastern Air Line strike and on El Salvador "is mostly the same." The media falsify the human and political realities of unions and of El Salvador in ways that favor US official and elitist doctrines and programs.

851. Cockburn, Alexander. "The US and the Death Squads." Corruptions of Empire. London: Verso, 1987. 364-65.

THE MEDIA

Failure of mainstream press to report that El Salvador's death squads were "built up by the officials from the State Department, A.I.D., CIA and other agencies and managed with their cooperation through six Administrations over the last twenty years."

852. Cockburn, Alexander. "Watergate: The 1984 Version." Na 239 (Dec. 8, 1984) 606-7.

"The failure of the U.S. press to report on the true state of the [Reagan-Bush] economy in the second half of 1984 must rate as one of the great journalistic lapses of the last twenty years."

853. Cockburn, Alexander. "What Did You Do in the Cold War, Daddy?" Corruptions of Empire. London: Verso, 1987. 385-88.

Official and media misinformation about Yalta is analyzed.

854. Cockburn, Alexander, and Richard McKerrow. "Black Holes." LOOT 1.7 (July 1990) 14-15.

The killed Jackson State students are media "black holes."

855. Coffin, Tristram. "A Look at the News Media." WS 14.4 (Feb. 15, 1988) 1-3.

Many examples of uncritical acceptance of official lies and propaganda.

856. Cohen, Jeff, and Martin A. Lee. "Media Put Reagan Spin on Arias Plan." Extra! 1.3 (Aug.-Sept. 1987) 1, 5-6.

The media follow the administration's lead in reporting Nicaragua and other Central American countries.

857. Cohen, Richard M. "Censorship Works." NR 198.23 (June 6, 1988) 13-15.

South Africa's ban on media coverage of police actions has succeeded due to the American media's cowardice: journalists and news organizations have passed on either watered-down stories or no story at all.

858. Cohen, Stanley, and Jock Young, eds. The Manufacture of News: Social Problems, Deviance, and the Mass Media. Beverly Hills, CA: Sage, 1981. 506.

Explores how media provide the images and myths for social order and control, especially conceptions of deviance and social problems.

859. Colhoun, Jack. "Activists Take 'Steps' to Break 'Conspiracy of Silence.'" Guard 41.5 (Oct. 16, 1988) 3.

Nationwide demonstrations to confront the "information blockade" that prevents people from knowing about the repression in El Salvador.

860. Colhoun, Jack. "Media Wink as Republicans Reelect Racist Leader." Guard 41.12 (Dec. 14, 1988) 7.
"USA Today: The Television Show" for 2 months delayed an interview of Rep. Bob Michel (R-IL) in which he made several racist comments, and the major media gave the story "short shrift."

861. Commoner, Barry. "Talking to a Mule." CJR 19.5 (1981) 30-31.
On media disregard of third parties.

862. "Communicating Risk: The Media and the Public." JoC 37.3 (Summer 1987) 10-108.
A symposium of seven essays.

863. Curry, Jane Leftwich, and Joan R. Dassin. Press Control Around the World. New York: Praeger, 1982. 283.
Essays on Western democracies, the communist press, and the developing world. One essay on "the suppression of information" that is "built into the very organization of the news media" in the US.

864. Daly, Charles, ed. The Media & the Cities. Chicago: U of Chicago Center for Policy Study, 1968. 90.
Eight essays inspired by the 1967 riots and the Kerner Commission report. The authors were asked to address the relationship between media, race, and violence. The basic issue was the fact that the media "still are almost exclusively shaped for the taste--some would say the prejudices--of white audiences."

865. "Danger of Worldwide Nuclear Accidents." SLJR 16.106 (May 1988) 12.
In the US "there have been more than 23,000 mishaps" since the Three Mile Island meltdown in 1979, and "the number is increasing," but reactor accidents are one of the most neglected stories, according to Project Censored.

866. Davidov, Marv. "Doors Close on Dan and Jane." TCJR 3.2 (Feb.-Mar. 1975) 14-15.
The visit by Jane Fonda, Daniel Ellsberg and Holly Near to the Twin Cities in October 1974 to tell about how the US was blocking peace in Vietnam was suppressed by much of the TC media.

867. Daviss, Bennett. "Touching Up Reality: New Technologies Shake Old Beliefs in News Photography." M&V 50 (Spring 1990) 10-11.
"Technology's ability to change images into electronic information has destroyed the photograph as a reliable record of reality."

867a. Dorman, William. "The Chemical Weapons Crisis: A Debate Denied." Deadline 4.2 (Mar.-Apr. 1989) 1-2, 10-12.

"For nearly five months, major news organizations failed to inform their audience" that under international law it was not illegal for Libya to produce chemical weapons. In contrast, they reported month after month on the Libyan "threat," so that the public easily accepted the armed confrontation initiated by the US off the Libyan coast.

868. Dorman, William. "Peripheral Vision: U.S. Journalism and the Third World." WPJ 3.2 (Summer 1986) 419-445.

"Knowledge of foreign affairs actually comes to us from a system of news-gathering deeply flawed by the subtle interplay of ideology, ethnocentrism, dubious professional practice, and economic forces. As a result, U.S. journalism is not the proudly independent institution it believes itself to be, but instead defers all too often to the established perspectives and formulations of the national security state."

868a. Dorman, William, and Ehsan Omeed. "Reporting Iran the Shah's Way." CJR 17.5 (1979) 27-33.

For many years the media have misinformed the public about Iran, giving undue weight to the Shah's perspective at the expense of his opponents.

869. Downing, John D.H. "Outside the Mainstream." JoC 37.2 (Spring 1987) 159-62.

Review of The Rise and Fall of the Bulgarian Connection by Edward Herman and Frank Brodhead, which assesses the methodological divergences by the authors from traditional news content analysis.

870. Duncan, Dayton. "Press, Polls, and the 1988 Campaign: An Insider's Critique." Cambridge, MA: Harvard U Barone Center, 1989. 10.

Governor Dukakis's press secretary finds the quality of political coverage "declining."

871. Edelman, Murray. Constructing the Political Spectacle. Chicago: U of Chicago P, 1988. 137.

News purveyors bolster existing inequalities and strengthen the dominant ideology by presenting news as spectacle to an irrational majority. "The spectacle constituted by news reporting continuously constructs and reconstructs social problems, crises, enemies, and leaders and so creates a succession of threats and reassurances" by which support or opposition for causes and policies are won (1). This hegemonic process of ideology maintenance is masked by the constructed myth that observers if properly trained can be objective about "facts." In fact, political events as news are creations of the groups concerned with them, and this reality makes control of the media essential to control of national priorities.

872. Epstein, Edward Jay. Between Fact and Fiction: The Problem of Journalism. New York: Vintage, 1967. 232.

Analyzes numerous cases to illustrate the problems of objective reporting: Watergate, Black Panthers, etc.

873. Ericson, Richard, Patricia Baranek, and Janet Chan. *Negotiating Control: A Study of News Sources.* Toronto: U of Toronto P, 1989. 428.

"In a society where knowledge is a principle of social hierarchy at least as important as property, the power of the news process is enormous. Sources and journalists can be seen as joining together to articulate the contours of 'the knowledge society,' reproducing the power/knowledge structures of bureaucratic life, and thereby, the authoritative apparatus of society." Chapters on "Negotiating the News," etc.

874. Ericson, Richard, Patricia Baranek, and Janet Chan. *Visualizing Deviance: A Study of News Organization.* Toronto: U of Toronto P, 1987. 390.

"Journalists join with other agents of control as a kind of 'deviance-defining elite,' using the news media to provide an ongoing articulation of the proper bounds to behaviour in all organized spheres of life. . . . In sum, journalists are central agents in the reproduction of order" (3). Journalists "inevitably concentrate on deviance and control, because designating deviance is itself so fundamental to articulations of culture. Our cultural identity, our sense of what we are, derives from pointing to what we are not: that which is bad, wrong, faulty, in error, straying, etc." (356). The authors are writing a second book about how some individuals, organizations and institutions gain power "both over and through the news media" (364). (See #873).

875. Fatemi, Ali. "The Shah's 'Democracy.'" *MO* 5.11 (Nov. 1963) 20-21.

The pro-Shah US press lied to the public that the recent election in Iran was democratic.

876. Faulkner, Francis. "Bao Chi: The American News Media in Vietnam, 1960-1975." Ph.D. Diss., U of Massachusetts, 1981. 823. *DAI* 41 (1981) 4875.

Coverage of Vietnam lacked investigative and analytical depth that would have engaged the uncritical assumptions underlying US involvement.

877. "Fear and Loathing at the Atlanta Convention." *Extra!* 2.1 (July-Aug. 1988) 4-5.

Reporters transformed the real economic special interests behind the Democratic party into the special interests of women, labor unions, senior citizens, gays and lesbians, and other minor constituencies.

878. Fehrenbach, T.R. *This Kind of War.* New York: Macmillan, 1963. 688.

Coverage of the Korean War was warped by ethnocentrism and patriotism.

879. Ferguson, LeRoy C., and Ralph H. Smuckler. *Politics in the Press: An Analysis of Press Content in 1952 Senatorial Campaigns.* East Lansing: Michigan State

THE MEDIA

UP, Gov. Res. Bur., 1954. 100.
Focuses on the inadequate reporting of the campaigns of Senators Joseph McCarthy and William Benton, which concentrated upon personalities instead of policies.

880. Fields, Echo. "Preachers, Press, & Politics: The Media Career of a Conservative Social Movement." U of Oregon, 1984. 411. DAI 45 (1985) 1903-A.
Portrayal of three New Christian Right organizations in major news media 1979-1981 both "legitimated and delegitimated" them. The movement's leaders and followers were undercut, while their political effectiveness was "portrayed as substantial."

881. Fishman, Mark. Manufacturing the News. Austin: U of Texas P, 1980. 180.
Maintains that news does not mirror or even distort objective, concrete reality. Rather, a news story is a separate constructed reality determined by the work routines of journalists highly dependent on bureaucratic sources. News consumers are led to see the world outside their firsthand experience through the eyes of the existing authority structure. Based on observations of news workers.

882. Frank, Jerome, et al. "American Indifference to Atrocities on Our Side." MO 8.6 (June 1966) 17.
One of the causes is the "voluntary self-censorship by most of the American correspondents in Saigon."

883. Friedman, Robert I. "Selling Israel to America." MJ 12.11 (1987) 21-26, 52.
On pressures to suppress stories critical of Israel.

884. Friedman, Sharon, Carole Gorney, and Brenda Egolf. "Reporting on Radiation: A Content Analysis of Chernobyl Coverage." JoC 37.3 (Summer 1987) 58-67.
Studies coverage during the first two weeks after the accident by the NYT, WP, PI, WSJ, and by ABC, NBC, and CBS news programs. Radiation coverage was "appropriate, even-handed, and conservative," but "there was not enough coverage, both of the actual situations and levels and of the explanatory information."

885. Fry, Don, ed. Believing the News. Poynter Institute Ethics Center Report. St. Petersburg, FL: Poynter Institute, 1985. 301.
A panel focused upon the press's unfairness, bias, arrogance, greed, rudeness, and especially upon televised presidential news conferences "as particularly damaging to the image of the press" (xx). The use of unnamed sources, collusion with government, mixing news with opinion, fragmentariness, and emphasis upon breaking news were discussed as additional reasons for suspicion by the public. The panelists suggested several reforms.

886. Galster, Steven R. "Afghanistan Atrocities: The Other Side of the Story." Extra! 2.7/8 (Summer 1989) 32-33.
While the US media have eagerly reported human rights violations by the Soviet-backed Kabul government, widespread abuses by rebels have been grossly underreported.

887. Gans, Herbert. "Are U. S. Journalists Dangerously Liberal?" CJR 24.4 (1985) 29-33.
A skeptical analysis of the study of journalists by Stanley Rothman, S. Robert Lichter, and Linda Lichter which claimed to reveal a liberal and left bias on the part of journalists. Journalists are not.

888. Gans, Herbert. Deciding What's News: A Study of "CBS Evening News," "NBC Nightly News," "Newsweek," and "Time." New York: Pantheon, 1979. 393.
Analysis of story selection concludes that considerations of story suitability internal to the news organization such as impact, novelty, the "enduring values" embraced by journalists, and gravitation toward certain (powerful) sources are the prime modifiers of the final news product. Part 3, "News Policy," analyzes the shortcomings of the present news structure (stressing the lack of diversity) and urges greater access for all levels of American society, with multiple points of view expressed: "multiperspectival news."

889. Gans, Herbert. "News Media, News Policy, and Democracy: Research for the Future." JoC 33.3 (Summer 1983) 174-184.
Media studies should pay less attention to those who gather the news and concentrate more on newsmakers, the audience, and the relationship between the media and political organizations.

890. Garbus, Martin. "The Sharon Verdict: Wrong Case, Wrong Place, Wrong Result." Freedom at Risk: Secrecy, Censorship, and Repression in the 1980s. Ed. Richard O. Curry. Philadelphia, PA: Temple UP, 1988. 335-340.
Analyzes Ariel Sharon v. Time Inc. as a disaster for democracy, since such libel trials will inhibit investigative journalism and will decrease information about public controversies.

891. [Cancelled]

892. Gerbner, George, and George Marvanyi. "The Many Worlds of the World's Press." JoC 27.1 (1977) 52-66.
A study of foreign news coverage, including the US press, in nine countries representing the capitalist, socialist, and "third" worlds. The authors drew several conclusions: there is an inverse relationship between commercial sponsorship and foreign news coverage; the American blindspot is Latin America; Soviets get more news about the US, Western and Eastern Europe than those readers get about the Soviet Union; and the regions of Africa, Australia and Oceania, and the Eastern

THE MEDIA   145

Socialist countries of China, Mongolia, and North Korea were barely visible in the 1970 world press.

893. Gervasi, Tom. "Charting the Double Standard in the Coverage of Chernobyl." Deadline 1.3 (1986) 1-5.
Media coverage was a self-righteous exercise in Cold War journalism.

894. Giese, Paula. "Covering Cambodia." TCJR 2.2 (Sept.-Oct. 1977) 4-11.
Cambodia, Nixon's invasion of Cambodia, and the antiwar strike at the U of Minnesota were distortedly reported by the US press. "American journalism is a bag of disconnected facts, mainly carrying messages of the ruling class while claiming all sides are presented."

895. Giese, Paula. "Wounded Knee: Bringing the War Back Home." TCJR 2.1 (Summer 1973) 14-19.
"The story the press told of Wounded Knee came mostly from government sources. For Twin Cities journalists, this must be a particular shame," since the American Indian Movement's national headquarters was in St. Paul. "There are obvious parallels with Vietnam."

896. Gitlin, Todd. The Whole World is Watching: Mass Media in the Making and Unmaking of the New Left. Berkeley: U of California P, 1980. 327.
A study of news frames, where they come from, why they appear natural and are taken for granted, why and how they are disputed, and why and how the New Left of the '60s was systematically denigrated. The author employs Gramsci's idea of hegemony to explain news as a complex system of power and the treatment of the New Left/student radical opposition to the Vietnam War as an illustration of that system.

897. Golding, Peter, and Philip Elliott. Making the News. London: Longman, 1979. 241.
Data drawn from Sweden, Ireland, and Nigeria shows how news "is shaped by a variety of organisational, cultural, and normative restraints. At the end of a tightly structured and highly organised production routine emerges a cultural package called news."

898. Goldstein, Tom. The News at Any Cost: How Journalists Compromise Their Ethics to Shape the News. New York: Simon and Schuster, 1985. 301.
Documents several types of means impersonally adopted to illegally, immorally, or, at best, questionably achieve news gathering ends.

899. Graber, Doris. Processing the News: How People Tame the Information Tide. New York: Longman, 1984. 241.
The twenty-one people studied for one year "blocked out most of what the news media told them," focusing on information that fit into their existing mental "schemas," i.e. that

900. Gray, William. "Nukes in the News: Mass Media Covers the Freeze Campaign." AltM 14.1 (Fall 1982) 9-11.
"In the media's eyes, political issues are best left to politicians, corporate leaders and assorted technocrats."

901. Green, Pippa. "South Africa's Toughest Censor." CJR 27.2 (July-Aug. 1988) 6, 8.
The US media reaction to South African repression of journalists has been largely one of self-censorship.

902. Grey, David. The Supreme Court and the News Media. Evanston, IL: Northwestern UP, 1968. 194.
Attributes the abysmal state of public knowledge of the criminal justice system partly to the news media, who are charged with "misinterpretations and shallowness of meaning." The press must provide not just accurate and ample facts and events, but "it must provide meaning."

903. Gwyn, Robert. "Political Dissent and the Free Market of Ideas: An Eight-Nation Study." Gaz 12 (1966) 187-200.
On the distortion and lack of coverage of the San Francisco to Moscow Peace Walk by the establishment press of both countries.

904. Hachten, William, and Harva Hachten. The World News Prism: Changing Media, Clashing Ideologies. 2nd ed. Ames: Iowa State UP, 1987. 162.
The principal emphasis is on communications satellites and computers. [Ideologically pro-US/Western].

905. Halaby, Ralph J. "Iraq's Actions Must Be Considered in Regional Context." AG (Aug. 16, 1990) 9B.
Media coverage of the Middle Eastern crisis of 1990 (Iraq's invasion of Kuwait and US troops to Saudi Arabia) was unbalanced, tended "to drum up support for the military over the political solution," and in general did the public a "disservice."

906. Hallin, Daniel C. "The American News Media: A Critical Theory Perspective." Critical Theory and Public Life. Ed. John Forester. Cambridge, MA: MIT P, 1985. 121-146.
Employs the concept of the "scientization of politics"--that US journalism takes "technical knowledge as a model for the reporting of news"--to examine the news media and the issue of "media's ability to legitimize the existing social order."

907. Hartley, John. Understanding News. New York: Methuen, 1982. 203.
Understanding news requires study of the commercial and governmental contexts of the production of news.

908. Hellinger, Dan. "Interviewing Western Reporters in Nicaragua." SLJR 11.65 (1984) 19-22.
Distortion of Nicaragua by US media.

909. Henry, William A. "News as Entertainment: The Search for Dramatic Unity." What's News: The Media in American Society. Ed. Elie Abel. San Francisco, CA: Inst. for Contemporary Studies, 1981. 133-158.
On the strengths and limitations of TV and print journalism.

910. Herbert, Wray. "Humanities and Journalism: Akin but Worlds Apart." Humanities Report 2.10 (Oct. 1980) 4-10.
Journalists report the humanities inadequately.

911. Herman, Edward. "Diversity of News: 'Marginalizing' the Opposition." JoC 35.3 (1985) 135-46.
Reporting of El Salvador and several other countries reflects national policies.

912. Herman, Edward. "Gatekeeper versus Propaganda Models: A Critical American Perspective." Communicating Politics. Ed. Peter Golding, et al. New York: Holmes & Meier, 1986. 171-196.
Explains the ability of the US government to mobilize a mostly compliant media around its preferred definitions of events and issues, especially in foreign affairs, where the media frequently conform to an official propaganda system. Illustrates his argument by the quite different reporting of the shooting down of KAL 007 by a Soviet fighter pilot in 1983 and the shooting down of a Libyan commercial airliner by Israel in 1973.

913. Herman, Edward. "U.S. Mass Media Coverage of the U.S. Withdrawal from UNESCO." Hope & Folly: The United States & UNESCO, 1945-1985. Minneapolis: U of Minnesota P, 1989. 203-284.
The mass media failed to treat the withdrawal impartially because they had "a conflict of interest" and followed the US government and multinational line. This failure followed "a long tradition of extremely biased and self-serving coverage of UNESCO." The evidence indicates that "the severity of bias of a commercial press would be difficult to surpass."

914. Herman, Edward, and Noam Chomsky. Manufacturing Consent: The Political Economy of the Mass Media. New York: Pantheon, 1988. 412.
Their purpose is to apply a "propaganda model" to the mass media of the US, following the belief, which the book supports in great detail, that the media serve to mobilize support for special interests (xi). Based upon the "guided market system" of government and corporate leaders in position to take significant initiatives to command access to the media, this is no conspiracy theory. In brief, "the media serve the ends of a dominant elite" (1), which exploits the "inequality of wealth

and power and its multilevel effects on mass-media interests and choices" (2) through a set of five news "filters" (Chapter 1, "A Propaganda Model"): "l) the size, concentrated ownership, owner wealth, and profit orientation of the dominant mass-media firms; 2) advertising as the primary income source of the mass media; 3) the reliance of the media on information provided by government, business and 'experts' funded and approved by these primary sources and agents of power; 4) 'flak' as a means of disciplining the media; and 5) 'anticommunism' as a national religion and control mechanism." This interlocking and mutually reinforcing system explains "the routes by which money and power" are able to filter the news, marginalize dissent, and dominate access (2). The remaining chapters and the 3 appendices apply and test the model, with particular focus on the "dichotomization in news coverage" that serves "power interests" (35).

915. Herman, Edward, and Noam Chomsky. "Propaganda Mill: The Media Churn Out the Official Line." Prog 52.6 (1988) 14-17.

Article adapted from **Manufacturing Consent**, showing how the mass media in the US, through self-censorship, bias, and co-opting experts, function to mobilize public support for special interests that dominate the symbiotic government private business sector.

916. Hess, Stephen. The Ultimate Insiders: U.S. Senators in the National Media. Washington, DC: Brookings, 1986. 114.

Senators who shape laws and seem to wield institutional power get most of the publicity.

917. Hoch, Paul. "Socialization for Consumption." Rip Off the Big Game: The Exploitation of Sports by the Power Elite. Garden City, NY: Doubleday, 1972. Chapter 7.

Sports news is described as mainly promotional, "the bribery of the mediamen by professional promoters has long been institutionalized" (137).

918. Holland, Max. "Nicaragua: A Despot Falls, the Press Stumbles." CJR 18.3 (1979) 46-7.

Biased reporting of popular revolutions.

919. "How to Analyze the News." QRD 15.1 (Oct. 1988) 9.

Opponents of the Contras have been "almost entirely ignored."

920. Huffman, John L., and Denise M. Trauth. "Freedom of the Press: An Eroding Legal Concept." FSY (1979) 58-66.

In recent decisions the Supreme Court has rejected the idea of "special status" for the press under the First Amendment, declaring that the press enjoys no rights not allotted to ordinary citizens.

THE MEDIA

921. Ibelema, Minabere. "Global News Flow Issues: Toward a Convergent Perspective." Ohio SU, 1984. 199. DAI 45 (Apr. 1985) 3021-A.
Thirty-eight journalists from developing countries were interviewed: US media cover other countries favorably or unfavorably depending upon the level of consonance between the US and the country covered, but given the constraints over journalistic independence in developing countries, the correspondents prefer Western news media "as the lesser evil."

922. Isaacs, Norman. Untended Gates: The Mismanaged Press. New York: Columbia UP, 1986. 258.
Owners and managers are to blame for the present disesteem of the press. Instead of using profits to enhance reporting in the public interest, owners sought increased ratings and circulation with trivia. Praises the Hutchins Commission report A Free and Responsible Press and the National News Council for their advocacy of a more responsible press.

922a. Jalbert, Paul. "Categorization and Beliefs: News Accounts of Haitian and Cuban Refugees." The Interactional Order: New Directions in the Study of Social Order. Ed. David T. Helm, W. Tim Anderson, A. Jay Meehan and Anne Rawls. New York: Irvington, 1989. 231-48.
A study in how the uses of particular categories of persons by government officials and print and broadcast reporters can mean the difference between the granting of asylum and deportation.

923. Jensen, Carl. The Top 25 Censored News Stories of 1989. Rohnert Park, CA: Censored, 1990. 71.
Contains synopses of each of the stories.

923a. Johnstone, John, et al. The News People: A Sociological Portrait of American Journalists & Their Work. Urbana: U of Illinois P, 1976. 257.
Their "most general conclusion" is "how very much modern newswork is a collective enterprise, and how very intricate is the process by which occurrences in the real world come to be translated into news stories" (182). Behind the news lies "centralizing trends" that have produced "greater homogenization in the news, have increased the control of national and regional news organizations over local outlets, and have integrated the news media even more firmly within the corporate nexus of American industry" (181). Chapters on education, careers, division of labor, etc.

924. "KAL 007 and Iran Air 655: Comparing the Coverage." Extra! 2.1 (July-Aug. 1988) 1, 6-7.
Media followed the KAL downing with vehement righteous indignation; they reported the Iran Air 655 shootdown with excuses and avoidance of fundamental issues.

925. Karetzky, Stephen, ed. The Media's War Against Israel.

New York: Shapolsky/Steimatzky, 1986. 423.
Nine essays, the longest of which is the editor's "The New York Times Propaganda War Against Israel" (29-119). Foreword by R.J. Isaac: "In reporting the war in Lebanon, the media behaved like a lynch mob" against Israel, employing "misstatement and calumny." Other essays focus on the TV networks and Time.

926. "Keeping Nicaragua Covered." BI 8.280 (Nov. 10, 1988) 3-4.
A veil of silence covers the continued atrocities committed by the contras against the civilian population of Nicaragua paid for by Congress' "humanitarian" aid, the increase of electronic surveillance flights over Nicaragua, and other illegal acts by the US.

926a. Kelly, Tom. "Ceremonial Media." C&C 50.16 (Nov. 12, 1990) 340-342.
Evaluates the "clear Gadarine tendencies" of the media over the Iraqi crisis, motivated by profit and "establishmentarian conformity."

927. King, Dennis. Lyndon LaRouche and the New American Fascism. New York: Doubleday, 1989. 415.
Unmasks the failure of some of the nation's biggest, most respected news organizations to tell the truth about LaRouche, despite plenty of evidence already printed in small magazines and alternative newspapers.

927a. Kinsella, James. Covering the Plague: Aids and the American Media. New Brunswick: Rutgers UP, 1989. 299.
"For the past decade, the AIDS story has challenged the ground rules of American journalism. It has forced reporters to acknowledge that their treatment of the news, far from being objective, is often shaped by their personal prejudices and their assumptions about their audience." "For example, almost no one who worked for the networks' nightly news broadcasts admitted to knowing a single person with the disease—and the television coverage reflected that lack of individual knowledge and concern. . . . [A]t least some of the blame for the ravages of AIDS in America must lie with members of the media who refused to believe that the deaths of gay men and drug addicts were worth reporting."

928. Kirk, Robin. "Behind the Cocaine Curtain: Dirty War Escalates in Columbia." Extra! 2.7/8 (Summer 1989) 12-13.
US coverage of Columbia tends to focus almost exclusively on violence committed by drug cartels or leftist guerrillas, rather than violence committed by right-wing death squads, often with the tacit approval or direct assistance of the military.

929. Klotzer, Charles. "Why Do the Mass Media Ignore Charges of a 1980 Election Steal?" SLJR 18.110 (Oct.

1988) 7.
Reports in ITT and Playboy that before the 1980 election the Reagan-Bush team made a deal with Iran to keep the 52 hostages past the inauguration in return for weapons have been ignored by the mass media.

930. Knight, G. "News and Ideology." CJC 8.4 (Sept. 1982) 15-41.
News reflects wider relations of power and tends to reproduce those relations uncritically. Since these relations are conflicting, news should represent that reality.

931. Knoll, Erwin. "Journalistic Jihad." Prog 54.5 (May 1990) 17-22.
CBS "faked and distorted" news about Afghanistan, and the WSJ refused to publish a thoroughly documented exposé of the facts, and the CJR toned down the exposé.

932. Krieghbaum, Hillier. Pressures on the Press. New York: Crowell, 1972. 248.
Explains "some of the real pressures on the press"--e.g., the Nixon administration--so that news "will have more significance for its 'consumers' and less bias and prejudice," for the press is "an essential social institution" in a democracy as "watchdog of government." The final chapter suggests ways to deal with the pressures and maintain the press's watchdog function, e.g. press councils.

933. Lafeber, Walter. "Covering the Canal or, How the Press Missed the Boat." MORE 8.6 (1978) 26-31.
Evaluates inadequate reporting of the Panama Canal Treaty.

934. Lambeth, Edmund B. "Beyond the Muckrakers." IREJ 11.3 (Summer 1988) 6-9.
Analyzes the ethical question of deception in investigative reporting and argues that news organizations should join together in determining what circumstances justify deception and just what degree of deception under those circumstances is ethical.

935. Lanouette, William. "The Half-life of the Tritium Story." Deadline 4.1 (Jan.-Feb. 1989) 1-2, 9-11.
Accidents and safety problems at government nuclear facilities were little reported until the Energy Department sought huge sums of money for repairs, new installations, and cleanup.

936. Lapham, Lewis. "A Political Opiate." Harper's 279.1675 (Dec. 1989) 43-48.
President Bush and the Congress have created a political war on drugs because it "requires them to do nothing difficult, and allows them to postpone, perhaps indefinitely, the more urgent and specific questions about the state of the nation's schools, housing, employment opportunities for young black men," etc. The media, eager to make money from the phony war,

dress it up in "theatrical devices" and "garish colors." The NYT, the WP, and the three television networks combined to produce 347 reports on the fraudulent crisis, by journalists most of whom knew nothing about it. One of the results is the "enormously enhanced powers of repression and control" by government.

937. Lawler, Philip. The Alternative Influence: The Impact of Investigative Reporting Groups on America's Media. Lanham, MD and Washington, DC: The Media Institute with UP of America, 1984. 93.
A rallying cry of alarm to the right wing against an alleged leftist takeover of the mass media.

938. Lederer, William. A Nation of Sheep. New York: Norton, 1961. 192.
Blames the government-media combine for the uninformed and apathetic public.

939. Lee, Martin A., and Gloria Channon. "Invisible Victims." Extra! 2.7/8 (Summer 1989) 11.
The US media tend to frame human rights within the civil-political arena, often ignoring violations of the social, economic and cultural rights expressed in the UN Universal Declaration.

940. Lee, Martin A., and Norman Solomon. Unreliable Sources: A Guide to Detecting Bias in News Media. New York: Lyle Stuart/Carol, 1990. 419.
Explains how and why news media are distorting current events--from the major TV networks and the NYT to public broadcasting. Covers such topics as taxes, social security, abortion, drugs, violence, environmental pollution, the SU, terrorism, and the Third World.

941. Lemert, James. Criticizing the Media: Empirical Approaches. Newbury Park, CA: Sage, 1989. 128.
Advocates social science techniques to evaluate and criticize the performance of the news media.

942. Lent, John. "Foreign News in American Media." JoC 27.1 (1977) 46-51.
Coverage and usage of much international news is determined by diplomacy, national government, and military policies. It is also affected by a dwindling corps of adequately-trained correspondents.

943. Leroy, David, and Christopher Sterling, eds. Mass News: Practices, Controversies, and Alternatives. Englewood Cliffs, NJ: Prentice-Hall, 1973. 334.
Twenty-six essays divided into 4 parts: I, "Context of Mass News" (brief introduction): II, "Practice of Mass News"; III, "Controversies in Mass News"; IV, "Alternatives in Mass News."

944. Lim, Sang. "Ideology and International Information

Flow: A Q-Methodological Study." U of Missouri, 1987. 221. DAI 48 (1988) 2479-A.
A study of the liberal, socialist, and conservative perspectives in conflict over the New World Information Order, primarily reducible to individual freedom vs. national development, the former defending the present order, the latter attacking it.

945. Lutz, William. "Notes Toward a Definition of Doublespeak." Beyond Nineteen Eighty-Four. Ed. William Lutz. Urbana, IL: NCTE, 1989. 1-10.
Four kinds of doublespeak (language used to deceive): euphemism, gobbledygook or bureaucratese, jargon, inflated language.

946. Lynch, Sheila. "We Seek Portrayal as Real People." SLJR (July 1982) 9.
The media "as a whole have not concerned themselves with doing anything regarding minorities other than placating them." (See SLJR [May 1982] for related article).

947. Lynn, Joyce. "Filed & Forgotten: Why the Press Has Taken Up New Issues." WJR 2.4 (1980) 32-37.
Inadequate coverage of social services by media.

948. Making Sense of the News: A Modern Media Institute Ethics Center Seminar. St. Petersburg, FL: Poynter Institute, 1983. 118.
Panel discussion of the superficiality of the news caused by the failure to explain "to tell how and why things happen," inspired by William Grider's article, "The Education of David Stockman."

949. Malakoff, David. "Separating Science Fact." NMA 16.3 (May-June 1986) 15.
Science reporting is inadequate in quantity and quality.

950. Manoff, Robert K., and Michael Schudson, eds. Reading the News. New York: Pantheon, 1987. 243.
Seven essays examine the "interaction between what the world is and how it gets reported," how the reporter "not only relates stories but makes them" (4). No "what," "why," "who," or "where" "gets asked without some [prior] assumption," some presupposed "platform for inquiry, a framework for interpreting answers." "The essays in this book hold that these platforms, frameworks, and rules organize the kind of news we read occupational routines of daily journalism, and literary forms that journalists work with" (5).

951. Marker, Dennis. "Who Killed Ben Linder?" Soj 16.7 (1987) 4-5.
If Ben Linder, murdered by Contras in Nicaragua, had been murdered "in France, Ireland, Lebanon, or many other countries around the world, the headlines would have screamed 'American Engineer Killed by Terrorists.'"

952. Marnell, William. The Right to Know: Media and the
       Common Good. New York: Seabury, 1973. 221.
   Surveys basic issues of First Amendment and the press.

953. "Mass Marketing Cold War Thrills." NT (June 1983) 26-7.
   Discusses books and TV programs which exploit fear of SU.

954. Massing, Michael. "After the Dictator." CJR 29.2
       (July-Aug. 1990) 48.
   Typical of reporting of Central America, after the US
   invasion of Panama the media ceased reporting that country: if
   "no controversy . . . no news."

955. Massing, Michael. "Remember El Salvador?" CJR 26.1
       (1987) 21-22.
   On media neglect of El Salvador even though the US was
   spending over $1 million a day there keeping the war going.

956. Matthews, Herbert L. The Cuban Story. New York:
       Braziller, 1961. 318.
   An effort "to present the Cuban side" of Castro's revolution
   in contrast to the "lack of balance and objectivity" by the US
   government and press. "Once the label of communism was pinned
   on Fidel and his regime . . . the hysteria that accompanies
   the American attitude toward communism worked its poison."

957. Maxwell, Robert A. "Television & Print Journalism: A
       Descriptive Study of Differences in the Reporting of
       a Controversial Public issue--the Trans-Alaskan Oil
       Pipeline." New York U, 1982. 298. DAI 43 (1982)
       1737-A.
   TV "tended to report the 'official' point of view" more than
   print, which offered more diversity. Neither provided any
   investigative stories.

958. Mayer, Martin. Making News. Garden City, NY:
       Doubleday, 1987. 348.
   Examination of the people who report, consume, publish, and
   air the news. Review of history of radio and television news
   and evolution of the "feelies." Discussion of problems of
   communicating fairly and convincingly. Detailed case studies
   of 1982 Tylenol poisonings and of 1984 presidential election
   to show how information is controlled.

959. McCarthy, Colman. "Euphemistic Language Makes the
       Gruesome Palatable." QRD 16.4 (July 1990) 7.
   Examines the distortions of reality through the distortions
   of language regarding eating animals.

960. "The Media and the Summit: Continuing the Cold War
       Legacy." Extra! 1.5 (Dec. 1987) 1, 4-5.
   "Despite the pretense of 'objective reporting,' coverage of
   the arms race has often resembled 'rooting for the home
   team.'"

THE MEDIA

961. "Media Coverage of Business and Labor: Who Serves?" TCJR 3.4 (Aug. 1975) 1-55.
Seven articles supported by the Fund for Investigative Journalism. Business and labor are underreported and superficially covered.

962. Merrill, John C. The Imperative of Freedom: A Philosophy of Journalistic Autonomy. New York: Hastings House, 1974. 228.
Maintains "American journalism is becoming so institutionalized and professionalized and so immured with the nascent concept of 'social responsibility' that it is voluntarily giving up the sacred tenet of libertarianism--'editorial self-determinism'--and is in grave danger of becoming one vast, gray, monotonous, conformist spokesman for some collectivity of society."

963. Merrill, John C. "Professionalization: Danger to Press Freedom and Pluralism." JMME 1.2 (Spring-Summer 1986) 56-60.
Professionalism will curtail individualism and diversity and increase narrowness and self-centeredness.

964. Mintz, Morton. "Holy Moses." CJR 17.3 (1978) 95.
The press failed to report adequately the corruption, secrecy, lies, and racism pervading the New York City public authorities run by Robert Moses.

965. Mitchell, Greg. "Media Cool to Message." NT 4.1 (Sept.-Oct. 1985) 11.
Leaders of the peace movement are studying how to become more effective through the media, which at present give the movement little access and a poor image.

966. Moghadam, Val. "The View from Kabul: Western Media Reports Are Misleading." Guard 41.25 (Mar. 22, 1989) 10-11.
Contrary to reports about Kabul, only some of the people are fearful, food is available, and many women strongly support the government.

967. "More Best-Censored Stories of 1988." SLJR 19.117 (June 1989) 8-9.
Cites huge federal subsidies of oil companies, toxins sent through the mail, Ronald Reagan's secret laws, and the booming business of adolescent mental institutions as some of the news stories overlooked or ignored by the US media.

968. "More Best-Censored Stories of 1988." SLJR 19.118 (Jul.-Aug. 1989) 10-11.
The abuse of women crossing the border illegally, the NYT's support of nuclear weapons, and the stalking of remote tribes by religious fundamentalists are some of the stories ignored by the mainstream media in 1988.

969. Morris, Roger. "Mexico: The U.S. Press Takes a Siesta." CJR 23.5 (1985) 31-36.
Mexico is reported very inadequately.

970. Morris, Roger. "This is the First and Last Article CJR Will Run About Press Coverage of Foreign Policy During the Presidential Campaign." CJR 18.6 (1980) 51.
How the press evades truly significant issues and focuses on the trivial instead.

971. Munoz, Julio E. "The New International Information & Communication Order." U of Minnesota, 1983. 220. DAI 44.2 (1983) 314-A.
This analysis of the conflict between the developed and Third World countries regarding control of the flow of news includes analysis of Western news agencies and US press coverage of the issues.

972. Muwakkil, Salim. "Black Journalists Hit U.S. Media Distortions." ITT 10.20 (1986) 6.
Delegates to a conference in Libya found much to admire there, none of which is reported by the mainstream media.

973. Naureckas, Jim. "Stop the Presses--Tear Down the Front Page." ITT 11.16 (Mar. 18, 1987) 18.
Reading the News, edited by Robert Manoff and Michael Schudson, refuses to see journalism "as embedded in a larger system where news is a commodity . . . and where publishers are powerful members of the establishment their papers report on." The essays by James Carey and Daniel Hallin are exceptions.

974. Nelkin, Dorothy. "The High Cost of Hype." ETC 45.3 (Fall 1988) 262-271.
Maintains that journalists tend to be less critical of scientists than of other professionals and that science reporting is characterized by distortion of events through dramatization.

975. Nelkin, Dorothy. "Selling Science: The High Cost of Hype." ScP 19.3 (1987) 16-21.
"Unaggressive in their reporting and relying on official sources, science journalists present a narrow range of coverage."

976. Newman, Robert, and Dale Newman. Evidence. Boston: Houghton, 1969. 246.
Examines the ideological bias and lying by government, corporations, and media.

977. "Nicaragua Update: What's in a Label?" Extra! 1.5 (Dec. 1987) 14.
Media coverage of Nicaragua favors the administration's policies and language.

THE MEDIA 157

978. Nielsen, Wayne. "The Second Indo-China War and the American Press." MO 6.10 (Oct. 1964) 11-16.
"The US press misrepresents every aspect of the Vietnam war, from the Geneva Agreements to the position of Ho Chi Minh. It acts as the Government's propaganda arm, not as a source of information."

979. Nietschmann, Bernard. "Third World War: The Global Conflict Over the Rights of Indigenous Nations." UR 30 (Nov.-Dec. 1988) 84-91.
Explains why journalists tend to oppose liberation movements.

980. Nigut, Bill, Sr. "The Cheapest Components in Our Very Expensive Military Machine." CMC (Aug. 1988) 2-6.
Thousands of US soldiers die in aircraft crashes each year because of defective equipment, yet the media and the political parties have not probed or protested.

981. Nigut, Bill, Sr. "How American Editors Withhold Important News." CMC (June-July 1989) 1-3.
Denounces inattention to the decline of democracy and bank failures.

982. Nigut, Bill, Sr. "Part Two: This Is a Time for Truth." CMC (Oct. 1988) 1-6.
The media have underreported "the Number One campaign issue --Ronald Reagan's $2 trillion" arms budget and failed to answer the question of "what did the nation get in exchange for the doubling of our national debt?"

983. Nigut, Bill, Sr. "Part Three: This Is a Time for Truth." CMC (Nov. 1988) 1-6.
On the failure of the media to report adequately Reagan's broken campaign promise of a balanced budget and the corruption of the stealth bomber program.

984. Nigut, Bill, Sr. "Was the Media's Reporting of the John Tower Fiasco Fair and Responsible?" CMC (Feb.-Mar. 1989) 1-6.
"Washington journalists and their editors back home did not report important facets of the Tower story that could be politically damaging or embarrassing to George Bush and the Republican party."

985. Nordenstreng, Kaarle, and Lauri Hannikainen. The Mass Media Declaration of UNESCO. Norwood, NJ: Ablex, 1984. 475.
US vs. UNESCO, the "New International Information Order," and the Declaration on Fundamental Principles Concerning . . . the Mass Media.

986. O'Dair, Barbara. "Anatomy of a Media Epidemic." AltM 14.3 (Fall 1983) 10-13.
Press coverage of AIDS "has consisted of sensationalistic

headlines and misinformation."

987. Oldham, Cheyenne. "An Analysis of the Frames Reporters Use to Identify Newsworthiness." U of Kentucky, 1986. 371. DAI 48 (1987) 769-A.
Examines 4 primary frames (competition, editors/newspapers, objectivity, and strategy) and four phases during the news construction process (prior to event, during, while writing the story, afterward).

988. O'Neal, Kathleen. "Northern Ireland: U.S. Media Peddles British Line." CS 7 (1983) 25-29.
Seemingly objective news stories about Northern Ireland project the British position and deny access to the Irish republican point of view.

989. Padwe, Sandy. "'Out' in Left Field." PJR 1.4 (July 1971) 2-3, 12.
Exposes the lack of coverage of Edward Herman's writings and speeches about the Vietnam war by Philadelphia media.

990. Parenti, Michael. Inventing Reality: The Politics of the Mass Media. New York: St. Martin's, 1986. 258.
A survey of information control by the "prestigious news media": namely, the three major networks--CBS, NBC, ABC--NYT, and WP, and to a lesser extent Time, Newsweek, WSJ, and LAT. Chapters 2-5 trace corporate power over news, chapters 6-9 deal with Sovietphobia, 10-12 on foreign affairs news, chapter 12 explains journalistic methods of misrepresentation, and the final chapter is about governmental manipulation and coercion.

991. Patterson, Oscar. "The Vietnam Veteran and the Media: A Comparative Content Analysis of Media Coverage of the War and the Veteran 1968-1973." U of Tennessee, 1982. 254. DAI 43 (1983) 2822.
Vietnam was the dominant topic on network news but not in the weekly news magazines studied. "Anti-war news reports received more coverage on a per-item basis on television and in news magazines than did combat."

992. Patton, Cindy. "AIDS Reporting: Rewriting the Myths." Zeta 2.3 (Mar. 1989) 102-105.
The media have been homophobic and duplicitous in disinforming the public about HIV and AIDS.

993. Paulos, John. Innumeracy: Mathematical Illiteracy and Its Consequences. New York: Hill and Wang, 1988. 135.
On how numbers are misunderstood and used to mislead, including polls and polling and statistics.

994. Peretz, Don. "Reporting Lebanon the 'Christian' Way." Middle East Insight 2.4 (1982) 46-52.
Press coverage of the 1982 Israeli invasion of Lebanon. The US media have tended to frame the strife in Lebanon in terms of valiant Israeli-backed Christians staving off attacks of

Soviet-backed Muslim terrorists, when in fact the conflict is very complex and not neatly divided along lines of religious belief.

995. Perkovich, George. "Conventional Balance Coverage: Reporters on the Record." Deadline 2.1 (1987) 1-2.
Reporters have taken for granted the superiority of the Warsaw Pact over NATO in conventional forces, despite considerable expert opinion that the US and its European allies possess an adequate conventional deterrent.

996. Perrin, Dennis. "China is Simple for U.S. Reporters." Guard 41.36 (June 7, 1989) 2.
Coverage of the Chinese student uprising revealed more about the distorted world-view of the reporters than about China.

997. Perrin, Dennis. "U.S. Media Declare War on Nicaragua." Guard 41.40 (Summer 1989) 4.
Reviews the media's poor reporting, distortion, and outright deception in its coverage of Nicaragua since the revolution.

998. Petrusenko, Vitaly. The Monopoly Press, Or How American Journalism Found Itself in the Vicious Circle of the "Crisis of Credibility." Trans. Vladimir Leonov. Prague: International Organization of Journalists, 1976. 143.
Portrays the press as an apparatus of the corporate state.

999. Phelan, Ann Marie. "A Textual Analysis of Apartheid in Selected News Periodicals." MA Thesis, California SU, 1985.
US press coverage of apartheid reflects US foreign policy aims.

1000. Pollock, John. The Politics of Crisis Reporting: Learning to Be a Foreign Correspondent. New York: Praeger, 1981. 221.
Statistical survey of 102 foreign correspondents who had covered Latin America in an attempt to determine how their attitudes had been shaped. The author assumes attitudes are shaped through hegemonic process, since political learning is cumulative. Reporters who accept US intervention generally, or conflict with the Soviet Union or "communism" specifically, exhibit diminished receptivity to change in the Third World, and are not judged highly "professional" in their reporting by this author.

1001. Pollock, John, and Michele Pollock. "The U.S. Press and Chile." DJ 4 (1975) 4-8.
The biased coverage of Chile.

1002. Postman, Neil. Amusing Ourselves to Death: Public Discourse in the Age of Show Business. New York: Viking, 1985. 184.
Analyzes what watching TV (as opposed to reading) does to

us, especially fragmenting our perception and thought, so that we are decreasingly well-informed.

1003. Preston, William, Jr., Edward Herman, and Herbert Schiller. Hope and Folly: The United States and UNESCO: 1945-1985. Institute for Media Analysis. Minneapolis: U of Minnesota P, 1989. 396.
Describes the history of relations between the US and UNESCO from its inception through the US withdrawal, and gives an analysis of the campaign of media disinformation against UNESCO which led to the US pullout, and an overview of US communications policy. (After contracting for the book, UNESCO tried to suppress the book, but an international outcry forced the organization to withdraw its threats.)

1004. Protzman, Bob. "Uncle Sam Has Some Real Live Heroes--Finally." TCJR 1.6 (Mar.-Apr. 1973) 3-8.
The media presented a mainly statistical treatment of killed and wounded Vietnam War GIs (over 50,000 dead, over 12,000 totally disabled) while turning the few hundred POWs into a "three-ring circus."

1005. Radosh, Ronald. "The Socialists Go To Washington." Na 231 (Dec. 27, 1980) 699-701.
Avoidance of reporting of socialist events.

1006. Reed, Ishmael. "Crime, Drugs, and The Media: The Black Pathology Biz." Na 249.17 (Nov. 20, 1989) 597-598.
Corporate crime far exceeds black crime. "The only difference between white pathology and black pathology is that white pathology is underreported."

1007. Retbøll, Torben, ed. East Timor, Indonesia and the Western Democracies: A Collection of Documents. Copenhagen: International Secretariat of the International Work Group for Indigenous Affairs, 1980. 138.
Includes discussion of US underreporting of atrocities in East Timor.

1008. Roach, Colleen. "The U.S. Position on the New World Information and Communication Order." JoC 37.4 (Fall 1987) 36-51.
The US attack on the New World Information and Communication Order (NWICO), a defense of US privatization, deregulation, and "free flow" doctrines, is rife with contradictions and derives partly from US global economic interests.

1009. Roberts, Steve. "Why Journalists Are Tools of the Establishment." RSCJ 2 (Fall 1971) 2-3, 13.
For many reasons journalists are not critical of the establishment: the myth of objectivity, the sheer weight of corporate and government access to media, government intimidation (Agnew), government-media elite identification, etc.

THE MEDIA

1010. Robinson, Michael, and Margaret Sheehan. Over the Wire and on TV: CBS and UPI in Campaign '80. New York: Sage, 1983. 332.
Attempts to distinguish the ways TV and print report campaigns and to assess the extent to which media are independent and critical.

1011. Rockwell, Paul. "Seeing Is Believing? The Strange Case of the Jackson-Arafat Photo." PR 3 (Winter 1988) 18-20.
Reveals how media framing of Jesse Jackson's 1979 visit with Yassar Arafat during the 1988 presidential campaign "helped transform a peace mission into an act of disloyalty" and contributed significantly to his defeat.

1012. Roeh, Itzhak, and Sharon Ashley. "Criticizing Press Coverage of the War in Lebanon: Toward a Paradigm of News as Storytelling." CY 9 (1985) 117-141.
Cites examples of perceived unfairness in media coverage of the Israeli invasion of Lebanon, then explains the distorted news reports as examples of journalistic "storytelling."

1013. Rosen, Jay. "Dilemma for National Security Reporters: Is Anybody Listening?" Deadline 3.6 (Nov.-Dec. 1988) 3-5.
Discusses the dark implications for democracy of "massive ignorance" on major issues by the public.

1014. Rosen, Jay. "Election Coverage as Propaganda." PR 2 (Summer 1988) 5-9.
The press chooses to cover the political "horse race" every four years and ignore the real story of public alienation.

1015. Rosen, Jay. "Václav Havel in Washington: The Media Encounter That Never Was." Deadline 5.3-4 (Summer 1990) 1-2, 10-13.
Analyzes Havel's beliefs and the difficulty the media and officials experienced in understanding them, so he was turned into a human-interest story and symbol.

1016. Roshco, Bernard. Newsmaking. Chicago: U of Chicago P, 1975. 160.
Explains how relationships the press maintains with other institutions determine what it defines and presents as news; how news content is shaped by the dominant values of US society; why the press developed a definition of "objectivity" that encourages distorted reportage; why individuals with high social standing are usually rated more newsworthy than those with less; why most news is managed and why that practice is so seldom reported; why reporters who cover news beats tend to become collaborators with their news sources; why long-lived social problems remain unreported except under special circumstances; etc.

1017. Rothmyer, Karen. "What Really Happened in Biafra?"

CJR 9.3 (1970) 43-47.
The news media responded excessively to pressures from people "with self-interests tied to one side." The use of public relations firms to affect foreign policy "is becoming more and more common."

1018. Rubin, Barry. "International News and the American Media." International News: Freedom Under Attack. Ed. Dante B. Fascell. Beverly Hills: Sage, 1977. 181-245.
Decries the underreporting of foreign events and nationalistic bias of the coverage.

1019. Rubin, Bernard. Media, Politics, and Democracy. New York: Oxford UP, 1977. 192.
The media should expose "unscrupulous power brokers," explain comprehensively "the relation between key events and vital political processes," set forth "the range of alternatives facing decision makers and the public they serve," etc. Five topics are analyzed: "communications objectivity, community value setting, media freedom, popular participation, and election trends" (xi-xii).

1020. Rubin, Bernard, ed. When Information Counts: Grading the Media. Lexington, MA: Lexington Books, 1985. 244.
The "fourth volume in a series of studies developed to enhance the First Amendment." The authors ask such questions as how well the media informed the public about diverse subjects, how biased were the media, how were the powerless treated, to what degree are the media manipulated by those in power? Chapter examples: "Women, Myth, and the Media," "A Spectrum of Press Watchers," and "Intellectual Foundations of Reagan's Soviet Policy."

1021. Rubin, David. "How the News Media Reported on Three Mile Island and Chernobyl." JoC 37.3 (Summer 1987) 42-57.
Official information following each accident was too optimistic, provided too few facts, suppressed too much crucial information, and thereby damaged official credibility in the eyes of both journalists and the public. But information was more rapidly and fully available in the US than in the SU.

1022. "Runner-ups to Best-Censored Stories." SLJR 17.107 (June 1988) 12-13.
Ten more under-reported issues identified by Project Censored at Sonoma State U: military aid to Honduras while their children starve, loss of life forms (gene pool), US violations of international law, Grenada since the invasion, etc.

1023. Russell, Dick. "The Media and the Environment: Redefining National Security." Extra! 1.8 (May-June 1988) 1, 8-10.
"There is a disturbing lack of attention and expertise being devoted to the environment by the mass media." When attention

THE MEDIA

is paid by the major media it is usually at effects instead of causes.

1024. Said, Edward. Covering Islam: How the Media and the Experts Determine How We See the Rest of the World. London: Routledge, 1981. 186.
An analysis of the inter-connection of institutions in the production and control of knowledge and information, here specifically about the Islamic world. The relationship between the Middle East and the West, particularly the US, is presented in terms of imagery, symbol, and information constructed by governments, corporations, the media, and the academy.

1025. Said, Edward. "Iran." CJR 18.6 (1980) 23-33.
On media bias against Iran and Islam. [Rejoinder by J.C. Hurewitz, CJR 19.1 (1980) 19-21].

1026. Said, Edward. "U.S. Media Portrays Palestinians as 'Terrorists,' not People." Guard 40.6 (Nov. 4, 1987) 19.
Media treat the Middle East as incomprehensible and doomed to disaster, and Palestinian victims as aggressors.

1027. Sale, Kirkpatrick. "Myth as Eternal Truths." MORE 3.6 (1973) 3-5.
Media coverage of the Students for a Democratic Society (SDS) was inaccurate.

1028. Salzman, George. "11:39:12 am EST." SciP 18.2 (1986) 27, 31.
Hyper-coverage of the Challenger shuttle disaster diverts the public from the major problems confronting the world.

1029. Schechter, Daniel. "Media Myopia." MORE 7.12 (Dec. 1977) 26-31.
The economics of apartheid and its US connections have been underreported.

1030. Schiller, Dan. "Transformations of News in the US Information Market." Communicating Politics. Ed. Peter Golding, et al. New York: Holmes and Meier, 1986. 19-36.
Government and big business are increasingly successful in managing images and information. Traditional "news" is disintegrating as new technological developments produce new organizations--e.g. newspaper chains linked into satellites and computer-based data banks. Also, privatization and price of commercialized information plus government limitations on information diminish public debate.

1031. Schwennesen, Don. "The Environmental Beat." MJR 19 (1976) 51-55.
An explanation of the problems of reporting ecological problems and an appeal for more and better coverage.

1032. Seltzer, Curtis. "The Pits: Press Coverage of the Coal Strike." CJR 20.2 (July-Aug. 1981) 67-70.
An example of blindness of journalists to rank-and-file views.

1033. Servan-Schreiber, Jean-Louis. The Power to Inform; Media: The Information Business. New York: McGraw-Hill, 1974. 297.
Shows "how well the Americans have done in some areas and how much room there is for improvement in other areas." In his final chapter, "The Urgent Need for a New Ethic," he projects increased public resistance to media monopoly "subject to no democratic process" and defending "only the interests of whoever owns them": "Access: People now realize that freedom of expression is useless without the means to exercise it" (275).

1034. Shaheen, Jack. "Media Coverage of the Middle East: Perception & Foreign Policy." Annals 482 (Nov. 1985) 160-175.
Describes false media coverage of Arabs.

1035. Shaw, Donald, and Maxwell McCombs. The Emergence of American Political Issues: The Agenda-Setting Function of the Press. St. Paul: West, 1977. 211.
Focuses on the 1972 presidential campaign. "By hypothesizing that there is an 'agenda-setting' function of the press, we have sought to discover what press audiences actually learn, and the conditions under which they learn." The news media not only "guide and direct" but they "structure our cognitions."

1036. "Shuttle to Carry Lethal Plutonium." SLJR 16.102 (May 1988) 13.
"NASA is pursuing plans to launch the Project Galileo shuttle space probe which will carry enough plutonium to kill every person on earth," yet the media have neglected the story, according to Project Censored.

1037. Sibbison, Jim. "Environmental Reporters: Prisoners of Gullibility." WM 16.2 (1984) 26-35.
An explanation of journalists' failure to report environmental and EPA news adequately because of their naive and uncritical acceptance of official sources.

1038. Siebert, Fred S., Theodore Peterson, and Wilbur Schramm. Four Theories of the Press: The Authoritarian, Libertarian, Social Responsibility, and Soviet Communist Concepts of What the Press Should Be and Do. Urbana: Illinois UP, 1956. 153.
"The thesis of this volume is that the press always takes on the form and coloration of the social and political structures within which it operates." Volume is concerned with "the philosophical and political rationales or theories which lie behind the different kinds of press we have in the world today."

1039. Sigal, Leon. Reporters and Officials: The Organization and Politics of Newsmaking. Lexington, MA: Heath, 1973. 221.
Official sources dominate the news by the essentially economic nature of the relations between news sources and reporters in that routine channels are cheaper than interviews or firsthand observation. These routine channels are heavily subsidized by news sources who want to control the availability and interpretation of information about issues.

1040. Skardon, James. "The Apollo Story: The Concealed Patterns." CJR 6.4 (1967) 34-39.
The media failed all along to scrutinize the safety of the Apollo project, which eventuated in the deaths of three astronauts. (See second article CJR 6.3 [1967] 11-15 on weak coverage of the disaster itself.)

1041. Smith, Stephen, and Cherri Roden. "CBS, The New York Times, and Reconstructed Political Reality." SSCJ 53.2 (Winter 1988) 140-158.
Examines coverage of the 1984 national election in the local newscasts of a CBS affiliate owned by the New York Times Company and discovers "a bias in both time of coverage and direction of favorability toward the Reagan-Bush campaign."

1042. Smolla, Rodney. Suing the Press. New York: Oxford UP, 1986. 277.
The proliferation of libel suits, in spite of the Sullivan ruling, has had a chilling effect on the press. The author suggests several remedies.

1043. Smyth, Frank. "El Salvador's Forgotten War." Prog 51.8 (1987) 22-24.
El Salvador is all but forgotten, "despite a resurgence of political violence and new evidence of U.S. complicity in assaults on human rights."

1044. So, Clement Y.K. "The Summit As War: An Analysis of Reporters' Use of Metaphors." Paper Submitted to the Political Communication Division of the 37th ICA Annual Conference in Montreal, 1987. 23.
In reporting the 1985 US-Soviet summit in Geneva, reporters used such metaphors as "war," "business," "game," etc., which contradicted its peaceful purpose.

1045. Solomon, Norman. "Behind the Scenes with the US Press Corps in Moscow." Extra! 1.5 (Dec. 1987) 9.
"Cold War assumptions . . . routinely filter vision, with windows on the world tinted red-white-and-blue. Meanwhile, 'objective' reporting on US-Soviet relations remains an absurd myth."

1046. Spence, Jack. "Second Time Around: How to Cover an Election." CJR 22.6 (1984) 41-43.
Media misrepresented the Salvadoran assembly elections of

March 1982 as a defeat for the left.

1047. Spofford, Tim. Lynch Street: The May 1970 Slayings at Jackson State College. Kent, OH: Kent State UP, 1988. 219.
While the Kent State killings have come to symbolize a generation's protest and sacrifice, few remember Phillip Gibbs and James Green, bystanders killed at Jackson State. The unequal reporting and memory of these deaths derive from a failure to understand the events at Jackson as an anti-war action and from racism.

1048. Stevenson, Robert L., and Donald L. Shaw, eds. Foreign News and the New World Information Order. Ames: Iowa State UP, 1984. 243.
Studies of the image of developing countries projected by news agencies and by news media. Discusses issues, research, patterns, Third World, cultural dependency, structural imperialism, etc.

1049. Stoler, Peter. The War Against the Press: Politics, Pressure and Intimidation in the 80's. New York: Dodd, Mead, 1986. 226.
Examines the widespread attack on the news media by government, the right wing, big business, the Reagan administration, conservative churches, conservative Congressmen, and even the public, and explores why. Exhorts the press to "print the news and raise hell."

1050. "Swept Away." CJR 19.6 (1981) 21.
On the jingoistic reporting of the return of the Iranian Embassy hostages.

1050a. Tasini, Jonathan. "Lost in the Margins: Labor and the Media." Extra! 3.7 (Summer 1990) 2-11.
The takeover by miners of the Pittston Coal mine, "the first major takeover of a plant since the 1937 sitdown strike by autoworkers" at Flint, MI, received a virtual news blackout.

1051. "The Ten Best Censored Stories of 1980." SLJR 7.42 (July 1981) 8-10.
The ten most under-reported stories according to Project Censored were El Salvador, the National Security Agency, censorship of nuclear issues, the Bendectin cover-up, conversion of agricultural lands in Third World countries to cash export crops by transnational firms, dangerous pesticides, nuclear space war plans, tobacco company censorship of magazines, oil company monopoly of solar industries, toxic chemical ruination of water and land. Selection is based upon both minimal press coverage and maximum national or international significance.

1052. "The Ten Best Censored Stories of 1981." SLJR 8.47 (July 1982) 12-13.
News that went largely unnoticed includes the US economic crisis, KKK murders in Greensboro, radioactive waste, world

hunger, water shortages, and the insanity of nuclear weapons.

1053. "The Ten Best Censored Stories of 1982." SLJR 9.52 (June 1983) 8-9.
Cites stories the mainstream press neglected to cover, including fraudulent safety testing, a super-secret intelligence court, the defoliant "Agent White," Central America, Ronald Reagan as censor, American industrialists who traded with the enemy in WWII, and the targeting of Indian lands by toxic waste firms.

1054. "The 10-Best Censored Stories in the U.S.A." SLJR 10.63 (June 1984) 10-15.
For 1983: Israel in Central America, US arms buildup, SU proposals for freezing nuclear weapons and condemning nuclear war, agri program (PIK) disaster, KAL 007, Central America, South Africa, naval nuclear safety, DNA in biological warfare, Pentagon's cost-plus contracting.

1055. "[Ten] Best Censored Stories." SLJR 12.75 (1985) 3.
For 1984: Reagan vs. civil liberties, Nicaragua's fair elections, etc.

1056. "The 10 Best-Censored Stories in the U.S.A." SLJR 13.86 (June 1986) 18-19.
Cites news stories ignored by the media at large in 1985, including genocide in East Timor, military toxic waste, a phony "Star Wars" test, and media merger mania.

1057. "The 10 Best Censored Stories of 1986." SLJR 15.97 (June 1987) 10-11.
Project Censored's ongoing project of identifying significant underreported issues or events. For 1986: FBI investigation of critics of Reagan, government censorship, FBI invasion of privacy, CIA-paid pro-Contra reporting, Reagan's approval of the far-right World Anti-Communist League, nerve gas production in residential areas, Contragate and Costa Rica, radiation experiments on humans, VA destroying evidence, plutonium fuel for space shuttle. (A second level of ten more underreported stories is also given by PC.)

1058. "The 10 Best Censored Stories of 1987." SLJR 17.106 (May 1988) 5, 12.
The most overlooked stories of 1987, marking the 12th anniversary of Project Censored at Sonoma State University: the information monopoly, US contra-drugs connection, danger of worldwide nuclear accidents, Reagan's mania for secrecy, Bush's role in Iran arms deal, biowarfare research increase, biased coverage of Arias peace plan, wastes dumped on Third World, space shuttle carrying plutonium, systematic torture in El Salvador.

1059. "The 10 Best-Censored Stories of 1988." SLJR 19.115 (May 1989) 10-11, 19.
News the media chose to ignore includes George Bush's "dirty

secrets," the risk of a nuclear disaster involving the space probe Galileo, irradiation of food, the effects of acid rain, a secret club which links most major police forces, and the growing likelihood of a new constitutional convention.

1060. "The 10 Top Under-Reported News Stories of 1989." SLJR 20.127 (June 1990) 8, 20.
Project Censored continues its exposure of the failure of the media to report significant subjects adequately. For 1989 it identified the growing threat of a handful of monopolistic global media lords, international toxic waste dumping in Africa, US support of holocaust in Mozambique, US deceitful war on drugs, Guatemalan repression on US hands, radioactive waste, etc.

1061. Terrell, Robert L. "Mass Media Collaboration Invites Public Condemnation." SLJR 20.127 (June 1990) 18-19.
"The mainstream news media in the U.S. are just as much a part of a system of elite domination as were the news media of Eastern Europe."

1062. Thompson, Betty. "'Pro-active' Press Relations Can't Change Deep Bias." C&C 44 (Nov. 26, 1984) 452-4.
Criticizes the prejudice newsmen project against clergymen visiting the Soviet Union for peace and reconciliation.

1063. Thompson, David C. "The Coverage of Canada in the U.S. News Media: A Study of 'Inadequacy.'" Carl JR, Spec. Ed. (Summer 1978) 1-24.
Covers wire services, WSJ, NYT, B Sun, CSM, MH, WP, LAT, SLP-D, Louisville Courier-Journal, and broadcasting. Conclusion: "The American public receives a rather poor quality of Canadian news coverage." More correspondents should be assigned to Canadian affairs, etc.

1064. Tismaneanu, Vladimir. "Civil Society: An Idea That Became a Story." Deadline 4.5 (Nov.-Dec. 1989) 9-12.
US coverage made liberations in eastern Europe seem sudden and inexplicable, when they resulted from a long struggle for a "civil society" by opposition activists.

1064a. Todd, Russell G. "Wasted Words? News Releases & the Making of Washington News." Stanford U, 1982. 169. DAI 43.8 (Feb. 1983) 2480-A.
Study of news releases received by Newsweek, LAT, and ABC World News concludes that media "do not rely on releases for individual stories" but releases and stories resemble each other in topics, sources, and structure. "The similarity in release and news flows probably stems from information and frames of reference shared among Washington journalists and sources."

1065. Traska, Maria. "Health is Sick." ChJR 7.7 & 8 (1974) 12-14.
Criticizes journalists for failing to report the efforts by

THE MEDIA

the Nixon administration to undermine the mental-health profession and system.

1066. Tuchman, Gaye. "The Exception Proves the Rule: The Study of Routine News Practices in the United States." Press Control Around the World. Ed. Jane L. Curry and Joan Dassin. New York: Praeger, 1982. 3-26.
The "suppression of information is built into the very organization of the news media" in the US--"the marriage, sometimes harmonious, sometimes embattled, between the news media and the centralized and legitimated institutions upon which reporters and editors rely for information and 'facts.' By discussing 'exceptions'--occasions when newsworkers depart from organizational and professional routines--it explores the general rules through which newsworkers frame their stories to uphold the dominant hegemony" (3-4).

1067. Tuchman, Gaye. Making News: A Study in the Construction of Reality. New York: Free, 1978. 244.
Ten chapters on "News as Frame," "Representation and the News Narrative," "The Topic of the Women's Movement," "News as a Constructed Reality," etc. A study of "the social construction of reality," the "structure of news," "how newsworkers decide what news is, why they cover some items but not others, and how they decide what I and others want to know." Since "the quality of civic debate necessarily depends on the information available," it is essential to know how "the news media set the frame in which citizens discuss public events" (ix).

1068. Tuchman, Gaye. "Objectivity as Strategic Ritual: An Examination of Newsmen's Notions of Objectivity." AJS 77.4 (1972) 660-79.
Journalists employ certain procedures or rituals to protect themselves from the risks of the trade, especially criticism.

1069. Varela, Carlos. "Uruguay's Referendum on Human Rights." Extra! 2.7/8 (Summer 1989) 14-15.
A national referendum in Uruguay to block a law giving immunity to human rights violators was poorly reported in the US; "coverage was often uninformed and, in some cases, blatantly misleading."

1069a. Warren, James. "Except for One Day a Year, Workers Get Short Shrift from the Media." CT (Sept. 2, 1990) 1, 4.
The working class are extremely underreported by the major newspapers and the networks.

1070. Watney, Simon. Policing Desire: Pornography, Aids, and the Media. Minneapolis: U of Minnesota P, 1987. 159.
The primary goal of AIDS reporting has not been educational, informational, nor even merely sensational, but is the current means of policing desire, of controlling unacceptable sexuality, and ultimately of stopping gay sex. Chapter 6, "Aids and the Press"; Chapter 6, "Aids on Television."

1071. Weaver, David, and G. Cleveland Wilhoit. The American Journalist: A Portrait of U.S. News People and Their Work. Bloomington: Indiana UP, 1986. 216.
A study based upon interviews during 1982-83, partly replicating the 1971 study by Johnstone, et al., The News People. Some conclusions: women journalists increased between 1971 and 1983; black, Hispanic, and Jewish journalists decreased; fewer journalists claimed to be left-of-center in 1982-3; more claimed to be centrist.

1072. Weingartner, Charles. "What Do We Know?" Beyond Nineteen Eighty-Four. Ed. William Lutz. Urbana, IL: NCTE, 1989. 29-45.
Generally judgment in the US rests upon misinformation, disinformation, semi-information and anti-information.

1073. Weiss, Carol. "What America's Leaders Read." POQ 38 (Spring 1974) 1-22.
"Major newspapers, news magazines, other general and specialized periodicals, and a few television newsmen provide inputs for top level debate and negotiation that America's leaders view as important in the resolution of national policy issues" (21). [Cited by Gandy as "powerful evidence of the subsidized news media's role in setting the agendas" of other public policy regulators.]

1074. Weiss, Philip. "Party Time in Atlanta." CJR 27.3 (Sept.-Oct. 1988) 27-34.
The Democratic Convention of 1988 demonstrated that "the more reporters are in a pack the greater the pack's attraction and the less inclined any individual is to go off on his or her own" (29). The Convention produced generally "stifled discourse and engineered unity" in a "celebratory" mood.

1075. Weschler, Lawrence. "The Media's One and Only Freedom Story." CJR 28.6 (Mar.-Apr. 1990) 25-31.
The media devoted tremendous attention to the liberations in eastern Europe, but paid little attention to similar events in Latin America, and the media referred constantly to SU interventions in their satellites but said nothing about US interventions in their client states.

1076. Whitaker, Brian. News Ltd: Why You Can't Read All About It. London: Minority Press Group, 1981. 176.
The value of the alternative press is its exposure of nationalistic, ethnocentric, class, racial, and gender assumptions which "colour the way all news is selected, written up and presented," in contrast to the established and particularly the popular press, "whose hallmarks are complacency, servility, triviality and the avoidance of controversial issues" (Preface).

1077. White, Edward M. "The Dangers of Singlespeak." Beyond Nineteen Eighty-Four. Ed. William Lutz. Urbana, IL: NCTE, 1989. 47-53.

THE MEDIA

Simpleminded ideas and language are as pernicious as doublespeak: patriotism, Sovietphobia (and all bigotries), etc.

1078. Wicker, Tom. On Press. New York: Viking, 1978. 271.
"The overwhelming conclusion I have drawn from my life in journalism . . . is that the American press . . . is not often 'robust and uninhibited' but is usually timid and anxious--for respectability at least as much as for profitability." The press is a little more challenging toward the government than it was in the 1950s, but it is still uncritical of business. He urges the press "to shake off the encumbrance of a falsely objective journalism and to take an adversary position toward the most powerful institutions of American life" (259).

1079. Wien, Barbara. "News and Numbers: Do They Measure Human Costs?" M&V 47 (Summer 1987) 8-9.
While economic trends affect us all, the public interest is poorly served by analysis of economic matters in the mass media, "where we never learn the fundamental causes and human impact of certain policy choices."

1080. Wilkins, Lee, and Philip Patterson. "Risk Analysis and the Construction of News." JoC 37.3 (Summer 1987) 80-92.
The news media "commit fundamental errors of attribution in their coverage of risk situations, by treating them as novelties, failing to analyze the entire system, and using insufficiently analytical language."

1081. Williams, Juan. "Simmering Anger at the White Press: A Black Reporter Tells Why." WJR 9.2 (Mar. 1987) 48-50.
Criticizes the "overwhelming trend in the American press today to stereotype black people negatively."

1082. Wills, Garry. "The Greatest Story Ever Told." CJR 18.5 (1980) 25-33.
During the Pope's visit to the US in October 1979, the press treated him uncritically and at times even with adulation and turned him into both "Santa Claus" and "Dr. Feelgood."

1083. Wolf, Louis. "Inaccuracy in Media: Accuracy in Media Rewrites the News and History." Freedom at Risk: Secrecy, Censorship, and Repression in the 1980s. Ed. Richard O. Curry. Philadelphia, PA: Temple UP, 1988. 355-377.
A history and analysis of the right-wing media organization Accuracy in Media.

1084. "World Forum: The U.S. Decision to Withdraw from UNESCO." JoC 34.4 (1984) 81-179.
While most US media organizations and allied countries favor the decision, most scholars are troubled by it. The symposium reflects the divergent views.

1085. "Wrong on Wright and Nicaragua." Extra! 2.2 (Sept.-Oct. 1988) 3.
Examples of media misinformation about Nicaragua.

1086. Wurst, Jim. "What the U.S. Media Failed to Mention About Namibia." ITT 13.24 (May 10-16, 1989) 10.
US reports of violation of the U.N. ceasefire in Namibia by SWAPO guerrillas were based on false information from the South African government, the true aggressor.

1087. Zogby, James. "Jewish Souls Arab Bones." PR 2 (Summer 1988) 15, 18-20.
"American media coverage of the Middle East is saturated with bias against Arabs."

II. A. 3. CORPORATIONS (1088-1214)

1088. Acosta, Leonarda. "Mass Media and Imperialist Ideology." Communication and Class Struggle: I. Capitalism, Imperialism. Ed. Armand Mattelart and Seth Siegelaub. New York: International, 1979. 141-58.
The mass media and their product, "mass-culture," function "as an ideological-industrial complex devoted to the justification and perpetuation of the capitalist system, and in particular, the North American financial-political-military complex that constitutes the core of yankee imperialism."

1089. Aufderheide, Pat. "If You Can't Beat Em . . . Buy 'Em." ITT 12.12 (Feb. 17-23, 1988) 21.
The entertainment oligopoly is now advancing vertically by purchase of theaters.

1090. Aufderheide, Pat. "Time Warner: Less Is More of the Same." ITT 13.18 (Mar. 29-Apr. 14, 1989) 19-20.
The merger of Time and Warner creates "the largest media and entertainment organization in the world." Time Warner "will have immense power to set the nation's agenda, and to influence the political and economic structures that shape it."

1091. Bagdikian, Ben. "The Empire Strikes." M&V 47 (Summer 1989) 4-6.
Summarizes the accelerating concentration of media ownership in recent years, a trend poorly reported by the media.

1092. Bagdikian, Ben. "Giant Owners, Small Ideas." World 2.5 (Sep.-Oct. 1988) 10, 57-58.
The concentrated ownership of the news media allows the perpetuation of a world-vision flawed by acceptance of the Cold War as right, of conservatism as morally superior to liberalism, and of the "automatic virtue of unfettered 'free enterprise.'"

1093. Bagdikian, Ben. "The Lords of the Global Village." Na 248.23 (June 12, 1989) 805-820.

THE MEDIA

Provides a briefing on the accelerating trend of media concentration, summarizing the activities and holdings of the five largest media conglomerates and revealing how much of the media "global village" is controlled by how few.

1094. Bagdikian, Ben. The Media Monopoly. 2nd Ed. Boston: Beacon, 1987. 274.
The growing monopoly concentration of media and the collapse of the traditional wall between the business and editorial departments is undermining the media's role as a watchdog for the public's interests against the interests of the corporations which own the media. The pace has continued so fast that 29 corporations now control most major media businesses, compared with 50 five years ago, a situation which motivated this second edition. "The antidemocratic potential of this emerging corporate control is a black hole in the mainstream media universe. . . . What the public learns is heavily weighted by what serves the economic and political interests of the corporations that own the media" (x).

1095. Bartimole, Roldo. "A Case Against Cleveland's News Media." PoV 11.17 (Mar. 17, 1979) 1-6.
The Cleveland media are being used by corporate interests to destroy the Kucinich administration.

1096. Bartimole, Roldo. "CEI Hosts 100 Reporters/Editors for Brunch, Drinks, Browns Game." PoV 10.8 (Nov. 12, 1977) 1-2.
The Cleveland Electric Illuminating Co. "spends lots of money and time catering to the needs of the news media"; "bribes are usually offered to people you expect will take."

1097. Bartimole, Roldo. "Press, WEWS-TV Treat Jim Carney Well, But Then They're Business Associates." PoV 4.2 (July 26-31, 1971) 1-2.
Cleveland Press and Channel 5 are Scripps-Howard operations, and mayoral candidate Carney is an associate with their officers in conflict of interest.

1098. Bartimole, Roldo. "Sohio: Buying Favor." PoV 13.12 (Jan. 10, 1981) 1-2.
Standard Oil of Ohio paid a high honorarium to three Cleveland news editors for a one-day seminar.

1099. Baxter, Richard. "Executives' Media Paranoia: Differences in the Selective Perceptions of Media Messages Exhibited by Business Leaders, Education Leaders & Other Elites." U of Tennessee, 1986. 178. DAI 47 (1987) 3601-A.
Business executives rated business news as "significantly more negative" than non-business news and "significantly more negative" than did non-business elites. Explains the pressure on media for favorable stories about business.

1100. Bellant, Russ. The Coors Connection: How Coors Family

Philanthropy Undermines Democratic Pluralism. Cambridge, MA: Political Research Associates, 1989. 96.
The Joseph Coors beer family has bankrolled a right-wing agenda of union-busting, sexism, racism, covert operations, and right-wing think tanks and media.

1100a. Bermann, Karl. "Filtering Out Health Issues." ITT 14.25 (May 16-22, 1990) 19.
An exhibition on "Smoke Signals: Cigarettes, Advertising, and the American Way of Life" at Richmond's Valentine Museum barely mentions tobacco's epidemic lethality. Philip Morris is "a regular donor to the Valentine," and is the city's "largest private employer."

1101. Bertrand, Claude-Jean. "Commercialism and U.S. Media Ethics." SLJR 16.105 (Apr. 1988) 8.
"Media ethics, thus, is always a reflection of the ethics of corporate leadership."

1102. Bishop, Ed. "More Business, Less News." SLJR 19.120 (Oct. 1989) 11.
Explains the negative effects of media concentration.

1103. Blumberg, Nathaniel. "The Media and Montana." MJR 21 (1978-79) 2-9.
During the author's 30 years of press analysis (he was Dean of the Montana School of Journalism 1956-1968), "the daily press and newsmagazines reflected essentially the views of the wealthy and the powerful--the corporations and the government," a one-party press committed to the status-quo of profit, basic issues and deepest problems unexamined, institutions "rarely investigated," etc.

1104. Brenkman, John. "Mass Media: From Collective Experience to the Culture of Privatization." ST 1 (Winter 1979) 95-108.
Wealth and corporations dominate the discourses and images that "regulate social life." Calls for resistance.

1105. Bringing GE to Light: How General Electric Shapes Nuclear Weapons Policies for Profits. Compiled by Infact. Philadelphia, PA: New Society, 1990. 146.
Several sections on aspects of GE public relations: "Behind GE's Public Relations" (its crimes), ch. 1-6 of Part III on GE's government and business connections, ch. 8 "Creating the Climate" on GE's participation in exaggerating the Soviet threat for its own profits and the continuation of a permanent war economy, ch. 9 "PACs and Honoraria--Pay for Access," etc.

1106. Brown, Les. "Reagan and the Unseen Network." Ch 1.4 (1981) 17-18.
The lengthening of broadcast license terms (decreasing accountability) was poorly reported.

1107. Burd, Gene. "The Civic Superlative: 'We're Number

THE MEDIA

One.'" TCJR 1.2 (Apr.-May 1972) 3-5, 24-25, 32.
"Analysis of the needs, effects and aesthetics of growth often takes a back-seat to applause of growth itself" by the media.

1108. Carey, Alex. "Reshaping the Truth: Pragmatists and Propagandists in America." Meanjin Quarterly (Aus.) 35.4 (1976) 370-378.
Asserts the "corruption of American democratic ideals and American power" and suggests how "it might be remediable."

1109. Carmo, Alberto. "International Telephone and Telegraph--A Gigantic Multinational Octopus." DJ 9 (1973) 15-18.
ITT's global power.

1110. Cirino, Robert. Don't Blame the People. New York: Random House, 1971. 339.
Twenty-two chapters illustrate and analyze unequal access to media regarding hunger, auto safety, smoking, over-population, etc. The wealthy, privileged, and powerful in and out of government dominate media and determine terms and boundaries of discussion.

1111. Cockburn, Alexander. "Murdoch's Long Shadow." Corruptions of Empire. London: Verso, 1987. 392-93.
Rupert Murdoch's expanding media empire is only a blatant manifestation of the rapidly advancing conglomeration in the US.

1112. Compaine, Benjamin, et al. Who Owns the Media? Concentration of Ownership in the Mass Communications Industry. 2nd ed. White Plains, NY: Knowledge, 1982. 529.
Chapters on newspapers, book publishing, magazines, theatrical film, television and radio broadcasting, cable and pay TV.

1113. Cowan, Paul. "Slicking Over the Oil Industry." MORE 1.1 (1971) 7.
Media fail to convey the scope and power of the industry.

1114. Craig, John R. "Federal Communications Commission v. National Citizens Committee for Broadcasting: The Courts Act on Crossownership." U of Missouri-Columbia, 1981. 155. DAI 43 (1982) 1736-A.
Traces the history of newspaper-broadcasting crossownership and FCC and the courts' opposition to crossownership.

1115. Crespi, Irving. "Polls as Journalism." POQ 4 (1980) 462-476.
Media corporations control public opinion polls.

1116. Douglas, Susan, and T.R. Durham. "Megamerger Makes Philip Morris a Krafty Monster in the Food Chain." ITT 13.3 (Nov. 16-22, 1988) 24.

The effort of Philip Morris Companies, Inc. to buy Kraft (Velveeta, Miracle Whip) for $13.5 billion has been badly reported.

1117. Dreier, Peter. "Capitalists vs. the Media: An Analysis of an Ideological Mobilization Among Business Leaders." MCS 4 (1982) 111-132.
Describes the efforts of big business to control the media and the resistance by the media.

1118. Dreier, Peter. "The Corporate Complaint Against the Media." American Media & Mass Culture. Ed. Donald Lazere. Berkeley: U of California P, 1987. 64-80.
On the "ultimate PR campaign" by business interests--"to persuade the public" that the media have "a leftist bias" (31). [See Lazere.]

1119. Dubro, Alec. "Media Monopoly." Z 1.4 (Apr. 1988) 44-45.
On the growing powers of the media barons and the need to organize resistance.

1120. Duckworth, Michael, et al. "The Bottom Line From the Top Down." CJR 29.2 (July-Aug. 1990) 30-32.
Data about the top media corporations: income, executive pay, minorities, etc. These conglomerates are run "predominantly by white, middle-aged, highly paid men, most of whom are from a business background--in short, companies not distinguishable . . . from the rest of corporate America."

1121. Ernst, Morris L. The First Freedom. New York: Macmillan, 1946. 316.
On the subversion of media freedom by the "cartelization of press, radio and movies."

1122. Eversole, Pam. "Concentration of Ownership in the Communications Industry." JQ 48 (1971) 251-60.
The steadily increasing monopoly of electronic media, especially when linked to the military, poses a threat to freedom.

1123. Ewen, Stuart. "The Bribe of Frankenstein." JoC 29.4 (1979) 12-19.
"The mass media, through the production and distribution of imagery, have reconciled widespread demands for a better life with the general priorities of corporate America."

1124. Foley, Joseph. "The Information Society: A New Threat to Freedom of Speech." FSY 1984. Ed. Henry Ewbank. Annandale, VA: Speech Communication Assoc. 51-57.
"As the generation and sale of information comes to be the dominant activity in the US economy, the very foundations of the ideal of a free flow of information are challenged."

1125. Franck, Peter. "First Amendment, Friend or Foe?" PR 3 (Winter 1988) 25-27.
The First Amendment is increasingly used as a shield to

protect corporate media interests. Some distinction must be made between the rights of individuals and the rights of enormous organizations.

1126. Friedman, Marilyn, and Larry May. "Corporate Rights to Free Speech." BPEJ 5.3 & 4 (1986) 5-22.
Disputes the Supreme Court's decision equating corporate speech with individual speech, stressing the distinction between the purpose and effect of the two kinds of speech, and pointing out that individual expression may suffer when corporate expression is given the same protection.

1127. Gandy, Oscar, Jr. "Information in Health: Subsidized News." MCS 2 (Apr. 1980) 103-115.
Presents the power of the health lobby in determining policy by influencing reporting.

1128. Gandy, Oscar, Jr. "The Political Economy of Communications Competence." The Political Economy of Information. Ed. Vincent Mosco and Janet Wasko. Madison: U of Wisconsin P, 1988. 108-124.
A "substantial and growing disparity in communications competence" is endangering democracy. The poor, especially among black and ethnic minority groups, are largely unable to utilize information resources to improve the quality of their lives." But as the "poor are losing ground," the rich, "the information elites find their competence enhanced at every turn" (109).

1129. Graber, Doris. "Media Giants." SLJR 8 (1982) 13-14.
Analyzes the trend toward concentration and uniformity and recommends several corrections.

1130. Harrington, Michael. "To the Disney Station." Harper's 258.1544 (Jan. 1979) 35-44, 86.
Disney World "embodies the current dream of American business" to solve problems and pursue profit free of government regulation.

1131. Herman, Edward. "Deepening Market (5): The Privatization of Government." Z 3.7/8 (July-Aug. 1990) 58-59.
Analyzes mainstream media treatment of the present "business regime."

1132. Herman, Edward. "Information Flow Threatened by Giant Merger." Guard 41.44 (Sept. 13, 1989) 11.
Explains why the merger of Time, Inc., and Warner Communications has "dealt a sharp blow to political democracy and cultural diversity in the U.S. and abroad."

1133. Hill, Andrew. "Rules of the News Gatekeepers: One American Equals Ten Others." Pr 8 (1980) 11-12.
The mass media provide distorted perceptions of what occurs particularly in international events.

1134. Hochberg, Lee. "Environmental Reporting in Boomtown
Houston." CJR 19.1 (1980) 71-74.
Houston media's pro-industry bias.

1134a. Hoffman, Nicholas von. "Nine Justices for Seven Dirty
Words." MORE 8.6 (June 1978) 12-15.
The author suggests that the mass media either choose incorporation and the regulation corporate status properly entails, or go private and enjoy none of the privileges of a corporation but have the rights of a citizen, including free speech.

1135. Hoyt, Michael. "Downtime for Labor." CJR 22.6 (1984) 36-40.
Labor reporting declining in quantity and quality.

1135a. Huebner, Albert. "The Worldwide Struggle Over Information." BSR 34 (1980) 59-62.
"Information is one of the world's most precious resources, and multinational corporations control it."

1136. "The Information Monopoly." SLJR 16.106 (May 1988) 5.
One of the most neglected stories of 1987 according to Project Censored--the rapidly increasing centralization and interlocking of media ownership.

1137. Joffe, Phyllis. "How Much Media Clout for One Company?" Ch 4 (1985) 14-15.
Dangers of media monopoly.

1138. Johnson, Nicholas. "The Media Barons and the Public
Interest: An FCC Commissioner's Warning." AM 221.6
(1968) 43-51.
Warns against media monopoly.

1138a. Kaplan, Sheila. "The Powers That Be Lobbying." WM
20.11 (Dec. 1988) 36-46.
The media lobby--broadcasters and publishers--is one of the most powerful. It lobbies mainly for its profit, not for the First Amendment, and it seldom reports on or investigates these lobbies. For example, the American Newspaper Publishers Assoc. (ANPA) helped defeat a proposal in Congress to ban cigarette ads in newspapers and magazines, and few newspapers covered the controversy.

1139. Kaufman, Richard F. "Letting the Justice Department
Off the Hook . . . Again." Deadline 3.6 (Nov.-Dec.
1988) 1-2, 9-10.
"Journalists covering the current round of procurement fraud once again failed to focus on the two key aspects of the scandal: the persistence of criminality in defense contracting and the inability of the legal system to competently prosecute those charged with breaking the law."

1140. Klotzer, Charles. "Here." SLJR 19.115 (Apr. 1989) 2.
The International Federation of Journalists at their recent

meeting in Sydney, Aus., approved the "Sydney Declaration," which condemned concentration of ownership and "the influence of corporate objectives over the presentation of news," and warned of "the danger of self-censorship" and the threat to diversity of information sources resulting from monopoly. In contrast, the "Code of Ethics" of the US Society of Professional Journalists (SPJ) is person-centered, with "absolutely nothing to say about business practices, media conglomerates, the concentration of ownership, and the decline in diversity of views. The 'Code,' updated in 1987, is frightfully outdated." [Klotzer is the editor of SLJR. Following his article he prints the full texts of both the "Sydney Declaration" and the "Code."]

1141. Kopkind, Andrew. "The Unwritten Watergate Story." MORE 4.11 (Nov. 1974) 5-6, 26.
Corporate involvement in Watergate was underreported.

1142. Kurtz, Howard. "Dr. Whelan's Media Operation." CJR 28.6 (Mar.-Apr. 1990) 43-47.
Corporate influence over science and health news via the corporate funded American Council on Science and Health.

1142a. Lange, David L., Robert K. Baker, and Sandra J. Ball. Mass Media and Violence: A Report to the National Commission on the Causes and Prevention of Violence. Vol. 11. Washington, DC: US Government Printing Office, 1969. 614.
The media "have shown an appalling lack of concern about the effects of particular media practices" and about how "they might do better." Control over the broadcasting system by only a few corporations is unacceptable in a society which values free expression. "If the ultimate in concentration of media control ever arrives, there is no reason to believe that government control would not be better. At least the government is apt to be more responsive than a self-perpetuating corporate management with such tremendous power. Today we are moving in that direction and one thing seems clear: the policies of the First Amendment can no longer be secured simply by keeping the government out" (vi). Part I an overview of the First Amendment and the media; Part II the news media; Part III TV entertainment.

1143. Laski, Harold. The American Democracy. New York: Viking, 1948. 785.
Chapter XIII, "Press, Cinema, and Radio in America": the purpose of these media "is not the communication of truth, but the making of profit; and the truth it can afford is rarely the whole truth, but so much of it as is compatible with profit-making" (617).

1144. Leapman, Michael. Arrogant Aussie. The Rupert Murdoch Story. Secaucus, NJ: Lyle Stuart, 1985. 288.
Details the media mogul's rise to power, his acquisitions of major news sources, and the resultant effects upon

journalistic quality.

1145. Lenski, Gerhard. Power and Privilege. New York: McGraw-Hill, 1966. 495.
"The schools and the mass media are dominated by the propertied, entrepreneurial and managerial classes, and while they permit a certain amount of criticism to be reported there, in the main these institutions are supportive of the system" (421).

1146. Lerbinger, Otto. "Corporate-Media Relations." Big Business and the Mass Media. Lexington, MA: Lexington, 1977. 63-95.
Exhorts both business and media to become "more open organizations" in their efforts to define media content.

1147. Levin, Jack. Power Ethics: An Analysis of the Activities of the Public Utilities in the United States. New York: Knopf, 1931. 191.
A digest of the twenty-six volumes of the FTC investigation of the electrical utilities, most of the contents dealing with efforts to control public opinion. Chapter 3 "Machinery of the Utility-Information Committees," 4 "The Publicity Director," 7-11 on "Private-Utility Propaganda," 12-14 "The Press," 19 "The Costs of Propaganda" ("The Consumer Pays").

1148. Lindstrom, Duane. "Concentration Is the Name of the Media's Game." ChJR 4.12 (1971) 3-6, 15.
Monopoly in Chicago.

1149. "Lords of the Air." Na 240.12 (1985) 355-6.
Increasing concentration of communications corporations: purchase of ABC by Capital Cities.

1150. Lynch, Roberta. "The Media Distort the Value of Labor Unions." ITT (July 15-28, 1981) 17.
"Media coverage of trade union activities is restricted to superficial reports of major national strikes."

1151. MacDougall, A. Kent. "A Business Problem: Bull Market in Bad News." WJR 2.6 (1980) 32-3.
Corporate strategies seek favorable media images.

1152. MacDougall, A. Kent. Ninety Seconds to Tell It All: Big Business and the News Media. Homewood, IL: Dow Jones, 1981. 154.
Generally makes the case that business and capitalism are treated favorably by the capitalist media. For example, Ch. 5 explains how weak was reporting of nuclear power until Three Mile Island; 6 describes the failure to investigate and expose corporate finances; 7 similar on corporate-caused environmental hazards; 8 on corporate PR as free advertising; etc.

1153. Mackenzie, Angus. "Drivin' in the Dark: The Lights Go Out on Product Safety." NaR 10.2 (1987) 3-4.

Corporate opposition to the release of data they submit to regulatory agencies on corporate mistakes.

1154. "The Media Business." UAW Ammo 25.8 (Nov. 1987) 1-32.
Described as "A Worker's Guide to the Media," questions whether the media represent the public interest as they claim. This number "looks behind the media business to examine its role in mass marketing, its increasing integration into the corporate world, and how its values have been shaped by commercial needs."

1155. Meehan, Eileen R. "Towards a Third Vision of an Information Society." MCS 6 (1984) 257-271.
A pessimistic forecast of "continued concentration, integration, and commoditization" of information.

1156. Miller, Arthur S. "On Politics, Democracy and the First Amendment: A Commentary on First National Bank v. Bellotti." WLLR 38.1 (1981) 21-41.
The implications of First National Bank v. Bellotti are that a majority of the Justices wish to protect their own social class. They are mainly interested in ensuring that the rich are able to maintain their status, political power and wealth.

1157. "The Mintz Legacy." IREJ 12.3 (Summer 1989) 20-22.
Offers excerpts from the works of investigative journalist Morton Mintz dealing with the nature of corporate crime and the media's failure to address it.

1158. Moody, Kim. "Campaign '88: A Clash of 'Economic Miracles.'" Extra! 1.8 (May-June 1988) 3.
On media failure to investigate and report the harm caused by Reaganomics.

1159. Mosco, Vincent. "Who Makes U.S. Government Policy in World Communications?" JoC 29.1 (1979) 158-64.
Fragmentation among government agencies--FCC, DOD, NTIA, ICA--strengthens the already large role of private industry--AT&T, ITT, RCA, WUI, COMSAT.

1160. Mosco, Vincent, and Janet Wasko, eds. The Critical Communications Review, Vol. 1: Labor, the Working Class, and the Media. Norwood, NJ: Ablex, 1983. 312.
The volumes in the series "challenge an established perspective in communications research" and "promote the transformation of the system by indicating how critical research can critique the system." This volume challenges the established approach to the criticism "of the media's representation of labor and the working class" and promotes change.

1161. Nichols, Dana M. "Striking Blows Against the Empire." MedF 10.4 (Aug.-Sept. 1989) 5.
Describes "the war America's largest newspaper chain [Gannett] is waging against labor unions."

1162. Ogden, Don. "Dollars Swamp Antinuke Voters." Guard 41.9 (Nov. 23, 1988) 6.
The utility companies of Massachusetts outspent opponents of nuclear energy 21-1 ($8.3 million to $400,000) to persuade voters to vote against a proposition that would have shut down the state's two nuclear reactors.

1163. Ohmann, Richard. "On Teaching About Mass Culture." Politics of Culture. Middletown, CT: Wesleyan UP, 1987. 205-211.
Advocates teaching mass culture, the "culture produced by a few for many, through which the few try to turn the many into masses, the more easily to sell us to advertisers and sell commodities and the American way to us."

1164. Parenti, Michael. "Does the U.S. Have a Free Press?" Wit 68 (Mar. 1985) 12-14.
The author claims the US does not have a "free and independent press" because of the extreme concentration of ownership of the media and because the media are corporations themselves. He suggests four remedies, including supporting alternative media.

1165. Parker, Richard. "Press Fiddles While Drivers Burn." CJR 18.2 (1979) 8, 13-14.
Impediments to reporting on oil shortage.

1166. Patton, William, and Randall Bartlett. "Corporate 'Persons' and Freedom of Speech: The Political Impact of Legal Mythology." WLR 1981 (1981) 494-512.
"What the Supreme Court did" in First National Bank of Boston v. Bellotti "was to preserve and protect a state-created amplification system [corporations], available only to a relatively few, which can effectively drown out the speech of other natural persons" (511).

1167. Pauly, John J. "Rupert Murdoch and the Demonology of Professional Journalism." Sage Annual Reviews of Communication Research. Newbury Park, CA: Sage, 1988. 246-261.
Maintains that the American press villainizes media mogul Rupert Murdoch not because of his economic and political power, but because he threatens their cherished myths: the imaginary line between news and entertainment, the supposed independence of editors, and the idea that the large newspapers represent and address the concerns of everyone.

1168. Phillips, Kevin. "Busting the Media Trusts." Har 255 (July 1977) 23-34.
Attacks media monopoly, advocates competition and diversity.

1169. Picard, Robert. The Press and the Decline of Democracy: The Democratic Socialist Response in Public Policy. Westport, CT: Greenwood, 1985. 173.
A critique of the impact on the media of concentrations of

THE MEDIA

economic power from the perspective of economic democracy. He encourages journalists to be aware and wary of the dominance of corporations over an industry which ideally values independence and is needed in a democracy for its independence. Democracy has declined because public participation in democratic decision making has been eroded by an elite economic control of the media and a journalistic profession in which "business" receives first priority. As remedy of the control of the marketplace of ideas by undemocratic economic activities, he advocates various interventions practiced in Western Europe.

1170. Picard, Robert. "State Intervention in Press Economics in Advanced Western Democratic Nations." U of Missouri, 1983. 194. DAI 44.10 (Apr. 1984) 2916-A.
Commercialization of the marketplace, concentration of ownership, and newspaper mortality have "reduced the outlets for diverse opinion that are required for the marketplace of ideas to operate freely" and have thereby reduced "effective popular democracy." Economic control of the marketplace is as devastating to press freedom as government control of the marketplace.

1171. "The Pinto Story: the Press in Low Gear." CJR 17.1 (1978) 24-25.
Weak reporting of Ford Motor Company's negligence.

1172. Pollock, Richard. "Is the Nuclear Industry Silencing the Press?" CMJ 3.4 (1977) 1,8.
How the Atomic Industry Forum pressures the media.

1173. Pollak, Richard. "Time + Dallas = ?" Na 248.12 (Mar. 27, 1989) 401.
Media coverage of the merger between Time Inc. and Warner Communications was notable for its celebration of the "big deal" and its lack of discussion of the impact such concentration has on media diversity and the national welfare.

1174. Porter, William. "The Media Baronies: Bigger, Fewer, More Powerful." What's News: The Media in American Society. Ed. Elie Abel. San Francisco, CA: Inst. for Contemporary Studies, 1981. 97-115.
On the dangers of the growing consolidation of media.

1175. Powell, Walter. "The Blockbuster Decades: The Media as Big Business." American Media & Mass Culture. Ed. Donald Lazere. Berkeley: U of California P, 1987. 53-63. (WP 7.2 [July-Aug. 1979] 26-36).
Delineates "the immense acceleration into the 1980s of corporate conglomeration and oligopoly in every phase of the culture industry" (30).

1176. Proceedings of the Symposium on Media Concentration, Dec. 14 and 15, 1978. 2 vols. Bureau of Competition, Federal Trade Comm. Washington, DC: GPO, n.d. 761.

Studies the impact of concentration on information flow, the First Amendment, competition, TV, newspapers, book publishing, and anti-trust policy.

1177. Raymond, Chris. "Whose Health and Welfare?" SciP 16.2 (1984) 24-29.
The mainstream media help maintain an unhealthy and unsafe nation by "failing to question" the corporate system that creates occupational hazards.

1178. Read, William H. America's Mass Media Merchants. Baltimore: Johns Hopkins UP, 1976. 209.
"Just as other U.S. institutions have thoroughly established themselves in foreign countries--prominent among them being the armed forces, multi-national corporations and banks--so too have the American print and visual industries. . . . So pervasive is the foreign dissemination of American commercial mass media that if one word must be chosen to describe this phenomenon it is, inescapably, ubiquitous" (1 & 3). The author focuses upon eight print media and two visual: AP, UPI, NYTNS, WP-LATNS; Time, Newsweek, Reader's Digest; motion pictures, telefilms. Read supports the economic and cultural expansion he details.

1179. Real, Michael. "The Disney Universe: Morality Play." Mass-Mediated Culture. Englewood Cliffs, NJ: Prentice-Hall, 1977. 44-89.
Disney's productions from films to Disneyland are popular expressions of the US. For example, How to Read Donald Duck by Dorfman and Mattelart found that Disney comic books indirectly or directly advocated consumerism, colonialism, classism, and imperialism. Disneyland exercises "an awesome degree of social control" by confirming and beautifying the status-quo.

1180. Rollings, Jerry. "Mass Communications and the American Worker." The Critical Communications Review. Volume I: Labor, the Working Class, and the Media. Ed. Vincent Mosco and Janet Wasko. Norwood, NJ: Ablex, 1983. 131-152.
Discusses the "barrage of biased and skewed reporting" of "the House of Labor by the corporate-owned and -controlled media" and the Union Media Monitoring Project organized to expose the media bias.

1181. Rome, Edwin, and William H. Roberts. Corporate and Commercial Free Speech: First Amendment Protection of Expression in Business. Westport, CT: Quorum, 1985. 269.
"A systematic, historical account of the relevant judicial decisions and a sketch of the impact of these decisions in a number of distinct fields of law," Part I the history, Part II the issues surrounding First National Bank of Boston v. Bellotti. Ch. 6 surveys "the application or non-application of the commercial speech doctrine in a multitude of areas:

THE MEDIA

billboards, "shopper" advertising newspapers, false commercial advertising, etc.

1182. Rosenau, Neal. "On Covering the Revolution." ChJR 3.9 (Sept. 1970) 3-4.
Commercial control of media prevents accurate coverage of the counter-establishment protests.

1183. Roshco, Bernard. "No Business Like News Business." CJR 7.4 (1968-69) 27-28.
Presents news as entertainment, the result of corporate profit goals.

1184. Ross, Karl, and Ed Bishop. "Who Owns the Local Media?" SLJR 19.120 (Oct. 1989) 1, 10.
The "majority of the media is owned by large media corporations with headquarters far from the markets in which they operate," and many of these corporations have links with government and industry "which would appear to compromise their journalistic integrity."

1185. Rubin, Bernard. "Advocacy, Big Business, and Mass Media." Big Business and the Mass Media. Lexington, MA: Lexington, 1977. 1-62.
Analyzes the increasing advocacy advertising by corporations, a trend "both good and bad" for the public welfare. The "stories of big business must be told," but the "power of big business should never be allowed to dominate the media." Big business and the press have "a lot to learn" from each other. [See II.B.3.]

1186. Rubin, Bernard, ed. Big Business & the Mass Media. Lexington, MA: Lexington/Heath, 1977. 185.
Five essays based upon "opinion surveys of reporters, business executives, and public relations practitioners" paid for by a grant from the Shell Oil Company; contributors are members of the Institute for Democratic Communication at Boston U. The studies "analyze current and traditional relationships between big business and the communications industry" to show "the interdependencies and antagonisms that exist between" them.

1187. Rucker, Bryce. The First Freedom. Carbondale, IL: Southern Illinois UP, 1968. 322.
Demonstrates the tendency toward monopoly in print and broadcasting.

1188. Sanders, Bob. "Corporate Free Speech in the Driver's Seat." AltM 15:1 (Spring 1985) 16-18.
Marxist and Socialist writers are suppressed by the corporate controlled press.

1189. Schiller, Anita, and Herbert Schiller. "Commercializing Information." Na 243.10 (1986) 306-09.

Describes efforts to increase the private ownership of information.

1190. Schiller, Dan. "An Historical Approach to Objectivity and Professionalism in American News Reporting." JoC 29.4 (1979) 46-57.
Objectivity and professionalism create a public defender image of the press, which serves to legitimate the real purpose of the press, to make a profit.

1191. Schiller, Herbert. "Behind the Media Merger Movement." Na 240.22 (1985) 696-98.
On the threat to democracy and the public interest by the growing concentration of media ownership.

1192. Schiller, Herbert. "The Corporate Capture of the Sites of Public Expression." Culture, Inc.: The Corporate Takeover of Public Expression. New York: Oxford UP, 1989. 89-110.
Museums, art galleries, shopping malls, city downtowns, streets, public events and celebrations, homes (television), etc., are manipulated by corporations.

1193. Schiller, Herbert. "Corporate Speech, Power Politics, and the First Amendment." The Independent 11.6 (July 1988) 10-13.
Recent legal interpretations of the First Amendment and free expression presently advocated by businesses like cable television enhance private corporations' access to new media technologies while limiting or eliminating that of individual members of society.

1194. Schiller, Herbert. Information and the Crisis Economy. Norwood, NJ: Ablex, 1984. 133.
Appraises the global struggle to control technology and communications by transnational corporations and governments, the growth of information as a commodity, and the widening information gap between rich and poor.

1195. Schiller, Herbert. "Information--A Shrinking Resource." Na 241.22 (Jan. 1986) 708-710.
The "commercial utilization of information has become a central force," yet the media are largely silent about it.

1196. Schiller, Herbert. "Information for What Kind of Society?" Telecommunications: Issues and Choices for Society. Ed. J. L. Salvaggio. New York: Longman, 1983. 24-33.
Communications research should focus on how telecommunications reinforces the military-industrial complex and privilege and prevents change. Communications workers should be critics of power.

1197. Schiller, Herbert. "Is There a United States Information Policy?" Hope & Folly: The United States

& UNESCO, 1945-1985. Minneapolis: U of Minnesota P, 1989. 285-312.
In spite of the diversity within the US corporate state and the absence of an official national information policy, such a policy does exist and in service to the "needs of a transnational corporate business system." This policy pursues three main goals: a world-market system, extension of US commercial media and data flows and products, and anticommunism.

1198. Schiller, Herbert. "Journalistic Fervor." JoC 37.3 (Summer 1987) 155-61.
A critique of Margaret Blanchard's Exporting the First Amendment by placing US "free flow" doctrine within the context of its "indispensability to the successful operation of a worldwide business system that requires, along with a free flow of [western] information, the free flow of capital, labor, and commerce."

1199. Schiller, Herbert. "Old Foundations for a New (Information) Age." Competing Visions, Complex Realities. Ed. Jorge Reina Schement and Leah Lievrouw. Norwood, NJ: Ablex, 1987. 23-31.
Analyzes the concentrated private economic control "over the entire information sector," transforming all information into commercial products, "accountable only to the calculus of profit and loss." "The message outputs that reach American eyes and ears are almost entirely corporate-inspired and under-written" (30).

1200. Schiller, Herbert. "Privatization and Commercialization of the Public Sector: Information and Education." Culture, Inc.: The Corporate Takeover of Public Expression. New York: Oxford UP, 1989. 66-88.
The Reagan administration reduced the information government had provided the public and via the principle of privatization attacked the principle of libraries for free and equal access to all users.

1201. Sibbison, Jim. "Covering Medical 'Breakthroughs.'" CJR 27.2 (July-Aug. 1988) 36-39.
Reporters eagerly provide the public with news of medical "breakthroughs," often on the basis of "no more than tentative findings" and without consideration of conflicting studies.

1202. Sibbison, Jim. "Pushing New Drugs--Can the Press Kick the Habit?" CJR 24 (July-Aug. 1985) 52-54.
News agencies and the media tend to report new drugs uncritically on the basis of press releases from the manufacturers.

1203. Simons, Howard, and Joseph W. Califano, Jr. The Media and Business. New York: Vintage, 1979. 227.
Proceeding of a 1977 seminar of leaders from the media and business, sponsored by the Ford Foundation. Discussion focused upon three hypothetical cases of business/media conflict in which businessmen and media representatives

exchange criticisms and defenses.

1204. Spiegelman, Robert. "Media Manipulation of the Movement." SocP 13.1 (Summer 1982) 9-16.
Economic interests partly motivate media misrepresentation and underreporting of the antinuclear movement.

1205. Sterling, Christopher, and Timothy Haight. The Mass Media: Aspen Institute Guide to Communication Industry Trends. New York: Praeger, 1978. 457.
Extensive data on media ownership and concentration.

1206. Turow, Joseph. "Corporate Planning and Media Culture." CY 7 (1983) 432-442.
Challenges the futurist view of an increasingly consumer-controlled media environment, maintaining that entertainment conglomerates and the public relations industry will resist diversity and struggle to maintain the present "mass media culture."

1207. "Union Says: Don't Mourn the Media, Organize!" Extra! 2.1 (July-Aug. 1988) 15.
A new booklet produced by the UAW, A Worker's Guide to the Media, explains how biased against unions and working people are the media.

1208. Wallace, Mike. "Mickey Mouse History: Portraying the Past at Disney World." History Museums in the United States: A Critical Assessment. Ed. Warren Leon and Roy Rosenzweig. Urbana: U of Illinois P, 1989. 158-180. (RHR 32 [1985] 33-57).
Compares the two historical perspectives represented by Disney World and EPCOT. The essay tracks "the transformation of Original Walt" (Disneyland and World) into "Corporate Walt" (EPCOT, built in alliance with other corporations, the creme de la creme of US multinationals), to explore the effects of corporate sponsorship of historical information. Urges museum curators to confront "the corporate commodification of history."

1209. Weiss, Kenneth. "PAC Journalism: Cash, Candidates and Conflict of Interest." WJR 6 (1984) 49-53.
Decries political conflict of interest by media companies.

1210. Welles, Chris. "Scooped by Stockman." CJR 20.5 (Jan.-Feb. 1985) 21-23.
Denounces the "woefully anemic state of much economics reporting."

1211. Wirth, Michael. "Economic Barriers to Entering Media Industries in the United States." Communication Yearbook 9. Ed. Margaret McLaughlin. Beverly Hills, CA: Sage, 1986. 423-442.
"The data provided in this essay provide strong support for the proposition that the economic barriers to entering the

daily newspaper business are considerably higher than are the economic barriers to entering the broadcasting business (either television or radio) across all three economic barriers to entry examined."

1212. Young, T.R. "Public Opinion, Mass Opinion, and Social Opinion: The Constitution of Political Culture in the Capitalist State." Popular Culture and Media Events. Ed. Vincent Mosco and Janet Wasko. (CCRev 3). Norwood, NJ: Ablex, 1985. 259-280.
Argues that corporate exploitation of human needs (love, community) and material resources (media technologies, advertising) creates a mass opinion comprised mainly of wasteful tendencies. Also, the State and private capital manipulate traditions and fears (patriotism, national security) to establish a consensus in order to maintain their own power.

1213. Zachar, George R. "Press Swallows Atom Industry Bait: Industry-Sponsored Tour of Soviet Union Nets Pro-Nuclear Coverage." CMJ 4.9 (1978) 8.
The industry sponsored the tour, and reporters returned with pro-nuclear stories.

1214. Zinn, Howard. A People's History of the United States. New York: Harper & Row, 1980. 614.
Sporadic comment on the media as agencies of the Establishment: for example, "television coverage of Senate Committee hearings on Watergate stopped before the subject of corporate connections was reached," and this was "typical of the selective coverage of important events by the television industry" which downplayed systemic wrongdoing, particularly of corporate crime and influence in government (535).

II. A. 4. GOVERNMENT (1215-1662)
(See I.A.3., I.A.4., and II.B.5.)

1215. Abraham, Nabeel. "Politics and Principle: The 'Days of Rage' Affair." LOOT 1.2 (Feb. 1990) 14-15.
PBS and NYT ideological reactions to the film about the Palestinian uprising.

1216. The Adversary Press: A Modern Media Institute Ethics Center Seminar. St. Petersburg, FL: Poynter Institute, 1983. 112.
An account of a panel discussion of the thesis stated by Michael J. O'Neill that "the press is too hostile in its relationship with government" (Preface). [In the context of the contents of this bibliography, the panel discussed a delusion.]

1217. Alexandre, Laurien. "War Without End: Propaganda and Public Diplomacy in the Reagan Era." Extra! 2.1 (July-Aug. 1988) 8-9.
"No administration has used high technology and high finance

to sell itself and its policies as the Reagan regime has."

1217a. Alexandre, Laurien. "In the Service of the State: Public Diplomacy, Government Media & Ronald Reagan." MCS 9.1 (Jan. 1987) 29-46.
Examines Reagan's aggressive "ideological offensive" based on a message of "fear of communism." The USIA/VOA uses partial coverage, deceit, and Sovietphobia "to disinform the world's people."

1218. Andersen, Robin. "Reagan's 'Public Diplomacy'." CAIB 31 (Winter 1989) 20-24.
Reveals how the CIA conducted the equivalent of a wartime propaganda operation within the borders of the US in order to build public support for the Nicaraguan contras.

1219. Anderson, Jack, and Carl Kalvelage. American Government . . . Like It Is. Morristown, NJ: General Learning, 1972. 117.
The press is a "Sleeping Watchdog," while government manipulates the public ("News Media and the Public").

1220. Archibald, Samuel. "Rules for the Game of Ghost." CJR 6.4 (1967) 17-23.
"In the cooperation--or conspiracy--between Washington reporters and unnamed government news sources, the public sometimes gets less candid news than it deserves."

1221. Arkin, William M. "New INF Numbers Cast Doubt on Standard Press Tallies." Deadline 3.3 (May-June 1988) 1-2, 9-11.
The government, private experts, and reporters have been wrong about many weapons matters.

1222. Armstrong, Scott. "Iran-Contra: Was the Press any Match for all the President's Men?" CJR 29.1 (May-June 1990) 27-35.
The Iran-Contra affair amounted to a significant alteration of our Constitutional system--the principle of separation of powers --and it involved a series of serious crimes. Yet press coverage was frequently passive, irrelevant, and myopic.

1223. Armstrong, Scott, and Jeff Nason. "Company Man." MJ 14.8 (Oct. 1988) 20-25, 42-47.
"George Bush has been on the scene of the biggest political scandals of the last two decades," and he has emerged relatively unscathed because of the decline of investigative journalism and the increase in the sycophant method of news gathering.

1224. Aronson, James. Deadline for the Media: Today's Challenges to Press, TV & Radio. Indianapolis: Bobbs-Merrill, 1972. 327.
Introduction and account of the Nixon administration's efforts to suppress media criticism, of newspeople's

THE MEDIA

responses--journalism reviews, alternative press of protest, rise of black and female journalists--and of the limited significance of the publication of the Pentagon Papers in a history of "the general acquiescence of the media" to government power. "The media condition the citizen to think the thoughts that are preferred by government, industry, the military and the educational establishment--and by the media themselves."

1225. Aronson, James. "A Matter of Privilege." Deadline for the Media. Indianapolis: Bobbs-Merrill, 1972. 20-38.
Condemns use of subpoenas against individual journalists by the Nixon administration to force newspeople to present news more favorably to the administration and to turn them into agents of the police.

1226. Aronson, James. "On Assignment from WFBI." Deadline for the Media. Indianapolis: Bobbs-Merrill, 1972. 39-61.
Humorous examples of police and governmental agents masquerading as news reporters to spy on dissenters.

1227. Aronson, James. "The Package as President." Deadline for the Media. Indianapolis: Bobbs-Merrill, 1972. 3-19.
An account of the Nixon-Agnew administration's efforts to curb media and popular criticism of the Vietnam War and of itself and of widespread media compliance and complicity.

1228. Aronson, James. "The Siege of Pentagonia." Deadline for the Media. Indianapolis: Bobbs-Merrill, 1972. 62-90.
On the Pentagon Papers (published by the NYT June 13, 1971) and the media, particularly the failure of the media to disclose to the public earlier the deceptions revealed by the Papers. In general the media did a poor job of informing the public about all sides of the issues about Vietnam.

1229. Atta, Dale V. "The Death of the State Secret." NR 192.7 (Feb. 18, 1985) 20-23.
"Reagan is now attempting to impose a new regime of secrecy."

1230. Auletta, Ken. "Covering Carter Is Like Playing Chess with Bobby Fischer." MORE 6.10 (1976) 12-22.
Jimmy Carter's campaign manipulation of the press.

1231. Autin, Diana M.T.K. "The Reagan Administration and the Freedom of Information Act." Freedom at Risk: Secrecy, Censorship, and Repression in the 1980s. Ed. Richard O. Curry. Philadelphia, PA: Temple UP, 1988. 69-85.
On the attempts by the Reagan administration to cripple the Freedom of Information Act.

1232. Baer, John W. "The Strange Origin of the Pledge of

Allegiance." PR 5 (Summer 1989) 36-37.
Asks why the flag instead of the Constitution is the patriotic center of the country.

1233. Bagdikian, Ben. Bagdikian On Political Reporting, Newspaper Economics, Law, and Ethics. Fort Worth: Texas Christian UP, 1977. 29.
Three lectures urging the importance of access to reliable information through an aggressively investigative press.

1234. Bagdikian, Ben. "Congress and the Media: Partners in Propaganda." CJR 12.5 (1974) 3-10.
Media too often report as news canned press releases or film from members of Congress.

1235. Bagdikian, Ben. "The Fruits of Agnewism." CJR 11.5 (1973) 9-21.
Because of the Nixon administration's war on the press, the 1972 election coverage was not substantially investigative but merely a propagandistic repetition of government news releases.

1236. Bagdikian, Ben. "Press Independence and the Cuban Crisis." CJR 1.4 (1962) 5-11.
Kennedy administration dominated news coverage of the Cuban missile crisis.

1237. Bagdikian, Ben. "What Did We Learn?" CJR 10.3 (1971) 45-50.
The Pentagon Papers taught us again the importance of freedom to investigate and expose secret power.

1238. Banks, Jack. "The Contradiction of a 'Free Press': An Analysis of U.S. Press Coverage of UNESCO." M.S. thesis, U of Oregon, 1985. 276.
Media were biased.

1239. Barbosa, Ruy, et al. "The CIA and the Press: Foreign Reactions to Disclosures of Media Manipulation." Atlas 25 (Mar. 1978) 22-25.
Reactions from Brazil, England, and Australia.

1240. Bass, Carole, and Paul Bass. "More Than Censorship, Irrelevance Troubles U.S. Journalists." SLJR 11 (Jan. 1985) 17-18.
Account of a writers' conference on legalistic and ideological censorship.

1241. Bayley, Edwin R. Joe McCarthy and the Press. Madison, WI: U of Wisconsin P, 1981. 220.
Examines Senator McCarthy's manipulation of the press and the media's craven complicity. "For a time, McCarthy was able to get almost anything he wanted from either of the media; only a few individual broadcasters and a relatively small number of newspapers resisted him. Gradually the media

stiffened, but it was not until 1954 that the networks and the mass of newspapers felt it safe to oppose him" (212-13), four years after he began his career of lies and smears.

1242. Bell, Dan. "Our Many Men in Washington: Two Views. 2. The Age of Agnew." UM 1.4 (Dec. 1970) 10-11.
Vice President Agnew's right-wing efforts to "turn down the volume" of dissent in US media were successful. Remedies suggested.

1242a. Bennett, James R. "Censorship by the Reagan Administration." IC 17.7 (1988) 28-32.
The Reagan administration has increased both direct censorship (prohibiting speech or action on threat of punishment) and indirect censorship (denying information, secrecy).

1243. Bennett, James R. "Doublethink and the Rhetoric of Crisis: President Reagan's October 22, 1983, Speech on Arms 'Reduction.'" Oldspeak/Newspeak Rhetorical Transformations. Ed. Charles W. Kneupper. Arlington, TX: Rhetoric Society of America, 1985. 54-66.
Black-white Sovietphobia dominates the language of the speech.

1243a. Bennett, James R. "Oceania and the United States in 1984: The Selling of the Soviet Threat." STP 10.3 (Fall 1984) 301-318.
Compares the permanent war, "Hate Week," "Two Minutes Hate," and other aspects of hate fomenting via the media in Orwell's 1984 and in the US.

1244. Bennett, James R. "President Reagan's Panegyric for the Marines Killed in Lebanon." NDQ 55.2 (Spring 1987) 35-48.
Self-exculpatory and Cold War strategies shape the panegyric.

1244a. Bennett, James R. "Recent Government Censorship: Selected Checklist & Bibliography." Arkansas Libraries 45.3 (Sept. 1988) 6-12.
Sixty categories.

1245. Berkman, Ronald, and Laura W. Kitch. Politics in the Media Age. New York: McGraw-Hill, 1986. 332.
Discerns a decline in press independence and rise in the power of politicians, the government, interest groups, and private interests to use media to their own ends. Focuses upon how the news media use the political world and how that world uses the media. Great attention to media as business corporations.

1245a. Bernstein, Carl. "The CIA & the Media." RS (Oct. 20, 1977) 55-67.
Exposes the large number of journalists who worked for the CIA during the Cold War, especially from NYT, CBS, and Time.

1246. Blanchard, Robert O., ed. Congress and the News Media. New York: Hastings, 1974. 506.
Part I (9 essays) deals with "Access and Accommodation," II (30 essays) with "Interdependence and Interaction," III (12 essays) with "Conflict and Cooperation."

1247. Blanchard, Robert O. "A Watchdog in Decline." CJR 5.2 (1966) 17-21.
The decay of the freedom of information movement and its chief Congressional adjunct, the Moss Committee.

1248. Bleifuss, Joel. "A Domestic Covert Operation." ITT 12.37 (Sept. 28-Oct. 4, 1988) 4-5.
The Reagan administration used CIA and Pentagon propaganda experts to illegally lobby Congress and manipulate the media in its successful spring 1986 effort to persuade Congress to give aid to the Contras.

1249. Block, Herbert. Herblock on All Fronts. New York: New American Library, 1980. 280.
The power of the military-industrial complex over the media and the First Amendment is scattered throughout this book of cartoons and comment by the cartoonist "Herblock." The chapter on "The Open and the Closed Society," for example, focuses upon government surveillance and other efforts to deny the public and its media the information they need. "In an open society the conduct of officials in their public duties has to be open for public inspection."

1250. Bogart, Leo. Premises for Propaganda: The U.S.I.A.'s Operating Assumptions in the Cold War. New York: Free, 1976. 250.
Based on 142 interviews, focuses on uncertainties and controversies in the theory and practice of international propaganda. Provides an inside view of a major US propaganda agency in the days of Senator McCarthy. An abridgment of a five-volume report written in 1954 but kept from publication for 20 years.

1251. Bonafede, Dom. "The President's Publicity Machine." WJR 2.4 (1980) 42-44.
On President Carter's news management.

1252. Bonafede, Dom. ". . . The Press." WJR 2.4 (1980) 48-50.
The White House press corps is conformist and complicit with power.

1253. Bonner, Raymond. Waltzing With A Dictator: The Marcoses and the Making of American Policy. New York: Times, 1987. 533.
Discussion of media treatment of Marcos throughout; e.g., Time and Newsweek covered his fraudulent election favorably along with Carter administration policy.

1254. Bonner, Raymond. Weakness and Deceit: U.S. Policy and
El Salvador. New York: Times Books, 1984. 408.
   Partly a history of false discourses, of official pronouncements and documents which conflicted with what was happening in El Salvador, of administration--both Carter's and Reagan's --concealments and distortions in statements to the press, to Congress, and to the public. The deceptions were designed to misrepresent all aspects of the civil war.

1255. Boot, William. "Capital Letter." CJR 25.4 (1986) 11-18.
   Reagan's press conferences are full of errors and lies.

1256. Boot, William. "Wading Around in the Panama Pool."
CJR 28.6 (Mar.-Apr. 1990) 18-20.
   After the press was excluded from the 1983 invasion of Grenada, the Pentagon set up the war pool concept to allow selected journalists to cover combat operations. The invasion of Panama proved the pool an instrument of continued exclusion. The censorship was hardly necessary, since the news organizations supported the invasion.

1257. Boudin, Leonard. "The Ellsberg Case: Citizen
Disclosure." Secrecy and Foreign Policy. Ed. Thomas Franck and Edward Weisband. New York: Oxford UP, 1974. 291-311.
   "The Ellsberg case was the first criminal prosecution in American history for disclosure to the American public of information classified as secret by the U.S. Government . . . and an attempt to incorporate into American law the doctrines of the British Official Secrets Act." The indictment was dismissed because of government excesses.

1258. Boyer, Brian. "Reporters Threatened by Subpoena
Actions." ChJR 3.3 (1970) 13-15.
   Appeal for resistance to growing abuse of subpoena to acquire confidential information.

1259. Boylan, James. "How Free is the Press?" CJR 26.3
(Sept.-Oct. 1987) 27-32.
   "An overview of Supreme Court decisions, which while charting new areas of freedom, have fenced them in."

1260. Branch, Taylor. "The Scandal That Got Away." MORE
3.10 (1973) 1, 17-20.
   Indicts the failure to report the massive, secret, and illegal bombings of Cambodia in 1969 until after they had ended.

1261. Brockriede, Wayne, and Robert L. Scott. Moments in the
Rhetoric of the Cold War. New York: Random House, 1970. 130.
   The art of rhetoric is a generative principle of Cold War politics, because it constitutes the central substance that requires serious attention if the Cold War is to remain cold and rhetoric is to continue to be used in place of instruments of death.

1262. Broder, David. "Political Reporters in Presidential Politics." WM 1 (Feb. 1969) 20-33.
On the subservience of reporters to Robert Kennedy's speech writers.

1263. Brodhead, Frank. "Elections in El Salvador: A Death Squad 'Democracy.'" Alert! 6.2 (Mar. 1988) 1, 6-7.
False coverage of the elections in El Salvador and Nicaragua, following the administration's line.

1264. Brodhead, Frank, and Edward Herman. Demonstration Elections: U.S.-Staged Elections in the Dominican Republic, Vietnam and El Salvador. Boston: South End, 1984. 270.
The media follow the government's false claims of electoral democracy in these client dictatorships.

1265. Burns, E. Bradford. At War in Nicaragua: The Reagan Doctrine and the Politics of Nostalgia. New York: Harper & Row, 1987. 211.
Exhibits the dishonesty with which this war has been portrayed to the public.

1266. The Bush Administration and The News Media. Washington DC: The Reporters Committee For Freedom of the Press, 1990. 42.
Summary and analysis of almost 100 actions by the Bush administration aimed at restricting public and media access to government information and intruding on editorial freedom.

1267. Butts, David. "Political Maneuvers: Texas's Top Citizen Holds a Cookout in a Warzone; Plays Paperweight Politics; and Takes the Press for a Ride. A Story of Exploitation." AltM 15:2 (Summer 1985) 17-20.
In order to boost his image among conservative Texans, the Democratic governor of Texas, Mark White, took a trip to Honduras with the press in tow and loudly praised the Reagan policy in Central America.

1268. Carlisle, Johan. "Drug War Propaganda." PR 6 (Winter 1990) 6-9, 43-44.
"How the Cold War became the Drug War and helped Bush invade Panama. The media's role in the creation of a new McCarthyism."

1268a. Chamorro, Edgar. Packaging The Contras: A Case of CIA Disinformation. New York: Inst. for Media Analysis, 1987. 78.
Describes his experience with the Nicaraguan counterrevolutionaries "to clarify how the CIA develops such projects, the importance it places on packaging and marketing its projects, and the role of disinformation in determining foreign policy, both covert and overt." The CIA contra policy depended on a vast disinformation program for its very existence, to make the public of the US believe in a "fantasy."

THE MEDIA

1269. Charles, Daniel. "Delta 181 Puts Reporters to the Test." Deadline 3.3 (May-June 1988) 5, 8.
Faced with inconclusiveness, many military reporters "either ignored the complexities" of an SDI experiment, "or pumped up the results."

1270. Chester, Jeff. "Reagan's Global Reach." CJR 23.6 (1985) 10-12.
Describes the Reagan administration's expanding propaganda operations under NSDD-130.

1271. Chittick, William. The State Department, Press, and Pressure Groups: A Role Analysis. New York: Wiley, 1970. 373.
Studies "the interactions among four key groups in the opinion-policy process: State Department policy officers; State Department information officers; foreign affairs reporters; and the leaders of nongovernmental organizations." Cooperation described but focus upon conflicts. The strongest antagonism is between policy officers and reporters.

1272. Chomsky, Noam. "Afghanistan and South Vietnam." The Chomsky Reader. New York: Pantheon, 1987. 223-26.
The Soviet newscaster Vladimir Danchev courageously labeled the Russian invasion of Afghanistan as an invasion. But there were no Danchevs in the mainstream US press to name the Vietnam invasion the invasion it also was.

1273. Chomsky, Noam. "Central America: The Next Phase." Z 1.3 (Mar. 1988) 11-21.
Many illustrations of how the media support the Reagan-Bush administration's repression in Central America.

1274. Chomsky, Noam. "Controlling 'Enemy Territory'" and "Freedom of Expression in the Free World." The Culture of Terrorism. Boston: South End, 1988. 199-202, 203-214.
Analyzes the Reagan administration's propaganda campaign against the US public called "Operation Truth" and elaborated by the State Department's Office of Public Diplomacy and other agencies designed to control the public mind. One aspect of the successful campaign is the "uniformity and obedience of the media" (204).

1275. Chomsky, Noam. The Culture of Terrorism. Boston: South End, 1988. 269.
A dissection of US imperialism which includes considerable analysis of the "manufacture of consent" by state apparatuses with the cooperation of the "ideological institutions" that serve the state's interests. Illusion and deceit produce a population disabled from independent perception and judgment. Sixteen chapters deal with I. "The Scandals of 1986," II. "Further Successes of the Reagan Administration," and III. "The Current Agenda."

1276. Chomsky, Noam. "Damage Control." The Culture of Terrorism. Boston: South End, 1988. 113-130.
The Reagan administration and US mainstream media have employed suppression, distortion, tunnel vision, and double standards to prevent the public from perceiving the government's international terror network.

1277. Chomsky, Noam. "El Salvador." The Chomsky Reader. New York: Pantheon, 1987. 339-50.
As of early 1981 the press conveyed the US government's false picture of a moderate El Salvadoran government caught between violent left and right, but the El Salvadoran army and death squads under President Duarte have committed state terror and mass murder against the people of the country. The US government is generally successful in setting the terms of media and public discussion.

1278. Chomsky, Noam. "'A Gleam of Light in Asia.'" Z 3.9 (Sept. 1990) 15-23.
Revelations of the US role in Indonesia reveal much about the relationship between foreign policy and the media.

1279. Chomsky, Noam. "Guatemala." The Chomsky Reader. New York: Pantheon, 1987. 363-7.
Under "the pretext of a Communist takeover, with the U.S. press loyally playing its part, the CIA engineered a coup in 1954, restoring military rule and turning the country into a literal hell on earth."

1280. Chomsky, Noam. "The Intelligence Identities Protection Act." CS 6.3 (1982) 27-31.
Chomsky views the Act as "a direct attack on the First Amendment" and a "threat" to "all of the media."

1281. Chomsky, Noam. Language and Politics. Ed. Carlos Otero. Montreal: Black Rose, 1988. 779.
Interviews on the use and misuse of political propaganda and how and why people not only fall victim to it but appear to be accepting it.

1282. Chomsky, Noam. "Nicaragua." The Chomsky Reader. New York: Pantheon, 1987. 351-61.
Official criticism of the Sandinistas, uncritically reported by the media, is both unfounded and hypocritical.

1283. Chomsky, Noam. "The Perils of Diplomacy." The Culture of Terrorism. Boston: South End, 1988. 131-63.
Analyzes official US arguments regarding Nicaragua and press support of those arguments.

1284. Chomsky, Noam. Radical Priorities. Ed. Carlos P. Otero. 2nd Rev. Ed. Montreal: Black Rose, 1981. 307.
Analyzes US propaganda, obediently reported by media, on Vietnam protests, East Timor, and other events.

THE MEDIA

1285. Chomsky, Noam. "Rejectionism and Accommodation." The Chomsky Reader. New York: Pantheon, 1987. 371-405.
"In news reporting as in editorial commentary" in the US, "the Camp David accords" between Egypt, Israel, and the Palestinians "are known simply as 'the peace process,'" which simply reflects a "tacit acceptance of the U.S. propaganda system by the media and scholarship" (389).

1286. Chomsky, Noam. "The Tasks Ahead III: Problems of Population Control." Z 2.11 (Nov. 1989) 11-18.
Examines the "government-media campaign" to indoctrinate or divert the public away from the major menaces facing the world.

1286a. "Church Opposes TV Broadcast to Cuba." SLJR 20.127 (June 1990) 3.
The Office of Communication of the United Church of Christ opposes TV Marti because it violates international treaty.

1287. Churchill, Ward. "Renegades, Terrorists, and Revolutionaries: The U.S. Government's Propaganda War Against the American Indian Movement." PR 4 (Spring 1989) 12-16.
The US government restricted media access to AIM activists and mounted a disinformation campaign to brand them as violent extremists lacking legitimacy.

1288. Churchill, Ward, and Jim Vander Wall. Agents of Repression: The FBI's Secret Wars Against the Black Panther Party and the American Indian Movement. Boston: South End, 1988. 509.
"We argue that the Bureau was founded, maintained, and steadily expanded as a mechanism to forestall, curtail and repress the expression of political diversity within the United States." The authors focus upon FBI operations conducted against the American Indian Movement at the Pine Ridge Sioux Reservation, South Dakota, during 1972-76. In Chap. 10, "The Disinformation Campaign," they stress, what they have shown throughout the book, that the FBI spreads false information to discredit its "enemies" and equally inaccurate positive images of itself and its "friends," "standard Bureau counterintelligence activities throughout its history."

1289. "CIA Admits Help from Twenty-Five in U.S. Media, But Won't Give Any Names." Br 90.3 (1976) 32-33.
Includes information about covert CIA production or subsidization of books.

1290. The CIA and the Media. Washington, DC: GPO, 1978. 627.
About the contractual and informal relationships with individual journalists, their intelligence gathering, assumption of journalistic cover by CIA agents, etc., practices that have undermined the impartiality and credibility of the press. Citizens have been "the victims of disinformation sown by

their own Government" (2). One of a series of hearings by the Pike Committee.

1291. "CIAntics." NR 169.24 (1973) 7-8.
On journalists as CIA undercover agents.

1292. "The CIA's Press Corps." CS 7 (Sept.-Nov. 1982) 4.
The CIA used journalists as agents to gather information, suppress unfavorable stories, and promote CIA-inspired or produced stories.

1293. "CIA Relations with Media--Official and Otherwise." CAIB 7 (1979-80) 21-22.
"The CIA has used major U.S. news organizations as cover for its officers" and "owned or funded over fifty news organizations. And it has sponsored, subsidized or produced more than 1,000 books."

1294. Clarke, Peter, and Susan H. Evans. Covering Campaigns: Journalism in Congressional Elections. Stanford, CA: Stanford UP, 1983. 151.
The book "reveals how journalistic habits favor the political status quo, seldom reporting challenges to existing institutional arrangements. Politics is an uncomfortable place for courageous and unfettered reporting" (2). Journalists follow routine methods that favor incumbents; "the content of press coverage provides a meager base for fueling vigorous public debate" (5).

1294a. Clift, Eleanor. "How the White House Keeps Reporters in Their Place." WJR 8.6 (1986) 9.
Reagan press conferences are thoroughly choreographed.

1295. Cockburn, Alexander. Corruptions of Empire: Life Studies and the Reagan Era. London and New York: Verso, 1987. 479.
The first part is mainly autobiographical but deals in part with the rise and death of liberal reform in the 1970s. The "role of the press in articulating and hence validating the concepts and imagery of the Reagan era is the story of the second part."

1296. Cockburn, Alexander. "The Coup d'Etat." Corruptions of Empire. London: Verso, 1987. 452-55.
Nixon and Reagan believed that "the rituals of democratic elections were only a necessary prelude to the actual seizure of power, institution of secret procedures and evasion of accountability," while the mainstream press kept its eyes shut.

1297. Cockburn, Alexander. "From Vietnam . . ." Corruptions of Empire. London: Verso, 1987. 308-310.
"The nation that forgets its massacres and atrocities this quickly is certainly going to repeat them" (310).

1298. Cockburn, Alexander. "Nicaragua: News From Nowhere."

THE MEDIA

Na 241.22 (1986) 702-703.
Much of the U.S. press appears to have abandoned all efforts to contradict or even to challenge the propaganda put forth by the White House, the contras and their U.S. allies."

1299. Cockburn, Alexander. "Our Fallen Friend." ITT 12.33 (Aug. 31-Sept. 6, 1988) 17.
After the death of Zia, dictator of Pakistan, the US press "followed the official line, portraying Zia as a man leading Pakistan toward 'democracy.'"

1300. Cockburn, Alexander. "The Phantom Planes." Na 239 (Nov. 24, 1984) 542.
How the lying leak by ultra-right members of the Administration about the possible arrival of MIG-21 fighter planes in Nicaragua was retailed by the media.

1301. Cockburn, Alexander. "The Plane That Never Was." Corruptions of Empire. London: Verso, 1987. 277-278.
How the Sovietphobic press fueled the chimerical $1 billion campaign to build a nuclear-powered plane.

1302. Cockburn, Alexander. "The Press and the Grenada Invasion." Corruptions of Empire. London: Verso, 1987. 341-46.
"Important sections of the US media surrendered without much of a struggle in the face of the US invasion of Grenada and the Reagan administration's propaganda barrage to justify this outrageous and illegal venture."

1303. Cockburn, Alexander. "The Press and Reaganism." TO 80.11 (June 3, 1988) 14-15.
On press complicity with Ronald Reagan and the general tendency of the press in recent years to exclude reality.

1304. Cockburn, Alexander. "Silence Is Golden." Na 242.18 (1986) 638.
On the Reagan administration's successful news management.

1305. Cockburn, Alexander. "The Smoking Gun That Doesn't Smoke." Corruptions of Empire. London: Verso, 1987. 463-65.
The ways the press avoids telling truths about corruption in high office, and inoculates the public against presidential crimes and lies.

1306. Cockburn, Alexander. "Superfiend." Corruptions of Empire. London: Verso, 1987. 411-14. (Na 242.16 [1986] 576-77).
The government/media campaign to demonize Qaddafi. "The U.S. press has given the Administration free rein in deploying Qaddafi fantasies in the past few years."

1307. Cockburn, Alexander. "Telling Lies About Nicaraguan Policy." Corruptions of Empire. London: Verso,

1987. 383-85.
In their campaign for more funds for the contras, President Reagan and Secretary Schultz "erect a mountain of lies . . . many of which the editorial writers and network pundits take as gospel."

1308. Cohen, Jeff. "Propaganda from the Middle-of-the-Road: The Centrist Ideology of the News Media." Extra! 3.1 (Oct.-Nov. 1989) 12-14.
Challenges the claim that there is "no such thing as propaganda of the center."

1309. Cohen, Jeremy. Congress Shall Make No Law: Oliver Wendell Holmes, the First Amendment, and Judicial Decision Making. Ames, IA: Iowa State UP, 1989. 149.
Examines Holmes and Schenck v. united States (1919), arguing that the First Amendment "must always be seen in league with other legal theories--property law, criminal law, and civil procedure."

1310. Cole, Leonard. Clouds of Secrecy: The Army's Germ Warfare Tests Over Populated Areas. Totowa, NJ: Rowman and Littlefield, 1988. 199.
Scattered comments on media collusion in disseminating lies.

1311. Coleman, Peter. The Liberal Conspiracy: The Congress for Cultural Freedom and the Struggle for the Mind of Postwar Europe. New York: Free, 1989. 350.
The Congress was an anticommunist "guerilla" group of European and American writers and intellectuals formed to oppose the SU. Includes an account of the organization's secret funding by the CIA.

1312. Colhoun, Jack. "White House Enslaves the 'Free Press.'" Guard 41.6 (Nov. 2, 1988) 17.
In praise of Hertsgaard's On Bended Knee, which shows how the media served as a cheerleader for the Reagan administration.

1312a. Colhoun, Jack. "U.S. Rattles Electronic Saber at Cuba." Guard 42.35 (June 27, 1990) 3.
On the planned escalation of TV Marti, the illegal US TV broadcasting station beamed at Cuba.

1313. Collier, Barney. Hope and Fear in Washington (the Early Seventies): The Story of the Washington Press Corps. New York: Dial, 1975. 254.
Studies the lives of about sixty reporters because "news is a point of view." He asked them questions about "who loves who and why, and how much money people get paid, and if they panic like I do, and how their mind works," etc.

1314. Collum, Danny. "The Iron Curtain of Secrecy." Soj 18.5 (May 1989) 5-6.
The Bush administration is struggling to bury the truth

about its operations in Iran and Central America. "Thus far the media are playing their part as loyal servants to the state of secrecy."

1315. "Congressional Publicity in Action." Congress and the News Media. Ed. Robert O. Blanchard. New York: Hastings, 1974. 345-398.
Seven essays on techniques for publicity, communicating members' messages to constituents, and carrying proceedings to the public.

1316. Cook, Blanche, and Gerald Markowitz. "History in Shreds: The Fate of the Freedom of Information Act." RHR 26 (1982) 173-78.
On the attempt by the Reagan Administration to eviscerate the Act.

1317. Cook, Faye, et al. "Media and Agenda Setting: Effects on the Public, Interest Group Leaders, Policy Makers, and Policy." POQ 47 (Spring 1983) 16-35.
Governmental response to the problem of home health fraud and abuse resulted from collaboration between investigative journalists and governmental policy makers, not because of an aroused public.

1317a. Cook, Timothy E. Making Laws and Making News: Media Strategies in the U.S. House of Representatives. Washington, DC: Brookings, 1989. 210.
Argues that the Capitol Hill press corps is passive, favors incumbents, and therefore is exploited by office holders. The result is 99 percent victory for incumbents. Focuses especially on the legislative process, during which the media are used to attract attention to a problem and then are avoided while the solution is worked out.

1318. Cormier, Frank. "Co-option of the Press." The White House Press on the Presidency. Ed. Kenneth Thompson. Lanham, MD: UP of America, 1983. 60-80.
Press friendliness with president undermines its role as public watchdog.

1319. Corn, David. "The Republicans' N.E.D. Conduit: Foreign Aid For the Right." Na 249.21 (Dec. 18, 1989) 744-746.
The National Endowment for Democracy distributes money ostensibly to promote democracy abroad mainly to four groups: the AFL-CIO, the U.S. Chamber of Commerce, the Democratic Party, and the Republican Party. A close look at the National Republican Institute for International Affairs, a recipient, explains why the N.E.D. "should be put out of business" for its unaccountable right-wing activities.

1319a. Cornwell, Elmer E., Jr. Presidential Leadership of Public Opinion. Bloomington, IN: Indiana UP, 1965. 370.

Surveys the methods available to the president for mobilizing support for policies and for popularity: press conference, White House PR staff, broadcasting, etc.

1320. Cox, Arthur M. "Secrecy & the Media." The Myths of National Security: The Peril of Secret Government. Boston: Beacon, 1975. 119-149.
Since the beginning of WWII, "Instead of assuming the role of public watchdog on matters of national security, most of the press developed a cozy working relationship with the government." The "Big Lie" technique to deceive the public worsened during the Johnson and Nixon administrations, a practice insufficiently exposed by the media.

1321. Crowell, George H. "After Geneva Sleight-of-Hand: Still A Chance for CTB." C&C 45.21 (1985) 510-511.
Failure of media to cover clearly the SU's desire for a Comprehensive Test Ban and US opposition.

1322. Daniel, Josh. "New York City's Big Secret: The Nuclear Homeport." Extra! 1.8 (May-June 1988) 6-7.
The Navy's plan to store nuclear missiles on ships docked at the Staten Island port is not being well-investigated or even reported, for many reasons. The NYT "has had a longstanding pro-nuclear editorial policy."

1322a. David, Michael, and Pat Aufderheide. "All the President's Media." Ch 5.3 (1985) 20-24.
New electronic technologies increase presidential power.

1323. Davison, W. Phillips. "Diplomatic Reporting: Rules of the Game." JoC 25.4 (1975) 138-146.
A network of friendships and mutual dependencies draws diplomats and correspondents into an elite community of foreign affairs specialists.

1324. Deakin, James. "The Problem of Presidential-Press Relations." The White House Press on the Presidency: News Management and Co-option. Ed. Kenneth Thompson. Lanham, MD: UP of America, 1983. 7-33.
Sets forth the government's propaganda machine designed to manipulate the press. Focuses on the Johnson and Nixon administrations, in which lying became consistent policy.

1325. Deakin, James. Straight Stuff: The Reporters, the White House, and the Truth. New York: Morrow, 1984. 378.
A White House correspondent surveys the issues: press secretaries, reporters, coverage, lying, etc. Analysis of the Washington press corps and their relationship with the president, especially with Reagan. Explains the uncritical reporting of Reagan's errors and falsehoods of his administration.

1325a. DeFrank, Thomas M. "Fine-Tuning the White House Press Conference." WJR 4.8 (1982) 27-29.

Reagan's press conferences, aired to appear spontaneous, are actually "elaborately choreographed exercises in damage control which now routinely include a pair of dress rehearsals in the White House theater, seating charts and photographs of reporters in attendance, guaranteed questions to several reporters" and "even an occasional planted question to a receptive journalist."

1326. Delgado, Richard. "The Language of the Arms Race: Should the People Limit Government Speech?" BULR 64.5 (1984) 961-1001.
Believes the government's systematic deception and secrecy about nuclear issues to be inherently irremediable by the marketplace of ideas, and suggests possible solutions.

1327. "I. Delusive Myths & Lethal Weapons in South Vietnam." MO 5.9 (Sept. 1963) 7.
On press parroting official lies about the Diem regime and the National Liberation Front.

1328. Demac, Donna. "Battleground of Ideas." JoC 36.2 (Spring 1986) 173-75.
Review of Allen Hansen's USIA. The book, written by a thirty-year employee of the agency, aims "to foster an image that glosses over and misstates important aspects of the agency's history and practices."

1329. Demac, Donna. "Hearts and Minds Revisited: The Information Policies of the Reagan Administration." The Political Economy of Information. Ed. Vincent Mosco and Janet Wasko. Madison: U of Wisconsin P, 1988. 125-145.
Reagan administration restrictions on information dulled national debate.

1329a. Denison, Dave. "Politics and Symbols: The Democratic Convention as Political Theater." TO 80.16 (Aug. 19, 1988) 6-10.
"Political symbols have now become the very essence of the modern convention." The party primaries, which have virtually eliminated the convention's deliberative process, and television have transformed the convention into "the political variety show."

1330. Denton, Robert, Jr., and Dan Hahn. "Communication Dimensions of the Presidency." Presidential Communication: Description and Analysis. New York: Praeger, 1986. 105-320.
Chaps 3-6 on interpersonal, intrapersonal, small group, and mass communication dimensions of the US presidency.

1331. Denton, Robert, Jr., and Dan Hahn. Presidential Communication: Description and Analysis. New York: Praeger, 1986. 332.
Studies the presidency systematically "from a purely commun-

ication perspective. It is the only text that focuses on communication variables in relation to the presidency" (xv). "Today, presidential rhetoric and communication activities are sources of tremendous power." Therefore a president "surrounds himself with communication specialists. Every act, word, or phrase becomes calculated and measured for a response" (xiv).

1332. Denton, Robert, Jr., and Dan Hahn. "The Rhetorical Presidency." Presidential Communication: Description and Analysis. New York: Praeger, 1986. 3-101.
Chaps. 1 and 2. Chap. 1 investigates three case studies, including "President Ford and the Mayaguez Affair" and "Richard Nixon and Presidential Mythology" Chap. 2 studies two case studies ("Reagan's Persuasiveness" and "The Watergate Strategies of Richard Nixon During the 1972 Campaign").

1333. Denton, Robert, Jr., and Gary Woodward. Political Communication in America. New York: Praeger, 1985. 364.
The second part of the book "focuses on communication within the institutions of the presidency, the Congress, and the mass media," ending with discussion of "communication, politics, and the public trust," which includes sections on how television pushes debate to "the ideological center" (334); how broadcasting has contributed to the increasing power of the president at the expense of Congress (338-39); and the four corruptions of political discourse: coercion, deception, mystification, and mystification by redefinition (339-352). Included throughout the book are disclosures of ruling power.

1334. De Zutter, Henry. "The Media's Mythical Scenario." ChJR 2.4 (1969) 4-5.
Media are reporting false police reports about conspiracy behind riots.

1335. Divine, Robert. Blowing on the Wind: The Nuclear Test Ban Debate, 1954-1960. New York: Oxford UP, 1978. 393.
Public was never made aware of how dangerous atomic testing was before the late 1950s or early '60s when some information was disseminated under Eisenhower. Starting with Truman the government suppressed the truth.

1336. Donovan, Brian. "The Sorry State of Official Energy Information." Pr 10.1 (1982) 34-5.
The executive branch of the federal government "for the past several years has repeatedly acted as a censor and crude propagandist in energy matters."

1337. Dorman, William A. "The Media: Playing the Government's Game." BAS 41.7 (Aug. 1985) 118-124.
Journalists claim to be objective, but they accept the ideology of the cold war and arms race, that is, of Washington's view of the world.

THE MEDIA

1338. Dorsen, Norman, and Stephen Gillers, eds. None of Your Business: Government Secrecy in America. New York: Viking, 1974. 362.
Explores damages done to democracy by executive privilege, classification system, pressures on press, etc.

1339. Downing, John. "Government Secrecy and the Media in the United States and Britain." Communicating Politics. Ed. Peter Golding, et al. New York: Holmes & Meier, 1986. 153-170.
In contrast to the national power of the Labour Party in Britain, "the dispersal of opposition" in the US "is less likely to threaten the prevailing power-structure, and is thus allowable." Both countries have "a strong apparatus of secrecy and news management in areas defined" as "national security" or "national interest."

1340. Emery, Michael. "All the President's Men." RSCJ 12 (Sept. 1974) 7.
Gives high credit to Woodward's and Bernstein's reporting of Watergate, but emphasizes the general failure of the Washington press corps to report the scandal and to relate it to history of presidential secrecy, lying, and authoritarianism.

1341. Emery, Michael. "Fear & Loathing in Nixon's Inner Circle." RSCJ 12 (Sept. 1974) 8-9.
Nixon's hatred of the media in the context of bugging, bombing, and plotting against the rights of the people.

1342. Entman, Robert. Democracy Without Citizens: Media and the Decay of American Politics. New York: Oxford UP, 1989. 248.
A critique of news media failure to offer in-depth quality journalism necessary for an informed citizenry. Discusses such topics as media-fed demagogy, the FCC's Fairness Doctrine, the sources and bias of the news.

1343. "Europe: Pieces of a Puzzle." CJR 20.1 (1981) 27-29.
Coverage of the European antinuclear movement is largely from the hostile viewpoint of NATO.

1344. Fain, Jim. "Incest Is Press Problem." AG (Mar. 13, 1985) 15A.
An incident relating to the "government/media revolving door."

1345. Falbaum, Berl. "The Secret Branch of Government." CJR 16.5 (1978) 14-16.
On the lack of analysis of judicial decisions.

1345a. Foreign Policy Implications of TV Marti. Hearing before the Subcommittees on International Operations and on Western Hemisphere Affairs of the Committee on Foreign Affairs, House of Representatives, Sept. 22, 1988. Washington, DC: GPO, 1988. 92.

Debate over the proposed project to broadcast US sanctioned news into Cuba by floating a balloon 10,000 feet above the Florida keys.

1346. Frankel, Max. "The 'State Secrets' Myth." CJR 10.3 (1971) 22-26.
Evidence government officials leak top secret information when it suits the government's interests.

1347. Franklin, H. Bruce. War Stars: The Superweapon and the American Imagination. New York: Oxford UP, 1988. 272.
Studies an idea that has beguiled the people of the US since the 18th century: that miraculous new weapons will somehow end war and bring global triumph to US goals. Explores over 200 movies, novels, and stories that influenced later decision-making. Offers also a thorough account of the government's 1940 ukase forbidding all media from mentioning anything about atomic energy, even the names of elements such as uranium.

1347a. Frederick, Howard. Cuban/American Radio Wars: Ideology in International Communications. Norwood, NJ: Ablex, 1986. 200.
The conflict (1979-1982) between the two countries is expressed intensely in the conflict between the Voice of America (VOA) and Radio Havana Cuba (RHC). "Despite protestations of objectivity on both sides," both news services view world events "from ideological vantage points" (2).

1348. Frederick, Howard. "Ideology in International Telecommunication: Radio Wars Between Cuba & the United States." 2 vols. Am. U, 1983. 722. DAI 45 (1984) (Oct. 1984) 979.
Compares Radio Havana Cuba (RHC) and the Voice of America (VOA) as weapons in the battle for the hearts and minds of populations in the hemisphere. Uses a theory of Ideological Propaganda State Apparatuses based upon the writings of Karl Marx, Louis Althusser, and Antonio Gramsci.

1348a. Frederick, Howard. "'La Guerra Radial': US/Cuba Radio Wars." Win 19.15-16 (1983) 18-21.
Both countries are expanding their radio propaganda capabilities. The US has the Voice of America and is building Radio Marti; the Cubans are expanding the scope of Radio Havana Cuba. The author opposes Marti's disinformation function and supports an alternative to these Cold War media--Radio Romero, named after the assassinated Salvadoran Archbishop Oscar Romero, a voice of reconciliation and co-existence.

1349. Frederick, Howard. "La Guerra Radiofonica: Radio War Between Cuba and the United States." The Critical Communications Review, Volume II: Changing Patterns of Communications Control. Ed. Vincent Mosco and Janet Wasko. Norwood, NJ: Ablex, 1984. 119-164.
A history of the US-Cuba struggle via the airwaves, from Radio Swan and the Bay of Pigs through decades of fencing

THE MEDIA

between Voice of America and Radio Havana Cuba, culminating with a discussion of the implications of the Reagan Administration's Radio Marti.

1349a. Free Speech, 1984: The Rise of Government Controls on Information, Debate and Association. New York: ACLU, 1983. 30.
"The effort to restrict, control, and manipulate information that should be available to the public is now emerging as the principle threat to First Amendment rights": restricting travel into and out of the country, expanding the executive branch power to censor and classify, etc.

1350. Friar, David. Conflict of Interest in the Eisenhower Administration. Ames: Iowa State UP, 1969. 238.
Partly explores how the news media under-covered corruption in this administration, which had promised a crusade against wrongdoing in government.

1350a. Friedman, Robert. "The Reporter Who Came in from the Cold." MORE 7.3 (Mar. 1977) 46-48.
Explores newsman Sam Jaffe's eighteen years as an unpaid FBI informant, his motives, and the consequences personally and for journalism.

1351. Fryklund, Richard. "Covering the Defense Establishment." The Press in Washington. Ed. Ray E. Hiebert. New York: Dodd, Mead, 1966. 166-181.
"We lose the fight all the time" for truth about the Pentagon, because "everything is classified," but "I am going to do all I can."

1352. Gelb, L.H. "The CIA and the Press: Bearing Out Seymour Hersh." NR 172.12 (1975) 13-16.
On the accuracy of investigative journalist Hersh's accusation that the CIA conducted illegal domestic covert operations.

1353. Gervasi, Sean. "CIA Covert Propaganda Capability." CAIB 7 (1979-80) 18-20.
An attempt to make a dollar estimate of CIA covert propaganda expenditures in 1978 around $265 million, making it the largest "news" organization in the world.

1354. Gervasi, Tom. The Myth of Soviet Military Supremacy. New York: Harper, 1986. 545.
Forty-five chapters divided into five parts: I. "Myth and Its Role in the Arms Race," II. "The Myth of Soviet Strategic Superiority," III. "The Myth of Soviet Nuclear Superiority in Europe," IV. "The Myth of Soviet Conventional Superiority," V. "Creating the Myth." Several chapters deal directly with media complicity in creating and sustaining the myth: Chap. 14, "The Machinery of Coercion," Chap. 15, "The Power of Information," Chap. 19, "Disseminating the Myth," Chap 31, "The Common Wisdom."

1355. Ginsburg, Carl. Race and Media: The Enduring Life of the Moynihan Report. New York: Institute for Media Analysis, 1989. 80.
Daniel Patrick Moynihan, an official in the Johnson administration, in 1965 argued that because the Negro family was so immersed in a virtually hopeless pathology the federal government should treat the situation with what was later called "benign neglect." This book opposes the policy and its promotion by "the corporate-owned media . . . over a 20-year period" (vii).

1356. Gitlin, Todd. "The Greatest Story Never Told." MJ 12.5 (June-July 1987) 27-31, 45-47.
How the media ignore the real issues of the arms race; e.g., Star Wars, the Soviet Test Moratorium. The media define the issues as the Establishment define them.

1357. Gitlin, Todd. "How the Center Shifted Right." Na 239 (Nov. 24, 1984) 545-46.
The press stays in the center, and "the center has veered to the [Reagan] right."

1357a. Gonzalez-Manet, Enrique. "Radio Aggression Against Cuba." The Hidden War of Information. Norwood, NJ: Ablex, 1988. 69-78.
Examines radio as an instrument of subversion, as illustrated by "Radio Marti," directed against Cuba as part of a "continent-wide ideological initiative to 'control Latin American minds and intellectuals'" (70).

1358. "Government and the Media." Readings in Mass Communication: Concepts and Issues in the Mass Media. Ed. Michael C. Emery and Ted Curtis Smythe. Dubuque, IA: Wm. C. Brown, 1974. 376-438.
Eight essays on Watergate, the president and the press, use of classified information, the Vietnam War, etc.

1359. "Government Secrecy: Signs of the Times." ORK (Summer 1982) 16-20.
Instances of refusals by government officials to furnish documents and information about their activities.

1360. Graber, Doris. Media Power in Politics. 2nd ed. Washington, DC: Congressional Quarterly, 1990. 416.
Thirty-seven selections in six sections each on "the influence of mass media on an important facet of U.S. politics": political opinions and preferences, presidential and congressional elections, participants within and outside the political power structure, and formation and implementation of domestic and foreign public policies. Part 6 examines efforts to control the impact of the mass media.

1361. Graber, Doris, ed. The President & the Public. Philadelphia: Institute for the Study of Human Issues, 1982. 310.

THE MEDIA   211

Ten chapters in four parts: "The Presidential Image," "Media
Portrayals," "The Electoral Connection," and "Appraisals of
Presidential Performance." The subject is the linkage between
"the single most important figure in American politics" and
his constituency, an interaction carried through the mass
media.

1362. Graber, Doris. "Press and TV as Opinion Resources in
       Presidential Campaigns." POQ 40 (Fall 1976) 285-303.
Media concentrate on personality rather than qualifications
and issues. Print media present more negative pictures than
TV; TV presents simple pictures.

1363. Graber, Doris. "The Press as Opinion Resource During
       the 1968 Presidential Campaign." POQ 35 (1971) 168-
       182.
Analysis of campaigning by personality and imagery instead
of issues and the dependence of media on information provided
by candidates.

1364. Graham, Fred P. Press Freedoms Under Pressure: Report
       of the Twentieth Century Fund Task Force on the
       Government and the Press. New York: Twentieth
       Century Fund, 1972. 193.
Prepared with a common concern "about governmental infringe-
ments" on the nation's press. Opposes press subpoenas
(supports news people's privilege to protect the flow of
information to the public), police posing as journalists, etc.

1365. Granato, Leonard. "Prior Restraint: Resurgent Enemy of
       Freedom of Expression." Ph.D. Diss., Southern
       Illinois U, 1973. 538. DAI 34 (1974) 5895-A.
Supreme Court erosion of the First Amendment is clarified by
a history of prior restraint.

1366. Gravois, John, and Walt Potter. "How the Press Misses
       the Beat." WJR 4.1 (1982) 29-32.
On media neglect of regulatory agencies.

1367. Green, Mark. "Amiable Dunce or Chronic Liar?" MJ 12.5
       (1987) 9-17.
Despite President Reagan's obvious ignorance and innumerable
"misstatements," until the Iran-contra affair the American
press was unwilling to undertake any significant criticism of
the popular leader.

1367a. Greenfield, Jeff. The Real Campaign: How the Media
       Missed the Story of the 1980 Campaign. New York:
       Summit, 1982. 319.
Factors other than the media shaped the outcome of the election: the Republican Party raised five times the money of the
Democrats, the steady rise of Republican voters, Reagan's
clear ideological values.

1368. Gresham, Jewell. "The Politics of Family in America."

Na 249.4 (July 24-31, 1989) 116-122.
The Moynihan Report (1964) blaming black families and calling for "benign neglect" has dominated government and media.

1369. Grossman, Michael, and Martha Kumar. Portraying the President: The White House and the News Media. Baltimore: Johns Hopkins UP, 1981. 358.
A study of NYT, Time, and CBS news reveals a "consistent pattern of favorable coverage of the President," a tribute to the "vast array" of presidential public relations.

1370. Grossman, Michael, and Martha Kumar. "It is Inevitable, Say Two Scholars on the White House. The Institution, Not the Men, Makes it So." WJR 2.4 (1980) 52-56.
News management is inherent in the executive branch.

1371. Grossman, Michael, and Francis Rourke. "The Media and the Presidency: An Exchange Analysis." PolSQ 91.3 (1976) 455-470.
Collaboration more than opposition characterizes presidency/press relations.

1372. Guatemala! The Horror and the Hope. Ed. Rarihokwats. York, PA: Four Arrows, 1982. 288.
US support of Guatemalan state terrorism includes repression of the media there and collusion by the media here.

1373. Guttman, Daniel, and Barry Willner. The Shadow Government. New York: Pantheon, 1976. 354.
The government-corporate complex functions partly through consultant corporations and think tanks funded by corporations. Introduction by Ralph Nader.

1374. Halliday, Fred. "Managing The News In The East And West." ITT 9.37 (1985) 17.
Describes the US as a propaganda and disinformation center.

1375. Hallin, Daniel. The "Uncensored War": The Media and Vietnam. New York: Oxford UP, 1986. 285.
Examines the NYT and network news coverage of the Vietnam War from 1961 to 1973, presidential constraints over the press, Cold War ideology shared by presidents and journalists, news conventions and news management, coverage of the Tet offensive, and the shifts in media as political climate changed. In general, official perspectives dominated the media.

1376. Halperin, Morton. "The CIA and Manipulation of the American Press." FP 3.5 (1978) 1-5.
On CIA covert use of and intrusion into the press.

1377. Halperin, Morton. "Secrecy and National Security." BAS 41 (Aug. 1985) 114-117.
Condemns increased executive and judiciary constraints on publication and debate.

1378. Hammitt, Harry. "The Breadth of National Security."
	IREJ 11.3 (Summer 1988) 18-19.
The US government continues to deny public access to the workings of government.

1379. Hammond, William. U.S. Army in Vietnam, Public
	Affairs: The Military and the Media, 1962-68.
	Washington, DC: Army Center of Military History, 1988. 413.
Not news media coverage but rising casualties and lack of a winning strategy led to erosion of public support for the war.

1380. Hansen, Allen. USIA: Public Diplomacy in the Computer
	Age. New York: Praeger, 1984. 250.
Surveys the agency's global organization, its media (radio, books, press, videotapes), and similar agencies in other countries.

1381. Hanson, C.T. "Gunsmoke and Sleeping Dogs: the Prez's
	Press at Midterm." CJR 22 (May-June 1983) 27-35.
"The White House press served with unusual frequency during Reagan's first two years as a kind of Pravda of the Potomac, a conduit for White House utterances and official image-mongering intended to sell Reaganomics."

1382. Hardt, Hanno. "Power--and the Courage to be Free."
	JoC 26.1 (1976) 141-47.
Six books dealing with the press and the First Amendment express a consensus that "power, in whatever form, corrupts and that a complacent public and a negligent professional attitude contribute significantly to the deterioration of personal and professional liberties."

1383. Harris, Richard. "The Strange Love of Dr. Kissinger."
	MORE 2.3 (1972) 1, 14-16.
How Nixon and Kissinger duped the compliant press regarding peace negotiations with North Vietnam.

1384. Hart, Roderick. The Sound of Leadership: Presidential
	Communication in the Modern Age. Chicago: U of Chicago P, 1987. 277.
A study of modern presidential communications (Truman through Reagan) that reflect "a new American presidency" affecting both leadership and citizenship in ways "manifestly unfortunate for the American people." Presidential speech-making has increased greatly since the 1940s, has provided the presidency with unprecedented power, until presidents now view speaking directly to the people as their greatest political asset (xxii). Hart sees the presidency and the mass media as "the two most powerful entities in the US today, together invincible" (111).

1385. Hart, Roderick. "Speech and Choice: The Presidential
	Election." The Sound of Leadership: Presidential Communication in the Modern Age. Chicago: U of

Chicago P, 1987. 155-189.
Analyzes the "rhetorical dimensions of the modern campaign." "Rhetoric is used to reclothe the presidency, to make it seem that even the crassest form of campaigning is nothing less than an institutional mandate"; nevertheless, "each of the last eight presidents has found a unique campaign style" in pursuit of power.

1386. Hart, Roderick. Verbal Style and the Presidency: A Computer-Based Analysis. Orlando, FL: Academic, 1984. 322.
A computer study of the speeches of presidents from Truman to Reagan. The symbiotic relationship between the media and the powerful speaking president necessitates the rhetorical study of the presidency.

1387. Hentoff, Nat. "How We Got an Official Secrets Act." Prog 53.3 (Mar. 1989) 10-11.
On October 19, 1988, the US Supreme Court refused to review the espionage conviction of Samuel Loring Morison, the first US citizen to be imprisoned for disclosing Government information to the press.

1388. Herman, Edward. "Disinformation & 'Defense' Limits on Free Speech." Z 1.11 (Nov. 1988) 10-12.
Explains state constraint of dissent and lying by people in power. "We can formulate two laws: a 'power law of access' and an 'inverse power law of truthfulness.'"

1389. Herman, Edward. "Mideast Cornucopia." Z 1.2 (Dec. 1988) 37-39.
"The Big Lie and Doublespeak are nowhere more pervasive than in U.S. discourse on Israel, the Palestinians, and Middle Eastern issues."

1390. Herman, Edward. "Moderates & Extremists." Z 1.3 (Mar. 1988) 29-31.
"Media doublespeak identifies as a 'moderate' anybody who will serve the interests of U.S. power."

1391. Herman, Edward. The Real Terror Network: Terrorism in Fact and Propaganda. Boston: South End, 1982. 252.
A survey of the state-sanctioned terror campaigns of US sponsored dictatorships and the mass media's failure to report them adequately and to analyze the contradictions of US terrorism policies.

1392. Herman, Edward. "Terrorism & Retaliation." Z 1.4 (Apr. 1988) 23-24.
Analyzes the government's doublespeak about retail and wholesale terror that obscures its support of state terrorism.

1393. Herman, Edward. "Toasting Morality." Z 1.2 (Feb. 1988) 36-7.
Mainstream media's soft treatment of Elliott Abrams, George

Bush, and Henry Kissinger illustrates how the powerful influence morality, language, law, and the press, and how liars and criminals in high places receive less severe attention and penalty.

1394. Herman, Edward. "Unesco and the Free Flow of Information." Z 1.10 (Oct. 1988) 41-43.
Analyzes how the media misrepresented the debate over the New World Information Order and the free flow of information.

1395. Herman, Edward, and Frank Brodhead. The Rise and Fall of the Bulgarian Connection. New York: Sheridan, 1986. 255.
US press uncritically transmitted false claims by the Italian secret service and a few US journalists linked to the CIA that Bulgarians attempted to assassinate Pope John Paul II.

1396. Hersh, Seymour. "From the Pentagon: (But Don't Tell Anyone I Told You)." NR 157.24 (1967) 13-14.
Pentagon press corps as propaganda conduit.

1397. Hertsgaard, Mark. "The Big Sellout." Esq 109.5 (May 1988) 78-91.
How the campaign press ignored the issues in 1984 and followed popularity polls, resulting in avoiding Reagan's "simplemindedness" and reflecting the opinions "of the governing political class of which it is a member." Adapted from the author's On Bended Knee.

1398. Hertsgaard, Mark. "Chronicle: The White House Press Takes a Stand." CJR 14.5 (1986) 8, 10.
Reagan administration restrictions on reporters encountered opposition over Foreign Minister Shevardnadze's visit.

1399. Hertsgaard, Mark. "How Reagan Seduced Us." VV (Sept. 18, 1984) 42.
Reagan's distortions and lies are not challenged by the media.

1400. Hertsgaard, Mark. "The Media Wrap Up Iran/Contra." Na 251.1 (July 2, 1990) 9-12.
The public is confused about the Iran/Contra scandal and the Poindexter trial, because the nation's "most influential news organizations have repeatedly failed to see the forest for the trees."

1401. Hertsgaard, Mark. On Bended Knee: The Press and the Reagan Presidency. New York: Farrar, Strauss, Giroux, 1988. 408.
About 175 interviews with journalists, news executives, and Administration officials expose the media as "profit-obsessed corporations" and cause the author to indict the media for failure to fulfill their role as watchdogs of US democracy. The mainstream press went soft in covering Reagan not because he was "the Great Communicator" but because favorable report-

ing of the popular president brought profits to media corporations and because of the unusual cunning of the president's media managers, particularly Michael Deaver and David Gergen.

1402. Hess, Stephen. The Government-Press Connection. Washington, DC: Brookings, 1984. 160.
On the symbiosis between the government PR officer and the press.

1403. Hess, Stephen. The Washington Reporters. Washington, DC: Brookings, 1981. 174.
This study of the domestic Washington press corps finds that they are more apolitical and have greater autonomy than is generally imagined. Reporters tend to follow excitement, which "biases news gathering in favor of certain institutions and certain types of newsmakers," generally choosing to cover the political rather than the permanent government.

1404. Hiebert, Ray E., ed. The Press in Washington: Sixteen Top Newsmen Tell How the News is Collected, Written, and Communicated from the World's Most Important Capital. New York: Dodd, 1966. 233.
Lectures by journalists representing the wire services, the broadcasting networks, and major newspapers and newsmagazines. Subjects: interpretive reporting, investigative reporting, secrecy, classified information, Washington press corps, wire services, newsletters, TV news, radio, covering the branches of government, etc.

1405. Himmelweit, Hilde, et al. How Voters Decide. Milton Keynes, Eng.: Open UP, 1985. 283.
[Although the study is based on British data, its conclusions are relevant to the US.] One conclusion is that the media are not performing responsibly because reporters are inadequately prepared to challenge politicians on the issues, allowing politicians to manage the news.

1406. Hinckle, Warren, and William Turner. The Fish Is Red: The Story of the Secret War Against Castro. New York: Harper & Row, 1981. 373.
Focuses on the CIA, Mafia, big business nexus, with some attention to media.

1407. Hochman, Sandra, and Sybil Wong. Satellite Spies: The Frightening Impact of a New Technology. Indianapolis: Bobbs, 1976. 212.
Describes the government's subsidies to corporations to assist them in gaining satellite domination, and warns of abuses to come.

1408. Hoffman, Nicholas Von. "Dining Out in Medialand." MORE 8.2 (1978) 24-5.
On the collaboration between the Washington press corps and government officials.

1409. Hooper, Alan. The Military and the Media. Brookfield, VT: Gower, 1982. 247.
Mainly from the author's British perspective, but with attention to US experience--e.g., the Vietnam War, the Iranian Embassy siege. Studies the relationship between the two professions and includes case studies of the news process in newspapers, TV, and radio.

1410. Hoyt, Ken, and Frances Leighton. Drunk Before Noon: The Behind-the-Scenes Story of the Washington Press Corps. Englewood Cliffs, NJ: Prentice-Hall, 1979. 418.
Mainly about journalists' private lives, methods, and ideologies, but also covers the Washington news scene--newspapers, newsletters, news bureaus, wire services, public relations firms, tv, etc.

1411. Hume, Brit. "The Invisible Bestseller." MORE 2.8 (1972) 3-4.
Challenges the Washington press corps to confront Robert Winter-Berger's The Washington Pay-Off.

1412. Hume, Brit, and Mark McIntyre. "Polishing Up the Brass. MORE 3.5 (1973) 6-8.
Pentagon press corps collaborates with the Pentagon.

1413. Isaacs, Norman E. "Beyond 'Caldwell'--1. 'There May Be Worse To Come From This Court.'" CJR 11.3 (1972) 18-24.
On June 29, 1972, the Supreme Court ruled that a reporter was without legal right in refusing to provide grand juries with confidential source data.

1414. Johnson, Haynes. "The Irreconcilable Conflict Between the Press & Government: 'Whose Side Are You On?'" Foreign Policy. Ed. Thomas Franck and Edward Weisband. New York: Oxford UP, 1974. 165-178.
Because of the Vietnam War, the press is under attack. But the press partly brought this repression upon itself, for during the Vietnam War "the press allowed itself to be used by the Government. By and large, it was a staunch supporter of government policies, particularly in foreign affairs."

1415. Johnson, M.B. The Government Secrecy Controversy: A Dispute Involving the Government and the Press in the Eisenhower, Kennedy, and Johnson Administrations. New York: Vantage, 1967. 136.
Arguments for and against censorship, the controversy revealing both the imperfections and the vigor of the nation.

1416. "Journalists and the C.I.A.: Should We Forget?" CJR 16.6 (1978) 22.
We should not forget that the CIA used journalists as an arm of propaganda in contempt of a free press.

1417. Kahane, Howard. Logic and Contemporary Rhetoric: The Use of Reason in Everyday Life. Belmont, CA: Wadsworth, 1971. 252.
A textbook on fallacies, not only all the logical fallacies, but also chapters on extended political arguments, selling candidates, managing the news, textbooks and indoctrination, and textbooks and fallacies.

1418. Kalven, Jamie. "At War With the First Amendment." BAS 45.1 (Jan.-Feb. 1989) 56-59.
Recounts the Reagan presidency's assault on freedom of speech, characterizing his program of secrecy and information control as the latest manifestation of a "shadow tradition" in American government which seeks to rule by controlling public discourse.

1419. Kaplan, Fred. "Going Native Without a Field Map." CJR 19.5 (1981) 23-29.
On the uncritical mentality of the Pentagon press corps, specifically regarding President Carter's PD59 (1980) on limited nuclear war.

1420. Karp, Walter. "All the Congressmen's Men: How Capitol Hill Controls the Press." Har 279.1670 (July 1989) 55-63.
Contrary to persistent myths of its "imperial" power, the press "does not act, it is acted upon"; investigative journalism is a rarity, dependence on official sources is the norm, and passive transmittal of their pronouncements in the name of "objectivity" is passed off as news.

1421. Keegan, Paul. "Press Misinterprets TMI Report." WJR 2.1 (1980) 7.
Media's failure to report the Three Mile Island Commission Report accurately as criticism of the nuclear power industry.

1422. Kelley, Kevin. "Broder Goes 'Behind the Front Page.'" Guard 40.4 (Oct. 21, 1987) 2.
David Broder in his book Behind the Front Page (1987) about the Washington Press corps does not challenge "or even perceive the mainstream media's underlying ideology," but he does criticize the press's "procedural failings," such as their coziness with the subjects of their coverage and their at times "gross superficiality."

1423. Kenworthy, Eldon. "Grenada as Theater." WPJ 1 (Spring 1984) 635-51.
Evaluates flaws in the administration's rationalizations for invading Grenada, generally accepted by the media.

1424. Kernell, Samuel. Going Public: New Strategies of Presidential Leadership. Washington, DC: Congressional Quarterly, 1986. 251.
Analysis of presidential activities to promote themselves and their policies before the American public throughout the

twentieth century, examining speeches, public appearances, and travel. Assessment of the role going public can play as a coercive weapon against Congress which forces him into an intensive public relations program.

1425. Kimery, Anthony. "Leak Control." CC 16.2 (Mar.-Apr. 1990) 16-20.
The Reagan administration instigated an intensified crackdown on information disclosures by government officials, and the Bush administration has continued the practice.

1426. Knightley, Phillip. The First Casualty: From the Crimea to Vietnam: The War Correspondent as Hero, Propagandist, and Myth Maker. New York: Harcourt, 1975. 465.
The Korean War (Chap. 14) was heavily censored, the Vietnam War was not (Chapters 16 and 17), but there was elaborate secrecy and news embargoes, especially about the air war (422). "Too few correspondents . . . probed beyond the official version of events to expose the lies and half-truths" (424).

1427. [Cancelled]

1428. Knoll, Erwin. "Communicator." Prog 52.11 (Nov. 1988) 40-41.
Although President Reagan "betrays abysmally muddled thinking," the media created him in the role of the Great Communicator.

1429. Kohn, Edward H. "Justice Seeks to Minimize Release of Information." SLJR 15.98 (1987) 11.
The Freedom of Information Reform Act of 1986 is being used by Federal agencies and departments to minimize access, maximize fees, and "ensure that their work and records will be shrouded by secrecy."

1430. Kondracke, Morton. "The CIA and 'Our Conspiracy.'" MORE 5 (May 1975) 10-12.
On CIA attempts to prevent publication of a story.

1431. Kornbluh, Peter. "Propaganda and Public Diplomacy: Selling Reagan's Nicaragua Policy." Extra! 2.7/8 (Summer 1989) 20-22. (Also PR 2 [Summer 1988] 25-28).
Details the propaganda campaign directed at the American people by the Reagan administration's Office of Public Diplomacy in order to win public support for Nicaraguan contras.

1432. [Cancelled]

1433. Kraus, Sidney, and Richard M. Perloff, eds. Mass Media and Political Thought: An Information Processing Approach. Beverly Hills: Sage, 1985. 350.
Recent thinking on political media processing: voters' ability and motivation, effect of political messages.

1434. Krepon, Michael. "The PR Administration." BAS 42.9 (1986) 6-7.
On the power of Reagan's PR, illogic, and disinformation over the media.

1435. Krinsky, Robert. "The Press Slices Up the Peace Dividend." Extra! 3.3 (Mar.-Apr. 1990) 1, 4.
The media are narrowing the money saved to deficit reduction only.

1436. Kumar, Martha, and Michael Grossman. "Images of the White House in the Media." The President & The Public. Ed. Doris Graber. Philadelphia: Inst. for the Study of Human Issues, 1982. 85-110.
Contrary to presidential complaints, media are overwhelmingly favorable to presidents. A study of Time, NYT, and CBS news.

1437. Lamperti, John. What Are We Afraid Of? An Assessment of the "Communist Threat" in Central America. Boston: South End, 1988. 109.
Chap. 1 discusses the multitude of misleading Sovietphobic speeches, articles, pamphlets, and books that for over forty years have blocked thought and dominated policy. Not only the government but the media have systematically fostered the discrepancy between alleged threat and reality.

1438. Lamperti, John. "Where the Thinking Stops." Fel 54.7-8 (July-Aug. 1988) 9-10.
How the media fosters Sovietphobia which in turn distorts US thinking about other nations and historical events.

1439. Landau, Jack C. "Harassing the Press." MORE 2.12 (1972) 8-9.
On government opposition to reporters.

1440. Landau, Jack C. "The State of the First Amendment." NmR 23.10 (1979) 18-24.
Government attacks on the press.

1441. Lane, Chuck. "Muscling the Media." NR 192.28 & 29 (1985) 22-25.
Documents the career of Richard V. Allen, advisor to President Reagan, who sent a menacing letter to the press urging them to cover him favorably.

1442. Lang, Gladys, and Kurt Lang. The Battle for Public Opinion: The President, the Press, and the Polls During Watergate. New York: Columbia UP, 1983. 353.
Media did not set the agenda of Watergate, but they helped build it by "responding to events" created by political insiders (both the Nixon administration and their opponents--Sirica, et al.) and "contributed to the unemotional response to the end" of the scandal. Each chapter uses a major event to shed light on a basic issue.

1443. Lanouette, William. "Tritium and The Times: How the Nuclear Weapons-Production Scandal Became a National Story." Cambridge, MA: Harvard U Barone Center, 1990. 43.
A massive nuclear waste story known in local and regional and specialized media did not become national news until 1988 through Energy Department leaks, Congressional hearings, and the NYT, which became interested through "a national-security angle based on the importance and scarcity of tritium" (23).

1444. Laurence, John. "In Politics a Joke Is No Laughing Matter." WJR 2.5 (1980) 16-18.
Pressures on reporters not to disclose one of Reagan's racist jokes.

1445. Lazarus, Simon. The Genteel Populists. New York: Holt, 1974. 303.
"In general, relations between the press and high officialdom move along well-grooved routines, if not amicably, then at least according to accepted conventions. . . . The official's command over information unquestionably gives him the upper hand in the relationship" (98).

1446. Lee, Martin A. "Human Rights and the Media: An Overview." Extra! 2.7/8 (Summer 1989) 2-10.
The US media's reporting of human rights violations worldwide "has often reflected the geopolitical priorities of the State Department"; i.e., it tends to ignore or downplay abuses by nations deemed useful to foreign policy objectives.

1447. Lee, Martin A., and Jeff Cohen. "U.S. Media on a Terrorist Tirade." Extra! 2.5 (Mar.-Apr. 1989) 1, 13.
In its current outcry against "international terrorism" the media hypocritically ignore the CIA's employment of Luis Posada, a man known to have bombed a Cuban airliner.

1448. Lens, Sidney. "The Secrecy Mill." Inq 6.12 (Nov. 1983) 14-16.
"The right to know has been increasingly curtailed since World War II under a steadily enlarged pall of official secrecy."

1449. Leonard, Thomas C. The Power of the Press: The Birth of American Political Reporting. New York: Oxford UP, 1986. 273.
Covers American political reporting to the heyday of muckraking.

1450. "Less Access to Less Information By and About the U.S. Government: A 1981-84 Chronology." Chicago: Association of College and Research Libraries, American Library Assoc., 1984 (with updates).
Describes the Reagan administration's systematic restriction of information.

1451. Leubsdorf, Carl P. "Winging it with Jimmy." CJR 17.2 (1978) 42-43.
Carter administration deception regarding solar energy funding.

1452. Lewis, Anthony. "Legacy of Suspicion Afflicts U.S. As Well." AG (July 12, 199) 9B.
Ideals of freedom and openness are curtailed by the "numberless ways American law and policy are built on fear of communism."

1453. Lewis, Carolyn. "A Reporter Feels the Heat." CJR 18.5 (1980) 34-37.
On the failure of the media to scrutinize the workings of the Three Mile Island Commission.

1454. "The Lie Detector." MO 9.2 (Feb. 1967) 26.
A regular report of official lies by parallel columns that demonstrate discrepancies. [See Albert Kahn's The Unholy Hymnal.]

1455. Lindee, Susan, and Dorothy Nelkin. "Challenger: The High Cost of Hype." BAS 42.9 (1986) 16-18.
On the media's failure to investigate NASA steadily and deeply.

1456. Linenthal, Edward. Symbolic Defense: The Cultural Significance of the Strategic Defense Initiative. Urbana: U of Illinois P, 1989. 139.
"SDI represents another of our periodic national efforts to regain, by semimagical means, that Edenic sense of perfect security"; it is a "secular 'symbol of deliverance.'" Analyzes the rhetorical strategies employed by SDI proponents that exploit the symbol in a vocabulary appropriated from the utopian New Age rhetoric and the peace movement.

1457. Linsky, Martin. Impact: How the Press Affects Federal Policymaking. New York: Norton, 1986. 260.
A study of how government elites manage the press and how the press affect policies by Harvard's Press-Politics Center, one of whose purposes is to assist policymakers to think strategically about the press. The reorganization of the Postal Department in 1969 and the neutron bomb deployment controversy of 1978 are discussed.

1458. Linsky, Martin, Jonathan Moore, Wendy O'Donnell, and David Whitman. How the Press Affects Federal Policymaking: Six Case Studies. New York: Norton, 1986. 373.
Intended to be read in conjunction with Impact: How the Press Affects Federal Policymaking by Linsky. The studies "demonstrate government officials reacting to and anticipating press coverage and using the press" (2). The cases: the reorganization of the Post Office, the resignation of Vice President Spiro Agnew, the neutron bomb, the Love Canal

THE MEDIA 223

relocation, President Reagan and tax exemptions for discriminatory schools, and television and the review of the disability rolls.

1459. Loader, Jayne, Kevin Rafferty, and Pierce Rafferty. The Atomic Cafe. Arlington, VA: Archives Project, 1982. 92 min.
A documentary collage exploration of government propaganda promoting the atomic bomb during the 1940s and '50s. [Also see Kevin Rafferty's The Atomic Cafe: the Book of the Film (Peacock/Bantam, 1982), 122.]

1460. Loory, Stuart. "The CIA's Use of the Press: a 'Mighty Wurlitzer.'" CJR 13.3 (Sept.-Oct. 1974) 9-18.
Newsmen were used as CIA agents to collect intelligence information to spread disinformation as part of Cold War animosity.

1461. Lyons, Gene. "Invisible Wars." Har 263.1579 (Dec. 1981) 37-52. Rpt. The Higher Illiteracy. Fayetteville: U of Arkansas P, 1988. 235-67.
The public relations, hype, and contradictions in the Pentagon's Chemical Warfare program.

1462. Mackenzie, Angus. "Press Fails to Report Reagan Censorship." SLJR 11 (Feb. 1985) 18.
"A White House move to censor the thoughts of three out of five government employees, initially blocked by Congress, has actually quietly been instituted anyway."

1463. Mackenzie, Angus. "Sabotaging the Dissident Press." The Campaign Against the Underground Press. Ed. Geoffrey Rips. San Francisco: City Lights, 1981. 159-170.
The attack was led primarily by the CIA, FBI, and the Army.

1464. Mahoney, Eileen. "Negotiating New Information Technology & National Development: The Role of the Intergovernmental Bureau for Informatics." Temple U, 1987. 633. DAI 48 (1987) 243-A.
Mainly a Third-World organization, the IBI ran aground in conflict with the developed nations, particularly the US, over issues of transborder data flow and technology transfer.

1465. Manoff, Robert K. "Covering the Bomb: Press and State in the Shadow of Nuclear War." War, Peace & the News Media. Ed. David Rubin and Ann Cunningham. New York: New York U, 1983. 197-237.
The media's statist (vs. ethical) assumptions have shaped the reporting of nuclear strategy. The state has established the boundaries of discussion and debate.

1466. Manoff, Robert K. "The Media: Nuclear Secrecy vs. Democracy." BAS 40.1 (1984) 26-29.
"Make no mistake about it: the press has become an essential

component in the epistemological apparatus of the nuclear regime" (29).

1467. Manoff, Robert K. "The Silencer." The Quill (Feb. 1984) 5-11.
Deplores the secrecy of the "nuclear régime" that began in WWII, because it subverts democracy.

1468. Manoff, Robert K. "State-Sponsored Journalism." Prog 50.6 (1986) 36.
The press is "captive to its government sources, its jingoistic rhetoric," and its general deference to government.

1469. Marchetti, Victor L., and John D. Marks. "Undercovering the CIA." MORE 4.4 (Apr. 1974) 8, 10, 14.
"Intelligence operations generally enjoy soft treatment by the press."

1470. Marro, Anthony. "When the Government Tells Lies." CJR 23 (Mar.-Apr. 1985) 29-41.
On how journalists might deal with official deceptions.

1471. Marwick, Christine M. "The Growing Power to Censor." FP 4.10 (1979) 1-5.
Secrecy expanding under Carter.

1472. Maslow, Jonathan Evan, and Ana Arana. "Operation El Salvador." CJR 20.1 (1981) 52-58.
The media docilely repeat administration falsehoods about El Salvador.

1473. Massing, Michael. "About-Face on El Salvador." CJR 22.4 (1983) 42-49.
Reagan's influence over media coverage of El Salvador is turning the press away from attention to death squads and land reform.

1474. Massing, Michael. "The Invisible Story." CJR 19.4 (1980) 51-54.
Failure of the media to investigate the Stealth aircraft. [In 1989 each bomber was estimated to cost over $1 billion, while evidence mounted of its failure to perform as publicized.]

1475. Mathews, Jay. "All the President's Men." CJR 20.4 (1981) 5-7.
Reporters are uncritical of Reagan.

1476. McCombs, Maxwell E., and Donald L. Shaw. "The Agenda-Setting Function of Mass Media." POQ 36 (1972) 176-187.
"In reflecting what candidates are saying during a campaign, the mass media may well determine the important issues--that is, the media may set the 'agenda' of the campaign."

THE MEDIA

1477. McGovern, George. "George McGovern: The Target Talks Back." CJR 23.2 (1984) 27-31.
Presidential hopeful McGovern describes himself as running on issues and blames the press for neglecting his candidacy and the issues.

1478. McGrory, Mary. "Nixon Now Celebrity, So Press Forgives All." AG (Jan. 9, 1989) 5B.
In spite of Nixon's contempt for the Constitution, law, and the press, he is now treated as an elder statesman celebrity by the media.

1478a. McNichol, Tom. "End-running the Networks." CJR 23 (Mar.-Apr. 1985) 20-23.
On the development of direct televised broadcasting from the White House to local stations, free of charge.

1479. "The Media Go to War--From Vietnam to Central America." Spec. no. of RA 17 (July-Aug. 1983).
On the administration's domination of news.

1480. "Media, Political Access and Social Change." Win 19.15 & 16 (1983).
On government uses of the media and speculations about a more democratic media; six essays.

1481. Michener, James A. "GOP's Methods Frightening." AG (Dec. 11, 1988) 1C, 6C.
Denounces George Bush's 1988 presidential campaign as "American-style fascism": using the "big lie," distorting national emotional symbols, accusing opponents of being unpatriotic, and racism.

1482. "Militarism: The Media Connection." M&V 39 (Spring 1987). 24.
Seven articles and eight notes. Four articles on relation of Sovietphobia and militarism.

1483. Miller, Arthur S. "Carter and the CIA." Prog 41.5 (1977) 9-10.
President Carter's tightening secrecy.

1484. Miller, Susan. "Reporters and Congressmen: Living in Symbiosis." JM 53 (Jan. 1978) 1-25.
The media are inextricably involved in the processes of government, serving both as an influence upon and an information conduit for lawmakers.

1485. Milligan, Bryce. "Chomsky: The Terrorism Within." TO 81.26 (Feb. 10, 1989) 18-19.
Review of The Culture of Terrorism. The US government has repeatedly revised the factual record in foreign events to satisfy national interests and ideology as those in power view them, regardless of truth and justice. His evidence is "abundant and well documented."

1486. Millman, Joel. "Narco-terrorism: A Tale of Two
 Stories." CJR 25.3 (1986) 48-51.
 Media reported uncritically the government's lie that the
Sandinistas were smuggling drugs, and underreported contra
drug smuggling.

1487. Millman, Joel. "Reagan's Reporters." Prog 48 (Oct.
 1984) 20-23.
 The press often does the Pentagon's spadework, conditioning
the American public to accept an aggressive US role in Central
America.

1488. Mink, Patsy. "The Cannikin Papers: A Case Study in
 Freedom of Information." Secrecy and Foreign Policy.
 Ed. Thomas Franck and Edward Weisband. New York:
 Oxford UP, 1974. 114-131.
 An account by a Representative of the efforts of some
members of Congress to acquire information about the Amchitka
nuclear tests, which President Nixon had denied in virtual
nullification of the FOIA of 1966 ("exemptions have been
interpreted so broadly by the Executive Branch as to render
the Act almost meaningless").

1489. Minor, Dale. The Information War. New York: Hawthorn,
 1970. 212.
 The growing use of secrecy by the government and its
widening activities in communications threaten a free press.
Chapters on US wars since WWII.

1489a. Moffett, Enoch. "Voice of America News: An Organizational Study of Its Struggle for Objectivity." U of
 Georgia, 1987. 256. DAI 48 (1987) 501-A.
 "Nearly all administrations have used VOA as an instrument
for implementing foreign policy," against its mandate to be
"accurate, objective, and comprehensive" and efforts of its
professional staff to be objective. Study of reporting the
Chernobyl nuclear accident, compared to German and British
coverage, supports the argument. Author recommends VOA become
"a nonpolitical independent agency."

1490. Mohr, Charles. "Once Again--Did the Press Lose
 Vietnam?" CJR 22.4 (1983) 51-56.
 Reporters mainly quoted senior officials.

1491. Moraes, Maria, and George Lawton. "Images of Chile in
 the U.S. Press." BS 4 (1974) 1-57.
 Compares hostile US coverage that parroted the government
with more diverse European counter-reporting.

1492. Morley, Morris, and James Petras. The Reagan Adminis-
 tration and Nicaragua: How Washington Constructs Its
 Case For Counterrevolution in Central America. New
 York: Institute for Media Analysis, 1986. 94.
 Exposes the falsehoods of the State Department's "Revolution
Beyond Our Borders": Sandinista Intervention in Central

THE MEDIA

America (1985) (34-84). Introduction by Noam Chomsky emphasizes media double standards and slanted coverage of Central America (1-31).

1493. Morris, Roger. "Reporting for Duty: The Pentagon and the Press." CJR 19.2 (July-Aug. 1980) 27-33.
Coverage of the Soviet invasion of Afghanistan served the Pentagon not truth.

1493a. Moyers, Bill. "High Crimes & Misdemeanors." Frontline. PBS (Nov. 27, 1990). 90 min.
Demonstrates President Reagan and Vice-President Bush and many of their highest national security officials committed felonies and lied systematically and continue to lie about the illegal sales of arms to Iran and diversion of the profits to the contras, and criticizes the media for failing to investigate and expose these crimes. What the officials did was "in effect a coup," the media allowed it to happen, and the conditions for a repetition of the subversion of the US democracy remain.

1494. Murphy, Jay. "Chomsky Exposes Media Distortions of Terrorism." Guard 39.25 (Apr. 1, 1987) 17.
Noam Chomsky's Pirates and Emperors is a "relentlessly researched compendium of government disinformation and lies that indicts the 'free press' as much as it does the policies of the Carter and Reagan administrations."

1495. Nader, Ralph. "Don't Let the Sunshine In." Na 233 (Nov. 7, 1981) 470-473.
Describes the increasing secrecy and censorship under the Reagan administration.

1496. Nessen, Ron. It Sure Looks Different from the Inside. Chicago: Playboy Press, 1978. 367.
Full of details about White House/press relations by President Ford's press secretary, who believed "the Ford administration was constantly scrutinized by the press through a lens of suspicion."

1497. "Nicaragua-Baiting." Na 239 (Nov. 24, 1984) 540.
The networks, newsmagazines, NYT and many other newspapers repeat President Reagan's "twisted truths and false claims."

1498. "Nicaragua's Drug Connection Exposed as Hoax." Extra! 2.1 (July-Aug. 1988) 14.
CIA allegations that the Nicaraguan government smuggled cocaine were widely reported; the disclosure that the allegations were fabricated was little reported.

1499. "Nicaragua in the News: Phantom Guns & Terror Plots." Extra! 2.3 (Nov.-Dec. 1988) 3.
Illustrations of media misrepresentation of Nicaragua.

1500. "Nicaragua and the US Media--A History of Lies."

Extra! 1.4 (Oct.-Nov. 1987) 1-16.
Entire issue on White House, State Department, and Pentagon lies about Nicaragua which are treated generally uncritically by the media.

1501. Nigut, Bill, Sr. "Will 1988 Be the Year of a U.S.-Iran Rapprochement?" CMC (Mar. 1988) 3-6.
At his February 24, 1988, news conference (his first in four months) Reagan was not asked about possibly the biggest news story of the year: a "U.S. and Iran rapprochement and the release of the Americans being held hostage."

1502. Nigut, Bill, Sr. "The Wounding of America by the Potomac Army of Press Pgymies." CMC (Apr.-May 1988) 4-6.
Denounces practice of anonymous sources.

1503. Nimmo, Dan. Newsgathering in Washington. New York: Atherton, 1964. 282.
"News results from the interaction of two processes" of government officials dispensing and journalists gathering information, the former seeking to influence, the latter serving as a filter. Focuses on public relations officers and news organizations. [See Chittick.]

1504. Noah, Timothy. "The Pentagon Press: Prisoners of Respectability." WM 15 (Sept. 1983) 40-45.
Another example of how poor is Pentagon reporting: whistleblower George Spanton.

1505. Ohmann, Richard. "Worldthink." Politics of Letters. Middletown, CT: Wesleyan UP, 1987. 187-97. (Rptd. Beyond Nineteen Eighty-Four. Ed. William Lutz. Urbana, IL: NCTE, 1989.)
The doublespeak of US nuclear confrontation and imperialism "has evolved through a complex process," including the "tendency for Pentagon-talk to become media language over a period of time."

1506. Orr, C. Jack. "Reporters Confront the President: Sustaining a Counterpoised Situation." QJS 66 (Feb. 1980) 17-32.
Critical questions at presidential press conferences tend to come at measured intervals; i.e. they are a ritual.

1507. O'Shaughnessy, Hugh. Grenada: An Eyewitness Account of the U.S. Invasion and the Caribbean History That Provoked It. New York: Dodd, 1984. 261.
Includes comment on the lies successfully dispensed by the government at the invasion in the absence of journalists.

1508. Osner, Audrey. "From Washington, a Chill Wind." UM 2.6 (Feb. 1972) 13-14.
Review of The Engineering of Restraint: The Nixon Administration and the Press by Fred Powledge, "an informal history of persecution of the press, starting with Agnew's November

THE MEDIA

1969 Des Moines speech."

1509. "Other Voices--On Grenada." CJR 22.5 (1984) 20-21.
On the news blackout during the invasion of Grenada.

1510. "Otto Reich: State Propagandist on Central America." Extra! 1.1 (June 1987) 3.
The State Department's Office of Public Diplomacy, launched in 1983, shapes media coverage of Central America.

1511. Packer, Kathy. "Freedom of Expression in the American Military: A Modeling Analysis." U of Minnesota, 1987. 413. DAI 48 (1987) 1047-A.
"No compelling proof of need exists for the degree of curtailment of expression existing in the military."

1512. Paletz, David, et al. "How the Media Support Governmental Authority." POQ 35 (Spring 1971) 80-92.
The authors identify "a number of mechanisms through which local print media reinforce the authority of local governing bodies."

1513. Paletz, David, and K. Kendall Guthrie. "The Three Faces of Ronald Reagan." JoC 37.4 (Fall 1987) 7-23.
The local newspaper through its wire service, the Associated Press, presents Reagan "most favorably." The NYT offers a more complex presidential picture, sometimes, like the local paper, serving "as a conduit" for Reagan's "version of events," but also presenting other sides. "CBS Evening News" "shows Reagan almost whenever he makes himself available." But none of these three media captures Reagan "beyond the clichés."

1513a. Panfilov, Artyom. Broadcasting Pirates, or Abuse of the Microphone: An Outline of External Political Radio Propaganda by the USA, Britain, & the FRG. Trans. Nicholas Bolrov. Moscow: Progress, 1981. 200.
A history of US, British, and West German "saboteur" radio propaganda during peace time.

1514. Panfilov, Artyom, and Yuri Karchevsky. Subversion by Radio: Radio Free Europe and Radio Liberty. Moscow: Novosti, 1974. 189.
History of the two CIA-financed radio stations in Europe.

1514a. Pearson, David. "The Media and Government Deception." PR 4 (Spring 1989) 6-11.
Explores the media's tendency to function as a conduit for government deception,

1515. Peck, Keenen. "A Freeze on Facts." Prog 49 (Apr. 1985) 28-30.
The new regulations "seem designed to hamper not saboteurs but Government watchdogs, historians, the news media, and users of the Freedom of Information Act."

1516. "The Pentagon Vs. The Press." Har 271.1626 (1985) 37-52.
A forum entitled "The Military and the News Media," held at Princeton University with representatives of the government and the media.

1517. Perkovich, George. "Is Defense Reporting a Martial Art?" Deadline 2.2 (1987) 7-8.
Increasingly, retired military officers are being hired by newspapers and magazines to cover defense news.

1518. Perrin, Dennis. "Stolid Right Jabs from the 'Con' Cartel." ITT 13.22 (Apr. 26-May 2, 1989) 19.
Evaluates Column Right: Conservative Journalists in the Service of Nationalism by David Burner and Thomas West, about five journalist spokespersons for Reaganism: George Will, William F. Buckley, Charles Krauthammer, Irving Kristol, and Jeane Kirkpatrick.

1519. Perry, Roland. Hidden Power: The Programming of the President. New York: Beaufort, 1985. 232.
Explains the various methods being used to enhance one's image--e.g., the opinion poll.

1520. Peterzell, Jay. "The Government Shuts Up: The Reagan Administration's Stonewalling Reporters." CJR 21.2 (July-Aug. 1982) 31-37.
The Administration restricts information in the name of national security and leaks such information when it suits its purpose.

1521. Petrusenko, Vitaly. A Dangerous Game: CIA and the Mass Media. Trans. Nicolai Kozelsky and Vladimir Leonov. Prague: Interpress, n.d. (ca. 1978). 190.
"Covertly and overtly [the intelligence service] seeks to use to its advantage newspapers, magazines, book publishing houses, the radio and television." Based entirely upon published materials from news media in the United States, Great Britain and other countries.

1522. Pettegrew, Loyd. "A Provocative Deliberation." JoC 37.2 (Spring 1987) 178-79.
Review of Daniel Hallin's The "Uncensored War": The Media and Vietnam. The book provides "compelling evidence" that the media "had a long-term legitimizing role in the deepening involvement in Vietnam," inspired by the commitment of newspeople to Cold War ideology. [See Dorman and Farhang, J. Fred MacDonald, and other books making the same case.]

1523. Picard, Robert. "Pentagon Manipulated Satellite Story." SLJR 11 (Feb. 1985) 9.
The media missed the real issues of the militarization of space and the Reagan administration's increasing efforts to control information.

1524. Pollard, James E. The Presidents and the Press. New York: Macmillan, 1947. 866.
A history of presidential communications as it developed into "the greatest sounding board in the land," with particular attention to the press conference.

1525. Polluting the Censorship Debate. Washington, DC: ACLU, 1986. 200.
An analysis of the constitutional and policy defects in Attorney General Ed Meese's attack on sexual material.

1526. Ponder, Stephen. "News Management in the Progressive Era, 1898-1909: Gifford Pinchot, Theodore Roosevelt, and the Conservation Crusade." U of Washington, 1985. 256. DAI 46 (1986) 2843-A.
The "system of executive branch news management" began and expanded "during the presidency of Theodore Roosevelt, 1901-1909," who employed press aides, commissions, and other devices to promote his ideas.

1527. Popkin, James. "Running the New 'Improved' FOIA Obstacle Course." CJR 28.2 (July-Aug. 1989) 45-48.
Under the changes that took effect in 1986 and 1987 obtaining government documents has become more difficult.

1528. Porter, William. Assault on the Media: The Nixon Years. Ann Arbor: U of Michigan P, 1976. 320.
Sets forth Nixon's campaign against the news media.

1529. Powe, Lucus A., Jr. "The Constitutional Implications of President Reagan's Censorship Directive 84." CM 17.2 (1984) 2-9.
Reagan's order requiring all officials with access to classified information to submit publications to government review thwarts the First Amendment and apes totalitarian methods.

1530. Powell, Jody. The Other Side of the Story. New York: Morrow, 1984. 322.
President Carter's press officer examines objectionable news stories and identifies media's commercial motive as the culprit. [See No. 1496].

1531. Powell, Lee R. J. William Fulbright and America's Lost Crusade: Fulbright's Opposition to the Vietnam War. Little Rock, AR: Rose Pub., 1984. 258.
Parts of this book deal with Fulbright's efforts to provide a forum for debate about the war as a counter to the government's domination of information through the media, secrecy, lying, etc.

1532. Powers, Richard. G-Men: Hoover's FBI in American Popular Culture. Carbondale: Southern Illinois UP, 1983. 356.
Account of the FBI's image and image-making, how a secret police and its mendacious director managed to become so

popular. Some chapters: "Hollywood and Hoover's Rise to Power," "The FBI Formula and the G-Man Hero," "Public Hero Number One: J. Edgar Hoover and the Detective Pulps."

1533. Powledge, Fred. The Engineering of Restraint: The Nixon Administration and the Press. Washington: Public Affairs, 1971. 53.
Nixon administration's attacks on the press amount to a massive attempt to undermine the First Amendment. [See No. 1528].

1534. "The Press's Own War Games." CJR 19.5 (1981) 19-21.
Pentagon reporters as extensions of the military.

1535. Preston, William, Jr. "The U.S., Nazis, and the U.N.: Media Bias in the Cold War." LOOT 1.7 (July 1990) 7-8.
Anticommunism and national self-interest produced covert operations in which "even war criminals were welcome," but the mainstream media failed to investigate and expose.

1536. Preston, William, Jr., and Ellen Ray. "Disinformation and Mass Deception: Democracy as a Cover Story." ORK (Spring 1983) 1-10.
Ronald Reagan manufactures disinformation on four levels: overt (e.g., the Voice of America), covert operations by the CIA (e.g., "blowback"), press manipulation (e.g., State Department "White Papers"), and use of disinformation peddlers (e.g., the Reader's Digest).

1537. Ragazzini, Giuseppe, Donna Miller, and Paul Bayley. Campaign Language: Language, Image, Myth in the U.S. Presidential Election 1984. Bologna: CLUEB, 1985. 370.
Several essays on aspects of language (JoC 37.1 [Winter 1987]).

1538. Raloff, Janet. "Coming: The Big Chill." Freedom at Risk: Secrecy, Censorship, and Repression in the 1980s. Ed. Richard O. Curry, Philadelphia, PA: Temple UP, 1988. 86-93.
Reagan administration's increased secrecy and censorship.

1539. "The Reagan Administration & the News Media." FYI Media Alert 1987 (Reporters Committee for Freedom of the Press), 1987. 50.
Lists 135 specific actions by which the Reagan administration and its supporters have restricted public and media access to government information: threatened prosecution, expulsion of foreign journalists, lie detectors, etc.

1540. "Reagan's Media for Secrecy Control." SLJR 16.102 (May 1988) 12.
The media have neglected Reagan administration information control.

THE MEDIA

1541. Reding, Andrew. "Under Construction: Nicaragua's New Polity." C&C 45 (July 22, 1985) 269-77.
In foreign affairs coverage, the media "tend to accept official guidance uncritically, as well illustrated by their reporting of Nicaragua.

1542. Relyea, Harold, et al. The Presidency and Information Policy. New York: Center for the Study of the Presidency, 1981. 216.
Essays cover a wide range of issues: openness v. secrecy, executive privilege, national security, media image, etc.

1543. Reston, James. "Politicians Worry About TV, Not Editors." AG (Apr. 18, 1985) 17A.
The American Society of Newspaper Editors assembled in Washington received more evidence that they were being "used as transmission belts to publish what officials [Ronald Reagan] say on television." Reagan is compared to Lenin.

1544. Rice, Jim. "A Clearly Present Danger." Soj 19.4 (May 1990) 44-7.
Tom Clancy's novels totally mirror militarist perspectives and in turn reinforce them among government and military officials.

1545. "Richard Nixon: By the Press Obsessed." CJR 18.1 (May-June 1989) 46-51.
A collection of internal memos of the Nixon White House reveals its campaign to intimidate the press.

1546. Rivers, William. The Opinion Makers. Boston: Beacon, 1965. 207.
An anecdotal overview of the Washington media/government complex providing insights into the relationships of journalists and public officials, highlights of the history of news management, and underscoring trends of change. Concludes that the public is "not abjectly at the mercy of opinion leaders, but that the mass media must face up to their involvement in public affairs."

1547. Rivers, William. The Other Government: Power and the Washington Media. New York: Universe, 1982. 240.
Explores the "double mirror" relationship between various sectors of government and the press, and analyzes the successes, failures, strengths, weaknesses and biases of Washington correspondents.

1548. Robinson, Michael, and Maura Clancey. "King of the Hill." WJR 5.6 (1983) 46-9.
A survey of senior congressional staff about their "news habits and the news habits of their bosses" found that the WP "totally dominates the daily news on Capitol Hill," the "CBS Evening News" runs second, and the NYT "a poor third."

1549. Rogan, Mary. "Increasing Secrecy in an Orwellian

1984." ORK (Spring 1984) 5-6.
"The Reagan administration, more than any other in recent memory, feels the need to divorce the people from the information required for an informed electorate."

1550. Romm, Joseph J. "The Defense Story of the Nineties: Shrinking Pains for the Peacetime Pentagon." Deadline 5.3-4 (Summer 1990) 3-6, 14.
Media's Pentagon and arms coverage extremely inadequate and often "seemed to accept the administration's own views."

1551. Rosen, Jay. "The Campaign Press and Nuclear Issues." Deadline 3.4 (July-Aug. 1988) 6-8.
The media contributed to public misinterpretation of Michael Dukakis's stand on the use of nuclear weapons.

1552. Rosen, Jay. Democracy Overwhelmed: Press and Public in the Nuclear Age. New York: New York U, Center for War, Peace, and the News Media, 1988. 45.
Nuclear weapons "overwhelm the means by which issues come to the attention of a democracy" (27). Nuclear weapons "make the watchdog function meaningless by encouraging citizens to evacuate the public realm, and acquiesce in the management of the nuclear question by government" (31), that is, by officials and technical (not ethical) experts.

1553. Rosenau, Neal. "The Secret Plan to End the War." ChJR 5.9 (1972) 3-5, 16-18.
On media failure to inform the public adequately about the Vietnam War--e.g. Nixon's increase of bombing.

1554. Rosenbaum, Robert, et al. "The Enlargement of the Classified Information System." Academe 69.1 (Jan.-Feb. 1983) 9a-12a.
An examination of EO 12356 (April 4, 1982), which prescribes a system for classifying information, imperils the freedoms it is meant to protect.

1555. Rubin, David. "Covering the 'Evil Empire.'" M&V 39 (Spring 1987) 7-8.
The US press has reported the SU as Washington saw it and wanted it.

1556. Rubin, David. "INF Inspections: U.S. and U.S.S.R. Quietly Limit Press Access." Deadline 3.5 (Sept.-Oct. 1988) 3-4.
"An ironic by-product of the INF treaty is that the two governments have teamed up to keep their respective publics in the dark about the details of the inspections."

1557. Russo, Anthony. "Inside the RAND Corporation and Out: My Story." Ram 10 (Apr. 1972) 45-55.
On the Pentagon Papers.

1558. Ryan, David. "United States vs. Marchetti and Alfred

THE MEDIA

A. Knopf, Inc. vs. Colby: Secrecy 2: First Amendment 0." HCLQ 3.4 (Fall 1976) 1073-1105.
Seeks a standard to protect both national security and the First Amendment.

1559. Ryan, Randolph. "When a Reporter Tries to Tell the Real Nicaragua Story." BG (Jan. 10, 1987) 11.
The Sandinistas rarely get the truth in the US media.

1560. Sableman, Mark. "Press Rulings Reveal Conservative Tilt." SLJR 19.119 (Sept. 1989) 15.
Recent key press decisions by the Supreme Court, Florida Star v. B.J.F. on the publication of information from public records and Harte-Hanks Communications v. Connaughton on libel, indicate a slight but significant shift toward restricting the press.

1561. Sanford, Bruce. "No Quarter from This Court." CJR 18.3 (1979) 59-63.
Analysis of four cases before the Supreme Court, three of which have "vast implications for access to the news and the freedom to print it": Gannett Co., Inc. v. DePasquale, Hutchinson v. Proxmire, and Wolston v. "Reader's Digest" (the fourth is Herbert v. Lando).

1562. Schaap, William. "Combat Coverage." ORK (Fall/Winter 1984-85) 11-12.
Pentagon and Reagan administration want to restrict reporting of military activities.

1563. Schiller, Herbert. "Journalistic Fervor." JoC 37 (Summer 1987) 155-161.
Evaluates Blanchard's Exporting the First Amendment: The Press-Government Crusade of 1945-1952 on the US/press efforts to obtain international agreement for US-style press practices, a reflection of the official view of cold war history and definitions.

1564. Schmidt, Benno, Jr. "The American Espionage Statutes and Publication of Defense Information." Secrecy and Foreign Policy. Ed. Thomas Franck and Edward Weisband. New York: Oxford UP, 1974. 179-201.
"Our statutes governing publication of defense information are an unacceptable morass," which deeply affects "our freedom to know about vital government decisions" (201).

1565. Schmidt, Benno, Jr. "A New Wave of Gag Orders." CJR 14.4 (1975) 33-34.
Cites examples of unjustified prior restraint of the press in criminal and civil cases.

1566. Schorr, Daniel. "Are CIA Assets a Press Liability?" MORE 8.2 (Feb. 1978) 18-23.
An account of Representative Les Aspin's hearings in 1977 on the issue of CIA involvement with the news media.

1567. Schuman, Frederick. "Cold War: The History of a Delusion." MO 8.1 (Jan. 1966) 16-17.
Ever since the end of WWI US leaders and the press have told the public the Communists are bent on conquering the world, but this is only false propaganda.

1568. "Scott Armstrong on the Media & Contragate." Extra! 1.2 (July 1987) 1, 8-9.
"The overall coverage of the [Iran-Contras] hearings has been poor--but that's an accurate reflection of what's going on in the hearings," in which lying is common.

1569. Scott, Peter D. "George Bush: The Teflon Candidate." Extra! 2.2 (Sept.-Oct. 1988) 1, 4-5.
The campaign patter "of 1980 and 1984 seems to be repeating itself. Instead of analyzing and exposing George Bush's tarnished record, the US press has coated the vice president with the same teflon which protected Ronald Reagan for the past eight years."

1570. Seldes, George. "Journalists and Cardinal Mindszenty." Witness to a Century. New York: Ballantine, 1987. 417-423.
The US press followed the government in misrepresenting as a hero this pro-Nazi, anti-Semitic Cardinal, the falsifications "one of the biggest fakes in U.S. press history."

1571. "Seymour Hersh on Government & Media." Extra! 1.1 (June 1987) 12.
Confronts the problems of White House lying and deceiving and media failure to investigate sufficiently.

1572. Shannon, William. "The Newlywed Game." MORE 4.9 (1974) 1, 19-20.
More instances of weakness of White House press corps.

1573. Sharkey, Jacqueline. "DisInformation, DatInformation: How the CIA Manipulates the Media." TM 20.5 (Dec. 1986-Jan. 1987) 23-28.
Deals with the US/contra invasion of Nicaragua and the ways the CIA indoctrinates and deceives regarding the invasion.

1574. Shils, Edward. The Torment of Secrecy: The Background and Consequences of American Security Policies. Glencoe, IL: Free, 1956. 238.
Demonstrates the destructiveness of secrecy and censorship and appeals for a pluralistic and tolerant society.

1575. "Showing the Flag." CJR 18.6 (1980) 19-20.
The media turned jingoist during the Iranian embassy hostage episode.

1576. Sibbison, Jim. "Dead Fish and Red Herrings: How the EPA Pollutes the News." CJR 27.4 (Nov.-Dec. 1988) 25-28.

THE MEDIA

On lack of vigorous media investigation of the corrupt EPA.

1577. Silver, Craig. "Warspeak." AltM 14.4 (Spring 1984) 14.
"Reaganthink" includes the systematic rationalization of violence, war, and imperialism.

1578. Silverman, Debora. "The Thoroughbred Inauguration: Reaganism and Vreelandian Culture, 1985." Selling Culture. New York: Pantheon, 1986. 137-161.
Compares Nancy and Ronald Reagan at the beginning of his second presidential term to the themes and style of Diana Vreeland's "Man and the Horse" show at the Metropolitan Museum of Art. Reagan's inaugural celebrations and Vreeland's show exhibited "social exclusivity, sartorial elegance, and media-commercial accessibility" (140).

1579. Silverstein, Ken. "The Panama Story, or Here We Go Again." CJR 27.1 (May-June 1988) 20.
Panama coverage "over the past several years demonstrates" how "the press allows the administration to set the nation's foreign news agenda."

1580. Simons, Howard. "Watergate As a Catalyst." MJR 18 (1975) 12-15.
The press was uncritically prepared for the breakin at the Democratic National Headquarters. Then when the WP began to take the story seriously, most other media disregarded it, because of popular credulity regarding the President and the lies and attacks from the White House.

1581. Simpson, Christopher. Blowback: America's Recruitment of Nazis and Its Effects on the Cold War. New York: Weidenfeld & Nicolson, 1988. 398.
US intelligence agencies knowingly hired Nazi criminals for their supposed intelligence value in the Cold War against the Soviet Union; they covered up the program for decades, and then publicly lied about its existence. A "convergence of powerful interests" has "kept this story buried," and US media have been complicit.

1582. Sklar, Holly. "And What's What." Z 1.11 (Nov. 1988) 24-26.
Media double-standard attends to anti-Semitism in the Black community and forgets the racists in the Bush administration and Republican Party.

1583. Sklar, Holly. "Bushwacking." Z 1.12 (Dec. 1988) 7-11.
"The big lie campaign prevailed in 1988 and gave the corporate-military-racist-and sexist complex another four years."

1584. Sklar, Holly. "Lick Low Intensity Conflict Doublespeak." Z 2.3 (Mar. 1989) 42-51.
Urges the media to defeat "LICspeak," since "Low Intensity Conflict" (the author always encloses the phrase in quotation marks) is a euphemism for large-scale atrocities.

1585. Sklar, Holly. "Washington's Contratortions." Z 1.2 (Feb. 1988) 30-35.
On the lies and illegalities of the Reagan Administration in its dealings with Nicaragua.

1586. Small, William. Political Power and the Press. New York: Norton, 1972. 423.
The job of the journalist is to scrutinize government, power, and privilege, to provide the public with the information it needs as citizens. Four ch. on the Pentagon Papers.

1587. Smith, Stephen. "Afraid of Ideas: From Plato to the P.L.O." JoCS 7.1 (1988) 27-37.
Examines government restrictions on the public's ability to receive and consider arguments and information which conflict with government policies. Focuses on 3 issues: three Canadian films excluded from the country, denial of entry visas to foreign speakers, and the closing of the Palestine Information Office.

1588. Snepp, Frank. Decent Interval: An Insider's Account of Saigon's Indecent End Told by the CIA's Chief Strategy Analyst in Vietnam. New York: Random House, 1977. 590.
Contains revelations of government "camouflage" and media complicity.

1589. Soley, Lawrence C. Radio Warfare: OSS and CIA Subversive Propaganda. New York: Praeger, 1989. 249.
Radio subversion practiced during and since WWII. "The CIA world view concerning the 'international Communist enemy' is the outgrowth of the postwar hysteria brought about by congressional opponents of the New Deal."

1590. Solomon, Norman. "Nuclear Weapons Plants: Media Report an Officially Sanctioned Scandal." Extra! 2.3 (Nov.-Dec. 1988) 1, 11.
Mass media "continue to function as accessories of the very nuclear weapons establishment they claim to be probing."

1591. "Some Dirty Dealing in Very High Places and the Media's Lack of Responsibility." ITT 12.39 (Oct. 12-18, 1988) 24, 22.
In spite of revelations in ITT in 1987 and in Playboy in 1988 of a deal between Reagan's 1980 campaign committee and Iran, the story has been avoided by the mainstream media.

1592. Sorensen, Thomas. The Word War: The Story of American Propaganda. New York: Harper, 1968. 337.
A chronologically arranged defense of US foreign propaganda.

1593. Speakes, Larry, and Robert Pack. Speaking Out: Inside the Reagan White House. New York: Scribner's, 1988. 322.
An insider's perspective of the Reagan administration by the

THE MEDIA

former press secretary. [See nos. 1530 and 1496.]

1594. Spear, Joseph. Presidents and the Press: The Nixon Legacy. Cambridge, MS: MIT Press, 1984. 349.
During the 1970s the chief executive's mastery of the media endangered the First Amendment. The author outlines the strategies of the presidential spokesmen, pollsters, image merchants, TV experts, media monitors and others who manipulate the press and public.

1595. Spence, Jack. "Media Coverage of El Salvador's Election." SocR 13.2 (Mar.-Apr. 1983) 29-57.
US media coverage of the March 1982 elections promoted the official US "guerrilla threat" theme and exaggerated the violence by the rebels, while omitting the issues the rebels were fighting for.

1596. Spragens, William. The Presidency and the Mass Media in the Age of Television. Washington: UP of America, 1979. 425.
Focuses especially "on the White House press secretaries and the White House press office, as well as the way in which television networks, metropolitan daily newspapers, wire services, magazines, and other components of the mass media handle news about the President and the Presidency."

1597. Spragens, William, and Carole Terwood. From Spokesman To Press Secretary: White House Media Operations. Washington, DC: UP of America, 1980. 243.
Contains biographical material about press secretaries, including some interviews, and views of press secretaries as both White House colleagues and correspondents perceived them.

1598. St. John-Stevas, Norman. "Art, Morality and Censorship." Ram 2.1 (1963) 40-48.
Defends a "basic principle of liberal society" that "the expression of opinion is free."

1599. Stapen, Candyce. "Radio Free Reagan." WJR 6.9 (1984) 10-11.
A summary of a study showing the favorable coverage of Reagan's weekly radio broadcast.

1600. "State of Siege." CJR 19.1 (1980) 25-26.
Criticizes media's support for the administration's weak human rights policy.

1601. Steele, Richard. "The Great Debate: Roosevelt, the Media, and the Coming of the War, 1940-41." JAH 71.1 (June 1984) 69-92.
How the Roosevelt Administration flooded radio, newspapers, and newsreel producers with the government's point of view. The broadcast and film industries became virtual propaganda arms of Roosevelt.

1602. Stein, Meyer. Under Fire: The Story of American War Correspondents. New York: Messner, 1968. 256.
Chap. 9 complains about US and S. Vietnam news manipulation.

1603. Steinberg, Charles S. The Information Establishment: Our Government and the Media. New York: Hastings, 1980. 366.
Deals with the structure and function of the press in three related and interlocking areas: "the government informational bureaucracy, the liaison between the mass media and the vast federal information apparatus, and the responsibilities and obligations of both the government and the media to each other and to the people" (ix).

1604. Stevenson, Robert L. Communication, Development, and the Third World: The Global Politics of information. New York: Longman, 1988. 223.
Even though the West and particularly the US extended "their political and economic influence as much as colonial powers had been in earlier centuries" out of Cold War fervor, he defends their mass media cultural expansion.

1605. Stone, I.F. "The Arms Lobby & LBJ's Great Society." IFSW 13.4 (Feb. 2, 1965) 1-2.
The White House-military contractors-Congressional-media complex used the old "bomber-gap" fear technique to push through new first-strike Poseidon missiles and other weapons.

1606. Stone, I.F. "The Crisis Coming for a Free Press." IFSW 19.14 (July 12, 1971) 1-4.
The increasing attempts "to prosecute for violation of the government's classification orders involves nothing less than the future of representative government."

1607. Stone, I.F. "The Danger to Liberty in the New Smith Act Decision." IFSW 2.38 (Oct. 25, 1954) 2.
Leading newspapers have not challenged the conviction of Elizabeth Gurley Flynn and the "second string" of Communist leaders, so powerful is the new US inquisition against heresy.

1608. Stone, I.F. "A Fateful Decision Nobody Talks About." IFSW 2.47-48 (Jan. 10, 1955) 1, 8.
Only one of 13 newspapers surveyed (the Louisville Courier Journal) protested the Circuit Court's upholding the McCarran Internal Security Act.

1609. Stone, I.F. "The Hoax That Cost a Trillion Dollars in 25 Years." IFSW 17.15 (July 28, 1969) 1, 4.
The media-supported myth of the Soviet threat has been "the mainstay of the military and the war machine."

1610. Stone, I.F. "How Jog the Numbed Conscience of the American Press?" IFSW 2.35 (Oct. 4, 1954) 2.
The efforts of the US Immigration and Naturalization Service to deport Cedric Belfrage, a writer and editor, for his

THE MEDIA

political views has caused little resistance or even response from the press.

1611. Stone, I.F. "It's Been a Faked Class B Movie from the Beginning." IFSW 13.3 (Jan. 25, 1965) 1, 4.
The government has deceived the public about the Vietnam War.

1612. Stone, I.F. "Jeffersonianism for Export Only." IFSW 14.13 (Apr. 4, 1966) 1, 4.
Police state tactics in US, while Congress and press denounce similar tactics in Hungary.

1613. Stone, I.F. "Little Attention Paid to First Test of New Thought Control Law." IFSW 2.39 (Nov. 1, 1959) 3.
The new Communist Control Act with its registration requirement and vague criteria for defining a Communist "singles out one party for outlawry." This government has set out "to police ideas," and the newspapers are "indifferent."

1614. Stone, I.F. "Mr. Molotov's Time-Bombs." IFSW 2.5-6 (Mar. 1, 1954) 1.
The Berlin Conference on German armament reunification was ill reported to the US public. "What the American public read" was "a 'line' handed out each day to the correspondents."

1615. Stone, I.F. "News Censorship & Nuclear Bombing Now Planned for Vietnam." IFSW 13.11 (Mar. 22, 1965) 2.
Already news blackouts occur.

1616. Stone, I.F. "Nixon, Agnew and Freedom of the Press." IFSW 18.11 (June 1, 1970) 1, 4.
Nixon and Agnew "seem increasingly to regard a free press as another privileged sanctuary" for enemies.

1617. Stone, I.F. Polemics and Prophecies, 1967-70. New York: Random House, 1970. 497.
Essays focused largely on the Vietnam War; illustrative chapters in Part II: "The Fraud with Which Bomb Resumption Was Excused," "The Mendacities Go Marching On, Truce or No Truce," "How TV and Press Were Led to Rehash Those Tet Supply Lies." Part IV on Nixon, Part V on militarism, Part VII on Tonkin Gulf, Part VIII on "Endless War," etc.

1618. Stone, I.F. The Truman Era: How the Cold War Started. New York: Random House/Vintage, 1972 (1953). 226.
A collection of Stone's newspaper columns to 1952 from PM, the New York Star, and the New York Daily Compass, and from The Nation magazine. Many of these essays expose the bigoted anti-Communist dogmas which shaped US policies and contributed to the Cold War. Stone sought to show that the government/ media campaign to paint the US as benevolent, defensive, freedom-loving, and above reproach, and the SU as the opposite, was belied by the facts: US leaders early employed

armed force and supported dictators against popular liberation movements, and they sought to destroy freedoms in the US. They incited fears of foreign attack and domestic subversion to justify global intervention and domestic repression.

1619. Stone, I.F. "What John F. Kennedy Never Understood About Freedom of the Press." In a Time of Torment. New York: Random House, 1967. 391-393.
Kennedy "deeply" resented press criticism and was "eager" to "put restraints on the press."

1620. Stone, I.F. "When the Government Lies, Must the Press Fib?" In a Time of Torment. New York: Random House, 1967. 388-91.
President Kennedy's appeal to the American Newspaper Publishers Association for self-censorship in the handling of news is a totalitarian point of view.

1621. Sussman, Barry. What Americans Really Think: And Why Our Politicians Pay No Attention. New York: Pantheon, 1988. 278.
A study of the political signification of polls.

1622. Swomley, John. Press Agents of the Pentagon. Washington, DC: National Council Against Conscription, 1953. 55.
Analyzes the Pentagon's public relations programs and their contribution to creating a militaristic nation.

1623. Tebbel, John, and Sarah Watts. The Press and the Presidency: From George Washington to Ronald Reagan. New York: Oxford UP, 1985. 583.
The growth of an "imperial presidency" and its accompanying public relations staff, secrecy, and disinformation threaten the First Amendment and democracy.

1624. "Terrorism." CAIB 26 (Summer 1986).
Several articles on the Reagan administration's capture of the definition of "terrorism," followed by the media.

1625. Thomas, Helen. "Ronald Reagan and the Management of the News." The White House Press on the Presidency. Ed. Kenneth Thompson. Lanham, MD: UP of America, 1983. 34-59.
Managed news by the presidency has increased dangerously: secrecy, limited access, photo opportunities, ritualistic press conferences, image consultants, etc.

1626. Thompson, Kate. "Media Disinformation on El Salvador: 'Psychological Warfare Operation' Targets U.S. Public." Alert! 6.10 (Dec. 1988-Jan. 1989) 12.
The Reagan administration's "public diplomacy" program designed to provide "evidence" to support its policies.

1627. Thompson, Kenneth, ed. The White House Press on the

THE MEDIA

Presidency: News Management and Co-option. Lanham, MD: UP of America, 1983. 81.
Speeches by Frank Cormier, James Deakin, and Helen Thomas opposed to presidential news management.

1628. Tracey, Patrick. "Inflating Soviet Star Wars." Extra! 1.5 (Dec. 1987) 7.
Media follow the Reagan administration's distortions of SU ballistic missile research.

1629. Tulis, Jeffrey. The Rhetorical Presidency. Princeton, NJ: Princeton UP, 1987. 209.
History and analysis of "the essence of the modern presidency--rhetorical leadership," in which "popular or mass rhetoric has become a principal tool of presidential governance." Whereas "pre-twentieth-century polity proscribed the rhetorical presidency as ardently as we prescribe it," the "modern rhetorical presidency marks a change in the American meaning of governance." (See 1384-1386.)

1630. Turner, Kathleen. Lyndon Johnson's Dual War: Vietnam and the Press. Chicago: U of Chicago P, 1985. 358.
Focuses on press interaction with Johnson's Vietnam War rhetoric, his manipulation, and his secrecy.

1631. Ungar, Sanford. "'This Is Your FBI'?" MORE 6.3 (1976) 19-22.
"The late J. Edgar Hoover proved a master at manipulating the media," using "enormous financial and human resources" to shape the agency's image.

1632. Ungar, Sanford. The Papers & the Papers: An Account of the Legal and Political Battle Over the Pentagon Papers. New York: New York UP, 1989. 352.
A history from their inception in 1967 through the Supreme Court's decision in June 1971 to permit their continued publication, and an indictment of the abuse of the government's classification system.

1633. "The United States Information Agency: Pushing the Big Lie." LAER 6.7 (1972) 1-31.
Surveys the diverse media methods of the USIA.

1634. Vaughn, Robert. Only Victims: A Study of Show Business Blacklisting. New York: Putnam's, 1972. 355.
Describes the House Committee on Un-American Activities' totalitarian attacks on writers and actors and freedom of thought and speech.

1635. Vaughn, Stephen. Holding Fast the Inner Lines: Democracy, Nationalism, and the Committee on Public Information. Chapel Hill: U of North Carolina P, 1980. 397.
About the US government's "first large-scale propaganda agency," the Creel committee. "The CPI proved spectacularly

successful in mobilizing public opinion behind the country's participation in the World War of 1917-18, popularizing the notion that the struggle was a great crusade to save democracy" (xi).

1636. Walker, Daniel. Rights in Conflict. Report Submitted to the National Committee on the Causes & Prevention of Violence. Chicago: Chicago Study Team, Nov. 18, 1968. Text 233; photog. 88. Rpt. New York: Dutton, 1968. 362.
A study of Democratic Party Convention week in Chicago, August 25-29, 1968, and the violent clash between dissenters against the Vietnam War and the Chicago Police. "Our purpose is to present the facts so that thoughtful readers can decide what lessons come out of them."

1637. Wallace, Jaime. "Freedom of Speech--Continued Erosion of a Fundamental Right." FSULOR 9.4 (1981) 682-692.
A defense of free speech against increasing restrictions.

1638. Wallace, Mike. "Hijacking History: Ronald Reagan and the Statue of Liberty." RHR 37 (Jan. 1987) 119-130.
The restoration and rededication of the Statue of Liberty was part of the Reagan administration's reconstitution of a structure of myths partly fractured in the 1960s and 1970s. This project was rife with historical distortions.

1639. Walters, Robert. "What Did Ziegler Say, and When Did He Say It?" CJR 13.3 (1974) 30-35.
The Nixon Administration for almost six years maintained a conscious policy of dispensing misleading, useless--and sometimes fraudulent--information to the media."

1640. Watkins, John. The Mass Media and the Law. Englewood Cliffs, NJ: Prentice-Hall, 1990. 642.
Designed for journalism and communications courses.

1641. Watters, Susan. "The Seduction of Hildy Johnson." WJR 2.3 (1980) 26-29.
Describes the social relations between media and government policy makers.

1642. Weaver, Carolyn. "When the Voice of America Ignores Its Charter: An Insider Reports on a Pattern of Abuses." CJR 27.4 (Nov.-Dec. 1988) 36-43.
E.g., the VOA is particularly biased in its coverage of Central America, closely following the Reagan policy agenda, "markedly hostile to the Sandinista government and strongly supportive of the contras." Another example: suppression of the Iran-contra scandal. [See CJR's editorial 21].

1643. Weeks, James L. "Comsat: The Technology for Ruling Global Communications." An End to Political Science: The Caucus Papers. Ed. Marvin Surkin and Alan Wolfe. New York: Basic, 1970. 215-240.

THE MEDIA

Examines the Communications Satellite Corporation, a government backed private monopoly corporation with enormous nationalistic power.

1644. Weinberg, Steve. "Creeping Secrecy." CJR 22.4 (1983) 31-32.
President Reagan's Executive Order 12356 radically increased secrecy.

1645. Weinberg, Steve. "Trashing the FOIA." CJR 23.5 (1985) 21-28.
Reagan administration weakening the FOIA.

1646. Weisman, Steven. "The President and the Press: The Art of Controlled Access." NYTM (Oct. 14, 1984) 34-37, 71-74, 80, 82-83.
Surveys various ways President Reagan controls journalists.

1647. Weiss, Philip. "The $220 Grease Job." CJR 27.1 (May-June 1988) 16-18.
The State Department's training school which hires journalists places reporters in conflict of interest; government officials-journalist collegiality--insiderism--"defangs" investigative reporting.

1648. Welch, Susan. "The American Press and Indochina, 1950-1956." Communication in International Politics. Ed. R.L. Merritt. Urbana: U of Illinois P, 1972. 207-31.
"The press . . . certainly did not contribute to the consideration of various alternative policies and their long-range implications." (224) The press "did play a crucial role in developing and sustaining mass and elite public acceptance of the Administration's view of the Indochina situation" (231).

1649. Welty, Gordon. "Deviations from the True Path: KAL 007 and the U.S. Mass Media." Anti-Communism: The Politics of Manipulation. Ed. Judith Joel and Gerald Erickson. Minneapolis: Marxist Educational P, 1987. 165-193.
"The 'Korean Airliner incident' was used to divert the public from several crises by identifying a scapegoat, to push for the MX missile and binary nerve gas, and to improve the president's popularity ratings.

1650. Wete, Francis. "The U.S., Its Press, and the New World Information Order." SLJR (July 1984) 20.
The free flow of information concept is part of "the strategy for U.S. global hegemony."

1651. White, Graham J. FDR and the Press. Chicago: U Chicago P, 1979. 186.
Roosevelt often opposed the press and consistently tried to manipulate it, especially through his press conferences. Most newspaper owners did oppose the New Deal. But Roosevelt praised reporters (but not columnists), using them to undercut

the owners.

1652. Whittemore, L.H. "The Plugging of the President." MORE 2.2 (1972) 4-6.
President Nixon employs the White House press conference to give his versions of reality and policy.

1653. Wiggins, Robert. "Access to the Mass Media: Public's Right or Publishers' Privilege?" Southern Illinois U, 1973. DAI 34 (1974) 5899-A.
The courts have rejected right of access for every viewpoint in recent cases, as in CBS, Inc. v. Democratic National Committee. Offers a "comprehensive treatment of the press access problem."

1654. Wilcott, Jim. "The CIA and the Media: Some Personal Experiences." CAIB 7 (1979-80) 23-24.
"During nine years of employment as an accountant with the CIA (from 1957 to 1966) I became familiar with the widespread use of the media by the CIA."

1654a. Windt, Theodore, Jr. Presidents and Protesters: Political Rhetoric in the 1960s. Tuscaloosa: U of Alabama P, 1990. 384.
From Kennedy's inaugural address to the Yippies, considers people in and out of power and their different rhetorical bases and political contexts, showing how they utilized every form of political discourse available.

1655. Wise, David. "Pressures on the Press." None of Your Business: Government Secrecy in America. Ed. Norman Dorsen and Stephen Gillers. New York: Viking, 1974. 217-250.
Focuses on secrecy and lying by the Johnson and Nixon administrations, and the legal sanctions--prior restraint and subsequent punishment--exerted against the press. Asserts the unqualified right of the press to report about the government.

1656. Witcover, Jules, et al. "The First Amendment on Trial." CJR 10.3 (1971) 7-53.
Seven discussions of the Pentagon Papers and the First Amendment.

1657. Witcover, Jules. "Surliest Crew in Washington." CJR 4.1 (1965) 11-15.
Pentagon press corps, public relations officers and secrecy.

1658. Witcover, Jules. "Washington: Focusing on Nixon." CJR 7.4 (1968-69) 11-17.
Despite Nixon's frequent promises of open government, his 1968 campaign reached a new height in managed news.

1659. Wolfson, Lewis. The Untapped Power of the Press: Explaining Government to the People. New York: Praeger, 1985. 202.

ADVERTISING AND PUBLIC RELATIONS

Surveys press coverage of the institutions and processes of American government and politics: presidency, Congress, judiciary, bureaucracy, elections, state and local government, and the freedom of information laws. Urges less reporting of events and more presentation of analysis and assessment.

1660. Yudof, Mark G. When Government Speaks: Politics, Law, & Government Expression in America. Berkeley: U of California P, 1983. 323.
Investigates the government's propaganda power. By 1975 the Federal Government was one of the nation's ten largest advertisers. Government restrictions on individual speech and even the enormous secrecy lack the danger to liberty posed by government indoctrination.

1661. Zarefsky, David. President Johnson's War on Poverty: Rhetoric and History. University: U of Alabama P, 1986. 275.
Explains how the "War" began, faltered, and failed and analyzes the arguments the politicians used to sell the program to the media and public.

1662. Zins, Daniel. "Nukespeak." Kentucky English Bulletin: Teaching English in a Nuclear Age 34.2 (Winter 1984-85) 74-84.
Because of official misuse and abuse of language about nuclear war, "not only is discussion and debate sharply limited, but our reliance on nukespeak and the language of the pre-nuclear era may preclude any meaningful discussion of these issues."

II. B. ADVERTISING AND PUBLIC RELATIONS

II. B. 1. THE MASS CONSUMPTION SYSTEM (1663-1818)

1663. Pollay, Richard W., comp. Information Sources in Advertising History. Westport, CT: Greenwood, 1979. 330.
Includes an "overview" essay by Pollay and three "bibliographic essays." Two directories identify archives and professional associations. The bibliography covers eleven topics, including histories, psychology and sociology, ethics, textbooks, and fiction.

1664. Adbusters Quarterly: The Magazine of Media & Environmental Strategies 1.1 (Summer 1989). Burnaby, BC, Canada V5B 3S2.
Its aim is to "break the spell that advertising has cast over our culture": in North America $100 billion is spent a year to encourage 6% of the people in the world to "consume one-third of its resources and produce half the non-organic wastes. Advertising encourages the voracious consumption that has already caused irreparable ecological damage."

1665. "Advertising." Readings in Mass Communication:

Concepts and Issues in the Mass Media. Ed. Michael C. Emery and Ted Curtis Smythe. Dubuque, IA: Wm. C. Brown, 1974. 315-340.
Three essays give analysis and remedies for abuses.

1666. Alexander, George. Honesty and Competition: False Advertising Law and Policy Under FTC Administration. Syracuse: Syracuse UP, 1967. 315.
Judicial history for lawyers.

1667. Allen, James S. The Romance of Commerce and Culture: Capitalism, Modernism, and the Chicago-Aspen Crusade for Cultural Reform. Chicago: U of Chicago P, 1983. 336.
The book "discloses the dynamics" of ambivalence toward modern "cultural disunity and spiritual aridity," industrial production, consumer capitalism, mass advertising, and public relations, and tells the story of some endeavors to resolve the ambivalence during the first half of the twentieth century among consumer capitalism, art and design, educational theory, cultural criticism, and "the making of Aspen, Colorado, as a center of cultural reform and of fraternization for America's intellectual, managerial, and political elites" (xii-xiii).

1668. Anderson, Michael H. Madison Avenue in Asia: Politics and Transnational Advertising. Cranbury, NJ: Fairleigh Dickinson UP, 1984. 353.
Transnational advertising agencies, particularly those of the US, "do exercise power over value forming institutions" and advertising "does exhibit the general interaction structure that Galtung's [imperialism] model hypothesized."

1669. Aronson, Steven. Hype. New York: Morrow, 1983. 399.
A study of celebrities and their creators, chapters on Cheryl Tiegs, film stars, hairdressers, plastic surgeons, publicists, Barbara Cartland, and others.

1670. Ascher, Carol. "Selling to Ms. Consumer." American Media & Mass Culture. Ed. Donald Lazere. Berkeley: U of California P, 1987. 43-52.
On "the corporate effort to engineer a shift in consciousness in middle-class women from homemaking to consuming" (30).

1671. Atlas, James. "Beyond Demographics: How Madison Avenue Knows Who You Are and What You Want." AM 254.4 (Oct. 1984) 49-58.
Explains VALS--Values and Lifestyles Program of SRI International in Menlo Park, CA. VALS divides US public into nine types grouped in four categories based on their self-images, aspirations, and products used, a research method utilized by advertising agencies to target specific consumers.

1672. Aufderheide, Pat. "The Interplay of Consuming Desires and Critical Masses." ITT 12.33 (Aug. 31-Sept. 6, 1988) 19.

ADVERTISING AND PUBLIC RELATIONS

Reviews Lazere's American Media and Mass Culture and Nelson and Grossberg's Marxism and the Interpretation of Culture. The commercial machinery of TV and Hollywood, toy and game manufacturers, fashion designers, and advertisers of all kinds produces the culture.

1673. Bagdikian, Ben. "The High Cost of Free Advertising." The Media Monopoly. 2nd ed. Boston: Beacon, 1988. 103-192.

Part II of the book, chapters 6-10, "deals with the influence of advertising on how journalism is performed," demonstrating that mass advertising is "the major cause of newspaper monopoly" and "deeply influences the subjects dealt with in the nonadvertising sections of newspapers and broadcast programs" (xi).

1674. Barthel, Diane. Putting on Appearances: Gender and Advertising. Philadelphia: Temple UP, 1988. 219.

Advertising's focus on the physical appearance of women (as opposed to the power of men) distorts their sense of self-esteem and assists in the creation of a generally superficial culture.

1675. Bennett, James R. "Saturday Review's Annual Advertising Awards." JBE 2.2 (1983) 73-78.

Saturday Review destroyed the credibility of its awards by fusing "public service" and "public relations" into one category, "public spirited ads."

1676. Berger, Arthur. "Women and Advertising: Selling with Sex." Television as an Instrument of Terror. New Brunswick, NJ: Transaction, 1980. 135-143.

Women continue to be exploited to sell commodities.

1677. Bernays, Edward. Crystallizing Public Opinion. New York: Liveright, 1961. 219.

Another edition of his 1923 book on public relations.

1678. Bernays, Edward, ed. The Engineering of Consent. Norman, OK: U of Okla. P, 1955. 246.

Eight essays on public relations and advertising as a science, edited by "the dean of the public relations profession."

1679. Birkhead, Douglas. "To Buy a Product is to Become a Product: Few Ads Pay the Piper Without Offending the Audience." SLJR 11.65 (Aug. 1984) 17.

How broadcasting companies sell audiences to business.

1680. Blyskal, Jeff, and Marie Blyskal. PR: How the Public Relations Industry Writes the News. New York: Morrow, 1985. 241.

The public relations industry in both business and government powerfully manipulates the media. Much of what one reads in the newspapers or sees or hears from broadcasting comes from slanted press releases written by people in the business of manipulating public opinion. For example, White House and Pentagon PR and not the truth was told the public about the invasion of Grenada.

1681. Bolinger, Dwight. "Power and Deception." Language, the Loaded Weapon: The Use & Abuse of Language Today. London: Longman, 1980. 105-124.
Analyzes the powerful institutions that produce linguistic distortions and evasions--advertising and government.

1682. Boorstin, Daniel. The Image: A Guide to Pseudo-Events in America. Rev. ed. New York: Atheneum, 1985. 315. (First ed. The Image; or, What Happened to the American Dream, 1961).
"We have used our wealth, our literacy, our technology and our progress to create the thicket of unreality which stands between us and the facts of life" (3). "The making of the illusions which flood our experience has become the business of America," not only through "advertising and public relations and political rhetoric," but "all the activities which purport to inform and comfort and improve and educate and elevate us" (3, 5). Advertising "has meant a reshaping of our very concept of truth" (205), from objectivity to an emphasis on credibility, believability, not "whether something is a fact" but whether it is "convenient" (212).

1683. Borsodi, Ralph. National Advertising Versus Prosperity: A Study of the Economic Consequences of National Advertising. New York: Arcadia, 1923. 303.
Advertising "creates wasteful conflicts, demoralizes distribution, changes the basis of profit from greater values to greater advertising resources and raises the producers' profits."

1684. Bowlby, Rachel. Just Looking: Consumer Culture in Dreiser, Gissing, and Zola. New York: Methuen, 1985. 188.
The novels of these writers reflect the merging of commerce and culture during the period. The rise of the department store and advertising drew women into a glamorous new culture, by which they were exploited by men as both consumers and commodities.

1685. Brown, Terry L. "The Way We Were." Adbusters 1.1 (Summer 1989) 26-29.
Quick history of advertising and its systematic creation of desires for commodities.

1686. Buhle, Paul, ed. Popular Culture in America. Minneapolis: U of Minnesota P, 1987. 271.
Thirty-three essays previously published in Cultural Correspondence "condemn the manipulative qualities of commercial culture" that integrates aesthetic production into general commodity production in an ever-expanding consumer market. But the blending of art and advertising exposes the reality.

ADVERTISING AND PUBLIC RELATIONS

"The triumph of the merchandizer, from the Oval Office to the corner video shop, has certainly flattened our reality. But the flatness permits a wide perspective," and "capitalism has become obvious in what it always was" (xxiv).

1687. Buxton, D. "Rock Music, the Star System, and the Rise of Consumerism." Popular Culture and Media Events. Ed. Vincent Mosco and Janet Wasko. Norwood, NJ: Ablex, 1985. 181-206.
The cultural expression of youths in the 1960s-1970s was largely oriented around the marketplace guided by heavily publicized habits of rock stars.

1688. Buxton, Edward. Promise Them Anything: The Inside Story of the Madison Avenue Power Struggle. New York: Stein, 1972. 302.
An exposé of advertising companies, what they know about the public and how they use that knowledge, how to get ahead in the business, advertising malpractices, etc.

1689. Cardona, Elizabeth de. "Multinational Television." JoC 25.2 (1975) 122-127.
Multinational corporations control television advertising in Columbia in order to open markets and establish consumer behavior.

1690. Carey, Alex. "Reshaping the Truth: Pragmatists and Propagandists in America." American Media & Mass Culture. Ed. Donald Lazere. Berkeley: U of California P, 1987. 34-42.
Studies "the origins of the industries of public relations and propaganda" (30).

1691. Cheskin, Louis. Basis for Marketing Decision Through Controlled Motivation Research. New York: Liveright, 1961. 282.
Plugs for Cheskin's research firms, the Color Research Institute, etc., and reports on several motivation research studies.

1692. Clark, Eric. The Want Makers, the World of Advertising: How They Make You Buy. New York: Viking, 1989. 416.
Raises many disturbing ethical questions about the industry and its practices in swaying public opinion. Probes why advertisers rarely try to sell the qualities of a product, but use sex, fame, fortune, and popularity instead, based upon exhaustive research into human motivation for purposes of manipulation. Examines the industry's ethics also in connection with its manipulation of people to buy products that are actually harmful to the buyers and to the world. A chapter on political advertising questions the benefits of swaying the populace with simplified and distorted messages, pointing out that the US is one of the few countries permitting its candidates to buy television time, most countries considering it

harmful to rational discussion of issues. Self-regulation by commercial and political advertisers has not worked. The remedy is greatly expanded education of consumers and the public by teaching critical thinking and exposing the manipulative devices employed by advertisers, and government regulation, for example following Britain's model of allocating network time free to all parties based on party size.

1693. Cockburn, Alexander, and Andrew Cockburn. "Flacks: They Clarify, They Edify, They Stupefy--They're PR Specialists and They Get Paid to Change Your Mind." Pb 34.1 (Jan. 1987) 98-102, 193-200.
From selling cigarettes, to selling the Soviet threat, to selling Reagan.

1694. Collins, Ronald K.L. "Sneakers That Kill: Kids and Conspicuous Consumption." Adbusters 1.3 (Spring 1990) 33-35.
Children have become so captive to commercialism that they "revel in conspicuous consumption." The author urges "a cultural reformation to counter" the erosion of values.

1695. Comanor, William, and Thomas Wilson. Advertising and Market Power. Cambridge: Harvard UP, 1974. 257.
Tells how heavy advertising can produce monopoly dominance.

1696. Cook, David A. "Your Money and Your Life." CJR 18.2 (1979) 64-66.
Americans think of television as free entertainment, but the real cost, in terms of wasted time and higher prices due to advertising, is quite high.

1697. Courtney, Alice E., and Thomas W. Whipple. Sex Stereotyping in Advertising. Lexington, MA: Lexington, 1983. 239.
Polls reveal that "the majority of consumers agree that advertising is insulting to women" (40). The criticism "leveled by feminists and other consumer groups during the 1970s has had only limited success" (41).

1698. Culley, James D., and Rex Bennett. "Selling Women, Selling Blacks." JoC 26.4 (1976) 160-74.
An update of advertising studies finds that negative stereotypes of women and blacks remain.

1699. Cummings, Gary. "When Advertisers Call the Shots." WJR 8.11 (Nov. 1986) 12.
On the breakdown of the separation between advertising sponsors and network programming, especially in children's and sports programming.

1700. Curran, James. "Capitalism and the Control of the Press, 1800-1975." Mass Communication and Society. Ed. James Curran, Michael Gurevitch, and Janet Woollacott. London: Arnold, 1977. 195-230.

"The period around the middle of the nineteenth century . . . did not inaugurate a new era of press freedom and liberty: it introduced a new system of press censorship more effective than anything that had gone before. Market forces [advertising, etc.] succeeded where legal repression had failed in establishing the press as an instrument of social control, with lasting consequences for the development of modern British society" (198).

1701. Della Femina, Jerry. From Those Wonderful Folks Who Gave You Pearl Harbor: Front-line Dispatches from the Advertising War. Ed. Charles Sopkin. New York: Simon and Schuster, 1970. 253.
Insider stories by the head of an agency who loves advertising. "The key is to find out which button you can press on every person that makes him want to buy your product over another product. What's the emotional thing that affects people?" (143).

1702. Dichter, Ernest. The Handbook of Consumer Motivation: The Psychology of the World of Objects. New York: McGraw-Hill, 1964. 486.
A promotional for the Institute for Motivational Research of which Dichter was the founder and president.

1703. Dos Passos, John. The 42nd Parallel. 1st ed. New York: Harper, 1930. 426.
A novel about J. Ward Moorehouse, public relations expert.

1704. Engelhardt, Tom. "Eternal Invasion of Privacy: the Good, the Ad and the Ugly." ITT 13.32 (Aug. 30-Sept. 5, 1989) 18-19, 21.
Analyzes the industry magazine, Advertising Age, as "a spectacle of the superficial, callow and peripheral."

1705. Evans, Charlotte. "Ad-ing Up the Past: New Museum Looks at American Society Through Advertising." SLJR 19.124 (Mar. 1990) 15, 18.
The Center for Advertising History at the Smithsonian's National Museum of American History has been documenting changes as reflected in ads since 1984.

1706. Ewen, Stuart. "Advertising and the Development of Consumer Society." Cultural Politics in Contemporary America. New York: Routledge, 1989. 82-95.
Provides an historical sketch of the "most overt form of commercial influence on culture."

1707. Ewen, Stuart. Captains of Consciousness: Advertising and the Social Roots of the Consumer Culture. New York: McGraw-Hill, 1976. 261.
Explains the development of the nineteenth century system of domination by Captains of Industry to include advertising to secure the mass consumption process and ward off hostility against big business.

1708. Ewen, Stuart, and Elizabeth Ewen. Channels of
Desire: Mass Images and the Shaping of American
Consciousness. New York: McGraw-Hill, 1982. 312.
Explains how a mass consumption ideology was created requiring a world view which divided humans from nature. The mass media played a crucial role in the saturation of mass images everywhere evident in our industrial, commodity, consumer society.

1709. Fejes, Fred. "The Growth of Multinational Advertising
Agencies in Latin America." JoC 30.4 (1980) 36-49.
A history of multinational expansion and a description of advertising's effect upon consumption patterns as well as consumerist values in Latin American culture.

1710. Fisher, John. The Plot to Make You Buy. New York:
McGraw-Hill, 1968. 209.
"The central theme of this book is that . . . North American marketing is moulding a selfish, materialistic, inward-looking society, whose standards are immoral in the context of world events. . . . The strongest opinion expressed here is that the buyers of Canada and the U.S. have been passive too long, and that they must educate themselves to exercise their power over manufacturers, making them their servants, not be their slaves in a program of planned obsolescence and consumption" (x); especially see Chapter 8, "What the Consumer Can Do."

1711. Fiske, John. "Miami Vice, Miami Pleasure." CSt 1.1
(Jan. 1987) 113-119.
Analysis of one segment of Miami Vice attempts to explain how the program itself promotes commodities and the values of consuming.

1712. Flitterman, Sandy. "The Real Soap Operas: TV
Commercials." Regarding Television. Ed. E. Ann
Kaplan. Frederick, MD: U Publications of America,
1983. 84-96.
Soap opera commercials promote a sense of infinitely prolonged desire in "an equation of material consumption with well-being."

1713. Fox, Richard, "Epitaph for Middletown: Robert S. Lynd
and the Analysis of Consumer Culture." The Culture
of Consumption. Ed. Richard Fox and T.J. Jackson
Lears. New York: Pantheon, 1983. 101-142.
Lynd, sharing the assumption of advertisers that people were thoroughly manipulable, sought to substitute disinterested administrators for corporate advertisers.

1714. Fox, Richard, and T.J. Jackson Lears, eds. The Culture
of Consumption: Critical Essays in American History
1880-1980. New York: Pantheon, 1983. 236.
The consumer culture is central to elite control of the country--promises of personal fulfillment through the corporate system.

ADVERTISING AND PUBLIC RELATIONS

1715. Fox, Stephen R. The Mirror Makers: A History of American Advertising & Its Creators. New York: Morrow, 1984. 383.
A historical study of the advertising industry, focusing on dominant firms and personalities. "It usually appeals to the less agreeable aspects of human nature: greed, vanity, insecurity, competitiveness, materialism. . . . But there it is, one of the dominant forces in twentieth-century America."

1716. Frappier, Jon. "Advertising: Latin America." RA 3.4 (1969) 1-11.
U.S. advertising in Latin America is expanding rapidly.

1717. Frederick, Christine. Selling Mrs. Consumer. New York: Business Bourse, 1929. 405.
A 1920's view of the vulnerability of women to advertising.

1718. Gaines, Jane, and Charlotte Herzog, eds. Fabrications: Costume and the Female Body. New York: Routledge Chapman & Hall, 1989. 256.
Weighs the pleasures women derive from consumer culture against social costs they have paid as wife, mother, and worker.

1719. Galbraith, John. The New Industrial State. 4th ed. Boston: Houghton Mifflin, 1985. 438.
"Advertising and salesmanship--the management of consumer demand--are vital for planning in the planning system." The wants created "ensure the services of the worker" by keeping them "slightly in excess of his income," which causes the worker to "go into debt," which in turn "adds to his reliability as a worker" (281).

1720. Gantz, Walter, et al. "Approaching Invisibility: The Portrayal of the Elderly in Magazine Advertisements." JoC 30.1 (1980) 56-60.
Only 6% of sample contained older people, and the uniform representations imply their devaluation as consumers.

1721. Geis, Michael. The Language of Television Advertising. New York: Academic, 1982. 257.
Advertisers should be held responsible not only for what they assert but for what they imply. Much advertising is deceptive and not only serves no human or societal good but actually harms people (e.g., cereal ads). Children are particularly susceptible to deceptive language. The NAB, the networks, and the government are failing to discipline the deceit endemic in the language of advertising.

1722. Gibson, Walker. "Sweet Talk: The Rhetoric of Advertising." Tough, Sweet and Stuffy: An Essay on Modern American Prose Styles. Bloomington, IN: Indiana UP, 1966. 71-89.
Linguistic features found in eight magazine ads.

1723. Gitlin, Todd. "Car Commercials and Miami Vice: 'We Build Excitement.'" Watching Television. Ed. Todd Gitlin. New York: Pantheon, 1987. 136-161.
 Auto ads sell not only cars but also the ideology of freedom and self-sufficiency through technological power, the Lone Driver entrepreneur myth, the Superpro, and the Supermanager, all in contrast to the realities of the US and the world. This myth helped bring on the Vietnam War and Star Wars.

1724. Glessing, Robert, and William P. White, eds. "Advertising." Mass Media: The Invisible Environment Revisited. Chicago: SRA, 1976. 122-141.
 Six essays--on sex, parity, etc.

1725. Gold, Phillip. Advertising, Politics, and American Culture: From Salesmanship to Therapy. New York: Paragon, 1987. 217.
 "Advertising, as a system of discourse, is a luxury this civilization can no longer afford" (xi), because it "represents the antithesis of rational discourse and public dialogue as these have been known in Western civilization" (xiii). Yet in addition to selling commodities whether people need them or not, advertisers also "redefine values and offer social and cultural guidance in ways calculated to spur consumption" (18), on behaviorist assumptions of the "irrationality, insecurity, and malleability" of the ordinary person.

1726. Goodman, Ellen. "Freedom to Drive at Stake." AG (Aug. 28, 1990) 9B.
 Analyzes the relationship between auto ads, President Bush, and the massive sending of troops to the Middle East against Iraq. (See 1723).

1727. Graebner, William. The Engineering of Consent: Democracy and Authority in Twentieth-Century America. Madison, WI: U of Wisconsin P, 1987. 265.
 Examines the rise of democratic social engineering (small group process) through consumerism, advertising, and public relations. In general a history of one form of authority, in specific comparing the Golden Age Clubs, agencies for the aged, with child-rearing theories and practices.

1728. Graves, Florence. "Taxpayers Foot B-1 Lobby Costs." CC 7.5 (1981) 7.
 Rockwell charged the government for its PR on the B-1 bomber.

1729. Gwyn, Robert J. "Education for Consumption: A Perspective on Commercial Broadcasting." TS 18.2 (1970) 23-26.
 On techniques used in news programs to attract and keep viewers to watch ads.

1730. Hanan, Mark. The Pacifiers: The Six Symbols We Live By. Boston: Little, Brown, 1960. 306.

Explores partly through advertising the symbols of sex, motherhood, success, youthfulness, sociability and sophistication.

1731. Hancock, G.B. "Commercial Advertisement and Social Pathology." SF 4 (June 1926) 812-19.
Advertising is an imbalanced struggle between the wealthy advertiser using scientific methods and the defenseless consumer. Argues that crime results from advertising to the poor.

1732. Haug, Wolfgang. Critique of Commodity Aesthetics: Appearance, Sexuality, and Advertising in Capitalist Society. Minneapolis: U of Minnesota P, 1986. 224. (Tr. Kritik der Warenästhetik, 1971).
Analysis of the student movement of the 1960s and its opposition to the consciousness- and behavior-shaping influence of the propagation of commodities for mass marketing seen as an instrument of repression.

1733. Havig, Alan. "Frederic Wakeman's The Hucksters and the Postwar Debate Over Commercial Radio." JB 28 (Spring 1984) 187-99.
The book and film challenged the commercialization of radio.

1734. Henninger, Daniel. "Worriers, Swingers, Shoppers, 'Psychographics' Can Tell Who'll Buy Crest, Who'll Buy Ultra Brite." The New Languages. Ed. Thomas H. Ohlgren and Lynn M. Berk. Englewood Cliffs, NJ: Prentice-Hall, 1977. 70-78. (NO [June 1972] 1, 19).
Analysis of segmental market research.

1735. Henry, Harry. Motivation Research: Its Practice and Uses for Advertising, Marketing, and Other Business Purposes. New York: Ungar, 1958. 240.
A textbook on the question of why people behave as they do; its aim is to enable advertisers to successfully persuade people to buy particular commodities.

1736. Henry, Jules. Culture Against Man. New York: Random House, 1963. 495.
In Chap. 3, "Advertising as a Philosophical System" (45-99), Henry describes advertising as the "pecuniary philosophy" with a new conception of truth as "pecuniary pseudotruth"--a statement is true if it sells products and false if it does not. Henry indicts advertising and capitalism for making acquisitiveness and not truth the moral imperative.

1737. Herman, Edward S. "The Deepening Market in the West 1: The Commodification Of Culture." Z 3.3 (Mar. 1990) 29-31.
Explores some of "the more pernicious aspects" of doublespeak: "The enlargement of the market, the growth of advertising, and commodification without limit."

1738. Himmelstein, Hal. "Advertising: The Medium Is the

Mirage." Television Myth and the American Mind. New
York: Praeger, 1984. 37-74.
"Nothing serves the cause of advanced capitalism more effectively . . . than does advertising. Ads are selling us not only a product or service or politician--they are selling us a way of life" (37). The issue is not ultimately advertisers' use of fear, greed, and hopes to deceive us into consuming what we do not need, but their turning acquisitiveness into a moral imperative as the chief guide to life. (See 1736).

1739. Hoch, Paul. "Coliseums & Gladiators." RSCJ 12 (Sept. 1974) 12-14.
The power of sports derives not from "any special idiocy" or "special deviousness" but from "the social relations of capitalist production itself."

1740. Horowitz, Daniel. The Morality of Spending: Attitudes Toward the Consumer Society in America, 1875-1940. Baltimore: Johns Hopkins UP, 1985. 254.
Presents the evolution of attitudes toward consumerism.

1741. Howard, John, and James Hulbert. Advertising and the Public Interest: A Staff Report to the Federal Trade Commission. New York: 1973. (Pagination by sections).
Explains the advantages the seller exerts over the buyer. Suggests ways to strengthen consumer power: greater adherence to truthfulness in ads (ad substantiation); more protection of children under six signals indicating shift from program to commercial; some programs free of commercials; corrective ads; a research bureau within FCC.

1742. Hoyt, Michael. "When the Walls Come Tumbling Down." CJR 28.6 (Mar.-Apr. 1990) 35-40.
Criticizes the increasingly blurred separation of advertising, editorials, and news, as journalism becomes more marketing oriented.

1743. Janus, Noreene. "Advertising and the Creation of Global Markets: The Role of the New Communication Technologies." The Critical Communications Review: Volume II: Changing Patterns of Communications Control. Ed. Vincent Mosco and Janet Wasko. Norwood, NJ: Ablex, 1984. 57-70.
"The expansion of transnational capital, the rapid flow of marketing 'know-how' from the headquarters of Madison Avenue advertising agencies to their branch offices around the world, the importance of the perpetual creation of demand for consumer products, and the rapid installation of the new communications infrastructure suggest that the new 'information age' will also be a 'commercial age' at the global level" (69).

1744. Janus, Noreene. "Advertising and Mass Media in the Era of the Global Corporation." Communication and Social Structure: Critical Studies in Mass Media Research. Ed. Emile McAnany, et al. New York: Praeger, 1981.

287-316.
 The increasing power of a small group of transnational ad agencies combined with the power of transnational corporations is forcing Third World mass media to adopt the transnational system.

1745. Jhally, Sut. "Advertising as Religion: The Dialectic of Technology and Magic." Cultural Politics in Contemporary America. Ed. Sut Jhally and Ian Angus. New York: Routledge, 1989. 217-229.
 Marketplace communication through advertising has "reinstated magic in everyday life." Traces the development of advertising through stages of idolatry, iconology, narcissism, and totemism, "a secular version of God."

1746. Jhally, Sut. The Codes of Advertising: Fetishism and the Political Economy of Meaning in the Consumer Society. New York: St. Martin's, 1987. 225.
 This is a consumer society. In earlier societies the meaning of products derived from knowledge of the producer. In capitalist society producer and object are separated, and products are emptied of meaning. Thus advertising provides the meaning; advertising fills the need for meaning. "That is why it is so powerful" (197): consumption has replaced religion, commodities have become the modern fetishism, within the larger religion of technology.

1747. Johnson, Roy, and Russell Lynch. The Sales Strategy of John H. Patterson. New York: Dartnell, 1932. 344.
 About the founder of National Cash Register, described as the "Napoleon of Modern Sales Promotion."

1748. Kavanaugh, John, SJ. "Idols of the Marketplace." M&V 37 (Fall 1986) 3-5.
 The economic/cultural system educates people to think and act in service to the "imperatives of the economic system itself," a system "founded upon continually expanding consumption, in a society that already has a surfeit of goods."

1749. Kehl, D.G. "How to Read an Ad: Learning to Read between the Lies." EJ 72 (Oct. 1983) 32-38. (Rptd. Beyond Nineteen Eighty-Four. Ed. William Lutz. Urbana, IL: NCTE, 1989.)
 A method of detecting pseudopurpose, pseudovoice, pseudologic, and other deceptive techniques of advertising.

1750. Kern, Marilyn. "A Comparative Analysis of the Portrayal of Blacks & Whites in White-Oriented Mass Circulation Magazine Advertisements During 1959, 1969, & 1979." U of Wisconsin, 1982. 122. DAI 43.8 (Feb. 1983) 2482-A.
 "Of 1431 ads examined, only 49 contained identifiable blacks."

1751. Key, Wilson Bryan. Media Sexploitation. New York:

Signet, 1976. 234.
The author's second book on subliminal persuasion. "Where his earlier book dealt primarily with visual deceit, this book continues not only with more examples of visual deceit, but also extensions into auditory and olfactory deception techniques." (See 1877).

1752. Key, Wilson Bryan. Subliminal Seduction: Ad Media's Manipulation of a Not So Innocent America. New York: Signet, 1973. 205.
The first of three books about "stimuli directed into" the "unconscious mind by the mass merchandisers of media," especially sexual stimulation. "It is fascinating to wonder how long this world--starving and impoverished as it is--will tolerate the incredible self-indulgence which has come to be known as the American Way of Life" (2).

1753. Keyser, S.J. "There is Method in Their Adness: The Formal Structure of Advertisement." NLH 14.2 (1983) 305-34.
Assesses the extent to which advertising makes use of the many formal devices of literature (305).

1754. Kirstein, George G. "The Day the Ads Stopped." The New Languages. Ed. Thomas H. Ohlgren and Lynn M. Berk. Englewood Cliffs, NJ: Prentice-Hall, 1977. 102-108. (Na [June 1964] 555-57).
Fictional story of results of the Supreme Court prohibition of advertising.

1755. Kline, Stephen, and William Leiss. "Advertising, Needs, and Commodity Fetishism." CJPST 2.1 (1978) 5-32.
A study of advertising to see if it presents "ambiguous 'messages' to consumers" as part of an investigation of whether ambiguity and confusion in the sense of "satisfaction" is being experienced in the consumption process (5).

1756. Krolak, Steven. "The Casino Society: They're Playing With America's Future." Adbusters 1.3 (Spring 1990) 81-82, 86-87.
Casinos reflect the society at large--show biz, fantasy parks, advertising, all offer the garden of earthly delights.

1757. Kunzle, David. "Scratching Our Revolutionary Itch: How Advertising Absorbs the Imagery and Slogans of Radicalism." Issues in American Society. Ed. Joseph Boskin. Encino, CA: Glencoe, 1978. 295-314.
Commercial advertisers have attempted to cover up serious social diseases and neutralize radical social change by manipulating the language of liberation, freedom, revolution, etc.

1758. Larson, Keith A. Public Relations, The Edward L. Bernayses and the American Scene: A Bibliography. Westwood, MA: F.W. Faxon, 1978. 774.
The writings of Bernays and his wife, Doris E. Fleischman,

ADVERTISING AND PUBLIC RELATIONS

with writings about them.

1759. Lasch, Christopher. The Culture of Narcissism: American Life in an Age of Diminishing Expectations. New York: Norton, 1978. 268.
Several chapters touch on the power of advertising.

1760. Lears, T.J. Jackson. "From Salvation to Self-Realization: Advertising and the Therapeutic Roots of the Consumer Culture, 1880-1930." The Culture of Consumption. Ed. Richard Fox and T.J. Jackson Lears. New York: Pantheon, 1983. 1-38.
Advertising exploited social fragmentation and alienation by promising self-realization.

1761. Leiss, William. The Limits to Satisfaction: An Essay on the Problem of Needs & Commodities. Buffalo, NY: U of Toronto P, 1976. 159.
Marketing is now the nation's main social bond, and increase of commodities the main source of values.

1762. Leiss, William, Stephen Kline, and Sut Jhally. Social Communication in Advertising: Persons, Products, & Images of Well-Being. New York: Methuen, 1986. 327.
"A single thread of argument is drawn through this book: In industrial societies in this century, national consumer product advertising has become one of the great vehicles of social communication" (3). Not only does it "promote goods and services" but it promotes values of the deepest concern to people, replacing church sermons, political oratory, and the words of elders as the privileged form of discourse. This discourse is about objects, about consumer goods, and it deeply conditions people's attitudes, expectations, and sense of identity. The things oriented public then become marketing targets.

1763. Lent, John A. "The Price of Modernity." JoC 25.2 (Spring 1975) 128-135.
Foreign enterprises in the US, Great Britain, and Canada increase control of mass media through advertising in Commonwealth Caribbean. Most radio and television shows are made in the US or Great Britain.

1764. Leymore, Varda L. Hidden Myth: Structure and Symbolism in Advertising. New York: Basic Books, 1975. 208.
A structuralist analysis of magazine and television ads which examines their signs and symbols and concludes that advertising functions as the modern equivalent of myth, constantly reinforcing the status quo by revealing the flaws of alternatives.

1765. Lois, George. George, Be Careful. New York: Saturday Review, 1972. 245.
An advertising executive tells about his commercial and political ads.

1766. MacDougall, A. Kent. "Half a Century of the Big Sell." CJR 15.4 (Nov.-Dec. 1976) 57-58.
Relates the manner in which advertising executives transformed the traditionally frugal public into a materialist bent on consuming more and more goods.

1767. Madeley, John. "The Worldwide Explosion in Cigarette Advertising." Pr 9.2 (1981) 15.
The seven major companies are spending "around $2,500 million a year on advertising" in the Third World.

1768. Mailer, Norman. "A Note on Comparative Pornography." Advertisements for Myself. New York: Putnam's, 1959. 431-33.
"Talk of pornography ought to begin at the modern root: advertising," for the US is a country "where almost every commodity is festooned with sexual symbol."

1769. Mailer, Norman. "From Surplus Value to the Mass-Media." Advertisements for Myself. New York: Putnam's, 1959. 434-37.
Capitalism depends upon "the creation in the consumer of a series of psychically disruptive needs," including "the desire for excessive security, the alleviation of guilt, the lust for comfort and new commodity, and a consequent allegiance to the vast lie about the essential health of the State."

1770. Mander, Jerry. "$30 Billion Questions." CJR 16.5 (Jan.-Feb. 1978) 57-59.
Analyzes all advertising as ideological advocacy ads.

1771. Mannes, Marya. But Will It Sell? Philadelphia: Lippincott, 1964. 240.
Warnings against the "money thinkers"; the first part of this collection of articles is on the supermarket and advertising.

1772. Marchand, Roland. Advertising the American Dream: Making Way for Modernity, 1920-1940. Berkeley: U of California P, 1985. 448.
Distortion in the advertising of the 1920s-30s derived from advertisers' desire to fuel "consumers' desires for fantasy and wish-fulfillment" and other factors. Advertisers provided class images and "upscale" settings for escape-minded consumers. "Most powerful of all in distorting advertising's social mirror were specific merchandising strategies" "not to reflect reality but to 'move merchandise'" (e.g., "the repeated depiction of women gazing spellbound into their open refrigerators"). In the process of selling specific products, advertisers also "communicated broad social values," especially an ideological bias toward business and consumption, and the American Dream through US advertising art of "Capitalist Realism" (xvii-xviii).

1773. Martin, Dennis. "Consumer Symbolicum: The Advertising

Legacy of Pierre Martineau." U of Illinois, Urbana, 1985. 219. DAI 46 (1985) 828-A.
Martineau advocated values and lifestyles research in his newspaper columns and his book, Motivation in Advertising, and taught the value of symbolic language theories of Ernst Cassirer and Suzanne Langer to advertising.

1774. McCartney, Laton. "How IBM Spindles the Media." MORE 3.9 (1973) 1, 19-21.
On the power over the press by corporate PR.

1775. McCracken, Grant. Culture and Consumption: New Approaches to the Symbolic Character of Consumer Goods and Activities. Bloomington, IN: Indiana UP, 1988. 192.
Anthropological explanation of how consumer goods become repositories of cultural and symbolic meaning.

1776. McGoldrick, Bernard E. "On Liberating the Middle Class: The Great American TV Ad Scam." Wit 70.3 (Mar. 1987) 20-22.
TV advertising participates in "the agenda of oppression."

1777. McLuhan, Marshall. The Mechanical Bride: Folklore of Industrial Man. Boston: Beacon, 1951. 157.
"Ours is the first age in which many thousands of the best-trained individual minds have made it a full-time business to get inside the collective public mind. To get inside in order to manipulate, exploit, control is the object now" (v).

1778. McMahon, A. Michal. "An American Courtship: Psychologists and Advertising Theory in the Progressive Era." AS 13 (1972) 5-18.
On the co-opting of academics by advertisers.

1779. Meyers, William. The Image Makers: Power and Persuasion on Madison Avenue. New York: Times Books, 1984. 242.
Carries forward Vance Packard's The Hidden Persuaders, arguing that the manipulative power of advertising has increased beyond what Packard described, through increasingly sophisticated psychographic techniques. "Vance Packard's stinging prophecy has, for the most part, come true. . . . Ad Alley's wizards have firmly established themselves as both the creators and the controllers of our consumer culture" (4-5), able to "dictate the foods we eat . . . the clothes we wear, the cars we drive, even the Presidents we elect" (4-5). And Madison Avenue contributes "little of tangible value to our society; its primary objective is to reap the financial rewards of the manic--and often unnecessary--public purchasing it induces" (5).

1780. Mintz, Morton. "The Smoke Screen: Tobacco and the Press: An Unhealthy Alliance." MM 8.7-8 (July-Aug. 1987) 15-17.

On the power of the tobacco industry over the media and the government.

1781. Mowry, George, ed. The Twenties: Fords, Flappers and Fantasies. Englewood Cliffs, NJ: Prentice-Hall, 1963. 186.
Business was coming to embrace advertising as the "ignition system of the economy, the dynamo of mass dissatisfaction and the creator of illusions in a most materialistic world" (15).

1782. Newman, Joseph W. Motivation Research and Marketing Management. Boston: Harvard Graduate School of Business, 1957. 525.
Six case histories.

1783. Ohmann, Richard. "Advertising and the New Discourse of Mass Culture." Politics of Letters. Middletown, CT: Wesleyan UP, 1987. 152-170.
Examines how magazine advertising and content legitimated capitalist development. [See Chenoweth.]

1784. Packard, Vance. "The Ad and the Id." The New Languages. Ed. Thomas H. Ohlgren and Lynn M. Berk. Englewood Cliffs, NJ: Prentice-Hall, 1977. 58-69. (Harper's [Aug. 1957] 8-14).
Critique of motivational research.

1785. Packard, Vance. "The Growing Power of Admen." AM 200 (1957) 55-59.
"Their power to do good or non-good is becoming massive, and many are using their power irresponsibly."

1786. Packard, Vance. The Hidden Persuaders. New York: McKay, 1957. 242. (Pocket Book, 1958; 242).
Explains how the social sciences were enlisted by advertising agencies--commercial and political--to manipulate people and direct them without their awareness. Called "motivational research" and the "depth approach" to persuasion, this antihumanistic and anti-democratic enterprise in the hands of unscrupulous public relations experts is dangerous and should be combatted.

1787. Payne, Richard J., and Robert Heyer. Discovery in Advertising. Paramus, NJ: Paulist P, 1969. 188.
Advertisers exploit human needs and desires. The book examines "how much our personal attitudes and values are influenced by the ever-present 'sell,'" and urges all people to learn the "grammar of advertising" in self-defense.

1788. Pingree, Suzanne, et al. "A Scale for Sexism." JoC 26.4 (1976) 193-200.
A majority of magazine ads either put women down or keep them in their place according to a "levels of consciousness" scale.

1789. Pollay, Richard, ed. & comp. Information Sources in Advertising History. Westport, CT: Greenwood, 1979. 330.
Annotated bibliography described by Leiss, Kline, and Jhally as the herald for "the maturing of advertising studies as a domain for serious research" (6).

1790. Pope, Daniel. The Making of Modern Advertising. New York: Basic, 1983. 340.
A history of the development of the institutions created to bring about national advertising mainly during the years before 1920, all in order to increase the consumption of goods. Advertisers deliberately sought to create and alter what consumers thought and bought, and they have now established and legitimized a gigantic propaganda industry with enormous power.

1791. Potter, David M. People of Plenty: Economic Abundance and the American Character. Chicago: U of Chicago P, 1954. 217.
Has a chapter on advertising with thesis that advertising's effects are not primarily economic but social--"the values of our society."

1792. Preston, Ivan. The Great American Blow-up: Puffery in Advertising and Selling. Madison: U of Wisconsin P, 1975. 422.
Legal puffery (false claims) gives the seller a powerful tool with which to deceive the consumer. Author seeks to eliminate it from the marketplace. This is the "story of legalized lying" of US advertising by a former FTC staff member.

1793. Quilter, Deborah. "P.R.'s Odd Man Out." CJR 27.5 (Jan.-Feb. 1989) 12.
On the pressures on news media from the new success-only fee system: clients pay the agency only when an item or story favorable to the client appears in print or on television.

1794. Quinn, Francis X., ed. Ethics, Advertising and Responsibility. Westminster, MD: Canterbury, 1963. 165.
Critical of media, advertisers, and governments. Criticism of advertising mainly from the point of view of business, media, and government officials who defend self-regulation.

1795. Rein, Irving. The Great American Communication Catalogue. Englewood Cliffs, NJ: Prentice-Hall, 1976. 217.
Focuses upon "institutional rhetoric" which empowers the producer at the expense of the consumer in an unfair contest" (4). By exposing both producer and consumer strategies the author hopes to encourage "less manipulative strategies."

1796. Reitz, Sara. "Oblivion for the Closest Thing to Consumer Protection." Pr 8 (Mar. 1980) 4.
Corporate public affairs offices in Washington exceed 500,

many of them working against FTC regulations.

1797. Roediger, David. "Sports for Sale." ITT 13.5 (Dec. 7-13, 1988) 5.
On the increasing identification of the commercial and the sport.

1798. Roncagliolo, Rafael, and Noreene Janus. "Advertising and the Democratization of Communications." Development Dialogue 2 (1981) 31-40.
"To a greater extent than anywhere else in the Third World, advertising serves in Latin America as the principal source of income for financing the media," and the dependence is growing. Advertisers "virtually control" the media, partly by punishing critics.

1799. Ross, Irwin. The Image Merchants: The Fabulous World of Public Relations. Garden City, NY: Doubleday, 1959. 288.
Discloses the extensive use of public relations in manipulating public opinion. At worst, success has involved the calculated exploitation of human ignorance. Urges greater vigilance by the public and more honesty by the advertiser.

1800. Rutledge, Kay Ellen. "Analyzing Visual Doublespeak: The Art of Duck Hunting." QRD 16.4 (July 1990) 1-3.
Presents ways to analyze visual data and images for distortion, misrepresentation, and lies.

1801. Schickel, Richard. Intimate Strangers: The Culture of Celebrity. New York: Doubleday, 1985. 299.
Celebrity can be considered "as the principal source of motive power in putting across ideas of every kind." "They are turned into representations" of "inchoate longings; they are used to simplify complex matters of the mind and spirit; they are used to subvert rationalism in politics . . . in every realm of public life." "The result is a corruption of that process of rational communication on which a democratic political system and a reasonable social order must be based" (viii-ix).

1802. Schudson, Michael. Advertising, The Uneasy Persuasion: Its Dubious Impact on American Society. New York: Basic, 1984. 288.
Explains the system of product advertising from production to marketing to the shaping of symbols, values, and life patterns for the public. Advertisers have done little social service: "no tradition of pro bono work," "no serious standards of condemnation" of shoddy work, nor have the universities done much to make advertising "more responsible" (242-43).

1803. Schuetz, Stephen, and Joyce N. Sprafkin. "Spot Messages Appearing Within Saturday Morning Television Programs." Hearth and Home: Images of Women in the Mass Media. Ed. Gaye Tuchman, et al. New York:

Oxford UP, 1978. 69-77.
Men predominate in the ads and in promoting products.

1804. Scitovsky, Tibor. The Joyless Economy: An Inquiry into Human Satisfaction and Consumer Dissatisfaction. New York: Oxford UP, 1976. 310.
Consumer behavior is an attempt to deal simultaneously with the conflicts of seeking both comfort and stimulation.

1805. "Selling the Dream: Advertising and the Consumer Economy." M&V 37 (Fall 1986) 24.
Seven articles and eight notes.

1806. Shames, Laurence. "What a Long, Strange (Shopping) Trip It's Been: Looking Back at the 1980s." UR 35 (Sept.-Oct. 1989) 65-71.
"Born to shop!" is "the motto of our modern era," and the "Reagan era raised the standards of gluttonous consumption to heights never before seen in human history."

1807. Silver, Hannah. "Shop Til You Drop." PR 6 (Winter 1990) 30-31.
"From Nordstrom's to K-mart, capitalism has created a consumerist mentality that has replaced citizenship."

1808. Van Allen, Judith. "Eating It! From Here to 2001." Ram 10 (May 1972) 26-33.
On the vast advertising organization of the food industry.

1809. Warren, Denise. "Commercial Liberation." JoC 28.1 (1978) 169-73.
In spite of surface changes in the appearance or activities of women, images of women in advertising leave power structures intact. Though masking itself as democratic and collective, advertising discourse, in fact, functions as a discourse of power and repression.

1810. Warren, Lynn. "Consolidated Edison Company of New York v. Public Service Commission: Freedom of Speech Extended to Monopolies--Is There No Escape for the Consumer?" PLR 8 (1981) 1087-1110.
An attack on the Supreme Court's extension of "full first amendment protection to the free speech of a corporate monopoly despite the resulting encroachment upon the privacy interest of its captive consumer."

1811. Wassmuth, Birgit. "Art Movements & American Print Advertising: A Study of Magazine Advertising Graphics 1915-1935." U of Minnesota, 1983. 288. DAI 44.11 (May 1984) 3197-A.
Studies the use of Art Deco in Magazine ads, the rise of the commercial artist, and the inclusion of fine art as an "integral part of the advertising message."

1812. Webster, Frank. "Advertising the American Dream." MCS

9 (1987) 111-117.
Reviews three books on advertising, two espousing the "functionalist" view of advertising as socially integrative (Roland Marchand, Michael Schudson), the third presenting the "critical" or historical study of corporate capitalism's efforts to silence criticism and to stimulate consumption by creating dissatisfaction (David Nye).

1813. Weiss, Ann. The School on Madison Avenue: Advertising and What It Teaches. New York: Dutton, 1980. 131.
Analyzes the driving aim of business to make profit through growth, which requires more purchasers, which necessitates advertising to induce consumption.

1814. Welles, Chris. "Business Journalism's Glittering Prizes." CJR 17.6 (1979) 43-45.
Some awards support corporations.

1815. Wicke, Jennifer. Advertising Fictions: Literature, Advertisement, and Social Reading. New York: Columbia UP, 1988. 193.
Examines advertising "as a language and a literature in its own right--as a preeminent discourse of modern culture." Ever since advertising began as an institution in the nineteenth century it has intertwined with the novel (Dickens, James, Joyce, and others), and neither can be "fully read without reference to the other" (1-2).

1816. Williamson, Judith. Decoding Advertisements: Ideology & Meaning in Advertising. London: Marion Boyars, 1978. 180.
Ads sell products but also create structures of meaning, thereby replacing the traditional function of religion or art/literature. Human need for meaning and identity is exploited for profit by teaching people to identify not with what they produce but with what they consume. This has the additional function of obscuring the realities of class differences.

1817. Williamson, Judith. "Woman Is an Island: Femininity & Colonization." Studies in Entertainment. Ed. Tania Modleski. Bloomington: Indiana UP, 1986. 99-118.
Femininity in advertising is an expression of "otherness that capitalism works to destroy" (xvii). "Woman" functions as the main vehicle (along with foreigners) for this process of diverting attention from "social inequality and class struggle" (101).

1818. Wooding, Edmund, ed. Advertising and the Subconscious: Advertising Conference Contributed Papers. Ann Arbor, MI: U of Michigan, Bureau of Business Research, 1959. 84.
Paper by Packard discussed by others.

II. B. 2. PRODUCT ADVERTISING (1819-1952)

1819. Alderson, Jeremy. "Confessions of a Travel Writer." CJR 27.2 (July-Aug. 1988) 27-28.
Travel industry publications shun investigative journalism for fear of angering advertisers, and reporters routinely accept free trips from the businesses they write about.

1820. Allen, Margaret. Selling Dreams: Inside the Beauty Business. New York: Simon and Schuster, 1981. 286.
History and evaluation of the cosmetics industry.

1821. Altman, David, Michael Slater, Cheryl Albright, and Nathan Maccoby. "How an Unhealthy Product Is Sold: Cigarette Advertising in Magazines, 1960-1985." JoC 37.4 (Fall 1987) 95-106.
"The tobacco industry has portrayed smoking in advertisements in a misleading manner--as adventuresome, healthy, safe, and erotic, images in stark contrast to voluminous data implicating smoking as a factor in ill health."

1822. "Amicus Brief in Chemlawn False Advertising Suit." NRDCN 6.3 (July-Aug. 1988) 2.
NRDC's support of the New York State's Attorney General's suit against Chemlawn's claim that its pesticide is as safe as aspirin or coffee.

1822a. Andrén, Gunnar. "The Rhetoric of Advertising." JoC 30.4 (1980) 74-80.
Through content analysis, the author explores advertisement strategies which reveal less than the truth. He uses the following criteria: an ad must correspond to facts; be comprehensive; offer support; be semantically intelligible; and assert a proposition.

1823. Andrews, David. "Wholesome Good Foodness, Fiber War." ITT 14.25 (May 16-22, 1990) 18.
How "ad pros have long manipulated health concerns" by "predatory advertising."

1823a. Arlen, Michael. Thirty Seconds. New York: Farrar, Straus, & Giroux, 1980. 211.
Examines the 30-second commercial, its production from conception through all stages to final airing.

1824. Atkin, Charles, et al. "Teenage Drinking: Does Advertising Make a Difference?" JoC 34.2 (1984) 157-167.
"Survey evidence shows that exposure to alcohol advertising is significantly associated with [increased] drinking behavior and intentions." "Those young people who say they have seen more television and magazine ads for beer, wine, and liquor generally drink more or expect that they will begin drinking."

1824a. Atwan, Robert, Donald McQuade, and John W. Wright.

Edsels, Luckies, & Frigidaires: Advertising the American Way. New York: Dell, 1979. 363.
Large, full-page photographs of ads in chronological order. In Part I the ads trace the stereotypes of "the aspirations, fears, and desires of the the American public" which interact with other media "to reinforce acceptable modes of behavior" (xiv) in a consumer society. Part II turns to "the objects of consumption themselves," and III "shows how effective advertising frequently depends on several basic human concerns: fear, fame, and sex."

1825. Auerbach, Stevanne. The Toy Chest: A Sourcebook of Toys for Children. Seecaucus, NJ: Carol, 1986. 256.
Discusses advertising pressures on parents to indulge their children with the newest and best. Offers alternatives to buying toys or provides guidance to quality toys.

1826. Aufderheide, Pat. "Slaves to the Market: Cultural Death by Consumption." ITT 14.1 (Nov. 1-7, 1989) 20-21.
On the proliferation and power of product marketing and its corporate sponsors.

1827. Badhwar, Inderjit. "What Do Doctors Recommend." ChJR 4.9 (1971) 9-10.
The National Association of Broadcasters has failed to restrain false ads.

1827a. Baker, Samm. The Permissible Lie: The Inside Truth About Advertising. Cleveland: World, 1968. 236.
A mixture of information about fraud and deception by advertisers and exhortations and methods to fight back. Agencies must follow their own codes of veracity, citizens must protest more through organizations, and the government "will necessarily have to play a more intrusive role in preventing fraud."

1828. Baran, Stanley J., and Vincent J. Blasko. "Social Perceptions and the By-Products of Advertising." JoC 34.3 (1984) 12-20.
Advertising, apart from any direct effects, influences consumers' perceptions of social reality to the extent that a brand of toothpaste and a make of car determine behavioral predictions. For example, a "young man was expected to be more or less 'forward' at the end of a date, depending upon the type of car he drove and toothpaste he used."

1829. Barmash, Isadore. The World Is Full of It: How We Are Oversold, Overinfluenced, and Overwhelmed by the Communications Manipulators. New York: Delacorte, 1974. 269.
Examines many ways the public is manipulated and misled, and how people's "own subconscious desires, psychic, emotional and economic needs" are used against them by the "value manipulators," the advertisers and public relations businessmen. Solution: autonomous individuals.

1830. Barnouw, Erik. The Sponsor: Notes on a Modern
		Potentate. New York: Oxford UP, 1978. 220.
	The communication system is "in trouble" because the sponsor, "the merchant," is in control (182). Part 1 sketches the rise of the sponsor in radio and then television; part 2 examines the impact of this power on programming; part 3 assesses what this dominance means and may mean for our society.

1830a. Bartimole, Roldo. "Editor Feels Consumer Reporting
		Would Help Credibility, But Would Hurt Press'
		Profits." PoV 4.6 (Sept. 27-Oct. 2, 1971) 2.
	The advertiser is far more important to the Cleveland press than the consumers.

1831. Beauchamp, Tom L. "Manipulative Advertising." BPEJ
		3.3 & 4 (1984) 1-22.
	Advocates replacing manipulative by persuasive advertising, and criticizes the excessive drift to a free-enterprise model of marketing unrestrained by rules of evidence and disclosure. "The freedom to compete has been confused with the freedom to deceive in the 'free-enterprise' model."

1831a. Berger, Arthur. "1984--The Commercial." Television in
		Society. New Brunswick, NJ: Transaction, 1987. 29-40.
	Shot-by-shot analysis of the "1984" commercial for Apple computers based upon Orwell's 1984 and shown during the 1984 Superbowl. It cost $500,000 to make and $800,000 air time.

1832. Berger, Arthur. "Pale Horse, Pale Bather: An Analysis
		of the White Horse Advertisement with the Lady in the
		Bath." Television as an Instrument of Terror. New
		Brunswick, NJ: Transaction, 1980. 129-133.
	Analyzes the contradictions in an ad of a young lady sitting in a bath with a glass of White Horse Blended Scotch Whiskey.

1833. Berger, Arthur. "The Wednesday Specials as Theatre of
		the Absurd." Television as an Instrument of Terror.
		New Brunswick, NJ: Transaction, 1980. 145-148.
	On supermarket advertisements, which are aimed mainly at women.

1834. Blair, Gwenda. "Shoot-Out in Marlboro Country." MJ
		9.1 (Jan. 1979) 33-35.
	Discusses the film Death in the West, which exposes the lethality of smoking and the deception of cigarette ads.

1835. "Brand Names Go to the Movies: Companies Pay Large Sums
		to Get Their Products in Films." AG (Mar. 1, 1988)
		3C.
	Product placement in films (the alien in E.T. learns to like Hershey's "Reese's Pieces") "is becoming a serious multi-million-dollar business." (See 1875.)

1836. Brandt, Steve. "Small Paper Dies." TCJR 3.1 (1974) 8-
		11.

The key to small newspaper survival is avoiding unpleasant news and coddling the advertiser.

1836a. Brumberg, Joan Jacobs. Fasting Girls: The Emergence of Anorexia Nervosa as a Modern Disease. Cambridge: Harvard UP, 1988. 366.
Examines the diverse causes of anorexia: biological, psychological, and cultural. The cultural analysis includes the relentless selling of slimness by magazines, a product of capitalist consumerism.

1837. Carson, Thomas L., Richard E. Wokutch, and James E. Cox, Jr. "An Ethical Analysis of Deception in Advertising." JBE 4.2 (Apr. 1985) 93-104.
"This paper examines several issues regarding deception in advertising. Some generally accepted definitions are considered and found to be inadequate. An alternative definition is proposed for legal/regulatory purposes and is related to a suggested definition of the term deception as it is used in everyday language. Based upon these definitions, suggestions are offered for detecting and regulating deception in advertising."

1837a. Cashill, John R. "Packaging Pop Mythology." The New Languages. Ed. Thomas H. Ohlgren and Lynn M. Berk. Englewood Cliffs, NJ: Prentice-Hall, 1977. 79-90.
Analyzes various myths exploited by the mass media: manifest destiny, white superiority, the frontier, anti-intellectualism, etc.

1838. Chaplan, Debra. "Multinationals: New Blacklisters of the 80s." ORK (Summer 1982) 9.
Corporate sponsorship controls program content, e.g., Kimberly-Clark's withdrawal of sponsorship of the Lou Grant TV program.

1839. Chase, Stuart, and F.J. Schlink. Your Money's Worth: A Study in the Waste of the Consumer Dollar. New York: Macmillan, 1927. 285.
The first of the exposés which helped to create the Consumer Research Union and other efforts for reform.

1840. Chester, Jeffrey, and Kathryn Montgomery. "Counterfeiting the News." CJR 27.1 (1988) 38-41.
Lifting the FCC ban on program-length commercials has subjected the consumer to a barrage of thirty-minute commercials which pretend to be news reports.

1841. "Cigarette Ads and the Press." Na 244.9 (1987) 283-89.
A symposium on the relationship between the press and tobacco advertising, weighing the need for regulation of public health hazards against the dangers of censorship.

1842. Clark, Blake. The Advertising Smoke Screen. New York: Harper, 1944. 228.

ADVERTISING AND PUBLIC RELATIONS

A criticism of the ethics of American consumer advertising based in large part "on complaints, stipulations and orders issued by the Federal Trade Commission" (vii). A great deal of information pertaining to false and misleading advertising is available to the public due to the efforts of the FTC, but much of this information is disregarded by the media.

1843. Clark, David G., and William B. Blankenburg. "Advertising: It Loves Us, But Is It Our Friend?" You & Media. San Francisco, CA: Canfield, 1973. 155-168.
A critique of advertising for promoting unneeded commodities and stimulating "materialistic drives and emulative anxieties."

1844. Clay, Floyd. Coozan Dudley LeBlanc: From Huey to Hadacol. Gretna, LA: Pelican, 1973. 264.
Annotated history of the last of the great patent medicine promoters.

1845. Coleridge, Nicholas. The Fashion Conspiracy: The Dazzling Inside Story of the Glamorous World of International High Fashion. New York: Harper & Row, 1988. 330. (A Remarkable Journey Through the Empires of Fashion. London: Heinemann, 1988).
About two conspiracies: the unwearable nature of many couture garments and the disparity in the fortunes of those who design them and those who make them, for the top designers live like Renaissance princes, while the garments are made in sweatshops around the world.

1846. Cook, James. Remedies and Rackets: The Truth about Patent Medicines Today. New York: Norton, 1958. 252.
Exposé of false advertising.

1846a. Craig, Robert L. "The Changing Communicative Structure of Advertisements, 1850-1930." U of Iowa, 1985. 312. DAI 47 (1986) 699-A.
Early ads were informational, but modern advertisement creates images to persuade customers the product "will fulfill some human desire." These advertisers "sought to mislead the public" to lead them "to make irrational decisions in purchasing products." This activity constitutes the "ideology of consumer capitalism, i.e., a belief that human needs and desires can be fulfilled through the purchase of consumer goods."

1847. Crisp, Roger. "Persuasive Advertising, Autonomy, and the Creation of Desire." JBE 6.5 (July 1987) 413-418.
"It is argued that persuasive advertising overrides the autonomy of customers, in that it manipulates them without their knowledge and for no good reason. Such advertising causes desires in such a way that a necessary condition of autonomy--the possibility of decision--is removed."

1847a. Cummins, Ken. "The Cigarettemakers: How They Get Away With Murder . . . With the Press an Accessory." WM

16.3 (Apr. 1984) 14-24.
"In the 1960s and early 1970s, the tobacco industry grew more defensive [in advertising] as an avalanche of studies confirmed the link with lung cancer and identified cigarettes as a major cause of heart diseases, emphysema, and strokes."

1848. Deeb, Gary. "ABC's Censors Remove 'Barney Miller' References to Dow, Dupont." AG (Dec. 22, 1978) 10B.
References to corporate crime were excised from one program in the series.

1849. Dispenza, Joseph. Advertising the American Woman. Dayton, OH: Pflaum, 1975. 181.
Collection of 285 advertisements directed toward women in the 20th century, with discussion. (See 1777).

1850. Dodge, Larry. "Let's Get Together to Get It All Together." TCJR 2.2 (Sept.-Oct. 1973) 20-25.
On advertiser control of journalism and ways it can be restrained for the public good.

1851. Earnshaw, Stella. "Advertising and the Media: The Case of Women's Magazines." MCS 6.4 (Oct. 1984) 411-21.
"The dependence of women's magazines on advertising subsidy" induces magazines "to produce material to meet the needs of advertisers." The indirect pressures from advertisers over magazine content are "substantial" (421).

1852. Eco, Nicolo. "Driving Us Crazy: A History of Auto Ads, Part 1." Adbusters 1.3 (Spring 1990) 37-39.
Assesses diverse techniques, the rise of credit buying, etc.

1853. Egan, Jack. "Press Encounters." MORE 8.1 (1978) 38-40.
On the $7 million PR for Close Encounters of the Third Kind.

1854. Ehrenreich, Barbara. "Laden with Lard." Z 3.7/8 (July-Aug. 1990) 46-47.
Focuses attention on all the social goods and needs that are never offered or even mentioned by advertisers.

1854a. Ehrenreich, Barbara. "Put On A Happy Face." MJ 12.4 (1987) 60.
Writers for magazines operate under "capitalist censorship," i.e., they are forced to write articles tailored for the tastes of the "yuppie overclass" being targeted by advertisers.

1855. Emamalizadeh, Hossein. "The Informative and Persuasive Functions of Advertising: A Moral Appraisal--A Comment." JBE 4.2 (Apr. 1985) 151-153.
"The paper argues that the informative and persuasive dichotomy of advertising is an empty concept. All advertising messages perform only one function and that function is to persuade."

ADVERTISING AND PUBLIC RELATIONS

1855a. Ewen, Stuart. "Woman's Place in the Advertising Culture." BSR 27 (Fall 1978) 61-64.
"The rise of modern mass production, and of the advertising industry which has enshrined it since the twenties, has had a devastating effect on the home and, at the same time, upon women who remained in the home."

1856. Fallows, James. "The Cigarette Scandal." WM 7.12 (1976) 4-16.
A comment on the events which have happened in the world of cigarette advertising since the Federal Trade Commission took both pro- and anti-cigarette commercials off the air in 1971. More people are dying from lung cancer, yet cigarette sales are up 30 percent, because public policy no longer tries to help smokers, and magazines and newspapers which helped to get cigarette ads off the airwaves are printing cigarette ads.

1856a. Ferrick, Thomas, Jr. "Billboards Target Young, Poor Blacks." AG (Feb. 7, 1988) 5C.
Blacks are being targeted for products that are killing them.

1857. Field, Roger. "The Fluffy Toilet Paper War." Science Digest (Mar. 1976) 87-89.
Procter & Gamble's Charmin tissue ad (in 1976 the longest running TV commercial ever produced) persuaded people to buy fewer sheets of toilet paper for more money by puffing up single-ply paper.

1858. Freedman, David H. "Why You Watch Some Commercials-- Whether You Mean to or Not: Madison Avenue Has a New Bag of Tricks to Keep Viewers From Turning Off its Ads." TVG (Feb. 20, 1988) 3-7.
On advertising agencies' new tricks to keep viewers from turning off ads.

1859. Freeman, John. "The Real Thing. 'Lifestyle' & 'Cultural' Appeals in Television Advertising for Coca-Cola, 1969-1976." U of North Carolina, 1986. 640. DAI 47 (1987) 3223-A.
The ads presented myths and symbols of lives as they should be, in contrast to the more discordant reality presented by television news, in order to make Coca-Cola enticing. Some of the appeals used were attractive males and females, nostalgia, prestige, and patriotism.

1859a. Frundt, Henry. "Fat Latin Profits for Agribusiness." BSR 34 (1980) 15-20.
"With the aid of modern marketing techniques, U.S. agribusiness is pressing for more control of the Latin American food supply."

1860. Gaines, Jane M. "The Popular Icon as Commodity & Sign: The Circulation of Betty Grable, 1941-45." Northwestern U, 1982. 625. DAI 43.8 (Feb. 1983) 2476-A.

Knowledge of Grable resulted from concentrated advertising campaigns by Twentieth-Century Fox Studio timed with the release of each of her films. Also studies her fans in a framework of class and ideology.

1860a. Goldsen, Rose K. "The Great American Consciousness Machine: Engineering the Thought Environment." JSR 1.2 (Apr.-June 1980) 87-102.
The author opposes First Amendment protection for tv commercials, which derive from market-research, depth-psychology and every device for engineering viewers' consciousness--absence of prices and terms, vague and ambiguous product descriptions and ingredients, suppression of real corporate owners, rigged demonstrations, etc. The FCC's obligation is to protect the public from this systematic, massive deception. It might begin by requiring weekly half-hour prime-time programs that disclose the behind-the-scenes production of commercials.

1861. Goldstein, Tom. A Two-Faced Press. Twentieth Century Fund: Priority Publications, 1988. 54.
Argues that news organizations should refuse to run cigarette advertising.

1862. Goodman, Walter. The Clowns of Commerce. New York: Sagamore, 1957. 278.
Satirical treatment of "the motives and morals of the professional persuaders."

1863. Gossage, Howard. "The Fictitious Freedom of the Press." Ram 4.4 (1965) 31-36.
On advertiser control of news.

1864. Grant, Mark. "I Got My Swimming Pool by Choosing Prell Over Brand X." MORE 6.11 (1976) 24-28.
A critique of endorsement ads.

1865. Hammitt, Harry. "Advertising Pressures on Media." Freedom of Information Center Report No. 367. Columbia, MO: School of Journalism, U of Missouri, Feb. 1977.
Ways corporations keep media pro-business.

1866. Hecker, Sidney, and David Stewart, eds. Nonverbal Communication in Advertising. Lexington, MA: Lexington, 1988. 296.
Sixteen chapters on theories, techniques, impact, relationship of program and education, music, art, etc.

1867. Hennessee, Judith. "Can Television Save Detroit?" Ch 1.1 (1981) 76-80.
Analyzes Detroit's small car ad campaign.

1868. Hiaassen, Carl. "Heritage Goes Up in Smoke." AG (Nov. 26, 1989) 3C.
Decries the deal between the National Archives and Philip

Morris Company that allows Morris to exploit the Constitution in slick patriotic ads of the 200th anniversary of the Bill of Rights.

1869. "The High Cost of Television Advertising." QRD 14.3 (Apr. 1988) 10.
Presents the costs of 30-second spot ads, both averages and for individual programs.

1869a. Hill, Doug. "Don't Make Your Bath Water Too Hot . . ." TVG (Apr. 5, 1986) 32-4.
On the failure to balance alcohol ads with public service spots on the dangers of drinking.

1870. Himmelstein, Hal. "Kodak's 'America': Images From the American Eden." JFV 41.2 (Summer 1989) 75-94.
Analyzes one spot, "America," of the nine-spot TV ad campaign for Eastman Kodak, "Because Time Goes By," by J. Walter Thompson. The ad employs patriotic and restorative themes. [Follow-up article JFV 41.3 (Fall 1989)].

1871. Hirsch, Marina. "Point and Click." PR 2 (Summer 1988) 46.
Pepsi ads associate the drink with the fantasy that reality is only the click of the remote control device.

1872. Holbrook, Stewart. The Golden Age of Quackery. New York: Macmillan, 1959. 302.
On patent medicines.

1873. Hook, Donald D. "Spitzer and Key Revisited: The Artfulness of Advertising." L&S 19.2 (Spring 1986) 184-195.
Fuses some of Leo Spitzer's techniques and some of Wilson Bryan Key's to examine "the effective combination of health and sex in a single ad."

1873a. How They Sell: The Successful Marketing Techniques of 13 Major American Corporations. New York: Dow Jones, 1965. 208.
Includes Muntz TV, Mattel (Barbie Dolls), Heinz, and Electrolux.

1874. Huebner, Albert. "Tobacco's Lucrative Third World Invasion." BSR 35 (1980) 49-53.
"Big tobacco companies are starting to make big money by promoting their dangerous products in the Third World."

1874a. Hulteen, Bob. "Just What Is Grumman Selling?" SoJ 19.10 (Dec. 1990) 2.
Military contractors are hyping their big weapons in expensive ad campaigns in spite of detente and pressing social needs, hoping we will accept continued weapons expenditures.

1875. Jacobson, Michael. "In Today's Movies, Art Imitates

Advertising." AG (Jan. 14, 1989) 5B.
On the increasing commercialization of films by product-placement. (See 1835.)

1876. Kelley, Thomas P., Jr. The Fabulous Kelley: Canada's King of the Medicine Men. Don Mills, Ont.: General, 1974. 149.
Reminiscences by the son of the man who sold Shamrock Nerve Tablets and other nostrums in a medicine show from 1890 to 1931, best known for his lecture to sell his New Oriental Discovery.

1877. Key, Wilson Bryan. The Clam Plate Orgy: And Other Subliminal Techniques for Manipulating Your Behavior. New York: Signet, 1980. 209.
The third in the series on the use of unconscious techniques in ads. All three books express concern for a population "anaesthetized toward reality" by ads and media--"a perverse, destructive manipulation into fantasies of instant gratification, endless sensual indulgences, and purposeless consumption just for the sake of consumption" (195). (See 1751 & 1752.)

1878. Kuletz, Valerie. "The Tasteless Intrigue." PR 2 (Summer 1988) 45.
Sexist ad for Drambuie makes the female model "the equivalent of the gift-wrapped bottle of liquor she holds."

1879. Lang, Annie. "Involuntary Attention and Physiological Arousal Evoked by Structural Features and Emotional Content in TV Commercials." Comm R 17.3 (June 1990) 275-299.
Structural features (commercial onsets, cuts, zooms, edits, etc.) and content/emotion affect TV viewer's arousal and attention.

1880. Leff, Arthur Allen. Swindling and Selling. New York: Free Press, 1976. 200.
Compares bunco and legitimate selling to demonstrate the difficulties of the law to control such activities.

1881. Levenstein, Alan. "Can This 48½-inch Kid Make You Eat Cake for Breakfast?" MORE 6.9 (1976) 22-28.
ITT-Continental uses children to sell non-nutritious food identical to competing products.

1882. Levesque, Cynthia. "Drug Advertising: How Eli Lilly Used the Media to Sell a Dangerous Drug." SLJR 10.61 (Apr. 1984) 22-23.
An account of the promotion of Oraflex.

1883. Levin, Myron. "A Filter Made Partly of Asbestos." SLJR 16.105 (Apr. 1988) 12-13.
Analyzes the false and deadly filter claims by tobacco companies. Focuses on Lorillard Co.'s Kent cigarette's "Micronite" filter, which contained "a particularly dangerous

form of asbestos," crocidolite.

1883a. Liebman, Bonnie. "Nouveau Junk Food: Consumers Swallow The Back-to-Nature Bunk." BSR 51 (Fall 1984) 47-51.
"Many products promoted as health food are nutritional junk."

1884. Lohof, Bruce. "The Higher Meaning of Marlboro Cigarettes." JPC 3.3 (Winter 1969) 441-450.
The Marlboro Man is "a symbol of irretrievable innocence."

1885. Magnuson, Warren G., and Jean Carper. The Dark Side of the Marketplace: The Plight of the Consumer. Englewood Cliffs, NJ: Prentice-Hall, 1968. 240.
Explains "how poorly the American consumer is protected and how he is exploited by the unscrupulous and irresponsible few of the business community."

1886. Mahler, Richard. "Tipsy Take on Ads For Beer and Wine." ITT 9.24 (May 15-21, 1985) 14.
Describes Project SMART's campaign against broadcast advertising for beer and wine and the resistance by manufacturers and the media.

1887. Margolius, Sidney. The Innocent Consumer vs. The Exploiters. New York: Trident, 1967. 240.
Discusses the whole range of consumer spending--medicines, cosmetics, foods, rugs, furniture, home improvements, etc.-- explaining the legal and illegal methods used by businessmen to extract money from buyers.

1888. Maslow, Jonathan. "Beer Wars." SR 6.14 (July 7, 1979) 50-51.
Describes the competition among beer manufacturers through sporting events, using advertising blitzes, payoff, kickback, and illegal cash inducements.

1889. McGrath, Roger. "AD/PR Notes." SLJR 18.112 (Dec. 1988) 13.
Describes a misleading ad campaign by a bank.

1890. McGrath, Roger, and Ed Bishop. "May Co. Store Ads Under Siege." SLJR 19.118 (July-Aug. 1989) 1, 6.
The May Department Stores Co. has been in the news across the country, charged with misleading advertising, but so far newspapers in St. Louis, where May is headquartered and its local chain is a major advertiser, have not carried the story.

1891. McNamara, Brooks. Step Right Up: An Illustrated History of the American Medicine Show. Garden City, NY: Doubleday, 1976. 233.
The medicine show was once "widespread and influential, especially in rural areas," and "it was a unique and complicated theatrical form." (See Young's Toadstool Millionaires.)

1892. Meisler, Andy. "Playing to Your Fears--and Your Funny Bone." TVG (Mar. 10, 1984) 17-22.
"Some of the most successful commercials these days comically exploit anxieties about looking dumb or making a mistake."

1893. Meyers, William. "Falling Arches: America Gets Burger Fatigue." The Image-Makers: Power and Persuasion on Madison Avenue. New York: Times, 1984. 104-126.
Analyzes the problems fast-food chains are having with the Societally Conscious Achievers, while the chains continue to stress appeals to Belongers and family togetherness. A history of McDonald's and its founder, Ray Kroc.

1894. Meyers, William. "Giant-Killer: Philip Morris Takes on the Marketing Establishment." The Image-Makers: Power and Persuasion on Madison Avenue. New York: Times, 1984. 64-83.
"One of the corporations that benefited most dramatically from the psychographic advertising revolution of the 1970s was Philip Morris"--Miller Beer, Merit Cigarettes, and the Seven-Up line of soft drinks.

1895. Meyers, William. "Patriots on Wheels: Detroit Starts to Fight Back." The Image-Makers: Power and Persuasion on Madison Avenue. New York: Times, 1984. 84-103.
The main difference between Japanese and US cars is the advertising. The Japanese ads have successfully appealed to the "increasingly powerful Societally Conscious Achievers."

1896. Miller, Roger W. "Critiquing Quack Ads." SLJR 12.73 (1985) 17.
Exposes fraudulent health ads.

1896a. Moog, Carol. "Are They Selling Her Lips?": Advertising and Identity. New York: Morrow, 1990. 236.
Analyzes new strategies used to manipulate a more sophisticated consumer. In case after case she asks what is really being sold, how the advertiser wants us to react, and how the ad shapes our image of ourselves.

1897. Morton, John. "This is Not an Advertorial." WJR 10.5 (June 1988) 12.
Exposes and denounces advertisements disguised as news.

1898. Mowbray, A.Q. The Thumb on the Scale: Or the Supermarket Shell Game. Philadelphia: Lippincott, 1967. 201.
Based on the congressional hearings for the Hart bill for "truth in packaging."

1899. Murphy, Joan. "Rolling Over For Detroit: Why Hundreds of Thousands of Dangerous Vehicles Remain on America's Roads." PC 10.1 (Jan.-Feb. 1990) 10-11, 19, 20.
American Motors Corporation used many methods to defend and

sell its lethal Jeep, including celebrity ads.

1900. Muwakkil, Salim. "Uptown Cigarettes Promote Downtown Health Problems." ITT 14.12 (Feb. 7-13, 1990) 6.
Cigarette and alcohol companies advertise in black publications and donate sums of money to the black community, which restrains black criticism of "vice ads."

1901. Nakayama, Tom. "'Stale Roles & Tight Buns': Video Examines Images of Men in Advertising." M&V 48 (Fall 1989) 17.
Reviews a video and slide-show project of the men's cooperative OASIS (Men Organized Against Sexism and Institutionalized Stereotypes).

1902. Navasky, Victor. "Substantiating the 'Permissible Lie.'" MORE 2.12 (Dec. 1972) 5-7.
Urges the FTC and journalists to increase exposure of deceptive ads.

1903. Nicholas, Jeff. "Nuclear Friction." Pr 8 (Jan. 1978) 8-9.
Don Widener's film, Plutonium, Element of Risk, was rejected by PBS apparently because of pressure from corporate sponsors. Widener's earlier documentary on nuclear energy was attacked by the nuclear corporations.

1904. Nilsen, Don L.F. "Subliminal Chainings: Metonymical Doublespeak in Advertising." Beyond Nineteen Eighty-Four. Ed. William Lutz. Urbana, IL: NCTE, 1989. 147-152.
Explains a subtle linguistic process that produces multiple meanings conveyed unconsciously.

1905. Nunes, Maxine, and Deanna White. The Lace Ghetto. Toronto: New P, 1972. 152.
Advertisements, comic strips, bits out of love magazines, etc., form the basis for discussions of aspects of women's lives (fashion, sexuality, etc.)

1906. Oliver, Thomas. The Real Coke, The Real Story. New York: Random House, 1986. 195.
A history of an institution that began in 1885 and became a symbol of US life. Particular attention to the furor that arose when new management in 1985 changed the taste of Coke.

1907. O'Reilly, William. "The King of Endorsement." MORE 6.9 (1976) 52-3.
Critique of endorsements of House Beautiful by famous people.

1908. Owen, David. "The Cigarette Companies: How They Get Away With Murder." WM 17.2 (1985) 48-54.
Criticizes tobacco advertising and magazines which are afraid to criticize smoking for fear of losing ad money.

1909. Perrin, Dennis. "O'Donoghue's Edgy Humor is Edged Out of the Mainstream." ITT 14.7 (Dec. 20, 1989-Jan. 9, 1990) 20.
Michael O'Donoghue (National Lampoon, Saturday Night Live) tells about corporate censorship and the reluctance of comedians to attack major institutions.

1909a. Peterson, Robin T. "Bulemia and Anorexia in an Advertising Context." JBE 6.6 (Aug. 1987) 495-504.
Reports on "a survey of college students which was designed to provide insights into associations of advertising with the eating disorders of anorexia nervosa and bulemia."

1910. Pollock, Richard. "Atom Firms Block TV Program: Show on Radiation Perils Blacked Out by Industry Pressure." CMJ 4.12 (1979) 7.
Pressure from the nuclear industry caused several PBS stations to refuse to show "Paul Jacobs and the Nuclear Gang."

1911. Pollock, Richard. "The Nuclear Industry . . . Silencing the Media." CMJ 3.10 (1978) 3, 10.
The nuclear industry has banded together to persuade corporations to cease producing and airing critical programs.

1912. Porter, Bruce. "The Scanlon Spin." CJR 28.3 (Sept.-Oct. 1989) 49-54.
Tells how public relations man John Scanlon has manipulated the media on behalf of clients ranging from tobacco companies to racist student journalists to the media themselves.

1913. "Procter & Gamble Co. Angry at Folger Attack." AG (May 13, 1990) 4A.
The company pulled its advertising from a Boston TV station which broadcast commercials against buying Folger's coffee grown in El Salvador because it contributes to "misery, destruction and death."

1913a. Quinn, John F. "Moral Theory and Defective Tobacco Advertising and Warnings (The Business Ethics of Cipollone v. Liggett Group)." JBE 8.11 (Nov. 1989) 831-840.
"Traditional moral theories help corporate decision-makers understand what position consumers, like Rose Cipollone, in Cipollone v. Liggett Group, will take against cigarette manufacturers who fail to warn of the dangers of smoking, conceal data about addiction and other dangers from the public, as well as to continue to neutralize the warnings on cigarettes by deceptive advertisements."

1914. Rand, Ellen. "Why Are Real Estate Ads So Bleh?" QRD 8.2 (1982) 3.
Real estate advertising is plagued by "short, clipped phrases, with code words like 'security' and 'a short distance from the midtown theater district.'"

ADVERTISING AND PUBLIC RELATIONS

1915. [Cancelled]

1916. Regan, Tom, ed. Just Business: New Introductory Essays in Business Ethics. New York: McGraw, 1983. 363.
Includes an essay on truth in advertising.

1917. "Reporter as Scapegoat, Advertiser as King." RSCJ 5 (Aug. 1972) 5.
An interview of a local Nazi member was suppressed by the publisher of the San Gabriel Sun because advertisers thought it would offend their customers.

1918. Robertson, Thomas, et al. Televised Medicine: Advertising and Children. New York: Praeger, 1979. 175.
"Although children's usage of proprietary medicines is firmly controlled by parents," medicine ads "have a modest short-run stimulating effect on their dispositions toward proprietary drugs" (134).

1919. Rosenthal, Herma. "Beware of News Clips Massaging Your Opinions." TVG (Apr. 12, 1984) 4-9.
Corporations now send out press releases on video cassettes that are often passed on to readers as news.

1919a. Rowen, James. "How to Keep Them Buying Even Though They Know You're Lying." WM 5.2 (1973) 55-60.
A study of the advertising campaign of Wonder Bread from the 1950s to the present--focusing on the 1971 "Wonder Bread Case" in which the Federal Trade Commission charged the Continental Baking Company with deception, both in promotion and marketing.

1920. Sableman, Mark. "New Law Targets Comparative Advertising." SLJR 19.120 (Oct. 1989) 15.
Lying comparative ads are now restrained along with all false advertising, by allowing suits.

1921. Sanderson, Samantha. "The Advertiser's Woman." Adbusters 1.1 (Summer 1989) 12-17.
Assesses the harms of the "advertiser's woman" (generic, passive, powerless); individual ads are examined.

1922. Sargent, Lydia. "Home for the Holidays." Z 1.11 (Nov. 1988) 51-54.
Satirical treatment of traditionalist ads directed to women.

1923. Schrag, Peter. "The Powers That Be." MORE 6.1 (1976) 26, 28.
Since he produced a documentary critical of the nuclear power industry, Powers That Be, Don Widener has not been employed by network television.

1924. Schrank, Jeffrey. "Advertising: The Engineers of Illusion." Snap, Crackle, and Popular Taste. New York: Dell, 1977. 83-108.

"Advertising has left millions of Americans 'freely' choosing to spend millions among various brands of a product about which they know nothing; their decision has been reduced to the level of pseudo-choice" (89).

1925. Schrank, Jeffrey. "Packaging: The Unstudied Medium." QRD 9.1 (1983) 10-11.
Examines the "packaging" and other ways products are sold to consumers.

1926. Shimek, John. Billions of False Impressions: An Anthology of Deception. Chicago: Concepts of Postal Economics, 1970. 256.
Criticism of "junk mail" publicity by newspapers and direct mailers.

1927. Silverblatt, Arthur. "Families and Fries That Bind: Fast Moods and Fast Foods." ITT 14.8 (Jan. 10-16, 1990) 21.
The central character in a series of Hardee's ads, Marty, "is the persona that worked so successfully for Ronald Reagan --a genuine, folksy, caring father figure."

1928. Silverman, Milton, and Philip Lee. Pills, Profits and Politics. Berkeley: U of California P, 1974. 403.
Analyzes drug industry product, image, and advocacy advertising.

1929. Silverstein, Brett. Fed Up! The Food Forces That Make You Fat, Sick and Poor. Boston: South End, 1984. 200.
Denounces false food commercials.

1930. Simon, Roger. "What's Red, White and Blue--and Makes Madison Avenue See Green?" TVG (July 13, 1985) 36-7.
On use of patriotism to sell products.

1931. Skolimowski, Henry K. "The Semantic Environment in the Age of Advertising." The New Languages. Ed. Thomas H. Ohlgren and Lynn M. Berk. Englewood Cliffs, NJ: Prentice-Hall, 1977. 91-101. (ETC [Mar. 1968] 17-26).
Real messages concern content; advertising presents pseudo-messages which depersonalize human relations by applying emotions to commodities instead of to humans.

1932. Smith, Ralph L. The Bargain Hucksters. New York: Crowell, 1962. 236.
"Everywhere there is a rising undercurrent of resentment and a growing distrust of business among ordinary citizens who have been duped time and time again."

1933. Smith, Ralph L. The Health Hucksters. New York: Crowell, 1960. 248.
Patent medicine advertising.

1934. Stephenson, William. "The Infantile vs. the Sublime in Advertisements." JQ 40 (Summer 1963) 181-86.
Finds more infantile mechanisms in current full-page ads than 30 years ago.

1935. Stern, Sydney, and Ted Schoenhaus. Toyland: The High-Stakes Game of the Toy Industry. Chicago: Contemporary, 1990. 320.
About the $12 billion a year toy industry, including its marketing methods.

1936. Stone, I.F. "How the 'Truth in Packaging' Bill Was Gutted by an Industry Lobby." IFSW 14.31 (Oct. 10, 1966) 4.
On resistance to Senator Hart's bill to prohibit deceptive labels and promotions.

1937. Sullivan, Andrew. "Flogging Underwear: The New Raunchiness of American Advertising." NR 198.3 (Jan. 18, 1988) 20-24.
On the exploitation of sex in advertising.

1938. Taylor, Peter. Smoke Ring: The Politics of Tobacco. London: Bodley Head, 1984. 328.
"My purpose is to consider why governments place wealth before health, and to examine the political and economic mechanisms of the power of tobacco" (xi). Chapter 3, "The Media Gets the Message": "Advertising is a vital link in the Smoke Ring." Chapter 7, "Polishing the Image," on using the arts. Chapter 10, "Unfair and Deceptive Practices," analyzes ads.

1939. "Toothpaste Wars." QRD 8.2 (1982) 8.
Denounces advertising for virtually identical products.

1939a. Trauth, Denise, and John L. Huffman. "New U.S. Supreme Court Philosophy on Advertising Faces Opposition." JQ 56.3 (Fall 1979) 540-545.
"Court ruling in two cases that commercial advertising has First Amendment protection is in conflict with actions of agencies on behalf of consumers."

1940. Turow, Joseph. Media Industries: The Production of News and Entertainment. New York: Longman, 1984. 213.
Profit determines which programs will receive support from advertisers and which will not survive (52), in magazines, for example, determined by costs per thousand to an advertiser to reach buyers. "The continual interactions of producers and primary patrons [advertisers] play a dominant part in setting the general boundary conditions for day-to-day production activity" (51).

1941. "Vail Spanked by Strawbridge." PoV 16.3 (Sept. 3, 1983) 2.
Pressure on the Cleveland Plain Dealer by its largest advertiser, Higbee's, is further evidence that advertisers try to

compel the news media into sympathetic coverage.

1942. Vestergaard, Torben, and Kim Schroder. The Language of Advertising. Cambridge, MA: Basil Blackwell, 1985. 256.
Uses over fifty ads from such magazines as Cosmopolitan and Penthouse to expose the arsenal of visual and verbal techniques sellers aim at specifically targeted buyers. Special attention to exploitation of sex, social prejudices, and cultivated materialism.

1942a. Wagner, Susan. Cigarette Country: Tobacco in American History and Politics. New York: Praeger, 1971. 248.
Much on advertising, especially the 1950s and '60s.

1943. Waide, John. "The Making of Self and World in Advertising." JBE 6.2 (Feb. 1987) 73-79.
It is a criticism of associative advertising. "Briefly, associative advertising induces people to buy (or buy more of) a product by associating that market product with such deepseated non-market goods as friendship, acceptance and esteem from others, excitement and power even though the market good seldom satisfies or has any connection with the non-market desire."

1943a. Wanderer, Robert. "She's 70: At Least She Will Be 35 Years From Now." ETC 45.3 (Fall 1988) 281-282.
Analyzes a false ad by a new health magazine for the elderly.

1944. Weir, Walter. Truth in Advertising and Other Heresies. New York: McGraw-Hill, 1963. 224.
An advertising executive advocates truthfulness.

1945. Weis, William, and Chauncey Burke. "Media Content and Tobacco Advertising: An Unhealthy Addiction." JoC 36.4 (Autumn 1986) 59-69.
The media under-report the risks of smoking because of the economic influence of tobacco advertising. "The tobacco industry has a history of [successfully] exerting financial pressure" to suppress information "that would impair tobacco sales."

1946. Welch, Barbara. "Being-in-the-Body: A Reflection Upon American Self-Medication Drug Advertising." U of Iowa, 1984. 412. DAI 45 (1985) 2293-A.
The history of this advertising illustrates Ivan Illich's theory that the individual has become more dependent upon mass produced goods and services and less autonomous.

1947. Wernick, Andrew. "Vehicles for Myth: The Shifting Image of the Modern Car." Cultural Politics in Contemporary America. Ed. Sut Jhally and Ian Angus. New York: Routledge, 1989. 198-216.
The automobile is a powerful symbol that has undergone

significant changes under advanced capitalism. The car's "disruptive dominance" is part of the implosion of technology and culture.

1948. Wesson, David. "Product Salience, Puffery, & Perceived Deceptiveness: A Comparative Treatments Experiment." U of Tennessee, 1983. 105. DAI 44.10 (Apr. 1984) 2919-A.
A study of perceived deceptiveness "in advertisements employing social or psychological product benefits as their primary appeal."

1949. White, Larry C. "Nicotine S.D.I." Na 247.10 (Oct. 17, 1988) 333.
Analyzes R.J. Reynolds' new hi-tech "cigarette," "Premier," its advertising, and Reynolds' power with the government.

1950. Whiteside, Thomas. Selling Death: Cigarette Advertising and Public Health. New York: Liveright, 1971. 153.
Includes a lengthy account of the PR struggle by companies in opposition to banning cigarette ads on TV.

1951. Young, James H. The Medical Messiahs: A Social History of Health Quackery in Twentieth Century America. Princeton: Princeton UP, 1967. 460.
The history of laws and prosecution for misleading advertising and the maneuvers of the medicine men to avoid prosecution. (Sequel to Toadstool Millionaires).

1952. Young, James H. The Toadstool Millionaires. Princeton: Princeton UP, 1961. 282.
History of patent medicines and selling.

II. B. 3. CORPORATE IMAGE AND ADVOCACY ADVERTISING (1953-2034)

1953. Adams, Gordon. "Moving the Public: Advertising and the Grass Roots." The Politics of Defense Contracting: The Iron Triangle. New Brunswick, NJ: Transaction, 1982. 185-198.
Military contractors "spend large sums" to persuade the public to support the military-industrial system and to put pressure on the Executive and Congressional policy-makers. Since all military industry advertising is political and often manipulative (identifying corporate interests with national needs), at least it should not be tax deductible.

1954. Albritton, Robert B., and Jarol B. Manheim. "Public Relations Efforts for the Third World: Images in the News." JoC 35.1 (1985) 43-59.
U.S. public relations firms prove instrumental in improving media images in the New York Times of Argentina, Indonesia, Korea, the Philippines, Turkey, and their rulers.

1955. "Alert." Safe Energy Communication Council, 1984.

Pamphlet exposes the $35 million campaign for nuclear power by the nuclear industry.

1955a. Alexander, Larry D. "The Seven Deadly Sins of Corporate Doubletalk." BSR 48 (Winter 1984) 41-44.
Ignoring major social problems, scapegoating, discrediting critics, suppressing information, PR campaigns, denial, firing troublemakers.

1956. Asher, Thomas. "Smoking Out Smokey the Bear." MORE 2.3 (1972) 12-13.
Analyzes the Advertising Council's pro-business "public service" ads.

1957. Astor, Gerald. "The Gospel According to Mobil." MORE 6.4 (1976) 12-15.
On Mobil Oil's aggressive energy advocacy.

1958. Bartimole, Roldo. "CEI Subverts Willing News Media with Plans to Brainwash Community." PoV 4.15 (n.d.) 4.
A 34-page memo from the public information office of Cleveland Electric Illuminating describes how to use the mass media to weaken the anti-pollution and consumer movements.

1959. Bartimole, Roldo. "Junk Makers Want to Make Us Junk Collectors While They 'Dirty Up America' for Fat Profit." PoV (Oct. 23-28, 1972) n.p.
The ad campaign "Keep America Beautiful" paid for by the Ad Council and companies which use non-returnable containers (soft drinks, beer) deceives the public into thinking recycling programs by individuals will solve the junk waste problem, when non-returnable (profitable) containers must be stopped.

1960. Bennett, James R. "An Analysis of Corporate Ideology Advertising." JACR 7 (1979) 23-29.
Examines a corporate ideology ad by a combination of methods.

1961. Bennett, James R. "Corporate Sponsored Image Films: Are They Better Than Ever?" JBE 2.1 (1983) 35-41.
Analyzes Chesebrough-Pond's image film, Family.

1962. Bennett, James R. "A Lesson in Doublespeak." FM 13 (1979) 14-16.
Analyzes Mobil Oil's ads that praise big business and Mobil Oil and condemn government regulation of industry.

1963. Bennett, James R. "The Westinghouse Broadcasting Company's 'Corita' Advertising Campaign." FSN 51 (June 1981) 3-8.
Analyzes the discrepancies between Group W's ad claims and company behavior.

1964. Bennett, James R., Dennis Jackson, and Leonard White. "Mobil Oil in the Land of King Sam the Avuncular."

Etc. 37 (1980) 6-16.
Exposes the biases and techniques in Mobil Oil's "Observations" advocacy ads which appear in Sunday supplements.

1965. Bonafede, Dom. "We're the Good, Rich Guys." WJR 1.5 (1979) 26.
On the extensive and well-financed pro-business image and advocacy advertising campaign.

1966. Brown, William R., and Richard Crable. "Industry, Mass Magazines, and the Ecology Issue." QJS 59.3 (Oct. 1973) 259-272.
Analyzes industrial corporate advertisements about the environment in magazines. The corporate ads followed two strategies: contending that industrial innocence had been retained and that innocence had been regained. The corporate voices--industrial and journalistic--"blended harmoniously"; the journals "in no way found the problem to be basically one of corporate greed or capitalistic cupidity."

1966a. Capitman, William G. "The Selling of the American Public." BSR 2 (1972) 42-46.
"Like its clients, the advertising industry is feeling the pressure of social discontent. The public is questioning the adman's world view which is continually foisted upon them and their children."

1967. Cassidy, Robert. "Stripping Out the Facts." MORE 2.4 (Apr. 1972) 3-5.
On deceptive ads by coal strip mining companies.

1968. Cerra, Frances. "Countering the Oil Slick." MORE 4.8 (1974) 12-15.
On oil companies' propaganda.

1969. Charlton, Linda. "Upwardly Mobil." Ch 1 (Aug.-Sept. 1981) 28-32.
Profile of Mobil Oil's public relations V-P, Herb Schmertz.

1970. Cloherty, Jack. "Seven Flacks for Seven Sisters." WJR 1.2 (1978) 29-35.
On the oil industry's efficient public relations organization.

1971. Connor, Michael. "Selling Capitalism." WSJ (Aug. 4, 1976) 32.
The business-supported Advertising Council with funding from the Commerce Department has begun a three to five year campaign to sell capitalism to the American people.

1972. Conrad, Thomas. "Winning Hearts and Minds for the All-volunteer Military Force." Prog 41.9 (1977) 28-31.
The recruiting program employs deceptive ads and exploits the public schools.

1973. Dadd, Debrah Lynn, and Andre Carothers. "A Bill of Goods?: Green Consuming in Perspective." Green 15.3 (May-June 1990) 8-12.
"Navigating the misleading claims of opportunistic advertisers is just one of the difficulties facing the consumer intent on 'ecologically correct' shopping."

1974. Dionisopoulos, George. "Corporate Advocacy Advertising as Political Communication." New Perspectives on Political Advertising. Carbondale and Edwardsville: Southern Illinois UP, 1986. 82-106.
Examines the nuclear power industry's public relations campaign in newspaper advertisements to counteract the negative publicity from the Three Mile Island accident.

1975. Dodge, Charlie. "Should Corporate Advertisers Be Allowed to Sell Ideas?" Ch 1.6 (1982) 52-4.
Debate over advocacy ads.

1976. Doyle, Jack. "'Enviro Imaging' For Market Share: Corporations Take to the Ad Pages to Brush Up Their Images." NMA 20.2 (Apr.-May 1990) 10-11.
"Major corporations that have had particularly bad environmental press in recent years" are "making a special effort to clean up their image."

1977. "Empirical Uses of Rewritten History." AG (June 4, 1983) 12A.
The "Revitalize America" advertising campaign by the Chamber of Commerce and corporations is a great con job.

1978. Fair, Elizabeth. "AP&L Pledges $500,000 for PR Push." AG (May 27, 1983) 1A.
The Arkansas Power & Light Company's support of the industry's $25 million public relations TV ads.

1979. "Fighting Power Companies." Aquarian (Apr. 25-May 9, 1974) 6, 10.
Consolidated Edison (and other utilities) advertises itself as an "investor-owned utility," but this disguises its control by the banks, its largest stockholders.

1980. "Free Enterprise Kits a Hit in High School." IW 198.6 (1978) 48-52.
The US Chamber of Commerce sponsors a pro-free-enterprise program in the public schools made up of films, worksheets and teachers' manuals. The materials are paid for by companies.

1981. Friedman, Robert. "How America Gets Up in Arms." NT 1 (Mar. 1983) 19.
Military contractors write off the cost of advertising weapons systems.

1982. Gerbner, George. "The Crack in the Tobacco Curtain, or the Bill of Rights Disinformation Campaign." FS 66

(Spring 1990) 2-5.
The tobacco industry has used its advertising clout (now over $3 billion a year) to obstruct information about tobacco lethality ever since 1938. The industry's latest strategy is to associate tobacco with civil liberties and free speech; currently it is pushing a $60 million "Bill of Rights" ad campaign intended to stop or blunt anti-smoking bills in Congress.

1983. Gerrard, Michael. "This Man was Made Possible by a Grant from Mobil Oil." Esq 89.1 (Jan. 1978) 62-64, 142-146.
Herbert Schmertz, Mobil Oil's vice president for public affairs, exerts a great influence on the media through which the company advertises, and also on the public television programs it sponsors.

1984. Golden, L.L.L. Only By Public Consent: American Corporations Search for Favorable Opinion. New York: Hawthorne, 1968. 386.
Shows how four major businesses--AT&T, Standard Oil of New Jersey, General Motors, and DuPont--make use of public relations to influence media, schools, the government, and the public at large.

1985. Green, Mark. "The Faked Case Against Regulation." PC (Spring 1975) 5.
The flood of business advertisements, speeches, and films against government are self-serving and not for the public good.

1986. Guerra, Joe. "Nuclear Industry May Need $42 Million to 'Set the Record Straight.'" CMJ 8.2 (1982) 11.
On nuclear industry TV propaganda.

1987. Guerra, Joe. "Selling Nuclear Power: A Look at the Industry's 'Foolish' Ad." CMJ 7.4 (1981) 6-7.
The ad shows teenagers going off to a war over oil because nuclear power is undeveloped.

1987a. Harty, Sheila. "Big Business in the Classroom." BSR 38 (1981) 36-39.
Criticizes "corporate pedagogy"--image, advocacy, and product advertising in the schools. [See Education].

1988. Harty, Sheila. "Who Produced These Teaching Materials?" TE 67 (1978) 62-64.
Corporate free materials are often designed not for education but for market advertising or corporate image or ideology.

1989. Henry, J.S. "From Soap to Soapbox: The Corporate Merchandising of Ideas." WP 7.3 (1980) 55-57.
Analyzes advocacy ads, which have become widespread.

1990. Hirsch, Glenn. "Only You Can Prevent Ideological Hegemony: The Advertising Council and Its Place in the American Power Structure." IS 5 (1975) 64-82.
Explains the Ad Council as a tool of the corporations.

1991. Foward, Bruce. "The Advertising Council: Selling Lies . . ." Ram 13 (Dec. 1974-Jan. 1975) 25-26, 28-32.
The Ad Council, controlled by business interests, monopolizes public service ads for the military-industrial complex.

1992. Kaplan, Jeremiah. "How the Power of Money Beats the Power of Positive Thinking." ITT 12.33 (Aug. 31-Sept. 6, 1988) 7.
Attempts to close nuclear plants by the ballot have failed because of the enormous amount of money the nuclear industry spends on discourses of all kinds.

1993. [Cancelled]

1994. Knelman, Dr. Fred H. "Nukespeak." Adbusters 1.2 (Winter 1989-90) 81-84.
"Nukespeak and Nukethink for the unique sub-culture of Nuclearism, part technology, part ideology, and part theology."

1995. Ladd, Anthony. "Corporate Energy Futures: A Dumbo Ride Through Epcot Center." SciP 18.2 (1986) 21-26.
Disney's Experimental Prototype Community of Tomorrow sells corporations as the saviors of progress.

1996. Lasn, Kalle, and Cat Simril, eds. "Tubehead: the Campaign Against TV Addiction." Adbusters 1.3 (Spring 1990) 16-20.
Because TV above all lacks a free market-place of ideas (it is almost totally dominated for and by advertisers), this magazine seeks to create a TV "where differing voices finally have a chance to speak," through the creation of TV "tubehead" spots critical of the present anti-democratic system.

1997. Lipman, Harry. "The Selling of the Atom." ITT (Mar. 23-29, 1983) 24.
Utilities gearing up a TV blitz to resuscitate the nuclear industry's image.

1998. Lutz, William. "'The American Economic System': The Gospel According to the Advertising Council." CE 38 (1977) 860-65.
Corporations promote their own interests through the Ad Council's public service ads.

1998a. Lutz, William D. "Corporate Doublespeak: Making Bad News Look Good." BSR 44 (1983) 19-22.
"As profits go down, business doublespeak goes up."

1999. MacDougall, A. Kent. "The Credibility Gap." WJR 3.6

(1981) 20-25.
On the increasing efforts by business to mold public opinion.

2000. Mackenzie, James. "A Critical Review of the Printed Ads of the U.S. Committee for Energy Awareness." CMB 1.12 (1984) 3-6.
These ads are paid for by the nuclear industry to push nuclear power.

2001. MacKenzie, James. "Critique of U.S. Committee for Energy Awareness TV Ad: 'Tomorrow.'" Wash., DC: Union of Concerned Scientists, 1984. 9.
Exposes falsehoods in the film.

2002. Mastro, Randy M., Deborah C. Gostlow, and Heidi P. Sanchez. Taking the Initiative: Corporate Control of the Referendum Process Through Media Spending and What to Do About It. Washington, DC: Media Access Project, 1980. 71.
How corporate advertising changes voters' minds.

2003. Mayer, Allan, and Pamela Simons. "Advertising: Selling Free Enterprise." Newsweek (Sept. 20, 1976) 74.
Examines the pro-business publication, The American Economic System, a joint publication of the Ad Council and the Commerce Department.

2003a. Mead, Nathaniel, and Ray Lee. "Nukespeak." Prog 54.12 (Dec. 1990) 18-21.
The drive to revive nuclear power as the clean alternative to fossil fuels is expressed in manipulative messages to make us forget Chernobyl and Three Mile Island.

2004. [Cancelled]

2004a. Mouat, Lucia. "Big Corporations Slip Into U.S. Classrooms." CSM 70 (Aug. 16, 1978) 16.
The chief problem with the free materials that private business offers public schools is "the mix of accuracy and bias in much of the material."

2005. Nelson, Joyce. "The Power of PR." TM 18.3 (Aug. 1984) 17-19.
On the billions of dollars being spent by corporations and government in North America to "readjust minds."

2006. Nelson, Joyce. "The Time of the Hangman." Adbusters 1.2 (Winter 1989-90) 87-92.
The murderous Argentine junta hired one of the top PR firms, Burson Marsteller, to improve its image. The lesson is that the US and its allies will give massive support to torture regimes so long as they maintain stability for corporate interests.

2006a. Nixon, Will. "An 'On-The-Air' War Over El Salvador." ITT 14.39 (Oct. 17-23, 1990) 21.
CISPES ad opposing funds to the El Salvadoran dictatorship is being rejected by many TV stations partly because of its sponsor, which many media executives consider political (but corporate ads not).

2007. Norrgard, Lee. "Special Ed." CC 11.3 (1985) 11.
The pro-MX Education Bureau was funded by military contractors and the right-wing American Security Council.

2008. Nye, David. Image Worlds: Corporate Identities at General Electric 1890-1930. Cambridge, MA: MITP, 1985. 188.
Studies GE's use of photographs between 1890 and 1930 as a part of modern capitalism's effort to increase profits, to spread consumerism and to silence criticism of the system.

2009. O'Driscoll, Mary. "'Nukespeak' in America: The 1989 Harlan Page Hubbard 'Lemon' Award." Adbusters 1.2 (Winter 1989-90) 85-86.
The U.S. Council for Energy Awareness has again won the award for "the most deceptive energy advertisement of the year."

2010. Ohmann, Richard. "Free messages, Messages of Freedom." Politics of Letters. Middletown, CT: Wesleyan UP, 1987. 198-204.
How the Advertising Council uses "public service" ads to advocate the corporate status quo.

2010a. Ohmann, Richard. "Language, Power, and the Teaching of English." CEAF 6 (Oct. 1975) 1-9.
Analyzes the pro-business ideology of the Ad Council.

2011. Olasky, Marvin. "Chemical Giant Hoodwinks the Press." BSR 54 (1985) 60-63.
"Experienced PR men know that few reporters have the time or understanding to dig deeper if at first glance everyone is smiling."

2011a. Olasky, Marvin. "Inside the Amoral World of Public Relations: Truth Molded for Corporate Gain." BSR 52 (1985) 41-44.
Exposes the manipulation and lies by people who believe there are only interests waiting to be served.

2012. Olasky, Marvin. "The 1984 Public Relations Scam Awards." BSR 51 (Fall 1984) 42-46.
"Corporate PR departments set up elaborate smokescreens."

2012a. Paletz, David, Roberta Pearson, and Donald Willis. Politics in Public Service Advertising on Television. New York: Praeger, 1977. 123.
The authors make the case that PSAs are propaganda for

powerful ruling interests. Chap. 12 discusses prospects for change (not good) and ways to include excluded groups, dissent, and structural criticism of society.

2013. Regna, Joseph. "How Do You Spell Deception?" ScP 20.3 (July-Aug. 1988) 3.
The nuclear industry's U.S. Council for Energy Awareness (USCEA) will spend $340 million in 1988 to "emphasize good news about nuclear energy."

2014. Rice, Ronald, and Charles Atkin, eds. Public Communication Campaigns. 2nd ed. Newbury Park, CA: Sage, 1989. 416.
Essays on the art of public relations campaigns--community, political, service (anti-smoking), etc.

2015. Ridgeway, James. "Exploits of 'The New Adventurers.'" MORE 2.7 (July 1972) 1, 18-19.
Analyzes Standard Oil of New Jersey's ad on off-shore drilling.

2016. Ridgeway, James. "Trying to Catch the Energy Crisis." MORE 4.1 (1974) 1, 15-17.
Analyzes energy companies' campaign to persuade the people there is an energy shortage and it was caused by the government.

2017. Ris, Thomas. "Report Card on Industry's Educational Materials." PRJ 33 (1977) 8-11.
"Over one-half of the educators queried stated that industry-sponsored education programs are not factual."

2018. Rubin, David. "Anatomy of a Snow Job." MORE 4.3 (1974) 18-22.
On PR for David Rockefeller and the Chase Manhattan Bank.

2019. Samuelson, Robert J. "The Oil Companies and the Press." CJR 12.5 (1974) 13-20.
The energy crisis and growing environmental concerns diminished the political clout of the oil companies and led them to undertake a massive campaign of "image advertising."

2020. Savage, J.A. "The Corporate Communicators." PR 2 (Summer 1988) 47-8.
The "flak"'s job is partly to prevent the truth from being told by journalists.

2021. "Say It Ain't So, Annie." ITT 8.36 (Sept. 26-Oct. 2, 1984) 4.
Details about the propaganda blitz by the energy companies and connected industries.

2022. Schroeder, Pat. "The Fairness Doctrine: Embroiled in Oil." UM 4.7 (1974) 13-14.
A critique of the third of a billion dollars deductible

advertising blitz by the oil industry to convince the public that the real culprits for the energy crisis are environmentalists, consumers, and the government.

2023. "Scuzzy Fuzzy." ITT 13.24 (May 10-16, 1989) 5.
Nestlé hired Ogilvie and Mather to improve the image of its subsidiary Carnation, and the PR firm designed a combination of strategies--a National Homework Help Line, a fund for AIDS victims, and spies to infiltrate Nestlé's opponents.

2024. Sethi, S. Prakash. Advocacy Advertising and Large Corporations: Social Conflict, Big Business Image, the News Media, & Public Policy. Lexington, MA: Lexington, 1977. 355.
Defends corporate self-regulation, but warns that well-financed corporate advocacy campaigns can "overwhelm" alternative views (292), and concedes that self-regulation has not worked in the past (296). Proposes diverse meliorations of present corporate domination of access to persuasion.

2025. Sethi, S. Prakash. "Business and the News Media." CMR 19.3 (Spring 1977) 52-62.
Mainly about corporate advocacy advertising, defending its prohibition on radio and television and recommending the establishment of a National Council for Public Information to provide ad space and air time for alternative viewpoints.

2025a. Sharplin, Arthur, and Robert Martin. "At Ashland, More Than Their Oil is Crude." BSR 68 (Winter 1989) 29-32.
An account of Ashland Oil, Inc.'s efforts to cover its corruption with public relations.

2026. Sibbison, Jim. "Pushing New Drugs--Can the Press Kick the Habit?" CJR 24.2 (1985) 52-54.
Methods used by the pharmaceutical industry to manipulate the media.

2026a. Slavin, Peter. "The Business Roundtable: New Lobbying Arm of Big Business." BSR 16 (1975-76) 28-32.
"Largely overlooked by the press and little known by the public, the Roundtable has become a political force" using "public relations and lobbying" as its principal tools: research, position papers, monitoring legislation, speeches, lobbyists, etc.

2027. Smith, David Horton. "'United Way' Is the Name, Monopoly Is the Game." BSR 25 (1978) 30-34.
The United Way "maintains a pervasive monopoly on payroll deduction fundraising" because it maintains "order and efficiency in the workplace."

2027a. Smith, J. Andy, III. "Committee for Energy Awareness: Fronts for Nuclear Power." BSR 50 (Summer 1984) 51-57.
"A trade group masquerades as an educational organization,"

ADVERTISING AND PUBLIC RELATIONS

when it is actually touting the nuclear industry with "factually incorrect and partial information."

2028. Sourcebook on Corporate Image and Corporate Advocacy Advertising. Subcommittee on Administrative Practice & Procedure, Committee on the Judiciary, U.S. Senate, 95th Congress, 1978. 2133.
Documents relating to the Subcommittee's inquiry into FTC, FCC, and IRS jurisdiction over corporate image and advocacy advertising and commercial speech.

2028a. Stephenson, Lee. "Prying Open Corporations: Tighter than Clams." BSR 8 (1973-74) 43-49.
"Here is a rating of 43 major corporations based on their willingness to release information on corporate responsibility."

2029. Sternberg, Steve. "The Drug Companies' Media Campaign to Extend the Patent Monopolies." Pr 9.4 (1981) 50.
Describes the intense campaign by the pharmaceutical industry to ensure the passage of a bill in Congress.

2029a. Stridsberg, Albert. Controversy Advertising: How Advertisers Present Points of View in Public Affairs. New York: Hastings, 1977. 188.
Sponsored by the International Advertising Association, mainly descriptive; pp. 100-147 duplicate examples of advocacy ads in the US.

2030. Wartick, Steven L. "Big Oil's Flawed Propaganda." BSR 36 (1980-81) 43-45.
What the oil companies tell us about their profits and what they are actually doing are different.

2030a. Weinstein, Henry. ". . . And Selling Truth." Ram 13 (1974-1975) 27, 64-65.
Criticizes the Ad Council.

2031. Weinstein, Michael. "No Surprise: The Business Roundtable Likes Business." BSR 17 (1976) 45-48.
Analyzes the deceptions in a series of articles on US capitalism published in Reader's Digest in cooperation with the Business Roundtable.

2031a. Weisman, John. "Why Big Oil Loves Public TV." TVG (June 20, 1981) 4-10.
Huge grants from energy companies go far in creating public and government favor.

2032. Wertheimer, Fred. "What Mobil Didn't Tell You." CC 10 (Nov.-Dec. 1984) 46.
Criticizes Mobil Oil ads which attack Common Cause opposition to PACs.

2033. Williams, Ted. "The Metamorphosis of Keep America

Beautiful." Au 92.2 (Mar. 1990) 124-134.
Explains how the can and bottle industry has used public service advertising, Congress (campaign contributions), and every method they can to prevent a national bottle bill or any other method of placing the blame for the garbage crisis on its source. Comments also on the failure of the media to give sustained attention to environmental problems.

2034. Young, Cameron. "Managing the Forest in Your Mind." Adbusters 1.2 (Winter 1989-90) 60.
The forest industry's misleading ads convey a Fantasy Forest without problems.

II. B. 4. CHILDREN AND ADVERTISING (2035-2057)

2035. Action for Children's Television.
An educational and activist organization that produces, sponsors, and promotes publications on the subject. They also appear frequently before the FTC with testimony, petitions, and commentary which are published.

2036. Adler, Richard P., et al. The Effects of Television Advertising on Children. Lexington, MA: Lexington, 1980. 367.
TV ads are effective but in diverse ways.

2037. Advertising Directed at Children: Endorsements in Advertising. Washington, DC: OECD, 1982. 64.
An international study that criticizes the use of endorsements and endorsers.

2038. Ascheim, Skip. "Channel One." Z 2.5 (May 1989) 101-04.
Reveals the hazards of Whittle Communications' Channel One, a program in which school administrators agree to expose children to commercials in exchange for free TV sets, a satellite dish and 12 minutes a day of catchy, shallowly presented news.

2039. Atken, Charles, and Gary Head. "The Content of Children's Toy and Food Commercials." JoC 27.1 (1977) 107-114.
A descriptive quantification of advertising strategies during the Saturday morning cartoon hour, intended as the basis for studies on the effects of commercial viewing.

2040. Barcus, Earle, and Rachel Wolkin. Children's Television: An Analysis of Programming and Advertising. New York: Praeger, 1977. 218.
Content analysis of children's weekend commercial TV, after-school commercial TV, and advertising. Recommends eliminating or strictly regulating food and toy commercials and the use of premiums. In general argues that TV should serve the public over economic interest.

2041. Blumenthal, Deborah. "Psychologists, Dermatologists

Take Aim at 'Kiddie Cosmetics.'" AG (June 2, 1988) 5E.
Cosmetic companies are now targeting small children.

2042. Broadcast Advertising and Children. Hearings Before the Subcommittee on Communications of the Committee on Interstate and Foreign Commerce, HR, 94th Cong. Washington, DC: GPO, 1976. 495.
Children's advocates vs. broadcasters (industry advertisers refused to participate).

2043. Charren, Peggy. "Protect Our Kids From '900' Exploitation." USA Today (Aug. 21, 1989) 8A.
"Action for Children's Television has petitioned the Federal Trade Commission asking that AT&T be required to offer a refund for all calls to child-oriented recordings made without parental knowledge and consent."

2044. Frideres, James S. "Advertising Buying Patterns and Children." JAR 13.1 (Feb. 1973) 34-36.
TV commercials of toys persuaded kids, who then persuaded their parents to buy certain brands.

2045. FTC Staff Report on Television Advertising to Children. Federal Trade Commission. Washington, DC: GPO, Feb. 1978. 346+.
Discusses "remedies calculated to undo harms arising out of television advertising to children" and recommends the Commission "should commence rulemaking proceedings under the Magnuson-Moss FTC Improvements Act" to ban all TV product ads seen by audiences composed "of a significant proportion of children," ban TV ads of sugared products seen by older children, and balance sugared product ads "by nutritional and/or health disclosures funded by advertisers" (245-46).

2046. Gussow, Joan. "Counternutritional Messages of TV Ads Aimed at Children." Journal of Nutrition Education 4.2 (1972) 48-52.
Children "are being urged on television to eat foods which produce neither present good health nor healthful lifetime food habits," and parents "are failing to stem the tide."

2047. Kunkel, Dale. "From TV Dial to Shopping Aisle." M&V No. 37 (Fall 1986) 15-16.
On the deception and manipulation of children by TV ads.

2048. Liebert, Diane E. et al. "Effects of Television Commercial Disclaimers on the Product Expectations of Children." JoC 27.1 (1977) 118-24.
"The standard disclaimer used in two different commercials was totally ineffective in communicating to children in the age range for which it was intended" (118).

2049. Mahler, Richard. "Ad Nauseam: Whittle-ing Away of the State of Young Minds." ITT 14.2 (Nov. 8-14, 1989) 20-21.

Condemns the Whittle Communications' "Channel One" scheme to inject commercial advertising into the classroom by giving away TV sets.

2050. Melody, William, and Wendy Ehrlich. "Children's TV Commercials: Policy and Research." JoC 24.4 (Autumn 1974) 113-144.

Whereas the Canadian Radio and Television Commission has removed advertising to children on CBC programs, the FCC sides with the broadcasting and advertising industries.

2051. Robertson, Thomas S., Scott Ward, Hubert Gatignon, and Donna M. Klees. "Advertising and Children: A Cross-Cultural Study." CommR 16.4 (Aug. 1989) 459-485.

Children who view TV more make more product requests resulting in more parent-child conflict. This family subversion is greater in the US than in Japan or England.

2052. Schmidt, Steven B. "Kids n' Food." PC 9.4 (July-Aug. 1989) 12-14.

"Advertorials" which blur the distinction between editorial material and advertisement are the latest in a series of innovations aimed at exploiting the commercial vulnerability of children.

2053. Stipp, Horace H. "Children as Consumers." AD 10.2 (Feb. 1988) 26-32.

On the expanding markets for pre-teens, who both buy and influence buying. The more than 20 million four- to twelve-year olds "have a combined disposable income of $4.7 billion a year," and advertisers know it.

2054. Tyner, Kathleen. "Adwatch--Commercials in the Classroom." PR 5 (Summer 1989) 38-40.

Arguments against Whittle Communications program to place commercial advertising in public schools in exchange for equipment and curricular material.

2055. [Cancelled]

2056. Ward, Scott. Effects of Television Advertising on Consumer Socialization. Cambridge, MA: Marketing Science Institute, 1974. 66.

Studies "children's reactions to TV advertising." Recommends that "something needs to be done to insure that very young children are not misled or confused by TV advertising" (46).

2057. Ward, Scott, Daniel Wackman, and Ellen Wartella. How Children Learn to Buy: The Development of Consumer Information-Processing Skills. Beverly Hills: Sage, 1977. 271.

Consumption skills "can be taught to very young children" especially by mothers' direct interaction; older children learn or fail to learn by observing their parents consume wisely or foolishly.

II. B. 5. POLITICAL ADVERTISING (2058-2115a)
(See II.A.4.)

2058. Aufderheide, Pat. "And Don't Forget, We're Paying For It." ITT 10.24 (1986) 14.
Data about the enormous public relations budgets of government agencies, the Pentagon's the largest of all.

2058a. Berkovitz, Tobe. "Political Television Advertising Objectives: The Viewpoint of Political Media Consultants." Wayne State U, 1985. 203. DAI 46 (1985) 1117-A.
Media consultants seek name identification foremost and voter comprehension of issues "rarely."

2059. Bettencourt, Michael. "The Language of Military Recruitment." QRD 15.1 (Oct. 1988) 6-7.
The armed services have made themselves into a virtuous Corporation whose product is "defense" and whose method is the language of business (career opportunities, etc.) and heroism.

2060. Bloom, Melvyn. Public Relations and Presidential Campaigns: A Crisis in Democracy. New York: Crowell, 1973. 349.
"To the degree that presidential campaigning is now essentially a process of communication to broad publics, the public relations man and other related professionals hold sway" (242-3). Studies the thinking, skills, techniques, and relationships with political figures and organizations. Chap. 3 on the two Eisenhower campaigns (1952 and 1956), Chap. 4 on the 1960 campaign, Chap. 5 on 1964, and Chap. 6 on 1968, with an Afterword on 1972.

2061. Blumenthal, Sidney, ed. The Permanent Campaign: Inside the World of Elite Political Operatives. Boston: Beacon, 1980. 264.
"The permanent campaign is the political ideology of our age. It combines image-making with strategic calculation . . . to sustain an elected official's public popularity. It is the engineering of consent with a vengeance" (7). The way to political victory is now through political consultants, who are "the new power within the American political system," rising as the political parties decline (1). "The consultant must stimulate the public's wish fulfillment for the candidate through manipulation of symbols and images, enticing voters to believe that the candidate can satisfy their needs" (5).

2062. Bonafede, Dom. "Uncle Sam: The Flimflam Man?" WJR 1.3 (1978) 65-71.
On the president's large public relations staff both to persuade and hide information.

2063. Buford, Daniel. "Marketing the Military." M&V 39 (Spring 1987) 12-15.

Military recruitment cost $1.7 billion in 1986-87.

2064. Byrne, Hugh. "El Salvador Subway Sign Censored in New York." Alert! 6.4 (May 1988) 5.
The New York Subways Advertising Company refused to display subway signs sponsored by the Winning Democracy Campaign questioning US policy in Salvador. (Also Alert! 8.6 [Oct. 1990] 8).

2065. Caldwell, Terry. "Air Force Takes the Media to Europe." AG (Aug. 6, 1982) 13A.
On USAF PR tours of Europe for media and community leaders.

2066. Carlisle, Johan. "Marketing Reagan." PR 1 (Winter 1987-88) 9-12.
Scrutinizes President Reagan's pollster, Richard Wirthlin, who may be the chief source of Reagan's success in marketing his policies.

2067. Chester, Lewis, et al. An American Melodrama: The Presidential Campaign of 1968. New York: Viking, 1969. 814.
Scattered analysis of advertising (see Index).

2068. "The Circus of a Press Conference." MO 8.3 (Mar. 1966) 6-7.
Presidential press conferences are rigged and dishonest.

2069. Cleghorn, Reese. "Reagan's New Bypass Operations: The White House News Service and Interviews by Satellite." WJR 7.5 (1985) 17-20.
The White House News Service is a partisan government propaganda service going directly to local broadcasting stations and newspapers and bypassing press analysis.

2070. Congressional Record. Washington, DC: GPO, December 1, 2, 4, and 5, 1969.
Documents and newspaper articles placed by Senator J. William Fulbright giving details about the Pentagon propaganda machine.

2071. Dertouzos, James N. The Effects of Military Advertising: Evidence From The Advertising Mix Test. Santa Monica, CA: Rand, 1989. 37.
The annual $80 million expenditures by the services in support of the all-volunteer force "appear to be very effective."

2072. Devlin, L. Patrick. "Campaign Commercials." Television in Society. Ed. Arthur Berger. New Brunswick, NJ: Transaction, 1987. 17-28.
On the functions, kinds, and mid-campaign changes in political advertising.

2073. Diamond, Edwin, and Stephen Bates. The Spot: The Rise of Political Advertising on Television. Rev. ed.

Cambridge, MA: MIT Press, 1988. 425.
New material on the use of 30- and 60- second TV ads from 1948 to the present includes the Hart-Mondale-Reagan campaigns of 1984 and the 1986 midterm elections. Authors probe the strategy, planning, creation, and execution of these brief TV ads, explain the diverse rhetorical kinds of such ads: the ID spot, the aura spot, etc., and the 5 cinematic styles: verité, video news, etc.

2074. Douglas, Sara U. "Organized Labor & the Mass Media." U of Illinois, Urbana-Champaigne, 1983. 450. DAI 44.7 (Jan. 1984) 1963-A.
This study of "the public relations efforts of the Amalgamated Clothing and Textile Workers Union during its lengthy confrontation with the J.P. Stevens Co." concludes that while accurate labor information has increased that information is shaped and dominated by "private corporations that own media industries."

2075. Firestone, O.J. The Public Persuader: Government Advertising. Toronto: Methuen, 1970. 258.
Criticizes partisan use of media particularly by the Executive (Canadian).

2076. "The Great American Bureaucratic Propaganda Machine." USNW 87 (Aug. 27, 1979) 43-47.
A survey of the extent and expenditure of public relations, public affairs and information efforts by government agencies. One study revealed at least 4,926 public-affairs personnel with total salaries of 109 million dollars, but that is "only a fraction of the payroll." [The article does not acknowledge the public's need for the information the regulatory agencies can provide, nor the Reagan administration's successful campaign to limit that information.]

2076a. Greenfield, Jeff. The Real Campaign: How the Media Missed the Story of the 1980 Campaign. New York: Summit, 1982. 319.
Factors other than the media shaped the outcome of the election: the Republican Party raised five times the money of the Democrats, the steady rise of Republican voters, and strong support of Reagan's clear ideological values.

2077. Hale, Katherine, and Michael W. Mansfield. "Politics: Tastes Great or Less Filling." Politics in Familiar Contexts: Projecting Politics Through Popular Media. Ed. Robert L. Savage and Dan Nimmo. Norwood, NJ: Ablex, 1990. 75-95.
Analyzes the political content of TV commercials and expresses concern for the trivializing of human problems in advertising that has helped produce a people who are "political adolescents."

2078. Hans, Dennis. "Just Good Friends." C&C 45 (Mar. 4, 1985) 55-7.

On US government and CIA misleading public relations regarding support for "democratic elements" and "pluralistic tendencies" in foreign lands.

2079. Hiebert, Ray, et al., eds. The Political Image Merchants: Strategies in the New Politics. Washington: Acropolis, 1971. 312.
Sections on "Television and Image Making," "The Science of Polling and Survey Research," "New Managers for the New Techniques," etc. A central theme is the high cost of campaigns.

2080. Hoffman, David. "At Home: The Candidate, Packaged and Protected." WJR 6.7 (1984) 37-41.
On "how Reagan controls his coverage."

2081. Jamieson, Kathleen. "The Evolution of Political Advertising in America." New Perspectives on Political Advertising. Ed. Lynda Lee Kaid, Dan Nimmo, and Keith R. Sanders. Carbondale and Edwardsville: Southern Illinois UP, 1986. 1-20.
From torch light parades to TV. Earlier messages from banners, songs, partisan newspapers, etc., "were often more brief, more extreme, and less substantive than those of today's sixty second spot advertisements" (xiii).

2082. Jamieson, Kathleen. Packaging the Presidency: A History of Criticism of Presidential Campaign Advertising. New York: Oxford UP, 1984. 505. (Rptd. 1988).
A "chronicle of the schemes and strategies presidential candidates and their ad executives have employed to sway the hearts and ballots of sometimes unsuspecting voters. Focusing on each presidential election from 1952 through 1980, it explains how presidential advertising came to be and what it has become, how candidates have shaped it and been shaped by it, what it has contributed, and the ways in which it has contaminated the political process" (viii).

2083. Joslyn, Richard. "Political Advertising and the Meaning of Elections." New Perspectives in Advertising. Ed. Lynda Lee Kaid, Dan Nimmo, and Keith R. Sanders. Carbondale and Edwardsville: Southern Illinois UP, 1986. 139-183.
Examines four methods for understanding elections (benevolent leader, ritual, etc.), concluding that TV campaign commercials limit perceptions to personas and icons rather than expanding understanding of policies.

2084. Kaid, Lynda Lee, Dan Nimmo, and Keith R. Sanders, ed. New Perspectives on Political Advertising. Carbondale and Edwardsville: Southern Illinois UP, 1986. 386.
Thirteen articles present "some of the latest thinking" on such topics as presidential TV commercials, corporate advocacy advertising, TV political spots, image formation, hidden myths in TV ads.

2085. Kaid, Lynda Lee, Keith R. Sanders, and Robert O. Hirsch. Political Campaign Communication: A Bibliography and Guide to the Literature. Metuchen, NJ: Scarecrow Press, 1974. 206.
Publications about campaigns from 1950 through 1972, emphasis on "source and channel variables," but some attention to message and receiver.

2085a. Keisling, Phillip. "Mis-led and Under-worked: Life in Today's Air Force." WM 16.1 (1984) 28-37.
Air Force "bait & switch" ads deceive recruits.

2086. Kern, Montague. 30-Second Politics: Political Advertising in the Eighties. New York: Praeger, 1989. 237.
Analyzes presidential, congressional, and state-level ads, news coverage, campaign managers, and media consultants. Political advertising has changed greatly since the 1970s: much shorter and more keyed to emotional appeals like commercial messages. Public relations and advertising executives are now at the center of political campaigns, i.e. "in determining who the nation's top leadership will be" (207). Commercial advertising principles are now "routinely used in high-budget, competitive campaigns" (208).

2087. Konda, Tom, and Lee Sigelman. "Ad-Versarial Politics: Business, Political Advertising, and the 1980 Election." Politics in Familiar Contexts: Projecting Politics Through Popular Media. Ed. Robert L. Savage and Dan Nimmo. Norwood, NJ: Ablex, 1990. 97-117.
About the intervention of commercial advertising in the electoral process, focusing on the presidential election of 1980.

2088. Kosterlitz, Julie, and Lee Norrgard. "The Selling of the Pentagon." CC 10 (Nov.-Dec. 1984), 14-19.
Describes the Pentagon's fall 1984 media campaign to counter charges of mismanagement.

2088a. The Made for TV Election. Washington, DC: News Analysis Associates, 1988.
Film hosted by Martin Sheen uncovering the ways "show-biz, network hype and the race for ratings" have transformed US presidential campaigns into "just another TV mini-series."

2089. Mark, Norman. "A Reporter's Guide to Military PR." ChJR 2.9 (Sept. 1969) 5.
Questions the honesty of a Pentagon press team.

2090. Martel, Myles. Political Campaign Debates: Images, Strategies, and Tactics. New York: Longman, 1983. 193.
Includes a case study of the 1980 presidential debate between Reagan and Carter. Body of book on goals, tactics, formats, etc.

2091. Matusow, Barbara. "Turning Up the Volume On Advocacy Ads." WJR 8.10 (Oct. 1986) 20-23.
Political advocacy ads are increasing during the Reagan-Bush administration. The American Conservative Trust, for example, spent $4.1 million on advertising attacking the Sandinistas and supporting the Contras.

2092. Mauser, Gary A. Political Marketing: An Approach to Campaign Strategy. New York: Praeger, 1983. 304.
Politics today "has changed from an art into a partial science. Today's candidates are turning to powerful modern marketing research tools--those used by large corporations to understand a market's needs, develop the right products, and communicate and distribute them in the most effective ways. . . . The other major change is the growing importance of electronic media, especially television."

2093. McGinniss, Joe. The Selling of the President 1968. New York: Trident, 1969. 253.
Analyzes Nixon's 1968 TV campaign and the alliance of politicians and advertising experts in political campaigns.

2094. Mechling, Thomas B. "PR Firms Who Work for Dictators." BSR 29 (Spring 1979) 15-21.
On PR firms employed to give atrocious regimes a good image.

2094a. Mickelson, Sig. From Whistle Stop to Sound Bite: Four Decades of Politics and Television. New York: Praeger, 1989. 186.
The first president of CBS News gives his personal account of the rise of television as the crucial element in modern political campaigns.

2095. Mickelson, Sig. The Electric Mirror: Politics in an Age of Television. New York: Dodd, 1972. 304.
TV is "the newest, the most expensive, the most intimate, the most widely followed" medium and "probably has the sharpest impact." Chapters on government and TV, the TV debate, convention coverage, costs, etc.

2095a. Miles, William. The Image Makers: A Bibliography of American Presidential Campaign Biographies. Metuchen, NJ: Scarecrow, 1979. 254.
Works that attempt, "through a recounting of the lives of candidates . . . to assist in the process of persuading the electorate to nominate and elect contenders."

2096. Miller, Mark C. "Massa, Come Home." Boxed In: The Culture of TV. Evanston, IL: Northwestern UP, 1988. 30-39.
Compares a 1977 ad for the country of Jamaica with a revision of the ad that reflects political changes in the country and employs infantile images to appeal to the "perfect consumer."

2097. Morrison, David. "Energy Department's Weapons Conglomerate." BAS 41 (Apr. 1985) 32-37.
On military contractors' nuclear promotion and against a nuclear freeze.

2098. Morrissette, Walt. "Recruiters Hit the Road in Cinema Vans." ArT (Sept. 30, 1985) 22, 32.
Details about the Army's expensive high school recruiting program.

2098a. Nesbit, Dorothy D. Videostyle in Senate Campaigns. Knoxville: U of Tennessee P, 1988. 193.
A study of how TV has changed the presentation of self, specifically about three pairs of candidates for the US Senate and their media consultants, the interactions of competing candidates, and the interactions between candidates and their producers during a campaign.

2099. Nimmo, Dan. The Political Persuaders: The Techniques of Modern Election Campaigns. Englewood Cliffs, NJ: Prentice-Hall, 1970. 214.
Analyzes campaign management through the new technologies of politics, the modern tactics of mass persuasion.

2100. Nimmo, Dan, and Arthur J. Felsberg. "Hidden Myths in Televised Political Advertising: An Illustration." New Perspectives in Advertising. Ed. Lynda Lee Kaid, Dan Nimmo, and Keith R. Sanders. Carbondale and Edwardsville: Southern Illinois UP, 1986. 248-267.
Examines the deep structure of the ads in a single statewide gubernatorial contest in which the Self-Made Man contested Mr. Clean (who won).

2101. Norrgard, Lee, and Joe Rosenbloom. "The Cold Warriors." CC 11.4 (1985) 14-19.
On the American Security Council's support of arms and the military-industrial complex through films, books, and ads.

2102. Paine, Christopher. "The Selling of the B-1." CC 8 (Oct. 1982) 16-23.
Describes the successful Pentagon/Rockwell International campaign to force the B-1 bomber through Congress.

2103. Pringle, Peter. "The Army Wages Propaganda for Chemical Warfare." Pr 10.2 (Apr. 1982) 14.
Exposes the Army's "massive propaganda campaign" for new chemical weapons.

2104. Pringle, Peter. "How the Pentagon Tried to Stifle Missile Debate." Ob 16 (Oct. 3, 1983) 14.
Describes the Pentagon's propaganda campaign for deploying missiles in Europe.

2104a. Rauch, Tom. "Merrie Go-around at KOA-TV." UM 3.7 (Mar. 1973) 4.

Difficulties experienced by Clergy and Laity Concerned to get some anti-war filmspots on TV in Denver.

2105. Real, Michael. "CRP Media Campaigning: All the President's Ad Men." Mass-Mediated Culture. Englewood Cliffs, NJ: Prentice-Hall, 1977. 140-151.
Nixon's 1972 campaign and his Committee to Re-elect the President (CRP) illustrate how much political campaigns are "increasingly modeled after the mass culture style of advertising" which erodes thought and anesthetizes evaluation. At the base of these campaigns is corporate money, which possesses "the power to shape campaigns and popular culture."

2106. Richman, Sheldon. "Bathtub Navy." Inq 6 (July 1983) 48.
Evaluates the Navy/Bath Iron Works propaganda campaign for a 600-ship navy.

2107. Schipper, Henry. "Armed Forces Deal Dirty to Recruits." Take Over 118 (Nov. 9, 1979) 25-28.
About Pentagon recruiting fraud since the inception of the All Volunteer Force in 1973 through misleading "contracts" and ad campaigns and even forged records.

2107a. Schram, Martin. The Great American Video Game: Presidential Politics in the Television Age. New York: Morrow, 1987. 328.
Explores the powerful role of TV news in presidential campaigns and the symbiosis between TV news and the people it covers. Analyzes the strategies used by the Mondale and Reagan campaign staffs to get their messages across and the cooperation they get from TV journalists.

2108. Schreiber, Mark E. "Civil Liberties in the Green Machine." CLR 3.2 (1976) 34-47.
Criticizes false recruitment ads.

2109. Sherrill, Robert. "The Selling of the FBI." Investigating the FBI. Ed. Pat Watters and Stephen Gillers. Garden City, NY: Doubleday, 1973. 3-32.
The public relations campaign for J. Edgar Hoover's image was "the most successful job of salesmanship in the history of Western bureaucracy."

2110. Shyles, Leonard. "The Televised Political Spot Advertisement: Its Structure, Content, and Role in the Political System." New Perspectives in Advertising. Ed. Lynda Lee Kaid, Dan Nimmo, and Keith R. Sanders. Carbondale and Edwardsville: Southern Illinois UP, 1986. 107-138.
There are "unique image and issue codes operating in political advertising" (127).

2111. Shyles, Leonard, and Mark Ross. "Recruitment Rhetoric in Brochures Advertising the All Volunteer Force." JACR 12.1 (Spring 1984) 34-49.

ADVERTISING AND PUBLIC RELATIONS

Ads stress "instrumental rewards" in contrast to traditional "intrinsic satisfactions," which "may explain in part" the "poor retention of skilled careerists." The authors recommend changes.

2111a. Smith, Hedrick. The Power Game: How Washington Works. New York: Random House, 1988. 793.
In Washington, to be a player is "to have power or influence on some issues." Part 1, the nature of power. Part 2, the playing field and strands of power: Congressional campaigns, Pentagon politics, lobbies, staff power, etc. Part 3, presidential agenda setting, coalitions, etc. Part 4, why the system doesn't work better. Chapter 12, "The Image Game: Scripting the Video Presidency," explains the power of public relations, with TV coverage of the president increasing and of Congress decreasing. The last chapter (pp. 392-450) is mainly about President Reagan, who "played the image game unabashedly" (402).

2112. Spero, Robert. The Duping of the American Voter: Dishonesty and Deception in Presidential Television Advertising. New York: Lippincott & Crowell, 1980. 232.
Criticizes TV political advertising for flattening the complex into the simple and the thinker into the sloganeer. TV political advertising emphasizes violent action, show business, stereotypes. The result is declining voter turnout for national elections since 1964. Focuses on the campaign spot. As solution he advocates town meetings.

2113. Sullivan, William. My 30 Years in Hoover's FBI. New York: Norton, 1979. 286.
Chap. 5, "Flacking for the Bureau": "The FBI's main thrust was not investigations but public relations and propaganda to glorify Hoover."

2113a. Swartz, James. "The Professionalization of Pentagon Public Affairs: The Evolution of a Role in the United States Federal Government, 1947-1967." U of Iowa, 1985. 320. DAI 47 (1986) 702-A.
Describes the shift in public affairs management "from one of coordinator to one of manager spokesman."

2114. Swerdlow, Joel L. Beyond Debate: A Paper on Televised Presidential Debates. New York: Twentieth Century Fund, 1984. 89.
Analysis of presidential debates with the conclusion that whoever has power to broadcast the debates should not be allowed to stage them.

2114a. Taylor, Paul. See How They Run: Electing the President in an Age of Mediaocracy. New York: Knopf, 1990. 320.
Analyzes the 1988 presidential campaign and media representation of it--simplistic, conflict-oriented, moralistic, picture-driven. His remedies include less emphasis upon

polling, greater analysis of the past, more exposure of false ads, and free network time to candidates.

2115. Vitale, Joseph. "Chasing the Political Ad Dollar on TV." Ch 8.2 (Feb. 1988) 91-3.
Deals with political advertising on television: how important it is to the stations and the politicians. Gives list of expenditures for House and Senate races from 1978-88.

2115a. Wyckoff, Gene. The Image Candidates: American Politics in the Age of Television. New York: Macmillan, 1968. 274.
Personal view of the sometimes decisive impact of TV on politics under the control of public relations experts, and an evaluation of the image-makers. Reviews several campaigns: Nixon's presidential in 1960, the 1964 presidential primaries, etc. Television has become such a powerful factor in political campaigning that it may become nearly impossible for the viewers to get behind the facade of the "image candidate."

II. C. ELECTRONIC MEDIA (2116-3219)

II. C. 1. a. COMMERCIAL BROADCASTING: REGULATION (2116-2182)

2116. Agosta, Diana. "Do Touch That Dial! The FCC and Citizens Involvement in Broadcasting." Media 2.3 (n.d.) 12-15.
Outlines the structure of the Federal Communications Commission, notes the rush to deregulation during the Reagan years, and tells what citizens can do to reverse the trend and influence media policy.

2117. Archer, Gleason. Big Business and Radio. New York: American Hist. Soc., 1939. 503.
An account of how a few corporations gained control of radio. (Also see his History of Radio to 1926).

2118. Arieff, Irwin. "Profits or a Free Press: The Effects of Broadcast Regulation." WJR 1.1 (1977) 40-44.
Regulation results in more profits for the networks than diversity.

2119. Aufderheide, Pat. "Free Speech for Broadcasters Only." Na 239 (Sept. 1, 1984), 140-42.
Defends the Fairness Doctrine.

2120. Aufderheide, Pat. "Madman Mark Fowler's Final FCC Show." ITT 11.22 (1987) 12-13, 22.
The head of the FCC recently announced a more strict definition of indecency for the airwaves after years of crusading against the Fairness Doctrine on the grounds that it restricts broadcasters' freedom of speech.

2121. Aufderheide, Pat. "Public Interest, Private Principal."

ELECTRONIC MEDIA

ITT 13.22 (Apr. 26-May 2, 1989) 20.
Since the FCC abandoned the Fairness Doctrine in 1987, public affairs programming has dwindled sharply.

2122. Aufderheide, Pat. "Shut Up and Watch." ITT 10.13 (1986) 14.
Criticizes Mark Fowler, FCC head, who regards corporations more highly than the public interest.

2123. "Backtalk." UM 2.2 (Oct. 1971) 12-14.
A survey of protests pending before the FCC regarding Colorado TV and radio stations, more challenges than ever before.

2124. Baughman, James L. Television's Guardians: The FCC and the Politics of Programming, 1958-1967. Knoxville: U of Tennessee P, 1985. 311.
Explains and justifies the weakening of the FCC to regulate in the public interest (e.g. excessive commercials) because of its potential for totalitarian abuse. The FCC failed to check the increasing commercialization of broadcasting and consequent decline of programming diversity and quality. Chapters 1 historical background, 2 television, 3 1950s, 4 "The Minow Years," etc. (eleven chapters).

2125. Besen, Stanley, et al. Misregulating Television: Network Dominance and the FCC. Chicago: U of Chicago P, 1985. 202.
A study of how and why the large networks dominate television, providing recommendations for more effective regulation by the FCC in order to create a broadcast system incorporating "competition, diversity, and localism."

2126. Bittner, John R. Broadcast Law and Regulation. Englewood Cliffs, NJ: Prentice-Hall, 1982. 441.
A comprehensive textbook with sections on I "The Regulatory Framework," II "Programming and Policy," III "Broadcast and Cable Operations," IV "Citizens, Self-regulation, and Legislation," and V "The Legal System and Legal Research." Designed for readers "outside the law school curriculum" by offering 2 perspectives: 1) that of the academician and legal scholar, and 2) that of the broadcasting industry itself. Analyses of important cases appear at the end of most of the 13 chapters.

2127. Bollier, David. "The Strange Politics of 'Fairness.'" Channels 5.5 (1986) 47-49, 52.
Overview of the Fairness Doctrine in television news.

2128. Brown, Les. "The Buck Starts Here." Channels 3 (Sept.-Oct. 1983) 22.
Describes the close relationship between the FCC and the industry it is supposed to oversee in the public interest.

2129. Brown, Les. "Fear of Fowler." Channels 1.5 (1981-82) 21-22.
Indicts the FCC chairman, Mark Fowler, for failing to

support the public's interest.

2130. Brown, Les. Keeping Your Eye on Television. New York: Pilgrim, 1979. 84.
Guide for citizens who wish to be actively involved in the regulatory process.

2131. Brown, Les. "The New Impresarios of Politics." Channels 4 (Mar.-Apr. 1984) 21-22.
Condemns FCC failure to uphold the Aspen Rule and Equal Time Rule.

2132. Brown, Les. "Who's Really Running the FCC--and Is It Legal?" Channels 3 (Jan.-Feb. 1984) 38-39.
The Reagan administration runs the FCC through its chairman, Mark Fowler.

2133. Byler, Robert. "The Broadcast Ascertainment Process-- 1971 to 1981." Bowling Green SU, 1982. 516. DAI 43.1 (July 1982) 8-A.
FCC intention to guide broadcasters in determining community needs for public interest programming was good, but the process failed because of imprecise objectives and weak enforcement. Deregulation has increased broadcasters' discretion.

2134. Chisman, Forrest P. "Public Interest and FCC Policy Making." JoC 27.1 (1977) 77-84.
In view of new technologies and communications regulations which should but do not serve the public interest, the author discusses the relationship between citizen strategies for intervention in policy-making and the revolving door of communications regulators without a long background in the field.

2135. Clark, Jeff. "The Media Control the Democratic Process." Pr 10 (1982) 10-11.
Corporate opposition to the Fairness Doctrine and Equal Time Provision.

2136. Cole, Barry, and Mal Oettinger. "Covering the Politics of Broadcasting." CJR 16.4 (Nov.-Dec. 1977) 58-63.
FCC commissioners "come and go, but the power of the broadcast trade press" continues to influence regulators and to suppress problems within the industry.

2137. Cole, Barry, and Mal Oettinger. Reluctant Regulators: The FCC and the Broadcast Audience. Reading, MA: Addison, 1978. 310.
A study of the FCC mainly during the 1970s with sections on the "players" (commission members, broadcasters, lobbyists, trade press, public), the process of communications with the citizenry, relations with Congress and licensees, citizen power through "petition to deny," and children's television (a case study of FCC response to a citizen group, Action for Children's Television).

2138. Coons, John E., ed. Freedom and Responsibility in Broadcasting. Evanston, IL: Northwestern UP, 1961. 252.
The contributors debate whether free economic competition will produce the best system, or government controls are needed, based on a public-utility analogy. Newton Minow's "The Public Interest" is one of the selections.

2139. Corn, Robert. "The F.C.C. Cleans Up the Airways." Na 245.19 (Dec. 5, 1987) 679-681.
Conflicts between the FCC and stations over alleged obscenity.

2140. Curtis, Cia. "The Incredible Shrinking Newscast." RRJ (Spring 1988) 6-7.
Deregulation of radio in the US has caused many stations to become "little more than free jukeboxes." "In 1986 alone . . . 2,000 full-time positions in radio news disappeared."

2141. Diamond, Edwin, Norman Sandler, and Milton Mueller. Telecommunications in Crisis: The First Amendment, Technology, & Deregulation. Washington, DC: Cato, 1983. 113.
Relates the FCC's current efforts to de-regulate telecommunications, then proposes the abolishment of the FCC in favor of a free market system.

2142. Douglas, Susan. Inventing American Broadcasting, 1899-1922. Baltimore: Johns Hopkins UP, 1987. 363.
Traces the falsehoods of radio history from Marconi, through the various patent battles, to the final dominance of governmental and business interests, especially by the Marconi Wireless Company and later the Radio Corporation of America, which co-opted and controlled production of radio receivers as well as programming. The falsehoods she examines (e.g., that consumerism equals freedom) legitimated and perpetuated the established corporate state.

2143. Du Boff, Richard B. "The Rise of Communications Regulation: The Telegraph Industry, 1844-1880." JoC 34.3 (1984) 52-66.
The history of this early mass communications technology established the "scenario of centralization" that would characterize consolidation and monopoly of later communications media.

2144. Edlavitch, Susan. "Fairness Doctrine and Access to Reply to Product Commercials." ILJ 51.3 (1976) 756-782.
The FCC should apply the Fairness Doctrine "to certain categories of product commercials."

2145. Ellemore, R. Terry. Broadcasting Law and Regulation. Blue Ridge Summit, PA: TAB, 1982. 496.
Concerned with "the selection of licensees" by the FCC, a

"practical guide to obtaining and retaining a license to broadcast." The author believes that the FCC has an "awesome responsibility" because licensees "must be chosen with great wisdom and discrimination" (vi). Chap. 10 "Political Broadcasting and the Fairness Doctrine," Chap. 11 "Advertising Regulation," etc.

2146. Emery, Walter B. "The Craven Dissent on Proposed Rule-Making." JB 3 (1959) 153-160.
Discusses licensing and censorship.

2147. Fore, William F. "Deregulation Is the Name, Grand Larceny the Game." C&C 43.15 (1983) 355-359.
After deregulation stations will have no public service obligations and will be completely free to do whatever makes the most money.

2148. Friendly, Fred. The Good Guys, The Bad Guys, and the First Amendment: Free Speech vs. Fairness in Broadcasting. New York: Random, 1976. 268.
A history and analysis of the conflict between First Amendment protection for freedom of speech in broadcasting and FCC regulations supported by Supreme Court rulings, in particular the Fairness Doctrine requiring broadcasting licensees to operate in the public interest by attending to controversial issues and contrasting views. Friendly hopes the doctrine will wither away as cable and satellite end the scarcity of channels and provide the diversity sought by the doctrine.

2149. Gill, Ann M. "Broadcast Deregulation and the First Amendment." FSY 24 (1985) 85-93.
Analyzes the arguments for deregulation presented by broadcasters and members of the FCC on the basis of First Amendment rights; concludes that such arguments are inconsistent with generally held views of free expression and can only prevail if the airwaves are considered as ownable property.

2150. Howell, Rex G. "Fairness . . . Fact or Fable?" JoB 8 (1964) 321-330.
Opposes the Fairness Doctrine.

2151. Jencks, Richard, and Robert Lewis Shayon. "Does the Fairness Doctrine Violate the First Amendment?" PTR 2 (Dec. 1974) 46-55.
Jencks says it does, Shayon no.

2152. Johnson, Mark. "The FCC: The Urge to Censor." FSY (1978) 73-81.
Tells how the Supreme Court's decision in the case of WBAI of New York's broadcast of George Carlin's "Seven Four-Letter Words" provided the FCC with the precedent it needed to fully assume the role of government censor in cases of obscenity or indecency.

2153. Kahn, Frank. Documents of American Broadcasting. 3rd

ed. Englewood Cliffs, NJ: Prentice-Hall, 1978. 638.
Laws, decisions, reports in their original form.

2154. Kaidy, Mitchell. "Prime-Time Numbers." Na 239 (Sept. 22, 1984) 226.
Deregulation means less public affairs programming.

2155. Kelley, David, and Roger Donway. Laissez Parler: Freedom in the Electronic Media. Bowling Green, OH: Social Philosophy & Policy Center of Bowling Green SU, 1982. 49.
Argues for complete deregulation of radio, television, cable television, and the telephone industry on the grounds of constitutional rights and improved efficiency.

2156. Kinsley, Michael. Outer Space and Inner Sanctums: Government, Business, and Satellite Communication. New York: Wiley, 1976. 280.
Exposes the takeover of Comsat satellite communication by ATT, ITT, and other corporations with government help, for private profit rather than public good (e.g., PBS). A case study of the capture of a regulatory agency by the regulated interests that extends to the highest levels of government.

2157. Konecky, Eugene. The American Communications Conspiracy. New York: Peoples Radio Foundation, 1948. 167.
Indicts monopoly domination of communications and its instrument the FCC.

2158. Krasnow, Erwin, and Lawrence Longley. The Politics of Broadcast Regulation. New York: St. Martin's, 1973. 148.
Studies who gets what, when and how, "those activities leading to decisions about the allocations of desired goods." Believes the FCC "more than an 'inert cash register' whose actions are dictated by the most politically powerful forces" (138).

2159. Krasnow, Erwin, and Samuel Simon. "Does the Public Own the Airwaves?" Channels 2 (Sept.-Oct. 1982) 66-67.
Krasnow justifies private ownership, Simon argues public.

2160. Labunski, Richard. The First Amendment Under Siege: The Politics of Broadcast Regulation. Westport, CT: Greenwood, 1981. 184.
Defends limited regulation such as the Fairness Doctrine, under the authority of the First Amendment.

2161. Lancaster, John. "Red Alert at CNN." CJR 25.1 (1986) 14.
Ted Turner vs. FCC over transmitting Soviet TV news.

2162. Lashner, Marilyn. "A Free Electronic Press the Key to a Vigorous Republic." Feedback 19.3 (1977) 1-4.
An attack upon government regulation of broadcasting from a

Libertarian point of view. The author would eliminate the Fairness Doctrine.

2163. Levin, Harvey. Fact and Fancy in Television Regulation: An Economic Study of Policy Alternatives. New York: Sage, 1980. 505.
"This book examines the licensing of television stations." Licensing originally was intended to ensure diversity of ideas, but its unintended result was extraordinary profits for owners. "The divergence of public and private advantage is therefore unmistakable" (156).

2164. Levin, Harvey. "U.S. Broadcast Deregulation: A Case of Dubious Evidence." JoC 36.1 (Winter 1986) 25-40.
Questions the FCC plan to increase the number of broadcasting stations owned by one corporation.

2165. Litman, Barry R. "Is Network Ownership in the Public Interest?" JoC 28.2 (1978) 51-59.
Economic analysis shows that divesting networks from owned stations will force the affiliated stations to act independently in their programming decisions and hence more closely conform to their fiduciary responsibility.

2166. Matusow, Barbara. "When Push Comes to Shove." Channels 1 (1981) 33-39.
Describes the power of the broadcast lobby in avoiding regulation by government and gaining protection from government.

2167. McGrew, Thomas J. "The Future of the First." Inq 6.12 (1983) 41-2.
We must ask important questions about the degree of government regulation.

2168. Meeske, Milan D. "The Deregulation of Radio and Television: First Amendment Implications." FSN 12.2 (1986) 6-9.
Explores the history of broadcast regulation and the First Amendment ramifications of regulating content.

2169. Morgenstern, Barbara. "The Federal Communications Commission's Commercial Radio Deregulation Role." Bowling Green SU, 1982. 356. DAI 43.7 (Jan. 1983) 2146-A.
Deregulation did not promote diversity, but it "would most probably contribute to greater profits for the major broadcasters."

2170. Nelson, Harold, and Dwight Teeter. Law of Mass Communications: Freedom and Control of Print and Broadcast Media. 3rd ed. Mineola, NY: Foundation, 1978. 675.
Part one deals with libel, copyright, privacy, free press-fair trial, and obscenity; part two with access rights, advertising regulation, antitrust laws, and licensing.

2171. Persky, Joel. "Self-Regulation of Broadcasting--Does It Exist?" JoC 27.2 (1977) 202-210.
Analysis of the National Association of Broadcasters (NAB) Code Authority and of changes in the Television Code since 1952 suggests that "the self-regulatory argument . . . is untenable."

2172. Pool, Ithiel de Sola. Technologies of Freedom. Cambridge, MA: Harvard UP, 1983. 299.
Because the diverse media are converging into one electronic medium, Pool is concerned about the regulatory environment not only surrounding present broadcasting technology but with the previously unregulated communications such as newspapers (once they become part of teletext systems).

2173. Prisuta, Robert H. "The Impact of Media Concentration and Economic Factors on Broadcast Public Interest Programming." JoC 21.3 (1977) 321-332.
Seeking to test his theory that public interest programming was a function of economic success and media concentration, the author surveyed network-affiliated stations in the top 50 SMSA markets in the US and found instead that public interest programming is a function of increased competition.

2174. Ray, William. FCC: The Ups and Downs of Radio-TV Regulation. Ames, IA: Iowa State UP, 1990. 193.
A history of the FCC, an understaffed and politically sensitive agency, and its bent and broken rules.

2175. Read, William. "The First Amendment Meets the Information Society." Telecommunications: Issues and Choices for Society. Ed. Jerry Salvaggio. New York: Longman, 1983. 78-84.
Advocates elimination of government regulation.

2176. Rose, Ernest. "Moral and Ethical Dilemmas Inherent in an Information Society." Telecommunications: Issues and Choices for Society. Ed. Jerry Salvaggio. New York: Longman, 1983. 78-84.
Favors regulation as in the public interest versus concentrated corporate media advantage.

2177. Rowan, Ford. Broadcast Fairness. New York: Longman, 1984. 214.
Analyzes the Fairness Doctrine, its development, intent, application; presents a case study of its use; weighs strengths and weaknesses.

2178. Rowland, William D., Jr. "The Federal Regulatory and Policy-making Process." JoC 30.3 (1980) 139-49.
Federal regulations "will continue to be influenced more substantially by the struggles among much larger political and economic forces than by . . . analysis of the needs of the enterprise."

2179. Schwartz, Louis B. "The Cultural Deficit in
Broadcasting." JoC 26.1 (Winter 1976) 58-69.
The concept of balanced programming should consider varying
levels of taste. Because free-market broadcasting is monopolistic and because PBS is underfinanced and politically
vulnerable, the FCC must intervene to insure representative
diversity.

2180. Simmons, Steven. The Fairness Doctrine and the Media.
Berkeley: California UP, 1979. 285.
Argues for repeal. [See N. Johnson's critique, CJR (May-June 1979) 63-66].

2181. Walters, Ida. "Deciding TV's Future." Inq 2.4 (Feb.
5, 1979) 16-20.
On some dangers of regulation.

2182. Wuliger, Gregory. "The Fairness Doctrine in Its
Historical Context: A Symbolic Approach." U of
Illinois, Urbana, 1987. 744. DAI 48 (1988) 1573-A.
The Doctrine as a symbol resembles the myths of "freedom of
expression," "free enterprise," and "the marketplace of
ideas," none of which possesses "objective reality, but are
simply social constructions" which legitimize corporate monopoly. Not free speech/enterprise and fairness but the profit
motive rules. And government uses the Doctrine to limit expression of unpopular ideas. "What suffers dramatically is
the level of public debate."

II. C. 1. b. COMMERCIAL BROADCASTING: GENERAL (2183-2275)

BIBLIOGRAPHIES

2183. Cooney, Stuart, Kenneth Gompertz and Richard Tuber. "A
Bibliography of Articles on Broadcasting in Law
Periodicals 1920-1968." Journal of Broadcasting 14
(1969-70) 83-156.
Entries are in both alphabetical and subject order; includes
articles on Federal Communications Commission and censorship.

2184. Kittross, John M. A Bibliography of Theses and
Dissertations in Broadcasting 1920-1973. Washington,
DC: Broadcast Education Association, 1978. 240.

2185. McCavitt, William, comp. Radio and Television: A
Selected, Annotated Bibliography. Metuchen, NJ &
London: Scarecrow, 1978. 229.
Divided into 21 sections: 1. Surveys, 2. History, 3. Regulation, 4. Organization, 5. Programming, 6. Production, 7.
Minorities, 8. Responsibility, 9. Society, 10. Criticism, 11.
Public Broadcasting, 12. Audience, 13. Cable Television, 14.
Research, 15. Broadcasting Careers, 16. International, 17.
Technical, 18. Bibliographies, 19. Annuals, 20. Periodicals,
21. References. 1,100 listings spanning 1920 to 1976.

ELECTRONIC MEDIA

2186. McCavitt, William. Radio and Television: A Selected, Annotated Bibliography, Supplement One: 1977-1981. Metuchen, NJ & London: Scarecrow, 1982. 155.
Adds six new sections on news, advertising, corporate video, home video, videotext, satellites.

GENERAL

2187. Arlen, Michael. The Living Room War. New York: Viking, 1969. 242.
A collection of 36 articles, all written by Arlen, dealing with the "other reality of television--television observed not merely as a box . . . dispensing such commodities as information or entertainment, but as . . . something we are doing to ourselves." Many of the articles reveal Arlen's observations of how the Vietnam war was being portrayed on the screen, compared to how others saw it in their own living rooms.

2188. Barnouw, Erik. A Tower in Babel. A History of Broadcasting in the United States. Vol. I--to 1933. New York: Oxford UP, 1966. 344.
The radio industry determined the structure of broadcasting --private over public interest.

2189. Barnouw, Erik. The Golden Web: A History of Broadcasting in the United States. Vol. II--1933 to 1953. New York: Oxford UP, 1968. 391.
On development of US broadcasting leading to global hegemony.

2190. Barnouw, Erik. The Image Empire: A History of Broadcasting in the United States. Vol. III--from 1953. New York: Oxford UP, 1970. 396.
The conversion of the public's air waves into "a private power system" based on advertising enabled the military-industrial-media complex to dominate the nation and expand globally. (N.B. 2188-2190 listed in chronological order.)

2191. Barnouw, Erik. Tube of Plenty: The Evolution of American Television. New York: Oxford UP, 1975. 520.
A History of Broadcasting condensed and updated, an account of how broadcasting became an integral part of the corporate state.

2192. Barrett, Marvin, ed. Survey of Broadcast Journalism 1968-1969. Alfred I. duPont-Columbia U Survey of Broadcast Journalism 1. New York: Grosset and Dunlap, 1969. 132.
Emphasizes "pollution" of the "relentless search for profits." This is the first annual survey of conditions in the industry, all volumes covering a wide variety of data and topics. (N.B. 2192-2199 listed chron. by publication date.)

2193. Barrett, Marvin, ed. Survey of Broadcast Journalism

1969-1970: Year of Challenge, Year of Crisis. Alfred I. duPont-Columbia U Survey of Broadcast Journalism 2. New York: Grosset and Dunlap, 1970. 156.

2194. Barrett, Marvin, ed. A State of Siege: Survey of Broadcast Journalism 1970-71. The Third duPont/Columbia U Survey of Broadcast Journalism, 1970-71. New York: Grosset and Dunlap, 1971. 183.

2195. Barrett, Marvin, ed. The Politics of Broadcasting. Alfred I. duPont-Columbia U Survey of Broadcast Journalism 4. New York: Crowell, 1973. 247.
Mainly examines the 1972 election.

2196. Barrett, Marvin, ed. Moments of Truth?. The Fifth Alfred I. duPont-Columbia U Survey of Broadcast Journalism. New York: Crowell, 1975. 274.

2197. Barrett, Marvin, ed. Rich News, Poor News. The Sixth Alfred I. duPont-Columbia U Survey of Broadcast Journalism. New York: Crowell, 1978. 244.
Surveys 1976-77.

2198. Barrett, Marvin, and Zachary Sklar, eds. The Eye of the Storm. Alfred I. duPont-Columbia U Survey of Broadcast Journalism 7. New York: Lippincott, 1980. 240.
Covers 1977-78.

2199. Barrett, Marvin, ed. Broadcast Journalism 1979-1981. Alfred I. duPont-Columbia U Survey of Broadcast Journalism 8. New York: Everest, 1982. 256.

2200. Biryukov, N. S. Television in the West and Its Doctrines. Tr. Yuri Sviridov. Moscow: Progress Publishers, 1981. 207.
A critique of "free flow of information" doctrine in conflict with Third World aims and needs.

2201. Brady, Ben. "What Watergate Reveals About Broadcast Journalism." RSCJ 8 (July 1973) 7-8.
Watergate was an attempt to dissolve constitutional process and establish a dictatorship, partly by control of information. [See Iran-Contra].

2202. Brendze, Ruth. Not to Be Broadcast: The Truth About the Radio. New York: Vanguard, 1937. 310. (Rptd. 1974).
By commercialization of radio, control by the "power trust," the people have "surrendered freedom of speech to Big Business" (7). Recommends limiting ownership of stations, disclosing holdings of major stockholders on prime time, disclosing major contributors to programs other than for product advertising, etc.

ELECTRONIC MEDIA

2203. Brown, Les. "G.E. Raises the Stakes." Channels 5.6 (1986) 23.
GE's purchase of RCA, parent of NBC, increases the control of the military-industrial complex over the media.

2204. Brown, Les. "Throwing the Bull in Barcelona." Channels 3 (Sept.-Oct. 1983) 21-22.
Reagan administration conservatism at an international TV conference.

2205. Clippinger, John H. "The Hidden Agenda." JoC 29.1 (1979) 197-203.
As the Third World calls for a New World Information Order at the upcoming World Administrative Radio Conference, it will be in the US interest to foreground and provide technical assistance to developing countries and to downplay the Pentagon's major consumption of the satellite spectrum.

2206. Cochran, Thomas C. "Media as Business: A Brief History." JoC 25.4 (Autumn 1975) 155-165.
A look at US media as centralized organizations with marketplace values. Electronic media brought a radical advance in business influence. The institution of advertising, unlike religion and education, lacked social goals and responsibilities besides the maintenance of profitable markets.

2207. Crump, Kathy. "The Jean Muir Case in Retrospect." MJR 21 (1978-79) 17-20.
An account of the blacklisting of the actress of "The Aldrich Family" and other media employees as the result of attacks by Counterattack and Red Channels, anticommunist publications which spread false accusations and intimidated corporate sponsors.

2208. Diamond, Sara. "Politics New Aim of Religious Right." SLJR 13.84 (1986) 19.
The 43rd annual National Religious Broadcasters Convention revealed a "new foreign and military emphasis" in support of the Reagan administration's anti-Soviet and anti-Nicaraguan policies and its arms proposals.

2209. Dizard, Wilson. The Coming Information Age: An Overview of Technology, Economics, and Politics. New York: Longman, 1982. 213.
An overview of new technologies, the industry of electronic communications, political debates within the government, and the evolving "universal electronic information network," connected by the argument that the US must restructure its communications policies for greater coherence and unity to meet the challenges posed by Japan and other competitors.

2210. Fejes, Fred. Imperialism, Media, and the Good Neighbor: New Deal Foreign Policy and United States Shortwave Broadcasting to Latin America. Norwood, NJ: Ablex, 1986. 193.

Advances the "media imperialism" thesis, including a history of the increasing cooperation between US media business and the US government as mutual benefits of penetrating Latin American media markets were recognized.

2211. Ferguson, Marjorie, ed. New Communication Technologies and the Public Interest: Comparative Perspectives on Policy and Research. London: SAGE, 1986. 197.
Eleven essays explore a "common concern" of whether or not technology "will serve the general public interest or only the particular interests of those who stand to gain."

2212. Foley, Karen Sue. The Political Blacklist in the Broadcast Industry: The Decade of the 1950s. New York: Arno, 1979. 498.
History of the industry's participation in the hunt for communists in the entertainment business. [Parallel in education: Schrecker].

2213. "Forms of Cultural Dependency: A Symposium." JoC 15.2 (1975) 121-93.
Nine essays explore aspects of US cultural imperialism.

2214. Freund, Charles. "License Hunters." CJR 20.5 (1985) 7-8.
Describes right-wing attacks on Pacifica radio, subscriber radio in San Francisco and other cities.

2215. Friendly, Fred. "The Campaign to Politicize Broadcasting." CJR 11.6 (1973) 9-18.
Warns against allowing federal funding to compromise programming.

2216. Gandy, Oscar H., Jr., et al., eds. Proceedings from the Tenth Annual Telecommunications Policy Research Conference. Norwood, NJ: Ablex, 1983. 406.
Twenty-two essays by people from government, industry, university, and nonprofit research centers discuss such subjects as the Justice Department's antitrust case against AT&T and the movement toward deregulation of the industry led by the FCC.

2217. Goldsen, Rose K., and Azriel Bibliowicz. "Plaza Sésamo: 'Neutral' Language or 'Cultural Assault'?" JoC 26.2 (1976) 124-25.
These authors are concerned that the international broadcast of largely standardized cultural material will reduce the cultural diversity within Latin America. They criticize claims of neutrality by a centralized source of production on the grounds that language cannot be acultural because language is culture.

2218. Gonzalez-Manet, Enrique. The Hidden War of Information. Tr. Laurien Alexandre. Norwood, NJ: Ablex, 1988. 173. (Written in 1985; first pub. in Span. 1987).

Argues that modern colonialism is the "monopolization of the design, production and marketing" of communication and electronic technologies "by a shrinking number of corporations" (9). Specifically, the US is the leading neocolonialist in its "efforts to impose global domination and information-dependency," and the commercial media reveal little about this development. The author undertakes to overcome "this atomization of vital information and the mystification of transnational corporate strategy" (xix).

2219. Goodman, Julian. "Network News: Running Shackled?" TQ 15.3 (1978) 41-44.
Instances of court censorship.

2220. Gunter, Jonathan F. "An Introduction to the Great Debate." JoC 28.4 (1978) 142-56.
The author summarizes the historical development and issues behind the current UNESCO General Conference and the next year's World Administrative Radio Conference in relation to the world "information order."

2221. Hadden, Jeffrey, and Charles Swann. Prime Time Preachers: The Rising Power of Televangelism. Reading, MA: Addison-Wesley, 1981. 217.
On the rising power of religious broadcasting, its personalities, business concerns, program styles, and political involvement. Special attention to the Moral Majority.

2222. Haigh, Robert, George Gerbner, and Richard Byrne, eds. Communications in the Twenty-First Century. New York: Wiley-Interscience, 1981. 240.
On the future of interactive communications, free-flow of information, media outlets, and public policies, communication breakthroughs versus public ignorance, humans in the service of machines or vice versa. The "next fifteen years will be critical in terms of decisions that can be expected to alter totally the course of communications" (xi).

2223. Hale, F. Dennis. "Why Limit Broadcaster's Rights?" TQ 16.4 (1979-80) 65-67.
Results are given of a survey among college students, in which the students supported tv reporters' rights to the same freedoms as newspaper reporters.

2224. Hanhardt, John, ed. Video Culture: A Critical Investigation. Layton, UT: Smith, 1986. 296.
Focuses on issues of electronic art and technology and the definition of a "video culture." Contains seminal essays by Walter Benjamin, Bertolt Brecht, Louis Althusser, Hans Enzensberger, and Jean Baudrillard; five essays on video and TV; and four essays on video and film.

2225. Herman, Edward S. "The Deepening Market in the West: (3) Commercial Broadcasting on the March." Z (May 1990) 63-4.

On the decline of public service broadcasting.

2226. Himmelstein, Hal. On the Small Screen: New Approaches in Television and Video Criticism. New York: Praeger, 1981. 206.
"Are there no clearly defined critical approaches to television? Are television critics clearly lacking when compared with literary, visual arts, and contemporary film critics? The book highlights the television and video critics John O'Connor, Bernie Harrison, Horace Newcomb, David Ross, and Douglas Davis.

2227. Hobbs, Fred. "Short Circuit." UM 2.2 (Oct. 1971) 9.
"A common practice in Denver newsrooms" is to pretend that a wire service report has originated at the station. "Electronic journalists often compromise integrity and build false images" in the name of "show biz."

2228. Hoover, Stewart. Mass Media Religion: The Social Sources of the Electronic Church. Newbury Park, CA: Sage, 1988. 256.
Interviews viewers of Pat Robertson's 700 Club within the historical context of the development of fundamentalism, neo-evangelism, and religious broadcasting.

2229. Hudson, Heather. "Implications for Development Communications." JoC 29.1 (1979) 179-86.
This synopsis of World Administrative Radio Conference issues focuses on developing countries' access to reliable, affordable communication technology appropriate for their development needs.

2230. Hudson, Heather. "Satellite Communications in the United States." Satellite Broadcasting: The Politics and Implications of the New Media. Ed. Ralph Negrine. London: Routledge, 1988. 216-233.
A history.

2231. Hurley, Neil P., S.J. "University Satellite for Latin America." JoC 25.2 (1975) 157-164.
An American priest narrates his experience in trying to establish a university-controlled system of TV broadcasting in order to help Chile avoid cultural dependency on foreign programming.

2232. Hurwitz, Donald. "Broadcast 'Ratings': The Rise & Development of Commercial Audience Research & Measurement in American Broadcasting." U of Illinois, 1983. 305. DAI 44.6 (Dec. 1983) 1615-A.
Ratings methodologies have been "more a product of economic, social, political, and cultural motives than of the pursuit of truth or better service."

2233. Jacobson, Robert. "The Hidden Issues: What Kind of Order?" JoC 29.3 (1979) 149-155.

In the regulatory debate over "free flow," Jacobson advocates a moratorium on the growth of transnational data flow (TDF) systems by transnational corporations, governments, and military organizations.

2234. Jacobson, Robert. "Who Gets What in the Information Society? Distributional Aspects of Communications Policymaking." Telecommunications Policy and the Citizen. Ed. Timothy Haight. New York: Praeger, 1979. 29-54.
Examines current legislation designed to revise the Communication Act of 1934. "One thing is clear: the tough questions of how to secure 'information equity' in America, and how to allow more Americans to participate in the shaping of their information environment, are not being addressed in the present debate" (51).

2235. Kletter, Richard, Larry Hirschhorn, and Heather Hudson. "Access and the Social Environment in the United States of America." Access: Some Western Models of Community Media. Ed. Frances J. Berrigan. Paris: UNESCO, 1977. 27-83.
Two general uses of communications technology are discussed: mass information/entertainment and delivery of specific services (education, health care, library service, etc.). Focus is upon the "narrow information path" of TV, its "embarrassingly limited view of life" (30), with public TV not much more diverse than commercial because of government and corporate pressures. Much of the article gives case studies of successful alternatives to mainstream media that contribute to a pluralist, participative society.

2236. Koch, Neal. "Power in the Shadows." Channels 8.6 (June 1988) 66-71.
The "power of business-affairs executives is clearly on the rise."

2237. Luther, Sara Fletcher. The United States and the Direct Broadcast Satellite: The Politics of International Broadcasting in Space. New York: Oxford UP, 1988. 230.
Studies the political economy of international telecommunications particularly as it relates to national sovereignty. The "free flow of information" doctrine has served US strategic needs, in opposition to the less industrialized nations' demand for "prior consent" before receiving satellite transmission.

2238. Lynch, William. The Image Industries. New York: Sheed & Ward, 1959. 159.
TV and motion pictures dangerously mix reality and fantasy in exploiting people's desire for entertainment.

2239. McQuail, Denis. "Diversity in Political Communication: Its Sources, Forms & Future." Communicating Politics.

Ed. Peter Golding, et al. New York: Holmes & Meier, 1986. 133-49.
Advocates expansion of choices open to the citizen audience. Diversity at present comes from special interest or oppositional media and from public broadcasting. Public broadcasting, however, privileges established political organizations. McQuail supports an open diversity that strives for equal access to all serious viewpoints.

2240. Meehan, Eileen. "Neither Heroes Nor Villains: Towards a Political Economy of the Rating Industry." U of Illinois, 1983. 305. DAI 44.6 (Dec. 1983) 1615-A.
A study of the "texts in which the ratings industry and its two client industries defend their practices before governmental bodies." Concludes that ratings firms "exercise considerable discretion in selecting measurement practices . . . for market control" and the "manufacture of the commodity audience."

2241. Mendelsohn, Harold. "Delusions of Technology." JoC 29.3 (1979) 141-43.
Contrary to hope that new technology will maximize information exchange among all people, Mendelsohn warns that "the new language of contemporary telecommunications makes possible serious global interchange only among and between selected groups of scientists, engineers, technocrats, and military strategists."

2242. Miller, Merle. The Judges and the Judged. Garden City, NY: Doubleday, 1952. 220.
An account of political blacklisting following WW II.

2243. Mitchell, Lee M. "Government as Broadcaster, Solution or Threat? Diversity in Broadcasting." JoC 28.2 (1978) 69-76.
Since the commercial broadcast system offers little information on the processes of government, government broadcasting could fill this void, but attempts to set up government broadcasting have met with fears of propaganda. Ironically such fears have led to a situation in which a few leaders have the "ear" of the media and dominate the information flow.

2244. Moberg, David. "Chicago's Fine Arts Station Fights Corporate Erosion." ITT 14.14 (Feb. 21-27, 1990) 6.
On the account of difficulties facing Chicago's WFMT-FM, "considered by many to be the best fine arts [radio] station in the country."

2245. Monson, Gary. "The War of the Well(e)s." JoC 29.3 (1979) 10-20.
A metaliterary analysis of Welles' famous radio broadcast explores the power of the mass media to exploit conditions and confuse the line between fact and fiction.

2246. Mosco, Vincent. Broadcasting in the United States:

Innovative Challenge and Organizational Control. Norwood, NJ: Ablex, 1979. 153.
Beginning with the reality that TV is controlled by "powerful people," this book "focuses on the fate of attempts to expand the radio/television world," on innovations obstructed by "the structure that governs it." Mosco seeks a system "more responsive to public needs, more open to the expression and control of more people" (126), and in his last chapter he offers a number of remedies.

2247. Mosco, Vincent. Pushbutton Fantasies: Critical Perspectives on Videotex and Information Technology. Norwood, NJ: Ablex, 1982. 195.
Examines four popular fantasies in terms of videotex, a technology which draws on major new developments in microelectronics for information processing and communication. Attacks the FCC for abandoning the public to the interests of large corporations, deregulation an instrument to increase power of centralized capitalism. Final chapter discusses alternatives.

2248. Nordenstreng, Kaarle, and Herbert Schiller, eds. National Sovereignty and International Communication. Norwood, NJ: Ablex, 1979. 286.
Fourteen essays in four Parts: 1 "Communication and National Development," 2 "Direct Satellite Broadcasting: Exemplar of the Challenge to National Sovereignty," 3 "International Law," 4 "International Communication in Transition: The New Global Balance." The world business system, of which the US is a major center, works through transnational corporations. TNCs "have a decisive role in determining--largely through advertising--the content of media flows and, consequently, the social consciousness prevailing in society, propagating the system's values."

2249. Ploman, Edward. Space, Earth, & Communication. Westport, CT: Quorum, 1984. 237.
Places satellite communications within political, economic, military, and technological contexts. Warns against hegemonic militarization of outer space and the anachronism of national sovereignty, and urges international cooperation.

2250. Powe, Lucas A., Jr. American Broadcasting and the First Amendment. Berkeley, CA: U of California P, 1987. 295.
Attacks licensing, which is likely to lead to censorship. Describes ways the FCC has harassed broadcasters who deviated from what it saw as acceptable social doctrine (editorials, Nixon vs. the WP, etc.). A comprehensive survey of what has happened in the 60 years of government regulation of broadcasting, which has often violated free-press ideals.

2251. Ridenour, Ron. "The Continuing Saga of KPFK: Media Support Is Waning." RSCJ 13-14 (Fall and Winter 1974-75) 3-4.
On LA police and grand jury harassment of radio station KPFK

over confidential news sources.

2252. Riegle, Barbara. "Something Is Missing in Broadcasting: The Majority Sex." RSCJ 6 (Dec. 1972) 8-12.
Women are seldom part of the electronic news-gathering and reporting system.

2253. Robinson, Glen, ed. Communications for Tomorrow: Policy Perspectives for the 1980s. New York: Praeger, 1978. 526.
Policy implications of the new communications technology.

2254. Salvaggio, Jerry, ed. Telecommunications: Issues and Choices for Society. New York: Longman, 1983. 182.
Ten essays discuss corporate monopoly, invasion of privacy, censorship, access, control of new technologies, etc.

2255. Schiller, Herbert. Mass Communications and American Empire. Boston: Beacon, 1969. 170.
Surveys the militarization of domestic communications and global expansion of commercial electronics, and offers suggestions for a more democratic system.

2256. Schiller, Herbert. Who Knows: Information in the Age of the Fortune 500. Norwood, NJ: Ablex, 1981. 187.
Just as international trade consists of goods and services produced by a handful of business firms, so information is created, managed, transmitted, stored, and retrieved by specific corporations and groups of people for profit. The author concentrates on the exploitation of new forms of communication by private enterprises controlled by US capital, the newly emerging information order.

2257. Schwartz, Tony. Media: The Second God. Garden City, NY: Anchor, 1983. 169.
This public relations expert "describes powerful processes which can be used to create social harm as well as social good" (Introduction). The electronic media are the second god because they are omnipresent, ubiquitous, all-knowing, and extraordinarily influential. "I shall try to demonstrate that people can make positive use of the power of this god" (6).

2258. Seldes, Gilbert. The Great Audience. Westport, CT: Greenwood, 1950. 299. (Rpt. 1970).
Examines "the conditions in which our entertainments are created--the way major studios conduct the business of making and showing movies, the economics of sponsored radio and television," and the effects on people. Seeks to preserve the strengths of the popular arts without retaining their vices, the chief of which is their uniformity. He would "make the popular arts serve free men trying to secure a free society."

2259. Siepmann, Charles. Radio's Second Chance. Boston: Little, 1946. 282.
Indicts radio's failure to function in the public interest.

2260. Skornia, Harry. Television and Society: An Inquest and Agenda for Improvement. New York: McGraw, 1965. 268.
The present system is the result of the pursuit of profits. The public interest would be served better by other arrangements. He recommends a mixed system to balance the commercial. "So far broadcasting has been controlled instead of released. It needs to be unshackled and used in other new ways by scores of different kinds of groups" (225).

2261. Skornia, Harry, and Jack Kitson, eds. Problems and Controversies in Television and Radio. Palo Alto, CA: Pacific Books, 1968. 503.
Fifty-four essays, including "The Role of the Commentator as Censor of the News" and "Reporting or Distorting." Part I offers economic and historical background, "Frames of Reference"; Part II "Criticism"; III deals with the conflicts between free speech and the US sponsorship structure; IV on educational broadcasting; etc. for ten sections.

2262. Smith, Anthony. The Shadow in the Cave: The Broadcaster, His Audience, and the State. Urbana: U of Illinois P, 1973. 351.
An examination of the existing relationships and struggles between broadcasters, audiences, and the state, as well as a study of their roles throughout broadcasting history.

2263. Smith, Robert Rutherford. "Corporate Access to the Electronic Media." Big Business and the Mass Media. Lexington, MA: Lexington, 1977. 97-133.
On the conflicts among corporations, the government, and public interest groups for access.

2264. Starowicz, Mark. "Slow Dissolve: The Death of Public Broadcasting." TM 19.1 (Apr. 1985) 4-8, 32.
While radio has maintained a national Canadian character, television has become a US monopoly and Canadian citizens part of "video-America."

2265. Sussman, Leila A. "Labor in the Radio News." Mass Media and Mass Man. Ed. Alan Casty. New York: Holt, 1968. 241-242.
Labor is treated negatively over radio.

2266. Sy, Demba. "Capitalist Mode of Communications, Telecommunications Underdevelopment & Self-reliance: An Interdisciplinary Approach to Telecommunications History & Satellite Planning on a Pan-African Scale." Howard U, 1984. 638. DAI 45 (June 1985) 3474-A.
Western capitalist telecommunications strategies for Africa "aggravate the continent's economic and technological dependency."

2267. Telecommunications and Democracy: How the Information Revolution Affects Our Lives and Politics. New York: Democracy Project, December 1984. 70.

Presents two papers and two panels, the first on the political implications and the second on social consequences. Most citizens are uninformed of how much is at stake, since the main source of information has been corporate advertising, which conveys an optimistic picture.

2268. Tolstedt, Mark. "Micronesian Broadcasting & U.S. Strategic Interests: The Evolution of a Dependency." Northwestern U, 1986. 298. DAI 47 (1986) 1916-A.
Radio and television in Micronesia, a US trusteeship under the United Nations, developed into forms which "promoted the interests" of the US.

2269. Traub, James. "Radio Without Rules." CJR 20.5 (1982) 36-38.
Public affairs programs will decrease with deregulation.

2270. Tuchman, Gaye. "Professionalism as an Agent of Legitimation." JoC 28.2 (1978) 106-113.
"The growth of the mass media is so intertwined with the emergence of modern capitalism that the media serve as the cultural arms of the capitalist industrial order." And the methods of journalistic professionalism--coverage of already legitimated institutions to name one--have become "a means not to know" (107).

2271. Tuck, Jay Nelson. "Unholy Alliance: AFTRA And The Blacklist." Na 181 (Sept. 3, 1955) 187-189.
The AFTRA would blacklist any actor or actress who was controversial.

2272. Wasco, Janet. "Trade Unions & Broadcasting: A Case Study of the National Association of Broadcast Employees & Technicians." The Critical Communications Review. Vol. I: Labor, The Working Class, & the Media. Norwood, NJ: Ablex, 1983. 85-113.
Studies the history and current status of the broadcast union as compared to other unions and guilds in the industry. Broadcast unions "today represent reinforcement for the existing structure and no real element of change" (110).

2273. Wicklein, John. Electronic Nightmare: The New Communications and Freedom. New York: Viking, 1981. 282.
Describes the growing danger of totalitarianism resulting from the concentration of communications and information within the military-industrial complex.

2274. Williams, Frederick. The Communications Revolution. New York: Mentor, 1983. 291.
The development of new technologies recently ranks with other social revolutions.

2275. Witty, Susan. "The Citizens Movement Takes a Turn." Channels 1.2 (June-July 1981) 68-73.
Explains why the media reform movement has weakened.

II. C. 1. c. (1). COMMERCIAL TELEVISION: GENERAL (2276-2448)

2276. Cassata, Mary, and Thomas Skill. Television: A Guide to the Literature. Phoenix: Oryx, 1985. 148.
Ten bibliographical essays divided into three categories: I. "Test Patterns": "A broad overview of the communication/mass communication process, a history of television, and reference sources for information about television" (3 chaps.); II. "The Environment": "the research of the field, first in broad brush strokes, then in a more specialized mode, focusing on such areas as television and children, television news, and television and politics" (4 chaps.); III. "Directions": "covers the literature of the television industry and television criticism and ends with a number of thought-provoking collected works" (3 chaps.).

2277. Adam, Barry. The Rise of a Gay and Lesbian Movement. Boston: Twayne, 1987. 203.
Lesbians and gay men are shunted aside by corporate and state communications channels (163).

2278. Allen, Jeanne. "The Social Matrix of Television: Invention in the United States." Regarding Television. Ed. E. Ann Kaplan. Frederick, MD: U Publications of America, 1983. 109-119.
Explores the discussion of how TV might be used in the two decades before it was marketed to show how the present one-way system was early standardized by economic interests.

2279. Allen, Robert, ed. Channels of Discourse: Television and Contemporary Criticism. Chapel Hill: U of North Carolina P, 1987. 310.
The authors recognize "the institutional nature of television" whose primary purpose is to translate mass viewing "into a commodity that can be sold to advertisers" (6), to produce quantities of viewers for profit for the owners. Thus these writers treat as texts not only programming but commercials, station promotions, network logos, and the flow of all elements designed to maintain and increase quantities of viewers. Programs are "only 'pre-texts' for the real content of television--advertising messages" (8).

2280. Altheide, David, and Robert Snow. Media Logic. Beverly Hills, CA: Sage, 1979. 256.
People equate TV programs with the real world, when TV does not so much reflect society as attempt to establish meanings and norms.

2281. Aronowitz, Stanley. "Working Class Culture in the Electronic Age." Cultural Politics in Contemporary America. Ed. Ian Angus and Sut Jhally. New York: Routledge, 1989. 135-150.
Examines the way "working-class identity is defined now, "almost entirely through its representation in the media,"

particularly TV. "From the mid-1970s," there are "no direct representations of working-class males (much less women) in television" (146).

2282. Aronson, James. "TV: Eyeball to Eyeball." Deadline for the Media: Today's Challenges to Press, TV and Radio. Indianapolis: Bobbs-Merrill, 1972. 143-161.
On network and corporate censorship of program content.

2283. Asante, Molefi Kete. "Television and Black Consciousness." JoC 26.4 (1976) 137-41.
The television medium transmits symbols which fail to represent the multi-ethnic composition of American society.

2284. Bagdikian, Ben. The Information Machines: Their Impact on Men and the Media. New York: Harper, 1971. 359.
The power held by those who control new technological instruments of communication is enormous, but the consumer can increase "control over what information he receives." Ch. 8 "Broadcast News as a Corporate Enterprise" recognizes the problems of controlled news.

2285. Bagdikian, Ben. "Television--'the President's Medium'?" CJR 1.2 (1962) 34-38.
TV provides presidents "awesome power," which the press must check.

2286. Ball-Rokeach, Sandra J., Milton Rokeach, and Joel W. Grube. The Great American Values Test: Influencing Behavior and Belief Through Television. New York: Free, 1984. 190.
Demonstrates the power of TV to manipulate viewers.

2287. Barber, Benjamin. "The Second American Revolution." Channels 1.6 (1982) 21-25, 62.
Corporations are gaining control of the potential pluralism of the new communications technology.

2288. Barrett, John R. "Will Bureaucracy Finally Kill Art?" TQ 8.3 (1969) 16-21.
Deplores the lack of originality in commercial TV.

2289. Barton, Laurence. "Coverage of the 1980 Olympic Boycott: A Cross-Network Comparison." Television Coverage of International Affairs. Ed. William Adams. Norwood, NJ: Ablex, 1982. 129-142.
Describes the homogeneity of reporting the boycott in terms of the Cold War.

2290. Berger, Arthur. Television as an Instrument of Terror. New Brunswick, NJ: Transaction, 1980. 83-98.
By terror he means "disorientation, paralysis, confusion, debilitation, as well as fear," the "goals of terrorists." Television "has created the man with commodities who is without qualities."

2291. Berger, Arthur. The TV-Guided American. New York: Walker, 1976. 194.
The influence of TV, "the most important socializing force in America," is malign, feeding our alienation by promoting "a life of ceaseless consumption" and life as a succession of "murderers and hunters of murderers, moral grotesques, nitwits, fools, and clowns" (187). TV is this way because it is controlled by businessmen whose sole aim is to attract viewers to commercials for profit (188).

2292. Berger, Arthur, ed. Television in Society. New Brunswick, NJ: Transaction, 1987. 282.
Eight sections divided into two sections: I. commercials, ceremonial events, series, and II. issues and topics (violence, values, education, technology, freedom of the press).

2293. Binzen, Peter. "The Annenberg School of Communications." Change 10.3 (Mar. 1978) 52-53.
Describes the work of the School under Dean George Gerbner in examining TV's abuses, its superficiality, and its tendency to shield itself behind the First Amendment.

2294. Blumenthal, Sidney. "Expose FBI-WBZ Links." MORE 7.5 (May 1977) 6-7.
A WBZ newscaster and a Westinghouse executive "appear to have cooperated in 1967 with the [FBI] counter-intelligence program aimed at discrediting the anti-war movement."

2295. Boddy, William. "'The Shining Centre of the Home': Ontologies of Television in the Golden Age." Television in Transition. Ed. Phillip Drummond and Richard Patterson. London: BFI, 1986. 125-134.
Challenges the conception of TV in the 1950s as a golden age. A "preferable broadcasting order might have been put in place" (5).

2296. Bogart, Leo. The Age of Television: A Study of Viewing Habits and the Impact of Television on American Life. 3rd ed. New York: Ungar, 1972. 515.
Thirteen chapters on programming, viewing patterns, TV and reading, TV and movies, spectator sports, advertisers, etc.

2297. Botein, Michael, and David Rice, eds. Network Television and the Public Interest: A Preliminary Inquiry. Lexington, MA: Lexington, 1980. 223.
The central concern of these New York Law School conference papers is the concentration of network power and the inability of other-than-major advertisers to buy time.

2298. Breen, Myles P. "Severing the American Connection: Down Under." JoC 25.2 (Spring 1975) 183-186.
Australian broadcasting industry hopes to prevent total "Americanization."

2299. Brown, Les. "Living in a Nielsen Republic." Channels

2.1 (1982) 20-21.
The corporate state has used TV to transform the populace into consumers more interested in material things than political rights.

2300. Brown, Les. Television: The Business Behind the Box. New York: Harcourt, 1971. 374.
"The game of television is basically between the network and the advertiser, and the Nielsen digits determine what the latter will pay for the circulation of his commercial. . . . In day-to-day commerce, television is not so much interested in the business of communications as in the business of delivering people to advertisers. People are the merchandise, not the shows. The shows are merely the bait." (15-16).

2301. Browne, Nick. "The Political Economy of the Television (Super) Text." Television, The Critical View. Ed. Horace Newcomb. 4th ed. New York: Oxford UP, 1987. 585-99.
Looks at large patterns of programming, at the schedule itself, as a text for analysis in the context of TV's roots in large-scale US economic practices.

2302. Brush, Judith M., and Douglas. Private Television Communications: An Awakening Giant. Boston: Herman, 1977. 160.
Describes the growth of corporate TV used for a multitude of internal purposes.

2303. Bunce, Richard. Television in the Corporate Interest. New York: Praeger, 1976. 150.
This book exposes the ineffectiveness of FCC policy, as well as discusses corporate control over television. In addition, it examines the inability of broadcasting owners to represent diversities in interests, needs, and priorities.

2304. Cantor, Muriel. The Hollywood Television Producer: His Work & His Audience. New Brunswick, NJ: Transaction, 1988. 256.
Television producers are "some of the most powerful but least known men in television." This book describes the types of people that become TV producers and how; their training, ways in which they deal with issues such as network censorship, obstacles to creativity and other constraints of the networks.

2305. Carey, James W., ed. Media, Myths, and Narratives: Television and the Press. Newbury Park, CA: Sage, 1988. 264.
Subjects range from television as a contemporary expression of popular culture and journalists as constructors of news stories to media stardom and the transformation of social reality.

2306. Castro, Janice. "Women in Television: An Uphill

ELECTRONIC MEDIA

Battle." Channels 8.1 (Jan. 1988) 42-52.
Deals with difficulties women face in the television industry, from the acting to executive levels.

2307. Catton, Bruce. "One Party Television--It's Big Money . . ." Na 177 (Aug. 15, 1953) 132-133.
Sketches further recent events in the "trend toward corporate domination" of TV.

2308. "CBS-CIA Connection Confirmed by Salant." Br 92.3 (May 30, 1977) 22-23.
CBS News cooperated with the CIA during 1950s and 1960s, allowing them access to incoming reports, outtakes, blow-ups, etc.

2309. "Coming of Age: Media and the Mature Audience." M&V 45 (Winter 1989) 1-24.
Special number on media and aging, gerontophobia perpetuated by anti-aging marketing campaigns, targeting elders as consumers, etc.

2310. Conrad, Peter, ed. Television: The Medium and Its Manners. London: Routledge, 1982. 180.
TV induces escape and triviality, but above all it serves capitalism to induce us to spend and consume regardless of need.

2311. Corcoran, Farrel. "Television as Ideological Apparatus: The Power & the Pleasure." CSMC 1 (1984) 131-45.
Studies "the ways in which mass communication fulfills an ideological mission by legitimating this power structure."

2312. Cowan, Geoffrey. See No Evil: The Backstage Battle over Sex and Violence on Television. New York: Simon & Schuster, 1979. 323.
Personal account of power relations within TV corporations.

2313. Cross, Donna. Mediaspeak: How Television Makes Up Your Mind. New York: Putnam, 1983. 254.
In all of its programming--from talk shows to the evening news--TV reinforces establishment values.

2314. D'Agostino, Peter, ed. Transmission: Theory and Practice for a New Television Aesthetics. New York: Tanam, 1985. 326.
This book of essays "offers a broad framework for the study of television, one which encompasses television aesthetics, social commentary and applications of new technologies."

2315. Diamond, Edwin. "The Atrocity Papers." ChJR 3.8 (1970) 3-4, 12-14.
Pentagon pressure on CBS.

2316. Diamond, Edwin. Sign Off: The Last Days of Television. Cambridge, MA: MIT P, 1982. 273.

The third volume produced by the News Study Group at MIT (The Tin Kazoo [1975] and Good News, Bad News [1978]). This book examines various major institutions through their TV representation: hype, labor, Three Mile Island, political campaigns, the Iranian Embassy hostages, etc. The "last days" refers to the incoming cable-satellite order.

2317. Dominick, Joseph R., and Millard C. Pearce. "Trends in Network Prime-Time Programming, 1953-1974." JoC 26.1 (1976) 70-80.
A study of four aspects of the broadcasting system--instability, diversity, homogeneity, and equilibrium--indicates that economic oligopoly among the networks has led to action/adventure domination since 1957 accompanied by a decline in reality programs (news, public affairs, interview/talk).

2318. Downing, John. "The Political Economy of U.S. Television." MR 42.1 (May 1990) 30-41.
Surveys "the leading indicators of flux in the television business" (decline of networks, rise of cable and other alternatives, etc.), changes in the advertising industry, attack on labor, and political implications of these changes.

2319. Drummond, Phillip, and Richard Paterson, eds. Television in Transition. London: BFI, 1986. 280.
Two emphases: political economy focusing on a "world communication order which is profoundly unequal" and textual analysis of "value systems and formal characteristics." Covers three broad areas: "political economy and cultural imperialism; the development of American television; and the relationship of television to the viewer."

2320. Eisler, Benita. Class Act: America's Last Dirty Secret. New York: Watts, 1983. 352.
Analyzes media representation of the US as a single-class nation and the systematic suppression of wide economic and social differences.

2321. Elgin, Duane. "Television and the Environment." Adbusters 1.3 (Spring 1990) 10-11.
TV presents a sustained message in support of life-styles of consumption.

2322. Ellis, John. Visible Fictions. Boston: Routledge & Kegan Paul, 1982. 295.
The distinctiveness of TV derives from the necessity of keeping the viewer watching, hence the importance of self-promotion, direct address, and sound, all rhetorical strategies to attract and retain viewers. Especially through the device of direct address (presenters, newscasters, talk-show hosts, etc.) TV poses as an institution functioning on behalf of the viewers.

2323. Ellis, Kate. "Queen for One Day at a Time." CE 38.8 (Apr. 1977) 775-781.

Prime time TV offers programs that both let women imagine a larger space and return women to the corner of their childhood. Programs about women stir up anxiety to get people interested and then contain the anxiety, reassuring the audience.

2324. Ellison, Harlan. The Glass Teat: Essays of Opinion on the Subject of Television. New York: Jove/HBJ, 1975. 317. (Ace, 1970).
This and The Other Glass Teat offers a variety of essays on government pressure on TV (Nixon), responses of young people, etc.

2325. Esslin, Martin. The Age of Television. San Francisco: Freeman, 1982. 138.
TV presents dangers with longterm consequences: the least intellectual people dictate content, it induces a schizophrenic state of mind, it is "a branch of the advertising industry," etc. Calls for an "adequately funded public television service."

2326. Ettema, James, and Charles Whitney. Individuals in Mass Media Organizations: Creativity and Constraint. Beverly Hills, CA: Sage, 1982. 259.
A study of the organizations producing the symbols of contemporary culture, with essays concerning "the way symbol-producing organizations shape the form, content and meaning of their products." The dominant view expressed is that the constraints imposed by these organizations upon the autonomy or freedom of individuals is extremely powerful, and often destructive.

2327. "Exxon, Ford, Domino's Pizza: Guardians of the First Amendment." Extra! 3.1 (Oct.-Nov. 1989) 16.
"In a medium which entrusts the First Amendment to big business, timidity, self-censorship and sponsor pull-outs have become commonplace."

2328. Faulk, John. Fear on Trial. New York: Simon, 1964. 308.
The author was fired from his CBS job and blacklisted for six years over false allegations he was pro-communist.

2329. Fiske, John. "British Cultural Studies and Television." Channels of Discourse: Television and Contemporary Criticism. Ed. Robert C. Allen. Chapel Hill: U of North Carolina P, 1987. 254-289.
Conceives of culture and therefore of TV as an arena of struggle between "those with and those without power" (15). Examines Madonna's music-video texts and audience responses.

2330. Fiske, John. Television Culture. London: Methuen, 1987. 353.
Partly about the relationship between how TV "is made meaningful and pleasurable" by its viewers (its cultural

dimension) and TV's status as "a commodity in a capitalist economy." TV functions as a cultural agent that produces meanings for "the dominant ideology" (1).

2331. Fiske, John, and John Hartley. Reading Television. London: Methuen, 1978. 223.
Employs linguistics and semiotics to analyze TV programs and examines the place of TV in society in chaps. on content analysis, the signs, codes, and functions of TV, audiences, etc.

2332. Frank, Robert. "The IAS [Institute for American Strategy] Case Against CBS." JoC 25.4 (1975) 188-189.
Unfavorable review of Lefever's TV and National Defense.

2333. Franzwa, Helen. "The Image of Women in Television: An Annotated Bibliography." Hearth and Home: Images of Women in the Mass Media. New York: Oxford UP, 1978. 272-299.
Documents the false portrayals of women that suggest little has changed "in the last twenty years" (273).

2334. Friedman, Leslie. "Broadcast Media." Sex Role Stereotyping in the Mass Media. New York: Garland, 1977. 99-143.
Entries cover a wide range of topics--passivity, emotionalism, etc.

2335. Galbraith, John K. A Tenured Professor. Boston: Houghton Mifflin, 1990. 197.
Because he requires his TV stations to give equal time to promoters of peace for every pro-military story, the owner is stripped of his company by the SEC for being un-American.

2336. Gerbner, George, et al. "The Demonstration of Power: Violence Profile No. 10." JoC 29.3 (1979) 177-96.
A heightened sense of fear and inequity caused by TV violence, and validated by one or two in a thousand real-life events, may lead people to welcome repression in the name of security.

2337. Gerbner, George. "The Dynamics of Cultural Resistance." Hearth and Home: Images of Women in the Mass Media. Ed. Gaye Tuchman, et al. New York: Oxford UP, 1978. 46-50.
TV's treatment of women is "more repressive than ever"; the subordinate picture of women "undermines existing social and economic advances of women and reinforces cultural repression" (42).

2338. Gerbner, George, and Larry Gross. "Living with Violence: The Violence Profile." JoC 26.2 (Spring 1976) 173-199.
While TV may incite the imitation of criminal violence in some viewers, it is more likely, through a heightened sense of risk and insecurity, to encourage dependence upon an

established authority and to legitimize police force.

2339. Gerbner, George, Larry Gross, Michael Morgan, and Nancy Signorielli. "Charting the Mainstream: Television's Contributions to Political Orientations." American Media & Mass Culture. Ed. Donald Lazere. Berkeley: U of California P, 1987. 441-464.
TV "transmits a predominantly middle-class, middle-of-the-road worldview that is both congenial to its corporate producers and effective in maximizing audiences," but this mainstream "tends to run toward the political right" (409).

2340. Gitlin, Todd. "Television's Screens: Hegemony in Transition." American Media & Mass Culture. Ed. Donald Lazere. Berkeley: U of California P, 1987. 240-265.
On the ways the dominant ideology, indirectly and unintentionally, permeates TV, while TV simultaneously contains contradiction and opposition.

2341. Gitlin, Todd, ed. Watching Television. New York: Pantheon, 1987. 248.
Seven essays on "Network News," "Soap Operas," "Children's TV," "Music Videos," "Car Commercials and Miami Vice," "Simulations" (wrestling, The People's Court, etc.), and "Prime Time." Because TV is the "principal circulator of the cultural mainstream," "or more precisely" what "the appointed seers think we need or want to know," because it is a "wasteland that grows vaster" by the year, it "bears special watching." The essays focus on forms, genres, and Reaganism.

2342. Goldsen, Rose. "The Great American Consciousness Machine: Engineering the Thought-Environment." JSR 1.2 (1980) 87-102.
TV serves the networks and their clients for profit and social control.

2343. Goldsen, Rose. The Show and Tell Machine: How TV Works and Works You Over. New York: Dial, 1977. 427.
"The power to dominate a culture's symbol producing apparatus is the power to create the ambience that forms consciousness itself. It is a power that we see exercised daily by the television business as it penetrates virtually every home." "The unanticipated outcome of it all is that the United States of America enjoys the dubious distinction of having allowed the television business to score . . . the first undertaking in mass-behavior modification by coast-to-coast and intercontinental electronic hookup."

2344. Green, Timothy. The Universal Eye: The World of Television. New York: Stein, 1972. 276.
Because of advertiser/profit domination, TV offers little variety (Chapter 2).

2345. Hanson, Jarice. Understanding Video: Applications,

Impact and Theory. Newbury Park, CA: Sage, 1987. 135.
A brief history of video development, some current applications of video forms and their impact on society, and a theory of video communication.

2346. Hardin, Herschel. Closed Circuits: The Sellout of Canadian Television. Vancouver: Douglas & McIntyre, 1985. 339.
A history of the Americanization of Canadian television and the failure of the Canadian government to pursue the official policy of a national broadcasting system.

2347. Harris, Ian. "Horatio Alger Revisited: Media Myths & the Reality of Men's Work." M&V No. 48 (Fall 1989) 12-13.
Condemns popular "American Dream" myths on TV (money is success, etc.) and calls for the creation of new myths for men as "concerned human beings promoting a better life for all creatures on this planet."

2348. Hawes, William. "TV Censorship: Myth or Menace?" TQ 4.3 (1965) 63-73.
Corporate sponsors, government, and religious groups seek to censor TV.

2349. Heath, Stephen, and Gillian Skirrow. "An Interview with Raymond Williams." Studies in Entertainment. Ed. Tania Modleski. Bloomington, IN: Indiana UP, 1986. 3-17.
Makes a distinction between mass culture and popular art, discusses role of TV in serving human needs, elaborates on his concept of "flow" for TV analysis, and other topics.

2350. Himmelstein, Hal. Television Myth and the American Mind. New York: Praeger, 1984. 336.
The author asks how close the US approximates Huxley's Brave New World where television runs without cessation, industrialists are deities, and the citizens are contentedly drugged. The book studies "the conceptual frames for today's television images," which "thrust an unending stream of commodities at us and assure us our way of life is both defensible and unthreatened." But "a careful deconstruction of the myths will cast doubt on their inevitability and simultaneously open our vision to oppositional conceptions of social formation."

2351. Howard, Herbert, and S. L. Carroll. Subscription Television: History, Current Status, and Economic Projections. Knoxville, TN: U of Tennessee, 1980. 178.
Covers both over-the-air and cable: a regulatory, technical, and economic nuts-and-bolts study asking no questions about cultural or political value.

2352. Johnson, Nicholas. "The Corporate Censor." Language Awareness. Ed. Paul Eschholz, et al. New York: St.

Martin's, 1974. 173-182.
On corporate secrecy and censorship.

2353. Johnson, Nicholas. How To Talk Back to Your Television Set. Boston, MA: Little, Brown, 1970. 228.
Diverse subjects but especially on corporate domination of TV and the FCC. For example, like "virtually all regulatory agencies," the FCC is bombarded daily by industry representatives to create industry orientation. The final chapter explains specifically how to fight back and reform TV for the public good.

2354. Johnson, Nicholas. "Out of the Wasteland." ChJR 3.5 (1970) 7-10.
FCC Commissioner Johnson attacks FCC for ignoring "decades of first amendment law" in its crusade against obscenity.

2355. Johnson, Nicholas. Test Pattern for Living. New York: Bantam, 1972. 154.
On the power of the corporate state as expressed through and reinforced by TV. Much of the book offers alternatives to corporate values.

2356. Johnson, Paul. "TV Tattler Books Hold Wide Appeal." AG (June 16, 1988) 4B.
Books by Peter Boyer, Ed Joyce, Gwenda Blair, and Jim Spence argue that TV is "purely show business, with an emphasis on the business," which is a "chilling prospect."

2357. Kaplan, E. Ann, ed. Regarding Television: Critical Approaches--An Anthology. American Film Institute Monograph Series. Frederick, MD: U Publications of America, 1983. 147.
On live TV, TV news, TV sports, daytime TV and women, soap opera (3 essays), movies made for TV, etc. Mainly papers presented at a conference intended to make available new theoretical approaches--semiology, psychoanalysis, structuralism, etc.

2358. Karp, Walter. "The Life of TV's Political Power." Channels 3 (May-June 1983) 37-40.
Television's power derives from those in power. It and "the parties are the closest of collaborators."

2359. Kellner, Douglas. "Network Television and American Society: Introduction to a Critical Theory of Television." TSoc 10.1 (Jan. 1981) 31-62.
Seeks a "media politics to try to bring about more diverse, pluralistic programming, public access to the media, and an end to censorship, by government or business, of controversial programming" (54) so that democracy and not monopoly capitalism dominates life in the US.

2360. Kellner, Douglas. Television and the Crisis of Democracy. San Diego: Westview, 1990. 287.

Analyzes the relationships among TV, the state, and business, emphasizing its social, economic, and political power. TV both serves the interests of the powerful but also on occasion offers important social criticism.

2361. Kemper, Vicki. "Fairness in Media?" Soj 14 (May 1985) 6.
CBS is a major bulwark of the corporate state, contrary to Senator Helms' claims it is too "liberal."

2362. Klein, Paul, et al. Inside the TV Business. New York: Sterling, 1979. 223.
Each essay addresses the bottom-line realities of one aspect of the industry: programming, sports, news, etc. [A mild picture of commercial control compared to Brown's Television and Barnouw's The Sponsor].

2363. Korzenny, Felipe, and Kimberly Neuendorf. "Television Viewing and Self-Concept of the Elderly." JoC 30.1 (1980) 71-80.
As television viewing increases, negative self-concept and feelings of alienation increase.

2364. Kosinski, Jerzy. Being There. New York: Harcourt Brace Jovanovich, 1971. 142.
Novel about a man named Chance, whose whole reality was TV.

2365. Kuhns, William. Exploring Television: An Inquiry/ Discovery Program. Chicago, IL: Loyola UP, 1971. 240.
Designed to help people "understand, analyze, criticize, evaluate, and judge the experiences they have had in front of the TV set." Divided into three parts: "The Medium," "The Message" (programs, commercials, news, situation comedies, etc.), and "The Massage" (ideological impact on nation).

2366. Kupferberg, Seth. "Union Monitors Static in Labor's TV Image." CJR 19.1 (1980) 13-14.
On TV bias against working class and unions.

2367. Langer, John. "Television's 'Personality System.'" MCS 3 (1981) 351-365.
TV reproduces the "ideological field" and the "structure of domination" by linking personalities with ideas, especially that people are free agents rather than part of the relations of class, gender, race, institutions, and interest groups.

2368. Larsen, Otto N., ed. Violence and the Mass Media. New York: Harper & Row, 1968. 310.
All of the articles in this book are concerned with "how the nature and incidence of real violence might be affected by exposure to mass media violence."

2369. Lindsay, John. "TV's Faltering Vision." IREJ 12.4 (Fall 1989) 12-13.
Discusses TV's trend toward more entertainment and briefer

ELECTRONIC MEDIA   343

reporting in its news stories.

2370. Littell, Joseph F., ed. Coping with Television.
         Evanston: McDougal Littell, 1973. 213.
     Essays divided into "Impact," "Production," "Content,"
"Ratings," "Advertising," and public resistance. For example,
one essay exposes the censorship of writers hired to work on
the FBI series, another exposes how TV teaches a philosophy of
life--"conspicuous consumption, chemical, corporate life
style."

2371. Lodziak, Conrad. The Power of Television: A Critical
         Appraisal. New York: St. Martin's, 1986. 217.
     Chapters 2-4 examine and question TV's ideological role in
contemporary Western societies in maintaining "the prevailing
social order with all its inequalities and injustices."

2372. Logan, Ben, and Kate Moody, eds. Television Awareness
         Training: The Viewer's Guide for Family and Com-
         munity. New York: Action Research Center, 1979. 280.
     Self-help guides to a deepened awareness of TV and the
world, covering controversial issues and offering workshop
exercises.

2373. Luke, Timothy. Screens of Power: Ideology, Domination,
         and Resistance in Informational Society. Urbana: U
         of Illinois P, 1989. 264.
     An exploration into "how cultural meanings, political insti-
tutions, and social relations are affected by the power flow-
ing through the new systems of symbols used in data process-
ing, telecommunications, and the electronic mass media" (4).
Some chapter titles: "From Fundamentalism to Televangelism,"
"Discourses of Charisma and Televisual Electoral Politics,"
"History as an Ideopolitical Commodity: the 1984 D-Day
Spectacle."

2374. MacDonald, J. Fred. Television and the Red Menace: The
         Video Road to Vietnam. New York: Praeger, 1985. 277.
     Commercial TV "conditioned the American people for almost
two decades to tolerate an unwanted and unexplained [secret,
illegal, and undeclared] land war" in southeast Asia. Through
black-white, good-evil simplicities, misrepresentation, glori-
fying militaristic values, TV "led the American people toward
that battle" (Preface).

2375. Mander, Jerry. Four Arguments for the Elimination of
         Television. New York: Morrow, 1978. 371.
     "Corporations are inherently uninterested in considerations
aside from the commercial"; since they have control over television and since the experience of television produces passivity, the conditions for autocracy are established. "Every
day, a handful of people speak, the rest listen. . . . In many
ways, television makes the military coup and mass arrests of
my imagination unnecessary."

2376. Mankiewicz, Frank and Joel Swendlow. Remote Control: Television and the Manipulation of American Life. New York: Times, 1978. 308.
Chapters on violence, family hour, news, race, sex, children, consumers, and alienation. Underlying these issues is "the business of television. This national medium is, at bottom, not a way to purvey news and public affairs to the viewers, not a way to entertain millions of Americans with comedy, drama, and music, not a way to educate and inform--but the most profitable method ever devised by man to deliver huge audiences to advertisers, who then deliver their commercial messages" (11). Each chapter shows how this profit orientation relates to the issues--e.g., the defeat of the family hour concept. "In the end, it all comes down to ratings" (217).

2377. Marc, David. "Understanding Television." AM 254.2 (Aug. 1984) 33-38, 41-44.
TV must be understood as an agency of capitalism designed for increased consumption of commodities. Thus we see the "schlockumentary magazine (Real People, That's Incredible!)," news as a "vaudeville show of history," etc.

2378. McAnany, Emile. "Television, Mass Communication and Elite Controls. " Television in Society. Ed. Arthur Berger. New Brunswick, NJ: Transaction, 1987. 203-213.
Explains how "a few senders dominate the present television system" globally and urges the US to "share satellite and communication technology with other nations."

2379. Megrowitz, Joshua. No Sense of Place: The Impact of Electronic Media on Social Behavior. New York: Oxford UP, 1985. 416.
Radio, telephone, computer, TV, etc., have undermined old privileges and have removed old obstructions, e.g., of masculinity vs. femininity, old vs. young, freeing people from the bondages of physical place, class, gender, race, and the print media.

2380. Mehling, Harold. The Great Time-Killer. Cleveland: World, 1962. 352.
"We have been robbed--deliberately, there is no doubt of that--by the television networks, by sponsors and their Madison Avenue advertising agencies, and by the hired hands in the Hollywood laugh-laugh mills." Instead of serving the public good, "television today is a national soma-dispenser delivering a population into blissful vacuousness, teaching automatic response to the Pavlovian command to buy, buy, buy" (14). Final chapter suggests remedies.

2381. Miller, Mark. Boxed In: The Culture of TV. Northwestern UP, 1988. 349.
The sole purpose of TV is to sell the audience to advertisers, and it does so through the very irony some see as proof of a critical, independent perspective. The pervasive irony

on TV is a symptom of the medium's complete capitulation to its function as a purveyor of commodities. This extends to news, since the marketing/profit orientation permits only a "timid majoritarianism" in news programs, reporters straining to follow opinion polls, seeking like advertisers the blend of superficial novelty and underlying conventionality that will sell goods to the most people.

2382. Miller, Mark. "Prime Time: Deride and Conquer." Watching Television. Ed. Todd Gitlin. New York: Pantheon, 1987. 183-228.
TV's stratagems "for keeping its more 'sophisticated' audience hooked" (7).

2383. Minow, Newton, et al. Presidential Television. New York: Basic, 1973. 232.
TV has increased presidential power and subverted the Constitutional balance of power.

2384. Moore, Ray. "Brave New Television World." TQ 2.4 (1963) 24-29.
TV is controlled by the corporate state. Exceptions noted.

2385. Morgan, Michael. "Television and Democracy." Cultural Politics in Contemporary America. Ed. Ian Angus and Sut Jhally. New York: Routledge, 1989. 240-253.
Shows "the affinity of television watching and right-wing politics" (166) that challenges democratic principles and practices. TV is becoming "the true twentieth-century melting pot."

2386. Neff, Lyle. "Walking in the New World." Adbusters 1.3 (Spring 1990) 27-29.
Since TV is now the "first curriculum" for most people, while in the second curriculum of the high school dropout rates are approaching one-third, training in media literacy is urgently needed.

2387. Nelson, Joyce. "CanCon Conundrum." TM 19.5 (Dec. 1985) 18-19.
Reviews Herschel Hardin's Closed Circuits: The Sellout of Canadian Television (1985), an "exposé of regulatory betrayal, private broadcasters' hypocrisy, and the overall sellout of Canadian television's potential."

2388. Nelson, Joyce. "Caught in the Webs: Political Economy of TV." JC 20 (May 1979) 31-33.
Explores the ways in which US media corporations dominate the world marketplace and explains how the financial structure of American broadcasting encourages them to do so.

2389. Nelson, Joyce. "The Global Pillage." The Perfect Machine: TV in the Nuclear Age. Toronto: Between the Lines, 1987. 117-128. (Expansion of same title, TM 13.2 [May-June 1979] 32-6.).

"Perhaps even more powerfully than its military supremacy, this techno-imperialism over the airwaves and the imaginations of the world's population has caused, and still causes, extraordinary rifts and tensions" (128).

2390. Nelson, Joyce. "The New World of the Bomb." The Perfect Machine: TV in the Nuclear Age. Toronto: Between the Lines, 1978. 29-39.
On the relationships between the rise of TV and the development of the nuclear bomb and industry.

2391. Nelson, Joyce. The Perfect Machine: TV in the Nuclear Age. Toronto: Between the Lines, 1987. 187.
Argues that "television has been crucial to the dissemination of that 'anti-people climate' in which investment in death-technologies and practices has become the norm. The first part of the book traces the parallel historical development of television and the nuclear industry, both nuclear weapons and nuclear power. . . . As technological cataract, television has been at the forefront of disseminating an ideology of technological omnipotence, the sign of which is surely the bomb itself."

2392. Newcomb, Horace, ed. Television: The Critical View. 2nd ed. New York: Oxford UP, 1979. 557.
Twenty-nine essays confront numerous aspects of television--soaps, news, ideology, etc., practical and theoretical.

2393. Newcomb, Horace, ed. Television: The Critical View. 3rd ed. New York: Oxford UP, 1982. 549.
This edition contains 30 essays, fourteen of them not in the second edition. Some topics covered: TV soaps, class, The Fonz, Laverne & Shirley, Mary Hartman, MASH, Lou Grant, Star Trek, The Waltons, Super Bowl, network news, TV commercials, 60 Minutes.

2394. Newcomb, Horace, ed. Television: The Critical View. 4th ed. New York: Oxford UP, 1987. 647.
All four editions organized identically into three parts: I "Seeing Television" about "specific program types," II "Thinking About Television" in search of TV's "meaning in the culture," and III "Defining Television" comparing the medium to other media. [Twenty essays in the 2nd edition, 19 of them new; 30 essays in the 3rd edition, 14 new; 32 essays in the 4th edition, 20 new.]

2395. Newcomb, Horace. TV: The Most Popular Art. New York: Oxford UP, 1974. 272.
Analyzes situation comedies, westerns, mysteries, adventure shows, soap operas, and news shows as art forms that distort the relationship between TV world and the real world.

2396. Newcomb, Horace, and Robert Alley, eds. The Producer's Medium: Conversations with Creators of American TV. New York: Oxford UP, 1983. 262.

Interviews of well-known TV producers glimpse hearts and minds.

2397. Pearce, Alan. "The TV Networks: A Primer." Joc 26.4 (1976) 54-59.
Basic information about the three major networks--reasons for existence, economic structure, profitability and power.

2398. Pearl, David. "Violence and Television." Television in Society. Ed. Arthur Berger. New Brunswick, NJ: Transaction, 1987. 105-172.
The "number of violent acts per program has increased" since 1967, and heavy viewers are "more likely to view the world as a mean and scary place" and "exhibit more fear, mistrust, and apprehension than do light viewers."

2399. Phelan, John. Disenchantment: Meaning and Morality in the Media. New York: Hastings House, 1980. 191.
Discusses three major contexts of moral awareness in the mass media: functionalism, the alliance of censorship consumerism, and technological determinism. We "virtually live within a 'mediaworld' whose factitiously concocted morality is unconsciously shared, and abetted, by the great audience, which used to be known as the public."

2400. Pollan, Michael. "The Businessman on the Box." Channels 1.4 (1981) 47-50, 60.
The corporate-financed The Media Institute and various corporations are complaining about business portrayal on TV. But whatever image they have, they reap extraordinary profits.

2401. Pollan, Michael. "The Season of the Reagan Rich." Channels 2.4 (1982) 14-15, 86.
Prime time TV presents the self-made man of Reaganism.

2402. Postman, Neil. Amusing Ourselves to Death: Public Discourse in the Age of Show Business. New York: Viking, 1985. 184.
The medium of television, despite cries that "it's not that bad," is degrading public discourse in the US, creating a shallow culture void of historical sense and reflective thought.

2403. Primeau, Ronald. The Rhetoric of Television. New York: Longman, 1979. 275.
A guide to watching TV critically to enable viewers to "take control" of this "permanent house guest." This guide employs classical rhetoric to study communication theory, strategies, and the different types of TV shows.

2404. Quinlan, Sterling. The Hundred Million Dollar Lunch: The Broadcasting Industry's Own Watergate. Chicago: O'Hara, 1974. 241.
An account of the death of a TV station and a newspaper, resulting from the fight for Boston's Channel 5 TV license.

The larger issue is media concentration.

2405. Quinlan, Sterling. Inside ABC: American Broadcasting Company's Rise to Power. New York: Hastings, 1979. 290.
A generally admiring history of ABC by a former member of the "inner circle."

2406. Rapping, Elayne. Looking Glass World of Nonfiction TV. Boston: South End, 1987. 201.
Examines the national news, documentaries, game shows, talk shows, news magazines, docudramas, commercials, local news, etc. TV "was developed by the powerful specifically to pursue" their interests. "And if, in the process, it also became a medium for creating and projecting collective dreams, those dreams take a particular form, in large part because of the political and economic forces which allow them to exist. There is a constant tension, then, between . . . the impulses to address and change what is bad and wrong, and the overriding need for those in power to manage and limit the range, scope and texture of those impulses. . . . It is this process which I am interested in analyzing" (5).

2407. Ravage, John. Television: The Director's Viewpoint. Boulder, CO: Westview, 1978. 184.
Interviews of twelve leading directors. Ravage criticizes programming's domination by corporations for commercials. "Seldom are humans shown as they come to grips with real issues, or with themselves as fallible creatures, trying to understand the difficult questions life poses" (10).

2408. Reel, Frank A. The Networks: How They Stole the Show. New York: Scribner's, 1980. 208.
Opposes network monopoly power over programming. Sees some hope in the switch to UHF (70 channels).

2409. Reidy, John S. "The Players: Powers That Be." Channels 2.4 (1982) 64-68 field guide.
The leading TV companies.

2410. Rollin, Roger, ed. The Americanization of the Global Village. Bowling Green, OH: Bowling Green State UP, 1989. 154.
About the "McDonaldization" of the world in 3 parts: foreign reactions to US popular culture, foreign adaptations, and mass culture as common ground. Essays on popularity of US game shows with French TV audiences, influences on Soviet TV, etc.

2411. Rollings, Jerry. "Mass Communications and the American Worker." The Critical Communications Review: Vol. I: Labor, the Working Class, and the Media. Ed. Vincent Mosco and Janet Wasko. Norwood, NJ: Ablex, 1983. 131-152.
An account of the Machinists Union's Media Monitoring Project initiated in 1979 by the union's president, William

Winpisinger. The project discovered that TV was "one, if not the chief, culprit in the decline of American trade unions and workers' self-esteem" (135).

2412. Sahin, H., and J. P. Robinson. "Beyond the Realm of Necessity: Television and the Colonization of Leisure. MCS 3.1 (1981) 35-95.
Free time has become free time for TV which has been appropriated by corporations to sell commodities.

2413. Schrank, Jeffrey. "There are No Mass Media: All We Have Is Television." Snap, Crackle, and Popular Taste. New York: Dell, 1977. 17-40.
TV is an addiction that functions as "a powerful means of social control" in the service of corporations.

2414. Schrank, Jeffrey. TV Action Book. Evanston, IL: McDougal, Littell, 1973. 128.
Explains "some of the broadcaster's legal obligations" to the public and "provides procedures for effective action to improve programming." Chapters: "You Own the Channels," "Television Programming," "The Fairness Doctrine," "Ownership of Broadcast Stations," "Television as a Shaper of Values," etc.

2415. Shaheen, Jack. "American Television: Arabs in Dehumanizing Roles." The American Media and the Arabs. Ed. Michael Hudson and Ronald Wolfe. Washington, DC: Georgetown U, 1980. 39-44.
Denounces TV for its "belligerent anti-Arab bias."

2416. Shaheen, Jack. "Images of Arabs on the Screen." Extra! 1.6 (Jan.-Feb. 1988) 13.
TV portrays Arabs stereotypically and negatively.

2417. Shaheen, Jack. "On the Tube, All Arabs Are Evil." Guard 41.42 (Aug. 16, 1989) 10. ("The Arab Image in American Film and TV," Cineaste 17.1).
Denounces the stereotypes of Arabs as terrorists.

2418. Shaheen, Jack. The TV Arab. Bowling Green, OH: Bowling Green State U Popular P, 1984. 146.
Studies "over 100 different popular entertainment programs, cartoons and major documents . . . nearly 200 episodes" relating to Arabs. Most presented negative stereotypes, "billionaires, bombers and belly dancers" (4). The cause is partly the ignorance and prejudice of TV executives and writers, but it partly derives from US foreign policy.

2419. Shayon, Robert L. The Crowd-Catchers: Introducing Television. New York: Saturday Review, 1973. 175.
Questions the value of a medium that emphasizes entertainment and profit over all other values.

2420. Shear, Marie. "Double-standard Reporting: Nicaragua and the Networks." CJR 23 (Jan.-Feb. 1985), 17-18.

How the networks conformed to the Reagan administration's view of the Nicaraguan elections of November 4, 1984.

2421. Simonson, Solomon. Crisis in Television: A Study of the Private Judgement and the Public Interest. New York: Living, 1966. 230.
An appraisal of the good and bad in TV to enable viewers to select the good. [Another study that fails to confront the real relations of TV and the corporate state.]

2422. Skornia, Harry. "TV Debases Everything It Touches . . . and TV Touches Everything." ChJR 7.12 (1974) 16-27.
TV has produced a nation of zombie consumers.

2423. Smith, Desmond. "RCA and GE: Going for the Globe." WJR 8.3 (Mar. 1986) 37.
Possible results of the purchase of RCA by GE, both immense military contractors.

2424. Smith, Robert R. Beyond the Wasteland: The Criticism of Broadcasting. Falls Church, VA: Speech Communication Assoc., 1976. 105.
Smith decries the lack of a systematic "humane and civilizing" criticism of TV and presents several critical approaches to the medium--e.g. 1) the mythological, 2) public policy.

2425. Smith, Sally Bedell. In All His Glory: William S. Paley, the Legendary Tycoon and His Brilliant Circle. New York: Simon & Schuster, 1990. 784.
During the radio years Paley lobbied successfully against a federal plan to create educational radio stations, flooded CBS with escapist programs and commercials, cut back on classical music, and turned over control of programming to ad agencies and thus to sponsors. After WWII he approved a blacklist and loyalty oath at CBS during the McCarthy era, allowed the CIA to screen CBS news reports and eavesdrop on correspondents' telephone conversations, submitted to President Nixon's pressure to stop analysis of his speeches immediately following their broadcast, etc.

2426. Steenland, Sally. "Prime Time Kids: An Analysis of Children and Families on Television." Washington, DC: National Commission on Working Women, ca. 1985. 11.
TV presents an unreal world, playing down real-life bigotry, evading need for child care services, etc.

2427. Streeter, Thomas. "Policy Discourse and Broadcast Practice: The FCC, the US Broadcast Networks and the Discourse of the Marketplace." MCS 5 (July-Oct. 1983) 247-62.
Network broadcasting exemplifies the oligopolistic corporate state.

2428. Taylor, Arthur R. "Dangers in our Midst." TQ 11.3 (1974) 54-59.

ELECTRONIC MEDIA 351

A summary of the "unprecedented erosion" of the independence of TV by agencies of the state.

2429. Television and Social Behavior: 5 vols. Washington, DC: US GPO, 1972.
"A Technical Report of the Surgeon General's Advisory Committee on Television and Social Behavior." V. 1, Media Content and Control; V. 2, Television and Social Learning; V. 3, Television and Adolescent Aggressiveness; V. 4, Television in Day-to-Day Life; V. 5, Television's Effects.

2430. Thayer, Lee. Ethics, Morality, and the Media. New York: Hastings House, 1980. 302.
Wide in scope--public opinion polling, news, entertainment, advertising, public relations, etc.

2431. Torre, Marie. "Labor Looks at Television--and Vice Versa." TQ 21 (1984) 25-31.
On AFL-CIO's efforts to gain more coverage of working class.

2432. Tuchman, Gaye, ed. The TV Establishment: Programming for Power and Profit. Englewood Cliffs, NJ: Prentice, 1974. 186.
Describes the many ways the networks manipulate programming for corporate values and profits: programming for advertising, talk shows, children's shows, news, etc.

2433. Turow, Joseph. Media Industries: The Production of News and Entertainment. New York: Longman, 1984. 213.
Investigates continuity and change and the extent to which the public can effect change in the mass media. "The structure of a mass media industry ultimately reflects the overall power relations of the society in which it emerges and develops. . . . Those vested interests will not allow the basic industrial relationships and perspectives that shape the shared messages of the society to deviate fundamentally from mainstream industrial relationships and perspectives" (38).

2434. United States Commission on Civil Rights. Window Dressing on the Set. Washington, DC: GPO, 1977. 181. (An Update, 1979).
Data on how TV programming fails to portray women and minorities adequately and accurately. Also data on trends from 1950s to 1970s.

2435. Van Horn, Carl, Donald Baumer, and William Gormley. Politics and Public Policy. Washington, DC: Congressional Q, 1989. 346.
How diverse institutions affect policy-making, including business, education, and TV's power to focus public attention on social issues.

2436. Varis, Tapio. "Global Traffic in Television." JoC 24.1 (1974) 102-109.

The US and UK dominate sale of TV programs to Europe and Third World.

2437. Varis, Tapio. "The International Flow of Television Programs." JoC 34.1 (1984) 143-152.
A study of 69 countries reveals the continued dominance of a few exporting nations, with the US leading, but with a trend toward greater regional exchanges. If money is the primary indicator, the gap between access and influence, despite new technology, will likely increase.

2438. Velez, Hector. "Television & Culture: The Case of Puerto Rico." Cornell U, 1983. 236. DAI 44.9 (Mar. 1984) 2615-A.
A study of the cultural colonization of Puerto Rico by the US: there is "little in Puerto Rican television which could be called autochthonous or reflective" of island culture. The author calls for "cultural balance" and "preserving a Puerto Rican identity."

2439. Wander, Philip. "Antidote to Textbooks." JoC 36.2 (Spring 1986) 152-55.
Review of J. F. MacDonald's Television and the Red Menace. "The strength of MacDonald's book lies in its effort to implicate TV news, entertainment, children's programming . . . in an ideological formation favorable to mindless interventionism."

2440. Watson, Mary A. "Commercial Television and the New Frontier: Resistance and Appeasement." U of Michigan, 1983. 185. DAI 44.2 (1983) 315-A.
President Kennedy's appointment of Newton Minnow as chairman of the FCC and his efforts to regulate the "vast wasteland" angered the broadcasting industry, which reacted "with a mixture of bitter resistance and protective appeasement." But Minnow became a hero to the public. Includes a study of "the editorial and advertising copy of the trade press."

2441. Weinberg, Meyer. TV in America: The Morality of Hard Cash. New York: Ballantine, 1962. 311.
On greed and crimes by TV corporations (e.g. quiz scandals) and the failure of self-regulation.

2442. Weisman, John, and Jeff Greenfield. "Public Interest & Private Greed." CJR 29.1 (May-June 1990) 46-48.
In separate articles, Weisman decries the equation of greed with good under the deregulatory policies of the Reagan administration and the FCC's chairman, Mark Fowler. Greenfield urges support of diversity against the "steady growth of concentrated power," especially in the cable industry.

2443. Wells, Alan. Picture-Tube Imperialism? The Impact of U.S. Television on Latin America. Maryknoll, NY: Orbis, 1972. 197.
Describes the many destructive features of US consumerist

ELECTRONIC MEDIA 353

capitalism projected into Latin America by TV.

2444. White, Mimi. "Ideological Analysis and Television." Channels of Discourse: Television and Contemporary Criticism. Ed. Robert C. Allen. Chapel Hill: U of North Carolina P, 1987. 134-171.
Analyzes the relation between viewers and the "enormous institution that makes the pleasure we derive from watching television the basis for our transformation into commodities" (14).

2445. White, Ned. Inside Television: A Guide to Critical Viewing. Palo Alto, CA: Science and Behavior Books, 1980. 161.
A textbook for a course on viewing TV critically.

2446. Williams, Huntington. Beyond Control: ABC and the Fate of the Networks. New York: Atheneum, 1989. 290.
An account of the decline and sale of ABC to Capital Cities conglomerate, by a former speechwriter for ABC founder Leonard Goldenson. He praises the early years of ABC for encouraging innovation and originality.

2447. Williams, Raymond. Television: Technology and Cultural Form. New York: Schocken, 1975. 160.
Contains some comparisons between British and US practice regarding the relationships between TV as a technology and TV as a cultural form. Chapters on the technology, the institutions of the technology, the forms of TV, programming, effects, and alternative technology and uses.

2448. Withey, Stephen, and Ronald Abeles, eds. Television and Social Behavior: Beyond Violence and Children: A Report of the Committee on Television and Social Behavior Social Science Research Council. Hillsdale, NJ: Erlbaum, 1980. 356.
There is an essay on violence but most of the essays are on topics other than violence and children--e.g., racism in TV.

II. C. 1. c. (2). TELEVISION ENTERTAINMENT (2449-2550)

2449. Adler, Richard, ed. "All in the Family": A Critical Appraisal. New York: Praeger, 1979. 322.
The program portrayed the family as a political arena that grappled with what was happening during the 1960s, and the "show's ultimate message was positive." "In the final analysis, the series represented an affirmation of the power of the family to endure" (xxxix).

2450. Allen, Robert C. Speaking of Soap Operas. Chapel Hill: U of North Carolina P, 1985. 245.
Examines the soap opera "as narrative form, cultural product, advertising vehicle, and source of aesthetic pleasure" for millions of viewers (4), by studying how various

perspectives--broadcasting, aesthetics, and social science--
have interpreted soaps. Chap. 3, "The Soap Opera as Commodity
and Commodifier," argues that TV "transforms viewers into
units of economic exchange," the program only the bait to
attract and retain the viewer for the commercial.

2451. Anderson, Kent, ed. Television Fraud: The History and
Implications of the Quiz Show Scandals. Westport,
CT: Greenwood, 1978. 226.
Fixed quiz shows increased ratings and therefore profits.

2452. Ang, Ien. Watching "Dallas": Soap Opera and the Melo-
dramatic Imagination. Trans. Della Couling. New
York: Methuen, 1986. 148. (Rev. Het Geval Dallas,
1982).
A study of how the TV program Dallas is "received and consumed." The commercial culture industry "sells its products
by propagating the idea that everyone has the right to his or
her own taste and has the freedom to enjoy pleasure in his or
her own way" in contrast to the scholarly study of mass
culture and Dallas, which ignores or overlooks pleasure in
their study of ideology.

2453. Aufderheide, Pat. "Music Videos: The Look of the
Sound." Watching Television. Ed. Todd Gitlin. New
York: Pantheon, 1987. 111-135.
The "glitz and simulated dreaminess of music video . . .
mirror the commodity-mindedness and shifting identities of
this shopping-mall age" (7).

2454. Bazalgette, Cary. "Regan and Carter, Kojak and
Crocker, Batman and Robin?" SE 20 (1976) 54-65.
Compares and contrasts the ideology and techniques found in
the US Kojak series with the British The Sweeney series--e.g.
the class conflict in The Sweeney.

2455. Bedell, Sally. Up the Tube: Prime Time TV and the
Silverman Years. New York: Viking, 1981. 313.
Greed dominated the networks during the 1970s, commercials
increased and program quality declined.

2456. Bedway, Barbara. "The Russians Are Coming." NT 4.3
(1986) 16-18.
A look at the controversial TV program Amerika, which
concerns America after a Soviet takeover.

2457. Berger, Arthur. "The Six Million Dollar Man."
Television as an Instrument of Terror. New
Brunswick, NJ: Transaction, 1980. 113-116.
Austin's mythic, heroic, masculine qualities (male ego
ideal) and his "good Frankenstein" qualities (reconciling life
and technology, Austin part human, part machine) have made him
a culture hero.

2458. Berk, Lynn M. "The Great Middle American Dream

Machine." JoC 27.3 (1977) 27-31.
Network programming cultivates the myth of middle-class America in which working class means the ignorance and bigotry of Archie Bunker. No bias is so thoroughly supported by networks and so ignored by critics and viewers as the bias of class.

2459. Blair, Karin. Meaning in "Star Trek". Chambersburg, PA: Anima, 1977. 159.
Spock is the key to the program, for he represents the mission of the Enterprise "to explore new worlds, to contact new life forms, to reach out to the alien" both within ourselves and in the universe. "Difference is not condemned but embraced as IDIC: infinite diversity in infinite combinations" (9).

2460. Boddy, William. "Operation Frontal Lobes Versus the Living Room Toy: The Battle Over Programme Control in Early Television." MCS 9 (1987) 347-68.
"Precisely when network hegemony was achieved . . . the precipitous decline of 'Golden Age' programming began," as in "the death of live anthology drama."

2461. Brown, Mary Ellen, ed. Television and Women's Culture: The Politics of the Popular. Newbury Park, CA: Sage, 1990. 256.
Investigates how different genres, such as game shows, soap operas, and police fiction, offer women opportunities for negotiation of their own meaning and aesthetic appreciation.

2462. Budd, Mike, Steve Craig, and Clay Steinman. "'Fantasy Island': Marketplace of Desire." JoC 33.1 (Winter 1983) 67-77.
Fantasy Island reinforces dominant cultural values, and the program is used by those who control the mass media to "manipulate this process in a general way for their own purposes." Entertainment exists on commercial television "only to support an audience for advertising."

2463. Burnett, Betty. "Kidvid is Violent and Vapid." SLJR 10.61 (Apr. 1984) 5.
Children's TV creates Cold Warriors and "zombie consumers."

2464. Butler, Jeremy G. "The Politics of Monogamy and Romance: Ideology and the Soap Opera." Politics in Familiar Contexts: Projecting Politics Through Popular Media. Eds. Robert L. Savage and Dan Nimmo. Norwood, NJ: Ablex, 1990. 139-158.
Soap series reflect traditional middle-class values but they also present some dissidence toward the dominant ideology.

2465. Butsch, Richard. "The Simpsons: A Breath of Fresh Air Mixed With Old Pollutants." ITT 14.30 (July 18-31, 1990) 19.
The picture of the father as buffoon seems yet another anti-working-class theme. In contrast is Roseanne, another

working-class sitcom, which treats both parents favorably.

2466. Buxton, David. "Rock Music, the Star-System and the Rise of Consumerism." Popular Culture and Media Events. Ed. Vincent Mosco and Janet Wasko. (CCRev 3). Norwood, NJ: Ablex, 1985. 181-206.
The linkage of star, rock music, and advanced technology facilitated the development of rock stars as consumer role models for consumption of records, clothes, etc. The author urges creation of alternative cultural forms outside the capitalist commodity circuit.

2467. Cantor, Muriel. Prime Time Television: Content & Control. Beverly Hills: Sage, 1980. 143.
"Both the form and actual content of prime-time programs depend on social and political controls which exist outside the creative process. At present, the networks have the greatest power over the creators," but social action groups, court decisions, and new technologies have influenced or can influence network power (21).

2468. Cargas, Harry James. "America is Saturated by Violence." SLJR 19.122 (Dec. 1989-Jan. 1990) 16-17.
The violence deeply embedded in US history and character is reinforced by TV programming (rapist heroes) and advertising.

2469. Carlson, James. Prime Time Law Enforcement: Crime Show Viewing and Attitudes Toward the Criminal Justice System. New York: Praeger, 1985. 219.
Attempts to demonstrate that crime and violence on TV help maintain the social and political order and legitimate the dominant power structure of society. TV conveys a "crime control" (vs. due process) point of view, suggesting that TV may be helping erode support for civil liberties.

2470. "Censorship Dateline: Video, Hollywood." NIF 37.5 (Sept. 1988) 155.
MTV refused to air a music video by Neil Young that lampoons rock performers who promote soft drinks and beer.

2471. Chandler, Joan. Television and National Sport: The United States and Britain. Urbana: U of Illinois P, 1988. 240.
A response to Benjamin Rader's attack on the commercial degeneration of sports. This study of baseball, football, cricket, soccer, and tennis as televised in the US and Britain argues that TV "has revealed to sports fans on both sides of the Atlantic the business skeleton beneath the mythic clothing, and in so doing shattered the illusions on which professional promoters have long based their profits" (xiii). A related argument is that the meaning of the sports is shaped in advance in each society by media.

2472. Clawson, Suzanne. "The Industry Behind the Wasteland: Television and Hollywood Scriptwriters." Cornell U,

1986. 388. DAI 47 (1986) 337-A.
"F.C.C. policies promote neither diversity, freedom of expression, nor democracy." Studies of scriptwriters "show a picture of corporate control down to the most individual level, where writers censor themselves because they have learned what the networks will buy."

2473. Cohen, Dan. "Workers Slandered--When They Appear At All." Guard 40.44 (Aug. 31, 1988) 10.
With few exceptions, workers are either completely absent from the world of fictional TV or are cast negatively or in an unrealistic manner.

2474. Cowan, Geoffrey. See No Evil: The Backstage Battle over Sex and Violence on Television. New York: Simon & Schuster, 1979. 323.
Money controls television, whose programming is "a highly competitive game, played in large measure by essentially insecure executives who are obliged to be more concerned about ratings and sales than about television's true potential." Television "is too powerful a tool to be left to a process so crass and mindlessly competitive. But that is the commercial television system, and it isn't likely to change" (310).

2475. Deeb, Gary. "ABC's Censors Remove 'Barney Miller' References to Dow, DuPont." AG (Dec. 22, 1978) 10B.
ABC's corporate lawyers deleted two references to Dow Chemical Co. and the DuPont company.

2476. Edmundson, Mark. "TV's Celebration of Itself." Channels 5.3 (1985) 67-8.
Escapism of Entertainment Tonight.

2477. Engelhardt, Tom. "Children's Television: The Shortcake Strategy." Watching Television. Ed. Todd Gitlin. New York: Pantheon, 1987. 68-110.
Children's programs are "protracted commercials for violent and saccharine toys" (7).

2478. Gerbner, George, et al. "Aging with Television: Images on Television Drama and Conceptions of Social Reality." JoC 30.1 (1980) 37-47.
Underrepresented groups include the old and the young. Children are devalued, women age faster than men, and the old people are vanishing.

2479. Gibson, Bill. "Tour of Duty: Vietnam War Returns to TV." Extra! 1.5 (Dec. 1987) 13.
The CBS series mythicizes and abstracts the Vietnam War, distancing it from political and historical realities and suppressing all questions about the rightness of the intervention.

2480. Gitlin, Todd. Inside Prime Time. New York: Pantheon, 1983. 369.

There is little diversity of substance, and there will be less and less. "The workings of the market give Americans every incentive to remain conventionally entertainment-happy. Conglomeration proceeds apace. . . . Technology opens doors, and oligopoly marches in just behind, slamming them" (332). "Democracy requires an active, engaged citizenry committed to determining and seeking the public good. As it is, the bulk of commercial television (along with most of the other media) reminds us to think of ourselves as consumers first and foremost" (334).

2481. Gitlin, Todd. "Prime Time Ideology: The Hegemonic Process in Television Entertainment." Television, The Critical View. 4th ed. Ed. Horace Newcomb. New York: Oxford UP, 1987. 507-532. (SP 26.3 [Feb. 1979]).
Defines hegemony to show how the structures of TV by limiting TV's capacity to criticize maintain the political status quo.

2482. Gitlin, Todd. "Prime-Time Whitewash." AF 9.2 (1983) 36-38.
The major television networks are reluctant to air programs featuring minorities, especially blacks and Jews.

2483. Goldman, Robert. "Hegemony and Managed Critique in Prime-time Television: A Critical Reading of 'Mork & Mindy.'" TSoc 11.3 (May 1982) 363-388.
The popular TV series Mork and Mindy "accounts for social contradictions and manages social critique within certain ideological and institutional limits" (364).

2484. Goldstein, Jeffrey H., and Brenda J. Bredemeier. "Socialization: Some Basic issues." JoC 27.3 (1977) 154-59.
Increased TV coverage of certain sports has led to a professionalization of amateur athletics which emphasizes winning over the process of participation.

2485. Gray, Herman. "Television and the New Black Man: Black Male Images in Prime-Time Situation Comedy." MCS 8.2 (1986) 223-42.
"Television's idealization of racial harmony, affluence and individual mobility" deflects attention "from the persistence of racism, inequality and differential power."

2486. Grossberg, Lawrence. "MTV: Swinging on the (Postmodern) Star." Cultural Politics in Contemporary America. Ed. Ian Angus and Sut Jhally. New York: Routledge, 1989. 254-268.
On how music TV has changed the ways rock & roll and TV works in our culture as economics and as communication.

2487. Gunther, Marc and Bill Carter. Monday Night Mayhem: The Inside Story of Monday Night Football. Ramparte Path, MI: Beech Tree, 1989. 384.

From the beginning, "Monday Night Football" was prime-time television. It displayed the stardom, the backbiting, and the politics of big-money commercialism.

2488. Gutierrez, Felix. "Chico & the Racist." RSCJ 13-14 (Fall and Winter 1974-75) 1-3.
"Chico and the Man" is network TV's "latest assault on the Chicanos."

2489. Heeger, Susan. "Why Lou Grant got the Ax." ITT 6.26 (May 26-June 1, 1982) 2.
Ed Asner's high visibility liberal politics (opposition to military aid to El Salvador, etc.) caused the show to be cancelled.

2490. Heilbronn, Lisa. "Domesticating Social Change: The Situation Comedy as Social History." U of California, Berkeley, 1986. 333. DAI 47 (1987) 2353-A.
Television sitcoms do not promote social change, but they express the audience's changing concerns about change, and "for which it most requires comic relief."

2491. Hesse, Petra, and Ted Stimpson. "The World is a Dangerous Place: Images of the Enemy on Children's Television." PR 5 (Summer 1989) 22-25.
Cites common characteristics of the "enemy" in cartoons (the enemy is different looking, the enemy is evil for evil's sake) and explains how GI Joe's depiction of the struggle against Cobra Commander in black/white terms reinforces the ideology of US patriotism.

2492. Himmelstein, Hal. "TV Religion & the TV Game Show." Television Myth and the American Mind. New York: Praeger, 1984. 253-77.
The religious show and the game show "are similar in many ways, not the least important of which is their promise of instant salvation" by money, donated or won.

2493. Himmelstein, Hal. "The TV Talk Show: Commodification and the Individual." Television Myth and the American Mind. New York: Praeger, 1984. 279-304.
The talk show uses "celebrities from the entertainment, sport, literary, political, and lifestyle world of image marketing" and ordinary people who "ascend to ephemeral celebrity status, to be used up and quickly discarded, in television's continual pecuniary search for the glamorous, the exotic, and the bizarre" (283).

2494. Hofeldt, Roger. "Cultural Bias in 'M*A*S*H.'" Television in Society. Ed. Arthur Berger. New Brunswick, NJ: Transaction, 1987. 71-77.
The characters in the program represent institutions of society in microcosm in a structure that affirms traditional values and institutions in a "bulwark against change and social criticism."

2495. Hynes, James. "The Big Shill?" ITT 12.36 (Sept. 21-27, 1988) 24 and 22.
Letterman has become "a licensed jester" for corporate power.

2496. Intintoli, Michael. Taking Soaps Seriously: The World of "Guiding Light." New York: Praeger, 1984. 248.
Explains how decisions are made, how the story line and writing are created, how the musical and visual conventions create a stylized version of reality, and how the commercials (romanticized domesticity) support the domestic romance of the soap world, all within the context of corporate need for profit.

2497. Jackson, Harold. "From 'Amos 'N' Andy' to 'I Spy': Chronology of Blacks in Prime Time Network Television Programming, 1950-1964." U of Michigan, 1982. 138. DAI 43.2 (Aug. 1982) 297-A.
"Blacks did have a role and did participate on television during the period of this study."

2498. Johnson, Paul. "NBC's 'Road to Seoul' Full of Credibility Potholes." AG (June 8, 1988) 4B.
Having spent between three and five hundred million dollars on rights to televise the Olympic Games, NBC is now protecting its investment through features showing Seoul as a vacation wonderland, omitting references to its repressive government.

2499. Kaplan, E. Ann. "Feminist Criticism and Television." Channels of Discourse: Television and Contemporary Criticism. Ed. Robert C. Allen. Chapel Hill: U of North Carolina P, 1987. 211-253.
Focuses on music videos and their arrangement as a continuous flow of programming to demonstrate the particular gender addressed in the flow.

2500. Kaplan, E. Ann. "A Post-Modern Play of the Signifier? Advertising, Pastiche and Schizophrenia in Music Television." Television in Transition. Ed. Phillip Drummond and Richard Paterson. London: British Film Inst., 1985. 146-63.
Examines "the tension between MTV's [commercial] context of production and its avant-garde techniques." In MTV capitalism exploits adolescent fears and desires for profit, but youthful energy and creativity "also have an effect on hegemonic culture" (161).

2501. Kaplan, E. Ann. Rocking Around the Clock: Music Television, Postmodernism and Consumer Culture. New York: Methuen, 1987. 196.
Focuses on the formative years of cable channel MTV between 1982 and 1985 with the central idea that "MTV reproduces a kind of decenteredness, often called 'postmodernist,' that increasingly reflects young people's condition in the advanced stage of highly developed, technological capitalism evident in

ELECTRONIC MEDIA

America" and that keeps them "endlessly consuming."

2502. Karman, Peter. "Amerika: Checking the Red (White and Blue) Menace." ITT 11.2 (1986) 24.
Compares the "incorporeal Commies" of ABC's Amerika with real communists, who "finally bored America to death."

2503. Klatell, David, and Norman Marcus. Sports for Sale: Television, Money, and the Fans. New York: Oxford UP, 1988. 253.
"We have evolved a system which virtually demands a highly structured, centrally controlled edifice of commerce to function properly. Television, once an observer of that edifice, has become an indispensable bulwark of the structure itself" (22). Some chapters: "TV Cameras Don't Blink, Only Advertisers Do," "Money Talks," "Who Shot the Messenger." The latter chapter describes the woefully uncritical state of TV sports journalism.

2504. Lemon, Judith. "Dominant or Dominated? Women on Prime-Time Television." Hearth and Home: Images of Women in the Mass Media. Ed. Gaye Tuchman, et al. New York: Oxford UP, 1978. 51-68.
In crime dramas (action-adventure shows) men dominate women the majority of times, but less so in situation comedies, where women are shown mainly in the family, men at work.

2505. Levinson, Richard, and William Link. Stay Tuned: An Inside Look at the Making of Prime Time Television. New York: St. Martin's, 1981. 253.
Behind-the-scenes operations of personalities, business, and conflict. The authors, Emmy-winning writers/producers, attempted to create quality TV about human relations in current social conditions (My Sweet Charlie, The Gun).

2506. Lewis, Andrea. "NBC Presents the 1988 Corporate Games." Guard 41.4 (Oct. 19, 1988) 6.
NBC's coverage of the 24th Olympic Games over-emphasized commercialism and nationalism. Michael Weisman, the producer of NBC Sports, said: "I guess we learned that jingoism sells."

2507. Lopate, Carol. "Daytime Television: You'll Never Want to Leave Home." FemS 3.3/4 (Spring-Summer 1976) 70-82.
Daytime television promotes the illusion that the "family can be everything" instead of realization of the individual self beyond the family.

2508. MacDonald, J. Fred. "The Cold War as TV Entertainment." Television and the Red Menace. New York: Praeger, 1985. 101-146.
TV, the most important information source regarding the Cold War and the SU, provided mainly stereotypes, fear, and automatic, unquestioning belief. "The Anti-Communist Spy as TV Entertainer" treats US spies as heroes in 2 parts: 1) govern-

ment and military spies ("I Led Three Lives," "The Man Called X") and 2) patriotic civilian spies ("Biff Baker, USA"), etc.

2509. Marc, David. Comic Visions: Television Comedy and American Culture. Boston, MA: Unwin Hyman, 1989. 239.
Discusses how old stereotypes have been exploited in TV situation comedies in the late twentieth century and new ones created: WASPs, blacks, women, etc. Between the comedy of social consciousness of a Lenny Bruce and the comedy of consensus of Bob Hope is the "oceanic middle" of the sitcom. Its purpose in capitalist USA is not merely to sell products but to sell an existing order, "a mythopoeic loss leader in the supermarket of national consciousness" (161).

2510. Mayerle, Judine. "The Development of the Television Variety Show as a Major Program Genre at the National Broadcasting Company: 1946-1956." Northwestern U, 1983. 288. DAI 44.11 (May 1984) 3195-A.
Studies "Your Show of Shows," "Colgate Comedy Hour," and other programs, and concludes that although TV can be brilliantly innovative, "the sponsor ratings/mass audience fix the guidelines within which commercial television must exist."

2511. Mellencamp, Patricia. "Situation Comedy, Feminism, & Freud: Discourses of Gracie & Lucy." Studies in Entertainment. Ed. Tania Modleski. Bloomington: Indiana UP, 1986. 80-98.
Analyzes two TV situation comedies, The George Burns & Gracie Allen Show and I Love Lucy to explain how they function as ideological apparatuses.

2512. Morse, Margaret. "Sport on Television: Replay and Display." Regarding Television: Critical Approaches --An Anthology. Ed. E. Ann Kaplan. Frederick, MD: U Publications of America, 1983. 44-66.
Effect of TV on sports, especially regarding scopophilia, the erotic pleasure of gazing.

2513. Olivier, Gwendolyn. "A Critical Examination of the Mythological and Symbolic Elements of Two Modern Science Fiction Series: Star Trek and Doctor Who." LSU, 1987. 272. DAI 48 (1987) 1347-A.
Following the theories of Carl Jung and Joseph Campbell, the author identifies the mythological function the two programs fulfill.

2514. Ornelas, Kriemhild. "The Depiction of Sexuality in Daytime Television Melodrama." Bowling Green State U, 1987. 255. DAI 48 (1987) 1347-A.
Soap operas follow traditional values regarding sexual intercourse (best in marriage), abortion (discouraged), and other activities.

2515. Parente, Donald E. "The Interdependence of Sports and

Television." JoC 27.3 (1977) 128-132.
As sports have become an integral part of the advertising and entertainment industries, and as the federal government has made decisions to favor the three major networks and sports franchises, the playing of sports has changed to make them a more marketable commodity.

2516. Patton, Phil. Razzle-Dazzle: The Curious Marriage of Television and Professional Football. Garden City, NY: Dial/Doubleday, 1984. 230.
Officials of the system uphold the "fiction that it was selling a game," but it actually sells "the audience that the game drew. It was an advertising device" that "offered a collective ritual" that made fabulous fortunes for a few.

2517. Powers, Ron. The Beast, the Eunuch, and Glass-Eyed Child: Television in the '80s. New York: Harcourt Brace Jovanovich, 1990. 382.
Explorations into the meaning of TV programs--MTV, "Entertainment Tonight," "The Morton Downey Jr. Show," etc.--and what they reveal about the US. For example, MTV is "the LSD of the Reagan Revolution," an administration based on "greed and assertion," a program "of feckless, pointless montage."

2518. Powers, Ron. Supertube: The Rise of Television Sports. New York: Coward-McCann, 1984. 288.
On the transformation of TV and sports by each other, using anecdote and observation to reveal the struggles over ratings, money, etc.

2519. Powers, Thomas. "It's as Simple as ABC, Amerika: The TV Russians Are Coming." Deadline 1.5 (1986) 3, 4, 6.
ABC's mini-series Amerika's suggestion that we are in imminent danger of Soviet invasion is absurd.

2520. Rader, Benjamin. In Its Own Image: How Television Has Transformed Sports. New York: Free; London: Collier, 1984. 228.
Television has changed the ethos of sports. "To seize and hold the attention of viewers and thus maximize revenues, the authenticity of the sporting experience has been contaminated with a plethora of external intrusions" which has "diminished the capacity of sports to furnish heroes, to bind communities, and to enact the rituals that contain, and exalt, society's traditional values" (5-6). [See Chandler].

2521. Real, Michael. "Marcus Welby and the Medical Genre." Mass-Mediated Culture. Englewood Cliffs, NJ: Prentice-Hall, 1977. 118-139.
US TV reflects "the institutional structure of the political-economic system of private property, capital, enterprise, and profit" and health care "illustrates the underlying structural symmetry between media image and social reality." "Welby" reflects a society in which medical care is excellent for those who can afford it, and which is first in the world

in per capita military expenditures but only fifth in health care, thirteenth in infant mortality rate and seventeenth in ratio of physicians to total population.

2522. Real, Michael. "The Super Bowl: Mythic Spectacle." Mass-Mediated Culture. Englewood Cliffs, NJ: Prentice-Hall, 1977. 90-117.
Explains why the Super Bowl is "the most lucrative annual spectacle in American mass culture" by focusing on the telecast 1974 Super Bowl VIII. "The Super Bowl recapitulates in miniature and with striking clarity certain dominant strains in the society": nationalism, militarism, violence, racism, aggression, competition, technology, and money.

2523. Real, Michael. "Understanding Oscar: The Academy Awards Telecast as International Media Event." Popular Culture and Media Events. Ed. Vincent Mosco and Janet Wasko. (CCRev 3). Norwood, NJ: Ablex, 1985. 153-180.
The Academy Awards promote US nationalism, the Hollywood star system, sexism, and mass spectacle, while their overwhelming concern is commercial.

2524. Reeves, Jimmie. "Star Discourse & Television: A Critical Approach." U of Texas, Austin, 1984. 251. DAI 45 (1985) 1904-A.
Studies stardom as a complex social phenomenon that represents "a strategic socio-ideological worldview," within television's role as "our culture's central processor of social reality."

2525. Robinson, Lillian. "What's My Line? Telefiction and the Working Woman." Sex, Class, and Culture. Bloomington: Indiana UP, 1978. 310-42.
TV's message about working women is that "their sex is its most important component."

2526. Rosen, Ruth. "Soap Operas: Search for Yesterday." Watching Television. Ed. Todd Gitlin. New York: Pantheon, 1987. 42-67.
"Takes us beneath the coincidences and melodrama of the soap opera to its deep, stabilizing verities--the underlying ethic of Ronald Reagan's romantic small-town America" (7).

2527. Rothenbuhler, Eric. "Media Events, Civil Religion, & Social Solidarity: The Living Room Celebration of the Olympic Games." U of Southern California, 1985. DAI 46 (1986) 2476-A.
Viewers of the 1984 Games possess a class-oriented set of values and symbols that constitutes "a civil religious dimension to thinking about the games."

2528. Salamon, Jeff. "This Show Will Self-Destruct in a Few Weeks--Good Luck, Jim." ITT 13.5 (Dec. 7-13, 1988) 19.

A comparison of the old and new television series Mission: Impossible (ABC). The old program "bristled" with Cold War "paranoia"; the revival has little Sovietphobia, which the author attributes to Reagan's cooled rhetoric regarding the "Communist Menace."

2529. Schudson, Michael. "The Politics of 'Lou Grant.'" Television in Society. Ed. Arthur Berger. New Brunswick, NJ: Transaction, 1987. 79-82.
The program takes a "liberal, reforming stand" on many issues, and it tries to relate problems individuals have with institutions--personal problems in relation to social structures--but the structures are left unresolved, and individuals are shown to have little power over institutions and issues.

2530. Schwichtenberg, Cathy. "The Love Boat: The Packaging and Selling of Love, Heterosexual Romance, and Family." MCS 6 (1984) 301-311.
Personal relations and love are packaged for the commodity structure of capitalism. The Love Boat represents "commercial television par excellence" (310).

2531. Seiter, Ellen. "The Hegemony of Leisure: Aaron Spelling Presents Hotel." Television in Transition. Ed. Phillip Drummond and Richard Paterson. London: BFI, 1986. 135-145.
Reviews the work of Aaron Spelling Productions (Charlie's Angels, Dynasty, etc.) through Gramsci's theory of hegemony to formulate categories of coercion by force (Mod Squad, Starsky and Hutch, etc.) and coercion by consent (The Love Boat, Fantasy Island, etc.).

2532. Seiter, Ellen. "Love Boat and Fantasy Island: Television Utopias." JC 32 (1987) 9-11.
While Love Boat and Fantasy Island may seem to offer hedonism and escape, they in fact reinforce traditional values and tell the audience that true happiness lies in marriage, conventionality, and resignation to one's fate in life.

2533. Shaw, David. "Danger! Please Don't Mix Facts With Fiction." TVG (Apr. 20, 1985) 5-7.
Too many TV docudramas "misinform and mislead."

2534. Sklar, Robert. Prime Time America: Life On and Behind the Television Screen. New York: Oxford UP, 1980. 200.
The designed conventionality of sitcoms for ratings and profits.

2535. Sorkin, Michael. "Simulations: Faking It." Watching Television. Ed. Todd Gitlin. New York: Pantheon, 1987. 162-182.
A new genre ranges from "wrestling to Mr. T, lip-synching contests to The People's Court, all obscuring the boundaries

between the real and the copy, the authentic and the put-on" (7).

2536. Stein, Ben. "Fantasy and Culture on Television." Television in Society. Ed. Arthur Berger. New Brunswick, NJ: Transaction, 1987. 215-227.

Programming is optimistic about life, none "challenges the assumption that the unexamined life is the only life worth living"; all are "clean and neat"; and all problems are "cured before the show is over." This social and psychic fantasy land reflects the markup of the Hollywood TV producers and writers who create the programs.

2537. Sugar, Bert. "The Thrill of Victory": The Inside Story of ABC Sports. New York: Hawthorn, 1978. 342.

Sympathetic history of ABC's sports division, which contributed significantly to ABC's rise from third in the ratings to first by 1977.

2538. Suls, Jerry, and John Gastorf. "The Incidence of Sex Discrimination, Sexual Content, and Hostility in Television Humor." JACR 9.1 (Spring 1981) 42-49.

There is "some support for the charge of sex discrimination."

2539. Sweeper, George. "The Image of the Black Family & the White Family in American Prime-Time Television Programming 1970 to 1980." New York U, 1983. 325. DAI 44.7 (Jan. 1984) 1964-A.

While "the old Black stereotypes have to a large extent been eliminated, the broadcast industry has replaced them with a new crop of equally demeaning characterizations of Black people, the Black family, and the Black experience, while maintaining its predominantly positive image and portrayal of White culture and the White family."

2540. Taylor, Gabriela. "All in the Work-Family: Imagery of Family and Workplace in Television Entertainment in the 1970s." Brandeis U, 1985. 219. DAI 46 (1985) 1432-A.

Prime time series presenting home and workplace as family and an ethic of "people's professionalism" serve "as a critique of corporate power and an alternative vision of public authority."

2541. Trumbo, Dalton. "Hail, Blithe Spirit!" Problems and Controversies in Television and Radio. Ed. Harry Skornia and Jack Kitson. Palo Alto, CA: Pacific, 1968. 97-102. (Na Oct. 24, 1959).

The quiz shows fraud scandal leads to general analysis of TV: "the calculated falsity of practically all televised commercials, or the arrogant greed of men who have appropriated the free air and turned it into a witches' bazaar of howling peddlers hawking trash" (100).

ELECTRONIC MEDIA

2542. Tuchman, Gaye. "Assembling a Network Talk-Show." The TV Establishment. Englewood Cliffs, NJ: Prentice, 1974. 119-135.
On the role of the talk-show in promoting products.

2543. Tuchman, Gaye. "Mass Media Values." Television in Society. Ed. Arthur Berger. New Brunswick, NJ: Transaction, 1987. 195-202.
"Contemporary television programming helps maintain the existing political, economic, and social arrangements" by affirming the "structure of society, the appropriate distribution of goods and power" and by "refusing to question basic American assumptions about social arrangements," particularly those of property and sex roles.

2544. Turner, Richard. "Changes Made in Toxic-leak Film by ABC." TVG (Feb. 22, 1986) A-2.
A fiction film with a Bhopal leak plot was censored by the network to spread the blame.

2545. "U.S. Army Routinely Censors CBS Program." NCTVN 9.3-4 (Mar.-Apr. 1988) 3-4.
The military provides many cost-saving privileges to the CBS Tour of Duty Vietnam prime-time TV series, for which it is allowed to review all scripts and reject stories.

2546. Valdez, Armando. "The Economic Context of U.S. Children's Television: Parameters of Reform?" Communication and Social Structure: Critical Studies in Mass Media Research. Ed. Emile McAnany, et al. New York: Praeger, 1981. 145-180.
Capitalist marketplace motives dominate children's TV programming.

2547. Vincent, Richard C., et al. "Sexism on MTV: The Portrayal of Women in Rock Videos." JQ 64.4 (Winter 1987) 750-755.
"Depiction of gender roles is fairly traditional and sexism is high."

2548. "We Are Teaching Barbaric War Ethics, Dressed in 20th Century Clothing." SLJR 13.84 (1986) 19.
TV programming of war cartoons is increasing.

2549. White, Mimi. "Engendering Couples: The Subject of Daytime Television." Popular Culture, Schooling, and Everyday Life. Ed. Henry Giroux and Roger Simon. Granby, MA: Bergin and Garvey, 1989. 244.
Focuses on the couple in daytime, nonfiction TV--"The All New Dating Game," "Love Connection," "The New Newlywed Game," "Perfect Match," etc. These programs provide both the social control of the consumer culture and grounds for counter-hegemonic resistance.

2550. Zynda, Thomas. "The Mary Tyler Moore Show and the

Transformation of Situation Comedy." Media, Myths, and Narratives: Television and the Press. Ed. James W. Carey. Newbury Park: Sage, 1988. 126-145.
The first period of TV history, from 1948 to 1970, is the transformation of "a medium of great creative potential by the dominant economic forces" (networks, major studios, major advertisers) into a "culturally conservative money-making machine." But beginning in 1970 three situation comedies created a TV watershed: All in the Family, M*A*S*H, and Mary Tyler Moore Show. These programs dealt with contemporary social issues and in varying degrees realistically, but "sanitized in the interest of inspiration toward a better world."

II. C. 1. c. (3). TELEVISION NEWS (2551-2885)
(See II.A.2., II.C.3.b., and II.D.)

2551. Smith, Myron, Jr., comp. U.S. Television Network News: A Guide to Sources in English. Jefferson, NC: McFarland, 1984. 233.
An annotated guide of 3,215 citations to "99% U.S." sources from the late 1940s through 1982 with an Addendum through fall 1983. It is "not definitive" but it "attempts comprehensiveness in that virtually all factors concerning network television news are covered," and diverse published material: "books and monographs, scholarly papers, periodical and journal articles, government documents, doctoral dissertations, and masters theses. . . . Excluded materials include fiction, children's works, newspaper articles (unless reprinted in other works), poetry, and book reviews."

2552. Adams, Adam, and Phillip Heyl. "From Cairo to Kabul With the Networks, 1972-1980." Television Coverage of the Middle East. Ed. William C. Adams. Norwood, NJ: Ablex, 1981. 1-39.
A quantitative overview of network coverage of the Middle East: first a summary, then Afghanistan, and finally the hostages in Teheran.

2553. Adams, William, ed. Television Coverage of International Affairs. Norwood, NJ: Ablex, 1982. 253.
Thirteen essays explore the versions of world news offered by the networks: Global, Third World, Presidential Diplomacy, Southeast Asia, and Audience.

2554. Adams, William, ed. Television Coverage of the Middle East. Norwood, NJ: Ablex, 1981. 167.
Explains the diverse reasons why the government's policies gain dominant access.

2555. Adams, William, and Michael Joblove. "The Unnewsworthy Holocaust: TV News and Terror in Cambodia." Television Coverage of International Affairs. Ed. William Adams. Norwood, NJ: Ablex, 1982. 217-26.
The authors struggle inconclusively to explain why

television (and US media in general and two presidents) was so silent during four years of "one of the most bizarre and brutal revolutions of this century."

2556. Adams, William, and Fay Schreibman, eds. Television Network News: Issues in Content Research. Washington: School of Public and International Affairs, George Washington U, 1978. 231.
Research and methodological essays.

2557. Adatto, Kiku. "Sound Bite Democracy: Network Evening News Presidential Campaign Coverage, 1968 and 1988." Cambridge, MA: Harvard University, John F. Kennedy School of Government, January 1990. 35.
Explores the danger to democracy when "political discourse is reduced to sound bites, one-liners, and potent visuals."

2558. Adoni, Hanna, and Akiba A. Cohen. "Television Economic News and the Social Construction of Economic Reality." JoC 28.4 (1978) 61-70.
Exposure to television news about economic issues can give viewers a false impression of understanding when, in fact, they may not even understand the analytical concepts.

2559. Ajuonuma, Livi. "U.S. Television News Coverage of Crisis in the Third World: The Case of the Sub-Saharan Hunger Crisis." U of Minnesota, 1987. 153. DAI 48 (1988) 2754-A.
During 1984-85 the three major networks reported Ethiopia "in polarized East-West terms."

2560. Almaney, Adnan. "International and Foreign Affairs on Network Television." JoB 14 (1970) 499-509.
Network TV is largely dominated by domestic news, and international and foreign affairs are reported only when they reach the "crisis" point.

2561. Altheide, David. Creating Reality: How TV News Distorts Events. Beverly Hills: Sage, 1976. 220.
Examines the diverse influences that produce the news: economics, politics, organization.

2562. Altheide, David. "Iran vs. US TV News: The Hostage Story Out of Context." Television Coverage of the Middle East. Ed. William C. Adams. Norwood, NJ: Ablex, 1981. 128-157.
Generally TV supported the government's positions and rarely made independent investigation or offered alternative ways of interpreting events. Network correspondents "tended to be spokespersons for State Department and other governmental officials."

2563. Andersen, Robin. "On Panama, Press Does Bush's Work: Administration Demands Veto Over TV Images." Guard 42.13 (Jan. 24, 1990) 4.

"Chauvinism and racism are at least part of the reason for the overwhelming bias."

2564. Anderson, David. "Blackout in Lansing." CJR 12.6 (1974) 26-29.
Gross Telecasting, Inc., a multi-media corporation in Lansing, Michigan, is accused of news blackouts, especially of political enemies.

2565. Asi, Morad. "Arabs, Israelis, and TV News: A Time-Series, Content Analysis." Television Coverage of the Middle East. Ed. William C. Adams. Norwood, NJ: Ablex, 1981. 67-75.
"While coverage in 1979 was a long way from being generally pro-Arab, it was a far cry from the pro-Israeli approach of earlier periods."

2566. Attansio, Paul. "Muckraking for Millions." CJR 23.4 (1984) 55-57.
Axel Madson's book, 60 Minutes, celebrates the successful news program, glossing over the show's serious journalistic shortcomings which result from the enormous profitability of the program as presently organized--a small-town focus that seldom touches upon big power or the system of power.

2567. [Cancelled]

2568. Aufderheide, Pat. "TV's Hidden Money Games: Missing Link in Global Links." CJR 27.1 (May-June 1988) 41-42.
Public TV station WETA co-produced a documentary on economic development with the World Bank, Global Links, but it failed to mention the Bank's conflict of interest.

2569. Bader, Eleanor J. "Study Finds Men Dominate News Media." Guard 41.31 (May 3, 1989) 2.
Junior Bridge's Media Tracking Project found that staffing and story selection still reflect a definite male bias.

2570. Bagdikian, Ben. "Murdoch and the Corporate Media Clan." Extra! 1.6 (Jan.-Feb. 1988) 1, 3.
Murdoch's successful circumvention of anti-monopoly laws partly derives from the failure of the mainstream news media to "report with fairness and balance the pros and cons of deregulation and monopoly development."

2571. Bagnied, Magda, and Steven Schneider. "Sadat Goes to Jerusalem: Televised Images, Themes, and Agenda." Television Coverage of the Middle East. Ed. William C. Adams. Norwood, NJ: Ablex, 1981. 53-66.
The favorable coverage of Sadat's trip to Jerusalem did not indicate a change in TV's generally favorable treatment of Israel over the Arab nations.

2572. Bailey, George. "Interpretive Reporting of the Vietnam

War by Anchormen." JQ 53.2 (1976) 319-324.
Network anchormen summarized with little interpretation and no adversary interpretation.

2573. Bailey, George. "The Vietnam War According to Chet, David, Walter, Harry, Peter, Bob, Howard, & Frank: A Content Analysis of Journalistic Performance by the Network Television Evening News Anchormen, 1965-1970." Wisconsin, 1973. 451. DAI 34 (1974) 4182-A.
Anchormen mainly read press releases from the government, though some criticism appeared near the end of the war.

2574. Bailey, George, and Lawrence W. Lichty. "Rough Justice on a Saigon Street: A Gatekeeper Study of NBC's Tet Execution Film." JQ 49 (1972) 221-229, 238.
A "cybernetic gatekeeping model" analysis concludes that the telecasting of General Loan's summary execution of a prisoner resulted from complex organizational norms.

2575. Barber, James David. "Not The New York Times: What Network News Should Be." WM 11.7 (Sept. 1979) 14-21.
Analyzes the flaws of network news: blanked-out history, inadequate follow-up, lack of comprehensiveness and linkage past-present-future, opinion emphasized over evidence, 90-second patness, docudramas, etc. Gives eight recommendations for improvement.

2576. Barron, Jerome. "'The Selling of the Pentagon': Partisan Involvements & Antagonisms." Congress & the News Media. Ed. Robert O. Blanchard. New York: Hastings, 1974. 406-410.
Analysis of controversy between Congress and CBS over the latter's examination of Pentagon propaganda. Danger of broadcasting's trustee responsibility: Congress used it to override possible First Amendment protection of its editing process.

2577. Bartimole, Roldo. "Claude Blair Destroys Credibility of Banks; Ch. 8 Retraction Mocks Concept of Free Press." PoV 11.9 (Nov. 25, 1978) 1-3.
Illustrates corporate "economic power over the news media" in Cleveland.

2578. Bartimole, Roldo. "Television: Bad News." PoV 13.1 (July 19, 1980) 1-2.
Shallow reporting and constant self-promotion help Cleveland's three TV stations make $20 million combined profit a year. [Also see 13.8 (Nov. 15, 1980)].

2579. Bartimole, Roldo. "Television: Fail, Fail, Fail." PoV 13.5 (Oct. 4, 1980) 1-2.
Cleveland's three TV stations were not reporting the city's anti-trust suit against Cleveland Electric Illumination Co., which had tried to destroy the city's Municipal Light System, and the newspapers had to be dragged into covering the story.

2580. Bartimole, Roldo. "Virgil Dominic Looks for Glib Tongue at Ch. 8 Where News Must Draw Youth, Earn More Bucks." PoV 10.24 (June 24, 1978) 1-2.
TV news "can't be taken seriously" because the managers "seek the lowest possible level" of "superficiality."

2581. Batscha, Robert M. Foreign Affairs News and the Broadcast Journalist. New York: Praeger, 1975. 254.
Studies the behavior of TV newsmen, concluding that the "artificial policy considerations of time and structure" (preference for stories that offer current and compelling visuals, the desire for simplicity at the expense of depth, the targeting of a "middle audience") produce "superficial reflections of world events." The "physical event" of a problem is presented, but underlying causes and alternatives for action are often lacking in network news stories.

2582. Beck, Andee. "A Bigger Chill." IREJ 13.4 (Fall 1990) 17-19.
"The terrifying trend to clamp down on advertiser-sensitive reporting in television." "Stations all around the country are under pressure to water down or kill consumer stories that name names."

2583. Benjamin, Burton. Fair Play: CBS, General Westmoreland, and How a Television Documentary Went Wrong. New York: Harper, 1988. 218.
The author found the documentary on Westmoreland to be unbalanced and unfair.

2584. Berkowitz, Dan. "TV News Sources and News Channels: A Study in Agenda Building." JQ 64.2-3 (Summer-Fall 1987) 508-513.
"Routine sources build the television news agenda."

2585. Bernstein, Dennis. "TV Reporters' Self-Censorship Helps Explain the Missing Pieces in Network News." ITT 12.39 (Oct. 12-18, 1988) 24, 22.
(This article was originally written for Newsday, but days before it was to run as a cover story it was killed.) Budget and staff cutbacks and corporate owner influence have created pervasive self-censorship. (See also Extra! 2.2 [Sept.-Oct. 1988] 1, 8-9.)

2586. "Better Living through Public Relations." Extra! 1.3 (Aug.-Sept. 1987) 6.
A CBS 60 Minutes report by Ed Bradley suppressed damning evidence against Union Carbide and its disaster at Bhopal, India.

2587. Biryukov, N.S. Television in the West and Its Doctrines. Trans. Yuri Sviridov. Moscow: Progress, 1981. 207.
A skeptical view of the impartiality and "free flow of information" of capitalist television. "The rich variety of

forms, genres, techniques used by programme-makers reveals a set of definite ideological guidelines and principles of Western television, i.e. the main tasks assigned to it by the ruling class in the ideological sphere" (88).

2588. Blair, Gwenda. Almost Golden: Jessica Savitch and the Selling of TV News. New York: Simon & Schuster, 1988. 352.
Biography of the rise and fall of a woman who became a network anchor at thirty-one, and an examination of a business that hired her to boost ratings and then abandoned her when she disintegrated.

2589. Bleifuss, Joel. "They've Got a Line on News." ITT 13.13 (Feb. 15-21, 1989) 5.
Between 1985 and 1988 ABC's Nightline with Ted Koppel had 89% male guests, 92% white, 80% professionals, government officials, or corporate representatives, only 5% representatives of public-interest groups, and less than 2% labor or racial ethnic leaders.

2590. Blume, Keith. The Presidential Election Show: Campaign 84 and Beyond on the Nightly News. South Hadley, MA: Bergin, 1986. 352.
TV has unwittingly transformed participatory democracy into a spectator sport. Interweaving newscast transcripts with commentary, the author illustrates the tendency of TV news to report on image, poll results, and campaign strategy rather than on the important issues. [See II.B.5.]

2591. Bohn, Thomas W. "Broadcasting National Election Returns, 1952-1976." JoC 30.4 (1980) 140-153.
TV, while enhancing the drama of candidate competition, has created a new ritualistic contest--complete with heroes, villains, and fools--in which the networks struggle for the Presidential pick. [See II.B.5.]

2592. Boot, William. "Campaign '88: TV Overdoses on the Inside Dope." CJR 27.5 (Jan.-Feb. 1989) 23-29.
TV news coverage of the '88 election campaign was stagemanaged to a large degree by the Bush campaign. Evaluations of both candidates dealt more with techniques of campaigning than with substance. [See II.B.5.]

2593. Boyer, Peter J. Who Killed CBS? The Undoing of America's Number One News Network. New York: Random, 1988. 361.
A history of CBS News and its decline during the 1980s into a "profit center in cutthroat competition for ratings" (5). Under Van Sauter's "draconian cutbacks" in news-gathering CBS News turned to "reach-out-and-touch-someone Sauterism, the television of moments": West 57th, 48 Hours, the Northshield program, Lack's True Stories, consisting of "commercial primetime shows designed to attract a wide audience. And the Evening News had finally become the broad-reaching video

tabloid Sauter had wanted" (345).

2594. "The 'Brawlcast' at CBS: Bush Got Off Easy." Extra! 1.6 (Jan.-Feb. 1988) 2.
The brief conflict between Dan Rather and presidential candidate Bush on CBS Evening News (Jan. 25, 1988) resulted in wide criticism of Rather, when in fact he had been easy on Bush's record.

2595. Breen, Myles. "Australia on American Television News: Coverage of the Invisible Continent." Television Coverage of International Affairs. Ed. William Adams. Norwood, NJ: Ablex, 1982. 167-178.
Criticizes the inadequate coverage of Australia.

2596. Brown, James, and Paul L. Hain. "Reporting the Vote on Election Night." JoC 28.4 (1978) 132-38.
The News Election Service (NES), formed by the three major networks and two main wire services, decides who will be covered by the media on election nights and how well, who the "serious" candidates are, to the exclusion of many minor party candidates.

2597. Campbell, Richard. "Narrative, Myth, & Metaphor in 60 Minutes: An Interpretive Approach to the Study of Television News." Northwestern U, 1986. 403. DAI 47 (1987) 2783-A.
60 Minutes is not neutral journalism but constructs social norms via narrative formulas to resolve tensions between individuals and institutions, etc., and thereby to maintain a mythology of the US as a place where contradiction and complexity are overcome.

2598. Campbell, Richard. "Securing the Middle Ground: Reporter Formulas in 60 Minutes." CSMC 4 (Dec. 1987) 325-350.
By portraying the reporters on 60 Minutes as "detectives, analysts, and tourists" in combat against evil in support of mainstream values, the program remains popular.

2599. Carter, Bill. "Whatever Happened to TV Documentaries?" WJR 5.5 (1983) 43-46.
Low Nielsen ratings--i.e. low profits--undermine network stated commitment to investigative reporting.

2600. Castro, Nelson Notario. "Electronic War Against Panama." Granma 25.18 (May 6, 1990) 11.
On the use of the SGN TV network at the US base at Clayton to advocate its views.

2601. Cater, Douglass. "A Strategy for Political Broadcasting." JoC 26.2 (Spring 1976) 58-64.
Discusses proposals for government, broadcasters, candidates and campaign advisers, and voluntary citizen organizations to

improve the completeness and fairness of campaign broadcasting in 1976.

2602. Celente, Gerald. "The McBraining of North America." Adbusters 1.3 (Spring 1990) 24-26.
Denounces the poor quality of news from broadcasting and tabloid newspapers, which give us headline and junk news mainly, crises and disconnection.

2603. Chauncey, Tom. "An Editorial." TQ 10.3 (1973) 4-5.
Governmental influence over TV is creating confusion and lack of confidence toward both the government and the media.

2604. Cockburn, Alexander. "Ashes & Diamonds." ITT 12.30 (July 20-Aug. 2, 1988) 17.
TV supported the government's rationalizations of the Navy's shooting down of an Iranian civilian airbus on a regular flight killing 290 people.

2605. Cockburn, Alexander. "Collapse of Free Press." Na 240 (Mar. 9, 1985) 262-3.
Two examples of TV newsmen acting as mouthpieces for US foreign policies: Reagan's declaration of war on Nicaragua and treatment of the fortieth anniversary of the Yalta agreement.

2606. Cockburn, Alexander. "How I Spent My Thanksgiving Vacation." ITT 14.7 (Dec. 20-Jan. 9, 1990) 17.
Networks spent enormous sums to cover Soviet miners on strike but paid no attention to the miners striking the Pittston Coal Group or to popular protests to US Central American politics.

2607. Cockburn, Alexander. "Perfect Executioners." ITT 10.24 (1986) 12.
The networks are generally arms of the military-industrial complex.

2608. Cockburn, Alexander. "TV and the Palestinians." ITT 13.5 (Dec. 7-13, 1988) 5.
"Network coverage of the Palestine National Council's announcement from Algiers [of Palestinian sovereignty] was generally better than that of the print media," particularly that of NBC and CBS, but in general the press took the Israeli side.

2609. Cockburn, Andrew. "Pictures from the Pentagon." Channels 2 (June-July 1982) 15-16.
Network news serves the military.

2610. Cohen, Akiba, Hanna Adoni, and Charles Bantz, et al. Social Conflict and Television News. Newbury Park, CA: Sage, 1990. 320.
Examines how social conflicts are constructed for the news and then understood by the public, a five-nation study.

2611. Cohen, Jeff. "Television's Political Spectrum."
Extra! 3.6 (July-Aug. 1990) 1, 6-7.
"TV's spectrum is clearly slanted in favor of the right."

2612. Cohen, Richard. "Good Morning, Journalism." MJ 13.6
(July-Aug. 1988) 12, 14.
Tells how CBS president Van Gordon Sauter trivialized the network's news programs in his quest for higher ratings.

2613. Cohen, Richard. "The Yelling of the President." NR
196.15 (Apr. 13, 1987) 34-36.
Sam Donaldson's confidence in the power of words is not borne out in TV, where pictures dominate and the networks are "co-conspirators" with the Reagan White House for high ratings.

2614. Collum, Danny. "15 Seconds Over Manila." Soj 15.5
(1986) 48-50.
Preceding the fall of the Marcos regime, network TV framed the story in US foreign policy doctrines.

2615. Cook, Mark, and Jeff Cohen. "The Media Go to War: How
Television Sold the Panama Invasion." Extra! 3.2
(Jan.-Feb. 1990) 1, 3-8.
Panamanian praise for the invasion dominated TV news; opposition received virtually no coverage. The networks served this invasion by "uncritically dispensing huge quantities of official news and views."

2616. Cooper, Anne. "Third World News on Network Television:
An Inclusion/Exclusion Study of Violence." U of
North Carolina, 1984. 194. DAI 45 (1985) 2291-A.
Television neglects 79 countries, while concentrating on a few, and covers only a few continuing Third World stories: Israel-Arab conflict, the threat of socialism/communism, and violence in sub-Saharan Africa.

2617. Cooper, Marc, and Lawrence Soley. "All the Right
Sources." MJ 15.2 (Feb.-Mar. 1990) 20-27, 45-48.
A two-year study (1987-1989) documents how limited, homogeneous, and conservative are the experts invited to comment on TV news.

2618. Corry, J. TV News and the Dominant Culture.
Washington, DC: The Media Institute, 1986. 54.
This New York Times reporter discusses how TV news reflects the liberal point of view, based on an analysis of TV news coverage 1963-66.

2619. Craft, Christine. Too Old, Too Ugly, and Not
Deferential to Men. Rocklin, CA: Prima, 1988. 211.
Story of the author's fraud and sex discrimination suit against Metromedia and its TV station in Kansas City.

2620. Croan, Melvin. "TV's Take on the Germanies: Media's

Metaphors and Mantras Go Awry at the Wall." Deadline
5.1 (Jan.-Feb. 1990) 3-5, 10.
The liberation of eastern Europe was reported through the filters of ingrained US "cultural assumptions."

2621. Cummings, Gary. "Invasion of the People Meters." WJR 9.3 (Apr. 1987) 12.
The new "People Meter" from Nielsen and AGB of England (combining meter and diary for immediate demographic data) may pervert news content.

2622. Cummings, Gary. "The Rising Threat of Tabloid TV." WJR 9.2 (Mar. 1987) 16.
Warns of a dangerous trend toward sensational video journalism as exemplified by A Current Affair (the product of Rupert Murdoch's WNYW in New York) and Tabloid TV, a program which "candidly declares it is not interested in 'truth, accuracy, or ethical journalism.'"

2623. Dahlgren, Peter. "The Modes of Reception: For a Hermeneutics of TV News." Television in Transition. Ed. Phillip Drummond and Richard Paterson. London: BFI, 1986. 235-249.
Examines the conditions of cognition and the ambiguity of perception of images for researchers as well as ordinary viewers.

2624. Dahlgren, Peter. "Network TV News and the Corporate State: The Subordinate Consciousness of the Viewer-Citizen." The Grad. Center, City U of New York, 1977. 199. DAI 38.8 (Feb. 1978) 4426.
Explains the method employed by the corporate state to ensure "a quiescent mass loyalty."

2625. Dahlgren, Peter. "TV News as a Social Relation." MCS 3 (1981) 291-302.
TV news format illustrates how network news serves the corporate state.

2626. Dahlgren, Peter. "TV News and the Suppression of Reflexivity." Mass Media and Social Change. Ed. Elihu Katz and Tamás Szecskö. London: Sage, 1981. 101-114.
TV news should "enable the public to develop critical self-knowledge of their society and of TV news as well," and lead to mobilization instead of passivity or paralysis as at present.

2627. Dahlgren, Peter, with Sumitra Chakrapani. "The Third World on TV News: Western Ways of Seeing the 'Other.'" Television Coverage of International Affairs. Ed. William Adams. Norwood, NJ: Ablex, 1982. 45-66.
TV presents the Third World ideologically, in terms of expansionist and hegemonic goals.

2628. Diamond, Edwin. "All the News that Isn't News." AF 6 (Oct. 1980) 74-76.
On TV news hype, making news more dramatic and exciting for ratings and profits. Also analyzes the newsbreak, "another program in which to insert commercials."

2629. Diamond, Edwin. "How Bad Reporting Scared America." TVG (Oct. 22, 1983) 4-8.
TV reported the beginnings of the AIDS epidemic poorly.

2630. Diamond, Edwin. "The Miami Riots: Did TV Get the Real Story?" TVG (Aug. 30, 1980) 18-22.
Coverage of the riots and of "the major continuing American story of our time" is inadequate.

2631. Diamond, Edwin. Sign Off: The Last Days of Television. Cambridge, MA: MIT P, 1982. 273.
Discusses a wide range of news reporting to support his belief that TV news is "shaped by perceived national interests" (106): Three Mile Island, Iranian Embassy hostages, labor, etc.

2632. Diamond, Edwin. The Tin Kazoo: Politics, Television, and the News. Cambridge, MA: MIT P, 1975. 269.
Critical of TV journalism as not comprehensive and relevant enough. For example, the four administrations manipulated the media about Vietnam.

2633. Dilley, Raymond. "A Comparison of the Cronkite, Huntley-Brinkley News Broadcasts." MJR 7 (Spring 1964) 29-30.
"The most significant finding of the content analysis was the similarity of the two programs."

2634. Dominick, Joseph R. "Geographic Bias in National TV News." JoC 27.4 (1977) 94-99.
Fascination with Washington, D.C., over fifty percent of the national news focus, characterizes network service. The author recommends a bicameral newscast which allocates time systematically to regional reports.

2635. Donaldson, Sam. Hold On, Mr. President. New York: Random House, 1987. 260.
ABC's White House correspondent during the Carter and Reagan administrations sees his goal "to find out what's really going on at the White House." The job of the reporter is "to challenge the president, challenge him to explain policy, justify decisions, defend mistakes, reveal intentions for the future, and comment on a host of matters," in contrast to the president and his aides, who want to "emphasize their successes, minimize or hide their blunders, send only the messages they think will advance their interests . . . and generally use the press."

2636. Douglas, Susan J. "Tubular Hells: Tabloid TV Makes the Move Uptown." ITT 13.34 (Sept. 13-19, 1989) 20-21.

ELECTRONIC MEDIA 379

Criticizes two new network news-magazines, NBC's Yesterday, Today, and Tomorrow and ABC's Prime Time Live, as being "top-heavy with overpaid, complacent stars and more concerned with style and form than substance."

2637. Dowie, Mark. "How ABC Spikes The News." MJ 10.9 (Nov.-Dec. 1985) 33-39, 53.
About what you weren't told by ABC News in 1984 about three powerful Republicans: US Information Agency Director Charles Wick, Nevada Senator Paul Laxalt, and then Secretary of Labor Raymond Donovan. This was an election year and ABC had financial reasons for wanting a Reagan victory.

2638. Dreifus, Claudia. "Marlene Sanders: The Networks Aren't Looking for Journalists. They're Looking for Attractive Personalities." Prog 54.10 (Oct. 1990) 36-38.
Interview of Sanders, whose recent book, Waiting for Prime Time, tells about the struggles of women in broadcasting news.

2639. Duberman, Martin. Paul Robeson. New York: Knopf, 1988. 804.
Describes how an appearance by Paul Robeson on Eleanor Roosevelt's television show was canceled by NBC, which further vowed that he would never appear on the network, "thereby making him the first American to be officially banned from television."

2640. Dunn, Max. "Network Television Coverage of U.S. Supreme Court Decisions: A Study of Information Flow." U of Virginia, 1985. 234. DAI 46 (1986) 2846-A.
Network treatment is "highly standardized."

2641. Edgar, Patricia, ed. The News in Focus: The Journalism of Exception. London: MacMillan, 1980. 213.
Analyzes the determining factors in the manufacture of news that contributes to the status quo and social control. Focuses on TV.

2642. Entman, Robert, and David Paletz. "The War in Southeast Asia: Tunnel Vision on Television." Television Coverage of International Affairs. Ed. William Adams. Norwood, NJ: Ablex, 1982. 181-201.
TV undermined official policy during the first half of 1968, "but before and after that, it legitimized presidential actions" in "deeper entrapment in the quagmire."

2643. Epstein, Edward. News From Nowhere: Television and the News. New York: Random, 1973. 321.
Studies the methods of selecting and organizing information into news reports by the three network news services, particularly at NBC. The author observed news operations and editorial conferences, interviewed newspeople, studied records, and examined logs and scripts. News is a "product of an organization" that functions within diverse constraining contexts or pressures--economics, government regulation, etc.

2644. Fang, I.E. TV News. Rev. New York: Hastings, 1972. 478.
Explains twenty aspects of TV news: reporting, sound, film editing, etc. Relevant to this bibliography: "Television News as News," "Editorials," "The Law," and "The Profession."

2645. Fant, Charles H. "Televising Presidential Conventions, 1952-1980." JoC 30.4 (1980) 130-139.
Cooperation between major parties and networks, in the form of financial support and prime advertising slots, has altered the confrontational structure of conventions in a way that stresses superficial emotion over critical political consciousness.

2646. Fauhy, Edward. "The Public Is Not Getting the News It Deserves." TQ 19.4 (1983) 61-64.
"Veteran White House reporters say they have never seen information as difficult to come by as it is in this [Reagan] administration."

2647. Feldman, Samuel, and Joseph Webb. "How TV Networks Covered Agnew's 'Day of Infamy.'" RSCJ 10 (Winter 1974) 9-10.
The networks presented "remarkably different portraits" of Vice-President Agnew at the time of his resignation over criminal charges.

2648. Fields, Howard. "The White House Versus the News Media." TRA 32 (Nov. 26, 1984) 44-46, 80-82.
Correspondents "acknowledge that they may be pawns being moved about on a chessboard at the whim of the White House. All, to one degree or another, believe things are only going to get worse during the second Reagan administration."

2649. Fong-Torres, Ben. "Why Are There No Asian Male News Anchors?" M&V No. 48 (Fall 1989) 14-16.
The WWII image of Japanese males stereotypes male Asian newsmen and excludes them from top anchor jobs.

2650. Friendly, Fred W. "The Assault on Broadcast Journalism." Britannica Book of the Year, 1972. Chicago: Encyclopedia Britannica, 1972. 664-666.
About government intervention and pressure mainly, with focus on CBS's "The Selling of the Pentagon."

2651. Friendly, Fred W. Due to Circumstances Beyond Our Control.. New York: Random, 1967. 325.
A memoir and a book about CBS, the author and Edward R. Murrow, and broadcast journalism, by the former president of CBS News who lost his job in a conflict over news vs. the bottom line. The last chapter presents noncommercial alternatives to the profit-dominated commercial networks, especially for independent funding for public broadcasting.

2652. "From the Folks Who Gave Us the Reagan Myth . . . Here's Ollie." Extra! 1.3 (Aug.-Sept. 1987) 3.

On the easy treatment accorded Col. North by TV.

2653. Funt, Peter. "Television News: Seeing Isn't Believing." SR (Nov. 1980) 30-32.
Summarizes ways TV news pictures are edited, altered, and manipulated.

2654. Gallantz, Michael. "The China Syndrome: Meltdown in Hollywood." JC 22 (May 1980) 3-4.
The second major theme of the film is TV news' preference for entertainment over information and the controlling influence of the ratings. The film, "unfortunately," treats "nuclear power with the same shallowness . . . and manipulativeness that it exposes in the television medium."

2655. Gans, Herbert. "How Well Does TV Present the News?" NYTM (Jan. 11, 1970) 31, 32, 35, 38, 40, 43, 46.
Journalists generally perceive the world through the dominant ideology and management's business interests.

2656. Gibson, W. "Towards a Theory of Network Television News." ST 3 (1980) 88-111.
Studies the familiar structural components of a network news broadcast, its "code, text, and intertext" which "establish patterns of meaning" and are shaped by the network both economically and politically.

2657. Gitlin, Todd. "Elevating Moderate Alternatives: The Moment of Reform." The Whole World Is Watching. Berkeley: U of California P, 1980. 205-232.
Describes the stages by which the TV networks gradually adopted the "frame of moderation-as-alternative-to-militancy" in response to the conflicting internal and external pressures of constructing news. Network corporate censorship and self-censorship significantly influenced the coverage of the Nixon-Moratorium-Mobilization perspectives toward the war.

2658. Gitlin, Todd. "Media Routines & Political Crises." The Whole World Is Watching. Berkeley: U of California P, 1980. 249-282.
Employs a theory of news "frames" derived from Gramsci to explain TV coverage of the anti-Vietnam War movement. News derives from "the force field" of intersecting, conflicting organizational and political pressures.

2659. Gitlin, Todd. "Spotlights and Shadows: Television and the Culture of Politics." CE 38 (1977) 791-96.
How TV news legitimizes the actions of the dominant power and deligitimizes opposition.

2660. Gitlin, Todd. "The War on Drugs and the Enlisted Press." CJR 28.4 (Nov.-Dec. 1989) 17-19.
Most TV coverage of drug addiction focuses on the superficialities of the "war" rather than the difficult problems of causes and cures.

2661. Gitlin, Todd. The Whole World Is Watching: Mass Media in the Making and Unmaking of the New Left. Berkeley: U of California P, 1980. 327.
Analyzes the networks, especially CBS, as part of the capitalist established order. The mass media protect and perpetuate the oligopoly by blacking out news that challenges corporate and political elites and by "disparaging movements that radically oppose the system" (4-5).

2662. Glasgow University Media Group. Bad News. London: Routledge & Kegan Paul, 1976. 310.
On news filters, including ideology, a pressure that affirms the status quo of the corporate/government complex. [About British television. Also see their More Bad News (1980).]

2663. Goldberg, Robert, and Gerald J. Goldberg. Anchors: Brokaw, Jennings, Rather and the Evening News. Secaucus, NJ: Birch Lane/Carol, 1990. 320.
Profiles of the anchors, an account of their competition, and how the evening news is created.

2664. Good, Paul. "Is Network News Slighting the Minorities?" TVG (Mar. 5, 1977) 4-8.
The answer is yes; for example, "documentaries about minorities have virtually ceased to exist."

2665. Gould, Stanhope. "Coors Brews the News." CJR 13.6 (1975) 18-29.
Tells how reporters of Colorado beer king Joseph Coors' Television News Inc. were subject to "ideological pressure by management" and how some journalists were fired for not toeing the conservative line.

2666. Graham, Fred. Happy Talk: Confessions of a TV Journalist. New York: Norton, 1990. 352.
Anecdotal account of the decline of TV news into corporate-led lightweight entertainment.

2667. Greeley, Bill. "Nixon--'Out of Sync' and (At Last) Off the Tube." TQ 12.1 (1974) 51-55.
Nixon's efforts to control TV news.

2668. Griffith, Thomas. "Television, The Wealthy Eunuch." TQ 11.3 (1974) 5-12.
On limitations of network news.

2669. Grossman, Lawrence K. "Reflections on Television's Role in American Presidential Elections." Cambridge, MA: Harvard University, John F. Kennedy School of Government, January 1990. 10.
On the misuse of TV by networks and politicians and six remedies (e.g., expanded public TV and C-SPAN). [See II.B.5.]

2670. Gunther, Marc. "White Males Dominate TV News." AG (June 27, 1990) 2E.

Few women correspondents and fewer blacks appear on daily network evening newscasts.

2671. Haile, Reesom. "Africa on Television: U.S. Network Television Coverage of African Affairs, 1977-1980." New York U, 1987. 145. DAI 48 (1987) 1346-A.
During the Carter administration, ABC, CBS, and NBC reported African nations in frequency according to their political and economic relations with the US. The networks covered a similar geography and generally the same countries. [See Onwochei.]

2672. Halberstam, David. "CBS: The Power & the Profits." AM 237.1 (Jan. 1976) 33-71; 237.2 (Feb. 1976) 52-91.
Part I "showed how the medium" and CBS in particular "became both a shaper and a creature of politics, both a maker and a prisoner" of power. Part II "tells how three Presidents influenced and were influenced by TV, how TV made Vietnam into an electronic war, and how, reluctantly, it dealt with the Watergate tragedy."

2673. Halberstam, David. "Medals--and Demerits--for Performance Under Fire." TVG (Apr. 20, 1985) 32-34.
TV could not explain the complexities of the Vietnam War, yet it played its part "brilliantly" by stimulating people to be better informed.

2674. Halberstam, David. The Powers that Be. New York: Knopf, 1979. 771.
Has a chapter on CBS and its owner Paley. [See No. 2672.]

2675. Hallin, Daniel. "Network News: We Keep America on Top of the World." Watching Television. Ed. Todd Gitlin. New York: Pantheon, 1987. 9-41.
A comparison of morning news, which is mainly entertainment, and evening news, which is journalism within entertainment. Television has "a special role in assigning ideological meaning to political events," an ideology that is reformist and populist but also conservative and nationalist, and its ultimate effect is reassuring. The news presents the world "as a great and simple battle ground between good and evil, with America as the unique embodiment of good."

2676. Hallin, Daniel. "Summit 1985: Washington Set the Tone." Deadline 2.3 (Sept.-Oct. 1987) 1-2, 7, 10.
Both the Soviet and the US media are nationalistic, "can be highly partisan in their coverage of the other side," and both shift tone with prevailing winds, as the Geneva summit coverage reveals.

2677. Hallin, Daniel. "Whatever Happened to the News? When Hard News Goes Soft, Entertainment Takes Over." M&V 50 (Spring 1990) 2-4.
The decline of TV hard news programs carries the danger of creating an even larger public ignorant of national and global

issues and history.

2678. Hallin, Daniel, and Paolo Mancini. "Political Structure and Representational Form in U.S. and Italian Television News." T&S 13 (1984) 829-850.
TV conventions obstruct analysis and boost reporting of officials.

2679. Hans, Dennis. "This Week With David Brinkley: ABC-TV." C&C 43 (Feb. 20, 1984) 45-6.
Analyzes a pro-US program on Central America.

2680. Harris, Mark. "Docudramas Unmasked: We May Be Paying a Heavy Price for TV's Distorted Portraits of Kennedy, Chessman, Custer and Others." TVG (Mar. 4, 1978) 6-10.
Docudrama oversimplifies and falsifies history.

2681. Hart, Roderick. "Speech and Drama: The President Versus the Mass Media." The Sound of Leadership: Presidential Communication in the Modern Age. Chicago: U of Chicago P, 1987. 111-154.
The media "make the American presidency an extraordinarily entertaining show": likewise the president "spends much of his time trying to outthink the media": "The result is the most plentiful and most skillfully choreographed speech the nation has known." "Perhaps the most distressing aspect of this 'mediazation' of the presidency is how preoccupied with image reporters and presidents have become."

2682. Haydock, John. "Innovative TV News Format Runs Counter to Accepted Standards." SLJR 13.82 (1986) 24.
Examines CBS's new news program, West 57th, that in turn looks at television journalism.

2683. Herman, Edward. "Anatomy of a Smear: Ed Bradley & '60 Minutes' on UNESCO." Hope & Folly: The United States & UNESCO, 1945-1985. Minneapolis: U of Minnesota P, 1989. 328-337.
Bradley's commentary on UNESCO "never once departed from the State Department line" and "demonstrates well both the strongly conformist tendencies of network television and its power to enhance the effects of animus and bias."

2684. Hess, Stephen. "Television Reporting: Self-fulfilling News." IREJ 12.4 (Fall 1989) 13.
Warns of a shift of control of news from reporters to "news processors."

2685. Hickey, Neil. "In an Era of Frantic Muckraking in the Press . . . Is Television Doing its Investigative Reporting Job?" TVG (Apr. 2, 1977) 2-6.
The answer is no. "It's clear that the actual volume of investigative reports" is "miniscule in view of the legendary resources" of TV journalism.

2686. Himmelstein, Hal. "Television News and the Television Documentary." Television Myth & the American Mind. New York: Praeger, 1984. 197-232. (Rptd. Television, the Critical View. Ed. Horace Newcomb. 4th ed. New York: Oxford UP, 1987. 255-91.)
Attempts to assess the impacts of cultural ideology, organizational imperatives, and individual biases in the presentation of news and documentaries. "News organizations and the corporate chiefs to whom they must report have developed identifiable ideological perspectives that at least indirectly impact on the newsgathering process." Both organizations and individuals "operate in cultures which at any given moment provide certain dominant ideological frames that impact on reportage as they set limits to the journalistic discourse and determine the relationship of the journalistic apparatus to the government in power" (198).

2687. Hitchens, Christopher. "Blabscam: TV's Rigged Political Talk Shows." Har 274.1642 (Mar. 1987) 75-6.
Explains the "phony homage to the notion of unfettered exchange," The McLaughlin Group, for example, canvassing "all opinions from the extreme right to the moderate right."

2688. Hofstetter, C. Richard. Bias in the News: Network Television Coverage of the 1972 Election Campaign. Columbus, OH: Ohio State UP, 1976. 207.
"Very little evidence was found to establish the presence of partisan bias in network coverage of the 1972 presidential campaign" (197).

2689. Horowitz, Andrew. "Playing Monopoly with the News." MORE 5 (1975) 16-17, 23.
Network TV's disdain for independent news film makers.

2690. Howell, Leon. "CBS, Westy, and Us." C&C 45.7 (1985) 152-4.
Discusses funding of libel by conservatives and the negative impact on investigative reporting.

2691. Hoynes, William, and David Croteau. "All the Usual Suspects: MacNeil/Lehrer and Nightline." Extra! 3.4 (Special Issue) 1-15.
A "comparative analysis of the guest lists of ABC's Nightline and PBS's MacNeil/Lehrer NewsHour for a six month period (2/6/89 to 8/4/89)." The NewsHour's "guest list represented an even narrower . . . political spectrum than Nightline's," which is limited almost entirely to white male elites. "By and large the promise of broad, in-depth coverage on MacNeil/Lehrer remains unfulfilled," just as it is in Nightline. What we get is white, male government officials, conservative think tank experts, and corporate executives.

2692. Hoynes, William, and David Croteau. "Are you on the Nightline Guest List?" Extra! 2.4 (Jan.-Feb. 1989) 1-15.

Entire issue devoted to Ted Koppel's Nightline, a condensation of the original 45-page study. The study shows that the program is heavily stacked "in favor of government spokespersons" and overwhelmingly "white, male representatives of powerful institutions." Nightline functions as gatekeeper for "those who pull the levers of corporate and government power."

2693. Hunter-Gault, Charlayne. "News Blackout." New York: MacNeil/Lehrer NewsHour, Oct. 26, 1988.
Because of South African government press restrictions since 1985, US media now play down South African news in "video appeasement."

2694. "If at First You Don't Succeed . . . Cheat." BI 8.278 (Oct. 13, 1988) 4.
TV stations in Los Angeles and San Francisco falsely reported the arrival in the US of Sandinista FSLN terrorists dedicated to killing highway patrol officers.

2695. "Interview with Abbas Criticized." AG (May 7, 1986) 1A.
The State Department accused NBC of "encouraging terrorism by televising an interview" with "the suspected master mind of the Achille Lauro ship highjacking," who accused President Reagan of becoming "enemy No. 1."

2696. "Iran & the Press in Retrospect." WJR 3.4 (1981) 23-38.
Four essays on the Embassy hostages, one on the biased network coverage.

2697. Iyengar, Shanto, and Donald R. Kinder. News that Matters: Television and American Opinions. Chicago: U of Chicago P, 1987. 187.
Attempts to explain why and how TV news is "an educator virtually without peer" through experiments on the importance of agenda setting, the ability of TV news to establish among viewers a hierarchy of concerns, and the importance of "priming" (chapters 7-11), determining what comes to the citizen's mind and what does not.

2698. Iyengar, Shanto, Mark D. Peters, and Donald R. Kinder. "Experimental Demonstrations of the 'Not-So-Minimal' Consequences of Television News Programs." APSR 76.4 (1982) 848-858.
Two experiments "show that television news programs profoundly affect which problems viewers take to be important. The experiments also demonstrate that those problems prominently positioned in the evening news are accorded greater weight in viewers' evaluations of presidential performance."

2699. Jalbert, Paul. "'News Speak' About the Lebanon War." JPS 14.1 (Fall 1984) 16-35.
Analysis of television network news of the Israeli invasion of Lebanon in 1982 demonstrates a clear pro-Israeli bias in the reportage.

2700. Jalbert, Paul. "Structures of 'News Speak': U.S. Network Television Coverage of the Lebanon War, Summer 1982." Boston U, 1984. 214. DAI 45 (1984) 1563-A.
A systematic study of the ABC, NBC and CBS treatment of this invasion. The networks were clearly pro-Israeli and anti-Palestinian.

2701. Jamieson, Kathleen. Eloquence in an Electronic Age: The Transformation of Political Speechmaking. New York: Oxford UP, 1988. 301.
A book about political eloquence, especially about how TV has changed it, and the new importance of the speechwriter, the decline of training in schools, the replacing of words by images. Special attention to explaining why Ronald Reagan remained popular despite his unpopular policies.

2702. Jamieson, Kathleen, and David Birdsell. Presidential Debates: The Challenge of Creating an Informed Electorate. New York: Oxford UP, 1988. 264.
A history, critique, and set of recommendations for improving the debates. They suggest a conversational mode or a direct form of confrontation would be better than the present form of candidates answering questions from the press, and they urge the networks to provide expert commentators to immediately expose lies and evasions by the candidates.

2703. Jensen, Klaus. "News as Ideology: Economic Statistics and Political Ritual in Television Network News." JoC 37.1 (Winter 1987) 8-27.
Attempts to show "how television network news in the United States is constructed by a particular ideological vision of the U.S. economic system in which a small set of explanations [private enterprise, e.g.] is offered to account for economic developments and political interventions into the economy."

2704. Johnson, Paul. "Beware the Authenticity of News Videotapes, at Least on ABC." AG (Aug. 4, 1989) 6E.
On faked news events.

2705. Johnson, Paul. "Jessica Savitch: The Portrait's Not a Pretty One." AG (June 14, 1988) 1B, 8B.
Savitch rose to NBC anchorwoman because she understood the job was showbusiness, money, and power, and she had the ability to relate to a TV camera.

2706. Joyce, Ed. Prime Times, Bad Times. New York: Doubleday, 1988. 561.
Former president of CBS News gives his account of his rise and fall with criticism of corporations and journalists.

2707. Kaid, Lynda Lee, and Joe Foote. "How Network Television Coverage of the President and Congress Compare." JQ 62.1 (Spring 1985) 59-65.
"Availability of live coverage of House does not seem to

have led to more network coverage. President still dominates network news."

2708. Kalter, Joanmarie. "Even if It's Not Visual: Please. Risk it. Bore Me with Reality." TVG (Nov. 17, 1984) 24-25.
Important issues--e.g., hunger and other systemic, structural programs--are underreported and underexamined on TV.

2709. Kalter, Joanmarie. "The Untold Stories of Africa: Why TV is Missing Some Big Ones." TVG (May 24, 1986) 2-12.
"A look at network blind spots that keep us from understanding the true problems of a continent rich in potential."

2710. Kanter, Elliot. "Powers That Be: The NBC Documentary You Never Got to See." Ram 13 (Aug. 1974) 28, 57-60.
Pacific Gas and Electric has prevented the national showing of this "frightening" TV documentary on the dangers of nuclear reactors. Its director, Don Widener, acclaimed creator of environmental documentaries, has lost his contract for more films.

2711. Karp, Walter. "Subliminal Politics in the Evening News." Channels 2.1 (1982) 23-27, 56.
Compares network coverage of martial law in Poland.

2712. Kaye, Tony. "The 27th Soviet Party Congress As Seen on U.S. Television." Deadline 1.2 (1986) 10-11.
Sovietphobia of ABC and CBS reporting.

2713. Kelly, John. "CBS as CIA." CS 5.1 (1980-81) 3-4.
The forthcoming CBS program The CIA "is a premeditated whitewash for a CIA beleaguered by public exposure of its misdeeds" similar to the The FBI TV show.

2714. Kelly, John. "CBS Aids Pentagon Cover Up." CS 3.2 (Dec. 1976) 55-62.
On Col. Anthony Herbert, Vietnam war crimes, and 60 Minutes.

2715. Kern, Montague. "The Invasion of Afghanistan: Domestic vs. Foreign Stories." Television Coverage of the Middle East. Ed. William C. Adams. Norwood, NJ: Ablex, 1981. 106-127.
Coverage was slanted in favor of the president and against the enemies of the US; allies who disagreed with the US were "largely ignored." In addition to patriotism, commercialism influenced coverage (popularity of simple and familiar conflict values). Network TV will not allow a foreign government to challenge the president during times of crisis.

2716. Kervin, Denise. "Structure & Meaning: A Semiotic Analysis of Network Television News." U of Wisconsin, Madison, 1985. 288. DAI 47 (1986) 701-A.
News coverage of the war in El Salvador from 1977 through

ELECTRONIC MEDIA   389

1981 by all three TV networks was dominated by official views and policies.

2717. King, Larry. "Rating the Sunday Morning News Shows." TVG (Jan. 26, 1985) 6-9.
The talk shows are uniform with the same or similar officials and experts. Rarely does any show "step out of the mainstream."

2718. Kowet, Don. A Matter of Honor: General William C. Westmoreland versus CBS. New York: Macmillan, 1984. 317.
Criticizes The Uncounted Enemy: A Vietnam Deception, a film about lying by the military.

2719. Kraus, Sydney. Televised Presidential Debates and Public Policy. Hillsdale, NJ: L. Erlbaum, 1988. 184.
"The purpose of this book is to review and explore what we have learned about televised presidential debates, consider the impact of such encounters on the election process, and apply that knowledge to questions of policy." [See No. 2702.]

2720. Landau, Saul. "The ABC's of Network News." SD 1.11 (1977).
Entire issue devoted to interview of Castro by Barbara Walters.

2721. Landay, Jerry M. "The Fall of the House of Murrow." CJR 26.2 (1987) 56-58.
A review of two recent books on CBS News' descent into mediocrity, "a cumulative indictment of an uncreative management that felt it necessary and possible to distort news and information into amusement."

2722. Lang, Gladys, and Kurt Lang. Politics and Television Re-Viewed. Beverly Hills, CA: Sage, 1984. 221.
A "much changed and updated version" of the authors' Politics and Television. Eight studies intended to help explain how television creates a symbolic environment "through which people largely experience the political world": General MacArthur's homecoming from Korea, the first televised presidential debate, Watergate, and more. The distortion derives from the institutional bias of television, which is "a natural extension of the social and political Establishment to which it is tied" (200).

2723. Lang, Kurt, and Gladys Lang. Politics and Television. Chicago: Quadrangle, 1968. 315.
They "look at the ways in which television, through its presentation of events, shapes public images of political life and personalities." Case studies: MacArthur Day in Chicago, the 1952 conventions, the Kennedy-Nixon debates, etc.

2724. Lanouette, William. "The Atom and the U.S. Press." WQ

9.5 (1985) 106-7.
TV's pro-nuclear coverage, at least before Three Mile Island (1979).

2725. Larson, James. "International Affairs Coverage on US Evening Network News, 1972-1979." Television Coverage of International Affairs. Ed. William Adams. Norwood, NJ: Ablex, 1982. 15-44. See next entry.

2726. Larson, James. "International Affairs Coverage on U.S. Network Television." JoC 29.2 (1979) 136-147.
Coverage of underdeveloped nations is inadequate, crisis-oriented, and ideologically biased.

2727. Larson, James. "Television and U.S. Foreign Policy: The Case of the Iran Hostage Crisis." JoC 36.4 (Autumn 1986) 108-130.
Prior to the hostage crisis coverage of Iran reflected US policy. The hostage seizure thrust US TV into very active participation in the foreign policy process.

2728. Larson, James. Television's Window on the World: International Affairs Coverage on the U.S. Networks. Norwood, NJ: Ablex, 1984. 195.
Examines US television network news "as a frame which delineates a particular view of the world" during the early 1970s and through the early 1980s. Conclusions: network coverage of international affairs is virtually identical; crises predominate; a few nations receive most of the coverage; television is a "principal forum" for government officials; there continued to be a "strong symbiotic relationship" between reporters and officials; etc. Larson advocates structural changes "to provide a more open and inclusive view of the world."

2729. Lashner, Marilyn A. The Chilling Effect in TV News: Intimidation by the Nixon White House. New York: Praeger, 1984. 296.
Reveals how, in response to anti-media criticism from the Nixon administration, television news commentary "dampened its censure" during the Watergate period. In contrast, the print media, subject to the same anti-media assault, became even more vigorous in their commentary--the critical difference in effect being broadcasting regulated status.

2730. Lefever, Ernest W. "CBS and National Defense, 1972-73." JoC 25.4 (Autumn 1975) 181-185.
A summary of the study by The Institute for American Strategy (IAS), which accused CBS news of bias in its failure to present antagonistic viewpoints.

2731. Leonard, Bill. In the Storm of the Eye: A Lifetime at CBS. New York: Putnam's, 1987. 240.
The former CBS News president tells his version of how the organization has evolved through the years and how it is now

trading away "its aspirations and its high standards for quick fixes."

2732. Lesher, Stephan. Media Unbound: The Impact of Television Journalism on the Public. Boston: Houghton, 1982. 285.
Journalistic news errors are magnified by TV, as illustrated by the reporting of the Afghanistan war.

2733. Levine, Grace. "'Learned Helplessness' and the Evening News." JoC 27.4 (1977) 100-105.
Newscasts are seemingly designed to heighten drama and to emphasize disaster, chaos, and unpredictability.

2734. Lewis, Florence, and Peter Moss. "The Tyranny of Language." "Nineteen Eighty-Four" in 1984: Autonomy, Control and Communication. Ed. Paul Chilton and Crispin Aubrey. London: Comedia, 1983. 45-57.
Summarizes how the media control "some of the ways in which we think about and assess the world" (47), how media downplay events which derogate national leaders and institutions, and how television resembles Orwell's telescreen in his novel 1984.

2735. Lichter, S. Robert. "America and the Third World: A Survey of Leading Media and Business Leaders." Television Coverage of International Affairs. Ed. William Adams. Norwood, NJ: Ablex, 1982. 67-78.
Businessmen are "considerably less likely to criticize" American policies and practices toward the Third World than are journalists (70).

2736. Lichter, S. Robert. "Media Support for Israel: A Survey of Leading Journalists." Television Coverage of the Middle East. Ed. William Adams. Norwood, NJ: Ablex, 1981. 40-52.
"Pro-Israeli sentiment within the media elite appears to extend well beyond the levels of support for Israel found among the general public" but this does not prove bias in reporting.

2737. Lindsay, John. "TV's Faltering Vision." IREJ 12.4 (Fall 1989) 12.
On TV's "trend toward more entertainment and briefer reporting" of news.

2738. Linsky, Martin, ed. Television and the Presidential Elections: Self-Interest and the Public Interest. Lexington, MA: Lexington, 1983. 137.
Account of a series of forums involving network executives and academics at the Institute of Politics at Harvard's John F. Kennedy School of Government, dealing with a wide range of issues: presidential debates, conventions, networks as candidate makers, managers managing the media, etc. [See II.B.5.]

2739. Lofton, John. "The News Media Shun Debate." SLJR 15.96 (May 1987) 14.

"What we get from the major news media is an imposed political dogma in the sense that opinion varying widely from the establishment line is largely ignored by the major media, especially by the commercial TV networks, from which most people now get their information on public affairs."

2740. Lower, Elmer. "Needed: An Hour of Network News Every Night." TVG (Mar. 15, 1980) 36-40.
"It is not debatable that a well-informed electorate is the linchpin" of democracy, and TV news "plays the leading role in keeping citizens informed" or misinformed.

2741. Lyford, Joseph. "The Pacification of the Press." TQ 10.3 (1973) 15-22.
Government determines or guides the news.

2742. Lyman, Francesca. "Introduction." Green Gems, 1986. 4-6.
Green Gems is a guide to the best films, videotapes, and slide shows on environmental and energy issues, produced by Environmental Action of Washington, D.C., and New York's Media Network.

2743. MacDonald, J. Fred. "Cold War Politics in News and Information Programming." Television and the Red Menace. New York: Praeger, 1985. 13-100.
This study "of the nonfiction programming from the late 1940s and into the 1960s clearly illustrates that video road to the Vietnam War was paved in part by the distorted understanding of the nation and world transmitted by nonfiction television" (14).

2744. MacDonald, J. Fred. "From Cold War to Hot War: The Video Road to Vietnam." Television and the Red Menace. New York: Praeger, 1985. 147-221.
J. F. Kennedy used television and anticommunism to build his popular image. From 1960 until his death he brought "his determination to fight" Communism in South Vietnam to the public via TV. Thus TV participated, though not conspiratorially, in "brainwashing" the public to accept the war. When Johnson succeeded Kennedy and escalated the war, TV "was crucial in persuading" the public to accept "protracted, undeclared war" (212).

2745. MacNeil, Robert. The Right Place at the Right Time. Thorndike, ME: Thorndike P, 1982. 352.
An insider's look at TV journalism by the co-anchor of PBS' MacNeil/Lehrer News Hour. Scattered comments about control: NBC sanitized the Vietnam War by censoring atrocious scenes (cutting off ears of Vietcong); an account of Nixon's assault on the independence of PBS; etc.

2746. Madsen, Axel. 60 Minutes: The Power & the Politics of America's Most Popular TV News Show. New York: Dodd, Mead, 1984. 255.

Studies the ethics and techniques of "one of the most influential and controversial programs" on TV. 60 Minutes is both the "most informative" and "most entertaining prime time information show on the air," but it typically concentrates upon individual or petty events or problems undirected at the system behind the symptoms.

2747. Manheim, Jarol B. "Can Democracy Survive Television?" JoC 26.2 (Spring 1976) 84-90.
The low level of psychological involvement required to learn political information from television and the non-intellectual content of political discourse on TV discourage active participation in the political process.

2748. Manoff, Robert Karl. "The Bipartisanship Boomlet: Reporters Covering the Government All Too Often Succumb to the Urge to Run It." Deadline 4.2 (Mar.-Apr. 1989) 7-9.
Analyzes the predominantly "statist" journalism ("operates within parameters largely established . . . by the state") predominating in the US. "Vibrant journalism cannot exist with national security managerialism," nor can "democratic politics." Gives five "managerial rules."

2749. Manoff, Robert Karl. "The 'Nightline' Line." Prog 50.12 (1986) 41.
In interviews on NBC's Nightline, Ted Koppel relentlessly interrogates ordinary guests, but takes on a tone of deference when US officials or leaders of friendly governments appear.

2750. Marton, Kati. The Polk Conspiracy: Murder and Cover-Up in the Case of CBS News Correspondent George Polk. New York: Farrar, Straus & Giroux, 1990. 369.
Polk was murdered in 1948 in Greece, perhaps the first casualty of the Cold War, because of his independent coverage of Greece's civil war. The affair was covered up by Greek and US officials, and CBS itself failed to investigate adequately.

2751. Mashat, Soraya. "A Rhetorical Analysis of the Image of Saudi Women in Two Specific Cross-Cultural Media Messages." Pennsylvania State U, 1985. 195. DAI 46 (1985) 1431-A.
"Death of a Princess" (PBS) and "Saudi Women Behind the Veil" (ABC) reveal stereotyping and misrepresentation.

2752. Massing, Michael. "Blackout in Television." CJR 21.4 (1982) 38-44.
"Despite minority group gains, power in TV news is still a white monopoly" with no pressure to change.

2753. Massing, Michael. "CBS: Sauterizing the News." CJR 24.6 (Mar.-Apr. 1986) 27-37.
The new CBS News president Van Gordon Sauter is stressing soft news. "CBS often seemed like a network version of local television."

2754. Massing, Michael. "Ted Koppel's Neutrality Act." CJR 27.6 (Mar.-Apr. 1989) 30-34.
Exposes the ideological conservatism and narrowness of Nightline with its guestlist of "political clones."

2755. Matthews, Christopher. "Boss Tube." NR 193.25 (Dec. 16, 1985) 14-16.
The TV news networks "have absorbed many of the democratic functions traditionally held by political parties."

2756. Matusow, Barbara. "Sunday Best: The Race to Beat ABC's David Brinkley." WJR 7.6 (1985) 23-37.
Sunday morning TV news shows are useful to politicians and officials.

2757. McAnany, Emile. "Television and Crisis: Ten Years of Network News Coverage of Central America, 1972-1981." MCS 5 (1983) 199-212.
News about Central America is stereotyped and biased in favor of government views, rarely presenting dissident or rebel perspectives.

2758. McCabe, Peter. Bad News at Black Rock: The Sell-Out of CBS News. New York: Arbor House, 1987. 302.
A former producer of the CBS Morning News tells of the politics and in-fighting involved in the operation of a network news show.

2759. McCabe, Peter. "The Sellout of CBS News." Playboy 34.4 (Apr. 1987) 64-66, 76, 161-166.
"An insider's account of how Phyllis George and troupe of dancing TV execs turned morning journalism [CBS Morning News] into breakfast mush."

2760. McNulty, Thomas. "Network Television Documentary Treatment of the Vietnam War, 1965 to 1969." Indiana U, 1974. DAI 35 (1974) 2210.
Explains how ABC and CBS treatment of the war gradually became less dependent upon the US government.

2761. McNulty, Thomas. "Vietnam Specials: Policy and Content." JoC 25.4 (1975) 173-180.
A description of CBS programming on Vietnam 1965-1969. [Although McNulty refers to the socialization of correspondents who learn acceptable bounds of reporting, he does not consider it censorship.]

2762. Meyer, Karl E. "Cover-up at ABC." SR 5.1 (Feb. 4, 1978) 46.
Difficulties the author experienced over getting a response to a complaint he made to an ABC affiliate. He is filing a formal complaint with the National News Council.

2763. Meyer, Karl E. "Skimming the Surface of Political Spectacle." SR 3.19 (June 26, 1976) 52-53.

ELECTRONIC MEDIA

TV lacks detailed, independent analysis of substantive issues.

2764. Mickiewicz, Ellen. "Soviet and American Television: A Comparison of News Coverage." NmR 39 (1985) 7-11.
SU's Vremya (Time) devotes much more time to the US than ABC World News Tonight devotes to the SU.

2765. Millman, Joel. "The Managua Twist." CJR 23.2 (1984) 9-10.
False reporting of Nicaragua by ABC World News Tonight.

2766. Minow, Newton N., John B. Martin, and Lee M. Mitchell. "The President and the Air Waves." TQ 11.1 (1973) 59-70.
The authors take the position that the equal time law and the fairness and political party doctrines "do not meet the problems" created by presidential monopoly of television.

2767. Morales, Waltraud. "Revolutions, Earthquakes and Latin America: The Networks Look at Allende's Chile and Somoza's Nicaragua." Television Coverage of International Affairs. Ed. William Adams. Norwood, NJ: Ablex, 1982. 79-116.
Coverage of Latin America is generally nationalistic, ethnocentric, and crisis-ridden, but mainly those countries are ignored or seldom reported.

2768. Morgan, Edward P. "Who Forgot Radio?" Problems and Controversies in Television and Radio. Ed. Harry Skornia and Jack Kitson. Palo Alto: Pacific, 1968. 117-126.
Condemns the commercialization of the media "with its endless commercials and idiotic entertainment" and appeals for information and "intelligent controversy."

2769. Morse, Margaret. "The Television News Personality and Credibility." Studies in Entertainment. Ed. Tania Modleski. Bloomington: Indiana UP, 1986. 55-79.
Examines appearance of TV network news anchor as engaged in dialogue and subjective journalism.

2770. Nelson, Joyce. "TV News: A Structure of Reassurance." The Perfect Machine: TV in the Nuclear Age. Toronto: Between the Lines, 1978. 98-104.
Adrift in a sea of information without historical context, "we are meant to find reassurance" in "the institution that sees and frames all others" (104).

2771. Nessen, Ron. "The Washington You Can't See On Television." TVG (Sept. 20, 1980) 9-12.
Numerous events occur in government never shown or mentioned by TV but which are as important as those that are.

2772. "Nightline Shoots Down Objectivity." Extra! 2.1 (July-

Aug. 1988) 7.
Contrasts Koppel's handling of the shooting down of the KAL 007 by the Soviets and the shooting down of Iran Air 655 by the US.

2773. Nigut, Bill, Sr. "A War Both Sides Deserved to Lose." CMC (Sept.-Oct. 1990) 1-8.
The media have not enabled the public to deliberate regarding troops to Saudi Arabia, but have mainly transmitted the Bush administration's propaganda.

2774. Nimmo, Dan, and James E. Combs. "'The Horror Tonight': Network Television News and Three Mile Island." JoB 25 (1981) 289-293.
"A content analysis of television network news coverage of the accident at the nuclear plant at Three Mile Island in 1979 reveals contrasting reporting styles of both anchors and correspondents."

2775. Nimmo, Dan, and James E. Combs. "What's Happening? TV News Reports the Unexpected." Mediated Political Realities. New York and London: Longman, 1983. 23-47.
The inadequacies of TV news. "Television news is an acquaintance medium not a source of knowledge. The headline service that is nightly network news calls things to viewers' attention and tells a neatly packaged tale about them" (45).

2776. Nimmo, Dan, and James E. Combs. Nightly Horrors: Crisis Coverage by Television Network News. Knoxville, TN: U of Tennessee P, 1985. 216.
Explains the production of crisis news from definition and selection to the diverse rhetorical framing of "vision" by the three networks.

2777. Nix, Mindy. "Meet the Press Game." MORE 3.2 (1973) 12-14.
The networks' Sunday interview programs mainly serve the corporate state.

2778. "Nuclear Broadcasting Company?" Extra! 1.1 (June 1987) 5.
On NBC News documentary "Nuclear Power: In France It Works" that "could have passed for a lengthy nuclear power commercial." No mention that NBC's owner, GE is the US's second largest nuclear power salesman.

2779. O'Connor, John. "Grunts and Groans." CJR 21.1 (May-June 1982) 62-63.
Review of Teague's Live and Off-Color: News Biz, which decries "triviality, banality, and gimmicky." Teague would remove newscasts from the traditional ratings system in order to distance them from sponsor control, but the reviewer considers this remedy hopeless, given the profits involved in ratings for advertising.

ELECTRONIC MEDIA

2780. Ohmann, Richard. "TV and the Sterilization of Politics." Politics of Letters. Middletown, CT: Wesleyan UP, 1987. 171-186.
This news-commercial format is part of the "mind industry" system of control that sells not only products but the existing order.

2781. Onwochei, Gil. "U.S. Television Coverage of Africa: Geopolitical, Economic, and Strategic Policy Implications." U of Oklahoma, 1987. 255. DAI 48 (1988) 2755-A.
US television coverage from 1970 to 1985 was "significantly in priority agreement with U.S. government foreign policy toward these countries," especially regarding a country's strategic minerals and location. [See Haile].

2782. Oppenheimer, Jerry. Barbara Walters: An Unauthorized Biography. New York: St. Martin's, 1990. 352.
Analyzes TV's famous celebrity interviewer, friend to ex-McCarthy aide Roy Cohn, Henry Kissinger, and Richard Nixon, a person who wants to be remembered as a journalist but who also seeks powerful friends, and will probably be remembered as part of the turn of broadcast news toward celebrity.

2783. Orenstein, Peggy. "Women on the Verge of a Nervy Breakthrough." MJ 14.5 (June 1989) 28-31, 46.
Four of TV's top female journalists comment on how far women have progressed in the medium and the inequities that still exist, including a double standard of physical beauty, continuing disparities in pay, and the scarcity of women in foreign correspondent positions.

2784. Ornstein, Norman, and Michael Robinson. "The Case of Our Disappearing Congress." TVG (Jan. 11, 1986) 4-10.
Network evening news paid little attention to Congress in 1985.

2785. Packwood, Senator Bob. "Protecting First Amendment Freedoms in the Age of the Electronic Revolution." TQ 20.4 (1984) 51-55.
Advocates repeal of the "Fairness Doctrine."

2786. Paletz, David, et al. "Terrorism on TV News: The IRA, the FALN, and the Red Brigades." Television Coverage of International Affairs. Ed. William Adams. Norwood, NJ: Ablex, 1982. 143-165.
Right-wing terror is seldom shown and the justice of terrorist aims seldom considered.

2787. Paraschos, Manny, and Bill Rutherford. "Network News Coverage of Invasion of Lebanon by Israel in 1982." JQ 62 (1985) 457-464.
Reporters on the three major networks, although predominantly neutral, made nearly 5 times as many negative as they did positive statements regarding Israel. In contrast, they made

half as many positive as negative statements about the PLO.

2788. Parenti, Michael. "Pack Pluralism." LOOT 1.5 (May 1990) 15.
Public affairs programming on TV for January 20, 1990, offered many voices but little political diversity.

2789. Patterson, Oscar. "An Analysis of Television Coverage of the Vietnam War." JoB 28.4 (1984) 397-404.
Nightly news was not filled with horrible pictures of destruction.

2790. Patterson, Thomas E., and Robert D. McClure. The Unseeing Eye: The Myth of Television Power in National Politics. New York: Putnam, 1976. 218.
Studies the TV commercials of the Nixon-McGovern contest of 1972 and the three nightly network news programs. Questions the effectiveness of TV in affecting elections. [See II.B.5.]

2791. Patterson, Tim. "Eyewitless News: An Amusing Aid to Digestion." JC 20 (May 1979) 30.
Bemoans the new formula of local news programs: investigative journalism and thoughtful commentary are being discarded in favor of photogenic anchors, happy talk, and action footage in a nationwide quest for higher ratings.

2792. Payne, Les. "For 20 Minutes, Apartheid Vanished." C&C 45 (Feb. 4, 1985) 40-44.
Examines a misleading 60 Minutes segment about South Africa.

2793. Pollock, Richard. "The Nuclear Industry . . . Silencing the Media." CMJ 3.10 (1978) 3, 10.
Nuclear industry efforts to censor investigative documentaries.

2794. Postman, Neil. "Television News Narcosis." Na 230.8 (Mar. 1, 1980) 245-46.
"All events on TV come completely devoid of historical continuity or any other context, and in such fragmented and rapid succession [softened by music and displaced by ads] that they wash over our minds in an undifferentiated stream."

2795. Powe, Lucas, Jr. American Broadcasting and the First Amendment. Berkeley: U of California P, 1987. 295.
Evaluates the safeguards imposed by the Communications Act to prevent abuses by the Federal Communications Commission. These safeguards have failed, "abuses have occurred with unfortunate frequency" and "have existed almost since the beginning," an "inevitable by-product of the decision to license and to supervise the licensees."

2796. Powers, Ron. The Newscasters: The News Business as Show Business. New York: St. Martin's, 1977. 243.
"By the 1970s, an extravagant proportion of television news --local news in particular--answered less to the description

ELECTRONIC MEDIA

of 'journalism' than to that of 'show business'" (1). "Instead of striving to impart information to the viewers, the salesmen-managers of television stations were engaged in a tacit conspiracy to extract information from the viewers" in order to "maximize audience size and thereby profits" (2). And newspapers followed (3).

2797. Powers, Ron. "Nonstop News Is Here." *TVG* (Aug. 16, 1980) 8-12.
Some praise for the pioneering efforts of the Cable News Network, at least "by existing TV-news standards," but CNN is missing "an historic change to open up new vistas" especially in reporting context, "of what is vital and why."

2798. Powers, Ron. "Where Have The News Analysts Gone?" *TVG* (Oct. 4, 1980) 4-10.
News commentary at the networks "is almost nonexistent."

2799. Prescott, Peter. "The Small Picture." *MORE* 2.11 (1972) 1, 13-17.
On one week of the Nixon-McGovern race. "Network news, this week" gave us "for the most part a week's worth of muddled newscasting." [See II.B.5.]

2800. "Print Media Protect Rather: Biased Afghan Coverage at CBS." *Extra!* 3.1 (Oct.-Nov. 1989) 1, 11.
CBS News' advocacy of the Afghan mujahideen in the guise of news has created a scandal which is not being reported adequately by other media.

2801. *Proceeding Against Frank Stanton & the Columbia Broadcasting System, Inc.: Report.* 92nd Cong., 1st Sess. Washington, DC: GPO, 1971. 272.
CBS refused to release materials relating to its documentary, "The Selling of the Pentagon."

2802. "A Program-by-Program Guide to TV's Political Spectrum." *Extra!* 3.6 (July-Aug. 1990) 8-10.
Explains the conservative bias of TV's political analysis shows.

2803. Ranney, Austin. *Channels of Power: The Impact of Television on American Politics.* New York: Basic, 1983. 207.
Focuses on network of news, benefits and limitations, and future.

2804. Rapping, Elayne. "Knee Deep in the Big Muddy." *JC* 30 (Mar. 1985) 17-18.
Review of the "serious flaws" in Todd Gitlin's *Inside Prime Time*. What Gitlin conveyed in his earlier *The Whole World Is Watching* about the hegemonic functions of media in liberal capitalist societies "is all but forgotten or denied here."

2805. Riordan, Teresa. "Beam Me Up, Scotty: I Wanna Be on

the Six O'Clock News." CC 12.4 (1987) 13-15.
Increasingly, incumbent legislators are sending satellite press releases (SPRs) that show them "in action" to home state television stations.

2806. Robins, J. Max. "Too Close For Comfort." Channels 9.4 (Mar. 1989) 24.
Miami TV station SPLG's Eye on Crime is symptomatic of a recent trend toward "policeocentric" news coverage of crime, raising questions as to whether or not the participating journalists' objectivity and integrity are being compromised.

2807. Robinson, John, Mark Levy, et al. The Main Source: Learning from Television News. Beverly Hills, CA: Sage, 1986. 272.
Questions the belief that TV is the main source of news in the US. Demonstrates that informationally TV is not the best source: e.g., news items are presented "in such a short, fleeting, or nonredundant manner that the items make less impression on the audience's memory than having encountered the same information in the print media."

2808. Robinson, Michael. "Future Television News Research: Beyond Edward Jay Epstein." Television Network News: Issues in Content Research. Ed. William Adams and Fay Schreibman. Washington, DC: School of Public and International Affairs, George Washington U, 1978. 197-211.
Presents models of network news other than Epstein's in News from Nowhere, which leads to a consideration of new approaches to using the Vanderbilt Television News Archive.

2809. Robinson, Michael, and Maura Claney. "Network News, 15 Years After Agnew." Channels 4 (Jan.-Feb. 1985) 34-35, 38-39.
Network news has no liberal bias.

2810. Roeh, Itzhak. "Israel in Lebanon: Language and Images of Storytelling." Television Coverage of the Middle East. Ed. William C. Adams. Norwood, NJ: Ablex, 1981. 76-88.
TV coverage of Israel's invasion of southern Lebanon in the summer of 1979 was generally structured on a narrative of "aggressors versus victims."

2811. Rose, Tom. Feeding the Whales: How the Media Created the World's Greatest Non-Event. Ed. Hillel Black. New York: Birch Lane, 1989. 252.
Instead of investigating the scandals at the Department of Housing and Urban Development or some other significant problem, the networks invested a massive effort in reporting on three whales trapped under the polar ice pack in 1988. TV is more interested in pictures than in issues.

2812. Rothmyer, Karen. "Westmoreland v. CBS." CJR 24.1

(1985) 25-30.
Concerns the charge by Westmoreland that CBS libeled him.

2813. Rubin, Barry. Paved with Good Intentions. New York: Penguin, 1981. 426.
Appendix A, "The Role of the Media," discusses the shortcomings of media coverage of Iran prior to, during and following the revolution and urges "more specialization by reporters, along with basic reading and research regarding the countries and regions they are likely to cover" (363).

2814. Rubin, David. "ABC's Walter Rodgers: Maverick in Moscow." Deadline 2.2 (1987) 1-2, 11.
To a great extent news from Moscow on ABC consists of the cold warrior viewpoint of correspondent Walter Rodgers.

2815. Rubin, David. "Television Signs An INF Pact." Deadline 2.4 (Nov.-Dec. 1987) 10-11.
The Reagan administration's announcement of the decision to remove medium- and short-range weapons from Europe was framed in "the best possible light for the administration."

2816. Rutkus, Denis S. "Presidential Television." JoC 26.2 (Spring 1976) 73-78.
Assuming that independent journalists should be able to judge the importance of events and what is "news," the author questions the independent judgment of television networks who routinely grant live air time to Presidents on request and thereby allow the chief executive to determine what gets coverage.

2817. Saldich, Anne. "Access to Television's Past." CJR 15.4 (Nov.-Dec. 1976) 46-49.
Although "access to records is the lifeblood of accountability," network news organizations resist opening their records to study. The Television News Archive at Vanderbilt U challenges their secrecy.

2818. Saldich, Anne. Electronic Democracy: Television's Impact on the American Political Process. New York: Praeger, 1979. 122.
TV is a powerful negative force in politics as an instrument of government public relations, as gatekeeper of issues discussed and thought about, causing campaigns to be prohibitively expensive, personalizing power and undermining other political institutions, and helping to create a vast passive, ill-informed audience, etc. But TV also democratizes by depicting mass protests.

2819. Saldich, Anne. "Video Invasion: Afghanistan, 1979-1983." When Information Counts: Grading the Media. Ed. Bernard Rubin. Lexington, MA: Lexington/Heath, 1985. 185-97.
The networks "did a creditable job of putting events [of the Soviet invasion] in their social and political context,"

because they had been expelled a month after the invasion, forcing the networks to produce often balanced micro- and mini-documentaries instead of merely Sovietphobic action pictures. And sources of the films were better identified than in the past.

2820. Salisbury, Harrison. "What's Missing from TV's Reports on the Soviets." TVG (July 10, 1982) 2-6.
Criticism of US media coverage of the SU.

2821. Sanders, Marlene, and Sandra Rock. Waiting for Prime Time: The Women of Television News. Urbana: U of Illinois P, 1988. 214.
Chronicles the struggle of women to gain legitimacy and recognition in the male-dominated world of network news.

2822. Sarnoff, Robert W. "Must We Accept Government Intimidation?" TQ 10.4 (1973) 71-75.
Sarnoff urges television networks to take a stand against governmental interference.

2823. Schieffer, Bob and Gary Gates. The Acting President: Ronald Reagan & the Men Who Helped Him Create the Illusion That Held America Spellbound. New York: Dutton, 1989. 397.
Reagan gave his best performance as president, seeing himself and acting as a star, surrounded by aides who wrote the script and set the scenes. The influence of TV on political campaigns as seen through the packaging of Reagan for TV is the central part of the book. [See II.B.5.]

2824. Schneiders, Greg. "The 90-Second Handicap: Why Tv Coverage of Legislation Falls Short." WJR 7.6 (1985) 44-46.
Network TV coverage of Congress has decreased sharply during the past ten years.

2825. "Schorr Assails TV's Show Business News." AG (Mar. 4, 1976) 12A.
Daniel Schorr describes TV news as a "visual entertainment medium."

2826. Schorr, Daniel. Clearing the Air. New York: Berkeley, 1978. 367.
Essays on "central conflicts involving government, the news media, and society," spanning his twenty-three year career at CBS and showing the pernicious influence of government and its officials on broadcast journalism.

2827. Schorr, Daniel. "The Establishment Press." CM 12.4 (1979) 2-8.
Recounts the author's battles with the CBS hierarchy, explaining how network contractual clauses tend to squelch free expression.

2828. Schorr, Daniel. "Harvest of Sham." Channels 5.6 (1986) 57-59.
A critique of docudramas.

2829. Schorr, Daniel. "Where Have All the Leaders Gone?" M&V 44 (Summer-Fall 1988) 2-4.
Television news coverage rewards blandly charismatic candidates who mold themselves for the occasion and discourages true leadership.

2830. Schrag, Peter. "The Powers That Be." MORE 6.1 (1976) 26, 28.
On Don Widener's struggles with PG&E and network TV.

2831. Selig, Michael. "Conflict and Contradiction in the Mass Media." JC 30 (Mar. 1985) 19-20.
Describes the dilution of a film on nuclear power.

2832. Shaheen, Jack. "Images of Saudis and Palestinians: A Review of Major Documentaries." Television Coverage of the Middle East. Ed. William Adams. Norwood, NJ: Ablex, 1981. 89-105.
The Middle East is often caricatured by Hollywood and primetime TV, but some documentaries have provided more accurate and comprehensive portrayals of Arab nations (CBS's The Saudi's and The Palestinians, ABC's Terror in the Promised Land).

2833. Sims, Ward. "Covering the Opening of the Pipeline." MJR 21 (1978-79) 21-24.
Difficulties experienced by this reporter in reporting the trans-Alaska oil pipeline operation in the summer of 1977 because of secrecy by the Alyeska Pipeline Service co., the builder of the line.

2834. Singer, Benjamin. "Violence, Protest and War in Television News: The U.S. and Canada Compared." POQ 34.4 (1970-71) 611-616.
US coverage contains more aggression than Canadian programs.

2835. Skornia, Harry. Television and the News: A Critical Appraisal. Palo Alto: Pacific, 1968. 232.
"Instead of the open market place of ideas, broadcasting has too often become a controlled arena in which only certain kinds of problems are presented under the spotlight of public attention. Indeed there is some evidence that the proprietors of the electronic media and their corporate friends and sponsors, whenever possible, would prefer to present facts that will not adversely disturb their status quo--those facts which they find it profitable to present."

2836. Smith, Fred Leslie. "CBS Reports: The Selling of the Pentagon." Mass News. Ed. David Leroy and Christopher Sterling. Englewood Cliffs, NJ: Prentice, 1973. 200-210.

On the controversy over CBS Reports' The Selling of the Pentagon.

2837. Smith, Fred Leslie. "The Selling of the First Amendment: An Analysis of Congressional Investigation of Four CBS Television Documentary Projects." Florida SU, 1972. DAI 33 (1972) 2964-A.
Attempts by Congress to censor one network.

2838. Smith, Henry. "An Analysis of Network Evening News Coverage of Religion and Politics in the 1984 Presidential Campaign." Ohio SU, 1987. 313. DAI 48 (1987) 1048-A.
Use of content dramatistic analysis discloses a pattern of black-white dichotomies, polarized viewpoints, and actions rather than analysis. Ronald Reagan was portrayed as the "Keeper of the Faith," Walter Mondale as the "Ineffectual General," in a general metaphorical structure of "Holy War Games." [See II.B.5.]

2839. Smith, Myron, Jr., comp. "The Selling of the Pentagon." U.S. Television Network News. Jefferson, NC: McFarland, 1984. 32-35.
Twenty-eight items on the CBS program based upon Fulbright's The Pentagon Propaganda Machine.

2840. Smith, Norma. "Mystery MiGs Fly into the U.S. Press." NicP 10 (Spring-Summer 1985) 18-20.
Reagan's lies about Nicaragua were reported uncritically by the media.

2841. Smith, Robert. "Mythic Elements in Television News." JoC 29.1 (1979) 75-82.
A view of television as a structuring agent emphasizing certain kinds of narratives, with government investigations providing the single largest subject, government officials the most frequent actors, "man decides" the most common narrative sequence, and helplessness or injustice the most recurrent themes.

2842. Smith, Stephen, and Cherri Roden. "CBS, 'The New York Times,' and Reconstructed Political Reality." SSCJ 53.2 (Winter 1988) 140-158.
A CBS affiliate (owned by The New York Times Company) revealed significant bias in favor of the 1984 Republican ticket of Ronald Reagan and George Bush. [See II.B.5.]

2843. "Sorry, Pat, Sorry, Ron." CJR 25.1 (1986) 23.
Reagan administration pressure on ABC News to eliminate certain kinds of criticism of the administration.

2844. Sperber, A. M. Murrow: His Life and Times. New York: Bantam, 1987 (Freundlich, 1986). 795.
Biography of US's foremost broadcast journalist after WWII. His radio and TV work for CBS, especially his TV documentaries

See It Now set the standard. His confrontation with Senator Joseph McCarthy helped bring him down. The opening Prologue focuses upon his speech on Oct. 15, 1958, to the Radio-Television News Directors Association in Chicago which attacked broadcasting as "a money-making machine" at the expense of quality, programs "being used to distract, delude, amuse and insulate us." For this speech he was soon expelled from CBS.

2845. Stam, Robert. "Television News and Its Spectator." Regarding Television. Ed. E. Ann Kaplan. Frederick, MD: U Publications of America, 1983. 23-43.
Offers several reasons why people watch TV news: narcissism, newscasters as stars, news as stories, a construction equipped with "reality-effects," cinematic methods, music, predictability, etc.

2846. Stanley, R. H. "Television News: Format as a Form of Censorship." ETC 35 (Winter 1978) 433-441.
For profits TV emphasizes visual entertainment. "As a result, most television news reporting does little, if anything, to develop our potential to analyze, think independently, or learn from grasping overall social patterns in the unfolding of events."

2847. "The Statesman from NBC News." CJR 16.6 (1978) 23.
NBC's documentary special "Henry Kissinger: On the Record" concealed the fact that Kissinger was an employee of NBC News.

2848. Stein, Robert. "Telling It Like It Is." TQ 10.2 (1973) 48-52.
On the dependence of TV news on official sources, and other government pressures.

2849. Stevenson, R. L., et al. "Untwisting The News Twisters: A Replication of Efron's Study." JQ 50.2 (Summer 1973) 211-219.
A reply to Edith Efron's analysis of TV network coverage of the 1968 presidential election, which claimed massive prejudice against Richard Nixon. "Analysis of CBS coverage of the 1968 campaign finds coverage of each candidate was positive and sees no advantage for any one presidential candidate."

2850. Stone, I. F. "What Rusk Did Not Say About that Dominican 'Constitutional Controversy.'" IFSW 13.22 (June 7, 1965) 2.
"Secretary Rusk was his most specious on Meet the Press May 30," and "none of the reporters on the panel effectively challenged him."

2851. "Study Aftermath: Fair Debates MacNeil/Lehrer." Extra! 3.5 (May-June 1990) 14-15.
Further discussion of the MacNeil/Lehrer's ideologically narrow, white, male dominated, government-oriented, conservative Newshour.

2852. Subpenaed Material RE Certain TV News Documentary Programs, Committee on Interstate and Foreign Commerce, HR, 92nd Cong., First Session. Washington, DC. 373.
On efforts to censor CBS and NBC.

2853. Swerdlow, Joel. "The Decline of the Boys On the Bus." WJR 3.1 (1981) 15-19.
TV neglects the significant issues of political campaigns.

2854. Szulc, Tad. "Isn't Latin America Important Too?" TVG (Sept. 29, 1979) 37-38.
More complaint about inadequate coverage of Latin America.

2855. Talmey, Paul. "What Is Denver Watching?" UM 2.7 (Mar. 1972) 5-12.
TV news in Denver is "superficial": "Some stories are ignored completely, and others are covered inadequately or inaccurately."

2856. Teague, Bob. Live and Off-Color: News Biz. New York: A & W, 1982. 239.
An "indictment of network and local TV news" because "hard news is becoming more 'infotainment.'" The "news biz" is being turned into "show biz for higher ratings" for higher profits.

2857. "Television News and Objectivity." Readings in Mass Communication: Concepts and Issues in the Mass Media. Ed. Michael C. Emery and Ted Curtis Smythe. Dubuque, IA: Wm. C. Brown, 1974. 440-495.
Six essays on selection, bias, production, etc.

2858. Television News Resources: A Guide to Collections. Washington, DC: Television News Study Center, George Washington University Library, n.d. 19.
Offers finding aids to TV news and documentary programs, collections (Vanderbilt TV News Archive, National Archives, Library of Congress, House Broadcast System), archives, local news, information organizations.

2859. Townley, Rod. "The Wars TV Doesn't Show You--And Why." TVG (Aug. 18, 1984) 3-5.
Most armed conflicts remain invisible.

2860. Truse, Kenneth. "The Children Are Dying--But, First, Here's a Commercial." TQ 11.1 (1973) 53-57.
Commercials dissipate impact of documentaries.

2861. Tuchman, Gaye. "The Technology of Objectivity: Doing 'Objective' Television News." Urban Life and Culture 2 (1973) 3-26.
Reconstructs TV newsmen's "theory of cinematic objectivity" by cataloging conventional techniques "through which a filmed story may appear to be objective to newsmen."

2862. Turow, Joseph, and Lisa Coe. "Curing Television's Ills: The Portrayal of Health Care." JoC 35.4 (1985) 36-51.
At a time when medical policy must address long-term chronic illnesses as opposed to short-term acute illnesses, TV heavily emphasizes acute illnesses which cure easily with drugs and machines.

2863. "TV Journalism--Air-Wave Pollution." PoV 2.14 (Feb. 2-7, 1970) n.p.
Because of self-censorship for profit and exclusion of the ordinary citizen, "free press" means that "the same old institutions and their representatives are allowed to peddle the same old meaningless propaganda." (By Roldo Bartimole.)

2864. U.S. Commission on Civil Rights. "Women and Minorities in Network News." Issues and Trends in Afro-American Journalism. Ed. James Tinney and Justine Rector. Washington, DC: UP of America, 1980. 289-304.
Minorities and women "were considered to be neither significant nor important" by network news, which "suggests to the nation that minorities and women may not matter" (304).

2865. "U.S. Media Distort Relocation Story." NicP 11 (Fall 1985) 16-17.
More disclosure of network Reaganite bias against the Sandinistas.

2866. Varis, Tapio. "Patterns of Television Program Flow in International Relations." Communication and Domination: Essays to Honor Herbert I. Schiller. Norwood, NJ: Ablex, 1986. 55-65.
"The author examines the international exchange pattern of TV program materials, using the same methods applied 10 years ago in his 1973 study, 'Television Traffic--A One-Way Street?' The main conclusion is as interesting as it is depressing. There has been no structural change in the last 10 years in the global trends of a one-sided information flow, especially in the field of entertainment shows" (54).

2867. "Viewers Protest TV Talkshow Line-Up." Extra! 2.3 (Nov.-Dec. 1988) 2.
The talkshows are shifting further to the right.

2868. Vidal, Gore. "Cue The Green God, Ted." Na 249.5 (Aug. 7-14, 1989) 1, 170-174.
Because of our corporate power, anti-communism, and militarism, we have "no opposition media." "The corporate grip on opinion in the United States is one of the wonders of the Western world," and the "principal dispenser of the national religion is Ted Koppel."

2869. Wafai, Mohamed. "Political Behavior, Legitimation, & Social Control: U.S. Senators, the Mideast, & TV News." U of Minnesota, 1983. 237. DAI 44.9 (Mar. 1984) 2615-A.

Legitimation is "a social control mechanism" to "maintain the political system." Legitimate (conventional) issues combined with a legitimate spokesman (e.g., a powerful Senator) enforces the status quo. Conventional issues are reported more than unconventional. The author reads the NYT motto, "all the news that's fit to print," as news that supports established power.

2870. Walsh, Mary Williams. "Mission: Afghanistan." CJR 28.5 (Jan.-Feb. 1990) 27-36.
The story of CBS contract reporter, Kurt Lohbeck, who was also "a partisan of the mujahideen and of one guerilla leader in particular, Abdul Haq, for whom he served in effect as a publicist."

2871. Warrior, Robert. "NBC's Wounded Knee: Media Ignores Organizing in American Indian Communities." Soj 19.2 (Feb.-Mar. 1990) 30-31.
Indicts the NBC Nightly News report "Tragedy at Pine Ridge" for its negative image of the Lakota people in South Dakota.

2872. Weaver, Paul. "Is Television News Biased?" Pub I 26 (Winter 1972) 57-74.
TV news is biased because of the limitations of its themes and forms. The remedy is "an enlargement of the journalistic imagination."

2873. Webb, Joseph. "The SLA, NBC, and the FCC." RSCJ 12 (Sept. 1974) 5.
Account of the author's frustrating attempts to reply to a KNBC editorial which claimed there were no classes or class warfare in the US.

2874. Weisbaum, Herb, and Silvia Gambardella. "Advertisers Fight Back: Consumer Reporters Tested." IREJ 13.4 (Fall 1990) 18-19.
"Everyone is feeling the sting of economic self-censorship." "Important decisions about story coverage are now being based on financial considerations, rather than journalistic merits."

2875. Weisman, John. "Behind The Pressures To Keep Stories Off The Air." TVG (Oct. 30, 1982) 48-52.
"Corporations and government have subtle--and not so subtle --ways of keeping correspondents from doing their jobs."

2876. Weisman, John. "Blind Spot In The Middle East: Why You Don't See More Palestinians on TV." TVG (Oct. 24, 1981) 6-14. (Continued TVG [Oct. 31, 1981] 10-14).
Palestinian perspectives are underreported and often distorted.

2877. Weisman, John. "Left! Right! The Gang of Five Throws Nothing But Political Haymakers." TVG (July 20, 1985) 11-12.

About a right-wing political talk show financed by Edison
Electric Institute.

2878. Weisman, John. "'60 Minutes'--How Good Is It Now?"
TVG (Apr. 16, 1983) 4-14.
Generally in praise, but points out that most of the
programs deal with insignificant subjects in simple terms.

2879. Weisman, John. "Stories You Won't See on the Nightly
News." TVG (Mar. 1, 1980) 4-8.
Substantial ongoing issues--e.g., government regulatory
agencies--are barely reported because they lack dramatic and
visual issues.

2880. Weisman, John. "What TV Didn't Tell Us About The
Energy Crisis." TVG (Mar. 6, 1982) 4-12.
Describes a new study of "disturbing omissions" from network
coverage.

2881. Whitworth, William. "An Accident of Casting." NY
44.24 (Aug. 3, 1968) 34-42, 44-60.
Focuses upon Huntley-Brinkley but also the nature of television news and the differences between CBS and NBC.

2882. Wicker, Tom. "Reagan Gets Away with Twisting Facts."
AG (Feb. 17, 1986) 11A.
Reagan's press conference lies go unchallenged.

2883. Williams, Wenmouth, Jr., and William D. Semlak.
"Structural Effects of TV Coverage on Political
Agendas." JoC 28.4 (1978) 114-19.
Refutes the idea that news coverage is simply the reporting
of facts; it is more likely an interpretation of the "facts."

2884. Wills, Garry. "TV Can Make a Difference." TVG (July
26, 1986) 2-8.
Praises documentaries, advocates more of them.

2885. Wittebols, James. "'Terror' Across the Border: U.S.
and Canadian Use of a Buzzword." Extra! 3.5 (May-
June 1990) 11.
The three networks use the loaded terms "terror,"
"terrorism," and "terrorist" much more often than CBC, and "in
line with U.S. government practice" the networks "portrayed
terrorism" as emanating from enemies in the Middle East:
Palestinians, Libya, Iran, etc.

II. C. 1. c. (4). CABLE TELEVISION (2886-2899)

2886. Adler, Richard, and Walter S. Baer, eds. The
Electronic Box Office: Humanities and Arts on the
Cable. New York: Praeger, 1974. 139.
"The essays in this volume examine the potential of cable
for increasing the diversity and quality of television

programming," by exploring "how the arts and humanities can stake a claim on the new communication's technologies." In addition, five conditions are proposed which must be met "if the cable is to serve as a pipeline for high culture."

2887. Aufderheide, Pat. "We Don't Have to Care, We're the Cable Company." Prog 55.1 (Jan. 1991) 28-31.
"Cable companies have become the arrogant bullies of consumer television."

2888. Barnes, John A. "Why Cable Costs Too Much." WM 21.5 (June 1989) 12-17.
Advocates elimination of so-called natural monopolies by permitting competition. "Local monopolies have fostered waste and corruption" and high service costs.

2889. Beck, Kirsten. Cultivating the Wasteland: Can Cable Put the Vision Back in TV? New York: American Council for the Arts, 1983. 249.
Guide to existing and future program possibilities for cable.

2890. Brown, Les. "Whose First Amendment Is It, Anyway?" Channels 2.3 (1982) 24-25.
On reluctance of cable companies to provide outlets for expression.

2891. Brunner, Ronald D., and Chen, Kan. "Is Cable the Answer?: Diversity in Broadcasting." JoC 28.2 (1978) 81-84.
Cable television could become a viable alternative to the network-dominated broadcast medium. Unfortunately the true innovations cable might offer (interactive television, hundreds of channels to choose from) are slow in coming, and the networks are moving to dominate cable as well.

2892. Drale, Christina. "The Elusive Public Interest: Mass Media & the Dialectic of the Common Good." U of California, San Diego, 1985. 274. DAI 46 (1985) 1430-A.
Analysis and history of idea of the public interest and application of definitions to mass media, particularly to cable television.

2893. Hollander, Richard. Video Democracy: The Vote-From-Home Revolution. Mt. Airy, MD: Lomond, 1985. 161.
Gives a pessimistic picture of the impact of TV on politics because of presidential direct advertising and packaging (selling Nixon in 1968, Reagan in 1980 and 1984), but is qualifiedly optimistic about the ability of new interactive technologies, such as videotex, to revive direct democracy. But the new technology could isolate people from politics more.

2894. LeDuc, Don R. Cable Television and the FCC: A Crisis in Media Control. Philadelphia: Temple UP, 1973. 289.

Criticizes the FCC for its "protective policy toward the industry it regulates" and argues for "an impartial mediator to protect the rights" of the public for "the quantity and quality of future media services."

2895. Meehan, Eileen. "Technical Capability Versus Corporate Imperatives: Toward a Political Economy of Cable Television and Information Diversity." The Political Economy of Information. Ed. Vincent Mosco and Janet Wasko. Madison: U of Wisconsin P, 1988. 167-187.
Study of corporate imperatives reveals "how capitalism systematically limits and slants the claims, images, and outlets available to people despite the technological potential for diversity." The essay examines one technology whose performance "generally failed to meet its promise": interactive cable tv (QUBE).

2896. Parsons, Patrick. "Cable Television & the First Amendment." U of Minnesota, 1984. 368. DAI 45 (May 1985) 3234-A.
Various models of cable rights--Print, Broadcast, Public Utility, and Public Forum--are "incapable of the necessary balancing of rights." A "Full Projection Model" would provide "an equitable balance" between cable operator and community.

2897. Peck, Diana. "Programming the Cable Television Channels: The Promise of Diversity." Columbia U Teachers C, 1983. DAI 44.6 (Dec. 1983) 1615-A.
Cable's diversity is "less than it might appear" and will decrease with government deregulation.

2898. Price, Monroe, and John Wicklein. Cable Television: A Guide for Citizen Action. Philadelphia: Pilgrim, 1972. 160.
This book discusses the potential of cable television, its controllers, and ways in which citizens can influence its development. In addition, it contains advice for private corporations interested in obtaining time on cable television for public interest programming.

2899. Smith, Doug. "Cable Firms Wield Unregulated Clout." AG (Sept. 30, 1989) 7B.
Since Congress deregulated cable, the companies have become "unregulated monopolies."

II. C. 1. c. (5). CHILDREN & TELEVISION (2900-2942)

2900. Alperowicz, Cynthia. "Toymakers Take Over Children's TV." BSR 49 (Spring 1984) 47-51.
"Saturday mornings are one long commercial," and "weekdays are no better."

2901. Anastaplu, George. "Education, Television, and Political Discourse in America." (Interview). CM

19.4 (1986) 20-26).
Television undermines the education of today's young people, deceiving them into thinking they are informed and "lowering the level of political discourse."

2902. Atkin, Charles, John Murray, and Oguz Nayman, eds. Television and Social Behavior: An Annotated Bibliography of Research Focusing on Television's Impact on Children. Rockville, MD: Public Health Service, 1971. 150.
A "by-product of a research program . . . under the guidance of the Surgeon General's Scientific Advisory Committee on Television and Social Behavior."

2903. Barber, Susanna. "When I Grow Up: Children and the Work-World of Television." M&V 47 (Summer 1989) 15-17.
Television tends to present children with a negative and unrealistic view of the working world.

2904. Barcus, Francis. Children's Television: An Analysis of Programming and Advertising. New York: Praeger, 1977. 218.
Content study of children's commercial weekend TV (programs, advertising) and after school TV. TV programming must serve the interests of children as well as the financial interests of broadcasters and advertisers.

2905. Bogart, Leo. "Warning: The Surgeon General has Determined that TV Violence is Moderately Dangerous to Your Child's Mental Health." POQ 36 (Winter 1972-73) 491-521.
An analysis of the Surgeon General's Study of Television and Social Behavior concerning how children are affected by viewing televised violence concludes with agreement with the Surgeon General, to whom the "causal relationship between televised violence and antisocial behavior is sufficient to warrant appropriate and immediate remedial action."

2906. Carlsson-Paige, Nancy, and Diane Levin. Who's Calling the Shots? How to Respond Effectively to Children's Fascination with War Play and War Toys. Philadelphia, PA: New Society, 1990. 188.
Indicts Reagan era FCC deregulation for making the program-length commercial legal, which increased war play.

2907. Cater, Douglass, and Stephen Strickland. TV Violence and the Child: The Evolution and Fate of the Surgeon General's Report. New York: Russell Sage Foundation, 1975. 167.
Examines Television and Growing Up: The Impact of Televised Violence (Jan. 1972), which found tentative indications of a causal relation between viewing televised violence and aggressive behavior but could not say how many children were affected or what should be done. "What ensued was even more dis-

turbing." The report was "grossly misinterpreted by The New York Times and other organs of the media" (2-3). Two years later little to nothing had been done to curb TV violence.

2908. Charren, Peggy. "Children's TV: Sugar and Vice and Nothing Nice." BSR 22 (1977) 65-70.
Commercial children's TV "proves that the nation's children are not as important as the bottom line."

2909. Choate, Robert B. "How Television Grabs Kids for Fun and Profit." BSR 7 (1973) 21-25.
"An average of twenty-two messages per hour is pumped out over the airwaves during children's viewing hours, adding up to 220 minutes of pure commercials seen by the average television-watching child in one week."

2910. Consumer Education Materials Project. Six Texts: Early Childhood Consumer Education, Elementary Level Consumer Education, Secondary Level Consumer Education, Consumer Education in Jr. and Community College/Postsecondary Vocational and Technical, Preparing the Consumer Educator, Adult Consumer Education in the Community. New York: Consumers Union of the US, 1973.
Books on consumer education from childhood to adulthood.

2911. Cullingford, Cedric. Children and Television. New York: St. Martin's, 1984. 239.
Emphasizes the complexity of the issues. Children's attention and recall decline as viewing increases, but advertisements "provide a disproportionate amount of material that they recall, not in terms of the quality of the product, but in the jingles, songs or catch-phrases that they promote. Television becomes for children propaganda for itself, for ease of entertainment, for the fulfillment of the same expectations in a variety of different ways" (181). Generally children imitate adults in their tastes and habits, "with a pervasive desire for entertainment that fulfills familiar norms" (180).

2912. Dorr, Aimee. Television and Children: A Special Medium for a Special Audience. Beverly Hills: Sage, 1986. 160.
Covers the nature of children's TV, the child audience, the nature of the influence process, the history of the debate about programming and effects, etc.

2913. Fischer, Stuart. Kid's TV: The First 25 Years. New York: Facts on File, 1983. 289.
Children's TV was transformed from participation shows to increasingly sophisticated programs by the demands of advertisers, "sparked by the recognition that children were an important target" for selling commodities. "Television had always been used to sell merchandise to children . . . but in the mid-1960s characters created for advertising figured prominently in children's programs."

2914. Goulart, Ron. The Assault on Childhood. Los Angeles: Sherbourne, 1969. 278.
Attacks the commercial exploitation of children by business executives who encourage selfishness and prejudice in order to make profits.

2915. Gross, Larry, and Suzanne Jeffries-Fox. "What Do You Want To Be When you Grow Up, Little Girl?" Hearth and Home: Images of Women in the Mass Media. Ed. Gaye Tuchman, et al. New York: Oxford UP, 1978. 240-265.
Very tentative conclusions that heavier TV watching lowers children's educational motivation and that TV induces sexist attitudes more in boys than girls (227).

2916. Hays, Kim, ed. TV, Science, & Kids: Teaching Our Children to Question. Reading, MA: Addison-Wesley, 1984. 210.
The contributors are "depressed by the generally low quality of what television has accomplished so far" but are also exhilarated by "the things that can be done" in teaching science by TV.

2917. Hesse, Petra, and Ted Stimpson. "Images of the Enemy on Children's TV." PR 5 (Summer 1989) 22-25.
Examines the kinds of enemies on eight of the most highly rated children's cartoon shows that teach children "some of the key elements of US patriotism"--e.g., peace through strength not negotiation.

2918. Hodge, Robert, and David Tripp. Children and Television: A Semiotic Approach. Stanford, CA: Stanford UP, 1986. 233.
A study of Australian children using British "cultural studies approach" and "Marxist theories of society and the state, allied to various forms of structuralism" (9). Presents "ten theses on children and television," among which are: "Children's television typically carries dominant ideological forms, but also a range of oppositional meanings," and "general ideological forms have an overall determining effect on interpretations of television" (215-17).

2919. Kaye, Evelyn. The Family Guide to Children's Television: What to Watch, What to Miss, What to Change and How to Do It. New York: Pantheon, 1974. 194.
Written under the guidance of Action for Children's Television; includes discussions of violence, commercials, programming, and their relation to the business of broadcasting.

2920. Kotch, Jonathan. "The FCC and The First Amendment Facade: A Rejoinder." PTR 6.2 (1978) 34-37.
Defends regulation of children's programming.

2921. Leifer, Aimee Dorr, Neal J. Gordon, and Sherryl Browne Graves. "Children's Television: More than Mere Entertainment." HER 44.2 (1974) 213-245.

ELECTRONIC MEDIA 415

Some conclusions: TV socializes children. Pursuit of profit outweighs "concern for the public in the choice of programming." Remedies are more diversity of TV content and more parental guidance in choosing and viewing programs.

2922. Liebert, Robert, and Joyce Sprafkin. The Early Window: Effects of Television on Children and Youth. 3rd ed. Elmsford, NY: Pergamon, 1988. 312.

Chapter 7, "Twenty Years of TV Violence Research": "There is causal link between TV violence and aggression or other antisocial behavior" (135). Chapter 8, "Television Advertising and Children": "young children are often confused, misled, and taken in by TV commercials," but the TV and advertising industries "counterattacked successfully" through pressure on members of Congress. Industry self-regulation, always weak, is weaker today. Other chapters on TV as a business, etc.

2923. Mattelart, Michéle. "Education, Television and Mass Culture: Reflections on Research into Innovation." Television in Transition. Ed. Phillip Drummond and Richard Patterson. London: BFI, 1986. 164-184.

Uses Sesame Street to attack "systemism," which "she regards as the kernel of technocratic thought, which in turn is an ideology that underpins the new channels of communication." Sesame Street, a product of positivism, "is structured around the quantifiable."

2924. Melody, William H. Children's Television: The Economics of Exploitation. New Haven: Yale UP, 1973. 164.

Present exploitation of children by corporations for profit must get worse under present arrangements and (lack of) regulation. Children need special protection from commercial TV, which should be compelled to live up to their licenses as public trustees.

2925. Packard, Vance. "Warning: TV Can Be Hazardous to Children." Reader's Digest 128.769 (May 1986) 217-220.

Recommends against children's unsupervised access to TV and suggests ways to make TV a "life-enhancing force" for them.

2926. Paine, Lynda Sharp. "Children as Consumers: An Ethical Evaluation of Children's Television Advertising." BPEJ 3.3 & 4 (1984) 119-139.

Proposes "ethical reasons" why "advertisers should refrain from directing commercials to young children."

2927. Palmer, Edward L., Milton Chen, and Gerald S. Lesser. "Sesame Street: Patterns of International Adaptation." JoC 26.2 (Spring 1976) 109-124.

An historical and economic account of the co-production process and the methods by which foreign countries have adapted the US curriculum programming to the cultural values and needs of their regions.

2928. Polsky, Richard M. Getting to Sesame Street: Origins of the Children's Television Workshop. New York: Praeger, 1974. 139.
   In the late 1960s, the manipulators of commercial television were not creating quality programs for children, but the Children's Television Workshop took the financial and creative risk.

2929. Potter, Rosemary Lee. The Positive Use of Commercial Television with Children. Washington, DC: National Education Assoc. of the U.S., 1981. 126.
   Offers teachers a "teaching and learning" guide that will raise awareness and help children become more critical.

2930. Rogers, Fred M. "Television and Individual Growth." TQ 9.3 (Summer 1970) 14-19.
   Commercial television does not encourage self-esteem or self-understanding in children, whereas "'Mister Rogers' Neighborhood' realizes that the real drama is going on within them."

2931. Rowland, W. D. The Politics of TV Violence. Beverly Hills, CA: Sage, 1983. 320.
   Politicians, government officials, and TV network executives all exploit the TV violence issue, the former by portraying themselves as highly concerned about the welfare of children and the quality of television without ever running the risk of being forced into legislative action, the latter by sponsoring biased or flawed research which creates the impression of being cooperative while diverting attention from its vast profits and enormous political power.

2932. Rutstein, Nat. "Go Watch TV!" What and How Much Should Children Really Watch? New York: Sheed and Ward, 1974. 213.
   Discussing such aspects of television as violence, racism, sexism, and materialism, this book attempts to warn parents of television "dangers," as well as to help them gain control of the television viewing in their homes.

2933. Schwartzberg, Neala. "What TV Does to Kids." Parents 62.6 (June 1987) 101-104.
   Among other things it makes children more violent and cynical.

2934. Shankar, Shobana. "TV Reinforces Racism, Sexism in Boys and Girls." AG (Aug. 20, 1990) 3E.
   Children's programs are racist, sexist, and militarist.

2935. Sprafkin, Joyce N., and Robert M. Liebert. "Sex-typing and Children's Television Preferences." Hearth and Home: Images of Women in the Mass Media. Ed. Gaye Tuchman, et al. New York: Oxford UP, 1978. 228-239.
   Attacks the predominance of male-oriented programs. Children of each sex "prefer to watch characters of their own

gender," and "children model their sex-role behaviors after stereotyped television portrayals" (226).

2936. Steenland, Sally. "Prime-Time Girls Just Want To Have Fun." M&V 49 (Winter 1989) 5.
"Study shows TV's teens are preoccupied with shopping, grooming and dating, not the real world of school, family and work."

2937. Television and Behavior: Ten Years of Scientific Progress and Implications for the Eighties. Vol. I. Rockville, MD: U.S. Dept. of Health and Human Services, 1982. 94.
Studies research since the Surgeon General's report of 1971, Television and Growing Up: The Impact of Televised Violence.

2938. TV News & Children. Cambridge, MA: ACT, 1987. 25.
Explores ways to help children deal with the news and encourages production of news shows for kids.

2939. Valdez, Armando. "The Economic Context of U.S. Children's Television: Parameters for Reform?" Communication and Social Structure. Ed. Emile McAnany, et al. New York: Praeger, 1981. 145-180.
Children's TV is a microcosm of "the domination of the nation's economic order by a few major conglomerates"; the commercials mirror the "hegemony that characterizes the social order as one defined by narrow and limited personal options for clothing, transportation, housing, and food products," catering to impulse gratification for economic gain by corporations (manufacturers and media).

2940. Williams, Frederick, Robert LaRose, and Frederica Frost. Children, Television, and Sex-Role Stereotyping. New York: Praeger, 1981. 161.
"Pervasive stereotyping characterizes the ways in which sex roles are portrayed on television. . . . Women are seriously underrepresented on television; they are portrayed in very limited occupational roles (if at all); and they are shown as typically deriving their identity from relationships with others," while "men give orders more frequently" and "their orders are obeyed more often" (v).

2941. Winick, Mariann, and Charles Winick. The Television Experience: What Children See. Beverly Hills, CA: Sage, 1979. 215.
"Our central finding is that on aspects of television experience, such as expectancy and developmental readiness to be aware of certain kinds of content, children differ from adults"; furthermore, children are "a series of different groups" according to age (186-7). This understanding is then related to societal and corporate aims and ideology in programming--the way TV presents violence in contrast to other countries.

2942. Winn, Marie. The Plug-In Drug. New York: Viking, 1977. 231.
An investigation of the television experience among middle-class families in New York and Denver which concludes that "parents need to think about television in a new way, and need to consider the role it plays in their children's lives and in their lives together as a family." Covered are such topics as television addiction, television violence, and television's effects on children and the family.

II. C. 1. c. (6). TELEVISION: RELIGION (2943-2961)

2943. Abelman, Robert, and Gary Petty. "How Political is Religious Television?" JQ 65.2 (Summer 1988) 313-319.
Political content is increasing.

2944. Alexandre, Laurien. "Church and Media: Lots to Learn." C&C 50.17 (Nov. 26, 1990) 378-381.
Discusses three books on the electronic church and religion's use of TV. William Fore's Television and Religion (1987) and Mythmakers (199) are intended to be read together; Goethals' The Electronic Golden Calf complements them. Their general subject is the power of TV to create meaning and that religious values oppose "media values based on consumption, property, and wealth."

2945. Anderson, John W. "A Heavenly Home for TV Preachers." Na 246.10 (Mar. 12, 1988) 338-340.
On the growing use of direct broadcast satellites (DBS) by televangelists.

2946. Ferré, John. Channels of Belief: Religion and American Commercial Television. Ames, IA: Iowa State UP, 1990. 152.
Six scholars assess the central role played by commercial TV in the communication of religion. Topics include: religious myths in the genre of TV narratives, the attitude of "democratic humanism" among writers and producers, religious events and persons on network news, religious public service announcements, and influence upon TV by religious watchdog groups.

2947. Fore, William. Mythmakers: Gospel, Culture and the Media. New York: Friendship, 1990. 156.
See the following entry.

2948. Fore, William. Television and Religion: The Shaping of Faith, Values and Culture. Minneapolis: Augsburg, 1987. 220.
His central thesis in both books is that Christian worldviews are fundamentally opposed to those of Western television culture, which is an expression of capitalism, that turns everything into a commodity. The mass media worldviews from a

Christian perspective are: happiness is the end of life and it consists in obtaining material goods; sexuality is sex appeal; self-respect is pride; will-to-live is will-to-power; etc.

2949. Frankl, Razelle. Televangelism: The Marketing of Popular Religion. Carbondale: Southern Illinois UP, 1987. 204.
Concentrates on the commercial and political implications of the electric church. In Part 3: "The Television Industry and Religious Broadcasting" and Part 4: "The Electric Church."

2950. Gerbner, George. "Television: The New State Religion?" ETC. 34.2 (June 1977) 145-50.
"Television provides an organically related synthetic symbolic structure which once again presents a total world of meanings for all. It is related to the State as only the church was in ancient times" (149).

2951. Goethals, Gregor. The Electronic Golden Calf: Images, Religion and the Making of Meaning. Boston: Cowley, 1990. 223.
Examines the values and techniques of the media and the economic system which produces them, from the belief that TV values oppose Christian values. Wishes to provide skills to demystify media messages: identifying ownership and control, demystifying consumerism, etc. (Also see her The TV Ritual).

2952. Hadden, Jeffrey, and Charles Swann. Prime Time Preachers: The Rising Power of Televangelism. Reading, MA: Addison-Wesley, 1981. 217.
"Merely to contemplate its potential power is staggering." Appraises the Christian Right on TV.

2953. Harrell, David. Oral Roberts: An American Life. Bloomington: Indiana UP, 1985. 622.
"Roberts's second major influence on modern Christian history stems from his innovative use of the media, particularly television"; he "prepared the way for the modern electronic church" (viii).

2954. Horsfield, Peter. "Evangelism by Mail: Letters from the Broadcasters." JoC 35.1 (1985) 89-97.
A study of religious broadcast mailings concludes that the primary goal of correspondence is not referral to local churches but an appeal for membership and financial support of the "electronic church."

2955. Horsfield, Peter. Religious Television: The American Experience. New York: Longman, 1984. 197.
A survey of the wide range of religious TV to expose the "marked imbalance in the presentation of American religious faith and culture" in favor of the evangelical and fundamentalist traditions," the main cause of which is "the economic and functional interests of the commercial television industry" (Preface xiv).

2956. Karp, Walter. "Big Business and the Little Minister." Channels 1.4 (1981) 12-14.
On Rev. Don Wildman's right-wing, pro-corporate Coalition for Better Television.

2957. Lader, Lawrence. Politics, Power, and the Church: The Catholic Crisis and Its Challenge to American Pluralism. New York: Macmillan, 1987. 273.
Chap. 8, "Money, Power, and the Media." "The religious conservatives saw that the media was essential to control, and much of their money and power has concentrated on shaping public opinion through radio and television" (113). "Money and media control have proved to be the foundation of the Fundamentalist-Catholic alliance and have brought it to a peak of power" (120).

2958. McLaren, Peter, and Richard Smith. "Televangelism as Pedagogy and Cultural Politics." Popular Culture, Schooling, and Everyday Life. Ed. Henry Giroux and Roger Simon. Granby, MA: Bergin & Garvey, 1989. 147-173.
Examines televangelism in the US and Australia in the context of a general "retreat from liberalism and emancipatory social reform," focusing on "the appeal of televangelism as a product of the consolidated forces of the New Right."

2959. "Mobilizing 'God's Army': The Media Power of the Christian Right." Extra! 3.1 (Oct.-Nov. 1989) 4-5.
"Televangelism has been the single most important ingredient in the rise and enduring political clout of the Christian Right," which the secular media is not examining as it should.

2960. Shepard, Charles E. Forgiven: The Rise and Fall of Jim Bakker and the PTL Ministry. New York: Atlantic Monthly, 1989. 635.
A generally critical biography from boyhood to the present by the Pulitzer-winning author of a newspaper series on Bakker and Hahn.

2961. Thomas, Sari. "The Route to Redemption: Religion and Social Class." Joc 35.1 (1985) 111-122.
A content analysis of religious TV programming, under the headings of salvation, materialism, and secularism, finds that religious teachings follow class lines and rationalize social class positions.

II. C. 2. PUBLIC & SUBSCRIBER BROADCASTING (2962-3034)

2962. Bennett, James R. "The Public Broadcasting System: A Bibliography of Criticism." JPFT 15.2 (Summer 1987) 85-92.
One hundred and twenty entries accompanied by a subject index. [Most of these items are not repeated in the present bibliography.]

2963. Ainbinder, Hollie. "MacNeil/Lehrer Program More Biased Than Nightline." SLJR 20.127 (June 1990) 4.
Both MacNeil/Lehrer Newshour and Koppel's Nightline are ideologically narrow--white, male, government-oriented, conservative--but MacNeil/Lehrer is the worse of the two.

2964. Alter, Jonathan. "Network Documentaries on the Blink." WM 17.12 (Jan. 1986) 35-36.
The decline of documentaries on PBS.

2965. Aronowitz, Stanley. "The American Worker: A PBS Endangered Species?" SLJR 20.129 (Sept. 1990) 14.
"The business and social elite are vastly overrepresented and workers are nearly invisible on PBS."

2966. Aufderheide, Pat. "The Corporatization of Public TV: Why Labor's Voice is Seldom Heard on PBS." Extra! 2.3 (Nov.-Dec. 1988) 12-13.
Appeals for a public TV "with priorities set by the public interest, not by the pocketbooks of the powerful."

2967. Aufderheide, Pat. "Network Failure." ITT 13.3 (Nov. 16-22, 1988) 12-13, 22.
During the Reagan era public TV became "ever tamer" because "ever more the corporate minion in search of program dollars." But the 100th Congress provided some potentially good news by its creation of the Independent Program Service as part of the Public Broadcasting Act of 1988.

2968. Aufderheide, Pat. "Propaganda and Public TV." ITT 9.27 (1985) 21.
The Corporation for Public Broadcasting is shifting further right under Reagan's appointees.

2969. Aufderheide, Pat. "Public TV: Commercialization and Its Discontents." ITT 7.23 (1983) 8-9.
Examines public television's growing commercialism and its negative implications for programming diversity and quality.

2970. Aufderheide, Pat. "Public TV Tunes Out the Big Picture." ITT 14.9 (July 4-17, 1990) 19-21.
If public TV cannot "make its reputation on its civic rather than entertainment function" it may not survive, since commercial TV is too competitive for the kind of programming now dominating PBS--nature, arts, how-to shows, and old movies.

2971. Aufderheide, Pat. "Sapping Public TV's Political Power: Nixon's the One." ITT 14.9 (July 4-17, 1990) 21.
Recounts President Nixon's long-lasting attempt to control PBS.

2972. Aufderheide, Pat. "Television with a Point of View." Prog 54.7 (July 1990) 36-38.
Describes and praises PBS's new documentary series P.O.V., which "demonstrates that the independent artist engaged with

2973. Aufderheide, Pat. "What Makes Public TV Public: It Gets Harder and Harder to Tell." Prog 52.1 (Jan. 1988) 35-38.
A gloomy look at PBS. For example, "Public-affairs programming is not designed to raise public debate," because of corporate control. Several solutions are described.

2974. Avery, Robert K., and Robert Pepper. "An Institutional History of Public Broadcasting." JoC 30.3 (1980) 126-38.
A 60-year history of organizational and technological changes paying much attention to political conflicts between PBS and CPB over programming content and perspective.

2975. Barnouw, Erik. "PBS Takes Control." BAS 46.5 (June 1990) 40.
Discusses the film Losing Control? about possible accidental nuclear war that was rejected by PBS because it was too critical of the US.

2976. Barrett, Marvin, ed. "Where the Action Was: Government and Public Broadcasting." Moments of Truth. (The Fifth Alfred I. DuPont/Columbia U Survey of Broadcast Journalism). New York: Thomas Crowell, 1975. 127-136.
On White House pressures against PBS by limiting its independence and funding.

2977. Bennett, James R. "The Public Broadcasting System." FSN 13.1 (Summer 1987) 3-5.
Summarizes the struggle for a public broadcasting system free of corporate and government control.

2978. Birnie, Heather. "Consideration of the Commercial Advertisement as a Means of Financing Public Radio & Television: 1896-1986." U of Wisconsin, 1986. 900. DAI 47 (1987) 2783-A.
Historical survey.

2979. Blakely, Robert. To Serve the Public Interest: Educational Broadcasting in the United States. Syracuse, NY: Syracuse UP, 1979. 274.
A history beginning with the 1950-51 struggle to mobilize educational institutions to the potential of TV. Traces the first four faltering years, development 1956-63, 1963-67 years of federal funding leading up to the Carnegie Commission, etc.

2980. Bolton, Roger. "The Problems of Making Political Television: A Practitioner's Perspective." Communicating Politics. Ed. Peter Golding, et al. New York: Holmes & Meier, 1986. 93-114.
This study of government and self-censorship in BBC applies to public broadcasting in the US.

ELECTRONIC MEDIA 423

2981. Brennan, Timothy. "Masterpiece Theatre and the Uses of
Tradition." American Media & Mass Culture. Ed. Donald
Lazere. Berkeley: U of California P, 1987. 373-383.
Traces "a recurrent motif celebrating the marriage of
British imperial rule to American bourgeois entrepreneurship"
that is "congenial to the corporate sponsors of PBS" (326).

2982. "The BS in PBS." Prog 54.8 (Aug. 1990) 9.
PBS favors power and privilege and "slights critics of U.S.
Government policies."

2983. Cantor, Muriel S. "Where are the Women in Public
Broadcasting?" Hearth and Home: Images of Women in
the Mass Media. Ed. Gaye Tuchman, et al. New York:
Oxford UP, 1978. 78-89.
The ways women are stereotyped and isolated in public broadcasting.

2984. Cantor, Muriel. "Women and Public Broadcasting." JoC
27.1 (1977) 14-19.
A summary of the CPB Report of the Task Force on Women.
Integration of women into programming and upper level positions within the industry is unlikely in the presence of male
dominance everywhere else.

2985. Carmody, John. "President Vetoes Funding Bill for
Public Broadcasting." WP (Aug. 30, 1984) C1.
Reagan favors decreasing PBS funding.

2986. Cater, Douglass, and Michael Nyhan, eds. The Future of
Public Broadcasting. New York: Praeger, 1976. 372.
Essays on policy issues by "middle range visionaries," each
identifying problems and proposing solutions.

2987. Clarkson, Fred. "Moon, the Contras & PBS." Extra! 1.3
(Aug.-Sept. 1987) 9.
The pro-contra film "Nicaragua Was Our Home" produced by
Rev. Moon's CAUSA International Films was shown on PBS shortly
before the 1986 Congressional vote for $100 million in contra
aid.

2988. Cockburn, Alexander. "The Tedium Twins." Corruptions
of Empire. London: Verso, 1987. 199-206.
"The spectrum of opinion thus offered [by the McNeil-Lehrer
NewsHour] is one that ranges from the corporate right to
cautious center-liberal. One should not be misled, by the
theatrical diversity of views deployed on the program, into
thinking that a genuinely wide spectrum of opinion is
permitted" (204).

2989. Cumming, Robert. "New Hope for Television: Educational
TV." The Responsibility of the Press. Ed. Gerald
Gross. New York: Fleet, 1966. 416.
"NET has accomplished wonders in only ten years" and is
"soaring to great heights."

2990. Emerson, Steven. "The System that Brought You Days of Rage." CJR 28.4 (Nov.-Dec. 1989) 25-30.
The difficulty PBS has in producing independent documentaries is highlighted by its program on young Palestinians: its "constant thirst for funding and its muddled sense of its mission" cause it to lower its standards or to avoid controversial documentaries.

2991. Evenson, Debra. "Cuba: PBS Airs Two Views." Guard 42.38 (Aug. 1, 1990) 24.
PBS would not show Saul Landau's "The Uncompromising Revolution," a film that mixes praise and blame, without juxtaposing it with "Nobody Listened," an indictment of Castro's political prisons, even though the latter testimony was of incidents no later than the 1960s.

2992. Gever, Martha. "SOS From Independent Public Broadcasting Producers." Extra! 1.8 (May-June 1988) 12-13.
An appeal for a National Independent Programming Service to produce documentaries and other films, as the 1979 Carnegie Commission report urged.

2993. [Cancelled]

2994. Gibson, George H. Public Broadcasting: The Role of the Federal Government, 1912-1976. New York: Praeger, 1977. 236.
A history and critique of federal policies toward noncommercial broadcasting, describing the work that presidents, members of Congress and the FCC, the Commissioner of Education, HEW, foundations, and educational broadcasters have done to make public broadcasting "a fundamental institution" in our culture.

2995. Gladstone, Brooke. "Emergency at NPR: This is Not a Test." ITT (May 4-10, 1983) 9.
Severe budgetary restrictions limit the potential of NPR.

2996. Griffen, Bill. "The PBS Version of the Viet Nam War: A Flawed History." AN 15.6 (Winter 1983) 17.
The film is part of the US propaganda effort to reestablish use of force worldwide as part of its "messianic crusade against evil Communism."

2997. Grossman, Lawrence. "Let's Keep All Our Educational Channels." TVG (Aug. 13, 1983) 32-34.
Opposes the FCC plan to turn over part of instructional TV frequencies to commercial TV.

2998. Harper, Sandra. "A Content Analysis of Public Broadcasting Service Television Programming." North Texas SU, 1985. 191. DAI 47 (1986) 8-A.
Females, Blacks, and Hispanics are "underrepresented." Some gains have been made in children's programming, but "minorities in major segments of PBS programming" are virtually excluded.

ELECTRONIC MEDIA   425

2999. Harrison, S. L. "Prime Time Pablum, How Politics and
          Corporate Influence Keep Public TV Harmless." WM
          17.12 (Jan. 1986) 33-39.
       Outside political and corporate interference impose as many
   constraints on public TV as commercial sponsors have on the
   networks.

3000. Herken, Gregg. "Early Takes on PBS's Nuclear Age: As
          History Direct Hits, Soft Targets." Deadline 4.1
          (Jan.-Feb. 1989) 1-2, 9-11.
       PBS's War and Peace in the Nuclear Age, a thirteen-part
   series, well exposes the secrecy about nuclearism enforced by
   succeeding administrations, but its treatment is "so shy of
   controversy" and "so determinedly middle of the road" that "it
   adds disappointingly little to the nuclear debate that was
   discouraged for so long" by that secrecy.

3001. Herman, Edward. "Toasting Morality." Zeta 1.2 (Feb.
          1988) 36-37.
       Uses the double standard employed by the MacNeil-Lehrer News
   Hour to demonstrate the media's policy of deference to corrupt
   authority while scrutinizing "'enemies' or the weak."

3002. Hezel, Richard T. "Public Broadcasting: Can It Teach?"
          JoC 30.3 (1980) 173-78.
       Given that PBS is perceived as an educational medium, it
   should establish goals and objectives in advance, present
   material to attract and maintain a target population, and
   schedule programs when that audience is most available. Otherwise, public television risks informing the already informed.

3003. Hood, Stuart. "Broadcasting and the Public Interest:
          From Consensus to Crisis." Communicating Politics.
          Ed. Peter Golding, et al. New York: Holmes & Meier,
          1986. 55-56.
       A study of public broadcasting in Britain and the US under
   attack by the deregulators and the censors. He calls on Right
   and Left to find a new rationale for public broadcasting.

3004. Johnson, Nicholas. "Carter Looks at Public Broadcast-
          ing." Access 57 (Nov. 1977) 8.
       Praises President Carter's support of PBS.

3005. Jones, Jeff. "Right Revises PBS' Korea Series." Guard
          43.5 (Nov. 21, 1990) 17.
       Under pressure from Accuracy in Media, PBS altered its
   series "Korea: The Unknown War," especially suppressing North
   Korea's perspective regarding the initiation of the war.

3006. Kopkind, Andrew. "MacNeil/Lehrer's Class Act." CJR
          18.3 (Sept. 1979) 31-38.
       While the MacNeil/Lehrer Report may seem to be an intelli-
   gent and objective alternative to commercial news programs,
   it "fails to open up the debate to non-instrumentalist ideologies" and serves primarily as a daily briefing for the new

managerial class.

3007. Larson, Mary. "A Content Analysis of National Public Radio's 'All Things Considered.'" Northern Illinois U, 1985. 191. DAI 46 (1986) 1769-A.
The program from 1974 to 1983 stressed legal, political, international, scientific, environmental, and health issues, and neglected social welfare and education.

3008. LeRoy, David J. "Who Watches Public Television?" JoC 30.3 (1980) 157-63.
Presents an audience profile of a well-educated, affluent minority which enjoys elitist programming.

3009. Levin, Harvey. "The Use of Scarcity Rents to Fund Public Broadcasting." Fact and Fancy in Television Regulation. New York: Sage, 1980. 385-412.
Considers "alternative techniques for recapturing television's scarcity rents to fund public broadcasting." Also see "The Potential Role of Public Television" (250-273). At the basis of the argument for commercial TV support of public broadcasting is the author's belief that "FCC licensing and allocation policies more often operated to bolster industry profits and rents than to channel them into local, cultural, or informational service" (343).

3010. Lewis, Anthony. "Palestinian Views Deserve Showing." NYT (May 5, 1989) 11B.
On the difficulties the makers of a documentary on the Palestinian uprising have had getting it shown, and a discussion of the First Amendment as intended to protect "strong views."

3011. Macy, John Jr. To Irrigate a Wasteland: The Struggle to Shape a Public Television System in the United States. Berkeley, CA: U of California P, 1974. 186.
Sets forth ways to create a viable system in the public interest, to deliver programs for the public good, and to finance the system without commercials.

3012. Manoff, Robert Karl. "Quick-Fix News: MacNeil/Lehrer Plays It Safe." Prog 51.7 (1987) 15.
The MacNeil/Lehrer News Hour ignores those who want to discuss "root causes and systemic solutions."

3013. Marable, Manning. "Liberation Radio Shut Down." Guard 41.41 (Aug. 2, 1989) 2.
A 1-watt radio station for news about blacks and music was shut down by the police because it interviewed victims of police brutality.

3014. Markham, David. "Federal Censorship of National Open Forum Radio." FSY (1971) 36-42.
After a controversial poem was read on Pacifica Foundation radio station KPFK in Los Angeles, several US Senators tried to pressure the FCC into denying further licenses to the

ELECTRONIC MEDIA

listener-sponsored network.

3015. Mason, William A. "The Use of Minority Advisory Panels in Public Television: Cooptation or Cooperation." Harvard U, 1982. 143. DAI 43 (1982) 1737-A.
An account of the struggle for greater minority representation.

3016. Miley, Michael. "Speak No Evil." PR 2 (Summer 1988) 34-37.
Denunciation of the FCC's latest harassment of Pacifica Foundation's KPFK radio stations, this time over obscenity at its Los Angeles station. The larger danger is political harassment by the FCC in collusion with right-wing evangelical groups.

3017. Mills, Kay. "This Broadcast Will Be Delayed." MORE 4.4 (1974) 5-7.
FCC harassment and censorship of the Pacifica subscriber radio company.

3018. Muchnik, Melvyn M. "Responsibility and Survival: Free Expression and Political Broadcasting on Public Radio and Television Stations." FSY (1973) 38-50.
Suggests that public broadcasting has fallen short of its potential in the area of political programming due to the uncertain legal climate surrounding such programming and the difficulty in insulating its funding base from political maneuvering.

3019. Mullally, Donald P. "Radio: The Other Public Medium." JoC 30.3 (1980) 189-97.
Coverage area, limited audience size, local-national organization, and a lack of funding present four problems public radio must solve in order to maintain its alternative programming.

3020. "New Plan for Public TV Aired at NCAC Luncheon." CN 30 (Winter 1989) 2.
Because of political and commercial pressures on PBS, a forum, "Save Public Broadcasting--A National Treasure at Risk," called for an independent funding base for non-profit programming.

3021. "No Place for Labor on PBS?" Extra! 3.7 (Summer 1990) 13.
Explains why so few programs about labor are produced and shown, in contrast to the many pro-business programs.

3022. Phipps, Steven. "The Federal Government & Radio Piracy." U of Missouri, Columbia, 1986. 200. DAI 48 (1987) 1048-A.
A study of the government's actions to silence unlicensed broadcast operations.

3023. Pollack, Richard. "Atom Firms Block TV Program: Show on Radiation Perils Blacked Out by Industry Pressure." CMJ 4.12 (1979) 7.
About pressures on PBS not to show "Paul Jacobs and the Nuclear Gang."

3024. Porter, Bruce. "Has Success Spoiled NPR?" CJR 29.3 (Sept.-Oct. 1990) 26-32.
High praise for National Public Radio, ending with discussion of on-going problems, such as sponsor influence, excessive attention to minutiae of Washington to the neglect of significant stories (savings and loan scandal), etc.

3025. Rassbach, Elsa. "Elites Dominate Public TV, Charge Labor Leaders." SLJR 20.129 (Sept. 1990) 14.
PBS neglects working-class concerns and life.

3026. Roman, James. "Programming for Public Television." JoC 30.3 (1980) 150-56.
Corporate underwriting, mainly by oil companies, marks a preference for cultural programming, prime-time slots, and foreign-produced programs.

3027. Rubin, Nan. "Radio's Golden Future." AM 11.2 (1979) 7-10.
While commercial stations are increasingly more uniform, "public radio is on the verge of a new era in program diversity," because of the growth of independent producers, though money is scarce.

3028. "The Saga of Lucky Seven." CJR 17.2 (July-Aug. 1978) 22-23.
Underground TV vs. FCC. [See entries 3013, 3022].

3029. Seawell, Buie. "The Challenge of 'Public' TV." UM (Winter 1975) 6.
Public television arose because broadcasting had failed to serve the public interests, as the Communications Act of 1934 says it must. Yet public TV is extremely limited because most publics lack money, technical expertise, and courage.

3030. Shaheen, Jack. "Death of a Princess." The TV Arab. Bowling Green, OH: Bowling Green State U Popular P, 1984. 71-82.
"The docudrama solidifies" Arab stereotypes and "exploited the Saudis."

3031. Simon, Paul, Senator. "Uneasy About PBS." SLJR 18.111 (Nov. 1988) 3.
Fears corporate sponsorship will erode independence; urges "adequate appropriations."

3032. Steinberg, Charles. "Has Public TV Become Corporate TV?" CJR (Sept.-Oct. 1977) 14-17.
Dependence on corporate underwriting for quality programs

causes public TV to steer away from controversy and investigative journalism.

3033. Winston, Brian. "And Now a Word from Our Sponsor." AF 11.8 (1986) 33-5.
More and more PBS stations are running commercials on a limited basis, prompting questions about public broadcasting's future as an alternative medium and possibly endangering funding from government sources.

3034. Zuckerman, Laurence. "Has Success Spoiled NPR?" MJ 12.5 (June-July 1987) 32.
The trials and tribulations of NPR, which has won "every significant award in broadcast journalism."

II. C. 3. a. ECONOMICS OF FILM AND THEATER (3035-3052)
(See II.A.3. and II.B.2.)

3035. DeBauche, Leslie. "Practical Patriotism: The United States Film Industry in World War I." U of Wisconsin, Madison, 1987. 262. DAI 48 (1988) 1913-A.
During WWI the film industry aided the government while "acting in their own best interest," in accordance with the practice of other business.

3036. Dombrowski, Dennis. "Film & Television: An Analytical History of Economic & Creative Integration." U of Illinois, 1982. 468. DAI 43.3 (Sept. 1982) 576-A.
"The major firms in each medium have attempted to control those in the other, resulting in regulatory proceedings and antitrust litigation. Yet government actions preserve concentration and shift power merely from one oligopoly to another, maintaining the very features of the system that cause market dysfunction. Tendencies toward concentration in the film and television industries reflect deeper attributes of the economic system at large."

3037. Eckert, Charles. "Shirley Temple and the House of Rockefeller." American Media & Mass Culture. Ed. Donald Lazere. Berkeley: U of California P, 1987. 164-177.
Contrasts "the financial and social bases of the film industry with the ideology purveyed by the Hollywood dream factory in its classic period of the thirties" (157).

3038. Guback, Thomas. "Film and Cultural Pluralism." JAE 5.2 (1971) 35-51.
US domination of European film production and distribution.

3039. Guback, Thomas. "Film as International Business." JoC 24.1 (1974) 59-70.
Domination through co-production arrangements.

3040. Guback, Thomas. "Hollywood's International Market."

The American Film Industry. Rev. ed. Ed. Tino
Balio. Madison: U of Wisconsin P, 1985. 463-486.
"American film companies have forged a new empire rivaling
those of former days based on spices and minerals, an empire
in constant evolution, stretching around the world, and worth
billions of dollars" (486). Commercial aspects of film
"govern production" and "support dominant thought patterns"
(463). The "exploitation of foreign markets" brings in needed
revenue and conveys "values and myths" (465).

3041. Guback, Thomas. The International Film Industry:
Western Europe and America Since 1945. Bloomington:
Indiana UP, 1969. 244.
Studies US domination of the film industry and the economic
and ideological stake that influences the content of films,
particularly for the West German market.

3042. Izod, John. Hollywood & the Box Office, 1895-1986.
New York: Columbia UP, 1988. 240.
"Profits have always, from the earliest days, been the primary objective of the American film industry," which means the companies usually try to produce the conventional. Innovation "does take place" but "in line with certain developments in the movie business"--for example, The Godfather. "It is on this kind of business-led innovation that this book concentrates"--innovation often through efforts "to reorganize the market" (ix).

3043. Kaufman, Jim. "Corporate Drama." Zeta (Sept. 1988)
77-82.
Investigates how corporate support affects nonprofit theater, focusing upon Boston. For one thing, "ties between the art sector and corporate sponsors are becoming more complex."

3044. Kerr, Paul, ed. The Hollywood Film Industry. London
and New York: Routledge & Kegan Paul/Methuen, 1986.
290.
Examines the classic Hollywood cinema in terms of the industrial structures and strategies surrounding it.

3045. Klaprat, Cathy. "The Star as Market Strategy: Bette
Davis in Another Light." The American Film Industry.
Rev. ed. Ed. Tino Balio. Madison: U of Wisconsin P,
1985. 351-376.
The star system enabled the producer to charge higher prices
and to maximize profits. To maintain this function, all
departments of the studio were employed. But the star was
more than marketing strategy, for the economic imperatives of
the industry "shaped the very nature of the product itself"
(376), which included strict contractual controls over the
stars by the studio.

3046. Nielsen, Michael. "Toward a Workers' History of the
U.S. Film Industry." The Critical Communications
Review. Vol. I: Labor, The Working Class, & the

Media. Ed. Vincent Mosco and Janet Wasko. Norwood, NJ: Ablex, 1983. 47-84.

These authors offer a "bottom-up perspective" which merges "the idea of film as collaborative art with the notion of film as an industrial process," that is, "film as the product of human labor," analysis of structures combined with "real life stories of those most affected by the workings of the industry --the workers themselves."

3047. Pendakur, Manjunath. Canadian Dreams and American Control: The Political Economy of the Canadian Film Industry. Detroit: Wayne State UP, 1989. 352.

Canada struggles to serve its citizens with films autonomously conceived, produced, distributed, and exhibited, against US capital's drive to shape the Canadian film industry in its own image. Examines the relations between the monopoly and competitive sectors, state institutions in both countries, and the workers in the Canadian film industry.

3048. Pendakur, Manjunath. "Dynamics of Cultural Policy Making: The U.S. Film Industry in India." JoC 35.4 (1985) 52-72.

The tug-of-war history of the US film cartel (MPEAA) and the Indian government involving US film distribution and Indian theater revenues.

3049. Phillips, Joseph D. "Film Conglomerate 'Blockbusters.'" JoC 25.2 (Spring 1975) 171-182.

The author offers a four-part thesis: (1) a small number of film companies dominate the US and international film industry outside socialist countries; (2) domination is the result of size, historical advantage, and the nature of film; (3) these circumstances lead to concentration, centralization, and product homogenization; (4) the result is cultural bias, distortion, and instability.

3050. Thompson, Kristin. Exporting Entertainment: America in the World Film Market 1907-1934. Champaign: U of Illinois P, 1986. 238.

Since WWI, US films and companies have dominated the global trade in theatrical films. The US industry forced foreign competitors to share their domestic markets with US films while excluding the foreigners by vertically integrated majors and collusive trade practices.

3051. Wasko, Janet. Movies & Money: Financing the American Film Industry. Norwood, NJ. Ablex, 1982. 247.

Relationships between the film industry and the banking community have "inherently involved elements of influence, control, and, ultimately, power," with banks generally holding "the more powerful position" (216). But this power has been seldom overtly exercised because the managers and corporate directors of the film industry have generally accepted the "overall goals and policies" of bankers (217). The "various participants are bound by the general interests of capital" (218).

3052. Wasko, Janet. "The Political Economy of the American Film Industry." MCS 3 (1981) 135-153.
On control of film industry by bankers.

II. C. 3. b. FILM ENTERTAINMENT & NEWS (3053-3185)
(See II.A. and II.B.1. & 2.)

3053. Anderson, Carolyn. "Documentary Dilemmas: An Analytic History of Frederick Wiseman's Titticut Follies." U of Massachusetts, 1984. 335. DAI 45 (1984) 1556-A.
A study of the censorship of Wiseman's documentary made at a Massachusetts Correctional Institution.

3054. Arkin, William. "At the Movies." BAS 42.5 (1986) 6-7.
"Military action movies are big again," selling US nationalism, anti-Sovietism, and the image of the US as underdog. Many are fantasies about refighting and winning the Vietnam War, others deal with wars as yet undeclared.

3055. Arthur, Paul. "Shadows on the Mirror: Film Noir & Cold War America, 1945-1957." New York U, 1985. DAI 46 (1986) 2107-A.
Examines eighty-three Hollywood crime films for their contribution to the popular anticommunism and Sovietphobia of the period.

3056. Aufderheide, Pat. "Alan Parker Plays with Fire in Mississippi Burning." ITT 13.7 (Dec. 21, 1988-Jan. 10, 1989) 20-21.
The film covers up FBI harassment of the SCLC, SNCC, Martin Luther King, Jr., and the civil rights movement in general, and its support of vigilantism "builds a case for a secret government of the kind George Bush knows from the inside."

3057. Auster, Albert. "In Defense of the Working Class: Hollywood and Its New Labor Films, 'Blue Collar' and 'F.I.S.T.'" RHR 18 (1978) 136-141.
Hollywood's failure to represent the working class and labor unions accurately.

3058. Barnouw, Erik. Documentary: A History of the Non-Fiction Film. New York: Oxford UP, 1974. 332.
US films: 1930s depression (111-27), WWII (143), corporate promotional (213, 216-28), Vietnam (272-83). Examples of filmic service to master institutions: Robert Flaherty's Louisiana Story sponsored by Standard Oil of New Jersey focused on the unspoiled wilderness and de-emphasized oil with the message: "the wilderness is safe," a theme repeated in "countless oil-sponsored films and television commercials" (216-219). The government secretly subsidized Fox and MGM-Hearst newsreels during the 1950s (272). Etc.

3059. Bartosch, Bob. "Peggy Sue Got Married and Invited Charlie to Dinner." JC 32 (1987) 3-4.
The film "Peggy Sue Got Married" is a female melodrama in which the heroine sacrifices herself for her kids in a world of commodities. But the film also portrays her imagining a different life choice, which operates as a countercurrent to patriarchy.

3060. Basinger, Jeanine. The World War II Combat Film: Anatomy of a Genre. New York: Columbia UP, 1986. 373.
Establishes a definition of the US World War II combat genre and traces the evolution of the genre. The genre has a basic "story" of repeated elements, with the intent of producing in the audience the feeling they are "ennobled for having shared" the combat experiences of the actors. Contains an "Annotated Filmography of World War II and Korean Combat Films."

3061. Bennett, Tony, et al., eds. Popular Television and Film: A Reader. London: British Film Inst., 1981. 353.
All of the twenty-five essays are concerned with "the ideological and political significance" of the two media. Although mainly about British media, the methods are relevant to the study of US media.

3062. Benson, Thomas W., and Carolyn Anderson. The Films of Frederick Wiseman. Carbondale: Southern Illinois UP, 1988. 480.
One chapter covers the legal battle over filmmaker Wiseman's Titticut Follies, a graphic documentary of conditions at the Massachusetts Correctional Institution at Bridgewater, during which one judge ordered the film destroyed.

3063. Bentley, Eric. "The Political Theatre of John Wayne." Theatre of War: Comments on 32 Occasions. New York: Viking, 1972. 306-312.
McCarthyite attacks on the entertainment industry in the 1950s worsened in the 1960s, and John Wayne typifies the militarism, imperialism, racism, and repression of the times.

3064. Biskind, Peter. Seeing Is Believing: How Hollywood Taught Us to Stop Worrying & Love the Fifties. New York: Pantheon, 1983. 371.
Studies the messages in Hollywood films "of the cold-war years, roughly from Harry Truman's victory in 1948 to the beginning of the Kennedy presidency in 1960." "Every movie that was produced, no matter how trivial or apparently escapist, was made in the shadow of the anticommunist witchhunt. . . . Similarly, most movies stressed the virtues of conformity and domesticity." But the fifties and their films also reflected "contradiction," and it is "these conflicting cultural messages that his book attempts to decode."

3065. Biskind, Peter. "The Politics of Power in On the Waterfront." American Media & Mass Culture. Ed.

Donald Lazere. Berkeley: U of California P, 1987. 184-200. (Orig. Film Quarterly, Fall 1975.)
 Movie a paradigm of the 1950s: organized labor identified with crime and communism, reversion from collective to individual problems and solutions, etc.

3066. Biskind, Peter, and Ehrenreich, Barbara. "Machismo and Hollywood's Working Class." American Media & Mass Culture. Ed. Donald Lazere. Berkeley: U of California P, 1987. 201-215.
 Traces the "ever more depoliticized incarnations of the working-class hero" viewed "through middle-class lenses as noble savages of purely individual defiance" (158).

3067. Britton, Andrew. "Blissing Out: The Politics of Reaganite Entertainment." Movie 31-32 (Winter 1986) 1-42.
 Films such as "The Towering Inferno" and "Friday the 13th" made in the late 1970s and 1980s project a Reaganite ideology victorious though empty.

3068. Buck, Jerry. "Skerritt Warms to Cold War Role." AG (Nov. 25, 1989) 6E.
 As the Cold War winds down, films about the SU change accordingly.

3069. Byars, Jackie. "Gender Representation in American Family Melodramas of the Nineteen-Fifties." U of Texas, Austin, 1983. 220. DAI 44.4 (Oct. 1983) 893-A.
 Especially examines methodologies for the analysis of gender representation in films: genre, "the gaze," ideology, etc.

3070. Callenbach, Ernest. "The Great Chaplin Chase." Na 183 (Aug. 4, 1956) 96-99.
 Charlie Chaplin was the object of lies and vicious propaganda by the press and reactionary groups because he "was constantly puncturing approved ideas and behavior."

3071. Campbell, Craig. Reel America and World War I: A Comprehensive Filmography and History of Motion Pictures in the United States, 1914-1920. Jefferson, NC: McFarland, 1985. 303.
 Examines the whole Hollywood industry, concentrating on those films that had as their themes "diplomatic intrigue, the military, preparedness and/or war." One chapter gives an annotated list of anti-"Bolshevik" films 1919-1920. "Every type of film produced, from cartoons, documentaries and newsreels to shorts and features, was increasingly throughout this time engaged in placing images of war in front of the public" (25). [See entry 3179].

3072. "Can-Do Crusaders: Rallying Around the Wrong Stuff." Soj 12.11 (Dec. 1983) 38-39.
 The Right Stuff, a film about the astronauts, reflects the intensified Cold War, nationalism, and militarism of the Reagan administration.

3073. Cardwell, David. "Raoul Walsh." U of Southern
California, 1985. DAI 46 (1986) 2107-A.
Walsh accommodated himself to the Warner Brothers house style, but his world view was at times "deeply subversive of societal values."

3074. Ceplair, Larry, and Steven Englund. The Inquisition in Hollywood: Politics in the Film Community, 1930-1960. Garden City, NY: Doubleday, 1980. 536.
A history of persecution of radicals.

3075. Cholodenko, Alan. "The Films of Frederick Wiseman."
Harvard U, 1987. 291. DAI 48 (1988) 2749-A.
Wiseman's films "constitute the most significant and sustained examination" of US institutions in the cinema—prison, school, army, monastery. He reveals "the ways in which these institutions interlock as part of a normalizing disciplinary regime." Intervention is his subject, and nonintervention his "ethic, aesthetic, and principle of being."

3076. Clark, Michael. "Remembering Vietnam." CulC 3 (Spring 1986) 46-78.
Recent films about Vietnam reflect the Reagan administration's efforts to reaffirm US global intervention.

3077. Cogley, John. "HUAC: The Mass Hearings." The American Film Industry. Rev. ed. Ed. Tino Balio. Madison: U of Wisconsin P, 1985. 487-509.
Pp. 92-117 of the author's Report on Blacklisting I: The Movies.

3078. Colgan, Christine. "Warner Brothers' Crusade Against the Third Reich: A Study of Anti-Nazi Activism & Film Production, 1933 to 1941." U of Southern California, 1985. DAI 47 (1986) 1907-A.
Jack and Harry Warner were the first studio leaders to oppose Nazism actively; they exerted pressure on the Roosevelt administration to take more forceful action against Germany.

3079. Collum, Danny. "The War in Our Heads." Soj 13.10 (Nov. 1984) 35.
The film Red Dawn projects the Sovietphobia of the Reagan administration.

3080. Cooper, Marc. "Oh, Say You Won't See . . . Amerika."
TM 20.3 (Aug.-Sept. 1986) 13-14.
On the paranoid, Russian-bashing film about the Soviet takeover of the US, a plot that conforms closely "to the ideology of the current American right."

3081. Copjec, Joan. "Apparatus & Umbra: A Feminist Critique of Film Theory." New York U, 1986. 199. DAI 47 (1987) 4212-A.
Opposes the deterministic tendency in past theory which makes women the "casualty."

3082. Corn-Revere, Robert. "Putting the First Out of Business." Na 247.7 (Sept. 26, 1988) 234-38.
The "bureaucratic drive to censor [obscenity] continues unabated" now strengthened by the Racketeer Influence and Corrupt Organizations Act (RICO) forfeiture provision.

3083. Davies, Philip, and Brian Neve, eds. Cinema, Politics and Society in America. New York: St. Martin's, 1981. 266.
Essays on topics from the American Western to blacks' appearance in film focus on the impulse of films to address the "social significance" of standard thematic patterns.

3084. De Lauretis, Teresa. Alice Doesn't: Feminism, Semiotics, Cinema. Bloomington: Indiana UP, 1984. 220.
Cinema transforms women into myths of women. Examines various theoretical relations to feminist analysis of film: structuralism, perception theory, Foucault, narratology, and Freudianism. Articulates a politically open theory of the contradictions of cultural form, in which feminine resistance and subversion are found within male oppression and suppression.

3085. Dick, Bernard. The Star-Spangled Screen: The American World War II Film. Lexington, KY: UP of Kentucky, 1985. 294.
The WWII film (made during the war mainly) "has its own themes, plots, and iconography," with clear statements of good and evil, patriotism, valor, and duty. [See 3087].

3086. Doherty, Thomas. Teenagers and Teenpics: The Juvenilization of American Movies in the 1950s. Boston: Unwin Hyman, 1988. 275.
"American motion pictures today are not a mass medium"; rather, they "reflect teenage, not mass--and definitely not adult--tastes," in contrast to the movies prior to the mid-1950s. The "teenpic" has become "the industry's flagship enterprise" (3), "a version of the exploitation film."

3087. Donald, Ralph. "Hollywood and World War II: Enlisting Feature Films as Propaganda." U of Massachusetts, 1987. 286. DAI 48 (1988) 2186-A.
Studies five kinds of persuasive appeals used in 37 films to propagate support for the war: Guilt, Satanism, Victory, Apocalypticism, and Territoriality. Satanism was the most frequent technique. [See 3085].

3088. Dworkin, Marc. "The Jewish Collective Fantasy in American Film." U of Southern California, 1986. DAI 48 (1988) 1560-A.
A key to understanding films made by Jews is their immigrant background and "struggles to emerge from poverty and to become tycoons in Hollywood." Focuses on period 1927-1950.

3089. Ellsworth, Elizabeth. "The Power of Interpretive Communities: Feminist Appropriations of Personal

Best." U of Wisconsin, Madison, 1984. DAI 45 (1984) 1225-A.
Studies responses of the feminist community to the sexist film Personal Best as "political struggle to construct feminist viewing pleasures" and strategies in opposition to male regulation of "critical debate and dissent."

3090. Engelhardt, Tom. "Ambush at Kamikaze Pass." American Media & Mass Culture. Ed. Donald Lazere. Berkeley: U of California P, 1987. 480-498.
Examines media stereotypes of foreigners, racism, nationalism, and ethnocentrism.

3091. Falkenberg, Pamela. "Rewriting the 'Classic Hollywood Cinema': Textual Analysis, Ironic Distance, and the Western in the Critique of Corporate Capitalism." U of Iowa, 1983. 587. DAI 44.12 (June 1984) 3522-A.
"As a representational institution, the cinema can only model the corporate capitalism that has 'created' it." Analyzes four Westerns and their "production of meaning under corporate capitalism," through the "endlessly interchangeable" "circulation of desires, signifiers, and commodities."

3092. Faller, Greg. "The Function of Star-image and Performance in the Hollywood Musical: Sonja Henie, Esther Williams, & Eleanor Powell." Northwestern U, 1987. 508. DAI 48 (1988) 2475-A.
Stars function hegemonically as "managers of cultural and ideological contradictions and as role models."

3093. Fenwick, Steven. "Hearts & Minds: A Case Study of a 'Propaganda' Film." U of Michigan, 1982. 625. DAI 43.2 (Aug. 1982) 290-A.
Analyzes this 1975 Academy Award winning film critical of US activities in Vietnam.

3094. Fielding, Raymond. The American Newsreel, 1911-1967. Norman, OK: U of Oklahoma P, 1972. 392.
Because the producers of newsreels were mainly profit oriented, misrepresentation and fraud were frequent. Newsreels "failed, in almost every way" to "fulfill the promise" open to them.

3095. Fielding, Raymond. The March of Time, 1935-1951. New York: Oxford UP, 1978. 359.
From its beginning The March of Time newsreel was constructed on ideological purposes--against fascism, communism, demagogues, quacks. During the Cold War, MOT attacked communism "consistently, systematically, and vigorously" (290). Its popularity also derived from its problem-solving optimism.

3096. "Films." NIF 37.5 (Sept. 1988) 169.
The USIA's unconstitutional efforts to regulate foreign distribution of documentary films.

3097. Fleener, Nickie. "'The Worst Case of Racial Equality
He Ever Saw': The Supreme Court, Motion Picture
Censorship, and the Color Line." FSY (1979) 1-15.
Reviews Supreme Court decisions dealing with censorship of
films on the basis of racial content, underscoring the lack of
any definite stand by the Court on this issue.

3098. Fore, Steven. "The Perils of Patriotism: The Hollywood
War Film as Generic & Cultural Discourse." U of
Texas, Austin, 1986. 377. DAI 47 (1987) 3215-A.
Studies nine films about WWII, the Korean War, and the
Vietnam War, tracing their development from WWII propaganda
genre to adaptations to the increasingly complex and confusing
Korean and Vietnam wars.

3099. Gabler, Neal. An Empire of Their Own: How the Jews
Invented Hollywood. New York: Crown, 1988. 502.
A group biography of the Jewish immigrants who founded and
came to dominate the film industry: Adolph Zukor, Carl
Laemmle, Louis B. Mayer, the Warner brothers, Harry Cohn.
These men created an image of the nation that so shaped its
myths, values, traditions, and archetypes that this country
came to be largely defined by its movies.

3100. Galerstein, Carolyn. "Hollywood's Rosie the Riveter."
JC 32 (1987) 20-21.
Explores the sexism and racism of WWII films about women
workers. The films are totally white, classless, romanticized
versions of war factories, avoiding the many serious problems
facing women--e.g., the lack of child care.

3101. Gibson, William. "Sub Par: Tom Clancy's High-Tech
Warriors Surface in the Wake of the Cold War." ITT
14.17 (Mar. 21-27, 1990) 24.
Describes Sovietphobic, militarist novels and films and the
Reagan administration's approval of them.

3102. Gliserman, Marty. "Watch Out, Chicago." JC 5 (Jan.-
Feb. 1975) 7-8.
Films like Death Wish, which portray crimes by lower social
classes, reaffirm the hierarchy of power.

3103. Haines, Harry. "Mediated Vietnam: The Politics of
Postwar Representations." U of Utah, 1987. 257.
DAI 48 (1988) 1571-A.
Describes the struggle occurring within the media to assign
meaning to the war, especially the warrior hero myth repre-
sented by such films as Rambo and Accuracy in Media's
Television's Vietnam: The Real Story in conflict with
"informant, or witness" mediation.

3104. Hess, Judith. "Genre Films & the Status Quo." JC 1
(1974) 1, 16.
Westerns, horror, gangster, and sci-fi films serve the
ruling class by evading social and economic problems.

3105. Hirano, Kyoko. "The Japanese Tragedy: Film Censorship and the American Occupation." RHR 41 (Spring 1988) 67-92.
US officials in post-war Japan first supported, then banned The Japanese Tragedy as policy regarding the Emperor changed on account of fears of communist influence.

3106. Holmlund, Christine. "New Cold War Sequels & Remakes." JC 35 (Apr. 1990) 85-96.
During the 1980s a new Cold War raged on movie screens (Top Gun, etc.), while "less overtly xenophobic and chauvinistic" Sovietphobic films also projected hostility. But some of these films contain contradictory and self-subverting contents. Examines Down and Out in Beverly Hills, Rocky IV, and Aliens.

3107. Howe, Russell W. "Asset Unwitting: Covering the World for the CIA." MORE 8 (May 1978) 20-27.
Forum World Features, the press syndicate headed by John Hay Whitney and then Richard Scaife, was secretly funded by the CIA.

3108. Jaffe, Susan. "Why the Bomb Didn't Hit Home: Atomic Film Cover-Up." NT 1.5 (Mar. 1983) 10-15.
Tells of Herbert Sussan's struggle to obtain documentary footage he shot in Hiroshima and Nagasaki shortly after the use of the a-bomb. AEC's efforts to keep it from the public.

3109. Jowett, Garth. "The Concept of History in American Produced Films: An Analysis of the Films Made in the Period 1950-1961." JPC 3.1 (Summer 1969) 799-813.
Study of over 3,000 films reveals few historically accurate plots and little deviation from mainstream social values, both tendencies in the interest of commercial profit.

3110. Kael, Pauline. "On the Future of the Movies" (1970). Mass Media: The Invisible Environment Revisited. Ed. Robert Glessing and William White. Chicago: SRA, 1976. 66-70.
Gives causes for blatancy and nihilism of recent popular films: advertising, producers and profit, etc.

3111. Kanfer, Stefan. A Journal of the Plague Years. New York: Atheneum, 1973. 306.
The story of the blacklisting of the Hollywood Ten.

3112. Kerr, Paul, ed. The Hollywood Film Industry. New York: Routledge, 1987. 256.
A collection of case studies that confront the traditional perspective of Hollywood and focuses on the correlation between the organization of the industry and its products.

3113. Klinger, Barbara. "Cinema & Social Process: A Contextual Theory of the Cinema & Its Spectators." U of Iowa, 1986. 144. DAI 47 (1987) 2772-A.

Opposes cinematically specific approaches to spectator response, emphasizes social process and institutions. Draws upon the ideas of the Frankfurt School, Bakhtin, Foucault, Eco, and Tony Bennett to study interpretations ("reading formations") of Written on the Wind, a 1950s Hollywood melodrama.

3114. Koppes, Clayton, and Gregory Black. Hollywood Goes to War: How Politics, Profits and Propaganda Shaped World War II Movies. New York: Free, 1987. 374.
Account of how the tremendous pressure on Hollywood by the Office of War Information to turn out propaganda, combined with the industry's own economic aspirations, created not only false depictions of the enemies but false pictures of allies and of the US public.

3115. Kunzle, David. "Introduction to How to Read Donald Duck." American Media & Mass Culture. Ed. Donald Lazere. Berkeley: U of California P, 1987. 516-529.
Locates capitalist and imperialist values in Disney's production of the American Dream and in US culture in general.

3116. "Last Temptation of Christ: Censorship Holy War." NIF 37.6 (Nov. 1988) 195, 212-214.
An account of the efforts by fundamentalist Christians to prevent the showing of the film.

3117. Lawson, John H. Film in the Battle of Ideas. New York: Masses & Mainstream, 1953. 126. Rptd. New York: Garland, 1985.
Describes the film industry as an instrument of ruling ideology.

3118. Linz, Daniel, Edward Donnerstein, and Steven Penrod. "The Effects of Multiple Exposures to Filmed Violence Against Women." JoC 34.3 (1984) 130-147.
As men repeatedly view depictions of violence against women, the violence become normalized and more acceptable.

3119. Lytle, Stewart. "The Military Cultivates Its Hollywood Connection." Pr 8.6 (1980) 9.
On Pentagon methods for controlling the contents of war movies.

3120. MacDonald, Scott. A Critical Cinema: Interviews with Independent Filmmakers. Berkeley: U of California P, 1988. 410.
Surveys North American films known as "underground," "New American," "experimental," and "avant-garde." Many of these filmmakers view the dominant commercial cinema and TV "as a set of culturally conditioned and accepted approaches to cinema--a cultural text--to be analyzed from within the medium of film itself," placing our acceptance of commercial films "into crisis."

3121. Maland, Charles. Chaplin and American Culture: The

ELECTRONIC MEDIA

Evolution of a Star Image. Princeton, NJ: Princeton UP, 1989. 442.
Includes an account of the government's conspiracies against Chaplin, through trumped-up charges, selected leaks, spying, and allegations of un-American activities, until Chaplin left the US for a twenty-year exile in Switzerland.

3122. Marchetti, Gina. "Action-Adventure as Ideology." Cultural Politics in Contemporary America. New York: Routledge, 1989. 182-197.
Although the action-adventure genre is open to contradictory responses from audiences, it privileges the dominant white, male, bourgeois ideology.

3123. May, Lary. "Movie Star Politics: The Screen Actors' Guild, Cultural Conversion, and the Hollywood Red Scare." Recasting America: Culture and Politics in the Age of Cold War. Chicago: U of Chicago P, 1989. 125-153.
Hollywood became the agency for a new identity "rooted in consensus and consumption. To accomplish that ideological conversion," Hollywood leaders like Eric Johnston "drew on a new form of anticommunism to discredit opposition to monopoly capital and generate support for building a new world order" (148).

3124. May, Lary. Screening Out the Past: The Birth of Mass Culture & the Motion Picture Industry. New York: Oxford UP, 1980. 304.
Rebellion against Victorian mores was catalyzed by the emergence of America's motion picture industries which altered societal moral visions leading to "moral experimentation."

3125. McWilliams, Carey. "Hollywood Gray List." Na 169.21 (1949) 491-492.
Many actors who were in the past politically active were put on a "gray," or probationary list by the film industry and were not offered employment.

3126. Mellencamp, Patricia, and Philip Rosen, eds. Cinema Histories, Cinema Practices. Frederick, MD: The American Film Inst., 1984. 150.
Film exerts a political, social, and economic control that is "unseen." This is due to the fact that style, technology, and ideology are interrelated.

3127. Miller, Mark C., ed. Seeing Through Movies. New York: Pantheon, 1990. 266.
The movies "now are made deliberately to show us nothing, but to sell us everything." Corporate monopolies have resulted in an "image-generating system" that includes television production companies and syndication firms, cable distribution networks, record companies, and numerous merchandising operations--as well as publishing companies, major magazines, and many newspapers.

3128. Modleski, Tania. "The Terror of Pleasure: The Contemporary Horror Film & Postmodern Theory." Studies in Entertainment. Ed. Tania Modleski. Bloomington: Indiana UP, 1986. 155-166.
Compares popular "slasher" films and high art as opposition to bourgeois ideology.

3129. Moore, Thomas W. "The Images of the Hard-Boiled Detective in American Film Since 1941." U of Maryland, 1983. 299. DAI 44.12 (June 1984) 3523-A.
Examines the films' changing social and cultural contexts to reveal "how different eras' definitions of beliefs like law, order, and justice and the amount of confidence in the individual's power to uphold these beliefs can influence a film."

3130. Murray, Lawrence L. "Monsters, Spies, and Subversives: The Film Industry Responds to the Cold War, 1945-1955." JC 9 (Oct.-Dec. 1979) 14-16.
Studies the effect of the Cold War on Hollywood's product, citing four types of films symptomatic of the post-war anticommunist frenzy.

3131. Musser, Charles. "Before the Nickelodeon: Edwin S. Porter & the Edison Manufacturing Company." New York U, 1986. 636. DAI 47 (1987) 4213-A.
Porter's films emphasized family and condemned the city and large-scale capitalism. Because he opposed the standardization, specialization, and hierarchization demanded for faster production, he was fired by the company.

3132. Navasky, Victor. Naming Names. New York: Viking, 1980. 482.
A study of the informer in Hollywood during the McCarthy period of the Cold War.

3133. Nelson, Joyce. The Colonized Eye: Rethinking the Grierson Legend. Toronto: Between the Lines, 1988. 197.
An account of John Grierson, founder of Canada's National Film Board, as champion of film as public-relations vehicle for the corporate state and multinational capital's goal to integrate world markets.

3134. Nimmo, Dan, and James Combs. "The View from Sunset Boulevard: The Political Fantasies of Hollywood." Mediated Political Realities. New York: Longman, 1983. 105-123.
Brief history of film as "mediated political melodramas." "Hollywood makes movies for profit by telling stories. These stories are fantasies about the American Dream" (106).

3135. Parry-Giles, Trevor. "The Banning of Hail Mary at the University of New Mexico." FSN (Summer 1987) 13.
The banning of the film Hail Mary by the Regents was eventually reversed.

3136. "Pentagon Links Change in Script, Eastwood Aid." AG
 (May 26, 1986) 6A.
 On military manipulation of film contents.

3137. Polan, Dana B. "Daffy Duck and Bertolt Brecht: Toward
 a Politics of Self-Reflexive Cinema?" American Media
 & Mass Culture. Ed. Donald Lazere. Berkeley: U of
 California P, 1987. 345-356.
 A critique of the attack on representation by Continental
semiology, Althusserian Marxism, and Lacanian psychoanalysis.

3138. Polan, Dana B. The Political Language of Film and the
 Avant-Garde. Ann Arbor, MI: UMI Research P, 1985.
 141.
 Overview of the political aesthetics of the avant-garde, the
alternate political film culture. Polan examines both
American experimental film and classic Hollywood cinema--
including Warner Brothers cartoons and musicals. Brecht,
Eisenstein, and Oshima are among the major figures discussed.
Presents a record of the accomplishments--and failures.

3139. [Cancelled]

3140. Quart, Leonard. "Frank Capra and the Popular Front."
 American Media & Mass Culture. Ed. Donald Lazere.
 Berkeley: U of California P, 1987. 178-83.
 Evaluates Frank Capra's films in the context of opposition
to fascism.

3141. Randall, Richard. "Censorship: From The Miracle to
 Deep Throat." The American Film Industry. Rev. ed.
 Ed. Tino Balio. Madison: U of Wisconsin P, 1985.
 510-536.
 In spite of the Burstyn v. Wilson (1952) case that gave
First Amendment protection to motion pictures, movies have
continued to generate censorial attacks.

3142. Randall, Richard. Censorship of the Movies: The Social
 & Political Control of a Mass Medium. Madison: U of
 Wisconsin P, 1968. 280.
 Relates legal doctrines to the operating controls. Chaps.
2-4 examine the laws of movie censorship, particularly
obscenity; chaps. 5-6 governmental prior censorship--state,
city, and Bureau of Customs; chaps. 7-8 criminal prosecution,
self-censorship, etc. Almost all censorial standards except
obscenity have been eliminated, and obscenity objections have
been liberalized.

3143. Rapping, Elayne. "Women in film in the '80's: Fatal
 Omission: Feminism." Guard 40.23 (Mar. 9, 1988) 11.
 Current films portray women in ways that "undermine a lot of
important feminist values."

3144. Renov, Michael. Hollywood's Wartime Woman: Representation and Ideology. Ann Arbor, MI: UMI Research P,

1988. 275.

Analyzes 170 woman-centered films of the WWII era, concentrating on the pressures and limits government supervision exerted on wartime artistic practice.

3145. Ritt, Martin, interviewed by Pat McGilligan. "Ritt Large." FC 22.1 (Jan.-Feb. 1986) 32-37.

Fifties blacklist victim and film director Ritt recalls his experiences as one of the censored directors.

3146. Rogin, Michael P. "Kiss Me Deadly: Communism, Motherhood, and Cold War Movies." "Ronald Reagan," the Movie. Berkeley: U of California P, 1987. 236-271.

The Cold War introduced the "third movement" in US demonology (following Indian-Black and working class).

3147. Rogin, Michael P. "'Ronald Reagan,' the Movie." "Ronald Reagan," the Movie. Berkeley: U of California P, 1987. 1-43.

The presidential Reagan was produced in 1940s Hollywood "from the convergence of two substitutions that generated cold war countersubversion in the 1940s and underlie its 1980s revival--the political replacement of Nazism by Communism, from which the national-security state was born, and the psychological shift from an embodied self to its simulacrum on film" (3).

3148. Rosenberg, Howard L. "For Our Eyes Only." AF 8.9 (1983) 40-43.

In order for an educational or documentary film to enter another country without paying the duties required of "films for profit" it must receive a "Certificate of International Educational Character" from the USIA (United States Information Agency). Certificate control is thus an effective potential form of censorship for films that vary from official views.

3149. Rosenthal, Alan, ed. New Challenges for Documentary. Berkeley: U of California P, 1988. 615.

Innovations today--in point of view, political content, relations with broadcasting bureaucracies, etc.

3150. Rosenthal, Alan. The New Documentary in Action: A Casebook in Film Making. Berkeley: U of California P, 1972. 287.

Provides "insight into the day-to-day pressures on film-makers," focusing upon the creation of specific films and their producers and directors.

3151. Rossell, Deac. "Irreplaceable Experiences." When Information Counts: Grading the Media. Lexington, MA: Lexington/Heath, 1985. 131-38.

On the inadequate and unrealistic treatment of minorities by Hollywood, contrasted to the "true minority film" by independent film-makers.

3152. Ryan, Michael, and Douglas Kellner. Camera Politica: The Politics and Ideology of Contemporary Hollywood Film. Bloomington: Indiana UP, 1988. 328.

Focuses "on the relationship between Hollywood film and American society from 1967 to the mid-eighties, a period characterized by a major swing in dominant social movements from Left to Right," when Hollywood film increasingly promoted "the new conservative movements on several fronts, from the family to the military to economic policy" (xi). But not entirely, for "the social movements of the sixties carried over into the seventies and eighties" in "significant cinematic statements against social injustice, nuclear weapons, and U.S. foreign policy" (War Games, Missing, Silkwood, Under Fire, Salvador) (11).

3153. Savage, Robert L. "The Stuff of Politics through Cinematic Imagery: An Eiconic Perspective." Politics in Familiar Contexts: Projecting Politics Through Popular Media. Ed. Robert L. Savage and Dan Nimmo. Norwood, NJ: Ablex, 1990. 119-137.

Discusses "commercial motion pictures" as both reflections and purveyors of societal values, through their narrative structuring of myths, particularly the "romantic quest for a political paradise lost" (124), the search for the "American Dream."

3154. Sayre, Nora. Running Time: Films of the Cold War. New York: Dial, 1982. 243.

Analyzes how the cultural Cold War restored uncontested hegemony to the traditional mythology of capitalism in films. Chapter on "The Private Sector" traces the reduction of social conflict in fifties films to unhappy family life or the inability to love or communicate.

3155. Schumach, Murray. The Face on the Cutting Room Floor: The Story of Movie and Television Censorship. New York: Da Capo, 1975. 305.

Evaluates the Motion Picture Production Code and pleads for voluntary classification of films. Assesses government censorship (e.g. McCarthyism) and pressure groups. In general opposes all forms of censorship but believes in voluntary restraint by classification.

3156. Scott, Ronald. "Interracial Relationships in Films: A Descriptive & Critical Analysis of Guess Who's Coming to Dinner? and Watermelon Man." U of Utah, 1984. 443. DAI 46 (1985) 10-A.

Even though the films affirm the primacy of feelings over stereotypes and equality over prejudice, "both films end up by showing that whites are still in control," that accommodating blacks will be accepted but "at the cost of denying their blackness," and that blacks who refuse will be rejected by white society.

3157. Shain, Russell E. "Effects of Pentagon Influence on

War Movies, 1948-70." JQ 49.4 (Winter 1972) 641-647.
"War movies for which the Pentagon provided assistance are
more likely to emphasize military professionalism than films
made without such help. This tendency became more marked
between 1963 and 1970."

3158. Sharrett, Christopher. "Apocalypticism in the Contemporary Horror Film: A Typological Survey of a Theme in the Fantastic Cinema, Its Relationship to Cultural Tradition & Current Filmic Expression." New York U, 1983. 333. DAI 44.12 (June 1984) 3523-A.
Studies the vision of the "pervasive insanity and fragmentation" of "a now-dead social order" in fifteen apocalyptic horror films.

3159. Shindler, Colin. Hollywood Goes to War: Films & American Society 1939-52. London: Routledge, 1979. 152.
A social history, since the films "were shaped by . . . various social, political and ideological stimuli"--e.g., anticommunism, Nazism, patriotism.

3160. Shohat, Ella, and Robert Stam. "The Cinema After Babel: Language, Difference, Power." Screen 26 (May-Aug. 1985) 35-58.
"Inscribed within the play of power, languages are caught up in artificial hierarchies rooted in cultural hegemonies and political oppression. English, for example, as a function of its colonizing status, became the linguistic vehicle for the projection of Anglo-American power, technology and finance. Hollywood, especially, came to incarnate a linguistic hubris bred of empire."

3161. Short, K.R.M., ed. Film & Radio Propaganda in World War II. Knoxville: U of Tennessee P, 1983. 341.
Ch. 5: "Racial Ambiguities in American Propaganda Movies," 6: "Hollywood Fights Anti-Semitism, 1940-45," and 7: "'Why We Fight': Social Engineering for a Democratic Society at War."

3162. Sikov, Edward. "Laughing Hysterically: American Screen Comedies of the 1950s." Columbia U, 1986. 247. DAI 47 (1986) 689-A.
The comedies of Hawks, Wilder, Hitchcock, and Tashlin provided social criticism of the repressive and fragmenting era.

3163. Simone, Sam. Hitchcock as Activist: Politics and the War Films. Ann Arbor, MI: UMI Research P, 1985. 203.
During WWII Hitchcock's films "champion the United States" and democracy against the Nazis through "melodrama and suspense" (Preface).

3164. S.K. "The World According to Wick." CC 14.2 (Mar.-Apr. 1988) 7.
On USIA censorship of films critical of the US, blocking overseas distribution.

3165. Sklar, Robert. Movie Made America: A Social History of American Movies. New York: Random House, 1976. 340.
Movies formed the mores of the American consciousness and simultaneously were shaped by them.

3166. Smolla, Rodney, and Stephen A. Smith. "Propaganda, Xenophobia, and the First Amendment." OLR 67.2 (1988) 253-285.
Opposes Meese vs. Keene, which upheld Justice Department censorship of foreign films.

3167. Sofia, Zoë. "Exterminating Fetuses: Abortion, Disarmament, and the Sexo-Semiotics of Extraterrestrialism." Diacritics 14.2 (Summer 1984) 47-59.
Examines the "New Right's cult of fetal personhood and a 1968 science fiction film, 2001: A Space Odyssey" as "aspects of an ideological apparatus which addresses extinction fears only to distract us from the exterminist practices of the military-industrial complex."

3168. Soroka, Laurence. "Hollywood Modernism: Self-Consciousness & the Hollywood-on-Hollywood Film Genre." Emory U, 1983. 189. DAI 44.8 (Feb. 1984) 2275-A.
A study of the range of self-critical awareness in "Hollywood Modernism," the combination of traditional Hollywood illusionism with modernist self-consciousness, focusing on Sunset Boulevard, Singin' in the Rain, and The Last Movie.

3169. Springer, Claudia. "Cultural Projections: Traditions of Cross-Cultural Representation in Ethnographic, Educational, and Contemporary Hollywood Cinema." Northwestern U, 1986. 176. DAI 47 (1987) 2773-A.
Filmic constructions of the Third World reflect the dominant US ideology by their creation of a threat or mystery emanating from Third World settings which is then explained or defeated.

3170. Springer, Claudia. "Military Propaganda: Defense Department Films from World War II and Vietnam." CulC 3 (Spring 1986) 151-67.
Contrasts Frank Capra's films about WWII to films about the Vietnam War.

3171. Sragow, Michael. "Gross Projections." MJ 15.1 (Jan. 1990) 23-27.
"The true story of how Reagan and Television ate Hollywood's brain"; i.e., films during the Reagan era were mainly mediocre and escapist.

3172. Steven, Peter G. "Hollywood's Depiction of the Working-Class from 1970 to 1981: A Marxist Analysis." Northwestern U, 1982. 333. DAI 43.10 (Apr. 1983) 3142-A.
There was an upsurge of films in the 1970s about the working-class, and many of these films challenged the notion

of a classless society.

3173. Stone, Jennifer. Mind Over Media: Essays on Film and Television. Berkeley, CA: Cayuse, 1988. 167.
Our own culture is one of consumerism ("our national religion"), pornographic (all "things and people can be had"), and "sado-militarist" (Rambo etc.), all reflected in popular art. Yet there is art too that is "morally stunning," an art "which changes the world" (167).

3174. Suid, Lawrence. "The Film Industry and the Vietnam War." Case Western Reserve U, 1980. 296. DAI 41 (1981) 3164.
After 1977 films have portrayed the war more negatively.

3175. Taylor, Richard K. "The Greatest Argument for Peace the World Has Ever Seen." Soj 12.2 (1986) 19-21.
The story of Herbert Sussan's film record of the destruction of Nagasaki and Hiroshima.

3176. "This Property Is Condemned." Na 171.22 (1950) 485.
Censorship and conformity imposed upon the "Hollywood Ten" and other media employees.

3177. Virilio, Paul. War and Cinema: The Logistics of Perceptions. Trans. Patrick Camiller. London: Verso, 1989. 95.
Calculated cinematic techniques become "a war of pictures and sounds" espousing certain military perspectives thereby becoming the "logistics of perception" which will eventually replace nuclear weapons.

3178. Walker, Janet. "Couching Resistance: Women, Film, & Psychoanalytic Psychiatry from World War II Through the Mid-1960s." U of California, L.A., 1987. 399. DAI 48 (1988) 1561-A.
Employs Michel Foucault's "archaeological analysis" to delineate the network of relationships between film and psychoanalytic discourses, showing that psychiatry was "a set of institutions and practices that embodied, addressed, and sometimes even challenged the very contradictions of patriarchy."

3179. Ward, Larry. The Motion Picture Goes to War: The U.S. Government Film Effort during World War I. Ann Arbor, MI: UMI Research, 1985. 176.
The government's Committee on Public Information (CPI) and the film industry worked together to produce propaganda films.

3180. Waugh, Thomas, ed. "Show Us Life:" Toward a History and Aesthetics of the Committed Documentary. Metuchen, NJ: Scarecrow, 1984. 508.
In order to view reality in documentary films as opposed to the kisses, sighs, and killings of commercial films, producers of documentaries must be activists presenting specific political ideologies "not only about people . . . but with and for

those people as well."

3181. Whillock, David. "The Fictive American Vietnam War Film: A Structural Analysis of Myth Based on the Theories of Claude Lévi-Strauss." U of Missouri, Columbia, 1986. 197. DAI 47 (1987) 3592-A.
The Green Berets, Apocalypse Now, and The Killing Fields "contain identical underlying structures" of "binary Nature/ Culture opposition."

3182. Wood, Robin. Hollywood from Vietnam to Reagan. New York: Columbia UP, 1986. 328.
Analyzes how films dramatize cultural conflicts of class, wealth, gender, and race. Particular attention to sex and capitalism to explain how dominant institutions are maintained. The author is committed to "the struggle for liberation" through socialism and feminism.

3183. Wood, Robin. "Ideology, Genre, Auteur." Film Genre Reader. Ed. Barry Grant. Austin: U of Texas P, 1986. 59-73.
Discusses the values and assumptions of US capitalist ideology which pervade classic Hollywood films and convey contradictions that support myth and neglect reality.

3184. Woodward, H. Mark. "The Formulation and Implementation of U.S. Feature Film Policy in Occupied Germany, 1945-1948." U of Texas, Dallas, 1987. 297. DAI 48 (1987) 1341-A.
The War Department with the cooperation of the film industry created an occupation feature film program to "re-educate" the German people away from Nazism and toward US values. The program "failed" to achieve this goal, "at least at a conscious level."

3185. Zheutlin, Barbara, and David Talbot. Creative Differences: Profiles of Hollywood Dissidents. Boston: South End, 1978. 370.
The title refers to the euphemism employed in the entertainment industry when someone is fired. "This book examines the lives of sixteen people" who have been fired from the industry for criticizing the industry.

II. C. 4. COMPUTERS (3186-3219)

3186. Beniger, James R. The Control Revolution: Technological and Economic Origins of the Information Society. Cambridge, MA: Harvard UP, 1986. 493.
The "Control Revolution" is "a complex of rapid changes in the technological and economic arrangements by which information is collected, stored, processed, and communicated and through which formal or programmed decisions can effect societal control" (427). "Perhaps most pervasive of all rationalization is the increasing tendency to regulate inter-

personal relationships in terms of a formal set of impersonal, quantifiable, and objective criteria, changes that greatly facilitate control by both government and business" (435).

3187. Brown, Ben. "Trouble in Paradise." AF 7.9 (1982) 61-62.
Danger of data banks controlled by corporations and government.

3188. Burnham, David. The Rise of the Computer State. New York: Vintage, 1984. 273.
In his Foreword Walter Cronkite evokes the threat of totalitarianism in Orwell's 1984 to contrast the actual shape of the threat that would exist in 1984: "the ubiquitous computer and its ancillary communication networks" that increasingly invade privacy.

3189. Burnham, David. "Tales of a Computer State." Na 236.17 (1983) 527, 537-541.
Warns of the widespread computerized surveillance by government and industry.

3190. Deibel, Mary. "Mr. Zip Takes the Measure of America." Pr 10.4 (Aug. 1982) 14.
Describes a direct marketing company.

3191. Dennis, Everette E. Reshaping the Media: Mass Communication in the Information Age. Newbury Park, CA: Sage, 1989. 210.
New communication technologies--cable TV, satellites, VCRs, computers, on-line data bases, etc.--have fundamentally altered communication.

3192. Drey, Leonard. "Media Ignore Possible Hazards of VDT's, Research Continues." SLJR 19.124 (Mar. 1990) 8.
Scientific research, particularly the Kaiser Permanente study, questions the safety of video display terminals. Yet main media ignore this controversy.

3193. Elsworth, Peter C. T. "The Menace of the Machine." Channels 3 (Sept.-Oct. 1983) 68-72.
Government compiling and access to computer files on individuals raise the dangers suggested by Orwell in 1984.

3194. Forester, Tom, ed. The Information Technology Revolution. Cambridge, MA: MIT P, 1985. 674.
Essays debate the advantages versus the sociological and economic dangers of the new computer-based technology. Part 4, "Implications for Society," discusses "Social Problems," "Global Issues," and "Parameters of the Post-industrial Society."

3195. Frantzich, Stephen. Computers in Congress: The Politics of Information. Beverly Hills: Sage, 1982. 285.
Assesses computers as a major source of power, which promoters in Congress well understand.

ELECTRONIC MEDIA 451

3196. Garson, Barbara. The Electronic Sweatshop: How Computers are Transforming the Office of the Future into the Factory of the Past. New York: Simon & Schuster, 1988. 288.
Indicts the increasing computer monitoring of workplaces in business and government, especially by the military.

3197. Gelbspan, Ross. "Computers Bring '1984' Closer." AG (Dec. 15, 1985) 1C, 7C.
Various levels of government together possess records on half the population, without counting the secret records held by intelligence agencies.

3198. Gordon, Diana, and Mae Churchill. "Interstate I.D. Index: 'Triple I' Will Be Tracking Us." Na 238.16 (1984) 497, 513-515.
Flaws and dangers in the FBI's arrest data bank.

3199. Krass, Peter. "Computers That Would Program People." BSR 37 (1980-81) 62-64.
The growing "spectre" of subliminal communication.

3200. Le Mond, Alan, and Ron Fry. No Place to Hide. New York: St. Martin's, 1975. 278.
Surveys the bugging, tapping, watching, and data filing on a host of people without their consent performed by businesses and the government.

3201. Linowes, David F. "How Databanks Get the Goods on Everybody." BSR 26 (1978) 54-57.
Warns of the increasing computerized integration of information about people, shared "often without the knowledge of the individual concerned."

3202. Miller, Arthur R. The Assault on Privacy: Computers, Data Banks, and Dossiers. Ann Arbor, MI: Michigan UP, 1971. 333.
"The Changing Face of Information Handling" (National Data Center, computers, credit bureaus, checks and cash, I.Q. and other tests, electronic schools, regulation), "The Handling of Personal Information by the Federal Government" (Census Bureau, information transfer among government agencies, Freedom of Information Act, wiretapping, etc.), etc.

3203. Ritchin, Fred. In Our Own Image: The Coming Revolution in Photography. New York: Aperture Foundation, 1990. 158.
Computers enable people to alter and even create photographs of "real" people and scenes that are completely false. So good is this new technology that the photographs it creates are totally undetectable as being forgeries. From now on we cannot know if a photograph has been altered or even completely fabricated.

3204. Roszak, Theodore. The Cult of Information. New York:

Pantheon, 1986. 220.
Examines the manipulation of the concept of information by
powerful business and political forces, involving the role of
new communication technologies in social control. Also
explores the economic implications of computerization--e.g.,
the absence of unions, unequal distribution of and access to
computers in rich and poor classrooms.

3205. Schiller, Dan. Telematics and Government. Norwood,
NJ: Ablex, 1982. 237.
Government has always furthered the progress of telematics
"under corporate guidance" as part of corporate "control over
not merely information technology--but our economy and society
as a whole" (xv). Divided into three parts: I "the evolution
of postwar policy . . . in parallel with growing corporate
demand for merged computer-communications services put to
private use," II same argument extended to "international
sphere, because the structure of corporate enterprise is now
essentially transnational," and III government's role "as a
market for telematics equipment and services."

3206. Schiller, Herbert. "Computer Systems: Power for Whom
and for What?" JoC 28.4 (1978) 184-93.
Examines the increasingly concentrated structures and
relationships underlying and determining new computer instrumentation and communications.

3207. Schiller, Herbert. "Information for What Kind of
Society?" Telecommunications: Issues and Choices for
Society. Ed. J. L. Salvaggio. New York: Longman,
1983. 24-33.
Communication and information technology is under the
control of the military-industrial complex.

3208. Siegel, Lenny, and John Markoff. The High Cost of High
Tech: The Dark Side of the Chip. New York: Harper &
Row, 1985. 235.
Warns of the anti-democratic, militaristic uses of computerization. Today, a small number of experts, bureaucrats, and
business executives control high technology. In response, he
advocates "computer citizenship"--"knowing enough about the
social, political, environmental, and military implications of
computer technology to make personal and public choices."

3209. Smith, Robert E. Privacy: How to Protect What's Left
of It. Garden City, NY: Doubleday, 1979. 346.
Examines all kinds of government and business intrusion,
including record keeping.

3210. Sorkin, Michael. "The FBI's Big Brother Computer." WM
4.7 (1972) 24-30.
On the FBI's arrest data bank.

3211. Surveillance, Dataveillance, and Personal Freedoms: Use
and Abuse of Information Technology. Fair Lawn, NJ:

Burdick, 1973. 247. (Orig. pp. 1-235 of Columbia Human Rights Law Review 4.1 [1972]). Eight essays on privacy, surveillance of dissidents, computers, data banks, etc. "Americans today are scrutinized, measured, watched, and quizzed more than at any time in our history" (11).

3212. Toles, Terri. "Video Games and American Military Ideology." Popular Culture and Media Events. Ed. Vincent Mosco and Janet Wasko. Norwood, NJ: Ablex, 1985. 207-226. (CCRev 3).
A content analysis of 100 video games and their use in leisure time activity and military training. On the psychological level, obedience to rules that promote aggressive action is rewarded; on the cultural level, two dominant values are affirmed: technology and militarism as appropriate means of conflict resolution.

3213. Turkle, Sherry. The Second Self: Computers and the Human Spirit. New York: Simon and Schuster, 1984. 362.
Examines what is happening to humans as the result of computer toys, computers in the classroom, video game players, home computer systems, programmers, artificial-intelligence research, etc. Computers are creating a philosophic interest in the idea of self as a machine. [Makes no inquiry into the relation between personal relations with computers and the corporate system which produces and advertises them.]

3214. Van Houten, Margaret. "The Politics and Proliferation of Data Banks." CS 2.3 (Spring-Summer 1975) 21-26.
On the danger to democracy by the growing centralization of information collecting.

3215. Vinson, Eva. "Cultural Images of Technology: The Depiction of Computers in Feature Films." Boston U, 1987. 479. DAI 48 (1988) 1560-A.
"Films consistently portray computers as autonomous, fearsome, powerful, threatening entities which are used for evil purposes as often as not."

3216. Weizenbaum, Joseph. "Not Without Us: A Challenge to Computer Professionals to Use their Power to Bring the Present Insanity to a Halt." Fel 52.10-11 (Oct.-Nov. 1986) 8-9.
Calls upon scientists and especially computer experts to insist that new developments be "immune from the greed of the military."

3217. Weizenbaum, Joseph. "Once More, the Computer Revolution." The Computer Age: A Twenty Year View. Ed. Michael Dertouzos and Joel Moses. Cambridge, MA: MIT P, 1979. 439-459.
Skeptical about benefits to public of developments in computer technology because of the military domination of it.

3218. Wiener, Hesh. "Why Police States Love the Computer." BSR 22 (1977) 38-43.
Several US companies sell large computers to dictatorships, and IBM dominates the business--all fully aware of what they are involved in.

3219. Wirbel, Loring. "Somebody Is Listening: There's a Computer on the Line." Prog 44.11 (1980) 16-22.
The threat to liberty from the National Security Agency and its computer system.

II. D. PRINT MEDIA (3220-4126)

II. D. 1. NEWS AGENCIES/WIRE SERVICES (3220-3269)

3220. Ainslie, Rosalynde. The Press in Africa: Communications Past and Present. New York: Walker, 1967. 264.
The US especially, the SU, the UK, and France dominate foreign news in Africa.

3221. Arno, Andrew, and Wimal Dissanayake. The News Media in National and International Conflict. Boulder and London: Westview, 1984. 250.
Several of the essays deal with news agencies, e.g., chs. 7 and 11.

3222. Aronson, James. The Press and the Cold War. New York: Monthly Review P, 1990. 342.
Discusses the AP and UPI throughout (see Index). The wire services have a mixed record. During the Vietnam War, for example, they exposed the real nature of the Diem regime and US support for Diem, but on the other hand they were being used by the military, as in the case of the fake "Vietcong camp" in Cambodia created to whip up the public to favor US invasion.

3223. Barnes, Peter. "The Wire Services in Latin America." Media Casebook. Ed. Peter Sandman, et al. Englewood Cliffs, NJ: Prentice-Hall, 1972. 179-84. (Rpt. NmR March 1964).
The wire services grossly underreport Latin America, generally unable "to see the relevance" of that region.

3224. Baum, Dan. "How to Make It as Your Own Foreign Correspondent." CJR 27.2 (July-Aug. 1988) 48-49.
The author and his wife set up their own free-lance news bureau in Harare, Zimbabwe.

3225. Beaubien, Michael. "Telling it Like it Isn't: U.S. Press Coverage of Zimbabwe." SA 13.6 (July-Aug. 1980) 2-4, 21.
Despite the great change from Rhodesia to Zimbabwe, reporters continued writing from a colonial perspective.

PRINT MEDIA   455

3226. Boyd-Barrett, Oliver. The International News Agencies.
            London: Constable; Beverly Hills: Sage, 1980. 284.
    AP and UPI are discussed in Chap. 3, pp. 130-151. "Formal
collusion . . . can be less important than coincidence of
value, and there is scope for argument that a government-
pursued policy of cold war was eventually successful in
shaping the attitudes of agency foreign correspondents, and of
the average newspaper editors who received agency services and
attended agency conferences" (149).

3227. Brown, Cynthia. "How UPI Spells Relief." CJR 20.3
            (Sept.-Oct. 1981) 6-7, 9.
    The UPI passed on government disinformation that humanitar-
ian agencies were helping to arm the El Salvadoran guerrillas.

3228. Browne, Malcolm W. "VietNam Reporting: Three Years of
            Crisis." CJR 3.3 (1964) 4-9.
    S. Vietnamese and US authorities sometimes interfered with
truthful reporting.

3229. Cockburn, Alexander. "Frame-Up Abroad and at Home: The
            A.P. and Nolan." Na 249.2 (July 10, 1989) 42.
    The AP falsely reported that the governments of Nicaragua
and Vietnam supported the massacre of students in Beijing.

3230. Dorman, William. "The Image of the Soviet Union in the
            American News Media: Coverage of Brezhnev, Andropov
            and MX." War, Peace, & the News Media. Ed. David
            Rubin and Ann Cunningham. New York: New York U,
            1983. 44-76.
    Like US newspapers and popular magazines, the AP and the UPI
have consistently presented a hostile picture of the SU, the
official point of view of the US government, and have thereby
"helped to make crisis a permanent aspect of the American
consciousness, and to create a garrison state of mind."

3231. Dykstra, Peter. "High Wire Act: UPI Defies Death, But
            Is Teetering." Extra! 2.2 (Sept.-Oct. 1988) 12.
    Laments the decline and possible demise of the UPI.

3232. Edgar, Patricia, ed. The News in Focus: The Journalism
            of Exception. Melbourne, Aus.: Macmillan, 1980. 213.
    Chap. 5, "The Rip and Read Service: AAP, a Study of a News
Agency" and "Overseas News in the Australia Press" analyze the
Australian Associated Press.

3233. Emery, Edwin, Phillip Ault, and Warren Agee. "Press
            Associations." Mass News: Practices, Controversies,
            and Alternatives. Englewood Cliffs, NJ: Prentice-
            Hall, 1973. 57-68.
    "Critical Views of the Agencies" (66-68) discusses the
dangers of uniformity and conformity, lack of context and
depth, preoccupation with the two major parties, and emphasis
on crises, but argues the services are improving and praises
reporting of the Vietnam War.

3234. Ezcurra, Ana Maria. Ideological Aggression Against the Sandinista Revolution: The Political Opposition Church in Nicaragua. Tr. Elice Higginbotham and Bayard Faithful. New York: New York CIRCUS, 1984. 233.
Ch. 4 "focuses on the papal visit to Nicaragua: the events of March 4 in Managua, John Paul II's speeches, and the ways in which AP and UPI recounted the events from the perspective of North American foreign policy propaganda." Pp. 136-154: "North American News Agencies and the Papal Visit to Nicaragua": AP and UPI underscored official US doctrine that Christianity and revolution were opposed and represented Sandinistas and the popular church negatively.

3235. Fenby, Jonathan. The International News Services. New York: Schocken, 1986. 275.
AP and UPI are "really U.S. enterprises that operate on an international scale. . . . they must be American organizations, subject to American pressures and requirements" (74). Chapter 9, "Secondhand News," discusses "the limitations that affect the shape and content of the news services." Chapter 10 surveys issues of UNESCO, the new world information order, and ideology.

3236. Giffard, C. Anthony. "Developed and Developing Nation News In U.S. Wire Service Files to Asia." JQ 61.1 (Spring 1984) 14-19.
"There is more negative news coverage of the less developed countries."

3237. Giffard, C. Anthony. "Inter Press Service: News from the Third World." JoC 34.4 (1984) 41-59.
A descriptive history and assessment of the Inter Press Service in relation to UNESCO and the New World Information Order. IPS officials have in common a perception of structural inequities in the flow of information and claim that their agency is an alternative source of Third World News.

3238. Golding, Peter, and Philip Elliott. Making the News. London: Longman, 1979. 241.
"Swedish and Nigerian journalists were concerned, in different ways, at pro-Western bias in the wire agencies, particularly the American agencies" (104). News production depends upon news agencies, that is, on news already selected, a process necessarily ideological.

3239. Hall, Peter. "What's all the fuss about InterPress?" CJR 22.5 (Jan.-Feb. 1983) 53-57.
US opposition to UNESCO and NWIO includes the Inter Press Service (IPS).

3240. Harris, Phil. Reporting Southern Africa: Western News Agencies Reporting from Southern Africa. Paris: UNESCO, 1981. 168.
Examines the pro-Western bias of Reuters, AP, and UPI.

PRINT MEDIA   457

3241. Heacock, Roger. UNESCO and the Media. Geneva:
      Institut U de Hautes Études Intern., 1977. 62.
   Comparison of US and Latin American newspaper coverage of
UNESCO activities in the communication area during the years
1974-76. "The US media reflected the views of interests which
felt threatened, particularly those of the news agencies, AP
and UPI, but also the importance of lobbying groups" (37).

3242. Johnson, Robert, Jr. "Covering the Nixon Resignation."
      MJR 18 (1975) 40-45.
   The author, managing editor of the AP at the time, explains
the difficulties faced by the press in reporting the death
knell of the Nixon administration because of the "widespread
distrust of the press" resulting from administration attacks.
He gives an account also of AP's transmission of the full
transcripts of the taped conversations in Nixon's office.

3243. Kennedy, Tom. "UPI Shuns Hot Ford Story." MORE 6
      (Dec. 1976) 6.
   UPI reporters uncovered the relationship of steel price
hikes and campaign donations and free vacations President Ford
received from the steel companies, but UPI refused to tell the
story until Jack Anderson put it on the air five weeks later.

3244. Kruglak, Theodore. "Suggestions for Improvement." The
      Foreign Correspondents: A Study of the Men and Women
      Reporting for the American Information Media in
      Western Europe. Geneva: Droz, 1955. 116-121. (Rpt.
      Greenwood, 1974).
   The news agencies should pay their correspondents more, hire
more correspondents, hire more experienced correspondents, and
print foreign stories in greater depth.

3245. Lee, Philip, ed. Communication for All: New World
      Information and Communication Order. Maryknoll, NY:
      Orbis, 1986. 158.
   Eight contributors defend NWICO as part of the long decolonization process. As it is sometimes called, the New
International Information Order (NIIO) seeks information as a
right, the autonomy of indigenous cultures, a balance in the
flow of news and other cultural products, etc.

3246. Lent, John A. "Foreign News in American Media." JoC
      27.1 (1977) 46-51.
   National interests, crisis-reporting, foreign censors, and a
shrinking corps of correspondents constrain international
coverage in US media.

3247. Lepowicz, Alice. "Wire Services the Key to Polish
      Coverage." SLJR 7.45 (Mar. 1982) 13.
   Compares and evaluates St. Louis Post and Globe "extensive"
coverage and their news agency sources.

3248. MacDougall, A. Kent. "Wire Services: AP and UPI." The
      Press: A Critical Look from the Inside. Ed. A. Kent

MacDougall. Princeton, NJ: Dow Jones, 1972. 106-118.
The reporters "work under pressure, and they make a lot of mistakes." Because their clients are politically diverse, they "try to be as neutral and fair--some say bland--as possible." "The wire services have the power to shrink an event into insignificance or blow it up into fame or infamy."

3249. Massing, Michael. "Inside the Wires' Banana Republics." CJR 18.4 (Nov.-Dec. 1979) 45-49.
The Spanish-language services of the AP and UPI support the status quo in Latin America.

3250. McCaskell, Lisa. "Nicaragua Through U.S. Eyes: Why the Star Leaves It to AP." RRJ (Spring 1987) 7-8.
The Toronto Star depends upon the wire services, especially AP, for its hard news on Nicaragua, even though AP is biased in favor of the Reagan administration's position.

3251. Millman, Joel. "The Brave New World of Spanish Language Television." Extra! 1.3 (Aug.-Sept. 1987) 10-11.
The new Univision all-Spanish news organization has "a distinct rightwing bias."

3252. Murphy, Mary Pat. "The United States vs. the AP." MJR 17 (1974) 40-46.
An account of the Department of Justice's successful suit against the Associated Press under the Sherman Anti-Trust Act, alleging the AP restricted freedom of the press. The First Amendment "rests on the assumption that the widest possible dissemination of information from diverse and antagonistic sources is essential to the welfare of the public."

3253. "The News from Latin America: Excerpts from a Report to the Center for the Study of Democratic Institutions." CJR 1.3 (1962) 49-60.
The New York Times was better than the AP and UPI, but all, especially the UPI, fell short in quantity and breadth.

3254. Robinson, Michael, and Margaret Sheehan. Over the Wire and on TV: CBS and UPI in Campaign '80. New York: Sage, 1983. 332.
Assesses how well UPI (compared to CBS) reported the campaign, according to the standards of "objectivity, fairness, seriousness, and comprehensiveness." Wire reports are less mediating, political, personal, critical, and cynical than network news (9).

3255. Schwarzlose, Richard. The American Wire Services: A Study of Their Development as a Social Institution. New York: Arno, 1979. 453.
Policy-making "increasingly involves questions of what the market will bear or what technical devices are feasible and profitable rather than what is journalistically a tenable approach to news gathering in a democratic society. . . . The consumer newspaper and the consumer public have become the

principal targets of wire-service operations" (336-7).

3256. Seelye, Katharine, and Lawrence Roberts. "UPI's Disaster Story." CJR 24.3 (1985) 25-33.
Criticizes the "haphazard management" of the agency during "the last three years."

3257. Seldes, George. Can These Things Be! Garden City, NY: Garden City P, 1931. 433.
Contrasts the extreme hostility toward the Soviet Union to the more favorable treatment of fascism by US newspapers, in "Fascism Corrupts the World Press," "European Press Corruption and America," and "Bunkum in the American Press" and other sections.

3258. Seldes, George. "A.P.: Our Main Source of News." Freedom of the Press. Garden City, NY: Garden City, 1937. Chap. X.
Criticizes corruption in the AP.

3259. Sheehan, Neil. A Bright Shining Lie: John Paul Vann and America in Vietnam. New York: Random House, 1988. 861.
Sheehan, who went to Vietnam in 1962 as a correspondent for UPI, discloses the gung-ho attitude of the first US troops and of the journalists who had been sent to report it: "We regarded the conflict as our war too. We believed in what our government said it was trying to accomplish in Vietnam, and we wanted our country to win this war just as passionately as Vann and his captains did."

3260. Smith, Anthony. The Geopolitics of Information: How Western Culture Dominates the World. London: Faber and Faber, 1980. 192.
The two main subjects are the domination of the southern countries by the northern and domination of the world by the US. The author supports the movement for a New Information Order (the "free flow" of information "enhances freedom only between equals"). But he does not recommend international censorship.

3261. Steinert, Sylvia. "AP Carrier Pigeon." Deadline (Mar.-Apr. 1986) 6.
The credulous AP military writer reported the Pentagon's alarming reports of the new Soviet aircraft carrier uncritically.

3262. Swinton, Stanley M. "Barbed Wires." (Letter). CJR 18.5 (1980) 63.
Replies by officials of the companies to Massing's criticism of AP and UPI Latin American desks.

3263. Thomas, Helen. Dateline: White House. New York: Macmillan, 1975. 298.

UPI reporter Thomas recollects her experiences, especially the "lack of candor" and secrecy in opposition to a democratic society.

3264. Tunstall, Jeremy. "US News Agencies: Peron, Pinilla and Allende as Villains." The Media Are American. New York: Columbia UP, 1977. 178-182.
"Presidents Peron, Pinilla and Allende are all portrayed as villains, and in each case a complex political situation was presented to the world's press simplistically. Each President threatened newspapers which in turn was a threat to revenue (of the news agencies) and to newspapers which were used by Anglo-American journalists as news sources" (181).

3265. Weaver, David H., et al. The News of the World in Four Major Wire Services. Schools of Journalism, Indiana U and U of North Carolina, 1980.
Examines stories in AP, UPI, Reuters, and Agence France-Presse during two weeks in 1979.

3266. "What Is the Alternative Press Syndicate?" AltM 9.6 (Winter 1978) 26-30.
An explanation of APS and a list of participating magazines.

3267. Whitton, John, and Arthur Larson. Propaganda: Towards Disarmament in the War of Words. Dobbs Ferry, NY: Oceana, 1964. 305.
The entire book appeals directly or indirectly to the news agencies (and to all media) to report the news from the point of view of international peace. Chap. 16 offers "A Code of Ethics for International Communicators."

3268. Wilhoit, G. Cleveland, and David Weaver. "Foreign News Coverage in Two U.S. Wire Services: An Update." JoC 33.2 (1983) 132-148.
Since most foreign news covered in smaller newspapers is supplied by AP and UPI, conflict, whether violent or non-violent, dominates world news.

3269. Williams, Francis. Transmitting World News: A Study of Telecommunications and the Press. Paris: Unesco, 1953. 95.
Sections on "World News Agencies," "National News Agencies," and related topics. Urges the responsibility of world news agencies to report news from and to the Third World as a public service.

II. D. 2. PRINT MEDIA, GENERAL: NEWSPAPERS & MAGAZINES (3270-3346)

3270. Baker, Glenn. "The Myth of Soviet Conventional Superiority." Extra! 1.5 (Dec. 1987) 6.
Media continue to exaggerate Soviet military superiority in Europe.

3271. Becker, Robert, et al. "The Change of the Right
Brigade: The New Right is Spreading its Message
through its own Alternative Press." WJR 3.9 (1981)
21-25.
On the growth and power of the right-wing press.

3272. Bennett, James R. "Reporting the El Salvador Civil
War." FSN 8 (Dec. 1981) 11-15.
Newspaper and popular news magazine coverage of El Salvador
during 1981 supported official US policies.

3273. Bennett, James R., et al. "Reporting Poverty and
Hunger in 1980." FS 54 (Oct. 1982) 2-6.
Wire service, newspaper, magazine, and TV reporting of world
hunger was extremely inadequate.

3274. Bennett, James R., and Christopher Gould. "Reporting
the Embassy Hostage Crisis." IR 2.2 (May 1980) 6-16.
Mainstream print media expressed intense prejudice against
Iran during the hostage crisis.

3275. Bennett, James R., and Jimmie Thomas. "Nicaragua in
Our Back Yard and on Our Doorstep: Madison, the First
Amendment, and a Free Press." FS 55 (Dec. 1982) 6-15.
Official government views dominate the news about Nicaragua
in the three magazines and three newspapers surveyed.

3276. Bennett, James R., and Jimmie Thomas. "Reporting Tio
Sam's 'Free World' Dictatorships in the Caribbean
Basin." CRPV 5.4 (1982) 218-39.
A comparison of the broad media support of Reagan Administration's enmity toward the Nicaraguan government and the
minimal coverage of much more oppressive governments only
because they are allied with us by their anti-Soviet ideology.

3277. Bernstein, Dennis. "The New, Improved, Moderate Arena
Party." Extra! 2.7/8 (Summer 1989) 26-29.
The US press chose to forgive and forget the death squads
and repression of the Arena party in its coverage of Dan
Quayle's recent visit to El Salvador.

3278. Blumberg, Nathan. "A Study of the 'Orthodox' Press:
The Reporting of Dissent." MJR 11 (1968) 2-9.
An indictment of general press support of the status quo and
of government policies, with focus on the Vietnam War.
"Perhaps it is too much to expect . . . that a press with an
undeniable stake in the economic and political system would
report fairly on those who are fundamentally dissatisfied with
the status quo."

3279. Bollinger, William, and Daniel Lund. "Gallup in
Central America: Mixing Polls and Propaganda." Na
246.18 (May 7, 1988) 635-638.
Intimate ties between Gallup's foreign affiliates and the
government pose serious ethical problems.

3280. Boot, William. "Bonding with Baker." CJR 28.3 (Sept.-Oct. 1989) 20-22.
Discloses how necessary access is to report the State Department, but acquiring access brings one "all too close to joining the diplomatic team," and criticism may result in denial of access.

3281. Bram, Steven. "What Reporters Think About Arms Control." Deadline 2.4 (Nov.-Dec. 1987) 1-2, 7.
The majority of those polled believed verification possible, opposed the MX, supported a first-use policy, etc.

3282. Brockmann, Stephen. "Only a Few Shape U.S. View of Greens." SLJR 12.75 (June 1985) 18-19.
Criticizes print media coverage of the emergence of the West German Green Party in the early 1980s, citing ludicrous comparisons with the rise of the Nazis, etc.

3283. Chomsky, Noam. "The Tasks Ahead IV: Post-Cold War Cold War." Z 3.3 (Mar. 1990) 8-18.
Analyzes how the government is shifting its rationalizations for foreign intervention as the result of the decline of Cold War conflict, and how the media shifts in agreement. "On critical issues, there is tactical debate within the mainstream, but questions of principle rarely arise."

3284. Chorbajian, Levon. "All the News That Fits: Media Coverage of the 1976 and 1980 Olympic Boycotts." The Critical Communications Review, Volume III: Popular Culture and Media Events. Ed. Vincent Mosco and Janet Wasko. Norwood, NJ: Ablex, 1985. 113-151.
Compares Time and New York Times coverage of the 1976 Olympic boycott (by nations protesting South Africa's participation) with their stories about the US boycott of the 1980 Moscow Olympics, showing how the myth of apolitical international competition, much-touted in 1976, was abandoned in deference to US foreign policy considerations.

3285. "CIA, the Press and Central America." CAIB 21 (Spring 1984) 7-23.
Two essays on US-sponsored terrorism and its pro-US coverage in NYT, Time, and Newsweek.

3286. "CIA Relations with Media--Official and Otherwise." CAIB 32 (Summer 1989) 63-64.
Several articles published previously in CAIB.

3287. Cline, Timothy R., and Rebecca J. Cline. "Gaining Access to the Media: Some Issues and Cases." FSY (1975) 35-56.
Deals with the attempts of groups and individuals to win the same right of access to print media as provided for broadcast media under the Fairness Doctrine. Includes the rationale of the court decisions denying such access.

3288. Cockburn, Alexander. "Bandits." Na 244.23 (1987) 790.
While reporters for NYT and WP provided "rapturous accounts of contra prowess," Newsweek's reporters accompanied the US backed guerrillas on a patrol and found them to be undisciplined, cowardly bandits.

3289. Cockburn, Alexander. "The Press & the 'Just War.'" Na 252.6 (Feb. 18, 1991) 181, 186-88, 201.
Journalists annul the history behind the war in a "depthless present" of trivial minutiae that functions both as censorship and as moral persuasion that "the war is fought by decent people for honorable objectives." But the press has suppressed "Iraq's negotiating positions."

3290. Cockburn, Alexander. "Remember El Salvador?" Corruptions of Empire. London: Verso, 1987. 394-96.
The ferocious aerial bombing of El Salvador has received "not one coherent report" of its "extent, viciousness or consequences" by "any major U.S. newspaper or magazine."

3291. "Covering the Gulf Crisis." Deadline 6.1 (Jan.-Feb. 1991) 1-15.
A dozen media critics "assess the media's handling of the early stages of the world's first post-Cold War crisis." Hertsgaard criticizes the bellicose saber-rattling, Kipper the demonizing of Hussein and lack of historical perspective, Klare the failure to disclose the Reagan-Bush alliance with Hussein, etc.

3292. Dorfman, Ariel. The Empire's Old Clothes: What the Lone Ranger, Babar, and Other Innocent Heroes Do to Our Minds. New York: Pantheon, 1983. 223.
Analyzes the ideological influence of US media and cultural symbols--Reader's Digest, Donald Duck, etc.--particularly in spreading consumerism.

3293. Dorfman, Ariel, and Armand Mattelart. "The Great Parachutist." American Media & Mass Culture. Ed. Donald Lazere. Berkeley: U of California P, 1987. 530-539.
On racist stereotypes in media and US cultural imperialism through Third World eyes. "Disneyfication is Dollarfication: all objects" and actions "are transformed into gold." [From How to Read Donald Duck.]

3294. Dorfman, Ariel, and Armand Mattelart. Trans. David Kunzle. How to Read "Donald Duck": Imperialist Ideology in the Disney Comic. New York: International, 1975. 112.
Explains the values promulgated by Disney productions throughout the world--e.g. the natural separation of rich and poor.

3295. Dorman, William. "The Image of the Soviet Union in the American News Media: Coverage of Brezhnev, Andropov,

and MX." War, Peace, and the News Media. Ed. David Rubin and Ann Cunningham. New York: New York U, 1983. 44-76. (Summarized SLJR 9.56 [1983] 17-20).
Demonstrates how Sovietphobia has tainted media coverage of the SU.

3296. Dorman, William. "Soviets Seen Through Red-Tinted Glasses." BAS 41.2 (1985) 18-22.
Reporting of the SU systematically biased.

3297. Dorman, William, and Ehsan Omeed. "Reporting Iran the Shah's Way." CJR 17.5 (1979) 27-33.
The media have misinformed the public about the Iranian conflict.

3298. Dorman, William, and Mansour Farhang. The U.S. Press and Iran: Foreign Policy and the Journalism of Deference. Berkeley: California UP, 1987. 272.
"Our thesis is this: The major shortcoming of American press coverage of Iran for twenty-five years was to ignore the politics of the country. This failure was rooted in the assumption that the political aspirations of Iranians did not really matter. This was an assumption shaped and reinforced by the foreign policy establishment and was given credence by highly West-centered preconceptions and an internalized cold-war-oriented ideology" (13).

3299. Douglas, Susan. "Twenty Years of Media Strikes Against Feminism." ITT 14.33 (Aug. 29-Sept. 11, 1990) 18-19.
An account of media misrepresentations of the feminist demonstrations Aug. 26, 1970, and of other feminist actions, and assessment of the costs of "one-dimensional stereotypes" that pervade the media.

3300. Eshenaur, Ruth. "Censorship of the Alternative Press: A Descriptive Study of the Social and Political Control of Radical Periodicals (1964-1973)." Southern Illinois U, 1975. 371. DAI 36 (1976) 7705.
History of harassment of oppositional newspapers and magazines by government and civilian censors.

3301. Ewen, Stuart, and Elizabeth Ewen. "The Bribe of Frankenstein." The Critical Communications Review, Volume I: Labor, the Working Class, and the Media. Ed. Vincent Mosco and Janet Wasko. Norwood, NJ: Ablex, 1983. 3-22. (Rptd. from Channels of Desire.)
The industrial revolution meant class conflict over the means of communication. The Ewens concentrate on the technology of the word: printing presses housed in print factories that advance both capitalist profit and the control of language and culture.

3302. Fauvet, Paul. "New York Times Reporter's Trip Aids MNR Bandits' Dirty War." Guard 40.43 (Aug. 17, 1988) 17.
A right-wing organization, Freedom Inc., trying to spruce up

the image of the Mozambique National Resistance, arranged for reporters from the NYT, WP, and Newsweek to travel to Africa and interview the rebels' leader.

3303. Friedman, Leslie. "Print Media." Sex Role Stereotyping in the Mass Media. New York: Garland, 1977. 167-183.
Fifty-five bibliographical entries on women's portrayal in magazines, newspapers, and print journalism.

3304. Friedman, Sharon, Sharon Dunwoody, and Carol Rogers. Scientists and Journalists: Reporting Science as News. New York: Free P, 1986. 333.
Several essays discuss the proper relationship between scientists and journalists in accomplishing the purpose of informing the public.

3305. Gerald, J. Edward. The Social Responsibility of the Press. Minneapolis: U of Minnesota P, 1963. 214.
"The mass media, in theory, are expected to maintain freedom of speech and discussion, but they are also under heavy pressure from interest groups . . . to bolster and sustain bias as if it were truth" (3-4).

3306. Hallin, Daniel. "Cartography, Community, and the Cold War." Reading the News. Ed. Robert K. Manoff and Michael Schudson. New York: Pantheon, 1987. 109-145.
In "Geopolitics: The American Image of the World from the 1960s to the 1980s," Hallin describes "much of the rhetoric of the cold war, as it appeared in the press in this period" as "so strident that it appears absolutely lunatic to us today." And this Sovietphobic worldview "remains very great" (135).

3307. Hartman, Thomas. "Reporting for Service: The Big Guns of the Military Press." WJR 6 (July-Aug. 1984) 29-32.
Differentiates among the various military-industrial media.

3308. Herman, Edward S. "Who Will Contain Us?" Z 3.2 (Feb. 1990) 44-45.
On the failure of the media to examine US double standards.

3309. Hertsgaard, Mark. "Covering The World; Ignoring The Earth." Green 15.2 (Mar.-Apr. 1990) 14-18.
The press "has an obligation to illuminate the dimensions and roots of the environmental crisis," but in general it has presented too little too late.

3310. "HUD, the Dud that Exploded." CJR 28.3 (Sept.-Oct. 1989) 4, 6.
The failure of the press to investigate the HUD scandal earlier than it did demonstrates how passive is the press and how subservient to government agencies.

3311. Ivie, Robert. "Inviting an American Backlash? A New Cold War Parable in The Post-Cold War Press." Deadline 5.1 (Jan.-Feb. 1990) 1-2, 8-9.

Reporting of Eastern Europe has followed the orthodox view of the cold war as freedom's victory over communism, the media once again functioning in its role as "a principal conveyor of American political culture."

3312. Kennerly, Evelyn. "Mass Media & Mass Murder: American Coverage of the Holocaust." JMME 2.1 (Fall-Winter 1986-87) 61-70.
Supports arguments by historians David Wyman and Deborah Lipstadt that the US media provided inadequate coverage of Holocaust developments and thereby helped create public apathy and inadequate responses by the Roosevelt administration.

3313. Keyssar, Alex. "Reporting the Revolution: Portugal and the American Press." NmR 29.2 (Summer 1975) 3-7.
"The American press has filtered the Portugal news through a prism of Cold War anti-Communism," and has "distorted facts, used cheap stylistic devices," etc.

3314. Klose, Roland. "Our Mass Media Runs the Risk of Mirroring the Soviet Union's Parrot Press." SLJR 11.66 (Sept. 1984) 2.
The nation's press reported the Reagan administration's version of the Soviet downing of a KAL civilian plane in fierce imitation of Reagan's Sovietphobia.

3315. Krinsky, Robert. "Media March to Bush War-Budget Beat." Guard 42.43 (Sept. 26, 1990) 4-5.
"Press coverage of Operation Desert Shield displays the mainstream media's eagerness to shore up the political power of the country's war-making institutions and help them regain a strong foothold in the federal budget."

3316. Lanouette, William. "The Half-Life of The Tritium Story." Deadline 4.1 (Jan.-Feb. 1989) 1-2, 9-11.
Print journalists were indifferent to the health and safety problems throughout the weapons network, but they became interested when the nuclear arsenal seemed to be running short of tritium, the hydrogen isotope in H-bombs.

3317. Leff, Donna. "Journalists and Jurists: The Evolution of Reporter's Privilege After Branzburg." U of California, Berkeley, 1982. 191. DAI 43.8 (Feb. 1983) 2480-A.
In Branzburg vs. Hayes the Supreme Court held that "reporters had no constitutional privilege to refrain from cooperating in criminal justice proceedings." But journalists are not exposing their confidential sources; subpoenas have failed as government policy. Appeals to government to "exercise great restraint in subpoenaing journalists."

3318. Liebovich, Louis. "The Press and the Origins of the Cold War, 1944-1947." U of Wisconsin, Madison, 1986. 371. DAI 47 (1987) 4222-A.
NYHT, CT, SFC, and Time had rejected friendship with the SU

by 1947, mirroring the Truman administration's antagonism.

3319. MacDougall, A. Kent. "Boring Within the Bourgeois Press: A Postscript." MR 41.8 (Jan. 1990) 15-27.
"Reporters not only in Western Europe but even in the Soviet Union have considerably more freedom than I ever enjoyed to sum up what facts they have gathered suggest. . . . A similarly healthy infusion of glasnost is called for in the increasingly concentrated American press" (26-7).

3320. Mackenzie, Angus. "Sabotaging the Dissident Press." CJR 19.6 (Mar.-June 1981) 57-63.
Describes the systematic and illegal government efforts (CIA, FBI, Army, etc.) to silence antiwar publications.

3321. Massing, Michael. "The Libel Chill: How Cold Is It Out There?" CJR 24.1 (1985) 31-43.
Examines the increase in libel suits directed toward the media, noting a New York trial lawyer's comment that the "chief effect of the recent flood of libel judgments has not been greater accuracy in the media but greater timidity."

3322. Miraldi, Robert. "Scaring Off the Muckrakers with the Threat of Libel." JQ 65.3 (Fall 1988) 609-614.
"Some major muckrakers took council of their fears of being sued."

3323. "The News Ethic: Defining News to Reach the Masses." You & Media. Ed. David G. Clark and William B. Blankenburg. San Francisco, CA: Canfield, 1973. 83-102.
Mainly about the development of print journalism practices.

3324. "On the Trail of a Secret War." CJR 19.6 (Mar.-Apr. 1981) 22-23.
On illegal police harassment of antiwar publications.

3325. O'Toole, Michael. "Disarming Criticism." Language and the Nuclear Arms Debate: Nukespeak Today. Ed. Paul Chilton. London and Dover, NH: Frances Pinter, 1985. 183-96.
Describes the linguistic devices by means of which the movie The Day After was neutralized politically in a review; claims that this is typical of commentary on the anti-nuclear movement.

3326. Pauly, John. "Rupert Murdoch and the Demonology of Professional Journalism." Media, Myths, and Narratives: Television and the Press. Ed. James W. Carey. Newbury Park: Sage, 1988. 246-261.
Analyzes the hostility toward Murdoch by US journalists. "What he threatens is the social legitimation and psychological repose of professional journalism" (252).

3327. Perrin, Dennis. "Stolid Right Jabs from the 'Con'

Cartel." ITT 13.22 (Apr. 26-May 2, 1989) 19.
Review of Column Right: Conservative Journalists in the Service of Nationalism, by David Burner and Thomas West, about George Will, William F. Buckley, Charles Krauthammer, Irving Kristol, and Jeane Kirkpatrick.

3328. Platt, Tony, ed. Tropical Gulag: The Construction of Cold War Images of Cuba in the United States. San Francisco, CA: Global Options, 1987. 263.
Documents the biased discourse about Cuba, gives the background of US-Cuban relations in the Reagan era, the organization and ideology of the anti-Cuba lobby, the US "human rights" campaign against Cuba, and analyzes press coverage of Cuba in 1986 (eight newspapers and eight magazines), plus bibliography, charts, and graphs.

3329. Pollak, Richard. "The Trial of Donald and Si Newhouse." Na 248.10 (Mar. 13, 1989) 1, 342-345.
Perhaps the biggest estate tax case ever--the Newhouse family accused of dodging more than $1 billion in taxes--has not been well covered by the press.

3330. Purvis, Hoyt. "Media Misinterpretation: The Supreme Court's Legislative Veto Decision." SMCJ 1.1 (1985) 29-40.
Explains the "oversimplified and sensationalized handling of the legislative veto story because of the media's 'winners and losers' approach."

3331. Quigley, Margaret. "Media on Peru: Turning Counter-insurgency into 'Drug War.'" Extra! 3.6 (July-Aug. 1990) 4-5.
On deceptive reporting of an alleged guerrilla/farmers/drug traffickers alliance.

3332. Reston, James. The Artillery of the Press: Its Influence on American Foreign Policy. New York: Harper & Row, 1966. 116.
On the conflict between reporters and makers of US foreign policy, and the necessity of the press to better inform the public.

3333. Riser, James V. "Cotton Candy Journalism." SM 18.4 (Dec. 1990) 57-58.
Urges the press to "go back to printing the news and raising hell."

3334. Rossie, Dave. "Iran-Contra Now History, But We Didn't Learn Much." AG (Dec. 9, 1990) 4C.
With "very few exceptions" the national press corps failed to report the constitutional crisis adequately or critically."

3335. Seltzer, Curtis. "How the Press Covered the Coal Strike." Unpublished (Aug. 1979). Summarized by Parenti, Inventing Reality, 81-83.

Media coverage of the 1977-78 coal strike was extremely biased against the United Mine Workers and unions in general.

3336. Shapiro, Walter. "Wilbur Mills: The Ways and Means of Conning the Press." WM 6.10 (Dec. 1974) 4-13.
Describes media development of this powerful Congressman's "statesmanlike image" while overlooking corruption, and analyzes "why our leading journalists have so often steered us wrong about the character of public officials."

3337. Shilts, Randy. And the Band Played On: Politics, People, and the AIDS Epidemic. New York: St. Martin's, 1987. 630.
A critique of the homophobia in all of the institutions involved in the AIDS crisis as it developed, including the media.

3338. Smith, Neil. "How the Press Gentrifies." Extra! 1.6 (Jan.-Feb. 1988) 5.
Media are collaborating "with glee" over the refurbishing of urban neighborhoods despite its displacement of people.

3339. Solomon, Norman. "Gulf Crisis Propaganda Spree." Guard 43.3 (Nov. 7, 1990) 4.
The mainstream media have beat the administration's war drums against Iraq and limited the debate.

3340. Spangler, Lynn. "Information about Television in Selected Major Newspapers and TV Guide Compared to Four Critical Television Viewing Skills Curricula." Wayne State U, 1983. 373. DAI 44.3 (Sept. 1983) 604-A.
The public "is not getting enough information in any of the sources studied to develop critical television viewing skills."

3341. Spurr, David. "Writing off Third World Issues." ITT (Apr. 14-20, 1982) 11.
The "major U.S. media often dismiss the third world point of view through the language they employ."

3342. Stillman, Don. "Tonkin: What Should Have Been Asked." CJR 9.4 (Winter 1970-71) 21-27.
Indicts media jingoism over the falsified Tonkin Gulf incident and Congressional "Tonkin resolution." "Perhaps the worst excesses in reporting were committed by Time and Life," but newspaper editorials "almost universally supported the President." He calls on the Fourth Estate to become "far more independent and critical."

3343. Treitler, Betsy D. "The Soviet Rubber Fleet Sails the Pacific." Deadline 2.3 (Sept.-Oct. 1987) 3.
The media exaggerate the size of the Soviet Pacific fleet.

3344. Turnbull, George, Jr. "Reporting of the War in Indo-China: A Critique." JQ 34 (1957) 87-89.

Analyzes the inadequate and distorted reporting of the Vietnam War in three newspapers and Time from 1946 to 1954.

3345. Welles, Chris. "Business Journalism's Glittering Prizes." CJR 17.6 (Mar.-Apr. 1979) 43-46.
Some business-sponsored awards are self-serving.

3346. Woodmansee, Dave. "There." SLJR 14.88 (Sept. 1986) 2.
Criticizes reporting of military/space shuttle program.

II. D. 3. NEWSPAPERS (3347-3817)

II. D. 3. a. NEWSPAPERS: GENERAL (3347-3511)

3347. Anderson, David. "The Press and the Spies." ChJR 4.4 (1971) 3-4, 12-13.
Although journalists knew about Army intelligence spying on civilians long before a former Army intelligence man disclosed it to Sen. Sam Ervin, they did not report it, but instead sought information from the intelligence units.

3348. Anderson, Douglas. A "Washington Merry-Go-Round" of Libel Actions. Chicago: Nelson-Hall, 1980. 351.
Examines the litigation against Drew Pearson and Jack Anderson, as authors of the syndicated column "Washington Merry-Go-Round," the effects of the column on libel law, the effects of libel law on the column, and other subjects.

3349. Anderson, Tom. "High School Journalism After Tinker." MJR 21 (1978-79) 10-16.
Discusses the decision, subsequent court decisions, effects on public school students, publications advisors and school administrators, and high school journalists in Montana.

3350. Arvidson, Cheryl. "The FBI Bears Down." CJR 22.3 (1983) 5-6.
FBI harassment of a Canadian reporter.

3351. Bagdikian, Ben. "Conglomeration, Concentration, and the Media." JoC 30.2 (1980) 59-64.
A number of trends in the media industry have reduced not only economic competition but truly antagonistic perspectives as well. An increase in subscription support may be the only solution.

3352. Bagdikian, Ben. "Journalism's Wholesalers." CJR 4.3 (1965) 27-33.
An inside look at and history of the syndicated columnist industry.

3353. Bagdikian, Ben. "Newspaper Mergers--the Final Phase." CJR 15.6 (Mar.-Apr. 1977) 17-22. Rptd. CongR (Apr. 6, 1977) 2126.
Tells how the desire of newspaper chains to expand makes

them vulnerable to takeovers by larger chains, with
deleterious effects on journalistic freedom and diversity.

3354. Bagdikian, Ben. "The Politics of American Newspapers."
CJR 10.6 (1972) 8-13.
Contrary to the accusations of Vice President Agnew, surveys
show that the news media are biased in favor of conservatism
not liberalism.

3355. Baram, Robert. "Newspapers: Their Coverage and Big
Business." Big Business and the Mass Media.
Lexington, MA: Lexington, 1977. 135-168.
Exhorts both corporations and journalists to strive for high
standards of reporting the full truth about important events
and issues. For example, condemns the underreporting of the
failure of the Franklin National Bank of New York.

3356. Barnett, Stephen R. "Monopoly Games--Where Failures
Win Big." CJR 19.1 (1980) 40-47.
The Newspaper Protection Act benefited owners financially
but not competition.

3357. Barnett, Stephen R. "Monopoly Marches On." CJR 27.4
(Nov.-Dec. 1988) 21-22.
New legal moves to reduce newspaper competition.

3358. Barnett, Stephen R. "Newspaper Monopoly and the Law."
JoC 30.2 (1980) 72-80.
The author focuses on both anti-competitive economic practices and government intervention in the industry. First, he
opposes the legality of combination rates. Second, he opposes
the 1970 Newspaper Preservation Act legalizing joint operation
of same-city newspapers in exemption of anti-trust laws.

3359. Berlet, Chip. "Student Editors Fight Back." UM 1.4
(Dec. 1970) 3-5.
Criticizes the widespread censorship of collegiate newspapers that is now more visible because campus newspapers are
revolting against "bulletin board journalism."

3360. Bishop, Bill. "Owning Your Own Weekly." WJR 10.4
(1988) 25-32.
The four-year rise and fall of an independent weekly Texas
newspaper forced to sell because mass merchandising now shapes
newspaper ownership, here in the form of Wal-Mart.

3361. Blumberg, Nathan. "The 'Orthodox' Media Under Fire:
Chicago and the Press." MJR 12 (1969) 38-60.
"What happened in Chicago [at the 1968 Democratic National
Convention] was that incidents of repression that in the past
almost always had been kept hidden from the public were
reported [for a few days] in detail," only because of the
police assaults on journalists and other attempts at censorship by Mayor Daley. Then the newspapers fell back into their
usual support of the establishment.

3362. Bogart, Leo. Press and Public: Who Reads What, When, Where, and Why in American Newspapers. Hillsdale, NJ: Lawrence Erlbaum, 1981. 285.
Provides data "on readers and on the changes in their tastes and habits" compiled by Bogart's Newspaper Advertising Bureau. "All the research reported here has been supported by the newspaper business and its Establishment."

3363. Bordewich, Fergus. "Supermarketing the Newspaper." CJR 16.3 (1977) 24-30.
Increasing preoccupation with profit is resulting in decreasing quality news.

3364. Brown, Jane Delano, et al. "Invisible Power: Newspaper News Sources and the Limits of Diversity." JQ 64.1 (Spring 1987) 45-54.
"Newspapers relinquish control of news to routine channels with male government executives as typical sources."

3365. Canadian Press Coverage of the Food Debate. Toronto: Canadian News Synthesis Project, 1975. 23.
How eleven big Canadian newspapers "covered" the World Food Conference in Nov. 1974.

3366. Chandler, Christopher. "The Exposé That Staggered Into Print." ChJR 2.6 (June 1969) 3, 14.
On the investigative reporting by a small newspaper outside of Chicago of a corporate crime in Chicago, which indicates how "extremely difficult" it is "for a story that attacks powerful interests in Chicago to see the light of day in the Chicago press."

3367. Chiasson, Lloyd. "An Editorial Analysis of the Evacuation & Encampment of the Japanese-Americans During World War II." S. Illinois U, 1983. 214. DAI 44 (1984) 1959-A.
". . . not one of the [27] newspapers editorially opposed mass evacuation and all but two supported either mass evacuation or mass encampment."

3368. Chile and the Canadian Press. Toronto: Canadian News Synthesis Project, n.d. (1974?) 1-29.
Canadian news reporting of the Chile coup Sept. 11-25, 1973.

3369. Chomsky, Noam. "Double Standard on Press Freedom." Extra! 2.7/8 (Summer 1989) 50-51.
While outrage at the Sandinistas' closing of the Nicaraguan opposition paper La Prensa (which received funding from the US government) was universal in the mainstream US press, far worse repression of the media by US client states and allied governments went largely unnoticed.

3370. Clarke, Bill. "Whacking TV's Critics." UM 1.12 (Aug. 1971) 8-9.
Film and television critics depend too much upon publicity

PRINT MEDIA

handouts.

3371. Clarkson, Fred. "New Right Money Finances New Student Papers." SLJR 12.74 (1985) 19.
Conservative campus newspapers are funded by business.

3372. Clarkson, Fred. "The Republicans, Reverend Moon and the Media." Extra! 2.2 (Sept.-Oct. 1988) 6-9.
The media should examine Rev. Sun Myung Moon's activities more.

3373. Cockburn, Alexander. "The Assassination of Ben Linder." Na 244.19 (1987) 636.
Mainstream newspaper coverage of Ben Linder's assassination by the Contras tried to mitigate the facts.

3374. Cockburn, Alexander. "Their Miners and Ours." Na 249.6 (Aug. 21-28, 1989) 194-195.
Were United Mine Workers strikes held in the SU "they would be assured of rather more generous coverage than they've been getting in the papers here."

3375. Cockburn, Alexander. "The Need to Tell: The Psychopathology of Journalism." Corruptions of Empire. London: Verso, 1987. 181-186.
Newspaper reports of foreign war events generally turn out to be "unrelievedly mendacious."

3376. Cohen, Bernard. The Press and Foreign Policy. Princeton, NJ: Princeton UP, 1963. 288.
A study of newspaper agenda-setting through interviews of reporters and government officials. Newspapers control reality by telling people what to think about.

3377. "Conglomerates and Press Freedom: A Canadian View." CJR 20.4 (1981) 55-57.
Criticizes the growing monopoly ownership of the newspaper industry.

3378. Cranberg, Gilbert. "What Baker and Quayle Told ASNE." CJR 28.3 (Sept.-Oct. 1989) 12, 14.
While the American Society of Newspaper Editors was quick to protest restrictions imposed on journalists by the Chinese government, the body was less outspoken when Secretary of State Baker and Vice-President Quayle defended the Bush administration's refusal to allow Castro and Daniel Ortega to enter the US and talk with reporters.

3379. Cros, Michele, and David Nugent. "The Hunger Story: An Unbalanced Diet." CJR 20.5 (Jan.-Feb. 1985) 51-54.
Explains why reporting hunger is so inadequate, ignorant, and biased.

3380. Daley, Patrick, and Beverly James. "Framing the News: Socialism as Deviance." JMME 3.2 (Fall 1988) 37-46.

Explores newspaper coverage of the nomination in Alaska of a socialist commissioner of environmental conservation and concludes that "news today is systematically biased" for "established positions of power and privilege."

3381. Daugherty, David. "Group-Owned Newspapers vs. Independently-Owned Newspapers: An Analysis of the Differences & Similarities." U of Texas, Austin, 1983. 215. DAI 44.4 (Oct. 1983) 899-A.
The two kinds of newspapers are "extremely similar."

3382. Dertouzos, James, and Kenneth Thorpe. Newspaper Groups: Economies of Scale, Tax Laws, and Merger Incentives. Santa Monica, CA: Rand, 1982. 125.
Produced for the Small Business Administration to explain the continued decline in the number of independently owned daily newspaper firms.

3383. Domhoff, G. William. "The Women's Page as a Window on the Ruling Class." Hearth and Home: Images of Women in the Mass Media. Ed. Gaye Tuchman, et al. New York: Oxford UP, 1978. 161-175.
Women's pages reveal the exercise of power because they present women "as satellites of the powerful" (144).

3384. Dreier, Peter. "The Position of the Press in the U.S. Power Structure." SP 29.3 (Feb. 1982) 298-310.
The institutional affiliations of the directors of the nation's 24 largest newspaper-owning companies reveal the interlock between the US power elite and the press.

3385. Dreier, Peter, and Steve Weinberg. "Interlocking Directorates." CJR 18.4 (Nov.-Dec. 1979) 51-68.
On the danger to an independent press of directors of newspapers who also sit on boards of other corporations which the papers cover. And these other companies are overwhelmingly corporate, not labor or public interest.

3386. Dzerzhinsky, D. "Dissidents, American-Style." AM 11.2 (1979) 28-30, 42.
Difficulties experienced by alternative presses in prison.

3387. Epstein, Cynthia F. "The Women's Movement and the Women's Pages." Hearth and Home: Images of Women in the Mass Media. Ed. Gaye Tuchman, et al. New York: Oxford UP, 1978. 216-221.
Argues against placing news of the women's movement on the women's page because it isolates the issues from men and thereby impedes liberation.

3388. Forcade, Thomas K. "Obscenity, Who Really Cares?" AM 11.1 (1979) 37-40.
The US "dictatorial structure cannot withstand an atmosphere of free speech. So they're constantly trying to stomp it out."

PRINT MEDIA   475

3389. Fraser, Laura. "The Earth First Bombing." LOOT 1.7
         (July 1990) 17.
   The FBI's message to the news media is that "radical
activists are guilty until proven innocent."

3390. Freimuth, V.S., et al. "Covering Cancer: Newspapers and
         the Public Interest." JoC 34.1 (Winter 1984) 62-73.
   Coverage of this fear-arousing subject lacks specific detail
about incidence, prevention, or control.

3391. Frye, Jerry K. "American Newspapers vs. Agnew's 1970
         Political Campaign." JACR 4.1 (Apr. 1976) 25-38.
   Vice-President Spiro Agnew's claims of distorted and unfair
reporting cannot be supported.

3392. Gersh, Debra. "A Code of Professional Ethics." SLJR
         19.121 (Nov. 1989) 2.
   The new code by the Newspaper Research Council.

3393. Ghiglione, Loren, ed. Chain Reactions: The Buying and
         Selling of America's Newspapers. indianapolis: Berg,
         1984. 200.
   Chain ownership generally decreases the quality of local
newspapers.

3394. Goldenberg, Edie N. Making the Papers: The Access of
         Resource-Poor Groups to the Metropolitan Press.
         Lexington, MA: Lexington, 1975. 164.
   Discusses "the conditions under which these groups seek and
gain access to newspapers, the dynamics of the access process
itself, and the characteristics and implications of the group-
newspaper relationships that result."

3395. Gomsrud, Lowell. "Dehumanizing the Inhuman." TCJR 1.4
         (Sept.-Oct. 1972) 3-17.
   US newspapers "have generally shown little serious, continuing interest" in telling "what Vietnam has been like for GIs,"
and the St. Paul-Minneapolis newspapers have been typical.

3396. Greene, Felix. "'China'--an Image of Conditioned
         America." MO 7.5 (May 1965) 10-16.
   A chapter from Greene's A Curtain of Ignorance (1964) about
the hostile and false propaganda by the US government and
media that China is the "most belligerent" nation in the world.

3397. Grimshaw, Tom. "The Beam in the Publisher's Eye." UM
         1.3 (Nov. 1970) 20-21.
   A survey of low ethical standards at newspapers and "contradictions between the public editorial utterances of newspapers
and their own performance." Advocates commissions and ombudsmen to stimulate better journalistic professionalism.

3398. Grodzins, Morton. Americans Betrayed: Politics and the
         Japanese Evacuation. Chicago: U of Chicago P, 1949.
         444.

The majority of Pacific coast editorials about the undemocratic and unnecessary evacuation of Japanese-Americans to concentration camps supported the action.

3399. Grossman, Karl. "Nuclear Dumping Scheme Buried by Media." Extra! 3.6 (July-Aug. 199) 14.
NRC's deregulation of "low level" radioactive waste was underreported.

3400. Hall, Bob. "The Brown-Lung Controversy." CJR 16.6 (1978) 27-35.
The textile industry has prevented the investigation and reporting of byssinosis.

3401. Hammett, Dashiell. "Introduction." The Communist Trial: An American Crossroads. By George Marion. New York: Fairplay, 1950.
On the trial of the leaders of the Communist Party U.S.A. in 1948-49 for conspiracy before Judge Harold Medina. The press handled this political trial with "inept dishonesty."

3402. Herman, Edward. "Unesco's Politicization." Zeta (Z) (Sept. 1988) 30-32.
Reasons given by the US government and media for withdrawal from Unesco are "fine illustrations of Doublespeak" and "hypocrisy" (30).

3403. Hirschorn, Michael. "University Efforts to Censor Newspapers Are on the Increase, Student Editors Say." CHE 33.32 (Apr. 22, 1987) 35-37.
A report on a study of 18 campuses sponsored by the Gannett Foundation and of the work of the Washington-based Student Press Law Center.

3404. Hoch, Paul. The Newspaper Game: The Political Sociology of the Press. London: Calder & Boyars, 1974. 217.
How the media serve the ruling class and their corporations: the Cold War, Vietnam War, militarization, "news," advertising, press "freedom," etc. The book "examines the politico-economic socialization mechanisms that ensure that the publisher and his staff will act "responsibly"--i.e. in the interest of corporations. For example, the NYT will usually "insist on the policy most in the interest of the corporate business class, without having to be lobbied, threatened or controlled" (11).

3405. Hochheimer, John. "A Comparative Spatial Analysis of International News Coverage by U.S. Newspapers & Wire Services." Stanford U, 1986. 253. DAI 47 (1986) 335-A.
Newspapers and wire services are biased in favor of the US and its allies: mentioned more frequently than Socialist and Third World countries and more often mentioned first. News stories are "Americanocentric."

3406. Hook, Glenn D. Roots of Nuclearism: Censorship and Reportage of Atomic Damage in Hiroshima and Nagasaki. La Jolla, CA: U of California Inst on Global Conflict and Cooperation, 1988. 23. (Also Multilingua 7.1-2 [1988] 133-158).
Study of the Japanese national daily, the Asahi Shimbun, from Aug. 1945 to Oct. 1949 reveals that the Occupation censors reduced the quantity and perverted the quality of information on the atomic damage by restricting criticism of the US, denying after-effects from nuclear exposure, and suppressing victims' accounts.

3407. Howell, Leon. "April 25: The Real Story." C&C 47.8 (1987) 179-80.
Print media news coverage of the April 25th "mobilization" in Washington focused on possible "communist domination" of the event and ignored the real story: that the American people are largely opposed to the Reagan administration's actions in Central America.

3408. Hynds, Ernest. American Newspapers in the 1970s. New York: Hastings, 1975. 349.
Ch. 6 discusses government intrusion.

3409. Johnson, Barbara, and Rich Yurman. "Central America Committee's Cause and Effect." MedF 10.4 (Aug.-Sept. 1989) 9.
Account of monitoring Bay area coverage of Central America, focusing especially on newspaper dependence upon official Salvadoran and US sources.

3410. Jones, Charlotte. "The Penny Press & the Origins of Journalistic Objectivity: The Problem of Authority in Liberal America." U of Iowa, 1985. 279. DAI 47 (1986) 700-A.
The penny press developed the neutral press model to correct the ills of faction while preserving Jeffersonian goals by emphasizing aggressive news gathering and advertising.

3411. Judis, John B. "K Streets Rise to Power of Special Interest to U.S." ITT 14.1 (Nov. 1-7, 1989) 7.
Although power shifted "dramatically" to "lawyers, lobbyists, public-relations flacks and policy experts, many of whom work at offices on or near K Street" in Washington, DC, the press "has been slow" to investigate and report them.

3412. Karp, Stan. "Sit Down and Shut Up!" Zeta (Z) (Sept. 1988) 88-93.
A summary of court rulings and school practices curbing the freedom of the high school press today, and a history of the high school press from the 1960s to the present.

3413. Kaufman, Richard. "Letting the Justice Department Off the Hook . . . Again." Deadline 3.6 (Nov.-Dec. 1988) 1-2, 9-10.

"A public realm that cannot produce for citizens even an acquaintance with the president's positions on nuclear issues has broken down completely."

3414. Kelley, Kevin J. "One Reason Why Press Coverage Fails." AltM 15.1 (Spring 1985) 22-23.
In the newsrooms of American newspapers "in-house apartheid is a dominating practice." In 1980 5 percent of professional journalists were non-whites at the same time that US population was 20% Blacks and Latinos.

3415. Kevelson, Roberta. The Inverted Pyramid: An Introduction to a Semiotics of Media Language. Bloomington: Indiana U, 1977. 137.
How to understand "the relationships between the overt content of the news, the social context from which the news transaction springs, and the underlying value judgments of editors who choose certain marked structures of word order to convey their editorial policies which reflect, largely, the myth of the great venturing hero" (vii).

3416. "Killing the Messenger." SPLCR 9.3 (Fall 1988) 34-37.
Student journalists "need not cave in" to university administrators because "case law leading up to Hazelwood has consistently sided in favor of college press freedom" and applies only to high schools.

3417. Knight, Al. "A Final Word." UM 1.12 (Aug. 1971) 10.
TV critics are "more a part of the broadcast 'business' than independent of it."

3418. Knopf, Terry. "Race Riots and the Press." UM 2.3 (Nov. 1971) 7-10.
"The press has borne a major responsibility for needlessly increasing racial tensions . . . conducive to violence."

3419. Krieghbaum, Hillier. Pressures on the Press. New York: Crowell, 1972. 248.
Explores government efforts--public relations, image building, harassment, secrecy--to control the news media and to undercut the press's role as a watchdog for the public. Focuses on the Nixon administration.

3420. Kuhn, Ferdinand. "Blighted Areas of Our Press." CJR 5.2 (1966) 5-10.
In newspapers' real estate sections commercialism is thinly disguised as news, and the real issues and problems of metropolitan areas are not addressed: gentrification displacing the poor, availability of affordable housing, traffic and parking problems, etc. [See 3469, 3546].

3421. Kushner, Sam. "News Item: Communist Reporter on the Loose!" RSCJ 13-14 (Fall-Winter 1974-75) 10-11.
Government persecution and public and media attack are a way of life for reporters for Communist publications.

3422. Landau, Jack C. "The State of the First Amendment." NmR 33.1 (Spring 1979) 18-25.
Discusses the Pentagon Papers, from Branzburg to Farber, Stanford Daily, The Reporters Committee vs. AT&T, state shield laws, secrecy in the courts, and concludes that the judiciary is hostile to the press. The "time has come for the press to stop being moderate and reasonable . . . and to fight with every tool at our disposal."

3423. Laqueur, Walter. "Foreign News Coverage: From Bad to Worse." WJR 5.5 (1983) 32-35.
Foreign news reporting is poor compared to other Western media.

3424. Lemert, James B., and Jerome P. Larkin. "Some Reasons Why Mobilizing Information Fails to Be in Letters to the Editor." JQ 56.3 (Fall 1979) 504-512.
"Both reluctance of writers to provide and newspaper policies account for low level of mobilizing information in letters to editor."

3425. LeoGrande, William. Uneasy Allies: The Press and the Government During the Cuban Missile Crisis. New York, NY: New York U, 1987. 53.
"As soon as the press discovered the existence of the missiles, it abandoned its role as a forum for differing opinions on Cuba, and began acting at the behest of the administration" (3). The crisis revealed how much the Cold War "had compromised the press's independence from the state" (44-5).

3426. Lewis, Anthony. "The Critical Role of the Press: Issues of Democracy." NmR 38.1 (Spring 1984) 10-14.
"New and subtle dangers threaten the freedom of the American press"--e.g., libel suits, presidential censorship.

3427. Liebling, A.J. "A Free Press?" The Press. New York: Pantheon, 1981. 15-26. (Dartmouth Alumni Magazine, 1947).
US has a free press--if you have enough money to own a newspaper. And newspaper owners are generally ideologues: against unions, against government intervention except for mailing subsidies, against property taxes, xenophobic, Sovietphobic, pro-business, pro-advertisers, pro-profit.

3428. Liebling, A.J. The Press. New York: Pantheon, 1981. 555. (Orig. 1961).
Section 1, "Toward a One-Paper Town," five skeptical essays regarding the "free press" in the US, particularly because of the increasing monopoly ownership by ideological conservatives.

3429. Lippman, Theo, ed. A Gang of Pecksniffs, and Other Comments on Newspaper Publishers, Editors and Reporters by H.L. Mencken. New Rochelle, NY: Arlington House, 1975. 206.

More of Mencken's attacks on "homo boobus" as journalist, but to make journalism better.

3430. Lofton, John. The Press as Guardian of the First Amendment. Columbia: U of South Carolina P, 1980. 358.
Survey of more than 175 years of press reaction to free speech issues reveals that "established general circulation newspapers have tended to go along with efforts to suppress deviations from the prevailing political and social orthodoxies of their time and place rather than to support the right to dissent" (279). Yet an avowed commitment to the principle of free expression "has survived" (xii).

3431. "The Los Angeles Newspaper Guild." RSCJ 11 (May 1974) 1-9.
Several articles examine the Guild and organized labor in the journalism industry.

3432. Lyle, Jack. News in Megalopolis. San Francisco: Chandler, 1967. 208.
In two parts, an overview (historical, statistics, news vs. comment, news media and the public) and a case study of Los Angeles. Chapter 2 looks at charges of bias and standardization in the news.

3433. MacDougall, Curtis. Superstition and The Press. Buffalo, NY: Prometheus, 1983. 616.
A multitude of examples of credulity by and in newspapers.

3434. Marion, George. Stop the Press! New York: Fairplay, 1953. 224.
One of the first books to place the newspaper industry thoroughly within the context of the system of American monopoly capital. Marion had to publish the book himself, so inhospitable were publishers to radical authors at the time of Senator Joe McCarthy's maximum influence. Vol. I of The Next Hundred Years.

3435. Marquez, F.T. "How Accurate Are the Headlines?" JoC 30.3 (1980) 30-36.
Given that many readers only scan for headlines, a study of four metropolitan dailies finds that headlines frequently mislead or confuse readers about the story content, especially in local papers.

3436. Marzolf, Marion. The Danish-Language Press in America. New York: Arno, 1979. 276.
The broad context of the book is the role of the ethnic press in US cultural diversity, subject to the strong influences of assimilation.

3437. Mauro, Tony. "What Did Reporters Know?" WJR 9.2 (Mar. 1987) 20-22.
Exposes the failure of newspapers to investigate the Iran-Contra crimes early and aggressively; nor have they yet delved

PRINT MEDIA

deeply and thoroughly.

3438. McCartney, James. "Starting War Is Easy; Staying Out Is Harder." AG (Sept. 29, 1990) 7B.
Observes how so many newspapers advocate war over Kuwait; asks why war is so attractive to them.

3439. McGrory, Mary. "Nixon New Celebrity, so Press Forgives All." AG (Jan. 9, 1989) 5B.
In spite of his persecution of the press, his illegal wiretapping and spying, his attempts to cover up his crimes, and his long history as a rabid Red-baiter, the Gridiron Club, an organization of print reporters, invited him to their annual banquet.

3440. McIntyre, Mark. "Muting Megaphone Mark." MORE 3.7 (1973) 5-6.
Trudeau's Doonesbury satire of Nixon and Mitchell was censored by some newspapers.

3441. McKerrow, Richard. "Central America Spiked." LOOT 1.8 (Aug. 1990) 18.
Despite continued atrocities by governments in Central America, newspapers decreased coverage, but maintained official US perspectives.

3442. Medsger, Betty. "Asbestos: The California Story." CJR 16.3 (1977) 41-50.
The major California newspapers have failed to report asbestos hazards adequately.

3443. Molotch, Harvey. "The News of Women and the Work of Men." Hearth and Home: Images of Women in the Mass Media. Ed. Gaye Tuchman, et al. New York: Oxford UP, 1978. 176-185.
Newspapers reveal men's power over women by presenting events and issues through male perspectives.

3444. Molotch, Harvey, and Marilyn Lester. "Accidental News: The Great Oil Spill as Local Occurrence and National Event." AJS 81 (1975) 235-60.
A study of newspaper coverage of the Santa Barbara oil spill by Union Oil reveals that "federal officials and business spokesmen have greater access to news media than conservationists and local officials" and that "symbolic topics and not topics with implications for distribution of wealth receive preponderant coverage."

3445. Morse, Randy, and Larry Pratt. Darkness at the End of the Tunnel: A Radical Analysis of Canadian-American Relations. Toronto: New Hogtown P, 1975. 39.
On US commercial and cultural domination: marketing, advertising, news flow. Some pages on US domination of Canadian newspaper content.

3446. Mundkowski, Walt. "Screening the Critics." UM 1.8 (Apr. 1971) 10-11.
Commercial and institutional pressures prevent good film reviewing. "The mass culture game has made the arts profitable for newspapers, but only so long as everybody keeps buying."

3447. Naureckas, Jim. "Media on the March: Journalism in the Gulf." Extra! 3.8 (Nov.-Dec. 1990) 1, 3-5, 7-9.
"From the beginning of the Persian Gulf crisis, most of the mainstream media went into war mode: The main mission seemed to be to create a national consensus in support of the U.S. military build-up."

3448. Nelson, Jack. Captive Voices. The Report of the Commission of Inquiry into High School Journalism. New York: Schocken, 1974. 264.
Denounces censorship of student publications, which along with other restrictions hold students in adolescent custodial care. Appeals for an educational environment of "democratic citizenship."

3449. "Newspapers Mustered as Air Force Defends B1B." WP (Apr. 3, 1987) A-25.
"The Air Force has ordered nearly 300 base newspapers to carry a free advertisement defending the controversial B1B bomber and chastising its critics." (USAF had 277 newspapers in 1987, as compared with 140 in 1979.)

3450. "Oliver North & Co. Banned from Costa Rica." Extra! 3.1 (Oct.-Nov. 1989) 1, 5.
Media have underreported the barring of Oliver North and other major contragate figures from Costa Rica.

3451. "Oliver North: Journalist's Friend." Extra! 1.3 (Aug.-Sept. 1987) 4.
Criticizes journalists for relying on "unnamed 'national security' sources who are partisan and unreliable."

3452. Parsons, Patrick. "Economics of the Newspaper Industry: A Marxian Analysis." M.A. Thesis, California SU, Northridge, 1978.
Newspaper readers do not determine the marketplace of ideas and content, because the market commercial newspapers seek is not readers but advertisers.

3453. Pearson, Ted. "Coverage of Chile: 'preconceived, wishful view.'" ChJR 6.10 (1973) 3-5.
The Chicago press sided with the White House in the overthrow of the elected Allende-government.

3454. Peterson, Robert A. "Attitudes of Newspaper Business Editors and General Public Toward Capitalism." JQ 61.1 (Spring 1984) 56-65.
"Business editors have more favorable attitudes toward capitalism than does the general public."

3455. Picard, Robert G. "Bottom-Line Profit Not Public Service Rules News Industry." SLJR 19.120 (Oct. 1989) 12.
Pursuit of short-term profit is undermining news quality.

3456. Pilat, Oliver. Pegler, Angry Man of the Press. Boston: Beacon, 1963. 288.
A reform-minded social critic and gadfly journalist, Westbrook Pegler wound up a reactionary McCarthyite writing for the John Birch Society.

3457. Pollock, Francis. "Knight-Ridder Wants to Know the Real You." CJR 16.5 (1978) 25-28.
Employment based upon personality tests.

3458. Pratte, Alf. "Terms of Endearment, Owner Ethics, JOAs, and Editorial Independence." JMME 2.1 (Fall-Winter 1986-87) 30-40.
Discussion of media ethics may be of little value until owner ethics becomes a major issue. This case study explores the conflict of interest problem for owners lobbying for special interest legislation, which erodes the independence of newsrooms.

3459. Pride, Armistead. "Negro Newspapers: Yesterday, Today, and Tomorrow." JQ 28 (Spring 1951) 179-188.
Believes that Negro newspapers will continue to be published and continue "as special pleaders for the rights of minority groups."

3460. Randall, Willard. "Cancer Country: Where Newspapers Fear to Tread." CJR 18.3 (1979) 67-71.
Contrasts three books on the environmental causes of cancer and newspaper failure to explore the issue.

3461. Ridenour, Ron. "The Alternative Press Fell Victim to Inequities It Purported to Oppose." RSCJ 9 (Fall 1973) 5-7.
Gives the many reasons why the "underground" press declined, with special attention to the Los Angeles Free Press. The main or a chief cause was advertiser pressures.

3462. Ridenour, Ron. "In Prison, Salvador Rights Panel Works On." SFE (Nov. 14, 1986) A8.
Reports the Marin Interfaith Task Force compilation of the report by the Human Rights Commission of El Salvador of torture in Mariona prison in El Salvador, which was sent to wire services and major newspapers but was little reported. [See "The 10 Best Censored Stories of 1987"].

3463. Ridenour, Ron. "Ridenour's Own Story." RSCJ 6 (Dec. 1972) 12-13.
Journalist Ridenour photographed the beating of a protesting paraplegic Vietnam veteran by policemen outside Nixon's Los Angeles headquarters. He was arrested and charged with various

crimes, and convicted by a jury for interfering with police.

3464. Rips, Geoffrey. The Campaign Against the Underground Press. PEN American Center Report. San Francisco: City Lights, 1981. 176.
A history of how the FBI's COINTELPRO and the CIA's CHAOS programs harassed the dissident media during the late 1960s and early 1970s. These agencies "were mobilized to crush constitutional rights" of people who opposed the Vietnam War and other opponents of government policies. Government police committed unlawful searches and seizures, trashed offices, destroyed mailing lists, made illegal arrests, and hassled the newspapers and their printers in litigation.

3465. Rips, Geoffrey. "Dirty Tricks on the Underground Press." IC 10.2 (1981) 47-50.
Extent and variety of official pressure exerted against alternative publications during the Vietnam War period.

3466. Rosenau, Neal. "No Cease-Fire in Chicago Press." ChJR 6.5 (1973) 3-8.
Chicago newspapers report the Vietnam War mainly from official US and South Vietnam perspectives.

3467. Ross, Karl. "Everywhere: Women Underrepresented on Post Front Pages." SLJR 20.127 (June 1990) 3.
Representation of women on page one of newspapers has increased, but is still low.

3468. Rosse, James N. "The Decline of Direct Newspaper Competition." JoC 30.2 (1980) 65-71.
An economic analysis of newspaper failure attributed to the competition of new media, changes in retailing and advertising, and movement to the suburbs.

3469. Rubin, Gail, et al. "For Sale or Rent." Center for Study of Responsive Law, 1978. Rev. CJR 17.2 (1978) 79.
Newspapers' real estate sections seldom provide readers with adequate consumer information; instead, they tend to be little more than press releases for agents and developers. [See 3420].

3470. Sablemen, Mark. "Publishing Threatened by String of New Laws." SLJR 18.114 (Mar. 1989) 11.
Expanded tort and contractual liabilities restrict publishers. "One of the most ominous threats is the federal 'RICO' (Racketeer Influenced Corrupt Organizations) Act."

3471. Sadeghi, Mansour. "National Differences & International Crisis Reporting: A Gatekeeper Study of the 1985 TWA Hostage Crisis." U of Southern California, 1987. DAI 48 (1987) 771-A.
Five newspapers from five countries (US, Israel, Mexico, Iran, and SU) exhibit national ideological allegiances in

reporting the event, by the criteria of space allotted, placement of story, selection of pictures, and choice and usage of words.

3472. Sandman, Peter, David Rubin, and David Sachsman. "Coverage of Specialized News." Media Casebook: An Introductory Reader In American Mass Communications. Englewood Cliffs, NJ: Prentice-Hall, 1972. 177-184.
Criticizes the uncritical irresponsibility of the business, travel, religion, real-estate, sports, women's entertainment, and science sections.

3473. Scardino, Albert. "A Look at the Conservative Alternative." CJR 25.3 (1986) 35-39.
Corporations and foundations are funding conservative college journalism.

3474. Schudson, Michael. Discovering the News: A social History of American Newspapers. New York: Basic, 1978. 228.
Recounts the emergence of objectivity as American journalism's overriding concern, and explains the factors which led to its preeminence. An account of the rise of the "adversary culture" of the 1960s reveals limitations of objectivity: it serves to mask the political assumptions of journalists, creates a format which "incorporates its own bias" and "constructs a reality which reinforces official viewpoints."

3475. Schumer, Fran. "The New Right's Campus Press." Na 234 (Apr. 3, 1982) 395-98.
On the forces behind the rise of conservative university-affiliated newspapers in the US.

3476. Scripps, Edward W. Damned Old Crank: A Self-Portrait of E. W. Scripps. Ed. Charles McCabe. New York: Harper, 1951. Rptd. Westport, CT: Greenwood, 1971. 259.
A sympathetically edited compilation of Scripps' autobiographical writings. At his death Scripps owned newspapers in fifteen states, Acme Newsphotos, United Feature Syndicate, and many other enterprises.

3477. Seldes, George. Freedom of the Press. Garden City, NY: Garden City, 1937. 380.
Complains of censorship and distortion of news by "big money and big business," but recognizes stellar examples of press opposition to "corrupting powers."

3478. Seldes, George. Lords of the Press. New York: Blue Ribbon, 1941. 408.
Attacks the American Newspaper Publishers Association: "the American public knows nothing about what the rulers of public opinion annually decide for it." Part I discusses the owners, Part II the employees, and III proposes ways to fight back.

3479. Senter, Richard, Jr., Larry Reynolds, and David
Gruenenfelder. "The Presidency and the Print Media:
Who Controls the News?" SQ 27.1 (1986) 91-105.
A study of the Nixon administration's criticism of the
press: 843 daily newspapers published in 1970 demonstrate that
"the newspapers often did change their policies in ways
desired by the Nixon Administration."

3480. Shaw, David. Press Watch: A Provocative Look at How
Newspapers Report the News. New York: Macmillan,
1984. 312.
Varied content: how front page story decisions are made, the
overuse of unnamed sources, awarding Pulitzer Prizes, etc.
Reprints of articles in the LAT 1977-1983, updated.

3481. Silverstein, Ken. "Brazil, the Bankers, and the U.S.
Press." CJR 27.3 (Sept.-Oct. 1988) 22-23.
US reporting of Brazil's declaration of a moratorium on its
debt payments to commercial banks "revealed a profound concern
for the plight of the bankers."

3482. Sneed, Don, and Harry W. Stonecipher. "More Freedom
for the Prison Press: An Emerging First Amendment
Issue?" JQ 63.1 (Spring 1986) 48-54.
"Supreme Court has dealt with related issues, but not specifically with rights of prison press."

3483. Sorensen, Jeff, and Jon Swan. "VDTs: The Overlooked
Story Right In the Newsroom." CJR 19.5 (Jan.-Feb.
1981) 32-38.
Health dangers of video display terminals are underreported.

3484. Spence, Jack. "Color It Undemocratic: Nicaraguan
Election Coverage." RA 19 (Jan.-Feb. 1985) 10-12.
Denounces the invidious comparison of the elections in
Nicaragua with the elections in El Salvador by major US
dailies functioning as conduits of official US policy.

3485. Steele, Richard W. "News of the 'Good War': World War
II News Management." JQ 62.4 (Winter 1985) 707-716.
"FDR managed the news with (mostly) press support and
thereby generated favorable public opinion."

3486. Steger, Tina. "Freedom of the Press." Q&S 59.1 (1984)
14-16.
On censorship of a newspaper at a private school.

3487. Stone, Gerald. Examining Newspapers: What Research
Reveals About America's Newspapers. Newbury Park,
CA: Sage, 1987. 152.
Includes a chapter on the selection of newspaper content.

3488. Stone, I.F. "Freedom of the Press & the CIA." IFSW
14.21 (June 13, 1966) 1, 4.
Pres. Kennedy scolded newspaper editors for revealing too

much secret information, yet he admitted the Bay of Pigs defeat might have been avoided had they disclosed more.

3489. Stone, I.F. "Harrison Salisbury's Dastardly War Crime." In a Time of Torment. New York: Random House, 1967. 393-396.
Harrison Salisbury's disclosures that the US bombed residential areas in Hanoi, instead of being praised by the press for truthtelling, "evoked as mean, petty and unworthy a reaction as I have ever seen in the press corps" eager to defend the war.

3490. Stone, I.F. "How the U.S. Press Covered Up New Revelations About the Pueblo." IFSW 16.9 (Apr. 29, 1968) 4.
Few newspapers carried the revelation that the USS Pueblo, captured by N. Korea, was within that country's 12-mi. limits.

3491. Stone, I.F. The Hidden History of the Korean War. New York: Monthly Review, 1952. 364. (2nd ed. 1969).
Partly a study of the propagandistic reporting of the Korean War. For example, for two weeks in 1951 the US reported thousands of atrocities against US prisoners, accusations never corroborated and then dropped, "but while it lasted the American press as a whole took it at face value." (Ch. 46, "Weird Statistics").

3492. Stone, I.F. "A Military Junta Rigs an Election Plain Enough for All to See, & the American Press Hails It as a Triumph of Democracy!" IFSW 14.28 (Sept. 19, 1966) 2-3.
S. Vietnam rulers did not allow freedom of the press during the election for the Assembly, but no "major Eastern seaboard newspapers I read" mentioned it.

3493. Stone, I.F. "The Witch Hunt Hits the Factory Worker." IFSW 2.45 (Dec. 13, 1954) 1, 4.
Even though the anticommunist hysteria has begun to engulf industrial workers, CIO President Walter Reuther's annual report is extremely timid, and the press largely ignored it.

3494. Sullivan, Denis F. "Comprehensiveness of Press Coverage Of a Food Irradiation Proposal." JQ 62.4 (Winter 1985) 832-837.
"Press coverage of the FDA's food irradiation proposal failed to give the public the information necessary for an informed decision."

3495. Swomley, John. "Panama Was the Central Clearing House For Nicaragua's Foreign Commerce." SLJR 19.124 (Mar. 1990) 2.
The media did not investigate the invasion of Panama but accepted the "official Pentagon/White House" explanation.

3496. Swomley, John. "U.S. News Coverage of Panama Invasion Not Representative of a Free Press." The Human Quest

(Mar.-Apr. 1990) 10-11.
"The media accepted the pretexts for the invasion but never examined the . . . reasons for it, which remain hidden from the American people."

3497. Terry, Janice, and Gordon Mendenhall. "1973 Press Coverage on the Middle East." Journal of Palestine Studies 4.1 (Autumn 1974) 120-33.
While news coverage in several major newspapers had improved over earlier years, editorials and features still exhibited pro-Israel and anti-Arab bias.

3498. Thrift, Ralph R., Jr. "How Chain Ownership Affects Editorial Vigor of Newspapers." JQ 54.2 (Summer 1977) 327-331.
"Study of matched groups of chain and independent papers on West Coast shows chain papers have fewer argumentative editorials in controversial contexts on local topics."

3499. Trillin, Calvin. "U.S. Journal: Kentucky." NY 45 (Dec. 27, 1969) 33-36.
Weeklies fear economic power.

3500. Tuchman, Gaye. "The Newspaper as a Social Movement's Resource." Hearth and Home: Images of Women in the Mass Media. New York: Oxford UP, 1978. 186-215.
On the difficulties faced by female and especially by feminist reporters.

3501. Underwood, Doug. "Retail Stores and Big-City Papers: Old Partners Fall on Tough Times." CJR 29.8 (Sept.-Oct. 1990) 33-35.
On difficulties newspapers have reporting their advertisers critically.

3502. Underwood, Doug. "Why the Cheering Should Stop." CJR 28.6 (Mar.-Apr. 1990) 49-50.
The "sports page of the average newspaper is still largely a place for boosterism," but the new The National, a nationwide sports daily, plans to emphasize investigative reporting.

3503. Walton, Richard. Henry Wallace, Harry Truman, and the Cold War. New York: Viking, 1976. 388.
Chapter 9, "The Press and Henry Wallace": The press treated Wallace and his supporters "much as the Soviet press treated dissent in Russia" (324). There is "great uniformity in the American press."

3504. Ward, Olivia. "Getting Past the Gatekeepers." Populi 13.3 (1986) 4-9.
Explains why development issues such as population are underreported, citing editors' preference for breaking stories and "hard news," as opposed to analysis and background reporting.

PRINT MEDIA

3505. Washburn, Patrick. "The Federal Government's Investigation of the Black Press During World War II." Indiana U, 1984. 438. DAI 45 (1984) 1231-A.
Concerned about complaints about injustices and discrimination, seven government agencies investigated the black press "extensively" and suppressed "a small number of black publications." A "strong undercurrent of anti-libertarianism existed in the government during the war," but no sedition indictments were initiated.

3506. "What's Unfair About the Fairness Doctrine?" Extra! 1.3 (Aug.-Sept. 1987) 2.
Newspapers "were virtually unanimous in opposing the Fairness Doctrine," and many failed to acknowledge their conflict of interest ownership or parent-company ownership of broadcasting stations.

3507. Whitaker, Brian. News Limited: Why You Can't Read All About It. London: Minority Press Group, 1981. Series No. 5. 176.
About reporting in Britain but applicable to US. Part I, "News Limited," deals with the established and popular press, whose hallmarks are nationalism, "complacency, servility, triviality and the avoidance of controversial issues." In contrast, Part II, "News Unlimited," gives an account of the "minority or alternative press," which exposes the limiting assumptions of the establishment and offers choices, investigates, opposes.

3508. Williams, Herbert. The Newspaperman's President: Harry S. Truman. Chicago: Nelson Hall, 1984. 243.
Explores President Truman's special relationship with newspaper reporters, including numerous excerpts from press conferences, letters to newspapermen and publishers, and his criticism and philosophy concerning the press.

3509. Worthy, William. "Déjà Vu All Over Again?" LOOT 1.7 (July 1990) 15-16.
Recalls how US media "played footsie with Washington for a full half year prior to the Bay of Pigs fiasco."

3510. Zagoria, Sam. "Equal Breaks for Labor News." CJR 6.3 (1967) 43-45.
"Not only do newspapers fail to give labor news attention comparable to that accorded business, but they neglect important parts of labor reporting in favor of crisis."

3511. Zion, Sidney. Read All About It! The Collected Adventures of a Maverick Reporter. New York: Summit, 1982. 362.
Accounts of newspaper accommodation to corporate and government power.

II. D. 3. b. NEWSPAPERS: INDIVIDUAL (3512-3696)

3512. Albert, Jan. "The Trial of New York's Daily News." CJR 26.2 (1987) 27-33.
In the "first civil rights case to be brought by journalists against a publication to reach open court," four employees gained a verdict of guilty from a jury, and settled with the paper for $3.1 million.

3513. Alderman, Jeffrey. "The Army Way: News Management at Fort Hood." CJR 7.4 (1968-69) 22-24.
The Army censored the Fort Hood post newspaper by burning 12,000 copies.

3514. Alexandre, Laurien. "TV Martí: An Electronic Bay of Pigs." LOOT 1.4 (Apr. 1990) 20.
VOA's anti-Castro TV station is "unquestionably interventionist," but it received "minimal coverage" in NYT, LAT, and WP during the ten months they were surveyed.

3515. Alsbury, Ray. "Boulder Battle: Maverick vs. 'The Voice of Growth.'" UM 3.4 (1972) 6-7.
The Boulder Camera is a house organ for business interests, but it is being opposed by a county weekly, the Town & Country Review.

3516. Ambrosio, Angela. "It's in the Journal. But This Is Reporting?" CJR 18.6 (1980) 34-35.
WSJ uses corporate press releases as news stories.

3517. Anderson, Jack. "'Stars and Stripes' News Censored." NAT (Dec. 4, 1988) 4.
US troops in the Pacific are "fed a diet of censored and sanitized news in the Pacific 'Stars and Stripes' newspaper."

3518. Anderson, Ronnene. "Press Coverage of Women." MJR 17 (1974) 2-19.
Study of women as they were treated in January and February, 1973, in five daily newspapers: NYT, WP, SFC, CT, SP-I. The five newspapers "have reported a change in women, but they cling in many ways to the traditional views of women as housewives, mothers, ornaments and sexpots. . . . The five newspapers are schizophrenic."

3519. Armstrong, Gerald. "The Business Jungle--Who's Covering?" UM 2.5 (Jan. 1972) 5-8.
Denver lacks critical coverage of business. Cervi's, the Denver Post, and the Rocky Mountain News distribute corporate publicity as news.

3520. Aronson, James. "A Radical Journalist in the 1950s." NmR 29.1 (Spring 1975) 34-38. (Part 1 of a 2-part series 29.2 [1975] 16-21).
An autobiographical account of the author's founding, with Cedric Belfrage, of the National Guardian, its opposition to

PRINT MEDIA

McCarthyism, etc.

3521. Bacon, Jack. "Register Moves Right." UM 1.2 (Oct. 1970) 3-4.
Right-wing executive (Schick Safety Razor, Technicolor Corp.) Patrick Frawley's Twin Circle Publishing Co. has purchased the Catholic The National Register to add to his far right media complex. This leaves "only one national Catholic paper with a liberal policy."

3522. Badran, Badran. "Editorial Treatment of the Arab-Israel Conflict in U.S. & European Newspapers: 1980-1982." U of Mass., 1984. 350. DAI 45 (Apr. 1985) 3021-A.
The WP, The Times, Le Monde, and Corriere Della Sera reflected "to a large extent the basic positions held by the policymakers in the United States, Britain, France, and Italy."

3523. Bagdikian, Ben. "Case History: Wilmington's 'Independent' Newspapers." CJR 3.2 (1964) 13-17.
DuPont determines the content of both Wilmington, Del., newspapers.

3524. Bagdikian, Ben. "The Wall Street Journal's Split Personality." WJR 3.6 (1981) 35-39.
"The Journal editorial page may be the most conservative and doctrinaire in a world full of conservative and doctrinaire newspaper editorial pages," yet it occasionally exposes corporate scandals and embarrassments.

3525. Barnett, Stephen. "The News-Free Press Case: Preserving Newspapers or Monopoly?" Na 249.15 (Nov. 6, 1989) 513, 530-32.
Examines the joint-operative agreement between The Detroit News and the Detroit Free Press. JOAs "have increased the homogenization of metropolitan dailies."

3526. Bartimole, Roldo. "Another Reporter Becomes Victim of News Media Attempt to Stifle Debate on Muny Light-CEI." PoV 22.13 (Jan. 20, 1979) 1-3.
Censoring of reporters regarding coverage of the Cleveland Electric Illuminating Co. [For many years Bartimole was Cleveland's gadfly.]

3527. Bartimole, Roldo. "Cartoonists: Following Management's Line." PoV 11.15 (Feb. 17, 1979) 1-2.
Patrick Victory's cartoons attacking Cleveland Mayor Kucinich (who is in conflict with the establishment) can be traced to his dependence upon Cleveland corporations and foundations and to newspaper support of corporations.

3528. Bartimole, Roldo. "Censorship at the Press." PoV 10.17 (Mar. 18, 1978) 1-2.
A sportswriter for the Cleveland Press who wrote a column critical of the conflict of interest between three TV sportscasters and the owner of the Cleveland Browns will henceforth

have his columns screened by four editors.

3529. Bartimole, Roldo. "Come to Columbus and Discover America--& the Wolfe Family." PoV 3.22-23 (May 31-June 5, 1971) 1-8.
"But more than any other Wolfe power is the death-tight vice the Wolfes apply on the media of Columbus" by inflaming fear of a communist invasion and reciting "right-wing gunk."

3530. Bartimole, Roldo. "Courage Department." PoV 3.21 (May 3-8, 1971) 2-3.
The Cleveland Plain Dealer editor talks on both sides of his mouth about the environment, claiming to be concerned while dropping the consumer reporting beat and refusing to use the name of offending businesses.

3531. Bartimole, Roldo. "CWRU Dean Hosts Meeting of Corporate Heads to Greet New PD Business Editor Privately." PoV 9.6 (Oct. 16, 1976) 1, 4.
Under the sponsorship of Case Western Reserve University's School of Management, Cleveland's Corporate Who's Who met with the business editor of the Cleveland Plain Dealer to demand more favorable treatment of business than they already get, which is very favorable."

3532. Bartimole, Roldo. "Diamond-Shamrock Payoffs Reveal News Bias." PoV 9.9 (Nov. 27, 1976) 3.
The revelation of Diamond-Shamrock Corp. paying $270,000 to bribe foreign customs officials was relegated to a brief article on B-8 and without mentioning the words bribery or payoffs.

3533. Bartimole, Roldo. "Editors Try to Discredit Former Star Reporter, Manage to Tar PD: Media Blacks Out Story." PoV 4.17 (Feb. 28-Mar. 4, 1972) 1-4.
The Cleveland Plain Dealer is trying to prove Joe Eszterhas was fired for professional irresponsibility, when he was fired for criticizing the PD.

3534. Bartimole, Roldo. "Garbage Gulping at PD." PoV 4.2 (July 26-31, 1971) 5.
The Cleveland Plain Dealer's boosting of plastic bags provided free publicity to Mobil Oil, whose ad agency created the material. Mobil makes Hefty garbage bags.

3535. Bartimole, Roldo. "H.A.D.C. Ripped by P.D. Lies, White Elites Protected." PoV 2.20 (Apr. 17-May 2, 1970) 1-4.
"The Cleveland Plain Dealer's vendetta against the Hough Area Development Corp." is "a cover-up of white business elites" and reflects PD's inability "to deal honestly with anything that has to do with black people."

3536. Bartimole, Roldo. "Hirschfeld Again Offers Comfort to Perk, Kills Article About Finance Director Putka." PoV 5.6 (Sept. 11-17, 1972) n.p.

PRINT MEDIA

Self-censorship at the Cleveland Plain Dealer again covers up questionable behavior by a member of the Perk Administration.

3537. Bartimole, Roldo. "Notes." PoV 2.19 (Apr. 13-18, 1970) 1-2.
PoV, critic of Cleveland journalism, gets "little exposure in the mass media," and the Press refused even PoV's offer to buy an ad.

3538. Bartimole, Roldo. "PD Fires Joe Eszterhas for Criticizing His Boss, Silencing Free Speech Again." PoV 4.5 (Sept. 13-18, 1971) 1-4.
"Gagging has become policy at the PD."

3539. Bartimole, Roldo. "PD Reporters Bend Nicely." PoV 1.15 (Feb. 16-20, 1970) 1-2.
The Cleveland Plain Dealer has pushed out another of its best reporters for being a "troublemaker," and his colleagues and the American Newspaper Guild "accepted the PD repression without a whimper."

3540. Bartimole, Roldo. "PD's Princiotto Attacks Own Reporter to Protect CEI's Nuclear Power Project." PoV 3.16 (Feb. 22-27, 1971) 1.
The managing editor of the Cleveland Plain Dealer has been "sabotaging" his environmental reporter.

3541. Bartimole, Roldo. "Plain Dealer?" PoV 2.7 (Oct. 20-25, 1969) n.p.
The Cleveland Plain Dealer editor, Tom Vail, suppressed an article written by two of his reporters because it was critical of the interlocking directorships between business foundations and the racist and right-wing Educational Research Council of America.

3542. Bartimole, Roldo. "Sohio Execs Secret Meeting with PD Editors Unreported." PoV 10.3 (Sept. 3, 1977) 1-2.
Sohio's $21 million tax abatement was barely reported by Cleveland media, and the secret meeting between the Plain Dealer publisher and editors and Sohio execs was not covered by the media.

3543. Bartimole, Roldo. "Toppling a Mayor." PoV 11.4 (Sept. 16, 1978) 1-4.
The Cleveland Plain Dealer has done "the dirty work of established" power in trying to recall Mayor Kucinich, who opposed the establishment.

3544. Bartimole, Roldo. "Worst Fire in 30 Years Forgotten by Press, PD: Poor & Blacks Don't Rate Attention." PoV 9.15 (Feb. 12, 1977) 1-2.
Two city street blocks and 28 houses containing 50 mainly poor black families were leveled but the two main Cleveland newspapers, the Press and the Plain Dealer, did not keep

abreast of the disaster, its victims, and the unanswered questions, nor did they support fund drives or rallies for victims.

3545. Bennett, James R. "Newspaper Reporting of U.S. Business Crime in 1980." NRJ 3 (Fall 1981) 45-52.
Newspapers underreport corporate wrongdoing.

3546. Bennett, James R. "Newspapers Neglect Car Safety." SLJR 18.110 (Oct. 1988) 14.
Newspapers serve their auto advertisers and not the public in their coverage of automobiles. [See entry 3420].

3547. Bennett, James R. "Page One Sensationalism and the Libyan 'Hit Team'" NRJ 4.1 (Fall 1982) 34-38.
Unsubstantiated Reagan administration claims that Gaddafi had sent an assassination team to the US were given prominent coverage by newspapers.

3548. Bennett, James R., and Christopher Gould. "Reporting the CIA: National Security or Civil Liberties?" FSN 7 (June 1981) 3-12.
Newspaper coverage of administration and intelligence efforts to increase the power of the intelligence agencies was insufficient and too slanted for well-informed judgment by readers.

3549. Berlet, Chip. "Woodstock West: Press Coverage of the Student Ghetto." UM 1.1 (Sept. 1970) 8-11.
Examines coverage of 1970 Vietnam War events and student response, and finds the papers one-sided against the students.

3550. "Biased Coverage of Arias Peace Press." SLJR 16.106 (May 1988) 13.
The NYT and other newspapers showed how much they shared the Reagan administration's biased obsession with Nicaragua in their treatment of the regional peace proposal signed by five Central American nations.

3551. Bishop, Bill. "Selling the Paper: Hard Times for an Independent Weekly in the New Rural Economy." TO 80.11 (June 3, 1988) 1, 6-8.
The former co-owner of a small Texas weekly tells how the incursion of chain merchandisers into his county cut his advertising revenues and forced him to sell.

3552. Bleifuss, Joel. "Picayune Minds." ITT 12.32 (Aug. 17-30, 1988) 4.
New Orleans Times-Picayune columnist Ronnie Virgets was fired after he refused to re-write a story critical of a media party held prior to the Republican National Convention.

3553. Blinken, Tony. "The Consumer News You Never See." WM 17.6 & 7 (1985) 33-36.
"By failing to take on the problem of defective products in a systematic way, the [Washington] Post has passed up an

PRINT MEDIA

opportunity to expose the corporate culture which tolerates risks to consumers and shamelessly covers up dangerous failures."

3554. Bonelli, William. Billion Dollar Blackjack. Beverly Hills, CA: Civic Research Press, 1954. 230.
An exposé of the LAT's kingpin and citymaker.

3555. Boot, William. "Captain Al Explores Planet Earth." CJR 27.3 (Sept.-Oct. 1988) 18-21.
USA Today chairman Allen Neuharth's global "JetCapade" reporting provides "mind candy" for Mr. Sixpack, focusing on celebrities, clichés, US patriotism, and trendy, fragmentary contemporaneity.

3556. Boot, William. "The Empire Strikes Back." CJR 20.1 (May-June 1981) 44-45.
Tom Dowling's attack on The Empire Strikes Back and on the film industry's commercialism caused him to be fired.

3557. Boot, William. "Time Inc.'s 'Unbiased' Satellite." CJR 20.1 (May-June 1981) 43-48.
Time Inc.'s Washington Star favors the Reagan administration and corporations and censors its reporters.

3558. Branch, Taylor. "The Scandal-Maker Stakes." MORE 5 (Mar. 1975) 18, 20-21.
On Seymour Hersh's coverage of the CIA operation that gathered surveillance information on at least 10,000 Americans during Nixon's presidency.

3559. Bray, Howard. The Pillars of the Post: The Making of a News Empire in Washington. New York: Norton, 1980. 308.
Studies the intricacies of this major mainstream newspaper, sometimes critic of the corporate state it generally represents.

3560. Bridge, Junior. "No News is Women's News." M&V 49 (Winter 1989) 11-13.
A study of "10 major, general-interest newspapers" revealed that "women are still not considered 'worth it.'"

3561. Brown, Pamela A. "Constructing the Cultural Curtain: The Meaning of Cold War in York, Pennsylvania Daily Newspapers, 1947-1962. U of Iowa, 1983. 454. DAI 44.12 (June 1984) 3529-A.
Although one of the two newspapers studied was liberal and the other conservative, they were alike in their treatment of Cold War themes, especially the "mission" of the US against the SU. These newspapers "helped to construct the American version of the iron curtain."

3562. Carter, Charles. "The Poor Get Theirs . . . Again." UM 1.7 (Mar. 1971) 4-6.

The special emphasis newspeople place upon "welfare chiseling" by the poor instead, say, of corporate corruption, in comparison to which welfare fraud is miniscule, is illustrated by a series in The Pueblo Chieftain.

3563. Chaney, Lindsay, and Michael Cieply. The Hearsts: Family and Empire: The Later Years. New York: Simon and Schuster, 1981. 410.
A study of William Randolph Hearst, his heirs, and his business enterprises.

3564. Chang, Tsan-Kuo. "The News & U.S.-China Policy, 1950-1984: Relationships with the Government & Public Opinion." U of Texas, Austin, 1986. 365. DAI 47 (1987) 4221-A.
Studies thirty-five years of the NYT and WP, presidential documents, and public opinion polls. The newspapers expressed a "pro-government direction in their coverage" and affected public opinion. The government influenced the newspapers' editorial position, "not vice versa."

3565. Clarkson, Fred. "Behind the Times: Who Pulls the Strings at Washington's #2 Daily?" Extra! 1.3 (Aug.-Sept. 1987) 8.
Complains of the media's failure to expose the ownership of the Washington Times by Reverend Sun Myung Moon's right-wing Unification Church and its support of autocratic and fascist individuals and groups.

3566. Clifford, George. "The Church Was in Control, and Everybody at the Times knew it." SLJR (Oct. 1984) 18.
On The Washington Times, owned by Rev. Moon.

3567. Cockburn, Alexander. "Beat the Devil." Na 242.4 (1986) 102-3.
The NYT and WP follow the official line in support of nuclear testing.

3568. Cockburn, Alexander. "How SWAPO Got Framed." Na 248.17 (May 1, 1989) 582-583.
Reveals how the NYT and the WP passed on as fact self-serving South African "intelligence briefings" about events in Namibia, transforming an ambush of peaceful returnees by the South African police into a foiled invasion.

3569. Cockburn, Alexander. "Me Bwana, and You?" Na 247.7 (Sept. 26, 1988) 226-7.
On the inadequate coverage of Burundi, Burma, and Afghanistan by the NYT and the WSJ.

3570. Cockburn, Alexander. "Return of Dracula" and "Miami Vices." ITT 12.32 (Aug. 17, 1988) 17.
Recent support of Reagan administration machinations against Nicaragua by NYT and WP.

PRINT MEDIA

3571. Cockburn, Alexander. "Smears Exposed." Corruptions of Empire. London: Verso, 1987. 293-95.
On red-baiting by a WP editorial writer.

3572. Cockburn, Alexander. "Working-Class Heroes at Home and Abroad." Corruptions of Empire. London: Verso, 1987. 268-70.
The contradictory way the NYT and WP reported the air traffic controllers' strike in the US and the shipworkers' strike in Poland.

3573. Collier, Peter. "A Press Dynasty Topples in Oakland." MORE 7.9 (Sept. 1977) 32-40.
On the rise and decline of the conservative Republican newspaper owned by the Knowland family, the Oakland Tribune.

3574. Cooper, Marc. "The Press and the Panama Invasion." Na 250.24 (June 18, 1990) 850-54.
A review of "more than 300 articles and editorials" about the invasion shows that the US press "did little more than parrot the Bush Administration's transparent legal justifications for the invasion." The coverage was "generally uncritical, superficial, often jingoistic."

3575. "The Death of Fred Hampton: A Special Report." ChJR 2.12 (Dec. 1969) 16 pp.
Criticism of police accounts of the killing of Black Panther Party leaders in Chicago, and of media reporting of the incident.

3576. Dorfman, Ron. "What You Can Do About Watergate." ChJR 6.6 (1973) 3-4.
Chicago's Tribune and American were "virtual megaphones" for the Chicago police Red Squad, when they should have been exposing and denouncing it.

3577. Dorman, William, and Mansour Farhang. "The U.S. Press & Lebanon." SAIS 3 (Winter-Spring 1983) 65-81.
Media coverage of Arab-Islamic world since World War II has followed official Washington's lead. "The press has, for the most part, exempted Israel's behavior and motives from scrutiny while dehumanizing Israel's antagonists" (67). During the first week of Israel's invasion of Lebanon on June 6, 1983, the same pattern prevailed.

3578. Dorman, William, and Daniel Hirsch. "Chernobyl, the Emerging Story: The U.S. Media's Slant." BAS 43.1 (Aug.-Sept. 1986) 54-56.
The early reporting of Chernobyl, which turned the disaster into "a morality tale" of the superiority of the US over the SU, was dominated by official sources.

3579. "Eclipse in Baltimore." MORE 4.3 (1974) 8-9.
VP Agnew pressured the Baltimore Sun to kill an article.

3580. Emery, Mike. "How the Times Picked Dick." RSCJ 6 (Dec. 1972) 5-7.
Despite its recognition of Richard Nixon's "creeping fascism," the LAT endorsed Nixon for president. "Joseph Pulitzer would be ashamed."

3581. FitzPatrick, Terry. "T. Boone Takes on the Press." WJR 9.2 (1987) 10, 12. (Also TO [Jan. 15, 1988] 8-9).
Angry over the Amarillo Globe-News's coverage of his company, Mesa Ltd. Partnership, Texas oilman T. Boone Pickens asked his 400 Mesa Petroleum employees in Amarillo to cancel their subscriptions to the newspaper.

3582. Flippo, Chet. "Gushing Over Oil in Houston." MORE 4.1 (Jan. 1974) 10-11, 14-15.
The Post and Chronicle are virtually public relations arms of the oil industry.

3583. Freedman, Allan. "Fundamental Split Divides Baptists Over Freedom of the Press." ITT 12.16 (Mar. 16-22, 1988) 18.
Jack Harwell, editor of The Christian Index for twenty-one years, was voted out because he reported events even when they opposed the values of fundamentalist Baptists.

3584. Friedman, Robert. "The Freedom of the Press Under Siege." NewT 11.12 (Dec. 11, 1978) 35-50.
Discusses recent attacks on the First Amendment.

3585. Gillenkirk, Jeff. "On Central America, U.S. Dailies Parrot Reagan Line." SFBG (Jan. 6, 1987) 7, 9-11.
Stories about the Arias peace plan in seven major dailies followed the Reagan administration's direction.

3586. Gitlin, Todd. The Whole World Is Watching: Mass Media in the Making and Unmaking of the New Left. Berkeley: U of California P, 1980. 327.
The NYT and newspapers in general are part of the "oligopolized, privately controlled corporate economy and its intimate ally, the bureaucratic national security state" (9). In consequence, "increasingly the impression was conveyed that extremism was rampant and that the New Left was dangerous to the public good" (29).

3587. Gordon, Douglas E. "The Great Speckled Bird: Harassment of an Underground Newspaper." JQ 56.2 (Summer 1979) 289-295.
"Despite selective enforcement of obscenity and traffic laws, this underground newspaper outlived its constituency."

3588. Gottlieb, Robert. "The Forgotten History of the Los Angeles Times." RSCJ 10 (Winter 1974) 2-7.
An account of the LAT's ferocious drive to create and maintain its monopoly.

PRINT MEDIA

3589. Gottlieb, Robert, and Irene Wolt. Thinking Big: The Story of the "Los Angeles Times," Its Publishers, and Their Influence on Southern California. New York: Putnam's, 1978. 576.
Los Angeles has always been a commodity, something to be advertised and sold to the public, and the LAT bought and sold the commodity at the same time. The LAT was an essential part of the speculation and expansion of LA, and whatever got in its way it trampled on. Its owner once owned 2 million acres and numerous businesses all inseparable from LAT editorial policies, and this power decided who would be elected to public offices. But in 1960 it began to change from a right-wing parochial rag to the major newspaper it is today.

3590. Gould, Christopher, and James R. Bennett. "A Comparison of Press Coverage of Communist & Pro-Western Dictatorships." FSN 6 (June 1980) 3-11.
Coverage in 1979 downplayed pro-Western atrocities while accentuating communist faults and weaknesses.

3591. Grossman, Karl. "New Improved Nukes: The Press Pushes the Nuclear Option." Extra! 3.5 (May-June 1990) 1.
Newspapers mirror nuclear industry "falsehoods and half-truths: Nukespeak 1990s-style."

3592. Gruchow, Paul, and Paul Berg. "3M: Coverage of a Scandal . . . or Scandalous Coverage?" TCJR 3.4 (Aug. 1975) 11-15.
Coverage of the Minnesota Mining and Manufacturing Company's illegal political campaign fund by the four Twin Cities daily newspapers was ineffective.

3593. Haddigan, Michael. "Showdown at Pine Bluff." CJR 26.2 (1987) 16-18.
Donald Mace Williams was fired from his job as editor of the Pine Bluff Commercial after the paper was taken over by the Donrey Media Group and he clashed with the new general manager over story content.

3594. Hanrahan, John. "The Union-Busing Post." Prog 53 (Feb. 1989) 18-25.
Once regarded as perhaps the nation's leading liberal newspaper, WP has systematically undermined the unions in its shop. "This swing to the right in labor relations has been marked by a corresponding rise in conservatism in Post editorials and on the op-ed pages."

3595. Hansen, Evelyn. "Attica: Truth Was One of the Hostages." TCJR 1.1 (Feb. 1972) 20-26.
Reporting of the riot at Attica Correctional Facility in New York during September 1971 by the St. Paul Pioneer Press and Dispatch was poor in quality.

3596. Hellinger, Daniel. "Sun International Coverage Offers Less of the Same." SLJR 19.121 (Nov. 1990) 1, 8.

Competition does not mean diversity. St. Louis' Sun and Post "operate within a narrow ideological framework in their news coverage," dominated by Democratic and Republican party "official" sources.

3597. Helvarg, David. "San Diego: Newsline's Bottom Line." CJR 23.2 (1984) 4, 6.
San Diego Newsline "earned a reputation for skilled investigative reporting," but its financial support by two wealthy, political investors who went bankrupt, and its failure to report the scandal, damaged its reputation.

3598. Henwood, Doug. "Dow Jones: Going for the Glitz?" Extra! 3.5 (May-June 1990) 8-10.
A critique of the WSJ and its editor, Norman Pearlstine, under whom the paper's "business coverage has grown notably fluffier."

3599. Henwood, Doug. "The Washington Post: The Establishment's Paper." Extra! 3.2 (Jan.-Feb. 1990) 9.
The Post's "hard foreign policy line," union-busting, etc.

3600. Herzog, James. "From Inside, Beacon Journal Not All That Good." PoV (Nov. 27-Dec. 2, 1972) n.p.
The Akron Beacon Journal is heavily influenced by local corporations.

3601. Holk, Richard. "Print Coverage of Military Conflict: The Los Angeles Times and the Vietnam War (A Content Analysis, 1964-1972)." MA Thesis, California SU, Fullerton, 1979. 88. MA 18.1 (1980) 41.
Anti-war and military spending were least reported.

3602. Hoyt, Michael. "Publish and Perish in Ohio." CJR 23.6 (Mar.-Apr. 1985) 14-16.
The Wheeling-Pittsburg Steel Co. suppressed the union newspaper.

3603. "In Bed Together." Na 247.5 (Sept. 3, 1988) 152-53.
Attorney General Edwin Meese granted a joint operating agreement to two chain newspapers in Detroit (the Detroit News and the Free Press) under the Newspaper Preservation Act, creating an "instant monopoly" and stifling competition.

3604. Johnson, Flora. "Stampede on Page One." CJR 18.5 (1980) 8, 12.
Chicago Sun-Times and Tribune reported Ford Motor's Pinto auto fires and coverup two years after Mother Jones published Mark Dowie's exposé.

3605. Joseph, Nadine. "Water, Water Everywhere." CJR 19.5 (Jan.-Feb. 1981) 8-9.
LAT's economic self-interest prejudices its reporting on the state's water system.

PRINT MEDIA

3606. Katel, Peter. "Plugging In to the Power Company." CJR 19.3 (1980) 13, 15.
Arizona electric utility attacked the Albuquerque Journal for its critical reporting.

3607. Kayser, Jacques. One Week's News: Comparative Study of 17 Major Dailies for a Seven-Day Period. Paris: Unesco, 1953. 102.
Includes the New York Daily News. Gives data about structure (percent copy, advertising, illustrations) and content.

3608. Keeler, Robert F. "Newsday: A Candid History of the Respectable Tabloid." IREJ 13.4 (Fall 1990) 6-8.
"An excerpt from the newly published book by Robert Keeler" that illustrates the investigative reporting by the newspaper.

3609. Kelly, Tom. The Imperial Post: The Meyers, the Grahams, and the Paper That Rules Washington. New York: William Morrow, 1983. 320.
A history of the Washington Post. After the triumph of Watergate reporting, the Post "grew increasingly reckless and arrogant" in its "Metro" and "style" sections and "its credibility went down" (301). Perhaps Donald Graham can "make it what it has always claimed to be--complete, accurate, well written, well edited and fair" (303).

3610. Kern, Montague, et al. The Kennedy Crises: The Press, the Presidency, and Foreign Policy. Chapel Hill: U of NC Press, 1983. 290.
Studies "press-presidential interaction and day-to-day coverage in five important newspapers during four major crises in which the Kennedy administration was involved: Laos and Berlin in 1961, Cuba in 1962, and Vietnam in 1963." Newspapers examined: NYT, WP, CT, SFE, SLP-D. Kennedy "was able in the latter stages of each of the four crises to eclipse rival influences and achieve a dominant position in the press" (195). Issues "did not originate in the press, but rather stemmed from the politically significant forces at work on the issues. In this vital sense, the press during these years was largely a reflective institution" (196).

3611. Kim, Seung. "Information Flow: A Critical Approach from a World-System Perspective." U of Missouri, 1986. 307. DAI 47 (1987) 2785-A.
The NYT and WP not only actively opposed Third World ideas of the balanced flow of international information, UNESCO, and leaders of the New International Information Order (NIIO) movement, but they sought to undermine them by distorting their arguments.

3612. Kluger, Richard. The Paper: The Life and Death of the "New York Herald Tribune." New York: Knopf, 1986. 801.
In 1945 the Tribune under Ogden Reid was at "its apex of power and prestige," excelled only by the NYT in "quality of

content." But it closed in 1966 not because of its staff but because of the Tribune company--newspapering as big business. Much comparison with the NYT.

3613. Knight, G. "Strike Talk: A Case Study of News." CJC 8.3 (June 1982) 61-79.
The strike by postal employees in 1980 was reported by two Toronto dailies mainly in terms of the disruptiveness of the workers and the negative impact of strikes on the public. Virtually no attention was paid to the workers' issues behind the strike.

3614. Knoll, Erwin. "Shaping Up CBS: A Case Study in Intimidation." Prog 34 (July 1970) 18-22.
Links criticism of CBS's Vietnam coverage by the Des Moines Register to a White House Advisor.

3615. Knoll, Erwin. "Through the Looking Glass." Prog 49 (Feb. 1985) 4.
WP reactions to government censorship are contradictory.

3616. Kopkind, Andrew. "Tools of Power." MORE 8.2 (1978) 30-34.
Two books examine the LAT and WP in terms of the impact of economic and political conditions upon reporting.

3617. Kreig, Andrew. Spiked. 2nd ed. Old Saybrook, CT: Peregrine, 1988. 245.
An account of the decline in quality of the Hartford Courant after it was acquired by the Times Mirror Co. of Los Angeles.

3618. Kwitny, Jonathan. Endless Enemies: The Making of an Unfriendly World. NY: Congdon and Weed, 1984. 435.
A press criticism book designed to "highlight a common fallacy of approach in the reporting of foreign relations that has caused great harm to the country." The focus is mainly on the WSJ, the WP, and the NYT. Chap. 21 in its entirety exposes the NYT/government alliance.

3619. Lalehparavaran, Parvin. "A Content Analysis of The New York Times and St. Louis Post-Dispatch Coverage of the Arab-Israeli Conflict from June 6, 1982 - February 12, 1983." Oklahoma SU, 1984. 107. DAI 45 (June 1985) 3469-A.
Studies news coverage of Arabs and Israelis before, during and after the Beirut Massacre of Palestinian refugees during September 1982. Both newspapers were more positive toward Israel prior to the Massacre, and more positive toward Arabs afterward. Neither newspaper provided sufficient background to understand the conflict.

3620. Lekachman, Robert. "Playing Inflation Down the Middle." CJR 17.6 (1979) 35-39.
The NYT, WP, and WSJ reported only mainstream opinions of President Carter's economics program and "failed abysmally to

clarify causes and assess cures" for inflation.

3621. Logan, Robert. "USA Today's Innovations and Their Impact on Journalism Ethics." JMME 1.2 (Spring-Summer 1986) 74-87.
The newspaper prefers packaging, marketing, and graphics to in-depth reporting and engagement with the nation's ethical challenges.

3622. Lowenstein, Douglas. "Covering the Primaries." WJR 2.7 (1980) 38-42.
Newspaper (WP, NYT, CT) reporting of political campaigns is deficient; offers five remedies. [See II.B.5.]

3623. Lyons, Gene. "The Other Carters." NYT (Sept. 18, 1977) 14-16, 76-100. Rpt. The Higher Illiteracy (Fayetteville: U of Arkansas P, 1988) 114-34.
In praise of Hodding Carter and his son Hodding III and The Delta Democrat-Times of Greenville, Miss., the "conscience of Mississippi."

3624. MacDougall, A. Kent. "Boring from within the Bourgeois Press: Part One." MR 40.6 (Nov. 1988) 13-24.
Describes how as a journalist for the WSJ and LAT he was "a well-paid, privileged member of that fast-growing corps of information workers who mass-produce news, disseminate official proclamations, standardize information and ideas, reinforce institutional viewpoints, legitimize dominant values, and help secure the compliance of the populace."

3625. MacDougall, A. Kent. "Boring from within the Bourgeois Press: Part Two." MR 40.7 (Dec. 1988) 10-24.
The author's experiences as a radical working for the LAT, writing about the contradictions in capitalism, and constantly struggling with censoring editors.

3626. MacDougall, A. Kent. "Taking Stock of Dow Jones." CJR 21.4 (1982) 59-63.
A review of two books on The Wall Street Journal: Lloyd Wendt's The Wall Street Journal and Jerry Rosenberg's Inside the Wall Street Journal. "Neither book ever quite gets a handle on the newspaper's news product" because "both books are based mainly on the records and recollections of Dow Jones management and are practically devoid of independent appraisals of the Journal." Wendt's book "is a company history commissioned by Dow Jones."

3627. MacMichael, David. "The Brenneke Trial." LOOT 1.8 (Aug. 1990) 3.
The significant trial of Richard Brenneke related to the release of 52 Embassy hostages in Iran was barely mentioned by the NYT and WP.

3628. Maroe, Jim. "Newsday and the F-14 Debate: What's Good for Grumman . . ." Deadline 5.1 (Jan.-Feb. 1990) 6-8.

Exposes the alliance between the Times-Mirror newspaper Newsday on Long Island and the Grumman Corporation also on Long Island, which builds the F-14 fighter.

3629. Martin, Josh. "Placid News Makes Headlines." ITT (Mar. 2-8, 1983) 14.
USA Today offers "slick presentations and lifestyle essays" over "investigative reporting."

3630. Massing, Michael. Euromissiles and the Press. New York: New York U, 1987. 37. Center for War, Peace, and the News Media, Occasional Paper No. 2.
The media served as the administration's public relations arm during the negotiations about the cruise and Pershing II deployment.

3631. Massing, Michael. "The Missouri Compromise." CJR 20.4 (1981) 35-41.
The St. Louis Post-Dispatch has become less critical of business for reasons of profit.

3632. McAuliffe, Kevin. The Great American Newspaper: The Rise and Fall of the "Village Voice." New York: Scribner's, 1978. 486.
Traces the transition of VV from a vital "voice to voiceless people" to a subdivision of a corporation.

3633. McCarthy, Colman. "Lock Stepping Media & Military." WP (Dec. 31, 1989) F2.
"Editorial page war-whooping . . . was heard on Dec. 21, the day after the U.S. rape of Panama." Not one of ten major newspapers dissented.

3634. McCartney, James. "The Washington 'Post' and Watergate: How Two Davids Slew Goliath." CJR 12.2 (1973) 8-22.
Tells how WP reporters unscrambled the puzzle of the Watergate break-in despite significant pressure from the Nixon administration and little support from their peers in the media.

3635. McKerrow, Richard. "Editing Out Salvadoran Torture." LOOT 1.3 (Mar. 1990) 5.
Compares NYT reporting of torture to that of the Seattle Post-Intelligencer to show how the NYT "habitually obfuscates" evidence of US-sponsored torture.

3636. Meeker, Richard. Newspaperman: S.I. Newhouse and the Business of News. New Haven: Ticknor and Fields, 1983. 294.
Biography of "the greatest buyer of newspapers America has ever known." "Newhouse began his life in newspapers with one goal--to accumulate capital." For Newhouse, "a newspaper was not a newspaper at all. It was a package whose purpose was to carry advertising" (252-53). The legacy of Newhouse is "modern journalism."

PRINT MEDIA

3637. Metzger, H. Peter. "Wanted: Rocky Mountain Post." UM 1.3 (Nov. 1970) 3-5.
On the failure by Colorado newspapers to report radioactive and chemical dangers caused by federal agencies.

3638. "Miami Vice." Na (Feb. 27, 1988) 260.
Condemns a MH editorial on Nicaragua as "violent in tone and disdainful of truth."

3639. Milton, Joyce. The Yellow Kids: Foreign Correspondents in the Heyday of Yellow Journalism. New York: Harper, 1989. 412.
Joseph Pulitzer's World and William Randolph Hearst's Journal engaged in fierce competition for readers by producing ever more sensational accounts of Cuba's struggle for independence. Their part in the war-mongering that led to US involvement is a stunning example of media irresponsibility and power that has disturbing echoes in our own day.

3640. Moore, Michael. "How to Keep 'Em Happy in Flint." CJR 24.3 (1985) 40-43.
Criticism of GM by the editor of the Flint newspaper caused his dismissal.

3641. Morris, Roger. "Reporting the Race War in Rhodesia." CJR 17.6 (Mar.-Apr. 1979) 32-34.
Media coverage of the insurrection in NYT and WP carries "racial overtones" by favoring the white government's point of view and by stressing black guerrilla savagery.

3642. Muchnick, Irvin. "The Bizarre Career of Jacque Srouji, Alias Lelia Hassan." MORE 6.10 (Oct. 1976) 26-30.
How a cub reporter was persuaded by her editor to cooperate with the FBI in covering the New Left, the KGB, and Karen Silkwood.

3643. Nigut, Bill, Sr. "The Media & the 'Evil' Empire' on the Potomac." CMC (July 1988) 4-6.
Decries underreporting of crimes by military contractors.

3644. Nigut, Bill, Sr. "The Media's Scandalous Reporting of the S&L Scandal." CMC (Aug. 1990) 1-8.
The media overlooked and hid the scandal for ten years and sold out the nation "to George Bush's rich friends."

3645. Noah, Timothy. "The Washington Post: Monopoly Profits and Broken Promises." WM 15 (Jan. 1984) 14-33.
Criticizes WP's devotion to profits over responsiveness to the community.

3646. Nocera, Joseph. "Making It At The Washington Post." WM 10.10 (Jan. 1979) 10-22.
WP falls short of its great potential by its lack of mission which causes the insufficiency of in-depth, thoughtful analysis.

3647. Norden, Eric. "The Prophet Honored." MO 5.12 (Dec. 1963) 18-19.
The award of the 1962 Nobel Peace Prize to Dr. Linus Pauling shocked the US Establishment and its press, which had "vilified and derided" him "for over a decade."

3648. O'Brien, Sue. "Unsatisfied Women." UM 3.3 (Nov. 1972) 1.
A sex discrimination suit against the Boulder Camera by Patricia Hodgins.

3649. Perl, Peter. "Asbestos: The Connecticut Story." CJR 16.3 (1977) 50-54.
The serious asbestos health problems at Electric Boat submarine shipyard were underreported by four daily newspapers, even after 22 deaths were revealed.

3650. Petras, James. "Editing the Op-Ed Page: NYT and CSM." LOOT 1.4 (Apr. 1990) 5-6.
Examples of "dishonesty" by editors of the two newspapers.

3651. "A Political Press." CJR 21.1 (May-June 1982) 20.
On WSJ support of US foreign policy toward El Salvador.

3652. Pollack, Richard. "Trying to Remember Vietnam." MORE 3.3 (1973) 8-9.
On WP refusal to print anti-war and anti-Nixon ads.

3653. Pollock, Francis. "The Common Cents Approach to Consumer Reporting." CJR 16.3 (1977) 37-38.
Common Cents, self-described as a consumer oriented newspaper supplement, "will offend no advertiser."

3654. Pollock, John, and David Eisenhower. "The New Cold War in Latin America: The U.S. Press and Chile." The Chilean Road to Socialism. Ed. Dale L. Johnson. Garden City, NY: Anchor, 1973. 71-86.
Newspapers' hostility toward Allende mirrored government policy.

3655. Price, Sean. "View from the Right at UT." TO 79.7 (1986) 13-14.
U of Texas at Austin students publish a conservative newspaper, the Texas Review.

3656. Prichard, Peter. The Making of McPaper: The Inside Story of "USA Today." Kansas City, MO: Andrews, McMeel & Parker, 1987. 370.
An authorized history of the first five years of USA Today by the newspaper's deputy editorial director, who had broad access to corporate records.

3657. Quigley, Margaret. "The Anti-Semitic Roots of Eastern European Nationalism." Extra! 3.5 (May-June 1990) 6-7.

Newspapers have failed to "provide adequate historical context concerning the anti-Semitic and fascist currents in eastern European nationalism."

3658. Ramsey, William. "Journalists Affect the Outcome of Events They Cover--A Burden They Cannot Shed." SLJR 19.123 (Feb. 1990) 9.
First in a 3-part study of the SLP-D's coverage of the Central American peace process. The SLP-D narrowed its sights on Nicaragua and overlooked the issue in other countries, following White House policy of discrediting the Arias peace plan.

3659. Ramsey, William. "Post Leans Towards Dependence on U.S. Sources, Media Survey Reveals." SLJR 19.124 (Mar. 1990) 13.
SLP-D coverage of Central America has been strongly biased toward the official White House/CIA position. For example, of 54 articles on Nicaragua, only one used Nicaraguan sources.

3660. Ramsey, William. "Post Articles Favor U.S. Line Over Central American Peace Plan." SLJR 19.125 (Apr. 1990) 6.
A survey of 217 SLP-D articles published during the six months following the Central American peace plan signed by five Central American countries reveals a highly uncritical treatment of US misrepresentations about Nicaragua, El Salvador, and the plan.

3661. Rosenberg, Jerry M. Inside the Wall Street Journal: The History and the Power of Dow Jones & Company and America's Most Influential Newspaper. New York and London: Macmillan, 1982. 335.
Generally approving, based mainly on the records and recollections of Dow Jones management [like Wendt's book].

3662. Ross, Robert, and Sally Power. "Protest Coverage Assessed." TCJR 1.6 (Mar.-Apr. 1973) 16-18.
Newspaper coverage by each of the four metropolitan dailies of student unrest at the U of Minnesota in May of 1972 tended to "ignore what students are protesting for." [See No. 3586].

3663. Rutland, Robert. "Newspaper Antitrust: 'Trade Copy' Only?" CJR 6.3 (1967) 46-7.
The LAT failed to report an anti-trust trial in which it was a defendant to camouflage their expansion efforts.

3664. "Salvadoran Disinformation in the Miami Herald?" Extra! 3.5 (May-June 1990) 3.
El Salvadoran military disinformation planted in US newspapers, this time to influence a crucial vote in Congress on military aid.

3665. Scharff, Edward. Worldly Power: The Making of "The Wall Street Journal." New York: Beaufort, 1986. 305.

Conversations with "scores of Journal employees" provide the basis for this account of "the most popular newspaper in the country" that is read by "the cream of American society" ("average household income of $107,800 a year in 1985") and that "sets forth the intellectual agenda for the nation" (xi). As the nation's "financial paper of record," it also "in some respects behaves like an arm of government, an extension of the Securities and Exchange Commission" (xii). [Puffery, no analysis of WSJ as reflection of elite power.]

3666. Schillinger, Elisabeth, and Joel Jenswold. "Three Olympiads: A Comparison of Pravda and the Washington Post." JQ 64.4 (Winter 1987) 826-833.
The Post was more nationalistic and partisan than Pravda, which emphasized "universal ideals."

3667. "Search Warrants and the Effects of the Stanford Daily Decision." House Committee on Government Operations. Washington, DC: US GPO, Aug. 21, 1978.
Criticizes the ruling as a threat to a free press and recommends restraints on search warrants.

3668. "Seattle Times Muzzles Latin America Expert." Extra! 2.1 (July-Aug. 1988) 13.
The Times has barred its Latin American expert from working on his specialty possibly because of right-wing opposition to his views.

3669. "'Self-Dealing,' 'Double-Dealing.'" PoV 1.21 (May 6-11, 1969) n.p. [By Roldo Bartimole].
"The mass media play a large role not only in covering up the real activities" of Cleveland business foundations "but in helping push their programs, often for selfish reasons."

3670. Semmel, Andrew. "Foreign News in Four U.S. Elite Dailies: Some Comparisons." JQ 53.4 (1976) 732-36.
The NYT, MH, CT, and LAT "inequitably" apportion foreign news by focusing upon "a very small number of elite countries which are the major political and economic powers."

3671. Shahin, Jim. "Austin Redux: The Kathleen Sullivan Mystery." CJR 27.2 (July-Aug. 1988) 14-16.
Austin American-Statesman reporter Sullivan was fired after she insisted on writing stories about safety hazards in hi-tech industries.

3672. Sheridan, Terry. "Letters & Another Point of View (Or Is It?)" PoV 3.19 (Apr. 5-12, 1971) 1-2.
While Cleveland and the US fester with significant problems, the Cleveland Plain Dealer published a series on how a handful of black servicemen were a threat to the harmony of Okinawa.

3673. Sigal, Leon. Reporters and Officials: The Organization and Politics of Newsmaking. Lexington, MA: Heath, 1973. 221.

PRINT MEDIA

Studies why and how officials make use of the press, through studies of newspeople and officials, the political science literature of specific examples, and the newsrooms of the NYT and WP. News is produced out of conventions, institutions, hierarchies, interaction of bureaucracies, organizational politics, economic imperatives (particularly pressure from advertisers), and ideology. This process legitimates the procedures and authenticates the news.

3674. Simurda, Stephen. "Can the Stripped-Down Monitor Stay Afloat?" CJR 27.6 (Mar.-Apr. 1989) 42-45.
Because of continued deficits, a move to end the CSM resulted in drastic cuts in its newsgathering staff and the length of the newspaper.

3675. Solomon, Norman. "U.S. Media Does An Ugly Job on Iran." Guard 40.41 (July 20, 1988) 11.
"News coverage of the Iranian airliner shootdown" reveals the "chilling unity between U.S. mass media and the state."

3676. Stone, I.F. "The Need for a Double Jeopardy Clause in Loyalty Proceedings." IFSW 2.41 (Nov. 15, 1954) 4.
The NYHT editorialized in favor of national security over constitutionality.

3677. "Systematic Torture in El Salvador." SLJR 16.102 (May 1988) 13.
Torture is systematic in the Mariona men's prison, but major US media have disregarded it (NYT, WP, BG, LAT, and wire services), according to Project Censored, except for the SFE's two articles.

3678. Tate, Cassandra. "Gannett in Salem: Protecting the Franchise." CJR 20.2 (July-Aug. 1981) 51-56.
On Gannett's effort to kill a competing newspaper.

3679. Tate, Cassandra. "Letter from 'The Atomic Capital of the Nation.'" CJR 21.1 (May-June 1982) 31-35.
Richland, Washington's newspaper boosts its nuclear power company.

3680. Tharp, Marty. "Sour Notes from a House Organ." UM 1.8 (Apr. 1971) 8-9.
An editor of the National Catholic Register was fired for criticizing the newspaper's turn to "ultra-conservative" under its new owner, the Twin Circle, another Catholic newspaper.

3681. "Timber! Did Industry Cut Down a Crusading Reporter? The War Over the Woods." CJR 28.5 (Jan.-Feb. 1990) 11-12.
Complaints from industry officials about Richard Manning's reporting on the environment caused the Missoulian to reassign him to another beat.

3682. Trice, Robert. "The American Elite Press and the Arab-

Israeli Conflict." The Middle East Journal 33.4 (Summer 1979) 304-26.
Although there has been more criticism of Israel than other researchers had found, editorial positions in eleven elite newspapers over the 1966-74 period revealed overwhelming anti-Arab and anti-Palestinian opinion. All 11 papers were found to be moderate to strong supporters of US policy.

3683. Underwood, Doug. "The Boeing Story and the Hometown Press: When it Comes to Covering the Neighborhood Giant, Seattle's Dailies Keep Dropping the Ball." CJR 27.4 (Nov.-Dec. 1988) 50-56.
Seattle's newspapers are pro-Boeing and upbeat about the company's serious problems. The nation deserves a "more aggressive business press."

3684. Veblen, Eric. The "Manchester Union Leader" in New Hampshire Elections. Hanover, NH: UP of New England, 1975. 205.
Examines the influence of William Loeb's newspaper on election campaigns and outcomes. Loeb was a militant anticommunist who perceived a dangerous communist conspiracy both from abroad and domestically, supporting Senator Joseph McCarthy and opposing Senator McGovern as "a tool of the conspiracy."

3685. Virgets, Ronnie. "How I Wrote Myself Out of a Job." Extra! 2.1 (July-Aug. 1988) 16.
The author was fired by the New Orleans Times-Picayune for writing a report "on the foibles and excesses of the national press" at the Democratic Convention at Atlanta, because the editor had planned a media party at the Republican convention in New Orleans similar to the kind Virgets ridiculed.

3686. Warsh, David. "The Stars & Stripes Flap." ChJR 2.10 (Oct. 1969) 3-4.
Army censorship of the Pacific Stars & Stripes.

3687. Weinberg, Steve. "The Mob, the CIA, and the S&L Scandal: Does Pete Brewton's Story Check Out?' CJR (Nov.-Dec. 1990) 28-36.
Takes seriously the Houston Post's reporting of CIA involvement in S&L failures and criticizes the nation's media for not following up the investigation.

3688. Weiss, Philip. "Invasion of the Gannettoids." NR (Feb. 2, 1987) 18-22.
The "Gannett formula" satisfies corporate profit but does not produce a good newspaper.

3689. Weiss, Philip. "Muzzled in Minneapolis." CJR 23.1 (1984) 10, 12.
A critical sports columnist was censored.

3690. Weiss, Philip. "Rolling Back the Radicals in Iowa City." CJR 25.3 (1986) 39-41.

PRINT MEDIA

The right-wing campus newspaper at the U of Iowa, the Campus Review, attacks the Soviet Union, evolution, lesbians, humanists, feminism, the ACLU, and everything "left."

3691. Welch, Susan. "Vietnam: How the Press Went Along." Na 213.11 (Oct. 11, 1971) 327-330.
Examines four newspapers--NYT, WP, CT, and SFC--to show how the press helped the Truman and Eisenhower administrations establish the rhetoric and policy of good versus evil regarding Indochina.

3692. Wendt, Lloyd. The Wall Street Journal. The Story of Dow Jones & the Nation's Business Newspaper. Chicago: Rand McNally, 1982. 448.
A company history commissioned by Dow Jones to commemorate its 100th anniversary.

3693. Whitcover, Jules. "Two Weeks That Shook the Press." CJR 10.3 (1971) 7-15.
On newspaper struggles to publish the Pentagon Papers.

3694. Whitman, David. The Press and the Neutron Bomb. Cambridge, MA: Kennedy School of Government, Harvard U, 1983. 170.
Plans by the Carter administration to build the neutron bomb were disclosed by Walter Pincus on the front page of the WP, which inspired protests in the US and throughout Europe. The CIA then began a covert program to sell the bomb to the European press.

3695. "The Word from Olympus." UM 1.8 (Apr. 1971) 3.
The Denver Post strongly supports the 1976 Winter Olympics and suppresses the objections expressed by environmentalists.

3696. Young, Virginia. "Smaller Jeff City Press Corps Adequate on Spot News, Poor on Investigations." SLJR 16.106 (May 1988) 8-9.
The decline in number of full-time reporters (drastic reduction in UPI staff, death of the St. Louis Globe-Democrat) has caused a decline in "quality and diversity of news coverage."

II. D. 3. c. NEWSPAPERS: **THE NEW YORK TIMES** (3697-3817)

3697. Abraham, Nabeel. "Iraqi and Other Aggressions." LOOT 1.9 (Sept. 1990) 5-6.
"International crises invariably bring out the servile nature of the U.S. establishment press." Compares NYT on Iraq's invasion of Kuwait and Israel's invasion of Lebanon.

3698. Abraham, Nabeel. "The Times Frames a Massacre." LOOT 1.8 (Aug. 1990) 5-6.
Except for one article, the NYT (and most newspapers) treated the murder of seven Palestinian workers by a lone Israeli as the work of a deranged person seeking revenge unrelated to

the "atmosphere or racism and fascism" in Israel.

3699. Alcalay, Glenn. "Purging Politics from the Fiji Coup." Extra! 1.2 (July 1987) 3.
On the inadequate and biased coverage of the military coup in Fiji by the NYT.

3700. Arnoni, M.S. "The News That's Not Fit to Print in The New York Times." MO 6.8 (Aug. 1964) 20-21.
Despite a press release to the AP, UPI, and the NYT about an exclusive article by President Ho Chi Minh of North Vietnam in the magazine The Minority of One, none of them published one word about Ho's statements.

3701. Aslam, Abid. "Election Violence in Nicaragua." LOOT 1.2 (Feb. 1990) 6-7.
The NYT reported Sandinista mobs provoked fighting and killed one person during the elections of Dec. 1989, but UN, OAS, and other observers deny the report.

3702. Barranco, Deborah A., and Leonard Shyles. "Arab vs. Israeli News Coverage in the New York Times, 1976 and 1984." JQ 65.1 (Spring 1988) 178-181.
"Israel receives substantially more coverage than its Arab neighbors."

3703. Bowles, William. "It's a Proxy World: Reporting the War in Angola." Extra! 2.3 (Nov.-Dec. 1988) 6.
"A deep-rooted cold war bias has skewed US media coverage of the war in Angola and, more recently, the Southern Africa peace talks."

3704. Braley, Russ. Bad News: The Foreign Policy of the "New York Times." Chicago: Regnery, 1984. 678.
The newspaper has given its readers a false view of the world. [Braley expresses a Sovietphobic point of view].

3705. Brammer, Gale. "Editorial Attitude of the New York Times Toward Labor." MJR 4 (1961) 32.
Summary of student's research. Fifty-two editorials from 1929 to 1959 show the NYT editorials more noncommittal than critical or favorable.

3706. Charles, Jeff, et al. "The New York Times Coverage of Equatorial and Lower Africa." JoC 29.2 (1979) 148-155.
Analysis of the NYT index shows that coverage is limited to a few African nations, trade being a good predictor for media attention. Though not covered in the news generally, violence will most likely make the front page.

3707. Chomsky, Noam. "Letter from Lexington." LOOT 1.5 (May 1990) 9-10.
Analyzes the propaganda techniques of an article on Israel in the NYT.

PRINT MEDIA

3708. Chomsky, Noam. "Letter From Lexington." LOOT 1.8 (Aug. 1990) 7-9.
On the ambiguous and hypocritical stance of the NYT toward terrorism.

3709. Cirino, Robert. "Auto Safety: A Deadly, Crippling, Disfiguring Silence." Don't Blame the People. New York: Vintage, 1971. 14-20.
The auto industry influenced the media to suppress safety problems. The NYT is studied for illustration.

3710. Cockburn, Alexander. "The Cat's Meo." Corruptions of Empire. London: Verso, 1987. 231.
NYT gave easy treatment to General Vang Pao, formerly of the Royal Laotian Army, now a Montanan rancher, by omitting his former operation of a heroin factory and theft of his soldiers' pay.

3711. Cockburn, Alexander. "The Discourse of Fascism." Na 247.17 (Dec. 5, 1988) 591.
Press "willful or reflexive ignorance and racism in its coverage of Israel and the Palestinians" is illustrated by the writings of Thomas Friedman, until recently NYT's correspondent in Israel.

3712. Cockburn, Alexander. "Dropping the Big One." Na 251.7 (Sept. 10, 1990) 226-27.
The biased difference between reporting Israel's nuclear arsenal and Saddam Hussein's potential single bomb.

3713. Cockburn, Alexander. "Hello History, Get Me Rewrite: The Ongoing Case of Grenada." ITT 13.7 (Dec. 21, 1988-Jan. 10, 1989) 17.
The NYT's reporter Joseph Treaster continues to represent the disaster to Grenada as a godsend.

3714. Cockburn, Alexander. "A Million Here, A Million There." Na 248.9 (Mar. 6, 1989) 294-5.
The NYT reported on page one "Major Soviet Paper Says 20 Million Died As Victims of Stalin." The truth is somewhere between hundreds of thousands to several million.

3715. Cockburn, Alexander. Nahhalin: From March 1954 to April 1989." ITT 13.24 (May 10-16, 1989) 17.
Compares the NYT's distorted reporting of an Israeli attack on a Palestinian village with its coverage of a similar raid thirty-five years ago.

3716. Cockburn, Alexander. "The Poisoned Well." Na 247.3 (July 30-Aug. 6, 1988) 83.
NYT reporter James LeMoyne's crowd estimate of a May Day march in San Salvador (one-sixth of wire services' estimate) left an inaccurate impression of dwindling support for the F.M.L.N. guerrillas.

3717. Cockburn, Alexander. "The Tricoteuse of Counter-revolution." Corruptions of Empire. London: Verso, 1987. 474-77.
The NYT's Shirley Christian exemplifies the "rightward swerve of mainstream journalism."

3718. Cockburn, Alexander, and Richard McKerrow. "The New York Times Sets the Table and Serves the Appetizers." ITT 14.14 (Feb. 21-27, 1990) 12.
"The Times coverage [of the Nicaraguan elections] has been heavily weighted toward Chamorro and UNO."

3719. "The Company They Keep." CJR 19.6 (Mar.-Apr. 1981) 22.
The Washington press corps' intimacy with their sources prevents independent investigative and critical reporting, as illustrated by the NYT's Richard Burt.

3720. Denison, Dave. "Reporter Non Grata." TO 76 (Oct. 26, 1984) 18-19.
Interview of Raymond Bonner, NYT correspondent who was recalled from Central America and reassigned to domestic affairs after complaints by the White House about his reporting.

3721. Diamond, Sara, and Richard Hatch. "Moonshine." LOOT 1.7 (July 1990) 11.
The NYT policy of selling space on the Op-Ed page to Rev. Sun Myung Moon's International Security Council, "a think tank of Moon-linked militarists," without adequate identification should be stopped.

3722. El Zein, Hassan M. "The New York Times's Coverage of Africa: A Descriptive Analysis of the Period 1976-1985." Ohio U, 1986. 129. DAI 47 (1987) 2349-A.
Out of a total of 51 nations only 25 got coverage and five of these dominated. On page one crisis and negative news predominated.

3723. Engler, Robert. "From Heads to TOES: A Tale of Two Summits." LOOT 1.9 (Sept. 1990) 9-10.
To provide another perspective to the Economic Summit of the Group of Seven (major powers) in Houston, The Other Economic Summit was organized to focus on conditions of the 85 percent of the world's people not represented by the industrial leaders. Coverage of this counter-summit was virtually nonexistent in the mass media.

3724. Ensign, Tod. "Flacking for Dow." LOOT 1.6 (June 1990) 8-9.
On the NYT's coverage of Agent Orange that supports Dow Chemical and the other manufacturers.

3725. Eshghi, Fleurin. "The New York Times's Image of Iran in Crisis: A Content Analysis." Columbia U Teachers College, 1983. 163. DAI 44.5 (Nov. 1983) 1232-A.
Not inspected.

PRINT MEDIA   515

3726. Evenson, Debra. "Fossil Cold Warriors: The Times on
       Cuba." LOOT 1.2 (Feb. 1990) 16.
   More examples of NYT "distortions and errors." "Cuban
politics are as complex and as dynamic today as ever. The
Times ignores this reality; it opts instead for the famil-
iarity of invalid Cold War schematics."

3727. Evenson, Debra. "The Times's Relentless Assaults on
       Cuba." LOOT 1.5 (May 1990) 11.
   On the unbalanced handling of 2 events prejudicial to Cuba.

3728. "Ex-General Reports Victory that Never Was." Extra!
       1.3 (Aug.-Sept. 1987) 16.
   A false pro-contra story in the NYT was written by Bernard
Trinor, NYT's military correspondent and former Marine Corps
general.

3729. Fisk, Mark, and Jonathan Scott. "The Times on People's
       Park." LOOT 1.9 (Sept. 1990) 3-4.
   On NYT misrepresentation of the People's Park on the
Michigan State University campus.

3730. Flanders, Laura. "Anti-Gay Violence: Off the New York
       Times' Agenda." Extra! 3.6 (July-Aug. 1990) 14.
   The NYT "no longer prints the word gay only in quotation
marks, but it still has a long way to go to represent gay and
lesbian reality."

3731. Francis, Carolyn. "The Year of Dangerous Reporting:
       Indonesia Bloodbath, New York Times Whitewash."
       Extra! 3.6 (July-Aug. 1990) 16.
   NYT's refusal to report a news study of US complicity in
"one of the most horrifying stories of the Cold War"--the
massacre by the Indonesian military of possibly a half million
communists.

3732. Gemma, Gavrielle. "Greyhound and the Media." LOOT 1.4
       (Apr. 1990) 7.
   In reference to the 1990 Greyhound Lines strike, "the role
of the media has become clear to every Greyhound worker: to
turn the public against the union in support of the company's
positions." The NYT "has been the real media culprit."

3733. George, Alexander. "On the Desert and Democracy."
       LOOT 1.10 (Oct. 1990) 3-4.
   NYT and media coverage of the Iraqi invasion of Kuwait
mirrors "the contempt many of our political leaders have for
democratic ideals" (the secret week-end decision by Bush and a
handful of advisors to commit the largest force since Vietnam,
which the media accepted).

3734. Geyer, Alan. "The NCC Takes Another Beating." C&C 44
       (Oct. 1, 1984) 349-52.
   Complains about the coverage of efforts by US churches to
find a meeting ground with Soviet Christians, a coverage by

gross caricature and misrepresentation, particularly in the NYT.

3735. Gitlin, Todd. The Whole World Is Watching: Mass Media in the Making & Unmaking of the New Left. Berkeley: U of California P, 1980. 327.
The antiwar movement, writing outside NYT's ideological and news production frames, put together an accurate picture of the US hegemonic process, "amassing a strong case that American policy was systematically neocolonial, racist, and criminally targeted on the civilian population; but the Times did not cover these revelations and analyses at the time" nor retroactively.

3736. Goldin, Marion. "Father Times: Who's on the Op-Ed Page?" MJ 15.1 (Jan. 1990) 51.
The NYT is "a bastion of male chauvinism."

3737. Goodwin, David. "Was There a Ghastly Ending to Allies' So-Called Good War?" ITT 14.17 (Mar. 21-27, 1990) 18-19.
A review of Other Losses: An Investigation into the Mass Deaths of German Prisoners at the Hands of the French and Americans After World War II by James Bacque. These deaths were not reported by the press, which supported the government's secrecy, a process "perpetuated by historians who sanitize" US history.

3738. Goulden, Joseph C. Fit to Print: A.M. Rosenthal and His Times. New York: Carol, 1988. 504.
A negative picture of the NYT's editor.

3739. Griffin-Nolan, Ed. "From Strongman to Santa Claus: The Selling of General Pinochet." Extra! 2.3 (Nov.-Dec. 1988) 4-5.
NYT misrepresentations of Chilean politics.

3740. Grossman, Karl. "New York Times' Nuclear Obsession: The Shoreham Debacle." Extra! 2.6 (May-June 1989) 10-11.
Despite Shoreham nuclear plant's sad history of defects and mushrooming costs, the nation's "paper of record" has consistently presented the project and nuclear power in general in a positive light and has censored the work of its reporters.

3741. Gunn, Herb. "Contra Blast Kills Thirty-Two, Kinzered by the Press." Voice 7.5 (1986) 2.
Media buried or distorted the contra murders of thirty-two Nicaraguan civilians.

3742. Gusamão, Ivna, and Alan Benjamin. "The New York Times' Coverage of El Salvador." New York: El Salvador Information Office, 1981.
NYT a foreign policy arm of the government in its coverage of El Salvador.

PRINT MEDIA

3743. Henwood, Doug. "Third World Debt and the Mexico 'Breakthrough.'" Extra! 1.6 (Jan.-Feb. 1988) 6-7.
The NYT does not ask "sharp questions" about "debt crisis, massive inequalities, and the huge US trade deficit."

3744. Herman, Edward. "Disinformation as News Fit to Print." CAIB 31 (Winter 1989) 65-69.
Tells how NYT reporter James Lemoyne served as a conduit of US government disinformation by serving up as truth a confession obtained under torture.

3745. Herman, Edward. "Explaining Regulatory Failure." LOOT 1.9 (Sept. 1990) 15.
Despite the S&L debacle, the mass media cannot acknowledge the class and corporate interest in the Reagan administration's attack on regulation.

3746. Herman, Edward. "Gruson on Guatemala: An Update." LOOT 1.8 (Aug. 1990) 15-16.
Analyzes NYT's Lindsey Gruson's biased reporting of Guatemala.

3747. Herman, Edward. "Hiding South Africa's Role in Mozambique." LOOT 1.5 (May 1990) 7.
Condemns the South African "terrorist state" and the NYT's support of lenient US policy.

3748. Herman, Edward. "How Paul Lewis Covers UNESCO." LOOT 1.6 (June 1990) 17.
Lewis's twenty-two articles in the NYT about UNESCO are biased against the organization. "Lewis's close adherence to the U.S. government's premises and frames of reference has never faltered."

3749. Herman, Edward. "Keeping Propaganda Themes Alive: The Bulgarian Connection." LOOT 1.7 (July 1990) 10-11.
More illustration of NYT and US media Sovietphobia, which requires "neither credibility nor a news peg."

3750. Herman, Edward. "Labor Abuses in El Salvador and Nicaragua: A Study of New York Times Coverage." Extra! 2.7/8 (Summer 1989) 24-26.
NYT has made much of Sandinista suppression of strikes and demonstrations while minimizing the murderous acts of the contras and Salvadoran death squads.

3751. Herman, Edward. "Lemoynespeak." Z 1.5 (May 1988) 39-40.
The NYT's "bias is so massive and systematic that the paper is properly viewed as an organ of state propaganda." Focuses on the "preestablished framework" of propaganda and doublespeak used by reporter James LeMoyne.

3752. Herman, Edward. "Lindsey Gruson on Guatemala: In the Great Tradition." LOOT 1.3 (Mar. 1990) 12-14.

NYT reporter Lindsey Gruson writes about Guatemala within the paper's biased attitude toward that country, which fits official US policies.

3753. Herman, Edward. "The New York Times on the 1984 Salvadoran and Nicaraguan Elections." CAIB 21 (Spring 1984) 7-13.
The NYT and the mass media in general "follow a patriotic agenda."

3754. Herman, Edward. "The New York Times on the South African Election of September 6, 1989." LOOT 1.2 (Feb. 1990) 17-19.
NYT handling of the pre-election protests by blacks in 1989 is more evidence of the uncritical treatment of the South African apartheid government.

3755. Herman, Edward. "Playing to the Home Audience: Media Myths Uphold U.S.-Sponsored Demonstration Elections." NicP No. 18 (Winter-Spring 1990) 17-20.
"In their approach to foreign elections, the U.S. establishment and mainstream media also operate out of a structure of myths."

3756. Herman, Edward. "The Times on the Nicaraguan Election." LOOT 1.4 (Apr. 1990) 10-11.
The NYT "used an agenda and selected information in perfect accord with the Reagan administration's effort to delegitimize the Nicaraguan government."

3757. Hester, Hugh. "Does God Preside Over the U.S. Cabinet?" MO 7.7 (July 1965) 11-12.
In a column in the NYT James Reston presented the US as "God's Plenipotentiary" on earth. To the contrary, US foreign policies consistently reflect US self-interests.

3758. Hinchberger, Bill. "Expects More Pressure on Sandinistas." SLJR 11 (Feb. 1985) 21.
An interview of former NYT correspondent Ray Bonner, who was recalled from El Salvador because of criticism of his reporting from US Embassy and military officials there.

3759. Howell, Sharon. Reflections of Ourselves: The Mass Media and the Women's Movement, 1963 to the Present. New York: Peter Lang, 1990. 194.
"The purpose of this study is to trace the evolution of the female identity through an analysis of the dominant metaphors emerging in the course of the contemporary women's movement" (15): woman as nigger, object, persona, and victim. The NYT serves as focus for media analysis.

3760. Hunter, Jane. "Covering Africa." LOOT 1.5 (May 1990) 8.
Accuses the NYT of racist reporting of Africa.

3761. Hunter, Jane. "Ignoring Zaire." LOOT 1.8 (Aug. 1990) 9-10.
On Zaire the NYT and "the Bush administration have been right in step with each other."

3762. Karman, Peter. "Paper of Record, Paper of Recipes." ITT 13.22 (Apr. 26-May 2, 1989) 18.
Rev. of Goulden's book on A. M. Rosenthal and the NYT.

3763. Kennedy, Daniel D. "The Bay of Pigs and the New York Times: Another View of What Happened." JQ 63.3 (Autumn 1986) 524-29.
Contrary to popular belief, the NYT did not suppress news of the Bay of Pigs invasion, but provided all the reliable information available to the newspaper at the time.

3764. Kirby, Laurie. "Non-Truth at the New York Times." CS 7 (June-Aug. 1983) 30-32.
Distortion of NYT coverage of a symposium resembles those of Ronald Reagan and advertising.

3765. Koschwitz, Hansjürgen. "The Case 'New York Times.' The Pros and Cons of Freedom of the Press." Gaz 18 (1972) 235-244.
The disclosures of the Pentagon papers "acquired fundamental importance" because they raised basic issues of the relation between government, the public, and the press.

3766. Kriesberg, Martin. "Soviet News in the New York Times." POQ 10 (1946) 540-64.
NYT hostile to SU during early Soviet years, more objective later, relapsing after end of WW II.

3767. Kupferberg, Seth. "Loyalty Test at The New York Times?" CJR 22.2 (1983) 41-44.
The NYT is trying to prevent one of its reporters from having a book published elaborating on some articles he originally wrote from the Times.

3768. Leggett, John, et al. Allende, His Exit & Our "Times." New Brunswick, NJ: New Brunswick Cooperative, 1978. 79.
Exposes NYT's counterrevolutionary ideology, preferring fascist over left-wing governments, as in the case of Chile under Allende.

3769. Lindorff, Dave. "East Germany Report: It's Who You Know." LOOT 1.7 (July 1990) 6-7.
The NYT has reported economic conditions in Eastern Germany inadequately.

3770. Loory, Stuart. "Stalin's Apologist." CJR 29.2 (July-Aug. 1990) 52-4.
Review of Stalin's Apologist: "The New York Times"'s Man in Moscow, by S.J. Taylor. "The problem that Taylor personalizes

in her book is really institutional and therefore much more serious"--mass media support of the establishment.

3771. Lyford, Joseph. "The 'Times' and Latin America." Columbia, MO: School of Journalism, U of Missouri, Freedom of Information Center Publication No. 93, 1963. 1-6.
The NYT's coverage during Feb. 1962 was "geographically very uneven and restricted in subject matter," yet "it has done a far better job than any other American newspaper: and this is the most ominous fact of all."

3772. Marks, John D. "The Story that Never Was?" MORE 4.6 (June 1974) 20-22.
On NYT suppression of exposé of planned US/S. Vietnam invasion of Cambodia.

3773. Mathurin, Victor. "A Content Analysis of Vietnam War News in The Times of London, Using The New York Times Content as a Basis for Comparison." MA Thesis, American U, 1967. 63. MA 5 (1967) 12.
The Times gave a generally negative view of the US; the NYT showed the US militarily and morally superior.

3774. Matthews, Herbert L. A World in Revolution: A Newspaperman's Memoir. New York: Scribner's, 1971. 462.
Because of its Sovietphobia and Castrophobia, the NYT has not reported Cuba fairly.

3775. McGuire, Colleen. "New York Times Disguises Palestinian Success as Setback." Extra! 2.2 (Sept.-Oct. 1988) 13.
The NYT's coverage of Jordan's King Hussein turning Palestinian matters over to the PLO contrasted sharply with the international press.

3776. "Mental War Targets." MO 9.1 (Jan. 1967) 4-5.
Harrison Salisbury's revelations of bombings of Hanoi civilians for the NYT were already known and available, but because the truths came from people labeled "subversive" they were not reported or they were attacked, and the NYT has been guilty of the practice.

3777. Mintz, Morton. "Holy Moses." NmR 31.2 & 3 (Summer-Autumn 1977) 13-22.
For decades Robert Moses wielded "truly fantastic power" in NYC, and his policies contributed to the deterioration of that city and many others. Because the press was idolatrous of Moses, they failed to tell the public "what it needed to know in the longer run."

3778. Mintz, Penny. "Miscovering the Environment." LOOT 1.6 (June 1990) 12.
The "earth's ailments carry little weight" at the NYT.

3779. "Mock Newspapers Expose U.S. War in El Salvador."

PRINT MEDIA   521

Alert! 7.1 (Feb. 1989) 10.
A "People's Edition" of the NYT publicizes "some of the news
the Times does not see fit to print."

3780. Moghadam, Val. "Limited Sources in the Afghan
       Conflict." LOOT 1.10 (Oct. 1990) 4-5.
   "Over the years, what Americans have learned of the Afghan
conflict has come from unbalanced reportage, the Mujahideen
viewpoint, and the perspectives of the U.S. administration."

3781. Morris, Roger. "A Bullish Pulpit: The NYT's Business
       Desk." CJR 20.1 (May-June 1981) 31-37.
   On the biased and scanty coverage of financial news.

3782. Mumble, Dennis. "The Times Miscovers the ANC." LOOT
       1.5 (May 1990) 4-5.
   The NYT still covers South Africa through the prism of
apartheid's view."

3783. Mysak, Joseph. "Air Attack." MORE 7.1 (Jan. 1977) 7.
   Describes McDonnell Douglas' attempt to intimidate a
reporter and the NYT by a libel suit.

3784. Nader, Ralph, and Steven Gold. "Unfit to Print?" CJR
       27.3 (Sept.-Oct. 1988) 56-7.
   NYT bias in favor of the US-supported government of
Indonesia in its repression of East Timor is illustrated by
its selection of letters-to-the-editor.

3785. Naureckas, Jim. "No Hope for the Homeless at The New
       York Times." Extra! 3.3 (Mar.-Apr. 1990) 16.
   The NYT tends to portray the homeless as "victimizers
deserving contempt."

3786. "The New York Times and the Nazis Among Us." Extra!
       2.1 (July-Aug. 1988) 14.
   The NYT review of Christopher Simpson's Blowback: America's
Recruitment of Nazis and Its Effects on the Cold War was "a
subtle apology for the Nazi recruitment effort." The reviewer
was possibly biased through his father who participated in the
CIA/Nazi spy operation.

3787. "New York Times Covers And Aids 1953 CIA Coup In Iran."
       CS 4.4 (Sept.-Oct. 1980) 1-6.
   It was through NYT correspondent Kennett Love and AP correspondent Dan Schwind that "the American people were kept in the
dark about a CIA operation."

3788. "The New York Times Recants." Extra! 2.2 (Sept.-Oct.
       1988) 2.
   The NYT exhibits "a deep-rooted bias" regarding El Salvador
"that reflects US government priorities rather than objective
reporting."

3789. "'No Quick Fix': An Annotated Editorial." Deadline 1.5

(1986) 12-13.
Takes apart a NYT editorial about the Reykjavik summit, with annotations by Kosta Tsipis that explain just how foolish the Times' assertions are.

3790. Norton, Chris. "US Media Promote Salvadoran Army Disinformation." Extra! 2.1 (July-Aug. 1988) 1, 12.
A NYT story on guerrilla violence by James LeMoyne "never happened." "The daily barrage of army and government disinformation has become a key component of the 8-year civil war in El Salvador."

3791. Perrucci, Robert, and Brenda Gunneman. "The New York Times Is Framing the Homeless." ITT 13.3 (Nov. 16-22, 1988) 12-13, 22.
Times readers learned little about the "systemic conditions that create and sustain homelessness," such as "the investment decisions of real estate developers working hand-in-hand with elected officials" to destroy "affordable housing."

3792. Pollock, John Crothers, and Christopher L. Buidette. "Mass Media, Crisis, and Political Change: A Cross-National Approach." CY 4 (1980) 309-324.
Compares the New York Times and Times of London's coverage of crises in Brazil, Chile, and South Africa, concluding that the "prior socialization" of a journalist is a more significant factor in determining the slant of news than whether or not the reporter's nation has a "distinct economic stake" in the crisis at hand.

3793. Ray, Ellen. "If They Win, It's Not Free." LOOT 1.7 (July 1990) 20.
The NYT "coverage of the June elections in Bulgaria went from optimism for an anticommunist victory to sour grapes."

3794. Ray, Ellen, and William Schaap. "Damage Control At the Times." LOOT 1.8 (Aug. 1990) 13-14.
NYT helps expunge the record of CIA criminal involvement in the massacre of communists in Indonesia.

3795. Rice, Michael, and James Cooney. Reporting U.S.-European Relations: Four Nations, Four Newspapers. New York: Pergamon, 1982. 120.
The NYT reports European news either as "a reflection" of US interests or the personal interest of some editor in NYC.

3796. Ross, Bonnie. "Interpretations of the Black Civil Rights Movement in the Black and White Press." U of California, Irvine, 1985. 203. DAI 46 (1986) 2848-A.
NYT under coverage and narrow framing of the movement differed greatly from the reality presented by the Chicago Defender and New York Amsterdam News.

3797. Saalfield, Catherine. "Close to Her Heart." LOOT 1.5 (May 1990) 17-18.

PRINT MEDIA

The heterosexist NYT misrepresents the sexual preference of victims of violent crimes.

3798. Salisbury, Harrison. *A Time of Change: A Reporter's Tale of Our Time*. New York: Harper, 1988. 353.
A collection of the author's recollections of the US from the mid-fifties to the 1970s, when he was a reporter for the NYT. The picture he gives is of the freedom of a reporter to discover and tell the truth and of big powers that would conceal or distort the truth.

3799. Salisbury, Harrison. *Without Fear or Favor: "The New York Times" and Its Times*. New York: Times, 1980. 652.
Mainly congratulatory but includes examples of NYT support of power, especially the CIA, and its share in the "system of hypocrisy."

3800. Scott, Jonathan, and Rashid Taher. "Double Standards." LOOT 1.8 (Aug. 1990) 6-7.
NYT's bias against the PLO and in support of Israel is revealed by comparing its coverage of the Palestinian raid of May 30, 1990, with its reporting on Israel's October 1985 bombing of PLO headquarters in Tunis.

3801. Seldes, George. *Freedom of the Press*. Garden City, NY: Garden City, 1937. 380.
A wide-ranging critique of the business-media complex: the NYT friend of established power and profit (214), enemy of labor (181-190), lying about the SU (174-181), advertiser corruption of news (Ch. 2), etc.

3802. Shoar-Ghaffari, Pirouz. "Iran in the *New York Times* and in the *Times*, 1968-78: A Comparative Study of the Relations of Press and National Interest." Syracuse U, 1985. 181. DAI 46 (1986) 2477-A.
Both newspapers stressed issues related to national interests, and both "relied heavily on official sources." But after the oil crisis of 1973-74 the NYT opposed official US policy toward Iran.

3803. "Shutting Up Schanberg." CJR 24.4 (1985) 24.
Sidney Schanberg's censorship by the NYT places him among a long list of censored journalists.

3804. Sklar, Holly. "*Times* Strikes Again." LOOT 1.8 (Aug. 1990) 11.
On the biased anti-Sandinista reporting by the NYT of a Sandinista-led strike.

3805. Small, Melvin. "The *New York Times* and *Toronto Globe and Mail* View Anti-Vietnam War Demonstrations, 1965-1969." P&C 14.3 (July 1989) 324-49.
The two newspapers reported US antiwar demonstrations similarly.

3806. Stockwood, Kristina. "Colombian History Rewritten." LOOT 1.3 (Mar. 1990) 9.
NYT reporting of leftwing guerrillas follows official Washington doctrines.

3807. "The Tricoteuse of Counterrevolution." Na 245.2 (1987) 44-45.
"All in all, in her stints at The Miami Herald and The New York Times, [Shirley] Christian has proved herself to be as rapturous an apologist for Latin American fascism as you will find writing in a major U.S. newspaper."

3808. "Trouble at the Times." Prog 49.11 (1985) 15.
NYT expresses a conservative ideology.

3809. Trumpbour, Jack. "Voices of Responsibility or Generation of Swine?" Z 1.10 (Oct. 1988) 26-30.
The NYT is afflicted by "Corruptions of Empire"--e.g., its approval of the illegal invasion of Grenada and Richard Thornburgh's replacement of Ed Meese as Attorney General. Legitimacy is reaffirmed by claiming "the system worked."

3810. "Vietnam and the Integrity of the N. Y. Times." MO 5.9 (Sept. 1963) 9.
The NYT attacked a letter it published from Bertrand Russell for lacking substantiating evidence for his allegations of US war crimes in Vietnam, when it had deleted the evidence from his letter.

3811. Wakin, Eric. "Dressing Down Ralph Lauren and the Times." LOOT 1.5 (May 1990) 6.
A NYT Arts article on Lauren's new "safari collection" and ad campaign serves "to apologize for racism and colonialism."

3812. Wallis, Victor. "East European and Global Realities." LOOT 1.7 (July 1990) 3-4.
The NYT pays constant attention to the collapse of communism in eastern Europe, but little attention to the breakdown of capitalism in other parts of the world.

3813. Webster, Katharine. "Deception in Guatemala: How the U.S. Media Bought a Cover-Up." Prog 54.2 (Feb. 1990) 26-28, 30, 32.
About the massacre at El Aguacate.

3814. Wolfe, Alan. "Defense Crisis at 'The Times.'" Na 231.16 (1980) 503-06.
A NYT series on the military was "filled with Pentagon propaganda."

3815. Womack, John, Larry Rohter, and Alan Riding. "Mexico: An Exchange." NACLA 22.6 (Mar. 1989) 8-10.
Womack, a historian of Mexico, calls the NYT's coverage of Mexico "no more than a tourist guide." Rohter and Riding reply.

PRINT MEDIA

3816. Worthy, William. "Murder Will Out." LOOT 1.8 (Aug. 1990) 12-13.
NYT perpetuates lies about the massacre of communists in Indonesia.

3817. Yang, Kisuk. "News Through a Distorting Prism: New York Times Coverage of UNESCO, 1970-1985." U of Texas, Austin, 1986. 291. DAI 47 (1987) 3604-A.
Times coverage of Unesco's alleged support of press curbs has been "narrow," "distorted," "intemperate and inflammatory," and it "relied too excessively and uncritically" upon official news sources.

II. D. 4. PRINT MEDIA: MAGAZINES (3818-3946)

II. D. 4. a. MAGAZINES: GENERAL (3818-3847)

3818. Canan, Craig. Progressive Periodicals Directory. Nashville, TN: Progressive Education, 1989. 35.
Annotations of 600 national social concerns magazines, newsletters and newspapers divided into fifteen categories from children to environment to health to religion.

3819. Berlet, Chip. "Private Spies of the Right: Reactionary Snoop Rags Are Watching YOU." AltM 14.1 (Fall 1982) 14-18.
Right-wing paranoid publications claim that ultra-leftists and even KGB agents are behind various events.

3820. Bird, Elizabeth S. "The Kennedy Story in Folklore and Tabloids: Intertextuality in Political Communication." Politics in Familiar Contexts: Projecting Politics Through Popular Media. Ed. Robert L. Savage and Dan Nimmo. Norwood, NJ: Ablex, 1990. 247-268.
A study of tabloids, which are extensions of urban folktales and graffiti, focusing on the life, death, and afterlife of John F. Kennedy.

3821. Brown, William, and Richard Crable. "Industry, Mass Magazines, and the Ecology Issue." QJS 59.3 (1973) 259-272.
Examines industry's mass magazine advertisement campaign 1970-1972 in defense of its environmental innocence. The "strategy was apparently effective in helping to hold public attacks at bay and to identify industry with social and ecological goals" (272).

3822. Butler, Matilda, and William Paisley. "Magazine Coverage of Women's Rights." JoC 28.1 (1978) 183-86.
Although the 1920s and the 1970s stand out in print media attention to women's rights, the long-term trend in coverage is not necessarily encouraging for those who believe that consistent, wide-ranging representation of women's issues is essential for equal political representation.

3823. Chang, Hyung. "The Emergence of the New International
        Information Order as a World Problem: A Communication
        Perspective." U of Washington, 1985. DAI 46 (1986)
        1767-A.
   Studies the ideology of articles published in international
journals from 1969 to 1983.

3824. Chernus, Ira, and Edward Linenthal, eds. A Shuddering
        Dawn: Religious Studies and the Nuclear Age. Albany,
        NY: SUNY P, 1989. 210.
   The authors ask why there are nuclear weapons and a continuing arms race, and some seek answers in the symbolic functions of nuclearism, including two chapters on magazines, "Nuclear Images in the Popular Press."

3825. Compaine, Benjamin M. "The Magazine Industry: Developing the Special Interest Audience." JoC 30.2 (1980)
        98-103.
   Though circulation remains stable, the variety of magazines is increasing. The result of specialization is an improved market outlet for advertisers.

3826. Earnshaw, Stella. "Advertising and the Media: The Case
        of Women's Magazines." MCS 6.4 (Oct. 1984) 411-21.
   See No. 1851.

3827. English, Deirdre. "Journalism: The Little Chill." MJ
        9 (Nov. 1984) 6.
   Decries government restrictions upon the free expression of non-profit publications.

3828. English, Deirdre. "Say It Isn't So, Uncle Sam." MJ
        8.1 (1983) 7.
   The IRS has tried to revoke Mother Jones's tax-exempt status in a thinly veiled attempt to squelch a major left-wing news source.

3829. Fenn, Donna. "Fashion Magazines: 99 Ways to Increase
        Your Security." WM 13.2 (Apr. 1981) 28-31.
   Although there are significant differences between the fashion magazines of the 1950s and the 1980s, they "continue to play on women's insecurities." In spite of the liberation movement, women "continue to view appearance and success as reflected by someone else's mirror."

3830. Ferguson, Marjorie. "Imagery and Ideology: The Cover
        Photographs of Traditional Women's Magazines."
        Hearth and Home: Images of Women in the Mass Media.
        Ed. Gaye Tuchman, et al. New York: Oxford UP, 1978.
        97-115.
   Analyzes covers of three traditional, highly ideological British women's magazines that "reject women as workers," suppress class realities, and present women as striving to please, stereotypes also found in US media.

3831. Graebner, William. "Coming of Age in Buffalo: The Ideology of Maturity in Postwar America." RHR 34 (Jan. 1986) 53-74.
The concept of "maturity" developed in the late 1940s as a method of social control of adolescents, was part of the Cold War search for a crusading faith, and it was class-conscious, separating working class from middle class.

3832. Greene, Theodore. America's Heroes: The Changing Models of Success in American Magazines. New York: Oxford UP, 1970. 387.
Surveys magazine biographies and profiles over more than a century. His chapter on the years 1894-1903, entitled "The Hero as Napoleon," argues that the typical hero is a response to the growing dominance of corporations that subverted the Horatio Alger ideal of entrepreneurial individualism and success, not in opposition to corporations but in ways that eased the transition to a corporate ad agency/mass consumption society.

3833. Honey, Maureen. Creating Rosie the Riveter: Class, Gender and Propaganda During World War II. Amherst: U of Massachusetts P, 1984. 251.
Analyzes the manner in which popular media, in this case women's magazines, were used to alter public opinion. The Magazine Bureau of the Office of War Information was established in 1942 to gain the cooperation of the magazine industry to help alter the traditional image of men as breadwinners and women as homebodies, and then at war's end to persuade women to return to their previous roles.

3834. Husni, Samir. "Success and Failure of New Consumer Magazines in the United States: 1979-1983." U of Missouri, Columbia, 1983. 284. DAI 45 (1984) 330-A.
One part of the study deals with the inseparable social and commercial functions of magazines in the US.

3835. Lundberg, Lea J. "Comprehensiveness of Coverage of Tropical Rain Deforestation." JQ 61.2 (Summer 1984) 378-382.
"Analysis of eight magazine articles shows almost half the pertinent information missing."

3836. Marquis, Donald, and Thomas Allen. "Communication Patterns in Applied Technology." AP 21 (1966) 1052-1062.
Explains the growing control over technology journals by businessmen.

3837. Mitford, Jessica. The American Way of Death. Greenwich, CT: Fawcett, 1963. 288.
Ch. 17, "Press & Protest," reveals how little investigative exposure of the funeral industry the media have provided, and how intense has been mortuary opposition to that scattered criticism.

3838. Nelson, Madeline. "Money Makes the Press Go 'Round." MORE 4.3 (Mar. 1974) 1, 10-11, 14-17.
Describes popular newspaper and magazine fawning over David Rockefeller.

3839. Ohmann, Richard. "Where Did Mass Culture Come From?" Politics of Letters. Middletown, CT: Wesleyan UP, 1987. 135-51.
"Magazines grew up in response to the capitalist manufacturers' power to shape consumer publics," and thus they contributed "notably to ideological domination" (150-51).

3840. Patterson, Oscar, III. "Television's Living Room War in Print: Vietnam in the News Magazines." JQ 61.1 (Spring 1984) 35-39.
"Coverage of Vietnam did not dominate from 1968 to 1973 and did not become more pictorially bloody."

3841. Pool, Gail, and Michael Comendul. "The Computer Magazines' Puffery Problem." CJR 24.3 (1985) 49-51.
Computer magazines often boost products unethically.

3842. Showalter, Stuart. "Coverage of Conscientious Objectors to the Vietnam War: An Analysis of the Editorial Content of American Magazines, 1964-1972." U of Texas at Austin, 1975. 173. DAI 36.10 (1976) 6351.
Many magazines treated conscientious objectors positively.

3843. Smith, R.C. "The Magazines' Smoking Habit." CJR 16.5 (Jan.-Feb. 1978) 29-31.
Magazines "that have accepted growing amounts of cigarette advertising have failed to cover tobacco's threat to health."

3844. Strodthoff, Glenn G., Robert P. Hawkins, and A. Clay Schoenfield. "Media Roles in a Social Movement: A Model of Ideology Diffusion." JoC 35.2 (1985) 134-153.
A study of environmentalism as a social movement charts media coverage in both special interest and general audience magazines through the stages of relevant yet unfocused information, to doctrine, to become unified substantive concerns.

3845. Whelan, Elizabeth, et al. "Analysis of Coverage of Tobacco Hazards in Women's Magazines." JPHP 2.1 (Mar. 1981) 28-35.
Because women's magazines are tied to the tobacco industry through advertising, they fail to report tobacco hazards adequately.

3846. Wilson, Christopher P. "The Rhetoric of Consumption: Mass-Market Magazines and the Demise of the Gentle Reader, 1880-1920." The Culture of Consumption. Ed. Richard Fox and T.J. Jackson Lears. New York: Pantheon, 1983. 39-64.
Around 1900 mass magazines transformed the ideal of the

PRINT MEDIA 529

self-made man into the practice of salaried employment. [See Chenoweth].

3847. [Cancelled.]

II. D. 4. b. MAGAZINES: INDIVIDUAL (3848-3946)

3848. Abrams, Floyd. "Progressive Education." CJR 18.4 (Nov.-Dec. 1979) 28-29.
Condemns the government's censorship of The Progressive magazine.

3849. Abramson, Howard. "National Geographic": Behind America's Lens on the World. New York: Crown, 1987. 279.
Exposes the magazine's relentlessly sunny attitude (approving articles on Nazi Germany in 1937 and South Africa in 1962), sexist and racist contents and corporate employment practices, and a dubious tax-exempt status.

3850. Abuelkeshk, Abdelkarim Ahmad. "A Portrayal of the Arab-Israeli Conflict in Three U.S. Journals of Opinion: 1948-1982." U of Wisconsin, 1985. 291. DAI 47 (1986) 694-A.
Israel has been more successful than the Arabs in winning their public relations battle, but the record of 3 journals in reporting the conflict is complex. For example, The Nation was pro-Israel until 1982, while the National Review was anti-Israel until 1982. (The third journal is The New Republic).

3851. "An Arbitrary Ruling." Na 168.23 (June 4, 1949) 627-268.
New York's Commissioner of Education's decision to uphold New York City's public schools' banning of The Nation "invites arbitrary censorship of any magazine that happens to offend a local school board."

3852. Aronson, James, and Cedric Belfrage. "Guardian Founders Recall the Rewards of Printing the Truth." Guard (Supplement to Oct. 19, 1988) 10-12.
Because of their stands on the Korean War, the Rosenbergs, and other cases, the FBI and Senator McCarthy intimidated the Guardian's subscribers, causing the magazine's circulation to drop from "about 54,000 to about 20,000."

3853. "Atomic Censorship." Na 170.14 (Apr. 18, 1950) 313.
The Atomic Energy Committee censored an article in Scientific American because it disliked the author.

3854. Belfrage, Cedric. "On Political Exile." Prog 41.8 (1977) 20-21.
The former editor of The National Guardian castigates the McCarran-Walter Act: Belfrage was deported for invoking the Fifth Amendment before Senator McCarthy.

3855. Bennett, James R. "TV Guide Bozzles America." QRD 9 (Oct. 1982) 3-4.
Analyzes the propaganda devices of a Sovietphobic article in TV Guide.

3856. "Bigger Than Us." Na 236.18 (1983) 562.
On Na's suit against the CIA for censoring an article.

3857. Bishop, Robert, and Helen Johnson. "Magazine Treatment of the Report." CJR 7.3 (1968) 53-56.
A survey of seven magazine treatments of the report on racism by the National Advisory Commission on Civil Disorders (Mar. 2, 1968). In general, this strong condemnation of US racial separatism was "filtered through white-oriented media."

3858. Bleifuss, Joel. "The Fifth Estates Fifth Column." ITT 14.34 (Sept. 12-18, 1990) 4-5.
War "psychosis" in Time and Newsweek over the Iraqi invasion of Kuwait.

3859. Boylan, James. "Reconstructing I.F. Stone." CJR 28.3 (Sept.-Oct. 1989) 46-47.
A tribute to the great "adversary of government and of the passive press."

3860. Chenoweth, Lawrence. The American Dream of Success: The Search for the Self in the Twentieth Century. North Scituate, MA: Duxbury/Wadsworth, 1974. 237.
Study of the Reader's Digest (1926-1969), The Saturday Evening Post (1917-1969), comic strips, and self-help books explains how free will and independence were transformed into obedience to the corporate state, and how individuals have become more passive as the nation has become "domestically more violent and internationally more arrogant" (viii).

3861. Christenson, Reo. "Report on the Reader's Digest." CJR 3.4 (1965) 30-36.
The Reader's Digest generally supports corporate values.

3862. Cirino, Robert. "The Reader's Digest: The Biggest Myth of All." Don't Blame the People. New York: Vintage, 1971. 222-233.
On its biases and falsehoods.

3863. Cockburn, Alexander. "The Labors of Leiken." Na 242.18 (1986) 639.
Robert Leiken's attacks on Nicaragua published in The New York Review reveal him to be a "monumental fraudmonger."

3864. Cockburn, Alexander. "Red Horror." Corruptions of Empire. London: Verso, 1987. 307-308.
On the paranoid Sovietphobia of an article in Look magazine of 1948 entitled "Could the Reds Seize Detroit?"

3865. "Congressional Aide Spies On Left." CS 3.1 (Spring

1976) 17-22.
The right-wing newsletter, Information Digest, edited by S. Louise Rees (Sheila O'Connor), is a fragment of a campaign of spying, dossier compiling, blacklisting, infiltration, and other activities to suppress dissent.

3866. Dan, Uri. Blood Libel: The Inside Story of General Ariel Sharon's History-Making Suit Against "Time" Magazine. New York: Simon & Schuster, 1987. 270.
Intense attack on Time by Sharon's media adviser. [Contrast Renata Adler's Reckless Disregard].

3867. DeVolpi, Alexander, et al. Born Secret: The H-Bomb, the "Progressive" Case and National Security. Elmsford, NY: Pergamon, 1981. 320.
Account of the government's censorship of an article on the H-bomb in The Progressive, the first case of extended prior restraint of the press in US history.

3868. "Does 'The Progressive' Have a Case?" CJR 18.1 (May-June 1979) 25-27.
Denounces both government efforts to impose prior restraint on an article and support of the government by many newspapers.

3869. Dorfman, Ariel. "The Infantilization of the Adult Reader." The Empire's Old Clothes: What the Lone Ranger, Babar, & Other Innocent Heroes do to Our Minds. New York: Pantheon, 1983. 135-173.
Analyzes the Reader's Digest in which common sense reality, stability, the establishment, and the status quo prevail.

3870. Doudna, Martin K. Concerned about the Planet: "The Reporter Magazine" and American Liberalism 1949-1968. Westport, CT: Greenwood, 1979. 197.
Doudna's book places the Reporter in US liberalism in this period.

3871. Douglas, Susan. "'Time' Does Jackson in with Subliminal Message." ITT 12.21 (Apr. 20-26, 1988) 16.
Analyzes the racist treatment of Jesse Jackson in the April 11 number of Time.

3872. Draper, Robert. Rolling Stone Magazine: The Uncensored History. Princeton, NJ: Princeton UP, 1990. 395.
An anecdotal history, a portrait of its owner, Jann Wenner, and an account of how a magazine works, of the conflict between editorial integrity and commercial imperatives (dependence upon record companies' ads), editorial censorship, and the eventual dominance of corporate over editorial priorities.

3873. Eisenberg, Carolyn. "Two Cheers for Reagan from Old Establishment." ITT 7.41 (Nov. 2, 1983) 18-19.
Reviews one volume of Foreign Affairs, published by the Council on Foreign Relations, which favors an imperial foreign policy.

3874. Elson, Robert. Time Inc.: The Intimate History of a
 Publishing Enterprise 1923-1941. Vol. 1. New York:
 Atheneum, 1968. 500.
 "This is the first of two volumes in a history of Time
Incorporated done by Time Inc. people. It is, in other words,
an 'authorized history.'"

3875. Elson, Robert. Time Inc.: The Intimate History of a
 Publishing Enterprise 1941-1960. Vol. 2. New York:
 Atheneum, 1973. 505.
 See No. 3918.

3876. Farhang, Mansour. U.S. Imperialism: From the Spanish-
 American War to the Iranian Revolution. Boston:
 South End, 1981. 190.
 The author's study of the reporting of Iran and Mossadeq
from 1951 to 1953 by Time, Newsweek, and USNWR discovered
extreme ignorance and bias. "This sad experience taught me
that the existence of freedom and resources does not
necessarily make the press coverage of human affairs fair or
intelligent" (4).

3877. Fisher, June, et al. "The Role of Popular Media in
 Defining Sickness and Health." Communication and
 Social Structure: Critical Studies in Mass Media
 Research. Ed. Emile McAnany, et al. New York:
 Praeger, 1981. 240-262.
 On reporting coronary heart disease, Ladies Home Journal,
Reader's Digest, and Time supported the status quo of
capitalist medicine.

3878. Flippo, Chet. "Time Inc.'s Sticky Wicket." MORE 4.4
 (Apr. 1974) 20-21.
 East Texas stockholders in Time, Inc., have influenced its
magazines to ignore a major conservation story in the area.

3879. Friedberg, Anne. "Writing About Cinema: Close Up 1927-
 1933." New York U, 1983. 372. DAI 44.12 (June
 1984) 3522-A.
 The film journal, Close Up, was avant-garde in artistic,
sexual, and racial progressiveness. "Writing about cinema is
an essential component of the cinematic apparatus."

3880. Friedman, Robert. "The United States v. The
 Progressive." CJR 18.2 (1978) 27-35.
 Condemns the government's censorship of a story about the H-
Bomb, suppression supported by the NYT and WP.

3881. Friel, Howard. "Covert Propaganda in Time and
 Newsweek." CAIB 21 (Spring 1984) 14-23.
 Strategies of support for the corporate state.

3882. Gervasi, Tom. "The Doomsday Beat." CJR 18.1 (1979)
 34-40.

PRINT MEDIA

Aviation Week is a conduit for the Pentagon and military contractors.

3883. Goodman, Sandy. "Can Newsweek Really Separate Fact from Opinion?" CJR 7.2 (1968) 26-29.
The magazine does not separate "fact from opinion" as its advertising claims.

3884. Grahame, Peter. "Criticalness, Pragmatics, and Everyday Life: Consumer Literacy as Critical Practice." Critical Theory and Public Life. Ed. John Forester. Cambridge, MA: MIT P, 1985. 147-174.
Examines kinds of critical literacy exemplified by Consumer Reports. Rationalizing "the circulation of goods by improving the conditions of personal choice" supports "possessive individualism."

3885. Guma, Greg, and Jeffrey Polman. "The News Magazines: A License to Interpret." Pr 8 (Aug. 1980) 10-11.
Time and Newsweek project the mainstream ideology of 2 corporate empires, Time, Inc., and the Washington Post Company.

3886. Hanson, C.T. "A Day of Disinformation." CJR 20.3 (Sept.-Oct. 1981) 19-20.
On the paranoia and intolerance of Accuracy in Media (AIM). According to AIM, most criticism of the military or of business "amounts to disinformation."

3887. Hartman, Thomas. "Reporting for Service: The Big Guns of the Military Press." WJR 6.6 (1984) 29-32.
Describes several pro-military magazines, the most important being Aviation Week & Space Technology.

3888. Hochschild, Adam. "Ramparts: The End of Muckraking Magazines." WM 6.4 (June 1974) 33-42.
The author's recollections of successes and gradual decline of the magazine.

3889. Holcomb, Betty. "Grounded At Harper's." CJR 21.4 (1982) 7-8.
"Who is in editorial control of the prestigious monthly," the Atlantic Richfield Corporation or the editor Michael Kinsley?

3890. Hoyt, Michael. "Earthly Editing: The Dirt on The New Yorker's Environmental Advertorial." CJR 29.2 (July-Aug. 1990) 8-11.
A hard-hitting essay on the environment was censored by the advertising execs, who turned it into "a high-school newspaper report."

3891. Keddie, Shirley. "Naming & Renaming: Time Magazine's Coverage of Germany & the Soviet Union During the 1940s." U of Massachusetts, 1985. 288. DAI 46 (1985) 1430-A.

Countries with interests parallel to those of the US receive more favorable coverage, are pictured as "like us," and have their negative qualities downplayed, with the reverse true for "enemies."

3892. Kelly, Tom. "'They're ba-a-ck': The IRD's 1989 Spring Offensive." C&C 11.14 (Aug. 14, 1989) 236-239.
Examines the Institute on Religion and Democracy's attack on C&C in their Religion & Democracy for not following the White House line on Cuba and other issues.

3893. Kimball, Penn. "The History of The Nation According to the F.B.I." Na 242.11 (1986) 399-426.
Examines the Nation's FBI file (started in 1918) and other FBI hostilities toward the magazine.

3894. Knoll, Erwin. "Bread-and-Butter Man." Prog 50.2 (1986) 4.
On the censorship of Howard Morland's article on the H-Bomb in The Progressive.

3895. Knoll, Erwin. "Filed But Not Forgotten: the F.B.I. and The Progressive." Prog 50.10 (1986) 24-25.
On FBI surveillance of the magazine for four decades.

3896. Koger, Daniel. "The Liberal Opinion Press and the Kennedy Years in Vietnam: A Study of Four Journals." Michigan SU, 1983. 171. DAI 44.9 (1984) 2612-A.
The Nation opposed the war, The New Republic began to oppose it in 1963, and The Reporter and The New Leader supported it.

3897. Kramer, Staci D. "Not Quite a JR." SLJR 18.112 (Dec. 1988) 3, 14.
A new magazine, Business & the Press, is devoted to assisting corporations in dealing with the press.

3898. Lacob, Miriam. "Reader's Digest: Who's in Charge?" CJR 23.2 (1984) 41-43.
The editor of the magazine was fired partly for criticism of the Reagan administration.

3899. Laurence, Philip, and Tracey Dewart. "The CIA Goes to College." NT 4.5 (1986) 21-2.
An article in Harvard's International Security journal was CIA-financed.

3900. Lazere, Donald. "Public Doublespeak: TV Guide's News Watchers." CE 37 (Mar. 1976) 694-697.
Discusses TVG's conservative writers of its "News Watch" column.

3901. Lee, Martin A., and Norman Solomon. "Unreliable Sources: Slick Coverage of the Exxon Valdez Spill." Extra! 3.3 (Mar.-Apr. 1990) 1, 6.

Newsweek and USNWR played down the disaster and Exxon's criminality.

3902. Lentz, Richard. "Resurrecting the Prophet: Dr. Martin Luther King, Jr., and the News Magazines." U of Iowa, 1983. 993. DAI 44.8 (Feb. 1984) 2279-A.
This study of Time, Newsweek, and U.S. News & World Report during the period, 1956-1968, argues that the three magazines "washed out much of the radicalism that King exhibited during the last years of his life."

3903. Lentz, Richard. Symbols, the News Magazines, and Martin Luther King. Baton Rouge: Louisiana State UP, 1990. 376.
Studies the changing representation of King in Newsweek, Time, and U.S. News & World Report as King shifted during the 1960s from reform to radicalism. The magazines faced a "crisis of symbols" when King no longer fit the mold the magazines had created for him.

3904. Lopate, Carol. "Jackie!" Hearth and Home: Images of Women in the Mass Media. Ed. Gaye Tuchman, et al. New York: Oxford UP, 1978. 130-140.
The treatment of Jackie Kennedy Onassis in twelve magazines is diverse, but one theme about women connects all of them: work outside the home is negative compared to wife and mother activities.

3905. MacDougall, A. Kent, ed. "Reader's Digest." The Press. Princeton, NJ: Dow Jones, 1972. 68-78.
Optimism, anticommunism, anti-labor, and anti-big government are favorite themes of the magazine.

3906. Mackenzie, Angus. "IRS Persecutes the Non-Profit Press." NaR (Fall 1987) 3-4.
Describes government harassment of Sojourners magazine.

3907. "The Man Who 'Stole' The Secret." CMJ 5.2 (1979) 4-5, 7.
Howard Morland relates the experiences which led to the suppression of his article for The Progressive magazine on the details of a nuclear bomb.

3908. Marlin, Cheryl L. "Space Race Propaganda: US Coverage of the Soviet Sputniks in 1957." JQ 64.2 & 3 (Summer-Fall 1987) 544-549.
"'Time' and 'US News' covered story in Cold War terms, while 'Newsweek' put emphasis on prospects for space exploration."

3909. McAuliffe, Kevin. The Great American Newspaper: The Rise and Fall of the "Village Voice." New York: Scribner, 1978. 486.
Favorable treatment of the early days of the journal under the editorship of Dan Wolfe; negative treatment of the opponents of Wolfe and the post-Wolfe years.

3910. Morland, Howard. The Secret That Exploded. New York: Random, 1981. 288.
Believing the secrecy surrounding nuclear weapons derived from a desire by the nuclear weapons industry to keep the public ignorant and passive, Morland wrote an article on the H-bomb based upon public sources for The Progressive magazine. The government went to great lengths to censor him and the magazine.

3911. Mujahid, Sharif al. "Coverage of Pakistan in Three U.S. Newsmagazines." JQ 47.1 (Spring 1970) 126-130.
Time, Newsweek, and USNWR, concerned primarily with Pakistan's foreign relations, provided inadequate coverage of domestic matters, and were generally neutral, factual, balanced.

3912. "Murray Bookchin Reads Time." New York: Paper Tiger TV, No. 20.
One of a series of critical commentaries on diverse media.

3913. Nadler, Eric. "Guiding TV to the Right." MJ 9.3 (Apr. 1984) 17-20.
In the early 1980s TVG became a "conservative critic of network news."

3914. Neier, Aryeh. "USA: 'Born Classified.'" IC 9.1 (1980) 51-54.
Condemns government efforts to censor a Prog article on nuclear bombs.

3915. Norris, Vincent P. "Mad Economics: An Analysis of an Adless Magazine." JoC 34.1 (1984) 44-61.
A case study of Mad magazine which proves that magazines can refuse to advertise and still be profitable.

3916. Owen, David. "A Final Word on The New Republic and Those Cigarette Ads." WM 17.5 (June 1985) 51-52.
On the disreputable behavior of NR toward the author out of fear of losing lucrative cigarette ads.

3917. Parham, Paul. "Vietnam 1958-1961: U.S. Newsmagazine Coverage." MA Thesis, U of Missouri, 1971. MA 10.1 (1972) 65.
On inadequate coverage of the war by Time, Newsweek, and U.S. News & World Report.

3918. Pendergast, Curtis. The World of Time Inc.: The Intimate History of a Changing Enterprise 1960-1980. Vol. 3. New York: Atheneum, 1986. 590.
Carries forward the authorized history begun by Elson.

3919. Perrin, Dennis. "The New Republic: The Center as Left." Extra! 3.6 (July-Aug. 1990) 7.
Describes NR as a conservative magazine.

PRINT MEDIA

3920. Peterson, Trev. "National Security Exception to the Doctrine of Prior Restraint." NLR 60.2 (1981) 400-415.
Decries the censorship of the Prog article by Howard Morland on nuclear bombs.

3921. Pfeiffer, Richard. "The Popular Periodical Press and the Vietnam War: 1954-1968." MA Thesis, U of Louisville, 1978. 106. MA 17.1 (1979) 56.
From 1965 Newsweek criticized the war and Time and USNWR supported it.

3922. Phillips, E. Barbara. "Magazine Heroines: Is 'Ms.' Just Another Member of the 'Family Circle'?" Hearth and Home: Images of Women in the Mass Media. Ed. Gaye Tuchman, et al. New York: Oxford UP, 1978. 116-129.
Family Circle and Ms. differ, the former purveying "images of housewifery and mothercraft," the latter emphasizing "women in political life and public service," but both share the traditional stress on women as helpers rather than ambitious (supposedly male).

3923. Prendergast, Alan. "The Boys in the Bush." CJR 22.4 (1983) 59-63.
On the relations between the Pentagon and the militarist magazine Soldier of Fortune.

3924. "The Progressive Case: Democracy Is Dangerous." CJR 18.2 (1979) 22-23.
To assume the risk of democracy is to assume the risk of free access to all kinds of information.

3925. "Quiddity." Z 1.11 (Nov. 1988) 6-7.
A picture of the different roles that various magazines of the Left might play, including criticism of Mother Jones for "too many People magazine-like articles."

3926. "The Review Slips on 'Banana Republics' Story." CJR 19.3 (1980) 81, 84-85.
The National News Council found an article on UPI published in CJR to have departed from "Sound journalistic standards."

3927. Reynolds, Paula K. "Opinion Journals and the Women's Movement, 1968-1977." U of Texas, Austin, 1982. 180. DAI 43.3 (Sept. 1982) 574-A.
Examination of three ideologies in six journals (The Atlantic, etc.) revealed that most coverage went "to issues and goals of the legalist branch, the most conservative of the ideologies," less coverage to the "more radical" separatists, and even less coverage to "the most radical" "androgynists," and this pattern intensified during the time period studied.

3928. Rosenzweig, Roy. "Marketing the Past: American Heritage and Popular History in the United States, 1954-1984." RHR 32 (1985) 7-29.

Describes the magazine as conservative and Establishment oriented, from transforming robber barons into statesmen to suppressing social conflict.

3929. Rowse, Arthur. "1. A Warning from the Mailman." CJR 6.4 (1967) 24-26.
Criticizes the Reader's Digest for not identifying pharmaceutical advertising as advertising.

3930. Rubin, David. "Surprise! TV Guide Is No Longer a Toothless Wonder." MORE 6.10 (Oct. 1976) 32-6.
Describes the magazine as an adjunct of commercial broadcasting.

3931. Ryan, Michael. "Changes: Split Level." CJR 17.3 (Sept.-Oct. 1978) 6.
American Enterprise Institute's Public Opinion magazine is ideologically skewed to the right.

3932. Schiller, Herbert. "Recreation & Entertainment: Reinforcement for the Status Quo." The Mind Managers. Boston: Beacon, 1973. 79-103.
TV Guide, National Geographic, and Walt Disney Productions promote dominant values and institutions.

3933. Seelye, Katharine. "TV Guide: The Shake-Up." CJR 28.4 (Nov.-Dec. 1989) 41-45.
"While the old TV Guide showed a bracing skepticism toward the industry, the new TV Guide [purchased by Rupert Murdoch] is clearly more eager to join the hype."

3934. Seldes, George. "The FBI and I." Prog 53 (Feb. 1989) 50.
Three instances in which the FBI or the Post Office for the FBI illegally spied on the author and his magazine, In Fact, which eventually "put In Fact out of business."

3935. Slater, Robert Bruce. "One Magazine We Can Do Without." BSR 60 (Winter 1987) 45-47.
Philip Morris magazine presents cigarettes as healthy, enjoyable, and glamorous.

3936. Smolla, Rodney A. Jerry Falwell v. Larry Flynt: The First Amendment on Trial. New York: St. Martin's, 1988. 51-53.
Tells the story of the evangelist's suit against the porn magazine, The Hustler, and its publisher, Flynt, which ended with victory for the latter and broadened the protections of the First Amendment.

3937. Sorkin, Michael. "Timespeak: Hidden Persuaders." MORE 8 (May 1978) 29-32.
The ways in which Time uses rhetorical devices to deprecate socialism and exalt capitalism.

PRINT MEDIA

3938. Staudenmaier, John, S.J. Technology's Storytellers: Reweaving the Human Fabric. Cambridge, MA: MIT, 1985. 282.
Studies the articles in the journal Technology and Culture from 1959 to 1980 as a single "text" which reveals the "world view of the new historical community," moving away "from case studies toward a contextual approach."

3939. Stillman, Don. "2. Attack on the Taxman." CJR 6.4 (1967) 26-27.
Criticism of Reader's Digest public affairs articles "that purport to be factual analysis, but actually contain highly debatable conclusions."

3940. Stokes, Geoffrey. "Follow the Money in Fortune Report of the Nestle Boycott." ITT (Feb. 18-24, 1981) 7, 10.
Influence of a foreign corporation.

3941. Suleiman, Michael. "American Mass Media and the June Conflict." The Arab-Israeli Confrontation of June 1967: An Arab Perspective. Ed. Ibrahim Abu-Lughod. Evanston, IL: Northwestern UP, 1970. 138-54.
Seven US newsmagazines were very reluctant to criticize Israel, while generally stereotyping the Arabs negatively regarding the 1967 war. Support for Israel and antagonism toward the Arabs were greater than in 1956.

3942. Suleiman, Michael. "An Evaluation of Middle East News Coverage in Seven American News Magazines, July-December, 1956." MEF 41 (Autumn 1965) 9-30.
Study of the 1956 Suez attack as reported in USNWR, Newsweek, Time, Life, Na, NR, and the NYT's "The Week in Review" reveals antagonism toward Arabs.

3943. Sullivan, John. "A Year of the New Maclean's: Import Substitution in the Ideology Market." TM 11.1 (Jan.-Feb. 1977) 5-9.
A discussion of Maclean's recent content and format change that makes it "an ideological force" to be "reckoned with" in conflict with US media, especially Time (Canada).

3944. Swanberg, W.A. Luce and His Empire. New York: Scribner's, 1972. 529. (New York: Dell, 1973).
A biography of Henry Robinson Luce and an account of his publishing empire, Time Inc., and of its enormous impact on the world. Swanberg sees Luce as an American chauvinist and megalomaniac who used his publications to advance the cause of US Christianity and capitalism.

3945. Tribe, Laurence H., and David H. Remes. "Some Reflections on The Progressive Case: Publish and Perish?" BAS 36.3 (1980) 20-24.
Howard Morland's article on the hydrogen bomb was published in The Progressive magazine after the federal government attempted for eight months to suppress it.

3946. Walljasper, Jay. "The Politics of Ecology." UR (July-Aug. 1988) 126-127.
On environmental magazines.

II. D. 5. PRINT MEDIA: BOOKS (3947-4026)

3947. Anawalt, H.C. "A Critical Appraisal of Snepp v. United States: Are There Alternatives to Government Censorship?" SCLR 21 (Summer 1981) 697-726.
Denounces the prior restraint of pre-publication review of Frank Snepp's book on the CIA.

3948. Anderson, Jack. "Guard Your Library Card!: FBI May Watch What You Read." NAT (Dec. 15, 1988) 4A.
Condemns the FBI's library surveillance program looking for foreign agents and subversives.

3949. Aufderheide, Pat. "Pantheon's Fall: Publish and Perish." ITT 14.16 (Mar. 14-20, 1990) 18-19.
A "major voice for human rights and diversity of expression was silenced when Pantheon Books was gutted by corporate managers."

3950. Bacon, Betty, ed. How Much Truth Do We Tell The Children? The Politics of Children's Literature. Minneapolis: MEP, 1988. 257.
Children's literature is a product of the social order within which it is written and usually expresses dominant social, political, ethical, and moral values. The values are those of the elite class within the capitalist system of England and the US. Racism, sexism, and national chauvinism are part of this class structure.

3951. Bagdikian, Ben. "Public Information As Industrial By-Product." The Media Monopoly. Boston: Beacon, 1983. 29-41.
Reports the suppression of several books.

3952. Barnett, Frank, and Carnes Lord. Political Warfare and Psychological Operations: Rethinking the US Approach. National Defense UP with National Strategy Information Center. Washington, DC: US GPO, 1989. 242.
Eight essays with responses on how the US can increase and make more effective its propaganda against the SU. All believe that the US "must upgrade its performance in the political-psychological arena." [NDUP publishes books about US national security.]

3953. "Between (and under) Covers." Prog 46.12 (1982) 13-14.
The CIA is "one of the world's largest [book] publishers," and perhaps the most secretive.

3954. Bob, Murray. "Cooking the Books: The Perils of Publishing." MR 42.4 (Sept. 1990) 22-28.

Condemns conglomerate book publishing and laments the firing of the editor of Pantheon by its new owner Newhouse Communications, which bought Random House of which Pantheon was a part.

3955. Brians, Paul. "Nuclear Fiction for Children." BAS 5.6 (July-Aug. 1988) 24-27.
Realistic books about war and peace are rare.

3956. "Chains, Mergers, & Marginalization: The Censorship of the Marketplace." South End Press Newsletter (1987) n.p.
The concentration of book publishing and retailing are reducing access of and to ideas.

3957. Chien, A.J. "Arab Stereotypes & the Limits of Honest Journalism." MR 42.5 (Oct. 1990) 55-61.
Lamb's The Arabs counteracts anti-Arab racism, but he is "a typically indoctrinated American."

3958. Churchill, Ward. "Goons, G-Men, and AIM: At Last the Story Will Be Told." Prog 54.4 (Apr. 28, 1990) 28-29.
On the attempted censorship of Peter Mattheissen's 1983 book, In the Spirit of Crazy Horse, "documenting FBI persecution of the American Indian Movement" at the Pine Ridge Sioux reservation in South Dakota during the mid-1970s. (Also see Na [Nov. 13, 1989] 564-7).

3959. Cockburn, Alexander. "The Blindness of Intellectuals." Z (Apr. 1990) 65-66.
Analyzes the illusions and misinformation in public letter of protest at the firing of the head of Pantheon (part of Random House which is owned by Newhouse).

3960. Cockburn, Alexander. "The Death of Herman Kahn." Corruptions of Empire. London: Verso, 1987. 326-27.
A critical look at Kahn, whose On Thermonuclear War (1960) was a plan and rationale for mass murder.

3961. Colby, Gerard. Du Pont Dynasty. Secaucus, NJ: Lyle Stuart, 1984. 968.
The first version of this book was partly censored by its publisher's reduction of advertising after pressure from Du Pont.

3962. Cole, David. "Deportation of a Poet." Na 246.25 (June 25, 1988) 892-95.
Chronicles the campaign by the Immigration and Naturalization Service to deport poet and author Margaret Randall.

3963. Croft, Jack. "Du Pont's Curtain to Be Opened in Court." PI (May 24, 1981) 1B.
On the censoring of a book on Du Pont because of pressure from that company.

3964. Cunningham, Ann Marie. "The Book That Came in from the

Cold." MORE 4.12 (Dec. 1974) 17-18.
On the difficulties Philip Agee had finding a US publisher for his book, Inside the Company: A CIA Diary.

3965. Denman, William M. "'Them Dirty, Filthy Books': The Textbook War in West Virginia." FSY (1976) 37-45.
Chronicles the protest in Kanawha County, West Virginia, following the adoption of textbooks considered by many to be unpatriotic, obscene, or disrespectful to religious beliefs. [This bibliography provides only a few entries on local censorship. See Newsletter on Intellectual Freedom].

3966. Efron, Edith, and Clytia Chambers. How CBS Tried to Kill a Book. Los Angeles: Nash, 1972. 187.
Tells how the media giant tried to squelch publication of the author's book, The News Twisters.

3967. Ellis, Kate. "Gimme Shelter: Feminism, Fantasy, and Women's Popular Fiction." American Media & Mass Culture. Ed. Donald Lazere. Berkeley: U of California P, 1987. 216-232.
Seeks "an analysis of women's popular fiction" that helps "to deepen our analysis of women's aspirations without jettisoning our critique of the institutions that support inequality" (218).

3968. Ezell, Macel D. Unequivocal Americanism: Right-Wing Novels in the Cold War Era. Metuchen, NJ: Scarecrow Press, 1977. 152.
By "right-wing" the author means "conservative, rightist, and patriotic," in general right of center used in "a non-condemnatory way." The book's "primary purpose is to provide bibliographical information and isolate some of the major themes in right-wing novels" (viii). Since they "consider themselves at war" against liberals and communists, right-wingers are apocalyptic, making "no apologies for their tactics," defending America "regardless of cost."

3969. Fast, Howard, and Meredith Tax. "What's Black & White & Red All Over? Anticommunism and American Literature." Anticommunism and the U.S.: History and Consequences Conference, Harvard U, Nov. 11-13, 1988.
Critical fiction about the social complex of the US declined after WWII.

3970. "The FBI Reviews A Book." Na 172.4 (Jan. 27, 1951) 86.
Describes attempts by the FBI and the House Un-American Activities Committee to block a book on the FBI by Max Lowenthal.

3971. "FBI Seizes Iranian Books from Reporters." CL 341 (Feb. 1982) 2.
The ACLU sued FBI and US Customs officials for seizing books on US involvement in Iran at Boston's Logan Airport. (Also SLJR 7.45 [1982] 10.)

PRINT MEDIA

3972. Franck, Thomas M., and James J. Eisen. "Balancing National Security and Free Speech." NYUJLP 14 (Winter 1982) 339-369.
Condemns the Supreme Court's support of the CIA's censorship of a book by Frank Snepp.

3973. Franco, Jean. "The Incorporation of Women: A Comparison of North American & Mexican Popular Narrative." Studies in Entertainment. Ed. Tania Modleski. Bloomington: Indiana UP, 1986. 119-138.
Compares Harlequin Romances and Mexican comic strip novels to demonstrate that mass culture "plots" women into the social order "according to their position in the division of labor" (xvii).

3974. Geismar, Maxwell. "Non-non Book Reviews." MO 5.12 (Dec. 1963) 13.
Discusses books which the US "free press" has "misrepresented" because the books "go against the tide of public opinion"--such as Edgar Snow's The Other Side of the River and Margaret Halsey's The Pseudo-Ethic.

3975. Goodrich, Chris. "Most Paperbacks Are in Chains." Na 240 (May 4, 1985) 523-25.
Avon books will sell only to chains now: "local bookstores, once the mainstay of book publishing, may soon go the way of mom and pop groceries."

3976. Goodrich, Chris. "Writers and the Market-II." Na 249.1 (July 3, 1989) 24-28.
Reviews four recent books about publishing, cites their shortcomings as evidence of the industry's decline into unadulterated commercialism.

3977. Herman, Edward. "Time Merger Kiss of Death for Mob Expose." Guard 42.29 (May 16, 1990) 5.
Time, Inc., owner of Little, Brown, killed the publication of Connections: American Business and the Mob by Roy Rowan and Sandy Smith, already listed in the company's catalog, probably because of certain contents of the book embarrassing to the impending merger of Time and Warner Communications.

3978. Horowitz, Irving Louis. Communicating Ideas: The Crisis of Publishing in a Post-Industrial Society. New York: Oxford UP, 1986. 240.
"Social science publishing operates within parameters set by American capitalism. The social system is the context within which social science survives."

3979. Huffman, John L., and Denise Trauth. "After Ginsberg and Tinker: Book Banning and Minors' First Amendment Rights." JQ 58.3 (Fall 1981) 434-438.
"Inherent ambiguity of Tinker has allowed two judicial philosophies to develop on banning books in schools."

3980. Hume, Britt. "The Cult of Censorship." MORE 4.4 (Apr. 1974) 9.
Explores the legal issues surrounding the censorship of Marchetti's and Marks' The CIA and the Cult of Intelligence.

3981. Judis, John B. "Book Biz Censors." ITT 7.38 (Oct. 12-18, 1983) 2.
On the censorship of Zilg's (Colby) Du Pont.

3982. Kahn, Albert E. The Matusow Affair: Memoir of a National Scandal. Mount Kisco, NY: Moyer Bell, 1987. 320.
Account of government suppression of a book on Harvey Matusow, a paid "expert" witness for the Justice Department and HUAC who gave false testimony against alleged communists.

3983. Kostelanetz, Richard. The End of Intelligent Writing: Literary Politics in America. New York: Sheed & Ward, 1974. 480.
Examines why certain tendencies dominate, how recognition develops, what is "literary power," and other questions previously considered "verboten." "It is obvious that in a state-supported literary society such as Soviet Russia, certain writers and styles are disseminated to the exclusion of others; yet too many of us remain oblivious to similar forces and pressures shaping the public life of American writing today" (xv).

3984. Krehm, William. Democracies and Tyrannies of the Caribbean. Westport, CT: Hill, 1984. 244.
The Foreword gives the history of the censorship of the original English version of this book and of the author as correspondent. Its story is US support of tyrannical and corrupt Central American governments.

3985. Landis, Fred. "Robert Moss, Arnaud de Borchgrave, and Right-Wing Disinformation." CAIB 10 (Aug.-Sept. 1980) 37-44.
Critique of the Sovietphobic novel The Spike.

3986. Lazer, Charles, and S. Dier. "The Labor Force in Fiction." JoC 28.1 (1978) 174-82.
Findings from a study of occupational roles in magazine short stories from 1940 to 1970 show that the proportion of working women in fiction has not increased over time, even though the proportion of women actually in the labor force has increased substantially.

3987. Levy, Harlan. "Some Big Boys Move Into Book Publishing." BSR 27 (Fall 1978) 44-47.
American authors fear that the increasing concentration within paperback publishing is "lending to the suppression of books of literary and intellectual quality."

3988. Lorimer, James. "Canadian Textbooks and the American 'Knowledge Industry.'" TM 5.3 (Summer 1971) 47-57.

US corporate purchase of Canadian publishing companies should be opposed because it leads to domination of reality by the corporations and to censorship.

3989. Lukenbill, Bernard W. "Who Writes Children's Books?" JoC 26.1 (Winter 1976) 97-100.
School librarians continue to determine children's access to divergent views.

3990. MacCann, Donnarae. "Militarism in Juvenile Fiction." IBCB 13.6-7 (1982) 18-20. (Rpt. How Much Truth Do We Tell the Children? Ed. Betty Bacon [1988]).
Lists scholarship and novels.

3991. Mandel, Ernest. Delightful Murder: A Social History of the Crime Story. London: Pluto P, 1984. 152.
The basic structure of individual conflict in detective stories maintains the ruling status quo. [A large bibliography could be compiled on the ideology of authors and genres. See my bibliography in BoB (Oct.-Dec. 1973 and Jan.-Mar 1980)].

3992. Marion, George. The Communist Trial: An American Crossroads. 2nd ed. New York: Fairplay, 1950. 192.
The trial of the leaders of the Communist Party U.S.A. for allegedly advocating the overthrow of the government, under the Smith Act. The author analyzes the trial as a text comparable to Alice in Wonderland in which the complex writings of Karl Marx were reduced to the level of children's fables in order to call the public activities of the Party a conspiracy.

3993. Miller, Warren. "Author's Note." The Sleep of Reason. Boston: Little, Brown, 1960. xi-xiv.
This attack on McCarthy and McCarthyites in the form of a novel was rejected by US publishers but was published in England in 1956.

3994. Mitgang, Herbert. Dangerous Dossiers: Exposing the Secret War Against America's Greatest Authors. New York: D.I. Fine, 1988. 331.
Account of the surveillance by the FBI over some of this country's most distinguished writers.

3995. Moody, Sid. "CIA Ex-agent, Author Stands on Principles, Continues to Play by Federal Rules." AG (Nov. 9, 1980) 18A.
An account of the difficulties Frank Snepp encountered following the publication of his book on the CIA in Vietnam, Decent Interval. The CIA sued and won a penalty of $140,580.

3996. Moore, Michael. "Stopping the Presses: The Anatomy of the Book Burning Business." MM 8.9 (Sept. 1987) 13-15. (Also see ITT 11.34 [Sept. 9-15, 1987] 20-21).
An account of the destruction of 20,000 copies of a book on Katharine Graham.

3997. Neier, Aryeh. "Frank Snepp: A Win for the CIA." IC 9.4 (1980) 51-56.
Condemns the censoring of Snepp's book, which will result in reduced whistle-blowing of government abuses.

3998. Neier, Aryeh. "A Sterling Vapor Gun." Na 232.18 (1981) 573-575.
Claire Sterling in The Terror Network "shows nothing to support the charge" that the Soviet Union "promotes terrorism."

3999. Pell, Eve. "Taking C.I.A. Critics to Court." Na 233.12 (1981) 371-72.
A CIA agent's libel suit against Donald Freed's Death in Washington is part of the suppression of information about illegal acts committed by the intelligence community.

4000. Peterson, Ted, and Jay W. Jensen. "The Case of General Yamashita: A Study of Suppression." JQ 28 (Spring 1951) 196-204.
An account of the suppression of a book critical of the US Army's execution of the general.

4001. Pless, Laurance. "Snepp v. United States--Short Shrift for the Prior Restraint Doctrine." NCLR 59 (1981) 417-427.
Denounces the prior restraint placed upon Frank Snepp's Decent Interval.

4002. Porter, Dennis. The Pursuit of Crime: Art & Ideology in Detective Fiction. New Haven, CT: Yale UP, 1981. 267.
"Works in the genre always take a stand in defense of the established societal order . . . even when . . . they uncover corruption among prominent citizens and public officials. . . . The point of view adopted is always that of the detective, which is to say, of the police, however much of an amateur the investigator may appear to be. In a detective story the moral legitimacy of the detective's role is never in doubt" (125). [See entry 3991].

4003. Powell, Walter. Getting Into Print: The Decision-Making Process in Scholarly Publishing. Chicago: U of Chicago P, 1985. 260.
Focuses on case studies of two commercial scholarly publishers (discussed under assumed names), one small, one large, using the methodology of the sociology of organizations. Gatekeeping factors include the large quantity of manuscripts, time limits, an editor's knowledge and contacts, and chance. [Does not discuss ideological and cultural influences.]

4004. "A Professor's Accident." MO 5.10 (Oct. 1963) 18-19.
Sidney Hook's distorted attack on Eugene Burdick's and Harvey Wheeler's Fail-Safe in The Fail-Safe Fallacy reveals his "blind hatred of Communism."

PRINT MEDIA

4005. Radecki, Thomas. "Newsweek Praises Militaristic, WW III Entertainment; Violent Fantasies Affect America's Leaders." NCTVN 9.6-7 (June-Oct. 1988) 4.
Newsweek gave a cover story to "best-selling militaristic fiction writer Tom Clancy," author of "extremely violent war novels" portraying the US "wiping out the Soviets."

4006. Renfro, Robert. "Three American Novelists at War: The World War II Journalism of Steinbeck, Caldwell, & Hemingway." U of Texas, Austin, 1984. 217. DAI 46 (1985) 289-A.
The writers "set aside" their novelist's goal of "telling the whole truth whatever the cost," because of press censorship, the "peculiar 'objectivity' of working newsmen, and the mood of the country."

4007. Richman, David. "CIA Silences a Whistle Blower." HR 10.1 (Winter 1982) 24-27, 48-52.
Condemns the censorship of Frank Snepp's Decent Interval by the CIA.

4008. Robinson, Michael J., and Ray Olszewski. "Books in the Marketplace of Ideas." JoC 30.2 (1980) 81-88.
An economic look at how consolidation at the levels of distribution and production, in addition to media mergers, makes it difficult for new authors and book publishers to provide diverse alternatives in an established market.

4009. Rosebury, Theodor. "Salesman for Chemical & Biological Warfare." MO 6.10 (Oct. 1964) 20.
Analyzes Tomorrow's Weapons--Chemical and Biological by Brig. Gen. J.H. Rothschild (Ret.), who "extols chemical warfare as humane, and biological warfare as desirable."

4010. Rubin, Trudy. "Stalking Beacon Press." MORE 2.9 (Sept. 1972) 5-7.
Decries government investigation of Beacon for publishing the Pentagon Papers.

4011. Safire, William. "CBS, Time Ignore Press Freedom in Effort to Suppress Book." AG (Oct. 29, 1986) 17A.
The attempted censorship of a book by Renata Adler on General Sharon's libel suit against Time.

4012. Schaar, John. "Review of Diana Trilling's We Must March My Darlings." Legitimacy in the Modern State. New Brunswick: Transaction, 1981. 39-98.
Explains the reactionary perspectives of the book, her lack of knowledge that "this society is ruled by elites of power." Takes apart the logic of her blaming anti-anticommunists for McCarthyism.

4013. Schiller, Herbert, and Anita Schiller. "Libraries, Public Access to Information, and Commerce." The Political Economy of Information. Ed. Vincent Mosco

and Janet Wasko. Madison: U of Wisconsin P, 1988. 146-166.
The steadily expanding commercialization of information is extending even into libraries and is threatening the fundamental principle of free access to information for a democracy.

4014. Schulzinger, Robert. The Wise Men of Foreign Affairs: The History of the Council on Foreign Affairs. New York: Columbia UP, 1984. 326.
This Council is part of the national security system.

4015. The Shelter Hoax and Foreign Policy. New York: Marzani, 1961. 96.
Critical of the Pentagon's 1962 pamphlet on fallout protection.

4016. "Snepp v. United States: The CIA Secrecy Agreement and the First Amendment." CLR 81.3 (Apr. 1980) 662-706.
CIA prior-approval requirement for publications undermines the First Amendment.

4017. Stone, I.F. "Biography as Facial Surgery." In a Time of Torment. New York: Random House, 1967. 46-50.
Review of William S. White's biography, The Professional: Lyndon B. Johnson (1964), one of five campaign "pseudo biographies" "tailored to the man's enormous vanity and to his need for a new liberal look."

4018. Stone, I.F. "How the Government Secretly Subsidizes Books as Foreign Policy Propaganda." IFSW 14.32 (Oct. 17, 1966) 3.
USIA pays for books controlled "from the very idea down to the final edited manuscript."

4019. Stone, I.F. "A Louis XIV--In All But Style." In a Time of Torment. New York: Random House, 1967. 62-68.
Review of Theodore White's The Making of the President: 1964, a "mawkish" and excessively flattering book. "To be able to write these books [White also wrote The Making of the President: 1960], and to get them serialized in Life magazine, White had to join the Establishment and to be circumspect about the deeper insights of which he is capable" (64).

4020. Taylor, Terri. "U.S. Customs Seizes Iran Books." ORK (Summer 1982) 18-19.
The FBI confiscated books the author bought in Iran and interrogated him.

4021. Tebbel, John. Between Covers: The Rise and Transformation of Book Publishing in America. New York: Oxford UP, 1987. 514.
A history mainly of trade publishing, a shortened version of the original four-volume work. Pp. 452-461 deal with censorship from 1940s to the present. "The struggle for freedom to read and view has never been more intense than from 1940 to

PRINT MEDIA

the present" (452).

4022. "Warmongering: Council on Foreign Relations." CS 5.4 (1981) 25-27.
Criticizes the CFR's The Soviet Challenge (paid for by the Ford Foundation) for its call to "unrestrained intervention."

4023. Weiner, Jon. "Inside the Nixon Library." Na 251.7 (Sept. 10, 1990) 242-246.
"The $21 million Nixon Library" "takes visitors on a twisted trip down memory lane . . . . the effort made here to reshape popular memory is more sweeping, more relentless, more sophisticated and more expensive than that undertaken by any other President."

4024. Whiteside, Thomas. The Blockbuster Complex: Conglomerates, Show Business and Book Publishing. Middletown, CT: Wesleyan UP, 1981. 207.
The last two decades of publishing have conspired to focus greater and greater emphasis on the few big money-makers the industry produces every season, and consequently to exclude from publication the aesthetically venturesome books that should be as important as profit.

4025. Williams, John. "Prior Restraints." Na 246.16 (Apr. 23, 1988) 574-577.
On racism in book publishing companies that results in censorship of Afro-Americans.

4026. Wilson, R. Jackson. Figures of Speech: American Writers and the Literary Marketplace, From Benjamin Franklin to Emily Dickinson. New York: Knopf, 1989. 295.
A "critique of bourgeois writers for adopting the individualist ethos of capitalism, and of capitalism for destroying earlier communal relations between writers and audiences." The "figure of radical selfhood through which writers adapted to the marketplace in some measure mirrors the very free enterprise and cash nexus they wanted to appear as opposing" (from review). [See my bibliographies in BoB (Oct.-Dec. 1973 and Jan.-Mar. 1980)].

II. D. 6. PRINT MEDIA: GOVERNMENT AND CORPORATE REPORTS (4027-4126)

This section even more than others offers merely illustrations of a kind of media control greatly needing research: State Department reports, commission reports, think tank reports, etc., all are under-studied as discourses of the corporate state.

4027. Ajemian, Peter, and Joan Claybrook. Deceiving the Public: The Story Behind J. Peter Grace and His Campaign. Washington, DC: Public Citizen, 1985. 110.

The Grace Commission's (eliminate waste) task force on the EPA was stacked with representatives of the industries regulated by the agency, including 20 criminal companies. Predictably, the group recommended lower quality regulation. Grace's own company is a major environmental polluter. [Commission reports are sometimes rituals of mystification in support of some administration's challenged policy or part of a politics of reassurance during crises, or attempts to cover up and avert questions about deeper individual and institutional crimes.]

4028. Anderson, Jack. "Overcrowding Woes: Prisons a Tough Chore for Bush." NAT (Jan. 26, 1989) 4.
A report on prison overcrowding was kept secret because it showed the shortcomings of the Reagan administration.

4029. Andregg, Michael. Low Intensity Conflict at the Hubert H. Humphrey Institute: A Report About Spies and Related Problems. Minneapolis, MN: Ground Zero MN, 1989. 32.
Investigates the Humphrey Institute's support of US interventionism.

4030. Andres, Monica. "The Quality of Censorship: What the CIA Defines as Damaging to the National Security." FP 5.7 (1980) 6-7.
Condemns CIA power to censor publications.

4031. Apple, Michael. "Producing Inequality: Ideology and Economy in the National Reports on Education." Practice 4.3 (Winter 1986) 70-94.
The military-industrial complex dominates high-level educational reports. The Report of the National Commission on Excellence in Education, A Nation at Risk, expresses President Reagan's education values. The reports are "as much political as they are educational documents," and their language requires rhetorical analysis (76). [See II.F.].

4032. Arnove, Robert E., ed. Philanthropy and Cultural Imperialism: The Foundations at Home and Abroad. Boston, MA: G.K. Hall, 1980. 473.
Foundations like the Carnegie, Rockefeller, and Ford foundations help maintain an economic and political order benefiting the ruling-class.

4033. Bartimole, Roldo. "Smokescreen Commission Tries to Polish UA, Manages Only to Tarnish Itself." PoV 3.17 (Mar. 8-13, 1971) 1-2.
The Cleveland Commission on Health and Social Service "was created by elites" to save the "United Appeal hoax" and themselves money by pretending to solve problems.

4034. Belle, William Van, and Paul Claes. "The Logic of Deterrence: A Semiotic and Psychoanalytic Approach." Language and the Nuclear Arms Debate: Nukespeak

PRINT MEDIA 551

Today. London and Dover, NH: Frances Pinter, 1985. 91-102.
The semiotic theory of A.J. Greimas and the psychoanalytic theory of J. Lacan are employed to explain the "narrative" of NATO deterrence and mirror image policies.

4035. Bennett, James R. "Managing Consensus: The Presidential Commission As an Indictment for Bureaucratic Policy Control." NPS 16-17 (Fall-Winter 1989) 155-178.
Rhetorical study of the biased Report of the National Bipartisan Commission on Central America (January 1984), chaired by Henry Kissinger, written as part of President Reagan's mobilization of support for his unpopular Central American policies. Calls for commissions which represent all sides of an issue.

4036. Bennett, Jonathan A. "Shuttlescam Story Still Buried." Guard 39.17 (1987) 8, 19.
The Rogers Commission, appointed to investigate the Challenger disaster, conspired with NASA officials to cover up the agency's decision to launch the space shuttle in low temperatures despite warnings from Morton Thiokol engineers.

4037. Berman, Edward H. The Ideology of Philanthropy: The Influence of the Carnegie, Ford, and Rockefeller Foundations on American Foreign Policy. Albany: State U of New York P, 1983. 227.
Explains foundations as partners in US foreign policy determination and cogs in state capitalism's support system.

4038. Blachman, Morris. "The Stupidity of Intelligence." Inside the System: A "Washington Monthly" Reader. Ed. Charles Peters and Timothy Adams. New York: Praeger, 1970. 271-79.
Explains why and how Air Force bombing reports in Vietnam were falsified.

4039. Burns, E. Bradford. "The Kissinger Report: Visions of History Through Alice's Looking Glass." LASAF 15 (Spring 1984) 13-15.
Kissinger's report on Central America is pervaded with the biases of the Reagan administration.

4040. Carfagno, Jacalyn. "Report Card Given on Annual Reports." AG (Aug. 16, 1988) 1C.
Sid Cato, author of "Sid Cato's Newsletter on Annual [Corporate] Reports," charged that "'some companies lie through their teeth' in reports to stockholders."

4041. Chace, James. Endless War: How We Got Involved in Central America and What Can Be Done. New York: Vintage, 1984. 144.
Questions the validity of the Kissinger Report (80-93).

4042. Cockburn, Alexander. "Their White Paper . . . and Ours." Corruptions of Empire. London: Verso,

1987. 282-83.
A response to a US State Department report on El Salvador guerrillas.

4043. Coffin, Tristram. "John Adams' Ghost, Richard Nixon's Revenge." WS 1.20 (Nov. 1, 1975) 1-4.
Senate Bill 1 (S-1) reflects the "paranoia of power" that grips the government. It will be an instrument for repression.

4044. Cohen, Warren. "Stop Falsifying U.S. History." Campus Watch 2.2 (Fall 1990) 6-8.
A critique of the State Department's recent volume on Iran, 1952-1954, which "grossly misinterpreted" US complicity in the overthrow of Prime Minister Mossadegh.

4045. Cohn, Carol. "Sex and Death in the Rational World of Defense Intellectuals." Signs 12.4 (1987) 687-718. (Abbr. version "Slick'ems, Glick'ems, Christmas Trees, and Cookie Cutters: Nuclear Language and How We Learned to Pat the Bomb." BAS [June 1987] 17-24).
The men (almost exclusively) who create and maintain the theory of US nuclear strategy are extraordinarily removed from reality by their "technostrategic" language. Not only is their world unreal but it is non-accountable.

4046. Cook, Richard. "The Challenger Report: A Critical Analysis of the Report to the President of the Presidential Commission on the Space Shuttle Challenger Accident." King George, VA: n.p., 1986. 137.
Condemns the Rogers Commission report on the Challenger shuttle disaster. (Condensed version WM 18.10 [Nov. 1986] 13-21).

4047. Critchlow, Donald T. The Brookings Institution, 1916-1952: Expertise and the Public Interest in a Democratic Society. DeKalb, IL: Northern Illinois UP, 1985. 247.
Analyzes the policies and discourses of this think tank in its relations with elite groups and capitalist ideology. Its opposition to the National Recovery Administration, Keynesian economics, and national health insurance, and support for the founding of the U.N. and extension of Social Security benefit payments place it in the middle to conservative orbit.

4048. Diamond, Sara, and Richard Hatch. "Operation Peace Institute." Z 3.7-8 (July-Aug. 1990) 110-116.
Explains how establishment, conservative, and military perspectives have gained control of the federally funded US Institute of Peace (USIP).

4049. "Doublespeak and Iran Air Flight 655." QRD 15.2 (Jan. 1989) 10-11.
Focuses on the inconsistencies and absurdities of the US Navy's report on the downing of an Iranian airliner by the USS Vincennes.

PRINT MEDIA

4050. Dye, Thomas. "Organizing Power for Policy Planning: The View from the Brookings Institution." Power Elites and Organizations. Ed. G. William Domhoff and Thomas Dye. Newbury Park, CA: Sage, 1987. 169-188.
A historical and ideological analysis of Brookings as contrasted to the American Enterprise Institute and the Heritage Foundation. Think tanks are an important part of the "highly structured set of relations" of the corporate state.

4051. "Education and Economics." Ed 36 (Oct. 1975) 10-19.
Several articles, e.g., "The Great American Dream Freeze": "The objective of the Carnegie Commission" is to "restructure higher education to reproduce the class structure as it is." Also: Frank Darknell, "The Carnegie Corporation: Directing Higher Education."

4052. Elias, Thomas. "President Reagan's Think Tanks Have a Plan for the Media." Pr 9.3 (Apr. 1981) 4.
On the Institute for Contemporary Studies and the Claremont Economic Institute.

4053. Engelhardt, Tom. "Love Bytes: Rhetorical Hacks and the Rhetoric Hackers." ITT 13.13 (Feb. 15-21, 1989) 18.
Satirical fantasy that Bush speechwriter Peggy Noonan does not exist, and Bush's speeches are written by a cliché computer.

4054. Epstein, Joshua. The 1987 Defense Budget. Washington, DC: Brookings Inst., 1986. 61.
Because the annual military budget is partly ideological advocacy and always geopolitically and technically disputable, the Brookings Institution publishes an annual analysis.

4055. Feld, Bernard T. "On 'Soviet Military Power.'" TR 85 (Jan. 1982) 63.
The Pentagon's annual assessment of Soviet Military Power is misleading.

4056. Fisher, Donald. "American Philanthropy and the Social Sciences: The Reproduction of a Conservative Ideology." Philanthropy and Cultural Imperialism. Ed. Robert Arnove. Boston: Hall, 1980. 233-268.
Explains the Rockefeller Foundation's contribution to maintaining class inequality in Britain.

4057. Garai, Josef. "The Psychopathology of the U.S. Position on a Nuclear Test Ban." MO 5.6 (June 1963) 9-12.
US paranoia regarding the SU is revealed in the Khrushchev-Kennedy correspondence about inspection sites.

4058. Gavshon, Arthur. "The Power and Influence Behind America's Right." MGW (Dec. 1, 1985) 9.
The power of the Heritage Foundation in pushing the nation rightward.

4059. Gervasi, Tom. "Soviet Military Power": The Pentagon's Propaganda Document, Annotated and Corrected. New York: Vintage Books, 1988. 159.

Analyzes the Pentagon's annual mendacious evaluation of Soviet military power, the purpose of which is to support another massive increase in military spending. It is part of the Pentagon's constant propaganda campaign to expand US military power.

4060. Ginsburg, Carl. Race and Media: The Enduring Life of the Moynihan Report. New York: Institute for Media Analysis, 1989. 100.

The condition of Blacks in America is still deeply affected by Daniel Patrick Moynihan's 1965 Labor Department report, "The Negro Family: The Case for National Action." The report called for "benign neglect" of the victims, and its legacy has permeated both the government and the major institutions of this country, not least the media, in consequence of which Blacks have become increasingly impoverished.

4061. "The Great American Dream Freeze." Ed 36 (Oct. 1975) 12-13.

The Carnegie Commission's report on higher education will help maintain the present class structure.

4062. Green, Stephen. "Questioning Pentagon Authority." CSM 81.171 (July 31, 1989) 19.

Examines the Pentagon's annual report entitled Soviet Military Power, "which hypes Soviet weapons systems in order to justify greater US weapons spending."

4063. Hall, Earl. "Mein Kampf Translated? The Ultra-Right Parallels Pre-Hitler Days in Germany." Chm 199 (Jan. 1985) 6-7.

Analyzes Mandate for Leadership II by the Heritage Foundation.

4064. Hatch, Richard, and Sara Diamond. "The World Without War Council." CAIB 31 (Winter 1989) 61.

Ostensibly an organization dedicated to world peace, the publications of the World Without War Council are in fact a conduit for US intelligence agencies, enabling them to propagandize the public concerning Central America and other issues.

4065. Hayter, Teresa. Aid As Imperialism. Baltimore, MA: Penguin, 1971. 222.

Appendix gives an account of the censorship of her study of the relationship between the World Bank and Latin America, because she traced the policy and process of leverage.

4066. Hester, Hugh. "Presidential Rhetoric & Presidential Action." MO 5.8 (Aug. 1963) 7-8.

"Hints by Mr. Kennedy of relatively conciliatory changes in foreign policy are drowned in torrents of bellicose language"

PRINT MEDIA

in his commencement address at American U in Washington on June 10th.

4067. Hitchens, Christopher. "Minority Report." Na 250.11 (Mar. 19, 1990) 370.
Appraises Establishment Kremlinology.

4068. Holden, Constance. "Heritage Foundation: Court Philosophers." Science 211.4486 (Mar. 6, 1981) 1019-1020.
"Conservative think tank feeds new [Reagan] Administration with continuous menu of ideologically palatable reports."

4069. Horowitz, David, and David Kolodney. "The Foundations: Charity Begins at Home." Ram 7.11 (Apr. 1969) 38-48.
On the importance of foundations to ruling power.

4070. Howe, Barbara. "The Emergence of Scientific Philanthropy, 1900-1920: Origins, Issues and Outcomes." Philanthropy and Cultural Imperialism. Ed. Robert Arnove. Boston: G.K. Hall, 1980. 25-54.
Examines the Walsh Commission hearings of 1915 about the power of foundations as instruments of corporate capitalism.

4071. Jaffe, Louis. "American Education And International Tensions (1949)." HER 20 (Winter 1950) 1-10.
Rejects a commission report that advocates national security and Cold War policies for public education.

4072. Judis, John B. "One Thousand More Points of Rhetoric." ITT 14.12 (Feb. 7-13, 1990) 3.
The budget report for fiscal year 1991 "represents a continuation of the Reagan administration's policy of increasing military expenditures and reducing social expenditures."

4073. Kidder, Rushworth. "Ideas Rain from Brainstorms in Think Tanks." RMN (Oct. 21, 1984) 83 (from the CSM).
On the large number of right-wing to conservative research organizations.

4074. Kiester, Sally. "New Influence for Stanford's Hoover Institution." Cg 13.7 (1981) 46-50.
The anticommunist business-supported Hoover has increasing influence.

4075. Kimery, Anthony. "Creative Editing at the State Department." ITT 13.18 (Mar. 29-Apr. 4, 1989) 5.
The Department's annual human rights report to Congress, Country Reports on Human Rights Practices, significantly and secretly altered Embassy reports--the bases of the final report--to play down "human rights abuses of U.S. allies." The original reports were classified to keep the falsifications from the public.

4076. Klare, Michael. "Building a Fortress America." Na 240.11 (Mar. 23, 1985) 321, 337-9.

The Pentagon's 1986 budget request is alarmist, Soviet-phobic, and interventionist.

4077. Lemann, Nicholas. "Defense Budget Games." NR 192.5 (Feb. 4, 1985) 16-18.
The Pentagon budget is deceitful.

4078. LeoGrande, William. "Through the Looking Glass: The Kissinger Report on Central America." WPJ (Winter 1984) 252-84.
Criticizes the falsities of the report.

4079. Linenthal, Edward. "War & Sacrifice in the Nuclear Age: The Committee on the Present Danger & the Renewal of Martial Enthusiasm." A Shuddering Dawn: Religious Studies in the Nuclear Age. Ed. Ira Chernus & Edward Linenthal. Albany: State U of New York P, 1989. 20-32.
Compares the ideas, writings, and strategies of the rightwing Committee for the Present Danger with those of Physicians for Social Responsibility.

4080. Lockwood, Dunbar. "Grudging Kindness, Gentle Exaggeration." BAS 45.10 (Dec. 1989) 4-5.
On the inaccuracies of the 1989 edition of the Pentagon's Soviet Military Power.

4081. Lutz, William. "Doublespeak, Accounting, and the Annual Report." QRD 9.4 (1983) 1-2.
The doublespeak of corporate annual reports.

4082. Marshall, Jonathan, Peter Scott, and Jane Hunter. The Iran-Contra Connection: Secret Teams & Covert Operations in the Reagan Era. Boston: South End, 1987. 313.
Corrects The Tower Commission Report, which offered "mystification" and "the politics of reassurance." "Contrary to the Tower presentation, the Iran-Contra connections were not anomalous expressions of U.S. foreign policy"; rather, they represent "a frightening, shocking story that shakes the foundations of the republic" (Preface vii-viii).

4083. "The Masotti Report or 'Neville's Novel.'" PoV (Aug. 11-17, 1989) n.p. (special issue).
A report by the Case-Western Reserve Civil Violence Center on a shoot-out between police and black militants was rewritten by a writer hired by the President's Commission on the Causes and Prevention of Violence, Anthony Neville. Neville's version, blaming the blacks, bore little resemblance to the original report.

4084. McCartney, James. "Pentagon's Obsession Fades," Budget Remains." AG (Oct. 1, 1989) 4C.
Although the Pentagon's 1989 Soviet Military Power praises Gorbachev and the word "threat" has been removed from the

cover, the book continues to defend a high and sacrosanct budget.

4085. McShane, Joseph. "Winthrop's 'City Upon a Hill' in Recent Political Discourse." America 159.8 (Oct. 1, 1988) 194-98.
How recent presidents have used John Winthrop's 1630 Puritan sermon "Model of Christian Charity." Winthrop celebrated God's election of the US as the second chosen people, but he emphasized equally their rigorous accountability. In the 1988 party conventions Mr. Dukakis focused upon community and love for unfortunates, mercy and justice, while, following President Reagan, Mr. Bush concentrated on the nation's external mission to light the world.

4086. Merbaum, Richard. "RAND: Technocrats and Power." NUT 3 (Dec.-Jan. 1963-64) 45-57.
On the military orientation of the Rand Corporation.

4087. Moglen, Helene. "Erosion in the Humanities: Blowing the Dust from Our Eyes." Profession 83. New York: MLA, 1983. 1-6.
The report of the National Commission on Excellence in Education, entitled A Nation at Risk, is "intensely nationalistic," stressing "mastery and competition," military and marketplace metaphors appropriate to the commission's sense of the country involved "in a deadly technological and economic war" with enemies abroad.

4088. Montgomery, Peter. "Official History." CC 16.5 (Nov.-Dec. 1990) 8.
The State Department's publication Iran, 1952-1954 is flawed by crucial omissions and by misinformation.

4089. Moss, Peter. "Rhetoric of Defence in the United States: Language, Myth, & Ideology." Language & the Nuclear Arms Debate: Nukespeak Today. Ed. Paul Chilton. London & Dover, NH: Pinter, 1985. 45-64.
Analysis of a speech by President Reagan, the armed services magazine SSAM, the discourse of post-nuclear survivalism, pseudonyms given to nuclear weapons, and the language of annual reports from the Pentagon show how language selection marginalizes dissent.

4090. Muro, Mark. "Heritage Redefines Think Tanks." AG (Feb. 23, 1986) 1C.
On the right-wing Heritage Foundation.

4091. Naureckas, Jim. "Drugs and the Contras: Washington Looks the Other Way." ITT 13.22 (Apr. 26-May 2, 1989) 5.
Reveals how Congressional reports are compromised. Sen. John Kerry's subcommittee on narcotics, terrorism and international operations report on contra drug smuggling and other examples of US "tolerance of narcotics trafficking" was

obstructed by "administration stonewalling" and other "political sabotage."

4092. Newberry, Mike. "The Head Hunters." MO 7.3 (Mar. 1965) 7-9.
Right-wing organizations and publications flourish in the US.

4093. Nichols, John Spicer. "The Power of the Anti-Fidel Lobby." Na 247.11 (Oct. 24, 1988) 389-392.
The Cuban American National Foundation, partly supported by public funds, attacks Castro through lobbying and reports.

4094. Noble, David. "Corporatist Culture Ministries: The Foundation Trap." Na 232.11 (Mar. 21, 1981) 321, 336-340.
Culture is a contested terrain over world views in which conservative agencies are gaining power. Focuses upon the German Marshall Fund of the United States and the National Humanities Center, both of which "participate in a concerted cultural offensive of multinational corporatism."

4095. Ott, George. "Now It's a 'Naval Gap.'" Prog 42.9 (1978) 22-24.
The Navy exaggerates the Soviet naval threat in order to inflate its own budget.

4096. Packard, Frank. "Literature as Big Business." BT (Fall 1980) 8-12.
Expresses anxiety that the growth of conglomerate ownership of book publishing with its profit orientation will decrease the number of aesthetically excellent books.

4097. Peschek, Joseph. Policy Planning Organizations: Elite Agendas and America's Rightward Turn. Philadelphia: Temple UP, 1987. 288.
Elites run the nation, and think tanks and foundations are apparatuses of elite power. Peschek studies five policy groups: The Brookings Institution, The Trilateral Commission, The American Enterprise Institute, The Heritage Foundation, and The Institute for Contemporary Studies.

4098. Pike, John. "Soviet Military Power, 1983, Illustrated Disinformation." CS 7 (June-Aug. 1983) 21-2.
This annual report is part of the Reagan administration's propaganda campaign against the SU.

4099. Piller, Charles. "Lethal Lies About Fatal Diseases." Na 247.8 (Oct. 3, 1988) 271-75.
The US Army lied when it said in a 1977 report that no one was harmed during its biological warfare testing program of the 1950s and 1960s at the Dugway Proving Grounds near Salt Lake City.

4100. Polluting the Censorship Debate: A Summary and Critique

of the Final Report of the Attorney General's Commission on Pornography. Washington, DC: ACLU, July 1986. 188.
The Commission has "polluted the debate over sexually explicit materials and censorship."

4101. "The RAND Papers." Ram 11 (Nov. 1972) 25-42, 52-62.
Examines Rand Corporation support of US Vietnam policies.

4102. "Reagan Ideology Sneaks in Through the Back Door." PC (Sept.-Oct. 1988) 7.
Reagan's use of powerful executive orders to circumvent Congress and the courts.

4103. Rice, Berkeley. "The Cold War College Think Tanks." WM 1.5 (June 1969) 22-34.
Discloses the close connection among corporations, the Nixon administration, hardline military policies, and research institutes at Stanford, Georgetown, and Philadelphia.

4104. Rothmyer, Karen. "Citizen Scaife." CJR 20.2 (July-Aug. 1981) 41-50.
On the tremendous financial support to right-wing causes provided by Richard Mellon Scaife.

4105. Sanders, Jerry. "Terminators." MJ 10 (Aug.-Sept. 1985) 36-40.
A survey of right-wing think tanks and foundations--the Heritage Foundation, etc.

4106. Shoup, Laurence, and William Minter. Imperial Brain Trust: The Council on Foreign Relations and United States Foreign Policy. New York: Monthly Review, 1977. 334. Foreword by G. William Domhoff.
Shows "through close analysis of hitherto little-noticed position papers, memos, and personal letters how the most sophisticated corporate capitalists of the thirties and forties used the Council on Foreign Relations to develop an aggressive and expansionist foreign policy for the post-World War II era." (Domhoff vii). In "The Council and the Media" the authors show the close relationships between the Council and NYT, WP, Newsweek, Time, CBS and NBC, and the leading magazine in foreign affairs, Foreign Affairs, is published by the Council (66-68).

4107. Smith, Philip. "Who Is Who at the Think Tanks." Pr 10.3 (June 1982) 22-25.
Discusses the four major right-wing to middle-of-the-road research institutes--Heritage, American Enterprise, Hoover, and Brookings.

4108. Stern, Sol. "The Defense Intellectuals." Ram 5.8 (Feb. 1967) 31-37.
Analyzes Rand Corporation's Cold War and Vietnam reports.

4109. Stone, I.F. "The Corruption of Scholarship by Our Well-Heeled Intelligence Establishment." IFSW 14.15 (Apr. 18, 1966) 3.
A CIA agent published in Foreign Affairs was not identified as having a conflict of interest.

4110. Stone, I.F. "The Fatal Lure of World Dominion." IFSW 13.18 (May 10, 1965) 1-2.
Army research projects related to world hegemony are more examples of the advancing military invasion of the State Dept.

4111. Stone, I.F. "From Mink to General Motors." IFSW 1.2 (Jan. 24, 1953) 1.
President Eisenhower's Inaugural Address was packed with clichés and generalities and nothing concrete about civil liberties or negotiations with the SU.

4112. Stone, I.F. "Half Barry Goldwater, Half Billy Graham." IFSW 13.15 (Apr. 19, 1965) 1-2.
President Johnson's speech at Baltimore exhibits his "genius at sleight of hand" in its combination of fierce hawkishness and Christian piety.

4113. Stone, I.F. "Ho Chi Johnson Mobilizes Little Old New Asia." In a Time of Torment. New York: Random House, 1967. 68-70.
A conference in Manila, which produced three lengthy pronunciamentoes, was a campaign ploy, and the documents based peace negotiations upon unconditional surrender.

4114. Stone, I.F. "How the State Dept. Tried to Explain Away the Use of 'Non-Lethal' Gases." IFSW 13.12 (Mar. 29, 1965) 2.
State Dept. cant and obfuscation of US violation of the Geneva Convention of 1925.

4115. Stone, I.F. "John Foster Dulles: Portrait of a Liberator." IFSW 1.2 (Jan. 24, 1953) 2.
Dulles' "prevarications" are "highly polished," while his real views on foreign policy are masked, especially his former pro-Axis sympathies and his hatred of the New Deal and social reform.

4116. Stone, I.F. The Killings at Kent State: How Murder Went Unpunished. New York: NY Review/Random, 1971. 158.
Attacks the Commission on Campus Unrest report for not exposing those responsible for the killings at Kent State.

4117. Stone, I.F. "Lyndon Johnson's Bay of Pigs." IFSW 14.2 (Jan. 17, 1966) 1, 4.
Analyzes Johnson's State of the Union and Johns Hopkins messages and the Mansfield Report on Vietnam.

4118. Stone, I.F. "On National Defense, Space and Foreign Policy the New G.O.P. Platform Reads as if Written by

PRINT MEDIA

General Dynamics for a New Arms Race." IFSW 16.17 (Aug. 19, 1968) 2-3.
The Republican Platform reflects the military industrial complex.

4119. Stone, I.F. "On Pentagon Propaganda About the U.S. Becoming a Second Rate Power." IFSW 19.19 (Nov. 15, 1971) 3.
The Pentagon disseminated the falsehood that the US had inadequate defense "to prepare the way for a bigger arms budget next year."

4120. Stone, I.F. "Time to Get a New Secretary of State." IFSW 13.30 (Sept. 20, 1965) 1-4.
Secretary Dean Rusk's ideas and writings have been consistently wrong and deceptive.

4121. Stone, I.F. "A Reply to the White Paper." IFSW 13.9 (Mar. 8, 1965) 1-2, 4. (Rpt. In a Time of Torment).
The State Department's report on North Vietnam support of South Vietnam guerrillas "withholds all evidence which points to a civil war" and does not mention US violations of the 1954 Geneva accords regarding unifying the country.

4122. Stone, I.F. "Mr. Truman's Farewell Evasions." IFSW 1.1 (Jan. 17, 1953) 1.
Truman doubletalked in his Farewell Address: a nuclear war was unthinkable, yet he refuses to negotiate with the Soviets except on our terms, etc.

4123. Tinker, Tony, Cheryl Lehman, and Marilyn Neimark. "Bookkeeping for Capitalism: The Mystery of Accounting for Unequal Exchange." The Political Economy of Information. Ed. Vincent Mosco and Janet Wasko. Madison: U of Wisconsin P, 1988. 188-216.
The essay studies 1) 40 years of financial statements by one multinational, 2) 60 years of General Motors annual reports, and 3) literary and research discourses published in professional journals. These three kinds of discourses are part of the capitalist state's "ideological apparatus for producing the social cohesion needed for capital accumulation."

4124. Tulis, Jeffrey, K. The Rhetorical Presidency. Princeton, NJ: Princeton UP, 1987. 209.
The promise of popular leadership is a "profound development in American politics," in contrast to the anti-rhetorical nineteenth century. Ch. 2 treats The Federalist papers, which proscribed popular leadership. Ch. 3 discusses the nineteenth century under the influence of Federalist theory, etc. Ch. 7 discusses general issues and Ronald Reagan's rhetoric.

4125. Zahn, Curtis. "Some Maverick Notes on the Disarmament Image." MO 6.1 (Jan. 1964) 28-29.
Analyzes the "more flagrant rationalizations" in a booklet entitled Arms Control and Disarmament by the Arms Control and

Disarmament Agency.

4126. Zinn, Howard, and Noam Chomsky, eds. The Pentagon Papers: Critical Essays. The Senator Gravel Edition, Vol. V. Boston: Beacon, 1972. 341 + 72.
Fifteen essays, a note on the three editions of the Papers, the Tonkin Gulf narrative and resolutions, and the indices and glossary for Vols. I-IV of the Gravel Edition. "The Media and the Message" by James Aronson (41-59) denounces the media for failing to "stand united in an adversary role to the government --the only proper stance for a free press in a democracy" (58).

II. E. ART AND MUSIC (4127-4171)

II. E. 1. ART (4127-4146)

4127. Berger, Arthur Asa. "Politics in the Comics." Television as an Instrument of Terror. New Brunswick, NJ: Transaction, 1980. 39-51.
Offers "a theory of the common man as found in comics" which follows the two main themes of his book: the abandoned child and rebel.

4128. Berger, Arthur Asa. The Comic-Stripped American: What Dick Tracy, Blondie, Daddy Warbucks, and Charlie Brown Tell Us About Ourselves. Baltimore, MD: Penguin, 1974. 225.
Groups three generations of comic strips (1900-20, 1920-60, 1960-present) as they reflect changes in national perspectives, fears, and archetypes.

4129. Cascone, Charles. "Comics: Society's Mirror, Part I." Aquarian (May 30-June 13, 1974) 10-11.
Commercial comics usually reflect society at any particular time--sexism, anti-Nazis, racism, anti-communism, etc. But Wonder Woman extolled women and Walt Kelley depicted Sen. Joseph McCarthy as a pig.

4130. Doss, Erika. "The Art of Cultural Politics: From Regionalism to Abstract Expressionism." Recasting America: Culture and Politics in the Age of Cold War. Ed. Lary May. Chicago: U of Chicago P, 1989. 195-220.
Studies the "radical shift in art" from that of Thomas Hart Benton's social realism to that of Jackson Pollock's abstract expressionism. Pollock's art, which expressed "personal anxieties," was politically appropriate for the Cold War purpose of promoting US "freedom" in "direct opposition to the Soviet Union's style of social realism." "Despite the aims of both men, their art was used for other purposes, to support commercial, political, and social ideologies that neither subscribed to" (216).

4131. Guilbaut, Serge. How New York Stole the Idea of Modern

ART AND MUSIC

Art: Abstract Expressionism, Freedom, and the Cold War. Chicago: U of Chicago P, 1983. 277.
"Faced with the annihilation of the individual in the totalitarian regimes and with the absorption of the individual into the mass of consumers in the capitalist regimes, the American left tried to stake out a middle ground from which the individual painter or artist could assert his independence of both left and right" (198).

4132. Haacke, Hans. Hans Haacke: Unfinished Business. Cambridge: MIT P, 1986. 303.
"Museums, Managers of Consciousness": Arts museums have been transformed into "public relations agents for the interests of big business and its ideological allies."

4133. Kelley, Kevin J. "Exposing the Hypocrisy of Art for Corporate Sake." Guard 39.16 (Jan. 21, 1987) 20, 17.
The increasing function of the large urban art museum is "to serve as a fancy setting for corporate promotions and to reinforce historical and political ignorance."

4134. Kennedy, Pagan. "P.C. Comics." Na 250.11 (Mar. 19, 1990) 386-389.
Some comics offer alternative perspectives, because they are produced by single individuals; the comic book is "inherently subversive."

4135. Lippard, Lucy R. "At the Eye of the Storm." Z 2.10 (Oct. 1989) 70-76.
Analyzes how the "Far Right agenda has trickled down to the arts" in attempts to control the Natl. Endowment for the Arts.

4136. Lippard, Lucy. "General Strike!" Zeta (Z) (Sept. 1988) 66-68.
The comic magazine World War 3 Illustrated (1980-) has provided "a microcosm for connected global struggles" and "the counter-history of the Reagan administration."

4137. Lumley, Robert, ed. The Museum Time-Machine: Putting Cultures on Display. London: Routledge, 1988. 241.
Examines the role of museums in representing their society's history, which is now widely debated. US discussed only in a few pages.

4138. Mattick, Paul, Jr. "Arts and the State." Na 251.10 (Oct. 1, 1990) 348-58.
"The N.E.A. reflects the state's responsibility for aspects of the good life not taken care of by market forces," and "the struggle is against the right-wing agenda itself." (See in same number: Bruce Shapiro, "Prudery and Power: From Comstockery to Helmsmanship").

4139. Mooney, Michael. The Ministry of Culture: Connections Among Art, Money, and Politics. New York: Wyndham, 1980. 427.

The federal government uses the arts to indoctrinate the people.

4140. Peterson, Deborah. "Corporate Sponsorship of the Arts: Texaco & the Metropolitan." Paper, 68th Speech Comm. Assoc. Convention, Louisville, KY, 1982.
As part of a panel on "Who Decides What You Get," this paper examines the dynamics of corporate control of arts programming via sponsorship. (Summary in CP 4.4 [Jan. 1983]).

4141. Phifer, Gregg, and Thomas R. King. "Do the Comics Go Too Far?" FSY 24 (1985) 59-66.
Focuses on comic strips as controversial speech, offering highlights of Doonesbury's run-ins with editors and public figures and the fracas over Beetle Bailey's Miss Buxley, along with a short history of comic censorship in general.

4142. Polan, Dana. "Brief Encounters: Mass Culture & the Evacuation of Sense." Studies in Entertainment. Ed. Tania Modleski. Bloomington: Indiana UP, 1986. 167-187.
Applies the kind of analysis Barthes developed in S/Z to a "Blondie" comic strip as part of his argument that some mass art employs deconstructive nonrealist techniques.

4143. Schiller, Herbert. "The Museum as Corporate Showcase." Culture, Inc. New York: Oxford UP, 1989. 91-98.
Museums of the arts are adjuncts of the consciousness industry in the service of corporations, while appearing to be a public resource and site of creativity.

4144. Schiller, Herbert. "Pitchers at an Exhibition." Na 249.2 (July 10, 1989) 37, 55-57.
The nation's museums are increasingly dependent on corporate sponsorship of exhibitions, a trend which "leads inevitably . . . to self-censorship."

4145. Silverman, Debora. Selling Culture. New York: Pantheon, 1986. 175.
See entry no. 741.

4146. Stevens, Mark. "Brushes with Politics." NR 195.19 (1986) 28-32.
Political artists today lack the ability to "address power powerfully" because they have fewer intellectual and artistic resources, and they have "retired into the personal and the idiosyncratic."

II. E. 2. MUSIC (4147-4171)

4147. Abelard, Tony. "Song Is Over for Paredon Records." Guard 41.3 (Oct. 12, 1988) 9.
Paredon Records, the US label that recorded liberation movement folk music, has closed.

ART AND MUSIC 565

4148. Buxton, David. "Rock Music, the Star-System, and the Rise of Consumerism." The Critical Communications Review. Volume III: Popular Culture and Media Events. Ed. Vincent Mosco and Janet Wasko. Norwood, NJ: Ablex, 1985. 181-205.
Analyzes rock as "one of the last bastions of pure, laissez-faire capitalism" and the rock star system as evidence of the "breakdown of traditional organic culture and the creation of a mass audience."

4149. Carter, Sandy. "Slippin' & Slidin'." Z 1.10 (Oct. 1988) 66-70.
Pop music is both rebellious and accommodative. "One of the distinguishing characteristics of advanced capitalism's mass culture" is that it drains specific groups "of their distinctiveness with each cycle of production-consumption."

4150. Dunaway, David. "Music as Political Communication in the United States." Popular Music and Communication. Ed. James Lull. Newbury Park: Sage, 1987. 36-52.
Definition, types, and functions. "Political music most successfully evokes not the bitterness of repression but the glory of a world remade."

4151. Eliot, Marc. Rockonomics: The Money Behind the Music. New York: Franklin Watts, 1989. 290.
Deplores big business domination of the music industry.

4152. Frith, Simon. "The Industrialization of Popular Music." Popular Music and Communication. Ed. James Lull. Newbury Park: Sage, 1987. 53-77.
A history of the economics of pop to the present crisis of the "death of black vinyl" as part of shifts in the organization of profit making, especially the "move from record sales to rights exploitation as the basic source of music income" that "roots rock in corporate America" (TV and advertising). But the commercialization of music has not ended "music as a human activity."

4153. Frith, Simon. "Rock and Popular Culture." American Media & Mass Culture. Ed. Donald Lazere. Berkeley: U of California P, 1987. 309-322.
Analyzes rock music of the 1960s as popular culture, as a form of mass communication with both positive and negative characteristics.

4154. Gendron, Bernard. "Theodor Adorno Meets the Cadillacs." Studies in Entertainment. Ed. Tania Modleski. Bloomington: Indiana UP, 1986. 18-38.
Evaluates the strengths and weaknesses of Adorno's analysis of standardization (interchangeability of parts and pseudo-individualization) indispensable to capitalist production by applying those concepts to the Cadillac automobile and the Cadillacs musical group and other musical groups and styles.

4155. Harker, Dave. One for the Money: Politics and Popular Song. London: Hutchinson, 1980. 301.
Popular music is neither imposed upon a passive audience or an example of popular sovereignty, but somewhere in between.

4156. Hemphill, Michael R., and Larry David Smith. "The Working American's Elegy: The Rhetoric of Bruce Springsteen." Politics in Familiar Contexts: Projecting Politics Through Popular Media. Ed. Robert L. Savage and Dan Nimmo. Norwood, NJ: Ablex, 1990. 199-213.
Springsteen's message generally emphasizes individualistic aspirations and hope without any particular political agenda.

4157. Kaplan, E. Ann. Rocking Around the Clock: Music Television, Postmodernism, and Consumer Culture. New York: Methuen, 1987. 196.
Analyzes MTV, the 24-hour video channel: advertising, production, techniques, avant-garde, ideology, adolescent desire, five types, gender address. MTV by carrying television to an extreme lays bare its essential foundations: above all "consumption on a whole variety of levels," far "more obviously than other programs" it is "one nearly continuous advertisement, the flow being merely broken down into different kinds of ads" (143).

4158. Lipsitz, George. "Working People's Music." American Media & Mass Culture. Ed. Donald Lazere. Berkeley: U of California P, 1987. 293-308.
Accentuates populist and working-class content in country music.

4159. Lomax, Alan. "Appeal for Cultural Equity." JoC 27.2 (1977) 125-138.
Music is symptomatic of a larger problem: an over-centralized electronic communications system which imposes a few standardized, mass-produced, and cheapened cultures everywhere. Offers a decentralist policy.

4160. Lull, James, ed. Popular Music and Communication. Newbury Park, CA: Sage, 1987. 268.
Essays 2-6 in Part I examine the making and distribution of music, i.e. the relations of industry and art, the "struggles among forces of control and resistance." Essays 7-12, Part II, study "music's audiences."

4161. Miller, Mark. "Gonna Hawk Around the Clock Tonight." MJ 13.9 (Nov. 1988) 38-42.
"TV has transformed rock into a new vehicle for the commodity fetish" and "denatured the music by turning it into spectacle," its rebellion against authoritarianism "sold out to advertising."

4162. Nowell, William. "The Evolution of Rock Journalism at The New York Times and The Los Angeles Times, 1956-

1978: A Frame Analysis." Indiana U, 1987. 115. DAI 48 (1987) 1045-A.
  The prevailing dominant cultural frames slowly shifted from "generally negative to generally positive." The author analyzes the resistance to change through the criticism of Adorno, Marcuse, Raymond Williams, and others.

4163. Perry, Steve. "Rocklisting: Lyric Restraint." ITT 10.4 (Nov. 27-Dec. 10, 1985) 13-14.
  The Parents Music Resource Center's campaign to censor rock lyrics is an attempt to check the growing political awareness of rock musicians.

4164. Pratt, Ray, and Carl Boggs. "The Blues Tradition: Poetic Revolt or Cultural Impasse?" American Media & Mass Culture. Ed. Donald Lazere. Berkeley: U of California P, 1987. 279-292.
  Examines "the historical role the blues have played in black oppositional culture and the changes in the political meaning of blues music as it has become commercialized and redirected toward white and middle-class black audiences" (234).

4165. Rodnitzky, Jerome. "The Evolution of the American Protest Song." JPC 3.1 (Summer 1969) 35-45.
  Views with alarm the transformation of the message song into the mood song, "the tendency to treat protest as a life-style, divorced from actual goals."

4166. Rothenbuhler, Eric. "Commercial Radio and Popular Music: Processes of Selection and Factors of Influence." Popular Music and Communication. Ed. James Lull. Newbury Park: Sage, 1987. 78-95.
  Given all the pressures of the business orientation of the popular music industry, "contemporary radio's influence on popular music must be limiting and conservative" (2).

4167. Santoro, Gene. "Book Note." Na 251.7 (Sept. 10, 1990) 251-252.
  Discusses Hit Men by Fredric Dannen, which focuses on "the institutionalization of payola" in the record industry.

4168. Shore, Laurence. "The Crossroads of Business & Music: A Study of the Music Industry in the United States & Internationally." Stanford U, 1983. 366. DAI 44.5 (Nov. 1983) 1233-A.
  Particularly focuses on the influence of transnational music corporations on indigenous music and music industries. "There is a predominantly one-way flow of recorded music from the U.S. to the rest of the world," but there is a significant lesser flow between other countries. Public tastes "are shaped not so much" by direct control but "by the exclusion of alternatives."

4169. Smith, Stephen A., and Jimmie N. Rogers. "Political Culture and the Rhetoric of Country Music: A

Revisionist Interpretation." <u>Politics in Familiar
Contexts: Projecting Politics Through Popular Media</u>.
Ed. Robert L. Savage and Dan Nimmo. Norwood, NJ:
Ablex, 1990. 185-198.
Country music tends to express an anarchistic or libertarian outlook on the issues of race, law and order, and economics.

4170. Sprague, Raymond, and Kathleen J. Turner. "Diary of a Generation: The Rhetoric of 1960s Protest Music." <u>Politics in Familiar Contexts: Projecting Politics Through Popular Media</u>. Ed Robert L. Savage and Dan Nimmo. Norwood, NJ: Ablex, 1990. 171-184.
Urban folk music followed three overlapping stages during the late 1950s and 1960s from idealism to disillusionment and escape to the country.

4171. Wadsworth, Anne Johnston, and Lynda Lee Kaid. "Political Themes and Images in Music Videos." <u>Politics in Familiar Contexts: Projecting Politics Through Popular Media</u>. Ed. Robert L. Savage and Dan Nimmo. Norwood, NJ: Ablex, 1990. 159-170.
The vision of the future is generally pessimistic, "its strongest and basic contention is that the average person's future is manipulated and controlled by powerful . . . political or authority figures" (169).

III. ALTERNATIVES 4172-4749

Introduction

A. Media 4172-4384

B. Advertising 4385-4399

C. Broadcasting & Film 4400-4557

D. Print 4558-4724

E. Art, Music, Literature 4725-4749

ALTERNATIVES TO MEDIA CONTROL

CORPORATE CAPITALISM AND THE CONSCIOUSNESS INDUSTRY

The writers in this section are endeavoring to strengthen political equality so that consent means more than electoral illusion. They study and write because of the steady expansion of corporate/government power in this century recently intensified by the increased secrecy, censorship, deception, and repression by the Reagan-Bush administration, whose actor leader declared at his election to France's Academy of Moral and Political Sciences that modern communications possessed the power to undo totalitarianism by giving all people access to information!

Robert Dahl contrasts the early fear by the Framers of the Constitution and by Jefferson that equality might undermine economic democracy, and by Tocqueville that equality threatened political democracy, to our present realization that the liberty of corporate enterprises has overwhelmed economic and political equality and created "a body of citizens highly unequal in the resources they could bring to political life" (4).

A recent critic to make the case of deepening authoritarianism in the US is Sue Jansen in Censorship. She argues that the libertarian myths created at the birth of our nation obscure the controlling reality of the corporate capitalist "Panopticon." The Promethean adversarial role of a free press and the watchdog press of democracy are metaphors only partly true; the historical record is a "socially structured silence" about the realities of "the business side of media institutions" dedicated to maximized profit (133). Liberty, consumer sovereignty, and similar metaphors "deflect attention away from the tightly controlled decision-making processes that actually determine what ideas will gain entry into the commodity system" (134). Instead of a market-place of ideas, which functions marginally, the nation follows a model of corporate "consciousness industry": the press, advertising, public relations, mass entertainment, and organized leisure "permit elites to rule but preserve the semiotic of democracy" (134).

The writers in this section recognize the extraordinary increase in sophistication and pervasiveness of propaganda today, the exploitation of "unprecedented technologies" of mass communications, and the "new relationship of powerlessness and cynicism between the rulers and the governed." "Propaganda has virtually merged with political discourse and popular consciousness--so much so, in fact, that its very ubiquity serves to conceal its pervasiveness and its danger as an obstacle to clear thinking and the preservation of democratic freedoms" (Stout).

But the authors gathered together in Part III also share the hope in a society emancipated from "the monologues--public relations, advertisements, and party lines--of the powerful"

ALTERNATIVES TO MEDIA CONTROL

(Jansen 298). Dahl proposes an alternative economic structure that would "strengthen political equality and democracy by reducing inequalities originating in the ownership and control of firms." Jansen would find ways to enable the people "to reclaim their own voices" and to expose "the technology of Panopticon control." The following authors offer a wealth of creative alternatives to the present corporate state. Of course, so have the authors in Parts I and II.

INVESTIGATING AND GAINING ACCESS

So what is to be done? One key is simple and familiar, through which we struggle for the democracy we desire; it is the contradiction between the promise and the practice of our nation regarding political liberty and equality for all. The evidence of this contradiction is also familiar to us, since it is systemic. The evidence is indeed so substantial that critics like John Downing see no hope of ever changing mainstream institutions. "Although the U.S. media have an official ethic of balance, of objectivity, of reproducing 'all the news that's fit to print' as the New York Times' masthead would have it, the reality is different and quite beyond popular control" (38). Yet the hypocrisy of press practice expressed in that masthead is a powerful leverage for change, for it links us not only with deep journalistic and literary repugnance for deceit but with the mainstream religion's hostility to cant powerfully expressed in the Sermon on the Mount (Matthew 6).

We must thus not only continue but significantly increase investigation of discrepancy, since the systems of control constantly develop and change form, and are intensifying, and since the struggle to investigate and expose, when opposed by the National Security juggernaut, is vulnerable to repression. For example, only two small publications watch the Pentagon (Recon, The Defense Monitor). We need more books on right-wing foundations and think tanks. Museums should serve people's needs.

But although data and theory are the essential beginning of resistance, we lack in neither. The technology and process of ideological control are known. The Domhoffs and Dyes, the Bagdikians and Chomskys have identified the chain of command. I do not mean there is no more to learn about the consciousness industry. But since thousands of articles, books, and films have already explained the contradiction of US democratic ideals and real US hegemony, our next urgent task is to find access to the public. We must expose the conflict between the corporate-government-military-education-media complex and the ideals of democracy and human emancipation in the Bill of Rights.

These writers and scholars not only gather data and elaborate theory about the US state capitalist propaganda system but they reaffirm our determination to expose its attempts to dominate naming, data, and definitions, and to find more effective ways to make the commanding structures visible to all.

Creating critical discourses to make the covert known, reclaiming independent voices as a way of helping others to do the same to make the seemingly natural hierarchy of power seen, is thus the second initiative after knowledge. Nothing new about this. Individuals and small groups have long voiced their knowledge of the US propaganda system. For Downing the only hope therefore lies in developing alternative communications by which to challenge and balance established media. The alternative press, in opposition to the monologs of power, have always understood it. The Progressive magazine is 80 years old. Two reporters created the National Security Archive to assist us in making FOIA requests. Individual public interest lobbyists and groups have fought and defeated powerful corporations and associations. People have learned how to oppose nuclear power successfully. Others have learned how to make films. Not all book publishers shore up corporate capitalism, as the publisher Lyle Stuart proved, and the South End Press and many others prove. George Seldes wrote and wrote, and Corliss Lamont, and I.F. Stone. In response to "Raygunism," Stuart Ewen, while writing books about the consumer culture, created a weekly poster as "a vehicle of human possibility and liberation." Tracy Chapman sings. We can all tell jokes about officials. We have had the critical analysis of The Washington Monthly, the Columbia Journalism Review, and the St. Louis Journalism Review, and now Propaganda Review and Extra! and Lies of Our Times extend our investigations and our insights. And we can all subscribe to these journals and others like them and work to get them in our local and college libraries. Month after month, year after year, Bill Nigut writes, types, prints, and distributes--speaks his own Chicago Media Critic against the consciousness industry.

There are today thousands of Bill Niguts and associations of Bill Niguts who understand that the media cultural arm of the elite complex possesses the power to define their reality if not opposed, and that a democratic reality depends upon opposition. This was James Aronson's five-decade message in powerful essays and books on the US National Security State.

One book in particular offers us many ideas for alternative communication: John Downing's Radical Media. Downing discusses innovations in Portugal, Italy, Eastern Europe, and the US. His main criterion for selection is "the overwhelming priority" of "linkage of various movements against oppression and inequality." The media given attention in his book have successfully developed "lateral media communication," an end that must be "infinitely better" (21). In the US he concentrates upon nine media, five of them print, four electronic. The newspapers and magazines are The National Guardian/Guardian, Union Wage, Akwesasne Notes, ERIN Notes, and NACLA: Report on the Americas. The broadcasters and film makers are KPFA radio, Berkeley, Third World Newsreel, California Newsreel, and independent film-making in Puerto Rico.

The critics in this section push for a grass-roots democracy. One number of Propaganda Review (Spring 1989), for example, included seven articles on such topics as media/government deception, repression of native Americans, and economic data as a propaganda tool, and six notes on such topics as polling and advertising--that is, the magazine x-rayed the methods of control. And FAIR exposed Ted Koppel's prejudiced Nightline, which was heavily biased in favor of official views of US policies.

CHANGING INSTITUTIONS

But there is another, more difficult method of achieving a more democratic political order, or at least to stop the slide into authoritarianism. And that is to change institutions themselves.

We must investigate and communicate our knowledge to as wide an audience as within our power. Hundreds of thousands of people write informed letters to newspapers every year; teachers present their research to classes; scholars and journalists investigate and reveal. Without thse efforts our world would be enormously more corrupt and totalitarian. But it is not enough. Until criticism can transform the principles and structures of institutions, the struggle for political equality will always lag far behind established power. For example, we have all heard and read a thousand times the convincing case that only 300 or so nuclear warheads are necessary to pose a credible threat to the Soviet Union, yet we have possibly 30,000 now and continue to produce more each day. Those who wish to stop the arms buildup correctly infer from this aggressively militaristic policy that in addition to criticism, exposure, imagining alternative "ways of world-making," and physical protest, we must expand our influence within the major reality-making institutions in order to change them.

Change the Pentagon? Rather ask how you can change the structures where you are. Don Lazere's outstanding anthology offers democratic socialist transformations of the conservative right to center liberal capitalist ideologies commanding the mass culture today. In his Introduction to five essays on "Alternatives and Cultural Activism" he recommends democratic socialist communications that would provide maximal "freedom of political and cultural expression, public participation, and dialogue and debate among a full range of ideological viewpoints" (555). Some of these essays tell about alternative media, but some deal with institutional structural change.

My own profession serves as a present example. The two editions of Robert Con Davis's anthology of literary criticism reveal significant changes within the study of literature. The first edition of Contemporary Literary Criticism (1986) began with "the call for form" and advanced through Marxism, feminism, depth psychology, structuralism/semiotics, reader response, and deconstruction. That is, he established in Parts I and II, containing essays published between 1917 and 1948, the modernist formalist preference for art over life as its political response to perceived cultural disintegration, a preference that, according to Terry Eagleton, "helped, wittingly or not, to sustain and reinforce" the corporate-military-media complex. In following sections he dramatized

the resurgence (Marxism, feminism, etc.) or the origination (deconstruction, etc.) of opposition to Russian formalism and the "New Criticism."
This challenge to the status quo of traditional power is reinforced in the revised edition of 1989, which conflates the modernist and formalist sections and increases the Marxist/ "new historical" and feminist perspectives. And of particular significance, a new section of seven essays, numerically the largest in the new anthology, "Canon, Profession, Ethics," relates literature to society, centers of power, and institutions. In this anthology we discern an evolution of literary studies more and more institutionally self-conscious, which amounts to a fundamental (though not irreversible) structural change. Literature will increasingly be taught from an growing diversity of conflicting descriptive and interpretive perspectives, the profession, its departmental structure, and the canon, all now being called into question, decreasingly an apparatus of the consciousness industry. Literature teachers cannot directly affect the Pentagon and other institutions of corporate capitalism/national security state, but by a commitment to a dialogic rather than an authoritarian model, and by self-reflexive analysis, one more pressure is added for change in the ruling institutions.

Of much more immediate importance is the reorganization of the institution of journalism and media. Evidence of the contribution of our "free press" to democratic and honest government amounts to an endless roll of honor: from the Virginia Pilot's nuclear alerts scoop and Appalachia's Mountain Eagle's crusades against strip mining, police harassment of youths, and secrecy in corporations and government, to the publishing of the Pentagon Papers and network investigative reporting. But the shortcomings and failures of the press to reach its potential in the public interest seem greater than its successes.

Efforts to reconstitute the press parallel my general model for change. For example, George Gerbner urges researchers to expose the dynamics of myth-making in the media and its control over people's lives. And Lee Brown, among other modes of access for investigation of journalism and the media, wants press councils. To Brown, criticism is "the single greatest corrective known to man" (92). The journalism of dissent, some of which has been called the "underground press," has provided extensive access to criticism of the press. Paper Tiger Television makes criticism of the information industry accessible to a television audience.

The third method for improving journalism and the media is again to change the structure of the institution, not merely to prune it with criticism. Without going into the economics of the media, the Commission on Freedom of the Press (the Hutchins Commission) suggested such sweeping changes in the way news was presented (events in context, "all sides of an issue," etc.) as to amount to a structural revolution. Phil Jacklin would extend the Fairness Doctrine (recently dropped from broadcasting regulation) to print media in wording ensuring access for all citizens. One way to accomplish this is to greatly expand space for letters to the editor. Christopher Jencks advocates nonprofit news production in the public service, shifting policy decisions from corporate stockholders and managers to the professional staff. Robert Cirino recommends adoption of the publicly owned "spectrum-sharing model" of broadcasting to guarantee diversity of views found in the Netherlands and being introduced into Italy, France, and Belgium. He proposes a United States Broadcasting Corporation that would consist of four separate and independent networks representing four different political positions. Douglas Kellner gives an enthusiastic account of the new possibilities in public access television based upon his experiences with "Alternative Views" TV in Austin, TX.

But, and here I swing back to Dahl's argument for economic equality as the foundation for political equality, many critics perceive the source of the Panopticon of control in the financial organization of the media under corporate capitalism. Donald McDonald condemns the commercial distortion of the media's role of informing the people. He offers a four-part plan to reorganize the institution: decentralization of ownership, facilitation of the entry of new media, opening up existing media channels, and improving the ethical and legal bases of the journalist's professional status. The major scholar of media monopoly's constriction of the ideals of a free, watchdog press in the public interest is Ben Bagdikian, our Cassandra of concentration. Twenty-nine corporations now control most major media businesses, compared to fifty five years ago. This economic control contains "built-in biases that protect corporate power" and "weaken the public's ability to understand the forces" that dominate the nation. Since reforming media power requires changing all corporate power, because major media and giant corporations are not only allies, "they are now a single entity" (233), "nothing truly significant will change" until there is a change in the "fundamental imbalance of power in society at large" (237).

Nevertheless, he remains hopeful, like Jansen (Chap. 10), that "small, minority voices today . . . can produce a change that will strengthen American democracy and validate the principle of a truly informed consent as the basis for a free society" (238). Mainly he urges us to pull ourselves together not only to stop further concentration but to create and encourage new media; acquirement would be curbed; diversity would be promoted. Policies and techniques in other countries should be studied and those in the public interest adopted (e.g., the diverse broadcasting in the Netherlands). New, small newspapers, magazines, and television should receive public financial support. Cable system access should be guaranteed to all political perspectives. Advertisers should pay a progressive tax increasing as the spending increases, to favor smaller enterprises. Corporate image and advocacy advertising should be taxed and not deducted as a business expense. Postal rates for non-advertising publications should be low. Small publications should pay lower postal rates than larger publications. News and editorial staffs should have a voice in the choice of editors, producers, and directors, and they should have an elected representative on corporate boards of directors. All financial secrecy by broadcast media should be abolished. Bagdikian, like Dahl for corporations in general, would open up, equalize, and democratize media power.

We can be further encouraged by the "Sydney Declaration," Unesco's "Declaration of Fundamental Principles," and other international efforts to strengthen journalism for the people. The International Federation of Journalists, meeting recently in Sydney, Australia, approved a code potentially capable of altering the economic structures of media. Whereas the US Society of Professional Journalists' "Code of Ethics" has nothing to say about business practices, media conglomerates, concentration of ownership, and the decline of diversity, the Sydney code warns against the influence of corporations over the presentation of news, the danger of self-censorship, and the threat to diversity, and recommends limits on ownership.

The Unesco Declaration offers a vision of mass media promoting peace and human rights instead of ethnocentric and nationalistic myths. The entire document upholds the highest principles of this country and thus challenges US media practice, especially in Article II, which affirms not only full freedom of opinion and expression, access to the diversity of information, freedom to report, participation of the public, and protection of journalists, but opposition to racism and war, and support of oppressed peoples. And there are eleven articles.

ALTERNATIVES (4172-4749)

III. A. ALTERNATIVES: MEDIA (4172-4384)
See II.

4172. Adler, Allan R. The 1990 Edition of Litigation Under the Federal Freedom of Information Act and Privacy Act. Washington, D.C.: ACLU, 1990. 492.
The 15th edition of the litigation manual for attorneys.

4173. Altschull, J. Herbert. Agents of Power: The Role of the News Media in Human Affairs. New York: Longman, 1984. 355.
Desires to raise global understanding and amity by explaining global press similarities of three types: market, Marxist, and developing world.

4174. Armstrong, David. A Trumpet to Arms: Alternative Media in America. Los Angeles: J.P. Tarcher; Boston: Houghton Mifflin, 1981. 384.
A history of the creation in the 1960s of dissident newspapers, magazines, video projects, radio stations, publishing companies, and film coops out of an awareness of the ability of the established media to perpetuate the status quo of privilege and power. The '60s manifested "an important rebellion against the accumulated rigidities of oppressive puritanism, commercialized culture, corporate power, warmaking, and race, class and sex prejudice" (from the Foreword by Ben Bagdikian).

4175. Aronson, James. "The Long Road." Deadline for the Media. Indianapolis: Bobbs-Merrill, 1972. 275-97.
On alternatives to commercial journalism: PBS, listener-sponsored radio (Pacifica Foundation), dissenting newspapers and magazines (the Bay Guardian).

4176. Aronson, James. "The Sting of the Gadfly." Deadline for the Media. Indianapolis: Bobbs-Merrill, 1972. 93-111.
A survey of critics of the press both within and outside the profession: Seldes, Marion, Liebling, Stone, the Hutchins Commission Report, press councils, and journalism reviews. They sought to come to grips with "the interweaving interests --financial and social--between the owners of the media and the dominant industrial and political figures" (103).

4177. Aumente, Jerome. Against Misinformation: A Media Action Program for Young People. New York: KTAV, 1973. 126.
The second part is a series of suggestions for young people to get to the truth.

4178. Bagdikian, Ben. "To Undo Excess." The Media Monopoly. 2nd ed. Boston: Beacon, 1987. 223-238.

Suggests ways to counteract concentrated media power and consequent uniformity of outlook and to restore "genuine competition and diversity."

4179. Barber, Benjamin. Strong Democracy: Participatory Politics for a New Age. Berkeley: U of California P, 1984. 320.
Suggests various methods by which citizens might wrest control back from the disproportionately powerful corporations: communications cooperatives, civic videotex services, etc.

4180. Barnet, Richard. The Rocket's Red Glare: When America Goes to War--the Presidents and the People. New York: Simon and Schuster, 1990. 476.
A primer on "how to create structures for subjecting foreign policy to democratic control," especially grassroots education about foreign countries supported by a network of new communication technologies.

4181. Barron, Jerome A. Freedom of the Press for Whom?: The Right of Access to Mass Media. Bloomington, Ind.: Indiana UP, 1973. 368.
"This book's basic argument is that the First Amendment should be restored to its true proprietors--the reader, the viewer, the listener. Freedom of the press must be something more than a guarantee of the property rights of media owners. The rise in court decisions and FCC proceedings supporting access to the media is set forth; a core idea is that the privately controlled media have a responsibility to provide opportunity for expression. Also portrayed are new ways of broadening public participation in the media through law and technology" (Preface).

4182. Benjaminson, Peter, and David Anderson. Investigative Reporting. 2nd ed. Ames, IA: Iowa State UP, 1990. 304.
From the purpose and ethics of investigating to specific procedures for selecting a subject, gathering data, and getting a story to the public. New chapters on computers and TV.

4183. Bennett, James R. "McCarran Goodthinkful." FS 60 (Fall 1986) 8-11.
Supports "Free Trade in Ideas" legislation.

4184. Bennett, W. Lance. The Political Mind and the Political Environment: An Investigation of Public Opinion and Political Consciousness. Lexington, MA: Heath, 1975. 207.
Identifies the kinds of political experiences that "can lead to the cognitive development necessary to deal with rhetoric and complex policy choices in a critical fashion." Hopeful about achieving a greater participatory democracy.

4185. Bergman, Kostia. "SftP and rDNA: Science for the People's Involvement." SciP 17.3 (1985) 50-52.

MEDIA 579

On public debate urgently needed concerning genetic engineering. (SftP is the acronym for Science for the People).

4186. Berry, Jeffrey M. Lobbying for the People: The Political Behavior of Public Interest Groups. Princeton: Princeton UP, 1977. 331.
Surveys 83 organizations and studies two intensively.

4187. Blanchard, Margaret A. "The Hutchins Commission, The Press and the Responsibility Concept." JM 49.4 (1977) 1-59.
An account of the Hutchins Commission on Freedom of the Press, its report, A Free and Responsible Press, and its impact.

4188. Bolinger, Dwight. Language--The Loaded Weapon: The Use and Abuse of Language Today. New York: Longman, 1980. 214.
In "An Ecology of Language" sets forth four rules for accuracy and honesty and for equal access.

4189. Bollinger, L.C., Jr. "Freedom of the Press and Public Access: Toward a Theory of Partial Regulation of the Mass Media." MLR 75.1 (1976) 1-42.
First Amendment goals "can be achieved by permitting legislative access regulation but sharply restricting it to only one segment of the mass media, leaving the choice of the area to Congress."

4190. Bosmajian, Haig, ed. The Principles and Practice of Freedom of Speech. Boston: Houghton Mifflin, 1971. 448.
Contains "Landmark Court Decisions" and recent essays in defense of free speech by Meiklejohn, Chafee, Emerson, Marcuse, et al. A "variety of arguments which have been used to explain and defend freedom of speech."

4191. Boylan, James. "First-rater." CJR 20.5 (Jan.-Feb. 1982) 59-61.
A favorable review of Franklyn Haiman's Speech and Law in a Free Society as a worthy continuation of Emerson's The System of Freedom of Expression.

4192. Boylan, James. "The Hutchins Report: A Twenty-Year View." CJR 6.2 (Summer 1967) 5-8.
An account of the creation and the text of A Free and Responsible Press: A General Report on Mass Communication: Newspapers, Radio, Motion Pictures, Magazines, and Books (1947).

4193. Boyte, Harry C., Heather Booth, and Steve Max. Citizen Action and the New American Populism. Philadelphia: Temple UP, 1986. 215.
An account of the tens of thousands of local people who write, speak, and organize for grass-roots defense of the

public good.

4194. Brand, Stewart. The Media Lab: Inventing the Future at MIT. New York: Viking Penguin, 1987. 285.
The goal of MIT's Media Lab is to enable the audience to take over and individualize mass media, to create a dialog between machine and humans to bring about ideas unrealizable by either alone. (Brand founded the Whole Earth Catalog and The Whole Earth Software Catalog.)

4195. Brennan, William J. "Why Protect the Press?" CJR 18.5 (1980) 59-62.
Part of an address by Associate Justice Brennan of the Supreme Court explaining the special protection accorded the press under the Constitution.

4196. Breslau, Andy. "Watchdogs Eye Mainstream Media." MA 1.3 (1986-87) 21-22.
Several new organizations have recently been formed to "challenge the mass media's uncritical acceptance of a conservative world view": FAIR (Fairness and Accuracy in Reporting), The Institute for Media Analysis, The Communicators Consortium, and GLAAD (Gay and Lesbian Alliance Against Defamation).

4197. Brown, Lee. The Reluctant Reformation: On Criticizing the Press in America. New York: McKay, 1974. 244.
A study of theories and the role of press criticism, a history of press criticism, a national press council, the ethics of press criticism, and future developments. Appendices on codes of ethics, press councils, etc.

4198. Budd, Richard W., and Brent D. Ruben, eds. Beyond Media: New Approaches to Mass Communication. Rochelle Park, NJ: Hayden, 1979. 292.
Makes a distinction between mass communication (the process) and mass media (the technologies--broadcasting, film, print) in order to expand the range of mass media to include architecture, museums, theater, and even restaurants and to broaden and redefine the systemic process of communication.

4199. "Build The Fifth State." CS 2.1 (Fall 1974) 17-18.
"What the American people need to help focus their mass resistance to technofascism and the conditions which produce it is an alternative intelligence community--a Fifth Estate." As a beginning, the creators of CS call themselves the "Fifth Estate."

4200. Buitrago, Ann Marie, and Leon Andrew Immerman. Are You Now or Have You Ever Been in the FBI Files? New York: Grove Press, 1981. 227.
A guide to obtaining documents from the FBI under the Freedom of Information Act, with a section on attempts by the FBI to weaken and circumvent the FOIA.

4201. Center for National Security Studies: A Report on Its

MEDIA

Functions and Activities. Washington, D.C.: Center for National Security Studies, 1989. 27.

Sponsored by the ACLU and the Fund for Peace "to resist incursions against civil liberties justified on national security grounds." One project is "Free Trade in Ideas" to eliminate legal barriers to the free flow of information and ideas across the border.

4202. Chamberlin, Bill, and Charlene Brown, eds. The First Amendment Reconsidered: New Perspectives on the Meaning of Freedom of Speech and Press. New York: Longman, 1982. 218.

Seven essays and the authors' Introduction, the essays organized in three categories: the role of the states, the twentieth-century search for the meaning of the freedom of the press, and the First Amendment in the 1980s. The essays are bound together by the concern for freedom of speech and press in a self-governing society.

4203. Christians, Clifford. "Reporting and the Oppressed." Responsible Journalism. Ed. Deni Elliott. Beverly Hills: Sage, 1986. 109-130.

Affirms the Hutchins Commission's call for the press to "present a representative picture of society's various groups" by constructing a theoretical foundation for the idea, concluding that "justice for the powerless stands at the centerpiece of a socially responsible press."

4204. [Cancelled]

4205. Cirino, Robert. Power to Persuade: Mass Media and the News. New York: Bantam, 1974. 246.

The author tentatively explores an alternative communication system (214-220), and until the time that system becomes a reality he suggests ways to improve the present system (221-225).

4206. Citizen's Media Directory. National Citizens Committee for Broadcasting, April 1977. 170.

Lists nearly 400 media reform groups, radio stations, news services, etc.

4207. Clurman, Richard. Beyond Malice: The Media's Years of Reckoning. New Brunswick, NJ: Transaction, 1988. 306.

"Book One: The News Media on Trial" discusses two trials that reveal the tensions in the press-public-government triangle. "Book Two: The News Media at Work" examines journalistic practices and ownership. Ending the tension is undesirable but it can be eased by increased coverage of, increased access to, and increased opportunity to reply to the media.

4208. Cox, Archibald. Freedom of Expression. Cambridge, MA: Harvard UP, 1981. 89.

Introduction to case law affecting regulation of content, conduct affecting publication, political campaigns, etc.

4209. Daley, Patrick. "Radical Currents in Twentieth Century American Press Criticism: Notes for the Future." U of Iowa, 1983. 283. DAI 44.7 (Jan. 1984) 1963-A.
Calls for "a radical intersubjectivity based on Habermas' communicative action" to counteract advertising and consumer mentality, chain journalism and uniformity, industrial/ commercial formulas, public relations, and propaganda.

4210. "Darts and Laurels." CJR.
Every number of CJR contains this section of rapid criticism and praise of media behavior.

4211. Dennis, Everette E., Donald M. Gillmor, and David L. Grey, eds. Justice Hugo Black and the First Amendment. Ames, IA: Iowa State UP, 1978. 204.
Twelve essays on Black's unequivocal support for the First Amendment as the foundation of the democratic process.

4212. Dennis, Everette E., and William L. Rivers. Other Voices: The New Journalism in America. San Francisco: Canfield, 1974. 218.
Ch. 1, an introduction; 2, "The New Nonfiction" (Tom Wolfe, et al.); 3, "The Modern Muckrakers"; 4, "Guarding the Guardians: The Journalism Reviews"; 5, "The Advocates" (Gloria Steinem, Pete Hamill, James Ridgeway, et al.); etc. (9 chs. in all). Not so much about "new" journalism as an account of "divergent journalistic voices" in the 1960s.

4213. Devol, Kenneth. Mass Media and the Supreme Court: The Legacy of the Warren Years. Hastings, 1971. 369.
Studies media rights by topics--e.g., censorship.

4214. Dorsen, Norman, and Stephen Gillers, eds. None of Your Business: Government Secrecy in America. New York: Viking, 1974. 362.
Part II discusses the foundations of open government--the press, the Freedom of Information Act, whistle blowing, etc.

4215. Downing, John. Radical Media: The Political Experience of Alternative Communication. Boston: South End, 1984. 340.
The "first comparative treatment in detail of the political experiences of organizing 'self-managed' media," radical in both values and organization. Covers the US (Guardian, KPFA, Union Wage, Akwesasne Notes, ERIN Bulletin, NACLA, Third World Newsreel, California Newsreel, independent film-making in Puerto Rico), Portugal, Italy, and Eastern Europe. By "self-managed," Downing means constructing and owning media "independently of capital, the state, the church, and other agencies of oppressive power." The polemical purpose of the book is "overcoming class, racism, sexism, other forms of subjugation" by discovering how the powerless "can communicate with one another" in order to understand the subjection and "how they can act together to create new social relations."

4216. Eliasoph, N. "Routines and the Making of Oppositional News." CSMC 5 (1988) 313-334.
A "deviant case study" which opposes the view that media's political complacency is the result of conventional news gathering. Rather, those common conventions can become oppositional tools.

4217. Elliott, Deni, ed. Responsible Journalism. Beverly Hills: Sage, 1986. 192.
Focuses on old debate over whether libertarianism or social responsibility should guide news media. John Merrill and Ralph Barney take the libertarian side, Theodore Glasser, Everette Dennis, and Clifford Christians take the side of responsibility. And other essays.

4218. Emerson, Thomas I. "Legal Foundations of the Right to Know." WULQ 1976.1 (1976) 1-24.
In defense of "the vital importance in a democratic society of the right to know."

4219. Emerson, Thomas I. The System of Freedom of Expression. New York: Random, 1970. 754.
Case applications of the author's Toward a General Theory of the First Amendment.

4220. Emery, Michael, and Ted Smythe, eds. "Increasing Access to the Mass Media," "Increasing Control of the Mass Media." Readings in Mass Communication. Dubuque, IA: Brown, 1972. 7-94.
These and other topics ("Creating Alternative Media for Minorities," etc.) provide a wealth of ideas for improving the media for the public good: press councils, ombudsmen, protecting news sources, muckraking, access to media as First Amendment right, community control of broadcasting, etc.

4221. Ewen, Stuart. "Youth Culture." Communication and Domination: Essays to Honor Herbert I. Schiller. Ed. Jörg Becker, et al. Norwood, NJ: Ablex, 1986. 89-95.
"Shows how the once truly oppositional culture, the counter culture, the 'youth culture,' was gradually transformed into the 'culture of youth'--no longer an expression of sensibility but a mere icon of commercial sensuality." However, "the visionary potential of a true 'youth culture,' a reappraisal of resistance, persists even today."

4222. FAIR. New York: Fairness & Accuracy in Reporting.
A media research organization especially intended to counter right-wing propaganda and domination of mainstream media. Publishes the journal Extra!.

4223. Feder, Timothy. "Native American Media Projects Fill Communications Vacuum." Access 52 (June 1977) 4-5.
Several Indian news and communications organizations are attempting to bring about "media rights to American Indians."

4224. Flippen, Charles C. Liberating the Media: The New Journalism. Washington: Acropolis, 1974. 212.
The nineteen essays focus on five areas: literary journalism, advocacy journalism, underground journalism, democracy in the newsroom, and public access.

4225. Franklin, Marc, and Ruth Franklin. The First Amendment and the Fourth Estate: Communication Law for Undergraduates. Mineola, NY: Foundation, 1977. 727.
Analyzes Supreme Court decisions.

4226. Freedom to Read Foundation. Chicago: American Library Assoc., 1969-.
A clearing house for litigation resisting censorship of libraries.

4227. Free Trade in Ideas: A Constitutional Imperative. Washington, DC: ACLU, 1984.
Opposition to the presidential power to prevent citizens from learning about what is going on in a foreign country. The president's power to require a license to invite foreign speakers to a public forum, to travel abroad, to subscribe to books and magazines published abroad, and to exchange unclassified information with foreigners violates the First Amendment.

4228. Friendly, Fred W. Minnesota Rag: The Dramatic Story of the Landmark Supreme Court Case that Gave New Meaning to Freedom of the Press. New York: Random, 1981. 243.
An account of J.M. Near v. State of Minnesota (1931) that infused "with life and spirit" the free-press clause of the First Amendment.

4229. Friendly, Jonathan. "NNC Folding." WJR 6.4 (1984) 11-12.
Because of lack of media and foundation support, the National News Council has ceased functioning.

4230. Fulbright, J. William. "Dangers of the Military Sell." The Pentagon Propaganda Machine. New York: Vintage/Random House, 1970. 166.
Recommends several ways to curb the militarism rising in America.

4231. Gaines, Jane. "Women and Representation: Can We Enjoy Alternative Pleasure?" American Media & Mass Culture. Ed. Donald Lazere. Berkeley: U of California P, 1987. 357-372.
Surveys "recent explorations in female erotica as liberatory alternatives to pornography" (326).

4232. Gambill, Joel. "Hugo Black: The First Amendment and the Mass Media." Southern Illinois U, 1973. DAI 34.9 (Mar. 1974) 5895-A.
"Black's staunch support for freedom of the press was unwavering in more than one hundred cases in which he participated."

MEDIA

4233. Gardner, Gerald. The Mocking of the President: A History of Campaign Humor from Ike to Ronnie. Detroit: Wayne State UP, 1988. 234.
Explores "the sweep of presidential campaign humor" from 1952 to 1984.

4234. Gerbner, George. "The Challenge Before Us." Communication and Domination: Essays to Honor Herbert I. Schiller. Ed. Jörg Becker, et al. Norwood, NJ: Ablex, 1986. 233-240.
Television is now the dominant culture organizer. "In such an era, communication research should, first and foremost, attempt (a) to understand and expose the dynamics of myth-making in society, and (b) to discover what happens when that process touches the lives of millions of people." Researchers must also cooperate with other organizations, such as churches and citizen groups "to build anew an independent basis for authentic public consciousness and philosophy."

4235. Ginger, Ann, and Eugene Tobin, eds. The National Lawyers Guild: From Roosevelt Through Reagan. Philadelphia: Temple UP, 1988. 468.
A history of an organization of lawyers who from "1937 to the present" has actively supported human rights, "finally spelled out in the United Nations Charter and Nuremberg Principles."

4236. Gitlin, Todd. "Conflicting Security Paradigms: A Contest for the Press to Cover." Deadline 5.2 (Mar.-Apr. 1990) 12-16.
Except for the opposition to the Vietnam War by media leaders following the Tet offensive in 1968 (and that was fueled by a mass protest movement), present dissent from the Bush administration's effort to continue the Cold War as usual is unprecedented since WWII.

4237. Glazer, Myron, and Penina Glazer. The Whistleblowers: Exposing Corruption in Government and Industry. New York: Basic, 1989. 286.
Accounts of "men and women of conscience who disclosed lawless acts in the workplace." Chapter 6, "Allies in the Struggle: The Press, Legislators, and Public-Interest Groups."

4238. Gleason, Timothy W. The Watchdog Concept: The Press and the Courts in Nineteenth-Century America. Ames: Iowa State UP, 1989. 160.
Shows how the watchdog concept evolved along with free press law of the 1800s.

4239. Glessing, Robert, and William P. White, eds. Mass Media: The Invisible Environment Revisited. Chicago: SRA, 1976. 241-257.
Three essays on technological education, community press councils, and students as media critics.

4240. Golove, David, and Michael Krinsky. "Congress Approves 'Free Trade in Ideas' with Havana." Guard 41.3 (Oct. 12, 1988) 6.
A new law allows the import from and export to Cuba of literature, films, and similar materials.

4241. Goodman, Julian. "It's Everybody's Freedom." TQ 11.4 (1974) 55-58.
An argument for the reinforcement of freedom of the press. "The real threat is and has been a gradual accumulation of regulations and restrictions on what journalists can and cannot report." Goodman was Chairman of the Board of NBC.

4242. Graham, Fred P., and Jack C. Landau. "The Federal Shield Law We Need." CJR 11.6 (1973) 26-35.
Problems and suggested solutions pertaining to the legislation are given.

4243. Green, Mark, et al., eds. "Alternatives to Business as Usual." The Big Business Reader. Rev. New York: Pilgrim, 1983. 443-511.
Seven essays on remedies to corporate domination of society.

4244. Grossman, Karl. Coverup: What You Are Not Supposed to Know About Nuclear Power. Sagaponack, NY: Permanent, 1980. 293.
Final two chapters explain how the public can resist corporate and government deception and blackmail.

4245. Grundfest, Joseph. "Participation in FCC Licensing." JoC 27.1 (1977) 85-88.
A survey finds that "the Commission could do much to create a regulatory environment based on a philosophy of cooperation and negotiation."

4246. "Guild Targets Limits on Press." SLJR 12.78 (Sept. 1985) 6.
At its annual convention the Newspaper Guild adopted two resolutions opposing Congressional and White House efforts to weaken the FOIA and to create an Official Secrets Act.

4247. Guimary, Donald. Citizens' Groups and Broadcasting. New York: Praeger, 1975. 170.
A survey of "citizen involvement in commercial broadcasting." Following a general background, "three case studies of three different citizens' groups are offered." The author believes in "the importance of citizen involvement in the broadcast industry" to challenge "licensees legally," participate in "renewal proceedings," and influence "programming, advertising, and employment policies of stations."

4248. Haiman, Franklyn. Citizen Access to the Media: A Cross-Cultural Analysis of Four Democratic Societies. Evanston, IL: Northwestern U, 1987. 66.
Recommends emulation of practices in Japan, France, and the

MEDIA   587

Netherlands for dealing with the problem of access for the
expression of diversity of information and opinion.

4249. Haiman, Franklyn. Freedom of Speech: Issues & Cases.
            New York: Random House, 1966. 207. (Rev. ed.
            Skokie, IL: National Textbook, 1977. 221.).
    Examines constraints over First Amendment rights.

4250. Haiman, Franklyn. Speech and Law in a Free Society.
            Chicago: U of Chicago P, 1981. 499.
    Seeks "a coherent set of guiding principles for the
resolution of conflicts between freedom of expression and the
competing interests with which it may clash" (425). Six
premises (6-7) and four principles (Part 6, 425-29) provide "a
more vigorous commitment to the values of a free society."

4251. Halperin, Morton. "Why Congress Must Past Free Trade
            in Ideas Legislation." CLA 9.3 (1986) 2.
    Bills have been introduced in Congress to remove restric-
tions on the right to invite foreign speakers, to travel
abroad, and to import and export information.

4252. Halperin, Morton, and Daniel N. Hoffman. Top Secret:
            National Security and the Right to Know. Washington:
            New Republic, 1977. 158.
    Chapters 4-6 set forth various solutions to the growing
secrecy in the nation.

4253. Halperin, Morton, and Daniel N. Hoffman. "Toward a
            More Open System." FP 3.2 (1977) 2-11.
    The article "outlines a reform program to structure the
secrecy system so that it protects only important secrets and
also guarantees public debate."

4254. Hedemann, Grace. "Making the Media Responsive and
            Responsible." NA 2.6 (1985) 4-7.
    On the War Resisters League's campaign to improve daily
media response to political issues.

4255. Held, Virginia. "Culture, Free Expression, and the
            Good Life." Rights and Goods: Justifying Social
            Action. New York: Free Press; London: Collier, 1984.
            215-232.
    US culture "is so thoroughly beholden to commercial
interests" that "any views seriously challenging the corporate
political economy" are undercut in diverse ways. Two rights
particularly need strengthening: "the rights of reporters to
gather news and the rights of citizens to have the means to
express themselves" (217).

4256. Hendricks, Evan. Former Secrets. Washington, DC:
            Campaign for Political Rights, May 1982. 200.
    A compilation of 500 Freedom of Information Act cases
arranged in broad categories--e.g., consumer product safety.

4257. Hentoff, Nat. American Heroes: In and Out of School. New York, NY: Delacorte, 1987. 126.
Librarians, singers (Joan Baez), and other upholders of the Bill of Rights.

4258. Hess, John. "Honorable Mentions." CJR 17.3 (Sept.-Oct. 1978) 56-57.
Investigative journalism is alive and well (as the submissions for the Pulitzer Prize show) but there are a lot of scandals out there yet to be exposed.

4259. Hess, John. "The Real Danger to Civil Liberties." MORE 6.3 (1976) 28-29.
The danger is suppression of free speech and press. The author urges more investigative journalism.

4260. Hulteng, John. "Holding the Media Accountable." What's News: The Media in American Society. Ed. Elie Abel. San Francisco, CA: Inst. for Contemporary Studies, 1981. 211-232.
Ways to improve media news.

4261. Immerwahr, John, Jean Johnson, and John Doble. The Speaker and the Listener: A Perspective on Freedom of Expression. New York: Public Agenda Foundation, 1980. 65.
Interviews of over a thousand media representatives and the public revealed a commitment to the right of free expression by the media people and a commitment to fair play by the public. The media interviewees opposed governmental interference because they perceived a danger to the First Amendment and free speech, while the public welcomed regulation in defense of First Amendment diversity.

4262. "Increasing Control of the Mass Media." Readings in Mass Communication: Concepts and Issues in the Mass Media. Ed. Michael C. Emery and Ted Curtis Smythe. Dubuque, IA: Wm. C. Brown, 1974. 50-87.
Diverse methods for increasing public influence: citizen review, a national news council, professional review, ombudsman, journalism reviews (magazines), shield law, muckraking, journalism schools, etc.

4263. Index/Directory of Women's Media. Washington, DC: Women's Institute for Freedom of the Press.
Annual, 1975- , "to aid networking." The 1985 number, ed. Martha Allen, lists 462 women's periodicals, 116 women's presses/publishers, 80 women's bookstores and mail order, etc.

4264. Jacklin, Phil. "A New Fairness Doctrine: Access to the Media." CM 8.3 (1975) 46-50.
Proposes a new Communications Act extending the fairness doctrine to print media and insuring access for all citizens, justifying such a plan by the decreasing number of print media sources and the lack of any real "competition of ideas."

MEDIA

4265. James, Beverly A. "Towards a Radical Humanist Perspective for Mass Communication Inquiry: Mihailo Markovic's Philosophy of Dialectical Praxis." U of Iowa, 1983. 195. DAI 44.8 (Feb. 1984) 2282-A.
   Seeks a "restructuring of media systems in the interests of human liberation." Examines the Frankfurt School, contemporary British cultural criticism, and Markovic's "democratic theory," and finds Markovic the best foundation for revolutionary change by confronting communication systems with "human needs and interests."

4266. Jellinek, J. Stephen. The Inner Editor: The Offense and Defense of Communication. New York: Stein & Day, 1977. 198.
   Deals "with some ways in which mass education and mass communication . . . can lead to a loss of individual integrity and to a loss of touch with reality," and "suggests ways of coping with these problems."

4267. Jencks, Christopher. "Should News Be Sold for Profit?" American Media & Mass Culture. Ed. Donald Lazere. Berkeley: U of California P, 1987. 564-567. (From WorkP July-Aug. 1979).
   Advocates news production on a nonprofit basis in the public service, which would shift policy decisions from corporate stockholders and managers to the professional staff. In TV the change could occur by leased time from existing commercial stations by nonprofits. (See Picard).

4268. Johnson, George C. "Special Privilege for an Autonomous Press: Justice Stewart's Structural Approach." Southern Illinois U, 1984. 273. DAI 45 (1985) 2288-A.
   Examines Stewart's belief that the framers of the Constitution intended to form a fourth institution separate from the three official branches of government, and that the First Amendment guarantees press privileges superior to protections afforded the general public.

4269. Johnson, Nicholas. Test Pattern for Living. New York: Bantam, 1972. 154.
   Most of the book explains how the author would counteract the negative influences of the US corporate state and its media tools.

4270. Joyce, Alisa. "Gunning for Respect in the Pentagon Press Corps." ITT 11.24 (1987) 12-13.
   Women reporters find it hard to be accepted by the "old boy network," but they will make an increasing contribution to "bringing national security back to the people it makes secure."

4271. Kahane, Howard. Logic and Contemporary Rhetoric: The Use of Reason in Everyday Life. 2nd ed. Belmont, CA: Wadsworth, 1976. 259.
   Intends "to raise the level of political argument and reason-

ing" by exposing the techniques "which drag that level down."

4272. Kahn, Douglas, and Diane Neumaier, eds. Cultures in Contention. Seattle, WA: Real Comet, 1986. 287.
Writers who protest against the mass culture of advertising, television, movies, popular music and the news media--Gabriel Garcia Marquez, Holly Near, Ernesto Cardenal, Abbie Hoffman, et al. Mainly essays, but many photographs of artwork, performances, and scenes from videotapes and media events. A collection of ideas and techniques for opposition to racist, sexist, and repressive behavior that parades as democracy.

4273. Kalven, Harry, Jr. A Worthy Tradition: Freedom of Speech in America. Ed. Jamie Kalven. New York: Harper & Row, 1988. 698.
A study of the First Amendment tradition through 1974.

4274. Kessler, Lauren, and Duncan McDonald. Uncovering the News: A Journalist's Search for Information. Belmont, CA: Wadsworth, 1987. 243.
A textbook on how to search out news, dig for facts, find and confirm a story, not only for aspiring journalists but for anyone seeking full and accurate information.

4275. Kirckhove, Derrick de. "On Nuclear Communication." Diacritics 14.2 (Summer 1984) 72-81.
The bomb inevitably resulted from technological "progress," but we should "stop cowering in apocalyptic clichés" and strive harder to turn around the danger of nuclear annihilation. The restructuring would come about through a revised national Constitution, education on all aspects of nuclear policy, abolition of secrecy regarding nuclear arms, etc.

4276. Kittrie, Nicholas, and Eldon Wedlock, Jr., eds. The Tree of Liberty: A Documentary History of Rebellion and Political Crime in America. Baltimore, MD: Johns Hopkins UP, 1986. 728.
A collection of more than 400 documents which recount the story of dissent and disobedience in America to show how challenges to government and authority have shaped the nation's thought, history, and freedom, on such topics as the treatment of native Americans, treason, domestic terrorism, religious protest, rights of women, rights of labor, and civil disobedience. Includes 46 illustrations, a concordance and user's guide, a complete table of court cases, an index to proper names, and an extensive bibliography.

4277. Knepler, Michael K., and Jonathan Peterson. "The Ombudsman's Uneasy Chair." CJR 17.2 (July-Aug. 1978) 54-57.
"Reader representatives" can improve news coverage by making sure those on both sides of an issue are heard.

4278. Kumar, Satish, ed. The Schumacher Lectures. New York: Harper & Row, 1980. 198.

Eight essays in honor of Fritz Schumacher, author of Small Is Beautiful and Buddhist Economics. Schumacher's two main principles are Intermediate Size and Intermediate Technology, or the division of states into modest administrative units to avoid industrial concentration, and the use of inexpensive and simple equipment to avoid the costly computerized, labor-saving machinery.

4279. Lambeth, Edmund B. Committed Journalism: An Ethic for the Profession. Bloomington, IN: Indiana UP, 1986. 208.
Ch. 3 "sets forth an eclectic system of journalism ethics," presenting five principles as an integrated whole: truth-telling, humaneness, justice, freedom, and stewardship. Of the five the first two are preeminent. Ch. 6 emphasizes "the potential for moral imagination and significant autonomy that journalists can and have exercised." Ch. 7 encourages media criticism as a First Amendment responsibility; etc.

4280. Lamont, Corliss. A Lifetime of Dissent. Buffalo, NY: Prometheus, 1988. 414.
The author's record of defiance of censorship and secrecy by the House Committee on Un-American Activities, the McCarthy Investigations, the U.S. Passport Office, and other agents of repression. "As we grow older, we dissenters should grow more militant rather than more timorous about the fundamental issues" of constitutional government, due process, free speech, and other democratic rights in opposition to tyrannical government run by demagogues.

4281. Lasswell, Harold D. National Security and Individual Freedom. New York: McGraw-Hill, 1950. 259.
Chapter 7, "What the Public Can Do" to defend a free press against the "Garrison-Police State."

4282. Lavin, Douglas. "Star Struck: Tracking Space Weapons." NT 4.3 (1986) 23.
Looks at a testing controversy over the nuclear powered laser for use in SDI.

4283. Lazare, Daniel. "Being FAIR to the Media." ITT 13.16 (Mar. 15-21, 1989) 12.
Jeff Cohen, executive director of Fairness and Accuracy in Reporting, comments on the media's concentration and connections with the military-industrial complex, the distortions and complicity of press during the Reagan years, and how FAIR came to be and operates.

4284. Lazere, Donald. "Alternatives and Cultural Activism." American Media and Mass Culture. Ed. Donald Lazere. Berkeley: U of California P, 1987. 555-618.
The editor's Introduction and five essays suggest what a communications system in a democratic socialist society would be like: maximal "freedom of political and cultural expression, public participation, and dialogue and debate among a

full range of ideological viewpoints" (55).

4285. Lazere, Donald. "A Selected Bibliography." CE 38.8 (Apr. 1977) 866-872.
A "sampling of works useful for developing a critical perspective on mass culture and political consciousness under capitalism."

4286. Leab, Daniel J. "Response to the Hutchins Commission." Gaz 16 (1970) 105-113.
"Little acclaim and much criticism greeted A Free and Responsible Press [1947] by the Commission on Freedom of the Press.

4287. Lee, Alfred, and Elizabeth Lee. "An Influential Ghost: The Institute for Propaganda Analysis 1936-1942." PR 3 (Winter 1988) 10-14.
Chronicles the short life and important contributions of Edward A. Filene's organization dedicated to enabling Americans to decode the barrage of propaganda aimed at them in the 20th century.

4288. Lehman, Tenney. "A Spectrum of Press Watchers." When Information Counts: Grading the Media. Ed. Bernard Rubin. Lexington, MA: Lexington/Heath, 1985. 103-129.
Discusses eight organizations that work for press freedom: Freedom House, the Inter American Press Association, the International Press Institute, Amnesty International, the Reporters Committee for Freedom of the Press, the Index on Censorship, the World Press Freedom Committee, and the Committee to Protect Journalists.

4289. Leroy, David, and Christopher Sterling, eds. Mass News: Practices, Controversies, and Alternatives. Englewood Cliffs, NJ: Prentice-Hall, 1973. 334.
Part Four, "Alternatives," recommends diverse remedies to present constrictions and distortions of news.

4290. Leslie, Larry. "Ethics as Communication Theory: Ed Murrow's Legacy." JMME 3.2 (Fall 1988) 7-19.
Murrow's strict morality, careful reporting, and integrity, his emphasis upon reporting as a trust before it is a business, remains a model for news reporting today.

4291. Lewels, Francisco J. The Uses of the Media by the Chicano Movement: A Study in Minority Access. New York: Praeger, 1974. 185.
A study 1) of how the US media contributed to keeping Mexican-Americans "in virtual isolation" and as "objects of systematic discrimination," 2) of the failure of the Mexican-American minority "to see the media's potential" for their own liberation and a just society, and 3) chiefly, of the Chicano Media Movement for equal access.

4292. Lewis, Anthony. "'Bad Time for Civil Liberties.'" MORE 2.12 (Dec. 1972) 9-10.

Praises Peter Bridge, the journalist who went to jail rather than answer grand jury questions about private information.

4293. Lewis, Anthony. "Press Power and the First Amendment." CLR 1.1 (Fall 1973) 183-85.
Argues against special immunity for the press against testifying in legal proceedings, and a defense of the new National News Council [now defunct].

4294. Lieberman, David. "Times Mirror in Hartford: Cross and Doublecross." CJR 18.6 (1980) 9, 13.
Connecticut regulators acted to break the Times Mirror Company's media monopoly in Hartford.

4295. Logan, Robert. "Jefferson's and Madison's Legacy: The Death of the National News Council." JMME 1.1 (Winter 1985-86) 68-77.
The demise of the Council derived not only from the refusal of the New York Times Co., Knight-Ridder, NBC, ABC, Times-Mirror, and Time-Life to support the Council's authority regarding complaints, but also from deep differences in ethical perspectives. There remains a great need for greater access for public complaints of journalistic quality.

4296. Looney, Michael. "A Public Service Communications Model." Union for Experimenting College/Union Grad. Sch., 1986. 264. DAI 47 (1987) 3603-A.
A guide for the social activist.

4297. MacBride, Sean, et al. Many Voices, One World: Communication and Society Today and Tomorrow. New York: Unipub, 1980. 312.
The final report of the International Commission for the Study of Communication Problems, which views freedom of information as a fundamental human right and which recommends reduction of the commercialization of communication as well as media concentration, and international cooperation in the form of a "new world information and communication order."

4298. Making Waves: The Politics of Communications. Ed. Radical Science Collective. London: Free Association, 1985. 173.
The eight essays "explore both the oppressive and liberatory possibilities of communications technologies." Some of the topics: community radio, alternative television via cable, Nicaraguan video.

4299. Maniquis, Robert. "Pascal's Bet, Totalities, & Guerilla Criticism." HiS 6.2-3 (Spring-Summer 1983) 133-38.
The solution to state domination is to be found in "guerilla criticism," a criticism from the political margin against totalities, logocentrism, historicism, totalitarianism, militarism, nuclear terror.

4300. Mann, Jim. "Open Season on Open Government." WP 9

(Mar.-Apr. 1982) 32-37.
Gives a brief history of the Act, describes how it works, and identifies the opponents of the Act (Reagan administration, the FBI, etc.).

4301. Marwick, Christine. Your Right to Government Information. New York: American Civil Liberties Union, 1985. 288.
From national issues to personal files, this guide tells how to obtain information from the federal government.

4302. Marzolf, Marion. Up From the Footnote: A History of Women Journalists. New York: Hastings House, 1977. 310.
The first two chapters bring the history through WWII, then chapters on "Post-World War II Pioneers," radio, TV, newspaper "women's pages, feminist press, journalism educators, and Europe.

4303. McCartney, James. "Must the Media be 'Used'?" CJR 8.4 (1969-70) 36-41.
New procedures are necessary to reduce managed news.

4304. McDonald, Donald. "The Media's Conflict of Interests." CM 9.6 (1976) 15-35.
Cites numerous examples of the media's failure to inform and offers a four-part plan to correct such problems: decentralization of ownership, facilitation of the entry of new media, opening up existing media channels, and improving the ethical and legal bases of the journalist's professional status.

4305. McWhorter, Darrell. "Birth of the National Security Archive: How Two Reporters Turned FOIA Nightmare into Simple Process." IREJ 12.2 (Spring 1989) 16-17.
Scott Armstrong and Raymond Bonner created a central repository which pools the efforts of many researchers in the area of US foreign policy.

4306. Media Access Action Package. Washington, DC: Media Access Project, 1980. 70.
Not examined.

4307. "Media for Minorities." Readings in Mass Communication: Concepts and Issues in the Mass Media. Ed. Michael C. Emery and Ted Curtis Smythe. Dubuque, IA: Wm. C. Brown, 1974. 288-312.
Three essays about new films, the Black press, and Chicano journalism.

4308. Media Network. New York: Alternative Media Information Center.
Promotes independent media producers and users. Produces a Media Information Database, media guides on films and videos for special events (Martin Luther King's Birthday, Hiroshima-Nagasaki, etc.), and publishes MediActive, a quarterly newspaper.

MEDIA

4309. Media Survival Kit. First Amendment Coalition, May 1978. 250.
This manual tells reporters what to do in various confrontational situations (i.e., closed courtrooms, judicial restraint, withholding of public records).

4310. Media Watch: Newsletter of the National Citizens Committee for Broadcasting.
The NCBB was founded in 1976 to "make media more responsive to the public interest." Its first chairperson was Nicholas Johnson, who served on the FCC.

4311. Mehra, Achal. "Free Flow of Information & the New International Information Order: Toward a Doctrinal Reconciliation." Southern Illinois U, Carbondale, 1985. 299. DAI 46 (1986) 2843-A.
Examines the US free flow doctrine and the Communist bloc and third world criticisms of it. Finds much in US constitutional law--even from a libertarian perspective--compatible with "the more moderate NIIO proposals."

4312. Meiklejohn, Alexander. Free Speech and Its Relation to Self-Government. New York: Harper, 1948. 107.
Explains the First Amendment as an absolute shield against suppression of ideas and speech.

4313. Mencher, Melvin. "The Arizona Project: An Appraisal." CJR 16.4 (Nov.-Dec. 1977) 38-47.
Praises the team of investigative reporters who investigated statewide corruption in the wake of a reporter's murder.

4314. Merrill, John C. The Imperative of Freedom: A Philosophy of Journalistic Autonomy. New York: Hastings House, 1974. 228.
"This whole book has attempted to stress the importance of freedom or journalistic autonomy--not only for the individual journalist, but also for the individual media and the press systems themselves."

4315. Merrill, John C., and Ralph D. Barney, eds. Ethics and the Press: Readings in Mass Media Morality. New York: Hastings House, 1975. 338.
A collection of essays in search of moral principles for journalistic action.

4316. Miller, Tim. "The Data-Base Revolution." CJR 17.3 (Sept.-Oct. 1988) 35-38.
Computers are extending reporting ability to gather, recall, organize, and perceive patterns in information.

4317. Mintz, Morton, and Jerry Cohen. Power Inc.: Public & Private Rulers & How to Make Them Accountable. New York: Viking, 1976. 831.
Proposes an accountability amendment to the Constitution to make all power centers accountable to the public.

4318. Morrissey, David. "Bombed by Mistake." IREJ 13.1 (Winter 1990) 14-16.
Describes how the FOIA was utilized to dig out the story of two separate accidental hydrogen bomb releases in the US.

4319. Mosco, Vincent, and Andrew Herman. "Critical Theory and Electronic Media." TSoc 10.6 (Nov. 1981) 869-896.
"The recent resurgence of radical and neo-marxist research on the world system, the capitalist state, its labor process, and private sphere challenge the dominance over the field of communications research of such conservative perspectives as developmentalism, pluralism, post-industrialism, and mass society" (892).

4320. Mosco, Vinnie, and Eileen Mahoney. "Media Monopoly and the Turn towards Democratic Communications." WIN 19.15-16 (1983) 4-6.
"The last five years have brought a number of organizations committed to democratic control over media production and distribution."

4321. Nader, Ralph, Mark Green, and Joel Seligman. Taming the Giant Corporation. New York: Norton, 1976. 312.
The book's thesis is that corporate law has not yet caught up with corporate power. The solution to the excessive power wielded by what are virtually large private governments is federal chartering.

4322. Neubauer, Mark. "Newsman's Privilege After Branzburg: The Case for a Federal Shield Law." UCLALR 24 (Oct. 1976) 160-192.
Supports the proposed federal shield legislation, "despite several weaknesses," because it assists newsmen "in protecting" confidence and sources.

4323. Neville, Richard. Play Power: Exploring the International Underground. New York: Random House, 1970. 325.
An account of the counter-culture--New Left, Underground, militant poor, etc.--which found its protest focus especially against the Vietnam War through play. One appendix gives a "Directory to the World's Underground Press."

4324. Nimmo, Dan, ed. Watching American Politics: Articles and Commentaries About Citizens, Politicians, and the News Media. New York: Longman, 1981. 314.
Intended to increase the independence of individual citizens as watch-dogs of power elites and their media.

4325. "1984: The Year in Review." PC (Spring 1985) 13-27.
What an informed consumer movement can do to combat the onslaught of corporate and government violation of human rights.

MEDIA

4326. O'Brien, Mark, and Craig Little, eds. Reimaging America: The Arts of Social Change. Philadelphia: New Society, 1990. 373.
A Voices of Dissent Project. "Foreword: Nurturing Resistance" by Bernice Reagon. Provides a forum for socially conscious artists to share their work, "to chart how culture is shaped, so that we can understand how it changes, and seize opportunities to alter it in ways that create possibilities for greater social justice" (9).

4327. Osner, Audrey. "Newsmen Need a Library." UM 1.9 (May 1971) 10-11.
A "24-hour 'information bank'" would help.

4328. Our Right to Know.
A quarterly magazine published by the Fund for Open Information and Accountability, Inc., for the dissemination of FOIA-related news, such as the New World Information Order vs. Cold War communications and combat coverage by the US media.

4329. Owen, Bruce M. Economics & Freedom of Expression: Media Structure & the First Amendment. Cambridge, MA: Ballinger, 1975. 202.
Since monopoly power is widespread in the communications industries and media companies are gatekeepers that control the flow of news and opinion to screen out ideas inimical to their economic interests, the author would break up networks, make newspaper printing plants common carriers, and other novel forms of government control for libertarian ends.

4330. Paletz, David, and John Ayanian. "Armageddon, the Pentagon and the Press." Communicating Politics. Ed. Peter Golding, et al. New York: Holmes & Meier, 1986. 197-210.
News coverage of false nuclear alerts reveal failures and opportunities. The Pentagon has immense power to impress its perspective on the media and the pubic, through a wide array of tools. But that power is not absolute, but can be challenged by more media investigating of the Pentagon, more issue-oriented reporters less restricted to the beat of breaking stories.

4331. Parenti, Michael. "Does the U.S. Have a Free Press?" The Witness 68 (Mar. 1985) 12-14.
The author believes we do not have an independent press and offers four remedies, e.g. supporting alternative media.

4332. Pertschuk, Michael. Giant Killers. New York: Norton, 1986. 252.
Celebrates the public interest lobbyist and chronicles the defeat in specific battles of such powerful private interest lobbies as the Tobacco Institute, the American Medical Association, and California's land and water developers.

4333. Pickard, Robert G. The Press and the Decline of

Democracy: The Democratic Socialist Response in Public Policy. Westport, CT: Greenwood, 1985. 176.
Sets forth the goal of economic democracy for the press-- the presentation of a diversity of views--against the dominance of concentrated power and the "business" of journalism. The rise of an elite-based economic control of the media has caused the decline of access to the process of democratic activity which in turn has caused the decline of democracy. His remedies are government support for economically weak newspapers and policies and regulations to encourage new forms of ownership by political, social, and racial groups. Media should not be private profit enterprises but public utilities serving the diverse public.

4334. Polanski, Jonathon, and Michael Singsen. Talking Back: Public Media Center's Guide to Broadcasting and The Fairness Doctrine For People Who Are Mad As Hell and Aren't Going to Take It Anymore. San Francisco: Public Media Center, 1983. 158.
Not examined.

4335. Powers, Ron. "A Modest Proposal." The Newscasters. New York: St. Martin's, 1978. 234-38.
In this age of "choreographed" news programs mixed with "Show Biz," the US needs more journalist and citizen monitors.

4336. "The Press and the Courts: Is News Gathering Shielded by the First Amendment?" CJR 17.4 (Nov.-Dec. 1978) 43-50.
Documents in the debate over whether journalists enjoy constitutional protection for their sources.

4337. The Public's Right to Know. Washington, DC: Editorial Res. Rpts., Cong. Quart., 1980. 196.
Covers numerous topics.

4338. Rank, Hugh, ed. Language & Public Policy. Urbana, IL: National Council of Teachers of English, 1974. 234.
The first of two collections of essays sponsored by the NCTE (see Dieterich) to counter dishonest and inhumane language by corporations and the government.

4339. Rank, Hugh. "The Need for Persuasion Analysis." QRD 9.2 (1983) 5-7.
English teachers need to work toward "a reorganization of the language curriculum" in order to confront powerful institutional propaganda.

4340. Rasor, Dina. The Pentagon Underground: A Group of Truth-Tellers in a Maze of Lies. New York: Times, 1985. 310.
The author is director of the Project on Military Procurement, an organization that helps dissenters in the Pentagon communicate to the press, a channel for whistleblowers who fear direct and public revelations.

MEDIA

4341. Reitman, Alan, and Trudy Hayden. "Should Government Impose the First Amendment on Media?" Mass News. Ed. David Leroy and Christopher Sterling. Englewood Cliffs, NJ: Prentice-Hall, 1973. 226-239.
Examines the idea that government has an affirmative obligation to ensure right of access to media.

4342. Rivers, William, Wilbur Schramm, and Clifford Christians. Responsibility in Mass Communications. 3rd ed. New York: Harper & Row, 1980. 378.
Offers three different perspectives; also discusses regulation and censorship, and suggests how the media can provide fair and truthful information along with diversity of entertainment.

4343. Rosen, Jay. "The Impossible Press: American Journalism & the Decline of Public Life." New York U, 1986. 491. DAI 47 (1987) 2779-A.
Examines the idea that it is the function of the press to inform the public, the notion of an "informed public," and the conditions enabling and inhibiting such a public.

4344. Rosen, Jay. "Is Anybody Listening?" Deadline 3.6 (Nov.-Dec. 1988) 3-5.
The press should become advocates, not of a particular point of view, but of general revitalization of "the public realm."

4345. Rossman, Michael. New Age Blues: On the Politics of Consciousness. New York: Dutton, 1979. 270.
On the rise of the "new age"/private consciousness movement and the alleged fall of "the many-branched social and political movement." But in fact the political Movement was stronger in the 1970s than in the 60s in support of freedom, democracy, and justice, and against authoritarianism and militarism. His aim is to integrate the personal and political movements to enlarge self-determination in the US.

4346. Rowe, James. "Ralph Nader Reconsidered." WM 17 (Mar. 1985) 12-21.
An account of Nader's full-time dedication to empowering the buying public. He is urging and teaching people how to build their own groups and institutions to deal with problems.

4347. Rubin, David. "Consider the Source: A Survey of National Security Reporters." Deadline (Mar.-Apr. 1986) 4-6.
Arms control journalists should search documentary evidence more [i.e., imitate I.F. Stone and other investigative journalists].

4348. Rucker, Bryce. The First Freedom. Carbondale: S Illinois P, 1968. 322.
Believing that "press freedom is a civil right accruing to news and information consumers, not a license granted media owners to enrich themselves at society's peril," the author

advocates the following remedies to media monopoly: tax laws to make selling to a chain unattractive; increase of postal subsidies for small, single ownerships; decrease or elimination of subsidies for large, multiple ownerships; formation of press councils; etc.

4349. Ryan, Charlotte. Prime-Time Activism: Media Strategies for Organizing. Boston: South End, 1990. 270.
Helps organizers apply their politics to their mass media campaigns by explaining how to deal with daily routines of news workers and organizations, how to gain greater access for their message, etc.

4350. Schement, Jorge Reina, et al. "The Anatomy of a License Challenge." JoC 27.1 (1977) 89-94.
The story of the legal dispute in San Antonio, Texas, between the Bilingual Bicultural Coalition on the Mass Media (BBC) and the FCC over the licensing of television station WOAI (since changed to KMOL).

4351. Schmidt, Benno, Jr. Freedom of the Press Versus Public Access. New York: Praeger, 1976. 296.
Surveys the arguments pertaining to publisher autonomy vs. right of access.

4352. Schonberg, Edward. "Search Warrants and Journalists' Confidential Information." AULR 25.4 (Summer 1976) 938-970.
Urges severe constraints over the use of search warrants to seize information from the press.

4353. Schudson, Michael. The News Media and the Democratic Process. New York: Aspen Institute for Humanistic Studies, 1983. 46.
The press needs to help facilitate the democratic process and get involved when that process appears not to be functioning.

4354. Science in the Streets. Report of the Twentieth Century Fund Task Force on the Communication of Scientific Risk. New York: Priority, 1984. 97.
Scientists and journalists make recommendations for better media coverage of technological controversy.

4355. Seiden, Martin H. "Access to the American Mind." TQ 12.1 (1974) 5-12.
On the importance of a privately controlled mass media as a check to big government.

4356. Seldes, Gilbert. The New Mass Media: Challenge to a Free Society. Washington, D.C.: Public Affairs, 1968. 100.
A study of "the trend to conformity of the mass media" and ways independence and free thought and action might be strengthened both directly in the media and through

MEDIA

"Countervailing Powers--voluntary associations, schools, newspapers, magazines--which can help to develop audience discrimination." "Independent thinking is essential to us as individuals and . . . a truly democratic system is safe only if the number of citizens able and willing to think for themselves is constantly increasing."

4357. Sherick, L.G. How to Use the Freedom of Information Act (FOIA). New York: Arco, 1978. 138.
Contains the full text as amended in 1974, a history of the act, case histories, etc.

4358. Shore, E., P.J. Case, Laura Daly, et al. Alternative Papers. Philadelphia: Temple UP, 1982. 521.
Its subtitle--"Stories, Events, & Issues that the Media Ignored, Distorted, Buried or Missed Altogether"--points to its contents on political repression, gay rights, antinuclearism, corporate power, and so on.

4359. Sichel, Berta. "Disinformation Lumps." ITT 9.27 (1985) 20-21.
An exhibit at New York's Alternative Museum exposes the disinformation pervading the nation.

4360. Smith, Robert M. "Why So Little Investigative Reporting?" MORE 3.11 (Nov. 1973) 7-9.
The author describes various impediments and proposes several ways to increase the number of good investigative reporters.

4361. "Some Who Did the Story Well: Winners of the 1987 Olive Branch Awards." Deadline 2.1 (May-June 1987) 4-6.
Awards for the best coverage of nuclear, arms control, and Soviet issues.

4362. Steinberg, Morton. "Only a Free Press Can Enable Democracy to Function." JQ 23 (Mar. 1946) 11-19.
Despite "red herrings," half-truths, suppression, etc., few controls should be put on the press.

4363. Steiner, Claude. "The PR Wizard Who Stopped Alar." PR 5 (Summer 1989) 14-19.
An interview with progressive media specialist David Fenton, who successfully overcame the bias of corporate media in his campaign to make the public aware of the hazards posed by the pesticide Alar.

4364. Stone, I.F. "Arthur Miller Sets an Example All Sensitive Americans Should Follow." IFSW 13.32 (Oct. 4, 1965) 3.
Miller refused to join the signing of the Arts and Humanities bill in protest of the Vietnam War.

4365. Taylor, Arthur R. "The Social Contract of the Free Press." TQ 12.2 (1975) 59-64.

Advocates the contract of "popular government with popular information."

4366. Tedford, Thomas. Freedom of Speech in the United States. New York: Random House, 1985. 473.
An explanation of what the First Amendment is, where it came from, and how it is currently being interpreted. Includes discussion of defamation, privacy, obscenity, commercial speech, prior restraint, free press/trial, copyright, broadcasting, and media access.

4367. Tedford, Thomas. "Freedom of Speech and Censorship: A Dozen Paperbacks for Teacher and Student." EJ 64.1 (Jan. 1975) 122-123.
An annotated bibliography of a dozen books on key opinions, documents, and analyses of First Amendment issues.

4368. Thompson, James C., Jr. "Resigning from Government and Going Public: The Costs and Benefits of Speaking Up and the Unwritten Vow of Silence." Secrecy and Foreign Policy. Ed. Thomas Franck and Edward Weisband. New York: Oxford UP, 1974. 385-98.
Analyzes the difficulties of whistleblowing by government officials.

4369. Townley, Rod. "They Watch the News--For Mistakes." TVG (Nov. 29, 1980) 8-12.
Praises the National News Council [now defunct].

4370. Ullmann, John. "Tapping the Electronic Library." IREJ (Summer 1983) 9-19.
Annotated list of data bases useful to investigative reporters.

4371. Walker, Samuel. In Defense of American Liberties: A History of the ACLU. New York: Oxford UP, 1990. 479.
Account of the organization whose purpose is to defend the Bill of Rights. Together the First Amendment and the ACLU provide a bastion against censorship.

4372. Weinberg, Steve. Trade Secrets of Washington Journalists: How to Get the Facts About What's Going on in Washington. Washington: Acropolis, 1981. 253.
Chaps. on Congress, the White House, the Cabinet departments, the agencies, the courts, private sector special interests, parties, and relevant legislation regarding reporting and investigating government.

4373. Weiner, Jon. "Pop and Circumstance." Na 249.15 (Nov. 6, 1989) 538-540.
Discusses No Respect: Intellectuals and Popular Culture by Andrew Ross, which "argues that popular culture provides a crucial political arena for challenging established authority."

MEDIA

4374. Weir, David, and Dan Noyes, eds. Raising Hell: How the Center for Investigative Reporting Gets the Story. Reading, MA: Addison-Wesley, 1984. 340.
Eight investigative magazine articles each followed by a how-we-got-the-story piece. The articles appeared between 1978 and 1982 in Mother Jones, New West, the Columbia Journalism Review, and the old New Times.

4375. Whitfield, Stephen J. Scott Nearing: Apostle of American Radicalism. New York: Columbia UP, 1974. 269.
Focuses "upon the intersection of his career" (over fifty books and pamphlets) "with the travail of dissent in this country." Nearing combined "the two strongest motifs in the heritage of American dissent, the agrarian and the socialist."

4376. Wicclair, Mark R. "A Shield Privilege for Reporters v. the Administration of Justice and the Right to a Fair Trial: Is There a Conflict?" BPEJ 4.2 (1985) 1-14.
Maintains that there is less of a conflict between the rights of reporters and the rights of the accused than is generally assumed.

4377. Wiethoff, William. "Milton's Viable Attack on Prior Restraint in the Areopagitica." FSY: 1984. Ed. Henry Ewbank. Annandale, VA: Speech Communication Assoc. 42-50.
Milton's argument "provides contemporary advocates of free speech with two ingenious premises."

4378. Wilcox, Fred, ed. Grass Roots: An Anti-Nuke Source Book. Trumansburg, NY: Crossing, 1980.
Ch. 10, "How to Use Television & the Press to Oppose Nuclear Power."

4379. Wills, Gary. "Is the Media Elite Enough?" MORE 8.1 (Jan. 1978) 32-34.
In praise of Murray Kempton, recipient of MORE's A.J. Leibling Award, and an argument for more knowledge and better writing by journalists.

4380. Wills, Gary. "A Revolution in the Church: And For Your Penance, Do Three to Five at Danbury . . . ." Pb 18.11 (Nov. 1971) 159-227.
On Catholic protesters for peace and justice and their opposition--the FBI and the Catholic Church. "One part of Catholicism is a captive of the state and the other part is trying to free it" (226).

4381. Wittner, Lawrence. Rebels Against War: The American Peace Movement, 1941-1960. New York: Columbia UP, 1969. 339.
Studies "the shifting pattern of support which the ideal of world peace elicited" between 1941 and 1960.

4382. Wolfson, Lewis W. The Untapped Power of the Press: Explaining Government to the People. New York: Praeger, 1986. 202.
Proposes various ways journalists can better explain government.

4383. Yinger, J. Milton. Countercultures: The Promise and the Peril of a World Turned Upside Down. New York: Free P, 1982, 371.
Examines countercultures as "important elements in the process of social change" and the struggle for a more just, peaceful, and ecologically balanced world.

4384. Zipes, Jack. "The Liberating Potential of the Fantastic in Contemporary Fairy Tales for Children." American Media & Mass Culture. Ed. Donald Lazere. Berkeley: U of California P, 1987. 384-420.
Studies the "writing and reception of fairy tales in different historical moments and class situations," and finds "alternative themes and structures that might transcend the shaping of genres to capitalist ideology" (328).

III. B. ALTERNATIVES: ADVERTISING (4385-4399)
See II.B.

4385. Atkin, Kenward. "Federal Regulation of Broadcast Advertising." JB 3 (1959) 326-340.
Recommends joint FTC/FCC regulation of advertising.

4386. Berger, Arthur Asa. "Analyzing the Advertisement." Television as an Instrument of Terror. New Brunswick, NJ: Transaction, 1980. 119-127.
A methodology for analyzing advertising.

4387. Dieterich, Daniel, ed. Teaching About Doublespeak. Urbana, IL: National Council of Teachers of English, 1976. 218.
Twenty-four essays on how to increase media awareness and to evaluate political statements, advertising, news, and entertainment. The second book sponsored by the NCTE's Committee on Public Doublespeak (see Hugh Rank).

4388. Ewen, Stuart. "Billboards of the Future: A Brief History." Communication & Domination: Essays to Honor Herbert I. Schiller. Ed. Jörg Becker, et al. Norwood, NJ: Ablex, 1986. 249-258.
"Ray-gunism"--right-wing militarism and rapacity--swept over the country in 1980 with media complicity. In response, the author, in addition to historical criticism of US consumer culture and mass media as vehicles of dominant political power, created a weekly poster as "a vehicle of human possibility and liberation."

4389. Green, Mark. "Talking back to the Hucksters." MORE

ADVERTISING   605

   3.10 (Oct. 1973) 6-9.
Advocates counter-commercials.

4390.   Keto, David B. "The Corporation and the Constitution:
           Economic Due Process and Corporate Speech." YLJ 90.8
           (July 1981) 1833-1860.
   Granting First Amendment rights to corporations "does not
serve any free expression interests . . . the Bellotti
decision was unwise and should be overturned."

4391.   Lamont, Corliss, ed. The Civil Liberties Campaign
           Against Secrecy in Government. New York: National
           Emergency Civil Liberties Committee, 1987.
   A collection of advertisements in the Sunday New York Times
that describe the violations of the American people's right to
know by the Nixon, Ford, Carter, and Reagan administrations.

4392.   Lasn, Kalle. "Tubehead: The Campaign Against TV
           Addiction." Adbusters 1.2 (Winter 1989-90) 17-21.
   Describes the magazine's anti-advertising 15- to 30-second
TV spots sent out free to people who will buy ad time. The
networks and CBC in Canada have refused to run the ads, for as
an ABC executive said, that would be "like shooting ourselves
in the foot."

4393.   "Make and Air Your Own TV Ad For Under $2,000."
           Adbusters 1.2 (Winter 1989-90) 45-47.
   A condensed version of the Do-It-Yourself Manual published
in the magazine's premier issue.

4394.   McGregor-Brown, Ian. "The Greening of Corporate
           America." Adbusters 1.2 (Winter 1989-90) 52-53.
   Expresses hope that advertising will become genuinely
sensitive to the environment, and not use the ecological
issues for more profits.

4395.   "NRDC Goes to Court in California to Close Loophole in
           Prop 65." NRDCN 6.3 (Jul.-Aug. 1988) 3.
   NRDC seeks warning labels on all products that contain toxic
substances.

4396.   Quinn, Jane Bryant. "Private Group Acts as Scold of
           Advertiser." AG (Sept. 12, 1984) 7D.
   The National Advertising Div. of the Council of Better Business Bureaus attempts to restrain ads of questionable accuracy.

4397.   Rank, Hugh. The Pitch. Park Forest, IL: The Counter-
           Propaganda Press, 1982. 207.
   Designed to help correct the "serious problem of inequality"
between "the average person and the 'professional persuaders.'" "This book is counter-propaganda. It will show
you, as the target of many persuaders, how to cope better with
the [advertising] blitz." Analyzes the five-part pattern of
the ads: attention-getting, confidence-building, desire-
stimulating, urgency-stressing, response-seeking. Includes

Rank's intensify-downplay schema and analyses of ads for common products and services.

4398. Schick, Suzanne. "Seeing Is Believing: The Use of Television Commercials to Develop a Model for Analyzing Visual Propaganda." New York U, 1983. DAI 45 (1984) 9-A.
Combines the Rank, Propaganda Institute, and Pseudo-Communication models for visual analysis.

4399. Schneider, Mary. "Training Skeptical Consumers: The Impact of Televised Public Service Announcements on Children." Adelphi U, 1983. 127. DAI 44 (1983) 9-A.
Experiments with PSAs giving either product information or customer dissatisfaction increased skeptical attitudes among first to fifth grade students, especially among the older children. The study supports use of PSAs to "bolster children's cautious buying habits."

III. C. ALTERNATIVES: BROADCASTING & FILM (4400-4557)
See II.C.

4400. Adler, Richard. The Humanistic Claim on the Cable. Palo Alto, CA: Aspen Program on Communications and Society, 1973. 60.
Assesses cable TV's future contributions "to solving some of our society's most pressing problems and to enhancing the quality of life in America" by challenging and expanding viewers' perceptions and providing the means to enrichment, in contrast to the typical commercial fare.

4401. Alderson, Jeremy Weir. "Everyman TV." CJR 19.5 (Jan.-Feb. 1981) 39-42.
Praise for public access television as "the world's only form of television in which no authority decides what can or cannot be televised." But the concept is threatened by hostility by cable TV corporations who won in the courts a ruling barring the FCC from requiring access.

4402. Allan, Blaine. "The New American Cinema & the Beat Generation 1956-1960." Northwestern U, 1984. 364. DAI 45 (1985) 1894-A.
Studies "a moment in the avant-garde cinema," whose films "explore suppressed or marginal parts of a society that represented itself as homogeneous, affluent, and normal."

4403. Armes, Roy. On Video. London: Routledge, 1988. 230.
Treats video as a technology distinct from film and TV. In contrast to the computer, which is increasingly perceived to be the defining technology of our age, individual and computer alone together, video offers "a complementary system of communication which will put men and women in touch with each other and with the world around them." "It has the potential to be truly the art of the twenty-first century."

4404. Arterton, F. Christopher. Teledemocracy: Can
Technology Protect Democracy? Newbury Park, CA:
Sage, 1987. 224.
Urges moving "onto center stage the discussion of the politics we want to emerge from the communications revolution"--cable TV, satellites, computer networks, videotex, etc. Examines several "teledemocracy projects" with the aim of safeguarding democracy by examining technology by "the values we hold dear" (27), that is, "representative processes and a pluralist conception of political interest" (204).

4405. Aufderheide, Pat. "Home Rules and the Video
Alternatives." ITT 13.12 (Feb. 8-14, 1989) 19.
Reviews six alternative documentary films available for VCR.

4406. Aufderheide, Pat. "Living-Room Screening Room: Making
Home Video an Issue." ITT 13.6 (Dec. 14-20, 1988) 19.
Begins regular coverage of independently produced video on social issues.

4407. Aufderheide, Pat. "Video Makers Primed for TV Success
Beyond Prime Time." ITT 14.24 (May 9-15, 1990) 21.
Camcorders and other forms of homemade video offer great potential for social reform and participatory democracy.

4408. Bazelon, David. "The First Amendment's Second Chance."
Channels 1.6 (1982) 16-17.
Urges use of antitrust laws to increase programming diversity.

4409. Berrigan, Frances J., ed. Access: Some Western Models
of Community Media. Paris: UNESCO, 1977. 229.
Studies new approaches to broadcasting and electronic media in the US, Canada, and Western Europe, on the assumption that "a diversity of experiences is important for future development" toward "more meaningful, more dynamic relationships between people and media channels and institutions."

4410. Bonner, Helen L. "The Jeannette Rankin Story." Ohio
U, 1982. 125. DAI 43.4 (Oct. 1982) 955-A.
Original screenplay of the life of a great female feminist and politician.

4411. Brokaw, Tom. "Network News--How We Can Do It Better."
TVG (July 6, 1985) 5-7.
Brokaw wants a one-hour network evening news program and more adequate examinations of the many sides of complicated subjects in a fuller context.

4412. Brown, Les. "A Question of Involvement." TQ 11.1
(1973) 72-78.
Ways to increase the public service of TV.

4413. Brown, Les. "Report Recommends New Structure, Fee for
Public Stations." AG (Feb. 1, 1979) 5B.

The Carnegie Commission on the Future of Public Broadcasting suggestions for a reorganized PBS that would shield the system from political interference.

4414. Browne, Donald R. "Citizen Involvement in Broadcasting: Some European Experiences." PTR 1 (Oct. 1973) 16-28.
How four countries have used national councils to meet the demand for audience participation.

4415. Browne, Donald R. Comparing Broadcast Systems: The Experiences of Six Industrialized Nations. Ames: Iowa State UP, 1989. 447.
Compares France, the Netherlands, the two Germanies, the Soviet Union, and Japan, to "allow students to see that there are many different ways to finance, supervise, and program the media" and to lead them "to reconsider the functions of the mass media" in the US.

4416. Brunsdon, Charlotte. Films for Women. London: British Film Institute, 1986. 236.
Book as whole an attack on white, male establishment sexism (and racism and elitism). Urges women to produce, distribute, and exhibit films for women.

4417. Cevoli, Cathy. "Ted Turner Has a Better Idea." NT 4.5 (1986) 14.
Turner, owner of the largest US cable network, has become one of the antinuclear movement's "most influential allies." He has organized the Better World Society to produce and acquire programming on arms control, population, and the environment, and will provide free air time on his WTBS station.

4418. Cirino, Robert. "An Alternative American Communications System." American Media & Mass Culture. Ed. Donald Lazere. Berkeley: U of California P, 1987. 568-576. (From CE 38.3 [1977]).
Contrasts the ideologically narrow US communications system to the wider pluralism in most other democracies. Some democracies do not permit private ownership of broadcasting, and the public system in the Netherlands follows a "spectrum-sharing model, with broadcasting access, technology, and production capacity divided [equally] among four different broadcasting societies, each representing a different basic viewpoint," with other views also given access but in smaller amounts. Italy, France, and Belgium are moving to this spectrum principle. In contrast, public broadcasting in the US is funded less than in other major democracies, and PBS does not provide the public with all points of view on a competing basis. The author proposes a United States Broadcasting Corporation (USBC) to supplement the commercial system. It would consist of "four separate and independent networks representing different positions--socialist, liberal, conservative, libertarian," each network with its own budget to hire staff and produce programs" (570). He believes "the

same system can equally well be extended to newspapers, magazines, books, and film" (569).

4419. Cockburn, Alexander. "Use It or Lose It: The Right to Make Your Own TV." ITT 11.20 (1987) 17.
Public access television provides an alternative to the "electronic propaganda system," but unless enough people take advantage of it and use it, the cable industry will withdraw the service.

4420. Cockburn, Alexander, and Richard McKerrow. "El Salvador: The Movie They Wouldn't Watch." ITT 14.25 (May 16-22, 1990) 17.
An account of a documentary, "El Salvador Human Rights Violations 1988-1989," and a booklet exposing the killings "done by government forces."

4421. Cohen, Dan. "Global Village Aims to Save 'Endangered Documentary.'" Guard 41.7 (Nov. 9, 1988) 17.
New York's Global Village sponsors documentary series particularly by or about women.

4422. Collum, Danny. "Cracks in the Tube: Dissident Films on Official Channels." Soj 18.8 (Aug.-Sept. 1989) 42-3.
In praise of public TV's POV (Point of View), an independent documentary film series on such subjects as racism, nuclearism, and unemployment. This is "the only regular national outlet for independent films."

4423. Czitrom, Daniel. "Bilko: A Sitcom for All Seasons." Popular Culture in America. Ed. Paul Buhle. Minneapolis: U of Minnesota P, 1987. 156-162.
Phil Silvers as Sgt. Bilko challenged military, authoritarian values, "endless variations on the theme of challenging authority."

4424. Day, Barbara. "How Black Filmmakers Fought Stereotypes." Guard 43.4 (Nov. 14, 1990) 19.
On the exhibit, "From Harlem to Hollywood: American Race Movies 1912-1948," at the American Museum of the Moving Image.

4425. Dean, Sidney W., Jr., and Robert Lewis Shayon. "Grabbing an Electronic Bonanza." Na 249.11 (Oct. 9, 1989) 370, 387-88.
Optical fiber technology could make "passive consumption a thing of the past" via interactive networks and a multiplicity of empowering information services, but this dream of universal communications may wither if the large communications carriers are allowed to supply content as well.

4426. Deep Dish Directory. New York: Paper Tiger T.V., 1986. 97.
Programs designed to strengthen public access TV by empowering individuals and groups against the increasing power of media corporations.

4427. Deep Dish T.V.
"Extends the concept of public access to a national scale, using satellites to distribute community and independent programs to access channels across the country." Example programs: "Biting the Hand That Leads Us: Humor and Social Change," "Good Things Come from Small Packages: Video by and for Young People," "A Dish of Central America." (See Paper Tiger TV).

4428. Dexter, Gerry. Muzzled Media: How to Get the News You've Been Missing! Lake Geneva, WI: Tiare, 1986. 96.
Shortwave international radio is the key to variety and amplitude of information in contrast to the meager fare of network TV.

4429. Diamond, Edwin. "Futures." Sign Off: The Last Days of Television. Cambridge, MA: MIT P, 1982. 273.
Discusses Turner's CNN, the diversification of magazines, the development of more activist/interactive viewers of TV, and the First Amendment/free press.

4430. Dor-Ner, Zvi. "How Television Reports Conflicts: Observations of an Unhappy Practitioner." NmR 31.2/3 (Summer-Autumn 1977) 23-26.
Appeals to journalists to avoid intensifying violence and to seek ways to facilitate peaceful resolution of conflicts.

4431. Downey, Roger. "The Pride of Dorothy S. Bullit." Channels 5.3 (Sept.-Oct. 1985) 45-6.
"The owner of Seattle's first television station has kept it creative and committed to public service."

4432. Downing, John. "California Newsreel." Radical Media. Boston: South End, 1984. 139-145.
An independent film company that focuses mainly on Southern Africa and the US labor movement.

4433. Downing, John. "KPFA, Berkeley." Radical Media. Boston: South End, 1984. 74-95.
Account of "the oldest of the listener-supported independent stations" (1949-).

4434. Downing, John. "Third World Newsreel." Radical Media. Boston: South End, 1984. 125-138.
A film company struggling against racism, sexism, and classism.

4435. Dyson, Michael. "Bill Cosby and the Politics of Race." Zeta 2.9 (Sept. 1989) 26-30.
Defends The Cosby Show's approach to race, maintaining that those who say the program ignores the problems of the black underclass expect too much; a non-stereotyped, non-clown black family in prime time is a real achievement.

BROADCASTING, FILM, VIDEO   611

4436.   "Electronic Media: Increasing Access." Readings in
        Mass Communication: Concepts and Issues in the Mass
        Media. Ed. Michael C. Emery and Ted Curtis Smythe.
        Dubuque, IA: Wm. C. Brown, 1974. 21-48.
   Three essays on how to increase public and community
control.

4437.   Emerson, Gloria. "Haskell Wexler Zooms in On
        Nicaragua." MJ 10 (Aug.-Sept. 1985) 30-35, 52.
   On the making of the movie about the Nicaraguan revolution,
Latino, by the Oscar-winner cinematographer Wexler, who put up
his own money and several years to persuade the people of the
US "we shouldn't be killing down there."

4438.   Esmonde-White, Patrick. "Mass Demonstrations and Mass
        Media. The 1983 March on Washington: A Case Study."
        Union for Experimenting Colleges/Union Grad. Sch.,
        1985. 272. DAI 46 (1985) 1430-A.
   Examines the March to identify factors for successful mass
demonstrations, especially the importance of alternate,
democratic forms of the electronic media, "if access to the
marketplace of ideas is to be open to the powerless."

4439.   Esplin, Fred. "Local Programming for Social Action."
        PTR 5.4 (1977) 24-27.
   WITF-TV of Harrisburg, PA spent its entire year's local
programming budget to a series designed to resettle refugees.
The manager of the station believes public TV ought to be
involved in social action and not merely information.

4440.   Etzioni, Amitai, Kenneth Laudon, and Sara Lipson.
        "Participatory Technology: The MINERVA Communications
        Tree." JoC 25.2 (Spring 1975) 64-74.
   The technology of telephone circuitry may enable mass
democratic participation in modern society.

4441.   "Fade-Out Censor." Na 246.23 (June 11, 1988) 812-813.
   Documentary filmmakers won a victory in court against the
USIA, which had blocked the export of films critical of the US
while accepting pro-US (pro-corporate) films made by corporations and religious groups.

4442.   Fisher, Marc. "Pacifica's Next Wave." MJ 14.4 (May
        1989) 51-52.
   The Pacifica alternative radio network, after years of
shrinking financial support and loss of key personnel to NPR,
is now making a comeback thanks to its gavel-to-gavel coverage
of the Iran-contra hearings.

4443.   Forest, Jim. "Tuning in on the World." Fel (July-Aug.
        1984) 15-16.
   Holland is a "media oasis" with its many stations representing many diverse political perspectives, and minimal advertising is presented in blocks before and after only some programs.

4444. Frank, Robert S. Message Dimensions of Television News. Lexington, MA: Lexington, 1973. 120.
How to do content analysis of TV news.

4445. Garnham, Nicholas. "The Media and the Public Sphere." Communicating Politics. Ed. Peter Golding, et al. New York: Holmes & Meier, 1986. 37-53.
Sees public service broadcasting as the only possible site for preserving communicative universality in the nation-state, and criticizes the limitations of journalistic professionalism in its knowledge-brokering role, arguing for wider access to media for diverse groups and views.

4446. Geltner, Sharon. "Matching Set: Brian Lamb and Cable's C-SPAN." WJR 6.7 (1984) 29-33.
The cable Satellite Public Affairs Network, which broadcasts government proceedings live, unedited and without commentary, is "the first true innovation in television since the cable revolution." Its head's objective is "getting more Americans involved in the political process."

4447. Gever, Martha. "Meet the Press: On Paper Tiger Television." Afterimage (Nov. 1983) 7-11.
A TV program that criticizes media monopolies and analyzes the politics of the communications industry.

4448. Gillespie, Gilbert. Public Access Cable Television in the United States and Canada: With an Annotated Bibliography. New York: Praeger, 1975. 157.
"This book is provided as a reference volume for persons who are involved with or planning to get involved with the production of community media programming," particularly "public access (community) cable television (PACT). In this volume the reader will find a survey of public access history and a discussion of the apparent impact of early experiments with the PACT idea. Someone has stated that the prime value of PACT is the decentralization of the sources of propaganda."

4449. Glass, Fred. "Organized Labor Struggles to Focus Its Clouded Media Vision." ITT 13.21 (Apr. 19-25, 1989) 20.
Recounts recent efforts by organized labor to reach the television audience, including a $13 million ad campaign and plans for a labor-oriented news program on PBS.

4450. Griffin, Julia. "Watching the Watchdogs. Can We Improve the Evening News?" Access 55 (Sept. 1977) 1, 4-5.
Discusses how to increase the quantity and diversity of news on TV, including the strengths and weaknesses of the National News Council.

4451. Guimary, Donald. Citizens' Groups & Broadcasting. New York: Praeger, 1975. 170.
Includes a history of citizens' groups, reactions of broadcasters to citizens' groups, reactions of the FCC and courts,

and an examination of three citizens' groups.

4452. Gunther, Marc. "Pacifica: Radio's Outlet for the Outrageous." WJR 5.4 (1983) 42-44.
This non-profit network of five stations has survived harassment by congressional committees hunting for communists, bombings by the KKK, and frequent attacks from conservatives and rightists for their strong expression of free speech from a left perspective.

4453. Gustafson, Julie. "De Antonio: He Made Film Out of Chaos." Guard 42.11 (Jan. 10, 1990) 20.
Emile de Antonio was one of the greatest political documentarians. Some of his work: Point of Order about the 1954 Army-McCarthy hearings, In the Year of the Pig about the Vietnam war, Milhouse: A White Comedy about Richard Nixon, In the King of Prussia about the Plowshares 8, Mr. Hoover and I about the government's view of himself.

4454. Haight, Timothy R., ed. Telecommunications Policy and the Citizen: Public Interest Perspectives on the Communications Act Rewrite. New York: Praeger, 1979. 266.
Eleven essays respond to H.R. 13015, a sweeping revision of the Communications Act, and additional bills, by teachers and lawyers "who have had practical experience with pleading citizens' positions for communication change."

4455. Haight, Timothy R., and Laurie R. Weinstein. "Changing Ideology on Television By Changing Telecommunications Policy: Notes on a Contradictory Situation." Communication and Social Structure: Critical Studies in Mass Media Research. Ed. Emile G. McAnany, et al. New York: Praeger, 1981. 110-144.
Traces "some of the history of the media reform movement, to assess the value of a strategy of influencing the formation of ideology in the mass media through changing government policy. In all, it is a tale of early hope curdling to later frustration, but in its telling we can not only learn better how hegemony functions in the related areas of mass communication and the state, but also perhaps how to continue to struggle against it" (111).

4456. Halleck, Deedee. "Paper Tiger Television: Smashing the Myths of the Information Industry Every Week on Public Access Cable." MCS 6 (1984) 313-318.
A description of the weekly series of media analyses transmitted on access channels to subscribers of Manhattan Cable in New York City. Halleck created the idea of the programs. "Each week Paper Tiger offers a critical reading of one publication" which includes "basic information on the economic structure of the corporation that produces the publication."

4457. Hanhardt, John G., ed. Video Culture: A Critical Investigation. Layton, Utah: Peregrine Smith, 1986. 296.

Focuses on new technology for alternative art and communications.

4458. "Help Unsell the War." New York: Clergy and Laymen Concerned, 1972.
A collection of 30- and 60-second TV and radio spots in opposition to the Vietnam War, produced by advertising executives and distributed by Clergy and Laymen.

4459. "Here, We Would Suggest, Is a Program for the FCC." Problems and Controversies in Television and Radio. Ed. Harry Skornia and Jack Kitson. Palo Alto: Pacific, 1968. 108-113. (Consumers Reports, Feb. 1960).
Twelve proposals to "guard against the abuse of broadcasting privileges and against corruption" in the FCC--e.g., a Consumers Council with full review powers.

4460. Hickey, Neil. "C-Span's Mission: Keeping an Eye on Our Democracy." TVG (Mar. 30, 1985) 26-29.
In praise of 24-hour non-profit cable live TV of the House of Representatives and House and Senate Committees, all kinds of seminars, etc.

4461. Hickey, Neil. "The Man Who Set the Standard." CJR 24.6 (Mar.-Apr. 1986) 54-57.
Praises Edward R. Murrow's news broadcasting.

4462. Hickey, Neil. "TV Must Create Rebuttal Time." TVG (June 22, 1985) 32-5.
"The medium still isn't doing enough to accommodate those who feel wronged or want to express views opposing what they see."

4463. Himmelstein, Hal. "Toward an Oppositional Television: Strategies for Change." Television Myth and the American Mind. New York: Praeger, 1984. 305-325.
A survey and evaluation of diverse oppositions to the "dominant centralized commercial and public television" in the US: community-based video documentary, criticism of media, etc.

4464. Hindman, James. "A Survey of Alternative Video II." AFI Education Newsletter 4.3 (Jan.-Feb. 1981) 5-8.
A model syllabus that surveys alternative video practice. The first installment offered perspectives on TV viewing, community video, and video by artists; this second syllabus focuses on the work of independent producers for public TV, on workplace video, and the video market and technology.

4465. Hollander, Richard. Video Democracy: The Vote-From-Home Revolution. Mt. Airy, MD: Lomond, 1985. 161.
Compares the democratic and the totalitarian potentialities in the new communication technologies. Interactive technologies, such as videotex, provide an unparalleled opportunity for reviving direct democracy, but they also tend to isolate individuals from the public sphere.

BROADCASTING, FILM, VIDEO   615

4466. Hudson, Heather E. "Divestiture and Deregulation in US
         Telecommunications: Consumer Policy Issues." MCS 7
         (1985) 71-84.
   "[T]elephone users will need to become well-informed consumers and active defenders of their own interests in order to
preserve access to affordable and reliable telecommunications."

4467. Hulser, Kathleen. "Access TV Addresses People, Not
         Nielsens." ITT 9 (Mar. 13-19, 1985) 20-21.
   "In the last decade, local TV production has quietly sprung
up in more than a thousand public access cable centers."

4468. Hulser, Kathleen. "Paper Tiger Television." AF 10.5
         (1985) 61-63.
   Profile of N.Y. public access cable program whose aim is to
make people think about the underpinnings of the information
industry.

4469. "If They Were Going to Make War on Us, We Were Going to
         Make War on Them." Take 118 (Nov. 9, 1979) 44-45.
   The film on the anti-war movement, The War at Home, counters
Hollywood Vietnam fantasies with the realities of the Dow
riot, the "grisly" destruction of Cambodia by US bombing, the
lying by officials, etc.

4470. "In the Public Interest." Washington, DC.
   A nationwide daily radio program intended to counter the
many right-wing radio programs throughout the country.

4471. Jankowski, Mike. "Alternative Television from Austin,
         Texas." Media 2.3 (n.d.) 3-4.
   Discusses the problems and successes of the public access
cable series Alternative Views.

4472. Jankowski, Nick. "Community Television: A Tool for
         Community Action?" Comm 7.1 (1982) 33-58.
   Assesses the workability of community produced television
and enumerates the requirements for its success, stressing
that public access will not necessarily produce activism in
the community.

4473. Jetter, Alexis. "Screen Test for the Left." MJ 10
         (Aug.-Sept. 1985) 10-11.
   Urges more filmic opposition to US foreign policies, such as
in Central America.

4474. Johnson, Nicholas. How to Talk Back to Your Television
         Set. Boston: Little, 1970. 228.
   Has two chapters on improving TV despite its control by
corporations.

4475. Johnson, Nicholas. "Introduction." Telecommunications
         Policy and the Citizen: Public Interest Perspectives
         on the Communications Act Rewrite. Ed. Timothy
         Haight. New York: Praeger, 1979. 1-7.

An appeal for a communications policy not in corporate special interests but in a "national interest, a public interest."

4476. Jubera, Drew. "'Sesame' Stars Launch Racism Attack." AG (Nov. 27, 1990) 6E.
Sesame Street will confront racial and ethnic differences and conflicts explicitly, turning away from the color-blind strategy.

4477. Kellner, Douglas. "Public Access Television: Alternative Views." American Media & Mass Culture. Ed. Donald Lazere. Berkeley: U of California P, 1987. 610-618.
Public access TV in Austin, TX, provides "weekly antinuclear programs, black and Chicano series, gay programs, countercultural and anarchist programs, an atheist program, occasional feminist programs, and a weekly left news magazine, "Alternative Views," which has produced over 250 hour-long videocassettes from 1978 to the present."

4478. Kelly, Tom. "Roger and US." C&C 50.2 (Feb. 19, 1990) 45-6.
Describes the documentary Roger and Me by Michael Moore about Roger Smith, chief executive officer of General Motors, the impact of GM plant closings, and how corporate dominance has created "two nations," separated by "class, race, and willful ignorance."

4479. Kerner, Jack. "KLZ-TV: The Shallow Channel." UM 1.8 (Apr. 1971) 4-6.
Denver's CBS outlet's license renewal was challenged by a citizen group because it sought profits prior to the public good.

4480. Kuntz, Jonathan. "The Films of George Cukor." U of California, LA, 1982. 250. DAI 43.4 (Oct. 1982) 955-A.
Cukor's films begin "a critique of the social repression of sexual identity" and "the inadequacy of male-dominated society in dealing with individual female sexuality."

4481. Lance, Peter. "The People v. the Wasteland." MORE 2.6 (June 1976) 8-10.
Citizen groups challenge TV stations for better programs.

4482. Lappé, Frances Moore. What to Do After You Turn Off the TV. New York: Ballantine, 1985. 197.
Family members can live happier and more fulfilled lives by putting the time normally spent watching TV to better use doing things with one another and learning about their world.

4483. Lesage, Julia. "Talkin' To Us." JC 5 (Jan.-Feb. 1975) 3-4.
The film Speaking Directly calls into question the ruling ideology.

BROADCASTING, FILM, VIDEO

4484. Lewin, Jackie. "TV on a Shoestring: Can the Little Guy Make It?" TVG (Nov. 29, 1980) 38-45.
A station in Broomfield, CO, struggles to prove it can.

4485. Making the News Fit. Dir. Beth Sanders; written by Randy Baker. 28 min., color, all video formats. New York: Cinema Guild, 1986.
Evaluates press coverage of El Salvador from 1980 to 1985 indicating a press corps often little more than a conduit for White House disinformation.

4486. Maland, Charles. "Dr. Strangelove (1964): Nightmare Comedy and the Ideology of Liberal Consensus." AQ 31 (Winter 1979) 697-717.
The film satirizes the bi-partisan Sovietphobia, male chauvinism, secrecy, mindless language and values, and violence of post-WWII US.

4487. Mandla, A. "South Africa Now." Z 2.5 (May 1989) 49-51.
An independent TV news program which fills the information gap left by South African censorship is presented as a "model for how news programming on a range of issues might be presented on television, if the system was open or could be opened to more diversity and to a wider range of perspectives."

4488. Manley, Paula. "Public Access--Local Static into Action." Win 19.15-16 (1983) 7-8.
Local public-access channels provide programs which "meet needs which cannot be met through traditional approaches to media."

4489. "Mary and Goliath." 60 Minutes. New York: CBS Television Network, 1985 (Sunday, Jan. 27). Transcript 17-21.
The story of Mary Sinclair's battle against Consumers Power Company's nuclear plant in Midland, Mich., the Nuclear Regulatory Commission, the local newspaper, Chamber of Commerce, and most of the citizens who wanted the plant in spite of questions about its safety.

4490. Massing, Michael. "Should Public Affairs Be the Networks' Private Domain?" CJR 19.1 (1980) 34-37.
Use of anti-trust laws by independent filmmakers to gain access to network TV.

4491. Matusow, Barbara. "NBC's Intrepid Investigators: Brian Ross and Ira Silverman." WJR 8.6 (1986) 18-22.
NBC's "premier investigative reporting team" won a duPont-Columbia award in 1985 for the ABSCAM story, exposing payola in the recording industry, and other exploits.

4492. Maurer, Marvin. "Screening Nuclear War and Vietnam." Television in Society. Ed. Arthur Berger. New Brunswick, NJ: Transaction, 1987. 257-267.

Analyzes the docudrama, "The Day After," and the thirteen-part documentary, "Vietnam: A Television History." Both "challenge American policies based on military strength" and question the US as "defender of democratic values."

4493. McGavin, Patrick Z. "Film Forecast on the Northern Front." ITT 15.2 (Nov. 14-20, 1990) 21.
"Toronto provides a corrective to Hollywood's venal distribution system, which effectively cancels out marginal or experimental films."

4494. "Media Resources on Central America." Media 2.4 (n.d.) 10-14.
Alternative views of Central America on video.

4495. Meeske, Mike. "Minority Ownership of Broadcast Stations: The Diversification Policy." FSY (1977) 81-86.
Examines court decisions which forced the FCC to give preference to minorities in station licensing.

4496. Meyer, Karl. "The Golden Giveaway." SR (Mar. 18, 1978) 58.
Advocates a franchise tax on commercial broadcasting for public broadcasting. At present commercial broadcasting freely exploits the national resource of air, which is in fact a public subsidy, as its "God-given right."

4497. Millman, Joel. "Covering Central America on a Shoestring." CJR 27.6 (Mar.-Apr. 1989) 10.
Noticiero Univision, the Spanish-language TV network based in California, offers news of Central America far broader and deeper than do the networks, and with a tiny staff.

4498. Mininberg, Mark. "Circumstances within Our Control: Promoting Freedom of Expression through Cable Television." HCLQ 11.4 (Summer 1984) 551-598.
If society is to attain the goals of the First Amendment, "it cannot rely solely on the commercial media. Rather, channels should be opened for public use: the screen must become the modern town square. . . . a general right of affirmative citizen access to cable television has become a practical and constitutional necessity" (595-6, 598).

4499. Mitzen, Jennifer. "Nuclear Radiation: Idaho's Nuclear Activists Get the Word Out." Media 2.4 (n.d.) 5.
A citizens' group makes films to inform the public of nuclear power plant hazards.

4500. "The Modest Price of Excellence." CJR 22 (July-Aug. 1983) 21.
Praise of National Public Radio's evening news program, All Things Considered.

4501. Morrow, Frank. "Alternative Views Has an Impact."

Community Television Review 9.1 (1986) 26.
An account of "one of the oldest social issues programs on public access" TV in Austin, TX.

4502. Morrow, James. "We Need a Nightly News Show on the Nuclear Arms Race." TVG (Mar. 8, 1986) 6-7.
"Daily coverage of the 'nuclear nightmare' may give us the power to end it."

4503. Mosco, Vincent. Broadcasting in the United States: Innovative Challenge and Organizational Control. Norwood, NJ: Ablex, 1979. 153.
Chapter 10 recommends ways of changing the entrenched structure of broadcasting.

4504. Murdock, Dave. "Farmers Speak Out: Video From the Heartland." Media 2.4 (n.d.) 7-9.
First in a series on rural independent media.

4505. Murrow, Edward R. "Murrow's Indictment of Broadcasting." CJR 4.2 (1965) 27-32.
The complete text is given of Murrow's October 15, 1958 speech at the Radio-Television News Directors Association convention. In it, Murrow argues that corporate sponsors of programming should occasionally finance educational programs or documentaries inserted into the regular time slots of popular programs.

4506. Not Top Gun. New York: Paper Tiger TV, 1986.
Explores the popular feature film/music video/soft drink advertisement/home video/children's toy to reveal the dissolving boundaries between entertainment and merchandising; also adds more evidence of Hollywood's contribution to militarism.

4507. "Now, About Those Facts . . ." ITT 11.2 (1986) 21.
A District Court Judge has ruled that the U.S. Information Agency cannot restrict the export of documentaries which show the US in a negative light.

4508. Ouellette, Dan. "The Great Reagan-Bush Coverup." WPN 5.5 (Nov.-Dec.-Jan. 1988-89) 3.
Review of the film Coverup: Behind the Iran Contra Affair by Gary Meyer, Barbara Trent, and David Caspar. The film documents the many illegal transactions at the highest echelons of government as part of a large-scale conspiracy, including a plan by FEMA and Ollie North to suspend the U.S. Constitution if Central American invaded by the US.

4509. Panitt, Merrill. "A New Vehicle for Television." TQ 1.3 (Aug. 1962) 55-60.
Seeks changes to prevent corporate control of programming.

4510. Paper Tiger Television. New York.
Uses video to look at the communications industry by examining print media over TV. Investigates both the contents of

print media and the corporate structures behind them.

4511. Paul Jacobs and the Nuclear Gang. Produced and directed by Jack Wills, Saul Landau, and Penny Bernstein. Center for Documentary Media Prcduction, 1978. 60 min., color.
Chronicles the government's attempt to suppress information about the health hazards of radiation. Winner of EMMY for best documentary of the year and the George Polk award for investigative journalism.

4512. Post, Steve. Playing in the FM Band: A Personal Account of Free Radio. New York: Viking, 1974. 230.
The story of the Pacifica Foundation listener-sponsored WBAI in New York City, a station free of profit-oriented commercial censorship and government efforts to dominate the media as a wing of government. It "tells the story of what radio can be when unfettered by accounting books, when it is almost monomaniacal about free speech." WBAI is "one of the few examples of freedom in action in the electronic media" (from Julius Lester's Foreword).

4513. Powers, Ron and Jerrold Oppenheim. "Is TV Too Profitable?" CJR 11.1 (1972) 7-13.
Networks make huge profits each year, yet are unwilling to devote prime time space to news programs or documentaries. The FCC should encourage prime-time network news through restrictions and bonuses.

4514. Price, Anders. "Peace TV." NT 6.6 (July-Aug. 1988) 15.
Tells about an independent film and video project in Berkeley, CA, the Educational Film and Video Project, that "produces and distributes films and works with activists to get peace programs onto the airwaves."

4515. Prowitt, Marsha. "Effective Public Action: Television and Radio." Mass News. Ed. David Leroy and Christopher Sterling. Englewood Cliffs, NJ: Prentice-Hall, 1973. 281-294.
Part of a manual for citizen action in broadcasting.

4516. Public Service Responsibility of Broadcast Licensees. Washington, DC: Federal Communication Commission, 1946. 59.
Known as the "blue book," this report castigated stations for failing to live up to the community obligations to provide quality programming which had justified their lucrative licenses in the first place.

4517. Rabinovitz, Lauren. "Radical Cinema: The Films & Film Practices of Maya Deren, Shirley Clarke, & Joyce Wieland." U of Texas, Austin, 1982. 352. DAI 43.12 (June 1983) 3736-A.
They approached filmmaking as a radically political activity.

4518. Raboy, Mark. "International Alternative Video Front Takes Shape in Montreal." The Democratic Communiqué 9.2 (Summer 1990) 9.
A conference on video for change with the intention to build a permanent international coalition.

4519. Raskin, Jamin. "The People's Mort." Z 2.2 (Feb. 1989) 67-71.
For all of his ultraconservative posturing and abuse of his radical guests, Morton Downey's show is actually superior to most TV news shows in that it does allow representatives of a broad range of political perspectives.

4520. Roe, Yale. The Television Dilemma: Search for a Solution. New York: Hastings, 1962. 184.
Suggestions for a better-quality TV by a network sales executive.

4521. Rosenthal, Alan, ed. The Documentary Conscience: A Casebook in Film Making. Berkeley: U of California P, 1980. 436.
About documentary "in the seventies," the "working methods and production problems . . . from financing and fund raising through restrictions such as censorship and personal pressures . . . the position of the networks both as sponsors and as end users." "In some of the interviews I have tried to probe the effects of the monopoly power of network transmission."

4522. Schwartz, Robert. "Public Access to Cable Television." HLJ 33 (Mar. 1982) 1009-1044.
Defends public access to cable systems and consequently denounces the Supreme Court's Midwest II ruling.

4523. Seeger, Peter. "The Air Belongs to Everyone." HAM (Apr. 28, 1969) 53-57.
As a corrective to the uniformity of television, the author proposes "requiring all commercial TV stations to donate 20 percent of their time to what would be called 'the public sector' of the air."

4524. Shamberg, Michael, and Raindance Corporation. Guerilla Television. New York: Holt, Rinehart, and Winston, 1971. 108.
Individual and group alternatives to network TV using home video cameras, expressing the hope that the power of commercial TV can be decentralized.

4525. Shannon, Kathleen. "Real Issues in a Reel World." M&V 49 (Winter 1989) 14-15.
"A feminist filmmaker describes how she makes films and uses them to bring about change."

4526. Shapiro, Andrew O. Media Access: Your Rights to Express Your Views on Radio & Television. Boston: Little, Brown, 1976. 297.

The author stresses the public interest standard for broadcasting, the idea of the licensee as a public trustee, as the basis for viewer and listener rights.

4527. Skornia, Harry. Television and Society: An Inquest and Agenda for Improvement. New York: McGraw-Hill, 1965. 268.
Chap. 9 offers "An Agenda for Change," detailed recommendations for the government and industry.

4528. Smith, Ralph Lee. The Wired Nation, Cable TV: The Electronic Communications Highway. New York: Harper & Row, 1972. 128.
A longer version of a special issue of Na (May 18, 1970). A case for civic, community, educational, and cultural use of cable TV, including a proposal for nonprofit ownership.

4529. Sola Pool, Ithiel de. "The Changing Flow of Television." JoC 27.2 (1977) 139-149.
As an alternative to a monolithic one-way flow of communication, new technology will disperse production centers and enrich viable cultures.

4530. Sola Pool, Ithiel de, ed. Talking Back: Citizen Feedback and Cable Technology. Cambridge, MA: MIT P, 1973. 325.
On the prospects of CATV: "copious numbers of channels, pay TV, and two-way communication"--"interactive on-demand telecommunication."

4531. Spark, Clare. "Pacifica Radio and the Politics of Culture." American Media & Mass Culture. Ed. Donald Lazere. Berkeley: U of California P, 1987. 577-590.
Summarizes the internal conflict in the radio station KPFK, between the drive to be a vanguard voice for left politics and the equally strong purpose to provide community access. Despite the difficulties, she is confident that "the struggle for alternative media and political visions is a valid one" (580), especially its anti-authoritarian aim to encourage an active, creative public.

4532. Stamets, Bill. "The Color of Money--That's Ecotainment." ITT 14.26 (May 23-June 5, 1990) 20-21.
An account of the Environmental Film Festival in Colorado Springs that attracted nearly 500 entries.

4533. Steinberg, Charles S., ed. Broadcasting: The Critical Challenges. New York: Hastings, 1974. 315.
Broadcasting should be regulated for the public interest.

4534. Straight, Michael. Trial by Television. Boston: Beacon, 1954. 282.
An account of the Senate hearing in 1954 over charges by the Army that Sen. Joseph McCarthy had sought preferential treatment for Pvt. G. David Schine, and McCarthy's countercharge

that the Army was seeking to defeat his exposure of Communist infiltration in the Army. TV exposed McCarthy's lies, slanders and bullyings to the American people and "hurt McCarthy."

4535. Stryker, Sean. "Networking for a Green Future." EIJ 2.2 (1987) 27-28.
"By putting the power of microelectronic information processing technology in reach of grassroots organizations, the desktop communication revolution can make it possible to empower local communities attempting to influence the actions of multinational institutions."

4536. Sullivan, Rob. "Hollywood Peaceniks." NT 6.5 (1988) 16-20.
Report on recent efforts to replace propagandized stereotypes of Russians in films by educating the industry about realities of life and politics in the Soviet Union.

4537. Symons, Howard. "Making Yourself Heard (and Seen): The Citizen's Role in Communications." Telecommunications Policy and the Citizen. Ed. Timothy Haight. New York: Praeger, 1979. 9-28.
Citizens need to understand the "extraordinary concentration of economic power" combined with "its twin, political power" if they are ever to transform the telecommunication industries into institutions that serve the national good.

4538. Talbot, David, and Barbara Zheutlin. Creative Differences: Profiles of Hollywood Dissidents. Boston: South End, 1978. 370.
An account of the left in Hollywood from the days before the blacklist to the present through profiles of 16 people whose work made a difference through their orientation to the public sphere rather than to the interests of class and privilege.

4539. Thelwell, Michael. "Pieces of the Dream." MJ 12.11 (Feb.-Mar. 1987) 58-60.
The six-part PBS series, Eyes on the Prize, is an attempt to present a full and clear recapitulation of the Civil Rights Movement of the 1960s.

4540. Van Houten, Carter. "'Faces of War' Confronts Television Bias." NicP 12 (Summer-Fall 1986) 11.
Tells about how Neighbor to Neighbor fought back against TV refusal to sell air time for its film Faces of War, interviews of US citizens living in Nicaragua and El Salvador and opposing US intervention.

4541. "A Video Which Claims to Tell All." SLJR 18.110 (Oct. 1988) 7.
The film Coverup indicts the Reagan administration for drug smuggling, weapons trading, assassinations, subversion of the Constitution, and other malfeasances and crimes going back to 1979.

4542. Vieira, Joao. "Hegemony & Resistance: Parody & Carnival in Brazilian Cinema." New York U, 1984. 253. DAI 46 (1985) 3-A.
  Brazilian narrative film resists the "hegemony of the North American film in the Brazilian market" via parody, carnivalesque musical comedies, and other satiric modes. Some of the US films mocked: Samson & Delilah, High Noon, Jaws, and King-Kong.

4543. Vogel, Amos. "Independents: Smashing Myths About the Information Industry." FiC 18 (Nov.-Dec. 1982) 76-77.
  Praises Paper Tiger TV, a video program that analyzes print media.

4544. Volpendesta, David. "Jennifer Stone Unturned from Her Always Critical Task." ITT 12.33 (Aug. 31-Sept. 6, 1988) 18.
  Stone especially opposes authoritarianism, sado-masochism and pursuit of death in her writing and radio commentary. For example, her criticism of Academy Award winning Platoon exposes its "megalomacho" glorification of death.

4545. Wasserman, Harry. "We Had to Destroy the Philippines to Save the Movie." Take 118 (Nov. 9, 1979) 46-47.
  About Coppola's Apocalypse Now, which "captures the irony" that thirty years (after stopping the fascists in WWII) the US has become "the fascist monster."

4546. Weinberg, Steve. "CNN Goes for the Gold: A Star-Studded Team is Now in Place. How's It Doing?" CJR 29.3 (Sept.-Oct. 1990) 21-24.
  An account of Ted Turner's plan "to mount the most pervasive investigative reporting effort in the history of broadcast (and maybe print) journalism."

4547. Weiss, Philip. "The Last, Best Hope for the TV Documentary." Channels 3 (Nov.-Dec. 1983) 85-9.
  Praises PBS's Frontline produced by David Fanning.

4548. Wenglinsky, Martin. "Television News: A New Slant." TQ 12.2 (1975) 38-45.
  The author urges reporters to emulate I.F. Stone, "who has shown how to develop immensely informative stories that get 'behind' the official facade by examining the handouts, briefings, and official data which constitute that facade."

4549. Westen, Tracy A. "Barriers to Creativity." JoC 28.2 (1978) 36-42.
  In response to the inherent conformity of the US broadcasting system driven to maximize profits, Westen suggests that one solution, analogous to the broadcast system in Holland, would be to separate the control of television programming from its financing.

4550. What's Wrong with this Picture? Changing the World on

BROADCASTING, FILM, VIDEO

Prime Time. 2 vols. Burnaby, Canada: PEPS, 1989. Vol. 1 papers on communication and social movements. Vol. 2 includes information on gaining access to media.

4551. Wicklein, John. "Technology Untamed." C&C 44 (Sept. 17, 1984) 335.
Praises a TV series that gives labor's perspective.

4552. Wicklein, John. "Wired City, U.S.A.: The Charms and Dangers of Two-Way TV." The Atlantic 243 (Feb. 1979) 35-42.
Appraises QUBE, a two-way interactive cable system in Columbus, OH.

4553. Winer, Laurie. "State-of-the-Art Criticism." CJR 23 (Mar.-Apr. 1985) 18-19.
A story about Paper Tiger Television, the award-winning public access show on New York's Manhattan Cable, each program of which tackles a single publication or medium. Tiger's purpose: "Investigation into the corporate structures of the media and critical analysis of their content" in order "to regain cultural pluralism and democratic control of information resources."

4554. Winett, Richard A., et al. "Reducing Energy Consumption: The Long-Term Effects of a Single TV Program." JoC 34.3 (1984) 37-51.
"Summer Breeze," a 20-min. TV program demonstrating conservation strategies and emphasizing personal benefits, resulted overall in a 10% energy savings.

4555. Wurtzel, Alan. "Public-Access Cable TV: Programming." JoC 25.3 (Summer 1975) 15-21.
"If made available, public-access channels can be used to increase communications at the grassroots" (21).

4556. Zito, Stephen. "The Lost Legacy of Edward R. Murrow." AF 2.5 (1977) 30-32+.
Edward R. Murrow's scathing documentary on Joseph McCarthy in the face of governmental disapproval is a reminder that "there may again come a time, as there was in the fifties, when the most important function of news commentators will be to speak out against prevailing notions."

4557. Zuckerman, Laurence. "The Raw-News Network Hits Its Stride." CJR 24.6 (Mar.-Apr. 1986) 42-44.
The non-profit, twenty-four hours a day Cable Satellite Public Affairs Network (C-SPAN) has developed a growing audience during its seven years in existence. C-SPAN presents House proceedings [and now Senate] "gavel to gavel" and speeches and conferences "in their entirety."

III. D. ALTERNATIVES: PRINT (4558-4724)
See II.D.

4558. Adkins, Jason. "An Interview with George Seldes." PC 6.5 (1986) 16-18.
The former muckraker is "still fighting for a free and responsible press."

4559. Alpern, Sarah. *Freda Kirchwey: A Woman of "The Nation."* Cambridge: Harvard UP, 1987. 319.
Biography of a leading feminist and editor from the 1920s to the 1950s.

4560. "The Alternative Press Awards." UR No. 35 (Sept.-Oct. 1989) 90-91.
The awards "call attention to the 2,000 or so low-profile publications" that "offer cutting-edge ideas, issues, and trends."

4561. Anderson, Jack, with George Clifford. *The Anderson Papers.* New York: Random House, 1973. 275.
Accounts of Anderson's investigative successes.

4562. Anderson, Jack, and James Boyd. "Un-American Activities." *Confessions of a Muckraker: The Inside Story of Life in Washington During the Truman, Eisenhower, Kennedy, & Johnson Years.* New York: Random House, 1979. 100-121.
On Drew Pearson's struggle against the House Un-American Activities Committee and other Sovietphobes.

4563. Armstrong, David. "San Francisco's Polyglot Muckraker." CJR 24.4 (1985) 16-17.
An account of one Laotian refugee's free neighborhood and muckraking newspaper.

4564. Armstrong, David. "A Thinking Approach to News." CJR 17.3 (1978) 61-64.
"The nonprofit Pacific News Service uses both reporters and scholars to uncover hidden issues."

4565. Aronson, James. "The Armed Forces Underground." *Deadline for the Media.* Indianapolis: Bobbs-Merrill, 1972. 198-226.
Describes the rise of the opposition to the Vietnam War within the military services carried on by numerous newspapers, and the military's efforts to suppress them.

4566. Aronson, James. "National Guardianship." *Deadline for the Media.* Indianapolis: Bobbs-Merrill, 1972. 229-52.
An account of the rise of the National Guardian newspaper edited by Aronson and Cedric Belfrage.

4567. Aronson, James. "One Man." *Deadline for the Media.* Indianapolis: Bobbs-Merrill, 1972. 112-22.

An account of Roldo Bartimole's Cleveland journal, Point of View (1968-), "perhaps the sharpest critique of the media--and the city it serves--being published anywhere.

4568. Aronson, James. "Rock 'N' Revolt." Deadline for the Media. Indianapolis: Bobbs-Merrill, 1972. 253-274.
A history of the underground press from its start in 1964 with the Los Angeles Free Press, and police harassment and repression.

4569. [Cancelled]

4570. [Cancelled]

4571. Bagdikian, Ben. "Why Journalists (And Not Businessmen) Should Run the Nation's Daily Newspapers." SLJR 9.52 (June 1983) 10-11, 13.
Cites increasing media concentration and indirect manipulation of the news to further owners' financial interests; suggests journalists "take responsibility for the news they produce" by negotiating for editorial control.

4572. Barbato, Joseph. "Black Sparrow: The House a Poet Helped to Build." Publishers Weekly 232.17 (Oct. 23, 1987) 26-27.
First of a series entitled "Independent Publishing" covering the publishing world outside the commercial mainstream. A "celebration of the vitality of these smaller publishers." This article tells about Black Sparrow Press.

4573. Barnes, Medill. "Alone in the Much." UM 2.2 (Oct. 1971) 3-4.
Investigative reporting by a Rocky Mountain News team about dealings between a Small Business Administration official and a convicted stock manipulator resulted in SBA dismissal of the official and an FBI investigation.

4574. Barsamian, David. "Media Madness." Z 3.4 (Apr. 1990) 75-78.
An interview of Jeff Cohen, Director of FAIR, Fairness and Accuracy in Reporting, publisher of Extra! magazine. One of FAIR's main purposes is to expose the conservative ideological bias of the mainstream media.

4575. Belfrage, Cedric, and James Aronson. Something to Guard: The Stormy Life of the "National Guardian" 1948-1967. New York: Columbia UP, 1978. 362.
An inside history by the former editors of a newspaper dedicated to the First Amendment and to the exposure of fanaticism and bigotry in individuals and institutions of power.

4576. Bennett, James R. "American Literature and the Acquisitive Society, Background and Criticism: A Bibliography." BoB 30 (Oct.-Dec. 1973) 175-184.

This bibliography was continued in BoB 37 (Jan.-Mar. 1980) 1-15, 32, and BoB 37 (Apr.-June 1980) 53-71, 79. Imaginative writers (along with journalists and theologians) have offered the most searching critique of the business ethos.

4577. Bennett, James R., and Christopher Gould. "Reporting the CIA: National Security or Civil Liberties?" FSN 7 (June 1981) 3-12.
In response to the conflict between those who would preserve America from the danger of external enemies and those who would preserve the country by upholding the Bill of Rights, newspapers might better clarify the issues in four ways.

4578. Berlet, Chip. "Counterspy: The Magazine Most Hated by the CIA." AM 9.5 (Jan.-Feb. 1977) 8-13, 30.
Founded by a group of ex-agents, the magazine exposes the identities of CIA operatives around the world.

4579. Berlet, Chip. "How the Muckrakers Saved America." AM 11.1 (1979) 4-7.
Youthful reporters with a commitment to changing society wrote far-reaching political exposes. The "underground" press first revealed the White House's dirty tricks operation and first exposed CIA illegalities. "The underground press was a solvent dissolving the lies."

4580. Berlet, Chip. "A Student Editor Wins One." UM 1.8 (Apr. 1971) 10-11.
A court ordered Ms. Trujillo reinstated after she was suspended as Managing Editor of her school's newspaper.

4581. Bernstein, Carl, and Bob Woodward. All the President's Men. New York: Simon, 1974. 349.
The story of exemplary investigative journalism.

4582. Bollier, David. How to Appraise and Improve Your Daily Newspaper: A Manual for Readers. Washington, DC: Disability Rights Center, 1978. 90.
Innovative editorial policies by leading papers are given along with a discussion of how readers can produce a report on their local newspaper that results in higher quality journalism for the community.

4583. Bollier, David. "Ralph Nader: News Creator." CJR 29.1 (May-June 1990) 51-53.
One of Nader's "most important influences has gone largely ignored--namely, his role in helping to transform some of the basic norms of daily journalism" by his combination of journalist activist.

4584. Bonafede, Dom. "Jack Muckraker Anderson." WJR 2.3 (1980) 40-46.
America's "foremost investigative reporter" sees himself as a defender of "the public weal."

PRINT

4585. Boylan, James. "New York Loses One." CJR 17.3 (Sept.-Oct. 1978) 12-16.
More, a New York-based magazine of journalistic criticism, folded in its seventh year due to financial problems.

4586. Brasch, Walter M. Forerunners of Revolution: Muckrakers and the American Social Conscience. Lanham, MD: UP of America, 1990. 208.
An account of how journalists at the turn of the twentieth century used investigative reporting to expose the widespread exploitation of lower- and middle-class people and to bring about social change.

4587. Brown, Lee. The Reluctant Reformation: On Criticizing the Press in America. New York: McKay, 1974. 256.
Believes that criticism of the press is "crucial and necessary" if it is to serve the nation effectively. The press has improved "much in the past two decades," but criticism is essential to its continued health.

4588. Burkhart, Ford. "Have Computer, Will Cover." CJR 24.6 (Mar.-Apr. 1986) 17-18.
Free-lancers reporting the sanctuary trial under the name of Desert West News received a duPont-Columbia University award.

4589. Burr, Beverly, and Neil DeMause. "Students Press Their Politics." Guard 41.22 (Mar. 1, 1989) 10-11.
Alternative campus newspapers are on the rise; "students at dozens of colleges and universities around the country" are "publishing newspapers calling themselves progressive, radical or leftist."

4590. Case, Patricia J, ed. The Alternative Press Annual, 1983. Philadelphia: Temple UP, 1984. 405.
The first of a series that collects articles and reviews from oppositional newspapers and magazines giving a radically different view of events and issues than found in mainstream media on such subjects as nuclear disarmament, civil rights, toxic waste, occupational hazards, AIDS, and the "new witch hunt."

4591. Case, Patricia J, ed. The Alternative Press Annual, 1984. Philadelphia: Temple UP, 1985. 316.
Second in an annual series of writings by organizations and individuals actively working for social change, including issues and events omitted or underreported by the mainstream media.

4592. Case, Patricia J., ed. The Alternative Press Annual, 1985. Philadelphia: Temple UP, 1986. 347.
Third volume in annual series.

4593. Case, Patricia J, ed. The Alternative Press Annual, 1986. Philadelphia: Temple UP, 1987. 366.
Fourth volume in annual series.

4594. The Commission on Freedom of the Press. A Free and Responsible Press. Chicago: U of Chicago P, 1947. 138.
A defense of diversity and participation by all in the marketplace of ideas; participation should not depend upon personal or corporate wealth, but access should be open to all. Dubbed the Hutchins Commission after the man who headed the enterprise, University of Chicago's chancellor Dr. Robert Maynard Hutchins, the group stressed, among other goals, that the press ought to provide "a truthful, comprehensive, intelligent account of the day's events in a context that gives them meaning," and "a forum for expressions on all sides of an issue."

4595. Conlin, Joseph R. American Anti-War Movements. Beverly Hills: Glencoe, 1968. 133.
Collection of writings mainly by pacifists and opponents of specific wars.

4596. Conlin, Joseph R., ed. The American Radical Press, 1880-1960, Vols. I and II. Westport, CT: Greenwood, 1974. 720.
Chronologically, generically, and topically organized from Wobbly papers to the communist press to "personal journalism," amounting to "a history of American radicalism itself."

4597. Cox, Archibald. "A Broad Look at Common Cause." CC 11.3 (1985) 42-43.
Common Cause has been intent on "making government work better--on making it more open, more honest and honorable, more accountable, more responsive to all the people, and more effective."

4598. Deitch, David. "The Political Economy of American Newspapers." ChJR 6.9 (1973) 29-31.
On how access to the media for working and disenfranchised people may be increased and the media made more accountable to the broad masses in society, focusing on "worker-professionals in the newspaper industry."

4599. Donelson, Ken. "Censorship in the 1970's: Some Ways to Handle It When It Comes (And It Will)." EJ 63.2 (Feb. 1974) 47-51.
Identifies eight categories of books under attack and proposes six defensive strategies by English departments.

4600. Downie, Leonard, Jr. The New Muckrakers. Washington, D.C.: New Republic, 1976. 292.
Each chapter tells about one or more investigative reporters who successfully revealed the truth about some problem to the public: Woodward and Bernstein, Seymour Hersh, et al. Final chapter attempts to explain why there are so few investigative reporters.

4601. Downing, John. "Akwesasne Notes and Erin Bulletin."

Radical Media. Boston: South End, 1984. 104-114.
The story of the liberation newspaper for Native American culture, Akwesasne Notes, published by the Mohawk Nation. The Erin Bulletin is an associated phone chain.

4602. Downing, John. "NACLA: Report on the Americas." Radical Media. Boston: South End, 1984. 115-124.
History of a magazine devoted to exposing conditions in Latin America, especially as they relate to US domination and intervention.

4603. Downing, John. "Union Wage." Radical Media. Boston: South End, 1984. 96-103.
An account of an organizing newspaper for women, Union Wage.

4604. Forcade, Thomas King, ed. Underground Press Anthology. New York: Ace, 1972. 191.
Twenty-two essays by Tim Leary, Huey Newton, Dick Gregory, Todd Gitlin, Jean Genet, Bernadine Dohrn, and others. The underground press "rose like a Phoenix" from nuclear bombs, "ashen lies," cops, drugs, consumption, imperialism, to bring mind expansion, ecology, and revolution.

4605. Fraser, Laura. "The Magazine with a Bad Attitude." CJR 23.3 (1984) 12-13.
Processed World delivers an alternative view of office work in "The Computer Age": it's boring.

4606. Fried, Emanuel. "Union Life and the Arts." Ed 27-28 (Dec.-Jan. 1974) 19-23.
Encourages the growth of labor theater.

4607. Fromartz, Samuel. "Open Secrets: What the Government Seeks to Conceal the National Security Archive Works Hard to Put on the Record." CJR 28.6 (Mar.-Apr. 1990) 32-34.
A private archive seeks to record government conduct to hold officials accountable.

4608. Fudge, William, and John English. "Emergence of the Fifth Estate: The Underground Press." Mass News. Ed. David Leroy and Christopher Sterling. Englewood Cliffs, NJ: Prentice-Hall, 1973. 274-280.
A rapid survey of oppositional newspapers.

4609. Georgakas, Dan, ed. Left Face: A Source Book of Radical Magazines, Presses and Collectives Actively Involved in the Arts. New York: Cineaste & Smyrna P, 1978. 1-16.
Thirty-one entries of US left magazines and newspapers which emphasize the visual arts, film, and literature.

4610. "George Seldes: Still Giving 'Em Hell." Extra! 1.3 (Aug.-Sept. 1987) 16.
A salute to the great muckraking journalist.

4611. Gleason, Timothy. The Watchdog Concept: The Press and the Courts in Nineteenth-Century America. Ames, IA: Iowa State UP, 1989. 160.
Traces the origin and development of the idea of the press as a defender of public interests and therefore deserving special legal protection.

4612. Glessing, Robert J. The Underground Press in America. Bloomington, IN: Indiana UP, 1970. 207.
The Underground Press is "a new brand of journalism in the making," holding "the possibility of initiating changes just as significant" as earlier watersheds (the Penny Press, etc.). This journalism enables "the dissenter, the little man, the innovator" to speak out for "political change" by using "new typesetting and printing processes" and by disregarding normal business expenses. This press is "spiritual in nature" particularly by asking persistent questions about the "nature of justice"--civil rights, social welfare, colonialism, peace, war, etc.

4613. Goldenberg, Edie. Making the Papers: The Access of Resource-Poor Groups to the Metropolitan Press. Lexington, MA: Lexington, 1975. 164.
Powerless groups need media to gain access to government more than groups possessing money and other means of direct access. Chapters on seeking and gaining access to newspapers.

4614. Goldwater, Walter. Radical Periodicals in America, 1890-1950: A Bibliography with Brief Notes. New Haven, CT: Yale UP, 1966. 51.
Contains also annotated list of radical groups and a genealogy of radical groups 1890-1950.

4615. Gore, LeRoy. Joe Must Go. New York: Julian Messner, 1954. 192.
The publisher of the weekly Sauk-Prairie Star in Sauk City, Wisconsin. The book is an expression of the movement in Wisconsin to recall Senator McCarthy, more than a third of a million qualified voters. The book is a critique of McCarthy and an account of the recall efforts.

4616. Green, Larry, and Wendy Leopold. "Reporting on Race in Chicago: Brash Newsletter Leads the Pack." WJR 9.5 (June 1987) 22-24.
In praise of The Chicago Reporter.

4617. Gruliow, Leo. "Notes from a Pravda-Watcher." AR 27.4 (Winter 1967-68) 440-457.
The editor of The Current Digest of the Soviet Press advocates more study of SU publications as a way both to inform and to decrease prejudices.

4618. Hanson, C.T. "Kitchen Table Journalism." CJR 21.3 (Sept.-Oct. 1982) 19-20.
FTC: Watch, a biweekly newsletter, keeps a close eye on the

PRINT

agency and advocates open government.

4619. Harry, M. The Muckraker's Manual: How To Do Your Own Investigative Reporting. Port Townsend, WA: Loompanics, 1984. 145.
A detailed guide of principles and practices: searching documents, keeping records, interviewing techniques, etc.

4620. "Hellbox." MORE 4.2 (Feb. 1974) 3.
Praise for The Philadelphia Inquirer series puncturing the oil companies' explanation of the so-called oil shortage.

4621. Hentoff, Nat. "Lifeline for the Underground." MORE 2.10 (Oct. 1972) 5-8.
The financial difficulties Liberation News Service is having, and the good it is doing for diversity and by muckraking.

4622. Hentoff, Nat. "Near and Dear." CJR 20.2 (July-Aug. 1981) 75-76.
A favorable review of Friendly's Minnesota Rag, a book about Near v. Minnesota of 1931, which strengthened press protection against prior restraint.

4623. Holder, Dennis. "The Little Journal That Did." WJR 6.3 (1984) 51-54.
An admiring appraisal of The Texas Observer, the "journal of free voices" against the Establishment and for social change created by Ronnie Dugger 30 years ago.

4624. Hollstein, Milton. "Are Newspaper Subsidies Unthinkable?" CJR 17.1 (1978) 15-18.
Government funding of the press (increasingly prevalent in Europe) might provide more diversity of expression than news-for-profit.

4625. Horowitz, Julie. "College Papers: New Life on the Left." CJR 28.3 (Sept.-Oct. 1989) 6, 8.
The number of leftist alternative campus papers is growing, providing forums for criticism of administration policies and local issues.

4626. Hymowitz, Carol. "Not The Pittsburgh Press." CJR 20.4 (Nov.-Dec. 1981) 12, 16.
The Mill Hunk Herald is a non-profit, grassroots alternative magazine aimed at "just about any working person who has something to say and needs a place to say it."

4627. The IRE Book. Columbia, MO: Investigative Reporters and Editors, 1984. 98.
The best investigative reports of 1983.

4628. The IRE Book II. Columbia, MO: Investigative Reporters and Editors, 1985. 107.
Best investigations of 1984.

4629. Isaacs, Norman E. "20 Years Later: 33 Ombudsmen." WJR 9.8 (Oct. 1987) 40.
Appraises the effectiveness of the newspaper ombudsmen.

4630. Jensen, Carl. "Three Cheers for George Seldes: One Cheer for the American Press." The Quill 75.8 (Sept. 1987) 14-20.
High praise for this First Amendment hero.

4631. Jess, Paul. "Antitrust Law: A New Approach to Access to the Media." U of Minnesota, 1972. DAI 33 (1972) 2964-A.
Recommends antitrust laws to resist concentration and open access.

4632. Johansen, Bruce E. "Readers Take on One-Paper Town." Prog 51.4 (1987) 16.
Some of its readers have come to feel that the Omaha World-Herald abuses its position as the only newspaper in town and have reacted by publishing a newsletter which criticizes the World-Herald's biased reporting and failure to cover important stories.

4633. Jones, Gregory M. "Confessions of a Reg Writer." QRD 7.4 (1981) 9.
Personal recollection of a writer of government gobbledygook. Notes what he finds to be the core of the problem of government doublespeak: "Bureaucrats writing for bureaucrats and not for the 220 million other Americans who support the government with their taxes."

4634. Joseph, Albert. "Physician, Heal Thyself." QRD 7.4 (1981) 8-9.
Advocates clear writing in the battle against doublespeak. Also examines why misrepresentation has contributed so much to public acceptance and insensitivity toward government and corporate doublespeak.

4635. Kempton, Murray. "Introduction." In a Time of Torment. By I.F. Stone. New York: Random House, 1967. vii-x.
The "average issue of I.F. Stone's Weekly is more illuminating than the average Sunday edition of the New York Times." Stone "always remembers the official lie of last month which is contradicted by the official lie of today," setting "the unremembering present in the history it neglects."

4636. Kessler, Lauren. The Dissident Press: Alternative Journalism in American History. Beverly Hills, CA: Sage, 1984. 160.
A history of the idea and sporadic practice of a marketplace of ideas. The aim is to allow expression of the diversity inherent in society. The history of dissent in the US, however, is a history of exclusion from the mainstream press. Chapters on the Black press, utopianists, feminists, immigrants, working class, war resisters, etc.

PRINT

4637. LaBrie, Henry G., ed. Perspectives of the Black Press. Kennebunkport, ME: Mercer House, 1974. 231.
Eighteen essays on such subjects as the black cartoonist and the black press as a catalyst for a democratic society.

4638. Lambeth, Edmund. Committed Journalism: An Ethic for the Profession. Bloomington: Indiana UP, 1986. 224.
Propounds five principles of a system of ethics for journalistic decision-making and criticism: truth telling, humaneness, justice, freedom, and stewardship. These principles are then applied and tested through a series of cases, including Seymour Hersh's My Lai story and Daniel Schorr's expose of CIA assassination plans.

4639. Lange, Timothy. "Joe College's Media." UM 1.11 (July 1971) 4-5.
Most college newspapers are controlled by faculty or administration and resemble high school productions. But in Colorado, "four student papers can be considered part of the alternate press." "In many ways" the college alternative press "is the only 'free' press in the country today."

4640. Leamer, Laurence. The Paper Revolutionaries: The Rise of the Underground Press. New York: Simon, 1972. 220.
Most of the chapters convey the achievements of this press in exposing problems and explaining causes.

4641. Lee, Alfred McClung. "George Seldes: Author Synonymous With Truth." CHQ (Aug.-Sept. 1987) 11-12.
Reviews Seldes' autobiography, Witness to a Century. Seldes spent his lifetime writing about subjects generally suppressed by the mainstream media.

4642. Leeper, Roy V. "Richmond Newspapers, Inc. v. Virginia and the Emerging Right of Access." JQ 61.3 (Fall 1984) 615-622.
"Eight of nine justices have supported idea of right of access in other cases."

4643. Lewis, Roger. Outlaws of America: The Underground Press and its Context. Harmondsworth: Penguin, 1972. 204.
An account of the alternative press in the 1960s in its battle against commercialism, war, and the cooperation of the mainstream press with big business and government.

4644. Mantooth, Sara. "The Electronic Newspaper: Its Prospects & Directions for Future Study." U of Tennessee, 1982. 198. DAI 44.10 (Apr. 1984) 2919-A.
The new technology "has the potential to eliminate geographic barriers, thereby opening the door to equalization of all information providers."

4645. Mathes, William. "Rediscovering China, The Blacked-Out Country." MO 6.8 (Aug. 1964) 17-18.
Discusses books about China that counteract US governmental

fantasies and ignorance.

4646. McGuire, Leo. "New Muckraker in Town." UM 3.7 (Mar. 1973) 3-4.
"More than any other single man, [Dr. H. Peter] Metzger has forced Colorado journalism to take a hard look at problems that traditionally had been ignored"--inadequate nerve gas storage at the Rocky Mountain Arsenal, plutonium dangers at the Rocky Flats AEC plant, radiation hazards in Grand Junction, etc.

4647. McNamara, Steve. "The Alternative Press: The New Stars on Newsprint." Pr 8.4 (May 1980) 9-10.
In praise of the alternative press's "three hallmarks": something to say, advocacy of alternative ways of life, and innovative techniques.

4648. McVey, Judy. "A Content Analysis of Mad Magazine." MJR 4 (1961) 29-30.
Summary of student's research finds Mad's top three objects of satire to be commercialization (cashing in on the evils, weaknesses, or desires of society), lack of professional ethics (mainly in medicine, politics, and advertising), and misrepresentation and lying. Religion and race were strangely absent from the magazine.

4649. McWilliams, Carey. The Education of Carey McWilliams. New York: Simon, 1979. 363.
An account of The Nation's long defense of civil liberties and uncensored news.

4650. Miller, Jack. "1969-70 Trib Revolt." TCJR 1.3 (July 1972) 19-23.
A small group of employees tried to open up the "oppressive, highly bureaucratic," and "autocratic" Minneapolis Tribune to greater employee control, but the effort failed, because newspapers are mainly "business first, newspapers second."

4651. Mills, Kay. A Place in the News: From the Women's Pages to the Front Page. New York: Dodd, Mead, 1988. 384.
Cites the achievements of women journalists past and present, stressing the difference they have made in the way the news is reported and what stories are covered.

4652. Mintz, Morton. "Seldes Hangs Up His Typewriter: A Muckraker at 100." Na 252.9 (Mar. 11, 1991) 300-302.
The dean of investigative reporters whose In Fact magazine was the model for I.F. Stone's Weekly.

4653. "Missouri Magazine Fights Racists, Fascists." SLJR (Mar. 1984) 19.
Describes The Hammer of Kansas City, a quarterly devoted to reporting the activities of racist and fascist organizations.

PRINT

4654. Moorhead, William. "Operation and Reform of the Classification System in the United States." Secrecy and Foreign Policy. Ed. Thomas Franck and Edward Weisband. New York: Oxford UP, 1974. 87-113.
Because all national administrations have classified information "in order to withhold it from the public and the Congress," Congress must enact guidelines providing for the flow of information essential to democratic government and for the public's right to know.

4655. Mungo, Raymond. Famous Long Ago: My Life and Hard Times With Liberation News Service. Boston: Beacon, 1970. 202.
A founder's personal account of the rise and fall in the late 1960s of the Liberation News Service. The LNS was named after the National Liberation Front because "after resistance comes liberation."

4656. Nader, Ralph, and Steven Gold. "Letters to the Editor: How About a Little Down-Home Glasnost?" CJR 27.3 (Sept.-Oct. 1988) 52-57.
Recommendations for strengthening letters-to-the-editor as an instrument for full and free discussion: increased space, right to reply, etc.

4657. The National Reporter (formerly Counterspy), Washington, D.C.
NR begins with vol. 9 (Winter 1985) and "will continue to report on the CIA and the intelligence agencies. These agencies' demonstrated capabilities to undermine the existence of the U.S. as a constitutional democracy makes such coverage essential."

4658. Navasky, Victor. "The Role of the Critical Journal." Na 240.22 (1985) 698-702.
"My thought is that we have a common interest in preserving and extending our right to be heard."

4659. "New Post Reader's Advocate Has Editor's Promise of Complete Freedom To Criticize." SLJR 20.130 (Oct. 1990) 1, 7-8.
An interview of the SLP-D's new Reader's Advocate (ombudsperson), of which there are about thirty now. Interviewed by the editor of SLJR.

4660. Osner, Audrey. "An Antidote for AEC Handouts." UM 2.4 (Dec. 1971) 12.
Books and reports counteract AEC and utility company propaganda regarding nuclear power.

4661. Osner, Audrey. "A Decade of Vigilance." UM 2.5 (Jan. 1972) 11-12.
Review of Our Troubled Press: Ten Years of the "Columbia Journalism Review" by Alfred Balk and James Boylan. CJR has "enhanced the collective sense of responsibility" on the part

of the press, and has contributed to democratic self-government.

4662. Patner, Andrew. I.F. Stone: A Portrait. New York: Pantheon, 1988. 174.
In praise of one of the nation's watchdogs, based upon conversations with Stone.

4663. Patterson, Margaret, and Robert H. Russell, eds. Behind the Lines: Case Studies in Investigative Reporting. New York: Columbia UP, 1986. 324.
Discusses six newspapers which sponsored investigations resulting in "modest reforms and heightened public sensitivity." The accounts "try to show the student of investigative reporting just what happens when an indepth project is undertaken."

4664. Peck, Abe. Uncovering the Sixties: The Life and Times of the Underground Press. New York: Pantheon, 1985. 364.
The author focuses mainly on the hip kinds of radical press (probing causes of conflicts, consciousness expansion, utopias, provocation) in contrast to the conventional radical press of the old-time populists and Socialists who organized the oppressed and ran for office and the establishment press reporting conflict as crime news.

4665. Peck, James. "Introduction." The Chomsky Reader. New York: Pantheon, 1987. vii-xix.
He shows that "there is a pervasive, omnipresent ideological process of indoctrination that permeates American life, makes us immune to the suffering all around us, and blinds us to what is all too obvious." Chomsky calls this network of intellectuals, technocrats, and propagandists, "whose task is to make the actions of the state palatable," the "secular priesthood."

4666. "The People's Voice." MJR 20 (1977) 2-15.
Three articles on The People's Voice, of Helena, Montana, published from 1939 to 1968, whose motto was: "the hottest places in Hell are reserved for those who in a time of moral crisis refuse to take a stand." The newspaper upheld civil liberties, attacked authoritarian organizations like the Birch Society, criticized corporate power.

4667. Peters, Charles and Taylor Branch. Blowing the Whistle: Dissent in the Public Interest. New York: Praeger, 1972. 305.
Chapter one distinguishes between the old tradition of muckraking by outsiders from Ralph Nader's methods and exposure by insiders. Remaining chapters describe individual whistleblowers. (Articles published originally in WM.)

4668. Peterson, Theodore. "A Trade Magazine that Hit Hard." CJR 4.1 (1965) 21-22.
The small trade magazine Fleet Owner researched and printed

PRINT

an article on amphetamine use by truckers, and helped spark federal regulation on the distribution of the drugs.

4669. Picard, Robert. *The Press and the Decline of Democracy: The Democratic Socialist Response in Public Policy.* Westport, CT: Greenwood, 1986. 168.

Democracy has declined because elites have gained control of decision making and the media (he concentrates on newspapers). Democracy means access to the diversity of ideas and the process of democratic activity. But now only the wealthy own media, which limits ideas for its own profit and perpetuation. Picard's remedies are government support for weak media ownership, especially ownership by political, social, and racial minorities. The ultimate goal is increased participation of citizens in all aspects of life. His model is the Scandinavian countries.

4670. Pilat, Oliver. *Drew Pearson: An Unauthorized Biography.* New York: Harper's, 1973. 332.

Chronicles the life and career of journalist Drew Pearson, revealing how he used his syndicated column, *Washington Merry-Go-Round*, to uncover corruption and wrongdoing (incurring hundreds of libel suits in the process) and also to advance his own political agenda.

4671. Pippert, Wesley G. *An Ethics of News: A Reporter's Search for Truth.* Washington, DC: Georgetown UP, 1989. 156.

"I believe that the ethical reporter committed to truth inevitably will be drawn to issues dealing with justice and peace, no matter what his or her assignment happens to be" (xii).

4672. Pollak, Richard, ed. *Stop the Presses, I Want to Get Off!* New York: Random House, 1975. 337.

Articles about the news business reprinted from *More* magazine, which was dedicated not only to finding rotten apples in the barrel, but to questioning the shape of the barrel itself.

4673. Primack, Joel, and Frank von Hippel. *Advice & Dissent: Scientists in the Political Arena.* New York: Basic, 1974. 299.

Government agencies ignore, distort, corrupt, or misuse scientific advice to defend their decisions, which could be countered by the proper resistance by scientific experts. On issues ranging from nerve gas to nuclear plant sitings, case studies show how campaigns can be won.

4674. "Print Media: Access and Reply." *Readings in Mass Communication: Concepts and Issues in the Mass Media.* Ed. Michael C. Emery and Ted Curtis Smythe. Dubuque, IA: Wm. C. Brown, 1974. 9-21.

On access to the press as a new concept of the First Amendment.

4675. Public Citizen. Washington, DC.
Founded by Ralph Nader to shift "power to people who need it"; includes Congress Watch, Health Research Group, and Litigation Group.

4676. "Quiddity." Z 2.2 (Feb. 1989) 6-8.
Uses the facsimile edition of the New York Times created by New Yorkers for a Free El Salvador as starting point for speculation on a future "hard-hitting radical media 'conglomerate'."

4677. Rabinowitz, Victor. "The Radical Tradition in the Law." The Politics of Law: A Progressive Critique. Ed. David Kairys. New York: Pantheon, 1982. 310-318.
An optimistic view of legal change for the benefit of the people.

4678. Rank, Hugh. "Ad Age in the Classroom." QRD 7.3 (1981) 6-7.
Rank discusses how he teaches systematic analysis of "the content of political language" through Advertising Age,"the ideal complement to keep up with certain issues in this fast changing area" of political and commercial advertising.

4679. Rank, Hugh, ed. Language and Public Policy. Urbana, IL: National Council of Teachers of English, 1974. 234.
The first book published by the NCTE's Committee on Public Doublespeak: thirty-seven pieces on Watergate, commercial and political deception, and the Committee's history.

4680. Reed, John D. "Toward a Theory of the First Amendment for the College Press." Southern Illinois U at Carbondale, 1986. 287. DAI 47 (1986) 695-A.
Affirms the editorial discretion approach to college press rights, which supports the "student journalist's press clause right to protection of the editorial-decision making process."

4681. Rhodes, Jane. "The Enduring Black Press." UR (May-June 1988) 111-112.
Discusses a few of the 150 magazines and newsletters.

4682. Ripston, Ramona. "Let's Return to Muckraking." RSCJ 7 (Apr. 1973) 10.
The Caldwell case weakening First Amendment protection to confidential sources, police licensing for press passes, the imprisonment of LAT Washington Bureau Chief John Lawrence and of Los Angeles' Free Press reporter Ron Ridenour call for sustained resistance via investigative reporting.

4683. Roberts, Nancy L. "Dorothy Day & The Catholic Worker, 1933-1982." U of Minnesota, 1982. 278. DAI 43.8 (Feb. 1983) 2480-A.
Assesses the "remarkably consistent editorial line, espousing communitarian Christianity, pacifism, nonviolent

social justice, and personal activism." Praises high quality contents and Day's work as editor and publisher.

4684. Roberts, Nancy L. "Journalism and Activism: Dorothy Day's Response to the Cold War." P&C 12.1-2 (1987) 13-27.
Analyzes Day's pacifism and her editorship of the Catholic Worker.

4685. Sableman, Mark. "Confidentiality of Sources Question of Ethics, Not Law." SLJR 15.98 (1987) 7.
A summary of the ethical and legal issues of reporter's confidential sources, noting the major court decisions for and against forced disclosure of sources and offering advice on how journalists can best "enhance the likelihood of legal protection."

4686. Saporita, Jay. "Publisher on a Hot Streak." AltM 11.2 (1979) 4-6.
An account of the publisher Lyle Stuart's opposition to secret police, censorship, and other antidemocratic institutions: Sex Without Guilt, The Rich and the Superrich, Dirty Works I, Spy Government, Inside the FBI, etc.

4687. Scheinin, Richard. "Retraining a Press Watchdog." WJR 6.1 (1984) 40-41.
On the difficulties experienced by the National News Council, the "press watchdog and voice for press freedom." It is opposed by some members of the press itself, and it has trouble finding funds.

4688. Schmidt, David. "Government By the People." PC 6.5 (1986) 12-15, 19.
Voters are writing new laws through initiative and referendum making the "democratic muscle" stronger.

4689. Schoonmaker, Mary Ellen. "Has the Alternative Press Gone Yuppie?" CJR 26.4 (Nov.-Dec. 1987) 60-64.
Focuses on three newspapers seriously devoted to news in North Carolina, Arkansas, and California.

4690. Scialabba, George. "What Are Intellectuals Good For?" Grand Street 7.3 (Spring 1988) 194-211.
What is needed is a new kind of intellectual to bring "more --and more precise--information" to bear on issues. Noam Chomsky and Alexander Cockburn represent this social critic who produces concrete criticism to protect the public against the manipulation by centers of power.

4691. "Scratching TUM." UM 1.12 (Aug. 1971) 7.
A critique of the journal The Unsatisfied Man, a review of Colorado journalism.

4692. Seldes, George. "Now It Can Be Told." Witness to a Century. New York: Ballantine, 1987. 345-352.

An account of Seldes' muckraking weekly newsletter, In Fact, its friends, and its enemies (the FBI, the most powerful business organizations, reactionaries and pro-fascists). The newsletter was crushed by government, business, and media red-baiting in revenge for Seldes' revelations of business and government corruption that the mainstream media would not print.

4693. Sellers, Leonard. "California Dredging." MORE 8.2 (Feb. 1978) 35-6.
How the San Francisco Bay Guardian kept a possibly corrupt Bay Area politician from becoming an assistant secretary of Interior in the Carter Administration.

4694. Shore, Elliott, Patricia J. Case, and Laura Daly, eds. Alternative Papers: Selections from the Alternative Press, 1979-1980. Philadelphia: Temple UP, 1982. 521.
Views of society different from those presented by the corporate press, especially by their questioning the legitimacy of established institutions. (See no. 4590).

4695. Smith, Anthony. "Is Objectivity Obsolete?" CJR 19.1 (1980) 61-65.
In the last two decades, journalists have come to realize that what used to be considered "objectivity" was actually tacit support of the status quo; in order to get at the truth, newsmen must be prepared to confront instead of just report.

4696. Smith, Jeffery. "Printers & Press Freedom: The Ideology of Early American Journalism." U of Wisconsin - Madison, 1984. 336. DAI 45 (May 1985) 3229-A.
Libertarian press theory in eighteenth-century America rejected "most of the press controls employed in England," including prior restraint and seditious libel.

4697. Sokolov, Raymond. Wayward Reporter: The Life of A.J. Liebling. New York: Harper & Row, 1980. 354.
Liebling "invented modern press criticism in his 'Wayward Press' columns in The New Yorker. He was the pioneer and the epitome of the art More [magazine] intended to practice."

4698. "Some Who Did the Story Well: Winner of the 1988 Olive Branch Awards." Deadline 3.3 (1988) 6-7.
Book awards going to Robert Del Tredici for At Work in the Fields of the Bomb, a photographic study of the nuclear weapons industry, and Sarah Pirtle for An Outbreak of Peace, a story of how a children's antinuclear group sparked awareness, and the lifetime achievement award to James Aronson for his five-decade-long reporting on the national security state.

4699. Spencer, Richard. "Leftist Thought Journal Moves East." SLJR 13.82 (Feb. 1986) 18.
The "internationally respected" journal Telos provides "alternative perspectives to English speaking people"

PRINT

interested in "broad-based theory of politics." The journal is moving from St. Louis to New York.

4700. Spiegelman, Bob. "George Seldes: Memory and the Cold War." LOOT 1.6 (June 1990) 10.
Seldes embodied the "struggle against historical amnesia" in his newsletter In Fact and his many books. He was banned by the NYT "for 50 years."

4701. Strada, Michael. "Kaleidoscopic Nuclear Images of the Fifties." JPC 20.3 (1986) 179-198.
Contrasts the pessimism of nuclear war fiction with the glib avoidance by political leaders.

4702. "Strategies for Political Publishing in the Reagan Era." SocR 15.4-5 (1985) 15-29.
A mini-forum by several authors generated out of the conference on the Journal of Critical Opinion convened by The Nation. "The purpose of the conference was to 'explore the role of the journal of critical opinion' in the 1980s."

4703. Swados, Harvey, ed. Years of Conscience: The Muckrakers. Cleveland: World, 1962. 409.
Articles published 1902-1912 to expose "the underside of American capitalism." [See Weinberg.]

4704. Swan, Jon. "Uncovering Love Canal." CJR 17.5 (Jan.-Feb. 1979) 46-51.
Praises the investigative courage of the Niagara Gazette in uncovering the Love Canal toxic waste dump.

4705. Tarbell, Ida M. All in a Day's Work: An Autobiography. New York: Seaview/Putnam, 1984. 286.
A great muckraker (1857-1944), Tarbell's History of the Standard Oil Company set the standards for investigative reporting. (See Kathleen Brady, Ida Tarbell: Portrait of a Muckraker. Toronto: General, 1984. 286.)

4706. Tate, Cassandra. "What Do Ombudsmen Do?' CJR 23.1 (1984) 37-41.
On readers' advocates, now at 36 papers.

4707. "30 Days in the County Pokey." UM 3.6 (Feb. 1973) 6-7.
Interview with Vi Murphy, who was sentenced to jail for refusing to disclose the source of an allegation against a judge.

4708. Thorkelson, Nick, and Jim O'Brien. Underhanded History of the USA from the Horse's Mouth. Somerville, MA: New England Free P, 1974. 64.
This comic book functions as a "counterbalance to America's widely-taught mythological 'history.'"

4709. Underwood, Doug. "The Desktop Challenge." CJR 18.1 (May-June 1989) 43-45.
Reveals how personal computer technology is "revolutionizing

the world of the small newspaper," sharply reducing the cash outlay required to become a publisher.

4710. Walljasper, Jay. "Is There Any Hope for the Mainstream Press?" UR 33 (May-June 1989) 126-27.
Cites examples of leftist journalists working within the rules of the mainstream press to convey their ideas to the American public.

4711. Warren, Lee. "Fighting the War of Ideas." NT 8.2 (Summer 1990) 40-44.
Discusses anti-militarist and pro-disarmament think tanks.

4712. Weinberg, Arthur, and Lila Weinberg, eds. The Muckrakers. New York: Putnam's, 1961. 449.
Significant magazine articles by reformers published 1902-1915. [See Swados.]

4713. Weinberg, Steve. "The Anderson File." CJR 28.4 (Nov.-Dec. 1989) 35-39.
Although Jack Anderson has made some mistakes, in general his muckraking investigative reporting has served the nation well.

4714. Weinberg, Steve. "The Press' Last Uncovered Story." WJR 3.4 (1981) 45-6.
On the necessity of constant press scrutiny of lobbyists.

4715. Wendland, Michael. The Arizona Project: How a Team of Investigative Reporters Got Revenge on Deadline. Kansas City: Sheed, Andrews, 1977. 276.
Some 36 reporters and editors from across the country banded together to tell the truth about the assassination of Phoenix newspaper reporter Don Bolles and the political corruption and organized crime in Arizona behind the murder.

4716. Whitaker, Brian. Here Is the Other News. London: Minority Press Group, 1980. 80. Series No. 1.
Describes approximately 80 newspapers in Britain which provide news on a monthly or less regular basis as alternatives to the established press.

4717. Whitman, David. The Press and the Neutron Bomb. Center for Press, Politics and Public Policy, Kennedy School of Government, Harvard University, 1983. 170.
Walter Pincus was widely praised for his stories about the neutron bomb during the summer of 1977, but the Pentagon criticized him for weakening US security. All agreed that Pincus' investigative reports forced the issue of deployment of the bomb in Europe to be discussed publicly.

4718. Wicker, Tom. "The Greening of the Press." CJR 10.1 (1971) 7-12.
In this "Age of Transformation" the Press must not rely on "official sources" but rather attract the best of writers to

ART, MUSIC, LITERATURE

translate the specific into the general in a humane way.

4719. Wicker, Tom. On Press. New York: Viking, 1978. 250.
The American press is "usually timid and anxious for respectability at least as much as profitability." The author gives several instances of journalistic courage and urges journalists "to take an adversary position toward the most powerful institutions of American life" ("cross-examining, testing, challenging").

4720. Williams, Brian. "Obsession with Media Turns Critic into Publisher." SLJR 12.77 (1985) 17.
Account of the editor and publisher of the Chicago Media Critic, Bill Nigut, Sr.

4721. Williams, Miller. "Why is a University Press?" Dialogue (June 1990) 3.
University presses publish books not financially attractive to commercial presses.

4722. Woito, Robert. To End War. New York: Pilgrim, 1982. 755.
A comprehensive bibliography with introductions to the ideas, books, and strategies which will help end war and accomplish change without violence.

4723. Wolseley, Roland E. The Black Press, U.S.A. 2nd ed. Ames: Iowa State UP, 1990. 453.
Studies chiefly newspapers, magazines, and news agencies, not including advertising. A record of this important part of "our national development" and a contribution to "fighting for justice for a still often unjustly treated human group."

4724. Zuckerman, Laurence. "Charlie Peters and His Gospel Singers." CJR 22.3 (1983) 40-44.
Peters and his magazine, The Washington Monthly, have gained respect for their reporting of the Washington bureaucracy.

III. E. ALTERNATIVES: ART, MUSIC, LITERATURE (4725-4749)

4725. Albert, Michael. "Rockin' Radical." Z 1.10 (Oct. 1988) 61-65.
Analyzes how radical song writers and musicians could promote their ideas more effectively.

4726. Aufderheide, Pat. "The Have-Nots of History Find a Place in Museums." ITT 12.32 (Aug. 17, 1988) 20-21.
Museum exhibits increasingly depict the history of minorities in the US for a broader and more analytical perspective. The Smithsonian Institution leads the way with exhibits about black migration and Japanese-American World War II experiences. Such exhibits, however, arouse hostility from right-wing groups.

4727. Berry, Wendell. "To a Siberian Woodsman." Fel 51.12 (1985) 16-17.
Poem on importance of human beings over governments and national glory.

4728. "Chapman's Message Reaches Millions." AG (Jan. 14, 1989) 1E, 2E.
Tracy Chapman sings about poverty, racism, inequality, and other social issues.

4729. Collum, Danny Duncan. "Eyes and Ears: Culture Watch." Soj 18.3 (Mar. 1989) 36.
On rap music as a democratic expression of black and Hispanic urban youth.

4730. Davis, R.G. "Rethinking Guerrilla Theater, 1971, 63 1985." American Media & Mass Culture. Ed. Donald Lazere. Berkeley: U of California P, 1987. 599-609. (From Performance 1.1 [1971] with 1985 postscript written for this collection).
A critical examination of guerrilla theater, agitprop theater, the Teatro Campesino, the San Francisco Mime Troupe, Yippie theater, and other radical agitational and cultural propaganda theater. The 1985 postscript gives a largely pessimistic survey of progressive theater and film since the 1960s.

4731. Denselow, Robin. When the Music's Over: The Story of Political Pop. London: Faber, 1989. 292.
"It is a story that has been marked by swings from apathy to rebellion, from wild attempts to change the system to support for particular parties or politicians. It involves the history of the civil rights movement, the anti-Vietnam protests, the student upheavals of the sixties, the seventies' anti-racism campaigns in Britain, and the anti-nuclear campaigns in the USA. It is a story that has become increasingly international."

4732. Farah, Joseph C. "The Role of the Creative Artist in Propaganda." PR 6 (Winter 1990) 19-22.
Analyzes Jasper Johns' painting "Moratorium Flag," which transforms a mass symbol into an individual experience for thought.

4733. Graff, Gary. "War, Not Love, Theme of Some Singers." AG (Apr. 15, 1986) 4B.
Songs about nuclear war are increasing, by Bob Dylan, Jackson Browne, Chicago, Sting, Rolling Stones, etc. Many songs resist the dehumanization of "enemies."

4734. Harvey, Joan, dir. A Matter of Struggle. New York: Parallel Films, 1985. 90 min.
Documentary of singer Richie Havens' efforts to encourage people to resist militarism.

4735. Hooks, Bell. "'When I Was A Young Soldier for The Revolution' Coming to Voice." Z 1.11 (Nov. 1988) 45-49.

ART, MUSIC, LITERATURE   647

The poetry of black and third world women participates in the global struggle to end domination.

4736. Lauter, Paul, et al. The Heath Anthology of American Literature. Lexington, MA: Heath, 1990. Vol. I, 2,835; Vol. II, 2, 615.
In addition to the canonical authors, this anthology devotes considerable space to gender, racial, and ethnic diversity, and thus offers a fuller and deeper picture of US culture past to present.

4737. Lieberman, Robbie. "People's Songs: American Communism and the Politics of Culture." RHR 36 (Sept. 1986) 63-78.
An account of People's Songs, Inc., created by singers and songwriters like Pete Seeger and Woody Guthrie to spread their left-democratic ideas.

4738. Lippard, Lucy R. "Recycled Images Redeem Memory." ITT 10.8 (Jan. 15-21, 1986) 20.
An art exhibit analyzes media misrepresentations.

4739. Lont, Cynthia. "Between Rock & a Hard Place: A Model of Subcultural Persistence & Women's Music." U of Iowa, 1984. 204. DAI 45 (Mar. 1985) 2684-A.
Redwood Records, a women's music recording company, has survived financially while penetrating "dominant cultural territory without taking on dominant values" by tapping various subcultures.

4740. MacCannell, Dean. "Baltimore in the Morning . . . After: On the Forms of Post-Nuclear Leadership." Diacritics 14.2 (Summer 1984) 33-46.
Studies the relationship between capitalists, nuclear weapons, and nuclear rhetoric. Nuclear weapons have long had the purpose in the West to perpetuate and extend "Free Enterprise" and reduce programs designed "to alleviate the negative consequences" of the exploitation of the poor by the rich. Literary critics have the skills to expose leaders who seek "administrative totalization"--i.e., "exclusionary and expansionist" tyranny--under the banner of "Free Enterprise."

4741. McCanles, Michael. "Machiavelli and the Paradoxes of Deterrence." Diacritics 14.2 (Summer 1984) 12-19.
The superpowers suppress the paradoxes embedded in their threatening texts and turn them into further arms build-ups. Literary criticism can play a vital role in "unmasking the paradoxes of deterrence" in superpower rivalry today by teaching us how to fight "against words," particularly the "self-binding structures into which words may lead us."

4742. McClure, Laura. "Impact Visuals." Z 3.6 (June 1990) 49-51.
Describes the work of progressive/left artists and photographers who seek to foster the creation of socially conscious

visual images.

4743. Muwakkil, Salim. "Tracy Chapman: An American Folk Tale." ITT 13.6 (Dec. 14-20, 1988) 24.
Inquires into the reasons for the popularity of this leftist singer "full of songs" about revolution, racial division, and misplaced priorities. "Her style bucks '80s materialism and glitter" to get her messages out.

4744. Nielson, Elizabeth. "The Public Sphere: Nuclear-Freeze Posters in a Commodity Culture." MR 40.2 (June 1988) 43-52.
Analyzes "the role of political posters in a commercially dominated society," using the "public spheres" theories of Benjamin Barber and Susan Sontag.

4745. Otis, Lauren H. "Artist Richard Roederer Dredges Up That Petrol Emotion." ITT 14.26 (May 23-June 5, 1990) 21.
Roederer's art is directed at preserving the environment, such as his sculpture about the Exxon Valdez, Memorial to Planet Earth (which was removed from its Houston restaurant location because of complaints by Exxon employees).

4746. Riordan, Teresa. "Art Imitates Politics." CC 13.4 (1987) 22-26.
"Political art seems for the first time since the 1930s to be enjoying a status in the 'mainstream' art world," offering an alternative to more controlled mediums of expression such as television.

4747. Secrets in the Sand. San Francisco Mime Troupe, 1989.
Because RKO Pictures made the film The Conqueror in a radioactive area of the Utah desert in 1954, and an extraordinary number of the film's actors and crew died from cancer, the movie studio and the government conspired to cover up the deaths and the cause. The play employs satire and buffoonery to expose the secret machinations.

4748. Sunness, Sheldon. "Political Comedy." Z 3.3 (Mar. 1990) 75-80.
On the present generation of political humorists, who "don't just lampoon, they harpoon": Will Durst, Barry Crimmins, Randy Credico, Jimmy Tingle.

4749. Von Blum, Paul. "The Public Art of Robbie Conal." Z 1.11 (Nov. 1988) 79-82.
Conal's satiric art about public figures constitutes a "guerrilla counterattack against the traditional mode of artistic creation and distribution of Western capitalism."

AUTHOR INDEX

(Note: Numbers refer to item and not page.)
Abel, Elie, 546
Abelard, Tony, 4147
Abeles, Ronald, 2448
Abelman, Robert, 2943
Abourezk, James, 767
Abraham, Nabeel, 1215, 3697, 3698
Abrams, Floyd, 3848
Abramson, Howard, 3849
Abuelkeshk, A. A., 3850
Achenbach, Joel, 547
Ackerman, Frank, 109
Ackley, Charles, 222
Acosta, Leonarda, 1088
Adam, Barry, 2277
Adams, Adam, 2552
Adams, Gordon, 1953
Adams, James, 110
Adams, William, 2554, 2555, 2556, 2557
Adato, Michelle, 167
Adatto, Kiku, 2557
Adkins, Jason, 4558
Adler, Allan, 4172
Adler, Renata, 768
Adler, Richard, 2036, 2449, 2886, 4400
Adoni, Hanna, 2558, 2610
Agee, Philip, 272
Agee, Warren, 3233
Agger, Ben, 111
Agosta, Diana, 2116
Ainbinder, Hollie, 2963
Ainslie, Rosalynde, 3220
Aitken, Hugh, 498
Ajemian, Peter, 4027
Ajuonuma, Livi, 2559
Albert, Jan, 3512
Albert, Michael, 4725
Albright, Cheryl, 1821
Albritton, Robert, 1954
Alcalay, Glenn, 3699
Alderman, Jeffrey, 3513
Alderson, Jeremy, 1819, 4401
Aldrich, Pearl, 548
Alexander, George, 1666
Alexander, Larry, 1955a
Alexandre, Laurien, 1217, 1217a, 2944, 3514
Al-Karni, Ali, 770

Allan, Blaine, 4402
Allen, James, 1667
Allen, Jeanne, 2278
Allen, Margaret, 1820
Allen, Robert, 2279, 2450
Allen, Thomas, 3836
Alley, Robert, 2396
Allman, T. D., 168
Almaney, Adnan, 2560
Alpern, Sarah, 4559
Alperovitz, Gar, 336
Alperowicz, Cynthia, 2900
Alsbury, Ray, 3515
Alter, Jonathan, 2964
Altheide, David, 549, 550, 771, 2280, 2561, 2562
Altman, David, 1821
Altschull, J. Herbert, 772, 4173
Ambrose, Stephen, 223
Ambrosio, Angela, 3516
Anastaplo, George, 2901
Anawalt, H. C., 3947
Andersen, Roberta, 773
Andersen, Robin, 1218, 2563
Anderson, Carolyn, 3053, 3062
Anderson, David, 2564, 3347, 4182
Anderson, Douglas, 3348
Anderson, Jack, 338, 1219, 3517, 3948, 4028, 4561, 4562
Anderson, John, 2945
Anderson, Kent, 2451
Anderson, Michael, 1668
Anderson, Ronnene, 3518
Anderson, Tom, 3349
Andrae, Thomas, 551
Andregg, Michael, 4029
Andrén, Gunnar, 1822a
Andres, Monica, 4030
Andrews, Bert, 339
Andrews, David, 1823
Ang, Ien, 2452
Angus, Ian, 551a
Apple, Michael, 437, 438, 439, 440, 4031
Arana, Ana, 1472
Archer, Gleason, 2117
Archer, Jules, 774
Archibald, Samuel, 1220
Arditti, Rita, 499

Arevalo, Juan, 340
Arieff, Irwin, 2118
Arkin, William, 1221, 3054
Arlen, Michael, 1823a, 2187
Armes, Roy, 4403
Armstrong, Dave, 775
Armstrong, David, 4174, 4563, 4564
Armstrong, Gerald, 3519
Armstrong, Scott, 1222, 1223
Arnett, Peter, 776
Arno, Andrew, 777, 3221
Arnoni, M. S., 3700
Arnove, Robert, 4032
Aronowitz, Stanley, 1, 441, 552, 2281, 2965
Aronson, James, 778, 779, 780, 1224, 1225, 1226, 1227, 1228, 2282, 3222, 3520, 3852, 4175, 4176, 4565, 4566, 4567, 4568, 4575
Aronson, Steven, 1669
Arterton, F. C., 4404
Arthur, Paul, 3055
Arvidson, Cheryl, 3350
Asante, Molefi, 2283
Ascheim, Skip, 2038
Ascher, Carol, 1670
Asher, Thomas, 1956
Ashley, Sharon, 1012
Asi, Morad, 2565
Aslam, Abid, 3701
Astor, Gerald, 1957
Atkin, Charles, 1824, 2014, 2039, 2902
Atkin, Kenward, 4385
Atkinson, Max, 169
Atlas, James, 1671
Atta, Dale, 1229
Attansio, Paul, 2566
Atwan, Robert, 1824a
Auerbach, Jerold, 416
Auerbach, Stevanne, 1825
Aufderheide, Pat, 1089, 1090, 1322a, 1672, 1826, 2058, 2119, 2120, 2121, 2122, 2453, 2568, 2887, 2966, 2967, 2968, 2969, 2970, 2971, 2972, 2973, 3056, 3949, 4405, 4406, 4407, 4726
Auletta, Ken, 1230
Ault, Phillip, 3233
Aumente, Jerome, 4177
Auster, Albert, 3057

Austin, Anthony, 341
Autin, Diana, 1231
Avery, Robert, 2974
Axelrod, Daniel, 241
Ayanian, John, 4330
Bacon, Betty, 3950
Bacon, Jack, 3521
Bader, Eleanor, 2569
Badhwar, Inderjit, 1827
Badran, Badran, 3522
Baer, John, 1232
Baer, Walter, 2886
Bagdikian, Ben, 553, 1091, 1092, 1093, 1094, 1233, 1234, 1235, 1236, 1237, 1673, 2284, 2285, 2570, 3351, 3352, 3353, 3354, 3523, 3524, 3951, 4178, 4571
Bagnied, Magda, 2571
Bailey, George, 2572, 2573, 2574
Baker, Glenn, 3270
Baker, Robert, 1142a
Baker, Samm, 1827a
Ball, Sandra, 1142a
Ball-Rokeach, Sandra, 2286
Ballard, Hoyt, 2
Bamford, James, 273
Banks, Jack, 781, 1238
Bantz, Charles, 2610
Baram, Robert, 3355
Baran, Stanley, 1828
Baranek, Patricia, 873, 874
Barbato, Joseph, 4572
Barber, Benjamin, 2287, 4179
Barber, James, 223, 554, 2575
Barber, Susanna, 2903
Barbosa, Ruy, 1239
Barcus, Earle, 2040
Barcus, Francis, 2904
Barmash, Isadore, 1829
Barnes, John, 2888
Barnes, Medill, 4573
Barnes, Peter, 3223
Barnet, Richard, 3, 112, 4180
Barnett, Frank, 3952
Barnett, Stephen, 3356, 3357, 3358, 3525
Barney, Ralph, 4315
Barnouw, Erik, 1830, 2188, 2189, 2190, 2191, 2975, 3058
Barranco, Deborah, 3702
Barrett, John, 2288

AUTHOR INDEX

Barrett, Marvin, 2192, 2193, 2194, 2195, 2196, 2197, 2198, 2199, 2976
Barron, Jerome, 2576, 4181
Barsamian, David, 555, 4574
Bartelt, David, 479
Barth, Alan, 342
Barthel, Diane, 1674
Bartimole, Roldo, 782, 783, 1095, 1096, 1097, 1098, 1830a, 1958, 1959, 2577, 2578, 2579, 2580, 3526, 3527, 3528, 3529, 3530, 3531, 3532, 3533, 3534, 3535, 3536, 3537, 3538, 3539, 3540, 3541, 3542, 3543, 3544, 4033
Bartlett, Randall, 1166
Barton, Laurence, 2289
Bartosch, Bob, 3059
Basinger, Jeanine, 3060
Bass, Carole, 1240
Bass, Paul, 1240
Bates, Stephen, 2073
Batscha, Robert, 2581
Baughman, James, 2124
Baum, Dan, 3224
Baumer, Donald, 2435
Baxter, Richard, 1099
Bayley, Edwin, 1241
Bayley, Paul, 1537
Bazalgette, Cary, 2454
Bazelon, David, 4408
Beaubien, Michael, 3225
Beauchamp, Tom, 1831
Beck, Andee, 2582
Beck, Hubert, 442
Beck, Kirsten, 2889
Beck, Melvin, 274
Becker, Robert, 556, 3271
Beckstrom, Maja, 784
Bedell, Sally, 2455
Bedford, Michael, 785
Bedway, Barbara, 2456
Belfrage, Cedric, 343, 3852, 3854, 4575
Belknap, Michal, 344
Bell, Dan, 1242
Bell, Daniel, 4
Bell, Richard, 653
Bellant, Russ, 1100
Belle, William, 4034
Bender, David, 224
Benét, James, 775
Beniger, James, 3186

Benjamin, Alan, 3742
Benjamin, Burton, 2583
Benjaminson, Peter, 4182
Bennett, James R., 113, 170, 225, 275, 786, 1242a, 1243, 1243a, 1244, 1244a, 1675, 1960, 1961, 1962, 1963, 1964, 2962, 2977, 3272, 3273, 3274, 3275, 3276, 3545, 3546, 3547, 3548, 3590, 3855, 4035, 4183, 4576, 4577
Bennett, Jonathan, 4036
Bennett, Rex, 1698
Bennett, Tony, 642, 3061
Bennett, W. Lance, 558, 787, 788, 4184
Bensky, Larry, 789
Bensman, David, 790
Benson, Thomas, 3062
Bentley, Eric, 345, 3063
Benet, James, 557, 755
Beres, Louis, 346
Berg, Paul, 3592
Berger, Arthur, 559, 560, 561, 1676, 1831a, 1832, 1833, 2290, 2291, 2292, 2457, 4127, 4128, 4386
Bergman, Kostia, 4185
Berk, Lynn, 707, 2458
Berkman, Ronald, 1245
Berkovitz, Tobe, 2058a
Berkowitz, Dan, 2584
Berle, A., 791
Berlet, Chip, 3359, 3549, 3819, 4578, 4579, 4580
Berlowitz, Marvin, 443
Berman, Edgar, 512
Berman, Edward, 4037
Berman, Jerry, 276
Bermann, Karl, 1100a
Bernays, Edward, 1677, 1678
Bernstein, Carl, 220, 347, 1245a, 4581
Bernstein, Dennis, 2585, 3277
Berrigan, Frances, 4409
Berry, Jeffrey, 4186
Berry, Wendell, 4727
Bertran, Claude-Jean, 1101
Besen, Stanley, 2125
Bettencourt, Michael, 2059
Betts, Richard, 226
Binzen, Peter, 2293
Bird, Elizabeth, 3820

Bird, George, 562
Bird, S. Elizabeth, 793
Birdsell, David, 2702
Brikhead, Douglas, 1679
Birkhead, Herbert, 563
Birnie, Heather, 2978
Biryukov, N. S., 2200, 2587
Bishop, Bill, 3360, 3551
Bishop, Ed, 1102, 1184, 1890
Bishop, Robert, 3857
Biskind, Peter, 3064, 3065, 3066
Bittner, John, 2126
Blachman, Morris, 4038
Black, Edwin, 794
Black, George, 564
Black, Gregory, 3114
Blackstock, Nelson, 277
Blair, Gwenda, 1834, 2588
Blair, Karin, 2459
Blakely, Robert, 2979
Blanchard, Eric, 795
Blanchard, Margaret, 4187
Blanchard, Robert, 1246, 1247
Blankenburg, William, 590, 591, 1843
Blasko, Vincent, 1828
Blaxall, Martha, 5
Bleifuss, Joel, 796, 1248, 2589, 3552, 3858
Blewett, Mary, 565
Blinken, Tony, 3553
Blits, Jan, 444
Block, Herbert, 1249
Bloom, Melvyn, 2060
Blumberg, Nathan, 3278, 3361
Blumberg, Nathaniel, 1103
Blume, Keith, 2590
Blumenthal, Deborah, 2041
Blumenthal, Sidney, 6, 2061, 2294
Blyskal, Jeff, 1680
Blyskal, Marie, 1680
Bob, Murray, 3954
Boddy, William, 2295, 2460
Bodenheimer, Thomas, 7
Bogart, Leo, 1250, 2296, 2905, 3362
Boggs, Carl, 4164
Bohn, Thomas, 652, 2591
Bolinger, Dwight, 1681, 4188
Bollier, David, 2127, 4582, 4583
Bollinger, L. C., 4189

Bollinger, William, 3279
Bolton, Roger, 2980
Bonafede, Dom, 1251, 1252, 1965, 2062, 4584
Bond, Patrick, 797, 798
Bonelli, William, 3554
Bonk, Kathy, 566
Bonner, Helen, 4410
Bonner, Raymond, 799, 1253, 1254
Boorstin, Daniel, 1682
Boot, William, 800, 801, 1255, 1256, 2592, 3280, 3555, 3556, 3557
Booth, Heather, 4193
Bordewich, Fergus, 3363
Borosage, Robert, 278
Borsodi, Ralph, 1683
Bosmajian, Haig, 567, 4190
Boss, Donna, 802
Botein, Michael, 2297
Bottome, Edgar, 348
Boudin, Leonard, 1257
Bowlby, Rachel, 114, 1684
Bowles, Samuel, 445
Bowles, William, 3703
Boyd, James, 4562
Boyd-Barrett, Oliver, 3226
Boyer, Brian, 1258
Boyer, Peter, 2593
Boyer, William, 227
Boylan, James, 568, 569, 1259, 3859, 4191, 4192, 4585
Boyte, Harry, 4193
Brady, Ben, 2201
Braestrup, Peter, 803, 804
Braley, Russ, 3704
Bram, Steven, 805, 3281
Brammer, Gale, 3705
Branch, Taylor, 1260, 3558, 4667
Brand, Stewart, 4194
Brandt, Steve, 1836
Brasch, Walter, 4586
Bray, Howard, 3559
Bredemeier, Brenda, 2484
Breed, Warren, 570
Breen, Myles, 2298, 2595
Brendze, Ruth, 2202
Brenkman, John, 1104
Brennan, Pat, 499
Brennan, Timothy, 2981
Brennan, William, 4195
Brenner, Daniel, 806
Breslau, Andy, 4196

AUTHOR INDEX

Brians, Paul, 3955
Bridge, Junior, 3560
Brinkley, David, 807
Britton, Andrew, 3067
Brockmann, Stephen, 3282
Brockriede, Wayne, 1261
Broder, David, 808, 1262
Brodeur, Paul, 115
Brodhead, Frank, 809, 1263, 1264, 1395
Brokaw, Tom, 4411
Brown, Ben, 3187
Brown, Charlene, 4202
Brown, Cynthia, 810, 3227
Brown, J. H. U., 513
Brown, James, 2596
Brown, Jane, 3364
Brown, Lee, 4197, 4587
Brown, Les, 1106, 2128, 2129, 2130, 2131, 2132, 2203, 2204, 2299, 2300, 2890, 4412, 4413
Brown, Mary, 2461
Brown, Pamela, 3561
Brown, Ralph, 349
Brown, Terry, 1685
Brown, Thomas, 571
Brown, William, 1966, 3821
Browne, Donald, 4414, 4415
Browne, Malcolm, 3228
Browne, Nick, 2301
Brownstein, Ronald, 171
Bruce, Steve, 480
Bruck, Peter, 714
Brumberg, Abraham, 811
Brumberg, Joan, 1836a
Brunner, Ronald, 2891
Brunsdon, Charlotte, 4416
Brush, Douglas, 2302
Brush, Judith, 2302
Buck, Jerry, 3068
Budd, Mike, 2462
Budd, Richard, 571a, 4198
Buford, Daniel, 2063
Buhle, Paul, 572, 1686
Buidette, Christopher, 3792
Buitrago, Ann Marie, 4200
Bunce, Richard, 573, 2303
Bunzl, Martin, 812
Burchett, Wilfred, 172
Burd, Gene, 1107
Burke, Chauncey, 1945
Burke, Chris, 813
Burkett, Warren, 814
Burkhart, Ford, 4588

Burnett, Betty, 2463
Burnham, David, 3188, 3189
Burnham, Philip, 574
Burns, E. B., 1265, 4039
Burr, Beverly, 4589
Burroughs, Bryan, 116
Burroughs, William, 575
Burt, Samuel, 446
Butler, Jeremy, 2464
Butler, Matilda, 3822
Butsch, Richard, 2465
Butts, David, 1267
Buxton, David, 1687, 2466, 4148
Buxton, Edward, 1688
Byars, Jackie, 3069
Byler, Robert, 2133
Byrne, Hugh, 2064
Byrne, Richard, 2222
Cady, Edwin, 531
Caldicott, Helen, 8, 816
Caldwell, Terry, 2065
Califano, Joseph, 1203
Callenbach, Ernest, 3070
Campbell, Craig, 3071
Campbell, Karlyn, 660
Campbell, Richard, 2597, 2598
Canan, Craig, 3818
Cannon, Lynn, 162
Cantor, Muriel, 2304, 2467, 2983, 2984
Capitman, William, 1966a
Cardona, Elizabeth, 1689
Cardwell, David, 3073
Carey, Alex, 1108, 1690
Carey, James, 2305
Carey, John, 817
Carfagno, Jacalyn, 4040
Cargas, Harry, 2468
Carleton, Don, 350
Carlisle, Johan, 1268, 2066
Carlson, James, 2469
Carlsson-Paige, Nancy, 2906
Carmo, Alberto, 1109
Carmody, John, 2985
Carnoy, Martin, 447, 448, 449
Carothers, Andre, 1973
Carp, Robert, 417
Carper, Jean, 1885
Carr, Robert, 351
Carroll, S. L., 2351
Carson, Thomas, 1837
Carter, Bill, 2487, 2599

Carter, Charles, 3562
Carter, Sandy, 4149
Cascone, Charles, 4129
Case, Patricia, 4358, 4590, 4591, 4592, 4593, 4694
Cashill, John, 1837a
Cassata, Mary, 2276
Cassidy, Robert, 1967
Castro, Janice, 2306
Castro, Nelson, 2600
Casty, Alan, 577
Cater, Douglass, 2601, 2907, 2986
Catton, Bruce, 2307
Caute, David, 352
Cavanaugh, John, 117
Cavrak, Steve, 499
Celente, Gerald, 2602
Ceplair, Larry, 3074
Cerra, Frances, 1968
Cevoli, Cathy, 4417
Chace, James, 4041
Chafets, Ze'ev, 818
Chaffee, Steven, 578
Chakrapani, Sumitra, 2627
Chamberlin, Bill, 4202
Chambers, Clytia, 3966
Chambliss, William, 9
Chamorro, Edgar, 1268a
Chan, Janet, 873, 874
Chandler, Christopher, 3366
Chandler, Joan, 2471
Chaney, David, 579
Chaney, Lindsay, 3563
Chang, Hyung, 3823
Chang, Tsan-Kuo, 3564
Channon, Gloria, 939
Chaplan, Debra, 1838
Chapman, Frank, 443
Charles, Daniel, 1269
Charles, Jeff, 3706
Charlton, Linda, 1969
Charren, Peggy, 2043, 2908
Chase, James, 4041
Chase, Stuart, 1839
Chauncey, Tom, 2603
Chen, Kan, 2891
Chen, Milton, 2927
Chenoweth, Lawrence, 3860
Chernus, Ira, 3824
Chernyavsky, V., 279
Cheskin, Louis, 1691
Chester, Jeff, 1270
Chester, Jeffrey, 1840
Chester, Lewis, 2067

Chiasson, Lloyd, 3367
Chien, A. J., 3957
Chirot, Daniel, 819
Chisman, Forrest, 581, 2134
Chittick, William, 1271
Choate, Robert, 2909
Cholodenko, Alan, 3075
Chomsky, Noam, 10, 173, 221, 582, 583, 584, 585, 820, 821, 822, 823, 824, 825, 826, 827, 837, 838, 839, 840, 841, 842, 843, 844, 845, 846, 847, 848, 849, 850, 851, 852, 853, 854, 914, 915, 1272, 1273, 1274, 1275, 1276, 1277, 1278, 1279, 1280, 1281, 1282, 1283, 1284, 1285, 1286, 3283, 3369, 3707, 3708, 4126
Chorbajian, Levon, 3284
Christensen, Jack, 586
Christenson, Reo, 3861
Christiano, David, 40
Christians, Clifford, 587, 4203, 4342
Churchill, Mae, 3198
Churchill, Ward, 280, 1287, 1288, 3958
Cieply, Michael, 3563
Cirino, Robert, 588, 828, 829, 1110, 3709, 3862, 4205, 4418
Claes, Paul, 4034
Clairmonte, Frederick, 117
Clancey, Maura, 1548, 2809
Clark, Blake, 1842
Clark, David, 590, 591, 1843
Clark, Eric, 1692
Clark, Jeff, 2135
Clark, Michael, 3076
Clarke, Bill, 3370
Clarke, Peter, 830, 1294
Clarkson, Fred, 2987, 3371, 3372, 3565
Clawson, Suzanne, 2472
Clay, Floyd, 1844
Claybrook, Joan, 4027
Cleghorn, Reese, 2069
Clifford, George, 3566, 4561
Clift, Eleanor, 1294a
Cline, Rebecca, 3287
Cline, Timothy, 3287
Clippinger, John, 2005
Cloherty, Jack, 1970
Clotfelter, James, 228

Cloward, Richard, 85
Clubb, O. Edmund, 353
Clurman, Richard, 831, 4207
Cobb, Jonathan, 96
Cochran, Thomas, 2206
Cockburn, Alexander, 118, 592, 593, 832, 833, 834, 835, 836, 837, 838, 839, 840, 841, 842, 843, 844, 845, 846, 847, 848, 849, 850, 851, 852, 853, 854, 1111, 1295, 1296, 1297, 1298, 1299, 1300, 1301, 1302, 1303, 1304, 1305, 1306, 1307, 1693, 2604, 2605, 2606, 2607, 2608, 2609, 2988, 3229, 3288, 3289, 3290, 3373, 3374, 3375, 3567, 3568, 3569, 3570, 3571, 3572, 3710, 3711, 3712, 3713, 3714, 3715, 3716, 3717, 3718, 3863, 3864, 3959, 3960, 4042, 4419, 4420
Cockburn, Andrew, 1693, 2609
Coe, Lisa, 2862
Coffin, Tristram, 229, 230, 855, 4043
Cogley, John, 3077
Cohen, Akiba, 2557, 2610
Cohen, Bernard, 3376
Cohen, Dan, 2473, 4421
Cohen, Jeff, 856, 1308, 1447, 2611, 2615
Cohen, Jeremy, 1309
Cohen, Jerry, 76, 77, 4317
Cohen, Richard, 857, 2612, 2613
Cohen, Stanley, 858
Cohen, Stephen, 354
Cohen, Warren, 4044
Cohn, Carol, 4045
Colby, Gerard, 3961
Cole, Barry, 2136, 2137
Cole, David, 3962
Cole, Leonard, 1310
Coleman, Peter, 1311
Colen, Donald, 11
Coleridge, Nicholas, 1845
Colgan, Christine, 3078
Colhoun, Jack, 859, 860, 1312, 1312a
Collier, Barney, 1313
Collier, Peter, 3573
Collins, Joseph, 135

Collins, Ronald, 1694
Collum, Danny, 1314, 2614, 3079, 4422, 4729
Comanor, William, 1695
Combs, James E., 93, 705, 706, 2774, 2775, 2776, 3134
Comendul, Michael, 3841
Commager, Henry, 174
Commoner, Barry, 861
Compaine, Benjamin, 1112, 3825
Conlin, Joseph, 4595, 4596
Connery, Robert, 450
Connor, Michael, 1971
Conrad, Peter, 2310
Conrad, Thomas, 1972
Conway, Flo, 481
Cook, Blanche, 12, 175, 1316
Cook, David, 1696
Cock, Faye, 1317
Cook, Fred, 231, 281, 355, 514
Cook, James, 1846
Cook, Mark, 2615
Cook, Richard, 4046
Cook, Timothy, 1317a
Cooney, James, 3795
Cooney, Stuart, 2183
Coons, John, 2138
Cooper, Anne, 2616
Cooper, Marc, 2617, 3080, 3574
Cooper, Thomas, 594
Copetas, A. Craig, 119
Copjec, Joan, 3081
Corcoran, Farrel, 2311
Cormier, Frank, 1318
Corn, David, 1319
Corn, Robert, 2139
Corn-Revere, Robert, 3082
Cornwell, Elmer, 1319a
Corry, J., 2618
Courtney, Alice, 1697
Cowan, Geoffrey, 2312, 2473
Cowan, Paul, 282, 1113
Cox, Archibald, 4208, 4597
Cox, Arthur, 356, 357, 1320
Cox, Harvey, 595
Cox, James, 1837
Cox, John, 325
Crable, Richard, 1966, 3821
Craft, Christine, 2619
Craig, John, 1114
Craig, Robert, 1846a
Craig, Steve, 2462

Cranberg, Gilbert, 3378
Crespi, Irving, 1115
Crew, Spencer, 657
Crisp, Roger, 1847
Critchlow, Donald, 4047
Croan, Melvin, 2620
Croft, Jack, 3963
Cros, Michele, 3379
Cross, Donna, 2313
Croteau, David, 2691, 2692
Crowell, George, 1321
Crump, Kathy, 2207
Culley, James, 1698
Cullingford, Cedric, 2911
Cumming, Robert, 2989
Cummings, Gary, 1699, 2621, 2622
Cummins, Ken, 1847a
Cunningham, Ann Marie, 3964
Cunningham, Ben, 596, 597
Curran, James, 598, 599, 642, 1700
Curry, Jane, 863
Curry, Richard, 13
Curti, Merle, 120
Curtis, Cia, 2140
Czitrom, Daniel, 4423
Dadd, Debrah, 1973
D'Agostino, Peter, 2314
Dahl, Robert, 14
Dahlgren, Peter, 2623, 2624, 2625, 2626, 2627
Daley, Patrick, 3380, 4209
Daly, Charles, 864
Daly, Laura, 4358, 4694
Dan, Uri, 3866
Daniel, Josh, 1322
Danielian, Noobar, 121
Daniels, Arlene, 755
Danielson, Michael, 15
Dardenne, Robert, 793
Darnovsky, Marcy, 600
Dassin, Joan, 863
Daugherty, David, 3381
David, Michael, 1322a
Davidov, Marv, 866
Davies, Philip, 3083
Davis, Dennis, 668
Davis, Kenneth, 16
Davis, R. G., 4730
Davison, Phillips, 1323
Daviss, Bennett, 867
Day, Barbara, 4424
Deakin, James, 1324, 1325
Dean, Sidney, 4425

DeBauche, Leslie, 3035
Deeb, Gary, 1848, 2475
DeFrank, Thomas, 1325a
Deibel, Mary, 3190
Deitch, David, 4598
De Lauretis, Teresa, 3084
Delgado, Richard, 1326
Della Femina, Jerry, 1701
Deluca, Donald, 724
Demac, Donna, 17, 176, 1328, 1329
deMause, Lloyd, 358
DeMause, Neil, 4589
Denison, Dave, 1329a, 3720
Denman, William, 3965
Dennis, Everette, 601, 3191, 4211, 4212
Denselow, Robin, 4731
Denton, Robert, 1330, 1331, 1332, 1333
Dertouzos, James, 2071, 3382
Devlin, L., 2072
Devol, Kenneth, 4213
DeVolpi, Alexander, 3867
Dewart, Tracey, 3899
Dexter, Gerry, 4428
De Zutter, Henry, 1334
Diamond, Edwin, 602, 2073, 2141, 2315, 2316, 2628, 2629, 2630, 2631, 2632, 4429
Diamond, Sara, 482, 2208, 3721, 4048, 4064
Dichter, Ernest, 1702
Dick, Bernard, 3085
Dickey, Glenn, 532
Dickson, David, 500
Dier, S., 3986
Dieterich, Daniel, 4387
Dilley, Raymond, 2633
Dionisopoulos, George, 1974
Dispenza, Joseph, 1849
Dissanayake, Wimal, 777, 3221
Divine, Robert, 1335
Dixon, Marlene, 18, 451
Dizard, Wilson, 2209
Dodge, Charlie, 1975
Dodge, Larry, 1850
Doherty, Thomas, 3086
Dombrowski, Dennis, 3036
Domhoff, G. William, 2, 19, 20, 21, 22, 23, 24, 25, 26, 3383
Dominick, Joseph, 2317, 2634
Donald, Ralph, 3087

AUTHOR INDEX

Donaldson, Sam, 2635
Donelson, Ken, 4599
Donner, Frank, 283, 284
Donnerstein, Edward, 3118
Donovan, Brian, 1336
Donovan, James, 232
Donway, Roger, 2155
Doob, Leonard, 603
Dorfman, Ariel, 604, 3292, 3293, 3294, 3869
Dorfman, Ron, 3576
Dorman, William, 867a, 868, 868a, 1337, 3230, 3295, 3296, 3297, 3298, 3577, 3578
Dor-Ner, Zvi, 4430
Dorr, Aimee, 2912
Dorsen, Norman, 1338, 4214
Dos Passos, John, 1703
Doss, Erika, 4130
Doudna, Martin, 3870
Douglas, Sara, 2074
Douglas, Susan, 1116, 2142, 2636, 3299, 3871
Dowie, Mark, 2637
Downey, Roger, 4431
Downie, Leonard, 4600
Downing, John, 605, 869, 1339, 2318, 4215, 4432, 4433, 4434, 4601, 4602, 4603
Downs, Hugh, 606
Doyle, Jack, 1976
Drale, Christina, 2892
Draper, Robert, 3872
Draper, Theodore, 27
Dreier, Peter, 1117, 1118, 3384, 3385
Dreifus, Claudia, 2638
Drew, Elizabeth, 177
Drey, Leonard, 3192
Drummond, Phillip, 2319
Duberman, Martin, 2639
Du Boff, Richard, 2143
Dubro, Alec, 1119
Duckworth, Michael, 1120
Dugger, Ronnie, 28, 29
Dunaway, David, 178, 4150
Duncan, Dayton, 870
Dunn, Max, 2640
Dunwoody, Sharon, 3304
Durham, T. R., 1116
Dworkin, Marc, 3088
Dye, Thomas, 26, 30, 31, 4050
Dykstra, Peter, 3231
Dynes, Wayne, 607

Dyson, Michael, 4435
Dzerzhinsky, D., 3386
Earnshaw, Stella, 1851, 3826
Easlea, Brian, 32
Easton, Nina, 171
Ecclestone, Jake, 598
Eckert, Charles, 3037
Eco, Nicolo, 1852
Edelman, Murray, 788, 871
Edgar, Patricia, 2641, 3232
Edlavitch, Susan, 2144
Edmundson, Mark, 2476
Edsall, Thomas, 33
Edwards, Richard, 122
Eells, Richard, 465
Efron, Edith, 608, 3966
Egan, Jack, 1853
Egleson, Nick, 282
Egolf, Brenda, 884
Ehrenreich, Barbara, 515, 1854, 1854a, 3066
Ehrenreich, John, 515
Ehrlich, Howard, 609
Ehrlich, Wendy, 2050
Eisen, James, 3972
Eisenberg, Carolyn, 3873
Eisenhower, David, 3654
Eisenstein, Zillah, 418
Eisler, Benita, 2320
Elgin, Duane, 2321
Elias, Thomas, 4052
Eliasoph, Nina, 610, 4216
Eliot, Marc, 4151
Ellemore, R., 2145
Elliott, Deni, 4217
Elliott, Philip, 897, 3238
Ellis, John, 2322
Ellis, Kate, 2323, 3967
Ellison, Harlan, 2324
Ellsworth, Elizabeth, 3089
Elson, Robert, 3874, 3875
Elsworth, Peter, 3193
El Zein, Hassan, 3722
Emamalizadeh, Hossein, 1855
Emerson, Gloria, 4437
Emerson, Steven, 233, 2990
Emerson, Thomas, 4218, 4219
Emery, Edwin, 611, 3233
Emery, Michael, 611, 612, 1340, 1341, 4220
Emery, Mike, 3580
Emery, Walter, 2146
Engelhardt, Tom, 1704, 2477, 3090, 4053
Engler, Robert, 3723

English, Deirdre, 3827, 3828
English, John, 4608
English, Robert, 613
Englund, Steven, 3074
Ensign, Tod, 3724
Entman, Robert, 614, 710, 1342, 2642
Epstein, Benjamin, 37
Epstein, Cynthia, 3387
Epstein, Edward, 179, 872, 2643
Epstein, Joshua, 4054
Erickson, Gerald, 374
Ericson, Edward, 34
Ericson, Richard, 873, 874
Ernst, Morris, 1121
Eshenaur, Ruth, 3300
Eshghi, Fleurin, 3725
Esmonde-White, P., 4438
Esplin, Fred, 4439
Esslin, Martin, 2325
Ettema, James, 2326
Etzioni, Amitai, 123, 4440
Evans, Charlotte, 1705
Evans, Susan, 1294
Evenson, Debra, 2991, 3726, 3727
Eversole, Pam, 1122
Ewen, Elizabeth, 1708, 3301
Ewen, Stuart, 616, 1123, 1706, 1707, 1708, 1855a, 3301, 4221, 4388
Ezcurra, A. M. 483, 3234
Ezell, Macel, 3968
Fackler, Mark, 587
Fackler, Paul, 617
Fain, Jim, 1344
Fair, Elizabeth, 1978
Falbaum, Berl, 1345
Falk, Richard, 234
Falkenberg, Pamela, 3091
Faller, Greg, 3092
Fallows, James, 1856
Fang, I. E., 2644
Fant, Charles, 2645
Farah, Joseph, 4732
Farber, Jerry, 452
Farhang, Mansour, 124, 3298, 3577, 3876
Fast, Howard, 3969
Fatemi, Ali, 875
Fauhy, Edward, 2646
Faulk, John, 2328
Faulkner, Francis, 876
Fauvet, Paul, 3302

Feder, Timothy, 4223
Fehrenbach, T., 878
Fejes, Fred, 618, 1709, 2210
Feld, Bernard, 4055
Feldman, Jonathan, 452a
Feldman, Paul, 711
Feldman, Samuel, 2647
Felsberg, Arthur, 2100
Fenby, Jonathan, 3235
Fenn, Donna, 3829
Fenwick, Steven, 3093
Ferguson, LeRoy, 879
Ferguson, Marjorie, 619, 2211, 3830
Ferguson, Thomas, 35, 36, 125
Ferré, John, 2946
Ferrick, Thomas, 1856a
Feuerlicht, Roberta, 359
Field, Roger, 1857
Fielding, Raymond, 3094, 3095
Fields, Echo, 880
Fields, Howard, 2648
Finnerty, Adam, 484
Firestone, O. J., 2075
Fischer, Stuart, 2913
Fisher, Donald, 4056
Fisher, Glen, 620
Fisher, John, 1710
Fisher, June, 3877
Fisher, Marc, 4442
Fishman, Mark, 881
Fisk, Mark, 3729
Fiske, John, 1711, 2329, 2330, 2331
Fitzgerald, A. Ernest, 235
FitzPatrick, Terry, 3581
Flake, Carol, 485
Flanders, Laura, 3730
Fleener, Nickie, 3097
Flippen, Charles, 4224
Flippo, Chet, 3582, 3878
Flitterman, Sandy, 1712
Foley, Joseph, 1124
Foley, Karen, 2212
Fom, William, 53
Fong-Torres, Ben, 2649
Fonzi, Gaeton, 621
Foote, Joe, 2707
Forcade, Thomas, 3388, 4604
Fore, Steven, 3098
Fore, William, 621a, 2147, 2947, 2948
Forest, Jim, 4443

AUTHOR INDEX

Forester, John, 622
Forester, Tom, 3194
Form, William, 53
Forster, Arnold, 37
Foster, Gregory, 271
Fox, Florence, 623
Fox, Richard, 1713, 1714
Fox, Stephen, 1715
Francis, Carolyn, 3731
Franck, Peter, 1125
Franck, Thomas, 3972
Franco, Jean, 3973
Francois, William, 623a
Frank, Jerome, 882
Frank, Robert, 2332, 4444
Frankel, Max, 1346
Frankl, Razelle, 2949
Franklin, H. Bruce, 459, 624, 1347
Franklin, Marc, 4225
Franklin, Ruth, 4225
Frantzich, Stephen, 3195
Franzwa, Helen, 2333
Frappier, Jon, 1716
Fraser, Laura, 3389, 4605
Frazier, Howard, 285
Frederick, Christine, 1717
Frederick, Howard, 1347a, 1348, 1348a, 1349
Fredin, Eric, 830
Freedman, Allan, 3583
Freedman, David, 1858
Freedman, Warren, 533
Freeman, John, 1859
Freimuth, V. S., 3390
Freund, Charles, 2214
Friar, David, 1350
Fricker, Mary, 149
Frideres, James, 2044
Fried, Emanuel, 4606
Fried, Richard, 360, 361
Friedberg, Anne, 3879
Friedman, Barbara, 625
Friedman, Leslie, 2334, 3303
Friedman, Marilyn, 1126
Friedman, Robert, 883, 1350a, 1981, 3584, 3880
Friedman, Sharon, 884, 3304
Friel, Howard, 3881
Friendly, Fred, 2148, 2215, 2650, 2651, 4228
Friendly, Jonathan, 4229
Frith, Simon, 4152, 4153
Fromartz, Samuel, 4607
Frost, Frederica, 2940

Frundt, Henry, 1859a
Fry, Don, 885
Fry, Ron, 306, 3200
Frye, Jerry, 3391
Fryklund, Richard, 1351
Fudge, William, 4608
Fulbright, J. William, 236, 4230
Funt, Peter, 2653
Fussell, Paul, 626
Gabler, Neal, 3099
Gaines, Jane, 1718, 1860, 4231
Galbraith, John, 126, 237, 1719, 2335
Galerstein, Carolyn, 3100
Gallantz, Michael, 2654
Galster, Steven, 886
Gambardella, Silvia, 2873
Gambill, Joel, 627, 4232
Gandy, Oscar, 38, 1127, 1128, 2216
Ganley, Gladys, 39
Ganley, Oswald, 39
Gans, Herbert, 887, 888, 889, 2655
Gantz, Walter, 1720
Garai, Josef, 4057
Garbus, Martin, 890
Gardner, Gerald, 4233
Garnham, Nicholas, 4445
Garrison, Jim, 362
Garrison, Omar, 286
Garrow, David, 287
Garson, Barbara, 3196
Garwood, Darrell, 288
Gastorf, John, 2538
Gates, Gary, 2823
Gatignon, Hubert, 2051
Gavshon, Arthur, 4058
Geis, Michael, 1721
Geismar, Maxwell, 3974
Gelb, L. H., 1352
Gelbspan, Ross, 3197
Gellhorn, Walter, 501
Geltner, Sharon, 4446
Gemma, Gavrielle, 3732
Gendron, Bernard, 4154
Georgakas, Dan, 4609
George, Alexander, 3733
Gerald, J. Edward, 3305
Gerard, Jeremy, 628
Gerbner, George, 628a, 629, 892, 1982, 2222, 2336, 2337, 2338, 2339, 2478, 2950, 4234

Gerrard, Michael, 1983
Gersh, Debra, 3392
Gerson, Joseph, 238
Gervasi, Sean, 1353
Gervasi, Tom, 893, 1354, 3882, 4059
Gever, Martha, 2992, 4447
Geyer, Alan, 3734
Ghareeb, Edmund, 630
Ghiglione, Loren, 3393
Gibson, Bill, 2479
Gibson, George, 2994
Gibson, W., 2656
Gibson, Walker, 1722
Gibson, William, 3101
Giese, Paula, 894, 895
Giffard, C. A., 631, 3236, 3237
Gill, Ann, 2149
Gillenkirk, Jeff, 3585
Gillers, Stephen, 328, 1338, 4214
Gillespie, Gilbert, 4448
Gillmore, Donald, 4211
Ginger, Ann, 40, 4235
Ginsberg, Benjamin, 41
Ginsburg, Carl, 1355, 4060
Gintis, Herbert, 445
Giroux, Henry, 441, 453, 454, 455
Gitlin, Todd, 632, 896, 1356, 1357, 1723, 2340, 2341, 2480, 2481, 2482, 2657, 2658, 2659, 2660, 2661, 3586, 3735, 4236
Glaberman, Martin, 127
Gladstone, Brooke, 2995
Glass, Fred, 4449
Glazer, Myron, 4237
Glazer, Penina, 4237
Gleason, Timothy, 4238, 4611
Glessing, Robert, 633, 1724, 4239, 4612
Gliserman, Marty, 3102
Goehlert, Robert, 415
Goethals, Gregor, 2951
Goggin, Malcolm, 502
Gold, Phillip, 1725
Gold, Steven, 3784, 4656
Goldberg, Gerald, 2663
Goldberg, Kim, 4450
Goldberg, Robert, 2663
Golden, L., 1984
Goldenberg, Edie, 3394, 4613
Goldin, Marion, 3736

Golding, Peter, 634, 897, 3238
Goldman, Robert, 2483
Goldsen, Rose, 1860a, 2217, 2342, 2343
Goldsmith, Barbara, 635
Goldsmith, Jeff, 516
Goldstein, Jeffrey, 2484
Goldstein, Richard, 636
Goldstein, Robert, 42, 181
Goldstein, Tom, 898, 1861
Goldston, Robert, 363
Goldwater, Walter, 4614
Golove, David, 4240
Gompertz, Kenneth, 2183
Gomsrud, Lowell, 3395
Gonzalez-Manet, E., 1357a, 2218
Good, Paul, 2664
Goodman, Ellen, 637, 638, 1726
Goodman, Julian, 2219, 4241
Goodman, Sandy, 3883
Goodman, Walter, 364, 1862
Goodrich, Chris, 3975, 3976
Goodwin, David, 3737
Gordon, Diana, 3198
Gordon, Douglas, 3587
Gordon, Neal, 2921
Gore, LeRoy, 4615
Gormley, William, 2435
Gorney, Carole, 884
Gossage, Howard, 1863
Gostlow, Deborah, 2002
Gottlieb, Robert, 486, 3588, 3589
Goulart, Ron, 2914
Gould, Christopher, 3274, 3548, 3590, 4577
Gould, Robert, 7
Gould, Stanhope, 2665
Goulden, Joseph, 3738
Graber, Doris, 899, 1129, 1360, 1361, 1362, 1363
Graebner, William, 43, 1727, 3831
Graff, Gary, 4733
Graham, Fred, 1364, 2666, 4242
Grahame, Peter, 3884
Granato, Leonard, 1365
Grant, Mark, 1864
Graves, Florence, 1728
Graves, Sherryl, 2921
Gravois, John, 1366

AUTHOR INDEX

Gray, Herman, 2485
Gray, William, 900
Greeley, Bill, 2667
Green, Larry, 4616
Green, Mark, 44, 45, 128, 419, 425, 1367, 1985, 4243, 4321, 4349, 4389
Green, Pippa, 901
Green, Stephen, 4062
Green, Timothy, 2344
Greenberg, Daniel, 503
Greenberg, Edward, 46
Greene, Felix, 3396
Greene, Theodore, 3832
Greenfield, Jeff, 13671, 2076a, 2442
Greenfield, Patricia, 639
Greer, Colin, 456
Gregory, Richard, 640
Gresham, Jewell, 1368
Grey, David, 902, 4211
Griffen, Bill, 2996
Griffin, Julia, 4450
Griffin-Nolan, Ed, 3739
Griffith, Robert, 365, 366
Griffith, Thomas, 2668
Grimshaw, Tom, 3397
Grodzins, Morton, 3398
Gronseth, Erik, 47
Gross, Bertram, 48
Gross, Gerald, 641
Gross, Larry, 628a, 2338, 2339, 2915
Grossberg, Lawrence, 2486
Grossman, Karl, 3399, 3591, 3740, 4244
Grossman, L., 2669, 2997
Grossman, Michael, 1369, 1370, 1371, 1436
Grove, Gene, 49
Gruchow, Paul, 3592
Gruenenfelder, David, 3479
Gruliow, Leo, 4617
Grundfest, Joseph, 4245
Guback, Thomas, 3038, 3039, 3040, 3041
Guerra, Joe, 1986, 1987
Guilbaut, Serge, 4031
Guimary, Donald, 4247, 4451
Guma, Greg, 3885
Gunn, Herb, 3741
Gunneman, Brenda, 3791
Gunter, Jonathan, 2220
Gunther, Marc, 2487, 2670, 4452

Gurevitch, Michael, 599, 642
Gusmão, Ivna, 3742
Gussow, Joan, 2046
Gustafson, Julie, 4453
Guthrie, Kendall, 1513
Gutierrez, Felix, 765, 2488
Guttman, Daniel, 1373
Gwyn, Robert, 903, 1729
Haacke, Hans, 4132
Haber, Samuel, 504
Haberer, Joseph, 505
Hachten, Harva, 904
Hachten, William, 904
Hadden, Jeffrey, 2221, 2952
Haddigan, Michael, 3593
Hahn, Dan, 1330, 1331, 1332
Haigh, Robert, 2222
Haight, Timothy, 643, 1205, 4454, 4455
Haile, Reesom, 2671
Haiman, F., 4248, 4249, 4250
Hain, Paul, 2596
Haines, Harry, 3103
Halaby, Ralph, 905
Halberstam, David, 644, 2672, 2673, 2674
Hale, F., 2223
Hale, Katherine, 2077
Hall, Bob, 3400
Hall, Earl, 4063
Hall, Peter, 3239
Hall, Ross, 129
Hall, Stuart, 645, 646
Halleck, Deedee, 4456
Halliday, Fred, 367, 1374
Hallin, Daniel, 906, 1375, 2675, 2676, 2677, 2678, 3306
Halperin, Jonathan, 613
Halperin, Morton, 182, 276, 289, 290, 1376, 1377, 4251, 4252, 4253
Halsell, Grace, 487
Halsey, A. H., 461
Hamelink, Cees, 50
Hamilton, Charles, 647
Hammett, Dashiell, 3401
Hammitt, Harry, 1378, 1865
Hammond, William, 1379
Hanan, Mack, 1730
Hancock, G. B., 1731
Hanhardt, John, 2224, 4457
Hannikainen, Lauri, 985
Hanrahan, John, 3594
Hans, Dennis, 2078, 2679
Hansen, Allen, 1380

Hansen, Evelyn, 3595
Hanson, C. T., 1381, 3886, 4618
Hanson, Elizabeth, 155
Hanson, Jarice, 2345
Hardin, Herschel, 2346
Harding, Sandra, 506
Hardt, Hanno, 1382
Harker, Dave, 4155
Harmer, Ruth, 517
Harper, Sandra, 2998
Harrell, David, 488, 2953
Harrington, Michael, 1130
Harris, Ian, 2347
Harris, Mark, 2680
Harris, Phil, 3240
Harris, Richard, 1383
Harrison, S. L., 2999
Harry, M., 4619
Hart, Roderick, 1384, 1385, 1386, 2681
Hartley, John, 907, 2331
Hartman, Thomas, 3307, 3887
Hartnett, Rodney, 457
Harty, Sheila, 1987a, 1988
Harvey, Joan, 4734
Hatch, Richard, 3721, 4048, 4064
Haug, Wolfgang, 1732
Hauser, Thomas, 534
Havig, Alan, 1733
Hawes, William, 2348
Hayden, Trudy, 4341
Haydock, John, 2682
Haynes, John, 335
Hays, Kim, 2916
Hayter, Teresa, 4065
Heacock, Roger, 3241
Head, Gary, 2039
Heale, M. J., 367a
Heath, Stephen, 2349
Hecker, Sidney, 1866
Hedemann, Grace, 4254
Heeger, Susan, 2489
Heilbroner, Robert, 130
Heilbronn, Lisa, 2490
Heise, Juergen, 239
Held, Virginia, 4255
Hellinger, Dan, 908
Hellinger, Daniel, 3596
Hellmann, John, 648
Helvarg, David, 3597
Helyar, John, 116
Hemphill, Michael, 4156
Hendricks, Evan, 4256

Hennessee, Judith, 1867
Henninger, Daniel, 1734
Henry, Harry, 1735
Henry, J. S., 1989
Henry, Jules, 1736
Henry, William, 909
Henslin, James, 89
Hentoff, Nat, 282, 1387, 4257, 4621, 4622
Henwood, Doug, 3598, 3599, 3743
Herbert, Wray, 910
Herken, Gregg, 368, 3000
Herman, Andrew, 4319
Herman, Edward, 10, 51, 131, 649, 650, 809, 911, 912, 913, 914, 915, 1003, 1131, 1132, 1264, 1388, 1389, 1390, 1391, 1392, 1393, 1394, 1395, 1737, 2225, 2683, 3001, 3308, 3402, 3744, 3745, 3746, 3747, 3748, 3749, 3750, 3751, 3752, 3753, 3754, 3755, 3756, 3977
Herner de Schmelz, I., 651
Hersh, Seymour, 183, 240, 1396
Hertsgaard, Mark, 52, 1397, 1398, 1399, 1400, 1401, 3309
Hertzke, Allen, 489
Herzog, Charlotte, 1718
Herzog, James, 3600
Hess, John, 4258, 4259
Hess, Judith, 3104
Hess, Stephen, 916, 1402, 1403, 2684
Hesse, Petra, 2491, 2917
Hester, Hugh, 3757, 4066
Heyer, Robert, 1787
Heyl, Phillip, 2552
Hezel, Richard, 3002
Hiaassen, Carl, 1868
Hickey, Neil, 2685, 4460, 4461, 4462
Hiebert, Ray, 184, 652, 1404, 2079
Higgs, Robert, 185
Hilgartner, Stephen, 653
Hill, Andrew, 1133
Hill, Doug, 1869a
Himmelstein, Hal, 1738, 1870, 2226, 2350, 2492, 2493, 2686, 4463
Himmelweit, Hilde, 1405

AUTHOR INDEX

Hinchberger, Bill, 3758
Hinckle, Warren, 1406
Hindman, James, 4464
Hippel, Frank von, 4673
Hirano, Kyoko, 3105
Hirsch, Daniel, 3578
Hirsch, Glenn, 1990
Hirsch, Marina, 1871
Hirsch, Robert, 2085
Hirschhorn, Larry, 2235
Hirschorn, Michael, 3403
Hitchens, Christopher, 654, 2687, 4067
Hobbs, Fred, 2227
Hoch, Paul, 535, 917, 1739, 3404
Hochberg, Lee, 1134
Hochheimer, John, 3405
Hochman, Sandra, 1407
Hochschild, Adam, 3888
Hodge, Robert, 2918
Hofeldt, Roger, 2494
Hoffman, Daniel, 182, 289, 4252, 4253
Hoffman, David, 2080
Hoffman, N. von, 1134a, 1408
Hoffman, Stanley, 369
Hofstetter, C. R., 2688
Holbrook, Stewart, 1872
Holcomb, Betty, 3889
Holden, Constance, 4068
Holder, Dennis, 4623
Holk, Richard, 3601
Holland, Max, 918
Hollander, Richard, 2893, 4465
Hollstein, Milton, 4624
Holmlund, Christine, 3106
Honey, Maureen, 655, 3833
Hood, Stuart, 3003
Hook, Donald, 1873
Hook, Glenn, 656, 3406
Hook, Sidney, 458
Hooks, Bell, 4735
Hooper, Alan, 1409
Hoover, Stewart, 2228
Horne, Gerald, 370
Horowitz, Andrew, 2689
Horowitz, Daniel, 1740
Horowitz, David, 371, 4069
Horowitz, Irving, 3978
Horowitz, Julie, 4625
Horsfield, Peter, 2954, 2955
Horton, James, 657
Howard, Bruce, 1991

Howard, Herbert, 2351
Howard, John, 459, 1741
Howe, Barbara, 4070
Howe, Russell, 3107
Howell, Leon, 2690, 3407
Howell, Rex, 2150
Howell, Sharon, 3759
Hoynes, William, 2691, 2692
Hoyt, Ken. 1410
Hoyt, Michael, 1135, 1742, 3602, 3890
Huber, Joan, 53
Hudson, Heather, 2229, 2230, 2235, 4466
Hudson, Michael, 658
Huebner, Albert, 1135a, 1874
Huffman, John, 920, 1939a, 3979
Hulbert, James, 1741
Hulser, Kathleen, 4467, 4468
Hulteen, Bob, 1874a
Hulteng, John, 4260
Hume, Brit, 1411, 1412, 3980
Hunt, Michael, 54
Hunter, Jane, 193, 3760, 3761, 4082
Hunter-Gault, C., 2693
Hurley, Neil, 2231
Hurwitz, Donald, 2232
Husni, Samir, 3834
Hymowitz, Carol, 4626
Hynds, Ernest, 3408
Hynes, James, 2495
Ibelema, Minabere, 921
Illich, Ivan, 518
Immerman, Leon, 4200
Immerwahr, John, 4261
Intinteli, Michael, 2496
Isaacs, Norman, 922, 1413, 4629
Ivie, Robert, 373, 3311
Iyengar, Shanto, 2697, 2698
Izod, John, 3042
Jacklin, Phil, 4264
Jackson, Dennis, 1964
Jackson, Harold, 2497
Jacobson, Michael, 1875
Jacobson, Robert, 2233, 2234
Jaffe, Louis, 4071
Jaffe, Susan, 3108
Jalbert, Paul, 922a, 2699, 2700
James, Beverly, 3380, 4265
Jamieson, Kathleen, 660, 2081, 2082, 2701, 2702

Jankowski, Mike, 4472, 4473
Jankowski, Nick, 4472
Jansen, Sue, 55
Janus, Noreene, 686, 1743, 1744
Jeffords, Susan, 661
Jeffries-Fox, Suzanne, 2915
Jellinek, J. Stephen, 4266
Jencks, Christopher, 4267
Jencks, Richard, 2151
Jensen, Carl, 923, 4630
Jensen, Jay, 4000
Jensen, Klaus, 2703
Jenswold, Joel, 3666
Jess, Paul, 4631
Jetter, Alexis, 4473
Jezer, Marty, 56
Jhally, Sut, 551, 1745, 1746, 1762
Joblove, Michael, 2555
Joël, Judith, 374
Joffe, Phyllis, 1137
Johannsen, Richard, 662
Johansen, Bruce, 4632
Johansen, Robert, 57
Johnson, Barbara, 3409
Johnson, Flora, 3604
Johnson, George, 4268
Johnson, Haynes, 1414
Johnson, Helen, 3857
Johnson, Loch, 301, 302
Johnson, Mark, 2152
Johnson, Miles, 1415
Johnson, Nicholas, 1138, 2352, 2353, 2354, 2355, 3004, 4269, 4474, 4475
Johnson, Paul, 663, 2356, 2498, 2704, 2705
Johnson, Robert, 3242
Johnson, Roy, 1747
Johnstone, John, 923a
Jones, Charlotte, 3410
Jones, Gregory, 4633
Jones, Jeff, 3005
Jorstand, Erling, 490
Joseph, Albert, 4634
Joseph, Nadine, 3605
Joslyn, Richard, 2083
Jowett, Garth, 664, 3109
Joyce, Alisa, 4270
Joyce, Ed, 2706
Joyce, James, 665
Jubera, Drew, 4476
Judis, John, 3411, 3981, 4072

Kael, Pauline, 3110
Kahane, Howard, 1417, 4271
Kahn, Albert, 375, 376, 3982
Kahn, Douglas, 4272
Kahn, Frank, 2153
Kaid, Lynda, 2084, 2085, 2707, 4171
Kaidy, Mitchell, 2154
Kairys, David, 420
Kaku, Michio, 241
Kalter, J., 2708, 2709
Kalvelage, Carl, 1219
Kalven, Harry, 4273
Kalven, Jamie, 1418
Kanfer, Stefan, 3111
Kanter, Elliot, 2710
Kanter, Rosabeth, 132
Kaplan, Craig, 460
Kaplan, E. Ann, 2357, 2499, 2500, 2501, 4157
Kaplan, Fred, 377, 1419
Kaplan, Jeremiah, 1992
Kaplan, Sheila, 1138a
Karabel, Jerome, 461
Karchevsky, Yuri, 1514
Karetzky, Stephen, 925
Karman, Peter, 2502, 3762
Karp, Stan, 3412
Karp, Walter, 58, 1420, 2358, 2711, 2956
Katel, Peter, 3606
Katz, Steven, 186
Katznelson, Ira, 59
Kaufman, Jim, 3043
Kaufman, Richard, 1139, 3413
Kavanaugh, John, 1748
Kaye, Evelyn, 2919
Kaye, Tony, 2712
Kayser, Jacques, 3607
Keddie, Shirley, 3891
Keegan, Paul, 1421
Keeler, Robert, 3608
Kefauver, Estes, 133
Kehl, D. G., 1749
Keisling, Philip, 2085a
Keller, William, 303
Kelley, David, 2155
Kelley, Kevin, 1422, 3414, 4133
Kelley, Thomas, 1876
Kellner, Douglas, 2359, 2360, 3152, 4477
Kelly, John, 2713, 2714
Kelly, Tom, 926a, 3609, 3892, 4478

AUTHOR INDEX

Kemper, Vicki, 2361
Kempton, Murray, 4635
Kennedy, Daniel, 3763
Kennedy, Duncan, 421
Kennedy, Pagan, 4134
Kennedy, Tom, 3243
Kennerly, Evelyn, 3312
Kenworthy, Eldon, 1423
Keracher, John, 666
Kern, Marilyn, 1750
Kern, Montague, 2086, 2715, 3610
Kernell, Samuel, 1424
Kerner, Jack, 4479
Kerr, Paul, 3044, 3112
Kervin, Denise, 2716
Kesselman, Mark, 59
Kessler, Lauren, 4274, 4636
Keto, David, 4390
Kevelson, Roberta, 3415
Key, Wilson, 1751, 1752, 1877
Keyser, S. J., 1753
Keyssar, Alex, 3313
Kidder, Rushworth, 4073
Kiester, Sally, 4074
Kim, Samuel, 234
Kim, Seung, 3611
Kim, Young, 304
Kimball, Penn, 3893
Kimery, Anthony, 1425, 4075
Kinder, Donald, 2697, 2698
King, Dennis, 60, 927
King, Larry, 2717
King, Thomas, 4141
Kinsella, James, 927a
Kinsley, Michael, 2156
Kirby, Laurie, 3764
Kirckhove, Derrick de, 4275
Kirk, Robin, 928
Kirstein, George, 1754
Kitch, Laura, 1245
Kitson, Jack, 2261
Kittrie, Nicholas, 4276
Kittross, John, 2184
Klapret, Cathy, 3045
Klare, Michael, 187, 242, 4076
Klatch, Rebecca, 61
Klatell, David, 536, 2503
Klees, Donna, 2051
Klein, Paul, 2361
Kletter, Richard, 2235
Kline, Stephen, 1755, 1762
Klinger, Barbara, 3113

Klose, Roland, 3314
Klotzer, Charles, 929, 1140
Kluger, Richard, 3612
Knelman, Fred, 62, 1994
Knepler, Michael, 4277
Knight, Al, 3417
Knight, G., 930, 3613
Knightley, Phillip, 1426, 1427
Knoll, Erwin, 196, 243, 244, 249, 931, 1428, 3614, 3615, 3894, 3895
Knopf, Terry, 3418
Koch, Nela, 2236
Koger, Daniel, 3896
Kohn, Edward, 1429
Kolodney, David, 4069
Konda, Tom, 2087
Kondracke, Morton, 1430
Konecky, Eugene, 2157
Kopkind, Andrew, 1141, 3006, 3616
Koppes, Clayton, 3114
Kornbluh, Peter, 64, 187, 242, 1431, 1432
Korzenny, Felipe, 2363
Koschwitz, Hansjürgen, 3765
Kosinski, Jerzy, 2364
Kostelanetz, Richard, 3983
Kosterlitz, Julie, 2088
Kotch, Jonathan, 2920
Kotz, David, 134
Kovel, Joel, 378
Kowet, Don, 2718
Kozol, Jonathan, 462
Kramer, Staci, 3897
Krasnow, Erwin, 2158, 2159
Krass, Peter, 3199
Krassner, Paul, 667
Kraus, Sidney, 668, 1433, 2719, 4417
Krehm, William, 3984
Kreig, Andrew, 3617
Krepon, Michael, 1434
Krieghbaum, Hillier, 932
Kriesberg, Martin, 3766
Krinsky, Michael, 4240
Krinksy, Robert, 1435, 3315
Krolak, Steven, 1756
Krueger, Marlis, 463
Kruglak, Theodore, 3244
Kuhn, Ferdinand, 3420
Kuhns, William, 2365
Kuletz, Valerie, 1878
Kull, Steven, 379

Kumar, Martha, 1369, 1370, 1436
Kumar, Satish, 4278
Kunkel, Dale, 2047
Kunstler, William, 422
Kuntz, Jonathan, 4480
Kunzle, David, 668a, 1757, 3115
Kupferberg, Seth, 2366, 3767
Kurland, Philip, 188
Kurtz, Howard, 1142
Kushner, Sam, 3421
Kutler, Stanley, 189, 380
Kwitny, Jonathan, 3618
LaBrie, Henry, 4637
Labunski, Richard, 2160
Lacob, Miriam, 3898
Ladd, Anthony, 1995
Ladd, Bruce, 190
Lader, Lawrence, 491, 2957
Lafeber, Walter, 65, 933
Lalehparvaran, Parvin, 3619
Lambeth, Edmund, 934, 4279, 4638
Lamont, Corliss, 4280, 4391
Lamperti, John, 1437, 1438
Lancaster, John, 2161
Lance, Peter, 4481
Landau, Jack, 1439, 1440, 3422, 4242
Landau, Saul, 66, 2720
Landay, Jerry, 2721
Landis, Fred, 3985
Lane, Chuck, 1441
Lang, Annie, 1879
Lang, Gladys, 669, 1442, 2722, 2723
Lang, Kurt, 1442, 2722, 2723
Lange, David, 1142a
Lange, Timothy, 4639
Langer, John, 2367
Lanouette, William, 935, 1443, 2724, 3316
Lapham, Lewis, 936
Lapp, Ralph, 245
Lappé, Frances, 135, 4482
Laqueur, Walter, 3423
Larkin, Jerome, 3424
LaRose, Robert, 2940
Larsen, Otto, 2368
Larson, Arthur, 3267
Larson, James, 2725, 2726, 2727, 2728
Larson, Keith, 1758
Larson, Mary, 3007

Lasch, Christopher, 136, 1759
Lashner, Marilyn, 2162, 2729
Laski, Harold, 1143
Lasko, Keith, 519
Lasn, Kalle, 1996, 4392
Lasswell, Harold, 4281
Laudon, Kenneth, 4440
Laurence, John, 1444
Laurence, Philip, 3899
Lauter, Paul, 4736
Lavin, Douglas, 4282
Lawler, Philip, 937
Lawson, John, 3117
Lawton, George, 1491
Lazare, Daniel, 4283
Lazarus, Simon, 1445
Lazer, Charles, 3986
Lazere, Donald, 671, 672, 3900, 4284, 4285
Leab, Daniel, 4286
Leamer, Laurence, 4640
Leapman, Michael, 1144
Lears, T. J., 1714, 1760
Lederer, William, 938
LeDuc, Don, 2894
Lee, Alfred, 4287, 4641
Lee, Elizabeth, 4287
Lee, Hyo-Seong, 673
Lee, Martin, 305, 856, 939, 940, 1446, 1447, 3901
Lee, Philip, 1928, 3245
Lee, Ray, 2003a
Leeper, Roy, 4642
Lefcourt, Robert, 423
Lefever, Ernest, 2730
Leff, Arthur, 1880
Leff, Donna, 3317
Leggett, John, 191, 3768
Lehman, Cheryl, 4123
Lehman, Tenney, 4288
Leifer, Aimee, 2921
Leighton, Frances, 1410
Leiss, William, 1755, 1761, 1762
Lekachman, Robert, 3620
Lemann, Nicholas, 4077
Lemert, James, 941, 3424
Lemon, Judith, 2504
LeMond, Alan, 306, 3200
Lens, Sidney, 66a, 67, 67a, 381, 1448
Lenski, Gerhard, 1145
Lent, John, 942, 1763, 3246
Lentz, Richard, 3902, 3903

LeoGrande, William, 3425, 4078
Leon, Warren, 674
Leonard, Bill, 2731
Leonard, Thomas, 1449
Leone, Bruno, 709
Leopold, Wendy, 4616
Lepowicz, Alice, 3247
Lerbinger, Otto, 1146
Lernoux, Penny, 137
LeRoy, David, 943, 3008, 4289
Lesage, Julia, 4483
Lesher, Stephan, 2732
Leslie, Lary, 4290
Lesser, Gerald, 2927
Lester, Marilyn, 3444
Leubsdorf, Carl, 1451
Levenstein, Alan, 1881
Levesque, Cynthia, 1882
Levin, Diane, 2906
Levin, Harvey, 2163, 2164, 3009
Levin, Henry, 449
Levin, Jack, 1147
Levin, Myron, 1883
Levine, Grace, 2733
Levine, Peter, 537
Levinson, Richard, 2505
Levy, Harlan, 3987
Levy, Mark, 2807
Lewels, Francisco, 4291
Lewin, Jackie, 4484
Lewis, Andrea, 2506
Lewis, Anthony, 1452, 3010, 3426, 4292, 4293
Lewis, Carolyn, 1453
Lewis, Florence, 2734
Lewis, Lionel, 382
Lewis, Roger, 4643
Leymore, Varda, 1764
Lichter, S. R., 2735, 2736
Lichty, Lawrence, 2574
Lieberman, David, 4294
Lieberman, Robbie, 4737
Liebert, Diane, 2048
Liebert, Robert, 2922, 2935
Liebling, A. J., 3427, 3428
Liebman, Bonnie, 1883a
Liebman, Robert, 492
Liebovich, Louis, 3318
Lievrouw, Leah, 729
Lifton, Robert, 246
Lim, Sang, 944
Lindblom, Charles, 674a

Lindee, Susan, 1455
Lindorff, Dave, 3769
Lindsay, John, 2369, 2737
Lindstrom, Duane, 1148
Linenthal, Edward, 1456, 3824, 4079
Link, William, 2505
Linowes, David, 3201
Linsky, Martin, 1457, 1458, 2738
Linz, Daniel, 3118
Lipman, Harry, 1997
Lippard, Lucy, 4135, 4136, 4738
Lippman, Theo, 3429
Lipsitz, George, 383, 675, 4158
Lipsky, Richard, 538
Lipson, Sara, 4440
Lipsyte, Robert, 539
Litman, Barry, 2165
Littell, Joseph, 2370
Little, Craig, 4326
Lloyd, Cynthia, 68
Loader, Jayne, 1459
Lockard, Duane, 192
Lockwood, Dunbar, 4080
Lodziak, Conrad, 2371
Lofton, John, 2739, 3430
Logan, Ben, 2372
Logan, Robert, 3621, 4295
Lohof, Bruce, 1884
Lois, George, 1765
Lomax, Alan, 4159
Longley, Lawrence, 2158
Lont, Cynthia, 4739
Looney, Michael, 4296
Loory, Stuart, 247, 1460, 3770
Lopate, Carol, 2507, 3904
Lord, Carnes, 3952
Lorimer, James, 3988
Lowenstein, Douglas, 3622
Lowenstein, Ralph, 694
Lowenthal, Max, 307
Lower, Elmer, 2740
Lowi, Theodore, 69
Luke, Timothy, 2373
Lukenbill, Bernard, 3989
Lull, James, 4160
Lumley, Robert, 4137
Lund, Daniel, 3279
Lundberg, Ferdinand, 138
Lundberg, Lea, 3835
Luther, Sara, 2237

Lutz, William, 676, 677, 945, 1998, 1998a, 4081
Lydenberg, Steven, 139
Lyford, Joseph, 2741, 3771
Lyle, Jack, 3432
Lyman, Francesca, 2742
Lynch, Roberta, 1150
Lynch, Russell, 1747
Lynch, Shelia, 946
Lynch, William, 2238
Lynn, Joyce, 947
Lyons, Gene, 678, 1461, 3623
Lytle, Stewart, 3119
MacBride, Sean, 4297
MacCann, Donnarae, 3990
MacCannell, Dean, 4740
Maccoby, Nathan, 1821
MacDonald, J. Fred, 2374, 2508, 2743, 2744
MacDonald, Scott, 3120
MacDougall, A. K., 679, 1151, 1152, 1766, 1999, 3248, 3319, 3624, 3625, 3626, 3905
MacDougall, Curtis, 3433
MacIver, Robert, 464
Mackenzie, Angus, 1153, 1462, 1463, 3320, 3906
Mackenzie, James, 2000, 2001
MacMichael, David, 3627
MacNeil, Robert, 2745
Macqueen, Graeme, 680
Macy, John, 3011
Madeley, John, 1767
Madsen, Axel, 2746
Maggin, Donald, 140
Magnuson, Warren, 1885
Mahler, Richard, 1886, 2049
Mahoney, Eileen, 680a, 1464, 4320
Mailer, Norman, 1768, 1769
Malakoff, David, 949
Maland, Charles, 3121, 4486
Maltby, Richard, 681
Mammitt, Harry, 1378
Mandel, Ernest, 3991
Mander, Jerry, 1770, 2375
Mandla, A., 4487
Manheim, Jarol, 1954, 2747
Maniquis, Robert, 4299
Mankiewicz, Frank, 2376
Manley, Paula, 4488
Mann, Jim, 4300
Mannes, Marya, 1771
Manno, Jack, 248

Manoff, Robert, 950, 1465, 1466, 1467, 1468, 2748, 2749, 3012
Mansfield, Michael, 2077
Mantooth, Sara, 4644
Marable, Manning, 3013
Marc, David, 2377, 2509
Marchand, Roland, 1772
Marchetti, Gina, 3122
Marchetti, Victor, 308, 1469
Marcus, Norman, 536, 2503
Margolius, Sidney, 1887
Marion, George, 3434, 3992
Mark, Norman, 2089
Marker, Dennis, 951
Markham, David, 3014
Markoff, John, 3208
Markowitz, Gerald, 1316
Marks, John, 308, 1469, 3772
Marlin, Cheryl, 3908
Marnell, William, 952
Maroe, Jim, 3628
Marquez, F. T., 3435
Marquis, Donald, 3836
Marro, Anthony, 1470
Marshall, Jonathan, 193, 4082
Martel, Myles, 2090
Martin, Dennis, 1773
Martin, Fenton, 415
Martin, John, 2766
Martin, Josh, 3629
Martin, Robert, 2025a
Marton, Kati, 2750
Marvanyi, George, 892
Marvin, Carolyn, 682
Marwick, Christine, 1471, 4301
Marzolf, Marion, 3436, 4302
Mashat, Soraya, 2751
Maslow, Jonathan, 1472, 1888
Mason, William, 3015
Massie, Robert, 128
Massing, Michael, 954, 955, 1473, 1474, 2752, 2753, 2754, 3249, 3321, 3630, 3631, 4490
Mastro, Randy, 2002
Mathes, William, 4645
Mathews, Anthony, 194
Mathews, Jay, 1475
Mathurin, Victor, 3773
Mattelart, Armand, 683, 684, 685, 3293, 3294
Mattelart, Michéle, 2923

AUTHOR INDEX

Matthews, Christopher, 2755
Matthews, Herbert, 956, 3774
Mattick, Paul, 4138
Matusow, Allen, 384
Matusow, Barbara, 2091, 2166, 2756, 4491
Maurer, Marvin, 4492
Mauro, Tony, 3437
Mauser, Gary, 2092
Max, Steve, 4193
Maxwell, Robert, 957
May, Elaine, 385
May, Lary, 70, 1126, 3123, 3124
May, Ronald, 338
Mayer, Allan, 2003
Mayer, Jane, 195
Mayer, Martin, 958
Mayerle, Judine, 2510
McAnany, Emile, 686, 2378, 2757
McAuliffe, Kevin, 3632, 3909
McCabe, Peter, 2758, 2759
McCanles, Michael, 4741
McCarthy, Colman, 959, 3633
McCarthy, Eugene, 687
McCartney, James, 3438, 3634, 4084, 4303
McCartney, Laton, 141, 1774
McCaskell, Lisa, 3250
McCavitt, William, 2185, 2186
McClure, Laura, 4742
McClure, Robert, 2790
McCombs, Maxwell, 688, 1035, 1476
McCracken, Grant, 1775
McDonald, Donald, 4304
McDonald, Duncan, 4274
McFadden, Judith, 243, 244
McGaffin, William, 196, 249
McGavin, Patrick, 4493
McGehee, Ralph, 309
McGinniss, Joe, 2093
McGoldrick, Bernard, 1776
McGovern, George, 1477
McGovern, James, 142
McGrath, Roger, 1889, 1890
McGregor-Brown, Ian, 4394
McGrew, Thomas, 2167
McGrory, Mary, 1478, 3439
McGuire, Colleen, 3775
McGuire, Leo, 4646
McIntyre, Mark, 1412, 3440
McIntyre, Thomas, 71

McKerns, Joseph, 766
McKerrow, Richard, 593, 854, 3441, 3635, 3718, 4420
McLaren, Peter, 2958
McLuhan, Marshall, 1777
McMahan, Jeff, 197, 386
McMahon, A. Michal, 1778
McManus, Doyle, 195
McNamara, Brooks, 1891
McNamara, Steve, 4647
McNichol, Tom, 1478a
McNulty, Thomas, 2760, 2761
McQuade, Donald, 1824a
McQuaid, Kim, 198
McQuail, Denis, 2239
McShane, Joseph, 4085
McVey, Judy, 4648
McWhorter, Darrell, 4305
McWilliams, Carey, 199, 3125, 4649
Mead, Nathaniel, 2003a
Mechling, Thomas, 2004, 2094
Medhurst, Martin, 689
Medsger, Betty, 3442
Meehan, Eileen, 1155, 2240, 2895
Meeker, Richard, 3636
Meeske, Mike, 4495
Meeske, Milan, 2168
Megrowitz, Joshua, 2379
Mehling, Harold, 2380
Mehra, Achal, 692, 4311
Meiklejohn, Alexander, 4312
Meisler, Andy, 1892
Mellencamp, Patricia, 2511, 3126
Melman, Seymour, 72, 250
Melody, William, 628a, 2050, 2924
Melosh, Barbara, 693
Mencher, Melvin, 4313
Mendelsohn, Harold, 2241
Mendenhall, Gordon, 3497
Meranto, Philip, 387
Merbaum, Richard, 4086
Merrill, John, 694, 962, 963, 4314, 4315
Merwin, Frederic, 562
Metzger, H. Peter, 3637
Meyer, Karl, 2762, 2763, 4496
Meyers, William, 1779, 1893, 1894, 1895
Michener, James, 1481
Mickelson, Sig, 2094a, 2095

Mickiewicz, Ellen, 2764
Miège, Bernard, 695
Miles, Michael, 73
Miles, William, 2095a
Miley, Michael, 3016
Miliband, Ralph, 388
Miller, Arthur, 74, 75, 424, 1156, 1483, 3202
Miller, Donna, 1537
Miller, Jack, 4650
Miller, Mark, 2096, 2381, 2382, 3127, 4161
Miller, Merle, 2242
Miller, Roger, 1896
Miller, Susan, 1484
Miller, Tim, 4316
Miller, Warren, 3993
Milligan, Bryce, 1485
Millman, Joel, 1486, 1487, 2765, 3251, 4497
Mills, C. Wright, 75a, 389
Mills, Kay, 3017, 4651
Milton, Joyce, 3639
Mininberg, Mark, 4498
Mink, Patsy, 1488
Minor, Dale, 1489
Minow, Newton, 2383, 2766
Minter, William, 4106
Mintz, Morton, 76, 77, 520, 964, 1780, 3777, 4317, 4652
Mintz, Penny, 3778
Miraldi, Robert, 3322
Mitchell, David, 390
Mitchell, Greg, 965
Mitchell, Lee, 2243, 2766
Mitford, Jessica, 3837
Mitgang, Herbert, 310, 3994
Mitzen, Jennifer, 4499
Moberg, David, 2244
Modleski, Tania, 696, 3128
Moen, Matthew, 493
Moffett, Enoch, 1489a
Moghadam, Val, 966, 3780
Moglen, Helene, 4087
Mohammadi, Ali, 605
Mohr, Charles, 1490
Mokhiber, Russell, 144
Mollenhoff, Clark, 200, 251
Molotch, Harvey, 3443, 3444
Monaco, James, 696a, 697
Monson, Gary, 2245
Montgomery, Kathryn, 1840
Montgomery, Peter, 4088
Moody, Kate, 2372
Moody, Kim, 1158
Moody, Sid, 3995
Moog, Carol, 1896a
Mooney, Michael, 4139
Moore, Jonathan, 1458
Moore, Linda, 698
Moore, Michael, 3640, 3996
Moore, Ray, 2384
Moore, Thomas, 3129
Moorhead, William, 4654
Moraes, Maria, 1491
Morales, Waltraud, 2767
Morgan, Edward, 2768
Morgan, Michael, 740, 2339, 2385
Morgan, Richard, 161, 311
Morgenstern, Barbara, 2169
Morland, Howard, 3910
Morley, Morris, 1492
Morris, Roger, 969, 970, 1493, 3641, 3781
Morrison, David, 2097
Morrissette, Walt, 2098
Morrissey, David, 4318
Morrow, Frank, 699, 4501
Morrow, James, 4502
Morse, Margaret, 2512, 2769
Morse, Randy, 3445
Morton, John, 1897
Mosco, Vincent, 78, 700, 701, 1159, 1160, 2246, 2247, 4319, 4320, 4503
Moskowitz, Milton, 145
Moss, Peter, 2734, 4089
Mouat, Lucia, 2004a
Mowbray, A. Q., 1898
Mowry, George, 1781
Moyers, Bill, 1493a
Muchnick, Irvin, 3642
Muchnik, Melvyn, 3018
Mueller, Claus, 702, 703
Mueller, Milton, 2141
Mujahid, Sharif al, 3911
Mullally, Donald, 3019
Muller, Ronald, 112
Mumble, Dennis, 3782
Mundkowski, Walt, 3446
Mungo, Raymond, 4655
Munoz, Julio, 971
Munson, Richard, 146
Muolo, Paul, 149
Murdock, Dave, 4504
Murdock, Graham, 634
Muro, Mark, 4090
Murphy, Jay, 1494
Murphy, Joan, 1899

AUTHOR INDEX

Murphy, Mary Pat, 3252
Murray, John, 2902
Murray, Lawrence, 3130
Murrow, Edward, 4505
Musser, Charles, 3131
Muwakkil, Salim, 972, 1900, 4743
Mysak, Joseph, 3783
Nader, Ralph, 425, 1495, 3784, 4321, 4656
Nadler, Eric, 3913
Nakayama, Tom, 1901
Nash, Bruce, 147
Nash, Roderick, 120
Nason, Jeff, 1223
Naureckas, Jim, 973, 3447, 3785, 4091
Navarro, Vicente, 521
Navasky, Victor, 1902, 3132, 4658
Nayman, Oguz, 2902
Neff, Lyle, 2386
Neier, Aryeh, 3914, 3997, 3998
Neimark, Marilyn, 4123
Nelkin, Dorothy, 252, 508, 974, 975, 1455
Nelson, Harold, 2170
Nelson, Jack, 3448
Nelson, Joyce, 2005, 2006, 2387, 2388, 2389, 2390, 2391, 2770, 3133
Nelson, Madeline, 3838
Nelson-Pallmeyer, Jack, 201
Nesbit, Dorothy, 2098a
Nessen, Ron, 1496, 2771
Neubauer, Mark, 4322
Neuendorf, Kimberly, 2363
Neumaier, Diane, 4272
Neuman, Robert, 976
Neve, Brian, 3083
Neville, Richard, 4323
Newberry, Mike, 4092
Newcomb, Horace, 2392, 2393, 2394, 2395, 2396
Newman, Dale, 976
Newman, Joseph, 1782
Newman, Robert, 976
Nicholas, Jeff, 1903
Nichols, Dana, 1161
Nichols, John, 4093
Nickson, Richard, 403
Nielsen, Elizabeth, 4744
Nielsen, Michael, 3046
Nielsen, Waldemar, 148

Nielsen, Wayne, 978
Niemi, Beth, 68
Nietschmann, Bernard, 979
Nigut, Bill, 980, 981, 982, 983, 984, 1501, 1502, 2773, 3643, 3644
Nilsen, Don, 1904
Nimmo, Dan, 93, 704, 705, 706, 1503, 2084, 2099, 2100, 2774, 2775, 2776, 3134, 4324
Nisbet, Robert, 253
Nix, Mindy, 2777
Nixon, Will, 2006a
Noah, Timothy, 1504, 3645
Noble, David, 509, 4094
Nocera, Joseph, 3646
Noll, Mark, 494
Norden, Eric, 3647
Nordenstreng, Kaarle, 985, 2248
Norrgard, Lee, 2007, 2088, 2101
Norris, Vincent, 3915
Norsworthy, Kent, 90
Norton, Chris, 3790
Novak, Michael, 540
Nowell, William, 4162
Noyes, Dan, 4374
Nugent, David, 3379
Nunes, Maxine, 1905
Nye, David, 2008
Nyhan, Michael, 2986
Oakley, Ann, 79
Oakley, Giles, 598
O'Barr, Jean, 506
Obert, John, 71
O'Brien, Conor, 80
O'Brien, Jim, 4708
O'Brien, Mark, 4326
O'Brien, Sue, 3648
O'Connor, John, 2779
O'Connor, Rory, 653
O'Dair, Barbara, 986
O'Donnell, Wendy, 1458
O'Driscoll, Mary, 2009
Oettinger, Mal, 2136, 2137
Ogden, Don, 1162
Ohlgren, Thomas, 707
Ohmann, Richard, 708, 1163, 1505, 1783, 2010, 2010a, 2780, 3839
Olasky, Marvin, 2011, 2011a, 2012
Oldham, Cheyenne, 987
Oliver, Thomas, 1906

Olivier, Gwendolyn, 2513
Olson, James, 541
Olszewski, Ray, 4008
Omeed, Ehsan, 869, 3297
O'Neal, Kathleen, 988
O'Neill, Terry, 709
Onwochei, Gil, 2781
Oppenheim, Jerrold, 4513
Oppenheimer, Jerry, 2782
O'Reilly, Kenneth, 312, 313
O'Reilly, William, 1907
Orenstein, Peggy, 2783
Orman, John, 202
Ornelas, Kriemhild, 2514
Ornstein, Norman, 2784
Orr, C. Jack, 1506
Oseth, John, 314
O'Shaughnessy, Hugh, 1507
Oshinsky, David, 391
Osner, Audrey, 1508, 4327, 4660, 4661
O'Sullivan, Gerry, 650
Otis, Lauren, 4745
O'Toole, Michael, 3325
Ott, George, 4095
Ouellette, Dan, 4508
Owen, Bruce, 4329
Owen, David, 1908, 3916
Pack, Robert, 1593
Packard, Frank, 4096
Packard, Vance, 81, 1784, 1785, 1786, 2925
Packer, Kathy, 1511
Packwood, Bob, 2785
Padwe, Sandy, 989
Paine, Christopher, 2102
Paine, Lynda, 2926
Paisley, William, 3822
Paletz, David, 614, 710, 711, 1512, 1513, 2012a, 2642, 2786, 4330
Palmer, Edward, 2927
Panfilov, Artyom, 1513a, 1514
Panitt, Merrill, 4509
Paraschos, Manny, 2787
Parente, Donald, 2515
Parenti, Michael, 82, 83, 392, 990, 1164, 2788, 4331
Parham, Paul, 3917
Parker, Richard, 1165
Parry-Giles, Trevor, 3135
Parsons, Patrick, 2896, 3452
Paterson, Thomas, 393
Patner, Andrew, 4662

Patrick, Kenneth, 465
Patterson, Margaret, 4663
Patterson, Oscar, 991, 2789, 3840
Patterson, Philip, 1080
Patterson, Richard, 2319
Patterson, Thomas, 2790
Patterson, Tim, 2791
Patton, Cindy, 992
Patton, Phil, 2516
Patton, William, 1166
Paulos, John, 993
Pauly, John, 1167, 3326
Payne, Les, 2792
Payne, Richard, 1787
Pearce, Alan, 2397
Pearce, Millard, 2317
Pearl, David, 2398
Pearson, David, 1514a
Pearson, Roberta, 2012a
Pearson, Ted, 3453
Peck, Abe, 4664
Peck, Diana, 2897
Peck, James, 4665
Peck, Keenen, 1515
Pell, Eve, 84, 495, 3999
Pelligrino, Edmund, 522
Pember, Don, 712
Pendakur, Manjunath, 3047, 3048
Pendergast, Curtis, 3918
Penrod, Steven, 3118
Pepper, Robert, 2974
Peretz, Don, 994
Perkovich, George, 995, 1517
Perl, Peter, 3649
Perloff, Richard, 1433
Perrin, Dennis, 996, 997, 1518, 1909, 3327, 3919
Perrucci, Robert, 3791
Perry, Mark, 254
Perry, Roland, 1519
Perry, Steve, 4163
Persky, Joel, 2171
Pertschuk, Michael, 4332
Peschek, Joseph, 4097
Peters, Charles, 4667
Peters, Mark, 2698
Peterson, Deborah, 4140
Peterson, Jonathan, 4277
Peterson, Robert, 3454
Peterson, Robin, 1909a
Peterson, Ted, 4000
Peterson, Theodore, 4668
Peterson, Trev, 3920

AUTHOR INDEX

Peterzell, Jay, 203, 1520
Petras, James, 1492, 3650
Petrick, Michael, 578
Petrusenko, Vitaly, 998, 1521
Pettegrew, Loyd, 1522
Petty, Gary, 2943
Pfeiffer, Richard, 3921
Phelan, Ann Marie, 999
Phelan, John, 713, 2399
Phifer, Gregg, 4141
Phillips, E. Barbara, 3922
Phillips, Joseph, 732, 3049
Phillips, Kevin, 1168
Phipps, Steven, 3022
Picard, Robert, 1169, 1170, 1523, 3455, 4669
Pickard, Robert, 4333
Pike, John, 4098
Pilat, Oliver, 3456, 4670
Piliawsky, Monte, 466
Piller, Charles, 4099
Pingree, Suzanne, 1788
Pippert, Wesley, 4671
Piven, Frances, 85
Pizzo, Stephen, 149
Platt, Toney, 3328
Pless, Laurance, 4001
Ploman, Edward, 2249
Poelchau, Warner, 315
Polan, Dana, 3137, 3138, 4142
Polan, Diane, 426
Polanski, Jonathan, 4334
Pollack, Richard, 3023, 3652
Pollak, Richard, 1173, 3329, 4672
Pollan, Michael, 2400, 2401
Pollard, James, 1524
Pollay, Richard, 1663, 1789
Pollock, Francis, 3457, 3653
Pollock, John, 1000, 1001, 3654, 3792
Pollock, Michele, 1001
Pollock, Richard, 1172, 1910, 1911, 2793, 3023
Polman, Jeffrey, 3885
Polsky, Richard, 2928
Ponder, Stephen, 1526
Pool, Gail, 3841
Pool, Ithiel de Sola, 2172, 4529, 4530
Pope, Daniel, 1790
Popkin, James, 1527
Porter, Bruce, 1912, 3024

Porter, Dennis, 4002
Porter, William, 1174, 1528
Post, Steve, 4512
Postman, Neil, 1002, 2402, 2794
Potter, David, 1791
Potter, Rosemary, 2929
Potter, Walt, 1366
Powe, Lucas, 1529, 2250, 2795
Powell, Jody, 1530
Powell, Lee, 1531
Powell, Walter, 1175, 4003
Power, Sally, 3662
Powers, Richard, 316, 1532
Powers, Ron, 2517, 2518, 2796, 2797, 2798, 4335, 4513
Powers, Thomas, 317, 2519
Powledge, Fred, 1533
Prados, John, 204, 255
Pratt, Larry, 3445
Pratt, Ray, 4164
Pratte, Alf, 3458
Prendergast, Alan, 3923
Prescott, Peter, 2799
Preston, Ivan, 1792
Preston, William, 1003, 1535, 1536
Price, Anders, 4514
Price, Don, 510
Price, Monroe, 2898
Price, Sean, 3655
Prichard, Peter, 3656
Pride, Armistead, 3459
Primack, Joel, 4673
Primeau, Ronald, 2403
Pringle, Peter, 2103, 2104
Prisuta, Robert, 2173
Protzman, Bob, 1004
Prouty, Leroy, 319
Prowitt, Marsha, 4515
Purpel, David, 455
Purvis, Hoyt, 3330
Quart, Leonard, 3140
Quigley, Margaret, 3331, 3657
Quilter, Deborah, 1793
Quinlan, Sterling, 2404, 2405
Quinn, Francis, 1794
Quinn, Jane Bryant, 4396
Quinn, John, 1913a
Quinney, Richard, 427
Rabinovitz, Lauren, 4517
Rabinowitz, Victor, 4677

Raboy, Marc, 714, 4518
Radecki, Thomas, 4005
Rader, Benjamin, 2520
Rader, Melvin, 394
Radosh, Ronald, 1005
Rafferty, Kevin, 1459
Rafferty, Pierce, 1459
Ragazzini, Giuseppe, 1537
Raloff, Janet, 1538
Ramsey, William, 3658, 3659, 3660
Rand, Ellen, 1914
Randall, Margaret, 715
Randall, Richard, 3141, 3142
Randall, Willard, 3460
Rank, Hugh, 1915, 4338, 4339, 4397, 4678, 4679
Ranney, Austin, 2803
Rapping, Elayne, 2406, 2804, 3143
Rappleye, Charles, 600
Rarihokwats, 1372
Raskin, Jamin, 4519
Raskin, Marcus, 86
Rasor, Dina, 4340
Rassbach, Elsa, 3025
Rauch, Tom, 2104a
Ravage, John, 2407
Rawick, George, 127
Ray, Ellen, 1536, 3793, 3794
Ray, William, 2174
Raymond, Chris, 1177
Raymond, Jack, 256
Read, William, 1178, 2175
Reagan, Barbara, 5
Real, Michael, 716, 717, 1179, 2105, 2521, 2522, 2523
Reardon, Betty, 87, 257
Rector, Justine, 753
Redekop, John, 395
Reding, Andrew, 1541
Reece, Ray, 150
Reed, Ishmael, 1006
Reed, John, 4680
Reel, Frank, 2408
Reese, Thomas, 496
Reeves, Jimmie, 718, 2524
Reeves, Thomas, 396
Regan, Tom, 1916
Regna, Joseph, 2013
Reich, Charles, 88
Reich, Michael, 122
Reidy, John, 2409
Rein, Irving, 1795
Reitman, Alan, 4341

Reitz, Sara, 1796
Relyea, Harold, 205, 1542
Remes, David, 3945
Renfro, Robert, 4006
Renov, Michael, 3144
Reston, James, 1543, 3332
Retbøll, Torben, 1007
Reynolds, Janice, 524
Reynolds, Larry, 89, 3479
Reynolds, Paula, 3927
Rhodes, Jane, 4681
Rice, Berkeley, 4103
Rice, David, 2297
Rice, Jim, 1544
Rice, Michael, 3795
Rice, Ronald, 2014
Richardson, Alan, 598
Richman, David, 4007
Richman, Sheldon, 2106
Ridenour, Ron, 2251, 3461, 3462, 3463
Ridgeway, James, 151, 467, 2015, 2016
Riding, Alan, 3815
Riegle, Barbara, 2252
Rifkin, Jeremy, 152
Riordan, Teresa, 2805, 4746
Rips, Geoffrey, 3464, 3465
Ripston, Ramona, 4682
Ris, Thomas, 2017
Riser, James, 3333
Rising, Richard, 258
Ritchin, Fred, 3203
Ritt, Martin, 3145
Rivers, William, 806, 1546, 1547, 4212, 4342
Roach, Colleen, 1008
Robbins, William, 153
Roberts, Lawrence, 3256
Roberts, Nancy, 4683, 4684
Roberts, Randy, 541
Roberts, Steve, 1009
Roberts, William, 428, 1181
Robertson, Thomas, 1918, 2051
Robins, J. Max, 2806
Robins, Kevin, 163
Robinson, Glen, 2253
Robinson, J. P., 2412
Robinson, John, 2807
Robinson, Lillian, 2525
Robinson, Michael, 1010, 1548, 2784, 2808, 2809, 3254, 4008
Robinson, William, 90

AUTHOR INDEX

Rock, Sandra, 2821
Rockwell, Paul, 1011
Rodberg, Leonard, 259
Roden, Cherri, 1041, 2842
Rodnitzky, Jerome, 4165
Roe, Yale, 4520
Roediger, Dave, 1797
Roeh, Itchak, 1012, 2810
Rogan, Mary, 1549
Rogers, Carol, 3304
Rogers, Fred, 2930
Rogers, Jimmie, 4169
Rogers, Joel, 35, 36, 125
Rogge, O. John, 397
Rogin, Michael, 91, 398, 719, 3146, 3147
Rohter, Larry, 3815
Rokeach, Milton, 2286
Rollin, Roger, 2410
Rollings, Jerry, 1180, 2411
Roman, James, 3026
Rome, Edwin, 428, 1181
Romm, Joseph, 1550
Roncagliolo, Rafael, 1798
Rose, Ernest, 2176
Rose, Tom, 2811
Rosebury, Theodor, 4009
Rosen, Jay, 1013, 1014, 1015, 1551, 1552, 4343, 4344
Rosen, Philip, 3126
Rosen, Ruth, 2526
Rosenau, Neal, 1182, 1553, 3466
Rosenbaum, Robert, 1554
Rosenberg, Emily, 720
Rosenberg, Howard, 3148
Rosenberg, Jerry, 3661
Rosenbloom, Joe, 2101
Rosenthal, Alan, 3149, 3150, 4521
Rosenthal, Herma, 1919
Rosenzweig, Robert, 399
Rosenzweig, Roy, 674, 3928
Roshco, Bernard, 1016, 1183
Rositzke, Harry, 320
Ross, Andrew, 721
Ross, Bonnie, 3796
Ross, Irwin, 1799
Ross, Karl, 1184, 3467
Ross, Mark, 2111
Ross, Robert, 3662
Ross, Thomas, 330, 331
Rosse, James, 3468
Rossell, Deac, 3151
Rossie, Dave, 3334

Rossman, Michael, 4345
Roszak, Theodore, 3204
Rothenbuhler, E., 2527, 4166
Rothmyer, Karen, 1017, 2812, 4104
Rotzoll, Kim, 587
Rourke, Francis, 206, 1371
Rovere, Richard, 400
Rowan, Ford, 321, 2177
Rowe, James, 4346
Rowen, James, 1919a
Rowland, W. D., 2931
Rowland, William, 2178
Rowse, Arthur, 3929
Ruben, Brent, 571a, 4198
Rubin, Barry, 1018, 2813
Rubin, Bernard, 722, 1019, 1020, 1185, 1186
Rubin, David, 727, 728, 1021, 1555, 1556, 2018, 2814, 2815, 3472, 3930, 4347
Rubin, Gail, 3469
Rubin, Nan, 3027
Rubin, Trudy, 4010
Rucker, Bryce, 1187, 4348
Rusher, William, 723
Russell, Dick, 1023
Russell, Robert, 4663
Russett, Bruce, 155, 260, 724
Russo, Anthony, 1557
Rutherford, Bill, 2787
Rutkus, Denis, 2816
Rutland, Robert, 3663
Rutledge, Kay, 1800
Rutstein, Nat, 2932
Ryan, Charlotte, 4349
Ryan, David, 1558
Ryan, Michael, 3152, 3931
Ryan, Randolph, 1559
Saalfield, Catherine, 3797
Sableman, Mark, 1560, 1920, 3470, 4685
Sachsman, David, 727, 728, 3472
Sadeghi, Mansour, 3471
Safire, William, 4011
Sahin, H., 2412
Said, Edward, 1024, 1025, 1026
St. John-Stevas, N., 1598
Salamon, Jeff, 2528
Saldich, Anne, 2817, 2818, 2819
Sale, Kirkpatrick, 725, 1027

Salisbury, Harrison, 2820, 3798, 3799
Saloma, John, 92
Salter, Liora, 726
Salvaggio, Jerry, 2254
Salzman, George, 1028
Sampson, Anthony, 156
Samuelson, Robert, 2019
Sanchez, Heidi, 2002
Sanders, Bob, 1188
Sanders, Jane, 401
Sanders, Jerry, 402, 4105
Sanders, Keith, 2084, 2085
Sanders, Marlene, 2821
Sanderson, Samantha, 1921
Sandler, Norman, 2141
Sandman, Peter, 727, 728, 3472
Sanford, Bruce, 1561
Santoro, Gene, 4167
Saporita, Jay, 4686
Sargent, Lydia, 1922
Sarnoff, Robert, 2822
Savage, J. A., 2020
Savage, Robert, 93, 3153
Sayre, Nora, 3154
Scales, Junius, 403
Scardino, Albert, 3473
Schaap, William, 1562, 3794
Schaar, John, 94, 4012
Schandler, Herbert, 207
Scharff, Edward, 3665
Schechter, Daniel, 1029
Scheer, Robert, 208
Scheinin, Richard, 4687
Schell, Jonathan, 209
Schement, Jorge, 729, 4350
Schick, Suzanne, 4398
Schickel, Richard, 1801
Schieffer, Bob, 2823
Schiller, Anita, 1189, 4013
Schiller, Dan, 1030, 1190, 3205
Schiller, Herbert, 157, 158, 429, 730, 731, 732, 1003, 1189, 1191, 1192, 1193, 1194, 1195, 1196, 1197, 1198, 1199, 1200, 1563, 2248, 2255, 2256, 3206, 3207, 3932, 4013, 4143, 4144
Schillinger, Elisabeth, 3666
Schipper, Henry, 2107
Schlesinger, Arthur, 95
Schlesinger, Philip, 634
Schlink, F. J., 1839

Schmidt, Benno, 1564, 1565, 4351
Schmidt, David, 4688
Schmidt, Steven, 2052
Schneider, Mary, 4399
Schneider, Steven, 2571
Schneiders, Greg, 2824
Schneir, Miriam, 733
Schneir, Walter, 733
Schnitman, Jorge, 686
Schoenhaus, Ted, 1935
Schonberg, Edward, 4352
Schoonmaker, M. E., 4689
Schorr, Daniel, 525, 1566, 2826, 2827, 2828, 2829
Schrag, Peter, 1923, 2830
Schram, Martin, 2107a
Schramm, Wilbur, 4342
Schrank, Jeffrey, 734, 735, 1924, 1925, 2413, 2414
Schrecker, Ellen, 404, 460
Schreiber, Mark, 2108
Schreibman, Fay, 2556
Schroder, Kim, 1942
Schroeder, Pat, 2022
Schudson, Michael, 950, 1802, 2529, 3474, 4353
Schuetz, Stephen, 1803
Schultz, Bud, 405
Schultz, Ruth, 405
Schulz, Muriel, 736
Schulzinger, Robert, 4014
Schumach, Murray, 3155
Schuman, Frederick, 1567
Schumer, Fran, 3475
Schwartz, Herman, 430
Schwartz, Louis, 2179
Schwartz, Robert, 4522
Schwartz, Tony, 2257
Schwartzberg, Neala, 2933
Schwarzlose, Richard, 3255
Schwennesen, Don, 1031
Schwichtenberg, Cathy, 2530
Scialabba, George, 4690
Scitovsky, Tibor, 1804
Scott, John V., 542
Scott, Jonathan, 3729, 3800
Scott, Peter, 193, 1569, 4082
Scott, Robert, 1261
Scott, Ronald, 3156
Scripps, Edward, 3476
Seawell, Buie, 3029
Seeger, Peter, 4523
Seelye, K., 3256, 3933

AUTHOR INDEX

Seiden, Martin, 737, 4355
Seiter, Ellen, 2531, 2532
Selcraig, James, 406
Seldes, George, 159, 737a, 1570, 3257, 3258, 3477, 3478, 3801, 3934, 4692
Seldes, Gilbert, 738, 2258, 4356
Selig, Michael, 2831
Seligman, Joel, 4321
Sellers, Leonard, 4693
Seltzer, Curtis, 1032, 3335
Semlak, William, 2883
Semmel, Andrew, 3670
Sennett, Richard, 96
Senter, Richard, 3479
Servan Schreiber, J., 1033
Sethi, S. Prakash, 2024, 2025
Shaheen, Jack, 1034, 2415, 2416, 2417, 2418, 2832, 3030
Shahin, Jim, 3671
Shain, Russell, 3157
Shamberg, Michael, 4524
Shames, Laurence, 1806
Shankar, Shobana, 2934
Shannon, Kathleen, 4525
Shannon, William, 1572
Shapiro, Andrew, 4526
Shapiro, Martin, 526
Shapiro, Walter, 3336
Sharkey, Jacqueline, 1573
Sharplin, Arthur, 2025a
Sharrett, Christopher, 3158
Shaskolsky, Leon, 431
Shaw, David, 2533, 3480
Shaw, Donald, 688, 1035, 1048, 1476
Shawcross, William, 210
Shayon, Robert, 2151, 2419, 4425
Shear, Marie, 2420
Shearer, Derek, 259
Sheehan, Margaret, 1010, 3254
Sheehan, Neil, 3259
Shepard, Charles, 2960
Sherick, L. G., 4357
Sheridan, Terry, 3672
Sherrill, Robert, 432, 2109
Shils, Edward, 1574
Shilts, Randy, 3337
Shimek, John, 1926
Shindler, Colin, 3159
Shivpuri, Pyare, 362
Shlain, Bruce, 305
Shoar-Ghaffari, P., 3802
Shohat, Ella, 3160
Sholle, David, 739
Shor, Ira, 468, 469
Shore, E., 4358
Shore, Elliott, 4694
Shore, Laurence, 4168
Short, K. R. M., 3161
Shoup, Laurence, 97, 4106
Showalter, Stuart, 3842
Shyles, Leonard, 2110, 2111
Sibbison, Jim, 1037, 1201, 1202, 1576, 2026
Sichel, Berta, 4359
Siebert, Fred, 1038
Siefert, Marsha, 629
Siegel, Lenny, 3208
Siegelaub, Seth, 685
Siegelman, Jim, 481
Siepmann, Charles, 2259
Sigal, Leon, 1039, 3673
Sigelman, Lee, 2087
Signorielli, Nancy, 740, 2339
Sikov, Edward, 3162
Siler, William, 527
Silver, Craig, 1577
Silver, Hannah, 1807
Silverblatt, Arthur, 1927
Silverman, Debora, 741, 1578, 4145
Silverman, Milton, 1928
Silverstein, Brett, 1929
Silverstein, Ken, 1579, 3481
Silvert, Frieda, 463
Simmons, Steven, 2180
Simon, Paul, 3031
Simon, Roger, 1930
Simon, Samuel, 2159
Simone, Sam, 3163
Simons, Howard, 1203, 1580
Simons, Pamela, 2003
Simonson, Solomon, 2421
Simpson, Christopher, 1581
Simril, Cat, 1996
Sims, Ward, 2833
Simurda, Stephen, 3674
Sinclair, Upton, 470
Singer, Benjamin, 2834
Singsen, Michael, 4334
Skardon, James, 1040
Skill, Thomas, 2276
Skirrow, Gillian, 2349

Sklar, Holly, 211, 1582, 1583, 1584, 1585, 3804
Sklar, Robert, 2534, 3165
Sklar, Zachary, 2198
Skolimowski, Henry, 1931
Skornia, Harry, 2260, 2261, 2422, 2835, 4527
Slack, Jennifer, 742
Slater, Michael, 1821
Slater, Robert, 3935
Slavin, Peter, 2026a
Small, Melvin, 3805
Small, William, 1586
Smigel, Erwin, 433
Smith, Anthony, 2262, 3260, 4695
Smith, Charles, 497
Smith, David, 471, 2027
Smith, Desmond, 2423
Smith, Doug, 2899
Smith, Dusky, 511
Smith, Fred, 2836, 2837
Smith, Hedrick, 2111a
Smith, Henry, 2838
Smith, J. Andy, 2027a
Smith, Jeffery, 4696
Smith, Larry, 4156
Smith, Myron, 212, 2551, 2839
Smith, Neil, 3338
Smith, Norma, 2840
Smith, Philip, 4107
Smith, R. C., 3843
Smith, Ralph, 1932, 1933, 4528
Smith, Richard, 2958
Smith, Robert, 2263, 2424, 2841, 3209, 4360
Smith, Ronald, 543
Smith, Sally B., 2425
Smith, Stephen, 743, 1041, 1587, 2842, 3166, 4169
Smolla, Rodney, 1042, 3166, 3936
Smuckler, Ralph, 879
Smyth, Frank, 1043
Smythe, Dallas, 98, 744
Smythe, Ted, 612, 4220
Sneed, Don, 3482
Snepp, Frank, 1588
Snow, Robert, 550, 745, 771, 2280
So, Clement, 1044
Sobel, Robert, 746
Sofia, Zoë, 3167

Sokolov, Raymond, 4697
Sola Pool (see Pool)
Soley, Lawrence, 1589, 2617
Solomon, Norman, 940, 1045, 1590, 3339, 3675, 3901
Sorensen, Jeff, 3483
Sorensen, Thomas, 1592
Sorkin, Michael, 2535, 3210, 3937
Soroka, Laurence, 3168
Spangler, Lynn, 3340
Spark, Clare, 4531
Speakes, Larry, 1593
Spear, Joseph, 1594
Spence, Gerry, 434
Spence, Jack, 1046, 1595, 3484
Spencer, Richard, 4699
Sperber, A. M., 2844
Spero, Robert, 2112
Spiegelman, Bob, 4700
Spiegelman, Robert, 1204
Spofford, Tim, 1047
Sprafkin, Joyce, 1803, 2922, 2935
Spragens, William, 1596, 1597
Spring, Joel, 472
Springer, Claudia, 3169, 3170
Sprague, Raymond, 4170
Spurr, David, 3341
Sragow, Michael, 3171
Sreberny-Mohammadi, A., 605
Stam, Robert, 2845, 3160
Stamets, Bill, 4532
Stanley, R. H., 2846
Stanley, Robert, 747
Stapen, Candyce, 1599
Stapp, Andy, 261
Starowicz, Mark, 2264
Starr, Paul, 528
Staudenmaier, John, 3938
Steele, Richard, 1601, 3485
Steenland, Sally, 2426, 2936
Steger, Tina, 3486
Stein, Ben, 2536
Stein, Meyer, 1602
Stein, Robert, 748, 2848
Steinberg, Charles, 747, 1603, 3032, 4533
Steinberg, Morton, 4362
Steiner, Claude, 600, 4363
Steinert, Sylvia, 3261
Steinman, Clay, 2462

AUTHOR INDEX

Stepan, Alfred, 260
Stephenson, Lee, 2028a
Stephenson, William, 1934
Sterling, Christopher, 943, 1205, 4289
Stern, Sol, 4108
Stern, Sydney, 1935
Sternberg, Steve, 2029
Steven, Peter, 3172
Stevens, Mark, 4146
Stevenson, R. L., 2849
Stevenson, Robert, 1048, 1604
Stevenson, Russell, 160
Stewart, David, 1866
Stidham, Ronald, 417
Stillman, Don, 3342, 3939
Stimpson, Ted, 2491, 2917
Stipp, Horace, 2053
Stockman, David, 213
Stockwell, John, 322
Stockwood, Kristina, 3806
Stokes, Geoffrey, 3940
Stoler, Peter, 1049
Stone, Gerald, 3487
Stone, I. F., 407, 1605, 1606, 1607, 1608, 1609, 1610, 1611, 1612, 1613, 1614, 1615, 1616, 1617, 1618, 1619, 1620, 1936, 2850, 3488, 3489, 3490, 3491, 3492, 3493, 3676, 4017, 4018, 4019, 4109, 4110, 4111, 4112, 4113, 4114, 4115, 4116, 4117, 4118, 4119, 4120, 4121, 4122, 4364
Stone, Jennifer, 3173
Stonecipher, Harry, 3482
Stout, Frederic, 600
Strada, Michael, 4701
Straight, Michael, 4534
Streeter, Thomas, 2427
Strickland, Stephen, 2907
Stridsberg, Albert, 2029a
Strodthoff, Glenn, 3844
Stryker, Sean, 4535
Suall, Irvin, 99
Sugar, Bert, 2537
Suid, Lawrence, 3174
Suleiman, Michael, 3941, 3942
Sullivan, Andrew, 1937
Sullivan, Denis, 3494
Sullivan, John, 3943

Sullivan, Rob, 4536
Sullivan, William, 2113
Suls, Jerry, 2538
Sunness, Sheldon, 4748
Susman, Warren, 749
Sussman, Barry, 1621
Sussman, Leila, 2265
Swados, Harvey, 4703
Swan, Jon, 3483, 4704
Swanberg, W. A., 3944
Swann, Charles, 2221, 2952
Swartz, James, 2113a
Sweeper, George, 2539
Swerdlow, Joel, 2114, 2376, 2853
Swinton, Stanley, 3262
Swomley, John, 262, 263, 264, 1622, 3495, 3496
Sy, Demba, 2266
Symons, Howard, 4537
Szulc, Tad, 2854
Taher, Rashid, 3800
Talbot, David, 161, 3185, 4538
Talmey, Paul, 2855
Tarbell, Ida, 4705
Tasini, Jonathan, 1050a
Tate, Cassandra, 3678, 3679, 4706
Tax, Meredith, 3969
Taylor, Arthur, 2428, 4365
Taylor, Gabriela, 2540
Taylor, John, 100
Taylor, Paul, 2114a
Taylor, Peter, 1938
Taylor, Richard, 3175
Taylor, Terri, 4020
Teague, Bob, 2856
Tebbel, John, 1623, 4021
Tedford, Thomas, 4366, 4367
Teeter, Dwight, 2170
Telander, Rick, 544
Terrell, Robert, 1061
Terry, Janice, 750, 3497
Terwood, Carole, 1597
Tharp, Marty, 3680
Thayer, Lee, 751, 2430
Thelwell, Michael, 4539
Theoharis, Athan, 323, 324, 325, 366, 408
Thomas, Helen, 1625, 3263
Thomas, Jimmie, 3275, 3276
Thomas, Sari, 2961
Thompson, Betty, 1062
Thompson, David, 1063

Thompson, James, 4368
Thompson, Kate, 1626
Thompson, Kenneth, 1627
Thompson, Kristin, 3050
Thorkelson, Nick, 4708
Thorpe, Kenneth, 3382
Thrift, Ralph, 3498
Tichi, Cecelia, 752
Tinker, Tony, 4123
Tinney, James, 753
Tirman, John, 265
Tismaneanu, Vladimir, 1064
Tobin, Eugene, 4235
Todd, Russell, 1064a
Toles, Terri, 3212
Tolstedt, Mark, 2268
Torre, Marie, 2431
Townley, Rod, 2859, 4369
Tracey, Patrick, 1628
Traska, Maria, 1065
Traub, James, 2269
Trauth, Denise, 1939a, 3979
Treitler, Betsy, 3343
Tribe, Laurence, 3945
Trice, Robert, 3682
Trillin, Calvin, 3499
Tripp, David, 2918
Trofimenko, Genrikh, 266
Trumbo, Dalton, 2541
Trumpbour, Jack, 3809
Truse, Kenneth, 2860
Tuber, Richard, 2183
Tuchman, Gaye, 754, 755, 1066, 1067, 1068, 2270, 2432, 2542, 2543, 2861, 3500
Tuck, Jay, 2271
Tulis, Jeffrey, 1629, 4124
Tunstall, Jeremy, 756, 757, 758, 3264
Turkle, Sherry, 3213
Turlington, Barbara, 399
Turnbull, George, 3344
Turner, Kathleen, 1630, 4170
Turner, Richard, 2544
Turner, Stansfield, 326
Turner, William, 1406
Turow, Joseph, 759, 1206, 1940, 2433, 2862
Tushnet, Mark, 435
Tyner, Kathleen, 2054
Ullmann, John, 4370
Underwood, Doug, 3501, 3502, 3683, 4709
Ungar, Sanford, 327, 1631, 1632

Ungurait, Donald, 652
Valdez, Armando, 2546, 2939
Van Allen, Judith, 1808
Van Horn, Carl, 2435
Van Houten, Carter, 4540
Van Houten, Margaret, 3214
Vanneman, Reeve, 162
Varela, Carlos, 1069
Varis, Tapio, 2436, 2437, 2866
Vaughan, Ted, 473
Vaughn, Robert, 1634
Vaughn, Stephen, 214, 1635
Veblen, Eric, 3684
Veblen, Thorstein, 474
Velez, Hector, 2438
Vestergaard, Torben, 1942
Vidal, Gore, 2868
Vieira, Joao, 4542
Vincent, Richard, 2547
Vinson, Eva, 3215
Virgets, Ronnie, 3685
Virilio, Paul, 3177
Vitale, Joseph, 2115
Voelker, Francis, 760
Voelker, Ludmilla, 760
Vogel, Amos, 4543
Volpendesta, David, 4544
Von Blum, Paul, 4749
Von Hoffman, Nicholas (see Hoffman)
Vyner, Henry, 101
Wackman, Daniel, 2057
Wadsworth, Ann, 4171
Wafai, Mohamed, 2869
Wagner, Susan, 1942a
Waide, John, 1943
Waitzkin, Howard, 529
Wakin, Eric, 3811
Waldman, Michael, 45, 128
Walker, Daniel, 1636
Walker, David, 758
Walker, Janet, 3178
Walker, Samuel, 4371
Wall, Jim, 280, 1288
Wallace, Jaime, 1637
Wallace, Mike, 1208, 1638
Walley, David, 761
Wallis, Victor, 3812
Walljasper, Jay, 3946, 4710
Walsh, Mary, 2870
Walters, Ida, 2181
Walters, Robert, 1639
Walton, Richard, 3503
Wander, Philip, 2439

AUTHOR INDEX

Wanderer, Robert, 1943a
Ward, Larry, 3179
Ward, Olivia, 3504
Ward, Scott, 2051, 2056, 2057
Warren, Denise, 1809
Warren, James, 1069a
Warren, Lee, 4711
Warren, Lynn, 1810
Warrior, Robert, 2871
Warsh, David, 3686
Wartella, Ellen, 2057
Wartick, Steven, 2030
Washburn, Patrick, 3505
Wasko, Janet, 78, 700, 701, 1160, 2272, 3051, 3052
Wasserman, Harvey, 102, 4545
Wasserstein, Bruce, 419
Wassmuth, Brigit, 1811
Waterman, Barbara, 529
Watkins, Arthur, 409
Watkins, John, 1640
Watney, Simon, 1070
Watson, Mary, 2440
Wattenberg, Martin, 216
Watters, Pat, 328
Watters, Susan, 1641
Watts, Sarah, 1623
Waugh, Thomas, 3180
Weart, Spencer, 762
Weaver, Carolyn, 1642
Weaver, David, 1071, 3265, 3268
Weaver, Paul, 2872
Webb, Joseph, 2647, 2873
Webster, Duncan, 763
Webster, Frank, 163, 1812
Webster, Katharine, 3813
Wedlock, Eldon, 4276
Weeks, James, 1643
Weinberg, Arthur, 4712
Weinberg, Lila, 4712
Weinberg, Meyer, 2441
Weinberg, Steve, 1644, 1645, 3385, 3687, 4372, 4546, 4713, 4714
Weiner, Jon, 4023, 4373
Weingartner, Charles, 1072
Weinstein, Henry, 2030a
Weinstein, Laurie, 4455
Weinstein, Michael, 2031
Weir, David, 4374
Weir, Walter, 1944
Weis, Lois, 440
Weis, William, 1945

Weisbaum, Herb, 2874
Weisberg, Barry, 103
Weisberger, Bernard, 410
Weisman, John, 2031a, 2442, 2875, 2876, 2877, 2878, 2879, 2880
Weisman, Steven, 1646
Weiss, Ann, 1813
Weiss, Carol, 1073
Weiss, Kenneth, 1209
Weiss, Philip, 1074, 1647, 3688, 3689, 3690, 4547
Weisskopf, Thomas, 122
Weissman, Steve, 104
Weizenbaum, J., 3216, 3217
Welch, Barbara, 1946
Welch, Susan, 1648, 3691
Welles, Chris, 1210, 1814, 3345
Wells, Alan, 2443
Wells, Ronald, 267
Welty, Gordon, 1649
Wendland, Michael, 4715
Wendt, Lloyd, 3692
Wenglinsky, Martin, 4548
Wenner, Lawrence, 764
Wernick, Andrew, 1947
Wertheimer, Fred, 2032
Weschler, Lawrence, 1075
Wesserman, Harry, 4545
Wesson, David, 1948
Westen, Tracy, 4549
Wete, Francis, 1650
Wheeler, Patricia, 3845
Whelan, Elizabeth, 164, 3845
Whillock, David, 3181
Whipple, Thomas, 1697
Whitaker, Brian, 1076, 3507, 4716
Whitcover, Jules, 3693
White, Deanna, 1905
White, Edward, 1077
White, Graham, 1651
White, Larry, 1949
White, Leonard, 1964
White, Mimi, 2444, 2549
White, Ned, 2445
White, Ralph, 217
White, Theodore, 218
White, William, 633, 1724, 4239
Whiteside, Thomas, 1950, 4024
Whitfield, S., 410a, 4375
Whitford, David, 545

Whitman, David, 1458, 3694, 4717
Whitney, Charles, 2326
Whittemore, L. H., 1652
Whitton, John, 3267
Whitworth, William, 2881
Wicclair, Mark, 4376
Wicke, Jennifer, 1815
Wicker, Tom, 1078, 2882, 4718, 4719
Wicklein, John, 2273, 2898, 4551, 4552
Wien, Barbara, 1079
Wiener, Hesh, 3218
Wieseltier, Leon, 268
Wiethoff, William, 4377
Wiggin, Gladys, 475
Wiggins, Robert, 1653
Wilcott, Jim, 1654
Wilcox, Clair, 411
Wilcox, Fred, 4378
Wiley, Peter, 486
Wilhoit, G. C., 1071, 3268
Wilkins, Lee, 1080
Williams, Brian, 4720
Williams, Francis, 3269
Williams, Frederick, 2274, 2940
Williams, Herbert, 3508
Williams, Huntington, 2446
Williams, John, 4025
Williams, Juan, 1081
Williams, Miller, 4721
Williams, Raymond, 2447
Williams, Ted, 2033
Williams, Wenmouth, 2883
Williams, William, 412
Williamson, Judith, 1816, 1817
Willis, Donald, 2012a
Willner, Barry, 1373
Wills, Garry, 105, 1082, 2884, 4379, 4380
Wilson, Christopher, 3846
Wilson, Clint, 765
Wilson, David, 476
Wilson, R. Jackson, 4026
Wilson, Thomas, 1695
Windt, Theodore, 1654a
Winer, Laurie, 4553
Winett, Richard, 4554
Winick, Charles, 2941
Winick, Mariann, 2941
Winn, Marie, 2942
Winston, Brian, 3033

Wirbel, Loring, 3219
Wirth, Michael, 1211
Wise, Arthur, 477
Wise, David, 219, 329, 330, 331, 1655
Witcover, Jules, 1651, 1656, 1657, 1658
Withey, Stephen, 2448
Witt, Elder, 436
Wittebols, James, 2885
Wittner, Lawrence, 413, 4381
Witty, Susan, 2275
Wofsy, Leon, 414
Wohl, Stanley, 530
Woito, Robert, 4722
Wokutch, Richard, 1837
Wolf, Louis, 1083
Wolf-Wasserman, Miriam, 478
Wolfe, Alan, 106, 3814
Wolfe, Ronald, 658
Wolfson, Lewis, 1659, 4382
Wolkin, Rachel, 2040
Wolseley, Roland, 4723
Wolt, Irene, 3589
Womack, John, 3815
Wong, Sybil, 1407
Wood, Robin, 3182, 3183
Wood, Scott, 2051
Wooding, Edmund, 1818
Woodmansee, Dave, 3346
Woodmansee, John, 165
Woodward, Bob, 220, 332, 4581
Woodward, Gary, 1333
Woodward, H. Mark, 3184
Woollacott, Janet, 599, 642
Worthy, William, 3509, 3816
Wright, John, 1824a
Wuliger, Gregory, 2182
Wurst, Jim, 1086
Wurtzel, Alan, 4555
Wuthnow, Robert, 492
Wyckoff, Gene, 2115a
Wyden, Peter, 333
Yakovlev, A., 269
Yakovlev, N., 334
Yang, Kisuk, 3817
Yarmolinsky, Adam, 270, 271
Yinger, J. Milton, 4383
Young, Cameron, 2034
Young, James, 1951, 1952
Young, Jock, 858
Young, T. R., 1212
Young, Virginia, 3696
Yudof, Mark, 1660

AUTHOR INDEX

Yurman, Rich, 3409
Zachar, George, 1213
Zagoria, Sam, 3510
Zahn, Curtis, 4125
Zarefsky, David, 1661
Zeigler, Harmon, 31
Zeitlin, Maurice, 107
Zelinsky, Wilbur, 108
Zheutlin, Barbara, 3185, 4538
Zilg, Gerard, 166
Zinn, Howard, 221, 1214, 4126
Zins, Daniel, 1662
Zion, Sidney, 3511
Zipes, Jack, 4384
Zito, Stephen, 4556
Zogby, James, 1087
Zuckerman, Laurence, 3034, 4557, 4724
Zullo, Allan, 147
Zynda, Thomas, 2550

SUBJECT INDEX

(Numbers refer to
entries not pages)

1950s, 56
1960s, 56, 636
1960s student movement, 1732
1968, 198
1970s, 4345
$1.98 Beauty Show, The, 2492
1984, 594, 676, 678, 2734
2,4,5-T, 3460
$5.20 an Hour Dream, The, 2316
$64,000 Question, The, 2492
ABC, 746, 759, 818, 860, 884, 925, 990, 1245a, 1401, 1530, 1569 1779, 2148, 2191, 2197, 2300, 2316, 2350, 2405, 2446, 2474, 2488, 2608, 2615, 2617, 2691, 2703, 2720, 2751, 2795, 2835
ABC: corporation, 2303
ABC coverup, 2762
ABC: EPA, 1576
ABC News, 630, 838, 1401, 2635, 2643, 2657, 2704, 3281
ABC News: Reagan, 2843
ABC News: Republicans, 2637
ABC News: Sovietphobia, 2814
ABC: Nicaragua, 2865
ABC Nightline (see also: Nightline), Nicaragua, 1500
ABC: nuclear weapons, 1443
ABC: Pentagon correspondent, 4330
ABC: sports, 541, 917, 2518, 2537
ABC television, 2544, 2679
ABC World News Tonight, 2712, 2764, 2765
ABM promotion, 236
A-Bomb (see also: nuclear), 2314
abortion, 480, 481, 482, 695aa
abortion: soap operas, 2514
Abrams, Elliott, 1254, 1275, 1283, 1393, 3001
Abrams v. United States (1919), 4190
Absence of Malice, 3171
abstract impressionism: cold war, 4130
abstraction, 4045
academic administrators, 382
academic freedom, 404, 443, 464, 4219, 4371, 4590
academic freedom: corporate state, 460
academic publishing, 3978
academic research: restrictions, 17
academic tenure, 2335
Academy Awards, 701, 2523
Acceptable Risks, 2544
access, 699, 760, 806, 889, 1009, 1032, 2119, 2148, 2160, 2176, 2239, 2241, 2303, 2359, 4220, 4224, 4254, 4306, 4309, 4333, 4341, 4351, 4363, 4366, 4407, 4454, 4550, 4598, 4631, 4636, 4674
access: broadcasting, 2235, 2795, 4409
access: cable, 4522
access: computer, 4535
access: economic restrictions, 78
access: powerless, 4438
access: government, 78, 660, 4301, 4305
access: laws, 1654
access: money, 1155
access: newspaper, 3394, 4613, 4632
access: print, 3287, 4264
access: public, 4349
access: Richmond Newspapers, Inc. v. Virginia, 4642
access: right of reply, 4207, 4248
access: rights, 2170
access: television, 2297, 4401, 4403, 4429, 4436, 4462, 4471, 4472, 4479, 4484, 4524
access: information, 1196, 1200
access: media, 1169, 4181, 4189, 4255, 4598
access: opposing views, 1963, 2024
access: power, 1388
access: Vietnam War, 2104a
access: working-class, 628a
accountability, 77, 4598

accountability: presidency (Reagan), 4102
accounting, 78, 4123
accounting corporations, 4081
Accounting Review, 4123
Accuracy in Media, 13, 733, 812, 1049, 1083, 1287, 1288, 2214, 2275, 3886, 4104
Accuracy in Media: PBS, 3005
ACCUtane case, 2026
Acheson, Dean, 4106
Acid from Heaven, 3166
acid rain, 128, 1059
Acid Rain: Requiem or Recovery?, 3166
ACLU, 2108, 2242, 3197, 3412, 4201, 4371, 4622
acquisitiveness, 1736, 1737
acronyms, 2734, 4045
Action for Children's Television (ACT), 2043, 2137, 2275, 2474, 2477, 2924, 4247
action: television, 2668
activism, 4349
ad agencies (see also: advertising), 1701
Ad Council, 1956, 1959, 1971, 1990, 1991, 1998, 2003
Adair, Devin (right-wing publisher), 3968
Adamson, John Harvey, 4715
Adbusters Quarterly, 1664, 4392
Adler, Larry, 2743
Adler, Mortimer, 1667
adolescence, 3831
adolescence: film, 3086
Adolph Coors Foundation, 3473
Adorno, Theodor, 673, 2381, 4154, 4162
Adventures of Rin Tin Tin, The, 2508
advertiser control (see also: II. B. sponsor), 1890, 3477, 3653
advertiser control: television news, 2796
advertising 1920s-1930s, 1772
advertising (II.B.), 43, 55, 112, 130, 548, 561, 591, 605, 611, 612, 616, 622, 652, 660, 664, 676, 677, 684, 694, 699, 707, 713, 716, 727, 728, 734, 735, 751, 756, 759, 772, 828, 914, 1032, 1163, 1193, 1206, 1667, 1669, 1681, 1682, 1695, 1707, 1721, 1725, 1739, 1772, 1795, 2186, 2191, 2192, 2258, 2279, 2318, 2350, 2403, 2406, 2422, 2441, 2455, 2462, 2501, 2534, 2835, 3363, 3400, 3546, 3551, 3839, 3846, 3881, 4173, 4266, 4271, 4284
advertising: advocacy (see also: advocacy advertising), 1117, 1212, 4620
Advertising Age, 1704, 1792, 4678
advertising: agencies, 1762, 1772, 1827a, 2191
advertising: alcohol, 1692, 1900
advertising: American Dream, 1812
advertising: amorality, 1843
advertising: analysis, 1762, 4386, 4397
advertising: news programs, 2796
advertising: anorexia, 1836a
advertising: anti-advertising ads, 4393
advertising: art, 1686
advertising: Art Deco, 1811
advertising: as tax, 1786
advertising: associative, 1943
advertising: autos, 1723, 1867
advertising: awards, 1675
advertising: "belongers," 1779
advertising: bibliography, 1789
advertising: blacks, 1856a, 1900
advertising: body, 1706
advertising: books, 3978
advertising: brands, 1802, 1828
advertising: breakfast cereal, 1721
advertising: broadcasting, 1679, 2190

advertising: broadcasting, film, 2258
advertising: campaign (see also: public relations), 1802
advertising: capitalist realism, 1802
advertising: children, 1699, 1721, 1881, 2909, 2914, 2919, 2924, 2926, 4399
advertising: children's television, 2904, 2913
advertising: cigarettes, 1767, 1900, 3843, 3935
advertising: claims, 1721, 1792, 1802
advertising: comparatives, 1721
advertising: consequences (II.B.), 1683
advertising: consumers, 1692
advertising: control, 3397
advertising: cosmetic, 559
advertising: costs, 1696
Advertising Council (see Ad Council)
advertising: debt, 1719
advertising: deceit, 1715, 1721, 1749, 1777, 1822a, 1831, 1792, 1800, 4338
advertising: depth psychology, 1725, 1773
advertising: desires, 1685
advertising: devices (see also: technique), 1753
advertising: disclaimers, 1721
advertising: drugs, 520, 1794
advertising: education, 2038
advertising: elimination, 1754
advertising: endorsements, 1907, 2037
advertising: entertainment, 1940
advertising: environment, 1973
advertising: ethics, 1837
advertising: exploitation, 1777
advertising: false (see also: deceit), 1666, 1762, 1769
advertising: false needs (see also: desires), 1769

advertising: family life, 1706
advertising: fantasies, 1787
advertising: fashions, 559
advertising: feminine douche, 1843
advertising: fetishism, 1762
advertising: films, 1835, 1875, 3110
advertising: First Amendment, 1860a, 1939a, 2263
advertising: food (see also: cereals), 1808
advertising: global, 629, 700, 1743, 1744, 1798
advertising: growth, 1813
advertising: history, 1762, 1790
advertising: ideology (II.B.), 1088, 1816
advertising: imagery, 1755
advertising: imperialism, 2443
advertising: industry (II.B.), 1779
advertising: investigation, 4678
advertising: jingoism, 2077
advertising: John Patterson, 1747
advertising: Latin America, 1709, 1716
advertising: law, 1666, 1792
advertising: lies (see also: deceit), 147
advertising: magazines, 3825
advertising: manipulation, 1785
advertising: market segmentation, 1762
advertising: Marxist critique, 1762
advertising: mass opinion, 1212
advertising: materialism, 2299
advertising: men, 1901
advertising: minorities, 1741
advertising: modernism, 1667
advertising: modernity, 1772
advertising: monopoly, 1094
advertising: motivation, 1804 (see also: motivation research)

advertising: MTV, 2453, 4157
advertising: Muntz TV, 1873
advertising: myths, 1764, 1777, 1791, 1816
advertising: narcissism, 1706
advertising: need creation (see also: desires), 2375
advertising: neoliberal critique, 1762
advertising: news, 1793, 1940, 2582, 2643, 3801
advertising: newspaper content, 1673
advertising: newspaper monopoly, 1673
advertising: newspapers, 1692, 1836, 3452, 3460, 3501, 3600
advertising: nonverbal, 1866
advertising: novels, 1684, 1815
advertising: nutrition (see also: food), 2046
advertising: oppression, 1776
advertising: parables, 1772
advertising: patriotism, 1930
advertising: PBS, 2978
advertising: political (see also: campaigns), 1417, 1692, 2060, 2096, 2100, 2110, 2115, 4324
advertising: pornography, 1768
advertising: prejudices (see also: bigotry), 1942
advertising: presidential, 2114a
advertising: pre-teens, 2053
advertising: products (II.B.2.), 1802, 1212
advertising: psychology, 1778
advertising: racism, 1698, 1750
advertising: regulation, 709, 1741, 1762, 1837, 2126, 2145, 2170, 4385
advertising: religion, 1745, 1746, 1816
advertising: research, 1692
advertising: rhetoric, 1722
advertising: rich v. poor, 1731

advertising: Richard Nixon, 2093
advertising: schools, 1987a, 2049
advertising: security, 1772
advertising: self-regulation, 2024
advertising: semiotic analysis, 559
advertising: sex, 559, 1676, 1692, 1937, 1942
advertising: sexism, 1697, 1698, 1788, 1803, 1878, 1921, 1922
advertising: soaps, 2450
advertising: social change, 1757
advertising: social needs, 1854
advertising: "societally conscious achievers," 1779
advertising: sponsor (see also: sponsor), 1908, 3404
advertising: sports, 1739, 1797, 2506, 2516, 3689
advertising: substantiation, 2024
advertising: sugared products, 2045
advertising: supermarkets, 1771
advertising: symbolic language, 1773
advertising: symbols, 1730, 1764
advertising: technique (II.B.), 1741, 1779, 1823a, 1831a, 1858
advertising: technology, 1745
advertising: television, 1696, 1776, 1879, 2291, 2296, 2301, 2381
advertising: television news, 2628, 2796
advertising: television spot, 2110
advertising: testimonials (see also: endorsements), 1864
advertising: elderly (see also: ageism), 2309
advertising: subconscious (see also: depth psychology), 1818
advertising: therapy, 1772

SUBJECT INDEX 689

advertising: tobacco (see also: cigarettes), 1692, 1780, 1843, 1938
advertising: toilet paper, 697
advertising: totalitarianism, 1786
advertising: triggers, 1786
advertising v. democracy and freedom (II.B.), 1790
advertising v. reason (II.B.), 1790
advertising: women, 1670, 1674, 1809, 1817, 1849, 1905
advertising: women's fashions, 3829
advertising: women's images (WWII), 3833
advertising: women's magazines, 1851, 3826
advertorial, 1742, 1840, 1897, 2052
advocacy advertising (see II.B.3.), 1117, 1118, 1146, 1152, 1193, 1245a, 1693, 1770, 1964, 1965, 1977, 1978, 1981, 1984, 1989, 1990, 2002, 2005, 2010, 2010a, 2012a, 2016, 2024, 2030a, 2064
advocacy journalism, 3309, 4212
AEC (Atomic Energy Commission), 2710, 3637, 4660
AEC: censorship, 3108
aerial bombing, 3290
Aetna Casualty and Surety Company, 1185
Afghanistan, 203, 966, 931, 1272, 1493, 2289, 2552, 2715, 2800, 3569
Afghanistan: NYT, 3780
Afghanistan: television news, 2819, 2870
Afghanistan: war, 2554, 2732
AFL-CIO, 285, 732, 2431
Africa, 204, 1446, 2266, 2559, 2728, 4032, 4432
Africa: NYT, 3706, 3722, 3760
Africa: television news, 2671, 2709, 2781
Africa: wire services, 3220
African Diaspora Images, 4424

AG (see also: Arkansas Gazette), 3545, 3546, 3547
Agca, Mehmet Ali (see also: Ali Agca), 809, 842, 1395
age: television, 2478
ageism: advertising, 1720
ageism: television, 2363
agenda setting, 38, 581, 688, 699, 990, 1035, 1039, 1073, 1317, 1360, 1442, 1522, 2376, 2698, 3376
agenda setting: NPR, 3007
agenda setting: television news, 2697
agenda setting: wire services, 3248
Agent Orange: NYT, 3724
Agents of Power (Altschull), 569
agents provocateurs, 280
aggression, 230, 762, 1295, 4089
aggression: film, 3122
aggression: video games, 3212
agitprop theater, 4730
Agnew, Spiro, 611, 612, 932, 1019, 1078, 1235, 1242, 1333, 1457, 1458, 1508, 1533, 1616, 2060, 2193, 2324, 2647, 2657, 2658, 2729, 2795, 3354, 3391, 3579
agribusiness, 129, 135, 4590
agricultural economics, 3379
Agronsky, Martin, 1241
AID (Agency for Internat. Devel.), 1254, 2027
AIDS, 927a, 986, 992, 1070, 3337, 4592
AIDS: television news, 2629
AIFLD (American Institute for Free Labor Devel), 1254
Aim High, 2059
air bags, 828
Air Force (see also: USAF), 762
Air Force propaganda, 236
air pollution, 1726, 3460
Air Power, 2439
air power propaganda, 1347
airline ads, 1784
airwaves (see also: censorship), 434
airwaves: ownership, 598, 2159, 2380
Akron Beacon Journal, 3600

Akwesasne Notes, 4215, 4601
Alas Babylon (Pat Frank), 762
Alaskan pipeline, 3821
Albano Report, 1395
Alcoa, 1966, 3821
alcohol advertising, 1692, 1824, 1869a, 1886, 1900
alcoholism, 828, 1832
Alexander, Holmes, 3968
Alfred A. Knopf v. Colby, 1558
Alger, Horatio, 3860
Algeria, 3369
Ali Agca, Mehmet, 842, 809
Alice, 2323
Alice in Wonderland, 3992
Alien and Sedition Acts, 91
alien invader films, 3146
alienation, 122, 716
Aliens, 3106
aliens, 719
Alka-Seltzer, 1705
All in the Family, 2316, 2350, 2425, 2449, 2473, 2474, 2480, 2550
All My Children (see also: soap opera), 588
Allen et al. vs. U.S.A.(radiation fallout), 101
Allen, Lew Jr., 273
Allen, Richard, 4541
Allende, Salvador, 202, 1282, 3368
Allende: NYT, 3768
Allman, T.D., 1277
All's Fair, 2323, 2534
Ally, The, 4565, 4612
Alpert, Arthur, 2282
Alpert, John, 4463
Alsop, Joseph, 1245a
Alsop, Stewart, 3396
alternative broadcasting (see also: III.), 4212
alternative journalists, 611
alternative media (see section III), 605, 923a, 2235, 4174, 4560, 4676
Alternative Media Center (NYU), 2235
Alternative Museum, 4359
alternative newspapers, 4563
alternative press, 943, 1076, 3300, 3465, 4501, 4542, 4605, 4640, 4647, 4694, 4716
alternative press: censorship, 3587
alternative press (see also: underground press), 4643
Alternative Press Service, 3266
alternative television via cable, 4298
Alternative Views, 4298, 4471
Althusser, Louis, 1347a, 1348, 2329, 2444, 3137, 4157
Altman, Robert, 3182
Altschull, J. Herbert (Agents of Power), 569
Alyeska Pipeline Company, 2833
AM radio, 2246, 4503
AMA, 524, 976, 1945, 2474
amateur sports, 543
Amchitka nuclear tests, 1488
America ad campaign, 1870
American Association of University Professors (AAUP), 382, 464
American Brands, 1874
American Brands: tobacco, 164
American Broadcasting Company (see also: ABC)
American Cancer Society, 1950
American Civil Liberties Union (see also: ACLU)
American Conservative Trust, 2091
American Dream, 616, 668a, 706, 720, 1772, 2350, 2480, 2534, 3099, 3134, 3135
American Electric Power Company, 2024
American Enterprise Institute (AEI), 6, 92, 2617, 3931, 4050, 4107
American Federation of Labor (see AFL), 719
American Football League, 917
American Gas Association, 3821
American Heritage, 3928
American Indian, 574
American Indian Movement, 280, 895

SUBJECT INDEX 691

American Indians: genocide, 584
American Indians: NBC news, 2871
American Initiatives Project, 4064
American Iron and Steel Institute, 3821
American Labor Party, 323
American Legal Foundation, 733, 2214
American Legion, 350, 361
American Library Association, 1242a, 1540
American literature: censorship (Sovietphobia), 3969
American Medical Association (see also: AMA), 517
American Mercury, 4092
American Opinion (Birch Society), 4092
American Petroleum Institute, 4103
American Revolution: children's literature, 3950
American Security Council, 7, 2101, 4105
American Way of Life, 733, 4221
Americanism (see also: patriotism), 71, 479
Americanization, 1160, 1708
Americas Watch, 1446
Americas Watch: "Free Fire," 3290
Amerika, 623, 1482, 2456, 2502, 2519, 3080
Amnesty International, 1446, 4288
Amway Corporation, 481
An American Romance, 3114
Anacin, 1715
Anaconda Company, 1103
anarchist press, 4636
anarchists, 307
Anaya, Herbert Ernesto, 3677
anchors: television news, 2663, 2705, 2769, 2770
Anderson, Jack, 1530, 3348, 3437, 4584, 4600, 4713
Anderson, John, 2076a
Anderson, Pepper (Policewoman), 2323
androgyny, 3927
Andy Griffith Show, 2350

Angleton, James (see also: CIA), 321
Angola: NYT, 3703
animals: cruelty to, 959
Annenberg, Moe, 118
Annenberg, Walter, 118, 621
anonymous sources, 1220, 2251, 3451
anorexia: advertising, 1836a, 1909a
anti-ballistics missiles (ABM), 348, 762
anticommunism: women, 61
anticommunism, 70, 155, 166, 174, 178, 181, 193, 313, 316, 319, 324, 328, 342, 343, 349, 353,, 388, 391, 394, 402, 408, 413, 443, 492, 596, 719, 778, 914, 1197, 1375, 1452, 1541, 1607, 1618, 2328, 2420, 2528, 2639, 2743, 2868, 3077, 3125, 3147, 3229, 3276, 3491, 3521, 3576, 3655, 3691, 3860, 3962, 4074, 4129, 4281, 4371, 4645, 4665, 4670
anticommunism: book censorship, 4021
anticommunism: children, 2508
anticommunism: Christian, 395
anticommunism: films, 3152
anticommunism: Hollywood Ten, 3176
anticommunism: labor, 3493
anticommunism: religion, 481
anticommunism: religious television, 2508
anticommunist hysteria, 409
anti-feminism, 482
anti-labor (labor repression), 166
anti-libertarianism, 3505
anti-nuclear movement, 1204, 1343, 3325
anti-Semitism, 60, 480, 3099, 4371
anti-Semitism: films, 3161
anti-Sovietism, 624, 1375
antitrust, 44, 1168, 1176, 2408, 4408, 4631
antitrust: Associated Press, 3252

antitrust laws, 2126, 2164, 2170, 2191, 3987
antitrust: sports, 533
anti-war advertising: WP, 3652
anti-war movement (see also: war), 3324, 3662
antiwar publications: harassment by government, 3320
Antonio, Emile de, 4453
anxiety advertising, 1892
anxiety exploitation, 1843
AP, 868a, 1245a,1513, 1576, 2734, 3220, 3229, 3233, 3235, 3240, 3241, 3248, 3258, 3261, 3273, 3281, 3295, 3298, 3419, 3437, 3477, 3578, 3586, 3787, 3801
AP: anti-trust, 3252
AP: Pentagon reporting, 4330
AP Review, 4176, 4569
apartheid, 901, 999, 1029, 2792
apocalypse, 762
Apocalypse Now, 648, 3169, 3173, 3174, 4545
Apollo program, 1040
Apollo Space Flight, 248
appearance (see also: advertising), 616
Apple Computer's "1984" ad, 1896a
Apple, R.W., 1274
Aquino, Corazon, 785
Arab countries, 818
Arab News, 3274
Arab stereotypes, 487, 750
Arab-Israel conflict, 584, 2316
Arab-Israeli war (June 1967), 3941
Arabs, 658, 767, 925, 1034, 1087, 2571, 3030, 3497, 3522, 3577, 3619, 3682, 3850, 3942, 3957
Arabs: documentary, 2832
Arabs: NYT, 3702
Arabs: television, 2415, 2416, 2417, 2418, 2565
Arafat, Yasser, 818
architecture, 616, 1667
archive, 2819
archives: television, 2858
archives: television news, 2556

Arden, Elizabeth, 1820
ARENA (Nationalist Republican Alliance, El Salvador), 1254
Arens, Egmont, 616
Argentina, 112, 193, 1600, 2004, 2006
Arias peace plan, 1275, 1276, 1283, 1585, 3550, 3585, 3658, 3660
aristocracy, 741
Arizona Daily Star, 4663
Arizona Project, 4715
Arkansas Gazette, 3273, 3274, 3275, 3276, 3545, 3546, 3547
Arledge, Roone, 2405, 2487, 2537
Arledge, Roone: sports, 541
Arlington (right-wing publisher), 3968
Armageddon, 62, 487, 762
arms, 2208
arms budget, 1550
arms control, 243, 649, 3281, 4125, 4361
arms control communications, 39
arms control: Reagan, 1434
arms control reporting, 4347
arms industry, 16
arms race, 8, 230, 249, 266, 1054, 1326, 1356, 1953, 1981, 4098
arms race: Sovietphobia, 379
arms reduction: Reagan, 1243
arms sales, 258
Armstrong, Hamilton Fish, 4106
Armstrong, Karl, 4469
Army, 240, 321
Army Counterintelligence Corps (CIC), 1581
Army intelligence, 321
Army: public relations, 1379
Army spying: civilians, 3347
Army-McCarthy hearings, 4453
Arnold, Danny, 2474
Arnold, Judge William A., 3584
Arnot, Charles, 2744
Aronson, James, 597, 3852
art, 670, 1667, 4738
art: corporations, 4133
art for control's sake, 616
art galleries, 1192

SUBJECT INDEX 693

art: government
indoctrination, 4139
art museums, 4143
art museums: corporations,
4132
art: politics, 4146, 4746,
4749
arts, 83, 744
As the World Turns, 2450
asbestos, 115, 128, 499,
3442, 3649, 4590
asbestos: cigarettes, 1883
Ashland Oil, 2025a
Ashmore, Harry, 1382
Asia, 2728
Asian Speakers Bureau, 3521
Asner, Ed, 2480, 2489, 2529
Aspen Institute for
Humanistic Studies, 1667
Aspin, Representative, Les,
1566
aspirin, 1201
assassination, 285, 288,
3677
Associated Press and United
Press International, 3253
Associated Press (see also:
AP)
Association of American
Universities, 382
A.T.& T. Telecommunications
and Information
Administration, 4425
A-Team, 2279, 2330, 3122
Atheneum, 4021
athletics (see also:
sports), 531
athletics: American Dream,
531
Athyn Group (news
consultants), 2796
Atlanta Constitution, 3430,
3506, 3545, 3560, 3682
Atlantic Monthly, 1960, 3821
atom bomb, 505
Atom Squad, The, 2508
atomic bomb, 336, 371, 762,
1347, 1459
Atomic Bomb Casualty
Commission, 101
atomic bomb secrets, 3615
atomic energy, 368
Atomic Energy Act, 3848,
3868
Atomic Energy Commission,
101, 762

Atomic Energy Commission
(see also: AEC), 101, 501,
762
Atomic Energy Commission:
censorship, 3853
Atomic Industrial Forum,
762, 1172, 1213, 1974
Atomic Power Today: Service
with Safety, 762
atomic radiation, 172
atomic test effects, 101
atomic war, 375
Atoms for Peace, 762
atrocities: Vietnam War,
1297
AT&T, 30, 115, 121, 1135a,
2156, 2191, 2216, 3188,
3205, 4454
AT&T: children, 2043
Attack!, 3064
Attica, 4521
Attica riot, 3595
Attorney General's Black
List, 501
audience commodity, 744
audience research:
television, 2350
audience: television news,
2845
audiences, 605, 2433, 2461
August 4, 1964, 341
Auletta, Ken: The
Underclass, 4203
Australia, 2298
Australia: children's
television, 2918
Australia: television news,
2595
Australian Associated Press,
3232
Australian, The, 3325
authoritarianism, 13, 55,
74, 482, 2469, 4345
authoritarianism:
corporation, 75
auto advertising, 1726,
1779, 1827a, 1852, 1895,
2341
auto industry, 44, 112, 1779
auto safety, 1110, 3546
auto safety: NYT, 3709
automation, 78, 265
automobiles, 734, 1682,
1723, 1781, 1802, 1867, 1947
autonomy: art, 673
avant-garde, 4402

avant-garde film, 3126, 3138
Avatar, 3388
Avco Corporation, 2303
Aviation Week and Space Technology, 3887
Avon books, 3975
AWACS, 787
Ayers, Frederick Jr. (right-wing novelist), 3968
B-1 bomber (see also: Rockwell), 1728, 1953, 2102, 3449
B-36, 348
Babar, 3292
bacteria (biological warfare), 1310
Baez, Joan: Bill of Rights, 4257
Bagdikian, Ben, 1546, 4706
Baker, Bobby, 1246
Baker, James, 1401, 1458
Bakhtin, Mikhail (Baxtin), 3113, 3160
Bakker, Jim, 480, 2350, 2492, 2952, 2960
Bakker, Tammy Faye, 480
Baldwin, Hanson, 3489
Baldwin, Roger, 4371
Ball, George, 4106
Ball, Howard, 1382
Ball, John (right-wing novelist), 3968
Baltimore Sun, 3336
banana republic, 235
bananas, 1859a
Bangladesh, 4561
bank failures, 981
bankers, 376, 2568, 3481
banks, 44, 112, 116, 128, 131, 137, 140, 699, 797
Banks and the Poor, 2686
banks: crime, 137
banks: drug traffic, 137
banks: film industry, 3052
banks: Hollywood, 3051
banks: radio, 2202
Banks, Dennis, 812
Banzhaf Case, 2263
Banzhaf, John, III, 1950
Baptists, 3583
Barber, Benjamin, 4744
Barbie dolls, 2914
Barbie, Klaus, SS Officer, 1581
Barfly, 2281
bargaining chip, 649

Barlett, Donald, 4600
Barnes, Joseph, 3612
Barney Miller, 2474
Barris, Chuck, 2350, 2492
Barron, Jerome, 2795
Barthes, Roland, 2330, 2373, 2716
Bartimole, Roldo, 3537, 4567
Barton, Bruce, 749, 1772, 3860
Baruch Plan, 505
baseball (see also: sports), 532, 532, 537, 559
BASIC, 3204
basic research: pure science, 503
basketball, 532
BAT, 1874
Bates, Ted, 2060
Bates, Ted: ad agency, 1692, 1715
Batman, 2291, 3127
Batten, Barton, Durstine and Osborne (BBD&O), 1772, 2060
Battle Line film, 2744
Baudrillard, Jean, 714, 2373
Bay Guardian, 4175
Bay of Pigs, 288, 319, 1000, 1078, 1320, 1349, 1619, 1620, 3488, 3509
Bay of Pigs: NYT, 3763
BBC, 2980
"Be all you can be" recruitment campaign, 1482
Beacon Press: Pentagon Papers, 4010
Bear in the Woods ad: Ronald Reagan (1984), 1896a
Beat Generation, 4402
Beatles, 4155, 4165
Beaty, John (right-wing novelist), 3968
Bechtel: CIA, 141
Bechtel Corporation, 28, 141, 4374
Bechtel: Reagan, 141
Bechtel: State Department, 141
Bechtel, Stephen D., Sr., 141
beer advertising, 1886, 1888
beer: Blatz, 1792
Beggs, James, 800
Begin, Menachem, 1285
behavior: monitoring, modification, 321

SUBJECT INDEX

behaviorism, 1725
Beijing student massacre
(see also: Tiananmen
Square), 3229
Beirut hostage crisis, 2675
Beirut marines, 1244
Beirut Massacre, 837
Belfrage, Cedric, 596, 1610, 4566
Belgian Congo, 3757
believability, 1682
Bell Telephone: radio, 2202
Bellotti (corporate speech), 435, 1156, 4390
Belonger (psychographics), 1894
Ben Linder, 835
"benign neglect," 1355, 1368
Benjamin, Walter, 616
Bennett, William, Secretary of Education, 936, 1283, 4094
Bennett, Tony, 3113
Benson, 2485
Benson, Robert, 4667
Benton, Thomas Hart, 4130
Benton, William, 879
Bereyso, Patti, 3185
Berkeley Barb, 4612
Berkeley, Martin, 3077
Berlin (1961): newspapers, 3610
Berlin: John Kennedy, 3610
Berlin Wall, 4236
Bermanzohn, Paul, 405
Bernays, Edward, 1108, 1758, 1786, 2061
Bernays, Edward: "The Engineering of Consent" (1947), 616
Bernbach, Doyle, Dane, 2060, 1715
Bernstein, Carl, 3634, 4600
Berrigans, 1226
Best Censored Stories (see also: Project Censored), 699
best-seller books, 1682
Better Business Bureau: advertising, 4396
Better World Society: Ted Turner, 4417
beverage industry, 117
Beverly Hillbillies, 2350
BG, 3633, 3677
Bhopal, 1080, 2544, 2586

bias (see also: bigotry), 777, 868a, 1419, 2776, 3523, 3605, 4266
bias: television, 2757
bias: television news, 2872
bias: wire services, 3249
Bible, 481
Bible Bowl, The, 2492
Bible study, 43
Bible v. media, 595
bibliography: broadcasting, 2184, 2185, 2186
bibliography: broadcasting law, 2183
bibliography: magazines, 3818
bibliography: network news, 2551, 2556
bibliography: political campaigns, 2085
bibliography: presidential biographies, 2095a
bibliography: television, 2276
Biddle, Attorney General Francis, 3505
Biff Baker, USA, 2508
Big Brother, 2287, 4591
big business (see also: corporations, monopoly), 744, 1186, 3419, 4304
big business control: press, 3477
big business elite, 104
Big Lie, 1481, 1585
Big Picture, The, 2508
Big Sleep, The, 3129
Bigart, Homer, 1228
Biggers, Virginia, 350
bigotry, 4, 7, 60, 62, 69, 91, 42, 343, 347, 355, 361, 375, 378, 389, 597, 628, 736, 959, 960, 1045, 1437, 1574, 1618, 1634, 2242, 2456, 2488, 2508, 2519, 2744, 2832, 3070, 3146, 3267, 3295, 3296, 3314, 3318, 3328, 3398, 3421, 3561, 3684, 4371, 4645, 4727
bigotry: Arabs, 487
bigotry: film, 3090
bigotry: Japanese-Americans (WWII), 3367
bigotry: language, 567
bigotry: newspapers, 3503

bigotry: (see also: Sovietphobia), 3306, 3311, 3855
bigotry: television, 2426
Bikini atoll nuclear tests, 762
Bilderberg Group, 699
Bilko, Sergeant: anti-militarism, 4423
Bill of Rights, 81, 328, 405, 1868, 3188, 3676, 4122, 4256, 4371
billboards, 616, 1856a
billboards: smoking, 1945
Billings, Reverend Robert: Ronald Reagan, 490
Billings, Warren: LAT, 3588
biological war (BW), 292, 792, 1054, 1058, 4099
biological warfare experiments, 1310
biotechnology, 4185
biotechnology: government, 502
bipartisanship, 2748
bipartisanship (Sovietphobia: incompetence), 389
birth control, 482
black bag jobs, 280, 291, 293, 324
Black Evangelicals, 489
Black, Justice Hugo, 627, 1110, 2795, 3252, 3430, 4211, 4232
Black Panther Party, 104, 280, 291, 316, 872, 1288, 3575
Black Sparrow Press, 4572
black-bag techniques, 273
blacklisting, 178, 352, 405, 624, 1241, 1634, 2192, 2207, 2212, 2242, 2328, 2425, 2743, 2835, 3819
blacklisting: films, 3145, 3155
blacklisting: radio and television, 2271, 2835
blacklisting: Hollywood, 3125, 3130, 4538
blacklistng: Hollywood Ten, 3111, 3193
Blacks, 647, 719, 3928
Blacks: advertising, 1856a
Blacks: blues music, 4164
Blacks: campaigns, 2060
Blacks: crime, 1006
Blacks: education, 447, 4032
Blacks: family, 4060
Blacks: film, 3083, 3114
Blacks: journalism, 779
Blacks: law, 419
Blacks: press, 612, 943, 3505, 4307, 4636, 4637, 4723
Blacks: rap music, 4729
Blacks: radicalism, 3152
Blacks: television, 753, 2485, 2496, 2543
Black-White view of world, 2675
blankness (a television style), 1723
Blass, Bill, 741
Blondie cartoon, 4142
Bloom, Allan, 3962
Bloom, Marshall, 3320
Bloomingdale's, 741
"blowback," 1536
Blue Book, 2124
Blue Thunder, 3076
blues music, 4155
Bluhdorn, Charles, 3185
Board of Studies Analysis and Gaming Agency (SAGA), 255
boards of trustees (see also: education), 466
Bob Jones University, 480, 1457
Bobbs-Merrill, 4021
body count, 1379
Body Snatchers, The (1956), 3146
Boeing Company, 3683
Bohemian Grove, 19, 141
Bolles, Don, 4715
Bollinger, Lee, 2795
Bolschwing, Otto Von, SS Officer, 1581
bomb shelters, 1459
bomber gap, 348, 377, 624
Bombers B-52: film, 624, 762
bombing, 210
bombing: Cambodia, 4252
bombs: clean, 4045
Bonanno, Joe, Jr., 4715
Bond, the, 4565
Bonelli, William: Billion Dollar Blackjack, 3588
Bonnanno, Joseph (Joe Bananas), 4715

Bonner, Raymond, 1401, 1473, 3651, 3758
Bonner, Raymond: censorship, 3720
book censorship, 1179, 2324, 3434, 3963, 3984, 4021
book chains, 3975
Book of the Month Club, 1090
book conglomerates, 4024
book popularization, 1682
book publishers, 4096, 3956, 4021
book publishers: CIA, 3953
book publishing, 611, 759, 1094, 2433, 4686
book publishing: censorship, 3983
book publishing: commercialism, 3976
book publishing: Newhouse (Random House), 3954
book publishing: racism, 4025
book publishing: USIA, 4018
book reviews, 3974
book reviews: censorship, 3434, 3974
book technology, 3978
books, 744
Boorstin, Daniel, The Image, 1108
boosterism, 1107, 3556, 3557, 3640, 3689
Booth Newspapers, 3353
bootlegging, 1781
Borchgrave, Arnaud de, 592, 3985
Bork, Robert, 430
Borman, Frank, 850
Born Losers, 3076
Boston Globe, 3229, 3281, 3633, 3677
Boudin, Louis, 4677
Bourdieu, Pierre, 721
bourgeois ideology, 3991
bourgeois ideology: film, 3128
bourgeois political parties, 85
Bowie, David, 4157
Bowman, Isaiah, 4106
Bowser, Pearl, 4424
boxing, 534
Boy Scouts, 43, 259
Boyd, James, 4667
Bradlee, Benjamin, 3996

Bradley, Ed, 2683, 2746
Braestrup, Peter, 583
brand name advertising, 1783, 1802, 1828
Brandeis, Justice, 321
Brandywine, 2148
Braniff, 1765
Branzberg, 3422
Branzburg v. Hayes, 3317, 3584
Braun, Wernher von, 248
Brave New World, 663
Brazil, 112, 3481, 3812, 3812
Brazil (film), 4542
Bread Loaf Writers' School, 678
breakfast cereals, 1881
breakfast food, 153
breakins (see also: FBI, Watergate), 283, 312, 329
Brennan, Justice, 4195
Brian's Song, 2394
bribery, 45, 220, 1096, 1098, 3606
bribing journalists (CIA), 211
bridal salon, 1795
Bridges, Harry, 361
Bright, Dr. Bill, 481
Brinkley, David, 1546, 2756, 2679
Britain: media, 598, 599, 642, 1700
Britain: public broadcasting, 3003
Britain: television, 2447
Britain: television news, 2662
British Official Secrets Act, 1320
broadband telecommunications, 2318
broadcast debates (see also: presidency), 2702
broadcasting, 591, 612, 872, 1360, 2126, 2136, 2186, 2191, 2192, 2193, 2195, 2198, 2199, 2242, 2254, 2421, 2427, 2581, 2795, 2957, 4213, 4351, 4356, 4503, 4537
broadcasting: access, 2126, 4409, 4451
broadcasting: access, Europe, 4409

broadcasting: advertising, 1679, 1762
broadcasting: audience participation, 4414
broadcasting: business, 2236
broadcasting: children, 2042
broadcasting: CIA, 1521
broadcasting: citizens' groups, 4451
broadcasting: citizens' rights, 2126
broadcasting: corporate sponsors, 1830
broadcasting: corporations' public responsibility, 4516
broadcasting: documentary, 4505
broadcasting: economics, 2260
broadcasting: education, 4505
broadcasting: entertainment, 2126
broadcasting: equal time, 2126
broadcasting: ethics, 2126
broadcasting: Europe, 4414
broadcasting: foreign systems, 4415
broadcasting: history, 2126, 2189, 2190
broadcasting industry v. education broadcasting, 2835
broadcasting: lack of diversity, 2243
broadcasting: law, 747
broadcasting: licensing, 1106, 2201, 2795, 4495
broadcasting: licensing, public trustee, 4526
broadcasting: listener rights, 4526
broadcasting: minority access, 4495
broadcasting: monopoly, 1187, 4537
broadcasting: national councils, 4414
broadcasting: Netherlands, 4443, 4549
broadcasting: Netherlands spectrum-sharing model, 4418
broadcasting networks, 1404
broadcasting: news, 2186
broadcasting: political programming, 2126

broadcasting: politics, 2094a
broadcasting: public interest, 2133, 2134, 2147, 2225
broadcasting: public service, 2257, 4526
broadcasting: regulation, 2250, 4533
broadcasting: self-regulation, 2126
broadcasting: technology, 2211
broadcasting: unions, 2272
broadcasting: US elitist model, 4418
Broadway theater, 749
Broder, David, 1422
Brodhead, Frank, 869
Brokaw, Tom, 2663
Bromley Heath radio, 2235
bronchitis: tobacco, 164
Brookings Institution, 26n, 4047, 4050, 4107, 4607
Brookings, Robert, 4047
Brooks, John, 3987
Brown & Williamson Tobacco Corporation, 164
Brown, Charlie, 4128
Brown, George E. Jr., 244
Brown, Hilary: Pentagon correspondent, 4330
Brown, Jerry, 2061
Brown, Sam, 2657
Browne, Malcolm, 1228
brown-lung disease, 3400, 4663
Brucker, Herbert, 1382
Brugmann, Bruce, 4175, 4600
Brzezinski, Zbigniew, 7, 1458, 4106
BS, 3633
Buchanan, Patrick, 1500, 3900
Buckley, William Jr., 6, 741, 1518, 3968, 4092
Buddhists, 1379
budget, 2882, 4072
budget: military, 4054
Budin, Elbert (television food commercials), 1738
bugging, 286, 306, 312
bugging: microphone surveillance, 324
bulemia: advertising, 1909a
Bulgaria: NYT, 3793

SUBJECT INDEX

Bulgarian Connection, 1395
Bundy, McGeorge, 232, 341, 1228, 2651, 4106
Bundy, William, 1228, 4106
Bunker, Archie, 2281, 2473
Bunker Hunt, 481
Burchett, Wilfred, 828, 1228
Bureau of Narcotics and Dangerous Drugs, 179
bureaucracy, 72, 75, 89, 678
bureaucracy: nuclear, 16
bureaucracy: entertainment, 713
bureaucracy: war, 3
bureaucratic schools, 477
Burger King, 1779
Burger King: "Herb" ad, 1896a
burglaries, 276
Burke, Kenneth, 673
Burma, 3569
Burnett, Leo, 1701
Burns, Allan, 2474
Burson-Marsteller, 2004
Burstyn v. Wilson (film censorship), 3141
Burt, Richard, 3719
Burton, Phillip, 244
Burundi, 3569
Bush, 211, 819, 1314, 1368, 1569, 1583, 2076a, 2773, 4085, 4508, 4541
Bush administration, 1266
Bush administration: racism, 1582
Bush: campaign 1988, 1481
Bush: campaign 1988: lying, 1583
Bush: campaigns, 2592
Bush, CIA Director, George, 1289
Bush: Cold War, 4236
Bush: drug war, 936
Bush, George, 1222, 1223, 1393, 3001
Bush, George: Iran-Contra, 3334
Bush: Iran arms, 1058
Bush: lying, 1493a
Bush: oil, 1726
Bush: Panama, 3574
Bush; prisons, 4028
Bush: secrets, 1059
Bush: speeches, 4053
Bush: taxes, 983
Bush v. Dan Rather, 2594

Bushnell, John, 1254
Bush: news conference (March 7, 1989), 1360
business, 24
Business and the Press, 3897
business: broadcasting, film, 2258
business: crime, 1880
business: domination, 4243
business: editors of pro-capitalist bias, 3454
business: image, 2024
business: journalism awards, 1814
business: management, 498
business: news, 546, 961, 1099, 1146, 1151, 1814, 2199, 3472, 3516, 3519
business: newspapers, 3630
business: press, 3683
business: propaganda, 1117
business: regime, 1131
Business Roundtable, 128, 2026a, 2031
business values v. writers, 4576
business v. workers, 162
Business Week, 1277, 3328, 3838, 3857, 4510
business-government complex, 1984
business-government-science complex, 510
businessman, 746
businessman's state, 191
businessmen: television, 2400
Butler, Major General, Smedley, 774, 1585
Butler, Major, General Smedley: Nicaragua, 1500
BW (offensive), 1310
Cabinet department agencies, 4372
cable, 2216, 2235, 3191
cable channel amplitude, 2148
cable regulation, 4454
cable television, 78, 587, 601, 697, 699, 759, 1090, 1779, 2126, 2185, 2197, 2199, 2318, 2351, 2423, 2795, 4194, 4289, 4400, 4404, 4409, 4498, 4503
cable television: access, 4522

cable television: free speech, 1193
cable television: interaction, 4530, 4552
cable television: local, 4407
cable television: lobbying, 1138a
cable television: nonprofit, 4528
cable television: public access, 4448, 4555
cable television: public service, 4528
cable television: regulation, 2145
Caddell, Patrick, 1519, 2061
Cadillac musical group, 4154
Cagney and Lacey, 2330, 2444
Cagney, James (G-Men), 1532
Caine Mutiny, The, (1954), 3146
Caldwell, 4682
Caldwell Case, 1533
Caldwell decision, 633, 1413
Caldwell, Earl, 779, 780
Caldwell, Earl (Black Panther subpoena), 1225
Caldwell, Erskine, 4006
Caldwell, Taylor, 3968
Calhoun, Lynda, 3185
Califano, Joseph, 1874
California Campaign to Enact Proposition 9, 2024
California campaigns, 2060
California Newsreel, 4215, 4432
Calkins, Earnest Elmo, 616
Callaway, Lois, Holland (ad agency), 1765
Calley, Lieutenant, 4279
calumny, 352
Cambodia, 183, 203, 204, 210, 285, 894, 1260, 2553, 2555
Cambodia bombing, 1320
Cambodia (bombing by US), 584
Cambodia: NYT, 3772¶
camcorders, 4407
Camel cigars, 116
Camil, Scott, 405
Camp David (Egypt, Israel), 1530, 2316
Camp, John, 4546

campaigns, 36, 133, 184, 817, 1010, 1230, 1537, 2084, 558, 2702, 3622
campaigns: 1952 (Eisenhower-Stevenson), 2060
campaigns: 1956 (Eisenhower-Stevenson), 2060
campaigns: 1960 (Kennedy-Nixon), 2060
campaigns: 1964 (Johnson-Goldwater), 2060
campaigns: 1980, 2076a
campaigns: 1984 (spot advertising), 2073
campaigns: advertising, 2076a
campaigns: broadcasting, 2601
campaigns: Bush, television
campaigns: consultants, 2060
campaigns: costs, 2060
campaigns: debates, 2076a
campaigns: donations, 3243
campaigns: elections, 2099
campaigns: ethics, 4671
campaigns: expensiveness: television, 2818
campaigns: finance, 4597
campaigns: financing, 177, 180
campaigns: management, 2099
campaigns: news: CBS, 3254
campaigns: news: incumbents v. challenger, 1294
campaigns: news selection, 1294
campaigns: news (UPI), 3254
campaigns: newsgathering resources, 1294
campaigns: newsgathering strategies, 1294
campaigns: photo opportunities, 547
campaigns: polling, 2099, 2632, 2722
campaigns: presidency, 970, 1035, 2590, 2719
campaigns: reporting, 870, 879, 1294
campaigns: spot, 2112
campaigns: television, 2373, 2591, 2601, 2631, 2829, 2853
campaigns: uniformity, 2688
Campbell's Soup, 1705, 1715
Campus Crusade for Christ, 481

SUBJECT INDEX 701

campus newspapers, 4625
campus press, 1533, 3690, 4181
Canada, 39, 451, 700, 714, 744, 1063, 1876, 1994, 2075, 2140, 3133, 3445
Canada: broadcasting, 2050, 2264
Canada: film, 3047, 3133
Canada: monopoly, 3377
Canada: newspapers, 3365
Canada: Nicaragua, 3250
Canada: television, 2346, 2387, 2389, 2834, 4409
Canada: textbooks, 3988
Canada/US nuclearism, 62
Canadian Broadcasting Company: access, 2235
cancer, 101, 153, 519, 762, 1201, 1945, 3390, 3460
cancer: tobacco, 164
cancer: women's magazines, 3845
candidate images: network news, 546
canned laughter, 697
canon: US literature, 4736
Canosa, Jorge Mas, 1312a
Canticle for Leibowitz, A, 624
canvassing, 4219
Canwell Committee (University of Washington), 199, 401, 394
Capital Cities Communications, 434
Capital Legal Foundation, 2690
capitalism, 46, 55, 106, 107, 111, 112, 122, 127, 130, 484, 622, 643, 681, 685, 695, 700, 775, 1117, 1686, 1706, 1736, 1805, 1817, 1945, 2218, 2237, 2299, 2486, 2530, 3625, 3839, 4032, 4388
capitalism: auto, 1947
capitalism: censorship, 1700
capitalism: democracy, 59
capitalism: environment, 103
capitalism: films, 3091
capitalism: Hollywood, 3182, 3183
capitalism: medicine, 3877
capitalism: newspapers, 3454
capitalism: NYT, 3812
capitalism: production, 4154
capitalism: realism, 1725
capitalism: television, 2587
capitalism: ultra, 55
capitalism: women, 61
Capitol Hill News Service, 4583
Capra, Frank, 3140, 3170
Captain America, 4129
Captain Kangaroo, 1826, 2474
Captain Midnight, 2508
Captain Video, 2439
captains of consciousness, 1707
Captive Voices, 3412
Cardinal Mindszenty, 1570
cardiovascular disease: tobacco, 164
care/caring humanism, 3860
Carey, James, 973
Caribbean, 248, 1763
Carlin decision (censorship), 2152
Carmichael, Stokely, 312
Carnation public relations, 2023
Carnegia, Andrew, 471
Carnegie Commission, 4051
Carnegie Commission: Educational Television, 2979, 2994
Carnegie Commission: Higher Education, 4061
Carnegie Commission: Future of Public Broadcasting, 4413
Carnegie, Dale, 3860
Carnegie Endowment Foundation, 148
Carnegie Foundation, 4032, 4037
Caro, Robert, 3608
Carr, Frank, 4534
cars (see also: automobile)
cartelization, 1121
Carter, Hodding, 678, 1277, 3623
Carter, Jimmy, 30, 31, 36, 205, 348, 377, 490, 602, 704, 706, 771, 808, 929, 1078, 1230, 1251, 1285, 1331, 1333, 1385, 1386, 1401, 1419, 1446, 1458, 1483, 1494, 1530, 2062, 2076a, 2111a, 2289, 2635, 2698, 3274, 3339, 3548, 3620, 3694

Carter Administration, 314, 321, 624, 1254, 1336, 1600
Carter administration: science, 500
Carter, Jimmy: PBS, 3004
Carter, Jimmy: speeches, 1384
Carter: press, 611
Carter: reporting of, 1342
Carter-Ford debates, 2702, 2722
Carter-Reagan debate, 2076a, 2702
Carter: 1980 State of the Union Address, 1330, 1331
Carter: energy messages, 1330
Carter: Playboy interview, 1330, 1331
cartoons, 2491, 3440, 3527
cartoons: Star Wars, 1456
Casey, William, 7, 193, 332, 1222
casino society, 1756
Cassirer, Ernst, 1773
Castro, 202, 288, 810, 2720, 4093
Catch 22, 1347
Catholic bishops pastoral letter: nuclear weapons, 1552
Catholic bishops pastoral letters, 489
Catholic Church, 491, 496, 2957
Catholic Church: Reagan administration, 483
Catholic protesters, 4380
Catholic Worker, 4683, 4684
Catledge, Turner, 3798
CATV: cable television, 2353
CAUSA: Confederation of Associations for the Unity of the Societies of America, 7
causation, 1079, 1080
caveat emptor, 1792
caveat emptor: children's television, 2546
Cavett, Dick, 2534
Caxton (right-wing publisher), 3968
CBS, 644, 787, 789, 818, 860, 896, 924, 925, 990, 1010, 1019, 1041, 1175, 1395, 1401, 1447, 1533, 1569, 1599, 1779, 1827a, 2148, 2191, 2197, 2202, 2300, 2316, 2328, 2350, 2361, 2425, 2449, 2474, 2480, 2496, 2594, 2608, 2615, 2617, 2658, 2661, 2667, 2675, 2690, 2703, 2713, 2714, 2743, 2750, 2795, 2826, 2835, 2844, 3254, 3419, 3966, 3987, 4011, 4099, 4106
CBS, 733, 746, 759, 884
CBS: censorship, 2827
CBS: CIA, 2308
CBS: corporation, 2303
CBS Evening News, 906, 1401, 1513, 1548, 2712, 2753, 2758
CBS Evening News: Nicaragua, 977
CBS Evening News: Walter Cronkite, 2291
CBS: General Westmoreland, 2583, 2718
CBS Inc. v. Democratic National Committee, 1654
CBS: libel, 1042
CBS Morning News, 4005
CBS Morning News: Nicaragua, 1500
CBS News, 650, 768, 900, 931, 1458, 2593, 2607, 2612, 2641, 2643, 2657, 2672, 2682, 2706, 2721, 2730, 2731, 2746, 2881, 3281
CBS News: Afghanistan, 2870
CBS News: arms race, 960
CBS news: presidency, 1370, 1436
CBS news: "The Vanishing Family: Crisis in Black America," 1355
CBS: Nicaragua, 2865
CBS: nuclear weapons, 1443
CBS: Paley, 2674
CBS: Pentagon, 2315
CBS radio, 2425, 2844
CBS Reports, 2651, 2844, 4289
CBS Reports: The Selling of the Pentagon, 2576, 2836
CBS: soaps, 2450
CBS: sports, 917, 2518
CBS television, 2425
CBS v. Congress, 2837
CBS v. government, 2801
CBS: Vietnam War, 2479

SUBJECT INDEX

CBS: Watergate, 1442
Cedric Belfrage, 3852
celebrities, 21, 547, 616,
681, 696a, 713, 741, 748,
756, 1669, 1682, 1687, 1757,
1801, 2350, 2394, 2466,
2486, 3045, 3439
celebrities: film, 3124
celebrities: illusion, 635
celebrities: rock star, 4148
celebrities: television,
718, 2524, 2782
celebrities: television
anchor, 2769
celebrities: television
news, 2796
censorship, 13, 17, 41, 42,
55, 94, 166, 199, 207, 239,
328, 352, 405, 411, 457,
501, 589, 612, 678, 709,
715, 782, 783, 806, 828,
834, 888, 931, 940, 943,
1003, 1016, 1019, 1061,
1076, 1121, 1229, 1237,
1240, 1242, 1242a, 1249,
1250, 1257, 1266, 1280,
1320, 1336, 1347, 1349a,
1377, 1379, 1418, 1443,
1466, 1467, 1495, 1508,
1539, 1634, 1644, 1827a,
1908, 1913, 1945, 2006a,
2064, 2150, 2161, 2190,
2207, 2212, 2214, 2251,
2288, 2348, 2353, 2354,
2359, 2474, 2480, 2505,
2639, 2657, 2659, 2665,
2695, 2710, 2743, 2835,
3053, 3114, 3142, 3319,
3320, 3350, 3385, 3388,
3400, 3408, 3412, 3430,
3434, 3460, 3470, 3479,
3486, 3507, 3517, 3526,
3537, 3538, 3539, 3541,
3552, 3556, 3579, 3581,
3584, 3587, 3597, 3615,
3625, 3637, 3667, 3683,
3685, 3686, 3686, 3693,
3817, 3848, 3867, 3868,
3920, 3924, 3934, 3962,
3964, 4011, 4133, 4183,
4226, 4227, 4249, 4251,
4271, 4280, 4289, 4304,
4328, 4342, 4358, 4371,
4461, 4575, 4580, 4622,
4671, 4682, 4686

censorship: advertising,
4392
censorship: AEC, 3108, 3853
censorship: alternative
press, 3300, 3587
censorship: art, 4135
censorship: atomic film,
4590
censorship: <u>Austin American-Statesman</u>, 3671
censorship: book publishing,
3983
censorship: books, 1179,
2324, 3951, 3958, 3961,
3963, 3966, 3971, 3977,
3984, 3996
censorship: books (CIA),
3964
censorship: books (Du Pont),
3981
censorship: books (FBI),
3970
censorship: books
(Sovietphobia), 3982
censorship: books (U.S.
army), 4000
censorship: broadcasting,
2120, 2146, 2795
censorship: CBS, 2827
censorship: CIA, 3972, 3999,
4001, 4016, 4030
censorship: CIA (books),
3980
censorship: CIA (Frank
Snepp), 3997, 4007
censorship: Cleveland PD,
3533
censorship: college
newspapers, 3359, 3403, 3416
censorship: comics, 4141
censorship: Congress, 2836
censorship: constituent and
regulative, 55
censorship: corporations,
1911, 3951
censorship: courts, 2219
censorship: Donrey Media
Group, 3593
censorship: <u>Doonesbury</u>, 3440
censorship: English
departments, 4599
censorship: environment,
3681
censorship: FBI, 3852, 4020

censorship: film, 3062, 3082, 3105, 3141, 3142, 3145, 3185
censorship: film reviews, 3446
censorship: film WWII, 3144
censorship: films, government, 3148
censorship: Foreign Agents Registration Act, 3166
censorship: Frank Snepp, 3995
censorship: government, 1244a, 1415, 1439, 1440, 1656, 2650, 2801, 2822t, 3947, 4391
censorship: Grenada, 1562
censorship: high school journalism, 3448
censorship: high schools, 3349
censorship: Hiroshima-Nagasaki, 3406
censorship: Hiroshima-Nagasaki film, 3175
censorship: Hollywood, 3074
censorship: Hollywood Ten, 3111, 3176
censorship: laws (film), 3142
censorship: letters to editors, 3424
censorship: libel, 3321
censorship: listener supported radio, 3014, 3016, 3017
censorship: local (textbooks), 3965
censorship: McCarran-Walter Act, 3854
censorship: McCarthyism, 3852
censorship: Motion Picture Production Code, 3155
censorship: museums, 693
censorship: New Republic (tobacco ads), 3916
censorship: news, 794
censorship: newspaper, 3440, 3556, 3640, 3803
censorship: Nicaragua, 4540
censorship: nuclear, 1172
censorship: nuclear bombs, 3907
censorship: nuclear corporations, 2793

censorship: NYT, 3720, 3758, 3767
censorship: obscenity, 3142
censorship: muckrakers, 3322
censorship: radicalism, 1188
censorship: Panama, 3496
censorship: PBS, 2971, 2975, 2976, 3023
censorship: pornography, 4100
censorship: presidency, 3426
censorship: prior restraint (Pentagon Papers), 4126
censorship: public schools, 3851
censorship: racism, 3097
censorship: Raymond Bonner, 3720
censorship: Reagan, 1462, 1529, 2843
censorship: Reagan administration, 1587
censorship: religion, 3116
censorship: rock music, 4163, 4592
censorship: schools (books), 3979
censorship: Seattle Times, 3668
censorship (see also: prior restraint, secrecy), 3880, 3898, 3947
censorship, self, 780
censorship: shield laws, 3422
censorship: Sovietphobia, 3993
censorship: Sovietphobia (books), 3982
censorship: sports writing, 2689, 3528
censorship: Supreme Court, 3972
censorship: television, 2327, 2370, 2384, 2470, 2475, 2482, 2489, 2545, 2650, 2831, 2875, 2880, 4474
censorship: textbooks, 3965
censorship: The FBI television series, 2109
censorship: The Progressive, 3914, 3945
censorship: USIA films, 3148
censorship: US/SU, 903
censorship: Vietnam War, 1426, 1588, 1602, 3228

SUBJECT INDEX 705

censorship: WWII, 4006
censure: McCarthy, 409
Census Bureau, 3188, 3202
Central America, 1275
Center for Auto Safety, 3546
Center for Defense Information, 4099
Center for Investigative Reporting, 4374
Center for Judicial Studies, 6
Center for Strategic and International Studies, 4103, 4104, 4105
Center for the Study of Public Choice, 6
Central America, 65, 173, 193, 204, 233, 346, 388, 714, 788, 799, 813, 825, 855, 856, 914, 915, 1053, 1054, 1058, 1273, 1276, 1357, 1401, 1437, 1446, 1479, 1487, 1492, 2208, 2585, 2606, 2679, 2692, 2757, 3285, 3407, 3409, 3441, 3659, 3660, 4035, 4039, 4041, 4064, 4078, 4105
Central America: censorship, 3984
Central America: dictatorships, 3276
Central America: Faces of War, 4473
Central America: news, 4497
Central America: Otto Reich, 1510
Central America: television news, 2691
Central America: universities, 452a
Central America: video, 4494
Central American Court of Justice, 584
Central Hudson Gas and Electric Corporation vs. Public Service Commission of New York (1980), 429
CEOs, 30
cereal advertising, 1795
cereals, 2046, 2914
Chad, 203
Chain, Lt. Gen., John, 1344
chain merchandising, 3551
chain ownership, 3393
chains, 697, 1187
chains: books, 3975

chains: Gannett, 3688
Chaka, Carol, 3185
Challenger shuttle disaster, 800, 904, 975, 1028, 1455, 4036, 4046
Chamber of Commerce, 128, 1977
Chamorro, Edgar, 211, 1500
Chancellor, John, 611
Chandler, 644
Chandler family, 3605
Chaney, James, 3056
change, 4326
channel scarcity, 2148
CHAOS, 1463, 3320
Chaplin, Charlie, 3070, 3121
Chaplinsky v. New Hampshire (freedom of expression, 3430
Chapman, Tracy, 4728, 4743
character assassinations, 280
charities, 2027
Charlie Brown, 3860
Charlie's Angels, 2534
Charlotte Observer, 4663
Charmin advertising, 1857
Charmin: Mr. Whipple, 697
Charren, Peggy: action for children's television, 1715
charters: corporations, 76, 4321
Chase, Harold, 1382
Chase Manhattan Bank, 137, 3838
chauvinism, 32, 532, 532, 655, 762, 2508, 2604, 3103, 3405
chauvinism: films, 3152
chauvinism: news agencies, 3223
chauvinism: newspapers, 3443
chauvinism: science, 503
Chavis, Ben, 405
chemical pollution, 4704
chemical warfare, 678, 1461, 2103, 4114
chemical warfare: Agent Orange, 3724
chemical warfare: Vietnam War, 4114
chemical weapons, 867a
chemical weapons research, 502
chemical-biological warfare (see CBW), 305, 4009

Chernobyl, 884, 893, 904, 1021, 1080, 1489a, 2373, 3578
Chernobyl coverage, 4593
Chesebrough-Pond, 1961
Cheskin, Louis, 1786
Chevron, 1973
Chicago 7, 1226, 1968
Chicago Bildungsideal, 1667
Chicago Daily News, 1608, 3361
Chicago Journalism Review, 4176, 4569, 4612
Chicago press, 3453, 3466
Chicago riot of 1968
Chicago Sun-Times, 1608, 3361, 3604
Chicago Tribune (see also:CT), 3281, 3317, 3318, 3361, 3419, 3428, 3576, 3604
Chicago's American, 3361, 3576
Chicanos, 2488, 4291
Chicanos: journalism, 612
Chicanos: press, 4307
Chico and the Man, 2291, 2488
child care, 2426
child labor, 431
children, 2191, 2376, 2433, 2900, 2914
children: advertising, 1721, 1741, 4399
children: Cold War, 375
children: cosmetics, 2041
children: fairy tales, 4384
children: fiction (nuclear war), 3955
children: FCC, 2137
children: food, 129
children: literature, 3989, 3990
children: media literacy, 4177
children: television, 686, 697, 755, 1699, 2035, 2166, 2276, 2341, 2474, 2477, 2491, 2912, 2913, 2916
children: TV, 2394
children: television: commercialization, 2900
children: television: profit, 2546
children: television: Sovietphobia, 2439

Children's Television Workshop, 2928
Chile, 57, 112, 183, 204, 278, 285, 290, 291, 730, 990, 1001, 1075, 1446, 2231, 2553, 2767, 3453, 3717, 3812
Chile: Allende, 3654
Chile: NYT, 3739, 3768
China, 2191, 3396, 3564, 4032, 4645
China: advertising, 1668
China: film, 3114
China: Laos (false US propaganda), 3396
China: student uprising, 996
China: television news, 2691
Chinaphobia, 3396
Chinatown (film), 3129
Chiquita Banana, 153
Chocolate Zestabs, 2046
choice: illusion, 731, 734, 737a
Choirboys, The, 3076
Chomsky, Noam, 592, 1485, 1494, 4359, 4665, 4690
Christian Science Monitor, 1581, 3328
Christian anticommunism, 395
Christian Broadcasting Network, 480, 481, 2492
Christian Broadcasting Network (CBN), 480, 481, 2208, 2492, 2952, 2955
Christian capitalism, 497
Christian fundamentalism, 485
Christian, George, 1597
Christian Right, 482, 487, 2952
Christian: right wing, 395, 493
Christian, Shirley, 1075, 3717, 3739
Christian, Shirley: NYT, 3807
Christian values: imperialism, 201
Christian Voice, 480, 492
Christianity, 719
Christianity: Reagan, 1638
Christianity: television (see also: electronic church), 2492
Christianity v. mass media, 2948

SUBJECT INDEX 707

Christianity v. televison, 2951
Christmas bombing, 183
Chromally American Corp., 1960
Chrysler, 112
Chrysler LeBaron ad, 2077
Church Committee (1975), 1585
Church Committee Hearings, 291
Church Committee Report, 299
Church, Senator Frank, 302
church-state relations, 480
church-state separation, 4371
CIA, 7, 77, 81, 104, 137, 180, 193, 202, 203, 204, 233, 266, 272, 273, 274, 276, 278, 283, 285, 288, 290, 291, 292, 293, 300, 301, 302, 305, 308, 309, 310, 311, 314, 315, 317, 319, 321, 322, 326, 329, 330, 331, 332, 334, 343, 481, 699, 786, 1218, 1222, 1223, 1229, 1239, 1242a, 1245a, 1247, 1248, 1254, 1268a, 1311, 1320, 1350, 1353, 1376, 1380, 1430, 1432, 1447, 1448, 1469, 1483, 1498, 1514, 1521, 1536, 1566, 1574, 1581, 1585, 1603, 1620, 1625, 1655, 2191, 2425, 2615, 2696, 2735, 2750, 3188, 3274, 3285, 3286, 3298, 3320, 3369, 3548, 3618, 3694, 3787, 3799, 3899, 4029, 4064, 4199, 4541, 4578, 4590, 4657, 4694
CIA: alternative press, 3464
CIA and the Cult of Intelligence, The, 3980
CIA assassination, 4638
CIA: banks, 137
CIA: book publishers, 3953
CIA: broadcasting, 1589
CIA: CBS, 2308
CIA: censorship, 3857, 3995, 3999, 4001, 4016
CIA: censorship (books), 3980
CIA: censorship (Frank Snepp), 3972, 3997, 4007
CIA: Chile, 298

CIA: computers, 3197
CIA: Contras, 1057, 1573
CIA: covert actions, 298, 301
CIA: Cuba, 333
CIA Directorate of Plans (dirty tricks), 1463
CIA: domestic operations, 1352
CIA: domestic surveillance, 2826
CIA: education, 304
CIA: false press stories, 315
CIA: Foreign Affairs, 4109
CIA journalists, 1290, 1291, 1292, 1293, 1420, 1460
CIA: media, 301, 1289
CIA: news, 3107
CIA: Nicaragua, 211, 1500
CIA: NYT, 3787, 3794
CIA: Philip Agee, 3964
CIA: press coverage, 4577
CIA: public relations, 2078
CIA: Ralph McGehee, 3857
CIA: right wing, 60
CIA: Sovietphobia, 1589
CIA: St. Louis, 3687
CIA: surveillance, 3558
CIA: television whitewash, 2713
CIA: The Secret World of the CIA, 4406
CIA: universities, 301
CIA: Vietnam War, 1588
CIA vs. civil liberties, 301
cigarette ads, 828, 4188
cigarette ads: deception, 1821
cigarette ads: sex, 1821
cigarette ads: youth, 1821
cigarette advertising, 1767, 1779, 1827a, 1834, 1841, 1842, 1847a, 1856, 1856a, 1861, 1900, 1949, 1950, 2191, 3843
cigarette labeling, 1885
cigarette lethality, 1834
cigarettes, 1100a, 1802, 1868, 1883
Cimino, Michael, 3182
CISPES, 2006a, 3290
citizen access, 2275, 4537
citizen action: broadcasting, 4515, 4451
citizen groups: FCC, 4459

citizen groups (see also: access, public access), 4451, 4481
citizen groups: television, 4479
citizen participation, 2234
citizen participation: regulation, 4537
citizen protest, 4632
Citizens Committee for Postal Reform (CCPR), 1458
Citizens Communications Center, 2275, 4247
citizenship, 4346
citizenship: computers, 3208
citizenship: education, 455
city upon a hill, 4085
civic texts, 4271
civic videotex services, 4179
civil defense, 375, 762, 1459, 3960
civil disobedience, 4276
civil liberties, 324, 352, 596, 3548, 4252, 4259, 4281, 4371, 4577, 4590, 4649
civil liberties: military, 2108
civil liberties: television, 2469
civil religion, 2527, 4085
civil rights, 4371, 4454, 4590
civil rights: FBI, 312
Civil Rights Movement, 489, 725, 3903
Civil Rights Movement: Eyes on the Prize, 4539
Civil Rights Movement: FBI, 316
Civil Rights Movement: NYT, 3796
civil rights: NYON, 3512
civil rights: television, 2864
civil rights: Underground Press, 4612
Civil Service, 352
civilian orientation tours, 259
civilization, 108
CJR, 922, 931, 3926
claims of advertising, 1721
Claire Sterling, 842
Clairemonte, Fredrick, 1874
Clancy, Tom, 1544, 3101
Clancy, Tom: Cold War, 1544
clandestine operations, 204, 319
clandestine services, 274
Clapton, Eric, 4161
Clarion (Denver University), 4639
Clark, Attorney General Tom, 328, 361
class: 1970s films, 3172
class, 21, 22, 24, 53, 83, 85, 96, 122, 127, 162, 437, 453, 479, 616, 642, 645, 685, 702, 719, 990, 1145, 1397, 1816, 2320, 2373, 2393, 2527, 2543, 2780, 2873, 3152, 3383, 3831, 3904, 4037, 4056
class conflict, 162, 559
class conflict: communication, 3301
class: education, 455
class: films, 3102, 3160
class: genre films, 3104
class: Hollywood, 3117
class: news, 2686
class: PBS, 2965, 2966
class struggle: language, 646
class: television, 2458, 2465, 2473, 2525, 2534
Classic Comics, 3521
classical realism: MTV, 4157
classical rhetoric, 2403
classification, 175, 219, 266, 653, 1320, 1338, 1349a, 1418, 1632, 4075, 4654
classified documents, 1254
classified information, 1404, 1520, 4282
classified system, 1242a
classism, 91, 4434
Cleveland, 782, 783
Cleveland Electric Illumination Company, 1096, 3540
Cleveland Foundation, 3669
Cleveland media, 1095, 1830a
Cleveland newspapers, 3669
Cleveland PD, 3526, 3527, 3531 3534, 3535, 3536, 3538, 3539
Cleveland PD: racism, 3544
Cleveland Plain Dealer, 580, 3542, 3543, 3633, 3636, 3672

SUBJECT INDEX 709

Cleveland Press, 1097, 3527, 3528
cliché, 3325
client state: dictatorships, 843, 1264, 3590, 3664
client state: terrorism, 1391
client state: torture, 3635
client states, 915
Client's Channel, 2796
Clifford, Clark, 2657
Clines, Thomas, 7, 193
clique journalism, 1422
Close Up, 3879
Closing of the American Mind, The, 3962
clothing, 681, 1708
clothing ads, 1827a
CNN, 1023, 2161, 2316, 2797, 3574, 4429, 4546
coal mining, 1032
Coalition for Better Television, 2956
Cobb, Lee, 3077
Coca Crystal, 4463
Coca-Cola, 112, 681, 1692, 1795, 1906, 1966a
Coca-Cola advertising, 1779, 1859
cocaine, 928, 1498
Cochran, Ron, 2744
Cockburn, Alexander, 4690
Cockburn, Andrew, 1419
Code of Ethics, 1140, 3267
codes (semiotics), 2279
codes (semiotics): television, 2330
coduit press, 1472
coffee, 1859a
Cohen, Jeff, 4574
Cohen, Larry, 3182
Cohen, Peter, 116
Cohen v. California, 4208
Cohn, Roy, 741, 4534
COINTELPRO, 104, 280, 287, 291, 293, 297, 316, 321, 325, 327, 2294, 3320
Colby, William, 1430
cold remedies, 1842
Cold War, 13, 39, 99, 204, 219, 226, 248, 249, 305, 321, 323, 324, 336, 342, 352, 371, 378, 386, 408, 412, 443, 624, 717, 719, 721, 732, 746, 824, 903, 1000, 1224, 1320, 1337, 1395, 1563, 1981, 2191, 2528, 2743, 3064, 3146, 3260, 3283, 3404, 3471, 3561, 3577, 3726, 3831, 4071, 4106, 4236, 4645, 4649, 4670
Cold War: art, 4130
Cold War: demagoguery, 689
Cold War: films, 3041, 3068, 3154
Cold War: magazines, 1536
Cold War: mirror-image of NSS, 3146
Cold War: news agencies, 3222, 3226
Cold War: news management, 1374
Cold War: novels, 1544
Cold War: rhetoric, 689, 1261, 4066
Cold War: science fiction, 3146
Colgate ads, 1792
Colgate-Palmolive, 1939
colleges: trustees, 457
colleges: football, 544
colleges: newspapers, 3416, 3655, 4589, 4639
colleges: newspaper censorship, 3359, 3403
colleges: conservative newspapers, 3475
colleges, 746
Collier's: Sovietphobia, 623, 1618
Collingwood, Charles, 2593, 2672
Collins, Peter, 2765
Collins, Phil, 4157
colonialism, 2217, 2218, 2743, 3160, 4032
colonialism (see also: imperialism)
Color Research Institute of America, 1786
Colorado, 3637
Colorado Daily (Colorado U-Boulder), 4639, 4661
Colorado journalism, 4691
Colorado: radio/tv, 2123
Colson, Charles, 104
Columbia: cocaine, 928
Columbia Journalism Review, 3419, 4569
Columbia: NYT, 3806
Columbo, 2505

Columbus, 584
Columbus Dispatch, 3529
Combat, 2439, 2744
comic books, 588, 2914, 4134
comic books: Sovietphobia, 375
comics, 561, 572, 760, 4127, 4128, 4129
comics: Blondie, 4142
comics: censorship, 4141
comics: minorities, 612
Commentary, 592, 658, 3927
commentary: television news, 2798
commentators: television, 2633
commercial: 1984, 1831a
commercial ads: public broadcasting, 2978
commercial broadcasters v. public broadcasting, 2979
commercial censorship, 1133
commercial culture, 675, 1686, 1694
commercial deception, 4679
commercial film (see also: Hollywood), 3120
commercial press, 4173
commercial purposes, 3506
commercial speech, 1126, 1134a, 1181, 1193, 1939a, 2028, 2263, 2342, 2343, 4366
commercial television, 434, 741, 2462, 2476
commercial use of telematics, 50
commercialism, 29, 572, 695, 1708, 1826, 2191, 2421, 4155, 4209, 4643
commercialism: broadcasting, 2124
commercialism: democracy, 55
commercialism: information, 616
commercialism: media, 1169, 1733
commercialism: news, 703, 2561, 2779
commercialism: (opposition to), 4174
commercialism: pop music, 4152
commercialism: television, 2780
commercialism: television news, 2791, 2811
commercialism: television (see also: advertising), 2381
commercials, 1860a, 2191
commercials: children, 2414
commercials: Fairness Doctrine, 2144
commercials: lying (see also: advertising), 1827
commercials (production process), 1738
commercials: program-length, 1840
commercials: television, 2455
commercial media, 1762
Commission on Freedom of the Press, 4594
commission report, 4031, 4033, 4035, 4036, 4039, 4041, 4078, 4082, 4083, 4084, 4087, 4116
commission report (see also: Pentagon commission reports)
commissions: education, 4051
commissions: journalism, 3448
Committee for a Free World, 6
Committee for Energy Awareness, 1955, 1986, 2000
Committee for the Preservation of Methodism, 350
Committee in Solidarity with the People of El Salvador, 280
Committee on Economic Development, 4061
Committee on Public Doublespeak, 4338, 4679
Committee on Public Information (WWI), 214, 1277
Committee on Sound American Education, 350
Committee on the Present Danger, 6, 7, 348, 402, 4079, 4104, 4105
Committee to Protect Journalists, 1276, 4288
Committee to Re-elect the President (see CRP), 180, 716
Committee for Public Justice, 323

SUBJECT INDEX

commodification, 1155, 1676, 1745, 1761, 1931, 2290, 2299, 2375, 2450, 2466, 2530, 2780, 3293, 3829
commodification: culture, 701, 3839
commodification: doublespeak, 1737
commodification: fetishism, 1746, 1755
commodification: feminine stereotypes, 2462
commodification: information, 1200
commodification: MTV, 2486
commodification: propaganda, 744
commodification: religion, 1746
commodification: self, 1725
commodification: television, 2350
commodification: trading, 119
commodification: worship, 1759
Common Cause, 2032
Common Law of Privacy, 3202
communication, 2209
communication: concentration (see also: monopoly), 4408
communication: cooperatives, 4179
communication: democracy, 556
communication: deregulation, 4537
communication: equity and democracy, 2234
communication: imperialism, 1643
communication: industrial, 2318
communication: satellites, 2249
communication: technology, 39, 78, 634, 2222, 2284, 4388
Communications Act, 2795
Communications Act of 1934, 2126, 2160, 4537
Communications Act of 1934 rewrite, 2234
Communications Act of 1978, 4454
communism: fear, 363

communism: Red Scare, 339
communism: reporters, 3421
Communist Party, 350
Communist Party: press, 4636
Communist Party USA (CPUSA), 291, 344, 352, 1634, 3401, 3992
communists, 4371
community, 3860
community access, 4409
Community Antennae Television (CATV), 4181
community broadcasting, 4220, 4409
community control: television, 4436
community radio, 4298
Community Television Center, 4463
competition, 1176, 2522
competition of ideas: lack of (see also: marketplace), 4264
compilation theory, 1378
complicity: media, 3652
Comprehensive Test Ban, 1321
computer: advertising, 1779
computer: grassroots communities, 4535
computer: campaigns, 2099
computer: investigative reporting, 4182, 4370
computer: magazines, 3841
computer: militarism, 3216, 3217
computer: monopoly, 3206
computer: networks, 4404
computer: news, 4316
computer: newspapers, 4709
computer: surveillance, 1128
computers, 39, 78, 163, 306, 321, 601, 605, 628a, 639, 680a, 904, 1196, 1200, 1779, 1947, 2209, 2216, 2256, 2345, 2916, 3188, 3202, 3214, 4194, 4278, 4605
COMSAT, 1159, 1643, 2156, 2249, 2255
Conal, Robbie, 4749
concentration: economic power, 46, 48, 88, 89, 683, 4631
concentration camps, 405, 3367, 3398
concentration: computers, 3205, 3206

concentration: ownership (see monopoly), 1169
concentration: power, 4281
concentration: (see also: monopoly), 3036, 3319
conditioned assent, 1329
Condon, Edward, 3676
Condon, Martin, 4092
Cone & Belding, 1715
confidential information, 1258
confidential sources, 3408
confidentiality: sources, 4685
conflict of interest, 1097, 1209, 1350
conflict of interest: newspapers, 3671
conflict of interests, 4304
conformity, 352, 453, 1078, 1242, 1708, 2190, 2287, 2658, 3292, 3499, 4356
conformity: campaigning, 2689
conformity: loyalty, 94
conformity: media, 3652
conformity: television, 2863
conformity: television news, 2624
conglomerate: book publishing, 3954
conglomerates, 553, 1168, 1184, 2303
conglomerates: NYT, 3767
Congress, 210, 283, 323, 341, 351, 352, 704, 1234, 1245, 1246, 1315, 1317a, 1360, 1377, 1420, 1458, 1484, 1659, 2102, 2191, 2805, 4181, 4281, 4371, 4372
Congress: anticommunism, 366
Congress: campaigns, 1294, 2115
Congress: censoring CBS, 2837
Congress: computers, 3195
Congress: Contras, 1585
Congress for Cultural Freedom, 1311, 4037
Congress: corporations, 45
Congress: investigative committess, 382
Congress: Iran-Contra, 3334
Congress: military, 232
Congress: military contractors, 249

Congress: president, 1331
Congress: press, 1603
Congress: public broadcasting, 2994
Congress: reports, 4091
Congress: research, 510
Congress: science, 500
Congress: Sovietphobia, 364
Congress: television (1985), 2784
Congress: television, 2098a, 2824
Conqueror, The film, 4747
conscientious objectors, 261, 3842
consciousness control, 2342
consciousness industry, 55, 744, 751, 1707
consciousness movement, 4345
consensus, 2082
consent: reflection vs. production, 646
conservatism, 6, 34, 614, 672, 1403, 2316, 2687, 3152, 3354, 3354, 4032, 4052
conservatism: foundations, 3371, 3473, 3475
conservatism: judges, 430
conservatism: newspaper owners, 3427
conservatism: NYT, 3808
conservatism: publications, 3371
conservatism: Reader's Digest, 3861
conservatism: talk shows, 2802, 2867
conservatism: television, 2611
conservatism: television news, 2617
Conservative Digest, 481
Consolidated Edison Company of New York, Inc. vs. Public Service Commission of New York (1980), 429
consolidation, 509
consorship, 172
conspicuous consumption, 616
conspiracy, 2, 6, 7, 8, 9, 10, 28, 30, 44, 104, 153, 180, 189, 193, 324, 328, 338, 374, 376, 990, 1334, 2142, 2156, 2157, 2793, 2796, 2812, 2815, 2830, 2833, 3320, 3400, 3404,

SUBJECT INDEX

3442, 3604, 3605, 3719,
3720, 3744, 3757, 3772,
3774, 3783, 3787, 3798,
3952, 3968, 3985, 4027,
4028, 4031, 4033, 4035,
4036, 4038, 4039, 4044,
4046, 4048, 4059, 4075,
4077, 4078, 4083, 4088,
4094, 4099, 4103, 4106,
4108, 4199, 4219, 4747
conspiracy: book censorship
(FBI and HUAC), 3970
conspiracy: book censorship
(government), 3983
conspiracy: censorship, 3984
conspiracy: CIA, 3997
conspiracy: films, 3152
conspiracy: Kent State, 4116
conspiracy: mentality, 706
conspiracy: PBS, 2981
conspiracy: (see also:
censorship), 2710, 2778,
2779, 2786, 2801
conspiracy: sexism, 2821
conspiracy: Sovietphobia,
censorship, 3969
conspiracy: television news,
2835
conspiracy: trials, 13
conspiracy: Vietnam War,
4121
Constitution, 210, 4371
constitution, 77
constitutional amnesia, 1418
constitutional law of
privacy, 3202
constitutional limits on
power, 289
Constitutionalizing the
Corporation, 4346
constructing reality, 871
consultants, 1373
Consumer Engineering (1932),
616
Consumer Reports, 3546, 3884
Consumer Research Union,
1839
consumerism, 43, 55, 70,
114, 163, 622, 681, 703,
741, 747, 749, 1578, 1664,
1672, 1687, 1688, 1694,
1706, 1708, 1713, 1745,
1748, 1761, 1727, 1766, 1772
1775, 1790, 1792, 1795,
1805, 1806, 1807, 1813,
1816, 1877, 1887, 2008,
2299, 2310, 2320, 2341,
2443, 2450, 2462, 2466,
2501, 3173, 3292, 3446,
3832, 3860, 3884, 4157
consumerism: advertising,
1757
consumerism: advocacy, 1830a
consumerism: capitalism,
1854, 1846a
consumerism: children, 2057,
2914, 2936
consumerism: children's
television, 2463
consumerism: choice, 1847
consumerism: commodities
(symbols), 1775
consumerism: credit, 1781
consumerism: culture, 1755,
1762, 1802, 2376, 4388
consumerism: culture
(Theodore Dreiser), 1684
consumerism: democracy, 616
consumerism: education, 478,
2910
consumerism: engineering,
616
consumerism: ethos, 4221
consumerism: films, 3124
consumerism: law, 419
consumerism: magazines, 3834
consumerism: medicine, 527
consumerism: movement, 4325,
4346
consumerism: MTV, 2453
consumerism: music, 4154
consumerism: myth, 2142
consumerism: news, 2193,
3362, 3553
consumerism: protection,
1796, 1839, 1885
consumerism: religion, 1746
consumerism: reporting, 625,
3653
consumerism: reporting
(sponsor control), 2874
consumerism: sex, 1676
consumerism: society, 1193,
1740
consumerism: sovereignty
myth, 55
consumerism: television,
2370, 2377, 2541
consumerism v. environment,
2321
consumption as religion,
1746

Contadora, 1276, 1282, 1492
Container Corporation of America, 1667
containment doctrine, 371, 585, 649
containment: SU, 266
containment/rollback, 62
content analysis, 1347a, 4444
content analysis: television news, 2556
Continental Airlines, 2012
Continental Baking Company, 1919a
Continental Oil Co., 580
Contra aid, 2987
contradictions, 127
Contragate, 7, 193, 1057, 3450, 3451, 4508
Contras, 7, 64, 233, 242, 482, 827, 833, 835, 919, 926, 1248, 1268a, 1275, 1282, 1283, 1298, 1431, 1447, 1500, 1585, 2959, 3288, 3741
Contras: Catholic Church, 483
Contras: drug smuggling, 1058, 1486, 4091
Contras: murder, 3373
Contras: PBS, 2987
control: history, 1540
conventions, 2279, 4266
Conyers, John, 244
Cook, Fred J., 2148, 4600
Cooper, Kent, 611
co-opting, 1534, 1627
Coors, Adolph, 4090
Coors, Joseph, 481, 1099, 2665
Coover, 721
Coppola, Francis, 3152, 3185, 4545
copyright, 2170, 3978, 4366
Corcoran Gallery, 4135
corporate cultural hegemony, 70
corporate directorates, 1094
corporate directors, 30
corporate elites, 31
corporate environmental advertising, 1973
corporate executives, 1099
corporate expansion, 29, 166
corporate expansion worldwide, 12

corporate farming, 3379
corporate films, 1961, 1984
corporate finances, 1152
corporate free speech, 427, 432, 1166
corporate greed, 2156
corporate hegemony, 1830, 2026a
corporate image, 1682
corporate image ads, 1961, 1966, 2028
corporate information control, 634
corporate law, 4321
corporate lawyers, 433
corporate lobbying, 128, 161, 1796
corporate medicine, 516, 530
corporate mistakes, 147
corporate names, 147
corporate news releases, 3546
corporate philanthropy, 1100
corporate power, 413
corporate power: technique, 1955a
corporate press kits, 3546
corporate press releases, 1202
corporate press releases: news, 3469
corporate propaganda, 2025, 2029a
corporate public relations, 611, 2026a
corporate public relations (see also: public relations), 1774,
corporate secrecy, 77, 160, 1153, 2833, 3678
corporate socialism, 44
corporate speech, 435, 1156, 1181, 1188, 1193
corporate speech (see also: commercial speech), 1810, 1860a
corporate sponsored conferences, 1928
corporate sponsors, 828, 1830, 1903, 2191
corporate sponsors: blacklisting (see also: blacklisting), 2207, 2212
corporate sports, 536
corporate state, 88, 89, 235, 998, 2270

SUBJECT INDEX

corporate state: art museums, 4132
corporate state: education, 438
corporate state: news, 1030
corporate state: religion, 479
corporate state: remedies (see also: III), 4269
corporate state: television, 2301
corporate state: television news, 2624, 2625
corporate television, 2302
corporate tyranny, 152
corporate unity, 26
corporate v. individual speech, 2176
corporate video, 2186
corporate violence, 1945
corporate-media interlock, 3740
corporate-government complex, 46, 48, 76, 507, 1373
corporate-newspaper collusion, 3443
corporate-university-newspaper complex, 3531
corporation, 24, 48, 81, 84, 125, 155, 402, 553, 553, 660, 730, 1978, 1986, 1989, 1990, 2000, 2197, 2288, 2361, 2690, 2868, 3404, 3602, 3645, 4106, 4155, 4346, 4694
corporation advocacy ads, 146
corporation: annual reports, 4081, 4123
corporation: art, 4133
corporation: broadcasting, 2190, 2196, 2206, 2348, 2353
corporation: censorship, 2327, 3523, 3602, 3606, 3951, 4181
corporation: computers, 3186
corporation: crime, 3963, 4663, 4704
corporation: education, 2017
corporation: environment, 1966
corporation: financial statements, 4123
corporation: free speech, 4390

corporation: image film, 3058
corporation: instrumental rationality, 2624
corporation: Masterpiece Theatre, 2981
corporation: museums, 4144
corporation: newspapers, 3385, 3523, 3606
corporation: PBS, 2969, 2973, 2981, 2999, 3026, 3031, 3032, 3033
corporation: pollution, 1966
corporation: presidents, 2105
corporation: press, 3801
corporation: press releases, 1919, 3516, 3519
corporation: propaganda, 4690
corporation: reports, 4040
corporation: sports, 1797
corporation: success dream, 3860
corporation: surveillance, 3200
corporation: television, 2278, 2579, 4509
corporation: think tanks and foundations, 4097
corporation v. consumer, 1958
corporation v. Fairness Doctrine, 2135
corporations, 7, 154, 160, 177, 306, 376, 509, 671, 712, 1049, 1214, 1355, 1633, 1708
corporations: advertising, 147, 1185, 1957, 1961, 1962, 1963, 1968, 1975, 1985, 1987, 1999, 2028
corporations: advocacy administration, 4244
corporations: annual reports, 78, 616, 1998a
corporations: arrogance, 2353
corporations: boards, 1136
corporations: bribery, 77
corporations: campaign contributors, 161
corporations: capitalism, 59
corporations: censorship, 1188, 1838, 1909
corporations: charters, 4321

corporations: crime, 9, 44, 101, 115, 119, 128, 137, 140, 144, 431, 434, 580, 775, 797, 798, 980, 983, 1006, 1134, 1139, 1153, 1157, 1171, 1177, 1848, 1882, 1887, 1888, 1919a, 1963, 1966, 2025a, 2124,2441, 2451, 2475, 3366, 3546, 3562, 3592, 3604, 3643, 3649, 3683, 3687, 3783, 4346
corporations: crime (asbestos), 3442
corporations: crime (auto industry), 3709
corporations: crime (Diamond-Shamrock Corporation), 3532
corporations: crime (Jeep), 1899
corporations: education, 26, 445
corporations: encyclopedia to, 145
corporations: film control, 2472
corporations: First Amendment, 435, 1166
corporations: free speech, 429
corporations: human rights, 4325
corporations: information, 729
corporations: law, 419
corporations: legal education, 421
corporations: mass media, 578
corporations: media, 1245
corporations: Montana, 1103
corporations: network control, 2585
corporations: press, 1169
corporations: satellites, 1407
corporations: Supreme Court, 424
corporations: television control, 2577
corporations: universities, 470
corporations v. labor, 3602
corporations vs. democracy, 55
corporations vs. free and critical press, 691
corporatism, 29
correspondents: television, 2581
corruption: government, 1350
Corruptions of Empire: A. Cockburn, 4690
Cosby, Bill, 717
Cosby Show, The, 2279, 2381, 4435
Cosell, Howard, 2518, 2537
cosmetic advertising, 559, 1827a
cosmetics, 1820
cosmetics: children, 2041
Cosmopolitan, 1851, 1945, 3826
cost overruns (military), 235
Costa Rica, 65, 585, 1492
Costa-Gravas, 3173
cotton industry, 3400
Council on Foreign Affairs, 4014
Council on Foreign Relations, 23, 97, 699, 3873, 4022, 4106
Council on Foreign Relations: Wall Street, 4106
Council on Hemispheric Affairs, 1276
Council on the Arts, 4606
Counterattack, 747, 1241, 2207, 2212, 2242
counter-commercials, 4389, 4392, 4393
counter-culture, 4323
counterculture, 636, 3152, 4383
counterculture journalism, 4212
"counterforce," 1662
counterinsurgency, 12, 242, 266, 321, 371, 3952
counterinsurgency (see low-intensity warfare), 187
counterintelligence, 274, 276, 327
Counterintelligence Program (see COINTELPRO), 277
counter-propaganda, 4397
counter-revolution, 57, 371, 719, 3152, 3768
counter-revolution: elections, 2255

SUBJECT INDEX 717

Counterspy, 4578
countersubversion, 3147
countersubversive
intelligence, 283
countervailing powers, 4356
country music, 4158, 4169
coup, 774, 1493a
coup d'etat, 179
court censorship, 2219
Court Martial of Billy
Mitchell, The, 3064
court reporting, 872
courts, 4372
courts: conservative judges,
430
coverage, 1600
covert action, 203, 278,
283, 290, 291, 1585
covert intelligence, 1338
covert military operations,
187
covert operations, 12, 193,
204, 211, 233, 288, 320,
332, 481, 789
covert propaganda, 1353
coverup, 104, 180, 240, 324,
940, 1443, 1585, 2750, 4704
cover-up: asbestos, 3442
Coverup film: Reagan
administration, 4541
coverup: public relations,
2020, 2025a
Cox news empire, 1094
CPB (Corporation for Public
Broadcasting), 2994
CPI, 3179
CPUSA, 361
Craig, Chief Federal Judge
Walter, 471
Craig, William (right-wing
novelist), 3968
creating news, 881
creation science, 480
creationism, 481, 678
credibility doctrine, 209
credibility gap, 1414
credibility (see
believability), 1682
credit, 1852
credit bureaus, 3202
credulity, 3433
Creel Committee, 1635
Creel, George, 214, 746,
3179
"creeping socialism," 350
crime, 9, 728, 1006, 1049

crime: advertising, 1731
crime by association, 1329
Crime Control Act, 3202
crime: corporations, 144
crime dramas, 2403
crime: FBI, 1532
crime films, 3102
crime films: Sovietphobia,
3055
crime: wealth, 138
crimes by the powerful, 1393
criminal justice, 420
criminal records, 3188
crises: wire services, 3233
Crisis at Central High, 2505
crisis news: labor, 3510
crisis reporting, 2728
crisis reporting:
international, 2715
crisis: rhetoric, 1331
Cristiani, Alfredo, 3277
critical journals, 4658
critical literacy, 468, 469
critical paradigm, 646
critical thinking, 453, 456,
652, 4284
Cronkite, Walter, 611, 2197,
2282, 2291, 2593, 2633,
2672, 2744, 2753, 2796
Crossfire, 2611
Crossroads, 2330
crosswords, 1781
Crozier, Brian, 592
cruise missile, 2104, 3630,
4590
cruise missile crash, 805
Crusade in Europe, 2508
Crusade in the Pacific, 2508
CSJ, 1395
CSM, 1277, 1443, 1608, 3281,
3298, 3311, 3316, 3423,
3437, 3481, 3550, 3577,
3585, 3650, 3674, 3682
C-SPAN (Satellite Public
Affairs Network), 4446,
4460, 4557
CS-T, 3644
CT, 1648, 3506, 3518, 3547,
3560, 3596, 3610, 3622,
3643, 3644, 3670, 3682, 3691
CT: cold war, 4236
CT: Sears Roebuck and
Company, 4304
Cuba, 183, 204, 315, 333,
371, 700, 715, 922a, 1282,
1286a, 1312a, 1345a, 1347a,

1348, 1348a, 1406, 2191,
3328, 3378, 3639, 3771,
3892, 4240
Cuba (1962): newspapers,
3610
Cuba and Castro Today (ABC),
2744
Cuba drug trade, 1536
Cuba: John Kennedy, 3610
Cuba: NYT, 3726, 3727, 3774
Cuba: PBS, 2991
Cuba (US invasion plans),
1315
Cuban exiles, 810
Cuban Missile Crisis, 1236,
1962, 3425, 4106
Cubana Airlines (1976
bombing), 1447
Cuestra, Mike (television
commercials), 1738
Cullen, Hugh Roy, 350
cultural change: film, 3124
cultural control, 1643
Cultural Correspondence, 572
cultural dependency, 744
cultural domination, 556,
1104, 3048, 3292
cultural expansion, 1178
cultural hegemony, 3076
cultural imperialism, 447,
605, 681, 683, 720, 730,
757, 2217, 2248, 3047, 3245,
3260, 3988, 4032, 4173
cultural imperialism:
Disney, 3294
cultural imperialism: music,
4168
cultural imperialism: news
agencies, 3264
cultural imperialism:
resistance, 4542
cultural propaganda, 4730
culture industry, 673
culture of consumption, 681
culural imperialism, 756
Cunningham, 405
CUNY, 468
Current Affair, A, 2622
Current Contents, 3465
Current Digest of the Soviet
Press, 4617
Currey, Fred, 3732
Cvetic, Matt, 719, 3146
cybernetic capitalism, 78
cybernetic news, 2796
cybernetics, 3202

Cycle World, 1821
Dagwood Splits the Atom, 624
Daily News, 1551
Daisy ad: Lyndon Johnson
(1964), 1896a
Daisy Girl, 2060
Daley, Mayor Richard, 3361
Dalkon Shield, 1157
Dallas, 2330, 2350, 2452,
2394, 2450
damage control, 1283
Danforth Foundation, 148
Danish newspapers, 3436
Danish pastry claims, 1792
Danskins, 559
Darrow, Clarence, 4371, 4677
data banks (see also:
computers), 3186, 3187,
3202, 3214
data banks: surveillance,
3187
data base, 601, 4316
data communications
networks, 50
data processing, 2256
database technology, 3978
D'Aubuisson, Roberto, 1254,
3277
Davies, John Paton Jr., 3676
Davis, Benjamin, 3992
Davis, Bette, 3045
Day After, The: nuclear war,
2748, 3325, 4492
Day, Dorothy, 611, 4683
Day the Earth Stood Still,
The 3064
Days of Rage: The Young
Palestinians (PBS), 1215,
2990, 3010
DBS, 2237, 2945
D-Day 1984, 2373
Dean, John, 104
Death in the West (cancer),
1834
Death of a Princess
(PBS)(see also: Arab), 2418,
2751, 3030
death penalty: documentary
films, 4405
death squads, 851, 1254,
3277, 3677, 3750
death squads: cocaine, 928
Death Wish: class fear, 3102
Deaver, Michael, 1401, 2111a
debates: presidency, 2702,
2719

SUBJECT INDEX

debt, 982
deceit, 182, 677, 1688, 1827a, 1837, 1945, 1967, 2326
deceit: advertising, 1831, 1860a, 1887, 1889, 1902, 1948
deceit: children, 2045
deceit: hucksterism, 1932
Decent Interval, 4001, 4016
deception, 202, 209, 1237, 1333, 1472
deception: advertising, 1721
deception: foreign policy, 57
deception: nuclear arms, 1326
deceptive advertising, 2342
deceptive drug advertising, 524
Declaration of Talloires, 772
deconstruction: nuclear texts, 4741
decoration, 616
Deep Dish Television, 4407, 4426, 4427
Deer Hunter, The, 3152
defamation, 2242, 4366
defense, 624, 1272, 1505, 1662
Defense Intelligence Agency, 321
deference to government, 1468
defining political issues, 1974
definition, 656
definition power, 55
definitions of words and politics, 1624
dehumanization: war films, 3087
Deitch, David, 4175
Delco corporation: 4123
DeLoach, Cartha, 313, 324, 327
Delta Force, 233
demagogue, 363
demagoguery, 361, 872, 1629
demand management, 55
DeMille, Cecil, 3124
democracy, 1467, 1786, 2235, 4353

democracy: communication (see also: citizen, diversity), 4404
democracy: computerization, 3208
Democracy Institute, 1536
democracy: media, 1170
"democracy" (Orwellian definition), 1277
democracy: procedural and substantive, 59
democracy: television, 2747, 2818
democracy: television news, 2755
democracy vs. capitalism, 55
democratic communications (see also: III), 714, 4179, 4440
democratic control: information resources, 4510
Democratic Convention 1988, 1329a, 1968, 2818
democratic culture, 701
democratic debate (failure of), 1552
democratic foreign policy, 4180
democratic media, 742
Democratic National Convention (Chicago, Aug. 1968), 3361
Democratic Party, 58, 216, 360, 877, 4085
Democratic Party: anticommunism, 361
Democratic Party: big business, 35
Democratic Party: conservatism, 35
Democratic Party Convention 1988, 1074
Democratic Party Convention (Chicago, 1968), 1636
Democratic Party: religion, 480
Democratic Party: the New Deal, 35
democratic socialism, 1169, 4333
democratic socialist communications system, 4284
demonology, 719
demonology (see also: enemy, Sovietphobia), 3146, 3147

demonstration election, 649, 1263
demonstration election (in client dictatorships), 1264
demonstrations, 1304, 4219, 4249
Dennis, Eugene, 3992
Dennis v. United States (1951), 3430, 4213, 4371
Denver Post, 3545, 3549
Denver television, 2855
deoxyribonucleic acid (see DNA), 499
Department of Agriculture, 153
Department of Energy, 3945, 4188
Department of Housing and Urban Development, 306
Department of Justice, 44
department stores, 114, 681, 741
deportation, 307, 352, 390, 405, 596, 1610, 3852, 3854, 3962
depth analysis, 707
depth approach to advertising, 1784
depth psychology, 616, 1785, 1786, 1846a
deregulation: broadcasting, 2147, 2168
deregulation: communications, 4537
deregulation: First Amendment, 2149
deregulation: media reform movement, 2275
deregulation: monopoly, 2164
deregulation of broadcasting, 1342
deregulation: public service, 2269
deregulation (see also: II.C.1.a.), 2121, 2133, 2135, 4454
deregulation v. public interest, 2154
Des Moines Register: Vietnam War, 3614
D'Escoto, Father Miguel, 483
Desert Shield, 3315
desire, 681
destroying public records, 276
Destry Rides Again, 3091

detective fiction, 3991, 4002
detective films, 3129, 3152
deterrence, 241, 4034
Detroit Free Press, 3419, 3603
Detroit News, 3603
deviance, 858
Devil Dogs, 2046
Devine, Frank, 1254
Dewey, Admiral (advertising), 1783
Dewey, John, 4343
Dewey, Thomas, 1552
Dial soap ads, 1896a
dichotomies: US/SU, 665
dichotomized thinking, 634
dichotomizing, 914
Dichter, Ernest, 1786
Dick, Philip (The Penultimate Truth), 624
Dickens, Charles, 1815
Dickinson, Emily, 4026
dictators, 137
dictators: public relations, 2094
dictators (US allies), 65
dictatorship, 74, 1222, 2006, 2201, 2496
dictatorship: New Right, 733
dictatorships: US clients, 3590
Diem, Ngo Dinh, 1228, 1327, 2744
Dies, Congressman Martin, 350, 361, 1634
digital telecommunications, 50
Ding, Loni (The Color of Honor), 2967
Dinges, John, 1277
dioxin, 3460
Direct Broadcast Satellite (DBS), 2216, 2237, 2248
direct marketing, 2273, 3190
direct marketing: computer, 3190
Dirksen, Senator Edward, 4534
dirty tricks (see CIA), 278
Dirty Works: CIA, 4686
disarmament, 816
disasters, 4591
disconnected news, 3555
discourse technology (computers), 321

discourse theory, 2703
discriminatory schools, 1458
disease: heart, 3877
dishonorable discharge, 352
disinformation, 266, 324, 676, 940, 1254, 1266, 1472, 1486, 1530, 1536, 2840, 3744, 3985, 4359
disinformation campaigns, 280
disinformation (gov't), 1264
Disney, 668a, 716, 731, 3293, 3932
Disney: American Dream, 3115
Disney comics, 1179
Disney: global, 3294
Disney (see also: Epcot), 1995
Disney World, 1130, 1208
Disneyland, 716, 1179, 2914
Disney's Davy Crockett, 2508
Disney's "Victory Through Air Power," 1347
disobedience, 4276
Dispatch News Service, 4600
disruption of New Left, 291
dissent, 405, 3430, 3503
dissent: film, 3185
dissent: filmmakers, 4538
dissent (reporting), 3278
dissent (see also: III), 4276, 4280
dissent: surveillance, 3211
dissent: Underground press, 4612
dissenters (Iran, SU), 868a
dissident media (see also: alternative media), 4174
dissident press: alternative press, 3464
diversity, 2148, 2160, 4261, 4333, 4429, 4596, 4636, 4669
diversity: cable television, 2891, 2897, 2898
diversity: children's television, 2921
diversity: external and internal, 2239
diversity: news agencies, 3252
diversity of programming (declining), 2124
diversity research, 2239
Division of I&E (WWII), 3161
DMN, 3682
DNA technology, 1310

Doctor Who, 2513
Doctorow, E. L., 721
doctors, 513, 519, 1795
doctors: continuing medical education, 519
doctors: profits, 519
doctors' wealth, 517
docudrama, 2505, 2533, 2406, 2680, 2828
documentaries: PBS, 2964, 2990, 2992
documentaries, 909, 2191, 2192
documentaries: lack of, 1840
documentary, 1459, 2406, 2599, 2686, 2751, 2830, 2837, 2844, 3053, 3094, 3095, 3149, 3150, 4406, 4434, 4453, 4490
documentary: Arabs, 2832
documentary: army, 3075
documentary: censorship, 3096
documentary: commercialsm, 2860
documentary: film, 3180, 4224, 4478, 4405, 4422, 4508, 4511, 4521
documentary: Frontline, 4547
documentary: General Westmoreland, 2583
documentary: Pamela Hill, 4546
documentary: PBS, 2972
documentary: prison, 3075
documentary: schools, 3075
documentary: television, 2394, 4513
documentary: USIA, 4441
documentary: Vietnam War, 2760
Dodd, Senator Christopher, 4021
DOE secrecy, 1515
dogma, 575
Dohrn, Bernardine, 725
Dolan, John Terry, 481
domestic intelligence, 283, 324
domestic spying, 311
domesticity: television, 2511
Dominican intervention, 976, 1489
Dominican Republic, 1000, 1264, 1302

Dominican Republic invasion, 1320
Dominican Republic invasion: NYT, 3757
Dominican Republic: NYT, 3757
Dominion Video, 2945
domino theory, 209, 2744
Donahue, 2493
Donald Duck, 3115, 3292
Donaldson, Sam, 1401
Donovan, Raymond, 2637
Donovan, William (Wild Bill), 2750
Doolittle, Hilda: film, 3879
doomsday, 487
Doonesbury: censorship, 3440
doo-wop, 4154
Dorfman, Ariel, (How to Read Donald Duck), 1179
Dorfman, Ron, 4176, 4569
Dos Passos, John, 3968
double jeopardy, 3676
double standard: NYT, 3712
double standard: PBS, 3001
double standards: foreign policy, 3308
Doubleday, 4021
doublespeak, 676, 677, 751, 945, 4081, 4338, 4387, 4398, 4634
doublespeak: corporations, 1998a
doublespeak: nuclearism, 11
doubling, 719
Douglas, Justice William, 2795, 3430
Dow Chemical: NYT, 3724
Dow, Dupont, 1848
Dow Jones, 1154
Dow Rocky Flats Atomic Plant, 3637
Dowling, Tom, 3556, 3557
Down and Out in Beverly Hills, 3106
Downey, Morton, 4519
DP, 3547, 3682
Dr. Spock: Star Trek, 2459
Dr. Stranglove film, 762, 1347
draft, 223, 263, 4590
Drambuie ad, 1878
Draper, Paul, 2743
Drayton, Arthur, 405
dream production, 756
dreams, 616

dreams and illusions, 1682
Dreiser, Theodore, 1684
drug abuse, 179
drug industry, 2029
drug promotion, 1928
drug scare, 13
drug traffic: banks, 137
drug war, 1060
drugs, 193, 520, 527, 1268, 1886, 1888, 1900, 1938
drugs: advertising, 1794, 1946
drugs: television, 2660
drugs: war on, 936
Drury, Allen, 3968
détente, 624
Du Pont, 166, 553
Du Pont: censorship, 3961, 3963, 3981
Duarte, José Napoléon, 769, 1254, 1275, 1277, 1393
dubbling (film), 3160
DuBoff, Richard, 989
DuBois, W.E.B., 370, 4575
Ducat, Craig, 1382
Duck and Cover, 624
Duckspeak, 2734
Dugger, Ronnie, 4600, 4623
Dugway Proving Grounds, 4099
Dukakis, Michael, 1329a, 1551
Dulles, Allen, 288
Dulles, J.F.: anticommunism, 393
Dulles, John Foster, 319, 4115
Dunham, Barrows, 405
DuPont, 3523
DuPont: nuclear hazards, 1443
Durkheim, Emile, 461
Durstine and Osborn (BBDO), 1772
Dutton, E.P., 4021
Dyer, Dallas, 350
Dylan, Bob, 4155, 4165, 4170
Dynasty, 2330
Eagleburger, Lawrence, 2617
Eagle's Talon, The, 2744
Eagleton, Senator Thomas, 2561
Earth Day, 2193
East Africa, 4037
East Europe: television, 2620
East Germany: NYT, 3769

SUBJECT INDEX   723

East Timor, 821, 822, 1007, 1056, 1284
East Timor: NYT, 3784
East Village Other, 4612
Eastern Europe, 1064, 1075, 2728, 3311, 3812
Eastman Kodak advertising, 1870
Eastwood, Clint, 3136
Ebey, George W., 350
Ebony, 1821
Eckhardt, Robert, 244
Eco, Umberto, 3113
ecology, 112, 223, 4590, 4592
ecology: NYT, 3778
ecology (see also: environment), 3821
economic blackmail, 4244
economic controls of information, 1169
economic crime, 44
economic democracy, 106, 152, 1169, 4333, 4669
economic expansion, 2735
economic imperialism, 1282
economic news: television, 2558
economic news; television orthodoxy, 2703
economic planning, 38
economic power, 30, 33
economic reporting, 1210, 1814, 3620
economic sanctions, 211
Economic Summit: NYT, 3723
economics, 415, 1079
economics: broadcasting, 2261
economics: children's television, 2546
Economics for Young Americans, 1980
economics: media, 546
economics: medicine, 513, 514, 515
economics news, 1146
economics (NYT), 3743, 3745, 3781
economics of media, 546
economics (see Reaganomics), 1158
economics: television, 2643
economy, 852
economy: military, 271

economy on television news, 2691
Edison Electric Institute, 1955, 1966, 2877, 3821
Edison Manufacturing Company, 3131
editing, 2643
editing: television news, 2644, 2653
Editor & Publisher, 3361
editorial autonomy, 962
editorial discretion, 4680
editorials, 1294
editorials: television news, 2644
editorials: Unesco, 631
editors, 1067
education, 15, 38, 81, 89, 120, 129, 199, 227, 252, 342, 352, 387, 394, 402, 411, 442, 444, 447, 448, 451, 453, 466, 471, 501, 509, 620, 678, 704, 716, 729, 732, 1808, 1980, 1999, 2292, 4031, 4032, 4037, 4071, 4284
education: advertising, 1987a, 1988, 2038, 2049
education: anticommunism, 404, 470
education authoritarianism, 454
education business government complex, 465
education centralization, 477
education: class, 455, 461
education: commissions, 4051
education: computers, 3213
education: conservative indoctrination, 441
education: consuming, 2910
education: corporate conformity, 449
education: corporate state, 452
education: corporations, 446, 450, 454, 461, 471
education: critical thinking, 586
education: democracy, 449
education: efficiency, 477
education: emancipation, 455
education for efficiency, 447
education: government, 478

education: hidden curriculum, 454
education: indoctrination, 455, 462, 472, 473, 2004a, 2017
education: journalists, 4379
education: law, 420
education: mass culture, 1163
education: militarism, 476
education: military, 263
education: nationalism, 4087
education: nuclearism, 4275
education: NYT, 3729
education: propaganda analysis, 4339
education: public television, 3002
education: race 437
education: racism, 462
education: racism, sexism, 478
education: robber barons, 471
education: ruling class, 471
education: ruling powers, 439
education: sports, 542, 543
education standardization, 477
education: status quo, 445
education: television, 2901, 2915, 2923
educational affairs, 3371
educational broadcasting, 2261, 2835, 2978, 2979
educational channels, 2979, 2997
Educational Film and Video Project, 4514
educational radio, 2157, 2425, 2979
educational television, 2443, 2989
educational television (ETV), 2979
Educational Televsion and Radio Center, 2979
educationese, 676
Edwards, Don, 244
Edwards, Stephanie, 2796
efficiency, 498, 504
Efron, Edith, 2849, 3900
Egypt, 1285
ethics, 1216
Eight Is Enough, 2534

Einstein, Albert, 505
Eisenhower, Dwight D., 12, 65, 141, 175, 200, 288, 341, 348, 350, 352, 371, 732, 808, 1279, 1331, 1333, 1385, 1386, 1786, 2060, 2192, 2795, 3691, 4534
Eisenhower administration, 1350
Eisenhower: anticommunism, 361, 393
Eisenhower: speeches, 1384
Eisenhower: FBI, 316
Eisenhower, President: Inaugural Address, 4111
Eisenhower: press, 611
Eisenhower: scientific-technological elite, 510
Eisenhower years, 3154
Eisenhower's "Atoms for Peace" speech, 689
Eisenhower's Executive Order 10501, 1448
Eisenhower's Farewell Address (1961), 249
El Nuevo Diario, 1500
El Salvador, 65, 193, 315, 769, 773, 787, 823, 838, 847, 850, 859, 868, 911, 914, 1043, 1051, 1254, 1263, 1264, 1275, 1276, 1277, 1283, 1360, 1392, 1401, 1446, 1472, 1473, 1492, 1505, 1838, 1913, 2006a, 2064, 2716, 3277, 3285, 3290, 3369, 3409, 3550, 3660, 3750, 3755, 3923, 4042, 4075, 4590, 4591, 4676, 4690
El Salvador: army disinformation, 3664
El Salvador: death squads, 851
El Salvador: elections, 1046, 1595
El Salvador: murders, 4420
El Salvador: news reporting, 4485
El Salvador: NYT, 3716, 3744, 3751, 3753, 3758, 3788, 3790, 3742, 3751
El Salvador: print journalism, 3272
El Salvador: torture, 1058, 3462, 3677

El Salvador: United Press
International, 3227
El Salvador: WSJ, 3651
elderly (see ageism), 1727
election campaign, 41, 706,
1360
election coverage, 1235
election endorsements, 1294
election news, 2596
election reporting, 1294,
2195
elections, 125, 817, 1014,
1019, 1659, 1980, 2086,
2087, 2192, 2199
elections in El Salvador,
1254
elections in Nicaragua and
El Salvador, 1274
elections: Nicaragua, 811
elections: rhetoric, 1384
elections: televisions, 633
Electric Boat, 3649
Electric Company, 2922
electric industry, 146
electrical power companies,
1966, 1979
electrical utilities, 1147
Electrolux, 1873a
electronic church, 481, 706,
2316, 2228, 2492, 2944,
2949, 2952
electronic church:
televangelism, 2955
electronic communications,
2273
electronic mail, 2345
electronic media, 1319a
electronic media:
consciousness industry, 55
electronic newspaper:
access, 4644
electronic religion, 2228
electronic surveillance,
273, 276, 321, 1128, 3188
electronic technology, 3197
electronic technology:
diversity, 2239
elite, 24
elite control, 22, 1110
elite culture, 616, 1667
elite: Democratic Party, 20
elite rule, 23, 25
elite social clubs, 19
elites, 25, 30, 710, 1186,
1714
elitism, 448, 1061

elitist theory: US
democracy, 31
Elle magazine, 616
Ellsberg, Daniel, 104, 866,
1257, 1320, 1564, 4667
Elton Rule, 2405
emancipation, 453
embassy hostages, 1025
Emergency Detention Act, 321
Emerson, Ralph Waldo, 4026
emphasis (selection,
placement), 3891
emphysema: tobacco, 164
employee obedience, 3860
employees, 132
Enders, Thomas, 1254
endorsements, 1907, 2037
enemies: songs, 4733
"enemy," 1505
enemy: war films, 3060, 3087
energy, 2021, 2742
energy consumption, 4554
energy corporations, 161
energy crisis, 1968
Energy Department, 2097,
3894
energy information, 1336
energy monopoly, 151
energy policy, 1726, 1957
energy: television, 2880
energy waste, 1726
engineering business
management, 498
engineering choice (see
also: advertising), 1924
engineering consent, 43,
1678, 1727, 1786
engineering desire, 1943
engineers, 509
English: clear, 4633, 4634
English Department:
propaganda analysis, 4339
English Departments, 678,
708
English departments:
censorship, 4599
Enlai, Zhou, 288
entertainment, 681, 696,
760, 2238
entertainment industry, 3063
entertainment: news, 2758,
2826
entertainment: television,
2825
entertainment: television
news, 2666, 2677, 2737

Entertainment Tonight, 2476, 2517, 2712
entrapment, 286
environment, 615, 1023, 1031, 1037, 1134, 1152, 2710, 2742, 3309, 3460, 4535
environment: advertising, 1973
environment: capitalism, 103
environment: censorship, 3681
environment: consuming, 1664
environment: corporations, 4394
environment: deterioration, 3361
environment: New Yorker, 3890
environment: news, 2193
environment: television news, 2691
environment: The Denver Post, Olympics, 3695
environment: Time, 3878
environmental art, 4745
Environmental Film Festival, 4532
Environmental Holocaust, 4745
environmental magazines, 3946
environmentalism, 3540
environmentalism: hypocrisy, 3530
environmentalism: magazines, 3835, 3844
EO 12356, 1231, 1554, 1644
EPA, 1037
EPA v. Mink, 1378
EPCOT (Experimental Prototype Community of Tomorrow), 1208, 1995
Equal Access Act of 1984, 489
equal employment opportunity, 4454
equal opportunities rule, 2002
equal opportunity, 477
equal rights, 415
Equal Time Rule, 828, 2131, 2135, 2766, 2795
equality: education, 461
equity: women, 5
ergonomics, 2345
ERIN Bulletin, 4215, 4601

Ernst, Morris, 4371
Ervin, Sam, 1246
espionage, 352, 501, 1564
Espionage Act, 1242a, 1387, 4190
Espionage Acts, 1329
espionage laws, 4252
Esquire, 1742
Esquivel, Adolfo Perez, 1274
Essene, 3075
Esso, 4103
established press, 4664
establishment (see corporate state), 1009
establishment viewpoint, 660
establishment/popular press, 3507
E.T., 1826
ethical issues, 4597
ethics, 184, 641, 662, 694, 727, 751, 898, 934, 1000, 1101, 1140, 1829, 1839, 2399, 3267, 3305, 4197, 4217, 4315, 4638
ethics: advertising, 1846a, 1855, 1916
Ethics and Public Policy Center, 6
ethics: economics, 3458
ethics: investigative reporting, 4182
ethics: journalism, 3392, 3397
ethics: media, 587, 595, 617
ethics: reporters, 4376
ethics: tobacco advertising, 1913a
Ethiopia, 2559
ethnic stereotypes, 2418
ethnocentrism, 91, 569, 569, 710, 868, 878, 908, 1045, 2743, 2772, 3481, 3684
ethnocentrism: newspapers, 3405
ethnocentrism: reporters, 4330
ethnocentrism: television news, 2595
euphemism, 945, 1333, 1662, 1681, 4045
euphemism: wars, 626
Europe: NYT, 3795
evangelicalism, 485, 490
evangelicalism: television, 2955
evangelicals, 489

SUBJECT INDEX 727

evangelicals: politics, 492
evening news, 2675, 2780
Everett Massacre, 405
evesdropping, 286
evidence, 976
exchange value: advertising, 1746
Exec. Order 11652, 4654
Execution of Private Slovik, The, 2505
executive branch, 24
Executive Order 12356, 1242a
executive orders: Reagan, 4102
executive privilege, 188, 200, 1338, 1542
Exemption 1, 1378
Exorcist, The, 3152
expectations, 1682
experimental film, 3138
experts, 14, 816, 914, 1373
experts (government by), 1552
experts (see also: officials), 2241
exploitation, 122
exploitation: advertising, 1829
exploitation: consumers, 1887
extermination: MIC, 3167
Extra!, 4574
Exxon, 30, 112, 1989
Exxon Valdez, 2663, 3901, 4745
F-14 fighter, 1953, 3628
Face the Nation, 2717, 2777
Faces of War: censorhsip, 4540
"fact," 881
Factor, Max, 1820
facts, 1067
fads, 616
Fail-Safe, 624
Fair Packaging Labeling Act, 1885
Fairbank, John King, 584
Fairchild, 1407
Fairness and Accuracy in Reporting (FAIR), 4196, 4222, 4574
Fairness Doctrine, 633, 722, 828, 1342, 2002, 2022, 2119, 2122, 2126, 2127, 2145, 2148, 2151, 2160, 2162, 2172, 2177, 2180, 2182, 2204, 2215, 2235, 2263, 2643, 2766, 2785, 2795, 2873, 3287, 3506, 4181, 4225, 4247, 4264, 4334, 4454, 4540
Fairness Doctrine: commercialism, 2144
Fairness Doctrine: newspapers, 3506
fallacies, 1417
fallout shelters, 4015
Fallows, James, 1419
FALN (Fuerzas Armadas de Liberacion Nacional), Puerto Rico, 2786
false ads, 4389
false advertising: law, 1920
false advertising (see also: advertising), 1827a, 1842, 1843
false documentation, 315
falsification, 210
Falwell, Jerry, 480, 481, 487, 492, 2208, 2492, 2945, 2952, 3936
Falwell, Jerry: libel, 1042
Family, 2534
family, 61, 89, 136, 2373
family: black, 4060
family: capitalism, 47
Family Circle, 3922
family farms, 4590
Family Feud, 2381
family hour, 2376
family: Sovietphobia, 385
family: television, 2540, 2942, 4482
Family Viewing Policy (Family Hour), 2474
famine, 3273
fanaticism, 62, 481, 4534
Fanning, David: documentaries, 4547
fantasy, 616
fantasy chain, 706
fantasy exploitation, 1756
fantasy films, 3152
Fantasy Island, 2462, 2531
Farber, Myron, 3422, 3584
FarmAid, 763
farmers, 4504, 4593
Farr, Finis (right-wing novelist), 3968
Farrar, 4021
Fascism, 3114

fascism, 48, 60, 291, 927, 4653
fascism: Eastern Europe, 3657
fascism: media, 594
fashion, 1708, 1845
fashion design, 616, 741
fashion magazines, 3829
Fast, Howard, 3434
fast-food industry, 1779, 1927
Fat Man (atomic bomb), 4045
Faulk, John Henry, 405, 2207, 2212
Faulkner, William, 3994
FBI, 13, 24, 77, 81, 91, 104, 180, 276, 277, 281, 282, 283, 287, 290, 291, 293, 297, 300, 302, 303, 306, 310, 311, 313, 314, 321, 323, 325, 326, 328, 329, 330, 339, 342, 343, 352, 403, 405, 895, 1057, 1226, 1287, 1288, 1533, 2294, 2508, 3056, 3188, 3197, 3214, 3320, 3350, 3575, 3584, 3642, 3971, 3994, 4200, 4282, 4300, 4453, 4561, 4606, 4664, 4686, 4692, 4734
FBI: AIM, 3958
FBI: alternative press, 3464
FBI: anticommunism, 361
FBI: breakin policy, 323
FBI: censorship, 3970, 4020
FBI: civil liberties, 4371
FBI: Cold War, 325
FBI: computers, 3198
FBI: data bank, 3210
FBI: Hollywood, 2109
FBI: illegal breakins, 325
FBI: illegal files, 325
FBI: image, 1532
FBI: library surveillance, 3948
FBI: Pine Ridge, 1288
FBI: public relations, 1631, 2109, 2113
FBI: radicals, 3389
FBI: spying, 3934
FBI Story, The (film), 2109
FBI: surveillance, 3895
FBI: The Nation, 3893
FBI: The Progressive, 3895
FBI, The (television series), 2109, 2282

FBI vs. Civil Rights Movement, 312
FBI vs. dissent, 325
FBI wiretapping, 316, 325
FCC, , 434, 628a, 686, 1019, 1094, 1175, 1190, 1366, 2118, 2120, 2122, 2124-2126, 2128, 2129, 2131, 2137, 2144-2146, 2148, 2150, 2156, 2157, 2160, 2164, 2166, 2169, 2191, 2192, 2193, 2204, 2215, 2223, 2246, 2250, 2254, 2343, 2353, 2354, 2376, 2414, 2427, 2440, 2472, 2474, 2643, 2795, 2835, 2890, 2920, 2924, 2978, 2979, 2997, 3014, 3016, 3022, 3028, 3205, 4385, 4454, 4495, 4503, 4513, 4537
FCC Blue Book, 4516
FCC: cable television, 2894
FCC: censorship, 2152, 3017
FCC: children, 2050, 2137, 2909
FCC: citizens groups, 4459
FCC: corporations, 2303
FCC: cross-ownership, 1114
FCC: deregulation (see also: deregulation), 2116, 2442
FCC: history, 2174
FCC: lobbying, 2137
FCC: petition to deny, 2137
FCC: public access, 2134
FCC: public interest, 2158, 2179
FCC: Ronald Reagan, 2132
FCC (see also: II.C.), 4181, 4245, 4247
FCC (see II.C.1.a.), 1792, 1869a, 2028, 2028a, 2042,
FCC: TV, 2380
FCC v. Midwest Video Corporation (Midwest II, 1979), 4522
FDA, 1928, 2026, 3494
fear, 1708, 3152
fear: advertising, 1738, 1784
fear (exploitation), 2456
fear of crime, 1532
Federal Bureau of Information (FBI), 273
federal case law, 4309
Federal Communications Commission (see FCC), 612

SUBJECT INDEX 729

Federal Depository Library Program, 1195
Federal Election Campaign Act Coverage, 4304
Federal Express, 1705, 1826
federal government, 4633
federal judiciary, 24
Federal Republic of Germany: broadcasting, 4415
Federal Reserve, 36
Federal Trade Commission, 4385
fee-for-service, 524
fee-for-service medical system, 517
FEMA, 638
female body: law, 418
female shape, 681
female stereotypes, 3922
femininity: advertising, 1817
feminism, 61, 111, 605, 655, 755, 2511, 3089, 3178, 3182, 3927, 4559, 4591
feminism: films, 3143
feminism: science, 506
feminism: television, 2461
feminist, 696
feminist criticism, 1860
feminist criticism: television, 2279, 2499
feminist demonstrations, 3299
feminist film theory, 3081
feminist films, 4416, 4421, 4517, 4525
feminist music, 4739
feminist press, 4636
feminist reporters, 3500
Ferrer, Jose, 3077
Ferrera, Sal, 1463
fetishism: advertising, 1746
fetishism: commodities, 1745
fiber optics, 4425
Field and Stream Magazine, 4304
fifth estate: underground press, 4289
"Fifth Freedom" 1274
Figueres, Jose (Pepe), 1274
Fiji coup: NYT, 3699
Filene, Edward, 4287
files, 283
files on dissidents, 285
film, 1, 560, 560, 605, 639, 684, 745, 746, 1121, 1178,
2258, 3047, 3134, 3178, 4284, 4402, 4437, 4538
film: 1930s, 3036, 3134
film: 1940s, 3134
film: 1950s, 3134, 3162
film: 1960s, 3134, 3152
film: 1970s, 3134, 3152
film: 1980s, 3152
film: A-bomb, 2314
film: A Gathering of Eagles, 762
film: Above and Beyond, 624, 762
film: advertising, 1835, 1875
film and documentaries: television, 2742
film: apocalypse, 3158
film: banks, 3052
film: censorhsip, 1587, 3062, 3082, 3135, 4213
film: Central America, 4494
film: computers (as subject), 3215
film criticism, 3370, 3879
film: documentary, 4508, 4478, 4511
film: economics, 3126
film: environment, 4532
film: escape, 3104
film: Faces of War, 4473
film: feminism, 3143
film: government subsidy, 3058
film: history (false), 3109
film: horror, 3158
film: independent (non-commercial), 3120
film: industry, 758
film: industry: labor unions, 3046
film: production, 3131
film: promotion, 1853
film: reviewing, 3446
film: Sovietphobia, 4536
film: television, 3036
film: Toronto Film Festival, 4493
film: underground, 4224
film: video, 2224
film: working class, 3046, 3057
film: WWI, 664, 3035
film: WWII, 3060, 3085
films, 259, 744, 747, 759, 1708, 4329, 4356

films: exploitation, 587
films: international, 2213
films: nuclear imagery, 762
films: smoking, 1945
films: Sovietphobia, 375
financial corruption, 775
financial reporting, 872
financing public
broadcasting, 2978
"Finpolity," 138
Firing Line, 2611
First Amendment, 84, 405,
546, 546, 602, 605, 623a,
627, 687, 709, 772, 806,
920, 932, 13, 405, 1020,
1042, 1078, 1193, 1195,
1224, 1225, 1242a, 1246,
1259, 1280, 1309, 1364,
1365, 1387, 1413, 1414,
1418, 1533, 1558, 1561,
1594, 1634, 1637, 1660,
1634, 1945, 2028, 2118,
2122, 2124, 2127, 2148,
2151, 2159, 2160, 2162,
2168, 2172, 2175, 2223,
2237, 2250, 2254, 2376,
2474, 2795, 2826, 2836,
3166, 3371, 3408, 3416,
3419, 3422, 3430, 3486,
3584, 3765, 3848, 3867,
3868, 3880, 3936, 3971,
3972, 4001, 4007, 4173,
4181, 4194, 4202, 4208,
4211, 4213, 4218, 4219,
4228, 4232, 4251, 4261,
4273, 4289, 4292, 4312,
4351, 4365, 4371, 4408,
4498, 4512, 4565, 4568,
4622, 4630, 4680
First Amendment: access,
4341, 4674
First Amendment:
advertising, 1860a, 1939a
First Amendment:
bibliography, 4367
First Amendment:
broadcasting, 2167
First Amendment: cable
television, 2890, 2896
First Amendment:
corporations, 428, 1125,
1126, 1134a, 1156, 1166,
1181, 1810, 4390
First Amendment:
deregulation of
broadcasting, 2149

First Amendment: obscenity,
3082
First Amendment:
pornography, 4100
First Amendment: press,
4195, 4225, 4268
First Amendment: television,
2837
First Amendment: The
Progressive, 3914
First Amendment: tobacco,
1982
First National Bank vs.
Bellotti(1978), 428, 429,
1181
First World: film, 3160
first-person plural pronoun:
we, 4089
Fitzgerald, A. Ernest, 4667
FitzGibbon, Constantine
(right-wing novelist), 3968
Fitzhugh, Gilbert, 4667
flackery, 1530
flag, 1232, 4732
flagpole sitters, 1781
flak (see public relations,
II), 2020
flappers, 1781
Flash of Darkness, 2508
Flexible Response (nuclear),
266, 348, 1551, 1552
Flight 191: television news,
2775
Flight 553, 104
Flintstones, 759
Florida Star v. B.J.F., 1560
flow, 4157
flow information, 1176
flow of information:
television, 2437
flow: television, 2349
Flying Leathernecks, 3064
Flynn, Elizabeth Gurley,
1607
Flynt, Larry, 3936
FM radio, 2157, 4503
FMLN (Farabundo Martí
National Liberation Front),
1254
FOIA, 239, 361, 707, 1049,
1153, 1229, 1242a, 1246,
1316, 1338, 1359, 1378,
1418, 1429, 1429, 1488,
1533, 1603, 1625, 1645,
1659, 3320, 3464, 3997,
4172, 4200, 4214, 4246,

SUBJECT INDEX

4256, 4300, 4301, 4305, 4318, 4328, 4337, 4357, 4372, 4607, 4654
FOIA abuses: Nixon and Reagan, 78
FOIA restrictions, 13
Folger's coffee, 1913
folk-song, 178
Foucault, Michel, 739, 3113
Fonda, Jane, 866, 3185
Fonz, the, 2393, 2534
food, 129, 135, 153, 734, 1682, 3365
food advertising, 1741, 1784, 1823, 1827a, 1929, 2036, 2039, 2040, 2052
Food and Drug Administration, 4668
food industry, 1808
food: irradiation, 1059, 3494
food monopoly, 128
food processing, 153
football, 5591, 716
football: advertising, 559
football: education, 544
football: Marxist analysis, 559
football: professional, 2522
football: semiotic analysis, 559
football: SMU, 545
football: television, 2291, 2516
Forbes, Malcolm, 3328
Ford Administration, 314
Ford Foundation, 148, 2651, 2979, 4022, 4032, 4037
Ford Foundation and Educational Television, 2994
Ford, Gerald, 30, 202, 1331, 1332, 1385, 1386, 3243
Ford Motor Company, 112, 128, 828, 1171
Ford recall reporting, 3546
Ford-Carter debates, 2702
<u>Foreign Affairs</u>, 3873, 4014, 4106
<u>Foreign Affairs</u>: CIA, 4109
foreign affairs news, 1323
foreign affairs: television, 2581
Foreign Agents Registration Act, 4251
foreign aid, 2735, 4065

foreign correspondent, 3224, 3244, 4671
foreign coverage, 2198
foreign exchange, 258
Foreign Intelligence Surveillance Act of 1978, 288
foreign news, 892, 912, 919, 921, 933, 938, 942, 1000, 1025, 1048, 1133, 1446, 1579, 3224, 3244, 3246, 3423, 3481, 3670
foreign news: television, 629, 2560
foreign news: wire services, 3268
foreign policy, 54, 57, 346, 724, 1264, 1271, 1278, 1648, 2420, 3298, 3332, 3376, 4105
foreign policy access, 4305
foreign policy discourse, 676
foreign policy: double standards, 3308
foreign policy experts, 650
foreign policy language, 1505
Foreign Policy Research Institute, 4103
foreign policy: television, 2781
foreign reporting, 911
foreign wars, 3375
foreigners: stereotypes, 3090
forests, 3058
format and formula, 2481
Fortress America, 3306
Fortune, 3328, 3336
<u>Fortune Magazine</u>, 2028, 3940, 4123
Forum World Features, 3107
Foster, William, 339, 3992
Foucault, Michel, 3178
foundations, 24, 30, 31, 148, 650, 699, 2690, 3669, 4032, 4037, 4056, 4069, 4070
foundations: tax exemption, 138
Fourth Amendment, 179, 291, 405, 3971
<u>Fourth Estate</u> (Colorado U-Denver), 4639
Fowler, Mark, 2120, 2129, 2132, 2442, 3016

Fox, Victor (right-wing novelist), 3968
fragmentation: television, 2794
frame analysis, 987, 2716
frame-ups, 280
framing reality, 4236
France, 4248
France: broadcasting, 4415
Frank, Reuven, 2643
Frankfurt School, 646, 673, 3113, 4669
Franklin, Benjamin, 4026
Franklin National Bank, 3355
Fraser, Donald, 244
fraud, 153, 235
fraud: military contractors, 235
fraud: products, 625, 1839
fraud (see also: crime, corporate crime), 1880
Frawley, Patrick, 3521
Free and Responsible Press, A (Hutchins), 3434, 4187, 4286, 4594
free election, 649
free elections: Vietnam War, 4121
free enterprise, 1831, 1945, 2182
free enterprise propaganda: schools, 1980
free flow, 628a, 692, 1008, 1124, 1178, 1198, 1394, 1464, 1563, 1650, 4311
free flow of information, 78, 730, 1197, 2200, 2218, 2222, 2229, 2233, 2237, 2248, 3823, 4297, 4454
free market, 1505
free market of ideas, 903
Free Press, 1463
free press, 627, 962, 3667, 3817, 4331, 4348, 4362, 4365, 4371, 4429
free press (see also: First Amendment), 4195, 4202, 4209, 4238, 4259
free press v. fair press (government regulation), 2316
free press: war, 3430
free press/trial, 4366
free speech, 84, 464, 590, 709, 806, 1124, 1193, 1587, 1634, 1637, 1963, 2119,
3135, 4191, 4202, 4213, 4225, 4249, 4259, 4261, 4273, 4280, 4312, 4356, 4371, 4377
free speech: antiwar protest, 4190
free speech: broadcasting sponsor, 2261
free speech: civil rights, 4190
free speech: corporations, 422, 439
free speech: law, 4250
free speech: libel, 3321
free speech: obscenity, 3388
free speech: press, 1561
free world, 649
Freed, Donald: Death in Washington, 3999
freedom, 3860, 4276, 4314
Freedom House, 1283, 4288
freedom: intellectual, 658a
freedom of belief, 4219
freedom of expression, 1598
freedom of information, 1560
Freedom of Information Act (see FOIA), 175, 3202
freedom of press (see also: free press), 1259, 2292, 3765, 4241, 4351
freedom of speech (see also: free speech), 420, 3765, 4219
freedom to drive, 1726
freeze movement, 816, 4590
Freud: advertising, 1779
Friedan, Betty: The Feminine Mystique (1963), 3833
Friedman, Milton, 6
Friedman, Thomas, 3339, 3711, 3800
Friendly, Fred, 2844
friendly witness, 1634
From the Ashes... Nicaragua Today, 3164
Fromm, Erich, 1738
"front" organizations (anticommunism), 1241
front page, 3480
frontier, 3182
frontier myth: television, 2350
frontier myths: advertising, 1837a
FTC, 1147, 1692, 1715, 1725, 1741, 1666, 1792, 1796,

SUBJECT INDEX

1827a, 1842, 1902, 1966a, 2028, 2042, 2045, 2126, 2342
FTC: chilren, 2909
FTC: cigarette ads, 1856
FTC Watch, 4618
Fuchs, Klaus, 501
Fulbright, J. William, 288, 304, 341, 732, 1379, 1531, 1611, 3342 3944, 4181
Fulbright, J.W.: The Pentagon Propaganda Machine, 2839
full employment, 456
Fulton, Robert, 1347
Fund for Adult Education, 2979
Fundamentalism, 34, 487, 489, 1574, 2228, 2952, 2955
Fundamentalism: broadcasting, 2957
Fundamentalist religion: television, 2492
Fundamentalist-Catholic alliance, 491, 2957
funeral industry, 3837
Funk & Wagnells, 1827a
future-war novels, 1347
Gaffney, Frank, Jr., 2617
gag orders, 1565
gag rule, 976
Gahdafi (see also: Qaddafi), 3547
Gall, Peter, 4667
Gallup Poll, 1442, 1786, 2099
Gallup polls: foreign affiliates, 3279
Galtung, Johan: imperialism theory, 1668
Gambill, Joel, 1365
game shows, 2403, 2406, 2444
game shows: women, 2461
gamesmanship, 1795
Gannett Co. Inc., v. DePasquale, 1561
Gannett Company, 1093, 1094, 1154, 3546, 3678, 3688, 4704
Gannett v. unions, 1161
Gans, Herbert, 2658, 2692
Garden-Plot detention program, 321
Garfield, John, 1634, 3077
garrison state, 222, 3230
Garrison v. Louisiana, 4208
Garth, David, 2061

Garvey, Marcus, 280
gatekeeper model, 634
gatekeeper vs. propaganda models, 634
gatekeeping, 652, 727, 728, 912
Gates, John, 3992
Gay and Lesbian Alliance Against Defamation (GLAAD), 4196
gay: NYT, 3730
gay sex, 1070
gays, 2277
gays: AIDS, 927a
gaze-scopophilia, 4157
GE Corporation, 112, 1094, 1772, 1812, 1966, 2008, 2191, 2203, 2423, 2495, 2585, 2778, 3473, 3821
GE: nuclear weapons, 1105
GE: radio, 2202
GE: Sovietphobia, 1105
Gelb, Leslie, 1344, 3694, 3719
Gelbart, Larry, 2474
Gemstone, 104, 180
gender, 437
gender: film, 717, 3069
gender: popular culture, 721
gender: television, 2330
General Dynamics, 800, 2607
General Electric (see GE), 165, 746
General Foods Corporation, 2242
General Hospital, 2450, 2496,
General MacArthur, 2722
General Motors (see also: GM), 78, 163, 790, 3640
General Motors: annual reports, 4123
general semantics, 4338
General Tire and Rubber Company, 2303
Genet, Jean, 4604
genetic engineering, 4185
genetics, 499
Geneva Accords: Vietnam War (1954), 1228, 1954, 1611, 4121
Geneva Radio Conference of 1963, 2255
Geneva Summit: Reagan and Gorbachev, 1321

genocide, 346, 574, 574, 820, 821
genre, 2279
genre films (westerns, honor, gangster), 3104
gentrification, 3338, 3420
George Burns and Gracie Allen Show, The, 2511
George Orwell Awards, 677
Georgetown Center for Strategic Studies, 6
Georgetown University, 4104
Georgetown University National Security Studies, 3952
Gerbner, George, 2293
Gergen, David, 1401
Geritol ads, 1792
German Democratic Republic: broadcasting, 441
German Marshall Fund, 4094
German occupation: film, 3184
Germans: films, 3114
Germans: WWII films, 3114
G.I. Joe, 2491, 2548
Gibbs, Phillip, 1047
Gilbey's London Dry Gin ad, 1751
Gilman, Carl, 1226
Ginsberg, 3979
Ginsburg, Douglas, 430
Gitlin, Todd, 2316, 2804, 4604
Glad garbage bags, 1973
Glamour, 3829
Glasgow University Media Group, 874
Glasser, Ira, 4371
Gleason, Gene, 3777
Gleason, Jackie (as Ralph Kramden), 2473
Gleichschaltung (control of media), 1227
global, 629, 680a, 686, 700, 1178, 1270, 1322a, 2866
global advertising, 1709
global coverage, 2553
global expansion, 683
global information flow, 2866
global media, 684
global propaganda, 1406, 1633
Globe, 3820
gluttony, 1664, 1806

GM, 112, 1772, 4478
GM: Roger and Me documentary, 4478
gobbledygook, 945
Gobots, 2548
God, 1682
Godfather II, 3185
Goebbels, Dr. Joseph, 481, 1481
"Going Native Syndrome," 1419
Goldenson, Leonard, 2405, 2537
Goldwater, Barry 341, 2060, 4019, 4092, 4715
Goldwater, Barry: campaign, 2099
Goldwater, Robert, 4715
Gong Show, The, 2492
Good Morning America (ABC), 2675
Good Times, 2534
good v. evil, 2439
Goodman, Andrew, 3056
Gorbachev, 960, 2663
Gore, Albert, 1551
Gospel Crusade, 2208
Gossage, Howard, 1715
Gottlieb, Dr. Sidney (CIA's MK-ULTRA), 305
Goulden, Joseph, 3342
Goure, Leon, 4101
governing elites, 31
governing rhetoric, 1384
government, 48, 81, 88, 122, 125, 172, 306, 553, 553, 660, 712, 777, 1224, 1358, 1512, 1543, 2150, 2192, 2690, 3474, 4300, 4314, 4355
government: advertising and information, 1660, 2075
government agencies, 1659
government agencies: television news, 2879
government: anticommunism complex, 2744
government: broadcasting, 2243
government: censorship, 1244a, 1439, 1440, 2314, 3014, 3164, 3378
government: censorship: Mother Jones, 3827
government: censorship (see also: I. A., CIA, FBI), 3982, 4001

government: censorship:
television news, 2646, 2852
government: commission, 3448
government: computers, 3186,
3193, 3205
government: control of
media, 1480
government: control of
television, 2576
government: control of
information, 1169
governmen:t co-option of
media, 1324
government: correspondents,
1547
government: corruption, 123,
1350, 4667
government: deception, 196,
219, 1470, 1514a
government: departments,
1603
government: disinformation,
1660
government: documents, 4634
government: doublespeak,
1492
government: harassment, 17
government: human rights,
4325
government: indoctrination,
1286
government: information,
1271, 1495
government: intimidation,
1432
government: loyalty
programs, 349
government: lying, 219,
1414, 1492, 1494, 1611, 1662
government manipulation,
1432
government manipulation of
news, 1528
government manipulation of
press, 1594
government: mass media, 712
government media, 756
government media complex,
1283
government: news, 1039
government officials, 1337
government officials:
definitions, 868
government officials: news,
868
government power, 185

government: press, 1216,
1233, 1445, 1586
government press complex,
1327
government press relations
officers, 1503
government press releases,
1264
government: propaganda, 214,
1218, 1237, 1349, 1431,
1660, 2076, 3744, 4690
government propaganda:
magazines, 3833
government: public
relations, 219, 2076
government: regulation, 36,
1130, 1364, 1366, 4669
government regulation:
corporations, 131
government regulation: news,
2199
government: regulation (see
also: regulation), 1964,
1985, 2193
government: reporting, 728,
4382
government reports, 1495
government: repression, 4640
government: satellites, 1407
government secrecy, 77, 186,
194, 196, 206, 219, 634,
1338, 1339, 1359, 1360,
1415, 1471, 1489, 1574, 4301
government sources, 1468
government surveillance, 324
government surveillance
(data banks), 3209
government: television
censorship, 2801
government: television news,
2741
government: television
programming, 2288
government white papers,
1277
government-corporate complex
(see also: corporate state),
2128, 3652, 4014
government-industrial-media
complex, 609
government-industrial-
military complex, 3361
government-press buddy
system, 1414
government-press complex,
1503

government-press complex (Guatemala), 1372
government-television complex, 2781
government news management, 1339
Grable, Betty, 1860
Grace Commission, 1450, 4027
Grace, J. Peter, 4027
graffiti, 1757
Graham, Billy, 644, 716, 990, 3860
Graham, Katharine, 30, 3996
Gramsci, Antonio, 420, 461, 535, 645, 721, 896, 990, 1347a, 1348, 2329, 2373, 2406, 2481, 2531, 2658, 2780
Grand Junction, 3637
Grand Junction Sentinel, 3637
grand juries, 283, 290, 405, 1413
Grant, Lee, 2474
grants, 464
graphics revolution, 1682
grass-roots, 4193
grassroots communications, 4179
Gray, Mike, 3185
Gray, Patrick III, 327
Great American Dream, 2492
Greater Cleveland Radio and Television Council, 4247
Greece, 371, 388, 824, 2750
greed, 1738, 2441
greed: television, 2455
green advertising, 1973
Green Berets, 648, 2744
Green Berets, The, 3174
Green, Bruce, 3185
Green, Gil, 405
Green, Gilbert, 3992
Green, James, 1047
Greenberg, Gary, 4667
Greene, Bob, 3608
Greenpeace magazine, 1023
Greensboro Massacre, 405
Greenwald, Robert, 2406
Gregg, Donald, 4541
Gregory, Dick, 4604
Grenada, national security, 1242a
Grenada, 584, 990, 1022, 1049, 1049, 1217, 1302, 1401, 1423, 1549, 1562, 3136, 3496, 4590, 4591

Grenada: imperialism, 3713
Grenada invasion, 1329
Grenada invasion (press censorship), 1418
Grenada news blackout (see also: censorship, militarism), 2111a
Grenada: NYT, 3713, 3809
Grenada: secrecy, 1509
Grenada: US lies, 1507
Grenada War, 803
Greyhound Lines, 3732
Grierson, John, 3133
Griffith, David, 3124
Griffith, D.W., (The Birth of a Nation), 719
Griffith, William, 1395
Grizzard, Lewis, 487
Grocery Manufacturers Association, 1936
groupthink, 706
growth, 112, 130
Gruening, Senator Ernest, 341, 978
Grumman Corporation, 1953, 1981, 3628
Gruson, Lindsey, 850
GTE Spring ad "Changing of the Guard," 2077
Guardian, 3586, 4215
Guatemala, 12, 65, 204, 288, 340, 371, 388, 834, 1060, 1275, 1276, 1279, 1283, 1372, 3369
Guatemala, 3658, 3755
Guatemala: NYT, 3746, 3752, 3813
guerrilla criticism, 4299
guerrilla television, 2314
guerrilla theater, 4730
guerrilla warfare, 4092
guerrilla/farmers/drug traffickers alliance, 3331
Guess Who's Coming to Dinner, 3156
Guggenheim Museum, 4133
Guiding Light, The, 2394, 2450, 2496
guilt by membership, 307
Guinn, Private First Class John, 3278
Gulf + Western, 1093, 1094, 1874, 3951
Gulf of Tonkin (1964), 2672
Gulf of Tonkin Resolution, 341

SUBJECT INDEX

Gulf Oil, 4103, 4104
Gulf War (1990-1991), 2773, 3291, 3339, 3438, 3447, 3858
Gulf War (1990-1991): NYT, 3733
Gulf War: just war, 3289
gullibility, 1419
Gulliver, Lemuel, 678
Gun, The, 2505
Gunsmoke, 2291, 2439
Gurfein, Murray, 3798
Guthrie, Arlo, 4170
Guthrie, Woody, 4737
Gwertzman, Bernard, 630
Haacke, Hans, 4133
Haber, Al, 725
Habermas, Jürgen, 622, 906
Hadacol, 1844
Hagar, Sammy, 4157
Hagerty, James, 1597
Haig, Alexander, 93, 1505
Haiti, 843, 922a
Halberstam, David, 761, 1228
Halberstam, David: The Powers That Be, 2316
Hall, Gus, 3992
Hall, Monty, 2492
Hall, Stuart, 2658
Halleck, DeeDee, 4543
Hallin, Daniel, 973
Halloran, Richard: Pentagon correspondent, 4330
Halperin v. National Security Council, 1378
Halsey, Margaret, 3974
Hammer, Armand, 4704
Hammett, Dashiell, 3994
Hampton, Fred, 3575
Hand doctrine (widening Holmes test), 3430
Hand, Judge Learned, 3430
handbills, 4249
Hanford Nuclear Reservation, 653, 1590, 4237
Hanna-Barbera, 759
happiness, 1179
Happy Days, 2534
Harcourt Brace : censorship, 3996
Harcourt Brace, 4021
Hardees, 1927
Hargis, Reverend, Billy James, 2148
Harlan County, USA, 4521

Harlequin Romance: sexism, 3973
Harper, 4021
Harper's, 3328, 3889, 3927
Harper's Bazaar, 3821, 3829
Harrington, Michael Rep., 285
Harris Survey, 1442
Harrison, Jim, 287
Harsch, Joseph C., 3577
Hart, Senator Gary, 1898, 1936, 3001
Hart to Hart, 2330
Harte-Hanks Communications v. Connaughton, 1560
Hartford Courant, 1137, 3617
Harvard University, 323, 464, 3899
Harvard's Press-Politics Center, 1457
Harvest of Shame, 2651, 2686, 2844
Harvey Girls, The: film, 3091
Hasbara Project, 883
Hate Week, 1243a
hatred, 1243a
Have Gun Will Travel, 2439
Havel, Václav, 1015
Hawaii 2000, 2234
Hawk, David, 2657
Hayden, Tom, 725
Haynes, Hilda, 3185
Hays Office, 3114
Hayward, Susan, 4747
Hazelwood v. Kuhlmeier, 3412, 3416
H-bomb, 348, 3316, 3848, 3867
H-bomb: humanitarian, 4045
headache remedies, 1842
headlines, 3435
health, 38, 716, 1847, 4590
health: advertising, 1869a, 1896, 1943a, 1951
health care, 525
health care profession (see medicine), 527
health care: television, 2862
health food, 1883a
health hazards: advertising, 1841
health insurance, 525, 528
health lobby, 1127
health news, 1142

health underdevelopment, 521
Hearst chain, 1245a
Hearst Corporation: McCarthy, 1241
Hearst, William Randolph, 1094, 1174, 1175, 3477, 3801, 3563
heart disease, 3877
<u>Heartbreak Ridge</u>, 3136
<u>Hearts and Minds</u>, 3093
Hebert, Representative Edward, 2836
Hefty garbage bags, 3534
hegemonic process, 453
hegemony (N.B. a concept basic to the biblio.), 2481, 2531, 2432, 2658, 2703
hegemony, 439, 583, 744, 990, 4037, 4236
hegemony: television, 2340, 2589, 2804, 2885
hegemony: televison news, 2627
Heilbroner, Robert, 1802
Heinz, 1873a
<u>Hell and High Water</u>, 624
Hellman, Lillian, 3077
Helms, CIA Director, Richard, 1333
Helms, Richard, 288, 317
Helms, Senator Jesse, 480, 481, 733, 1049, 2361
Helms, Senator Jesse: censorship, 4135
Helms-Hunt senate race, 2086
Hemingway, 310, 3994, 4006
Henry, E. William, 2124
Henry, Jules, 2350
Henze, Paul, 1395
Herbert, Colonel Anthony, 2714
<u>Herbert v. Lando</u>, 1561
heresy, 199, 1682
heresy trials, 405
Heritage Foundation, 6, 7, 92, 631, 733, 2690, 4050, 4058, 4063, 4068, 4073, 4090, 4094, 4104, 4105, 4107
Heritage Foundation: Catholic Church, 483
Herman, Edward S., 592, 989
Herman, Edward S.(<u>The Rise and Fall of the Bulgarian Connection</u>), 869
hero as patriarch, 3152

hero as warrior, 3152
heroes, 4129
heroes: capitalism, 1783
heroes: television sports, 2520
heroes: war films, 3060
heroes: WWII films, 3085
heroin, 179
heroism, 3103
Hersh, Seymour, 1223, 1352, 1571, 4600
Hess, Karl, 4092
heteroglossia, 3160
Hewitt, Don, 2746
hidden curriculum, 455
hidden persuaders (see advertising), 1725
hierarchy, 457
High Crimes and Misdemeanors, 3334
high school journalism, 3448, 3486
high school press, 3412
high school: Underground Press, 4612
high technology, 3194
high technology (microelectronics, avionics, etc.), 265
Hill & Knowlton, 2004
<u>Hill Street Blues</u>, 2330, 2480
Hilsman, Roger, 2744
<u>Hindustan Times</u>, 3274
Hinton, Deane, 1254
Hiroshima, 336, 653, 762, 1467, 3175, 3406
Hiroshima and Nagasaki, 172, 584
Hiroshima-Nagasaki: censorship, 3108
Hiroshima-Nagasaki: scientists, 505
Hispanics: rap music, 4729
Hiss, Alger, 323, 422
Hiss-Chambers case, 3974
historical memory, 675
history, 4738
history (distorted), 741, 3117
history: film (false), 3109
history museums, 674, 1208
history: newspapers, 3410
history: press criticism, 4197
history texts, 4271

SUBJECT INDEX 739

history: United States, 4708
Hitchcock: WWII films, 3163
hi-tech reporting, 3671
Ho Chi Minh, 1611
Ho Chi Minh: NYT, 3700
Hobby, Oveta, 350
Hochschild, Adam, 4667
Hoffman, Fred: AP, 4330
Hollenbeck, Don, 1570
Hollywood: 1980s, 3171
Hollywood, 352, 352, 706,
717, 747, 756, 758, 2191,
2326, 2472, 3045, 3057,
3073, 3092, 3114, 3117,
3124, 3126, 3134, 3146,
3152, 3160, 3178
Hollywood: banks, 3051
Hollywood: blacklisting,
3077, 3125, 3147
Hollywood: business, 3127
Hollywood: capitalism, 3123,
3183
Hollywood: censorship, 3074
Hollywood: commercialism,
3556
Hollywood: Communism, 2744
Hollywood: dissenters, 4538
Hollywood: FBI, 1532
Hollywood film: MTV, 4157
Hollywood film: heroes, 3182
Hollywood: ideology, 3117
Hollywood: industry, 3044,
3112
Hollywood: innovation, 3042
Hollywood: international
market, 3040
Hollywood: Jews, 3099
Hollywood: minorities, 3151
Hollywood musical: stars,
3092
Hollywood Red Scare, 70
Hollywood: social films,
4538
Hollywood: Sovietphobia,
3123, 3130, 3132
Hollywood Ten, 199, 405,
1634, 3111, 3139, 3176
Hollywood: the elderly, 2309
Hollywood v. underground
film, 3120
Hollywood: war films, 3098
Hollywood: women during
WWII, 3144
Hollywood: WWI, 3179
Holmes clear and present
danger test, 3430

Holmes, Oliver Wendell, 616,
1309
holocaust, 3312
holocaust: children's
literature, 3950
Holt, Henry, 4021
Holy State, 1282
home: advertising, 1855a
Home Box Office, 1090
home computers, 3213
home work, 78
homeless: NYT, 3785, 3791
homelessness, 848
homelessness: documentary
films, 4405
homophobia, 482, 628, 992,
3337, 4591, 4593
homophobia: NYT, 3730
homophobia: television, 2474
homosexuality, 607
homosexuality: television,
2474
Honda ads, 1792
Honda's "Dueling Banjos" ad,
2077
Honduras, 65, 1022, 1267,
1275, 1492
honesty, 139
Honeymooners, The, 2281,
2316, 2473
Hooker Chemical Company,
4704
Hoover Institution, 4073,
4074, 4103, 4104, 4107
Hoover Institution, 6
Hoover, J. Edgar, 280, 281,
287, 293, 306, 316, 324,
327, 328, 2242, 3934
Hoover, J. Edgar: A Study of
Communism, 2109
Hoover, J. Edgar: comic
strips, 1532
Hoover, J. Edgar: detective
pulps, 1532
Hoover, J. Edgar: Do Not
File Procedure, 324
Hoover, J. Edgar: G-Man
movies, 1532
Hoover, J. Edgar: Hollywood,
1532
Hoover, J. Edgar: ideologue,
2109
Hoover, J. Edgar: racism,
312
Hoover, J. Edgar: secret
files, 325

Hoover, J. Edgar: self-glorification, 2109
Hoover, J. Edgar: Sovietphobia, 2109
Hoover, Mike, 2800
Hopper, Dennis, 3168
Horn, Steve (television commercials), 1738
Horowitz, David, 1567
horror films, 3152, 3158
horse race reporting, 2094a
Horton, Myles, 405
Horton, Willie, 1368
hospitals, 519, 528
host shows, 588
hostages: Iran, 2552, 2554, 1562, 1776
hostages (Iran): television, 2631
Hostess Foods, 1881, 1919a
Hostess Twinkies, 2046
Hotel, 2531
hotels, 1682
Houghton Mifflin, 4021
Houghton, Dale, 1786
Hour of Power, The, 2492
House & Garden, 3831
House Beautiful, 1907
House Committee on Un-American Activities (see HUAC), 178
housewives, 79, 1676
housing, 3420
Houston Chronicle, 350, 3560
Houston newspapers, 3582
Houston Post, 3687
Houston, TX, 350, 1134
H.R. 2361, 4251
HTLINGUAL, 293
HUAC, 313, 324, 339, 342, 343, 345, 347, 350, 351, 361, 382, 364, 624, 737a, 3147, 4562, 4606
HUAC: censorship, 3970
HUAC: Charlie Chaplin, 3121
HUAC: FBI, 316
Huckleberry Finn, 3950
hucksterism (see also: advertising): television, 2492
hucksterism (see II.B.2), 1932
hucksters (see advertising), 1725
HUD scandal, 3310
Hudson Institute, 3960

Hughes, Howard, 4747
Human Events, 1536
human rights, 346, 939, 945, 1043, 1069, 1446, 1600, 3277, 3306, 4075
Human Rights Commission of El Salvador (CDHES), 3677
Human Rights Watch, 1446
humanism, 1786, 2399, 4400
humanism: market system, 511
humanism: medicine, 522, 523
"humanitarian" aid, 926, 977
humanities, 910
Humbard, Rex, 2952
humor, 4233
humorists, 4748
Humphrey, Hubert, 2067
Humphrey, Hubert: campaign, 2099
Humphrey, Hubert: Institute, 4029
hunger, 135, 829, 1052, 1110, 2559, 3273, 3379
hunger: television, 2708
Hunt for the Red October, 4005
Hunt, Howard, 180
Hunter Project, 293
Huntley, Chet, 2744
Huntley-Brinkley news show, 611, 2633, 2881
Hussein, King, 1483
Hussein, King (Jordan): NYT, 3775
Hussein, Saddam (see also: Saddam), 2773
Hustler, The, 3936
Huston Plan, 104, 180, 273, 291, 293, 301, 317, 321, 324, 327, 1320
Huston, Tom Charles, 293, 301
Hutchins Commission of Freedom of the Press, 606, 617, 772, 922, 1197, 4706
Hutchins Commission Report, 786, 1000, 4173, 4176, 4187, 4192, 4286, 4304, 4569, 4594, 4636
Hutchins, Robert Maynard, 1667, 4192, 4594
Hutchinson v. Proxmire, 1561
Huxley, Aldous: Brave New World, 2350
HYDRA, 321
hype, 616

SUBJECT INDEX 741

hype (see also:
advertising): television
news, 2628
I Can Hear It Now, 2651
I Led Three Lives, 2439,
2508
I Love Lucy, 2511
I Was a Communist for the
FBI (1951 film), 2109, 3146
iatrogenesis, 518
IBI, 112, 1464, 1682
IBM, 1774, 3206
ICA, 1159
ideals, 1682, 3077
ideological films: schools,
3169
ideological hegemony, 773
ideological history
textbooks, 443
ideological management, 616
ideological state apparatus
(press), 1238
ideological state
apparatuses, 1347a
ideology, 53, 155, 227, 453,
558, 558, 575, 575, 642,
645, 646, 660, 683, 772,
868a, 881, 976, 990, 1375,
1860, 1990, 2082, 2279,
3298, 3474, 3522, 3577,
3616, 3991, 4032, 4173
ideology advertising (see
advocacy advertising), 1770,
1960
ideology analysis, 1347a
ideology: journalists, 4289
ideology (see also:
hegemony): 2472, 2530, 2716
ideology: television, 2339,
2340, 2587
ideology: television news,
2641, 2655
If I Can't Dance You Can
Keep Your Revolution, 4463
I.F. Stone's Weekly, 3859
If You Love This Planet,
3166
ignorance, 737a, 1013
Iklé, Fred, 7, 4101
illegal arrests, 3464
illegal domestic covert
operations, 1248
illegal search and seizure,
3464, 3971
illegal wiretaps, 324
Illich, Ivan, 4278

illiteracy, 455, 1002
illusion, 616, 1682
image advertising (see
II.B.3), 1152, 1965, 1981,
1984, 2015
image consultants, 616
image control: Vietnam War,
1379
image film, 3058
image formation: political
campaigns, 2084
image industries, 2238
image management, 616
image/illusion, 741
images, 1795
images as reality, 1682
images: television, 2613
imagination, 575
immigrant press, 4636
immigrants, 1708
impeachment, 3334
imperial presidency, 1222,
1257, 1260, 1623
Imperial Tobacco, 1874
imperialism, 7, 8, 10, 12,
28, 29, 51, 54, 57, 58, 63,
64, 65, 66, 67, 90, 91, 122,
124, 127, 168, 173, 174 187,
197, 204, 230, 238, 242,
253, 258, 269, 271, 298,
299, 308, 336, 386, 479,
574, 604, 618, 651, 661,
671, 680a, 685, 692, 719,
720, 732, 756, 786, 799,
811, 813, 820, 823, 824,
825, 826, 832, 833, 834,
835, 836, 837, 838, 839,
841, 846, 851, 856, 866,
867a, 868, 868a, 875, 876,
878, 882, 894, 905, 908,
911, 931, 990, 1043, 1046,
1088, 1196, 1214, 1244,
1250, 1256, 1257, 1260,
1263, 1264, 1265, 1267,
1268, 1270, 1275, 1286a,
1295, 1297, 1306, 1312a,
1314, 1345a, 1347, 1357a,
1426, 1489a, 1500, 1514,
1577, 1585, 1588, 1618,
1620, 1651, 1689, 1709,
1716, 1723, 1726, 1743,
1744, 1763, 1767, 1798,
2078, 2104, 2106, 2190,
2191, 2200, 2205, 2217,
2218, 2220, 2229, 2231,
2233, 2237, 2248, 2249,

2298, 2374, 2378, 2420,
2439, 2479, 2553, 2600,
2604, 2672, 2715, 2716,
2743, 2744, 2750, 2868,
3167, 3234, 3239, 3240,
3259, 3276, 3278, 3281,
3285, 3314, 2927, 2987,
2991, 2996, 3005, 3055,
3063, 3076, 3318, 3328,
3331, 3334, 3342, 3369,
3373, 3395, 3396, 3481,
3489, 3490, 3492, 3503,
3521, 3547, 3564, 3574,
3611, 3633, 3651, 3652,
3658, 3677, 3684, 3741,
3750, 3751, 3753, 3757,
3766, 3768, 3772, 3787,
3952, 3968, 4029, 4032,
4035, 4038, 4039, 4041,
4042, 4044, 4054, 4055,
4059, 4065, 4071, 4076,
4077, 4078, 4084, 4085,
4088, 4093, 4101, 4110,
4126, 4483, 4492, 4508,
4540, 4545, 4590, 4645,
4740, 4741
imperialism: advertising,
1668
imperialism: Afghanistan,
2800
imperialism: Angola, 3703
imperialism: Bay of Pigs,
John Kennedy, 3488, 3509
imperialism: broadcasting,
2213
imperialism: Canada, 2346
imperialism: Central
America, 2679, 3407, 3409,
3550, 3585, 3659, 3660, 3720
imperialism: Chile, 3453,
3654, 3739
imperialism: Christian
values, 201
imperialism: CIA, neutron
bomb, 3694
imperialism: Council on
Foreign Relations, 4022
imperialism: Cuba, 3425,
3514
imperialism: Cuba (NYT),
3726, 3727
imperialism: cultural, 757,
2436, 3041, 3047, 3048,
3050, 3160, 3292, 3293
imperialism: Disney, 668a

imperialism: education,
452a, 4087
imperialism: El Salvador
(NYT), 3742, 3788, 3790
imperialism: film, 3038,
3039, 3040, 3054, 3093, 3170
imperialism: film
censorship, 3105
imperialism: Grenada, 1423,
3713
imperialism: Guatemala, 3752
imperialism: Hollywood, 3117
imperialism: intervention,
1276
imperialism: Iran, 3675,
3802
imperialism: Korean War,
3491
imperialism: LAT, 3601
imperialism: Latin America,
340, 2767, 4602
imperialism: Micronesia,
2268
imperialism: music, 4168
imperialism: network news,
2757
imperialism: Nicaraguan
election, 3484
imperialism: Nicaragua, 918,
919, 926, 2765, 3756, 4437
imperialism: Nicaragua
(NYT), 3728
imperialism: NYT, 3717, 3718
imperialism: Panama, 3495,
3496
imperialism: Pentagon, 4119
imperialism: Phillipines,
2614
imperialism: radio, 2210
imperialism: religion, 2208
imperialism: right-wing,
3985
imperialism: Sovietphobia,
412, 1354, 3106, 3561, 3590
imperialism: Spanish-
American War, 3639
imperialism:
telecommunications, 2266
imperialism: television,
2388, 2389, 2410, 2437, 2438
imperialism: television
news, 2627
imperialism: Time Inc., 3944
imperialism: Underground
Press, 4612

SUBJECT INDEX

imperialism: Vietnam War, 3103, 3466, 3691, 3724, 4113, 4121
imperialism: Vietnam War film, 3174
imperialism: Vietnam War, Lyndon Johnson, 4112
imperialism: Vietnam War (NYT), 3735, 3773
imperialism: war films, 3098
In Fact (G. Seldes), 3934, 4652, 4692, 4700
In Our Own Backyard, 4507
In the Year of the Pig, 4453
income, 15
independent, 649, 4308
Independent filmmakers, 4490
Independent Program Service, The, 2967
independent publishers: computers, 4709
Independent Publishing, 4572
independent radio, 3027, 4433
independent television, 4488
Index on Censorship, 4288
India, 57
Indian lands, 1053
Indians, 719
Indians: access (see also: Native Americans), 4223
Indians: Pequod, 820
Indians (see also: Native Americans), 91
individual autonomy, 673
individualism, 1723, 3832, 3860
individualism: television talk shows, 2493
individualism: Underground Press, 4612
Indochina, 1007, 1648, 1278, 3691
indoctrination, 173, 447, 469, 583, 666, 674a, 2091
indoctrination: education, 440, 455
indoctrination: education, research, 584
indoctrination: PSAs, 2012
Indonesia: advertising, 1668
Indonesia: NYT, 3784, 3794, 3816
Indonesia: Sovietphobia (NYT), 3731
industrial wastes, 130

industrialization, 1160
industry, 128
inequality, 15, 33, 46, 53, 59, 83, 96, 106, 107, 122, 192, 439, 448, 484, 517, 1817, 4056, 4061, 4728
inequality: computer technology, 3204
inequality (economic): women, 68
inequality: law, 416, 423, 425, 426, 427
inequality: medicine, 529
inequality: women, 79
INF treaty, 1556
infantilism: advertising, 1934
infiltrators, 280
inflammatory utterances, 4190
inflation, 3620
Info Digest, 3865
infomercials, 1840
informants, 276
informatics, 2218
information: access, 78
information: commercialization, 1030
information: commodity, 78, 1194
information economics, 1124
information elites, 1128
information flow, 944, 3245, 3610
information flow (global), 2866
information hegemony, 742
information: private ownership, 1189
information: privatization, 78
information production, 1124
information: rich v. poor, 1194
information society, 78, 2254, 2373
information systems, 2209
information technology, 163, 2267, 3205
information transfers: government, 3202
information workers (control of), 78
informed public, 4343
informers, 283, 306, 328, 352, 405, 3077, 3493

informers (Sovietphobia):
Hollywood, 3132
informing, 382
infotainment, 1183
infotainment: television
news, 616, 2856
inherited wealth, 138
initiative, 4688
innocence (environment),
3821
innuendo, 352
Inquiry, 3274
inquisition, 352, 380
inquisitional tribunal, 199
INS, 1610, 3962
Inside Media, 4176, 4569
inspirational books, 3860
installment buying, 1852
Institute for Comtemporary
Studies, 6, 4104
Institute for Educational
Affairs (IEA), 6, 3473,
3475, 3690
Institute for Educational
Affairs Institute for
Foreign Policy Analysis,
4104
Institute for National
Strategic Studies, 3952
Institute for Policy
Studies, 52
Institute for Propaganda
Analysis, 603
Institute for Religion and
Democracy, 4064
Institution for Motivation
Research, 1786
institutions (social
control), 734
insurance fraud, 4627
insurance industry, 434
Integrated Services Digital
Networks (ISDN), 2318
intellectuals, 463, 721
intellectuals in power, 30
intellectuals: resistance,
2373
intelligence agencies, 276,
300, 1196, 1516, 3430, 4657
Intelligence: Army, Navy,
Air Force, 306
intelligence: Church
Committee 1975, 302
Intelligence Identities
Protection Act, 1280

Intelligence Oversight Act
(1980), 302
intelligence: regulating,
314
intelligence service
systems, 3197
intelligence: theories, 443
INTELSAT, 1643, 2249, 2255
Inter American Press
Association, 4288
interactive communications,
2222
interactive television, 2314
interactive television
(QUBE), 2893, 2895
interactive video, 4465
Inter-American Press
Association, 3241
Intercessors for America,
492
interchangeability:
capitalist products, 4154
Interdepartmental Radio
Advisory Committee (IRAC),
2255
Intergovernmental Bureau for
Informatics (see IBI), 680a
interlocking directorates,
131, 699, 3740
interlocking newspaper
directorates, 3385
intermediate-range missiles,
4034
Internal Nationalization
Service (see INS), 715
internal security (see also:
FBI, HUAC, Sovietphobia),
327, 411, 4219
international, 39
International Broadcasting
Committtee (see also: IBC),
1217a
international
communications, 1190
International Electronic
Satellite (see INTELSAT),
628a
international law, 833,
867a, 1022, 1260, 1276, 2615
international law and covert
operations, 278
international news flow, 620
International Political
Committee, 1217
International Press
Institute, 4288

International Press Service
Third World News Agency,
3237, 3239
international reporting,
3267
International Revenue Office
(see also: IRS), 283
International
Telecommunications
Convention (1982), 1312a
International Telephone and
Telegraph, 1919a
International Workers of the
World (see also: IWW), 307
interpretive reporting, 1404
intervention, 259, 278, 371,
1279, 1620, 1279, 1620, 3283
interventionism (see also:
imperialism), 187, 204
intimidation, 328
intolerance, 31, 464
invasion of privacy, 286
Invasion of the Body
Snatchers, 3064
Invasion USA, 624
investigations: lack of,
1420
investigative, 3348
investigative journalism,
1317, 1342, 3604, 3696,
3859, 4182, 4258, 4274,
4282, 4313, 4316, 4318,
4335, 4360, 4372, 4374,
4382, 4546, 4581, 4573,
4579, 4584, 4586, 4588,
4619, 4620, 4627, 4628,
4635, 4682, 4693, 4695,
4697, 4703, 4704, 4712,
4713, 4719, 4720
investigative journalism:
PBS, 3032
investigative reporting,
602, 711, 725, 831, 934,
937, 1404, 15232192, 2199,
2690, 3502, 3597, 3671
investigative reporting: 60
Minutes, 2878
investigative reporting:
data bases, 4370
investigative reporting:
lack of, 1403, 1647, 3411
investigative reporting:
NBC, 4491
investigative reporting
(need for), 1233, 3310,
3336, 3372
investigative reporting:
neutron bomb, 4717
investigative reporting:
television, 2685
investigative reporting:
toxic waste, 1360
invisible censorhip
(ideological), 1240
invisible government, 4258
ionizing radiation (see
radiation), 101
Iowa 2000, 2234
IQ: 443
IQ: class, 461
IQ testing, 455
IRA, 2786
Iran, 193, 203, 204, 371,
868, 1024, 1025, 1501, 1530,
1591, 2813, 3297, 3787,
3876, 3971, 4020, 4044, 4088
Iran Air Flight 655, 924,
2604, 2772, 3675
Iran elections, 875
Iran Embassy hostages, 929,
1575, 3274, 4541
Iran Hostage crisis, 1360
Iran hostage: television
news, 2775
Iran: hostages, 1050, 1409,
2316, 2554, 2562, 2675,
2696, 2727, 2732
Iran: NYT, 3725
Iran Voice, 3274
Iran-Contra hearings
(Congress), 1585
Iran-Contra Report, 1585
Iran-Contra scandal, 7, 62,
193, 195, 233, 1218, 1222,
1223, 1305, 1314, 1400,
1401, 1642, 3334, 3437,
4082, 4508, 4541
Iran-Contragate, 198, 1493a,
1568
Iranian Revolution, 868a
Iraq 1990, 905, 926a, 1726,
3315
Iraq Crisis, 1990, 3339
Iraq: Kuwait, 3697
Iraq: NYT, 3697, 3712
Iron Eyes Cody (weeping
Indian ad), 2033
Iron Triangle, 128, 1953
Ironside, 2291

Iroquois, 1282
irradiation: food, 3494
IRS, 276, 286, 290, 291, 294, 306, 321, 1463, 2028, 4686
IRS: Mother Jones, 3828
IRS: Sojourners, 3906
Irvine, Reed, 1083
Irving, Washington, 4026
Isaac, Rael Jean, 592
Iser, Wolfgang, 2450
Islam, 658, 1024
Israel, 487, 767, 0925, 1087, 1282, 1285, 2571, 2608, 2736, 3369, 3497, 3619, 3682, 3708, 3850
Israel and Contras, 193
Israel: invasion of Lebanon, 994, 1012, 2699, 2787, 2810
Israel invasion of Lebanon (June 6, 1983), 3577
Israel (Iran-Contra), 1222
Israel: Iraq, 3697
Israel: Lebanon, 3697
Israel lobby, 883
Israel: NYT, 3698, 3702, 3707, 3708, 3711, 3712, 3715
Israel: PLO, 3800
Israel: television, 2565
Israel: terrorism, 3708
Israel-Arab conflict, 3522
Israeli invasion of Lebanon, Issues & Answers, 2777
It Came From Outer Space, 3064
ITT, 104, 156, 1109, 1159, 1881, 2156, 3273, 3274, 4561
Ivins, Molly, 4600
Jackson, Attorney General Robert, 328
Jackson, Jesse, 1011, 1329a, 3871
Jackson, Michael, 4157
Jackson State College, 1047
Jackson State killings, 593, 854
Jacoby, Russell, 4690
Jamaica, 2381
James, C.L.R., 572
Jameson, Fredric, 4157
Jankowski, Gene, 2706
Japan, 4000, 4248
Japan: broadcasting, 4415
Japan: film, 3105
Japanese: WWII films, 3114

Japanese-American evacuation: West Coast, 3398
Japanese-American repression WWII: free speech, 3430
Japanese-Americans: children's literature, 3950
Japanese-Americans (WWII), 3367
jargon, 676, 945, 4633
Javits, Sen. Jacob (campaign ads), 1765
JAWS, 3061
jazz, 4402
Jeep ads, 1899
Jeffersons, The, 2485, 2534
Jehovah's Child, 3014
Jenkins, Ray, 4534
Jennings, Peter, 630, 2663
Jensen, Carl, 1242a
Jesus, 484
Jesus Salvador Trevino, 3185
Jet Pilot (1951), 3146+
jet set, 21
Jewish film makers: myths, 3088
Jews, 489
Jews: Hollywood, 3099
Jimenez, Jose, 4291
jingoism, 1050, 1256, 1468, 1575, 2615, 2744, 3639, 3684
jingoism: commercial ads, 2077
jingoism (see also: patriotism), 2101
JOAs, 3525
job safety, 4590
jobs, 5
John Birch Bulletin, 4092
John Birch Society, 4, 49, 480, 4092
John Franklin Letters, The (right-wing novel), 4092
Johns-Manville, 115
Johnson & Johnson, 958
Johnson administration: Vietnam, 978
Johnson administration, 3798
Johnson: FBI, 316
Johnson, Lyndon, 29, 202, 207, 209, 232, 288, 324, 341, 348, 413, 644, 808, 1078, 1320, 1324, 1331, 1333, 1368, 1375, 1384, 1385, 1386, 1629, 1630, 1656, 2060, 2124, 2148, 2657, 2658, 2672, 2795,

3259, 4017, 4019, 4110,
4112, 4113, 4117, 4670
Johnson, Lyndon: campaign,
2099
Johnson, Lyndon: press
office, 1597
Johnson, Lyndon: public
broadcasting, 2994
Johnson, Lyndon: television
Cold Warrior, 2744
Johnson, Nicholas, 1225,
2128, 2204, 2585, 4181, 4310
Johnson, Ross, 116
Johnson, Senator Lyndon,
1246
Johnson: war on poverty,
1661
Johnson's 1965 State of the
Union Address, 1330, 1331
Johnson's April 7, 1965
Johns Hopkins speech, 1630
Joint Chiefs of Staff, 232,
254
joint operating agreements,
3603
Jones, Frank, 4667
Journal of Accountancy, 4123
journals of critical
opinion, 4702
Journal of Marketing, 1786
journalism, 563, 563, 708,
1376, 3870, 4162, 4314
journalism: business, 3305
journalism: capitalism, 3298
journalism: courage, 4719
journalism: ethics, 3392
journalism: methods of
verification, 881
journalism: news, 950
journalism: prizes, 3345
journalism reviews, 3537,
4212, 4262, 4632, 4691
journalism: self-criticism,
4295
journalism: Underground
Press, 4612
journalist autonomy, 874
journalistic work routines,
881
journalists, 352, 874, 887,
923a, 958, 1410
journalists: CIA, 1290
journalists: democracy, 4379
journalists: education, 2813
journalists: ideology, 1071
journals: opposition, 4658

Joyce, Ed, 2593
Joyce, James, 1815
JQ, 3545
judges, 417, 434
judiciary, 431, 802, 1345,
1659
judiciary: First Amendment,
1418
junk mail, 1926
Just Between Friends, 3143
justice, 4326, 4331
Justice Department, 1139,
3693
Justice Department: nuclear,
3413
Justice Department's Civil
Disturbance Group, 306
justice: inequality and
capitalism, 59
justice: Underground Press,
4612
justice system, 902
Kahn, Albert E., 3434
Kahn, Herman, 3960
KAL 007, 634, 912, 924, 990,
1054, 1217a, 1649, 2692,
2772, 3314, 3675
Kalb, Marvin, 842, 1395
Kalish, James, 4667
Kalmbach, Herbert, 104, 180
Kaplan, Fred, 3960
Kaplan, Sol, 3077
Kaross, Sonia, 405
Kastenmeier, Robert, 244
Kazan, Elia, 3077
KCS, 3545
Keep America Beautiful,
Inc., 2033
Kelley, Clarence M., 327
Kellogg Foundation, 148
Kellogg's Heartwise, 1823
Kemp, Jack, 6
Kennan, George, 371
Kennan: anticommunism, 393
Kennedy, John Fitzgerald,
65, 95, 202, 288, 324, 348,
371, 377, 571, 648, 706,
746, 808, 1078, 1279, 1331,
1333, 1375, 1384, 1385,
1386, 1611, 1619, 1620,
2060, 2124, 2672, 2722,
2744, 4066, 4670
Kennedy administration:
newspapers, 3610
Kennedy, Anthony, 430
Kennedy: FBI, 316

Kennedy, John: anticommunism, 393, 2744
Kennedy, John: campaign, 2099
Kennedy, John: nuclear atmospheric tests, 689
Kennedy, John: interventionist foreign policy, 2744
Kennedy, John: news conferences, 2744
Kennedy, John: Sovietphobia, 4057
Kennedy, John: tabloids, 3820
Kennedy, John: Vietnam War and television, 2744
Kennedy: press, 611
Kennedy, Robert, 287
Kennedy, Robert: campaign ads, 1765
Kennedy, Sen. Edward, 305, 2061, 1530, 2076a
Kennedy, Sen. Edward: campaign, 2099
Kennedy-Nixon debates, 2702, 2722
Kennedy's address at Yale, 1330
Kent cigarettes, 1883
Kent State, 1047, 4116
Kerner Commission Report (on 1967 riots), 864
Key, Wilson Bryan, 1873
Khomeini, 868a, 3274
kickbacks, 45
Kikoski, John, 1395
Kilpatrick, James, 3412
Kimberly-Clark corporation, 1838, 2480
King, Corita, 1963
King: FBI, 316
King, Martin Luther, Jr., 287, 290, 312, 3902, 3903
King of Prussia, 4453
King's Row, 3147
king's two bodies doctrine, 3147
Kintner, Robert, 1241, 2835
Kintner, William, 4048
Kinzer, Stephen: Kinzered, 3741
Kirchway, Freda, 4559
Kirkpatrick, Jean, 7, 27, 65, 592, 912, 1518

Kiss me Deadly (1955), 719, 3146
Kissinger: anticommunism, 393
Kissinger, Henry, 183, 210, 1254, 1393, 2617, 2754, 2692, 4005, 4035, 4039, 4483
Kissinger, Henry: NBC news, 2847
Kissinger Report: Central America, 4041, 4078
Kissinger Report on Central America, 2679
Kissinger: Vietnam War, 1383
Klare, Michael (American Arms Supermarket), 3437
Klein, Calvin, 559
Klein, Calvin: Obsession perfume ad, 1896a
Klein, Herbert, 1597
Klug, Terry, 4565
KNBC-TV (Los Angeles), 2710
Knight (newspaper chain), 1174
Knight Rider, 2341
Knight-Ridder, 3457
Knopf, 4021
Know Your Enemy--the Viet Cong, 3170
Koenig (see also: Papert, Koenig, Lois), 1715
Kojak, 588, 2454
Kool Aid, 2046
Kooning, Willem de, 4131
Koppel, Ted, 4005
Koppel, Ted (Nightline), 2691, 2692, 2748, 2749, 2754, 2772, 2868
Korea, 371, 2496
Korea: The Unknown War, 3005
Korean Airlines (see KAL 007), 374
Korean War, 388, 803, 878, 1489, 3490, 3491, 4575
Korean War: anticommunism, 361
Korean War: false reporting, 3491
Korean War: film, 3060, 3098
Korean War: PBS, 3005
Korean War: television, 2743
Kosinski, Jerzy, 2350
Koven, Ronald, 630
KPFA radio (Berkeley), 2235, 4215, 4433
KPFK, 2251

SUBJECT INDEX 749

KPOO (San Francisco), 2235
KQED, 2314
Kraft, 1116
Kramer v. Kramer, 3152
Krauthammer, Charles, 1518
Kravis, Henry, 116
Krazy Kat, 4128
Kristol, Irving, 6, 1518
Krogh, Egil "Bud," 104, 179, 293
Krushchev, Nikita, 4670
Ku Klux Klan, 719, 1052, 1781, 3056, 4371, 4663, 4734
Kubrick, Stanley, (Dr. Strangelove), 624
Kung Fu, 2291
Kuper, Peter, 4136
Kuralt, Charles, 2593
Kurtis, Bill, 2796
Kutcher, Jim, 405
Kuwait, 1845
Kwitny, Jonathan, 1277
LA Free Press, 4664
La Prensa, 813, 1217, 1276, 1282, 1500, 3369, 3550
labels: animals 959
labor, 127, 990, 1032, 1135, 1150, 1160, 1180, 3430, 3477, 3928, 4432
labor: anticommunism, 3493
labor: computer surveillance, 3196
labor films, 4406
labor: Hollywood, 3117
Labor Institute of Public Affairs, 4449
labor: judiciary, 431
Labor Media Network, 4449
labor movement, 2692
labor news, 961, 3335, 3510, 3613
labor: newspaper, 3602
labor: PBS, 3021
labor: press, 3801
labor (see unions), 1845, 2216, 2265
labor: strike, 1050
labor: television, 2316, 2411, 2431, 4551
labor: television news, 2631
labor theater, 4606
labor unions, 3277, 3750
labor unions: films, 3057
labor v. corporations, 3602
Lacan, 3137, 4157

Ladies Home Journal, 1821, 3877, 3904
Lady's Circle, 3904
Laffer, Arthur, 6
LaHaye, Tim, 480
Laing, R.D., 4278
Lamb, Brian: C-SPAN, 4460, 4557
Lamb, Edward, 405
Lamont, Corliss, 422, 4371
Lance, Bert, 771
land reform, 868a
Landau, Saul, 2991
Lane, Chuck, 850
Langer, Suzanne, 1773
language, 2682
language: bigotry, 567
language manipulation, 462
language: power, 1624
Laos (1961): newspapers, 3610
Laos, 202, 204, 233, 278
Laos (bombing by US), 584
Laos: John Kennedy, 3610
Laos: NYT, 3710
LAPD Red Squad, 405
Lardner, Frances, 405
Lardner, Ring, 339
Lardner, Ring, Jr., 405
LaRouche, Lyndon, 60, 927
Larsen, Roy, 3095
lasers, 4282
Last Temptation of Christ, 3116,
LAT, 97, 835, 990, 1009, 1023, 1094, 1277, 1401, 1443, 2251, 3273, 3281, 3298, 3306, 3311, 3316, 3328, 3342, 3432, 3437, 3481, 3545, 3547, 3550, 3554, 3560, 3574, 3578, 3585, 3586, 3588, 3589, 3616, 3624, 3625, 3633, 3647, 3657, 3658, 3670, 3677, 3682, 4162
LAT: antitrust, 3663
LAT: Nicaragua, 1500
LAT: Nixon, 3580
Late Night with David Letterman, 2493
Latin America, 791, 1000, 1075, 2213, 2217, 2443, 2553, 2728, 2767, 3668, 4065
Latin America: advertising, 1709, 1716, 1798

Latin America: Associated Press, 3249
Latin America: news agencies, 3223, 3253, 3262, 3264
Latin America: NYT, 3717, 3771
Latin America: television, 2854
Latin America: United Press International, 3249
Latin America: US media, 618
Latin America: US neurosis, 564
Lattimore, Owen, 361
laugh tracks, 2425
Lauper, Cyndi, 4157
Lauren, Ralph, 1845
Laurence, William L., 624
Laverne and Shirley, 2393, 2534
law, 89, 729
law: class, 431
law enforcement, 4043
law firms, 699
law: inequality, 426
law: mass media, 623a
law schools, 434
law: sexism, 420, 426
law: television news, 2644
law: women, 418
Lawrence, John, 4682
Lawrence Livermore Scientific Laboratory, 499, 4590
Lawrence, Ronald, 1226
laws: corporate state, 421
Lawson, John, Howard, 1634
lawyers, 30, 417, 434
Laxalt, Paul, 2637
laxatives, 1842
LC-J, 3682
Le Monde, 4175, 4650
Le Moyne, James, 3716
leaders, 26
leaks, 283, 1229, 1329, 1387, 1425, 1520
leaks: by government officials, 1414
leaks: government, 1346
Lear, Norman, 2449, 2474, 2480, 2534
Leary, Tim, 4604
Lebanon, 994, 1012, 1244
Lebanon: Israel, 2810
Lebanon: NYT, 3697

LeBlanc, Dudley, 1844
Ledeen, Michael, 592, 1395
Lee, Ivy, 1108
Lefcourt, Robert, 4677
Lefever, Ernest, 592
left, 1027, 1118
left v. right imperialism, 2692
legal change, 4677
legal education, 420
legal protest v. censorship, 4580
legislative committee meetings, 4219
legitimacy, 645, 703, 2657, 2659, 4094
legitimating myths, 191
legitimation: news, 906
legitimation: televison news, 2869
Lehrer, Jim, 1393, 2691
Leiken, Robert, 1274, 1275, 1298, 3863
leisure, 19, 681
leisure: television, 2412
Lemmon, Jack, 2710
LeMoyne, James, 1275, 1283, 3790, 3751, 3788
Lenkowsky, Leslie, 6
Lenzner, Terry, 4667
lesbians, 695a, 2277
Letelier, Orlando, 1223
Let's Make a Deal, 588, 2492
Letterman, David, 2493, 2495
letters-to-the-editor, 3784, 4656
leukemia, 101
leukemia: atomic testing, 4663
leveraged buy-out (LBO), 116
Levinson, Richard, 2350
Levison, Stanley D., 287
Lewis, Anthony, 584, 3577
Lewis, Neil, 1283
Lewis, Paul, 3402
Lewis, Samuel, 4048
Lewis, Sinclair, 3994
libel, 733, 768, 890, 1042, 1049, 1560, 1561, 2170, 2690, 2812, 2830, 3321, 3426, 3783, 3958, 4011
libel: attack on media, 13
libel: censorship, 3322, 3999
libel law, 3348
libel suits, 17, 4670

SUBJECT INDEX

liberal bias, 2361
liberal left, 887
liberal press establishment, 1224
liberal state, 303
liberal v. conservative news perspectives, 1227
liberalism, 719, 2316, 3152, 3870, 4265, 4326
liberals, 303
liberation: advertising, 1757
liberation movements, 979, 1075
Liberation News Service, 1463, 3320, 4568, 4600, 4608, 4612, 4621, 4655
liberatory learning, 468
libertarian press, 1038
libertarian press theory, 4696
Liberty Federation, 480, 2208
Liberty Lobby, 4092
liberty (negative, positive), 1169
liberty v. equality (see Dahl), 1169
librarians, 78, 352
librarians: Bill of Rights, 4257
libraries, 1189, 1200, 2216
libraries: commercialization, 4013
library: presidential (Nixon), 4023
library surveillance: FBI, 3948
Libya, 203, 825, 867a, 912, 972, 1217, 1296, 1468, 2607
Libya hit team, 3547
Libyan bombing, 763
"Libyan death squads," 1520
Licavoli, Peter, 4715
licensing, 509, 2170, 2201, 2250, 2303, 3022, 3028
licensing: broadcasting, 2146
Lichter, Robert, 1071
"LICspeak," 1584
Liddy, G. Gordon, 179, 180
lie detectors, 1539
Liebling, A.J., 4697
Liebman, Morris, 4048
lies by the powerful, 1393

Life, 1581, 3342, 3647, 3821, 3824, 3857, 3874, 3941, 3942, 3944
Life of Riley, 2316
Liggett & Myers, Inc.: tobacco, 164
limited nuclear war, 266, 1419, 1534, 4045
lindane, 4704
Lindbergh, Charles, 1781
Linder, Ben, 1393, 3373
Lindsay, Michael, 3396
Lindsey, Hal, 487
Link, Henry, 3860
Link, William, 2350
Lippman-Merz on NYT, 976
Lippmann, Walter, 371, 1546, 1552, 4343
liquor advertising, 1827a, 1832, 1856a
listener supported radio (see also: Pacifica), 2251, 4433, 4452, 4512, 4531
listening devices, 286
Listerine, 1715, 1772, 1842
literacy, 735, 3301
literacy: computer, 3204
literacy: young people, 4177
literature, 113, 708
literature: sexism, 3967
literature: social order, 3991
literature: technology, 752
Little Boy (atomic bomb), 4045
Little, Brown and Company, 3977, 4021
Little Orphan Annie, 3860
lobbying, 31, 123, 1138a, 1411, 1728, 1978, 2029, 2097, 2166, 4714
lobbying: public interest, 4186
lobbyists, 1441, 3411
local reporting, 4258
Lockheed, 800, 983, 1953, 2101
Lockheed loan, 23
Loeb, Philip, 2743
Loeb, William, 71, 3684
Loews Corporation: tobacco, 164
Lofton, John, 3900
Logan, Clara (reformer), 2380
logical fallacies, 1417

LOGO, 3204
Lohbeck, Kurt: CBS news, 2870
Lois, George, 1715
Lone Driver, 1723
Lone Ranger, The, 2508, 3292
loneliness, 3860
Long Beach (California) Independent, 4663
Long Island Lighting Company, 3740
Look magazine, 1581
Look magazine: Sovietphobia, 3864
Lord and Thomas, 1772
Lordstown, 1
Lorenzo, Frank, 850
Lorillard Company, 1883
Los Alamos Scientific Laboratory, 499
Los Angeles Free Press, 3463, 4600
Los Angeles Times (see also: LAT), 644, 3605, 4664
Losing Control?: PBS, 2975
Lou Grant, 1838, 2316, 2480, 2489, 2529
Louisville Courier-Journal, 922, 3430, 3584
Love Boat, The, 2394, 2530, 2531
Love Canal, 101, 128, 1457, 1458, 4704
Love Connection, 2549
Lovins, Amory, 4278
Low Intensity Conflict (LIC), 187, 201, 211, 242, 714
loyalty, 94, 324, 347, 353, 361, 397, 406, 2242, 4219, 4667
loyalty oath, 199, 352, 394, 401, 405, 457, 464, 2425, 3821
loyalty oaths: screening, 501
loyalty programs, 342
loyalty purges, 4122
LSD, 305
Lucas, George, 3152
Luce, Henry Robinson, 644, 3944, 4173
luck, 3860
Ludlum, Robert, 4005
lumber industry, 2034
Lumumba, Patrice, 288

lung cancer, 101
Luttwak, Edward, 592, 2617
lying, 183, 220, 266, 315, 341, 409, 637, 662, 677, 680, 998, 1241, 1298, 1320, 1324, 1325, 1388, 1393, 1448, 1454, 1486, 1649, 1656, 1736, 2882, 4116, 4534, 4561, 4635, 4704
lying (see also: related terms), 1945
lying: Vietnam War, 1531
Lynd, Robert, 1713
M16 Rifle controversy, 1379
MacArthur, General Douglas, 4670
Machiavelli, 4741
machine aesthetic, 616
machine communication, 4194
machines, 616
Mackenzie, Angus, 3324
Maclean's, 3943
MacMichael, David, 1276
MacNeil, Robert, 2691
MacNeil-Lehrer News Hour (see also: Lehrer), 1395, 2748, 2691, 2851, 2963, 2988, 3001, 3006, 3012
MacNeil-Lehrer News Hour: biased sources, 2982
Mad Magazine, 3915, 4338, 4648
Maddox, 341
Mademoiselle, 1821, 1908, 3829
Madgewick, Donald, 1382
Madison Avenue, 756, 1688, 1715
Madison Avenue in Asia, 1668
Madison Avenue (see also: advertising), public, 1779, 1813, 1984
Madonna, 2329, 2499, 4157
Mafia, 137
magazine ads, 1722, 1788, 1854a
magazines, 602, 728, 744, 745, 759, 765, 1033, 1238, 1682, 1783, 1819, 1966, 2316, 2433, 3833, 3839, 4329
magazines: advertising, 1762
magazines: bibliography, 3818
magazines: blacks, 4723
magazines: diversity, 4429
magazines: heroines, 755

SUBJECT INDEX 753

magazines: specialized, 3825
magazines: success, 3832
magazines: television news, 2636, 2686
magazines: Vietnam War, 3840
Magnum, P.I., 2279, 2394, 3103
Magruder, Jeb, 180
Mah John, 1781
mail intercepts, 288
mail opening, 276, 286, 291, 293
mail order, 1795
mail surveillance, 295
Malaysia: advertising, 1668
male chauvinism, 2534
Mallin, Jay, 976
malnutrition, 3273
Maltz, Albert, 3185
"Man and the Horse" show at Metropolitan Museum of Art, 741
Man Called X, The, 2508
managed news, 1251s, 1467
managed news: Nixon, 1658
Manchester Guardian, 3274
Manchester Union Leader, 3684
Manchurian Candidate, The (1962), 3146
Mandate for Leadership, 4063
Manhattan Institute, 6
Manifest Destiny, 266, 574, 1638
Manion, Daniel, 430
manipulation, 1241, 1912
manipulation (see also: related terms):
presidential, 2080
manliness, 4089
Mann, Thomas, 3994
Mano, D. Keith (right-wing novelist), 3968
mansions, 616
manuals, 4092
manufacture: news, 2641
manufacture of consent (see also: engineering of consent), 1275, 4665
manufacturing desire (see also: advertising), 1847
manufacturing news, 881
Mapplethorpe, Robert, 4135
Marcantonio, Congressman Vito, 323, 4575
March of Time, 3095

March on Pentagon (Oct 21, 1967), 3278
Marchand, Roland, 1812
Marchetti, Victor: CIA, 1320
Marconi Wireless Company, 2142
Marcos, Ferdinand, 1253
Marcus Welby, M.D., 716
Marcuse, Herbert, 3404, 4136, 4162, 4181, 4677
Marines, 227, 1244, 3136
Mariona men's prison (El Salvador), 3677
market economy, 511, 1760, 2373
market research, 2350, 2796
market system monolith, 55
marketeering society, 511
marketing, 616, 1710, 1725, 1782
marketing books, 3978
marketing: oppression, 1732
marketing politics, 2092
marketing: television, 2796
marketing v. production, 1786
marketplace of ideas, 41, 713, 2182, 4333
market-research (see motivational research), 1860a
Markovic, Mihailo, 4265
Marks and Marchetti, The CIA and the Cult of Intelligence, 3430
Marks, Leonard, 1592
Marlboro, 1705
Marlboro cigarettes, 1884, 1901
Marlboro Man, 1837a, 1884
Marley, Kemper, 4715
Marquez, 1240
Marshall Foundation, 6
Martin Marietta, 984
Martineau, Pierre, 1773
Marx, Karl, 420, 431, 479, 1348, 1860, 2412
Marxism, 111, 127, 451, 559, 645, 685, 699, 1746, 2918, 3452, 4162, 4319
Marxist analysis, 2444
Marxist analysis: films, 3172
Marxist critique: advertising, 1762
Marxist Guerillas, 3751

Mary Hartman, Mary Hartman, 2350, 2393
Mary Tyler Moore, 2394
Mary Tyler Moore Show, The, 2350, 2474, 2480, 2534, 2550,
masculinity, 661, 1901
masculinity: nuclear strategy, 32
M*A*S*H, 2350, 2393, 2474, 2494, 2550
mass adverting, 3404
mass communication, 571a
mass consumption, 70, 1707, 1739
mass consumption (see also: consumerism), 3404
mass consumption society, 3832
mass culture, 572, 572, 671, 704, 1206
mass culture: pop music, 4149
mass manipulation, 858
mass marketing, 744
mass media, 24, 686, 712, 744, 759, 760, 1178, 1362, 1363, 1476, 1512, 1708
mass media: access, 612
mass media: codes, 702
mass media: images, 858
mass media: leftists, 711
mass media: military, 578
mass media: propaganda, 738
mass media: religion (see also: electronic church), 2228
mass media: research, 740
mass media: rituals, 579
mass media: theory, 739
mass media: UNESCO, 985
mass murder, 1279
mass murder (see genocide), 584
mass news, 4289
mass passivity, 1552
mass produced music, 4159
mass protest: television, 2818
mass-consumption, 1761
massive retaliation, 266, 348, 389
mass-market magazines, 3846
mass-produced, 681
mass-produced fashion, 681

Mastermedia International, 3016
Masterpiece Theatre, 1969
Masters of Deceit, 2109
Matanza Part II, 1277
Material Girl (Madonna video), 2279, 2499
materialism, 1694, 1843, 1846a, 1854, 1871, 1877, 1942
materialism: advertising, 1766
Mattel (Barbie dolls), 1873a
Mattelart, Armand, (How to Read Donald Duck), 1179
Matusow, Harvey, 3982
Maude, 2474
Mayo, Elton, 1088
Mazariego, Joe, 3277
MCA, 1175, 1196, 1214, 1605, 1728, 4151
McBirnie, Reverend, 21
McCall's 3904
McCann Erickson ad agency, 1786, 1894
McCarran Act: Internal Security Act of 1950, 411
McCarran-Walter Immigration Act, 13, 1418, 1612, 3854, 3962, 4183, 4227, 4251
McCarthy, Senator Joseph, 181, 324, 338, 342, 343, 352, 355, 359, 360, 361, 363, 365, 366, 367a, 372, 384, 391, 396, 398, 400, 407, 409, 413, 737a, 738, 879, 990, 1241, 1634, 2191, 2651, 2844, 3852, 3993, 4534, 4556, 4562
McCarthy era censorship, 3155
McCarthy, Senator Eugene, 2067, 2657
McCarthy, Senator Joseph: recall movement, 4615
McCarthy, Senator Joseph: television, 1241, 2743
McCarthyism, 4, 34, 42, 323, 350, 535, 382, 408, 737a, 1268, 1634, 2425, 2639, 2835, 4649
McCarthyism: Hollywood, 4538
McCarthyism: press/speech freedom, 3430

SUBJECT INDEX 755

McCarthyism: Republican
Party, 398
McCarthyism (see bigotry,
Sovietphobia), 3870, 4012
McClellan, Senator John,
4534
McClure's: advertising, 1783
McCord, James, 180
McCormick, Colonel Robert,
1174, 3428
McDew, Chuck, 405
McDonald's, 1893
McDonald's: advertising,
1779
McDonnell Douglas
Corporation, 1981, 3783
McFarlane, Robert, 193, 1401
McGarvey, Patrick, 4667
McGee, John, 4667
McGill University, 451
McGovern, George, 244, 1611,
2688
McGowin, N. Floyd, 4092
McGraw-Hill, 1094
McIntire, Reverend Carl,
2148
McLaughlin Group, 2611
McLuhan, Marshall, 549
McMichael, R. Daniel (right-
wing novelist), 3968
McNamara, Secretary of
Defense, Robert, 232, 341,
1228
McSurely, Margaret H., 405
McWethy, John: Pentagon
correspondent, 4330
McWilliams, Carey, 4600
means and ends, 4266
media, 568, 575, 1466
media: access, 758, 1378,
4490
media: politics, 889
media: bureaucracy, 943
media: business, 748, 932,
1186, 1203
media: cartel, 756
media: CIA, 1289, 1291,
1292, 1293
media: cities, 864, 3432
media: citizen action, 726
media: class, 599
media: concentration, 712,
759, 3603
media: conservative, 672
media: consultant firms,
746, 1245

media: control mechanisms,
605
media: corporations, 716,
1120, 1164, 1245
media: criticism, 659
media: democracy, 1245
media: economics, 712
media: effects, 639
media: entertainment, 746
media: ethics, 587, 4342
media: ethics (see also:
ethics), 4203
media: fascism, 93, 594
media: formats, 549
media: gadfly, 4720
media: global, 684
media: ideology, 599, 772
media: images, 696a
media: imperialism, 612,
618, 1178
media: integration, 570
Media: Lab (MIT), 4194
media: law, 591, 722, 1245
media: manipulation, 1451
media: mergers, 1056
media: models, 2239
media: monopoly, 158, 747,
1195, 3603
media: myths, 1167
Media Network, 4320
media: objectivity, 555
media: politics, 551a
media: power, 30, 577
media: profits, 710
media: public utilities,
4333
media: racism, 864
media: regulation (for
access), 4189
media: restrictions, 1398
media: reviews, 4585
media: riots, 864
media: self-censorship, 589
media: sexism, 695a
media: shaping values, 577
media: social
responsibility, 772
media: strategies, 550
media: suburbs, 3432
Media Survival Kit, 4309
media: violence, 864
Media Watch, 4310
media: women, 557
MediActive, 4308
medicaid, 525

Medical Aid for El Salvador, 2480
medical authority, 528
medical care: indigents, 4663
medical ethics, 522
medical ideology, 3877
medical insurance, 517
medical journals, 1201
medical profession, 83, 518
medical specialization, 519
medicare, 89, 525, 521, 527, 528, 814
medicine, 1933, 1951, 2216
medicine ads, 1918
medicine: corporations, 528
medicine: dehumanization, 526
medicine: government, 528
medicine: power, 512
medicine: television, 2521, 2862
Medina, Judge Harold, 1607, 3430, 3992
Meese Commission Report on Pornography, 4100, 4593
Meese, Edwin: Iran-Contra, 3334
Meese, Edwin, 3603
Meese v. Keene, 3166
Meet the Press, 2717, 2777, 2850
Mehmet Ali Agca (see also: Agca), 1395
Meiklejohn, Alexander, 429
Meister Brau ad, 2077
Melady, Thomas, 1395
Melish, William H., 405
Mellencamp, John, 4157
Mellon, 2202
Mellon Bank, 4104
Mellon family, 4104
melodoxy, 713
melodrama, 706
melodrama: television news, 2775
memory hole, 653
Mencken, H.L., 3429
Mendlowitz, Harold, 3732
mental health profession, 1065
mercenaries, 285
merchandising, 616
merchandising metaphors (see also: advertising), 1884
Mercury program, 1040

merger, 44, 509
Meriam, Lewis, 4047
Merit Cigarettes, 1894
Merrill, John, 1382
Metronews, Metronews, 2686
Metropolitan Museum of Modern Art, 4133
Metzger, H. Peter, 4646
Mexican-Americans, 4291
Mexico, 969
Mexico: NYT, 3815
MGM, 3114
Miami Herald Publishing Company v. Tornillo, 4351
Miami Herald, 835, 838, 3317, 3328, 3437, 3481, 3506, 3560, 3574, 3633, 3664, 3670
Miami Herald: Nicaragua, 3638
Miami Herald v. Tornillo, 2254, 2795
Miami Vice, 1723, 2330, 2341
Miami Vice: advertising, 1711
MIC, 7, 8, 12, 16, 30, 31, 52, 56, 59, 62, 63, 67a, 72, 89, 95, 99, 122, 126, 223, 227, 228, 232, 235, 265, 731, 732, 983, 1953, 1991, 2097, 2101, 2106, 2203, 2390, 2439, 2607, 3167, 3307, 3404, 3643, 4103, 4118, 4720
MIC: Aviation Week, 3882
MIC: computers, 3207
MIC: news, 2744
MIC: space, 2255
Michel, Representative Bob, 860
Mickelson, Sig, 2672
Mickey Mouse, 681, 716
microcircuit technology, 2256
microelectronics, 2247
Middle East, 346, 585, 818, 825, 1026, 1034, 1390, 2552, 2554, 2715, 2728
Middle East: television news, 2869
middle-class women: WWII, 3833
Middleton, Drew, 3737
Mideast, 183

SUBJECT INDEX 757

Midwestern Universities
Reasearch Association (see
MURA), 503
midwives, 4590
Mikva, Abner, 244
Milhouse: A White Comedy,
4453
militarism: women, 61
militarism, 2, 3, 4, 6, 7,
8, 12, 16, 18, 28, 29, 32,
42, 48, 49, 60, 63, 65, 66,
67a, 73, 80, 95, 98, 99,
104, 187, 193, 210, 222,
223, 224, 225, 227, 228,
229, 230, 231, 232, 233,
233, 234, 236, 237, 241,
243, 246, 247, 250, 251,
254, 256, 258, 259, 260,
261, 263, 265, 268, 270,
271, 283, 291, 295, 297,
298, 299, 300, 308, 329,
337, 353, 375, 377, 378,
381, 408, 477, 482, 556,
624, 701, 714, 731, 732,
769, 773, 778, 780, 786,
789, 791, 792, 803, 816,
868, 878, 900, 1195, 1214,
1243, 1243a, 1244, 1254,
1256, 1322, 1329, 1347,
1351, 1354, 1356, 1435,
1448, 1482, 1517, 1544,
1564, 1574, 1609, 1622,
1651, 1708, 1726, 1728,
1874a, 1953, 2058, 2097,
2098, 2101-2103, , 2106,
2113a, 2191, 2201, 2203,
2212, 2242, 2249, 2255,
2294, 2315, 2335, 2338,
2374, 2439, 2479, 2491,
2508, 2522, 2548, 2607,
2675, 2692, 2744, 2868,
2906, 3063, 3064, 3114,
3146, 3167, 3188, 3189,
3259, 3315, 3320, 3324,
3334, 3339, 3342, 3367 3404,
3389, 3398, 3425, 3517,
3548, 3575, 3576, 3628,
3630, 3633, 3647, 3686,
3731, 3848, 3868, 3944,
3968, 3994, 4005, 4014,
4015, 4022, 4030, 4043,
4045, 4054, 4055, 4059,
4062, 4076, 4077, 4079,
4080, 4084, 4086, 4089,
4095, 4098, 4110, 4125,
4126, 4345, 4388, 4492,
4508, 4575, 4590, 4657,
4698, 4711, 4722, 4734
militarism: censorship, 3852
militarism: chemical and
biological warfare, 4009
militarism: children's
cartoons, 2917
militarism commission
report, 4046
militarism: computer
concentration, 3207
militarism: computer
records, 3197
militarism: computers, 3193,
3208, 3214, 3216, 3217,
3218, 3219
militarism: data banks (see
also: computers), 3200, 3202
militarism: drugs, 936
militarism: education, 475,
476
militarism: film, 3054,
3071, 3072, 3079, 3101,
3119, 3136, 3157, 3177,
3179, 3182
militarism: Gulf War, 3858
militarism: Hollywood, 3117
militarism: juvenile
fiction, 3990
militarism: Kent State, 4116
militarism: literature, 4593
militarism: magazines, 3882,
3887
militarism: Pentagon
propaganda, 4230
militarism: print
journalism, 3307
militarism: public
relations, 2839
militarism: Reagan
administration, 1577, 4541
militarism: religion, 2208
militarism: Republican
Platform, 4118
militarism: Reverend Moon,
3721
militarism: right wing, 34,
3985
militarism: Sergeant Bilko,
4423
militarism: sexism, 87, 257
militarism: Soldier of
Fortune, 3923
militarism: Sovietphobia,
392, 3106, 3230, 3306, 3676
militarism: space, 1523

militarism: space shuttle, 3346
militarism: sports, 535
militarism: technology, 501
militarism: television (children), 2934
militarism: think tanks, 4086
militarism: video games, 3212
militarism: Vietnam War, 1617, 3691
militarism: war films, 3103
militarized surveillance state, 3147
military, 1516, 4059
military advisors, 226, 243
Military Assistance Credit Account, 258
military budgets, 255
military bureaucracy, 271
military censorship, 4000
military censorship: Fort Hood, 3513
military: Congress, 228
military contractors, 235, 249, 265, 732, 800, 1039, 1054, 1981, 3315, 3643
military contractors: advertising, 1874a, 1953
military contractors: waste, 235
military: corporation, 2059
military costs, 4054
military doublespeak, 2059
military economy, 250
military equipment, 980
military industrial complex (see also: MIC), 501, 509, 4086
military intellectuals, 4045
military intelligence, 276, 290, 1226
military justice, 2108
military law, 419
military maneuvers, 709
military: mass media, 578
military: media, 228
military men: educators, 262
military misinformation, 1072
military: natural resources, 228
military newspapers, 3449
military: NYT, 3814
military: organized labor, 258
military: president, 228
military press, 3686
military propaganda, 99, 1622
military propaganda: schools, 262
military public relations, 1622
military recruiting ads, 2108
military recruiting (see also: Pentagon), 1544, 1972, 2059, 2063, 2098, 2107, 2111
military research, 262, 508
military schools, 262
military: science, 230, 500
military spending, 1435
military spies, 2508
military subversive lists, 3189
military surveillance, 283
military: television, 2545
military toxic waste, 1056
military-education complex, 249
military-university research, 500
Milius, John, 3079
Milk Fund, 180
Mill, John Stuart, 4181, 4636
Miller, Arthur, 1634, 4364
Miller Beer, 1894
Miller Brewing Company (owned by Philip Morris), 164
Miller, Jack, 405
Miller Lite, 1894
Miller Time, 1894
Mills, C. Wright, 461
Mills, Wilbur, 3336
Milton, John: Areopagitica, 4377, 4636
MINARET, 321
mine disaster, 580
miners, 2606
mines: unsafe, 128
miniseries, 2406
Minneapolis, 1107, 1850
Minneapolis Star, 3592
Minneapolis Tribune, 3592
Minnesota Mining and Manufacturing Company crimes, 3592

SUBJECT INDEX 759

minorities, 628a, 747, 828, 2185, 4220, 4307
minorities: Hollywood, 3151
minorities: journalists, 1071
minorities: PBS, 2998, 3015
minorities press, 611
minorities: television, 765, 2283, 2664
minority broadcasting, 686
Minow, Newton, 2124, 2380, 2424, 2440, 2441
Mintz, Morton, 1157, 3553
Minute Women of the USA, 350
Minutemen, 4092
Miranda, 3744
Miranda, Major Roger, 1585
misinformation, 1072, 1329, 4244
misinformation (Iran), 868a
Miskito Indians, 1282
misleading ads (see also: advertising), 1846a
misrepresentation, 4634
misrepresentation: ads, 1792
Miss America, 1676
missile gap, 348, 377
missile guidance systems, 252
Missing (film), 3173
Mission Impossible, 734, 2291, 2528
Mission to Moscow, 3114
Mississippi, 3056
Mississippi Burning, 3056
Missoulian, 3681
Misunderstanding China (ABC), 2418
Mitchell, Attorney General, John, 104, 1225, 4561
Mitchell, Billy, 1347
MK-ULTRA, 305
MLA, 736, 3465
Mobil Oil Company, 1094, 1185, 1957, 1962, 1964, 1969, 1983, 1989, 1999, 2032, 3543, 4103
Mod Squad, 2531
Model, 3075
moderates, 1390
modernism, 713, 2501
modernization theory, 3839
Moffitt, Ronnie, 1223
Mohole, 503
Mohr, Charles, 1228
Mondale, Walter, 2107a, 2838

Mondale-Reagan debates, 2702
Monday Night Football, 2487, 2537
money, 22, 53, 184, 2522, 3860
money: ideas and power, 41
money: politics, 20
Monior, Congressman David, 1500
monopolies: newspapers, 3356
monopolization, 44
monopoly, 24, 127, 128, 135, 697, 699, 727, 728, 758, 990, 998, 1019, 1032, 1058, 1060, 1089, 1090, 1091, 1092, 1093, 1094, 1102, 1104, 1111, 1112, 1116, 1119, 1121, 1123, 1129, 1132, 1136, 1137, 1138, 1140, 1155, 1164, 1167, 1168, 1169, 1170, 1173, 1174, 1175, 1176, 1184, 1187, 1199, 1205, 1342, 1695, 2119, 2156, 2164, 2182, 2191, 2218, 2254, 2273, 2275, 2287, 2297, 2303, 2404, 2408, 2423, 2570, 2835, 2887, 3036, 3353, 3357, 3428, 3525, 3551, 3617, 3645, 4178, 4294, 4304, 4329, 4348, 4425, 4490, 4537
monopoly: advertising, 1673
monopoly and regulation, 682
monopoly: atomic bomb, 368
monopoly: books, 3975, 3987
monopoly: broadcast news, 2442
monopoly: broadcasting, 2179
monopoly: cable television, 2888, 2899
monopoly campaigns, 1245
monopoly: Canada, 3377
monopoly: Capital Cities, 1149
monopoly: Capital Cities/ABC, 2446
monopoly capitalism, 55, 56, 117, 131, 133, 154, 157, 374, 673, 744, 1169, 2956, 3404, 4106
monopoly capitalism: sports, 535
monopoly: censorship, 3977
monopoly: Chicago, 1148

monopoly: communications, 1122, 4404
monopoly: computers, 3205, 3206
monopoly: conformity (books), 4008, 4024
monopoly: electronic communications, 2256
monopoly: film, 3049, 3127
monopoly: LAT, 3663
monopoly: newspapers, 1211, 3351, 3355, 3358, 3382, 3678
monopoly ownership, 4669
monopoly press, 3434
monopoly: radio, 2202
monopoly (see also: conglomerates), 3956, 4024
monopoly: technology, 4551
monopoly: telegraph, 2143
monopoly: TV, 2375
monopoly v. public interest, 2173
Monroe Doctrine, 65, 168
Monroe, Marilyn, 681
Montana, 4666
Montana Power Co., 1103
Moon landing, 248
Moon, Reverend: NYT, 3721
Moon, Reverend Sun Myung, 2987, 3372, 3565, 3566, 3721
Mooney, Tom: LAT, 3588
Moore, John Norton, 4048
Moore, Mary Tyler (see also: Mary Tyler Moore), 2323
moral absolutism, 490
Moral Majority, 92, 481, 490, 492, 2221, 2952
Moral Majority Inc., 480
morality: government, 1350
More, 4176, 4569, 4585, 4672
Morgan, 2202
Morgan Guaranty Trust, 1204
Morison case, 1329
Morison, Samuel, 1242a, 1418
Mork & Mindy, 2483
Morland, Howard (see also: nuclear bomb), 3615, 3848, 3867, 3868, 3880, 3906, 3914, 3924
Mormon Church, 486
morning news, 2675
Morning News (CBS), 2675
Morris, William, 616
Morse, Senator Wayne, 341, 978, 1246, 3342

Morton Downey Jr. Show, The, 2517
mosaic theory, 1378
Moscow press corps, 1045
Moses, Robert, 964, 3511
Moses, Robert: NYT, 3777
Mosqueda-Judd Case, 387
Moss, Robert, 592, 3985
Moss Subcommittee on Government Information, 190
Mossadegh, 4044
Mother Jones, 3604, 3925
Mother Jones: IRS, 3828
motherhood, 3146
Motion Picture Alliance for the Preservation of American Film, 307
motion pictures: racism, 3097
motion pictures (see also: film), 1682, 4249
motivation research, 1671, 1691, 1702, 1710, 1734, 1735, 1778, 1782, 1784, 1786, 1925
motivational analysis, 707
Moulton, Harold, 4047
Mount, Thom, 3185
Mount Weather, 321
Mountain States Legal Foundation, 4104
Mountains, 4092
Movie Mirror, 3904
movie review, 3325
movies: 2001, 3167
movies, 611, 712, 2433
movies: money, 3051
movies (see also: film), 1781
Moyers, Bill, 1302, 1368, 1597, 2593, 2884, 2973, 2999, 3334
Moyers, Bill: People Like Us (documentary), 4203
Moyer's The Vanishing Black Family-Crisis in Black America, 1368
Moynihan, Daniel Patrick: 1965 Report, 4060
Moynihan, Daniel Patrick, 821, 1368
Moynihan Report, 1355
Moynihan's "The Case for National Action," 1368
Mozambique, 1060, 3302
Mr. Hoover and I, 4453

SUBJECT INDEX

Mr. Rogers' Neighborhood, 2922, 2930
Mr. T sitcom, 2341
Ms. magazine, 695a, 1908, 3922
Ms. Shortcake, 2477
MTM, 2480
MTV: business, 2500
MTV: economics, 2486
MTV (music video), 2279, 2329, 2341, 2453, 2394, 2406, 2470, 2486, 2501, 2517, 4151, 4157, 4161
MTV pastiche, 4157
MTV: political themes, 4171
MTV: sexism, 2547
MTV types, 4157
MTV: white male stars, 2499
muckraking, 612, 772, 4558, 4563, 4579, 4586, 4600, 4608, 4600, 3859, 4262, 4610, 4619, 4621, 4639, 4646, 4667, 4692, 4705, 4713
muckraking journalism, 4212
muckraking: libel, 3348
Muir, Jean, 2207, 2212, 2242, 2743
multinational bank data flows, 50
multinational communications: Third World, 4298
multinational corporation, 112, 683, 939, 1744
multinational corporations: science, 500
multinationals, 481, 684, 730, 1838, 1995, 2213
Multiple Intercontinental Reentry Vehicle (see MIRV), 348
Mundt, Senator Karl, 2743, 4534
Mungo, Ray, 3320, 4600
Munsey's, 1783
Muntz TV, 1873a
murder, 280, 1254, 4715
Murder in the Air (Reagan), 624, 3147
murder mysteries, 559
Murder on the Orient Express: Marxist analysis, 559
Murder on the Orient Express: semiotic analysis, 559

Murdoch, Rupert, 1093, 1111, 1144, 1167, 2570, 2622, 3326, 3933
Murrow, Edward (October 15, 1958 speech), 2844
Murrow, Edward R., 1241, 1592, 2191, 2260, 2350, 2380, 2593, 2651, 2672, 2844, 4290, 4461, 4505, 4556
Murrow, Edward R.: Chicago (Oct. 15, 1958) speech, 2651
Murrow, Edward R. vs. McCarthy, 611, 689, 1241
Muselin, Pete, 405
museum, 574, 670, 1192, 1208, 4359, 4738
museum: monorities, 4726
Museum of Westward Expansion, 574
museums, 674, 741, 4137
museums: art, 4143
museums: censorship, 693
museums: corporations, 1100a, 4144
museums: multi-media discourses, 693
museums: women, 693
music, 572, 734, 758, 1682
music: blues, 4164
music: feminism, 4739
music: Paredon, 4147
music: politics, 4150, 4163
music video (see also: MTV), 2499, 4160
music: youth, 4221
musical films, 3152
Mustang car, 1931
mutinationals: television, 1689
Mutt and Jeff, 4128
Mutual Assured Destruction (see MAD), 266
MX missile, 1419, 2007, 4332
My Lai, 222, 239, 240, 612, 828, 1426, 4600, 4638
My Son John (1952), 3146
My Sweet Charlie, 2505
Myer, Dillon S., 91
Myerson, Seymour, 405
mystification, 1333
myth, 558, 704, 4271
myth analysis, 3182
myth-making: television, 4234

myths: Hollywood, 3099
myths: Soviet supremacy (see also: Sovietphobia), 1354
myths: US, 3099
NAACP, 370, 4371
NAB, 2124, 2474
NACLA, 4602
Nader, Ralph, 4346, 4583, 4667, 4675
Nagasaki, 3175, 3406
Namibia, 1086, 3341, 3568
naming power, 55
Nanook of the North, 3169
Napolitan, Joe, 2061
narcissism, 1708, 1759
narcotics intelligence (see also: drugs), 179
narrative, 2279
narrative conventions: television news, 2841
narrative: news, 793, 2780
narrative: television, 2597
NASA, 252, 800, 1028, 1040, 1455, 2585, 4046
NASA (see space shuttle), 1036
Nashville, 2326
Nashville Tennessean, 4663
NAT, 3545, 3548
Nation at Risk, A, 4031, 4087
Nation, The, 3896, 3927, 3941, 3942, 4559, 4600, 4649
National Academy of Sciences, 500, 503
National Aeronautics and Space Administration (see NASA), 248
National Association of Broadcasters, 1827, 2118, 4247
National Association of Manufacturers, 1936
National Association of Working Women (nine to five), 4320
National Cash Register, 1747
National Catholic Register, 3680
National Caucus of Labor Committee (NCLC, Lyndon LaRouche), 60
National Christian Action Coalition, 492
National Coalition on Television Violence, 2548
National Committtee to Abolish HUAC, 323
National Communications System (NCS): militarized, 2255
National Conservative Political Action Committee (NCPAC), 480, 481
National Council for Public Remedies, 2024
National Council of Churches, 4064
National Council of Teachers of English (NCTE), 4338, 4679
National Data Center, 3202
National Decency Forum, 3016
National Defense UP, 3952
National Educational Television (NET), 2979, 2989
National Endowment for Democracy, 1217
National Endowment for Democracy: Nicaragua, 3701
National Endowment for the Arts, 4135, 4138
National Enquirer, 3820
National Football League, 917
National Geographic, 731, 3849, 3932
National Guard, 258
National Guardian, 3520, 4566
National Humanities Center, 4094
National Institutes of Health, 502
National Law Enforcement Telecommunications System (NLETS), 3214
National Lawyers Guild, 323, 4235
National Layman's Digest (Church League of America), 3819
national liberation movements, 4105
National News Council, 922, 1603, 2762, 3926, 4293, 4295, 4369, 4687
National Park Service, 678
National Public Radio, 4500

SUBJECT INDEX

National Reconnaissance
Office, 1196
National Religious
Broadcasters, 2945
National Republican Campaign
Committee, 2084
National Review, 3273, 3850,
3927
National Science Foundation,
502, 503
national security, 13, 54,
66, 75, 86, 91, 182, 193,
204, 205, 219, 239, 260,
273, 283, 289, 308, 316,
321, 325, 326, 328, 336,
337, 353, 356, 378, 411,
508, 653, 709, 719, 728,
1078, 1231, 1270, 1310,
1320, 1377, 1378, 1418,
1430, 1443, 1505, 1514a,
1523, 1542, 1554, 1558,
1581, 1625, 3548, 3676,
3880, 3920, 3952, 4014,
4030, 4054, 4252, 4305, 4577
National Security Agency:
computers, 3219
National Security Agency
(see NSA), 273, 290, 291,
296, 321, 1196, 3188, 3350
National Security Agency of
1947, 204
National Security Archive,
4607
national security
bureaucracy, 410
National Security Council,
183, 187, 1218
National Security Council
Directive 77 (NSDD-
77)(1983), 1217
National Security Council
Document 68, 1448
National Security Council:
right wing, 60
National Security Council
(see NSC), 193
National Security Council's
Crisis Management Team, 1223
National Security Directive
84, 1242a
national security
establishment, 243
national security: free
speech, 3430
national security:
militarism (computers), 3219

national security: press
freedom, 3430
national security (see also:
militarism), 2242, 2373
National Security Seminars,
259
National Security State (see
also: NSS), 303, 868, 1337,
1372, 3945, 4199, 4201, 4698
National Student
Association, 330
National Telecommun. and
Information Admin. (NTIA),
2126
nationalism, 108, 475, 569,
569, 681, 800, 868, 913,
1018, 1179, 1455, 2248,
2552, 2675, 3146, 3327,
3522, 3773
nationalism: education, 475,
4087
nationalism: film, 3072
nationalism: jingoism, 2506
nationalism: news, 3405
nationalism: religion, 80
nationalism: reporters, 4330
nationalism (see
patriotism), 2743
nationalism: sports, 3666
nationalism: television
news, 2562
nationalistic newspapers,
3630
Native American culture,
4601
Native Americans, 1288,
4223, 4276
Native Americans: children's
literature, 3950
Native Americans: FBI, 3958
NATO, 348, 371, 995, 4034
Nautilus exercise system,
616
Navy, 1322, 2106, 3628
Navy Log, 2508
Navy propaganda, public
relations, 236
Nazi Germany, 3891
Nazis, 1535
Nazis: films, 3078
Nazis: NYT, 3786
Nazis: US intelligence, 1582
NBC, 746, 759, 842, 860,
884, 914, 925, 990, 1019,
1245a, 1395, 1401, 1530,
1569, 1599, 1779, 2148,

2191, 2202, 2203, 2300,
2316, 2350, 2380, 2439,
2474, 2480, 2495, 2510,
2608, 2615, 2617, 2661,
2695, 2743, 2778, 2795,
2830, 2835, 3966, 4106
NBC: censorship, 2639
NBC: corporation, 2303
NBC: infotainment, 2856
NBC: investigative
reporting, 4491
NBC: news, 2881
NBC News, 2588, 2643, 2657
NBC Nightly News, 813, 1401
NBC Nightly News: arms, 960
NBC Nightly News: Pine Ridge
(American Indians), 2870
NBC: nuclear weapons, 1443
NBC: Olympic Games, 2496
NBC: Pentagon news, 4330
NBC: soaps, 2450
NBC: Vietnam War, 2574
NBC: Waist Deep in the Big
Muddy (Pete Seeger), 4170
NBC: Watergate, 1442
NBC's "Nuclear Power: In
France It Works," 865
NCTE (Committee on Public
Doublespeak), 1662
Near, Holly, 866
Near v. State of Minnesota
(1931), 4228
Nearing, Scott, 405
NED, 1319
needs (see also:
advertising), 1786
neglect of alternatives,
1477
Negro press, 3432, 3459
Negroes, 463
Negroponte, Nicholas, 4194
Neier, Aryeh, 4371
Neiman-Marcus, 616
Nelson, Jack, 1533
neomania, 616
nerve gas, 3637
nerve gas storage, 4646
Nestlé, 4590, 4591
NET, 2191
Netherlands, 4248, 4624
Netherlands: broadcasting,
4415, 4443, 4549
Netherlands communication
system, 2277
network anchor reports, 2728
network bureaucracy, 2480

network news, 588, 707, 777,
940, 1023, 1078, 1224, 1350,
1443, 2197, 2219, 2289,
2341, 2393, 2575, 2581,
2607, 2636, 2675, 2767
network news: bibliography,
2551
network news: Canada, 1063
network news: conservatism,
2617, 2809
network news: presidential
campaigns, 2838
network news: presidents,
1360
network news: religion, 2946
network power, 2358
Network Project, 1407
network television, 652,
2124, 2559
network television news,
2716
network TV: monopoly, 1094
networking media, 2235
networks, 97, 434, 747, 990,
1302, 1375, 2124, 2125,
2191, 2197, 2260, 2316,
2318, 2350, 2408, 2420,
2445, 2455, 2554, 2604,
2647, 2659, 2661, 2672,
2686, 2698, 2795, 2796,
3578, 4289, 4490
networks: Afghanistan, 2819
networks: colonialism, 2614
networks: commercialism,
1154, 2300
networks: Congress, 2657
networks: corporations,
2303, 2657
networks: Israel and
Lebanon, 2700
networks: Panama invasion,
2615
networks: Sovietphobia, 3295
networks: television, 2585
Neuharth, Allen, 3555, 3688
Neutrality Act, 288
neutron bomb, 1457, 1458,
3694, 4045
Never Let Me Go (1953), 3146
New Age movement, 4345
New Christian Right, 492,
880
New Deal, 4047
New International Economic
Order (see NWIO), 684

SUBJECT INDEX   765

New International
Information Order (NIIO, see
also: NWIO), 4173
New Journalism, 748
New Journalism: objectivity,
4695
New Leader, The, 3896
New Left, 293, 635t, 725,
1027, 2373
New Orleans Times-Picayune,
3552, 3636
New Republic, The, 658,
2611, 3916, 3919, 3927,
3941, 3942
New Right, 62, 71, 92, 492,
2812, 3167
New Right: religion, 2958
New Right, the, 4374, 4592
New Solidarity (later The
New Federalist, Lyndon
LaRouche), 60
New World Information Order
(New International
Information Order) (see
NWIO=NIIO), 631
New World Information and
Communication Order (NWICO),
1197
new world order: Hollywood,
3123
New York City, 964
New York Daily Mirror, 3428
New York Daily News, 3607
New York Herald Tribune
(NYHT), 1581, 3428, 3647,
3676
New York Journal American,
3428
New York Metropolitan Museum
of Art, 741
New York Post, 1608, 3428,
3647
New York Review of Books,
3328
New York Times (see also:
NYT), 209, 288, 630, 632,
633, 634, 650, 695a, 741,
4676
New York Times: Arabs, 658
New York Times vs. Sullivan,
733
New York World's Fair, 749
New York World-Telegram,
4697
New York World-Telegram and
Sun, 3428

New Yorker, 3890, 4697
Newfield, Jack, 4600
Newhouse Chain, 3353
Newhouse Communications,
3954
Newhouse, S.I., 3636
Newhouse trial, 3329
Newlywed Game, The, 2492
Newman, Barbara, 4667
News & Views (Church League
of America, Wheaton, IL),
3819
news, 404, 591, 622, 634,
660, 706, 712, 727, 735,
746, 770a, 772, 787, 1682,
2192, 2643, 2880, 3432, 4343
news: accountability, 4260
news: action v. analysis,
3504
news agencies, 611, 620,
679, 684, 756, 932, 1000,
1048, 1094, 2553, 2726,
2728, 3239, 3274, 2026,
2200, 2220, 2227, 3477,
3801, 4271, 4655
news agencies: El Salvdor,
3462
news agencies: Liberation
News Service, 4621
news agencies: Unesco, 631
news: AIDS, 927a
news: alternatives, 4205
news analysis, 941
news analysis: method, 869
news anchor, 718, 2686
news as spectacle, 871
news authority, 874
news: balance (Washington v.
regional), 2634
news bias, 885, 950, 1110,
3432
news: bibliography, 766
news blackouts, 2564
news broadcasting, 704
news budget (wire services),
3248
news bureaucracy, 4289
news: business, 772, 815,
1183, 4289
news: capitalist analysis,
772
news: CBS, 2758
news: CIA, 3107
news: commentary, 2798
news: commercial, 907

news commercials (see also: infomercial), 1840
news: commodity, 973
news conferences, 1078
news: consultancy, 2199, 2796
news control, 873, 874
news control: Cold War, 4236
news conventions, 3673
news: corporations, 873
news council, 922, 4262
news credibility, 874
news: crime, 874
news: democracy, 4362
news: deviance, 874
news distortion by government, 196
news: diversity, 4624
news: economics, 2703, 3673
news editing, 874
news: El Salvador, 4485
news: elections, 794
news: entertainment, 771, 874, 1183, 2846
news: entertainment: television, 2533
news: established power, 3380
news: ethics, 898, 4290
news: fake, 2704
news: film, 3107
news filters, 914
news flow, 971, 3269
news: foreign, 921
news: Forum World Features, 3107
news fragmentation, 885, 4330
news frames, 793, 874, 896, 950, 987, 1064a, 1067, 2661, 3586
news: free flow, 39
news gathering: opposition, 4216
news: global, 897
news: government, 766, 873, 874, 907
news: government officialism, 3673
news: health, 1127
news: historical context, 819
news: ideology, 874, 1308, 2703, 3673
news institutions, 874
news: junk, 2602

news: Latin America, 791
news leaks, 3673
news: liberal?, 1342
news: local, 2406
news: local government, 3432
news magazines, 2406
news management, 660, 1078, 1236, 1318, 1375, 1405, 1414, 1417, 1473, 1546, 1625, 1627, 3474, 4303
news management by gov't., 1304
news managing, 4271
news: manufacture of, 794
news: Marxist analysis, 772
news media, 609, 709, 756
news media: Arabs, 658
news narratives, 1067
news: networks, 904
news objectivity, 3410
news: organization, 897, 1066
news: page-one, 3673
news photographs: propaganda, 3881
news: photography, 867
news: pictures, 2643
news: police, 874
news politics, 3673
news: poverty, 795
news: power, 930
news: print and television news, 2807
news process, 874
news: production, 907, 2643
news: profit, 772
news: propaganda, 3507
news: public, 874
news: public ignorance, 938
news: public service, 4267
news publishers, 3673
news: regional, 2634
news releases, 1064a
news reporters, 660
news reporting, 547
news reporting: information resources, 4327
news reporting methodology, 874
news routines, 1375
news: selection process, 2643
news semiotics, 3415
news: show business, 2705
news: social consensus, 874
news: social control, 874

news: sources, 873, 874, 885, 3673
news sources: confidentiality, 4685
news sources protection, 612
news sources: shield law, 4322
news sources: television, 2584
news: specialized, 3472
news: sponsors (see), 1863, 1940
news: sports, 917
news stories: propaganda, 3881
news structures, 788
news: subsidy v. profit, 4624
news: superficiality, 948, 1342
news: technology, 904, 906
news: television, 909, 2362, 2392, 4450
news: Third World analysis, 772
news, TV: UNESCO, 913
news: TV v. newspapers, 830
News Twisters, The, 3966
news uniformity, 710
news v. profit (newspapers), 3455
news values, 888
news: violence, 1142a
news: women, 1067
newsbreak, 2628
Newsday, 3608, 3628
newsletters, 1404
newsmakers, 889
newsmaking, 1682
newspaper ads: atomic power, 1974
newspaper: analysis, 4582
newspaper: blacks, 4723
newspaper: business, 3515
newspaper: campus, 4625
newspaper: censorship, 3359
newspaper: chains, 3678
newspaper: combination rates, 3358
newspaper: competition (see also: monopoly), 3468
newspaper: corporate complex, 3366
newspaper: directors, 3384
newspaper: editorial, 3325

newspaper: editorial control, 4571
Newspaper Editors, American Society of, 1000
newspaper: electronic, 4644
newspaper: government subsidies, 4624
Newspaper Guild (AFL-CIO), 1276, 3431
newspaper: letters-to-the-editor, 4656
newspaper: muckraking, 4563
newspaper: ombudspersons, 4629, 4659
newspaper: ownership, 4571
Newspaper Preservation Act, 779, 3356, 3358, 3603, 4175
newspaper: public access, 4613
Newspaper Publishers Association, 3478
newspaper: sponsor, 1941
newspaper support of business, 3781
newspaper weeklies, 3499
newspaper women's pages, 755
newspaper-business collusion, 3542
newspapers, 602, 603, 728, 745, 746, 747, 759, 765, 1167, 1174, 1233, 1238, 1543, 1682, 3323, 3363, 3474, 3548, 3558, 3573, 3586, 3597, 3604, 3645, 3653, 3719, 4194, 4271, 4329, 4669
newspapers: access, 3394
newspapers: advertising, 1762, 3452, 3501
newspapers: conformity, 3624
newspapers: conservative ideology, 3428
newspapers: government, 3564
newspapers: headlines, 3435
newspapers: ideological conformity, 3596
newspapers: intelligence agencies, 3576
newspapers: interlocking directorates, 3385
newspapers: McCarthy, 1241
newspapers: monopoly, 1094, 1187, 3356
newspapers: nationalism, 3405
newspapers: Nixon, 3479

newspapers: public opinion, 3564
newspapers: racism, 3414
newspapers: Truman, 3508
newspapers: Unesco, 631
Newspeak, 678, 847, 1049, 1277, 2734
newsreel, 3094, 3095
Newsweek, 97, 209, 634, 644, 678, 900, 914, 990, 1178, 1245, 1253, 1355, 1379, 1395, 1401, 1426, 1443, 1945, 3270, 3273, 3274, 3275, 3276, 3277, 3281, 3285, 3295, 3298, 3299, 3302, 3306, 3311, 3316, 3325, 3328, 3335, 3341, 3545, 3821, 3838, 3857, 3876, 3881, 3883, 3885, 3901, 3902, 3903, 3908, 3911, 3917, 3921, 3941, 3942, 4005, 4106
Newsweek: Angola, 912
Newsweek: Contras, 3288
Newsweek: Gulf War, 3858
Newsweek: KAL 007, 912
Newsweek: sexism, 695a
Newsweek: UNESCO, 913
Newsweek: women, 3904
newsworthiness, 881
Newton, Huey, 4604
NFL, 2487
Niagara Gazette, 4704
Nicaragua, 7, 64, 65, 90, 193, 203, 332, 346, 483, 582, 584, 585, 715, 719, 769, 787, 811, 813, 827, 832, 833, 836, 839, 841, 846, 868, 908, 918, 926, 977, 997, 1085, 1268a, 1275, 1276, 1282, 1283, 1296, 1298, 1300, 1401, 1431, 1446, 1486, 1492, 1498, 1499, 1500, 1541, 1559, 1584, 1585, 1642, 2091, 2553, 2605, 2692, 2765, 2767, 2840, 2865, 3229, 3275, 3276, 3285, 3369, 3373, 3378, 3550, 3585, 3658, 3659, 3660, 3717, 3741, 3863, 4029, 4062, 4437, 4540, 4591, 4593, 4690
Nicaragua: Associated Press, 3250
Nicaragua: Canada, 3250
Nicaragua: CIA, 1573
Nicaragua: Contras, 1307, 1573
Nicaragua (lies about), 64
Nicaragua: Miami Herald, 3638
Nicaragua: MiG scare, 2840
Nicaragua: news agencies, 3234
Nicaragua: NYT, 3570, 3701, 3718, 3728, 3741, 3750, 3753, 3755, 3758, 3804
Nicaragua: Reagan, 1497
Nicaragua: television, 2865
Nicaraguan election (1984): NYT, 3756
Nicaraguan election coverage, 3484
Nicaraguan elections: television, 2420
Nichols, Dan (television commercials), 1738
Nichols, Louis B., 31, 3243
Nielsen ratings, 2232, 2240, 2299, 2300, 2318, 2472, 2561
Nielsen ratings: news, 2621
Nigeria, 4037
Nightline, 2963
Nightline: Colonel North, 2652
Nightline (see also: Ted Koppel), 2589, 2691, 2692, 2748, 2749
Nigut, Bill, Jr., 4720
NIICO (see NWIO), 971
NIIO (see also: New World Information Order, NWIO), 556, 680a, 684, 985, 1197, 1604, 2218, 3610, 3823, 4311
Nixon: 1960 campaign, 2115a
Nixon: 1972 campaign, 1332, 2105
Nixon, Richard, 31, 42, 65, 104, 141, 174, 179, 183, 189, 202, 209, 210, 218, 219, 273, 293, 321, 324, 329, 348, 377, 413, 478, 541, 602, 611, 633, 644, 716, 719, 746, 780, 787, 808, 932, 1047, 1078, 1094, 1219, 1235, 1246, 1260, 1305, 1320, 1324, 1331, 1332, 1333, 1340, 1375, 1384, 1385, 1386, 1401, 1442, 1458, 1463, 1488, 1508, 1528, 1545, 1594, 1603, 1616, 1617, 1639,

SUBJECT INDEX

1656, 2060, 2062, 2067,
2093, 2099, 2111a, 2148,
2191, 2215, 2324, 2425,
2643, 2657, 2658, 2672,
2688, 2722, 3419, 3439,
3466, 3558, 3860, 3966,
4019, 4371, 4453, 4483,
4561, 4568, 4581
Nixon administration, 1224,
3018
Nixon: anticommunism, 393
Nixon: Associated Press,
3242
Nixon: celebrity, 1478
Nixon; censorship, 2729
Nixon: FBI, 316
Nixon: LAT, 3580
Nixon: mental health
profession, 1065
Nixon: news manipulation,
2681
Nixon: newspapers, 3479
Nixon: PBS, 2745, 2971,
2979, 2999
Nixon: perjury, 220
Nixon: public broadcasting,
2994
Nixon: anticommunism, 361
Nixon: press office, 1597
Nixon: television, 2849
Nixon: television news,
2667, 2729
Nixon v. Media, 1341
Nixon: Vietnam War, 1383
Nixon-Kennedy debates, 2702
Nixon-McGovern Campaign
(1972): television, 2790,
2799
Nixon's press, 1533
Nixon's press conferences,
1330
Nobel Peace Prize (Linus
Pauling), 3647
noble savage, 3169
Nolan, Martin, 3229
Non-Aligned Nations, 2237
nonviolent justice, 4683
Noonan, Peggy, 4053
Noriega, Manuel, 233, 2615
Norma Rae, 3143
North America Air Defense
Command (NORAD), 4330
North, Dr. Robert, 3396
North, Oliver, 7, 187, 193,
233, 332, 789, 1022, 1218,

1222, 1275, 1305, 1431,
1432, 3334, 3437, 3450, 3451
Northern Ireland, 988
Northrop, 983
NOT-P, 3685
NOVA, 2916
novel: advertising, 1815
novelists v. business, 4576
novels, 745, 1682
novels: Cold War, 1544
novels: sexism, 3986
novels: television, 2335,
2364
novelty, 616
Noyes, Crosby, 3489
NPR, 940, 2978, 3019, 3024,
3027, 3033
NPR: All Things Considered,
3007
NPR: budget, 2995
NR, 3274
NSA, 276, 293, 1051
NSC, 204, 233, 273, 789,
1432, 4281
NSC paper #68, 348
NSDD 84, 1231, 1329
NSDD 84 (nondisclosure
requirement), 1418
NSDD-130, 1270
NSS (national security
state), 1448, 3146, 3230,
3643
nuclear accidents, 1058,
4244
nuclear advertising, 1994
nuclear aircraft, 1301
nuclear alerts, 4330
nuclear Armageddon, 487
nuclear arms, 3824, 4344,
4590
nuclear arms: Better World
Society, 4417
nuclear arms: opposition,
1343
nuclear arms: secrecy, 1326
nuclear blast, 4015
nuclear bomb, 1448, 1617
nuclear bomb censorship,
3406
nuclear bomb: secrecy, 3108
nuclear bombs (Israel): NYT,
3712
nuclear censorship, 1051
nuclear deterrence, 209, 266
nuclear disarmament, 4221
nuclear energy, 762, 1360

nuclear energy plant construction, 141
nuclear euphemisms, 1994
nuclear experts, 1552
nuclear firestorms, 4015
nuclear freeze, 1054, 2097
nuclear freeze plot, 1536
nuclear freeze posters, 4744
nuclear health hazard, 4244
nuclear imagery, 762
nuclear industry, 1910, 1911, 1923, 1992, 1994, 1997, 3578
nuclear industry: censorship, 2793
nuclear industry: television, 2703
nuclear language, 656
nuclear missiles, 1322
nuclear peace movement, 700, 965
nuclear policy, 14, 1552
nuclear policy (public ignorance), 1552
nuclear power, 167, 265, 1021, 1152, 1162, 1172, 1213, 1336, 1421, 1903, 1955, 1978, 1986, 2000, 2001, 2003a, 2009, 2013, 2027a, 2778, 2724, 3413, 3540, 4244, 4489, 4660, 4694
nuclear power: censorship, 2831
nuclear power companies advocacy ads, 2084
nuclear power corporations, 52
nuclear power: newspapers, 3679
nuclear power: NYT, 3740
nuclear power: opposition, 4378
nuclear power: radiation, 4499
nuclear power safety, 2710
nuclear power: The China Syndrome, 2654
nuclear proliferation, 245, 3867
nuclear propaganda, 1459
nuclear radiation, 102
nuclear radiation: PBS, 3023
nuclear reactor accidents (France), 865
nuclear reactors, 762
nuclear regime, 1467

Nuclear Regulatory Commission (NRC), 167, 4489
nuclear reporting, 1465, 1552
nuclear safety, 167, 935, 1054
nuclear scientists: masculinity, 32
nuclear secrecy, 3894
nuclear semantics, 1505
nuclear shelters, 4015
nuclear shield, 624
nuclear: space, 1059
nuclear symbols, 762
nuclear test ban, 1335, 4057
nuclear testing, 960
nuclear testing: NYT, 3567
nuclear testing: secrecy, 1335
nuclear testing: WP, 3567
nuclear texts, 4741
nuclear war, 18, 62, 208, 238, 268, 269, 379, 762, 1051, 1662, 2314, 4015, 4079, 4486, 4698
nuclear war: children's books, 3955
nuclear war: fiction, 4701
nuclear war language, 11, 4338
nuclear war novels, 762
nuclear war: PBS, 2975
nuclear war: songs, 4733
nuclear war: Sovietphobia, 374
nuclear waste, 653, 1443, 2027a, 4244
nuclear weapon plants, 1590
nuclear weapons, 16, 66, 378, 656, 968, 1052, 1466, 1551, 1556, 1662, 3316, 4275, 4361, 4502
nuclear weapons: GE, 1105
nuclear weapons (public ignorance), 1552
nuclear weapons testing: atmospheric, 101
nuclear weapons: TV, 2390, 2391
nuclear winter, 348
nuclearism, 680, 995, 1443, 1456, 1590, 3907, 3910, 3945, 4511, 4590, 4591
nuclearism: PBS, 3000
nuclearism: secrecy, 3000
nukespeak, 653, 1505, 3591

SUBJECT INDEX 771

Nuremberg Principles, 4235
nutrition, 129, 2908
N.W. Ayer and Son, Inc.,
1772
NWIA, 904
NWICO, 4297
NWIO (see also: NIIO), 692,
944, 1003, 1008, 1084, 1238,
1394, 1650, 2200, 2205,
2220, 2229, 2233, 2237,
2249, 2728, 3237, 3239,
3241, 3245, 3260, 3269
NY Herald Tribune, 3318,
3612
NY Post, 3338, 3578, 3675
NY Sun, 3503
NYC, 1322
Nye, David, 1812
NYHT, 3425
NYON, 3512
NYT, 695a, 787, 813, 818,
842, 850, 855, 857, 860,
868, 884, 896, 900, 914,
924, 932, 940, 990, 1015,
1016, 1019, 1023, 1039,
1041, 1049, 1066, 1067,
1078, 1094, 1110, 1136,
1215, 1220, 1225, 1241,
1245a, 1253, 1274, 1275,
1276, 1277, 1283, 1299,
1305, 1320, 1322, 1337,
1344, 1355, 1375, 1379,
1393, 1395, 1399, 1400,
1401, 1443, 1447, 1458,
1482, 1497, 1500, 1505,
1513, 1530, 1546, 1548,
1550, 1552, 1569, 1570,
1581, 1599, 1603, 1607,
1608, 1648, 1954, 2555,
2658, 2795, 2907, 3253,
3261, 3273, 3275, 3277,
3281, 3284, 3285, 3298,
3299, 3302, 3306, 3309,
3313, 3316, 3328, 3335,
3336, 3338, 3339, 3341,
3342, 3343, 3344, 3396,
3402, 3404, 3419, 3423,
3425, 3428, 3430, 3434,
3437, 3438, 3477, 3481,
3489, 3503, 3506, 3510,
3518, 3545, 3547, 3548,
3550, 3558, 3560, 3564,
3568, 3569, 3570, 3572,
3574, 3675, 3677, 3682,
3691, 3693, 3732, 3781,
3783, 3784, 3801, 3838,
3868, 3880, 3907, 3910,
3945, 4511, 4590, 4591,
3942, 4106, 4162, 4236,
4553, 4575, 4583, 4600,
4635, 4664, 4697, 4700
NYT: Angola, 912
NYT: anticommunism, 3969
NYT: Arabs, 1087, 3619
NYT: arms race, 960
NYT: Canada, 1063
NYT: civil liberties, 4371
NYT: Contras, 3288
NYT: El Salvador, 3635
NYT: EPA, 1576
NYT: Iran, 3802
NYT: Israel, 925, 3619
NYT: James Lemoyne, 3744
NYT: John Tower, 984
NYT: KAL 007, 912
NYT: libel, 1042
NYT: Lippman-Merz on, 976
NYT: Nicaragua, 977, 1500
NYT: nuclear, 968
NYT: nuclear bombs, 1590
NYT: nuclear power, 3591
NYT: nuclear waste, 1590
NYT: Panama invasion, 3496
NYT: Pentagon reporting,
4330
NYT: presidency, 1370, 1436
NYT: Sovietphobia, 1555
NYT: "The Week in Review,"
3941
NYT: UNESCO, 913
NYT: unions, 3705
NYT v. National News
Council, 922
NYT v. Sullivan, 890, 3430
NYT v. U.S.S., 2795
NYT: Vietnam War, 978, 3735
NYT: Watergate, 1442
Oakland Tribune, 3573
OAS charter, 1302
oaths, 2242
Ober, Richard, (CIA), 1463
objectivity, 694, 778, 787,
828, 871, 888, 990, 1000,
1009, 1016, 1019, 1068,
1076, 1078, 1110, 1190,
1342, 1420, 1522, 2703,
3298, 4006, 4173, 4224, 4639
objectivity: news, 874, 2472
objectivity of news, 2658
objectivity: television,
2861

objectivity: television news, 2686, 2857, 2883
obscenity, 713, 1525, 1598, 2152, 2170, 2354, 3082, 3142, 3388, 4366
obscenity: broadcasting, 2139
obscenity: censorship (radio), 3016
Observer, The, 3274
obstructing justice, 220, 276
Occidental Petroleum Corporation, 4704
Ochs, Phil, 4170
O'Connor, Harvey, 405
O'Connor, Jessie, 405
O'Connor, Sandra Day, 30
O'Dell, Jack, 405
Odets, Clifford, 1634
OFCC, 2028a
Office of Drug Abuse Law Enforcement, 179
Office of Education, 2994
Office of Public Diplomacy, 855, 1274, 1431, 1432, 1500, 1510, 1583, 16265
Office of Public Diplomacy for Latin America, 1218
Office of Science and Technology, 503
Office of Telecommunications Policy, 4247
Office of War Information, 3114
Office of War Information (Women's Bureau), 3833
Officer and a Gentleman, 3143
official news sources, 3364
official optimism, 1490
Official Secrets Act, 1387, 4246
official sources, 1037, 1039, 1220, 1233, 1337, 1400, 1486, 1500, 1514a, 2757, 3466, 3578, 3691, 4718
official sources for news, 1512
official sources: television news, 2848
official viewpoint, 3474
official views, 1264
officials: television news, 2678, 2841

Ogilvy and Mather ad agency, 1692, 1715
oil, 894, 967, 1009, 1165, 1372, 2015, 2031a, 2198, 3298
oil companies, 128, 142, 151, 1094
oil companies coverage, 4304
oil companies: Department of Interior alliansce, 3444
oil energy, 1987
oil industry, 44, 1113, 1962, 1966, 1968, 2016, 2019, 2025a, 2030, 3058, 3355, 3477, 3582, 4620
oil industry: press, 3801
oil industry: public relations, 1970, 2022
oil: solar industry, 1051
oil spill, 3444, 3901
Old Time Gospel Hour, 2955
Oldsmobile "Rocket," 1947
oligarchy, 30, 58, 75, 138, 159, 3404, 4106
oligopoly (see also: monopoly), 24, 44, 143, 479, 1808, 2317, 2427, 2661
Olin Foundation, 6
Olive Branch Awards, 4361
Olympic Boycott of 1980, 2289
Olympic boycotts, 701, 3284
Olympic Games, 2506, 2527
Olympic Games: Seoul, 2496
Olympics, 1980 Moscow, 2553
Olympics, 1984: television, 2350
Olympics, 532, 532, 717, 3666
Olympics: environment, 3695
OMB (Office of Management and Budget), 13, 78, 1195, 1200, 1329, 1495, 1576
ombudsmen, 612, 922, 932, 3397, 4262, 4277
ombudspersons (see also: newspaper, readers' advocate), 4659, 4706
On the Beach, 624, 762
On the Waterfront, 3065
On Thermonuclear War, 3960
Once Upon a Time in the West: film, 3091
One Day at a Time, 2444, 2534
One on One, 2611

on-site inspection agency, 1556
open access principle (see also: access), 2239
open admissions, 468
Open Channel, 628a, 2235
Open Studio Television (KQED, San Francisco), 3035
openness v. secrecy, 1542
Operation Broiler, 241
Operation CHAOS, 321
Operation Elephant Herd, 1585
Operation Just Cause (see also: imperialism, Panama), 2615
Operation Shamrock, 273
Operation Truth, 1274
Oppenheimer, Dr. Robert, 505
opportunity, 15
opposition, 4280
oppositional news (III.), 4216
oppression: film industry, 3046
optical fiber, 4194
optimism, 3860
Oraflex, 1202
Oraflex: advertising, 1882
Orangeburg Massacre, 405
organization man, 3860
organized crime, 104
ornamentation, 616
orthodoxy (see also: conformity, ideology), 83, 324, 464, 575
orthodoxy: television economics, 2703
orthodoxy: television news, 2739
Orwell, George: 1984, 41, 93, 594, 649, 676, 678, 1234, 1243a, 1662, 2495, 3188, 3193, 4591
Oscar, 2523
OSHA, 1177, 3400, 4590
OT, 3585
Otepka, Otto, 4667
other-directedness, 3860
Our Friend the ATOM, 624
Outreach Group (Reagan admin. propaganda), 64
overpopulation, 1110, 3504
Overseas Development Institute, 4065

ownership, 619, 642, 697, 699, 914, 1112, 1114, 1205, 1603, 2149, 2303, 4348
ownership: airwaves, 598
ownership: chains, 3393
ownership: gatekeepers, 1133
ownership: information, 1189
ownership: news, 3458
ownership: newspapers, 3381
ownership: television, 2165
Pacific Legal Foundation, 4104
Pacific News Service, 4564
Pacific Stars and Stripes, 3686
Pacifica Foundation, 1224, 2251, 2152, 2795, 3014, 3016, 3017, 4175, 4433, 4512, 4531
Pacifica Radio (see also: KPFA), 671, 2214, 4442, 4452
pacification, 1379, 3259
pacifism, 4683
pack journalism, 710, 808, 1074, 1403, 2617
packaged entertainment, 734
packaging (see also: images), 616, 713, 1682, 1710, 1925
packaging truth, 1898
Packard, Vance: The Hidden Persuaders, 1779, 1818
Pac-Man, 2477
PACs, 45, 1209, 2032
Paepcke, Walter, 1667
Paik, Nam June, 2224
Palestinian uprising, 1446
Palestinians, 487, 1026, 1215, 1285, 1390, 2608, 2699, 2700
Palestinians: NYT, 3698, 3711, 3715
Palestinians: PBS, 2990, 3010
Palestinians: television, 2876
Paley, William, 644, 2191, 2425, 2474, 2651, 2672, 2826, 2835, 2844
Palma, Brian De, 3182
Palmer raids, 390, 405
Palo Alto Times, 3344
Pan Am Flight 103, 1447
Panama, 1268, 1579, 2600
Panama: Bush, 3574
Panama Canal treaties, 71

Panama Canal Treaty 1978, 933
Panama invasion, 2615, 3495, 3496
Panama: television, 2563
Panopticon, 616
Pantheon, 3949, 3954, 3959
Paper, The (Metro State College), 4639
Paper Tiger Television, 2314, 4426, 4447, 4456, 4463, 4467, 4468, 4506, 4510, 4542, 4553, 4738
Papert, Koenig, Lois (ad agency), 1715
Paperwork Reduction Act (1980), 1200
Parade: advertising, 1962
parades, 603, 1192
paradigm (see also: ideology), 4236
paramilitary operations, 193, 204
Paramount, 1094
paranoia, 60, 363, 1083
paranoia: Sovietphobia, 406, 410a, 3080, 3855, 4057
paranoid style, 91
Parenthood, 3171
parity advertising, 1724
parity products, 1881, 1939
Parker, Richard, 2061
Parks, Larry, 3077
participatory democracy, 4193
participatory democracy: media literacy, 4184
passive public: television, 2818
passivity, 1707, 2310
passports, 352, 1634, 4227, 4251
Pastore, Senator John, 2148, 2994
patent medicine, 1844, 1876, 1891, 1846, 1872, 1951, 1952
patent medicine advertising, 1933
patent monopoly, 509, 2029
patriarchy (see also: feminism), 32, 114, 719, 762, 923a, 1120, 2472, 3089, 3178
patriarchy: films, 3156
patriarchy: law, 420, 426
patriarchy: science, 506
patriarchy: Vietnam War, 661
patriotism (see also: nationalism), 71, 361, 464, 479, 574, 778, 800, 801, 878, 913, 1077, 1179, 1375, 1532, 1574, 1575, 1708, 2491, 2522, 2743, 3103, 3259, 3557, 4732
patriotism: advertising, 1859, 1870, 1987
patriotism: films, 3159
patriotism: journalism, 4006
patriotism: press, 3430
patriotism: war films, 3098
pattern-setting, 548
Paul Jacobs & the Nuclear Gang, 1910, 3023, 4511
Pauling, Linus, 3647
pay television, 2835
payoffs, 180
"Pay-per Society," 78
PBA, 2751
PBS, 434, 633, 842, 940, 1023, 1215, 1224, 1603, 1969, 2124, 2156, 2191, 2193, 2276, 2325, 2350, 2691, 2742, 2916, 3018, 3030, 4175, 4418, 4533
PBS: corporate sponsors, 1903
PBS: corporations, 1149, 1910
PBS: documentary, 4547
PBS: Eyes on the Prize (civil rights movement), 4539
PBS: Frontline, 4547
PBS: funding, 2994, 3009, 3020, 3031, 4413
PBS: McNeil/Lehrer, 2988
PBS: Point of View, 4422
PBS: political interference, 4413
PBS: Richard Nixon, 2999
PBS: working class, 2982
PCBs, 3460
PD 59, 377, 1419, 1534
peace, 3267, 4592
Peace Corps advertising, 1757
"Peace Is Our Profession," 762
Peace March, 4593
peace movement, 3282, 4381
Peace Television, 4514
Peace Walk, 903

SUBJECT INDEX 775

"Peacekeeper," 1505
Peale, Norman Vincent, 3860
Peanuts, 3860, 4128
Pearson, Drew, 1546, 3348, 4562, 4600
pedagogy, 453, 552, 4284
Peers Report, 240, 4600
Pegler, Westbrook, 3456
Pekar, Harvey, 2495
Peltier, Leonard, 405
penny press, 3410
Pentagon, 3, 24, 72, 89, 101, 190, 226, 233, 240, 249, 255, 256, 266, 402, 464, 732, 803, 828, 982, 1139, 1254, 1310, 1409, 1487, 1493, 1516, 1517, 1523, 1550, 1574, 1622, 1657, 1981, 2191, 2231, 2273, 2303, 2314, 2690, 3188, 3278, 3315, 3887, 3960, 3990, 4015, 4281, 4282, 4289
Pentagon and the press, 634
Pentagon Annual Report: Soviet military, 4055, 4062
Pentagon Annual Reports, 4089
Pentagon: Aviation Week, 3882
Pentagon: Beacon Press, 4010
Pentagon: budget, 4076, 4077
Pentagon capitalism, 250
Pentagon: CBS, 2315, 2714
Pentagon censorship: secrecy, 1256
Pentagon censorship (see also: militarism), 1511, 3517
Pentagon: commercial film, 3136, 3157
Pentagon corps, 1344
Pentagon: covert ops, 789
Pentagon film: "The Armed Forces Hour," 2508
Pentagon films, 236
Pentagon fraud, 4340
Pentagon news corps, 4270
Pentagon: NYT, 3814
Pentagon Papers, 221, 273, 553, 553, 611, 780, 806, 872, 932, 943, 1078, 1228, 1237, 1257, 1320, 1338, 1557, 1564, 1586, 1632, 1651, 2795, 3419, 3422, 3430, 3693, 3765, 4126, 4252, 4279, 4289
Pentagon Papers: NYT, 3765
Pentagon Papers: television news, 2632
Pentagon press, 1269, 1504, 4347
Pentagon press corps, 1396, 1412, 4330
Pentagon propaganda, 231, 232, 236, 249, 251, 264, 266, 1354, 1426, 4330
Pentagon: public affairs, 2113a
Pentagon: public relations, 239, 2058, 2065, 2070, 2071, 2088, 2089, 2576, 2609, 2839
Pentagon reporting: AP, 4330
Pentagon: research, 510
Pentagon: right wing, 60
Pentagon: satellite, 2205
Pentagon: science, 502
Pentagon: secrecy, 1351, 1515
Pentagon: Soldier of Fortune, 3923
Pentagon: Soviet Military Power (1983), 4080, 4084, 4098
Pentagon: Soviet Union report, 4059
Pentagon: State Department, 258
Pentagon: television, 2332
Pentagon, USA, 2508
Pentagon: war films, 3119
Pentagon: waste, 235, 4340
Pentagonese, 2734
Pentagon: Terrorist Group Profiles, 1447
Pentagon-talk, 1505
Pentagon-university research complex, 3952
Penwalt Corp., 823
People for the American Way, 1540
People's Court, The, 2341, 2406
People's Dreadnought, 3324
People's Songs, Inc. 4737
People's Voice, The, 4666
Pepperidge Farm cookies, 547
Pepsi advertising, 1871
Pepsi-Cola, 112, 1705, 1966a
Peretz, Martin, 592
Perle, Richard, 2617

permissible lie, 1787
persecution, 352
Pershing II: newspapers, 3630
Pershing missile, 2104
Persian Gulf War (see also: Gulf War), 3496
Personal Best, 3089
personality system, 2367
persuasion strategies, 1332
Peru, 3331
pesticide advertising, 1822
pesticides, 1053, 1201, 4363, 4591, 4593
Peter, Paul, and Mary, 4170
Pettis, Charles, 4667
Pfizer, 112
P&G (conservative foundation), 3473
PG&E (Pacific Gas and Electric), 2710, 2830
phallocentrism: law, 418
pharmaceutical companies: corruption, 520
pharmaceutical industry, 527, 1928, 2026
Pharmaceutical Manufacturer's Association, 2029
Philadelphia Inquirer, 4600, 4620
Philadelphia Journalism Review, 4176, 4569
philanthropy (see also: charity), 120, 1984, 4032, 4037, 4056, 4070
Philip Morris Co., 1100a, 1116, 1193, 1692, 1779, 1868, 1874, 1894
Philip Morris: tobacco, 164
Philip Morris magazine, 3935
Philippines, 785, 868, 2614
Philippines: election, 2882
Phillips, Howard, 480
Phillips, Kevin, 733, 2617, 3900
Phillips, Lynn, 3185
Phoenix Program in Vietnam, 285, 321
phone chain, 4601
phone monitoring, 3350
phone tapping (bugging), 306
photo opportunities, 1627
photo-bias, 773
photographs: computer fabrication, 3203
photography, 616, 867, 1011, 4742
photography: spying, 283
photon, 3471
Phyllis, 2323
Physicians for Social Responsibility, 4079
Pickens, T. Boone, 3581
picket signs, 4249
Pickford, Mary, 3124
Pickup on South Street (1953), 3146
pigishness, 1664
Pike Report, 2826
Pincus, Walter, 1457, 1458, 3694
Pine Ridge Sioux reservation, 1288, 3958
Pinochet, General: NYT, 3739
Pinto, 1171
pipeline technology, 265
Pipes, Richard, 7
Pittston Coal Co., 1050a
Pittston strike, 849, 3374
plane shot down, 3314
planned obsolescence, 616
plant relocations, 128
Playboy, 588, 707, 1734
Playhouse 90, 2425
pleasure: consumerism, 3860
pleasure: soap opera, 2452
Pledge of Allegiance, 1232
PLO, 925, 1447, 2787, 3577
PLO: NYT, 3775, 3800
Plowshares 8, 4453
plumbers (see also: Watergate), 183
plumbing fixtures conspiracy, 44
pluralism, 21, 4284
pluralist television, 2235
plutocracy, 123
plutonium: nuclear industry, 2793
plutonium (see also: radiation), 1903, 3637, 4646
plutonium: NASA space shuttle, 1036, 1057, 2585
Podhoretz, Norman, 6
poetry: liberation, 4735
Pogo, 4128
Poindexter, John, 193, 1400, 1585
Point of Order, 4453
Point of View, 3537, 4567, 4569

SUBJECT INDEX 777

Poland, 1446, 2711
Poland: news agencies, 3247
Poland, Reverend Larry, 3016
Poletown, 128
police: detective fiction, 3991, 4002
police: fiction, 3991
police: harassment, 3421
police: posing as journalists, 1364
police riot, 3361
police state, 324, 405, 1618, 3464, 4281
police state: computers, 1613, 3200, 3218
police television: women, 2461
policemen posing as newsmen, 1533
policy planning organization (think tanks), 4050
policy process, 38
policymakers: press, 1458
policymaking, 4086
political action, 4597, 4597
Political Action Groups (PACs), 92
political advertising, 1524, 1594, 1692, 1786, 1896a, 2084
political art, 4146, 4359
political campaign advertising, 2058a
political campaigns, 31, 1245, 2072, 2376
political celebrities, 706
political commercials, 2376
political consultants, 2061
political conventions, 2191
political coverage, 566
political crime, 4276
political discourse, 558, 1654a
political dissent: suppression, 91
political heresy: free speech, 3430
political humor, 4233
political language, 169, 676
political media consultants, 2058a
political music, 4150
political parties, 85, 216, 328
political police, 329
political poster, 4744

political prisoners, 405, 4276, 4565
political programming, 3018
political publishing, 4702
political satire, 1909
political science, 704
Political Science Association, 1618
political spot ads, 2084
political surveillance, 328
political symbols, 4085
political television, 2084
political trials, 42, 199, 344, 405, 1634, 3992, 4380
political warfare (POLWAR), 3952
political writing, 1417
politics: media, 551a
politics: presidency, 554
politics: religion, 494
Polk, George, 824, 2750
Pollock, Jackson, 4130, 4131
polls, 31, 41, 93, 603, 610, 713, 731, 751, 993, 1115, 1397, 1442, 1552, 1621, 2061, 2079, 2114a, 2430, 3931
polls: Reagan, 2066
pollsters, 704
pollution, 57, 1110, 1134
Polonsky, Abraham, 3185
polyarchy, 30
polygraph, 1329
Pond's "Angel Face," 1905
Ponzi, 1880
poor, the, 795, 3562
pop music, 4149
pop music: business, 4152
pop music: radio, 4166
Pope, 842, 914, 1082
Pope assassination, 990
Pope assassination plot, 649, 809, 990, 1536
Pope, John Paul II, 1395
Pope John Paul II: Nicaragua, 3234
Pope (plot against), 1536
Popeo, Daniel (head of ALF), 2214
popular culture, 591, 701, 713, 721, 748, 749, 3292, 4373
popular culture: education, 1163
popular fiction: sexism, 3967

popular leadership: president, 4124
popular music, 605, 4155, 4284
popular music: audiences, 4160
popular music: industrialization, 4160
Popular Science, 1821
popular television and film, 3061
populism, 2675
pornography, 612, 721, 1525. 1921, 4100, 4231, 4686
pornography: advertising, 1768
Porter, Edwin, 3131
Portugal, 3313, 3768
Posada, Luis, 1447
Posados de Puerto Rico v. Tourism Company, 1193
positive thinking, 1786, 3860
Posner, Vladimir, 2843
possessive individualism v. community, 4221
postal censorship, 4213
postal rates, 4348
Postal Service, 1457, 1458
posters, 4744
Postman, Neil, 663
postmodernism: MTV, 4157
post-nuclear surveillance, 4089
Potash, Irving, 3992
Potsdam, 336
P.O.V.: PBS documentary, 2971
poverty (see also: the poor), 15, 53, 127 , 192, 431, 456, 479, 796, 829, 848, 939, 1128, 1355, 3273, 4728
poverty: drugs, 936
poverty: Johnson's war, 1661
poverty: law, 419
poverty: television, 2426
Powell, Dick, 4747
Powell, Jody, 1230, 1597
power, 2433
power: abuse, 288
power: accountability, 4317
power: centralized in presidency, 4124
power: concentration, 30

power elite, 2, 23, 24, 25, 26, 28, 30, 33, 55, 58, 75, 82, 86, 89, 350, 433, 699, 1990, 4324
power elite and CIA, 21
power elite; domestic policy, 21
power elite; foreign policy, 21
power elite: law, 423
power elite: money, 100
power elite: newspapers, 3384
power elite: sports, 535
power: genre films, 3104
power in media, 759
power: knowledge, 55
power: language, 1624
power structure, 22
power structure analysis, 3616
power: success dream, 3860
Powers That Be (documentary), 2830
POWs (WWII): NYT, 3737
Practices, 4075
Praise the Lord (PTL) Club, 2492
Pravda, 3666, 4617
prayer in schools, 482
precision journalism, 4212, 4316
premiums ad techniques, 2040
prescriptions, 517, 527
presidency, 31, 170, 190, 200, 202, 205, 309, 553, 605, 712, 1245, 1322a, 1324, 1358, 1371, 1422, 1436, 1513, 1519, 1542, 1572, 1579, 1627, 1659, 2289, 3564
presidency: advertising, 1424
presidency: anticommunism, 366
presidency: biographies, 2095a, 4017, 4019
presidency: broadcasting, 2994
presidency: campaigning, 602, 771, 861, 929, 970, 1010, 1362, 1363, 1385, 1477, 1976, 1988, 2082, 2088a, 2099, 2112, 2114a, 2557, 2635, 2790, 2823, 2838
presidency: campaigning (corporations), 2105

SUBJECT INDEX

presidency: campaigning (network news), 2799
presidency: campaigning (television), 2590, 2591, 2592, 2669, 2744, 2829, 2849
presidency: commission, 1454
presidency: Congress, 1330, 1331, 1424
presidency: conventions, 2645
presidency: co-option of newsmen, 1318
presidency: corporations, 59
presidency: debates, 2090, 2114, 2702, 2719
presidency: diplomacy, 2553
presidency: documents, 175
presidency: elections, 870, 958, 1035, 1041, 1245, 1537, 2087, 2738
presidency: executive privilege, 205
presidency: images, 1384, 2681
presidency: libraries (Nixon), 4023
presidency: lying, 190, 1340, 3342
presidency: manipulation of news, 2635
presidency: mass media, 1331
presidency: metaphors, 1331
presidency: network news, 2681, 2707
presidency: news, 1370
presidency: news censorship, 1227
presidency: news conferences, 2635
presidency: news management, 190, 1227, 1526, 1619
presidency: newspapers, 3479
presidency: politics, 554
presidency: power, 174, 188, 320, 410, 1331, 1625, 2816, 4124, 4180
presidency: press, 1294a, 1318, 1324, 1330, 1331, 1506, 1596, 1597, 1623, 1627, 1652, 1653, 2715, 3508
presidency: propaganda, 309, 1623
presidency: public relations, 1361, 1370, 1424, 1597, 1625

presidency: rhetoric, 1331, 1332, 1384, 1629, 1654a
presidency: ruling class, 28
presidency: secrecy, 190, 202, 3263
presidency: speeches, 1424
presidency: staff, 1331
presidency: television, 1331, 2193, 2285, 2383, 2557, 2648, 2688, 2698, 2743, 2766, 2818, 2893
presidency: television news, 2107a, 2642, 2678
Presidential Directive #59 (see also: PD #59), 348, 709
presidents, 704, 1049, 1524
President's Science Advisory Committee, 503
press, 83, 1224, 1362, 1663, 553, 553, 744, 777, 1623, 4314, 4587, 4667, 4695
press: agents, 704
press: First Amendment access, 612
press: associations, 611, 4289
press: Britain, 3507
press: censorship, 3505
press: censorship (Grenada invasion), 1418
press: concentration, 747
press: conference, 196, 1255, 1319a, 1329a, 1524, 2068
press: conference: Ronald Reagan, 2111a, 2882
press: councils, 612, 932, 943, 2126, 4197, 4220, 4239, 4289, 4587
press: coverage: Chernobyl, 3578
press: criticism, 4587
press: fair trial, 2170
Press, Four Theories, 4669
press: freedom, 1121, 1169, 1364, 1413, 3369, 3422, 3477
press: freedom: organizations, 4288
press: freedom, (see also: free press), 920
press: government manipulation, 219
press: ideological state apparatus, 1238
press: intimidation, 1224
press: law, 4611

press: manipulation, 660
press: monitors, 4335
press: passes, 3463
press: privilege, 1364
press: release, 1202, 1234, 2026
press: release: corporations, 1919
press: release: news, 3516, 3519, 3841
press: release: real estate, 3469
press: responsibility, 4187, 4203
press: secretaries, 1325, 1639
press: self-censorship, 1426
press: sexism, 669
press: society, 562
press: subpoenas, 1364
press: status quo, 3361
press: suppression, 863
press: watchdog, 932
press-government alliance, 1648
press-government interaction, 1458
Press-Telegram, 4663
pressure groups, 2480
Price of Liberty, The film, 2744
price-fixing, 44
Priest, Roger Lee, 4565
prime time, 2317, 2487, 2488
prime time: access rule, 2125
prime time: Blacks, 2496
Prime Time Live, 2636
prime time: reporting, 2806
prime time: television, 2305, 2341, 2163, 2480, 2539, 2545
prime time: television (women), 2504
princess image (advertising), 1795
print media: access, 4264
print media: CIA, 1521
print media v. television, 639
printing press, 3301
prior restraint, 623a, 1320, 1564, 1565, 1651, 1656, 1965, 3408, 3615, 3693, 3848, 3867, 3868, 3880,
3894, 3924, 4213, 4228, 4252, 4366, 4377, 4622, 4696
prior restraint: CIA, 4001
prior restraint: Frank Snepp, 3947, 3972
prior restraint: The Progressive, 3910, 3914, 3945
prison newspapers, 3386
prison newspapers: First Amendment, 3482
Prisoner, 2330
prisons, 1061, 3595, 4028
privacy, 81, 289, 306, 714, 2254, 3188, 3200, 3202, 3211, 3667, 4213, 4366, 4371
Privacy Act, 4372
privacy: government employees, 4219
privacy: libraries, 3948
privacy (see also: computers), 3209
private censorship, 4181
private centers of power, 4219
private domain power, 2367
private schools, 26
privatization of information, 1200, 1329
privilege, 1145
procedural democracy, 59
Procter & Gamble, 1094, 1692, 1939, 2450, 2496
Proctor & Gamble advertising, 1779
Proctor & Gamble: Charmin, 1857
Proctor and Gamble Co., 1692
producers: television, 2581
product ads: feature films, 4592
product advertising, 1688, 1740
product fixing, 44
professionalism (see also: vocationalism), 963, 1067, 1190, 2270
professionalization, 528
Profile on Communism (NBC news), 2744
profit, 1190, 2191, 2753
profit: children's television, 2921
profit: films, 3110
profit motive, 1169, 2182, 2441

profit motive: television, 2455, 2835
profit: news agencies, 3255
profit: newspapers, 3455
profit system, 517, 1736
profit: television, 2578, 2863
profit: television news, 2655, 2846
profit v. truth, 1143
profit:news, 4267
programming, 2185, 2455, 3952
programming patterns, 548
progress, 2350
progressive law, 420
Progressive, The, 3615, 3848, 3867, 3868, 3880, 3894, 3907, 3924
Progressive, The: censorship, 3907, 3910, 3914
Progressive, The: FBI, 3895, 3920
Progressive, The: hydrogen bomb, 4279
Project Camelot, 2231
Project Censored, 699, 865, 923, 967, 968, 1022, 1051, 1052, 1053, 1054, 1055, 1056, 1057, 1058, 1059, 1060, 1242a, 2585, 2734
Project Democracy, 195, 1217
Project Galileo, 2585
Project Resistance, 1463
Project Rulison (AEC), 3637
Project Sandwedge, 180
pronouns, 4089
propaganda, 249, 343, 548, 548, 600, 603, 616, 664, 678, 694, 713, 1592, 1657, 1729, 2000, 2103, 4188, 4287
propaganda analysis, 4339
propaganda devices, 1217a, 3768, 3891
Propaganda Institute, 4398
propaganda machine, 259
"propaganda model," 585
propaganda model, 634, 912, 914, 915
propaganda models: (German, Soviet, Chinese, Fundamentalist), 481
propaganda of consumption, 1725
propaganda operation, 1401
propaganda system, 173, 770a, 1281
Proposition 65 (California), 4395
protest, 4276, 4299
protest demonstrations: television, 4438
protest journalism, 3333
protest movements: 1960s, 611
protest movements, 632, 769, 1182, 1360
protest: Vietnam War, 3662
Protestantism, 1760
PSAs, 1869, 2010
pseudo-choice, 1924
pseudo-debate: MacNeil/Lehrer News Hour, 2988
pseudo-events, 1682
pseudo-individualization, 4154
pseudo-poetry: advertising, 1931
psychiatry, 3178
psychiatry drugs, 519
psychoanalytic criticism, 559
psychographics, 707, 1738, 1779, 1893, 1894, 1895
psychological warfare, 1357a
psychological warfare (v. Nicaragua), 1500
Psychology Today, 1945
psychsell, 1779
PSYOP (psychological operations), 3952
PSYOP-POLWAR (psychological and political warfare), 3952
PTL Club, 92, 2952, 2955, 2960
public access, 2172, 4501
public access: cable television, 4555
public access: telecommunications, 4498
public access: television, 4401, 4419, 4488
public access television, 4542, 4553
public address: style vs. substance, 616
public affairs, 2062
public affairs coverage, 3363

Public Affairs Information Service, 3465
public affairs: PBS, 2973
public affairs programming, 2303
public affairs programming: television, 2788
public broadcasting, 609, 2979, 4418
Public Broadcasting Act of 1967, 2994
Public Broadcasting Act of 1988, The, 2967
public broadcasting: bibliography, 2962
public broadcasting: Britain, 3003
public broadcasting: Corporation for Public Broadcasting, 2974
public broadcasting: diversity, 2239
public broadcasting: funding, 2651
public broadcasting (see also: PBS), 2185, 2197
Public Broadcasting Service (PBS), 2979
Public Citizen, 4346
Public Citizen, 4675
Public Citizen's Health Research Group, 2026
Public Enemy (rap music group), 4729
public health, 528
public ignorance (nuclear), 1552
public information (euphemism for progaganda), 3166
public interest, 2160, 4265, 4324, 4383, 4587
public interest: cable television, 2892, 2894, 2896, 2898
public interest groups, 4186, 4206
public interest law firms, 419
public interest news, 4267
public interest: press, 4611
public interest programming, 2173
public interest: television, 4412
Public Opinion, 3931

public opinion, 603, 713
public opinion poll, 1519, 1826
public passivity, 4665
public protest, 2192
public relations, 43, 751, 756, 759, 1088, 1108, 1319a, 1410, 1519, 1552, 1680, 1710, 1862, 1912, 1978, 1984, 2011, 2111a, 2014, 2018, 3411, 4209, 4363
public relations ads, 1675
public relations: dictators (see also: Argentina), 2094
public relations: Edward Bernays, 1758
public relations: exploitation, 1799
public relations: FBI, 2113
public relations: foreign, 1017
public relations: GE, 1105
public relations industry, 1690
Public Relations Journal, 2028
public relations: military, 2839
public relations: nuclearism, 653
public relations: Pentagon, 2113a
public relations: politics, 2060, 2115a
public relations (see also: corporations), 1152, 1677, 1678, 1693, 1703
public relations: television, 2430
public relations: Third World, 1954
public schools, 456
public service, 4296
public service ads, 1675
public service ads (PSAs)(see also: Ad Council), 1956, 2012a, 4399
public service announcements: religion, 2946
public service: broadcasting, 4516, 4445
public service: television, 4431
public service time, 4523
public speaking, 4249

public sphere theory, 4744
public televison: audience, 3008
public teleivsion: programming, 2970
public television: financing, 3011
public television: public interest, 3011
public television (see also: PBS), 2163, 2235, 2568, 4289, 4409, 4464
public television: social action, 4438
public v. power, 4489
publications, 259
publicity, 1682
Public/Private Sector Report (1982), 1200
public's right to know, 239
publisher control, 3597
publishers: books, 4024
publishing: books (commercial), 4003
publishing: books (conformity), 4008
publishing companies, 2326
Puerto Rico, 285, 2786
Puerto Rico: cultural imperialism, 2438
puffery (see II.B.1, II.B.2), 1688, 1792, 1827a, 1948, 3781, 3841
Pugh, Robert (Minutemen), 4092
pulic relations, 1319a
Pulitzer, 1174
Pulitzer Prize, 3480, 4258
Punta del Este, 3771
purges, 352, 464
Putnam, 4021
Pyle, Christopher, 4667
pyramid scheme, 1880
Qaddafi, 1296, 1306, 1447, 3547
quackery (see II.B.2), 1794, 1932
quality of programming (declining), 2124
Quarterly Review of Doublespeak, 671
Quayle, Senator Dan, 4005
QUBE: capitalism, 2895
QUBE: interactive cable television, 4463, 4552
Quinn, Tom, 405

Quiz Kids, The, 2492
quiz scandals, 2441, 2451
quiz show scandals, 2124
quiz shows, 2651
R. J. Reynolds, Inc.: tobacco, 164
Rabble-Rousers Index, 321
race, 3152
race: popular culture, 721
race riot, Chicago, 1781
race riots, 3418
race riots: television news, 2630
racism, 1, 54, 91, 122, 443, 479, 482, 566, 566, 604, 605, 624, 640, 651, 657, 662, 671, 698, 719, 728, 736,. 753, 765, 820, 854, 860, 946, 1047, 1081, 1110, 1288, 1368, 1444, 1481, 1837a, 2283, 2316, 2350, 2433, 2488, 2496, 2664, 2792, 2871, 3056, 3063, 3090, 3293, 3361, 3367, 3398, 3418, 3505, 3512, 3535, 3541, 3641, 3672, 3684, 3760, 3782, 3796, 3957, 3968, 4060, 4083, 4157, 4266, 4272, 4291, 4434, 4476, 4495, 4537, 4590, 4653, 4728
racism: advertising, 1698, 1750
racism: book publishing, 4025
racism: Bush administration, 1582
racism: Chicago, 4616
racism: Cleveland, 3544
racism: Eastern Europe, 3657
racism: film censorship, 3097
racism: films, 3156, 3160, 4416
racism: Hollywood, 3151
racism: law, 420
racism: media, 864
racism: Nat. Adv. Comm. on Civil Disturbance Report (1968), 3857
racism: Native Americans, 3958
racism: Negro newspapers (see also: civil rights), 3459
racism: news anchors, 2649

racism: newspapers, 3414
racism: NYT, 3796, 3811
racism: PBS, 2998, 3015
racism: radio, 3013
racism: sports, 541
racism: television, 2448,
2482, 2485, 2539, 2752, 2864
racism: television news,
2630, 2632, 2670
racism: The Cosby Show, 4435
racism: Time, 3871
racism: Vietnam War (NYT),
3735
racism: WWII films, 3100,
3161
radiation, 101, 102, 653,
762, 884, 893, 935, 1057,
1467, 1910, 2710, 3406,
3637, 3910, 4499, 4511,
4592, 4646
radiation: nuclear test,
1335
radical arts, 4609
radical journalism, 3625
radical literature, 4609
radical media, 4215
radical music, 4725
radical periodicals, 4614
radical press, 779, 4566,
4596, 4609
radical press criticism,
4209
radical propaganda, 4730
radicalism, 324
radicals, 3430
radicals: repression, 3074
radio, 352, 572, 572, 603,
712, 744, 745, 746, 759,
765, 1121, 1135a, 1224,
1781, 2142, 2191, 2258,
2260, 2265, 2296, 2433,
3022, 3432, 4249, 4329, 4470
radio: access, 2235, 4409
radio: CBS, 2425
radio: censorship, 2271
Radio Columbia, 1500
radio: commercialization,
2768
radio: corporate control,
2117
radio: deregulation, 2169
radio: diversity, 2169
radio: fine arts, 2244
Radio Free Europe, 1514,
1581

Radio Havana Cuba, 1347a,
1348, 1348a, 1349
radio: history, 2188
Radio Impacto, 1500
radio: imperialism, 2210
Radio Liberation, 1500
Radio Liberty, 1514, 1581
Radio Lincoln, 1347a
radio: listener supported,
4531
radio: listener supported
(censorship), 3014
Radio Marti, 1217, 1347a,
1348a, 1349, 1357a
radio: monopoly, 1094, 2202
radio: music, 4166
radio: news, 559, 588, 2140,
2195, 2844
radio news: Marxist
analysis, 559
radio: NPR, 3027
radio: Orson Welles, 2245
radio: Pacifica (listener
supported), 4442, 4452,
4512, 4531
radio: profits, 2169
radio: propaganda, 1513a
radio: public interest, 2259
radio: religion, 481
Radio Romero, 1348a
radio: shortwave, 1347a,
4428
radio: spectrum, 2159
Radio Swan, 1347a, 1349
radio: underground racism,
3013
radio v. television and
print media, 639
radio: women & talk shows,
695a
radio: women, talk shows,
695a
radio: WWII, 3161
radioactive waste, 1052,
1060, 4627
radioactivity (see also:
radiation), 101, 1036, 1459,
2724, 3399, 4244, 4747
radon gas (radioactive),
101, 3637
Radosh, Ronald, 1277
Raging Bull, 3173
Raiders of the Lost Ark,
3169
rain forests: magazines,
3835

SUBJECT INDEX   785

Rambo, 2548, 3122, 3152
Rambo: First Blood, Part II, 3103
Ramparts, 1463, 3320, 3888
Ramparts We Watch, The film, 2744
"Rancheros Vistadores": elite club, 19
Rand, Ayn, 3968
RAND Corporation, 255, 377, 1557, 3960, 4086, 4101, 4107, 4108
Rand Corporation: Air Battle Model (& Sovietphobia), 255
Rand Corporation: Black Rock (wargame), 255
Rand Corporation: Carte Blanche (wargame), 255
Randall, Margaret, 405, 3962, 4183
Randolph, John, 405
Random House, 4021
Rank, Hugh, 4398, 4398
Rankin, Jeannette, 4410
rape, 695a
Rat, 4664
Rat Patrol, The, 2744
Rather, Dan, 1401, 2593, 2663, 2686, 2706, 2753, 2800
ratings, 2240, 2260, 2561, 2621, 2779, 2791, 2846
ratings: television news, 2628, 2654
rationality: nuclear weapons, 4045
Ray, Dixie Lee, 52
Raymond, Jill, 405
Raymond, Walter, 1218, 1431, 1432
RCA, 273, 434, 1094, 1159, 1175, 1407, 2142, 2202, 2203, 2303, 2380, 2423, 2439, 2510, 2743
RCA: FM, 2835
Roman Catholic Church: newspaper, 3680
reader-response, 2279
Reader's Digest, 679, 730, 828, 842, 914, 1154, 1178, 1536, 1787, 1827a, 1945, 2031, 3292, 3821, 3824, 3860, 3861, 3862, 3869, 3877, 3898, 3905, 3929 3939
readers: newspapers, 3362
reading by leaders, 1073

Reagan, Ronald, 7, 28, 30, 31, 33, 36, 48, 62, 84, 105, 125, 170, 176, 193, 211, 213, 233, 235, 348, 358, 377, 386, 414, 480, 481, 487, 490, 584, 624, 649, 719, 741, 763, 787, 808, 833, 840, 867a, 868, 929, 1222, 1229, 1243a, 1268a, 1270, 1275, 1277, 1280, 1294a, 1296, 1298, 1304, 1305, 1316, 1322a, 1325, 1325a, 1331, 1332, 1357, 1357a, 1360, 1367, 1368, 1377, 1381, 1384, 1385, 1386, 1397, 1418, 1428, 1444, 1446, 1458, 1473, 1475, 1479, 1486, 1487, 1494, 1501, 1513, 1520, 1530, 1536, 1554, 1591, 1593, 1623, 1624, 1625, 1627, 1629, 1644, 1645,, 1649, 1662, 1692, 1826, 1927, 1977, 2007, 2067, 2076a, 2080, 2099, 2107a, 2111a, 2316, 2341, 2480, 2526, 2528, 2635, 2646, 2695, 2711, 2773, 2952, 2956, 3076, 3080, 3147, 3182, 3188, 3276, 3407, 3658, 3873, 3898, 4005, 4028, 4031, 4035, 4058, 4063, 4068, 4074, 4082, 4085, 4089, 4136, 4359, 4371, 4388, 4391, 4508
Reagan, Ronald: Tom Clancy, 1544
Reagan administration, 13, 64, 203, 273, 314, 346, 500, 631, 914, 1195, 1217, 1218, 1231, 1242a, 1248, 1254, 1302, 1329, 1336, 1398, 1401, 1492, 1578, 1585, 4339, 4541
Reagan administration: Catholic Church, 483
Reagan administration: censorship, 1450
Reagan administration: engineering of consent, 616
Reagan administration: information policies, 78
Reagan administration: Iran-Contra, 3334
Reagan administration: lies, 1300

Reagan administration: nuclear war, 208
Reagan administration: PBS, 2967, 2968, 2985, 2999
Reagan administration: political imperialism, 2815
Reagan administration: right wing, 60
Reagan administration: second term, 195
Reagan administration: secrecy, 1450, 1523
Reagan administration: television, 2204, 2675, 2823
Reagan: anticommunism, 393
Reagan: arms control, 844
Reagan: big business, 28
Reagan: broadcasting, 1106
Reagan: budget, 983, 4072
Reagan: censorship, 1053, 1462, 1529, 1538, 1539, 1540, 1562, 1587, 2843
Reagan: Central America, 1283
Reagan: Christian right wing, 493, 495
Reagan: corporations, 495
Reagan: covert ops, 789
Reagan: deceit, 845, 968
Reagan: deregulation, 2116
Reagan Doctrine, 7
Reagan era, 116, 1295
Reagan era: films, 3171
Reagan: executive orders, 4102
Reagan: FCC, 2132
Reagan: Gahdafi, 3547
Reagan: government regulation, 3745
Reagan: imperialism, 197
Reagan: Iran hostages, 1022
Reagan: lies, 1399, 1493a, 1568, 1571, 2840, 2882
Reagan: McCarthyism, 28
Reagan: militarism, 1577
Reagan: military budget, 982
Reagan, Nancy, 741, 1578
Reagan: Nicaragua, 1497, 1500, 2840, 3570
Reagan: nuclear war, 28
Reagan: nuclear weapons, 268
Reagan: polling, 2066
Reagan: press, 611, 1312
Reagan: press conferences, 2882

Reagan press control, 1646
Reagan: propaganda, 1626
Reagan: public relations, 1434
Reagan: reporting of, 1342
Reagan: rhetoric, 4124
Reagan, Ronald, 480, 481, 490, 741, 1222, 1360
Reagan, Ronald: engineering of consent, 616
Reagan, Ronald: Iran-Contra, 3334
Reagan, Ronald: lies, 2840, 2882
Reagan, Ronald: PBS, 2967, 2968, 2985, 2999
Reagan, Ronald: television, 2675, 2823
Reagan, Ronald: Tom Clancy, 1544
Reagan: secrecy, 28, 967, 1058, 1243, 1418, 1538, 1540, 1549, 3079
Reagan: speeches, 1243, 1244, 2701
Reagan: Star Wars speech, 624
Reagan: Statue of Liberty, 1638
Reagan: television, 2204
Reagan: think tanks, 4052
Reagan v. arms agreements, 62
Reagan v. checks and balances, 62
Reagan v. Constitution, 62
Reagan v. due process, 62
Reagan v. press, 1049
Reagan: West Point speech, 638
Reagan-Anderson debate, 2076a
Reagan-Bush: advocacy ads, 2091
Reagan-Bush news, 1061
Reagan-Carter debate, 2076a, 2702
Reagan-Gorbachev Summit, 1321
Reaganism, 100, 654, 1295, 1723, 2675, 4027
Reaganism: films, 3067
Reaganite journalists, 1518
Reagan-Mondale debates, 2702
Reaganomics, 109, 852, 1158, 1381

SUBJECT INDEX

Reagan's 1982 strategies, 1330
Reagan's Executive Order (EO) 12333, 302
Reagan's officials, 171
Reagan's Political Information System, 1519
Reagan's weekly radio broadcasts, 1599
real estate advertising, 1914
real estate: news, 3469, 3472
real estate news: newspapers, 3420
reality, 706, 881
reality: avoidance, 4045
reality: construction, 727
reality: distortion, 2342
reality effect, 646
reality: television news, 2771
Reasoner, Harry, 2746
rebellion, 4276
Rebozo, Bebe, 104
reclassification of information, 1329
Record, Jeffrey, 4667
record (music) industry, 210, 759, 4167
recruiting, 2098
recruiting ads, 2085a
recruiting: military, 2107, 2108, 2111
recruitment, 1482
recycling, 1959
red baiting, 990, 1500, 1241
Red Brigades, 2786
Red Channels, 747, 1241, 2207, 2212, 2242, 2743, 2835
Red Dawn, 3079
Red Lion Broadcasting Company v. FCC, 943, 2126, 2148, 2254, 2263, 2795, 2836, 4181, 4213, 4289
Red Scare, 324, 350, 374, 390, 406, 585
Red Squads, 284, 1226, 3576
Red Storm Rising, 1544, 4005
red-baiting, 1241
redlining, 128
Reds (film), 3173
Reedy, George, 1597
Reeves, Rossen, 1701, 1715
referendum, 4688

referendum: contests and corporations, 2002
referendums v. Vietnam War, 3278
reform groups, 4383
reform organizations, 4206, 4383
refugees, 922a
regulation, 128, 137, 415, 619, 1928, 2156, 2223, 4556, 4568, 4575, 4694, 4734
regulation: advertising, 1841, 1869a, 2042
regulation: broadcasting (see II.C.1.a.), 2125, 2440
regulation: media, 4342
regulation: television, 2380, 2668
regulation: television ads & children, 2056
regulative censorship, 55
regulatory agencies, 24
regulatory-industrial complex, 419
Rehnquist, William, 430
Reich, Otto, 1432
Reid, Brown, 3612
Reid, Ogden, 3612
religion (I.B.3.,II.C.1.c.), 83, 84, 89, 1062, 2221, 2348, 2943, 4284
religion: broadcasting, 2199
religion: censorship, 3116
religion: commercial television, 2946
religion: politics, 706
religion: militarism, 4112
religion: nationalism, 80
religion: news, 2838, 3472
religion: political parties, 4085
religion: politics, 494
religion: Pope, 1082
religion: sports, 540
religion: television, 2948
religion: television and class, 2961
religious censorship, 3135
religious freedom, 4276
religious fundamentalism, 481, 3684
religious lobbying, 492
religious magazines, 612
religious PACs, 492
religious press, 3583, 3680

religious right, 62, 709, 880, 2959
Religious Roundtable, 492
Rembrandt/Rothmans group, 1874
Remington, William, 3676
reportage art, 2682
Reporter, The, 3870, 3896
reporters, 1067, 4309
Reporters Committee for Freedom of the Press, 1540, 4288
reporters: confidential sources, 4242
reporters: news processors, 2684
reporter's privilege, 3317
reporters: source protection, 4336
reporting dissent, 3361
reporting revolution, 1182
reporting the bomb, 1465
repression, 12, 13, 18, 42, 48, 56, 64, 66, 69, 73, 74, 86, 91, 181, 199, 209, 284, 303, 344, 352, 382, 394, 405, 408, 451, 464, 719, 1618, 2242, 2251, 2337, 2338, 2743, 3063, 3324, 3463, 3851, 3853, 4272
repression: academic, 401
repression: FBI, 297
repression: Sovietphobia, 380
repression: universities, 404
repressive pedagogy, 443
represson, 18
Republican bias: television news, 2842
Republican National Committee, 1441
Republican Party, 7, 58, 104, 216, 360, 482, 4085
Republican Party: ABC News, 2637
Republican Party: anticommunism, 361
Republican Party: Christian Right, 490
Republican Party: McCathy, 398, 1241
Republican Party: religion, 480, 481
Republican Platform: militarism, 4118

research, 444, 464
research development, 1451
research: government, 458
Reserve Officer Training Corps (ROTC), 227
"responsible free press," 1414
restaurants, 1893
Reston, James, 1224, 1276, 1546, 3757
restriction, 3430
Retin-A, 1201
Reuters news agency, 3250, 4298
Reuther, Walter, 3493
Review of Southern California Journalism, 4569
Revlon, 559
revolution, 412
revolution: advertising, 1757
revolution (opposition to), 54
revolving door, 249, 1517, 2128, 2744
revolving door: Pentagon, 732, 1344
Revson, Charles, 1820
Reykjavik summit: NYT, 3789
Reynolds Aluminum, 1966, 3821
Reynolds, R.J., 1874, 1949
rhetoric, 660, 1319a
rhetorical presidency, 1331
Rhoda, 2291, 2323, 2474
Rhodesian insurrection, 3641
Rhodesia: imperialism: news agencies, 3225
Rich, Marc, 119
rich v. poor (see also: poverty), 1845, 2320
Richardson Foundation, 4103
Richter, Robert (Hungry for Profit), 2973
Richter, Robert (Pesticides and Pills), 2967
RICO, 3082, 3470
Ridenour, Ron, 3677, 4682
Riding, Alan, 1473
Right Stuff, The, 3072
right to know, 84, 1377, 3408, 4218, 4252, 4337
right to lie, 1282
right to publish, 1598, 3408
right to travel (see also: visa), 1612

SUBJECT INDEX

right turn, 1357
right wing 1960s, 37
right wing, 4, 7, 13, 18, , 28, 31, 34, 49, 62, 73, 84, 92, 99, 193, 402, 487, 604, 810, 880, 927, 937, 990, 1049, 1083, 1099, 1242, 1337, 2091, 2101, 2214, 2361, 2480, 2665, 2690, 2956, 3271, 3327, 3521, 3886, 3898, 3931, 3968, 3985, 4090, 4092, 4105, 4063, 4073, 4592
right wing: bigotry, 3080
right wing: campus press, 2690, 3473
right wing: censorship (radio), 3016
right wing: Christian, 395, 493
right wing: conspiracy, 4058
right wing: Info Digest, 3865
right wing: media, 573
right wing: novels, 3968
right wing: publications, 3819, 4009
right wing: religion, 2208, 2987, 3892
right wing: students, 3655
right wing: TV, 2385
right wing: women, 61
rights: labor, 4276
rights: women, 4276
rightward shift, 724
right-wing conspiracy, 4058
right-wing: Info Digest, 3865
right-wing novels, 3968
right-wing publications, 3819, 4009
right-wing religion, 3892
right-wing students, 3655
Rintels, David W., 2282, 2474
riots, 1334, 3418
risk, 862
Risky Business, 3152
Rist Amendment, 2342
Ritt, Martin, 3145
ritual analysis, 718
rituals: mass media, 579
rituals: status quo, 579
Rivera, Geraldo, 2796
RJR Nabisco, 116
RKO pictures, 4747

robber barons, 3928
robber barons: education, 471
Roberts, Kokie, 3024
Roberts, Oral, 2945, 2952, 2953
Robertson, Dr. Marion "Pat," 480, 481, 487, 488, 2208, 2945, 2952, 2959
Robertson, Pat: 700 Club, 2228
Robeson, Paul, 1634, 2639
Robinson, James (NBC), 2755
Robinson, Pat, 2492
Robinson vs. Cahill, 477
Rochemont, Louis de, 3095
Rochemont, Richard de, 3095
rock and roll, 70, 681, 696, 4151, 4154, 4160, 4161, 4731
rock festivals, 681
rock music, 635, 675, 697, 701, 1687, 2466, 2470, 4148, 4153, 4157, 4162, 4593
rock music: censorship, 4592
rock music: MTV, 2500
rock music: television, 2486
rock stars: consumerism, 2466
rock video, 2501, 4161
rock video: women, 2461
Rockefeller Commission, 288
Rockefeller, David, 30, 3838
Rockefeller, David: Chase Manhattan Bank, 2018
Rockefeller Foundation, 148, 4032, 4037, 4056
Rockefeller interests, 3757
Rockefeller, John D., 2202
Rockefeller, John D.: education, 471
Rockefeller, Nelson, 179, 2067
Rockefeller, Nelson: campaign, 2099
Rockne, Knute, 3147
Rockwell Corporation, 1728
Rockwell International, 1953, 2102
Rocky and His Friends, 2508
Rocky IV, 3106
Rocky Mountain Arsenal, 3637
Rocky Mountain News, 3549
Rocky Mountain News: investigative reporting, 4573
Roederer, Richard, 4745

Rogers, Buck, 4128
Rogers Commission, 4036
Rogers, William P., 183
rollback, 7
rollback (see also: imperialism, Sovietphobia), 12
Rolling Stone Magazine, 1821, 3872
Rolling Thunder, 3076
Rollnet: global rollback network, 7
Rolodex, Golden, 2617
Roman Catholics, 480, 489
romance novels, 671
romance novels: WWII, 3833
Romancing the Stone, 3122, 3169
romantic confession magazines (WWII), 3833
Romero, Archbishop, Oscar, 914, 1254
Romero, George, 3182
Ronstadt, 4161
Rookies, The, 2531
Roosevelt, Franklin D., 807, 1601, 1652
Roosevelt administration: holocaust, 3312
Roosevelt, F.D.: civil liberties, 4371
Roosevelt, F.D.: news management, 3485
Roosevelt, Theodore, 1526
Roots, 697
Roquemore, Reverend Dallas, 4092
Rose, Don, 2061
Roseanne, 2465
Rosenberg, Mark, 3185
Rosenbergs, 721, 4575
Rosenthal, A.M., 1283, 1447, 3717, 3738, 3798, 3807
Rosenthal, A.M.: NYT, 3738, 3762
Rosenthal, Benjamin, 244
Rosenzweig, Harry, 4715
Roshwald, Mordecai (Level 7), 624
Rosie the Riveter, 655, 3833
Ross, Edward, 471
Rostow, Walter W., 232, 1228, 2744, 3396
ROTC, 259, 262
rote learning, 443
Rothko, Mark, 4131

Rothman, Stanley, 1071
"Roundup:" elite club, 19
routinization: news, 3364
Rowan, Carl, 1592, 1611
Rubinstein, Helena, 1820
Ruckelshaus, William D., 327
Rudd, Mark, 725
Ruder & Finn, 2004
ruling class, 22, 23, 24, 158, 484, 645, 699, 894, 2627, 3404, 4032
ruling class cohesiveness, 19
ruling legitimacy, 2658
ruling power, 58
Rusk, Dean, 232, 341, 1228, 1414, 2850, 4120
Russia: film, 3114
Russian MIGs in Nicaragua, 584
Russian wheat deals, 153
Russo, Anthony, 1320
Ryan, William, 244
Saatchi & Saatchi advertising agency, 1692
sabotage, 285
SAC, 255, 762, 4330
SAC: sex, 32
Sadat, Anwar, 1285, 2571
Saddam Hussein, 3339
Saddam Hussein: NYT, 3712
Safer, Morley, 2593, 2746, 2792
safety, 1177, 3553
safety: food, 3494
safety: industry, 3671
safety: labels, 4395
safety net, 649
safety: nuclear, 4489
safety: nuclear power, 2710
safety testing, 1053
safety: VDT, 3483
Saigon press corps, 1426
Saint Laurent, Yves, 741
Salant, Richard, 2308, 2672, 3966
sales promotion, 1710
salesmanship, 3860
Salinger, Pierre, 1597
Salisbury affair, 1379
Salisbury, Harrison, 1228, 3489
SALT, 183
SALT I, 348

SUBJECT INDEX 791

Salt Lake City Deseret News, 4663
salvation, 1760
Salzberg, Louis, 1226
San Diego Newsline, 3597
San Francisco Bay Guardian, 4600, 4693
San Francisco Chronicle, 1648, 3318, 3344, 3383, 3518, 3550, 3585, 3691
San Francisco Chronicle/Examiner, 3328
San Francisco Examiner, 3506, 3550, 3585, 3610, 3677
San Jose Mercury News, 3550, 3585
sanctuary, 4590
Sanctuary Movement, 13
sanctuary trial, 4588
Sandinistas, 1500, 2767, 3369
Sandinistas (demonized), 64
Sandler, Norman, 602
Santa Barbara News Press, 3444
Santa Barbara oil spill (1969), 3444
Sarnoff, David, 2743
satellite broadcasting, 2230, 2235, 2248
satellite communications, 1135a, 2156, 2237, 4194
satellite: public broadcasting, 2651
satellite: Soviet communications, 1523
satellite transmissions, 601
satellites, 39, 904, 1407, 2186, 2345, 2728, 2945, 3191, 4404
satire: art, 4749
Saturday Evening Post, 3833
Saturday Review, 1675, 3857
Saudi Arabia, 141, 1446, 2751, 3030
Saudi Women Behind the Veil, 2751
Sauter, Van Gordon, 2593, 2612, 2706, 2753, 2758
Savannah River, 1590
Savings and Loans, 775
Savio, Roberto, 3239
Savitch, Jessica, 2588, 2705
Scaife Foundation, 6, 2690, 3473

Scaife, Richard Mellon, 733, 1083, 2214, 2812, 4104, 4374
Scales, Junius, 403
Scalia, Antonin, 430
scandals, 2651
Scandinavian media, 1169
Schanberg, Sidney, 3803, 3808
Schanen, William, Jr., 4568
Schenck v. United States (1919), 4190, 4213
Schick Safety Razor Company, 2744, 3521
Schiller, Herbert I., 556, 4388
Schine, David, 4534
Schirfrin, André, 3954
Schlafly, Phyllis, 21, 480
Schlesinger, Arthur, 584
Schlesinger, James, 1419
Schmertz, Herbert, 1969
Schneider, Alfred, 2474
scholarly publications, 3978
scholarships: public relations, 1984
school prayer, 489
Schorr, Daniel, 760, 2653, 2732
Schudson, Michael, 1812
Schuller, Robert, 2492
Schultz, Michael, 3185
Schultz, Secretary, George, 1299
Schwartz, Tony, 2061
Schwerner, Michael, 3056
science, 83, 89, 265, 342, 411, 501, 509, 511, 744, 974, 1443, 4354
science: autonomy, 502
science: business, 508
science: corporations, 499, 500
science: democracy, 500
science: ethics, 505
science fiction, 624
science fiction films: Sovietphobia, 3130
Science for the People, 499, 4185
science: foreign policy, 500
science: government, 503, 508
science: military, 500
science: minorities, 499
science: news, 814, 949, 1142, 1201, 3304

science: not neutral, 499
science: programming, 2916
science: public control, 500
science: regulation, 500
science: Sovietphobia, 503
science: teaching, 499
science: technology, 36, 38
science: technology, democracy, 502
science: television, 2916
science: University of California, 499
science: women, 499, 506
science writing, 814
scientific research, 508, 1418
scientific research: money, 499
scientists, 352, 389, 402, 499
scientists: government, 4673
Sciolino, Elaine, 1305
Scopes Trial, 422
scopophilia, 2512
Scorsese, Martin, 763, 3182
Scowcroft, Brent, 2617
Scranton commission, 4116
Scribner's, 4021
Scripps, E.W., 3476
Scripps-Howard, 1094
scriptwriters, 2472
SDI (Star Wars), 1404, 1456, 2208, 4282
SDS (Students for a Democratic Society), 288, 293, 632, 725, 896, 1027, 3586
search and seizure v. privacy, 307, 2126
search warrants, 179, 3667, 4352
Seaspray, 233
Seattle Post-Intelligencer, 3518, 3635, 3683
Seattle Times, 3668
Seattle Times: Casey Ruud, 4237
SEC, 2028a
second strike counterforce, 348
Secord, General Richard, 193, 1305, 1585
secrecy, 12, 13, 17, 66, 77, 148, 172, 175, 176, 179, 182, 183, 187, 193, 200, 202, 204, 209, 210, 233, 239, 240, 266, 278, 280, 285, 288, 289, 291, 300, 303, 304, 308, 309, 316, 317, 319, 320, 322, 328, 342, 366, 368, 411, 451, 501, 508, 553, 612, 653, 709, 806, 1195, 1229, 1231, 1235, 1236, 1237, 1242a, 1245a, 1247, 1257, 1260, 1266, 1310, 1314, 1320, 1329, 1349a, 1350a, 1358, 1377, 1378, 1404, 1414, 1418, 1443, 1448, 1466, 1467, 1488, 1495, 1520, 1527, 1552, 1554, 1557, 1558, 1620, 1623, 1625, 1627, 1644, 1651, 1656, 2062, 2111a, 2314, 2646, 3637, 3765, 3787, 3867, 3880, 3924, 3972, 3995, 4075, 4088, 4099, 4214, 4244, 4252, 4253, 4280, 4281, 4300, 4301, 4328, 4391, 4581, 4607, 4663
secrecy: accountability, 356
secrecy: Angola, 4252
secrecy: anticommunism, 1452
secrecy: atomic bomb, 368
secrecy: classification system, 1606
secrecy: corporate state, 4199
secrecy: corporations, 1153, 2352, 2833
secrecy: DOE, 1515
secrecy: FOIA, 4256
secrecy: government (see also: secrecy: Grenada invasion), 186;, 194, 206, 998, 1359, 1415, 1425, 1429, 1471
secrecy: Gulf War, 3733
secrecy: Hiroshima-Nagasaki, 3175
secrecy: John Kennedy and Vietnam War, 2744
secrecy: NASA, 1040
secrecy: nuclear arms, 1326, 4275
secrecy: nuclearism, 893, 3000
secrecy: nuclear accidents, 865
secrecy: Pentagon, 1351, 1515, 4330

SUBJECT INDEX

secrecy: presidency, 190, 3263
secrecy: Reagan, 1418, 1538, 1549, 4028
secrecy: Vietnam War, 1588
Secret Agent, 2439
Secret Army Organization, 104
secret bombing, 183
secret cables, 1254
secret files, 324
secret government, 193, 233, 291, 300, 309, 1314
secret intelligence court, 1053
secret police, 179, 405
secret records, 307
Secret Service, 276, 1627
Secret Team, 319
secrets, 1229
Section 8 of the Organization of Eastern Caribbean States charter, 1302
secular humanism, 34, 480
secular priesthood, 4665
secular religion: nationalism, 108
secularization, 1760
security classifications, 1516
Security Council Directive 130 (communications), 1322
security leaks, 709
security officer, 352
sedition, 178, 4122, 4219
sedition laws, 311, 3505, 4190
seditious libel, 13, 4696
See It Now (CBS television), 2651, 2844
Seeger, Pete, 405, 4165, 4170, 4737
Segretti, Donald, 180
Seldes, George, 597, 774, 3434, 4558, 4610, 4652, 4692, 4700
self-censorship, 328, 649, 747, 888, 890, 915, 923, 990, 1016, 1066, 1078, 1090, 1140, 1157, 1242, 1508, 1514a, 1591, 1854a, 1890, 1909, 2585, 2657, 3385, 3460, 3499, 3511, 3649, 3652, 3963

self-censorship: apartheid, 901
self-censorship: film, 3142
self-censorship: Hollywood, 3130
self-censorship: newspapers, 3479
self-censorship: rock music, 4592
self-censorship: Sovietphobia, 3969
self-censorship: sponsor control, 2874
self-censorship: television, 2474
self-censorship: women's magazines (cancer), 3845
self-determination, 57, 649
selfhood, 1760
self-indulgence, 1877
self-realization, 1760
self-regulation: broadcasting, 2171
self-reliance, 3860
Sellers, Cleveland, 405
selling capitalism (see II), 1971, 2003, 2031
Selling of the Pentagon, The, 2282, 2650, 2658, 2686, 2801
Selling of the Pentagon, The: censorship, 2852
semantics, 4338
semiconductors, 265
semiotics, 559, 2279, 2330
semiotics: news (newspapers), 3415
Senate, 1246
Senate Bill 2263, 4251
Senate Foreign Relation Committee, 341, 1611
Senate Intelligence Committee, 273
Senate Internal Security Subcommittee, 324, 361, 382
Senate Select Committee on Intelligence Activities, 288
Senate, U.S., 916
Seneca Peace Encampment, 4590
sensationspeak, 676
sensuality, 1877
separation of form from substance, 616
Serling, Rod, 2508
Serrano, Andres, 4135

Sesame Street, 588, 2922, 2923, 2927, 2928
Sevareid, Eric, 2672
Seven Hundred Club, 2492
Seven Station Rule, 2164
Seventeen, 1676
Seven-Up Co. (Philip Morris), 164, 1894
sex: ads, 1734
sex: advertising, 707, 1676, 1692, 1724, 1732, 1751, 1752, 1784, 1787, 1859, 1873, 1937
sex magazines, 697
sex: soap operas, 2514
sex: television, 2474, 2525, 2534
sex: violence, 1829
sexism, 1, 32, 79, 91, 114, 122, 443, 566, 572, 572, 662, 755, 1708, 1803, 1809, 1905, 2252, 2333, 2334, 2433, 2472, 3089, 3143, 3146, 3299, 3383, 3560, 3648, 3829, 3830, 3904, 3922, 3967, 4231, 4272, 4434, 4480, 4486
sexism: advertising, 1670, 1674, 1698, 1788, 1849, 1878, 1921, 1922
sexism: education, 455, 468
sexism: film, 3059, 3069, 3081, 3084, 3122, 3126, 3178, 3182, 4416
sexism: film (violence), 3118
sexism: film WWII, 3144
sexism: Harlequin Romance, 3973
sexism: imperialism, 257
sexism: law, 418, 420, 426
sexism: magazines, 3822, 3833, 3467
sexism: mass media, 695a, 754
sexism: media, 695a
sexism: militarism, 87
sexism: MTV, 2547
sexism: national security, 4270
sexism: newspapers, 3387, 3443, 3500, 3518
sexism: novels, 3986
sexism: NYT, 3736, 3759, 3797

sexism: PBS, 2983, 2984, 2998
sexism: Pentagon press corps, 4270
sexism: press, 669
sexism: print, 3303
sexism: sports, 535
sexism: television, 2306, 2337, 2538, 2569, 2617, 2638, 2752, 2783, 2821, 2864, 2915, 2935, 2940
sexism: television news, 2670
sexism: WWII films, 3100
Sexton, Anne, 468
sex-typing, 755
sexual domination, 3118
sexual equality, 4221
Shackley, Theodore, 193
Shadegg, Stephen (right-wing novelist), 3968
Shah of Iran, 868a, 875, 3274, 3298
Shakertown Pledge, 484
Sharon, Ariel, 768, 831
Sharon v. Time Magazine, 890
Shavano Institute, 6
Shearson Lehman Hutton, 116
Sheehan, Neil, 1426
Sheen, Bishop Fulton (Life Is Worth Living), 2508, 3860
Sheldon, Roy, 616
Shell, 1989
Shepard, Sam, 763
Sheridan, Terry, 3539
Sherrill, Robert, 3783
shield law, 624, 1246, 4242, 4262, 4322, 4336, 4376
Shirer, William, 2844
shopping malls, 1192
Shoreham, 3740
show business, 352
shredding documents, 1305
Shultz, George, 141
Shultz, George (lying to Congress), 3677
shuttle: plutonium (see also: NASA, space shuttle)
Sider, Donald: Pentagon correspodent, 4330
Sidle Media Panel, 1562
Sidle Panel Report, 803
Signals Intelligence Act, 1223
Silkwood, Karen (nuclear industry), 2793, 3325

SUBJECT INDEX 795

Silverman, Fred, 2405, 2455, 2474, 2480
Simon & Schuster, 3951, 4021
Simon, Paul, 4165
Simon, William, 6
simplification, 4089
Simpsons, The, 2465
simulations: television, 2341
Sinclair, Mary, 4489
Singapore: advertising, 1668
Singlaub, John, 193
Single Integrated Operating Plan (see SIOP), 255
singlespeak (see doublespeak), 1077
SIOP, 241
sitcom, 2531, 2490, 2511, 2534
sitcom prime time television, 2530
Six Million Dollar Man, The, 2457
Sixty Minutes, 2279, 2393, 2406, 2566, 2597, 2598, 2653, 2686, 2690, 2714, 2734, 2746, 2792, 2878
Sixty Minutes: UNESCO, 2683
Sixty Minutes: Union Carbide, 2586
SJMN, 3585
Skag, 2316
Skybolt controversy, 3673
SLA-Hearst, 3768
slander, 1481, 2242, 4534
Slaughterhouse Five, 1347
slavery, 91, 3430
Slow Guillotine, The (air pollution), 2710
S&Ls, 110, 149, 798
smear, 60, 405
Smith Act (see also: bigotry, Sovietphobia), 91, 328, 344, 361, 1607, 3077, 3992, 4371
Smith, C. Arnold, 104
Smith, Howard, 2672, 2744
Smith, Terrence, 1447
Smith-Richardson Foundation, 6
Smithsonian Institution, 4726
Smokey and the Bandit, 2345
smoking (see also: cigarette, tobacco), 1110, 4592
Smoot, Dan, 21

SMU football, 545
Smythe, Tony, 1382
Snepp, Frank, 3972, 3995, 3997, 4001, 4016
Snepp, Frank: prior restraint, 3947
Snow, Edgar, 3974
Snyder, Tom, 2493, 2796
soap opera, 713, 2310, 2341, 2357, 2393, 2403, 2452, 2464, 2496, 2507, 2526
soap opera: advertising, 1712, 2450
soap opera: sex, 2514
soap opera: women, 2461
Social Abstinence, 3465
social clubs: power, 30
social contexts, 3113
social control, 50
social control: computers, 3204
social control: democracy, 584
social interpretation, 3931
social justice: journalism, 4203
social problem films, 3152
social process, 3113
social responsibility: press, 1038
Social Responsibility Theory, 617
social science, 70, 463, 511, 521, 947
social science: book publishing, 3978
social science: conservatism, 4032
Social Security Disability Reviews, 1457, 1458
Social Text, 3560
socialism, 1005, 3182
Socialist Party, 4371
socialist political candidates, 3380
socialist press, 4636
socialist realism: art, 4130
Socialist Workers Party, 291, 297
socialists, 3430
Society of Professional Journalists, 1140
sociobiology, 499, 975
sociological criticism, 559
sociology, 451, 511
soft news, 2753

Sohio, 3542
Sojourners: IRS, 3906
solar energy, 150, 161, 1336, 1451
Soldier of Fortune, 1268a, 1482, 3923
Someone to Watch Over Me, 2281
Somoza, 918, 2767
Sone, Robert (Radio Bikini), 2967
song lyrics, 707
Song My, 820
Sontag, Susan, 4744
sound bits, 2094a, 2557
source control, 729
sources, 1067, 1502, 3578
sources: administration, 3691
sources: anonymous, 3480
sources: confidentiality, 4707
sources: news, 3364
sources: NYT, 3719
sources: official, 895
sources: television news, 2848
South Africa, 346, 784, 857, 868, 901, 1029, 1086, 1069, 2693, 2792, 3240, 3568
South Africa: NYT, 3747, 3754, 3782
South Vietnam (see also: Vietnam), 1327
Southeast Asia, 2553
Southern Africa, 2692
Southern Baptists, 492
Southern California, 3589
Southern media, 743
Soviet aircraft carrier, 3261
Soviet bomb test moratorium, 1356
Soviet issues, 4361
Soviet Military Power, 3270
Soviet press, 4617
Soviet stereotypes, 1482
Soviet threat, 266, 356, 357, 362, 1243a, 1437
Soviet Union, 613, 1401
Soviet Union: broadcasting, 4415
Soviet Union: television news, 2676
Sovietphobia: 1970s-1980s, 367

Sovietphobia: 1980s (Reagan), 3106
Sovietphobia, 4, 7, 8, 12, 18, 29, 34, 40, 42, 56, 62, 66, 71, 93, 99, 101, 187, 193, 197, 199, 204, 230, 255, 259, 266, 273, 308, 313, 316, 324, 328, 347, 354, 357, 364, 367a, 369, 382, 383, 386, 402, 443, 482, 584, 597, 616, 624, 747, 762, 780, 791, 809, 842, 849, 853, 886, 903, 914, 924, 960, 990, 1045, 1057, 1062, 1083, 1217, 1226, 1228, 1243a, 1250, 1311, 1322a, 1354, 1401, 1401, 1437, 1438, 1452, 1472, 1482, 1489a, 1505, 1514, 1522, 1532, 1535, 1567, 1570, 1581, 1589, 1609, 1613, 1618, 1634, 1648, 1649, 2161, 2207, 2212, 2242, 2289, 2374, 2456, 2502, 2519, 2559, 2692, 2711, 2712, 2743, 2744, 2750, 2772, 2835, 3064, 3065, 3072, 3074, 3095, 3111, 3146, 3147, 3152, 3176, 3261, 3270, 3296, 3298, 3306, 3311, 3313, 3314, 3318, 3343, 3374, 3401, 3407, 3421, 3425, 3434, 3493, 3520, 3561, 3576, 3590, 3612, 3630, 3676, 3684, 3690, 3691, 3794, 3817, 3819, 3891, 3896, 3952, 3960, 3968, 3985, 3992, 3994, 4004, 4005, 4012, 4035, 4044, 4055, 4059, 4062, 4066, 4067, 4071, 4076, 4079, 4080, 4084, 4089, 4095, 4098, 4099, 4104, 4108, 4122, 4575, 4617, 4727, 4734
Sovietphobia: ABC news, 2814
Sovietphobia: Afghanistan, 2800
Sovietphobia: Amerika, 3080
Sovietphobia: Angola, 3703
Sovietphobia: blacklisting, 3145
Sovietphobia: book reviews, 3974

SUBJECT INDEX

Sovietphobia: censorship, 3969, 3970, 3993
Sovietphobia: Charlie Chaplin, 3121
Sovietphobia: children, 2463
Sovietphobia: family, 385
Sovietphobia: film, 3054, 3055, 3071, 3079, 3101, 3106, 3154, 3159, 4536
Sovietphobia: film censorship, 3105
Sovietphobia: history, 381
Sovietphobia: Hollywood, 3123, 3130
Sovietphobia: Hollywood Ten, 3139
Sovietphobia: Indonesia (NYT), 3731
Sovietphobia: INF pact on television, 2815
Sovietphobia: informers (Hollywood), 3132
Sovietphobia: Look magazine, 3864
Sovietphobia: missiles, 1628
Sovietphobia: networks, 2819
Sovietphobia: news, 3107
Sovietphobia: news agencies, 3226, 3230, 3257
Sovietphobia: newspapers, 3503
Sovietphobia: NYT, 3714, 3734, 3749, 3750, 3766, 3816
Sovietphobia: PBS, 2996
Sovietphobia: Reagan, 1020
Sovietphobia: repression, 380
Sovietphobia: television, 2620, 2820
Sovietphobia: The Terror Network, 3998
Sovietphobia: TV Guide, 3855
Sovietphobia: WP, 3571
space allotted, 3471
space shuttle, 248, 2585, 3615
space shuttle: militarism, 3346
space shuttle: plutonium, 1036, 4593
Spacek, Sissy, 763
Spain, 3369
Spanish-American War, 3639
speaker bans (see also: censorship), 401
speakers' bureaus, 259

Speakes, Larry, 1049, 1401
special intelligence, 1229
special interests, 58, 3411, 4372
special operations, 204
Special Operations Division, 233
special privilege, 58
specialization (see also: professionalism, vocationalism), 528
spectrum-sharing model, 4418
speech, 4249
speeches, 1384
speechwriters, 2701
Spencer, Stuart, 2061
Spielberg, Steven, 3152
spies, 1245a
spies: heroes, 2508
Spike, The (see also: Robert Moss, Arnaud de Borchgrave), 3985
spin control, 940
Spitzer, Leo, 1873
Spivak, John, 774
Spock, Benjamin, 405
sponsor, 1117, 1700, 1820, 1826, 1850, 1917, 2190, 3363, 3400
sponsor control, 729, 1733, 1838, 1840, 1851, 1854a, 1865, 1910, 1911, 1913, 1923, 1940, 1945, 2246, 2327, 2376, 2425, 2441, 2480, 2489, 2561, 2582, 2621, 2758, 2796, 2835l, 3446, 3709, 3826, 3916, 4509
sponsor control: arts, 4140
sponsor control: film, 3058
sponsor control: news, 1863, 2779
sponsor control: PBS, 3033
sponsor control: television, 2474, 2534
sponsor control: television (see also: advertising control), 2874
sponsor control: theater, 3043
sponsor: inflation, 3628
sponsor: newspaper, 1941
sports, 83, 532, 535, 572, 605, 671, 681, 705, 706, 716, 734, 764, 1739, 2191, 2296, 2506, 4284

sports: advertising, 1699, 2516
sports: antitrust, 533
sports: beer, 1888
sports: business, 539
sports: celebrity, 718
sports: censorship, 3689
sports: chauvinism, 3666
sports: Cold War, 541
sports: college, 543
sports: commercial, 2516
sports: commercialism, 543, 1797, 2471, 2520
sports: commodity, 2515
sports: crime, 541
sports: education, 542
Sports Illustrated, 4510
sports: journalism, 2503
sports: media, 531
sports: MNF, 2487
sports: news, 917, 3472, 3502
sports: Olympics, 3284
sports: professionalism, 533, 543
sports: programs, 2403
sports: racism, 541
sports: religion, 540
sports: sexism, 695a
sports: television, 536, 541, 1699, 2362, 2471, 2484, 2503, 2512, 2515, 2516, 2518, 2520, 2522, 2527, 2537
sports: tv, 2362
sports values, 538, 540, 542
sports writing: censorship, 3528
spot ads: political, 2094a
spot ads (see also: thirty-second ads), 1869
spot ads: television, 2073
Springfield, USA, 623
Springsteen, Bruce, 763, 4156
Sputnik, 371, 624
spying, 286, 306, 321, 324, 1407, 3347, 3576
spying: FBI, 3934, 3994
spying: libraries (FBI), 3948
SS 20s, 4034
SSAM: Soldier, Sailor, Airman, Marine Magazine, 4089
ST, 3560
St. Elsewhere, 2394

St. Louis, 3644
St. Louis: CIA, 3687
St. Louis Globe-Democrat, 3636
St. Louis Journalism Review, 4176, 4569
St. Louis newspapers, 3596
St. Louis Post Dispatch, 1608
St. Louis Post Dispatch, 3275, 3430, 3545, 3547, 3560, 3584, 3596, 3610, 3660, 3682, 3685
St. Louis Post Dispatch: business inflation, 3631
St. Louis Post Dispatch: Central America, 3659
St. Louis Sun, 3596
St. Paul Dispatch, 3592
St. Paul Pioneer Press, 3592
Stachel, Jacob, 3992
Staggers, Rep. Harley, 2836
Standard Oil of New Jersey, 2015, 3058
Standard Oil of Ohio, 1098
standardization, 498, 4154
standing army (see also: militarism), 222, 230
Stanford Daily, 3422, 3584, 3667
Stans, Maurice, 104
Stanton, Frank, 2425, 2474, 2651, 2672, 2801, 2836, 2844
Stapp, Andy, 4565
star as commodity, 1860
star system (films), 3045
star system (see also: celebrity), 1801, 2523, 3820
star system: Sonja Henie, 3092
Star Trek, 2291, 2393, 2459, 2513, 3152
Star Wars (SDI), 248, 624, 714, 1269, 1723, 4593
Star Wars rhetoric, 1456
Star Wars: US myths, 1456
stardom (see celebrity), 718
Stars and Stripes (Pacific), 3517, 3686
Starsky and Hutch, 2531, 2534
state capitalism (corporate state), 127, 4037
State Department, 339, 352, 1582, 1611, 1647, 4075, 4110

SUBJECT INDEX

State Department classification system, 27
State Department: Country Reports on Human Rights, 4075
State Department: diplomatic history, 4088
State Department: press, 1271
State Department: propaganda (Nicaragua), 1500
State Department: reports, 4042, 4044
State Department White Paper: El Salvador (Feb 23, 1981), 1277, 1472
State Department White Paper: Vietnam War (1965), 4121
State of Maine v. University of Maine, 3018
state propaganda, 1283
state religion, 583, 584
state religion: television, 2950
state terrorism, 7, 10, 51, 193, 233, 650, 1277, 1279, 1283, 1372, 1391, 1585
state violence, 91
statism, 1465, 1552, 3405
statist journalism, 2748
statistics, 976, 993
Statue of Liberty, 801, 1638
status, 616
status quo, 2481, 3104, 3991
Stealth aircraft, 1474
Stealth fighter, 983
steel industry, 44, 3243
Steele, James, 4600
Steinbeck, John, 3994, 4006
stereotypes (see also: bigotry), 616, 1482, 2366, 2418, 2534, 3090, 4129, 4291
stereotyping: foreign culture, 2751
sterilization, 499
Sterling, Claire, 592, 1395, 3717
sterotypes, 1482
Stevenson, Adlai, 2060
Stevenson, Adlai, and McCarthy, Joseph, 1241
Stewart, Justice Potter, 932
stock market, 616
Stockman, David, 6

Stone, I.F., 611, 1401, 3859, 4600, 4635, 4662
Stone, Jennifer, 4544
stonewalling, 2111a
Storm Warning (1951), 3146
story placement, 3471
story selection, 888, 4651
Storyteller, The, 2350, 2505
Strategic Air Command, 624, 762, 3064
Strategic Air Command (see SAC), 210
Strategic Defense Initiative (SDI, Star Wars), 60
Straus & Giroux, 4021
Strausz-Hupé, Robert, 4103
strikes, 769, 847, 849, 850, 1150, 2074, 3335, 3374, 3613, 3928
strikes: Greyhound, 3732
strikes: NYT and WP, 3572
strikes: US/SU, 2606
strip mining, 4405
strip mining ads, 1967
structualism: ads, 1764
Stuart, Lyle, 4686
student press, 4680
Student Press Law Center, 3412
student protest, 463
student rebellion, 387, 3152
students, 943
Students for a Democratic Society (see also: SDS), 288, 293, 632, 3586
students: media critics, 4239
Studies Analysis and Gaming Agency (SAGA), 255
style obsolescence, 616
stylization, 616
SU (see also: Soviet Union), 3298
subculture, 4402
subliminal advertising, 1877, 1904
subliminal communication, 3199
subliminal persuasion, 1751, 1752
submarine, 1347
subpoenas, 943, 1258, 1364, 2193, 3317, 4289, 4292
subpoenas: newspeople, 1414
subpoenas: Nixon administration, 1225

subscription television, 2246, 4503
subsidized information, 38
subversion, 325 , 351, 352, 411
subversion: accusations, 464
subversion: fear, 91
subversion: laws, 311
subversion of foreign governments, 288
subversives, 321
success, 3860
success: advertising, 1730
success dream: corporate ideology, 3860
success: magazines, 3832
success: women, 3829
suffragists, 4276
sugar, 1859a
Sullivan, William C., 287, 316, 324, 327
Sulzberger, Arthur, 3803
summit 1985, 1044
summits, 585
Sun Oil Company, 4103
Sunday network news, 2777
Sunshine Act, 4372
Super Bowl, 716, 1831a, 2393, 2521
superficiality: television news, 2846
Superman, 671, 2439, 2914, 3860
Superman: ahistorical exploits, 551
Superman II: Marlboro cigarettes, 1945
supermarket, 1795
supermarket ads, 1784, 1833
supersitition, 3433
superweapon, 624, 1347
supplement to wire service copy, 4564
suppression, 1657, 3523, 4281
suppression: ideas, 4312
Supreme Court, 902, 920, 932, 1245, 1259, 1365, 1413, 1560, 1603, 2198, 3097, 3330, 3419, 3422, 3667, 4213
Supreme Court: censorship, 3947, 3972
Supreme court: civil liberties, 4371
Supreme Court: corporations, 424

Supreme Court: history, 436
Supreme Court: network television, 2640
Supreme Court: religion, 480
Surgeon General's Report on Television Violence, 2922
surgeons, 519
surreptitious entry (see also: black bag), 278
surveillance, 17, 78, 81, 182, 276, 286, 287, 289, 306, 307, 310, 311, 352, 366, 1196, 1349a, 1407, 1418, 3146, 3189, 3202, 3320, 3350, 3576, 3994, 4200
surveillance: anticommunism, 1452
surveillance: computer records, 3200, 3201
surveillance: computers, 3186, 3193, 3197, 3205, 3211
surveillance: data banks, 3187
surveillance (data banks): corporations, 3209
surveillance: direct marketing, 3190
surveillance: election, 293
surveillance: FBI data bank, 3210
surveillance: illegal, 280
surveillance: Info Digest, 3865
surveillance: mail, 295
surveillance: police, 282
surveillance (see also: computers), 3211
"Surveillance State," 312
surveillance: workers, 3196
suspicion, 4281
Sussan, Herbert, 3108, 3175
Swafford, Thomas, 2474
SWAPO, 3568
swing bands, 70
Sydney Declaration, 1140
Sylvester, Arthur, 1320, 1414, 1448
symbol makers, 2326
symbols, 1884
symbols: political campaigns, 2086
Symington, Senator Stuart, 4534
syndicated columnists, 3348, 3352, 4670

SUBJECT INDEX
801

syndicated columnists:
Unesco, 631
System, 3126
system maintenance, 3991
tabloid news, 2682
tabloid television, 2636
tabloid television news, 714
Tabloid TV, 2622
tabloids, 3820
talk show, 695a, 2310, 2403, 2493, 2687, 2691, 2692, 2717, 2777, 2788, 2850, 4519
talk show: conservatism, 2802, 2867, 2877
talk show: news, 2756
talk show: sponsor control, 2877
talk show: television, 2687
talk show: radio, 695a
Tarbell, Ida, 4705
Target America: The Influence of Communist Propaganda on US Media (James L. Tyson), 733
targeted buyers, 1942
Tarkington, Booth (The Gentleman from Indiana), 1783
Tarzan, 651, 3169
Tashima, Judge Wallace, 4507
Tawney, R.H., 461
tax swindle: rich, 138
taxes, 1977
Taylor, Arthur, 2474
Taylor, Frederick, 498
Taylor, General, Maxwell, 232, 1379
Taylor, Robert, 3146
Taylor v. Department of Army, 1378
Taylorism, 163
teacher education, 455
teaching (see pedagogy), 708
technical magazines, 3836
Technicolor Corporation, 3521
technocracy, 4037
technofascism, 4199
technological information, 3836
technological language, 676
technological manipulation of advertising, 1762
technologies (converging), 4194

technology (see also: II.C.4.), 321, 424, 444, 502, 509, 605, 619, 624, 628a, 713, 762, 1407, 1760, 2172, 2209, 2218, 2222, 2239, 2241, 2247, 2253, 2273, 2292, 2399, 2457, 2916, 3191, 3193, 3194, 3204, 3212, 3215, 4278, 4404, 4694
Technology and Culture, 3938
technology as propaganda, 744
technology: auto, 1947
technology: books, 3978
technology: communications, 2274, 2284, 2284
technology: computers, 3186
technology: control, 158
technology: corporate control, 4551
technology: literature, 752
technology: news, 904, 906
technology: Pentagon, 4330
technology: press, 1552
technology transfer, 643
technology transfer: Third World, 1464
technology: TV, 2391
technology: video, 4403, 4457
technostrategic language, 4045
Ted Bates Advertising Company, 1881
teen magazines, 695a
teenage drinking, 1824
teenagers: advertising, 1787
teenagers: films, 3086
teflon, 1569
Telecom 2000, 2234
telecommunication technology, 2241
telecommunications, 744, 1196, 2254, 2256, 4425, 4466
telecommunications concentration, 4537
telecommunications: democracy, 2267
telecommunications: history, 2266
telecommunications policy, 4455
telecommunications regulation, 2176
teleconferencing, 2345

teledemocracy, 4404
telegraph: regulation, 2143
telegraphy, 3205
telematics (computer information technology), 50, 3205
telephone, 4466
telephone circuitry, 4440
telephone industry, 4537
telephony, 3205
televangelism (II.C.), 482, 487, 2221, 2373, 2943, 2944, 2945, 2948, 2949, 2953, 2958, 2959
televangelism: money, 2954
television (see also: TV), 184, 352, 553, 553, 560, 560, 572, 572, 602, 611, 639, 684, 690, 694, 712, 734, 744, 745, 746, 751, 758, 759, 872, 1224, 1362, 1374, 1401, 1682, 2127, 2191, 2195, 2204, 2258, 2276, 2310, 2314, 2318, 2324, 2342, 2343, 2350, 2361, 2366, 2367, 2379, 2472, 2495, 2703, 2480, 2914, 3432, 4329, 4356
television: 1950s, 2295
television: 1952 campaign, 611
television: 3-2-1 Contact, 2922
television: 700 Club, 2952, 2955
television: abuses, 2293
television: access, 2235, 2375, 2692, 4462
television: access, Canada, 4409
television: access, Europe, 4409
television: addiction, 1996
television ads as myths, 1738
television ads: children, 2048
television ads: frontier myth, 1738
television: advertising, 1779, 1827a, 1870, 1879, 2310, 2330, 2321, 2325, 2370, 2375, 2393, 2414, 2430, 2444, 2445, 2499, 2510, 2541, 2911, 2919

television advertising: children, 722, 2922, 2926
television advertising: Richard Nixon, 2093
television affiliates: news, 2643
television: age, 2478
television: Amerika, 2456
television: anticommunism, 2502
television: anti-democracy, 2375
television: Arab, 658, 2415, 2416, 2417, 2418
television: archives, 2817
television: arts and humanities, 2886
television: audience, 2331
television: audience as commodity, 2279
television: audience measurement, 2318
television: Blacks, 753
television: boys, 2477
television: Britain, 2447
television: business, 2356, 2362, 2402, 2419
television: Canada, 2387
television: cartoons, 2917
television: celebrity, 718
television: censorship, 1848, 2282, 2327, 2370, 2384, 2475, 2545, 2544
television: character types, 2481
television: children, 2035, 2051, 2276, 2350, 2394, 2426, 2477, 2935
television: children and advertising, 1721, 2913
television: cinematic analysis, 2279
television: class, 2330, 2458, 2473, 2525, 2543, 2961
television: codes, 2331
television: comedy, 2350
television: commercialism (II.C.1.c.[5]), 2911, 2295, 2908, 2909, 2939, 4412
television: commercialization v. public interest, 2904
television: commercials, 547, 2444
television commercials: children (see II.B.4), 2045

SUBJECT INDEX

television: community, 4427
television: conformity, 2532
television: congressional campaigns, 2098a
television: conservatism, 2339
television: consumerism, 2422, 2549
television: consuming, 2375, 2377
television: content analysis, 2331
television: conventionality, 2534
television: conventions (codes), 2279
television: corporate capitalism, 2939
television: corporate censorship, 4474
television: corporate control, 1996
television: corporate state, 2360
television: corporation, 2307, 2355, 2384, 2409, 2922
television: correspondents, 2643
television: crime, 2441
television: crime programs, 2279, 2469
television: criticism, 3370, 3417
television: cross-ownership, 2163
television: cultural imperialism, 2319, 2437, 2443
television: daytime, 2549
television: decentralization, 4524
television: decoding, 2330
Television Digest, 2136
television: directors, 2407
television: discourse, 2330
television: disorientation, 2290
television: docudrama, 2350
television: documentary, 2350, 2394, 4513, 4546
television: domesticity, 2511
television: dominant ideology, 645
television: drama, 2310, 2460

television: education, 639, 2235, 2901, 2915, 2989, 4409
television: Edward Murrow on Joseph McCarthy, 4556
television: effects, 2429
television: elderly, 2309, 2363
television: entertainment, 710, 2369, 2430
television: environment, 2321
television: establishment, 2313
television: evaluation skills, 3340
television: falsity, 2541
television: family, 2051, 2372, 2507, 2540, 2942
television: fantasy, 2536
television: feminist criticism, 2279, 2499
television: film, 3036
television: First Amendment, 2890
television: flow, 2349
television: foreign politics, 2418
television: fraud, 2451
television: game shows, 2279, 2410
television: gender, 2330
television: genre, 2481
television: global, 2388, 2389, 2391, 2410, 2436
television: government, 2427
television: hegemony, 2313, 2355
television: heroes, 2457
television: heroes and heroines, 2330, 2350
television: history, 2319
television: ideology, 2311, 2330, 2365, 2371, 2513, 2517, 2918, 4455
television: impact on audience, 2353
television: imperialism, 756
television: independence, creativity, 4549
television: independent, 4426, 4427, 4524
television: industry, 2276
television: influence, 2286
television: investigative reporting, 4182
television: Kojak, 2454

television: labor, 2316, 2431, 4551
television: Latin America, 2443
television: legitimizing, 2311
television: leisure, 2412
television: licensing, 2163
television: licensing (public interest), 4350
television: literacy, 2386
television: literacy (children), 2929
television: literary analysis, 2279
television: love and romance, 2530
television: marketplace of freedom, 2472
television: marriage, 2530, 2532
television: materialism, 2948, 2951
television: medicine, 2521
television: melodrama, 2350
television: militarism, 2934
television: military, 2545
television: minorities, 2283
television: monopoly, 2404
television: movies, 2357, 2406
television: mysteries, 2395
television: myth-making, 4234
television: myths, 2347
television narrowcasting, 759
television: national resource, 4496
television: network power, 2467
television: network regulation, 2163
television: networks, 1333, 2326, 2397, 2427, 2474, 2534, 2658
television: new technology, 4529
television: news, 605, 612, 706, 714, 748, 773, 1360, 1505, 2187, 2357, 2369, 2276, 2305, 2310, 2330, 2348, 2350, 2376, 2362, 2392, 2394, 2395, 2406, 2430, 2445, 2672, 2844, 4411

television: news activism, 2746
television: news as Show Biz, 2796
television news: business, 2197
television news: children, 2938
television: news, content analysis, 4444
television: news criticism, 2226
television: news, diversity, 4487
television news: hunger, 3273
television: news, I.F. Stone, 4548
Television News Inc., 2665
television news: Nielsen ratings, 2621
television news: presidential campaigns, 2107a
television: news programs, 2403
television news: Unesco, 631
television: newsgathering, 2686
television: novels, 2335
television: nuclear weapons, 2390
television: nuclearism, 2391
television: oppositional ideology, 2350
television: ownership, 2414, 4474
television: partriarchy, 2330
television: patriotism, 2917
television: patterns, 2296
television: peace, 4514
television: Pentagon, 2332
television: political advertising, 2086, 2100, 2112, 2115
television: political campaigns, 2079, 2083, 2094a, 2115a
television: political marketing, 2092
television: politics, 2095, 2276, 2373
television: presidency, 2383
television: presidential campaigns, 2276, 2893

television: presidents, 2114, 2284
television: prime time, 2401, 2467, 2483
television: profit, 2163, 2651, 2920, 2939
television: programming, 1830, 2317, 2321, 2330, 2348, 2365, 2392, 2395, 2414, 2445, 2889
television: programming, corporate control, 4509
television: programming diversity, 2163
television: programming, funding, 4549
television: propaganda conduit for government, 2316
television: public access, 2130, 4419, 4467, 4474, 4477, 4479, 4524
television: public interest, 2165, 2297, 2939, 4475
television: Puerto Rico, 2438
television: quality, 2460
television: race, 2922
television: racism, 2448, 2482, 2539, 2908, 2934
television: ratings, 2232, 2370, 2445
television: Reaganism, 2401
television: real life shows, 2406
television: reality, 2280
television: regulation, 2441, 2920, 2922
television: regulation for children, 2924
television: religion, 2228, 2350
television rhetorical vision, 706
television: right wing, 2385
television: Ronald Reagan, 2111a
television: salesmen, 2796
television: schedule, 2301
television: schizophrenia, 2325
television: science, 2916
television: science fiction, 2513
television (see also: II.C., III.), 4194, 4241, 4249, 4271, 4284

television: semiotics, 2279
television: setting, 2481
television: sex, 2525, 2922
television: sex, violence, 2312
television: sexism, 2306, 2337, 2538, 2934, 2935, 2940
television: sexism and racism, 2932
television: sex-typing, 2543
television: shopping, 2345
television: simulations, 2535
television: sitcom, 2279, 2394, 2395, 2403, 2509, 2511, 2550
television: slant, 2481
television: soap opera, 2279, 2392, 2393, 2394, 2395, 2401
television: social change, 2371
television: social class, 2350
television: social control, 2413
television: social issues, 2435
television: social purposes, 2441
television: social responsibility, 2347
television: Soviet Union, 2675
television: Sovietphobia, 2439
television: spectacles, 2406
television: sponsor control, 2350
television: sponsors, 1984, 2844
television: sports, 536, 541, 1739, 2350, 2357, 2362, 2471, 2484, 2503, 2512, 2515, 2516, 2518, 2520, 2522, 2527, 2537
television: spot advertising, 2073
television spot: political, 2110
television: spy programs, 2508
television: stardom, 2524
television "supertext," 2301
television: supervision, 2925

television: Surgeon General's Report, 2429
television: talk show, 2350, 2541
television: tax for public broadcasting, 4496
television: technique, 2322, 2382
television: tobacco, 1950
television: trivia, 2376
television: trust, 2322
television: uniformity, 2344, 4523
television: unions, 2411, 4449
television v. print media and radio, 639
television: values, 2260, 2936, 2944
television: variety shows, 2510
television: video, 2224
television: Vietnam War, 1379, 2186, 2374, 1426
television: viewers as commodity, 2444
television: viewers as consumer, 2444
television: violence, 690, 864, 2336, 2338, 2398, 2448, 2468, 2469, 2543, 2902, 2905, 2907, 2919, 2931, 2932, 2933, 2937, 2941, 2942, 4430
television violence: children, 2922
television: war, 2381, 2906
television: war cartoon programming, 2548
television: Watergate, 1442
television: westerns, 2350, 2395, 2508
television: women, 2426
television: work, 2412, 2540, 2903
television: working class, 2281
television: direct address, 2322
television networks, 1398, 1399
television: novels, 2364
television: reform, 2353
television: underground, 3028

televsion: multinationals, 1689
Telos, 4699
Temple, Shirley, 671
tenure, 457
terHorst, Gerald, 1597
terrorism, 51, 91, 204, 299, 346, 585, 592, 650, 713, 789, 825, 842, 979, 990, 1026, 1049, 1275, 1295, 1360, 1391, 1392, 1447, 1485, 1505, 1624, 2553, 2675, 2692, 2695, 2696, 2786, 3274, 3276, 3285, 4276, 4593
terrorism: broadcasting, 2197
terrorism: lies, 2694
terrorism: Nicaragua, 2694
terrorism: NYT, 3708
terrorism: television, 2691, 2885
Test Ban Treaty, 348
test oath, 199
testimonial ads, 1864
Tet crisis, 896, 2657, 2732
Tet Offensive, 207, 776, 804, 1375, 1379, 1426, 1490
Texaco, 1966, 3821
Texaco: Metropolitan Opera, 4140
Texas Observer, The, 4600, 4623
Texas Un-American Activities Committee, 350
textbooks, 1417, 4271
textile industrialization, 565
TGSB, 3587
That Certain Summer, 2505
The Mayaguez affair, 1332
The A-Team, 1723
The Atlantic, 3927
The Atlantic Council of the United States, 97
"The Atom Gives Up," 624
The Atomic City, 624
the "Big Lie," 1320
the big lie, 153
the body, 616
The Brookings Institution, 97
The Business Council, 97
The Business Roundtable, 97
The Car Book, 3546
The Chancellor Manuscript, 325
The Chomsky Reader, 4690

SUBJECT INDEX

The Committee on the Present Danger, 97
The Communicators Consortium, 4196
The Dartmouth Review, 3473
The Day After, 1360, 1552
The Day the Earth Stood Still, 624
The Denver Post, 3637, 3695
The Detroit News, 3503
The Empire Strikes Back, 3556
the flag, 1575
The Flint Journal, 3640
The German Ideology, 645
the "Great Communicator," 1428
The Guardian, 3852
The Hunt for Red October, 1544
The Institute for Media Analysis, 4196
The Institute for Propaganda, 4287
the Jolly Green Giant, 1701
The Kwitny Report, 2691
The Last Day, 624
The Lemon Times, 3546
the Los Angeles Times sports page, 588
"the medium is the message," 639
The Nation, 3274, 3850
The Nation: censorship (schools), 3851
The Nation: FBI, 3893
The National Catholic Press, 3521
The Negro Family: The Case for National Action (the Moynihan Report), 1355
The New Republic, 3850, 3857
The New York Times, 97
The New York World Telegram and Sun, 3777
The Office of Public Diplomacy, 64
the Plumbers, 180
The Protestant Ethic and the Spirit of Capitalism (Max Weber), 479
the "public realm," 1552
The Realist, 667
the rich, 33
The Saturday Evening Post, 3860

The Seattle Times, 3683
"The Selling of the Pentagon", 612, 624, 943, 1246
The Tower Commission Report, 193
The Wall Street Journal, 3838
The Washington Star, 3556, 3557
The Washington Times, 3566
the White House, 283
theater, 352, 1634, 4249
theater: nonprofit, 3043
Them! (1954), 3064, 3146
Thermidor (US)=corporate capitalism, 55
Thing, The, 3064
think tank, 92, 97, 232, 377, 402, 650, 699, 1373, 1990, 2101, 3873, 3931, 3952, 3960, 4014, 4022, 4029, 4047, 4050, 4058, 4068, 4073, 4074, 4090, 4097, 4103, 4105, 4107, 4108, 4711
think tank: elite rule, 4097
think tank: militarism, 4086
think tank: Reagan, 4052
third parties: the media, 861
Third World, 273, 868, 979, 1000, 1003, 1051, 1238, 1604, 2229, 2553, 3169, 3269, 3341, 3611, 3817, 4037, 4694
Third World: advertising, 1874
Third World communism, 680a
Third World coverage, 722
Third World: film, 3160, 3169
Third World: movies, 671
Third World: news agencies, 3265
Third World Newsreel, 4215, 4434
Third World: public relations, 1954
Third World: television, 2616, 272
Third World: televison news, 2627
Third World: tobacco, 1938
Third World: wire services, 3236

thirty-second commercial, 1823a, 1869
This Week with David Brinkley, 2635, 271
Thomas, Helen, 3263
Thomas, J. Parnell, 1634, 4562
Thomas, Norman, 4371
Thompson, J. Walter (ad agency), 1692, 1715, 1772, 1783, 1870
Thompson, Meldrin Jr., 3684
Thompson, Robert, 3992
Thompson, W. Scott, 4048
Thorn, 4569
Thornburgh, Richard, 3809
thought control, 307, 586, 715
Three Mile Island, 52, 893, 1021, 1421, 1974, 2084, 2198, 2316, 2724, 2732, 2775, 2776
Three Mile Island Commission, 1454
Three Mile Island: network news, 2774
Three Mile Island: television news, 2631
Three's Company, 2534
Tiananmen Square, 1446, 2663
Tibet, 204, 1320
timber industry, 1009, 3681
Time, 768, 818, 990, 1178, 1245a, 1253, 1821, 1908, 1945, 3273, 3275, 3276, 3284, 3285, 3295, 3298, 3299, 3309, 3313, 3874, 3876, 3877, 3881, 3885, 3902, 3903, 3908, 3911, 3912, 3917, 3921, 3937, 3941, 3942, 3943, 3944, 4011, 4106
Time, 97, 900, 925, 1023, 1049, 1379, 1395, 1443, 1546, 3316, 3318, 3328, 3336, 3338, 3341, 3342, 3343, 3344, 3425, 3545, 3556, 3557, 3821, 3824, 3838, 3857, 3866, 4330
Time: Angola, 912
Time: Gulf War, 3858
Time Inc., 644, 1094, 1136, 1173, 3875, 3885, 3918, 3944, 3977
Time Inc.: conservation, 3878

Time Inc.: history, 3874
Time: KAL 007, 912
Time: libel, 1042
Time: presidency, 1370, 1436
Time: racism, 3871
time study, 498
Time: UNESCO, 913
Time: Vietnam War, 1426
Time Warner, 1090, 1093, 1132, 1173, 3127
Time: women, 3904
Times Mirror Company, 3617
Tin Pan Alley, 4154
Tinker, 3349, 3979
Tinker, Grant, 2480
Titticut Follies, 3053, 3062, 3075
To Secure These Rights (1947), 199
tobacco, 517, 1157, 1942a
tobacco ads, 1751
tobacco: advertising, 1138a, 1193, 1692, 1780, 1843, 1913a, 1945
tobacco advertising: cancer, 3845
tobacco: companies, 1912
tobacco company censorship, 1051
tobacco: consumption, 1802
tobacco: industry, 1094, 1847a, 1908, 1938, 3916
tobacco industry: First Amendment, 1982
Tobacco Institute, 1945
tobacco: magazines, 1742
tobacco: television ads, 1950
Tobocman, Seth, 4136
Tolson, Clyde, 293
Tomorrow, 2493
Tonight Show, The, Johnny Carson, 2493
Tonkin Gulf, 340, 612, 1617, 2744
toothpaste, 1842
toothpaste ads, 1734, 1939
top 40, 588
Tornillo, 2148
torpedo, 1347
torture, 823
torture: El Salvador, 3462, 3635
torture: Philippines, 785
totalitarianism, 291, 990, 3634, 4092

SUBJECT INDEX

totalitarianism,: computers, 3193, 3218
Totenberg, Nina, 3024
Tour of Duty, 2479
tourism, 714
tourist promotion, 2213
Tower Commission (Iran-Contra), 1222
Tower Commission Report, 4082
Tower, John: Bush, 984
toxic agents, 291
toxic chemicals, 1051
toxic chlorinated hydrocarbons, 4704
toxic leak, 2544
toxic poisoning, 3460, 4592
toxic substances, 4395
toxic waste, 101, 128, 1060, 4590
Toyota, 1947
toys, 1935, 2548, 2914
toys: advertising, 1825, 2039, 2044, 2050
toys: computers, 3213
toys: television, 2477
toys: violence, 2341
Tracy, Dick, 4128
trade embargoes, 4251
trade unions, 1
trademarks, 1783
transborder data flow (see TDF), 680a
Transborder Data Flow: TBDF, 39
transnational ad agencies, 1668
transnational agribusiness, 1859a
transnational banks, 50
transnational business system, 78, 680a
transnational corporations, 143, 1194, 1197
transnational information, 2248
transnationals, 700
travel, 1349a, 1682, 4227
travel: news, 3472
travel restrictions (see also: visa denial), 1452, 1587, 1819
treason, 4276, 4667
Treaster, Joseph, 3713
Trenton Six, 397

Trevino, Jesus Salvador, 3185
trials, 434, 1565, 4304
Tri-City Herald, 3679
triggers (advertising), 1786
Trilateral Commission, 97, 348, 699, 4094, 4106
Trilling, Diana, 4012
tritium, 1443, 3316
triviality: television news, 2811
True Story, 3833
Trujillo and Dominican Republic, 2850
Truman, Harry S., 42, 200, 273, 324, 343, 352, 408, 413, 1331, 1385, 1386, 3318, 3503, 3508, 3691
Truman administration, 1618
Truman: anticommunism, 393
Truman: communism, 361
Truman Doctrine, 352, 824
Truman Doctrine: press, 4236
Truman: Farewell Address, 4122
Truman, Harry: Fair Deal, 4047
Truman, Harry: speeches, 1384
Truman's Executive Order 9835 ("Loyalty Order"), 347
Trumbo, Dalton, 1634
truth in packaging, 1898, 1936
truth vs. commercial truth, 616
truth=that which sells, 616
Tubehead (anti-advertising campaign), 1996, 4392
TUM, 4691
Tuohy, Albert, J., 3493
Turkey, 371, 1446
Turner, Admiral Stansfield, 326
Turner Broadcasting System, 1576, 1826
Turner Joy, 341
Turner, Robert, 4048
Turner, Ted, 4417, 4546
Turner, Tina, 4157
TV, 1002, 1049
TV: AIDS, 927a
TV: Army-McCarthy hearings, 1241
TV: escape, 635
TV: foreign news, 629

TV Guide, 731, 1821, 3273, 3340, 3900, 3913, 3930, 3932, 3933
TV Guide: Sovietphobia, 3855
TV Marti, 1286a, 1312a, 1345a, 3514, 4407
TV: McCarthy, 1241
TV: network 1950s, 675
TV networks, 943, 1110
TV news, 909
TV news: Unesco, 1238
TV Radio Talk, 3904
TV sponsor control, 1241
TW, 3545, 3547, 3548
TWA hostage crisis (1985), 3471
Twelve O'Clock High, 2744, 3064
Twentieth Century Fox, 1860
Twentieth Century, The (CBS Cold War series), 2744
Twenty/Twenty, 2406, 2746, 2751
Twin Circle Forum (right-wing radio program), 3521
Twin Circle Headline (right-wing television), 3521
Twin Circle Publishing Company (right-wing media), 3521
Two Minutes Hate, 1243a
two-party system, 58
Tylenol, 958
Tylenol poisonings, 2776
typography, 560
Tyson, James L., 733
U-2, 288, 319, 1320
UHF, 4533
UHF television, 4503
Ulasewicz, Tony, 180
UMT, 1622
UMW, 3374
Un-American Activities Committee, 4371
underground press, 611, 612, 748, 1224, 1463, 1533, 3388, 4224, 4323, 4600, 4608, 4612, 4643, 4664
underground press (protection from government harassment), 1364
underground press (see also: alternative press), 3461, 4568, 4579
Underground Press Syndicate, 4608

underground press: US Army, 4565
underground radio, 3013, 3022
underreporting, 4358
underreporting: television, 2708
unemployment, 4278, 4590
UNESCO, 39, 680, 680a, 684, 730, 781, 913, 1003, 1084, 1197, 1198, 1238, 1563, 1668, 1604, 2220, 2248, 3237, 3238, 3239, 3241, 3245, 3269, 3402, 3823, 4173
UNESCO: 60 Minutes, 2683
UNESCO: mass media, 985
UNESCO Mass Media Declaration, 2126
UNESCO: news agencies, 3235
UNESCO: NYT, 3748, 3817
unfriendly witness, 1634
uniformity, 2359, 4178, 4209
uniformity: broadcasting, film, 2258
union busting, 128
Union Carbide, 1083, 1976
Union for Democratic Communications, 1347a, 4320
Union Maids, 4521
Union Media Monitoring Project, 1180
union movement, 285
Union Oil Company, 3444
Union Pacific: film, 3091
Union Wage, 4603
unions, 46, 83, 307, 352, 390, 769, 850, 939, 1150, 1154, 1180, 1207, 2366, 2431, 3065, 3732, 4432, 4606
unions: anticommunism, 40
unions: broadcasting, 2272
unions: journalism industry, 3431
unions: NYT, 3705, 3732
unions: public relations, 2074
unions: repression, 40, 42
unions: television, 2411, 4449
unions v. Gannett, 1161
unions: WP, 3594
Unique War, The, 3170
United Airlines, 104, 147
United Appeal, 4033
United Electrical Workers, 352

SUBJECT INDEX 811

United Fruit Company, 340
United Mine Workers, 3335
United Nations, 352, 371, 3568
United Nations Charter, 1302, 4235
United Nations Charter Article 2(4), 288
United Nations Declaration of Rights, 939
United Nations Educational Scientific Cultural Organization (see UNESCO, 631
United Press International, 3220, 3227, 3231, 3233, 3235, 3240, 3241, 3243, 3248, 3254, 3256, 3259, 3263, 3281, 3295, 3298
United States Air Force (see USAF), 273
"United States Broadcasting Corporation," 588
United States Information Agency (see USIA), 611
United States Institute of Peace, 4064
United States literature: canon, 4736
United States Navy in Vietnam, The, film, 2744
United States of America v. Samuel Loring Morison, 1387
United Technologies, 4738
Universal Declaration of Human Rights, 1446
Universal Military Training (UMT), 263
universities, 24, 83, 285, 382, 387, 463, 466, 699, 746
universities: biological warfare, 792
universities: boards of trustee, 442, 470
universities: Central America, 452a
universities: corporations, 460, 467, 470, 474
universities: government, 458
universities: McCarthyism, 404
universities: military, 467
universities: power, 30
universities: power elite, 459

universities: science, 503
universities: Sovietphobia, 399
University of Arizona: football, 4663
University of California, 464
University of California loyalty oath, 199
University of California: science, 499
University of Southern Mississippi, 466
University of Texas (Austin), 3655
University of Washington: anticommunism, 401
University of Washington, Seattle, 387, 394
University of Wisconsin, 4469
university press, 4721
university research, 252
university trustees, 464, 474
Univision news agency, 3251
unnamed sources, 4347
Unsatisfied Man, The, 4176, 4569
Up In The Clouds, 4507
UPI, 838, 868a, 1245a, 1576, 2765, 3419, 3578, 3586
UPI: Pentagon, 4330
Upjohn, 2012
upper class, 21
upper class: governing class, 21
upper class women, 21
Upstairs, Downstairs, 697, 2291
uranium mining hazards, 101
urban riots, 321
urbanization, 15
Uruguay, 1069
U.S. Army, 3637, 4099, 4110
U.S. Army Counterintelligence Branch, 3320
U.S. Army Morale Branch (Information and Education, 3161
U.S. Army repression: dissent, 4565
U.S. Chamber of Commerce, 1980, 1999
US client states, 3276

US dreams: illusions, 1682
US Embassy hostages in Iran, 1591
US foreign policy, 1492, 4690
US global economic expansion, 1196
US global intervention, 3076
US global terrorism, 1276
US history, 3928
US history: captive (official), 55
US House Committee on Intelligence, 301
US Institute of Peace (USIP), 4048
U.S. Navy, 259, 2191, 4095
U.S. Navy report, 4049
U.S. Navy: Tom Clancy, 1544
U.S. News & World Report, 3270, 3273, 3274, 3275, 3276, 3316, 3328, 3341, 3857
US state religion, 4690
US Steel, 2012
U.S. Supreme Court, 4622
U.S. v. American Bond and Mortgage, 3022
U.S. v. Marchetti, 1558
U.S. v Reverend Carl McIntyre, 3022
U.S. Vincennes, 3675
USA, 1634
USA Today, 860, 3555, 3560, 3621, 3629, 3633, 3656, 3688
USAF, 259, 4038
USAF public relations, 2065
USCEA, 2021
USDA, 1874
use of force, 226
use value: advertising, 1746
USIA, 13, 976, 1217, 1217a, 1250, 1322a, 1328, 1357a, 1380, 1592, 1611, 1633, 1642, 2303, 2744, 3164, 3952
USIA: book publishing, 4018
USIA: censorship, 3096, 4441
USIA: censorship of films, 3148
USIA: "Worldnet," 1270
USN&WR, 976, 789, 1443, 3316, 3270, 3273, 3274, 3275, 3341, 3545, 3876, 3901, 3902, 3903, 3908, 3911, 3917, 3921, 3941, 3942
U.S.S. Pueblo, 3490

USSR (see also: SU, Sovietphobia), 334, 2191
utilities, 151, 1147, 1162, 3477, 3526
utilities: AP, 3801
utilities: corruption, 3606
utilities: press, 3801
utopia, 673
utopian press, 4636
utopian thinking: education, 468
UWA, 2027
Vader, John, 4089
Valenti, Jack, 3556
VALS (audience profiling)=Values and Lifestyles, 1671, 1738, 1779
VALS (consumer classification system), 1692
value manipulators, 1829
values, 2292
Values and Lifestyles Program (see VALS), 1671
Van Atta, Dale, 1222
Van Deerlin, Congressman Lionel, 2234
Van Doren, Charles, 2441
Vanderbilt Television News Archive, 2808, 2817, 2858
Vanishing Family: Crisis in Black America, The documentary, 2884
Vanity Fair magazine, 741
Vann, John Paul, 3259
variety shows, 2403
VCR, 601, 2318, 3191, 4194, 4406, 4409
VDT, 3483
vegetables, 1859a
Velde, Harold, 1634
Verrett, Jaqueline, 4667
VHF systems, 2408
VHF television, 2246, 4503
Viacom, 4151
Vicks cough medicines commercial, 2444
victims, 914
Victory at Sea, 2508
Vidal Sassoon, Inc., 2480
video, 4457
video activism, 4407
video art, 2224, 2345
video culture, 2224
video display terminals (VDT), 3192

SUBJECT INDEX 813

video games, 639, 7012345, 3213
video games: militarism, 3212
video: independent, 4406
video: issue oriented, 4407
video tape-recorders, 2235
video v. film, television, 4403
videocassette recorders, 2345
videodiscs, 2345
videotex, 2247, 2314, 2345, 2893, 4404
videotex: democracy, 4465
videotext, 2186
Vietnam, 10, 27, 168, 173, 174, 183, 190, 198, 204, 207, 209, 217, 232, 236, 240, 243, 244, 246, 248, 255, 261, 277, 285, 371, 413, 584, 876, 1264, 1272, 1375, 1392, 1426, 1522, 1611, 2553, 2690, 3229, 3466, 3652, 3691, 4121, 4483
Vietnam (1963): newspapers, 3610
Vietnam: A Television History: documentary, 4492
Vietnam antiwar movement, 632
Vietnam: John Kennedy, 3610
Vietnam, North: bombing, 978
Vietnam: Picking Up the Pieces, 4463
Vietnam: television news, 2775
Vietnam Veterans Against the War (see VVAW), 291
Vietnam Veterans Memorial in Washington D.C., 3103
Vietnam Village Reborn, 3170
Vietnam War, 54, 104, 301, 583, 611, 648, 661, 725, 776, 778, 780, 803, 804, 820, 826, 828, 892, 895, 896, 914, 943, 976, 989, 990, 991,1000, 1004, 1019, 1047, 1228, 1257, 1284, 1297, 1320, 1358, 1383, 1409, 1414, 1489, 1490, 1531, 1553, 1557, 1586, 1611, 1617, 1630, 1636, 1651, 1723, 2294, 2479, 2642, 2657, 2659, 2672, 2714, 2744, 2812, 3076,

3103, 3182, 3259, 3278, 3324, 3344, 3361, 3404, 3489, 3492, 3686, 3798, 3896, 3917, 3921, 3944, 3966, 4101, 4112, 4113, 4117, 4289, 4371, 4545, 4453, 4458, 4568, 4575, 4600, 4664
Vietnam War: access, 2104a
Vietnam War: Agent Orange, 3724
Vietnam War: alternative press, 3464
Vietnam War: Ben Suc, 1379
Vietnam War: bombing reports, 4038
Vietnam War: censorship, 1615
Vietnam War: censorship (news agencies), 3228
Vietnam War correspondents, 1426
Vietnam War: Council on Foreign Relations, 4106
Vietnam War coverage, 3395
Vietnam War crimes, 882
Vietnam War: Dak To, 1379
Vietnam War: Des Moines Register, 3614
Vietnam War: economic interests, 2744
Vietnam War: film, 3054, 3076, 3093, 3098, 3127, 3170, 3173, 3174, 3180, 4521
Vietnam War: film, The War at Home, 4469
Vietnam War: Kent State, 4116
Vietnam War: LAT, 3601
Vietnam War: Madison, WI, 4469
Vietnam War: magazines, 3840
Vietnam War: NBC, 2574, 2745
Vietnam War: network news, 2572, 2573
Vietnam War: networks, 2760
Vietnam War: news agencies, 3222
Vietnam War: news manipulation, 1602
Vietnam War: newspapers, 3466
Vietnam War: NYT, 3700, 3735, 3773, 3776, 3805, 3810
Vietnam War opposition, 2658
Vietnam War: PBS, 2996

Vietnam War: Pentagon Papers, 4126
Vietnam War: protest, 3662, 4565, 4323
Vietnam War: protest music, 4170
Vietnam War public relations, 1379
Vietnam War: television, 2282, 2789, 2818
Vietnam War: television news, 2642, 2673
Vietnam War: Underground Press, 4612
viewer passivity: televison news, 2626
Viguerie, Richard A., 480, 481, 492, 2061
Viking, 4021
Village Voice, 3632, 3909, 4600
Vincennes, 2604
Vinocur, John, 3282
violation: national and international law, 1312a, 1393
violation of law, 288
violence, 91, 222, 223, 230, 280, 375, 389, 612, 634, 747, 760, 828, 943, 1334, 1577, 1636, 2292, 2368, 2376, 2439, 2474, 2477, 2522, 2543, 2548, 2734, 3079, 4005, 4092, 4289, 4722
violence: children, 2414, 2463
violence: corporations, 144
violence: film (sexism), 3118
violence: media, 864
violence: television, 1142a, 2336, 2338, 2398, 2448, 2468, 2469, 2534, 2834, 2902, 2905, 2906, 2907, 2919, 2931, 2932, 2933, 2937, 2941, 2942, 4430
violence: television and children, 2922
violence: televison, toys, 2341
Violets Are Blue, 3143
Virginia Slims, 1734, 1757, 1921
Virginia-Pilot (nuclear alerts scoop), 4330

visa control (see also: McCarran-Walter), 715
visa denial, 3378, 4227
visual propaganda, 4398
visuals: television, 2557
vitamins, 1842
VOA: Edwin Warner, 1642
VOA: Reagan, 1642
vocationalism, 678
Vogue, 741, 3829
Voice of America, 611, 1217, 1217a, 1348, 1348a, 1357a, 1489a, 1500, 1536, 1633, 1642
Voice of America: Nicaragua, 2865
Voice of America's Spanish Service, 1347a
Volkswagen, 1765
voter decline, 2112
voting, 85, 1014, 1405
Voting Rights Act: 1982, 4332
Voyage to the Bottom of the Sea, 2744
Vreeland, Diana, 741, 1578, 4145
Vremya (Time), 2764
VVAW (see also: Vietnam veterans), 297, 405
wage labor, 3839
Wagner-Hatfield Amendment (broadcasting), 3506
Walden II (B.F. Skinner), 468
Walk on East Beacon (1952), 3146
Walker Report, 611
Wall Street, 116
Wall Street Journal (see also: WSJ), 97, 3516, 3524, 3618
Wall Street lawyers, 433
Wall Street: nuclear power, 52
Wallace, George, 2067
Wallace, Henry, 361, 3503
Wallace, Mike, 2746
Wal-Mart, 3551
Wal-mart: newspapers, 3360
Walsh, Jack, 2061
Walsh, Mary W., 931
Walsh, Raoul: films, 3073
Walter, Francis, 1634
Walters, Barbara, 611, 2197, 2720, 2782, 2796

SUBJECT INDEX

Waltons, The, 2393
war, 3, 72, 192, 217, 479, 625, 728, 762, 1708, 2548, 3361, 3375, 3395, 4643, 4722
War Advertising Council, 3833
war cartoons, 1482
war: civil liberties, 4371
war coverage, 1256
war crimes, 244, 584, 1260
war documentaries, 2508
war economy, 55
war: film, 1482, 3079, 3119, 3159, 3177, 3035, 3054, 3060, 3071, 3087
war games, 321
war: Gulf War, 3858
war: Iraq, 3438
war language, 1505
war: media, 771
war metaphors, 1044
war news, 2191
war: opposition, 4174, 4595
war: pacifism, 4595
war power, 174, 210, 1260, 1448
war propaganda, 3477, 3801
war resisters press, 4636
war (see also: individual US wars), 3491
war system, 238
war toy advertising, 1482
war toys, 1492, 2914
war toys: television, 2906
war: TV, 2381
war: Underground Press, 4612
Warbucks, Daddy, 4128
Warfare State, 665
wargames, 255
warmaking power, 341
war-mongering, 3267
Warner Brothers, 3114
Warner Brothers: anti-Nazi, 3078
Warner Brothers: Raoul Walsh, 3073
Warner Communications, 1173, 4151
Warner Time (see also: Time Warner), 3977
warrantless searches, 276
warranty, 1792
Warren, Ned, Sr., 4715
wars, 267
wars: television news, 2859

Washington correspondents, 4372
Washington, George: Farewell Address, 4122
Washington Legal Foundation, 6
Washington Monthly, The, 4724
Washington Post, 209, 630, 633, 634, 644
Washington Post Company, 3885
Washington press corps, 808, 1411, 1262, 1313, 1317a, 1323, 1340, 1351, 1381, 1396, 1400, 1403, 1408, 1410, 1422, 1503, 1546, 1547, 1641, 1646, 2648, 3719
Washington press corps: state department, 3280
Washington Times, 1536, 3565, 3633
waste: government, 4027
waste: militarism, 4054
waste: military contractors, 235
wastes, 130
watchdog press, 1019, 1040, 4238, 4611
water, 1052
water pollution, 3460
Watergate, 59, 104, 174, 180, 189, 198, 212, 215, 293, 306, 318, 587, 602, 611, 780, 787, 872, 934, 1019, 1049, 1049, 1246, 1305, 1331, 1332, 1340, 1358, 1360, 1414, 1442, 1580, 1639, 2201, 2561, 2667, 2672, 2722, 2826, 3634, 4279, 4338, 4581, 4600, 4671, 4679
Watergate: Associated Press, 3242
Watergate: corporations, 1141
Watergate: public opinion, 1442
Watergate: television news, 2632, 2667
Watermelon Man, 3156
Watson, John, 1786
Wayne, John, 3063, 4089, 4747
WBAI New York City, 4512

wealth, 30, 100, 107, 122, 616, 699
wealthy people: politics, 20
weapons data, 1221
weapons: sex, 4045
Weather Underground, 323
Webster, 2444, 2485
Wedding Day, 2492
Wedemeyer, General A.C., 4092
weight reduction remedies, 1842
Weinberger, Caspar, 141, 3261
Weisman, John, 3855
Weiss and Geller, 1786
Welch, Joseph, 4534
welfare, 3562
welfare: law, 420
welfare programs, 3860
Welles, Orson: radio, 2245
Wells, Mary, 1715
Wendy's, 616
Wertheimer, Linda, 3024
West 57th, 2682
West ad appeal, 1837a
West Bank, 487
West Germany, 1614
West Germany: films, 3041
West, Mafia, 4715
WESTAR, 1407, 2156
Western bias, 3240
western film, 707, 3083, 3091, 3152
western films: American Dream, 3153
western hero, 648
Western Union, 1407, 2156
Westinghouse, 1094, 1966, 1976, 2191, 3821
Westinghouse Broadcasting Company (Group W), 1963
Westinghouse Electric Corporation, 2303
Westinghouse: radio, 2202
Westmoreland, General, William, 768, 831, 1379, 1414, 1490, 2583, 2689, 2812
Westmoreland libel suit, 733
Wexler, Haskell, 3185, 4437
Weyrich, Paul, 481, 492
WGBH: television workshop, 2314
Wheaties, 1823
whistle blowing, 235, 1338
whistleblower, 4007, 4237

whistleblower: George Spanton, 1504
whistleblower: "pure" and "alumnus," 4667
whistleblowers: Pentagon, 4340
whistleblowing, 508, 4214, 4368, 4673
whistleblowing: CIA, 3997
White, Ambassador, Robert, 1277
white collar crime (see corporate crime), 431
white collar workers, 1
White House, 202, 1251, 1255, 1319a, 1524, 1530, 1623, 2160, 4247, 4372
White House broadcasting, 1478a
White House Communications Agency, 321
White House Conference on Library and Information Services, 1200
White House News Service, 2069
White House: newspaper, 3614
White House press, 1325, 1603, 1627
White House press conference, 1325a
White House press corps (see also: Washington press corps), 1252, 1369, 1475, 1530, 1572, 1653
White House press secretary, 1398, 4671
White House propaganda (Nicaragua), 1500
White House public relations, 2111a
White House tapes (not shredded), 1305
White, Justice, Byron, 1564
White, Mark, 1267
White Papers, 315, 153, 4042
"white propaganda," 1431, 1432
Whitehead, Clay, 1414
whitewash, 4116
Whitman, 4026
Whitney, John Hay (Jock), 3612
Whittle Communications, 1742
Whittle's "Channel One," 2038, 2049, 2054

Why We Fight (WWII film), 3161, 3170
Whyte, W.H., 1786
Wick, Charles, 1642, 2637
Wicker, Tom, 1283
Wide World of Sports, 2537
Widener, Don, 1903, 1923, 2709, 2830
Wiesbaum, Herb, 2582
Wieseltier, Leon, 1276
Wildmon, Reverend Donald, 2956
Wilkinson, Frank, 405
Will, George, 1518
will power, 3860
William Sloane Associates, 4021
Williams, Raymond, 439, 645, 2349, 2406, 2424, 4162
Williams, Tennessee, 3994
Williamson, John, 3992
Wilmington Ten, 405
Wilson, George: Pentagon correspondent, 3489, 4330
Wilson, Woodrow, 1629
"Wimp Factor," 1419
wine, 1779
wine ads, 1886
Winston Churchill-The Valiant Years, 2744
Winston, Henry, 3992
Winter, Carl, 3992
Winter-Berger, Robert, 1411
Winthrop, John, 4085
Winthrop, John: Model of Christian Charity, 4085
wire services (see also: news agencies), 699, 728, 800, 868, 943, 976, 1010, 1016, 1078, 1178, 1241, 1404, 1410, 1513, 3220, 3240, 3241, 3260, 3273, 3323, 3376, 3546, 3586, 3677, 3926, 4173, 4289
wire services, AIDS, 927a
wire services: Canada, 1063
wire services: official conduit, 4330
wire services: presidency, 1596
wire services: socialism, 3405
wire services: UNESCO, 913
wire services: Zimbabwe, 3225

wiretapping, 183, 220, 283, 312, 321, 324, 329, 3202
Wirthlin, Richard, 1519, 2066
Wise, David (The Politics of Lying), 1340
Wiseman, Frederick, 3053, 3062, 3075
witch hunt: Hollywood, 3074
witch hunt, 199, 1618, 2207, 2212, 3064
witch hunt: academia, 394
witch hunt anticommunism, 401
Witness to a Century, 4641
WNET/Thirteen: television lab, 2314
Wolston v. "Reader's Digest," 1561
womanhood, 3833
Woman's Day, 3904
Woman's Own, 1851, 3826
women, 61, 485, 715, 1020, 1067, 1779, 3928, 4603
women: advertising, 1674, 1697, 1717, 1809, 1833, 1849, 1855a, 1905, 1921, 1922
Women Against Violence Against Women, 1757
women: broadcasting, 2197
women: consumer culture, 1718
women: consumerism, 2461
women: corporations, 26
women: economics, 68
women: exploitation, 1676
women: films, 3152
women in home, 79
women in news, 695a
women: jobs, 5
women: journalists, 4302
women: law, 419
women: media, 557, 722
women: medicine, 521
women mobilized: WWII, 3833
women: museums, 4137
women: news, 695a
women: power, 30
women: print journalism, 4263
women: right wing, 61
women: science, 499
women: television, 755, 2426, 2461, 2504
women's liberation, 1832

women's liberation: advertising, 1757
women's magazines, 3826, 3904
women's magazines: advertising, 1851
Wonder Bread, 1919a
Wood, John, S., 1634
Wood, Robert, 2474
Woodbury, David (right-wing novelist), 3968
Woodward and Bernstein, 1340
Woodward, Bob, 1223, 3634, 4600
word choice, 3471
work place: toxic chemicals, 4627
work: television, 2540
work: television programs, 2350
worker control, 4650
worker surveillance: computers, 3196
working class, 1, 122, 127, 162, 1160, 2431, 2465, 2473
working class, 4606
working class education, 468, 471
working class films: 1970s, 3172
working class: films, 3046, 3057, 3066, 3152
working class magazine, 4626
working class: museums, 4137
working class: music, 4158
working class: PBS, 2965, 2966
working class (see also: labor), 1069a
working class (see also: labor): PBS, 3025
working class (see also: labor): television, 2473
working class: television, 2281, 2903
working journalist, 4585
working people: television, 2534
working women: novels, 3986
working women: television, 2525
working-class press, 4636
working-class women: WWII, 3833
workplace video, 4464

World Administrative Radio Conference: WARC '79, 39
World Affairs, 1581
World Anti-Communist League (WACL), 193, 482
World Bank, 2568, 4037, 4065
World Court, 584, 832, 1275, 1276
world markets, 258
world news, 3269
World Press Freedom Committee, 4288
World War I, 214
World War II, 807
Worldnet, 1322a
Wouk, Herman, 3987
Wounded Knee, 812, 895
Wounded Knee: television, 2818
WP, 679, 787, 797, 838, 860, 884, 900, 914, 925, 932, 990, 1015, 1019, 1023, 1039, 1049, 1066, 1067, 1078, 1094, 1220, 1337, 1241, 1253, 1275, 1276, 1283, 1320, 1379, 1399, 1400, 1401, 1414, 1443, 1458, 1530, 1548, 1569, 1599, 1607, 1608, 1648, 2555, 2795, 3270, 3273, 3276, 3281, 3302, 3309, 3316, 3328, 3335, 3336, 3341, 3342, 3343, 3419, 3423, 3430, 3437, 3481, 3489, 3503, 3518, 3522, 3545, 3547, 3553, 3558, 3559, 3560, 3564, 3568, 3569, 3570, 3572, 3574, 3577, 3578, 3586, 3591, 3609, 3610, 3611, 3616, 3618, 3620, 3622, 3627, 3630, 3633, 3646, 3652, 3657, 3658, 3666, 3673, 3675, 3677, 3682, 3691, 3868, 3880, 3996, 4005, 4106, 4510, 4575, 4581, 4583, 4600
WP: Arabs, 3619
WP: arms race, 960
WP: cold war, 4236
WP: Contras, 3288
WP: corporate state, 3599
WP: EPA, 1576
WP: Israel, 3619
WP: Nicaragua, 1500, 2865
WP: nuclear weapons, 1590
WP: profit orientation, 3645

SUBJECT INDEX

WP: red-baiting, 3571
WP: UNESCO, 913
WP: unions, 3594
WP: Watergate, 1442
WP: libel, 1042
wrestling, 2341
Wright, Jim, 797
writers: divergent disciplines, 4564
Writers Guild of America, 2474
writers v. business, 4576
Written on the Wind (film), 3113
WSJ, 787, 789, 838, 842, 884, 914, 931, 990, 1077, 1094, 1253, 1277, 1283, 1302, 1310, 1337, 1355, 1395, 1443, 1569, 1607, 1608, 1692, 3277, 3281, 3316, 3328, 3335, 3425, 3428, 3437, 3438, 3481, 3545, 3548, 3569, 3574, 3591, 3598, 3620, 3624, 3626, 3633, 3661, 3665, 3682, 3692, 4005
WSJ: El Salvador, 3651
WSJ: Nicaragua, 1500
WWI films, 3071, 3179
WWI propaganda, 1635
WWII, 389, 625, 803, 1842, 3398, 3505, 3833
WWII: advertising about women, 655
WWII film, 3060, 3085, 3087, 3098, 3114, 3134, 3161, 3170
WWII films: Hitchcock, 3163
WWII: films, women, 3144
WWII news: Franklin Roosevelt, 3485
WWII: NYT, 3737
WWII reporting, 4006
WWII: women, 655
WWIII, 1456, 4005
Wylie, Philip, 3146
Wylie, Philip (Tomorrow, 1954), 3146
xenophobia, 62, 91, 624, 1045, 1574, 3106, 3166
xenophobia: science, 503
Xerox, 1765
Yalta, 853, 2605
Yasui, Minoru, 405
Yates v. United States, 3430
Year of the Dragon, 3076
Yellow Fruit, 233

yellow journalism, 3639
"yellow rain," 990, 1310
Yesterday, Today, and Tomorrow, 2636
Yippie, 667
YMCA, 43
Young and Rubicam advertising agency, 1692, 1715, 1786, 1934
Young, Neil, 4161
Your Tour in Vietnam, 3170
youth: advertising, 1730
Youth Communication, 3412
youth: protest, 4221
"You've Come a Long Way, Baby," 1757
Zaire: NYT, 3761
Zero-1960, 2508
Zia El-Haq, Mohammed, 1299
Ziegler, Ronald, 1597, 1639
Zimbalist, Efrem, Jr., 1631, Jr., 2109
Zinn, Howard, 584
Zurcher v. Stanford Daily, 1561, 2126, 3584, 4208